EUROPEAN RESEARCH CENTRES

RELATED REFERENCE BOOKS AVAILABLE FROM LONGMAN GROUP LIMITED

Longman Reference on Research series

Aerospace Research Index
Agricultural Research Centres (supersedes Agricultural Research Index)
Directory of Scientific Directories
European Research Centres
European Sources of Scientific and Technical Information
Industrial Research in the United Kingdom
International Medical Who's Who
International Who's Who in Energy and Nuclear Sciences
Materials Research Centres
Medical Research Index
Pollution Research Index
Who's Who in Ocean and Freshwater Science
Who's Who in Science in Europe
Who's Who in World Agriculture
World Energy Directory
World Nuclear Directory

Longman Guide to World Science and Technology series

Science and Technology in China
Science and Technology in Eastern Europe
Science and Technology in the Indian Subcontinent
Science and Technology in Israel
Science and Technology in Japan
Science and Technology in Latin America and the Caribbean
Science and Technology in the Middle East
Science and Technology in South-East Asia
Science and Technology in the United Kingdom
Science and Technology in the USSR

Other reference books published by Longman

Financial Times Mining International Year Book
Financial Times Oil and Gas International Year Book
Financial Times Who's Who in World Oil and Gas
Medical Directory

EUROPEAN RESEARCH CENTRES

a directory of organizations in science, technology, agriculture, and medicine

Fifth edition

Volume 1 (International, Albania to Hungary)

Longman

EUROPEAN RESEARCH CENTRES: a directory of organizations
in science, technology, agriculture, and medicine

Published by Longman Group Limited, Professional and Information
Publishing Division, Sixth Floor, Westgate House, The High, Harlow,
Essex CM20 1NE, UK
Telephone: Harlow (0279) 442601

Distributed exclusively in the USA and Canada by Gale Research Company,
Book Tower, Detroit, MI 48226, USA

British Library Cataloguing in Publication Data
European Research Centres: a directory of organizations in science,
    technology, agriculture, and medicine.
    – 5th ed. – (Longman reference on research series)
    1. Research institutes – Europe – Directories
    I. Williams, Trevor I.
    001.4'025'4   Q180.E/

ISBN 0-582-90012-3

Printed in Great Britain by
William Clowes (Beccles) Limited, Beccles and London

FOREWORD

European Research Centres: a directory of organizations in science, technology, agriculture, and medicine is the successor to **European Research Index** and **East European Research Index.** These are both firmly established reference works, currently in their fourth and first editions respectively, but it is felt that the convenience of readers is now best served by amalgamating them. This would in itself have demanded a change of title, and the opportunity has been taken of adopting one that is more precisely descriptive of the scope of the work. This is not an index of all institutions and organizations concerned with scientific research in its broadest sense – including medicine, agriculture, and engineering – but more strictly with those at which research and/or development is actually carried out or directly funded. For example, some learned societies are direct sponsors of research, but the majority have as their remit the indirect promotion of research by publishing journals, organizing conferences and so on. Societies of the latter type are omitted here not because their contribution is judged unimportant – indeed, the whole progress of science depends on the existence of facilities for the prompt and effective dissemination of new knowledge – but because information about them is available elsewhere, and they do not fulfil the redefined criteria. Their inclusion, it is argued, is no more logical than the inclusion of the many commercial publishing houses which publish journals devoted to original research, conference proceedings, specialist monographs, and the like. For similar reasons, we have excluded consultancy organizations which offer a purely advisory service, as opposed to those which conduct research for clients on a contract basis. However several new industrial firms who have reacted to our appeal for information are represented. Again, we have omitted most of the professional bodies to which research workers belong, and the trade bodies which are peripheral to the research activities of their member firms. Nevertheless, the net has been cast wide and we include research centres in universities; in private industry and public corporations; and in government laboratories.

While no attempt has – or, indeed, could – be made to evaluate the quality of research, we have tried to indicate its scale. Where the information is available, entries show the number of graduates involved in full-time research; annual expenditure on research and development; whether research is undertaken for other organizations; and whether progress reports are published. Thus there is more information about most of the centres than was given in previous editions.

The amalgamation of the two earlier works has demanded complete resetting of the type. The opportunity has been taken to substitute a serif typeface for the previous IBM typing. A further improvement is the almost complete elimination of duplication, a consequence of storing information on magnetic discs. The usefulness of the work has also been greatly increased by the Subject Index, now included for the first time.

European Research Centres thus seeks to give a comprehensive picture of the centres throughout Europe which are actively promoting research. How far this has been successful is for the reader to judge. We have addressed ourselves to our task energetically and systematically, but in the last analysis we are very much in the hands of those to whom we send our questionnaires. Overall the response has been so high as to confirm us in the belief that there is a widespread and continuing need for an authoritative reference book of this kind. Not surprisingly, our greatest difficulties have been encountered in the countries of eastern Europe where the problems of language are particularly severe and are compounded by those of a political nature.

Where there have been unavoidable omissions, or entries are less than comprehensive, we hope that those concerned will be encouraged, in their own interests as much as those of others, to provide the necessary information when this is requested for future editions.

Trevor I. Williams　　　　　　　　　　　　　　　　　　　　　　　　　　　　Oxford
Consultant Editor　　　　　　　　　　　　　　　　　　　　　　　　　　　　July 1982

PUBLISHER'S INTRODUCTION

The publishers are proud to bring out the fifth edition of this directory. This edition carries the title **European Research Centres: a directory of organizations in science, technology, agriculture, and medicine**, and amalgamates details of research organizations in eastern and western Europe. The directory includes chapters on research centres in each of the major countries in Europe. For the purposes of this directory Europe has been taken to exclude the whole of the USSR; this view was influenced by the number of questionnaire responses received from that country. The subject coverage embraces science, technology, medicine and agriculture. Some research and development units, because of their range of activities, fall on the border between the humanities/social sciences area and the subject matter we cover; the reader will find included some industrial management and trade economic centres particularly where there is a technological content. Pure social sciences and humanities research centres have been omitted where there is no element of technological studies. The arrangement of the book is described below.

This European reference guide is arranged by countries in alphabetical order. Organizations spanning more than one country are listed in the opening chapter entitled 'International' establishments. This chapter, as well as providing details of research centres carrying out r&d projects, includes some international bodies influential in recommending research expenditure, because of their close links with research projects. Chapters incorporating entries on each research centre or research-funding organization follow. The criteria for inclusion in the country chapters are that an institute, centre or department carries out or finances research projects within the subject area.

To locate a particular organization, the reader can either refer directly to the country chapter, or use the Titles of Establishments Index. All organizations are listed in the Titles of Establishments Index by proper name, and, in the case of non-English institutes, by the English translation of their title. The English translations are printed in italic type. In some cases where the initial word of the establishment may not be the term looked up by the reader, establishment titles are also indexed by a keyword taken from the English version of the title.

The reader is advised to use the Titles of Establishments Index to speed location of an entry. The Subject Index, which completes the book, allows the reader to identify where specific research activities are being conducted. Thus this directory allows the reader to identify research and organizational details of establishments by country, by title, and by subject matter.

Each country chapter comprises research establishments and research-funding organizations arranged in alphabetical order in the language of that country. For countries which do not use the Roman alphabet, the title is given in English translation. Universities are entered under their proper title.

Each entry is introduced with the full title of the organization accompanied by its acronym if used. If the title is in a language other than English, a translation into English is supplied. It should be noted that the translated title is not a transliteration of the original language but is an English version intended to give an indication of the work of the particular body. The following details, where available, are given in an entry: full postal **address; telephone** number, and **telex** address; the heading **affiliation** or **parent body** indicates its administrative links or parentage; the name of the **research director**, director or head is given preceded by his official job title, which is given in its English version; the **sections**, departments or divisions provides the scope of the section followed by the name of the person leading that section, or that line of research; **graduate research staff** gives the number of graduates engaged in full-time research; annual expenditure on research is either given in terms of a cash sum or within a particular cash range; **activities** provides an outline of the research activities, which may include details of facilities owned, usual source of funding, and date of formation; **contract work** is followed by a 'yes' or a 'no' and indicates whether the organization is willing to undertake research work on behalf of other organizations; **publications** give titles and frequency of progress reports and publications issued on a regular basis, such as annual reports, year books and research reports. In this paragraph the introductory word or phrase given in the entry has been given in bold type. Occasionally other introductory words or phrases have been used in the entry but it is hoped that they are self-explanatory.

Overall the entry information is intended to indicate the size of the organization, its major personnel and an overview of its research activities, interests, and major projects, and its direct links with other organizations. The work of individual scientists and the scope of particular research projects, which may be of short duration, have not been included.

An asterisk (*) appearing after the title indicates that a reply was not received in time for inclusion in the book. However the Consultant Editor believes these organizations are conducting activities which fall within the scope of this directory, so they have been included. In these cases the entry contains data available from public sources.

The Titles of Establishments Index includes titles of all establishments listed in this reference book, and directs the user by country and entry number to the full information on that establishment. An establishment with a title in a language other than English is entered both under its original language title and its English translation, as given in the entry. Translated titles are printed in italic type. The acronyms of major establishments listed are also incorporated into this index.

The Subject Index is compiled primarily from the 'activities' section of each entry and allows the reader to identify where specific research activities are being carried out in Europe. The subject terms are based on the controlled vocabulary of the British Standards Institution's published *ROOT* (1981) Thesaurus. Entries in the index have largely been made as detailed as the information given will allow. The reader should therefore choose as specific a keyword as possible for the initial search, as broader terms have been used only where detail is not available or where activities are genuinely comprehensive over a given field.

This edition is the first Francis Hodgson reference directory to be typeset. We hope that readers find this redesigned format acceptable – a format which will allow browsing, and one which will readily allow readers to extract particular details which interest them. The change of format is a consequence of a system of computer-assisted compilation which is welcomed by the Francis Hodgson Editorial Team for not only can the Editor more easily compare similar organizations, but particular entries can be immediately linked to their parent or administering body. Furthermore this system allows all entries to be amended or updated right up to the time that the directory goes to press.

The continuing development of research programmes and investigative scientific, technical, medical and agricultural work means that any reference guide of this nature needs regular updating. Consequently it is hoped to produce revised versions of **European Research Centres** at regular intervals in the future. The publishers would appreciate hearing from users who may have suggestions to make for the improvement of future editions, or who are able to point out any errors of omission or commission.

Colin P. Taylor
Publisher

CONTENTS AND INDEX ABBREVIATIONS

INTERNATIONAL

Association Européenne Océanique 1

– Eurocean
[European Oceanic Association]
Address: Villa Richard, rue de l'Abbaye, Monaco-ville, Monaco
Telephone: (93) 304015
Telex: 469037
President: Dr H. Kippenberger
Director-General: B. Lachmann
Activities: A group of major industries from many European countries, organized to coordinate research, evaluation, development, and promotion of projects in the marine field. In particular, it deals with projects of large magnitude requiring international cooperation and coordination with (inter)national and (inter)governmental organizations. It also provides services of experts attached to the Association and an up-to-date information and documentation service.
Contract work: No
Publications: Eurocean technical reports, *Amer-Seamarks*, and information bulletins (for members only).

Atlantic Salmon Trust Limited 2

Address: 14 Downing Street, Farnham, Surrey GU9 7PB, United Kingdom
Telephone: (0252) 724400
Director: G.D. FitzGerald Hadoke
Activities: Support for the efficient management and conservation of Atlantic salmon and sea trout stocks in the national and international sphere; sponsorship of research into all economic and biological factors affect-ing these issues; providing background and detailed information on important matters affecting the development of salmon and sea trout stocks.
Contract work: No

Bureau International de l'Heure 3

– BIH
[International Time Bureau]
Address: 61 avenue de l'Observatoire, 75014 Paris, France
Telephone: 320 12 10
Telex: 270776
Affiliation: International Astronomical Union
Director: Bernard Guinot
Sections: Earth's rotation, M. Feissel; Atomic time, M. Granveaud
Graduate research staff: 6
Annual expenditure: £10 000-50 000
Activities: Determination of the Earth's rotation characteristics. Establishment of the worldwide basis for time.
Contract work: Yes
Publications: Annual report, monthly circular.

Carbon 14 Centralen 4

[International Agency for Carbon 14 Determination]
Address: Agern Allé 11, DK-2970 Hørsholm, Denmark
Telephone: (02) 86 52 11
Affiliation: Akademiet for de Tekniske Videnskaber - ATV

Institute Leader: Ann-Mari Bresta
Activities: C14C functions as an international centre for determination of primary production by the ^{14}C method, thus maintaining research, development, and standardization about methods for measuring photosynthesis rates. Special fields of activity: production of $NaH^{14}CO_3$ solutions in 1 ml ampoules; calibration of $NaH^{14}CO_3$ solutions; measurement of radioactivity of primary production rates in phytoplankton samples; supply of special equipment for collection and treatment of samples. Primary production measurement is used as a parameter for judging fish stocks, monitoring of eutrophication and test of toxicity in recipient investigations in natural phytoplankton as well as in phytoplankton cultures.
Contract work: No

Centre de Coopération pour les Recherches Scientifiques Relatives au Tabac   5

– CORESTA
[Cooperation Centre for Scientific Research Relative to Tobacco]
Address: 53 quai d'Orsay, 75340 Paris Cedex 07, France
Telephone: 555 91 50
Secretary General: Pierre Ray
Activities: Research activities are carried out by four study groups which deal with tobacco agronomy, phytopathology, technology, and smoke.
Contract work: No
Publications: Quarterly information bulletin.

Commission Internationale des Industries Agricoles et Alimentaires   6

– CIIA
[International Commission for Food Industries]
Address: 35 rue du Général Foy, 75008 Paris, France
Telephone: 2921924
President: Professor Hollo
President of the scientific council: Professor Carballo Caabeiro
Activities: Developing international cooperation on the promotion of agricultural and food industries.
Publications: Biannual bulletin; biannual calendar of international meetings related to food industries; biannual listing of international organizations associated with food industries.

Commission Internationale du Génie Rural/ Internationale Kommission für Technik in der Landwirtschaft   7

– CIGR
[International Commission of Agricultural Engineering]
Address: 17-21 rue de Javel, 75015 Paris, France
Telephone: 577 75 78
General Secretary: Michel Carlier
Sections: Land improvement and reclamation, Baquero De La Cruz
Agricultural buildings, structures and related equipment, Mr Henriksson
Agricultural machinery, Mr Manfredi
Electricity in agriculture, Mr Wakeford
Scientific organization of agricultural work, M Maton;
Activities: Organization of congresses and sections symposia on themes dealing with the various fields of agricultural engineering: sciences of soil and water in their application to the work of agricultural engineering; agricultural buildings and related equipment; agricultural machinery; rural electrification and agricultural applications of electricity; and scientific organization of agricultural work.
Contract work: No
Publications: Conference and congress papers; international farm machinery abstracts; indexes on farm work science; research reports; terminology in electricity supply economics.

Committee on Data for Science and Technology   8

– CODATA
Address: 51 boulevard de Montmorency, 75016 Paris, France
Telephone: 525 04 96
Telex: ICSU 630553 F
Affiliation: International Council of Scientific Unions
President: Professor M. Kotani
Executive Secretary: P. Glaeser
Activities: A scientific committee of ICSU concerned with the improvement of the quality, reliability and accessibility of scientific data. Task groups have been set up for computer use, key values for thermodynamics, fundamental constants, data for chemical kinetics, transport properties, presentation of data in the primary literature, accessibility and dissemination of data, and training courses in the treatment and critical evaluation of data.

Committee on Science and Technology in Developing Countries* 9

- COSTED

Address: (Secretariat): Department of Physics, Indian Institute of Technology, Madras 60036, India
Telephone: 4140 46
Telex: TECHMASMS (041) 7362
Affiliation: International Council of Scientific Unions
Chairman: Dr Y. Nayudamma
Secretary: Dr S. Radhakrishna
Activities: Established in 1966 by ICSU for the encouragement of science and technology in developing countries.

Committee on Space Research/Comité de la Recherche Spatiale 10

- COSPAR

Address: (Secretariat): 51 boulevard de Montmorency, 75016 Paris, France
Telephone: 5250679
Telex: ICSU 630553 F
Affiliation: International Council of Scientific Unions
President: Professor J.F. Denisse
Executive Secretary: Z. Niemirowicz
Activities: Fostering progress on an international scale of all fundamental research carried out with the use of balloons, rockets, and rocket-propelled vehicles. Interdisciplinary scientific commissions and independent panels have been set up on: space studies of the earth's surface; meteorology and climate; space studies of the earth-moon system; planets and small bodies of the solar system; space studies of the upper atmospheres of the earth and planets; space plasmas in the solar system, including planetary magnetospheres; research in astrophysics from space; life sciences as related to space; materials sciences in space; space research and developing countries; potentially environmentally detrimental activities in space; technical problems as related to scientific ballooning; and dynamics of artificial satellites and space probes.

Committee on the Teaching of Science* 11

- CTS

Address: (Secretariat): Malvern College, Malvern, Worcestershire, United Kingdom
Telephone: (06845) 61413

Affiliation: International Council of Scientific Unions
Chairman: Professor C.A. Taylor
Secretary: J. Lewis
Activities: Established in 1968 by ICSU to study all matters related to the teaching of science.

Commonwealth Advisory Aeronautical Research Council 12

Address: Ministry of Defence, Main Building, Room 2115, Whitehall, London SW1A 2HB, United Kingdom
Telephone: (01) 218 2344
Member Countries: Australia, Canada, Ghana, India, Federation of Malaysia, New Zealand, United Kingdom
Secretary: Gp Capt R.D. Hillary
Activities: The encouragement of joint aeronautical research by members of the British Commonwealth.
Contract work: No

Commonwealth Agricultural Bureaux 13

- CAB

Address: Farnham House, Farnham, Royal Slough, SL2 3BN, United Kingdom
Telephone: (02814) 2281
Telex: 847964
Chairman of Executive Council: R.B. Ryanga (Kenya)
Secretary to the Executive Council: N.G. Jones
Activities: The Commonwealth Agricultural Bureaux, founded in 1929, consists of four Institutes and ten Bureaux under the control of an Executive Council comprising representatives of the Commonwealth countries which contribute to its funds. CAB's main objective is to provide a scientific information service for agricultural research workers throughout the world. Secondary objectives include the provision of identification and biological control services. Each Institute and Bureau is concerned with its own particular branch of agricultural science and acts as an effective clearing house for the collection, collation and dissemination of information of value to research workers. The information, compiled from worldwide literature, is published in 45 abstract journals which have been produced by computer-assisted processes since January 1973; some 1 250 000 records are already on tape, and the number increases by 150 000 per annum.
In addition, three Institutes provide identification and taxonomic services and the fourth undertakes fieldwork in biological control in several parts of the world.

COMMONWEALTH INSTITUTE OF BIOLOGICAL CONTROL   14

Address: Gordon Street, Curepe, Trinidad, West Indies
Telephone: 662 4173
Director: Dr F.D. Bennett
Activities: Control of invertebrate agricultural pests and weeds by biological means.
Contract work: Yes
Publications: Biocontrol News and Information, CIBC Parasite Catalogue.

COMMONWEALTH INSTITUTE OF ENTOMOLOGY   15

Address: 56 Queen's Gate, London, SW7 5JR, United Kingdom
Telephone: (01) 584 0067
Director: Dr N.C. Pant
Assistant director: A.H. Parker
Activities: Research into insects, mites or ticks of importance in the agricultural, medical or veterinary fields, (related to work of the Insect Identification Service).

COMMONWEALTH INSTITUTE OF HELMINTHOLOGY   16

Address: 103 St Peter's Street, St Albans, Hertfordshire AL1 3EW, United Kingdom
Telephone: (0727) 33151
Director: Dr R.L.J. Muller
Sections: Plant nematology, Dr M.R. Siddiqi; helminthology, Dr L.F. Khalil
Annual expenditure: £10 000-50 000
Activities: Helminthology and plant nematology in public health, agricultural, medical and veterinary fields.
Contract work: Yes
Publications: Taxonomic monographs and keys to genera and species.

COMMONWEALTH MYCOLOGICAL INSTITUTE   17

Address: Ferry Lane, Kew, Richmond, Surrey TW9 3AF, United Kingdom
Telephone: (01) 940 4086
Director: A. Johnston
Sections: Herbarium, Dr B.C. Sutton; culture collection, Dr A.H.S. Onions
Graduate research staff: 11
Annual expenditure: £51 000-500 000
Activities: Microfungi and plant pathogenic bacteria; preservation of fungi in culture.
Contract work: Yes

Commonwealth Science Council   18

Address: Commonwealth Secretariat, Marlborough House, Pall Mall, London, SW1Y 5HX, United Kingdom
Telephone: (01) 839 3411
Telex: 27678
Activities: The Council coordinates research programmes carried out in the member states. The programmes can be grouped into four main subject areas: metrology and standards; renewable energy sources; natural products; and rural technology. Each programme is made up of several projects, for example the Caribbean Alternative Energy Programme includes projects on biogas, bagasse, solar and wind systems, biomass, and energy accounting. At present there are eight programmes (given with the date of inception); Caribbean Alternative Energy Programme, 1977; Asia/Pacific Metrology Programme, 1977; Asia/Pacific Rural Technology Programme, 1978; African Programme on Standardization and Quality Control, 1978; Caribbean Metrology Programme, 1978; Caribbean Natural Products Programme, 1978; African Energy Programme, 1978; African Natural Products Programme, 1981.
Member countries: Australia, Bahamas, Bangladesh, Barbados, Botswana, Britain, Canada, Cyprus, Ghana, Grenada, Guyana, India, Jamaica, Kenya, Lesotho, Malawi, Malaysia, Malta, Mauritius, New Zealand, Nigeria, Papau New Guinea, Seychelles, Sierra Leone, Singapore, Sri Lanka, Swaziland, Tanzania, Trinidad and Tobago, Uganda, Zambia, Zimbabwe
Contract work: Yes

Communautés Européennes   19

[European Communities]
Address: 200 rue de la Loi, B-1049 Bruxelles, Belgium
Member countries: Belgium, Denmark, France, Federal Republic of Germany, Greece, Ireland, Italy, Luxembourg, Netherlands, United Kingdom
Associate members: Turkey, Malta, Cyprus, 2 North African countries, 46 African, Caribbean and Pacific countries

COMMISSION OF THE EUROPEAN COMMUNITIES 20

Address: 200 rue de la Loi, B-1049 Bruxelles, Belgium
Secretary-general: Émile Noel
Sections: Industrial and technological affairs (DGIII), Fernand Braun; agriculture (DG VI), Claude Villain; scientific and technical information and information management (DG XIII), Raymond Appleyard; energy (DG XVIII), Leonard Williams; euratom supply agency, Jan-Baldem Mennicken

Joint Research Centre 21

Address: 200 rue de la Loi, B-1049 Bruxelles, Belgium
Telephone: 7350040; 7358030; 7358040; 7366000
Telex: 21877 COMEU B
Director-general: S. Villani
Director, Scientific Coordination: J.P. Contzen
Graduate research staff: 500
Annual expenditure: over £2m
Activities: Nuclear safety and the fuel cycle; reactor safety, plutonium fuels and actinide research, safety of nuclear materials, fissile materials control and management; new energies: solar energy, hydrogen production, energy storage and transport, thermonuclear fusion technology, high-temperature materials; study and protection of the environment: remote sensing from space; nuclear measurements; informatics; operation of large-scale installations.
Contract work: Yes
Publications: JRC Science News; Annual Status Report.

CENTRAL BUREAU FOR NUCLEAR MEASUREMENTS 22

Address: Steenweg op Retie, B-2440 Geel, Belgium
Director: Roland Batchelor
Activities: Programmes include research in nuclear metrology and reference substances.
Facilities: 150 million electronvolts linear accelerator; Van de Graaff generator.

EUROPEAN INSTITUTE FOR TRANSURANIUM ELEMENTS 23

Address: Postfach 2266, Linkenheim, D-7500 Karlsruhe, German FR
Director: Roland Lindner
Activities: Programmes include basic research on transuranium elements, especially plutonium, and applied research into their industrial uses.
Facilities: Tight hot cells.

ISPRA ESTABLISHMENT 24

Address: 21100 Ispra (Varese), Italy
Director: Roland Mas
Activities: A multidisciplinary research centre; programmes include reactor and nuclear plant safety, treatment and storage of radioactive wastes, hydrogen production by chemical cycles, solar energy, informatics, remote sensing of resonances, environment, standards and reference substances, training, etc.
Facilities: Loop Blowdown Investigator; ESSOR reactor; cyclotron.

PETTEN ESTABLISHMENT 25

Address: St Maartensburg, Petten, Noord-Holland, Netherlands
Director: Pieter Van Westen
Activities: Programmes include operation of the high flux reactor, research on high-temperature materials and standards, and reference substances.
Facilities: High flux reactor.

COUNCIL OF THE EUROPEAN COMMUNITIES 26

Address: 170 rue de la Loi, B-1048 Bruxelles, Belgium
Secretary-general: Niels Ersbøll

EUROPEAN PARLIAMENT 27

Address: Secretariat General: Centre Européen, Plateau du Kirchberg Case Postale 1601, Luxembourg
Parliamentary commissions: Energy research and technology, Hanna Walz; public health and the environment, Kenneth D. Collins

JET (JOINT EUROPEAN TORUS) JOINT UNDERTAKING 28

Address: Abingdon, Oxfordshire OX14 3EA, United Kingdom
Telephone: (0235) 28822
Telex: 837505 (JET EUR G)
Director of the JET Project: Dr Hans Otto Wüster
Departments: Construction, Dr P.H. Rebut; Scientific, R.J. Bickerton
Graduate research staff: 120
Annual expenditure: £30m
Activities: The JET Project is a principal part of the Fourth European Fusion Programme; ultimately it is hoped to make available for Europe a new source of energy, the energy released by the fusion of the nuclei of light atoms, the energy source of the sun. The JET Joint Undertaking's mandate is to construct, operate and exploit as part of the Euratom Fusion Programme and for the benefit of the participants in this programme a large torus facility of tokamak-type and its auxiliary

facilities in order to extend the parameter range applicable to controlled thermonuclear fusion experiments up to conditions close to those needed in a thermonuclear reactor. JET should commence operation in 1983 and will have a greater performance capability than any other tokamak in the world.
Contract work: Yes
Publications: Annual report.

STATISTICAL OFFICE OF THE   29
EUROPEAN COMMUNITIES

Address: Centre Européen, Plateau du Kirchberg, Luxembourg
Director-general: Aage Dornonville de la Cour

Confédération Européenne   30
des Industries du Bois

– CEI-BOIS
[European Confederation of Woodworking Industries]
Address: 109-111 Rue Royale, B-1000 Bruxelles, Belgium
Telephone: (02) 217 63 65
Telex: 61933 meubel b
General Delegate: E. Ronse

European Molecular   31
Biology Laboratory/
Europäisches Laboratorium
für Molekularbiologie/
Laboratoire Européen de
Biologie Moléculaire

– EMBL
Address: Postfach 10.2209, D-6900 Heidelberg, German FR
Telephone: (06221) 3871
Telex: 461613 embl d
Director-general: Sir John Kendrew
Divisions: Cell Biology; Biological Structures; Instrumentation
Graduate research staff: 100
Annual expenditure: over £2m
Activities: Research in fundamental biology. There are two EMBL outstations, at Grenoble, France and Hamburg, German FR.
Contract work: No

European Organization for   32
Research on Treatment of
Cancer

– EORTC
Address: Birchstrasse 95, CH-8050 Zürich, Switzerland
Telephone: (01) 312 44 56
Telex: 56659
Secretary General: Gisela Haemmerli
Project Groups and working parties: Gnotobiotic, D. van der Waaij, P.J. Heidt; antimicrobial therapy, J. Klastersky, H. Gaya; metastases, K. Hellmann; tumour invasion, P. Strauli, A. Hagenbeek; high let therapy, W. Duncan, J.J. Battermann; pharmacokinetics and metabolism, J.F. Smyth, H. Pinedo; choriocarcinoma, K.D. Bagshawe, E. Newlands; osteosarcomas, C. Jasmin; haemopathies P. Stryckmans; immunology and immunotherapy of cancer, R. Plagne, B. Serrou; breast cancer, A. Zwaveling, R. Scheerens; bronchial cancer, J. Klastersky, E. Longeval
Task Forces: Breast cancer, J.C. Heuson, W.H. Mattheiem; G.I. task force, A. Gerard, P. Kemps
Activities: Formerly Groupe Européen de Chimiothérapie Anticancéreuse (GECA), a transnational institution consisting of laboratories and clinical services situated in different countries (15 laboratories, 250 clinical services, and several hundreds of clinicians). Conducting, developing, coordinating, and stimulating research in Europe on the experimental and clinical bases of treatment of cancer and related problems. Extensive and comprehensive research in this wide field is often beyond the means of the individual European laboratories and hospitals and can be best accomplished through the joint efforts of the clinical and basic research groups of several countries. EORTC has initiated five major efforts in the field of cancer treatment: a screening programme of potential anti-cancer agents; the organization of clinical and preclinical cooperative groups aimed at carrying out controlled clinical trials with new therapeutic agents and regimens; the organization of collaborative research programmes; a fellowship programme, to enable clinicians and research workers to study and work in EORTC institutions outside their own country; and the initiation of symposia, courses and publications on the subject of cancer research and treatment. EORTC has a Council which plans and supervises the activities within the organization. Research is carried out by some 27 clinical and preclinical cooperative groups, cooperative research project groups, and working parties.
Facilities: Through the combined efforts of the collaborating laboratories of its members, the group has available a wide range of screening procedures for anti-tumour activity as well as a limited number of assay-systems for evaluating related activities. More than 6 000 new drugs are screened annually and through a close

cooperation with the US National Cancer Institute it is possible to test only those compounds which have not been tested previously in the American Programme. Primary tests are carried out in the three screening centres in Brussels, Milan and Paris.

Contract work: Yes

Publications: European Journal of Cancer, Newsletter, *EORTC Monograph Series,* edited by M. Staquet, *EORTC Cancer Chemotherapy Annual Series,* edited by H.M. Pinedo.

CLINICAL COOPERATIVE GROUPS 33

Address: Institut Jules Bordet, 1 rue Heger-Bordet, 1000 Bruxelles, Belgium
Telephone: 5385790
Telex: 22773
Coordinator: M. Staquet
Sections: Screening and pharmacology, F. Spreafico, P. Lelieveld; clinical screening, P. Cappeleare, M. Hayat; leukaemia and haematosarcoma, C. Haanen, M. Hayat; bronchial carcinoma, O. Monod, A. Depierre; breast cancer, E. Engelsman, W.H. Mattheiem; gastrointestinal tract cancer, J. Loygue, A. Gerard; urological cancer, M. Pavone-Macaluso, P.H. Smith; melanoma, E. Macher, F.J. Lejeune; radiochemotherapy, M. Hayat, E. van der Schueren; radiotherapy, E. van der Schueren, J.C. Horiot; head and neck, Y. Cachin, A. Jortay; brain tumours, L. Calliauw, J. Hildebrand; early clinical trials, H.H. Hansen, M. Hansen; cancer of the ovary, J.P. Wolff, A. Maskens; soft tissue and bone sarcoma, G. Bonadonna, H.M. Pinedo, A.T. van Oosterom
Activities: Carrying out collaborative work, aimed at the clinical evaluation of new drugs or new treatments for cancer. The studies are carried out in collaboration between radiotherapists, medical and surgical oncologists. Through this cooperation, data on therapeutic results from a large number of patients are collected at a much faster rate than within any of the clinical centres alone. The studies planned by the cooperative groups are reviewed by a Protocol Review Committee for evaluation and advice.

COORDINATING AND DATA CENTRE 34

Address: Institut Jules Bordet, 1 rue Heger-Bordet, 1000 Bruxelles, Belgium
Telephone: 5385790
Telex: 22773
Director: Dr M. Staquet
Activities: To provide central coordination for the activities of the EORTC groups and to make available to the groups a wide range of statistical and data processing expertise, including advice on study design as well as analysis and reporting of results, at a central, and hence economical location.

European Southern Observatory 35

– ESO
Address: Karl-Schwarzschild-Strasse 2, D-8046 Garching bei München, German FR
Telephone: (089) 320060
Telex: 05282820 es d
Director-general: Professor L. Woltjer
Graduate research staff: 30
Annual expenditure: DM40m
Member countries: Belgium, Denmark, France, German FR, Netherlands, Sweden
Activities: All fields of contemporary astronomy and astrophysics (including extragalactic studies, studies of radio and X-ray sources, studies of stars and the structure of our galaxy and interstellar matter).
Facilities: 10 telescopes with apertures ranging from 40 centimetres to 360 centimetres (located in Chile on the mountain La Silla, 600 kilometres north of Santiago); data-reduction and image-processing centre at headquarters building in Garching; facilities for the development of the auxiliary instrumentation.
Contract work: No
Publications: Annual report; *The Messenger,* quarterly.

European Space Agency 36

– ESA
Address: 8-10 rue Mario-Nikis, 75738 Paris Cedex, France 15
Telephone: 567 55 78
Telex: ESA 202746
Member Countries: Belgium, Denmark, France, Germany, Italy, Ireland, The Netherlands, Spain, Sweden, Switzerland, United Kingdom
Associate Member: Austria
Observer Countries: Canada, Norway
Chairman of Council: Jan Stiernstedt
Director General: Erik Quistgaard
Director, Administration: Georges Van Reeth
Director, Scientific Programme: Ernst Trendelenburg
Director, Applications Programme: Edmond Mallett
Director, Space Transportation Systems: Michel Bignier
Activities: Set up on 31 May 1975; ESA groups in a single body the complete range of European space activities previously conducted by ESRO and ELDO in their respective fields of satellite development and launcher construction. Under the terms of its Convention, the Agency's task is to provide for and promote, for exclusively peaceful purposes, cooperation among European States in space research and technology, with a view to their use for scientific purposes and for operation

space applications systems. ESA's current programme comprises: five scientific satellites - Exosat (for determination of the position and structure of celestial X-ray sources); Space Telescope (a joint ESA/NASA programme); ISPM (a joint ESA/NASA programme to explore the regions distant from the plane of the Earth's orbit, and in particular the space above the poles of the Sun); Giotto (a cometary mission), and Hipparcos (a satellite for astrometrical measurements). Seven applications satellites - Meteosat 2 (a meteorological satellite); Marecs A and B (for maritime comunications); Sirio 2 (for Earth observation); ECS 1 and 2 (for communications), and L-SAT (for direct broadcasting). Spacelab (a manned space laboratory, due for launch by NASA's Space Shuttle, for space research and applications in astronomy, solar physics, high-energy astrophysics, life sciences, earth resources survey, communications, weather observation, space processing and manufacturing, etc). Ariane (a heavy launcher, giving Europe a launch capability for its own applications and scientific satellites).

EUROPEAN SPACE OPERATIONS CENTRE   37

– ESOC
Address: Robert-Bosch Strasse 5, D-6100 Darmstadt, German FR
Telephone: (06151) 88 61
Telex: 419453 ESOC-D
Director: Dr R.O. Steiner
Sections: ESA computer, K. Debatin; ground systems engineering, B. Walker; meteorological data management, J.A. Jensen; mission analysis, Dr E. Roth; mission and technical coordination, Dr H. Kummer
Graduate research staff: 104
Annual expenditure: over £2m
Activities: All satellite operations and corresponding ground facilities and communications networks, including determination of spacecraft orbit and attitude; in-orbit satellite operation, including control and monitoring (of ESA and some non-ESA satellites), acquisition, processing and analysis of satellite data, and the storage, retrieval and distribution of data for the users community. Responsible for all computer facilities of ESA and production of the Agency's software. Research in various fields (satellite dynamics, satellite control, data processing, numerical methods, data transmission) mainly in view of future projects.
Facilities: Include a central control centre in Darmstadt and telemetry, tracking and control facilities at Michelstadt, Belgium, Spain, French Guiana and Australia; in addition to these sites, ground stations are being used by ESOC in Kenya, Italy, Sweden and Gran Canaria, Spain.
Contract work: Yes
Publications: Scientific papers and articles.

EUROPEAN SPACE RESEARCH AND TECHNOLOGY CENTRE   38

– ESTEC
Address: Zwarteweg 62, Noordwijk aan Zee, Netherlands
Telephone: 1719 86555
Telex: 39135-39098
Director: Massimo Trella
Activities: Responsible for the study, development, control and testing of spacecraft, which are built by European industry; carrying out the technological research programme for the preparation of future missions.

EUROPEAN SPACE RESEARCH INSTITUTE   39

– ESRIN
Address: Via Galileo Galilei, CP 64, 00044 Frascati Roma, Italy
Head: Tim Howell
Activities: Responsible for Earthnet activities (remote sensing of Earth resources) and for the Information Retrieval Service (IRS).
Several technical teams are located in national establishments for the conduct of certain programmes: the Earth Observations Programme Department in the CNES Space Centre at Toulouse (France); SPICE (Spacelab Payload Integration and Coordination in Europe in the DFVLR at Porz-Wahn (Germany); the Ariane Launch Site (ELA) at the Guiana Space Centre at Kourou (French Guiana). The Agency also has an office in Washington for liaison with NASA and plays an important role in the coordination of activities under the ESRANGE special project, relating to the launching of sounding rockets and balloons.

Eurotransplant Foundation/ Stichting Eurotransplant Nederland   40

Address: c/o Bloodbank, University Hospital, Rijnsburgerweg 10, 2333 AA Leiden, Netherlands
Telephone: (071) 147 222
Telex: 39266 eurtr nl
Research director: Professor J.J. van Rood
Administration director: B. Cohen
Sections: Transplantation; immunology
Graduate research staff: 4
Annual expenditure: £51 000-2m
Activities: Research on transplantation of donor organs, and immunology.

Federation of Astronomical and Geophysical Services* 41

– FAGS

Address: (Secretariat): Service de la Géodésie, IGN, avenue Pasteur 2, 94160 Saint Mandé, France
Telephone: 374 12 15
Affiliation: International Council of Scientific Unions
President: Dr H. Enslin
Vice-President: Professor E. Kejlsø
Secretary: C.D. Boucher
Permanent Services: Bureau International de l'Heure, Dr B. Guinot
International Service of Geomagnetic Indices, Dr D. van Sabben
International Polar Motion Service, Dr S. Yumi
Bureau Gravimétrique International, Dr J.J. Levallois
Quarterly Bulletin on Solar Activity, Dr F. Moriyana
Permanent Service for Mean Sea Level, Dr D.T. Pugh
International Centre for Earth Tides, Professor P. Melchior
International Ursigram and World Days Service, Dr P. Simon
Permanent Service on Fluctuation of Glaciers, Professor F. Müller
Activities: Established by ICSU in 1956 the Federation includes nine permanent services each of which operates under the authority of one or more of the interested Unions: IAU, IUGG and URSI.

General Fisheries Council for the Mediterranean/ Conseil General des Preches pour la Méditerranée 42

– GFCM

Address: FAO, Viale delle Terme di Caracalla, 00100 Roma, Italy
Telephone: 797 6616
Secretary: D. Charbonnier
Activities: To promote in the Mediterranean and the Black Sea the development, conservation, rational management and best utilization of living marine resources; to keep under review the economic and social aspects of the fishing industry and recommend any measures aimed at its development; to encourage, recommend and, as appropriate, undertake training, extension, research and development activities in all aspects of fisheries including the protection of living marine resources.

Group of Experts on the Scientific Aspects of Marine Pollution 43

– GESAMP

Address: 101-104 Piccadilly, London, W1V 0AE, United Kingdom
Telephone: (01) 499 9040
Telex: 23588 INMARCOR
Affiliation: IMCO, FAO, UNESCO, WMO, WHO, IAEA, UN, UNEP
Director: Y. Sasamura
Graduate research staff: 24
Annual expenditure: £51 000-500 000
Activities: The Group is composed of experts nominated by the Intergovernmental Maritime Consultative Organization (IMCO), the Food and Agriculture Organization (FAO), UNESCO, WMO, WHO, IAEA, UN and the United Nations Environment Programme (UNEP), to advise the organizations on the scientific aspects of marine pollution, especially those of interdisciplinary nature, and to consider the development of programmes on the oceanographic research aspects of marine pollution, including monitoring.
Contract work: Yes
Publications: Reports and studies.

Groupement Européen d'Études Spatiales 44

– Eurospace
[European Space Study Group]
Address: 16 bis, avenue Bosquet, 75007 Paris, France
Telephone: 555 83 53
Telex: 270 716 AIRLIQ
Director of Studies: Marcel Toussaint
Sections: Space technology; telecommunications; earth sciences; new energy sources
Activities: Conducting projects on space technology, satellites, telecommunications, earth sciences and meteorology for those organizations involved in space technology.
Contract work: Yes

Hochalpine. 45
Forschungsstationen
Jungfraujoch und
Gornergrat

[Scientific stations of Jungfraujoch and Gornergrat]
Address: Sidlerstrasse 5, CH-3012 Bern, Switzerland
President, International Jungfraujoch Foundation: Professor Hermann Debrunner
Activities: To facilitate research by scientists of all countries in all branches of science where high-altitude research is of importance.

ICSU Panel on World Data 46
Centres (Geophysical and
Solar)*

Address: (Secretariat): National Academy of Sciences, 2101 Constitution Avenue, Washington DC 20418, USA
Affiliation: International Council of Scientific Unions
Chairman: Sir Granville Beynon
Honorary Secretary: Dr E.R. Dyer
Activities: Established by ICSU in 1968 to advise the Officers of ICSU on the management of World Data centres, the Panel has members studying: meteorology, oceanology, polar research, solid earth geophysics, space and water research and has a steering committee on radioactive waste disposal.

COMMITTEE ON RADIOACTIVE 47
WASTE DISPOSAL*

Chairman: Dr J.M. Harrison
Activities: Steering Committee established to study radioactive waste disposal.

INCA-FIEJ Research 48
Association

– IFRA
Address: 1 Washingtonplatz, D-6100 Darmstadt, German FR
Telephone: (061) 5176057
Managing Director: Dr F.W. Burkhardt
Research Manager: Nils Enlund
Activities: Technical development of the newspaper industry: electronic production systems, development of newsprint, newsink, printing plates and newspaper printing processes; information and documentation service, symposia, annual congress and exhibition, advisory research, research and development.

Inter-Union Commission on 49
Frequency Allocations for
Radio Astronomy and
Space Science*

– IUCAF
Address: (Secretariat): 10 Clarence Drive, Egham, Surrey TW20 0NL, United Kingdom
Affiliation: International Council of Scientific Unions
Chairman: Dr J.P. Hagen
Secretary: Dr F. Horner
Activities: Set up in 1960 by ICSU to study and coordinate the requirements for radiofrequency allocations for radioastronomy and space science; to take action aimed at ensuring that harmful interference is not caused to radioastronomy or space science, operating within the allocated bands, by other radio services.

Inter-Union Commission on 50
Radio Meteorology*

– IUCRM
Address: (Secretariat): US Department of Commerce, NOAA/WRL, 325 Broadway, Boulder CO 80302, USA
Affiliation: International Council of Scientific Unions
President: Dr S. Wickerts
Secretary: Dr J.C. Kaimal
Activities: Set up in 1959 by ICSU to study meteorology and oceanography as they affect the propagation of electromagnetic waves in the earth's atmosphere and over its surface and through planetary atmospheres; to further the application of electromagnetic techniques to meteorology.

Inter-Union Commission on 51
Spectroscopy*

– IUCS
Address: (Secretariat): 51 boulevard de Montmorency, 75016 Paris, France
Affiliation: International Council of Scientific Unions
Members: Professor B. Edlen (IAU); Professor I. Kovacs (IUPAP); Professor M.A. Elyshevich (IUPAC)
Activities: Established by ICSU in 1966 the Commission works mainly by correspondence.

Inter-Union Commission on the Application of Science to Agriculture, Forestry and Aquaculture* 52

– CASAFA
Address: (Secretariat): 51 boulevard de Montmorency, Paris 75016, France
Telephone: 527 77 02
Affiliation: International Council of Scientific Unions
Chairman: Dr J.H. Hulse
Ad hoc Secretary: F.W.G. Baker
Activities: Established by ICSU in 1978 to study, research and report on the application of science to agriculture, forestry and aquaculture.

Inter-Union Commission on the Lithosphere* 53

– ICL
Address: (Secretariat): University of British Columbia, 2075 Wesbrook Place, Vancouver V6T IW5, Canada
Telephone: 228 4132
Telex: 04 54245
Affiliation: International Council of Scientific Unions
President: Professor A.L. Hales
Secretary-General: Professor R.D. Russell
Activities: Set up as a Commission on geodynamics (ICG) in 1969, to study the lithosphere through their working groups on: geodynamics; Earth's interior; tectonic, metamorphic and magmatic processes; global syntheses and paleoreconstructions; data centres; and exchange.

Intergovernmental Oceanographic Commission 54

Address: 7 place de Fontenoy, 75700 Paris, France
Telephone: 577 16 10
Telex: 204461 Paris
Affiliation: United Nations Educational, Scientific and Cultural Organization
Chairman: Dr A. Ayaia-Castañares
Secretary: Dr Mario Ruivo
Subsidiary bodies:
IOC Association for the Caribbean and adjacent regions (IOCARIBE), Dr M. Murillo
IOC Working Committee for Global Investigation of Pollution in the Marine Environment (GIPME), Dr V. Gruzinov
IOC Working Committee for Integrated Global Ocean Station System (IGOSS), J. Holland
IOC Working Committee for International Oceanographic Data Exchange (IODE), T. Winterfeld
IOC Working Committee for Training, Education and Mutual Assistance (TEMA), Dr U. Lie
Activities: The purpose of the Commission is to promote scientific investigation with a view to learning more about the nature and resources of the oceans through the concerted action of its members. Functions are: to define those problems the solution of which requires international cooperation in the field of scientific investigation of the oceans and review the results of such investigations; to develop, recommend and coordinate with interested international organizations, international programmes for scientific investigation of the oceans and related services which call for concerted action; to make recommendations to international organizations concerning activities of such organizations which relate to the Commission's programme; to promote and make recommendations for the exchange of oceanographic data and the publication and dissemination of results of scientific investigation of the oceans; to make recommendations to strengthen education and training programmes in marine science and its technology; to develop assistance programmes in marine science and its technology; to make recommendations and provide technical guidance as to the formulation and execution of marine science programmes of UNESCO; and to promote freedom of scientific investigation of the oceans for the benefit of all mankind, taking into account all interests and rights of coastal countries concerning scientific research in the zones under their jurisdiction. In carrying out its functions, the Commission bears in mind the special needs and interests of developing countries, including in particular the need to further the capabilities of these countries in marine science and technology.
Contract work: Yes
Publications: Biennial report of IOC, IOC manuals and guides series, technical workshop series.

Internasjonalt Massemedia Institutt 55

– IMMI
[International Mass Media Institute]
Address: Kongensgt. 2B, Postboks 650, 4601 Kristiansand S, Norway
Telephone: 042 24848
Telex: 21008 haaco-n
Director of training and research: Gudm. Gjelsten
Graduate research staff: 3
Annual expenditure: £10 000-50 000
Activities: Satellite broadcasting; media ethics; media and missions.
Contract work: Yes

Internatienaal Agrarische Centrum

56

– IAC
[International Agricultural Centre]
Address: Postbus 88, 6700 AB Wageningen, Netherlands
Telephone: (08370) 19040
Telex: 45888 NL
Affiliation: Netherlands Ministry of Agriculture and Fisheries; Netherlands Universities Foundation for International Cooperation
Director: Ir A.H. Haak
Sections: Development projects and experts, Ir L. Razoux Schultz; training, Ir B.J. Buntjer
Activities: Coordination of all agricultural expertise in the Netherlands in the interest of cooperation for development in the Third World. In this capacity IAC is an advisory body to the Ministers of Agriculture and Fisheries and of Development Cooperation.
Publications: Agricultural Science in the Netherlands.

Internationaal Bodenkundig Museum

57

– ISM
[International Soil Museum]
Address: Duivendaal 9, PO Box 353, 6700 AJ Wageningen, Netherlands
Telephone: (08370) 19063
Director: Dr W.G. Sombroek
Sections: Soils, J.H.V. van Baren; micromorphology, D. Creutzberg; laboratories, Dr L.P. van Reeuwijk
Graduate research staff: 3
Annual expenditure: £10 000-50 000
Activities: Centre for research and information, where background material and documentation on the soils of the world are available. The central aim is to collect and display illustrative sample material of the major soils. In addition, ISM is: gradually building up a systematic collection of soil maps; involved in international efforts to correlate soil classification systems; under the encouragement of the FAO, serving as a clearing house for new soil data with the intention of updating the *Soil Map of the World*; taking the initiative for a comparison of methods and procedures of laboratory methods for soil classification purposes, and considering the build up of a base-line collection of uncontaminated soil materials to be used as a reference for soil studies by generations to come.
Contract work: Yes
Publications: Annual reports, soil monolith papers, technical papers, monographs, history and programme of ISM.

International Agency for Research on Cancer/Centre International de Recherche sur le Cancer

58

Address: 150 cours Albert-Thomas, 69372 Lyon Cedex 2, France
Telephone: 75 81 81
Telex: 380023
Affiliation: World Health Organization
Director: Dr J. Higginson
Activities: To promote international collaboration in cancer research.

International Astronomical Union/Union Astronomique Internationale

59

– IAU
Address: 61 avenue de l'Observatoire, 75014 Paris, France
Telephone: 325 83 58
Affiliation: International Council of Scientific Unions
General Secretary: Professor Patrick A. Wayman
Assistant General Secretary: Dr Richard M. West
Annual expenditure: £10 000-50 000
Activities: The aims of the Union are largely achieved through the work of the following commissions; ephemerides; documentation; astronomical telegrams; celestial mechanics; positional astronomy; astronomical instruments; solar activity; radiation and structure of the solar atmosphere; fundamental spectroscopic data; physical study of comets, minor planets and meteorites; physical study of planets and satellites; rotation of the Earth; positions and motions of minor planets, comets and satellites; the light of the night sky; meteors and interplanetary dust; photographic astrometry; stellar photometry and polarimetry; double stars; variable astrometry; stellar photometry and polarimetry; double stars; variable stars; galaxies; stellar spectra; radial velocities; time; the structure and dynamics of the galactic system; interstellar matter and planetary nebulae; stellar constitution; the theory of stellar atmospheres; star clusters and associations; exchange of astronomers; radio astronomy; history of astronomy; close binary stars; astronomical observations from space; stellar classifications; the teaching of astronomy; cosmology; high-energy astrophysics; the interplanetary plasma and the heliosphere; and protection of existing and potential observatory sites.
Contract work: No
Publications: Information bulletins, symposia proceedings, transactions of the IAU.

International Atomic Energy Agency/Agence Internationale de l'Energie Atomique/Organismo Internacional de Energia Atomica

60

– IAEA
Address: Vienna International Centre, Wagramerstrasse 5, POB 100, A-1400 Wien, Austria
Director General: Sigvard A. Eklund
Divisions: Scientific and Technical Information, Harold E. Pryor; Nuclear Power and Reactors, Hans-Juergen Laue; Nuclear Safety and Environmental Protection, Syed Fareeduddin; Research and Laboratories, Vitaliy Frolov; Life Sciences, Krishna Sundaram; Development and Technical Support, Adolf von Baeckmann; Safeguards Information Treatment, Vladimir Shmelev; Operations (A), Frantisek Klik; Operations (B), Harumitsu Iwamoto; Technical Assistance, Svasti Srisukh
Activities: The Agency seeks to accelerate and enlarge the contribution of atomic energy to peace, health and prosperity throughout the world, and ensure, so far as it is able, that assistance provided by it or at its request or under its supervision or control is not used in such a way as to further any military purpose.
Member countries: Afghanistan, Albania, Algeria, Argentina, Australia, Austria, Bangladesh, Belgium, Bolivia, Brazil, Bulgaria, Burma, Byelorussian SSR, Cambodia, Cameroon, Canada, Chile, Colombia, Costa Rica, Cuba, Cyprus, Czechoslovakia, Denmark, Dominican Republic, Ecuador, Egypt, El Salvador, Ethiopia, Finland, France, Gabon, German DR, German FR, Ghana, Greece, Guatemala, Haiti, Holy See, Hungary, Iceland, India, Indonesia, Iran, Iraq, Ireland, Israel, Italy, Ivory Coast, Jamaica, Japan, Jordan, Kenya, Korea DPR, Korea (Republic of), Kuwait, Lebanon, Liberia, Libyan Arab Republic, Liechtenstein, Luxembourg, Malagasy, Malaysia, Mali, Mauritius, Mexico, Monaco, Mongolia, Morocco, Netherlands, New Zealand, Niger, Nigeria, Norway, Pakistan, Panama, Paraguay, Peru, Philippines, Poland, Portugal, Qatar, Romania, Saudi Arabia, Senegal, Sierra Leone, Singapore, South Africa, Spain, Sri Lanka, Sudan, Sweden, Switzerland, Syrian Arab Republic, Tanzania, Thailand, Tunisia, Turkey, Uganda, Ukrainian SSR, USSR, United Arab Emirates, United Kingdom, USA, Uruguay, Venezuela, Yugoslavia, Zaire, Zambia

DEPARTMENT OF RESEARCH AND ISOTOPES

61

Deputy Director-general: Maurizio Zifferero

Seibersdorf Laboratory

62

Address: A-2444 Seibersdorf, Nieder Osterreich, Austria
Telephone: 02254 2251
Telex: 1-12645
Head: Maurizio Zifferero
Head of Laboratory: G.G. Cook
Graduate research staff: 25
Activities: Plant/soil relationship (fertilizers); mutation plant breeding; entomology (SIT); analytical chemistry with special reference to uranium and plutonium analysis; isotope hydrology; nuclear medicine; dosimetry; electronics and absolute measurement of nuclear radiation.

DEPARTMENT OF SAFEGUARDS

63

Deputy director-general: Hans Gruemm

DEPARTMENT OF TECHNICAL ASSISTANCE AND PUBLICATIONS

64

Deputy director-general: Carlos Velez Ocon

DEPARTMENT OF TECHNICAL OPERATIONS

65

Deputy director-general: Ivan Zheludev

INTERNATIONAL CENTRE FOR THEORETICAL PHYSICS

66

Address: PO Box 586, Trieste, Italy
Director: Professor Dr Abdus Salam
Activities: Since 1970 the Centre has been operated jointly by IAEA and the United Nations Educational, Scientific, and Cultural Organization. It helps in fostering studies of theoretical physics in developing countries and conducts research in theoretical physics on a broad basis through visiting professors and fellows.
Date of foundation: 1964

INTERNATIONAL LABORATORY OF MARINE RADIOACTIVITY

67

Address: Oceanographic Museum, Monaco-Ville, Monaco
Head: Dr Alan Walton
Activities: Effects of radioactivity in the sea; effect of certain non-radioactive pollutants on the sea and on marine life.
Date of foundation: 1961

JOINT FOOD AND AGRICULTURE ORGANIZATION-IAEA DIVISION OF ATOMIC ENERGY IN FOOD AND AGRICULTURE   68

Director: Dr Maurice Fried
Activities: Promotion of use of radiation and radioisotopes in the soil sciences, plant breeding and genetics, animal production and health, insect and pest control, chemical residues and pollution, and in food preservation.
Date of foundation: 1964

International Commission of Sugar Technology/ Commission Internationale Technique de Sucrerie   69

– CITS
Address: 1 Aandorenstraat, B-3300 Tienen, Belgium
President of Scientific Committee: Professor F. Schneider
General Secretary: Dr R. Pieck
Activities: To promote scientific and technical research work in the sugar industry.

International Commission on Radiological Protection   70

– ICRP
Address: Clifton Avenue, Sutton, Surrey SM2 5PU, United Kingdom
Telephone: (01) 642 4680
Telex: 895 1244 ICRP G
Affiliation: International Congress of Radiology
Chairman: Professor B. Lindell
Vice-Chairman: D.J. Beninson
Scientific secretary: Dr F.D. Sowby
Sections: Radiation effects, D.J. Beninson; secondary limits, J. Vennart; protection in medicine, C.B. Meinhold; recommendation applications, H. Jammet
Annual expenditure: £40 000
Activities: Collection of data relevant to the establishment of recommendations on all aspects of protection against ionizing radiations. The policy adopted by the Commission in preparing its recommendations is to consider the fundamental principles upon which appropriate radiation protection measures can be based while leaving to the various national protection bodies the responsibility of formulating the specific advice, codes of practice, or regulations that are best suited to the needs of their individual countries. Much of the work of ICRP is performed by ad hoc task groups and studies include: a review of non-stochastic effects of irradiation; annual limits of intake for the general public; doses to patients from radiopharmaceuticals; radiation protection in medicine; protection of the patient in radiodiagnosis and therapy; protection of the patient in radionuclide investigation; principles of environmental monitoring; the assessment of internal contamination resulting from uptake of radionuclides; general principles of monitoring of radiation workers; optimization of radiation protection; practices that modify man's exposure to nature background; and protection of the public in the event of radiation accidents.
Contract work: No
Publications: Reports, *Annals of the ICRP.*

International Committee on Aeronautical Fatigue   71

Address: Delft University of Technology, Department of Aerospace Engineering, Postbus 5058, 2600 GB Delft, Netherlands
Secretary: Professor J. Schijve
Activities: Collaboration on aeronautical fatigue among institutes and laboratories having aeronautical interests by means of exchange of documents on all aspects of fatigue problems of aircraft structures and by organizing biannual conferences combined with symposia. A National Centre in each of the following twelve countries collects and distributes information: Australia, Belgium, Canada, France, Germany FR, Israel, Italy, Netherlands, Sweden, Switzerland, UK and USA.

International Copper Research Association   72

Address: Brosnan House, Darkes Lane, Potters Bar, Hertfordshire EN6 lBW, United Kingdom
Telephone: (0707) 44577
Telex: 27711 INCRA G
European director: Brian B. Moreton
Annual expenditure: £501 000-2m
Activities: Contract research management organization funding research relating to new products and end use markets for copper and copper alloys.
Contract work: No

International Council for the Exploration of the Sea/ Conseil International pour l'Exploration de la Mer

73

Address: Palaegade 2-4, DK-1261 København K, Denmark
Telephone: (01) 15 42 25
Telex: 22498 ices dk
Member countries: Belgium, Canada, Denmark, Finland, France, Germany DR, Germany FR, Iceland, Ireland, Netherlands, Norway, Poland, Portugal, Spain, Sweden, UK, USA, USSR
President: G. Hempel
General Secretary: Hans Tambs-Lyche
Activities: Coordinates marine scientific activities of member countries such as monitoring of commercially important fish stocks, basic marine research, and investigations of marine pollution. Sponsors symposia and publishes scientific literature. Runs regional (North Atlantic) data centres for physical and chemical oceanography and for fishery statistics.

International Council of Scientific Unions/Conseil International des Unions Scientifiques/Consejo Internacional de Uniones Científicas

74

– ICSU
Address: 51 boulevard de Montmorency, 75016 Paris, France
Telephone: (01) 527 77 02
Telex: ICSU 630553F
President: Professor D.A. Bekoe (Ghana)
Secretary-General: Professor J.C.I. Dooge (Ireland)
Treasurer: Professor T.F. Malone (USA)
Vice-President: G.K. Skryabin (USSR)
Activities: The principal objective of ICSU is to encourage international scientific activity for the benefit of mankind. It does this by initiating, designing and coordinating international scientific research projects: the International Geophysical Year and the International Biological Programme are probably the best known examples. ICSU acts as a focus for the exchange of ideas, the communication of scientific information and the development of standards in methodology, nomenclature, units, etc. The various members of the ICSU family organize, in various parts of the world, conferences, congresses, symposia, and meetings of experts, as well as General Assemblies and other meetings to decide

policies and programmes. In 1980 more than 300 were organized. Committees or Commissions of ICSU are created to organize programmes in multi- or transdisciplinary fields which are not completely under the aegis of one of the Scientific Unions, such as Antarctic, Oceanic, Space and Water Research, and Problems of the Environment. Activities in areas common to all the Unions such as teaching of science, data, science and technology in developing countries, are also coordinated by committees. ICSU maintains close relations and works in cooperation with a number of international governmental and non-governmental organizations, and in particular UNESCO (with which ICSU has taken the initiative in launching a number of international programmes such as the International Indian Ocean Expedition, the World Science Information System, International Geological Correlation Project, etc) and with WMO (with which ICSU has launched the Global Atmospheric Research Programme and the World Climate Research Programme).
Members: National research councils, principal scientific institutes and academies in 68 countries, together with the following international scientific unions (date of incorporation in parentheses):
International Astronomical Union - IAU (1919)
International Union of Biochemistry - IUB (1955)
International Union of Biological Sciences - IUBS (1923)
International Union of Crystallography - IUCr (1947)
International Union of Geodesy and Geophysics - IUGG (1919)
International Geographical Union - IGU (1923)
International Union of Geological Sciences - IUGS (1961)
International Union for the History and Philosophy of Science - IUHPS (1947-1956)
International Union of Immunological Societies - IUIS (1976)
International Mathematical Union - IMU (1952)
International Union of Nutritional Sciences - IUNS (1968)
International Union of Pharmacology - IUPHAR (1972)
International Union of Physiological Sciences - IUPS (1955)
International Union of Pure and Applied Biophysics - IUPAB (1966)
International Union of Pure and Applied Chemistry - IUPAC (1919)
International Union of·Pure and Applied Physics - IUPAP (1922)
International Union of Radio Science - URSI (1919)
International Union of Theoretical and Applied Mechanics -IUTAM (1947)
Committees and Commissions:
Scientific Committee on Antarctic Research (SCAR)
Committee on Data for Science and Technology (CODATA)
Scientific Committee on Genetic Experimentation - COGENE (1976)

Scientific Committee on Oceanic Research (SCOR)
Scientific Committee on Problems of the Environment (SCOPE)
Committee on Radioactive Waste Disposal (1978)
Committee on Science and Technology in Developing Countries (COSTED)
Special Committee on Solar Terrestrial Physics (SCOSTEP)
Committee on Space Research (COSPAR)
Committee on the Teaching of Science
Scientific Committee on Water Research (COWAR)
Inter-Union Commission on the Application of Science to Agriculture, Forestry and Aquaculture - CASAFA (1978)
Inter-Union Commission on Frequency Allocations for Radio Astronomy and Space Science (IUCAF)
Inter-Union Commission on the Lithosphere (ICL)
Inter-Union Commission on Spectroscopy (IUCS)
Inter-Union Commission on Radio Meteorology (IUCRM)
Permanent Service:
ICSU Abstracting Board - ICSU AB (1953)
Federation of Astronomical and Geophysical Services - FAGS (1956)
ICSU Panel on World Data Centres (Geophysical and Solar)
Note: Those Unions, Committees or Commissions with a secretariat in Europe have been given a separate entry under their English language title in this International section.
Contract work: No
Publications: Year Book.

International Electronic Publishing Research Centre   75

- IEPRC
Address: Pira House, Randalls Road, Leatherhead, Surrey KT22 7RU, United Kingdom
Telephone: (03723) 76161
Telex: 929810 PIRA G
Affiliation: Pira, the Research Association for the Paper and Board, Printing and Packaging Industries, United Kingdom
Chief executive: Brian Blunden
Research manager: Tony Johnson
Head of research programmes: Yuri Gates
Graduate research staff: 4
Annual expenditure: £51 000-500 000
Activities: Technology monitoring in electronic publishing and associated areas; techno-economic forecasting studies; socio-technical environment studies; producer/user interface studies; market studies; technology studies; education and training projects; demonstration projects; development of publishers' performance

specifications; software commissioning and evaluation. Priority subjects: techno-economic forecast of electronic publishing technology; study of relationship between user needs and technology options for a document delivery service; study of data capture in publishing leading to standards for electronic document exchange through common input language via a multi-purpose work station.
Contract work: Yes

International Energy Agency/Agence Internationale de l'Énergie   76

- IEA
Address: 2 rue André-Pascal, 75775 Paris Cedex 16, France
Telephone: 524 82-00
Telex: 630190 ENERG A
Affiliation: Organization for Economic Cooperation and Development - OECD
Chairman, Governing Board: Ambassador H. Miyazaki
Executive Director: Dr U. Lantzke
Activities: The IEA was established by decision of the OECD Council on 15th November, 1974 to carry out their International Energy Programme. Twenty-one countries have agreed to participate in the Agency, which is open to all of the OECD countries that are able and willing to meet the requirements of the programme, and is also open for accession by the European Communities. IEA has been granted a special status within the framework of the OECD in order to give the Agency an opportunity to draw upon the resources of an existing organization in which IEA's members had already established programmes for economic cooperation, and to create new operational capabilities within the OECD while expanding upon the existing institutional apparatus of the organization. By 1980, the collaborative research, development and demonstration programme involved cooperation by member countries in fifty projects covering the following twelve technology areas: energy systems analysis, energy conservation, coal technology, enhanced recovery of oil, nuclear reactor safety, geothermal energy, solar energy, biomass conversion, ocean energy, wind energy, fusion energy and production of hydrogen from water.

International Geographical Union* 77

– IGU
Address: (Secretariat): Geographisches Institut, Universität Freiburg, D-7800 Freiburg im Breisgau, Werderring 4, German FR
Telephone: (0761) 203 4419
Affiliation: International Council of Scientific Unions
President: Professor M.J. Wise
Secretary-General: Professor W. Manshard
Activities: The Union promotes the study of geography on an international level by research and through the activities of its seventeen commissions and eleven working groups on: history of geographical thought; international geographical terminology; geographical education; geographical data sensing and processing; geomorphological survey and mapping; field experiments in geomorphology; international hydrological programme; geoecology on mountains; geography of transport, population geography; national settlement systems; agricultural productivity and world food supplies; rural development; coastal environment; industrial systems, policies and environmental problems.

International Hospital Federation/Fédération Internationale des Hôpitaux (FIH)/Federación Internacional de Hospitales (FIH) 78

– IHF
Address: 120-126 Albert Street, London, NW1, United Kingdom
Telephone: (01) 267 5176
Director General: M. Hardie
Assistant Director: Dorothy Maitland
Annual expenditure: £10 000-50 000
Activities: An independent non-political body that aims to promote improvements in the planning and management of hospitals and health services through international conferences, study tours, training courses, information services, publications and research and development projects on community mental health, improvement of health care in big cities, and encouraging closer collaboration between hospitals and primary health care services.
Contract work: No
Publications: Quarterly journal.

International Immunology Training and Research Centre 79

– ITR
Address: Plesmanlaan 125, 1066 CX Amsterdam, Netherlands
Telephone: (020) 5123445
Telex: Blood nl 13159
Parent body: Netherlands Universities Foundation for International Cooperation
Director: Dr K.W. Pondman
Activities: Immunology of schistosomiasis, leprosy, cell-membrane; tumour-immunology. Courses are organized in collaboration with World Health Organization and Central Laboratory of the Blood Transfusion Service of the Netherlands.

International Institute for Aerial Survey and Earth Sciences 80

Address: Postbus 6, 7500 AA Enschede, Netherlands
Telephone: (053) 320330
Telex: 44525
Parent body: Netherlands Universities Foundation for International Cooperation
Rector: Dr Ir K.J. Beek
Sections: Photogrammetry, Professor Dr Ing H.G. Jerie; natural resources, Professor Dr Ir I.S. Zonneveld; social sciences, Professor Dr Ir A.H. Luning
Activities: Provision of courses in photogrammetry; aerial photography; cartography; geomorphological survey, applied geomorphology and geographical landscape analysis; soil, geological, forest, urban and rural surveys; remote sensing; mineral exploration and exploration geophysics; multidisciplinary investigations for development planning. Some research is also carried on in these areas.
Publications: ITC Journal, quarterly.

International Institute for Applied Systems Analysis 81

– IIASA
Address: Schloss Laxenburg, Schlossplatz 1, A-2361 Laxenburg, Austria
Telephone: (02236) 715210
Telex: 079137
Director: Dr Roger E. Levien
Sections: Energy systems programme, Professor Wolf

Haefele; food and agriculture programme, Professor Kirit Parikh; resources and environment area, Dr Janusz Kindler; human settlements and services area, Professor Andrei Rogers; management and technology area, Alec Lee; system and decision sciences area, Professor Andrzej P. Wierzbicki
Graduate research staff: 100
Annual expenditure: Sch143.65m
Activities: IIASA is an informational research institute whose members are not nations, but scientific institutions from each of the 17 participating nations. It applies modern analytic tools to major problems of global concern, seeking to strengthen international collaboration and contribute to the advancement of science and systems analysis. With research programmes on energy systems and food and agriculture, research areas are resources and environment, human settlements and services, management and technology, and system and decision sciences. Participating institutions include The Academy of Sciences of the Union of Soviet Socialist Republics, The National Academy of Sciences, United States of America, The Royal Society of London, United Kingdom, and The Swedish Committee for Systems Analysis.
Date of foundation: 1972
Contract work: Yes

International Institute for   82
Cotton, Technical Research
Division

Address: Kingston Road, Didsbury, Manchester M20 8RD, United Kingdom
Telephone: (061) 4458141
Telex: 669671
Affiliation: International Institute for Cotton
Activities: The International Institute for Cotton (ITC) was established in 1966, and funding is provided by a levy on net exports of raw cotton and cotton textiles by the member countries (Argentina, Brazil, Greece, India, Ivory Coast, Mexico, Nigeria, Spain, Tanzania, Uganda, and USA). Programmes of technical research are directed by the Technical Research Division which works to create new and improved cotton products to ensure the preferential use of cotton in modern textile machinery and to improve cotton-specific processes. Research programmes are carried out in ITC laboratories and at research institutes and universities worldwide.
Publications: Cotton Market International.

International Institute for   83
Hydraulic and
Environmental Engineering

– IHE
Address: Postbus 3015, 2601 DA Delft, Netherlands
Parent body: Netherlands Universities Foundation for International Cooperation
Director: Professor Ir L.J. Mostertman
Activities: Provision of 11-month courses in hydraulics, health technology and environmental management for graduate engineers from other countries; annual 6-week port-management seminar for port directors from around the world. The Institute was founded by Delft University of Technology and Netherlands Universities Foundation for International Cooperation.

International Institute for   84
Land Reclamation and
Improvement

– ILRI
Address: Postbus 45, 6700 AA Wageningen, Netherlands
Telephone: (08370) 19100
Telex: 75230 VISI
Affiliation: Netherlands Ministry of Agriculture and Fisheries
Director: Ir F.E. Schulze
Graduate research staff: 15
Annual expenditure: £10 000-50 000
Activities: Irrigation; drainage; reclamation; soil science.
Contract work: No
Publications: Annual report.

International Institute for   85
Sugar Beet Research/
Institut International de
Recherches Betteraviéres/
Internationales Institut für
Zuckerrübenforschung

– IIRB
Address: Rue Montoyer, 47, B-1040 Bruxelles, Belgium
Telephone: (02) 512 65 06
Telex: IIRB 21 287
President: J. Lemaitre
Vice Presidents: H. Doblhoff-Dier, R. Esteruelas

Secretary General: L. Weickmans
Sections: Breeding and genetics, M.H. Arnold; pests and diseases, R.A. Dunning; agronomy and weed control, J.E. Nilsson; quality and storage, P. Devillers
Activities: Free exchange of results and discussions, concerning sugar beet physiology, genetics, seed, agricultural techniques, plant protection, and the organization of joint trials; pests and diseases; industrial quality and storage, animal feeding with by-products, agricultural machinery. Coordination of joint programmes on an international level.
Contract work: No
Publications: List of members, reports of study groups, Proceedings of winter congresses.

International Institute of Refrigeration/Institut International du Froid   86

Address: 177 boulevard Malesherbes, 75017 Paris, France
Telephone: 227 32 35
Research director: M. Anquez
Sections: Cryobiology; thermodynamics; biology and food science; refrigerated storage and transport; air conditioning and energy recovery
Activities: The diffusion of knowledge concerning refrigeration science and technology. A major part of the activities is, therefore, associated with scientific and technical information.
Contract work: Yes
Publications: General books, guides and recommendations, basic data, proceedings of meetings of scientific and technical commissions, *Journal of Refrigeration.*

International Laboratory of Marine Radioactivity   87

Address: Musée Océanographique, Monaco-Ville, Monaco
Telephone: 30 15 14
Telex: 469037 REMONA
Affiliation: International Atomic Energy Agency; Government of Monaco; Institut Océanographique
Director: Dr Alan Walton
Sections: Biology, Dr S.W. Fowler; chemistry, Dr R. Fukai; geochemistry, Dr S.R. Aston
Graduate research staff: 18
Annual expenditure: £501 000-2m
Activities: Chemical, biological and geochemical behaviour of radioactive and non-radioactive substances in the oceans including sea water, suspended matter, biota

and sediments. Intercalibration and quality control studies for transuranic elements and some non-radioactive pollutants.
Contract work: Yes
Publications: Series on radioactivity in the sea (RITS), research reports and Congress papers.

International Mathematical Union*   88

– IMU
Address: (Secretariat): College de France, 11 rue Marcelin-Berthelot, 75005 Paris, France
Telephone: 954 9020
Affiliation: International Council of Scientific Unions
President: Professor L. Carleson
Secretary: Professor J.L. Lions
Activities: The Union promotes the study of mathematics through the work of its two commissions on: mathematical instruction; development and exchange.

International Organization for Biological Control Against Noxious Animals and Plants/Organisation Internationale de Lutte Biologique Contre les Animaux et les Plantes Nuisibles   89

– OIBC
Address: 1 rue Le Notre, 75016 Paris, France
Telephone: 52077 94
Affiliation: International Union of Biological Sciences (IUBS)
Secretary-General: Dr G. Mathys
Graduate research staff: 400
Annual expenditure: £10 000-50 000
Activities: To promote biological control and the development of pest management systems on a global level. Research on alternative methods for crop protection and vector control of human diseases.
Contract work: No
Publications: Entomophaga.

International Society for   90
Mushroom Science

Address: Institut für Bodenbiologie, Bundesforschungsanstalt für Landwirtschaft, Bundesallee 50, D-3300 Braunschweig, German FR
Affiliation: International Society for Horticultural Science; International Union of Biological Science
Executive Officer and Secretary-Treasurer: Dr Klaus Grabbe
Activities: Promoting research in the field of nutrition, preparation of substrate, environment, genetics, cost price, labour, marketing; cultivation of edible fungi.
Publications: Mushroom Science, Conference papers.

International   91
Telecommunication Union/
Union Intérnationale des
Télécommunications

– ITU
Address: Place des Nations, CH-1211 Genève 20, Switzerland
Secretary-General: Mohamed E. Mili
Deputy Secretary-General: Richard E. Butler
Technical bodies:
International Frequency Registration Board (IFRB), Chairman: Abderrazak Berrada; Vice-Chairman: Petr Sergeevich Kurakov
International Radio Consultative Committee (CCIR), Director: Richard C. Kirby
International Telegraph and Telephone Consultative Committee (CCITT), Director: Leon Burtz
Activities: The ITU, which is comprised of 154 member countries, aims to maintain and extend international cooperation for the improvement and rational use of telecommunication of all kinds; to promote the development of technical facilities and their most efficient operation with a view to improving the efficiency of telecommunication services, increasing their usefulness and making them, as far as possible, generally available to the public; and to harmonize the actions of nations in the attainment of these common ends. ITU works to fulfil these basic aims in three main ways: international conferences and meetings; publication of information; and technical cooperation.

International Tin Research   92
Institute

Address: Fraser Road, Perivale, Greenford, Middlesex UB6 7AQ, United Kingdom
Telephone: (01) 997 4254
Director: Dr D.A. Robins
Research manager: Dr C.J. Thwaites
Sections: Chemistry Division, Dr P.J. Smith; Metallurgy and Tinplate Division, Dr M.E. Warwick
Graduate research staff: 40
Activities: Development of tin-containing materials for new application areas in order to promote increased consumption of tin.
Facilities: Electron microscopy, X-ray analysis, activation analysis, trace element analysis, ultraviolet, infrared, nuclear magnetic resonance, Mössbauer, small foundry, rolling mill and wire drawing.
Contract work: No
Publications: Tin and its Uses (English, French, German, Italian, Spanish, Japanese).

International Union for the   93
History and Philosophy of
Science*

– IUHPS
Address: (Secretariat): History Department, University of Edinburgh, Edinburgh, United Kingdom
Telephone: (031) 667 1011
Affiliation: International Council of Scientific Unions
President: Professor A.T. Grigorian
Secretary-General: Professor E.G. Forbes
Divisions: History of Science, Professor A.T. Grigorian (President); Logic, Methodology and Philosophy of Science, Professor J. Los (President)
Activities: The Union promotes the study of the history and philosophy of science through the work of the Divisions committees and commissions on: publications, bibliography; scientific instruments; teaching; documentation; modern physics; mathematics; oceanography; science in the Renaissance; history of technology; historical metrology; science policy; and history of geography, astronomy, geological science.

International Union of Biochemistry* 94

– IUB

Address: (Secretariat): Biochemistry-UMED, PO Box 016129, Miami, FL33101, USA
Telephone: (305) 547 6265
Telex: 519308
Affiliation: International Council of Scientific Unions
Activities: Through its committees and groups the Union meets its objectives of promoting study and research into biochemistry on: biothermodynamics; bioenergetics; carbohydrate chemistry and biochemistry; metabolic regulation; nomenclature and coordination.

International Union of Biological Sciences/Union Internationale des Sciences Biologiques 95

– IUBS

Address: 51 boulevard de Montmorency, 75016 Paris, France
Telephone: 525 00 09
Telex: ICSU: 630553 F
Affiliation: International Council of Scientific Unions
President: Professor E. De Robertis (Argentina)
Secretary-General: Professor E.S. Ayensu (USA)
Executive Secretary: Dr Talal Younès (France)
Activities: The Union aims to promote international cooperation in the biological sciences through the work of its Divisions and Sections:
Division of Botany (with sections for palaeobotany, plant taxonomy, plant pathology, and horticultural science, and commissions on nomenclature, botanic gardens, palynology, algology, plant protection, mycology, bee botany, mushroom science and succulent lants).
Division of Zoology (with sections for general zoology, comparative endocrinology, entomology, ornithology, parasitology, palaeozoology and zoological nomenclature, and commissions on primatology, bryozoology, protozoology, invertebrate pathology, and social insects).
Division of Functional and Analytical Biology (with sections for cell biology, development biology, experimental psychology and animal behaviour, genetics, plant physiology, radiobiology, and plant growth substances, and commissions on biochemistry, biometry, ethology, photobiology, physiology, and biophysics).
Division of Environment (with sections for ecology, limnology, human biology, oceanography, and biological control and commissions on quaternary biology, plant geography and ecology, small-scale vegetation maps, and aerobiology).
Publications: Biology International.

International Union of Crystallography 96

– IUCr

Address: (Executive Secretary): 5 Abbey Square, Chester CH1 2HU, United Kingdom
Telephone: (0244) 428 78
Telex: 667325 COMCA G attention UNICRYSTAL
Affiliation: International Council of Scientific Unions
President: Professor N. Kato (Japan)
General-Secretary: Professor S.E. Rasmussen (Denmark)
Executive Secretary: Dr J.N. King
Activities: The Union promotes international cooperation in crystallography and its commissions include those for charge, spin and momentum densities; crystal growth; crystallographic apparatus, computing, data, and nomenclature; crystallographic studies at controlled pressures and temperatures; crystallographic teaching; electron diffraction, and neutron diffraction.
Contract work: No

International Union of Geodesy and Geophysics/ Union Géodésique et Géophysique Internationale 97

– IUGG

Address: Observatoire Royal de Belgique, Avenue Circulaire 3, B-1180 Bruxelles, Belgium
Telephone: (02) 374 38 01
Telex: 21565 OBS BEL
Affiliation: International Council of Scientific Unions
Secretary-General: Professor Paul Melchior
Associations:
International Association of Geodesy (IAG/AIG)
International Association of Seismology and Physics of the Earth's Interior (IASPEI/AISPIT)
International Association of Volcanology and Chemistry of the Earth's Interior (IAVCEI/AIVCIT)
International Association of Geomagnetism and Aeronomy (IAGA/AIGA)
International Association of Meteorology and Atmospheric Physics (IAMAP/AIMPA)
International Association of Hydrological Sciences (IAHS/AISH)
International Association for the Physical Sciences of the Ocean (IAPSO/AISPO)
Activities: To promote and coordinate physical, chemical and mathematical studies of the Earth and its immediate spatial environment. These studies cover the geometrical form (shape), gravitational and magnetic fields of the Earth, its internal structure and seismicity, volcanism whether on the surface or submarine, the

hydrological cycle and glaciers, the Earth's oceans, atmosphere, ionosphere, magnetosphere, solar terrestrial relation and similar problems as related to the Moon and other planets. The scope of the Union activities also embraces studies of the Earth by artificial satellites and by other techniques for deploying instruments at latitude above the ground. The IUGG has in the past been responsible for initiating the collaborative action that has led to such intensive worldwide cooperative research programmes as the International Geophysical Year (1957-58), the Upper Mantle Project (1964-70), and the Global Atmospheric Research Programme (1970-80). With 78 member countries, the IUGG cooperates with UNESCO in the study of natural catastrophes. It is also represented on the ICSU Committee for Science and Technology in Developing Countries, and gives particular emphasis to the scientific problems of such areas by sponsoring symposia relevant to the scientific needs of the Third World (eg Geodesy in Africa, International Water Resources, etc).
The Union also co-sponsors the Federation of Astronomical and Geophysical Services (FAGS) and is a partner with other Unions of ICSU in Inter-Union Commissions.
The Union itself comprises seven semi-autonomous Associations, each responsible for a specific range of studies within the overall scope of the Union's activities. Owing to the interactive nature of the subject fields managed by the Union's Associations, a number of Inter-Association Commissions have been established which serve the Union and the international geophysical community by promoting the study of particular interdisciplinary problems.
Contract work: Yes
Publications: The Union and the Associations publish information bulletins periodically as well as the proceedings of meetings of the Associations and of symposia sponsored by the Associations.

International Union of Geological Sciences/Union Internationale des Sciences Géologiques
98

– IUGS
Address: (Secretariat): Maison de la Géologie, 77 rue Claude Bernard, 75005 Paris, France
Telephone: (01) 707 9196
Telex: BRGM 780258 F BURGEOL
Affiliation: International Council of Scientific Unions
President: Professor E. Seibold
Secretary-General: Dr C.C. Weber
Treasurer: Dr J.A. Reinemund
Activities: To encourage and promote the study of

geological problems of a fundamental or applied character, of the Earth and of other planets where relevant data contribute to an increased understanding of the Earth; to facilitate the investigation of geological problems which require interdisciplinary and international cooperation and to promote such cooperation; to collaborate with the International Geological Congress, which provides a forum for individual geologists from all parts of the world for presentation and discussion of research in the geological sciences and its results, and to safeguard the long-established activities of the Congress. These objectives are realized through the work of its commissions and committees on: marine geology; meteorites; stratigraphy; systematics in petrology; experimental petrology; tectonics; geology teaching; geological documentation; storage, automatic processing and retrieval of data; history of geological sciences, publications; geoscience and man.

International Union of Immunological Societies*
99

– IUIS
Address: (Secretariat): Institute of Immunology and Rheumatology, Rikshopitalet University Hospital, Oslo 1, Norway
Telephone: (02) 201050
Affiliation: International Council of Scientific Unions
President: Professor M. Sela
Secretary General: Professor J.B. Natvig
Activities: Through its committees and regional organizations the Union meets its objective of promoting study and research of immunology on: clinical; education; nomenclature; standardization.

International Union of Nutritional Sciences/Union Internationale des Sciences de la Nutrition
100

– IUNS
Address: c/o Institute of Biology, 41 Queen's Gate, London, SW7 5HU, United Kingdom
Telephone: (01) 589 9076
Affiliation: International Council of Scientific Unions
Secretary-General: Miss D.F. Hollingsworth
Activities: Devoted to the study of nutrition and its applications, the union meets its objectives through its six commissions on: nomenclature, procedures and standards; operational programmes; human development with special reference to mother and child; diseases of special nutritional importance; nutrition education and training; and nutrition of animals.
Contract work: No
Publications: Newsletter (twice yearly), directory.

International Union of Pharmacology 101

– IUPHAR
Address: (Secretariat): Department of Pharmacology, The Worsley Medical and Dental Building, University of Leeds, Leeds, LS2 9JT, United Kingdom
Affiliation: International Council of Scientific Unions
Secretary-General: Professor A.M. Barrett
Sections: Clinical pharmacology, Dr F. Sjoqvist (Chairman); toxicology, Dr G. Zbinden (Chairman)
Activities: Promotion of the study of pharmacology on an international level by research, the dissemination of knowledge, and the organization of the International Congress of Pharmacology and other scientific meetings.

International Union of Physiological Sciences* 102

– IUPS
Address: (Secretariat): Experimental Research Department, Semmelweis Medical University, Üllöi ut 78a Budapest 1082, Hungary
Telephone: 343 162
Affiliation: International Council of Scientific Unions
President: Professor E. Neil
Secretary: Professor A.G.B. Kovach
Activities: Through its committees and commissions the Union meets its objectives of promoting study and research into physiological sciences on: cardiovascular; cell; comparative; environmental; gastrointestinal; gravitational; medical; muscle; oral; renal; respiratory; somatosensory; thermal; undersea medical, and on endocrinology; microcirculation and capillary transport; motor control; olfaction and taste; physiology of domestic animals, food and fluid intake; psychophysiology.

International Union of Public Transport/Union Internationale des Transports Publics/ Internationaler Verband für Öffentliches Verkehrswesen 103

– UITP
Address: 19 avenue de l'Uruguay, B-1050 Bruxelles, Belgium
Secretary-General: André J. Jacobs
Activities: To study all problems connected with urban and suburban transport, to promote its progress, both from the technical and economic standpoints and in the public interests. Activities include surveys and studies on traffic and urban planning, regional transport (railways, motorbuses, waterways), metropolitan railways, study of motorbuses (including standardization), automation, and economic policies in transport. Members represent the transport industries in 65 countries.

International Union of Pure and Applied Biophysics 104

– IUPAB
Address: (Secretariat): Institute of Molecular Biology and Biophysics, ETH-Hönggerberg, CH-8093 Zürich, Switzerland
Telephone: (01) 57 57 70
Telex: 54354 CH
Affiliation: International Council of Scientific Unions
Secretary-General: Professor K. Wüthrich
Activities: Promotion of international cooperation, dissemination of information, and advancement of biophysical knowledge through the work of its commissions: cell and membrane biophysics, biophysics of communication and control processes, education and development in biophysics, macromolecular biophysics, radiation and environmental biophysics, subcellular and macromolecular biophysics. Joint committees with other unions affiliated to the International Council for Scientific Unions have been set up for biothermodynamics, and comparative physiology.
Publications: Biophysics reviews (quarterly).

International Union of Pure and Applied Chemistry 105

– IUPAC
Address: (Secretariat): Bank Court Chambers, 2-3 Pound Way, Cowley Centre, Oxford OX4 3YF, United Kingdom
Telephone: (0865) 770125
Telex: 83147 IUPAC
Affiliation: International Council of Scientific Unions
Secretary-General: Professor G. Ourisson
Executive Secretary: Dr M. Williams
Activities: To promote the advancement of pure and applied chemistry in all its aspects. The Union is organized in seven divisions for: physical chemistry, inorganic chemistry, organic chemistry, macromolecules, analytical chemistry, applied chemistry and clinical chemistry. Each division is responsible for a number of commissions on: physicochemical symbols, terminology and units, thermodynamics,

electrochemistry, physicochemical measurements and standards, molecular structure and spectroscopy, and colloid and surface chemistry including catalysis; atomic weights and isotopic abundances, nomenclature of inorganic chemistry, high temperatures and refractory materials; nomenclature of organic chemistry, physical organic chemistry, photochemistry, and medicinal chemistry; macromolecular nomenclature, polymer characterization and properties; analytical reactions and reagents, michrochemical techniques and trace analysis, analytical nomenclature, spectrochemical and other optical procedures for analysis, equilibrium data, analytical radiochemistry and nuclear materials, solubility data; food chemistry, biotechnology, oils, fats and derivatives; atmospheric environment, pesticide chemistry, water quality, reclamation of solid wastes; automation, quantities and units, teaching, toxicology.

International Union of Pure and Applied Physics/Union Internationale de Physique Pure et Appliquée   106

– IUPAP
Address: Département de Physique, Université Laval, Québec PQ G1K 7P4, Canada
Telephone: 656 2528
Telex: 051 31621
Affiliation: International Council of Scientific Unions
Secretary-General: Professor Larkin Kerwin
Annual expenditure: $100 000
Activities: The Union realizes its aims of developing and promoting research into physics through the work of sixteen standing commissions for: symbols, units, nomenclature, atomic masses and fundamental constants; thermodynamics and statistical mechanics; cosmic rays; very low-temperature physics; publications; acoustics; semiconductors; magnetism; solid-state physics; particles and fields; nuclear physics; physics education; atomic and molecular physics and spectroscopy; plasma physics; quantum electronics; finance, and two affiliated commissions for: optics; general relativity and gravitation.
Publications: General and annual reports, bulletins.

International Union of Radio Science/Union Radio-Scientifique Internationale   107

– URSI
Address: (Secretariat): Avenue Albert Lancaster 32, B-1180 Bruxelles, Belgium
Telephone: (02) 374 13 08
Affiliation: International Council of Scientific Unions
Secretary-General: Professor J. Van Bladel
Activities: The Union realizes its aims of developing and promoting research into radio science through the work of nine standing commissions for: electromagnetic metrology, fields and waves, signals and systems, physical electronics, interference environment, wave phenomena in non-ionized media, ionospheric radio and propagation, waves in plasmas, and radioastronomy.

International Union of Theoretical and Applied Mechanics*   108

Address: (Secretariat): Chalmers University of Technology, Fack, S-40220 Gothenburg 5, Sweden
Telephone: (031) 810100
Affiliation: International Council of Scientific Unions
President: Professor F.I. Niordson
Secretary-General: Professor J. Hult
Symposia Panels: Fluid mechanics, Sir James Lighthill (Chairman); solid mechanics, Professor P. Germain (Chairman)
Activities: The Union promotes the study of theoretical and applied mechanics through the activities of its affiliated organizations and symposia panels.

International Vine and Wine Office/Office International de la Vigne et du Vin   109

Address: 11 rue Roquépine, 75008 Paris, France
Director: Gilbert Constant
Activities: Viticulture, vine pathology, grapes and raisins, oenology, wine making, analysis of wine, wine microbiology, economic problems, statistics.

International Whaling Commission 110

– IWC
Address: The Red House, Station Road, Histon, Cambridge CB4 4NP, United Kingdom
Telephone: (022023) 3971
Telex: 817960
Secretary: Dr R. Gambell
Annual expenditure: £51 000-500 000
Activities: Coordination and sponsorship of research into the biology, ecology and population dynamics of whales.
Contract work: No
Publications: Annual reports and special reports and research papers.

International Wool Secretariat/Secrétariat International de la Laine 111

– IWS
Address: Wool House, Carlton Gardens, London SW1Y 5AE, United Kingdom
Telephone: (01) 930 7300
Managing Director: Dr G. Laxer
Graduate research staff: 50
Annual expenditure: over £2m
Activities: Wool promotion and publicity; research and product and process development on wool and wool textiles.
Contract work: No
Publications: Wool Science Review.

IWS TECHNICAL CENTRE 112

Address: Valley Drive, Ilkley, Yorkshire LS29 8PB, United Kingdom
Telephone: (0943) 601555
Director, Research and Development: Dr K. Baird
Activities: Full pilot plant from scoured wool to making-up, and carpets.

Jernkontoret 113

Address: Kungstradgårdsgatan 10, Box 1721, S-111 87 Stockholm, Sweden
Telephone: 08-22 46 20
Telex: 10165 JERNGRC S
Research director: K-G. Bergh
Deputy research director: Jan Aselius

Sections: Ore-based metallurgy, refractory materials, ladle metallurgy, non-destructive testing, Hedi Brunner; powder metallurgy, Kerstin Fernheden; scrap-based metallurgy, casting and solidification, metallurgical history, Sven-Erik Johansson; heating and furnace technology, environmental control, energy, Birgitta Lindblad; properties - high-alloy steels, analytical chemistry, non-ferrous metals, Sven Sundberg; processing - flat products, processing - long products, properties - commercial steels, properties - carbon and low-alloy steels, Bengt Waller
Annual expenditure: SKr30m
Activities: Jernkontoret is the administrative centre for joint research activities in which steel works in Sweden, Denmark, Finland and Norway participate. Targets of research are determined by a Research Board made up of representatives of the Nordic steel industry, and financial grants are allocated to a number of Research Panels. Their field of activity embraces the entire chain of production from raw material to the finished product, as well as matters relating to energy and environmental control. The members of the Research Panels are specialists in the branch of technology with which the Panel is concerned. The Panels decide which particular research projects are to be pursued and distribute available finance between them. The actual research is monitored by committees and carried out by research engineers belonging to member companies, universities or the institutes and research plants closely associated with the joint research. Nearly 1 200 people are in one way or another engaged in these research activities.
Jernkontoret's joint research programme is financed by the participating 47 member companies and supported by grants from outside bodies, particularly the National Swedish Board for Technical Development - STU.
Publications: Jernkontorets Annaler - JkA, Swedish; *Scandinavian Journal of Metallurgy*, English; research reports, mainly in Swedish.

Ludwig Institute for Cancer Research/Ludwig Institut fur Krebsforschung/Institut Ludwig de Recherche sur le Cancer 114

Address: Neustadtgasse 7, CH-8001 Zürich, Switzerland
Telephone: (01) 251 53 77
Telex: 58 560
Medical director: Dr Carl G. Baker
Director, London Branch: Munro Neville
Director, Lausanne Branch: Jean-Charles Cerottini
Director, Sydney Branch: Martin Tattersall
Director, Brussels Branch: Thierry Boon

Interim Director, Bern Branch: Carl G. Baker
Director, Melbourne Branch: Anthony Burgess
Graduate research staff: 58
Annual expenditure: over £2m
Activities: A private, charitable institute, all research is into cancer: molecular biology; pharmacology; endocrinology; pathology; electron microscopy; immunology; tissue culture; genetic engineering. Direct operating branches in different parts of the world emphasize different aspects of cancer research: human cancer biology with emphasis on breast cancer; cancer immunology; therapy and pharmacology; cell genetics; clinical trials - breast and lung cancer; and biochemistry of cell differentiation.
Contract work: No
Publications: Research reports, reviews, abstracts and letters.

Miedzynarodowe Laboratorium Silnych Pol Magnetycznych i Niskich Temperatur   115

[International Laboratory of High Magnetic Fields and Low Temperatures]
Address: Ulica Próchnika 95, 53-529 Wrocław, Poland
Telephone: 07-61 27 21
Telex: 813929 intem pl
Affiliation: Polska Akademia Nauk
Director: Professor Dr W. Trzebratowski
Research director: Dr W. Shamray
Graduate research staff: 6
Annual expenditure: £51 000-500 000
Activities: Improvement of coreless electromagnet design; properties of superconductors; magnetic properties of materials in high magnetic fields; electronic properties of pure metals, alloys and compounds; methods of obtaining very low temperatures suitable for investigations in high magnetic fields.
Contract work: Yes
Facilities: Bitter magnets 20, 15, 10 T; superconducting magnet 15 T.

Nordforsk   116

[Nordic Cooperative Organization for Applied Research]
Address: Box 5103, S-102 43 Stockholm, Sweden
or: PB 181, SF-00181 Helsinki 18, Finland
Telephone: (08) 14 14 50
Telex: 19035 nordf s
Members: Danish Academy of Technical Sciences;

Council for Scientific and Technical Research (Denmark); Finnish Academy of Technical Sciences; Swedish Academy of Engineering Sciences in Finland; Finnish Research Council for Technical Sciences; National Research Council of Iceland; Royal Norwegian Council for Scientific and Industrial Research; Royal Swedish Academy of Engineering Sciences; Swedish Board of Technical Development.
Director: Erling Hagen
Sections: Copenhagen Secretariat, Eric Bornhøft; Helsinki Secretariat, Nils Mustelin
Annual expenditure: £501 000-2m
Activities: To promote and organize cooperation in the field of scientific and industrial research and in the utilization of research results between the five Scandinavian countries. Nordforsk sponsors cooperative research and a number of Scandinavian working groups, research committees, symposia, conference and liaison activities.

Nordic Council/Nordiska Rådet/Nordisk Råd/ Pohjoismaiden-Neuvosto/ Nordurlandarad   117

Address: Box 19506, S-104 32 Stockholm, Sweden
Telephone: (08) 14 34 20
Telex: 128 67 (nordpr s)
Member Countries: Denmark, Finland, Iceland, Norway, Sweden
Secretary of the Praesidium: Jan O. Karlsson
Deputy Secretaries: Gunnar Naesselund, Gudmund Saxrud
Head of Information: Inger Jägerhorn
Standing Committees of the Nordic Council: Legal Committee; Cultural Committee; Social and Environment Committee; Communications Committee; Economic Committee
Activities: An advisory body to the Nordic parliaments and governments, founded in 1952, the Council deals with questions concerning cooperation between the Nordic countries in the economic, legislative, social and cultural fields, and regarding environmental protection and communications. The Council acts through adopting recommendations at the annual sessions and through passing declarations of opinion. High priority is given to cooperation and collaboration between research institutions by the exchange of scientists, by the organization of conferences and symposia, and by exchange of scientific information and documentation. Committees have been established for: medical education; arctic medicine; research in medicine; humanities; social research; research in science; research in forestry; international politics (including peace and conflict research); scientific and technical information.

Note: The following institutes, among others, have been established due to recommendations from the Nordic Council: Institute of Theoretical Physics, Copenhagen; Institute of Maritime Law, Oslo; Institute of African Studies, Uppsala; Institute of Asiatic Studies, Copenhagen; Institute of Social Planning, Stockholm; Institute of Public Health, Gothenburg; Institute of Folklore, Turku; Institute of Volcanology, Reykjavik; Collegium of Marine Biology; Collegium of Game Research; Collegium of Physical Oceanography; Collegium of Terrestrial Ecology; Scandinavian Council for Applied Research - NORDFORSK. These institutes, however, must not be regarded as subsidiary to the Council.

NATIONAL SECRETARIATS OF THE NORDIC COUNCIL 118

Denmark 119

Address: Christiansborg Ridebane 10, DK-1218 København K, Denmark
Secretary-General: Axel Gormsen
Deputy Secretary: Niels Ove Gottlieb

Finland 120

Address: Eduskuntatalo, SF-00102 Helsinki 10, Finland
Secretary-General: Haakan Branders
Deputy Secretary: Dag Lindberg

Iceland 121

Address: Altinget, Reykjavik, Iceland
Secretary-General: Fridjon Sigurdson

Norway 122

Address: Stortinget, N Oslo 1, Norway
Secretary-General: Gudvin Laader Ve
Deputy Secretary: John Dale

Sweden 123

Address: Box 7765, S-10396 Stockholm, Sweden
Secretary-General: Christer Jacobson
Deputy Secretaries: Birgitta Malmros, Eric Hultén, Eva Smekal

Nordisk Forskningsinstitut for Maling og Trykfarver/ Nordiska Institutet för Färgforskning 124

– NIF
[Scandinavian Paint and Printing Ink Research Institute]
Address: Agern Allé 3, DK-2970 Hørsholm, Denmark
Telephone: (02) 57 03 55
Affiliation: Akademiet for de Tekniske Videnskaber - ATV
Director: Charles M. Hansen
Sections: Analysis, Karen Eng; coatings, Ago Saarnak; printing ink, William Hansen
Graduate research staff: 15
Annual expenditure: DKr 5 800 000
Activities: Coatings: studies of coatings during application and as dried films; studies of pigment dispersion and application properties, accelerated weathering in weather-meters, exterior exposures, corrosion resistance, dirt retention, etc; scanning electron microscope and computer applications to coatings. Printing inks: studies and test methods including determinations of optical, rheological, and printing properties of printing inks; colour measurement; pigment studies, and adhesion to plastic films. Analysis: chemical analysis of coatings and printing inks and their films; development of new analytical techniques in cooperation with international organizations.
Contract work: Yes

Nordisk Institut for Teoretisk Atomfysik 125

– NORDITA
[Nordic Institute for Theoretical Atomic Physics]
Address: Blegdamsvej 17, DK-2100 København Ø, Denmark
Telephone: 42 16 16
Chairman: Professor Haakon Olsen
Director: Professor Ben Mottelson
Activities: Established in 1957 as an institute jointly sponsored by the governments of the five Nordic countries (Denmark, Finland, Iceland, Norway and Sweden) and cooperating with the Niels Bohr Institute of the University of Copenhagen, for research and the provision of training of physicists from the Nordic countries; promotion of cooperation between member countries. Research fields include nuclear physics, high-energy physics, astrophysics, and solid-state physics.
Contract work: No
Publications: Nordita series.

Nordisk Institutt for Odontologisk Materialprøvning   126

– NIOM
[Dental Materials Institute of Scandinavia]
Address: Forskningsveien 1, Blindern, Oslo 3, Norway
Telephone: (02) 69 58 80
Affiliation: Governments of Denmark, Finland, Iceland, Norway and Sweden
Director: Dr Ivar A. Mjör
Sections: Biological/chemical: Ivar A. Mjör; physical/chemical: Dag Brune
Graduate research staff: 7
Annual expenditure: £51 000-500 000
Activities: The Institute tests dental materials available on the Scandinavian market to ensure that they are safe to use and that they fulfil the appropriate technological requirements. The Institute also carries out research, develops new materials and techniques, and supplies information about dental materials. The research projects cover areas such as physical/chemical test methods, studies of metals, dental polymer materials, cements, root filling materials and biological test methods.
Contract work: No
Publications: Niom-News, annual reports, scientific reports.

North Atlantic Treaty Organization/Organisation du Traité de l'Atlantique Nord   127

– NATO
Address: B-1110, Bruxelles, Belgium
Telephone: 241 00 40
Telex: 23867
Member Countries: Belgium, Canada, Denmark, France, Germany FR, Greece, Iceland, Italy, Luxembourg, Netherlands, Norway, Portugal, Turkey, United Kingdom, United States of America

ADVISORY GROUP FOR AEROSPACE RESEARCH AND DEVELOPMENT   128

– AGARD
Address: 7 rue Ancelle, 92200 Neuilly sur Seine, France
Director: J. Burnham

DEFENCE RESEARCH GROUP   129

Address: B-1100, Bruxelles, Belgium
Head, Defence Research Section: Ing Gl P. Naslin
Activities: Study and research of defence.

SACLANT ANTI-SUBMARINE WARFARE RESEARCH CENTRE   130

– SACLANTCEN
Address: Viale San Bartolomeo 400, 19026 La Spezia, Italy
Telephone: 560 940
Telex: 271 148 SACENT I
Director: B.W. Lythall
Groups: Applied oceanography; environmental acoustics; ambient noise; environmental modelling; operational research; assessment; experimental systems; signal processing
Graduate research staff: 40
Activities: Antisubmarine warfare research.

SCIENTIFIC AFFAIRS DIVISION   131

Assistant Secretary General for Scientific and Environmental Affairs: Professor R. Chabbal
Deputy Assistant Secretary General: P.W. Hemily
Science Committee:
Chairman: Professor R. Chabbal
Belgium, Professor Ph. Teyssié
Canada, Dr J. Tuzo Wilson
Denmark, Professor P.L. Ølgaard
France, Professor L. Néel
Germany FR, Professor Ing E. Pestel
Greece, Professor G. Contopoulos
Iceland, Dr Gudmundur E. Sigvaldason
Italy, Professor G. Sartori
Luxembourg, Professor A. Boever
Netherlands, Professor W.A. de Jong
Norway, Finn Lied
Portugal, Professor C.M. Alves Martins
Turkey, Professor Dr H.S. Oranç
UK, Professor Sir Geoffrey Allen
USA, Dr Edward E. David, Jr
Activities: The Science Committee is charged with the overall mission of stimulating and strengthening science within the Western Alliance, and of promoting contacts between scientists of the NATO member countries. The Assistant Secretary General for Scientific and Environmental Affairs, with the aid of a small scientific staff, is responsible for implementing the Committee's decisions, administering the various science programmes, and giving scientific and technical advice to the Secretary General of NATO.

Subsidiary Bodies/Scientific Programmes 132

NATO ADVANCED STUDY INSTITUTES PROGRAMME 133
Executive Officer: Dr M. di Lullo
Activities: Finances and coordinates international advanced study institutes in almost all areas of science. A duration of 2-3 weeks and a limited participation is aimed at in order to ensure treatment in depth of a specific subject.

NATO RESEARCH GRANTS PROGRAMME 134
Executive Officer: Dr A. Gomes
Activities: To promote collaboration among research groups working in the different member countries of NATO on common and specific projects. Fields are generally unrestricted with emphasis on basic science and fundamental aspects of applied science.

SCIENCE COMMITTEE CONFERENCE PROGRAMME 135
Activities: Research evaluation conferences in scientific areas that warrant specific attention.

SPECIAL PROGRAMMES 136
Information Officer: Dr P.W. Hemily
Programmes: Air-sea interaction; marine sciences; eco-sciences; materials science; human factors; systems science

STANDING GROUP ON SENIOR SCIENTISTS PROGRAMME 137
Executive Officer: Dr M. di Lullo
Activities: Supports lectureships, visiting professorships and senior fellowships.

SUB-COMMITTEE OF NATIONAL FELLOWSHIPS ADMINISTRATORS 138
Executive Officer: Dr B.A. Bayraktar
Activities: Finances NATO Science Fellowships for post-graduate and post-doctoral students in foreign countries. The programme is administered on a national basis.

SHAPE TECHNICAL CENTRE 139
– STC
Address: Postbus 174, s'Gravenhage, Netherlands
Director: E. Klippenberg

OECD Nuclear Energy Agency/Agence OCDE Pour l'Énergie Nucléaire 140

Address: 38 boulevard Suchet, Paris 75016, France
Telephone: 524 82 00
Telex: 630668 AEN/NEA
Affiliation: Organization for Economic Cooperation and Development
Member Countries: Australia, Austria, Belgium, Canada, Denmark, Finland, France, German FR, Greece, Iceland, Ireland, Italy, Japan, Luxembourg, Netherlands, Norway, Portugal, Spain, Sweden, Switzerland, Turkey, United Kingdom and United States of America
Director-General: I.G.K. Williams
Deputy Director-General: Dr W.H. Hannum
Deputy Director, Science and Development: Y. Motoda
Deputy Director, Safety and Regulation: P. Strohl
Nuclear Science Division: J.A.R. Rosen
Nuclear Development Division: W. Haüssermann
Radiation Protection and Waste Management Division: E. Wallauschek
Nuclear Safety Division: K. Stadie
Legal Section: P. Reyners
Committees and Working Groups:
Steering Committee, Chairman: H. Murata (Japan); Vice-Chairmen: J.D. Cunningham (Ireland); V.O. Eriksen (Norway)
Committee on the Safety of Nuclear Installations (CSNI)
Committee on Radiation Protection and Public Health (CRPPH)
Committee on Radioactive Waste Management (RWMC)
NEA Committee on Reactor Physics (NEACRP)
NEA Nuclear Data Committee (NEANDC)
Group of Governmental Experts on Third Party Liability in the Field of Nuclear Energy
Committee for Technical and Economic Studies on Nuclear Energy Development and the Fuel Cycle (FCC)
Activities: The Agency is an intergovernmental organization grouping 23 OECD countries. The main purpose of the Agency is to promote international cooperation within the OECD area for the development and application of nuclear energy for peaceful purposes. This it does through international research and development projects, and through the exchange of scientific and technical experience and information. The Agency also maintains under continual surveillance and, with the cooperation of other organizations in the field (notably the International Atomic Energy Agency, IAEA), world resources of nuclear fuels and the evolving estimates of future demand. An expanding part of the Agency's work is devoted to safety and regulatory aspects of nuclear energy, including the development of uniform standards

governing safety and health protection, and a uniform legislative regime for nuclear liability and insurance.

Publications: Activity reports, scientific, technical and legal publications, annual reports.

INTERNATIONAL PROJECT IN THE   141
FIELD OF FOOD IRRADIATION

Address: Institut für Strahlentechnologie, Postfach 3640, D-7500 Karlsruhe, German FR

Member countries: Australia, Austria, Belgium, Brazil, Canada, Denmark, France, Finland, German FR, Ghana, Hungary, India, Iraq, Israel, Italy, Japan, Netherlands, Norway, Portugal, South Africa, Spain, Sweden, Switzerland, United Kingdom, United States of America

Activities: Jointly sponsored by the NEA, the International Atomic Energy Agency, and the Food and Agriculture Organization (FAO) of the United Nations, the International Project came into being in 1971. The main objectives of the Project are wholesomeness testing of selected food products preserved by irradiation processes, together with investigations into the methodology of wholesomeness testing. Most of this work is being carried out under contract in specialist laboratories and institutions in the Project's participant countries.

NEA DATA BANK   142

Address: BP N 9 (Bâtiment 45), 91190 Gif sur Yvette, France

Head of Centre: J. Rosen

Activities: Set up at Saclay (France) in January 1978, taking over the tasks of two previously separate centres (the Computer Programme Library in Ispra, Italy, and the Neutron Data Compilation Centre at Saclay). The primary function of the NEA Data Bank is the collection, validation and dissemination of scientific and technical data and computer programmes needed for nuclear energy applications. The computer program services involve collecting programs from their authors, compiling and testing these programs, and distributing the program packages to users in OECD Member countries; this service is provided to other IAEA countries through an IAEA liaison officer stationed at the Data Bank. Nuclear Data services consist of the compilation of experimental and evaluated neutron data, and bibliographic information in this field, and their exchange with other nuclear centres throughout the world.

OECD HALDEN REACTOR PROJECT   143

Address: PO Box 173, Halden, Norway

Activities: The Halden experimental 20 MW boiling heavy water reactor first became a joint undertaking of the OECD Nuclear Energy Agency under an agreement

signed in June 1958 between the Norwegian Institute for Atomic Energy (now the Institutt for Energiteknikk, owner of the reactor) and Austria, the Danish Atomic Energy Commission, EURATOM, AB Atomenergi of Sweden, Switzerland, and the UK Atomic Energy Authority. The Finnish Atomic Energy Commission also took part in the Project under special bilateral arrangements with the Norwegian Institute. The Project has since continued under a series of further agreements, the latest of which covers the three-year period 1979-81. Signatories of the agreement are, the Norwegian Institutt for Energiteknikk, the Austrian Studiengesellschaft für Atomenergie, the Danish Atomic Energy Commission, the Finnish Ministry of Trade and Industry, the Italian Comitato Nazionale per l'Energia Nucleare, the Japan Atomic Energy Research Institute, Kernforschunganlage Jülich GmbH (representing a German group of companies working in agreement with the German Federal Ministry for Research and Technology), the Netherlands Energy Research Foundation, Studsvik Energiteknik of Sweden, the United Kingdom Central Electricity Generating Board and the United States Nuclear Regulatory Commission. Other organizations (the Electric Power Research Institute, Combustion Engineering Incorporated and General Electric Company all of the United States) are participating as associated parties.

Organisation des Nations   144
Unies pour l'Alimentation
et l'Agriculture/
Organización de las
Naciones Unidas para la
Agricultura y la
Alimentación

– FAO
[Food and Agriculture Organization of the United Nations]

Address: Via delle Terme di Caracalla, 00100 Rome, Italy

Telephone: 5797

Telex: 61181 FOODAGRI

Director-General: E. Saouma

Deputy Director-General: Ralph W. Phillips

Liaison Offices: Regional Office for Africa (Accra): Regional Representative, S.C. Sar

Regional Office for Asia and Far East (Bangkok): Regional Representative, D.L. Umali

Regional Office for Latin America (Santiago): Regional Representative, P. Moral López

Regional Office for Near East: Regional Representative, S. Jum'a

Regional Office for Europe (Rome): (vacant)
FAO Liaison Office for North America (Washington D.C.), D.C. Kimmel
FAO Liaison Office with the UN (New York City), T.N. Saraf
Office for Inter-Agency Affairs, A.G. Regnier
Office for Special Relief Operations (OSRO), K.P. Wagner
Office of Internal Audit and Inspection, K. Mehboob
Office of Programme, Budget and Evaluation, E.M. West
Legal Office, J.P. Dobbert
Activities: Established in 1945 as an autonomous agency in the United Nations system, with 147 member countries (whose representatives approve the main policy and programmes of the Organization at biennial sessions of the FAO Conference), the FAO aims are to raise levels of nutrition and standards of living, secure improvements of the production and distribution of all food and agricultural products, better the conditions of rural populations and thus contribute to an expanding world economy and ensure humanity's freedom from hunger. Working in the fields of fisheries and forestry as well as agriculture, the FAO acts as a world source of information in its various fields of concern and stimulates and services international consultation and negotiation in these fields. With funds received from international and national sources it gives technical advice and assistance to the developing countries; under a Technical Cooperation Programme financed from its own budget it is able to give speedy aid to countries facing sudden and unpredicted development problems. In cooperation with a number of financing agencies it helps to identify possibilities, and develop proposals, for investment in the developing world. It maintains a continuous watch on the food situation and warns of impending shortages and emergency situations. Through its Freedom from Hunger/Action for Development Programme it provides a possibility for individual citizens in member countries to play a part in development activities.
Publications: Reference IAEA Catalogue monographs, reports on conditions and trends in its various fields of concern; computer-based information retrieval service in these fields.
The fields in which FAO is active include the following Departments:

ADMINISTRATION AND FINANCE DEPARTMENT 145

Assistant Director-General: P.J. Skoufis

AGRICULTURE DEPARTMENT 146

Assistant Director-General: D.F.R. Bommer
Activities: Animal production and health, including programmes for the control of the international spread of the more serious livestock diseases; the various applications of atomic energy to agriculture, including food preservation, plant breeding and pest control; the development and conservation of land and water resources, including the efficient use of fertilizers and the improvement of irrigation; plant production and protection including development of seed production, conservation of plant genetic resources and control measures against pests such as the desert locust; farm management including farm mechanization, development of food and agricultural industries and of marketing and credit services and reduction of post-harvest losses through better storage and pest control.

Agricultural Operation Division 147

Director: C.H. Bonte-Freidheim
Sections: Regional operations service, Africa, L.W. Siry
Regional operations service, Asia and Far East, G.C. Juneja
Regional operations service, Near East, North Africa and Europe, A. Al-Jaff
Regional operations service, Latin America, R.A. Duarte-Torres
Management support service, I.C. Pokorny

Agricultural Service Division 148

Director: M.S.O. Nicholas
Sections: Marketing and credit service, J.C. Abbott
Agricultural engineering service, H. van Hülst
Food and agricultural industries service, E.A. Asselbergs

Animal Production and Health Division 149

Director: R.B. Griffiths
Sections: Animal health service, Y. Ozawa
Livestock research and education service, P. Mahadevan
Meat and milk development service, A. Charpentier

Joint FAO/IAEA Division of Atomic Energy in Food and Agriculture (Vienna) 150

Director: M. Fried
Deputy director: Dr Carl G. Lamm
Sections: Soil fertility, irrigation and crop production, Dr Y. Barrada
Plant breeding and genetics, Dr A. Micke
Animal production and health, Dr B.A. Young
Insect and pest control, Dr G. LaBrecque
Agricultural chemicals, Dr D.A. Lindquist
Food preservation, Dr J. van Kooij

Land and Water Development Division 151

Director: R. Dudal
Sections: Fertilizer and plant nutrition service, M. Mathieu
Water resources development and management service, H.M. Horning
Soil resources management and conservation service, F.W. Hauck

Plant Production and Protection Division 152

Director: O. Brauer
Sections: Crop and grassland production service, A. Bozzini
Plant protection service, L. Brader
Crop ecology and genetic resources unit, R.J. Pichel

DEVELOPMENT DEPARTMENT 153

Assistant Director-General: J. de Mèredieu
FFH/Action for Development: A. Pena Montenegro

Field Programme Development Division 154

Director: C. Beringer
Sections: Technical cooperation programme unit, G. de Lambilly
Field programme coordination service, U. Skullerud
Special programmes liaison service, H. Teunissen
Regional bureau for Africa, T. Taka
Regional bureau for Asia and Far East, M.L. Dewan
Regional bureau for Latin America, P. Lemos
Regional bureau for Near East and North Africa, S.A. El Shistawy

Investment Centre 155

Director: C. Fernando

ECONOMIC AND SOCIAL POLICY DEPARTMENT 156

Assistant Director-General: N. Islam
Sections: Global perspective studies unit, J.P. O'Hagan
Activities: Monitoring production and trade in agricultural commodities and facilitating international agreement on trade questions; assisting developing countries to develop food security measures; watching the food situation and warning of impending shortages; organization of agricultural cooperatives, rural employment, agricultural education and extension services, land tenure and settlement, population questions, home economics; nutritional needs and problems, food science and consumer protection; analysis of agricultural development trends and projections of future needs and possibilities; collection and dissemination of agricultural statistics, coordination of the decennial world censuses of agriculture, assistance to development of national statistical services.

Commodities and Trade Division 157

Director: A.G. Leeks
Sections: Basic foodstuffs service, B.P. Dutia
Raw materials, tropical and horticultural products service, J.G. Amoafo
Commodity policy and projections service, R.J. Perkins
Food security and information service, A.K. Binder
Food security assistance unit, B. van de Walle

Food Policy and Nutrition Division 158

Director: Z.I. Sabry
Sections: Food and nutrition assessment service, P. Lunven
Nutrition programmes service, J. Góngora y López
Food standards and food science service, G.O. Kermode

Human Resources, Institutions and Agrarian Reform Division 159

Director: R. Moreno
Sections: Agricultural education and extension service, K.A.P. Stevenson
Land tenure and production structure service, L.C. Arulpragasam
Home economics and social programmes service, R. Finney
Development organization and institutions service, M.R. El Ghonemy

Policy Analysis Division 160

Director: J.P. Bhattarcharjee
Sections: Situation and outlook service, vacant
Planning assistance service, J.B. Van As
Development policy studies and training service, H. Quaix

Statistics Division 161

Director: C.L. Quance
Sections: Statistical development service, D.C. Alonzo
Statistical analysis service, O.P. Aggarwal
Basic data unit, D. Basu

FISHERIES DEPARTMENT 162

Assistant Director-General: K.C. Lucas
Sections: Operations service, N. Kojima
Fishery information data and statistics service, E.F. Akyüz
Activities: Assessment and conservation of resources; improved technology such as gear and vessels, and processing of the catch; management of the new exclusive economic fisheries zones.

Fishery Industries Division 163

Director: A. Labon
Sections: Fish utilization and marketing service, W. Krone
Fisheries technology service, P. Gurtner

Fishery Policy and Planning Division 164

Director: J.E. Carroz
Sections: Fishery development planning service, J.P. Troadec
Fishery international institutions and liaison unit, J.J. Kambona

Fishery Resources and Environment Division 165

Director: H. Kasahara
Sections: Marine resources service, J.A. Gulland
Inland water resources and aquaculture service, H.F. Henderson

FORESTRY DEPARTMENT 166

Assistant Director-General: M.A. Flores Rodas
Sections: Operations service, M.K. Muthoo
Policy and planning service, S.L. Pringle
Activities: Measurement and conservation of resources, forest education and institutions, wildlife protection; forest industries including paper manufacture, forest logging and sawmilling and the processing of other forest products; development of community forests and production of fuel.

Forest Industries Division 167

Director: A.J. Leslie
Sections: Pulp and paper branch, B. Kyrklund
Mechanical wood products branch, J. Swidersky
Forest logging and transport branch, L.R. Letourneau

Forest Resources Division 168

Director: J. Prats Llaurado
Sections: Forest and wildlands conservation branch, T. Eren
Forest resources development branch, O. Fugalli
Forestry education, employment and institutions branch, H.A. Hilmi

GENERAL AFFAIRS AND INFORMATION DEPARTMENT 169

Assistant Director-General: A. Sylla

WORLD FOOD PROGRAMME 170

Executive Director: G.N. Vogel
Deputy Executive Director: B. de A. Brito

External Affairs and General Services Division 171

Director: E.E. Lühe

Project Management Division 172

Director: R.M. Cashin

Resources Management Division 173

Director: M. El Midani

Organisation Européenne d'Études Photogrammétriques Expérimentales 174

– OEEPE
[European Organization for Experimental Photogrammetric Studies]
Address: 350 Boulevard 1945, PO Box 6, 7500 AA Enschede, Netherlands
Telephone: (053) 320330
Telex: 44525
Member countries: Austria, Belgium, Denmark, Finland, France, Germany, Italy, the Netherlands, Norway, Sweden, Switzerland, United Kingdom
Secretary-General: Professor Ir J. Visser
Scientific Committees: Aerial Triangulation, Professor J. Talts, Sweden
Digital Height Models, M.G. Gros, France
Large-Scale Stereo-restitution, M. Jaakkola, Finland
Photogrammetric-cartographic Techniques for Topographic Mapping, Professor E. Spiess, Switzerland

Topographic Photo-interpretation, Dr J. Bernhard, Austria
Fundamental Problems of Photogrammetry, Professor H.G. Jerie, The Netherlands
Graduate research staff: 40
Annual expenditure: £51 000-500 000

Organisation Européenne et Méditerranéenne pour la Protection des Plantes   175

– EPPO
[European and Mediterranean Plant Protection Organization]
Address: 1 rue le Notre, 75016 Paris, France
Telephone: 5207794
Director-general: Dr G. Mathys
Activities: Intergovernmental organization principally involved in information exchange and harmonization of methods and regulations in the field of plant protection. EPPO promotes international cooperation in research in plant protection in Europe and the Mediterranean region and has a limited role in coordinating special international research projects.
Publications: EPPO Bulletin.

Organisation Européenne pour la Recherche Nucléaire   176

– CERN
[European Organization for Nuclear Research]
Address: CH-1211 Genève 23, Switzerland
or: Prevessin, 01631, CERN, Cedex, France
Telephone: (022) 834897/83; 836111
Telex: 23698 CH
President of the Council: J. Teillac
Executive director general: J.B. Adams
Research director general: L. Van Hove
Director general designate: H. Schopper
Committees: Finance, K.O. Nielsen; scientific policy, G. Stafford; proton synchrotron and synchrocyclotron, R. Klapisch; intersecting storage rings, G. Bellettini; super proton synchrotron experiments, B. Wiik

Activities: Pure and fundamental research conducted in the field of high-energy physics in order to increase knowledge of the ultimate constitution of matter by studying the sub-nuclear particles and the forces that govern their interaction. 625 universities and institutes from member countries have been involved in the experimental programmes, and 1550 physicists have drawn all or part of their research material from CERN.
Member countries: Austria, Belgium, Denmark, France, Federal Republic of Germany, Greece, Italy, Netherlands, Norway, Sweden, Switzerland, United Kingdom
Facilities: 560.5 hectares of land in France and Switzerland, housing three large particle accelerators: a 400 giga-electronvolts (Super Proton Synchrotron), a 28 giga-electronvolts proton synchrotron, a 600 million electronvolts synchrocyclotron, and the intersecting storage rings. From 1981, the Super Proton Synchrotron is scheduled to be used for the collision of high energy beams of protons and anti-protons.

DATA HANDLING RESEARCH DIVISION   177

Head: P. Zanella

EXPERIMENTAL PHYSICS FACILITIES RESEARCH DIVISION   178

Head: A. Minten

EXPERIMENTAL PHYSICS RESEARCH DIVISION   179

Head. E. Gabathaler

INTERSECTING STORAGE RINGS ACCELERATOR DIVISION   180

Head: F. Ferger

PROTON SYNCHROTRON ACCELERATOR DIVISION   181

Head: G. Munday

SUPER PROTON SYNCHROTRON ACCELERATOR DIVISION   182

Head: G. Brianti

THEORETICAL PHYSICS RESEARCH DIVISION   183

Head: J. Prentki

Organisation Européenne pour la Sécurité de la Navigation Aerienne/Europaische Organisation zur Sicherung der Luftfahrt/Europese Organisatie voor de Veiligheid van de Luchtvaart 184

[European Organization for the Safety of Air Navigation – EUROCONTROL]
Address: 2 rue de la Loi, B-1040 Bruxelles, Belgium
Telephone: (02) 2330211
Telex: 21173 EUROC B
President, Permanent Commission of Ministers: Lord Trefgarne
President, Committee of Management: R. Aucouturier
Director General: J. Leveque
Sections: Operations, J. van Elst; engineering, H. Flentje
Activities: Long-term requirements for air traffic control; definition of concepts for air traffic system including air traffic flow management; study and evaluation of air traffic control and air navigation procedures and equipment; operational research into air traffic systems development; fast time and real time simulations in support of air traffic control planning; studies of future air traffic systems concepts; applications of automation to air traffic control; primary and secondary radar signal processing and display; flight data processing, display and exchange; surveillance systems and aeronautical communications; study and development of new techniques (trajectory prediction, conflict detection and resolution, fuel conservation procedures).

EXPERIMENTAL CENTRE 185

Address: BP 15, 91220 Brétigny sur Orge, France
Director: D.D. Lipmen

Organization for Economic Cooperation and Development/Organisation de Coopération et de Developpement Économiques 186

– OECD
Address: 2 rue André-Pascal, 75775 Paris Cedex 16, France
Telephone: 524 8200
Member Countries: Australia, Austria, Belgium, Canada, Denmark, Finland, France, Germany, Greece, Iceland, Ireland, Italy, Japan, Luxembourg, New Zealand, Netherlands, Norway, Portugal, Spain, Sweden, Switzerland, Turkey, United Kingdom, United States of America, (Special status member, Yugoslavia)
Secretary-General: Emile van Lennep
Activities: Promotes economic and social welfare throughout the OECD area by assisting its member governments in the formulation of policies to this end and by coordinating these policies; stimulates and harmonizes its Members, aid efforts in favour of developing countries. Within the wide scope of its activities, OECD is also engaged in research, notably through the Committees.

CENTRE FOR EDUCATIONAL RESEARCH AND INNOVATION 187

– CERI
Chairman of the Governing Board: R. Grandbois
Activities: To promote, support and undertake research in education; to stimulate pilot experiments in order to test innovations in the educational system; and to encourage cooperation between member countries in the field of educational research and innovation.

COMMITTEE FOR SCIENTIFIC AND TECHNOLOGICAL POLICY 188

– CSTP
Chairman: J. Mullin
Activities: Utilization of science and technology in policy-making; interrelationships between science and technology and economic growth; technology and the structural adaptation of industry; science and technology in the management of natural resources; development and utilization of the social sciences; information, computer and communication policies; improvement of methodology used for research and development statistical surveys; scientific and technological relations between industrialized countries and developing countries.

DIRECTORATE FOR SCIENCE, TECHNOLOGY AND INDUSTRY   189

Director: Dr David Beckler
Activities: The Directorate services the Secretariat needs of the CSTP, CRR and various other committees and working parties.

DIRECTORATE FOR SOCIAL AFFAIRS, MANPOWER AND EDUCATION   190

Director: James Gass
Activities: The Directorate services the Secretariat needs of the Education Committee, the CERI and various other Committees and Working Parties.

EDUCATION COMMITTEE   191

– EDC
Chairman: D. Sette
Activities: Educational trends, statistics and interests; education and equality; education and employment; learning opportunities for adults; social demand for and admission policies to higher education; teaching resources; education and regional planning.

ENVIRONMENT COMMITTEE   192

Chairman: E. Lykke
Activities: To investigate the problems of preserving or improving man's environment with particular reference to their economic and trade implications; to review and confront actions taken or proposed in Member countries in the field of environment; to propose solutions for environmental problems that would as far as possible take account of all relevant factors, including cost effectiveness; and to ensure that the results of environmental investigations can be effectively utilized in the wider framework of the Organization's policy and social development. Study areas include: air management, water management, urban problems and chemicals, noise abatement and the environmental impacts of energy production and use.

Environment Directorate   193

Director: James MacNeill
Activities: The Directorate services the Secretariat needs of the Environment Committee and its various working groups.

STEERING COMMITTEE FOR ROAD RESEARCH   194

– CRR
Chairman: A. Silverleaf
Activities: Promotion of international cooperation in road construction and maintenance, safety, traffic and urban transports, the coordination of research facilities available in Member countries and the scientific interpretation of the results of joint experiments; organization of international Road Research Documentation, a cooperative scheme for the systematic exchange of information and of current research programmes in Member countries.

Scientific Committee on Antarctic Research   195

– SCAR
Address: (Secretariat): c/o Scott Polar Research Institute, Lensfield Road, Cambridge CB2 1ER, United Kingdom
Telephone: (0223) 62061
Affiliation: International Council of Scientific Unions
President: Professor G.A. Knox (New Zealand)
Executive Secretary: G.E. Hemmen
Activities: A scientific committee of ICSU concerned with all aspects of marine science in the southern oceans; promotion of international cooperation in scientific research in the Antarctic, through the working and specialist groups on: biology; geodesy and cartography; geology; glaciology; human biology and medicine; logistics; meteorology; oceanography; solid-earth geophysics; upper atmosphere geophysics; late cenozoic studies; living resources of the southern ocean; seals.
Contract work: No

Scientific Committee on Genetic Experimentation*   196

– COGENE
Address: (Secretariat): EMBO Postfach 1022, 40, D-6900 Heidelberg 1, German FR
Telephone: (06221) 387300
Affiliation: International Council of Scientific Unions
Chairman: Dr W.J. Whelan
Secretary: Dr J. Tooze
Activities: Created in 1976 by ICSU, to study genetics, the Committee has working groups on: guidelines; risk assessment; education and training; benefits and applications

Scientific Committee on Oceanic Research

197

– SCOR
Address: (Secretariat): Department of Oceanography, Dalhousie University, Halifax Nova Scotia B3H 4J1, Canada
Telephone: 902 424 3558
Telex: 019-21863 KELLOGLIB HFX
Affiliation: International Council of Scientific Unions
President: Professor E.S.W. Simpson
Vice-Presidents: Professor G. Siedler; Professor H. Charnock; Dr T. Wolff
Secretary: Dr A. Longhurst
Executive Secretary: Mrs E. Tidmarsh
Activities: A scientific committee of ICSU concerned with the furthering of international scientific activity in all branches of oceanic research. In discharging its function, SCOR cooperates with other international organizations which deal with scientific aspects of oceanic research (for example, SCOR presently advises UNESCO and the Intergovernmental Oceanographic Commission on marine sciences). Working groups and commissions are set up to consider scientific problems arising from international oceanic research programmes including, among others, the development of new methods and the standardization and inter-calibration of existing ones, on: oceanographic tables and standards; internal dynamics of the ocean; Baltic pollution; ocean-atmosphere materials exchanges; river inputs to ocean systems; oceanographic programmes; living resources in the southern ocean; prediction of El Niño; equatorial updwelling processes; coastal and estuarine regimes; arctic heat budget; mathematical models in biological oceanography; mangrove ecosystems; sedimentation processes on continental margins; carbon budget of the ocean; marine geochronological methods; oceanic atoll drilling; coastal-offshore ecosystems relationships; climatic changes and the ocean.

Scientific Committee on Problems of the Environment

198

– SCOPE
Address: (Secretariat): 51 boulevard de Montmorency, 75016 Paris, France
Telephone: 525 04 98
Telex: ICSU 630553 F

Affiliation: International Council of Scientific Unions
President: Professor G. White (USA)
Secretary-General: Dr F. Fournier (France)
Executive Secretary: Dr V. Smirnyagin
Annual expenditure: £10 000-50 000
Activities: A scientific committee of ICSU, SCOPE was created in 1969 to assemble, review and assess the information available on man-made environmental changes and the effects of these changes on man; to assess and evaluate the methodologies of measurement of environmental parameters; to provide an intelligence service on current research; and by the recruitment of the best available scientific information and constructive thinking to establish itself as a corpus of informed advice for the benefit of centres of fundamental research and of organizations and agencies operationally engaged in studies of the environment. Commissions and working groups have been set up on: biogeochemical cycles; renewable natural resources, environmental toxicology; simulation modelling; environmental monitoring; communication of environmental information and societal assessment and response, registry of potentially toxic chemicals in the environment; determination of potentially toxic substances in the environment; acoustics; environment and development; ecological effects of fire; environmental risk assessment of climatic changes.
Contract work: Yes
Publications: SCOPE brochure; SCOPE reports.

Scientific Committee on Water Research*

199

– COWAR
Address: (Secretariat): 51 boulevard de Montmorency, 75016 Paris, France
Telephone: 525 03 29
Telex: ICSU 630553 F
Affiliation: International Council of Scientific Unions
President: Professor J.C.I. Dooge
Executive Secretary: F.W.G. Baker
Activities: Joint ICSU-UATI Committee established in 1976 to carry out studies in water research.

Special Committee on Solar 200 Terrestial Physics*

– SCOSTEP

Address: (Secretariat): National Academy of Sciences, 2101 Constitution Avenue, Washington DC 20418, USA
Telephone: 3896401
Telex: 710 822 9589 (TWX)
Affiliation: International Council of Scientific Unions
President: Professor K.D. Cole
Vice-President: Dr J.W. King
Secretary: Dr E.R. Dyer
Activities: Established in 1966 (modified in 1972) by ICSU to study solar terrestial physics, with steering committees on magnetospherics; sun-earth environment monitoring; middle atmosphere; and sun maximum year.

Stichting Internationaal 201 Vlamonderzoek

[International Flame Research Foundation]
Address: c/o Hoogovens IJmuiden BV, Building 3G.25, Postbus 10 000, 1970 CA IJmuiden, Netherlands
Telephone: 02510 93064
Telex: 35211 Flames
President: M. Michaud
General superintendent of research: J.M. Beer
Director of research station: P.A. Roberts
Scientific manager: Dr G. Flament
Services manager: Ing. G. Holthuysen
Graduate research staff: 7
Annual expenditure: £501 000-2m
Activities: The IFRF is a cooperative research organization whose members meet to discuss problems and organize research in the area of technology relating to industrial heating processes which are based on flames as the source of energy. All aspects of combustion of fuels using turbulent diffusion flames are studied in depth in semi-industrial scale research furnaces; research centres on combustion characteristics of new fuels, high combustion efficiency with optimum heat transfer characteristics, minimizing environmental effects, and improved ability to scale-up investigation results.
Facilities: Research station situated within the steelworks of Hoogovens IJmuiden BV.
Date of foundation: 1948
Contract work: Yes

Stichting Technisch 202 Centrum Waalsteen

[Waalsteen Technical Centre]
Address: Nassausingel 4, Postbus 551, 6500 AN Nijmegen, Netherlands
Telephone: (080) 234041
Director: Dr P.C.F. Bekker
Graduate research staff: 4
Annual expenditure: £100 000
Activities: The Centre is a foundation established in 1955 and owned by a consortium of leading brick companies in The Netherlands, Belgium and Great Britain. It aims at promoting cooperation in the technological and operational field by transmission of knowledge and experience and carrying out research and development work into the manufacture and application of structural ceramics and a wide range of associated areas: brickmaking; factory design; water and air pollution; industrial noise and dust; demolition; reuse of demolition waste; feasibility studies for setting up of building materials industries.
Contract work: Yes

World Health 203 Organization/Organisation Mondiale de la Santé

– WHO
Address: Avenue Appia, CH-1211 Genève 27, Switzerland
Director-General: Dr Halfdan Mahler
Deputy Director-General: Dr T.A. Lambo
Activities: WHO encourages research in which a number of centres in different countries take part, provides grants for research purposes, facilitates international communication by arranging meetings of research workers and by seeking agreement on nomenclature and standardization of techniques, arranges for the international exchange of research workers and helps to increase the world's research potential by training research workers.

REGIONAL OFFICE FOR EUROPE/ 204 BUREAU RÉGIONAL DE L'EUROPE

Address: 8 Scherfigsvej, DK-2100 København Ø, Denmark
Telephone: 290111
Director: Dr Leo Kaprio
Activities: Promotion and development of health related research activities. Implementation of programmes takes place through advisory scientific groups and a network of collaborating centres at national level.

ALBANIA

AUSTRIA

Agrarwirtschaftliches Institut des Bundesministeriums für Land- und Forstwirtschaft

1

[Agricultural Economics Institute of the Federal Ministry of Agriculture and Forestry]
Address: Schweizertalstrasse 36, Postfach 32, A-1133 Wien
Telephone: 0222/823651
Research director: Dipl-Ing Hans Alfons
Sections: Agricultural policy and regional research: Dr W. Schwackhöfer; economics and market research: Dr R. Kreisl
Graduate research staff: 15
Annual expenditure: Sch10m
Activities: Farm economics; agricultural marketing; market forecasts; agricultural policies; rural regional research; rural sociology; documentation and information.
Contract work: No
Publications: Monatsbericht über die österreichische Landwirtschaft, monthly; *Schrifttum der Agrarwirtschaft,* bimonthly; *Schriftenreihe des Agrarwirtschaftlichen Institutes.*

Anstalt für Strömungsmaschinen GmbH

2

[Hydraulic Machines Institute]
Address: Reichsstrasse 68B, A-8045 Graz
Telephone: 0316/62112 and 61221
Research director: Dipl-Ing Dag Berglöff
Sections: Hydraulics, Dipl-Ing D. Berglöff; industrial processing engineering, Dr Dipl-Ing Alfred Weinmann,

Dipl-Ing Alois Wohlfarter
Graduate research staff: 16
Annual expenditure: £501 000-2m
Activities: The Institute is authorized by the Austrian Federal Government for turbomachine model and prototype testing; research and design of pumps; hydraulic research on inlet-outlet structures, trash racks, needle valves and gates of water power plants; and hydraulic and vibration research on nuclear components. Industrial processing engineering includes drying, mechanical de-watering techniques, water pollution, sludge and refuse recycling and debarking. Work is also carried out on ventilation of halls and vehicular tunnels.
Contract work: Yes
Publications: Research reports in yearbook.

Arbeitsgemeinschaft Österreichischer Entomologen

3

[Austrian Entomology Working Group]
Address: Ludo Hartman-Platz 7, 1160-A Wien
Activities: Life sciences; research into native insects.

Atominstitut der Österreichischen Universitäten

4

[Atomic Institute of the Austrian Universities]
Address: Schüttelstrasse 115, A-1020 Wien
Telephone: 0222/725136
Activities: Experiments with polarized neutrons; study of short-lived isometric nuclear conditions; study of neutron interferometry and neutron radiography: various separation methods for radioactive substances.

Development of reactor equipment; direct nuclear reactions, nuclear fission; study of physics of electron and X-ray radiation; study of colour centres in alkalihalides at minimum temperatures by optic methods and electron-spin resonance; dosimetry.

ELECTRON AND X-RAY PHYSICS SECTION   5

Director: Professor Dr Hannes Aiginger
Graduate research staff: 3

HEALTH PHYSICS SECTION   6

Director: Professor Dr Erich Tschirf
Graduate research staff: 1

NEUTRON AND SOLID-STATE PHYSICS SECTION   7

Director: Professor Dr Helmut Rauch
Graduate research staff: 5

NUCLEAR PHYSICS AND TECHNOLOGY SECTION   8

Director: Professor Dr Gernot Eder
Graduate research staff: 4

NUCLEAR TECHNOLOGY SECTION   9

Director: vacant
Graduate research staff: 4

RADIOCHEMISTRY SECTION   10

Director: Professor Dr Karl Buchtela
Graduate research staff: 2

AVL Professor List Ges mbH*   11

Address: Kleistrasse 48, A-8020 Graz
Telephone: 0316/9870
Telex: 31379
Research director: Dr Killmann
Sections: Combustion research, W. Cartellieri; fluid dynamics, Dr Mayer; stress, Dr J. Affenzeller; acoustics, Dr G. Thien; engine-testing, D. Schreiber
Total r&d staff: 450
Activities: AVL's primary objective in energy projects is the reduction of fuel consumption in internal combus-

tion engines. In the course of this work AVL has developed a combustion system with direct injection for light duty diesel engines giving a 20 per cent reduction in fuel consumption as compared with current indirect injection diesel engines. Further development work is being focused on meeting future demands in terms of fuel consumption, emissions, weight, and durability. Future research will therefore encompass the development of experimental and theoretical techniques for a better understanding of the air/fuel mixing and combustion processes, the reduction of weight with current or improved durability and the reduction of noise. In addition to these investigations, research is being done on alternative fuels such as natural gas, alcohol and methanol and on heat pumps and waste heat recovery.
Facilities: 26 engine test cells; chemical research laboratory; digital analysers for combustion processes; (computer) high-speed combustion photography; fluid dynamics laboratory; stress and strain laboratory; anechoic engine test-bed; various computer programs for prediction of air/fuel mixing.

BMW-Steyr Motoren Gesellschaft mbH   12

Address: Hinterbergerstrasse 2, Postfach 161, A-4400 Steyr
Telephone: 07252/63321
Telex: 28236 motges a
Affiliation: BMW AG Munich; Steyr-Daimler-Puch AG, Vienna
Research director: Dipl-Ing Ingomar Summerauer
Section head: Dr Ing Ferenc Anisits
Graduate research staff: 20
Annual expenditure: over £2m
Activities: Research and development of diesel engines and related components.
Contract work: No

RESEARCH CENTRE   13

Research director: Dipl-Ing Dr Tech Eugen Egger
Sections: Engine development, Dr Ing B. Mayr; combustion research and fuel injection, Dr Tech G. Schwarzbauer; components endurance test, Dipl-Ing F. Mundorf
Annual expenditure: over £2m
Activities: High speed engine design; direct injection - combustion research; fuel injection; exhaust gas turbine; emission and noise tests; component and engine endurance tests; vehicle emission tests.
Facilities: 24 engine test benches; emission control test beds; noise and climatic test benches; roller test benches; injection pump test bench.
Contract work: No

Boden- und Baustoffprüfstelle des Amtes der oü Landesregierung   14

[Upper Austria Building Materials Testing Centre]
Address: Kärtnerstrasse 12, A-4020 Linz
Telephone: 0732/584
Research director: Dipl-Ing Franz Pfaffenwimmer
Activities: Development and testing of materials used in the construction of roads, bridges, waterworks; research into protection against weather damage. Soil mechanics for foundations and road engineering.
Contract work: No

Bundesamt für Eich-und Vermessungswesen   15

– BAfEuV
[Federal Office of Metrology and Surveying]
Address: Friedrich Schmidt-Platz 3, A-1082 Wien 8
Telephone: 0222/435943
Telex: 07/5468
Affiliation: Federal Ministry of Construction and Technology
President: Dipl-Ing Friedrich Hudecek
Sections: Metrology, Dipl-Ing Dr F. Rotter; surveying, Dipl-Ing O. Kloiber (Vice-President), Dipl-Ing Dr J. Bernhard
Activities: Work on dosimetry; aerophotogrammetry: orthophototechnics, digital terrain models; basic surveying including projects on gravity and geoids.
Contract work: Yes

Bundesanstalt für Kulturtechnik und Bodenwasserhaushalt   16

[Federal Research Institute for Agricultural Engineering and Ground Water Economy]
Address: Pollnbergstrasse 1, A-3252 Petzenkirchen
Telephone: 07416/2108
Research director: Dipl-Ing Dr Franz Blumel
Sections: State waterworks and hydrology: Dipl-Ing Norbert Leder; Ground water economy and management, Dr Eduard Klaghofer
Graduate research staff: 2
Activities: New research is being carried out in the following areas: mechanization of drainage work (in laboratory and field); waterflow into drains and water

seepage; efficiency of ditch-clearing machines; chemical removal of weeds from ditches; soil erosion; soil compression; drainage pipes; ground water levels.
General topics of research include: ground physics; ground morphology; evapotranspiration.

Bundesanstalt für Künstliche Besamung der Haustiere   17

[Federal Institute for Artificial Insemination of Domestic Animals]
Address: Austrasse 10, Thalheim, A-4600 Wels
Telephone: 07242/7012
Affiliation: Federal Ministry for Agriculture and Forestry
Research director: Dr Franz Fischerleitner
Research graduate staff: 2
Annual expenditure: £10 000-50 000
Activities: Motility of spermatozoa; histochemistry of spermatozoa; cryobiological problems of deep freezing of spermatozoa; embryotransfers in cattle; artificial insemination in sheep; artificial insemination in horses.

Bundesanstalt für Lebensmitteluntersuchung und Lebensmittelforschung   18

[Federal Institute for Food Investigations and Research]
Address: Kinderspitalgasse 15, A-1090 Wien
Telephone: 0222/427661
Telex: 7/6000
Affiliation: Federal Ministry for Health and Environmental Protection
Research director: Dr Friedrich Petuely
Sections: Development of new analytical methods, Dipl-Ing E. Helwig; gas chromatography/mass spectrometry investigations, Dr H. Holzer; pesticides and heavy metals in food, Dr G. Beier; microbiological investigations, Dr G. Lindner
Graduate research staff: 8
Annual expenditure: £51 000-500 000
Activities: General food research, nutrition, food hygiene and microbiology, heavy metals in food, mycotoxins, pesticides, gas chromatography and mass spectrometry, flavours; use of centrifugal analyser for immunological and enzymatic methods.
Contract work: No

Bundesanstalt für Tierseuchenbekämpfung in Mödling

19

[Federal Institute for the Control of Diseases in Animals]
Address: Robert Koch Gasse 17, Postfach 75, A-2340 Mödling
Telex: 79-325
Affiliation: Federal Ministry for Health and Environmental Protection
Research director: Dr Wolfgang Krocza
Departments: Diagnostics, Dr Erich Scharfen; Serums and Vaccines, Dr Helmut Mathois
Graduate research staff: 9
Annual expenditure: £51 000-500 000
Activities: Research in the improvement and applicability of diagnostic methods: in serology, immunology of vaccines and serums, immunochemistry, bacteriology, epizootics and anthropozoonoses, rabies, Newcastle disease, ornithosis, salmonellosis, brucellosis, tuberculosis; diseases of Central European game, poultry and birds, and of young domestic animals.
Contract work: No

Bundesanstalt für Veterinärmedizinische Untersuchungen

20

[Federal Institute for Veterinary Research]
Address: Hans-Kudlich Strasse 27, Postfach 349, A-4021 Linz
Telephone: 0732/57531
Affiliation: Federal Ministry for Health and Environmental Protection
Research director: Dr Ernst Lauermann
Graduate research staff: 3
Contract work: No

Bundesanstalt für Virusseuchenbekampfung der Haustiere*

21

[Federal Institute for Virus Protection in Animals]
Address: Emil Behring-Weg 3, A-1231 Wien
Director: Professor Dr G. Kubin
Activities: Diagnosis of virus diseases; vaccine production.

Bundesanstalt für Wassergüte*

22

[Federal Institute for Water Quality]
Address: Schiffmühlenstrasse 120, Postfach 7, A-1223 Wien
Affiliation: Federal Ministry for Agriculture and Forestry
Director: W. Hofrat
Activities: Freshwater quality and wastewater treatment processes; influence of domestic, industrial and agricultural wastes from point and diffused sources; correlation between protection and corrective measures and water quality; research into herbicides and their toxicity to aquatic life-forms; research into fish diseases.

Bundesinsitut für Gewässerforschung und Fischerelwirtschaft

23

[Federal Institute for Water Research and Fisheries Management]
Address: Scharfling 18, A-5310 Mondsee
Affiliation: Federal Ministry for Agriculture and Forestry
Research director: Dr Jens Hemsen
Sections: Pond management: Dr Erich Kainz
Lake research: Dr Albert Jagsch

Fish diseases: Dr Manfred Rydlo
Trout feed bacteriology: Thomas Weismann
Water pollution in fisheries: Dr Ilse Butz
Crab farming: Dr Jens Hemsen
Graduate research staff: 5
Annual expenditure: Sch300 000-400 000
Activities: Salmonid and pike culture; experiments on artificial feeding; control of fish diseases; biological and chemical studies on lakes and streams; water pollution.
Contract work: No
Publications: Österreichs Fischerei, 8 issues per year.

Bundeslehr- und Versuchsanstalt für Milchwirtschaft*

24

[Federal Training and Research Institute for Dairy Farming]
Address: Wolfpassing, A-3261 Steinakirchen/Forst Niederösterreich
Affiliation: Federal Ministry for Agriculture and Forestry
Director: Dr B. Planckh
Activities: Experiments and development work in dairying.

Bundesministerium für Gesundheit und Umweltschutz 25

[Federal Ministry for Health and Environmental Protection]
Address: Stubenring 1, A-1010 Wien
Telephone: 0222/7500
Telex: 11780; 111780
Note: See separate entries for: Bundesanstalt für Lebensmitteluntersuchung und Lebensmittelforschung
Bundesanstalt für Tierseuchchenbekämpfung in Mödling
Bundesanstalt für Veterinärmedizinische Untersuchungen.

Bundesministerium für Wissenschaft und Forschung 26

[Ministry of Science and Research]
Address: Minoritenplatz 5, Postfach 104, A-1014 Wien
Activities: The Ministry coordinates and promotes Austrian research efforts generally; it has responsibility for activities within the universities and other institutes of higher education, and has direct authority for the Zentralanstalt für Meteorologie und Geodynamik (Meteorology and Geodynamics Centre).
See separate entry for:
Geologische Bundesanstalt
Naturhistorisches Museum Wien
Österreichische Gesellschaft für Sonnenenergie und Weltraumfragen GmbH.

Bundesversuchsanstalt und Forschungsanstalt Arsenal 27

[Federal Testing and Research Establishment, Arsenal]
Address: Franz Grill-Strasse 3, Postfach 8, A-1031 Wien
Director: Dipl-Ing Dr Erwin Hunter

ELECTRICAL ENGINEERING RESEARCH AND TESTING INSTITUTE 28

Address: Objekt 221, Arsenal, A-1030 Wien
Telephone: 0222/782531
Head: Dipl-Ing E. Böhm
Departments:
Electrical Machinery, Dipl-Ing R. Zillek
High Voltage, Dipl-Ing Dr R. Gös
Heavy Current, Dipl-Ing H.J. Hauer
Electrical Safety Criteria (including equipment in hazardous locations), Dipl-Ing H. Kuhl
Electrical Materials, Dr I. Gussenbauer
Electronics and Data Transmission for Railway Purposes, Dipl-Ing Dr A. Sethy
Applied Electronics, Dipl-Ing F. Oismüller
System Research, Dipl-Ing Dr H. Harich
Activities: The Institute offers testing facilities, laboratories and measuring and testing equipment for research and development work to all electricity supply undertakings, the electrical industry and the professional and trade organizations. Acceptance tests in accordance with any standards are executed. Personnel and equipment of the Institute are also available for systems studiesand investigation of failures in electrical networks.

GEOTECHNICAL INSTITUTE 29

Address: Franz Grill-Strasse 3, Postfach 8, A-1031 Wien
Head: Dr E. Schroll
Departments:
Analytical Geochemistry, Dr D. Sauer
Environmental Chemistry, H. Krachsberger
Applied Mineralogy and Petrology, Dipl-Ing Dr J. Ponahlo
Isotope Geophysics, Dipl-Ing Dr D. Rank
Hydrogeology and Applied Geology, Dr P. Hacker
Soil Mechanics, Dipl-Ing Dr E. Schwab
Road Construction Technique, Dipl-Ing Dr P. Wieden
International Road Research Documentation and International Cooperation in the Field of Transport Economic Documentation, Dipl-Ing H. Warmuth
Activities: The Institute offers testing and research facilities for industry, official bodies and other institutions in the fields of mineral, fuel and water resources and their applications, environmental impacts, soil investigation, pavement design, road building materials, construction and maintenance of road pavements.
The Institute cooperates with the Austrian Federal Geological Survey.

TECHNICAL INSTITUTE FOR MECHANICAL ENGINEERING 30

Address: Franz Grill-Strasse 3, Postfach 8, A-1031 Wien
Head: Dipl-Ing A. Diemling
Departments:
Vehicle Testing Facilities, Dipl-Ing G. Baumgartner
Acoustic and Vibration Measurements, Dipl-Ing G. Rauscher
Fluid Engineering, Dipl-Ing I. Krönke
Refrigeration and Acclimatization, Dipl-Ing G. Schuecker
Thermal Engineering, G. Ratschiner
Activities: Tests on vehicles (especially rail coaches and wagons) at a wide range of temperatures and wind velocities; also in simulated weather conditions. Aerodynamics tests in several wind tunnels; acceptance tests of pumps and ventilators according to standard rules; measurements of ventilation and acclimatization systems in office buildings, including refrigeration equipment; measurements of the efficiency of thermal power plants and of heat losses in buildings; vibration and noise measurements.

Chemiefaser Lenzing Aktiengesellschaft 31

Address: A-4860 Lenzing
Telephone: (07672) 2511
Telex: 026-606 lenfa a
Research director: Professor Dipl-Ing Hans Krässig
Departments: Viscose research, Dr J. Lenz; synthetics, Dr K. Weinrotter; physical research, Dr F. Puchegger
Graduate research staff: 20
Annual expenditure: over £2m
Activities: Viscose fibre research (small scale units and two tons per day pilot plant for viscose staple fibre; research on synthetic fibres and films (mainly polyolefines), pilot plant facilities for film and fibre extrusion; physical research in process automation and in fibre structure and testing.
Contract work: No
Publications: Biannual report.

Fonds zur Förderung der Wissenschaftlichen Forschung 32

[Austrian Science Research Fund]
Address: Garnisongasse 7-20, A-1090 Vienna
Telephone: 0222/421236-0
President: Professor Dr H. Tuppy

General Secretary: Dr Raoul F. Kneucker
Annual expenditure: Sch170m
Activities: The Fund has, in eleven years of existence, supported a wide programme of research in psychological, socio-medical, sociological, educational, linguistic, economical and scientific areas. The Fund has contributed considerably to the establishing of new scientific fields, such as immunology and allergology; and towards close collaboration between technology and medicine, especially in electronics. In this way research has been firmly established with electronic building components for transplants, biomaterials, artificial hearts, brain probes in human medicine, and the replacement of a non-functioning auditory nerve.
In 1979 the Fund promoted research in the natural sciences by Sch64.1m, in technology Sch36.1m, and in medicine Sch26.7m, with grants to various research centres, eg: University of Vienna; University of Graz; University of Innsbruck; University of Salzburg; Technical University of Vienna; Technical University of Graz; Montanuniversity Leoben; University for Soil Sciences, Vienna; Veterinary University of Vienna; Austrian Academy of Sciences; University of Linz.
Contract work: No
Publications: Annual report.

Forschungsgesellschaft für Wohnen, Bauen und Planen 33

[Housing, Building and Planning Research Association]
Address: Löwengasse 47, Postfach 164, 1030 Wien
Telephone: 0222/726251
Research director: Professor Dr Ewald Liepolt
Sections: Documentation and information, Oswald Horak; law, Dr J. Hrebec; planning, Dr Otto Ventruba; technical, Dr Ludwig Komoli; spatial design, Dr Hans Neuhofer
Annual expenditure: Sch2m
Activities: The Research Association was founded in 1962 and is especially interested in the practical application of new research projects. Work so far has been carried out in the area of town and village modernization and the problems of buildings in agricultural sectors. It is currently engaged in a three year project on prefabrication and variable building units, and in climate-oriented planning and building.
Contract work: Yes

Forschungsinstitut des Vereins der Österreichischen Zementfabrikanten 34

[Austrian Cement Manufacturers' Association Research Institute]
Address: Reisnerstrasse 53, A-1030 Wien
Telephone: 0222/756681
Research director: Dipl-Ing Dr Hermann Sommer
Graduate research staff: 7
Activities: Curing of concrete; self-levelling concrete floors; fatigue resistance of concrete and influence of porous aggregate; chloride corrosion of reinforcements; drainage of concrete pavements for roads; resistance of aggregates to polishing.
Publications: Zement und Beton, quarterly.

Forschungsinstitut für Technikgeschichte 35

[Research Institute for the History of Technology]
Address: Mariahilfer Strasse 212, A-1140 Wien
Telephone: 0222/833618
Affiliation: Technisches Museum für Industrie und Gewerbe
Activities: History of technology with special emphasis on Austrian contributions.
Contract work: No

Forstliche Bundesversuchsanstalt 36

– FBVA
[Federal Forest Research Station]
Address: Schönbrunn-Tirolergarten, A-1131 Wien
Telephone: 823638
Scientific director: Dipl-Ing J. Egger
Graduate research staff: 70
Annual expenditure: Sch1.5m
Contract work: Yes

FOREST OPERATIONS AND TECHNIQUES INSTITUTE 37

Head: Dipl-Ing Rudolf Meyr
Sections: Working technology and organization, E. Hauska; production technology, Rudolf Meyr; occupational hygiene and physiology, J. Wencl; testing laboratory for tools and machines, J. Eisbacher

FOREST PROTECTION INSTITUTE 38

Head: Dipl-Ing Dr Edwin Donaubauer
Sections: Entomology, H. Schmutzenhofer; phytopathology, E. Donaubauer; general forest protection, W. Stagl; forest chemistry and smoke damage, K. Stefan; forest insecticide testing, A. Egger

FOREST SITES INSTITUTE 39

Head: Dipl-Ing Dr Helmut Jelem
Sections: Climatology; soil and forest fertilization, W. Kilcan; forest vegetation, H. Jelem; forest stands mapping, K. Mader

MANAGEMENT SCIENCES INSTITUTE 40

Head: Dipl-Ing Otmar Bein
Sections: Biometrics, K. Schieler; photogrammetry, E. Mayer; documentation and publications, Otmar Bein; forest history, Otmar Bein

NATIONAL FOREST INVENTORY INSTITUTE 41

Head: Dipl-Ing Herbert Mildner
Sections: Organization, J. Triber; methods, K. Gratzl; evaluation, O. Niebauer; wood stock balance, J. Haszprunar; inventory interpretation, J. Kindermann

SILVICULTURE INSTITUTE 42

Head: Dipl-Ing Dr Günther Eckhart
Sections: Basic research, W. Rachoy; seed planting, J. Nather; forest planting and care, G. Eckhart; seed testing, J. Nather; testing garden, F. Müller

SUBALPINE FORESTRY RESEARCH 43

Address: 1 Rennweg, A-6020 Innsbruck
Telephone: (05222) 26993
Head: Professor Dr Walter Tranquillini
Sections: Soil biology, F. Göbl; forest plants ecology, I. Neuwinger; plant obstruction, H.M. Schiechtl; forest plant physiology, Walter Tranquillini; experimental glasshouses
Activities: Microclimate; ecophysiology of trees; soils and mycorrhiza; avalanche control; vegetation mapping; silviculture in subalpine forest; Patscherkofel experimental glasshouse; soil science laboratory.

TORRENT AND AVALANCHE RESEARCH INSTITUTE 44

Head: Dipl-Ing Dr Gottfried Kronfellner-Kraus
Sections: Geomorphology and excavations, F. Jeglitsch; hydrology and water science, G. Ruf; snow and avalanches, I. Merwald; control engineering, Gottfried Kronfellner-Kraus

TREE BREEDING AND GENETICS INSTITUTE 45

Head: Dipl-Ing Leopold Günzl
Sections: Basic nursery breeding, K. Holzer; applied breeding, L. Günzl; biological wood research, H. Krempl

YIELD AND ECONOMICS INSTITUTE 46

Head: Dipl-Ing Dr Josef Pollanschütz
Sections: Forest mensuration, K. Johann; yield and production research, H. Rannert; forest management, J. Pollanschütz; economics, J. Enk

Geologische Bundesanstalt 47

[Geological Survey of Austria]
Address: Rasumofskygasse 23, Postfach 154, A-1031 Wien
Telephone: 0222/72 56 74
Telex: 132927 GEOBA A
Parent body: Bundesministerium für Wissenschaft und Forschung
Director: Professor Dr F. Ronner
Sections: Geology, Dr W. Janoschek; applied earth sciences, Professor T. Gattinger
Graduate research staff: 50
Activities: Geological mapping, palaeontology, micropalaeontology, palynology, petrology, sedimentology; research in engineering geology, hydrogeology, mineral resources.
Contract work: No

Gesellschaft für Manuelle Lymphdrainage 48

[Manual Lymph Drainage Society]
Address: Innsbrucker Strasse 2, 6300 Worgl
Activities: Basic research into the application and effect of lymph drainage.

Höhere Bundeslehr- und Versuchsanstalt für Gartenbau* 49

[Federal Training and Research Institute for Horticulture]
Address: Grünbergstrasse 24, A-1131 Wien
Director: Dr L. Urban
Activities: Vegetable growing, variety trials, flowers and ornamentals, seed testing, landscaping, mechanization of horticulture.

Höhere Bundeslehr- und Versuchsanstalt für Wein- und Obstbau 50

[Federal Training and Research Institute for Viticulture and Fruit Growing]
Address: Wiener Strasse 74, Postfach 37, A-3400 Klosterneuburg
Affiliation: Federal Ministry for Agriculture and Forestry
Director: Professor Dipl-Ing Hans Haushofer
Activities: Vine breeding; viticulture; technology, analysis and microbiology of wine; fruit-culture; fruit processing (brandy, jam, juice, liqueur, nectar); plant protection.

Institut für Festkörperphysik - Erich-Schmid Institut 51

[Solid-State Physics Institute]
Address: Montanistische Hochschule, A-8700 Leoben
Affiliation: Austrian Academy of Sciences
Director: Dr Heinz Stüwe
Activities: Plasticity of materials at different temperatures and pressures; research into plastic deformation of metals; problems of fractures and crystal structure of layers of tinplate; diffusion-based enrichment of trace elements at interfaces; co-segregation of metallic and non-metallic impurities at interfaces.

Institut für Hirnforschung   52

[Brain Research Institute]
Address: c/o Neurological Institute of the University
of Vienna, Schwarzspanierstrasse 17, A-1090 Wien
Telephone: (0222) 431526
Affiliation: Austrian Academy of Sciences
Director: Professor Dr F. Seitelberger
Graduate research staff: 10
Annual expenditure: Sch80 000
Activities: Structure-function relation of the brain
especially the cerebral cortex; special micro-electroen-
cephalogram (EEG) methods for closer look at the
structural dependency of electrical activity; intra-corti-
cal aspects of rhythmicity in seizure patterns; action of
toxins, drugs, etc on the function of neuronal systems;
studies on ageing; neurochemistry of gangliosides; behaviour of brain ganglioside with Huntington's Chorea
and the 'Kainat Model' of this disease in the rat.
Studies on aphasias and cognitive brain functions; computer studies.
Member of the research team into epilepsy of the
Deutschen Forschungsgemeinschaft (German Research
Association). Neurochemical experiments are carried
out in collaboration with the Institut für Biochemische
Pharmakologie, Universität Wien, and the Clarke Institute of Psychiatry, Toronto, Canada.
Contract work: No

BRAIN PATHOLOGY DEPARTMENT   53

Address: Schwarzspanierstrasse 17, A-1090 Wien
Head: Professor Dr F. Seitelberger

NEUROPHARMACOLOGY   54
DEPARTMENT

Address: Währingerstrasse 132, A-1090 Wien
Head: Professor Dr Ch. Stumpf

NEUROPHYSIOLOGY AND   55
NEUROANATOMY DEPARTMENT

Address: Währingerstrasse 15, A-1090 Wien
Head: Professor Dr H. Petsche

Institut für   56
Hochenergiephysik

[High Energy Physics Institute]
Address: Nikolsdorfergasse 18, A-1050 Wien
Telephone: 0222/557328
Telex: 01-12628

Affiliation: Austrian Academy of Sciences
Head: Dr Walter Majerotto
Sections: Electronic experiments, Dr M. Regler; bubble chamber physics, Dr M. Markytan; electronics, Dr
W. Bartl; theory, Dr W. Majerotto; computing, Dipl-Ing
W. Mitaroff
Graduate research staff: 22
Annual expenditure: Sch7m
Activities: Interactions of elementary particles. The
two main experimental groups are concerned with the
analysis of bubble chamber data and the data from
electronic particle detectors respectively. Three smaller
groups are concerned with theoretical research,
electronics, and computing. The electronics group builds
wire chambers and other electronic devices for particle
detectors. Experiments are carried out in collaboration
with other foreign groups at the Super Proton
Synchrotron of CERN in Geneva. In particular the
Institute is involved in a major project for the An-
tiprotron-Protron Collider. Scattering experiments have
also been carried out in collaboration with the Sowjet
Laboratory Serpukhov.
Contract work: No

Institut für Limnologie,   57
Lunz*

[Limnology Institute, Lunz]
Address: A-3293 Lunz am See
Affiliation: Austrian Academy of Sciences
Director: Professor Dr Heinz Löffler
Activities: Limnological problems of Lunz lakes;
nutrients; light and wind conditions; thermic conditions;
hydrology; laboratory experiments; fauna; taxonomy of
trichoptera; anatomy and breeding behaviour of fish.

BIOLOGISCHE STATION LUNZ   58

[Biological Station Lunz]
Address: A-3293 Lunz am See
Telephone: 07486/330
Head: G. Bretschko
Projects: ÖEP, G. Schlott; RITRODAT Lunz, G.
Bretschko
Annual expenditure: £10 000-50 000
Activities: RITRODAT is the name of a master project
designed to combine the research efforts of the station
itself and other self-contained sub-projects funded by
private or public sponsors. The aim of the project is to
reach such a level of understanding that it becomes
possible to make scientifically sound forecasts. This is to
be achieved by a full analysis of the ecosystem on the
basis of the well known energy concept. The project
should last till the year 2003.

A detailed framework has been established by dividing the abiotic environment into six components according to functional and methodological relationships: catchment space, airspace, waterbody and sediment surface, bed sediments, groundwater space.

Ecosystem studies in running waters; study of the vertical distribution of brook fauna in the bed sediments as well as the description of this biotope. Lake; macrophytes; pollution.

Contract work: No
Publications: Yearbook.

Institut für Molekularbiologie 59

[Molecular Biology Institute]
Address: Billrothstrasse 11, A-5020 Saltzburg
Affiliation: Austrian Academy of Sciences
Head: J.V. Small
Sections: Physics; chemistry; biology
Activities: Physics: muscle contraction and cell movement; contraction mechanism of the smooth muscle, the muscle tissue of the inner organs of the body, such as digestive tract and urogenital tract, blood vessel walls, bronchia and various glands.

Chemistry: biosynthesis of a peptide 'Melittin', of the bee. Used as a model for the secretion and freeing of physiologically active polypeptides. Research into mechanism which triggers off the peptide 'Melittin' with its strong cyctoliptic effect in the cells of the venom gland.

Biology: cell division control and all differentiation by cell interaction. Three prototypes are used: nucleus-cytoplasma-interaction in heterocaryons, cell and tissue interaction of the embryonic organ development, and cell matrix interaction of epithelial tumours.

Institut für Radiumforschung und Kernphysik 60

[Neutron Physics and Radium Research Institute]
Address: Boltzmanngasse 3, A-1090 Wien
Telephone: 0222/342630
Affiliation: Austrian Academy of Sciences
Research director: Professor Herbert Vonarch
Graduate research staff: 15
Annual expenditure: £300 000
Activities: Study of fast neutron-induced nuclear reactions measurement of n,nI and n, alpha spectra, angular distributions and cross-sections using a pulsed neutron generator and multitelescope systems; development and application of nuclear model codes for calculation of cross-sections of all kinds in neutron-induced nuclear reactions; evaluations of neutron cross-sections; fast neutron activation analysis; dating of archaeological, palaeontological and geological objects, by means of nuclear methods (carbon 14, uranium-thorium and others); radiation dosimetry.

Contract work: Yes

Institut für Röntgenfein-strukturforschung 61

[X-Ray Fine Stucture Research Institute]
Address: Steyrergasse 17, A-8010 Graz
Telephone: 0316/71371
Telex: (3)1265 RZGRAZ
Affiliation: Austrian Academy of Sciences; Research Centre Graz
Activities: X-ray small-angle scattering methods as a structural clarification of colloid, especially macromolecular materials; special structural research of biological systems; lipoproteins of serum and micelle structures of lipids in biological membranes and in bile fluids.

Contract work: No

Institut für Weltraumforschung 62

[Space Research Institute]
Address: Halbärthgasse 1, A-8010 Graz
Telephone: 0316/31581-981; 77511-0
Telex: 31078 OBSLGZ A
Affiliation: Austrian Academy of Sciences; Karl-Franzens-Universität Graz
Acting director: Professor Dr O.M. Burkard
Graduate research staff: 36
Annual expenditure: £51 000-500 000
Activities: Measurements of the electron content of the ionosphere with satellites; ionophone measurements; theoretical work on magnetosphere and magnetopause; measurements of electron density in the ionosphere with balloons in polar regions; measurements with magnetometers and rockets in polar regions; satellite geodesy.

Contract work: No

EXPERIMENTAL SPACE RESEARCH DEPARTMENT 63

Address: Inffeldgasse 12, A-8010 Graz
Head: Professor Dr W. Riedler

PHYSICS OF THE NEARER SPACE DEPARTMENT 64

Address: Halbärthgasse 1, A-8010 Graz
Head: Professor Dr O.M. Burkard

SATELLITE GEODESY DEPARTMENT 65

Address: Rechbauerstrasse 12, A-8010 Graz
Head: Professor Dr K. Rinner

Interdisziplinäres Zentrum 66 für Forschung und Entwicklung in der Intensivmedizin

– IZI
[Intensive Medicine Interdisciplinary Centre of Research and Development]
Address: Spitalgasse 23, A-1090 Wien
Activities: Interdisciplinary research and development of intensive medicine.

ITT Austria Gesellschaft 67 mbH

Address: Scheydgasse 41, A-1210 Wien
Telephone: 0222/3800-0
Telex: 74573; 74579
Parent body: International Telephone and Telegraph Corporation, New York
Research directors: Dr Hermann Ebenberger, Dipl-Ing Peter Knezu
Graduate research staff: 22
Annual expenditure: Sch96m
Activities: Modern communication equipment, especially telephone switching systems (public and private automatic exchanges), railway signalling systems, and relevant components.
Contract work: Yes

Johannes Kepler Universität 68 Linz

[Linz University]
Address: Altenbergerstrasse 69, A-4040 Linz
Telephone: 0732/31381
Telex: 2/2323
Rector: Professor Dr Peter Oberndorfer

FACULTY OF TECHNICAL AND NATURAL SCIENCES 69

Dean: Professor Dr Bruno Buchberger

Analytical, Organic and Physical Chemistry Institute 70

Director: vacant
Senior staff: Professor Dr Heinz Falk, Professor Dr Hermann Janeschitz-Kriegl, Professor Dr Karl Winsauer

Chemical Technology of Inorganic Materials Institute 71

Director: Professor Dr Gerhard Gritzner

Chemical Technology of Organic Materials Institute 72

Director: Professor Dipl-Ing Dr Ernst Oltay

Experimental Physics Institute 73

Director: Professor Dr Paul Helmut
Senior staff: Professor Dr Dieter Bäuerle, Professor Dr Helmut Heinrich, Professor Dr Adolfo Lopez-Otero

Information Sciences Institute 74

Director: Professor Dr Arno Schulz
Senior staff: Professor Dr Peter Rechenberg, Professor Dr Ernst Rudolf Reiche, Professor Dr Jörg Mühlbacher

Mathematics Institute 75

Director: Professor Dr Günter Pilz
Senior staff: Professor Dr Bruno Buchberger, Professor Dr James Bell Cooper, Professor Dr Hans Knapp, Professor Dr Paul Otto Runck, Professor Dr Hannsjörg Wacker, Professor Dr Peter Weiss

Systems Analysis Institute 76

Director: Professor Dr Adolf Adam
Senior staff: Professor Dr Franz Pichler

Theoretical Physics Institute 77

Director: Professor Dr Wilhelm Macke
Senior staff: Professor Dr Franz Schwabl

Karl-Franzens-Universität Graz

78

[Graz University]
Address: Universitätsplatz 3, A-8010 Graz
Telephone: 0316/31581
Telex: 03 1662
Rector: Professor Dr Friedrich Hausmann
Director: Dr August Fetsch

FACULTY OF MEDICINE

79

Telephone: 0316/3850
Dean: Professor Dr Helmut Lechner

Anaesthiology Institute

80

Address: Auenbruggerplatz 5, A-8036 Graz
Telephone: 0316/3850
Director: Professor Dr Warner List

Anatomy Institute

81

Address: Harrachgasse 21, A-8010 Graz
Telephone: 0316/31581
Director: Professor Dr Walter Thiel

Dental Clinic

82

Address: Auenbruggerplatz 12, A-8036 Graz
Telephone: 0316/3850
Director: Professor Dr Heinrich Köle
Senior staff: Professor Dr Gerhard Plischka

Dermatology and Venereology Institute

83

Address: Auenbruggerplatz 8, A-8036 Graz
Telephone: 0316/3850
Director: Professor Dr Hans Kresbach
Senior staff: Professor Dr Anton Musger

Ear, Nose and Throat Clinic

84

Address: Auenbruggerplatz 20, A-8036 Graz
Telephone: 0316/3850
Director: Professor Dr Walter Messerklinger

Experimental and Clinical Pharmacology Institute

85

Address: Universitätsplatz 4, A-8010 Graz
Telephone: 0316/31581
Director: Professor Dr Fred Lembeck

Forensic Medicine Institute

86

Address: Universitätsplatz 4, A-8010 Graz
Telephone: 0316/31581
Director: Professor Dr Wolfgang Maresch

Functional Pathology Institute

87

Address: Mozartgasse 14, A-8010 Graz
Telephone: 0316/31581
Director: Professor Dr Horst G. Klingenberg

Gynaecology Clinic

88

Address: Auenbruggerplatz 14, A-8036 Graz
Telephone: 0316/3850
Director: Professor Dr Erich Burghardt

Histology and Embryology Institute

89

Address: Harrachgasse 21, A-8010 Graz
Telephone: 0316/31581
Director: Professor Dr Wilhelm Burkl

Hygiene Institute

90

Address: Universitätsplatz 4, A-8010 Graz
Telephone: 0316/31581
Director: Professor Dr Josef Möse

Medical Biochemistry Institute

91

Address: Harrachgasse 21, A-8010 Graz
Telephone: 0316/31581
Director: Professor Dr Anton Holasek
Senior staff: Professor Dr Gerhard Kostner, Professor Dr Walter Palm

Medical Biology and Human Genetics Institute

92

Address: Harrachgasse 21, A-8010 Graz
Telephone: 0316/31581
Director: Professor Dr Walter Rosenkranz

Medical Chemistry Institute

93

Address: Harrachgasse 21, A-8010 Graz
Telephone: 0316/31581
Director: Professor Dr Benno Paletta
Senior staff: Professor Dr Theodor Leipert

Medical Clinic

94

Address: Auenbruggerplatz 11, A-8036 Graz
Telephone: 0316/3850
Director: Professor Dr Siegfried Sailer
Senior staff: Professor Dr Werner Klein

Medical Physics and Biophysics Institute　　　95

Address: Harrachgasse 21, A-8010 Graz
Telephone: 0316/31581
Director: Professor Dr Helmut Tritthart

Medical Psychology and Psychotherapy Institute　　　96

Address: Auenbruggerplatz 23, A-8036 Graz
Telephone: 0316/3850
Director: Dr Walter Pieringer

Neurosurgery Clinic　　　97

Address: Auenbruggerplatz 5, A-8036 Graz
Telephone: 0316/3850
Director: Professor Dr Friedrich Heppner
Senior staff: Professor Dr Grigorios Argyropoulos

Ophthalmology Clinic　　　98

Address: Auenbruggerplatz 4, A-8036 Graz
Telephone: 0316/3850
Director: Professor Dr Hans Hofmann
Senior staff: Dr Helmut Hanselmayer

Paediatric Surgery Institute　　　99

Address: Heinrichstrasse 31, A-8010 Graz
Telephone: 0316/3850
Director: Professor Dr Hugo Sayer
Senior staff: Professor Dr Ronald Kurz

Paediatrics Clinic　　　100

Address: Auenbruggerplatz 30, A-8036 Graz
Telephone: 0316/3850
Director: Professor Dr Beat Hadorn

Pathological Anatomy Clinic　　　101

Address: Auenbruggerplatz 25, A-8036 Graz
Telephone: 0316/31581
Director: Professor Dr Max Ratzenhofer
Senior staff: Professor Dr Hans Becker, Professor Dr Kurt O. Schmid, Professor Dr Josef Zangger

Physiology Institute　　　102

Address: Harrachgasse 21, A-8010 Graz
Telephone: 0316/31581
Director: Professor Dr Thomas Kenner
Senior staff: Professor Dr Rudolf Rigler

Psychiatry and Neurology Clinic　　　103

Address: Auenbruggerplatz 22, A-8036 Graz
Telephone: 0316/3850
Director: Professor Dr Helmut Lechner
Senior staff: Professor Dr Wolfgang Walcher

Radiology Clinic　　　104

Address: Auenbruggerplatz 9, A-1036 Graz
Telephone: 0316/3850
Director: Professor Dr Erich Vogler
Senior staff: Professor Dr Gerhard F. Fueger, Professor Dr Ernst Kahr, Professor Dr Heribert Schreyer

Surgery Clinic　　　105

Address: Auenbruggerplatz 5, A-8036 Graz
Telephone: 0316/3850
Director: Professor Dr Julius Kraft-Kinz
Senior staff: Professor Dr Gerhard Friehs, Professor Dr Gerhard Hubner, Professor Dr Günther Koch, Professor Dr Leo Kronberger

FACULTY OF NATURAL SCIENCES　　　106

Dean: Professor Dr Ludwig Reich

Astronomy Institute　　　107

Address: Universitätsplatz 5, A-8010 Graz
Telephone: 0316/31581
Director: Professor Dr Hermann Haupt

KANZELHÖHE SUN OBSERVATORY　　　108
Address: Kärnten, 9520 Sattendorf
Telephone: 04248/2717

LUSTBÜHEL OBSERVATORY　　　109
Address: Lustbühelstrasse 46, 8042 Graz
Telephone: 0316/41358; 41316

Biochemistry Institute　　　110

Address: Halbärthgasse 5/I, A-8010 Graz
Telephone: 0316/31581
Director: Professor Dr Erwin Schauenstein
Senior staff: Professor Dr Hermann Esterbauer

Botany Institute　　　111

Address: Holteigasse 6, A-8010 Graz
or: Schubertstrasse 51A, A-8010 Graz
Telephone: 0316/31581
Director: Professor Dr Josef Poelt
Senior staff: Professor Dr Herwig Teppner

Experimental Physics Institute 112

Address: Universitätsplatz 5, A-8010 Graz
Director: Professor Dr Günther Porod
Senior staff: Professor Dr Franz Aussenegg, Professor Dr Ferdinand Gross

Geography Institute 113

Address: Universitätsplatz 2/II, A-8010 Graz
Telephone: 0316/31581
Director: Professor Dr Wilhelm Leitner

Geology and Palaeontology Institute 114

Address: Heinrichstrasse 26, A-8010 Graz
Telephone: 0316/31581
Director: Professor Dr Helmut Flügel

Inorganic and Analytical Chemistry Institute 115

Address: Universitätsplatz 1, A-8010 Graz
Telephone: 0316/31581
Director: Professor Dr Eugen Gagliardi
Senior staff: Professor Dr Edgar Nachbauer

Mathematics Institute 116

Address: Elisabethstrasse 11, A-8010 Graz
or: Halbärthgasse 1/I, A-8010 Graz
Telephone: 0316/36479
Director: Professor Dr Franz Kappel
Senior staff: Professor Dr Heribert Fieber, Professor Dr Peter Flor, Professor Dr Ludwig Reich

Meteorology and Geophysics Institute 117

Address: Halbärthgasse 1, A-8010 Graz
Telephone: 0316/31581
Acting head: Dr Reinhart Leitinger
See separate entry for: Institut für Weltraumforschung.

Mineralogy, Crystallography and Petrology Institute 118

Address: Universitätsplatz 2, A-8010 Graz
Telephone: 0316/31581
Director: Professor Dr Haymo Heritsch
Senior staff: Professor Dr Eva Maria Walitzi

Organic Chemistry Institute 119

Address: Heinrichstrasse 28, A-8010 Graz
Telephone: 0316/31581
Director: Professor Dr Erich Ziegler

Pharmaceutical Chemistry Institute 120

Address: Universitätsplatz 1, A-8010 Graz
Telephone: 0316/31581
Director: Professor Dr Gustav Zigeuner
Senior staff: Professor Dr Robert Ott

Pharmacodynamics and Toxicology Institute 121

Address: Universitätsplatz 2, A-8010 Graz
Telephone: 0316/31581
Director: Professor Dr Walter Kukovetz
Senior staff: Professor Dr Gerald Pöch

Pharmacognosy Institute 122

Address: Universitätsplatz 4, A-8010 Graz
Telephone: 0316/31581
Director: Professor Dr Theodor Kartnig

Physical Chemistry Institute 123

Address: Heinrichstrasse 28, A-8010 Graz
Telephone: 0316/31581
Director: Professor Dr Josef Schurz
Senior staff: Professor Dr Hans Leopold, Professor Dr Ingrid Pilz

Plant Physiology Institute 124

Address: Schubertstrasse 51, A-8010 Graz
Director: Professor Dr Franz Wolkinger
Senior staff: Professor Dr Irmtraud Thaler

Theoretical Chemistry Institute 125

Address: Mozartgasse 14, A-8010 Graz
Telephone: 0316/31581
Director: Professor Dr Rudolf Janoscheck

Theoretical Physics Institute 126

Address: Universitätsplatz 5, A-8010 Graz
Telephone: 0316/31581
Director: Professor Dr Heimo Latal
Senior staff: Professor Dr Kurt Bauman, Professor Dr Heinrich Mitter

Zoology Institute 127

Address: Universitätsplatz 2, A-8010 Graz
Director: Professor Dr Reinhart Schuster
Senior staff: Professor Dr Herbert Heran

Kuratorium für Verkehrssicherheit   128

[Road Safety Board]
Address: Olzeltgasse 3, Postfach 190, A-1031 Wien
Director: P. Manhardt
Sections: Traffic Engineering Institute, Professor Dr H. Knoflacher
Traffic Psychology Institute, Dr K. Höfner
Traffic Education Institute, Professor W.G. Kaan
Activities: A private association established and supported by insurance companies and automobile clubs. The aim of the Board is to improve traffic safety by means of research work in the three institutes and by following up the research results with practical measures. Tests and experiments are conducted at schools and teachers' training courses, and the mass media are informed about activities and cooperate in safety campaigns.

Laboratorium für Kunststofftechnik   129

– LKT-TGM
[Laboratory for Plastics Technology]
Address: Wexstrasse 19-23, A-1200 Wien
Telephone: 0222/353511-352106
Telex: 131824
Affiliation: Gesellschaft zur Förderung der Kunststofftechnik
Research director: Professor Dipl-Ing Dr Helmut Hubeny
Sections: Calendering, Professor Dr Josef Salhofer; chemistry, Professor Dr Ernst Wogrolly; computation, Professor Dr Franz Mayer; compounding, Herbert Wolonek: construction, Professor Dr Werner Jessenig; extrusion, Professor Dr Hans Revesz; foaming, Professor Dr Heinz Fischer; injection moulding, Professor Horst Grof; testing, Professor Dr Heinz Dragaun, Professor Dipl-Ing Dr Otto Horak, Erich Herbinger; thermoanalysis, Professor Dr Heinz Fischer
Graduate research staff: 9
Annual expenditure: £51 000-500 000
Activities: Technology, morphology and application of polymers; process analysis, polymer physics and chemical technology.
Main subjects: floor heating systems, latent heat storage systems, optimization of high quality floor coverings, pressure pipes, window profiles, packaging films; optimization of extrusion, injection moulding and foaming processes.
Facilities: Electronic universal testing machines, DSC-equipment, climate chambers, pipe and window testing stands, rheometers, injection moulding machines, extru-

sion sets, foaming machines, roll mills, presses, mixers, xenotest equipment, GC, IR-photometer.
Contract work: Yes
Publications: Annual report and *Österreichische Kunststoffzeitschrift.*

Landwirtschaftlich- Chemische Bundesversuchsanstalt Linz   130

[Federal Agricultural Chemistry Experimental Establishment]
Address: Wieningerstrasse 8, A-4025 Linz
Telephone: 0732/81261
Affiliation: Federal Ministry for Agriculture and Forestry
Research director: Professor Dipl-Ing Dr Walther Beck
Institutes: Analysis: Dipl-Ing Erwin Lengauer; agrarian biology: Dr Josef Gunsenleitner
Annual expenditure: £501 000-2m
Activities: Agricultural chemistry; biochemistry; pedology; agricultural microbiology; seed testing; fertility in cattle; field trials; biometrics; antibiotics; pesticides; mycotoxins; crop nutrition and fertilization; animal nutrition.
Contract work: Yes

Landwirtschaftlich- Chemische Bundesversuchsanstalt Wien   131

[Federal Experimental Station for Agricultural Chemistry]
Address: Trunnerstrasse 1, A-1020 Wien
Telephone: 0222/241511
Affiliation: Federal Ministry for Agriculture and Forestry
Research director: Professor Dipl-Ing Dr Walther Beck
Institutes: Analytics and biochemistry: Dr Peter Gunhold; plant nutrition and soil chemistry: Dr Hans-Erich Oberländer; wine and cellar economy: Dr Josef Schneyder
Graduate research staff: 6
Activities: Research in plant nutrition; soil chemistry; chemistry of feedstuffs; animal nutrition; fertilizers; minor elements; wines and spirits; use of isotopes.

Leopold-Franzens Universität Innsbruck* 132

[Leopold Franzens University, Innsbruck]
Address: Universitätsstrasse 2-6, 6020 Innsbruck
Telephone: 5222/33601

FACULTY OF CONSTRUCTION ENGINEERING AND ARCHITECTURE* 133

FACULTY OF MEDICINE* 134

Dean: Professor Dr K. Kryspin-Exner

FACULTY OF SCIENCE* 135

Dean: Professor Dr W. Wieser

UNIVERSITY AFFILIATED INSTITUTE* 136

Obergurgl Institute* 137

Address: Universitätsstrasse 4, A-6020 Innsbruck

Ludwig Boltzmann Gesellschaft- Österreichische Vereinigung zur Förderung der Wissenschaftlichen Forschung 138

[Ludwig Boltzmann Society - Austrian Association for the Promotion of Scientific Research]
Address: Hofburg, Postfach 33, A-1014 Wien
President: Professor Dr Rudolf Strasser
Directing member of the board: Dr Josef Bandion
Activities: The Society has set up and is now running 47 research institutes and 7 research units. The institutes and units are dealing with research in the natural sciences (solid-state physics, morphology, biochemistry, environmental sciences); in medicine (brain research, leukaemia, nervous system, andrology, surgery, endocrinology, rheumatology, acupuncture, metabolism, sexually transmitted diseases); in the social sciences and humanities.

ACUPUNCTURE INSTITUTE 139

Address: Allgemeine Polyklinik, Mariannengasse 10, A-1090 Wien
Telephone: 0222/425571
Activities: Treatments using acupuncture; training, and documentation; research into acupuncture, pain, and acupuncture-induced analgesia, and development of new methods and equipment, including laser and thermal devices, combined treatment forms, pharma-acupuncture, focal disturbances.
Contract work: Yes

ADDICTION RESEARCH INSTITUTE 140

Address: Stiftung Genesungsheim Kalksburg, Mackgasse 7-9, A-1237 Wien
Telephone: 0222/884137

AGE RESEARCH INSTITUTE 141

Address: II Medizinische Universitätsklinik, Garnisongasse 13, A-1090 Wien
Telephone: 0222/4289

ANDROLOGY INSTITUTE 142

Address: Krankenhaus der Stadt Wien-Lainz, Wolkersbergenstrasse 1, A-1130 Wien
Telephone: 0222/841616

APPLIED ENVIRONMENTAL AND HYDROTHERAPY INSTITUTE 143

Address: Badehospiz, A-5640 Badgastein
Telephone: 06434/2007

CIRCULATION OF THE BRAIN RESEARCH INSTITUTE 144

Address: Neurologisches Krankenhaus der Stadt Wien-Rosenhügel, Riedelgasse 5, A-1130 Wien
Telephone: 0222/882515

CLINICAL ENDOCRINOLOGY INSTITUTE 145

Address: II Medizinische Universitätsklinik, Garnisongasse 13, A-1090 Wien
Telephone: 0222/434348

CLINICAL NEUROBIOLOGY INSTITUTE　　146

Address: Krankenhaus der Stadt Wien-Lainz, Wolkersbergenstrasse 1, A-1130 Wien
Telephone: 0222/841616

CLINICAL ONCOLOGY INSTITUTE　　147

Address: Krankenhaus der Stadt Wien-Lainz, Wolkersbergenstrasse 1, A-1130 Wien
Telephone: 0222/841616

DERMATO-VENEROLOGICAL SERODIAGNOSIS INSTITUTE　　148

Address: Krankenhaus der Stadt Wien-Lainz, Wolkersbergenstrasse 1, A-1130 Wien
Telephone: 0222/841616

EXPANSION RESEARCH INSTITUTE　　149

Address: Österreichische Volksfürsorge, Allgemeine Versicherungs AG, Hohenstaufengasse 10, A-1010 Wien
Telephone: 0222/637216

EXPERIMENTAL ANAESTHESIOLOGY AND INTENSIVE THERAPY RESEARCH INSTITUTE　　150

Address: Institut für Anaesthesie und Allgemeine Intensivmedizin der Universität Wien, Spitalgasse 23, A-1090 Wien
Telephone: 0222/4289
Affiliation: Austrian Society for Anaesthesiology
Director: Professor Dr K. Steinbereithner
Graduate research staff: 15
Activities: Neurophysiological developments, haemodynamic studies; lung trauma; malign hyperthermia.
Contract work: No

EXPERIMENTAL AND GASTROENTEROLOGICAL SURGERY INSTITUTE　　151

Address: Landeskrankenanstalten, A-5020 Salzburg
Telephone: 06222/31581

EXPERIMENTAL PLASTIC SURGERY INSTITUTE　　152

Address: I Chirurgische Universitätsklinik, Alserstrasse 4, A-1090 Wien
Telephone: 0222/4289

EXPERIMENTAL TRAUMATOLOGY INSTITUTE　　153

Address: Lorenz-Böhler-Krankenhaus, Donaueschingenstrasse 13, A-1200 Wien
Telephone: 0222/335533

HEART SURGERY RESEARCH INSTITUTE　　154

Address: II Chirurgische Universitätsklinik, Spitalgasse 23, A-1080 Wien
Telephone: 0222/439229

HOMOEOPATHY INSTITUTE　　155

Address: Krankenhaus der Stadt Wien-Lainz, Wolkesbergenstrasse 1, A-1130 Wien
Telephone: 0222/841616

IMMUNOLOGICAL AND CYTOGENETIC RESEARCH IN DOMESTIC ANIMALS INSTITUTE　　156

Address: Veterinärmedizinische Universität Wien, Linke Bahngasse 11, A-1030 Wien
Telephone: 0222/735581

INSTITUTE FOR SOLID-STATE PHYSICS　　157

Address: Kopernikusgasse 15, A-1060 Wien
Telephone: 0222/563408; 563409
Graduate research staff: 14
Annual expenditure: Sch3m
Activities: Research into semiconductor physics: at low temperature ($4°K$); in strong magnetic fields (11 Testa); at high frequencies (microwave and farinfrared, $9-4O°$ GHz; lasers, HCN, Ar, Dye); research into solar cells.
Contract work: Yes

INSTITUTE FOR THE INVESTIGATION OF BRAIN DAMAGE IN CHILDREN　　158

Address: Neurologisches Krankenhaus der Stadt Wien-Rosenhügel, Reidelgasse 5, A-1130 Wien
Telephone: 0222/882515

INSTITUTE FOR THE INVESTIGATION OF DISEASES AND TUMOURS OF THE URINARY TRACT　　159

Address: Allgemeine Poliklinic der Stadt Wien, Mariannengasse 10, A-1090 Wien
Telephone: 0222/425571

INSTITUTE FOR THE INVESTIGATION 160
OF INFECTIOUS VENERO-
DERMATOLOGICAL DISEASES

Address: II Universitäts-Hautklinik Spitalgasse 2, A-1090 Wien
Telephone: 0222/4289

LASER SURGERY INSTITUTE 161

Address: Juchgasse 25, A-1030 Wien
Telephone: 0222/725661

LEUKAEMIA RESEARCH AND 162
HAEMATOLOGY INSTITUTE

Address: Hanusch-Krankenhaus, Heinrich-Collin-Strasse 30, A-1140 Wien
Telephone: 0222/942151

MEDICAL SOCIOLOGY INSTITUTE 163

Address: Institut für Höhere Studien und Wissenschaftliche Forschung, Stumpergasse 56, A-1060 Wien
Telephone: 0222/563601

METABOLIC DISEASES AND 164
NUTRITION INSTITUTE

Address: Krankenhaus der Stadt Wien-Lainz, 3 Medizinisches Abteilung, Wolkersbergenstrasse 1, A-1130 Wien
Telephone: 0222/841616

NUCLEAR MEDICINE INSTITUTE 165

Address: II Medizinische Universitätsklinik, Garnisongasse 13, A-1090 Wien
Telephone: 0222/4289

OBSTETRICS AND PREGNANCY CARE 166
INSTITUTE

Address: Ignaz-Semmelweis-Frauenklinik der Stadt-Wien, Bastiengasse 36, A-1180 Wien
Telephone: 0222/471515

PARADONTOLOGY INSTITUTE 167

Address: Theresienbadhaus, Kaiser-Franz-Ring 8, A-2500 Baden
Telephone: 02252/2407

RADIOCHEMISTRY INSTITUTE 168

Address: Institut für Theoretische Chemie und Strahlenchemie der Universität Wien, Währingerstrasse 38, A-1090 Wien
Telephone: 0222/347317

RADIOPHYSICAL TUMOUR 169
DIAGNOSIS

Address: I Medezinische Universitätsklinick, Lazarethgasse 14, A-1090 Wien
Telephone: 0222/4289

RECOVERY FROM INTERNAL 170
DISEASES INSTITUTE

Address: Rehabilitationszentrum, A-5760 Saalfelden
Telephone: 05682/3815

RESEARCH AND DEVELOPMENT OF 171
NEW ENERGY TECHNOLOGIES
INSTITUTE

Address: Auerspergstrasse 4, A-1080 Wien
Telephone: 0222/42800

RHEUMATOLOGY AND 172
BALNEOLOGY INSTITUTE

Address: Kurbadstrasse 10, A-1107 Wien Oberlaa
Telephone: 0222/681611

RHEUMATOLOGY AND FOCAL 173
DISTURBANCES INSTITUTE

Address: Theresienbadhaus, Kaiser-Franz-Ring 8, A-2500 Baden
Telephone: 02252/8138

SCIENCE RESEARCH INSTITUTE 174

Address: Lerchenfelder Strasse 44, A-1080 Wien
Telephone: 0222/481162

SOCIAL GERONTOLOGY AND LIFE 175
PATTERNS RESEARCH INSTITUTE

Address: Institut für Soziologie der Universität Wien, Alser Strasse 33, A-1080 Wien
Telephone: 0222/434679

SOCIAL PSYCHIATRY INSTITUTE 176

Address: Kriseninterventionszentrum, Spitalgasse 11, A-1090 Wien
Telephone: 0222/439595

VETERINARY ENDOCRINOLOGY 177 INSTITUTE

Address: Veterinärmedizinische Universität Wien, Linke Bahngasse 11, A-1030 Wien
Telephone: 0222/735581

Agricultural Biology Research Unit 178

Address: Rinnböckstrasse 15, A-1100 Wien
Telephone: 0222/743631

Biochemistry Research Unit 179

Address: Organisch-Chemisches Institut der Universität Wien, Währingerstrasse 38, A-1090 Wien
Telephone: 0222/344630

Computer Technology Systems 180 Research Unit

Address: Amstgebäude des Bundeskanzleramtes, Herrengasse 23, A-1010 Wien
Telephone: 0222/6615

Longterm Therapy and Rehabilitation 181 Research Unit

Address: 5 Medizinisches Abteilung, Wilhelminenspital der Stadt Wien, Montleartstrasse 37, A-1161 Wien
Telephone: 0222/952511

Rehabilitation Research Unit 182

Address: Orthopaedisches Spital, Speisinger Strasse 109, A-1130 Wien
Telephone: 0222/823611

Montanuniversität Leoben 183

[Leoben Mining University]
Address: Franz-Josef-Strasse 18, A-8700 Leoben
Telephone: 03842/2555
President: Professor Dr Hein-Peter Stüwe

INSTITUTE OF CHEMICAL AND 184 PHYSICAL TECHNOLOGY OF PLASTICS

Head: Professor Dr Jan Koppelmann

INSTITUTE OF DEEP MINING 185 CONSTRUCTION

Head: Professor Dr Georg Feder

INSTITUTE OF DEEP WELL DRILLING, 186 MINERAL DEPOSITS AND MINERAL OIL RECOVERY

Head: Professor Dr Manfred Lorbach

INSTITUTE OF DEFORMATION 187 SCIENCE AND FOUNDRY MACHINERY

Head: Professor Dr Werner Schwenzfeier

INSTITUTE OF ELECTRICAL 188 ENGINEERING

Head: Professor Dr Alfred Gahleitner

INSTITUTE OF FERROUS 189 METALLURGY

Head: Professor Dr Herbert Hiebler

INSTITUTE OF FOUNDRY SCIENCE 190

Head: Professor Dr Joseph Czikel

INSTITUTE OF GENERAL AND 191 ANALYTICAL CHEMISTRY

Head: Professor Dr Herbert Zitter

INSTITUTE OF GEOLOGY AND 192 MINERAL DEPOSITS SCIENCE

Head: Professor Dr Herwig Holzer

INSTITUTE OF GEOPHYSICS 193

Head: Professor Dr Franz Weber

INSTITUTE OF HEAT TECHNOLOGY AND INDUSTRIAL FURNACES AND ENERGY 194

Head: Professor Dr Max B. Ussar

INSTITUTE OF MATHEMATICS AND APPLIED GEOMETRY 195

Head: Professor Dr Franz J. Schnitzer

INSTITUTE OF MATHEMATICS AND STATISTICS 196

Head: Professor Dr Wilfried Imrich

INSTITUTE OF MECHANICAL DEVELOPMENT AND CONSTRUCTION SCIENCE 197

Head: Professor Dr Klaus-Jürgen Grimmer

INSTITUTE OF MECHANICAL ENGINEERING 198

Head: Professor Dr Gundolf Rajakovics

INSTITUTE OF MECHANICS 199

Head: Professor Dr Heinz W. Borgmann

INSTITUTE OF METAL PHYSICS 200

Head: Professor Dr Hein-Peter Stüwe
See entry for: Institut für Festkörperphysik - Erich-Schmid.

INSTITUTE OF METAL SCIENCE AND MATERIALS TESTING 201

Head: Professor Dr Hellmut Fischmeister

INSTITUTE OF MINERAL DEPOSITS, PHYSICS AND TECHNOLOGY 202

Head: Professor Dr Zoltan Heinemann

INSTITUTE OF MINERALOGY 203

Head: Professor Dr Eugen F. Stumpfl

INSTITUTE OF MINERALS SCIENCE 204

Head: Professor Dr Felix Trojer

INSTITUTE OF MINING SCIENCES 205

Head: Professor Dr Günter B. Fettweis

INSTITUTE OF PHYSICAL CHEMISTRY 206

Head: Professor Dr Heinz Gamsjäger

INSTITUTE OF PHYSICS 207

Head: Professor Dr Günther Bauer

INSTITUTE OF PLASTICS PROCESSING 208

Head: Professor Dr Werner Knappe

INSTITUTE OF PROSPECTING, DEPOSITS EXPLORATION AND MINERAL ECONOMY 209

Head: Professor Dr Walter J. Schmidt

INSTITUTE OF PURIFICATION AND REFINING TREATMENT 210

Head: Professor Dr Hans Jörg Steiner

INSTITUTE OF RAW MATERIALS RESEARCH 211

Head: Professor Dr Herwig Holzer

INSTITUTE OF TECHNOLOGY AND METALLURGY OF NON-FERROUS METALS 212

Head: Professor Dr Franz Jeglitsch

Naturhistorisches Museum   213
Wien

[Vienna Natural History Museum]
Address: Burgring 7, A-1014 Wien
Telephone: 0222/934541
Parent body: Bundesministerium für Wissenschaft und
Forschung
Director: Dr Oliver E. Paget
Departments: Mineralogy; Palaeontological Geology;
Botany; Zoology (vertebrates); Zoology (entomology);
Zoology (invertebrates); Anthropology; Prehistory
Graduate research staff: 37
Annual expenditure: Sch2m
Activities: Investigation of land molluscs, especially of
Greek Islands (Rhodes, Crete); participation in Euro-
pean invertebrate survey; cartography of land and fresh-
water molluscs.
Contract work: Yes
*Publications: Annalen des Naturhistorischen Museums;
Neue Denkschriften des Naturhistorischen Museums.*

Österreichische Akademie   214
der Wissenschaften

[Austrian Academy of Sciences]
Address: Dr Ignaz-Seipel-Platz 2, A-1010 Wien
Telephone: 0222/521586; 521580
Telex: 01-12628 oeaw a
President: Dr Herbert Hunger
Secretary-General: Professor Dr Leopold Schmetterer
Graduate research staff: 250
Annual expenditure: £501 000-2m
Activities: Individual research projects are planned and
carried out by the various scientific institutes and com-
missions of the Academy. The Academy has developed
from a purely learned society into a modern institution
for research. The special structure connects teamwork
on many different levels, large and small institutes,
scientific commissions with different numbers of people
engaged in research, with an emphasis on research by
the individual, especially by members of the Academy.
Contract work: Yes
*Publications: Tätigkeitsbericht der Österreichischen
Akademie der Wissenschaften*, comprehensive research
report, every second year. Individual reports are
published annually, and a more detailed categorization
and development of research projects is published every
five years in the *Forschungsprogramm Der Österreichischen Akademie der Wissenschaften.*
See separate entries for: Institut für Festkörperphysik -
Erich-Schmid

Institut für Hirnforschung
Institut für Hochenenergiephysik
Institut für Limnologie
Institut für Molekularbiologie
Institut für Radiumforschung und Kernphysik
Institut für Röntgenfeinstrukturforschung
Institut für Weltraumforschung.

MATHEMATICS AND NATURAL   215
SCIENCES SECTION
Head: Professor Dipl-Ing E. Plöckinger

Air Purification Commission   216

Chairman: George Stetter
Activities: Air pollution studies with particular
reference to the effect of carbon monoxide in humans;
carbon monoxide in the air and resulting carbox-
ihaemoglobin.

Arteriosclerosis and Thrombosis   217
Research Commission

Chairman: W. Auerswald
Activities: Morphological and functional aspects of
smooth muscle cells of the arterial wall of ar-
teriosclerosis; prostacyclic generation in arteriosclerotic
arteries; diet influences on lipoproteins and fatty acids in
man and possible influence on prostate gland synthesis;
fatty acid patterns in blood cells.

Ecology and Scope Commission   218

Chairman: Wilhelm Kühnelt
Activities: Morphological and physiological changes in
plants under the influence of lead; energy results of two
different types of park-ecosystems; influence of various
lead concentrations on unspecified enzymes of plants.

Quaternary Research Commission   219

Chairman: Julius Fink
Activities: Research into the quaternary of the fore-
lands of the Austrian Alps; stratigraphy; paleoclimatic
differentiation in sediments and soils; paleomagnetism.

Raw Mineral Materials Research   220
Commission

Chairman: Walter E. Petrascheck
Activities: Basic research into occurence, properties
and formation of mineral raw material, especially in
Austria; testing of alpinotype carbonate seams; cycles of
tertiary sea-level fluctuations and coal formation.

Österreichische Bundesbahnen 221

[Austrian Federal Railways]
Address: Elisabethstrasse 9, A-1010 Wien

ELECTRICAL TESTING INSTITUTE 222

Address: Zirl, Bahnhof Umgebung, Tirol
Director: Dipl-Ing Kurt Kaltenböck
Activities: New electrical and mechanical techniques in railway workshops; development of power-driven tools and apparatus.

MATERIALS TESTING INSTITUTE 223

Address: Landgutgasse 28, A-1100 Wien
Director: Dipl-Ing Karl Stiegler
Activities: Testing materials used in the construction and operation of the Austrian Federal Railways.

Österreichische Gesellschaft für Ernährungsforschung 224

[Austrian Society for Nutritional Research]
Address: Schwarzspanierstrasse 17, A-1090 Wien
Telephone: 0222/421215
Research director: Professor Dr Wilhelm Auerswald
Graduate research staff: 2
Activities: The Society acts as a promoter for the Federal Department of Research and Technology. It also acts as an advice and information centre. It is currently conducting a feasibility study on ways to improve the range of literature on nutritional research.
Contract work: Yes

Österreichische Gesellschaft für Geriatrie 225

[Austrian Society for Geriatrics]
Address: Hütteldorferstrasse 188, A-1140 Wien
Research director: Dr Walter Doberauer
Activities: Experimental gerontology; clinical geriatry; research into ageing processes and diseases.

Österreichische Gesellschaft für Gerichtliche Medizin 226

[Austrian Society for Forensic Medicine]
Address: Sensengasse 2, A-1090 Wien
Telephone: 0222/424761
Research director: Professor Dr N. Wölkart
Graduate research staff: 30
Annual expenditure: £51 000-500 000
Activities: Sudden death, violent death, battered child syndrome, histochemistry, immunohistology, anthropology, criminal law, civil law, paternity blood grouping, blood and other biological stains, blood alcohol (metabolism, determination), analysis of narcotics, toxicology.
Contract work: Yes

Österreichische Gesellschaft für Mikrochemie und Analytische Chemie 227

[Micro- and Analytical Chemistry Society]
Address: Getreidemarkt 9, A-1060 Wien
Affiliation: Verein Österreichischer Chemiker
Activities: Research projects in physics, chemistry, life sciences, earth and space sciences, agricultural sciences; medical sciences, technological sciences.
Publications: Microchimica Acta.

Österreichische Gesellschaft für Sonnenenergie und Weltraumfragen GmbH 228

– ASSA
[Austrian Solar and Space Agency]
Address: Garnisongasse 7, A-1090 Wien
Telephone: 0222/438177
Telex: 76560 assa a
Parent body: Bundesministerium für Wissenschaft und Forschung
Director: Dr Johannes Ortner
Graduate research staff: 5
Annual expenditure: £51 000-500 000

SOLAR ENERGY RESEARCH　　229

Head: Professor Dr G. Faninger
Activities: ASSA is engaged in the following areas of solar research: documentation, consultation, and distribution of information; coordination, planning, and evaluation of federal research projects at the Austrian test stations; participation in working groups on collector and system testing, meteorology, solar heating systems, solar power plants (including the 10 Kw Seibersdorf plant designed for Alpine conditions), photochemistry and photobiology, and photovoltaics; cooperation on projects under the International Energy Agency.

SPACE RESEARCH　　230

Sections: Telecommunications, Dr W. Lothaller; science and remote sensing, Dr E. Mondre
Activities: ASSA coordinates the development and construction of systems and technology in Austria for the Spacelab project with NASA and ESA; the planning and development of projects for the utilization of Spacelab during its first flight planned for 1983, including investigation of the plasma of the magnetosphere, and of brazing, and solidification of monotectic alloys, under zero-gravity conditions (these three projects are being developed in the scientific institutes of Austrian universities), as well as the planning of further Sacelab tests to be carried out on missions between 1983 and 1985. The Agency also participates in the telecommunications satellites programme of the ESA, which includes experimental broadcasting and television satellites, and the Advanced Systems and Technology programme.
ASSA also supervises independent space research activities at Austrian institutes, including the processing, analysis, and storage of data acquired over Austria by remote sensing methods such as the ESA Earthmet programme and the American LANDSAT satellites; other research activities cover the fields of wave propagation, ionosphere studies, gravimetry, meteorology, mineralogy of lunar materials.

Österreichische　　231
Gesellschaft zum Studium
der Sterilität und Fertilität

[Austrian Society for the Study of Sterility and Fertility]
Address: 1st Universitäts-Frauenklinik, Spitalgasse 23, A-1095 Wien
Telephone: 0222/4289; 4700
Research director: Professor Dr George Gasser
Graduate research staff: 3

Activities: Scientific research in the field of physiology and pathology of human reproduction; publications on animal and clinical experiments concerning gynaecological endocrinology.

Österreichische　　232
Gesellschaft zur
Bekämpfung der
Cystischen Fibrose

[Austrian Society for the Fight Against Cystic Fibrosis]
Address: Universitäts-Kinderklinik, Währinger Gürtel 74-76, A-1090 Wien
Activities: Research into cystic fibrosis; development of suitable examination and treatment methods.

Österreichischer　　233
Alpenverein - Sektion
Edelweiss, Gruppe für
Natur- und
Hochgebirgskunde und
Alpine Karstforschung

[Austrian Alpine Society - Edelweiss Section, Nature, Mountains and Karst Research Group]
Address: Walfischgasse 12, A-1020 Wien
Activities: Alpine research, especially karst research; alpine ecology; frost conditions; disclosure damages and sanitation possibilities.

Österreichisches　　234
Forschungszentrum
Seibersdorf GmbH

– FZS
[Austrian Seibersdorf Research Centre]
Address: Lenaugasse 10, A-1082 Wien
Telephone: 0222/427511
Telex: 07/5400
President, Supervisory Board: Dipl-Ing Dr Wilhelm Erbacher
Activities: Peaceful applications of nuclear energy and radiation; basic research in nuclear theory, reactor components, nuclear fuels, measuring, control and information techniques; environmental research; radiation protection; social diseases and pharmaceutics; isotope application.

SEIBERSDORF NUCLEAR RESEARCH CENTRE   235

Address: A-2444 Seibersdorf
Telephone: 02254/802313
Telex: 014/353
Research director: Professor Dr Hans Grümm
Sections: Astra Reactor
Reactor Development Institute
Isotope Applications Institute
Physics Institute
Chemistry Institute
Metallurgy Institute
Agriculture Institute
Mathematics Department
Electronics Institute
Radiation Protection Institute

Österreichisches Holzforschungsinstitut   236

[Austrian Wood Research Institute]
Address: Arsenal Franz-Grill-Strasse 7, A-1030 Wien
Telephone: 0222/ 782623
Affiliation: Austrian Society for Wood Research
Director: Professor Dr Herbert Neusser
Graduate research staff: 13
Annual expenditure: £501 000-2m
Facilities: Strength testing machines; microscopic equipment; laboratory production facilities for board-like materials and paper; equipment for wood and weathering tests; laboratory autoclave.
Publications: Wood journal published bimonthly, *Holzforschung und Holzverwertung* (Wood Research and Wood Utilization).

DEPARTMENT OF CHEMICAL TECHNOLOGY OF WOOD   237

Head: Professor Dr K. Kratzel
Activities: Chemistry of cell-wall substances and cellular materials; wood as a raw material for chemical products, foodstuff, etc; wood and bark for soil improvement, compost, etc; wastewater chemistry, wood pyrolysis; chemistry of wood preservatives, adhesives and varnishes; problems of corrosions; investigation into suitability and availability of wood for pulp and paper; environmental aspects (problems of pollution by air, dust and water); quality and quantity analysis; chemical or physical changes and effects in wood by storage.

DEPARTMENT OF MECHANICAL TECHNOLOGY OF WOOD AND WOOD MATERIALS   238

Head: Professor Dr Herbert Neusser
Activities: Wood as energy source; properties of wood, suitability for various application purposes; utilizing bark and wood chips; extraction and use of biomass, testing of adhesives and levels of resistance; quality control; classification, sizing, suitability for various industries, such as automotive, aerospace; architectural design, safety aspects and durability; wood preservation, damage by diseases; finishing techniques.

Österreichisches Institut für Formgebung   239

[Austrian Institute for Design]
Address: Salesianergasse 1, Zimmer 402-404, A-1030 Wien
Telephone: 725611
President: Arch Dipl-Ing Karl Mang
Secretary-General: Dr Charlotte Blauensteiner
Activities: Research and promotion in the field of industrial and environmental design; education and contacts.

Österreichisches Institut für Verpackungswesen   240

– OIV
[Austrian Packaging Science Institute]
Address: Gumpendorferstrasse 6, A-1060 Wien
Telephone: 0222/569686
Affiliation: Wirtschaftsuniversität Wien
Research director: Dr E.F. Ketzler
Graduate research staff: 4
Annual expenditure: £10 000-50 000
Activities: Technical research work, including investigation of transportation damage, protective packaging, and development of packaging for particular goods; economic research, including market research and environmental studies; testing of all packaging materials and methods.
Contract work: Yes
Publications: Verpackungsforschung; Selbstsbedienung.

FEDERAL AUTHORIZED RESEARCH CENTRE   241

Address: Franz Klein-Gasse 1, A-1190 Wien
Telephone: 0222/348244

Österreichisches Institut für 242 Wirtschaftsforschung

[Austrian Institute for Economic Research]
Address: Postfach 91, A-1103 Wien
Telephone: 782601
Research director: Helmut Kramer
Graduate research staff: 30
Activities: The Institute's research covers the full range of macroeconomic research.
Contract work: Yes
Publications: Monthly report.

Paris-Lodron-Universität 243 Salzburg

[Paris-Lodron Salzburg University]
Address: Residenzplatz 1, Postfach 505, A-5020 Salzburg
Telephone: 06222/44511
Rector: Professor Dr Wolfgang Beilner
University Director: Dr Raimund Spruzina

FACULTY OF LAW 244

Forensic Medicine Institute 245

Address: Ignaz-Harrer-Strasse 79, A-5020 Salzburg
Telephone: 33501
Director: Professor Dr Gerhart Harrer

FACULTY OF NATURAL SCIENCES 246

Botany Institute 247

Address: Freisaalweg 16, A-5020 Salzburg
Director: Professor Dr Dietrich Fürnkranz
Senior staff: Professor Dr Oswald Kiermayer, Professor Dipl-Ing Dr Heinrich Wagner

General Biology, Biochemistry and 248 Biophysics Institute

Address: Erzabt-Klotz-Strasse, A-5020 Salzburg
Director: Professor Dr Hans-Bernd Strack
Senior staff: Professor Dr Gerhard Czihak, Professor Dr Egon Pohl

Geography Institute 249

Address: Akademiestrasse 20, A-5020 Salzburg
Director: Professor Dr Helmut Riedl
Senior staff: Professor Dr Helmut Heuberger, Professor Dr Guido Müller, Professor Dr Josef Schramm

Geology and Palaeontology Institute 250

Address: Akademiestrasse 26, A-5020 Salzburg
Director: Professor Dr Günther Frasl

Psychology Institute 251

Address: Akademiestrasse 22 and 26, A-5020 Salzburg
Director: Professor Dr Erwin Roth
Senior staff: Professor Dr Wilhelm J. Revers, Professor Dr Kurt Eckel, Professor Dr Sepp Schindler

Zoology Institute 252

Address: Akademiestrasse 26, A-5020 Salzburg
Director: Professor Dr Hans Adam

Prüf- und Versuchsanstalt 253 der Elektrizitäts-werke Österreichs, Staatlich Authorisierte

[Testing and Research Institute of the Electricity Supply Works of Austria, Government Authorized]
Address: Obere Augartenstrasse 14a, A-1020 Wien
Telephone: 0222/331489
Telex: 131100 everb a
Administrative affiliation: Municipal Electricity Supply Works of Vienna
Research director: Dipl-Ing Dr Karl Sailer
Graduate research staff: 4
Activities: Research is only carried out in connection with the routine safety testing of electrical equipment for household and similar use; materials and appliances are type-tested to ensure they conform to standard.
Contract work: Yes

Psychiatrisch- 254 Neurologische Universitätsklinik

[University Clinic of Psychiatry and Neurology]
Address: Auenbruggerplatz 22, A-8036 Graz
Telephone: 0316/385385

WORLD NEUROLOGY ASSOCIATION 255 RESEARCH GROUP ON CEREBROVASCULAR DISEASE

Secretaries: Professor Dr H. Lechner, Professor Dr C. Loeb, Professor Dr J. Marshall, Professor Dr J.S. Meyer
Activities: Prevention, diagnosis and treatment of cerebral vascular disease and related disorders; investigation of clinical aspects of cerebral vascular disease and related disorders; a biennial conference for the discussion of recent results, information exchange and publication.
Contract work: No

Sonnblick-Verein 256

[Sonnblick Society]
Address: Hohe Warte 38, A-1190 Wien
Telephone: 0222/364453
Research director: Professor Dr Ferdinand Steinhauser
Activities: A non-profit association which has been in existence since 1886. It is the only weather centre in Europe to have a station 3 000 m above sea level. It provides invaluable information in the fields of meteorology, hydrology, glaciology and geophysics for both agriculture and industry. It also conducts research in the field of solar energy.
Contract work: Yes
Publications: Annual report.

Technische Universität Graz 257

[Graz Technical University]
Address: Rechbauerstrasse 12, A-8010 Graz
Telephone: 0316/77511
Telex: 31221

FACULTY OF ARCHITECTURE 258

Agricultural Buildings and Rural 259 Development Institute

Address: Rechbauerstrasse 12, A-8010 Graz
Director: Professor Dipl-Ing Arch Franz Riepl

Architecture and Design Institute 260

Address: Rechbauerstrasse 12, A-8010 Graz
Director: Professor Dipl-Ing Arch Anatol Ginelli

Artistic Design Institute 261

Address: A-8103 Stift Rein
Director: Professor Giselbert Hoke

Spatial Design Institute 262

Address: Rechbauerstrasse 12, A-8010 Graz
Director: Professor Dipl-Ing Arch Josef Klose

Superstructures Institute 263

Sections: Building construction and design, Professor Dipl-Ing Arch Werner Hollamey; building materials and construction, Professor Dipl-Ing Dr Wolfgang Fallosch; building construction and services, Professor Dipl-Ing Dr Horst Gamerith

Supporting Structures Institute 264

Address: Technikerstrasse 4, A-8010 Graz
Director: Professor Dipl-Ing Dr Harald Egger

Theory of Buildings and Domestic 265 Architecture Institute

Address: Rechbauerstrasse 12, A-8010 Graz
Director: Professor Dipl-Ing Arch Günther Domenig

Town and Country Planning Institute 266

Address: Rechbauerstrasse 12, A-8010 Graz
Director: Professor Dipl-Ing Dr Peter Breitling

FACULTY OF CIVIL ENGINEERING 267

Building Statics Institute 268

Address: Rechbauerstrasse 12, A-8010 Graz
Director: Professor Dipl-Ing Dr Peter Klement

Construction Economics and 269 Management Institute

Address: Technikerstrasse 4, A-8010 Graz
Director: Professor Dipl-Ing Norbert Raaber

General and Technical Mechanics 270 Institute

Address: Kopernikusgasse 24, A-8010 Graz
Director: Professor Dipl-Ing Dr Karl Wohlhart

General Geodesy and Photogrammetry 271
Institute

Address: Rechbauerstrasse 12, A-8010 Graz
Sections: Geodesy, Professor Dipl-Ing Dr Karl Runner; photogrammetry, Professor Dipl-Ing Dr Franz Leberl

Hydromechanics, Hydraulics and 272
Hydrology Institute

Address: Dietrichsteinplatz 15, A-8010 Graz
Sections: Hydromechanics, hydraulics and hydrology, Professor Dipl-Ing Dr Heinz Bergmann; theory of hydraulics experimentation and quantitive methods of hydrology, Professor Dipl-Ing Dr Ferdinand Wehrschütz

Industrial, Agricultural and Domestic 273
Waterworks and River Engineering
Institute

Address: Stremayrgasse 10, A-8010 Graz
Director: Professor Dipl-Ing Dr Ernst Paul Nemecek

Mathematical and Numerical Geodesy 274
Institute

Address: Technikerstrasse 4, A-8010 Graz
Section heads: Professor Dipl-Ing Dr Peter Meissl, Professor Dipl-Ing Dr Helmut Moritz

Railways and Traffic Institute 275

Address: Rechbauerstrasse 12, A-8010 Graz
Director: Professor Dipl-Ing Dr Karl Klugar

Reinforced Concrete and Solid 276
Structures Institute

Address: Technikerstrasse 4, A-8010 Graz
Director: Professor Dipl-Ing Dr Richard Küng

Road Building and Traffic Institute 277

Address: Rechbauerstrasse 12, A-8010 Graz
Director: Professor Dipl-Ing Dr Herbert Köstenberger

Soil and Rock Mechanics and 278
Foundations Institute

Address: Rechbauerstrasse 12, A-8010 Graz
Director: Professor Dipl-Ing Dr Heinz Brandl

Steel and Wood Structures and Load- 279
bearing Surfaces Institute

Address: Rechbauerstrasse 12, A-8010 Graz
Sections: Steel and wood buildings and load-bearing surfaces, Professor Dipl-Ing Dr Fritz Resinger; steel buildings and load-bearing surfaces, Professor Dipl-Ing Dr Richard Greiner; wood buildings, Professor Dipl-Ing Dr Richard Pischl

Superstructures and Industrial Building 280
Institute

Address: Rechbauerstrasse 12, A-8010 Graz
Director: Professor Dipl-Ing Arch Fritz Reischl

Water Resources and Construction 281
Works Institute

Address: Stremayrgasse 10, A-8010 Graz
Director: Professor Dipl-Ing Dr Helmut Simmler

FACULTY OF ELECTRICAL 282
ENGINEERING

Electrical Systems Institute 283

Address: Inffeldgasse 18, A-8010 Graz
Director: Professor Dipl-Ing Dr Richard Muckenhuber

Electro- and Biomedical Engineering 284
Institute

Address: Inffeldgasse 18, A-8010 Graz
Telephone: 0316/77511
Telex: 31221
Sections: Electro- and biomedical engineering, Professor Dipl-Ing Dr Stefan Schuy; computer engineering, Professor Dipl-Ing Dr Gert Pfurtscheller; general research and development, Professor Dipl-Ing Dr Paul Wach
Activities: Investigation and testing of electromedical equipment and electrical installations relating to medicine.

Electromagnetic Energy Conversion 285
Institute

Address: Kopernikusgasse 24, A-8010 Graz
Sections: Electric machines, Professor Dipl-Ing Dr Gerhard Aichholzer; electric railways, Professor Dipl-Ing Dr Manfred Rentmeister

Electronics Institute   286

Address: Inffeldgasse 12, A-8010 Graz
Director: Professor Dipl-Ing Dr Wilfried Fritzsche

General Electrical Engineering and   287
Electrical Measurement and Control
Engineering Institute

Address: Kopernikusgasse 24, A-8010 Graz
Sections: Control engineering, Professor Dr Gerhard Schneider; general electrical engineering and electrical measurement, Professor Dipl-Ing Dr Harald Weiss

High Voltage Technology Institute   288

Address: Inffeldgasse 18, A-8010 Graz
Director: vacant
Senior staff: Dipl-Ing Dr Hermann Egger, Dipl-Ing Ernst Feldner

Telecommunications and Transmission   289
Engineering Institute

Address: Inffeldgasse 12, A-8010 Graz
Director: Professor Dipl-Ing Dr Willibald Riedler

Theoretical and Fundamental Electrical   290
Engineering Institute

Address: Kopernikusgasse 24, A-8010 Graz
Director: Professor Dipl-Ing Dr Kurt Richter

FACULTY OF MECHANICAL   291
ENGINEERING

Flow and Gas Dynamics Institute   292

Address: Kopernikusgasse 24, A-8010 Graz
Director: Professor Dipl-Ing Dr Walter Gretler

General Mechanical Engineering and   293
Development Institute

Address: Kopernikusgasse 24, A-8010 Graz
Sections: Development and technical drawing, Professor Dipl-Ing Dr Kurt Bauer; components, Professor Dipl-Ing Dr Waldemar Jud

Hydraulic Equipment Institute   294

Address: Kopernikusgasse 24, A-8010 Graz
Director: Professor Dipl-Ing Dr Gerhard Ziegler

Internal Combustion Engines and   295
Thermodynamics Institute

Address: Kopernikusgasse 24, A-8010 Graz
Sections: Thermodynamics, Professor Dipl-Ing Dr Rudolf Pischinger; internal combustion engines, Head of Laboratory: Professor Dipl-Ing Dr Erich Huttmann; Professor Dipl-Ing Dr Gunter Krassnig, Professor Dipl-Ing Dr Gerhart Taucar
Hydrodynamics, Professor Dipl-Ing Dr Karl Pucher

Machine Tools and Manufacturing   296
Technology Institute

Address: Kopernikusgasse 24, A-8010 Graz
Director: Professor Dipl-Ing Dr Adolf Eduard Frank

Materials Resistance and Testing   297
Institute

Address: Kopernikusgasse 24, A-8010 Graz
Director: Professor Dipl-Ing Dr Ernst Tschech
Sections: Materials and welding techniques, Professor Dipl-Ing Theodor Povse; technology of building materials, Professor Dipl-Ing Dr Helmut Gemayer
Activities: Investigation and testing of materials used in the building and manufacturing industry and related fields; machine components and building structures.

Operational Economics Institute   298

Address: Kopernikusgasse 24, A-8010 Graz
Sections: Business management, Professor Dipl-Ing Dr Reinhard Haberfellner; operational economics, Professor Dipl-Ing Dr Walter Vect; industrial operation and economics, Professor Dipl-Ing Dr Josef Wohinz

Process Engineering Institute   299

Address: Kopernikusgasse 24, A-8010 Graz
Sections: Elements of process engineering, Professor Dipl-Ing Dr Franz Moser; apparatus construction and mechanical process engineering, Professor Dipl-Ing Dr Gernot Staudinger; process engineering, Professor Dipl-Ing Dr Otto Wolfbauer

Steam Engineering and Heat Institute   300

Address: Kopernikusgasse 24, A-8010 Graz
Director: Professor Dipl-Ing Dr Paul Viktor Gilli

Thermal Turbo-Engine and Machine   301
Dynamics Institute

Address: Kopernikusgasse 24, A-8010 Graz
Sections: Thermal turbo-engines, Professor Dipl-Ing Dr Herbert Jericha; thermal hydrodynamic engineering, Professor Dipl-Ing Dr Günther Zhuber-Okrog

FACULTY OF TECHNICAL AND NATURAL SCIENCES   302

Analytical Chemistry, Micro- and Radiochemistry Institute   303

Address: Technikerstrasse 4, A-8010 Graz
Sections: Analytical chemistry and trace elements, Professor Dipl-Ing Dr Günter Knapp; radioanalysis, Professor Dr Kurt Müller

Biochemical Technology, Microbiology and Waste Water Technology Institute   304

Address: Schlögelgasse 9, A-8010 Graz
Director: Professor Dr Robert Lafferty

Biochemistry and Food Chemistry Institute   305

Address: Schlögelgasse 9, A-8010 Graz
Director: Professor Dr Friedrich Paltauf

Experimental Physics Institute   306

Address: Rechbauerstrasse 12, A-8010 Graz
Director: Professor Dipl-Ing Dr Helmut Jäger

Geometry Institute   307

Director: Professor Mag rer nat Dr Hans Vogler

Information Processing Institute   308

Address: Steyrergasse 17, A-8010 Graz
Director: Professor Dr Hermann Maurer

Inorganic Chemical Technology Institute   309

Address: Stremayrgasse 16, A-8010 Graz
Sections: Inorganic chemical technology, Professor Dr Karl Kordesch; analytical chemistry, Professor Dipl-Ing Dr Friedrich Frenzel; physical chemistry, Professor Dipl-Ing Dr Gerhard Herzog; electrochemistry and corrosion science, Professor Dipl-Ing Dr Friedrich Hilbert

Inorganic Chemistry Institute   310

Address: Stremayrgasse 16, A-8010 Graz
Director: Professor Dipl-Ing Dr Edwin Hengge

Mathematics Institute   311

Sections: Mathematics, Professor Dr Karl Wilhelm Bauer, Professor Dr Rudolf Domiaty, Professor Dr Wolfgang Hahn, Professor Dipl-Ing Dr Rudolf Heersink; applied mathematics, Professor Mag rer nat Dr Helmut Florian

Nuclear Physics Institute   312

Address: Steyrergasse 17, A-8010 Graz
Director: Professor Dr Ludwig Breitenhuber

Organic Chemical Technology Institute   313

Address: Stremayrgasse 16, A-8010 Graz
Director: Professor Dipl-Ing Dr Klaus Hummel

Organic Chemistry Institute   314

Address: Stremayrgasse 16, A-8010 Graz
Director: Professor Dr Hans Wiedmann

Physical and Theoretical Chemistry Institute   315

Address: Rechbauerstrasse 12, A-8010 Graz
Sections: Physical chemistry, Professor Dipl-Ing Dr Karl Torkar; theoretical chemistry, Professor Dipl-Ing Dr Harald Paulson Fritzer; structural research, Professor Dipl-Ing Dr Harald Krischner

Solid-State Physics Institute   316

Sections: Applied physics, Professor Dr Hartmut Kahlert; surface area physics, Professor Dipl-Ing Dr Klaus-Dieter Rendulie

Statistics Institute   317

Address: Hamerlinggasse 6/VI, A-8010 Graz
Sections: Mathematical statistics, Professor Dr Ulrich Dieter; applied statistics, Professor Mag rer nat Dr Josef Gölles

Technical Geology, Petrography and Mineralogy Institute   318

Address: Rechbauerstrasse 12, A-8010 Graz
Sections: Petrography and mineralogy, Professor Dr Helmut Höller; geology, Professor Dr Gunter Adolf Riedmüller; rock technology, Professor Dr Erich Zirkl; hydrogeology, Professor Dr Josef Zötl

Theoretical Physics Institute 319

Address: Steyrergasse 17, A-8010 Graz
Sections: Theoretical physics, Professor Dr Ernst Ledinegg; mathematical physics, Professor Dr Bernhard Schnizer

STATE AUTHORIZED RESEARCH 320 INSTITUTES

High Voltage Technology Research 321 Institute

Address: Inffeldgasse 18, A-8010 Graz
Telephone: 0316/43780
Director: vacant
Senior staff: Dipl-Ing Dr Hermann Egger, Dipl-Ing Ernst Feldner
Activities: Testing centre covering all aspects of high voltage technology: characteristics of materials, behaviour of insulation, voltage regulation.

Paper, Cellulose and Fibres 322 Engineering Research Institute

Address: Kopernikusgasse 24, A-8010 Graz
Telephone: 0316/77511
Telex: 31221
Director: Professor Dipl-Ing Dr Helmut Stark
Activities: Testing of raw components and finished products of paper, cellulose and synthetic fibres, and related chemical investigation.

Reaktorinstitut des Vereines zur 323 Förderung der Anwendung der Kernenergie

[Reactor Institute of the Association for the Promotion of Applications of Nuclear Energy]
Address: Steyrergasse 17, A-8010 Graz
Telephone: 0316/77511
Telex: 3/1265
Research director: Professor Dr E. Ledinegg
Sections: Electrodynamics including wave propagation and quantum electrodynamics; reactor physics including reactor noise analysis, Dr F. Schürrer; energy physics, M. Heidler; mathematical physics, Professor B. Schnizer; quantum theory of superconduction, E. Schachinger; nuclear radiation measurements techniques, Hj. Müller
Graduate research staff: 14
Annual expenditure: Sch800 000
Activities: The scientific work of the Institute is carried out by members of the Institutes for Theoretical Physics and for Reactor Physics of the Technical University of Graz. Apart from fundamental research in the field of neutron and reactor physics, experimental and theoretical work is carried out on: liquid-cooled reactors with spherical fuel elements; cavitation by the use of radioactive isotopes; reactor noise analysis; improvement of multigroup cross sections, in cooperation with the Saclay and Cadarache research centres of the French CEA; determination of absorption cross sections and resonance integrals (pile-oscillator and danger coefficient); protection against nuclear radiation; coupled cores, correlation functions; nuclear radiation measurement techniques; electrodynamics, especially wave propagation; antenna theory; scattering theory; quantum mechanical coherence theory and mathematical quantum mechanics; and quantum theory of superconduction. Work is currently being carried out on the Siemens-Argonaut reactor.
Contract work: Yes
Publications: Various journals.

Technische Universität Wien 324

[Vienna Technical University]
Address: Karlsplatz 13, A-1040 Wien
Telephone: 0222/657641
President: Dr Wilfried Noebauer

FACULTY OF CIVIL ENGINEERING 325

Dean: Dr Walter Kemmerling

FACULTY OF ELECTRICAL 326 ENGINEERING

Dean: Dr Herbert Stimmer

FACULTY OF MECHANICAL 327 ENGINEERING

Dean: Dr Herbert Kazda

FACULTY OF NATURAL SCIENCES 328 AND TECHNOLOGY

Dean: Dr Alfred Schmidt

INSTITUTE OF AIRCRAFT 329 CONSTRUCTION

Address: Getreidemarkt 9, A-1060 Wien
Telephone: 0222/571651
Head: vacant

INSTITUTE OF ANALYTICAL CHEMISTRY 330

Address: Getreidemarkt 9, A-1060 Wien
Telephone: 0222/571651
Head: Professor Dr Hanns Malissa

INSTITUTE OF APPLIED AND TECHNICAL PHYSICS 331

Address: Karlsplatz 13, A-1040 Wien
Telephone: 0222/657641

INSTITUTE OF APPLIED BOTANY, TECHNICAL MICROSCOPY AND ORGANIC RAW MATERIALS 332

Address: Getreidemarkt 9, A-1060 Wien
Telephone: 0222/571651
Head: Professor Dr Engelbert Bancher

INSTITUTE OF BASIC PRINCIPLES AND THEORY OF ELECTRICAL ENGINEERING 333

Address: Gusshausstrasse 25-29, A-1040 Wien
Telephone: 0222/657641
Head: Professor Dr Hellmut Hofmann

INSTITUTE OF BIOCHEMICAL TECHNOLOGY AND MICROBIOLOGY 334

Address: Getreidemarkt 9, A-1060 Wien
Telephone: 0222/571651
Head: Professor Dr Max Röhr

INSTITUTE OF CHEMICAL TECHNOLOGY OF INORGANIC SUBSTANCES 335

Address: Getreidemarkt 9, A-1060 Wien
Telephone: 0222/571651

INSTITUTE OF CHEMICAL TECHNOLOGY OF ORGANIC SUBSTANCES 336

Address: Getreidemarkt 9, A-1060 Wien
Telephone: 0222/571651

INSTITUTE OF CHEMISTRY 337

Address: Getreidemarkt 9, A-1060 Wien
Telephone: 0222/571651

INSTITUTE OF ELECTRICAL MACHINERY 338

Address: Gusshausstrasse 25-29, A-1040 Wien
Telephone: 0222/657641
Head: Professor Dr Hans Kleinrath

INSTITUTE OF ELECTRONIC EQUIPMENT AND HIGH VOLTAGE TECHNOLOGY 339

Address: Gusshausstrasse 25-29, A-1040 Wien
Telephone: 0222/657641
Head: Professor Dr Herbert Stimmer

INSTITUTE OF ENERGY 340

Address: Wiedner Hauptstrasse 7, A-1040 Wien
Telephone: 0222/658731
Head: Professor Dr Peter Jansen

INSTITUTE OF ENGINE DYNAMICS AND TESTING TECHNOLOGY 341

Address: Karlsplatz 13, A-1040 Wien
Telephone: 0222/657641
Head: Professor Dr Alfred Slibar

INSTITUTE OF EXPERIMENTAL PHYSICS 342

Address: Karlsplatz 13, A-1040 Wien
Telephone: 0222/657641
Head: Professor Dr Hans Kirchmayr

INSTITUTE OF FABRICATION TECHNOLOGY 343

Address: Karlsplatz 13, A-1040 Wien
Telephone: 0222/657641
Head: Professor Dr Helmar Weseslindtner

INSTITUTE OF FLUID DYNAMICS AND HEAT TRANSFER 344

Address: Wiedner Hauptstrasse 7, A-1040 Wien
Telephone: 0222/658731
Head: Professor Dr Wilhelm Schneider

INSTITUTE OF FOOD CHEMISTRY AND FOOD TECHNOLOGY 345

Address: Getreidemarkt 9, A-1060 Wien
Telephone: 0222/571651
Head: Professor Dr Josef Washüttl

INSTITUTE OF GENERAL 346
ENGINEERING AND MECHANICAL DEVELOPMENT

Address: Getreidemarkt 9, A-1060 Wien
Telephone: 0222/571651
Head: Professor Dr Herbert Kazda

INSTITUTE OF HYDRAULIC POWER 347
PLANT AND PUMPS

Address: Karlsplatz 13, A-1040 Wien
Telephone: 0222/657641
Head: Professor Dr Heinz-Bernd Matthias

INSTITUTE OF HYDRAULICS, 348
HYDROLOGY AND HYDROECONOMY

Address: Karlsplatz 13, A-1040 Wien
Telephone: 0222/657641
Head: Professor Dr Werner Kresser

INSTITUTE OF INDUSTRIAL PROCESS 349
ENGINEERING AND FUEL TECHNOLOGY

Address: Getreidemarkt 9, A-1060 Wien
Telephone: 0222/571651
Head: Professor Dr Alfred Schmidt

INSTITUTE OF INORGANIC 350
CHEMISTRY

Address: Getreidemarkt 9, A-1060 Wien
Telephone: 0222/571651
Head: Professor Dr Viktor Gutmann

INSTITUTE OF INTERNAL 351
COMBUSTION ENGINES AND MOTOR VEHICLES

Address: Getreidemarkt 9, A-1060 Wien
Telephone: 0222/571651
Head: Professor Dr Hans-Peter Lenz

INSTITUTE OF MATERIALS AND 352
MATERIAL TESTING

Address: Karlsplatz 13, A-1040 Wien
Telephone: 0222/658731

INSTITUTE OF MATERIALS OF 353
ELECTRICAL ENGINEERING

Address: Gusshausstrasse 25-29, A-1040 Wien
Telephone: 0222/657641
Head: Professor Dr Gerhard Fasching

INSTITUTE OF MECHANICS 354

Address: Karlsplatz 13, A-1040 Wien
Telephone: 0222/657641
Head: Professor Dr Kurt Desoyer

INSTITUTE OF MINERALOGY, 355
CRYSTALLOGRAPHY AND STRUCTURAL CHEMISTRY

Address: Getreidemarkt 9, A-1060 Wien
Telephone: 0222/571651
Head: Professor Dr Anton Preisinger

INSTITUTE OF NUCLEAR PHYSICS 356

Address: Schüttelstrasse 115, A-1020 Wien
Telephone: 0222/725126
Head: Professor Dr Eder Gernot

INSTITUTE OF ORGANIC CHEMISTRY 357

Address: Getreidemarkt 9, A-1060 Wien
Telephone: 0222/571651

INSTITUTE OF PHYSICAL CHEMISTRY 358

Address: Getreidemarkt 9, A-1060 Wien
Telephone: 0222/571651
Head: Professor Dr Heinrich Noller

INSTITUTE OF PHYSICS 359

Address: Karlsplatz 13, A-1040 Wien
Telephone: 0222/657641
Head: Professor Dr Franz Viehböck

INSTITUTE OF PRECISION 360
ENGINEERING

Address: Karlsplatz 13, A-1040 Wien
Telephone: 0222/657641
Head: Professor Dr Helmut Detter

INSTITUTE OF SHIPBUILDING 361

Address: Getreidemarkt 9, A-1060 Wien
Telephone: 0222/571651
Head: Professor Dr Helmut Schwanecke

INSTITUTE OF STEAM AND GAS 362
TURBINES

Address: Getreidemarkt 9, A-1060 Wien
Telephone: 0222/571651
Head: Professor Dr Karl J. Müller

INSTITUTE OF TECHNICAL 363
ELECTROCHEMISTRY

Address: Getreidemarkt 9, A-1060 Wien
Telephone: 0222/571651

INSTITUTE OF TECHNICAL 364
THERMODYNAMICS

Address: Getreidemarkt 9, A-1060 Wien
Telephone: 0222/571651
Head: Professor Dr Wladimir Linzer

INSTITUTE OF THEORETICAL 365
GEODESY AND GEOPHYSICS

Address: Gusshausstrasse 25-29, A-1040 Wien
Telephone: 0222/657641

INSTITUTE OF THEORETICAL 366
PHYSICS

Address: Karlsplatz 13, A-1040 Wien
Telephone: 0222/657641

Tiroler Landesanstalt für 367
Planzensucht und
Samenprüfung

[Tyrolian Plant Breeding and Seed Testing Institute]
Address: A-6074 Rinn Tirol
Research director: Dipl-Ing Leonhard Köck
Activities: Cultivation of corn species in alpine areas, especially summer barley for feeding purposes; studies of feed crops for cultivation in meadowland, and fertilization of pasture land. Seed testing for the Tirol is carried out. Soil studies in relation to technical studies for crops are also undertaken.

Universität für Bodenkultur 368

[Vienna University of Agriculture]
Address: Gregor Mendel-Strasse 33, A-1180 Wien
Telephone: 0222/342500
Telex: 131066 z filt
Rector: Professor Dipl-Ing Dr Rudolf Frauendorfer

DEPARTMENT OF AGRICULTURE 369

Agricultural Economics and Nutrition 370
Institute

Heads: Professor Dipl-Ing Dr Johann Köttl, Professor Dipl-Ing Dr Otto Gurtner

Agricultural Engineering and Energy 371
Conservation Institute

Heads: Professor Dipl-Ing Dr Karl Vecsei, Professor Dipl-Ing Dr Helmut Rossrucker

Agricultural Plant Protection Institute 372

Head: Professor Dipl-Ing Dr Josef Weindlmayr

Animal Production Institute 373

Head: Professor Dipl-Ing Dr Alfred Haiger

Botanical Institute 374

Heads: Professor Dr R. Kandeler, Professor Dr Erich Hübl

Fruit Growing Institute 375

Head: Professor Dipl-Ing Dr Karl Duhan

Green Belt Planting and Horticulture 376
Institute

Head: Professor Dr Friendrich Weiss

Plant Cultivation and Breeding 377
Institute

Head: Professor Dipl-Ing Dr Otto Steineck

Political Economy, Agrarian Policy and 378
Legal Sciences Institute

Heads: Professor Frühwirth, Professor Dr Kurt Holzer, Professor Dr Manfried Welan

Universität Wien   404

[Vienna University]
Address: Dr Karl Lueger-Ring 1, A-1010 Wien

FACULTY OF MEDICINE   405

Dean: Professor Dr Wilhelm Auerswald

Anaesthesiology Department   406

Address: Spitalgasse 23, A-1090 Wien
Director: Professor Mayrhofer-Krammel

Anatomy Department I   407

Address: Währingerstrasse 13, A-1090 Wien
Director: Professor Helmut Ferner

Anatomy Department II   408

Address: Währingerstrasse 13, A-1090 Wien
Director: Professor Robert Mayr

Biochemistry Department   409

Address: Währingerstrasse 17, A-1090 Wien
Director: Professor Hans Tuppy

Blood Group Serology Department   410

Address: Spitalgasse 4, A-1090 Wien
Director: Professor Paul Speiser

Cancer Research Department   411

Address: Borschkegasse 82, A-1090 Wien
Director: vacant

Cardiological University Clinic   412

Address: Garnisongasse 13, A-1090 Wien
Director: Professor Fritz Kaindl

Children's Clinic of the University   413

Address: Währinger Gürtel 74-76, A-1090 Wien
Director: Professor Ernst Zweymüller

Dental Clinic of the University   414

Address: Währingerstrasse 152, A-1090 Wien
Director: Professor Koloman Keresztesi

Depth Psychology and Psychotherapy   415
Department

Address: Währinger Gürtel 74-76, A-1090 Wien
Director: Professor Hans Strotzka

Dermatological University Clinic I   416

Address: Alserstrasse 4, A-1090 Wien
Director: vacant

Diagnostic Radiology Department   417

Address: Alserstrasse 4, A-1090 Wien
Director: Professor Herbert Pokieser

Environmental Hygiene Department 418

Address: Kinderspitalgasse 15, A-1090 Wien
Director: Professor Manfred Haider

Forensic Medicine Department   419

Address: Sensengasse 2, A-1090 Wien
Director: Professor Holczabek

General and Comparative Physiology   420
Department

Address: Schwarzspanierstrasse 17, A-1090 Wien
Director: Professor Dr Astrid Kapka-Lützow

General and Experimental Pathology   421
Department

Address: Währingerstrasse 13, A-1090 Wien
Director: Professor Adolf Lindner

General Biology Department   422

Address: Schwarzspanierstrasse 17, A-1090 Wien
Director: Professor Dr Hans Joachim Becker

Histology and Embryology   423
Department

Address: Schwarzspanierstrasse 17, A-1090 Wien
Director: Professor Hans Schwarzacher

History of Medicine Department   424

Address: Währingerstrasse 25, A-1090 Wien
Director: Helmut Wycklicky

Hygiene Department   425

Address: Kinderspitalgasse 15, A-1090 Wien
Director: Professor Heinz Flamm

Immunology Department 426

Address: Borschkegasse 82, A-1090 Wien
Director: Professor Carl Steffen

Maxillo-Facial Surgery University Clinic 427

Address: Alserstrasse 4, A-1090 Wien
Director: Professor Siegfried Wunderer

Medical Chemistry Department 428

Address: Währingerstrasse 10, A-1090 Wien
Director: Professor Erich Kaiser

Medical Clinic of the University I 429

Address: Spitalgasse 23, A-1090 Wien
Director: Professor Erwin Deutsch-Kempny

Medical Clinic of the University II 430

Address: Alserstrasse 4, A-1090 Wien
Director: Professor Georg Geyer

Medical Physics Department 431

Address: Währingerstrasse 13, A-1090 Wien
Director: Professor Schedling

Medical Physiology Department 432

Address: Schwarzspanierstrasse 17, A-1090 Wien
Director: Professor Wilhelm Auerswald

Medical Statistics and Documentation Department 433

Address: Schwartzspanierstrasse 17, A-1090 Wien
Director: Professor Wohlzogen

Micromorphology and Electron Microscopy Department 434

Address: Schwarzspanierstrasse 17, A-1090 Wien
Director: Professor Leopold Stockinger

Neurological University Clinic 435

Address: Währinger Gürtel 74-76, A-1090 Wien
Director: Professor Herbert Reisner

Neurology Department 436

Address: Schwarzspanierstrasse 17, A-1090 Wien
Director: Professor Franz Seitelberger
Activities: Functions of the nervous vegetative system, biochemistry of neurotransmitters.

Neurophysiology Department 437

Address: Währingerstrasse 17, A-1090 Wien
Director: Professor Petsche

Neurosurgical University Clinic 438

Address: Alserstrasse 4, A-1090 Wien
Director: Professor Wolfgang Koos

Obstetrics and Gynaecology University Clinic I 439

Address: Spitalgasse 23, A-1090 Wien
Director: Professor Gitsch

Obstetrics and Gynaecology University Clinic II 440

Address: Spitalgasse 23, A-1090 Wien
Director: Professor Herbert Janisch

Ophthalmological University Clinic I 441

Address: Alserstrasse 4, A-1090 Wien
Director: Professor Karl Hruby

Ophthalmological University Clinic II 442

Address: Alserstrasse 4, A-1090 Wien
Director: Professor Hans Slezak

Orthopaedic Surgery University Clinic 443

Address: Alserstrasse 4, A-1090 Wien
Director: Professor Karl Chiari

Otorhinolaryngology University Clinic I 444

Address: Spitalgasse 23, A-1090 Wien
Director: Professor Novotny

Otorhinolaryngology University Clinic II 445

Address: Alserstrasse 4, A-1090 Wien
Director: Professor Burian

Pathological Anatomy Department   446

Address: Spitalgasse 4, A-1090 Wien
Director: Professor Holzner

Pharmacology Department   447

Address: Währingerstrasse 132, A-1090 Wien
Director: Professor Otto Kraupp

Psychiatric University Clinic   448

Address: Währinger Gürtel 74-76, A-1090 Wien
Director: Professor Berner

Radiotherapy University Clinic and   449
Department of Radiobiology

Address: Alserstrasse 4, A-1040 Wien
Director: Professor Kärcher

Research Institute for Laboratory   450
Animal Breeding

Address: Brauhausgasse 34, Himberg, Nö, Wien
Director: Professor Adolf Lindner

Specific Prophylaxis and Tropical   451
Medicine Department

Address: Kinderspitalgasse 15, A-1090 Wien
Director: Professor Gerhard Wiedermann

Surgical University Clinic I   452

Address: Alserstrasse 4, A-1090 Wien
Director: Professor Arnulf Fritsch

Surgical University Clinic II   453

Address: Spitalgasse 23, A-1090 Wien
Director: vacant

Urological University Clinic   454

Address: Alserstrasse 4, A-1090 Wien
Director: Professor Rummelhardt

Virology Department   455

Address: Kinderspitalgasse 15, A-1090 Wien
Director: Professor Kunz

FACULTY OF PHILOSOPHY   456

Dean: Professor Dr Giselher Guttman

Analytical Chemistry Department   457

Address: Währingerstrasse 38, A-1090 Wien
Directors: Professor Kainz, Professor Huber

Botany Department and Botanical   458
Garden

Address: Rennweg 14, A-1030 Wien
Directors: Professor Ehrendorfer, Professor Woess
Sections: Ultrastructure, Professor Dr Karl Carniel;
phytochemistry, Dr Harald Greger; cytology, Dr Dieter
Schweizer; lower plants, Professor Dr Elisabeth Woess;
phytogeography, Dr Harald Niklfeld; biosystematics,
Dr Manfred Fischer; numerical taxonomy, Professor Dr
Walter Titz; herbarium, Dr Eva Schonbeck-Temest
Graduate research staff: 22
Activities: Chromosome banding; systematics and
evolution of tropical woody angiosperms; phytochemis-
try and biosystematics of Compositae; mapping scheme
for the flora of Central Europe.
Contract work: No
Publications: Annual report.

General Biochemistry Department   459

Address: Währingerstrasse 38, A-1090 Wien
Director: Professor Hoffmann-Ostenhof

Geography Department   460

Address: Universitätsstrasse 7, A-1010 Wien
Directors: Professor Arnberger, Professor Fink,
Professor Troger, Professor Lichtenberger, Professor
Stiglbauer

Geology Department   461

Address: Universitätsstrasse 7, A-1010 Wien
Directors: Professor Exner, Professor Tollmann

Human Biology Department   462

Address: Van Swictengasse 1, A-1090 Wien
Director: Professor Zapfe

Inorganic Chemistry Department   463

Address: Währingerstrasse 42, A-1090 Wien
Directors: Professor Komarek, Professor Schönfeld

Logistics Department   464

Address: Universitätsstrasse 10/2/11, A-1090 Wien
Director: Professor Christian

Mathematics Department 465

Address: Strudlhofgasse 4, A-1090 Wien
Directors: Professor Hlawka, Professor Cigler, Professor Reiter, Professor Grosser, Professor Hejtmanek, Professor Sigmund

Meteorology and Geophysics Department 466

Address: Boltzmanngasse 5, A-1090 Wien
Directors: Professor Reuter, Professor Gutdeutsch

Mineralogy and Crystallography Department 467

Address: Dr Karl Lueger-Ring 1, A-1010 Wien
Director: Professor Zemann

Mineralogy and Petrology Department 468

Address: Dr Karl Lueger-Ring 1, A-1010 Wien
Director: Professor Wieseneder

Observatory 469

Address: Türkenschanzstrasse 17, A-1180 Wien
Director: Professor Meurers

Organic Chemistry Department 470

Address: Währingerstrasse 38, A-1090 Wien
Directors: Professor Schmidt, Professor Schlögel, Professor Kratzl, Professor Zbiral

Palaeontology and Palaeobiology Department 471

Address: Universitätsstrasse 7, A-1010 Wien
Directors: Professor Papp, Professor Thenius, Professor Zapfe, Professor Klaus

Pharmaceutical Chemistry Department 472

Address: Währingerstrasse 10, A-1090 Wien
Director: Professor Pailer

Pharmacodynamics and Toxicology Department 473

Address: Währingerstrasse 132, A-1090 Wien
Director: Professor Heistracher

Pharmacognosy Department 474

Address: Währingerstrasse 25, A-1090 Wien
Director: Professor Jentzsch

Physical Chemistry Department 475

Address: Währingerstrasse 42, A-1090 Wien
Director: Professor Nowotny, Professor Breitenbach, Professor Stickler, Professor Broda, Professor Kohler

Physics Department I 476

Address: Strudlhofgasse 4, A-1090 Wien
Directors: Professor Weinzierl, Professor Higatsberger, Professor Preining, Professor Warhanek

Physics Department II 477

Address: Strudlhofgasse 4, A-1090 Wien
Directors: Professor Lintner, Professor Schöck, Professor Seeger, Professor Stangler

Plant Physiology Department 478

Address: Dr Karl Lueger-Ring 1, A-1010 Wien
Directors: Professor Schindler, Professor Wendelberger, Professor Kinzel

Radium Research and Nuclear Physics 479 Department

Address: Boltzmanngasse 3, A-1090 Wien
Director: Professor Vonach

Theoretical Astronomy Department 480

Address: Türkenschanzstrasse 17, A-1180 Wien
Director: Professor Ferrari d'Occieppo

Theoretical Chemistry and 481 Radiochemistry Department

Address: Währingerstrasse 38, A-1090 Wien
Directors: Professor Getoff, Professor Schuster

Theoretical Physics Department 482

Address: Strudlhofgasse 4, A-1090 Wien
Directors: Professor Thirring, Professor Pietschmann, Professor Sexl, Professor Bartl

Zoology Department I 483

Address: Dr Karl Lueger-Ring 1, A-1010 Wien
Directors: Professor Schaller, Professor Riedl

Zoology Department II 484

Address: Dr Karl Lueger-Ring 1, A-1010 Wien
Director: Professor Löffler

Verband der Wissenschaftlichen Gesellschaften Österreichs

485

[Austrian Scientific Societies Federation]
Address: Lindengasse 37, A-1070 Wien
Telephone: 0222/934756
Telex: 1-34981
Secretary-General: Dr Rainer Zitta
Activities: Supports scientific and research projects through its member societies; represents the interests of scientific societies; publishes scientific works.

Verein Österreichischer Chemiker*

486

[Austrian Chemical Society]
Address: Eschenbachgasse 9, A-1010 Wien
Telephone: 0222/574249
Research director: Dr Jürenus Harms
Activities: Promotes research in chemistry by means of scientific and technical lectures and other means.
Publications: Österreichische Chemie Zeitschrift.

Vereinigte Edelstahlwerke Aktiengesellschaft

487

– VEW
Address: Postfach 10, A-8605 Kapfenberg
Telephone: 03862/24100
Telex: 036-612 and 613
Research centre within an industrial company
Research director: Professor Dr Ekkehart Krainer
Departments: Metallurgical, Dr Kulmburg, Dr Kohl, Dr Jäger, Dipl-Ing Machner
Welding, Dr Rabensteiner
Graduate research staff: 20
Annual expenditure: Schl20m
Activities: VEW were created by the mergers of Austria's special steel producers Böhler, Schoeller-Bleckmann and Styria, and have since also taken over the special steel business of Vöest-Alpine. With an annual turnover of Schl2 500m, VEW occupy a position among the world's leading alloy and special steel making companies in terms of both quality and size.
Research activities cover the whole range of their products: furnace metallurgy, development and upgrading of steel grades, special alloys and welding consumables, as well as steel technology for such critical and exacting fields of application as nuclear engineering, the fertilizer industry, etc.

They also contribute a considerable share to the advance of technology in a variety of industrial sectors. The present state of the art in electroslag remelting, continuous casting, the BEST process, vacuum technology, shaping of steel by the BSR process, forging of low ductility steels, precision forging, powder metallurgy and the manufacture of sophisticated new finished products, has to a large extent been achieved as a result of research and development work done by their metallurgists. They can offer technical assistance based on their own production activities, such as: for melting and processing special alloy steels, for precision forging of turbine blades, for the manufacture of welding consumables, pneumatic tools, sintered carbide products, tools, machine knives, files and for precision casting techniques.
Contract work: Yes

Vereinigte Metallwerke Ranshofen-Berndorf AG

488

Address: A-5282 Braunau-Ranshofen
Telephone: 0043/07722 and 23410
Telex: 27745x mwran a
Affiliation: Österreichische Industrie-verwaltungs-Aktiengesellschaft - ÖIAG
General Director: Dr Kurt Glaser
Sections: Aluminium
Metallurgy, Dipl-Ing Essl; technology, Dr Lang; surface and corrosion, Dr Meissner; metallography, Dr Matzner
Graduate research staff: 10
Annual expenditure: Sch25 000 000
Activities: Alloy development; materials properties; surface treatment; corrosion; technology for production of semi-finished aluminium (especially extrusions).
Facilities: Scanning electron microscope with microprobe assembly; continuous casting and extrusion press (900 tons) for research.
Contract work: No
Publications: Aluminium.

Vereinigung für Hydrogeologische Forschungen*

489

[Hydrogeological Research Association]
Address: Rechbauerstrasse 12, A-8010 Graz
Activities: Research projects into hydrogeology including karst and ground water.

Versuchsstation für das Gärungsgewerbe 490

[Fermentation Industry Experimental Station]
Address: Michaelerstrasse 25, Postfach 31, A-1182 Wien
Telephone: 0222/343673
Affiliation: Association of Testing Institutes for the Brewing Industry
Research director: Dipl-Ing Markus Liebl
Graduate research staff: 5
Annual expenditure: £51 000-500 000
Activities: Investigation of raw materials and production processes of brewing and malting; chemical analysis of raw materials; soft drinks; spirits, alcohol and yeast technology.

Veterinärmedizinische Universität Wien 491

[University for Veterinary Medicine, Vienna]
Address: Linke Bahngasse 11, A-1030 Wien
Telephone: 0222/735581
Rector: Professor Dr med vet Oskar Schaller
Sections:
Anatomy Institute, Professor Dr med vet Oskar Schaller
Animal Breeding and Breeding Hygiene Institute, Professor Dr med vet Walter Schleger
Animal Podology Institute, Professor Dr med vet Peter Knezevic
Bacteriology and Animal Hygiene Institute, Professor Dr med vet Hermann Willinger
Biochemistry Institute, vacant
Botany and Food Sciences Institute, Professor Dr Josef Hölzl
Domestic Animal Obstetrics and Gynaecology Clinic, Professor Dr med vet Kurt Arbeiter
Electron Microscopy Laboratory, Professor Dr med vet Harro Köhler
Histology and Embryology Institute, Professor Dr med Walther Lipp
Ichthyology Institute, Professor Dr med vet Walter Grünberg
Laboratory Animals Institute, Professor Dr med vet Walter Grünburg
Meat Hygiene, Meat Technology and Foodstuffs Institute, Professor Dr med vet Oskar Prändl
Medical Chemistry Institute, Professor Dr Maximilian Weiser
Medical Clinic and Clawed Animals, Professor Dr Erich Glawisching
Medical Clinic for Hoofed Animals, Small Animals and Poultry, Professor Dr med vet Walter Jaksch
Medical Physics Institute, Professor Dr Gertrud Keck
Milk Hygiene Institute, Professor Dr Dipl-Ing Ernst Brande
Nutrition Institute, Professor Dr Josef Leibetseden
Pathology and Forensic Medicine Institute, Professor Dr med vet Harro Köhler
Parasitology and General Zoology Institute, Professor Dr med vet Rudolf Supperer
Pharmacology Institute, vacant
Physiology Institute, Professor Dr med vet Alfred Kment
Radiology Institute, Professor Dr med vet Richard Pobisch
Surgery and Ophthalmology Clinic, Professor Dr Erich Eisenmenger
Virology Institute, Professor Dr med vet Franz Bürki

Vianova Kunstharz AG 492

Address: Leechgasse 21, Postfach 191, A-8010 Graz
Telephone: 0316/33578
Telex: 31 831 vialab a
Affiliation: Hoechst AG, Frankfurt
Research director: Dr Walter Knierzinger
Sections: Research: Dr H. Rauch-Puntigam; Development: Dr Franz Holzer; Information: Ing Kurt Zatloukal
Graduate research staff: 35
Annual expenditure: £2m
Activities: General research and development in synthetic resins; alkyds, acrylics, amino resins; specialized water soluble resins; unsaturated polyesters.
Contract work: No

BELGIUM

Agfa-Gevaert NV 1

Address: Septestraat 27, B-2510 Mortsel
Telephone: (031) 40 19 40
Telex: 31.223 a AGNVB
Affiliation: Bayer AG/Leverkusen, German FR
Research director: Dr J. Nijs
Sections: X-Ray products, Dr J. De Munck; graphic products, Dr H. Philippaerts; diffusion-transfer reversal products, Dr A. Poot; motion pictures and television products, Dr G. Benoy
Graduate research staff: 87
Annual expenditure: $138m
Activities: General photography: colour and black-and-white films and papers, chemicals for processing baths, cameras, flash guns, processors and apparatus for the photo-finishing laboratories; applied photography: films, papers, chemicals for processing baths, processors, auxiliary equipment; office systems: electrophotographic office copiers, complete systems for microfilm application; magnetic tapes for amateur and professional sound recordings.
Contract work: No

Association des Industriels 2 de Belgique

– AIB
[Association of Belgian Industrialists]
Address: 27-29 Avenue André Drouart, B-1160 Bruxelles
Telephone: (673) 80 90
Telex: AIBEL 23.166
Director: Jules Heirman
Laboratories: Mechanical Testing, Ir G. Jacques; Physical Testing, Dr W. Degraeve; Non-Destructive Testing, Ir M. Pintelon
Graduate research staff: 8

Annual expenditure: £51 000-500 000
Activities: Fatigue behaviour of metallic structures, such as railway and road vehicles; large size equipment, allowing full-size testing on trucks and wagons; occupational safety and health regulations; environmental pollution, especially air and noise; specific equipment for X-ray, X-ray and ultrasonic inspection.
Contract work: Yes

Association Royale des 3 Gaziers Belges/Koninklijke Vereniging der Belgische Gasvaklieden

[Royal Association of Belgian Gas Engineers]
Address: 4 avenue Palmerston, B-1040 Bruxelles
Telephone: (02) 230 43 85
Secretary-General R. de Tollenaere
Activities: Research on natural gas; labelling of gas appliances.

Bedrijfsvoorlichtingsdienst 4 voor de Tuinbouw

[Market Garden Research Centre]
Address: Liersesteenweg 32, B-2570 Duffel
Telephone: (015) 31 15 20
Director: Ludo Van der Linden
Graduate research staff: 15
Annual expenditure: £250 000
Contract work: Yes

VEGETABLE RESEARCH STATION 5

Address: B-2580 St Katelijne-Waver
Telephone: (015) 21 95 53
Activities: Variety and culture studies; chemical weed destruction; pesticide studies; insect and vegetable disease; parasitology; soil structure and improvement; plantation research; meteorology.
Political objectives - Belgian vegetable promotion; quality control; crop security; economic studies.

Belgonucléaire Société Anonyme 6

– BN
Address: 25 rue du Champ de Mars, B-1050 Bruxelles
Telephone: 513 97 00
Telex: 22187 NUCBRU B
Research director: Edouard Jonckheere
Graduate research staff: 50
Annual expenditure: over £2m
Activities: BN is an engineering office dealing with the development of energy resources, including solar and other renewable energies, as well as reactor development and waste treatment; it is in continuous contact with Belgian research centres and university laboratories on which it can rely for basic research when needed.
Contract work: Yes

Centre Belge d'Étude de la Corrosion 7

– CEBELCOR
[Belgian Centre for the Study of Corrosion]
Address: Avenue Paul Héger, Grille 2, B-1050 Bruxelles
Director: Antoine J.E. Pourbaix
Sections: Basic and applied research into corrosion, Antoine J.E. Pourbaix; advice on corrosion, Jacques Kissel
Graduate research staff: 5
Annual expenditure: £51 000-500 000
Activities: Research into corrosion in metals.
Contract work: Yes

Centre d'Enseignement et de Recherches des Industries Alimentaires et Chimiques 8

– CERIA
[Food and Chemical Industries Research and Education Centre]
Address: Avenue Émile Gryzon 1, B-1070 Bruxelles
Telephone: (02) 523 20 80
Director-general: Dr G. Chiltz
Activities: CERIA has a number of well-equipped laboratories. Routine work is carried out at the Research and Analysis Laboratory, fundamental research at the Research Institute and applied research in chemistry, biochemistry and the food industry at the Meurice Chemistry Institute.

COMMITTEE FOR THE PROMOTION OF SCIENTIFIC RESEARCH 9

– CPRS
President: Dr G. Chiltz
Research directors: Dr J.M. Piérard, N. Glansdorff
Graduate research staff: 42
Annual expenditure: £225 000
Activities: Infrastructure: personnel and equipment specializing in chemistry and biochemistry (food industries).
Contract work: Yes

FERMENTATION INDUSTRY INSTITUTE - MEURICE CHEMISTRY INSTITUTE 10

– IIF-IMC
Director: J.M. Piérard
Associate director: A. Blondeel
Graduate research staff: 25
Annual expenditure: £51 000-500 000
Activities: Applied research in all fields of chemistry, biochemistry, microbiology and chemical and biochemical engineering: yeasts; fermentation; substances with physiological activities; organic synthesis; catalysis; food technology; biochemical engineering.
Contract work: Yes

Analytical Chemistry Service   11

Head: Professor J. van Degans
Senior staff: Dr P. Delmine, J.P. Hartman, M. Jacqmain, J.P. Leemans
Activities: Quantitive analysis of trace metals; analysis of food products by chromatographic techniques; analysis by electrochemical, spectroscopic and chromatographic methods.

Biochemical Industries and   12
Fermentation Service

Head: Professor A. Devreux
Senior staff: Dr C.A. Mosschelein, Dr C. Jeunehomme
Activities: Metabolism of industrial yeasts; filtration process in brewing; flavour substances in brewery yeast; enzymatic synthesis of microorganisms.

Dietetics Service   13

Senior staff: G. Simoens, M. Woestyn, A.M. Steelens, D. Tamignioux, M. Thomas, E. Chantelot, J. Jungen
Activities: Food surveys; collective nutrition (children, adults, old people); dietary products.

Food Technology Service   14

Head: Professor D. Jacqmain
Senior staff: Chemical and biochemical engineering, Professor J. Lenges, Ph. Dricot
Activities: Technology - conservation, lipid chemistry, saccherose-calcium compounds; quality-freezing, oils and fats; tropical products - palm oil, cocoa, palmetto, butter-tree.

Microbiology - Biochemical Service   15

Head: Professor J. Bechet
Senior staff: H. Behr
Activities: Sensitivity and resistance to mycotoxins; synthesis of ribonucleic acids and ribonucleic acid polymerose in Saccheromyces cerevisiae.

Organic Chemistry and Natural   16
Substances Service

Head: Professor R.R. Smolders
Senior staff: Dr J. Honuise, A. Wafelaer, F. Jacquemotte, R. Coomans, N. Voglet
Activities: Structural study of natural products; organic analysis; general organic synthesis; structure of proteins; synthesis and pharmacological study of peptides; synthesis of molecules with physiological activity.

Physical Chemistry Service   17

Head: Professor P. Gosselain
Senior staff: J.P. Puttemans
Activities: Chemical kinetics; catalysis; mass spectrometry.

Physics - Electricity and Systems   18
Dynamics Service

Senior staff: J.P. Alle, J.C. Piret, P. Dekeyser C. Florquin, Dr G. Jonnes, F. Lepiemme, R. Wenders
Activities: Metrology; instrumentation; use of electronics and microelectronics in the field of control and command, mensuration; static modelling and dynamics of chemical processes; informatics; numeric and analogue simulation in chemical engineering and biochemistry.

PROVINCIAL INSTITUTE FOR THE   19
FOOD INDUSTRIES AND TOURISM

Director, French sections: J. Peeters
Director, Dutch sections: H. Gowie
Activities: Classification studies in the tourist and hotel trade; technology in the hotel trade; baking; pastry-making; confectionery; chocolate manufacture; butchery; food retailing.

RESEARCH AND ANALYSIS   20
LABORATORY

– SEA
Director: J. Bessemans
Graduate research staff: 10
Annual expenditure: £51 000-500 000
Activities: Malt; brewing; bacteria control. Chemical analysis for the food industries.
Contract work: Yes

Biochemical Industry Service   21

Head: R. Tilkens
Activities: Brewing, malt, lemonade; table water; juice, wine; glucosides; starches; fats and oils, chocolate; milk and related products; meat and fish products; vegetable and fruit products; animal food; tobacco; vitamins, food additives; food microbiology.

Chemical Industry Service   22

Head: A. Meurice
Activities: Paints and varnishes; high polymers; combustibles; solvents; lubricants; antifreeze products; cosmetics; minerals; metals; industrial waste water, pollution.

RESEARCH INSTITUTE   23

Director: Dr N. Glansdorff
Honorary director: Dr J.M. Wiame
Senior staff: Dr J. Bechet, Dr G. de Houwer, Dr E.
Dubois, Dr C. Legrain, Dr F. Messenguy, Dr E. Vander-
winkel
Activities: General cell biology; metabolic means of
catabolism of nitrogenized products among bacteria and
yeasts; molecular biology of bacteria and yeasts; experimental evolution; isolation and physiology of ther-
mophile bacteria; theoretical and experimental study of
enzyme catalysis; enzymes controlling cell division.

TECHNICAL INSTITUTE OF   24
DRYSALTERY, CHEMISTRY AND
PERFUMERY

Director, French section: W. Moons
Activities: Drysaltery and chemical products; pharmaceutical industries; perfumes and cosmetics.

Centre d'Étude de la   25
Population et de la
Famille/Centrum voor
Bevolkings: en
Gezinstudiën

[Population and Family Study Centre]
Address: Manhattan Center, Toren H2 Kruisvaar-
tenstraat 3, B-1000 Brussel
Telephone: (02) 219 54 00
Affiliation: Ministry of Public Health and Family
Welfare
Director: G. Hertecant
Graduate research staff: 74
Annual expenditure: BF55m
Activities: The study of population and family pro-
blems. Research topics include fertility; family planning;
ageing; demography.
Contract work: No
Publications: Annual report.

Centre d'Étude et de   26
Documentation de
l'Environnement

– CEBEDEAU
[Environment Study and Documentation Centre]
Address: 2 Rue Armand Stévart, B-4000 Liège
Telephone: (41) 52 12 33
Director: F. Edeline
Sections: Waste water, F. Edeline; L. Vandevenne; in-
dustrial water, J. Hissel
Graduate research staff: 4
Annual expenditure: BF25m
Activities: Research into water and corrosion technol-
ogy, including industrial and domestic water.
Contract work: Yes

Centre de Coopération   27
technique et pédagogique

– CECOTEPE
[Technical and Educational Cooperation Centre]
Address: Rue du Commerce 14, B-4100 Seraing
Telephone: (041) 367900
Director of research: Léon Beulen
Sections: Microcomputers, Paul Christophe; paper in-
dustries, Robert Saive; technological research, Victor
Ghys; educational technology, Léon Beulen
Graduate research staff: 4
Annual expenditure: £10 000-50 000
Activities: The Centre, with the cooperation of the
education authorities of Liège Province, contributes to
the growth of the economy in three ways: by cooperation
with industrial firms by testing and research related to
scientific specialities; by technological research (design,
production and adjustment of prototypes, and industrial
applications) in order to create new products and encourage new industries; and by educational technology
(design and application of educational methods) and
cooperation with national and international organizations.
Contract work: No

Centre de Recherche, d'Analyse et de Controle Chimiques   28

– CERACHIM
[Research, Analysis and Chemical Control Centre]
Address: Boulevard Sainctelette 55, B-7000 Mons
Director: Professor Gh. Lembourg
Activities: Foodstuffs control; analysis and control of mineral-oil products; industrial analysis; air and water pollution control and research.

Centre de Recherches Agronomiques de l'État Gembloux   29

– CRA
[National Agronomic Research Centre, Gembloux]
Address: 22 Avenue de la Faculté d'Agronomie, B-5800 Gembloux
Telephone: (081) 61 19 55
Telex: 591.65 CRAGX
Affiliation: Ministry of Agriculture
Director: R. Lecomte

AGRICULTURAL CHEMISTRY AND PHYSICS STATION   30

Address: 115 Chaussée de Wavre, B-5800 Gembloux
Director: G. Droeven
Activities: Physical, chemical and microbiological aspects of soil science; use of radio-isotopes and electron microscopy in agricultural research.

AGRICULTURAL ENGINEERING STATION   31

Address: 146 Chaussée de Namur, B-5800 Gembloux
Director: V. Dufey
Activities: Research and experiments on all types of agricultural machines.

ANIMAL HUSBANDRY RESEARCH STATION   32

Address: Liroux, B-5800 Gembloux
Director: P. Vandenbyvang
Activities: Mineral nutrition; preservation of forage crops; biological value of silage and hay; fattening; study of sterility caused by malnutrition.

APPLIED ZOOLOGY STATION   33

Address: 8 Chemin de Liroux, B-5800 Gembloux
Director: J. Bernard
Activities: Ethology, ecology, habits, and biocenotics of harmful animals and study of the most efficient methods of counteracting their influence in agriculture.

FOREST TECHNOLOGY STATION   34

Address: 6 Avenue Maréchal Juin, B-5800 Gembloux
Director: P. Roosen
Activities: Anatomical, physical, mechanical and technological research on wood and wood-based materials; wood preservation.

FRUIT AND VEGETABLE STATION   35

Address: 234 Chaussée de Charleroi, Grand-Manil, B-5800 Gembloux
Director: A. Monin
Activities: Applied genetics; selection; phytotechnology; seed production; preservation of fruits and vegetables.

HIGH BELGIUM STATION   36

Address: 48 Rue de Serpont, B-6600 Libramont
Director: L. Nys
Activities: The improvement of potato plants; plant production; prevention of mildew.

MILK RESEARCH STATION   37

Address: 24 Chaussée de Namur, B-5800 Gembloux
Director: P. Jamotte
Activities: The chemistry and physics, microbiology and technology of milk production.

PHYTOPATHOLOGY STATION   38

Address: 13 Avenue Maréchal Juin, B-5800 Gembloux
Director: G. Parmentier
Activities: Plant diseases and their amelioration; bacteriology, virology, mycology and teratology.

PHYTOPHARMACY STATION   39

Address: 11 Rue du Bordia, B-5800 Gembloux
Director: L. Detroux
Activities: Research into the composition, physicochemical and biological properties, and the rational use of insecticides, fungicides, herbicides, rodenticides, etc, used in agriculture, horticulture and forestry.

PHYTOTECHNOLOGY STATION 40

Address: Liroux, B-5800 Gembloux
Director: L. Rixhon
Activities: Study of cultural methods for obtaining the maximum economic production of crops.

PLANT BREEDING STATION 41

Address: 4 Rue du Bordia, B-5800 Gembloux
Director: L. Noulard
Activities: The improvement of forage crops, cereals, industrial plants and vegetables; research in cytogenetics and technology; seed production.

Centre de Recherches 42 Routières/ Opzoekingscentrum voor de Wegenbouw

[Belgian Road Research Centre]
Address: Boulevard de la Woluwe 42, B-1200 Bruxelles
Telephone: (02) 771 20 80
Director: Jean Reichert
Divisions: Research, Dr Jean Verstraeten; Application, Jean-Pierre Leyder; Operational Research, Pierre Becco
Graduate research staff: 35
Annual expenditure: over £2m
Activities: Design and construction of motorways, roads and airfield runways with a view to improved safety and efficiency, and reduced cost. Subjects studied include choice of road alignments, paving design, comfort and environment.
Contract work: Yes

Centre de Transposition 43 Semi-Industrielle de la Recherche Appliquée

[Centre for Semi-Industrial Transposition of Applied Research]
Address: Boulevard Roullier 1, B-6000 Charleroi
Telephone: (071) 322319; (071) 318130
Research director: Professor René Cypres
Sections: Chemistry and electromechanics, Mario Pilati
Graduate research staff: 2
Annual expenditure: BF5m
Activities: Development of ideas put forward by independent inventors to the point where they will be marketable; liaison with and choice of manufacturers interested in making and marketing the new product; super-

vision of payment to the owner of the patent, the original inventor.
Contract work: Yes

Centre National de 44 Production et d'Étude des Substances d'Origine Microbienne

– CNPEM
[National Centre for the Production and Study of Microbial Substances]
Address: 32 Boulevard de la Constitution, Liège
Affiliation: Ministère de l'Éducation Nationale
Director of Research: Dr L. Delcambe
Activities: Pilot-plant production and study of microbial enzymes, antibiotics, cell walls and bacterial viruses.

Centre National de 45 Recherches Scientifiques et Techniques pour l'Industrie Cimentière*

– CRIC
[National Centre of Scientific and Technical Research for Cement Industry]
Address: Rue César Franck 46, B-1050 Bruxelles

Centre Psycho-Medico- 46 Social

[Medical-Psychological-Educational Centre]
Address: Rue Pierre Decoster 115, B-1190 Bruxelles
Telephone: (02) 343 34 82
Affiliation: Commune de Forest; Ministère de l'Éducation Nationale
Director: Marcel Wouters
Activities: Educational psychology; guidance in primary schools; adjustment difficulties in school children.
Contract work: No

Centre Scientifique et Technique de la Construction/ Wetenschappelijk en Technisch Centrum voor het Bouwbedrijf　　47

– CSTC
[Scientific and Technical Building Centre]
Address:　Rue du Lombard 41, B-1000 Bruxelles
Telephone:　(02) 511 06 83
Director:　Alphonse Legros
Sections:　Research and Development, H. Motteu, J. Uyttenbroeck, T. Cuyckens, M. Stassart; management, J. Fassin; information, J. Reygaerts
Graduate research staff:　60
Annual expenditure:　over £2m
Activities:　Scientific and technical research and studies (engineering, building, main walls, foundations, heating, ventilation, air conditioning, plumbing, sanitary, joinery, glazing, painting, coating, insulation, acoustics, water- and air tightness), management of building contractors firms, technical assistance to contractors, information, documentation.

Centrum voor Bosbiologisch Onderzoek　　48

[Centre for Forest Biological Research]
Address:　Bokruk, B-3600 Genk
Telephone:　(011) 353583
Director of Research:　Antoon Huygh
Graduate research staff:　12
Annual expenditure:　BF20m
Activities:　Research on problems related to soil; water; agriculture; forestry.
Contract work:　No

Colgate-Palmolive Research and Development Incorporated　　49

Address:　Avenue du Parc Industriel, B-4411 Milmort
Telephone:　(041) 78 46 01
Telex:　42144 Palmrd b
Activities:　Research into detergents, diapers, household products, non-woven products.
See separate entry for:　Colgate-Palmolive Limited UK.

Comité National Belge de l'Éclairage/Belgisch National Comite voor Verlichtingskunde　　50

[Belgian National Lighting Committee]
Address:　Avenue de la Brabançonne 29, B-1040 Bruxelles
Telephone:　(02) 7349205
Affiliation:　Comité International de l'Éclairage, Paris
General Secretary:　A.F. Delizée
Graduate research staff:　1
Annual expenditure:　£10 000-50 000
Activities:　Advising on light and lighting.
Contract work:　No

Compagnie Intercommunale Bruxelloise des Eaux　　51

– CIBE
[Brussels Water Company]
Address:　Rue aux Laines 70, B-1000 Bruxelles
Telephone:　(02) 513 87 81
General Manager:　Ir M. Chalet
Electro-Mechanical Manager:　Ir L. Monin
Sections:　Chemical bacteriology, Dr Sc W. Masschelein; electronic teletransmission, M. Mostin; engineering, M. Atquet
Activities:　Questions concerning water collection, purification, treatment and distribution in industrialized and developing countries.
Contract work:　Yes

Diensten voor Programmatie van het Wetenschapsbeleid/ Services de Programmation de la Politique Scientifique　　52

– DPWB/SPPS
[Science Policy Progamming Services]
Address:　Rue de la Science 8, B-1040 Bruxelles
Telephone:　(02) 230 41 00
Telex:　PROSCIENJ BRU B 24501
Affiliation:　Office of the Prime Minister
Manager:　Walter Knuyt
Activities:　Financing research carried out in universities and other institutions; coordination of science policy.
Contract work:　No

École Centrale des Arts et Métiers 53

– ECAM
[Arts and Crafts Central School]
Address: 14 Rue du Tir, B-1060 Bruxelles
Telephone: (02) 5376986
Research director: A. Huylenbroeck
Laboratories: Metallography and materials testing, Professor Vanderbist; electronics, Professor Depauw; physics, Professor Heughebaest; chemistry, Professor Dupont; electrical, Professor Hennuy; mechanical, Professor Seynhaeve
Annual expenditure: £10 000-50 000
Activities: Technological problems of small and medium-sized industries.
Contract work: No

École Royale Militaire 54

[Royal Military College]
Address: Avenue de la Renaissance 30, B-1040 Bruxelles
Telephone: (02) 733 97 94-97
Commandant: Lieutenant-General G. Renson
Activities: The School combines military and academic training.

APPLIED CHEMISTRY 55

Head: Professor R.C. Meysmans

APPLIED MECHANICS 56

Heads: Professor A.L. Piret, Professor R.J. Jacques

ARMAMENTS 57

Head: Professor J.R. Dath

ARTILLERY 58

Head: Professor E. Celens

ASTRONOMY, GEODESY AND TOPOGRAPHY 59

Head: Professor U.L. Van Twembeke

CONSTRUCTION 60

Heads: Professor L.N. Belche, Professor A.E. Van Wambeke, Professor R.A. Bourgois

ECONOMY AND MANAGEMENT 61

Head: Professor A.H. David

ELECTRICITY AND ELECTROTECHNOLOGY 62

Heads: Professor P.P. Van Remoortere, Professor J.M. Archambeau

GENERAL CHEMISTRY 63

Heads: Professor R.F. Coekelbergs, Professor B. Kalitventzeff

GEOLOGY AND GEOGRAPHY 64

Head: Professor Colonel E. Wulms

MATHEMATICS 65

Heads: Professor T.P. Lamine, Professor P.E. Gennart, Professor M.A. Gobin

PHYSICS AND NUCLEAR PHYSICS 66

Head: Professor P.E. Vandenplas

PSYCHOLOGY 67

Head: Professor J.J. Van Buggenhout

RATIONAL MECHANICS 68

Head: Professor A.A. Callant

SOCIAL AND POLITICAL SCIENCES 69

Heads: Professor F.G. Lehouck, Professor M.M. Boeymaems

TELECOMMUNICATIONS 70

Heads: Professor J.E. Charles, Professor M. Verlinden

TRANSPORT MECHANICS 71

Head: Professor R.C. Van Laer

Electro-Navale et Industrielle Société Anonyme/Electrische Nijverheids - Installaties Naamloze Vennootschap 72

– ENI
Address: Kontichesesteenweg 25, B-2630 Antwerpen
or: Postbus 389, 2000 Antwerpen 1
Telephone: (031) 87 40 81
Telex: 31.598
Research director G. Noesen
Sections: Solar energy, G. Bertels; biomedical, W. Smets; H_2 production, A. Pauwels; nuclear energy, J.P. Rombaux
Graduate research staff: 9
Annual expenditure: £51 000-500 000
Activities: Thermal and photovoltaic solar energy systems; water electrolysers for H_2 production; air sterilizers for surgical applications; nuclear decontamination techniques; associated waste treatment processes.
Contract work: Yes

Faculté des Sciences Agronomiques de l'État 73

[State Faculty of Agronomy]
Address: Place St Guibert, 5800 Gembloux, Namur
Telephone: (081) 61 29 61
Rector: Professor Charles Bonnier
Publications: Annual report.

DEPARTMENT OF AGRICULTURAL FOOD SCIENCE AND FORESTRY 74

Head: Professor A. Mottet
Activities: Use of microdensitometry in forestry and technology of diverse species; study of lignocelluloses for panel fibres; study of improved utilization of the forest resources of the Walloon; forest management modelling; recycling of agricultural wastes; study of protein capacity; physico-chemistry of hydro-colloids in the food industry; meat technology; theoretical study of glyceride crystallization; production and conditioning of enzymes for the food industry; mycotoxins. Joint projects on the technological qualities of the Belgian spruce; statistical documentation of the Walloon forest; productivity of regional forest species; improvement of the physical and mechanical properties of paper paste and papers made from recycled material; applied study of glyceride crystallization; mathematical modelling of heat transfer in food production and improvement; pre-

paration, conservation and distribution of cooked dishes based on pork meat - hygiene and freezing; enzyme bioreactors; conception and preparation of new products; diversification and interchangeability of fat products; new methods of surveying forests; recycling of paper waste.

DEPARTMENT OF ANALYTICAL CHEMISTRY 75

Head: Professor P. Nangniot
Activities: Polarographic, spectrofluorometric, atomic absorption spectrophotometric study of different elements in plants, water and soil; study of percentage of pesticide residue in plants. Collaboration projects include: dispersion of herbicide in water and soil; pollution risk of underground water supplies situated near waste processing stations; characterization of purification systems; use of gas phase chromatography to separate and identify pesticides; analytical methods of measuring dosage in new products.

DEPARTMENT OF ANIMAL PHYSIOLOGY AND ZOOTECHNICS 76

Head: A. Antoine
Activities: Comparative study of male animals of the Blanc-Bleu-Belge and Pie Noire species. Joint projects on bovine enzootic leukaemia; phosphorus nutrition in ruminants; integral study of animal production in South Hainault; technological improvements to mixed farming in Northern Tunisia; indigestible markers to study the physiology of ruminent nutrition; effect of calcium peroxide on the growth of ruminants.

DEPARTMENT OF APPLIED ZOOLOGY 77

Head: Professor R. Breny
Activities: Distribution of nematodes harmful to maize; study of Ditylenchus radicicola; effect of pollution on aquatic biocenosis. Joint project on the documentation of entomologic enemies of the poplar.

DEPARTMENT OF EARTH SCIENCES 78

Head: Professor V. Tonnard
Activities: Thermal behaviour of phyllosilicates, radiocrystallographic analysis of clays; quaternary sedimentology; stratigraphical study of the Visé region.

DEPARTMENT OF ECOLOGY 79

Head: Professor A. Noirfalise
Activities: Transpiration and water balance in plants; ecological analysis of rural and forest areas; creation and management of nature reserves, forest reserves and natural parks in Belgium. Joint projects on associations and stations in Belgian forests; dendrometry, ecology and productivity of forests; biological management of water, riverine vegetation, aquatic mocrophytes; primary and secondary productivity of the Belgian grassland; establishment of a phytosociologic bank; ecological map of Belgium; evaluative methodology of environmental cartography; vegetation map of Europe and its subsequent revision.

DEPARTMENT OF FRUIT TREES AND 80 MARKET GARDEN CULTIVATION

Head: Professor A. Nisen
Activities: Photometric properties of horticultural buildings; construction techniques and use of horticultural buildings in relation to energy economics, ecoclimatological needs of different marsh plants. Joint projects include; recuperation of residual energy, productivity improvement in the Meuse valley; study of energy economics in protected cultures; technical, ecological and nutritive needs of marsh plants.

DEPARTMENT OF GENERAL AND 81 ORGANIC CHEMISTRY

Head: M. Severia
Activities: Joint projects on: nitrogen balance in leguminous plants; structure of whole or fractioned fats resulting from different technological treatment; influence of lipoproteins on the baking quality of different types of wheat, dosimetry of volatile acids and sugars; improvement of analytical methods for use in agronomic research.

DEPARTMENT OF GENERAL 82 ZOOLOGY AND FAUNISTICS

Head: Professor J. Leclercq
Activities: Sampling, determination, conservation and collection of insects, Isopoda, and the fauna of Belgium and other European countries; faunal documentation of Gembloux; documentation of Tenthredinidae; cartography and distribution of wasps and bees in Belgium; identification of Hymnoptera collected by British and American missions to South America, Africa and South East Asia; role of Diptera in human and veterinary parasitology; taxonomy and ecology of Protozoa and Ciliata; cave animals; identification of invertebrates for public or private individuals. Joint projects on the analysis of insect maps of Belgium; study of Franco-

Belgian and Diptera and their possible use to control Trematoda carrying molluscs; documentation of entomogenous fauna in the Pas de Calais.

DEPARTMENT OF GENETICS AND 83 PLANT IMPROVEMENT

Head: Professor A. Moes
Activities: Plant regeneration; Triticum alstivum.

DEPARTMENT OF MATERIALS 84 RESISTANCE AND RURAL CONSTRUCTION ENGINEERING

Head: Professor L. Sine
Activities: Joint projects related to rural roads and agricultural buildings, agricultural use and value of waste purification stations.

DEPARTMENT OF MATHEMATICS 85

Head: J.P. Lambotte
Activities: Extinction of branches in biology; application of stochastic processes to risk theories.

DEPARTMENT OF MICROBIOLOGY 86

Head: Professor C. Bonnier
Activities: Industrial use of enzymes; NAD recombination in Saccharomyces cerevisae; use of ATP to control purification stations and to measure soil fertility. Joint projects include: water and food bacteriology; microbiological and bacteriological aspects of waste products used for agriculture; rhizobium fixation; influence of rhizosphere microorganisms on soil fertility; recycling of agricultural waste by aerobic fermentation; production of species, forest management and ligneous production.

DEPARTMENT OF ORGANIC AND 87 BIOLOGICAL CHEMISTRY

Head: Professor J. Casimir
Activities: Study of amino acids in fungi and leguminous plants; qualitative and quantative evaluation of amino acids and peptide mixtures of Vigna radiata and Vigna mungo. Joint project on the alimentary value of lupine fodder crops.

DEPARTMENT OF PHYSICS AND PHYSICAL CHEMISTRY   88

Head: Professor J. Delfour
Activities: Student reasoning on elementary electrokinetics; solution strategies in elementary mechanics; docimology of multiple-choice questions; sociocultural handicaps in foreign students. Joint projects include: radioactive surveys and radiometric methods in agronomy; dispersion methods of agricultural products in rivers; isolation and dosimetric study of pesticides; percolation of radioactive isotopes and pesticides in soils; radiochemical study of the influence of Agrobacterium tumefeciens on the root penetration of rhizobium, optic and thermic properties of materials used in plant coverings and the effect on plants of different types of covering; evaluation of the amount of energy received by soils under different types of covering.

DEPARTMENT OF PHYTOPATHOLOGY   89

Head: Professor J. Semal
Activities: Role of lectins and toxins in phytopathology; study of the elm; effect of Cladosporium on the tomato plant; Uromyces phaseoli pests; effect of aluminium ethyl-phosphonines on the resistance of plants to fungal infections.

DEPARTMENT OF PHYTOTECHNOLOGY OF HOT ZONES   90

Head: J. Demol
Activities: Intergenomic study of Gossypium genus; characterization of descendants of the arboretum-thurben-hirsutum hybrid; taxonomy of Phasiolinae; transmission of peptides in hybrids; relation between the percentage of sulphur in plant mineral nutrients and the percentage of sulphur amino acids in Phaseolus vulgaris and Vigna mungo. Joint projects on cytogenetics of the cotton species, development of cotton fibres, hybridization of Phaseolus vulgaris and related species; genetic evaluation of Phaseolus lunatus L; determination of amino acid concentration in alimentary species, especially those of Rwanda, bibliographic research on alimentary species of minor or local importance.

DEPARTMENT OF PHYTOTECHNOLOGY OF TEMPERATE ZONES   91

Head: Professor R. Laloux
Activities: Cereals phytotechnology; fertilizers; popularization of cereal cultivation methods. Joint projects include; technological, alimentary and fodder value of oleaginous and protogynous plants; phytosanitary protection of cereals; varieties of fodder crops and maize.

DEPARTMENT OF PLANT BIOLOGY   92

Head: Professor P. Heinemann
Activities: Research into systematics and biology of higher mushrooms; industrial and urban plant life (pollution). Research carried out in collaboration with other organizations includes: interaction between sulphur pollutants in the atmosphere and mineral nutrition of plants by means of radioisotope detectors; cadmium air-plant and soil-plant interaction; ecology and management; waste purification; measurement of atmospheric pollution; study of the environment near main roads.

DEPARTMENT OF RURAL ECONOMICS   93

Head: Professor A. Ledent
Activities: Function of production in agriculture; agricultural management; agriculture and agro-alimentary complex of Walloon; agricultural integration in the European Economic Community; agricultural organization in black Africa; agro-alimentary markets and energy balance.

DEPARTMENT OF RURAL ENGINEERING I   94

Head: Professor E. Balligand
Activities: Hydrodynamic properites of agricultural substrata; study of water in non-saturated soils; irrigation by aspersion; drainage of agricultural land; evapotranspiration; surface hydrology of natural basins; theoretical and practical feasibility of drying agricultural products by solar energy. Joint projects on recuperation of residual energy for agriculture, modelling of the migration of soluble elements in soil; evaluation of the contamination risk by purification stations; hydro-agricultural management in Zaire; teledetection devices used in hydro-agricultural management.

DEPARTMENT OF SILVICULTURE 95

Head: Professor P. Roisen
Activities: Study of forest species in temperate countries; silviculture of high yield (poplar) and technologically interesting (American red oak) species; comparative study of diverse forestry techniques; phytogeographic forestry; forest management and nature conservancy. Joint projects on the characterization of forest soils and ecosystems; study of the reproductive method of the more noble forest species (wild cherry, ash); forest phytosociology, productivity of species; integral study of hydrological problems and forest on the north slope of the Haute-Fagnes region.

DEPARTMENT OF SOIL SCIENCE 96

Address: 27 Avenue Maréchal Juin, B-5800 Gembloux
Telephone: (081) 61 00 65
Head: Professor G. Hanotiaux
Centres: Soil cartography; forest soils; chemical fertility of soils; soil conservation
Graduate research staff: 12
Annual expenditure: £501 000-2m
Activities: Pedogenesis in geomorphology and geology. Joint projects include: pedological survey of Southern Belgian soils; fertilization of forest soils in Southern Belgium; soil nutrition; study of erosion in lime regions; dendrochronology of the Moroccan cedar in relation to its environment.
Contract work: No

DEPARTMENT OF STATISTICS 97

Head: Professor P. Dagnelie
Activities: Calculus service. Joint projects include: statistical analysis and consultation service; solution of problems.

DEPARTMENT OF TROPICAL FORESTRY 98

Head: Professor R. Pierlot
Activities: Study of natural forests in tropical countries; overseas artificial forest colonization; study of eucalyptus, pines and other exotics; adaptation of forest species to saline and arid environments.

EPIOUX SCIENTIFIC STATION 99

President: Ch. Gosper
Senior staff: M. Clignez, M. Locioix, M. Laurent
Activities: Ecology; fish production to repopulate rivers, influence of leafy and resinous forests on the hydrology of natural basins. Joint projects on the influence of game on the natural regeneration of forest species; simulation development of the colonization of resinous trees; sampling methods in forestry; coprophagous insects in forests and meadows; Epioux soils.

IMAGE ANALYSIS SECTION 100

Head: Professor L. Sine
Activities: Aerial and satellite photography; agronomy; chemistry.

PHYTOPHARMACEUTICAL SERVICE 101

Head: Professor J. Fraselle
Activities: Comparative study of chemical treatments against diseases affecting winter cereals; optimization of depots for phytosanitary products in treatment plants. Joint projects on the chemical fight against cereal diseases in Tunisia; studies on the protection of the cacao plant in Cameroun and the cassava plant in Rwanda; research on the improving of phytosanitary techniques.

Faculté Polytechnique de Mons 102

[Polytechnic Faculty of Mons]
Address: 9 Rue de Houdain, B-7000 Mons
Telephone: (065) 33 81 91
Rector: Professor R.E. Baland
Sections: Exploitation of mines, Professor G. Degueldre
Preparations of minerals and materials, Professor P. Moiset
Mineralogy and petrography, Professor A. Beugnies
Geology, Professor I. Godfriaux
General metallurgy and siderurgy, Professor Y. Riguier
Metallurgy of non-ferrous metals, Professor M. Jacob
Transformation metallurgy, Professor C. Pacque
Metallography, Professor A. Vilain
Thermodynamics, Professor J. Bougard
Mathematical physics, Professor J. Bougard
General chemistry I, Professor T. Doehaerd
General chemistry II, Professor H. Vander Poorten
Applied chemistry (analytical and industrial), Professor J.M. Levert
Chemical engineering, Professor S. Lefèbvre
Organic chemistry

General electricity, electrical measurements and electromagnetism, Professor P. Jacobs

Electrical engineering, Professor R. Baland

Electronics and radiocommunications, Professor M. Cogneaux

Transport and distribution of electricity, high voltage, Professor C. Grégoire

Industrial applications of electricity, Professor M. Crappe

Circuit theory, Professor R. Boite

Automation, Professor M. Mauroy

Applied mechanics, Professor J. Baland

Elasticity and stress analysis, Professor C. Meunier

Analytical mechanics, Professor S. Boucher

Heat technology, Professor H. Meunier

Description and construction of machines, metrology and technology I, Professor A. Leroy

Materials resistance, stability of buildings, general and industrial construction, Professor M. Save

Civil architecture, Professor J. Barthelemy

Civil engineering, technology of construction materials, Professor R. Berdal

Mathematical analysis and algebra, Professor W. Barbenson

Functional and numerical analysis, Professor E. Carton

Random mathematics and operational research, Professor M. Roubens

Computer science, vacant

Political economy and management of enterprises, Professor G. Labeau

General physics, Professor R. Quivy

Internal physics of materials and crystallography, Professor L. Danguy

Activities: Heat transfer - thermal conductivity of refractories at high temperatures, special heat transfer tube (finned tubes) for heat recovery exchangers; composite materials - effective moduli of isotropic two-phase elastic compositives, predictions in function of the shape of the inclusions; electrical properties - plastic insulators assessment, ageing insulators under severe atmospheric conditions, testing sample of materials and for field scale equipment up to 100 kV; sintering of iron ores - influence of chemical and structural composition on sinter and pellet properties, behaviour of these materials during reduction in the blast furnace; continuous casting of steel - reduction of occurrence of surface defects of continuous casting slabs; recycling and energy saving - utilization of steelmaking slags in manufacturing Portland Cement Clinker, new uses for steelmaking slags and dust.

Facilities: High voltage laboratory: equipment 1 megavolt, 50 hertz, 2.5 megavolt surge generator; thermal conductivity measurement facilities; laboratory testing sintering and pelletizing plants; test apparatus for evaluating iron ores, pellets and sinter.

Publications: Annual report.

Facultés Universitaires Notre-Dame de la Paix à Namur 103

[Notre Dame de la Paix University Faculties, Namur]
Address: Rue de Bruxelles 61, B-5000 Namur
Telephone: (087) 22 90 01
Telex: 59222 FAC NAM B
Rector: Professor R. Troisfontaines

MEDICINE FACULTY 104

Address: Place du Palais de Justice, B-5000 Namur
Telephone: (081) 22 90 61
Dean: Professor R. Wattiaux

Anatomy Department 105

Director: Professor J.-Y. Berben

Cell Physiology and Genetics Laboratory 106

Director: Professor J. Lammerant

Chemical Physiology Laboratory 107

Director: Professor R. Wattiaux

Histology and Embryology Laboratory 108

Director: Professor R. Leloup

Psychology Department 109

Director: Professor R. Troisfontaines

SCIENCE FACULTY 110

Address: 2 Rue Grafé, B-5000 Namur
Telephone: (081) 22 90 62
Dean: R. Paquay

Cell Biochemistry Unit 111

Senior staff: Professor J. Remacle

Cytology Unit 112

Senior staff: Professor M.-F. Ronveaux

Didactic Experimental Physics Unit 113

Senior staff: Professor G. Cardinael

Computing Centre   142

Director: J. Romaekers

Electron Microscopy Interfaculty Unit   143

Director: R. Leloup

Nuclear Reaction Laboratory   144

Director: G. Deconninck

Solid-State Interfaces Research   145
Institute

Address: 2 Rue Grafé, B-5000 Namur
Promoters: A. Lucas, R. Caudano, J.-M. Gilles
Activities: The Institute is run in collaboration with Mons University.

Fonds d'Études pour la   146
Sécurité Routière/
Studiefonds voor een Veilig
Wegverkeer

[Road Safety Research Fund]
Address: Chaussée de Haecht 1405, B-1130 Bruxelles
Telephone: (02) 241 87 76
Director: J.P. de Coster
Sections: Technical factors, L. de Brabander; human factors R. Dieleman
Graduate research staff: 10
Annual expenditure: £51 000-500 000
Activities: All aspects of road safety, including the psychology of road users, the driving licence, road safety statistics and opinion polls of road users.
Contract work: No

Fonds de la Recherche   147
Fondamentale Collective

[Fund for Collective Fundamental Research]
Address: Rue d'Egmont 5, B-1050 Bruxelles
Affiliation: Fonds National de la Recherche Scientifique
President of the Management Committee: F. Dethier
Activities: The Fund maintains contact groups for the following: mathematical sciences; physics; chemistry and earth sciences; biological sciences; applied sciences; moral and political sciences; agronomy; medical and pharmaceutical sciences.

Fonds de la Recherche   148
Scientifique Médicale

[Fund for Medical Scientific Research]
Address: Rue d'Egmont 5, B-1050 Bruxelles
Affiliation: Fonds National de la Recherche Scientifique
President of the Management Committee: P. Halter
Vice-President of the Management Committee: P. De Somer
Activities: The Management Committee of the Fund is helped in its task by five Commissions.

CANCER STUDIES COMMISSION   149

President: Professor W. Smets

CLINICAL RESEARCH COMMISSION   150

President: Dr M. Xhigne

EPIDEMIOLOGY AND PSYCHIATRY   151
COMMISSION

President: Professor M. Graffar

FUNDAMENTAL RESEARCH   152
COMMISSION

President: Dr J. Cuvelier

PHARMACEUTICAL SCIENCE   153
COMMISSION

President: Professor R. Vanden Driessche

Fonds National de la   154
Recherche Scientifique

[National Fund for Scientific Research]
Address: Rue d'Egmont 5, B-1050 Bruxelles
Telephone: (02) 512 58 15
Telex: 25498 BEREFO B
Secretary-General: Dr Paul Levaux
Activities: A public body which works to promote scientific research in Belgium. Revenues of the Fund are used in the following ways: grants are made to scholars and research workers; grants are made to young Belgians whose ability is brought to the Council's notice; subsidies are given to enable Belgian research workers to attend congresses abroad; and other subsidies may also be given at the discretion of the Council for purposes

related to the advancement of scientific research in Belgium. The Administrative Council of the Fund is helped in its task by 22 scientific commissions of which 17 are involved in scientific fields.

Publications: Annual report.

See separate entries for: Institut Interuniversitaire des Sciences Nucléaires; Fonds de la Recherche Scientifique Médicale; Fonds de la Recherche Fondamentale Collective.

AGRONOMY AND ZOOLOGY COMMISSION   155

President: Professor J. Heuts

ANIMAL BIOLOGY COMMISSION   156

President: Professor H. Meewis-Herlant

APPLIED CHEMISTRY AND METALLURGY COMMISSION   157

President: Professor A. Deruyttere

ASTRONOMY AND GEOPHYSICS COMMISSION   158

President: Professor P. Ledoux

BIOCHEMISTRY (NORMAL AND PATHOLOGICAL) AND MOLECULAR BIOLOGY COMMISSION   159

President: Professor L. Vandendriessche

CHEMICAL PHYSICS AND ELECTROCHEMISTRY COMMISSION   160

President: Professor V. Desreux

CIVIL AND MINING ENGINEERING COMMISSION   161

President: Professor E. De Beer

GENERAL MICROBIOLOGY AND MEDICAL IMMUNOLOGY COMMISSION   162

President: Professor P. De Somer

GEOGRAPHY, GEOLOGY AND MINERALOGY COMMISSION   163

President: Professor R. Tavernier

MATHEMATICS COMMISSION   164

President: Professor Paul Gillis

MECHANICS AND APPLIED ELECTRONICS COMMISSION   165

President: Professor M. Cogneaux

MINERAL AND ORGANIC CHEMISTRY COMMISSION   166

President: Professor G. Duyckaerts

NORMAL AND PATHOLOGICAL MORPHOLOGY COMMISSION   167

President: Professor E. Betz

NORMAL AND PATHOLOGICAL PHYSIOLOGY COMMISSION   168

President: Professor R. Vanden Driessche

PHYSICS COMMISSION   169

President: Professor Willy Dekeyser

PLANT BIOLOGY COMMISSION   170

President: Professor A. Louis

PSYCHOLOGICAL SCIENCES AND EDUCATION COMMISSION   171

President: Professor M. Verbist

Hôpital Militaire de Bruxelles 172

Address: Rue Bruyn, B-1120 Bruxelles

COMMISSION MILITAIRE POUR L'ÉTUDE ET LA PRÉVENTION DU SUICIDE 173

[Military Commission for the Study and Prevention of Suicide]
Telephone: (02) 267 99 10
Affiliation: Royal School of the Medical Service
Director: Dr G. Tallon
Annual expenditure: £10 000-50 000
Activities: Socio-psychiatric causes of absenteeism in the Belgian military forces: alcoholism, suicide, desertion; motivation and techniques of selection of members of the military.
Contract work: Yes

Institut Belge de la Soudure 174

[Belgian Welding Institute]
Address: 21 Rue des Drapiers, B-1050 Bruxelles
Telephone: 512 28 92
Director: Roger Vanden Eynden
Publications: Revue de la Soudre, in French and Flemish, 4 times a year.

RESEARCH CENTRE 175

Address: St Pieternieuwstraat 41, B-9000 Gent
Telephone: (091) 23382
Telex: 11344 ibsbil b
Head: Andre van Bernst
Activities: Weldability, study of welding materials; fracture mechanics; behaviour of welded constructions. Three research laboratories in England, Germany and Belgium have been proposed to study common problems of welding materials and techniques. The Research Centre offers technical advice.

Institut Belge pour l'Amélioration de la Beeterave/Belgisch Instituut tot Verbetering van de Biet 176

[Belgian Beet Research Institute]
Address: Molenstraat 45, B-3300 Tienen
Telephone: (016) 815171
Director of Research: M. Martens
Sections: Cultivation, N. Roussel; mechanization, A. Vigoureux; herbicides, J.M. Belien; pesticides, L. Vansteyvoort; laboratories, R. Vanstallen
Graduate research staff: 7
Annual expenditure: BF30m
Activities: Different varieties of beet, seed analysis, herbicides and pesticides.
Contract work: No
Publications: Quarterly journal, information bulletin.

Institut d'Hygiène et d'Épidémiologie/Instituut voor Hygiene en Epidemiologie 177

[Hygiene and Epidemiology Institute]
Address: Juliette Wytsman Street 14, B-1050 Brussel
Telephone: (02) 647 99 80
Telex: 21034 IHEBRU
Affiliation: Ministry of Public Health and Family Welfare
Director: A. Lafontaine
Sections: Environment, J. Bouquiaux; microbiology, E. Van Oye; pharmatoxicology, J. Gossele
Graduate research staff: 150
Annual expenditure: £14 285
Activities: The study of scientific problems related to the prevention and correction of factors capable of altering the health and wellbeing of man; the epidemiological study of the different factors that attack man and his environment, how they work and the ways and means to control them.
Contract work: No
Publications: Annual report.

Institut de Recherches Chimiques   178

[Chemical Research Institute]
Address: Museumlaan 5, B-1980 Tervuren
Telephone: (02) 767 53 01
Affiliation: Ministry of Agriculture
Director: J.R. Istas
Graduate research staff: 25
Contract work: No
Publications: Annual and biannual reports.

DEPARTMENT OF INORGANIC AND   179
PHYSICOCHEMISTRY

Head: R. De Borger
Sections: Pedology and physicochemistry, R. De Borger; geochemistry and spectrography, vacant
Activities: Interaction of soil-pollutants and soil-pesticides; biodegradation, adsorption, retention of pesticides and other chemicals; studies on the contamination of surface water; geochemical inventory of soils, plants, water; pollution of marine organisms and sediments by metals; spectroscopic studies on different materials.

DEPARTMENT OF ORGANIC AND   180
BIOLOGICAL CHEMISTRY

Head: X. Monseur
Sections: Biochemistry, M. Decleire; organic chemistry, X. Monseur; chemistry, vacant
Activities: Biochemical modifications in plants through the action of pesticides; metabolic changes in plants through the action of atmospheric pollutants; bioassays with pesticides; organic constituents in water and natural products, small traces; impact of organic volatile pollutants on vegetation; organometallic compounds in foods; utilization of agro-industrial waste; aerobic and anaerobic fermentation; chemical aspects of environmental pollution; soil and plant contamination by organic and inorganic pollutants; food contamination by in organic elements.

Institut Européen   181
d'Écologie et de Cancérologie

– INEC
[European Institute of Ecology and Cancer]
Address: Rue des Fripiers 24 Bis, B-1000 Bruxelles
Telephone: (02) 219-08 30
International Secretary General: Dr Émile-Gaston Peeters
Sections: Geocancerology; preventive medicine
Activities: Geocancerology: cancer seen in the context of subjects such as geography, geochemistry, hydrology and ecology as well as subjects such as biochemistry and comparative anatomy, to clarify the conditions of appearance and the causes of cancer and thus prepare for its prevention.
Contract work: No

Institut Interuniversitaire   182
des Sciences Nucléaires

[Interuniversity Institute of Nuclear Science]
Address: Rue d'Egmont 5, B-1050 Bruxelles
Telephone: (02) 512 58 15
Telex: 25498 BEREFO B
Affiliation: Fonds National de la Recherche Scientifique
Secretary-General: Dr Paul Levaux
President of the Administrative Council: Dr P. De Somer
Activities: Research in basic nuclear science is promoted at research establishments and higher education centres. The activities of the Institute are organized by three scientific commissions covering high-energy studies, low-energy studies and radiation and radiochemistry science.

Institut National de   183
Recherches Vétérinaires

[National Institute of Veterinary Research]
Address: 99 Groeselenberg, B-1180 Bruxelles
Telephone: (02) 3 544 55
Affiliation: Ministry of Agriculture
Director: Dr J. Levnen
Graduate research staff: 18
Activities: Microbiology; biology; toxicology; biochemistry; parasitology in relation to infectious animal diseases; control of biological products for veterinary use; production of foot-and-mouth vaccine.
Contract work: No
Publications: Annual report.

NUTRITION, BIOCHEMISTRY AND 184 TOXICOLOGY DEPARTMENT

Head: Dr P. Dekeyser
Sections: Toxicology, O. Antoine; immunochemistry, Dr A. Van Aert

PATHOLOGY OF LARGE DOMESTIC 185 ANIMALS DEPARTMENT

Sections: General bacteriology and plasmidology, Dr P. Pohl, Dr P. Lintermans; mycobacteria, leptospires and laboratory animals, Dr M. Desmacht, Dr G. Lecluselle; reproduction pathology and histopathology, Dr P. Dekeyser; hygiene and epidemiology, Dr L. Famerée

PATHOLOGY OF SMALL DOMESTIC 186 ANIMALS AND PARASITOLOGY DEPARTMENT

Head: Dr P. Halen
Sections: Pathology, Dr P. Halen, Dr G. Meulemans, Dr J. Peeters; parasitology, Dr C. Cotteleer

VIROLOGY DEPARTMENT 187

Head: Dr R. Strobbe
Sections: Pig viruses, Dr P. Biront; cattle viruses, Dr G. Wellemans, Dr E. Van Opdenbosch; foot-and-mouth disease, Dr R. Strobbe, Dr J. Debecq; leucoses, Dr M. Mammerickx; cellular cultures and electron microscopy, G. Charlier

Institut Pasteur du 188 Brabant/Instituut Pasteur van Brabant

[Pasteur Institute of Brabant]
Address: Rue du Remorqueur 28, B-1040 Bruxelles
Telephone: (02) 230 73 75
Affiliation: Province de Brabant
Research director: Professor F. De Meuter
Sections: Virology, Dr J. Content; microbiology, Professor F. De Meuter; immunology, Dr L. Thiry
Graduate research staff: 30
Annual expenditure: £51 000-500 000
Activities: Virology: Molecular bases of the mechanisms of action and induction of IFN; posttranslational modifications of proteins translated in vitro; study of retroviral expression in human placenta; humoral and cellular immune responses of different transformed simian oncornaviruses; role of oncornaviruses in human reproduction.

Microbiology: study of enzymatic activities of BCG; specific and non specific antifungal immunity; transmission of virulent Toxoplasma Gondii.
Immunology: purification of antibodies; immunostimulation; mediation of lymphocyte interactions.
Contract work: No

Institut pour 189 l'Encouragement de la Recherche Scientifique dans l'Industrie et l'Agriculture*

– IRSIA
[Institute for the Advancement of Scientific Research in Industry and Agriculture]
Address: 6 Rue de Crayer, B-1050 Bruxelles
Director: Dr Jean Van Keymeulen
Activities: The Institute grants financial assistance to research projects of a scientific and technical nature which are of interest to industry and agriculture. This assistance amounts to 50-80 per cent for industry and up to 100 per cent for agriculture.

Institut Royal des Sciences 190 Naturelles de Belgique/ Koninklijk Belgisch Instituut voor Natuurwetenschappen

[Royal Institute of Natural Sciences of Belgium]
Address: 31 Rue Vautier, B-1040 Bruxelles
Director: X. Misonne
Activities: To secure the conservation and the study of the collections of natural history specimens of Belgium, by scientific explorations of the territory, the administration of the collections, the presentation to the public of the results of those researches as well as the comparative scientific study of zoological and palaeontological documents from the whole world.

BIOLOGY DEPARTMENT 191

Head: G. Marlier
Sections: Hydrobiology; oceanography; ecology and protection of nature

MINERALOGY AND SEDIMENTOLOGY LABORATORIES 192

Head: R. Van Tassel

PALAEONTOLOGY DEPARTMENT 193

Head: P. Sartenaer
Sections: Primary invertebrates; secondary and tertiary invertebrates; vertebrate fossils; micropalaeontology and palaeobotany

ZOOLOGY DEPARTMENT 194

Head: X. Misonne
Sections: Anthropology and prehistory; vertebrates; invertebrates; entomology

Institut von Karman de Dynamique des Fluides 195

[Von Karman Institute for Fluid Dynamics]
Address: 72 Chaussée de Waterloo, B-1640 Rhode-Saint-Genèse
Telephone: (02) 358 19 01
Director: Professor J.J. Ginoux
Sections: Aeronautics/aerospace, J. Wendt; environmental and applied fluid dynamics, J. Ginoux; turbomachines, F. Breuselmans
Graduate research staff: 80
Annual expenditure: over £2m
Activities: Wind tunnels; instrumentation; data acquisition systems; fluid motion; ranges of velocities, pressures and temperatures.
Contract work: Yes
Publications: Technical notes.

Institution pour le Développement de la Gazéification Souterraine/ Instelling voor de Ontwikkeling van de Ondergrondse Vergassing 196

– IDGS
[Institution for the Development of Underground Gasification]
Address: Rue du Chéra 200, B-4000 Liège
Telephone: (041) 52 71 50
Telex: 41128 INIEX B
Affiliation: Ministry of Economic Affairs

Director: Pierre L.V. Ledent
Sections: Underground coal gasification, P. Ledent, Ch. Beckervordesandforth
Graduate research staff: 8
Annual expenditure: £501 000-2m
Activities: Trial underground coal gasification at great depth and high pressure.
Contract work: Yes

Instituut voor Tropische Geneeskunde Prins Leopold/Institut de Médecine Tropicale Prince Léopold 197

[Prince Leopold Institute for Tropical Medicine]
Address: Nationalestraat 155, B-2000 Antwerpen
Telephone: (031) 38 58 80
Director: Professor Dr L. Eyckmans
Sections: Bacteriology/virology, Professor Dr S.R. Pattyn; protozoology, Professor Dr M. Wéry; medical zoology, Professor Dr A. Fain; veterinary medicine, Professor Dr J. Mortelmans; zootechnics, Professor Dr J. Hardouin; haematology, Professor Dr G. Van Ros; immuno-haematology, Dr G. Helderweirt; anatomopathology, Professor Dr P. Gigase; serology, Professor Dr N. Van Meirvenne; mycology, Professor Dr Ch. De Vroey; nutrition, Professor Dr J. Vuylsteke; public health, Professor Dr P. Mercenier, Professor Dr H. Van Balen
Graduate research staff: 35
Annual expenditure: £501 000-2m
Activities: Tropical medicine and connected sciences; tropical public health; tropical veterinary medicine; zootechnics.
Facilities: There are 15 research laboratories in Antwerp and several overseas.
Contract work: Yes
Publications: Annual report.

Instituut voor Zeewetenschappelijk Onderzoek 198

– IZWO
[Institute for Marine Scientific Research]
Address: Prinses Elisabethlaan 69, B-8401 Bredene
Telephone: (59) 323715
Graduate research staff: 5
Activities: The institute is governed by a board of trustees, comprising delegates from 4 Belgian univer-

sities: the Free University of Brussels, the State University of Ghent, the University of Antwerp, and the Catholic University of Louvain, as well as representatives from national scientific institutes and the provincial government of the West Flanders and local interested persons. The institute provides facilities for scientists to use its laboratories and library and coordinates multidisciplinary research. The main research interest is marine biology, both fundamental and applied, but members are also working on other aspects of the marine environment such as geology and chemistry.
Contract work: Yes

Janssen Pharmaceutica NV* 199

BEERSE LABORATORIES* 200

Address: B-2340 Beerse
Research staff: 450
Activities: Research at Janssen centres on the following areas in both human and veterinary medicine: psychiatry, analgesia, anaesthesia, treatment of cardiovascular and gastrointestinal diseases, parasitology, mycology, bacteriology, immunology, chronic inflammatory diseases and endocrinology. Agrochemical research focuses on insecticides, herbicides, fungicides, acaricides, limacides, and growth regulators.

Katholieke Universiteit Leuven 201

[Catholic University of Louvain]
Address: Naamsestraat 22, B-3000 Leuven
Telephone: (016) 22 04 31

FACULTY OF AGRICULTURAL 202 SCIENCES

Address: Kardinaal Mercierlaan 92, B-3030 Leuven (Heverlee)
Dean: Professor Dr Ir J.B. Uytterhoeven

Department of Agricultural Economics 203

AGRICULTURAL ECONOMICS 204 RESEARCH CENTRE
– CLEO
Address: Kardinaal Mercierlaan 92, B-3030 Leuven (Heverlee)
Head: Professor Dr Ir G. Boddez

STATISTICS AND DESIGN OF 205 EXPERIMENTS UNIT
Address: Kardinaal Mercierlaan 92, B-3030 Leuven (Heverlee)
Head: Professor Dr Ir J. Wijnhoven

Department of Agricultural 206 Engineering

LABORATORY FOR AGRICULTURAL 207 BUILDINGS RESEARCH
Address: Kardinaal Mercierlaan 92, B-3030 Leuven (Heverlee)
Head: Professor Dr Ir V. Goedseels

LABORATORY OF FARM IMPLEMENTS 208 AND MACHINERY
Address: Kardinaal Mercierlaan 92, B-3030 Leuven (Heverlee)
Head: Professor Dr Ir R. Meire

LABORATORY OF SOIL AND WATER 209 ENGINEERING
Address: Kardinaal Mercierlaan 92, B-3030 Leuven (Heverlee)
Head: Professor Dr Ir J. Feyen

Department of Animal Sciences and 210 Management

CENTRE FOR ANIMAL HUSBANDRY 211
Address: Pastorijstraat 2, B-3040 Bierbeek (Korbeek-lo)
Head: Ir A. Moreels

F.A. JANSSENS MEMORIAL 212 LABORATORY FOR GENETICS
Address: Kardinaal Mercierlaan 92, B-3030 Leuven (Heverlee)
Head: Professor Dr Ir J. Heuts

LABORATORY FOR ECO-PHYSIOLOGY 213 OF DOMESTIC ANIMALS
Address: Kardinaal Mercierlaan 92, B-3030 Leuven (Heverlee)
Head: Professor Dr Ir H. Michels

Department of Bio-industries 214

LABORATORY OF AGRICULTURAL 215
INDUSTRIES IN THE TROPICS
Address: de Croylaan 42, B-3030 Leuven (Heverlee)
Head: Professor Dr Ir W. Van Pee

LABORATORY OF APPLIED 216
CARBOHYDRATE CHEMISTRY
Address: de Croylaan 42, B-3030 Leuven (Heverlee)
Head: Professor Dr Ir J. Casier

LABORATORY OF FOOD 217
PRESERVATION
Address: de Croylaan 42, B-3030 Leuven (Heverlee)
Head: Professor Dr Ir P. Tobback

LABORATORY OF INDUSTRIAL 218
MICROBIOLOGY AND BIOCHEMISTRY
Address: Kardinaal Mercierlaan 92, B-3030 Leuven
(Heverlee)
Head: Professor Dr Ir H. Verachtert

Department of Organic and Inorganic 219
Chemistry

LABORATORY OF ANALYTIC AND 220
MINERAL CHEMISTRY
Address: Kardinaal Mercierlaan 92, B-3030 Leuven
(Heverlee)
Head: Professor Dr Ir H. Bosmans

LABORATORY OF APPLIED ORGANIC 221
CHEMISTRY
Address: Kardinaal Mercierlaan 92, B-3030 Leuven
(Heverlee)
Head: Professor Dr Ir P. Dondeyne

Department of Soil and Plant Control 222

CENTRE FOR HORTICULTURAL SOILS 223
RESEARCH
Address: Kardinaal Mercierlaan 92, B-3030 Leuven
(Heverlee)
Head: Professor Dr Ir I. Scheys

LABORATORY FOR PLANT 224
PRODUCTION AND PLANT BREEDING
Address: de Croylaan 42, B-3030 Leuven (Heverlee)
Head: Ir R. Laeremans

LABORATORY OF PHYTOPATHOLOGY 225
AND PLANT PROTECTION
Address: Kardinaal Mercierlaan 92, B-3030 Leuven
(Heverlee)
Telephone: (016) 22 09 31
Head: Professor Ir C. Van Assche
Sections: Use of household waste in agriculture and
horticulture, Professor C. Van Assche; virology, Dr Ir J
Coosemans; bromide-residue, Ir G. Crauwels; pesticide-
residue analysis, Ir E. Van Wambeke; seed-treatment, Ir
P. Uyttebroeck
Graduate research staff: 5
Annual expenditure: £51 000-500 000
Activities: Study of biotic (viruses, bacteria, fungi) and
abiotic (household waste) factors in their relation to
healthy plant production; screening of new pesticides;
residue-analysis.
Contract work: Yes

LABORATORY OF SOIL FERTILITY 226
AND SOIL BIOLOGY
Address: de Croylaan 42, B-3030 Leuven (Heverlee)
Head: Professor Dr Ir K. Vlassak

Department of Surface and Colloid 227
Chemistry

CENTRE OF SURFACE AND COLLOID 228
CHEMISTRY
Address: de Croylaan 42, B-3030 Leuven (Heverlee)
Heads: Professor Dr Ir J.B. Uytterhoeven, Professor
Dr Ir A. Cremers

LABORATORY OF SOIL GENESIS AND 229
SOIL GEOGRAPHY
Address: de Croylaan 42, B-3030 Leuven (Heverlee)
Head: Professor Dr Ir J. D'Hoore

LABORATORY OF TROPICAL CROP 230
HUSBANDRY
Address: Kardinaal Mercierlaan 92, B-3030 Leuven
(Heverlee)
Head: Professor Dr Ir E. De Langhe

FACULTY OF APPLIED SCIENCES 231
Address: Arenbergkasteel, B-3030 Heverlee
Dean: Professor Dr Ir P. De Meester

Applied Mathematics and 232
Programming Section
Address: Celestijnenlaan 200A, B-3030 Heverlee

Department of Applied Chemistry   233

Chairman: Professor Ir A. Van Haute

CHEMICAL ENGINEERING SECTION   234
Address: de Croylaan 2, B-3030 Heverlee
Head: Professor Dr Ir M. Rijckaert

INDUSTRIAL CHEMISTRY SECTION   235
Address: de Croylaan 2, B-3030 Heverlee
Head: Professor Ir A. Van Haute

PHYSICAL CHEMISTRY SECTION   236
Address: Celestijnenlaan 200G, B-3030 Heverlee
Head: Professor Dr A. Neyens

Department of Construction   237

Chairman: Professor Dr Ir M. Van Laethem

ARCHITECTURE SECTION   238
Address: Kasteel van Arenberg, B-3030 Heverlee
Head: Professor Dr Ir J. Delrue

CIVIL ENGINEERING SECTION   239
Address: de Croylaan 2, B-3030 Heverlee
Head: Professor Dr Ir F. Mortelmans

INTERFACULTY INSTITUTE FOR   240
TOWN AND COUNTRY PLANNING
Address: Celestijnenlaan 131, B-3030 Heverlee

MINING SECTION   241
Address: de Croylaan 2, B-3030 Heverlee
Head: Professor Ir O. de Crombrugghe

Department of Electrical Engineering   242

Address: Kardinaal Mercierlaan 94, B-3030 Heverlee
Chairman: Professor Dr Ir G. François

ELECTRONICS, SYSTEMS,   243
AUTOMATIZATION, TECHNOLOGY
Senior staff: Professor Dr Ir R. Van Overstraeten

MICROWAVES AND LASERS   244
Senior staff: Professor Dr Ir P. Luypaert

POWER AND INDUSTRIAL   245
APPLICATIONS
Senior staff: Professor Dr Ir W. Geysen

Department of Mechanics   246

Chairman: Professor Dr Ir J. Peters

INDUSTRIAL MANAGEMENT SECTION   247
Address: Celestijnenlaan 300B, B-3030 Heverlee
Head: Professor Ir H. De Meulder

MECHANICS SECTION   248
Address: de Croylaan 2, B-3030 Heverlee
Head: Professor Ir Th. Van der Waeteren

THERMODYNAMICS AND ENERGY   249
CONVERSION SECTION
Address: Celestijnenlaan 300, B-3030 Heverlee
Head: Professor Dr Ir W. Dutré

WORKSHOP TECHNIQUES SECTION   250
Address: Celestijnenlaan 300B, B-3030 Heverlee
Head: Professor Dr Ir R. Snoeys

Department of Metal Sciences   251

Address: Institute Metaalkunde, de Croylaan 2, B-3030 Heverlee
Chairman: Professor Dr Ir E. Aernoudt

CHEMICAL AND EXTRACTION   252
METALLURGY
Senior staff: Professor Dr Ir J. Roos

MECHANICAL METALLURGY AND   253
NUCLEAR ENERGY
Senior staff: Professor Dr Ir P. De Meester

PHYSICAL METALLURGY AND   254
METALLOGRAPHY
Senior staff: Professor Dr Ir A. Deruyttere

Teaching Development Centre,.   255

Address: Celestijnenlaan 200A, B-3030 Heverlee

FACULTY OF MEDICINE   256

Address: Minderbroedersstraat 17, B-3000 Leuven
Dean: Professor P. De Moor

Biomedical Research Department   257

Address: Academische Ziekenhuis St-Rafael, Kapucijnenvoer 35, B-3000 Leuven
Chairman: Professor J. Bonte

ANATOMY LABORATORY   258
Heads: Professor G. Deneffe, Professor J. Bonte

ELECTROMYOGRAPHY AND   259
PHYSICAL MEDICINE LABORATORY
Head: Professor N. Rosselle

**GYNAECOLOGICAL CANCEROLOGY 260
AND EXPERIMENTAL RADIOTHERAPY
LABORATORY**
Heads: Professor J. Bente, Professor P. Ide

NUCLEAR MEDICINE LABORATORY 261
Head: Professor M. De Roo

**ONCOLOGY AND EXPERIMENTAL 262
RADIOTHERAPY LABORATORY**
Head: Professor A. Drochmans

**PULMONARY HISTOPATHOLOGY 263
LABORATORY**
Head: Professor J. Lauweryns

X-RAY DIAGNOSTICS LABORATORY 264
Heads: Professor A. Baert, Professor E. Ponette

Brain and Behaviour Research 265
Department.

Address: Onderwÿs en Navorsing Easthuisberg, B-
3000 Leuven
Chairman: Professor M. Callens

**NEURO- AND PSYCHO-BIOLOGY 266
DIVISION**
Heads: Professor J. Gybels, Professor M. Callens,
Professor G. Forrez, Professor M. Norré, Professor E.
Pillen, Professor A. Schaerlaekens, Professor J.
Tyberghein, Professor L. Velghe

**OTO-NEURO-OPHTHALMO-ANATOMY 267
DIVISION**
Heads: Professor R. Van den Bergh, Professor R.
Dom, Professor H. Carton, Professor L. Missotten,
Professor F. Ostyn, Professor C. Plets

PSYCHIATRY DIVISION 268
Heads: Professor F. Baro, Professor G. Buyse,
Professor R. Pierloot, Professor K. Pyck

Department of Human Biology 269

Address: Onderwÿs en Navorsing Gasthuisberg, B-
3000 Leuven
Chairman: Professor R. Casteels

BIOCHEMISTRY DIVISION 270
Address: Onderwÿs Navorsing Gasthuisberg, B-3000
Leuven
Heads: Professor W. Merlevede, Professor W. Rom-
bauts, Professor J. Dequeker, Professor W. De Loecker,
Professor H. De Wulf, Professor W. Stalmans

HUMAN HEREDITY DIVISION 271
Address: Minderbroedersstraat 12, B-3000 Leuven
Heads: Professor H. Van den Berghe, Professor J.
Corssiman, Professor E. Meulepas

MICROBIOLOGY DIVISION 272
Address: Rega Instituut, Minderbroedersstraat 10, B-
3000 Leuven
Heads: Professor P. De Somer, Professor H. Eyssen,
Professor M. Vandeputte, Professor J. Vandepitte,
Professor J. Desmyter, Professor A. Billiau, Professor E.
De Clereq

PHARMACOLOGY DIVISION 273
Address: Onderwÿs en Navorsing Gasthuisberg, B-
3000 Leuven
Heads: Professor P. De Schepper, Professor C. Denef,
Professor G. Mannaerts

PHYSIOLOGY DIVISION 274
Address: Onderwÿs en Navorsing Gasthuisberg, B-
3000 Leuven
Heads: Professor E. Carmeliet, Professor R. Casteels,
Professor R. Borghgraef, Professor W. Van Driessche

Development Biology Department 275

Address: Academische Ziekenhuis St-Rafael, Kapucijnenvoer 35, B-3000 Leuven
Chairman: Professor F. Van Assche

**CLINICAL AND EXPERIMENTAL 276
SURGERY DIVISION**
Head: Professor J. Gruwez

**EXPERIMENTAL ENDOCRINOLOGY 277
DIVISION**
Address: Rega Instituut, Minderbroedersstraat 10, B-
3000 Leuven
Heads: Professor P. De Moor, Professor O. Steeno,
Professor W. Heyns, Professor G. Verhoeven, Professor
R. Bouillon

**GYNAECOLOGY AND OBSTETRICS 278
DIVISION**
Address: Academische Ziekenhuis St-Rafael, Kapuci-
jnenvoer 35, B-3000 Leuven
Heads: Professor M. Renaer, Professor I. Brosens,
Professor P. Nijs, Professor F. Van Assche

PAEDIATRIC DIVISION 279
Address: Academisch Ziekenhuis Gasthuisberg, B-
3000 Leuven
Heads: Professor R. Eeckels, Professor E. Eggermont,
Professor L. Corbeel, Professor M. Van Daele, Professor
W. Proesmans, Professor M. Lodeweyckx, Professor P.
Casaer

Interfaculty Institute for Family and   280
Sex Studies

Address: Minderbroedersstraat 17, B-3000 Leuven
Chairman: Professor W. Dumon

Medical Research Department   281

Address: Onderwÿs en Navorsing Gasthuisberg, B-
3000 Leuven
Chairman: Professor K. Heirwegh

DERMATOLOGY LABORATORY   282
Head: Professor H. Degreef

GASTRO-INTESTINAL   283
PHYSIOPATHOLOGY LABORATORY
Heads: Professor G. Vantrappen, Professor J. Helle-
mans, Professor Y. Ghoos, Professor J. Janssens

HAEMATOLOGY AND VASCULAR   284
LABORATORY
Heads: Professor M. Verstraete, Professor R. Suy,
Professor J. Vermylen, Professor D. Collen

HAEMATOLOGY LABORATORY   285
Head: Professor R. Verwilghen

HISTOCHEMISTRY AND   286
CYTOCHEMISTRY LABORATORY
Heads: Professor V. Desmet, Professor Ch. De Wolf-
Peeters, Professor B. Van Dimme

LIVER PHYSIOPATHOLOGY   287
LABORATORY
Heads: Professor J. De Groote, Professor J. Fevery,
Professor K. Heirwegh

Pathophysiology Department   288

Address: Minderbroedersstraat 17, B-3000 Leuven
Chairman: Professor A. Amery

BACTERIOLOGY LABORATORY   289
Head: Professor L. Verbist

CARDIAC MORPHOLOGY   290
LABORATORY
Head: Professor L. Van der Hauwaert

CARDIOLOGY LABORATORY   291
Heads: Professor H. De Geest, Professor J.V.
Joossens, Professor H. Kesteloot, Professor J. Piessens

HYPERTENSION LABORATORY   292
Heads: Professor A. Amory, Professor R. Fapard,
Professor T. Reybrouck

IMMUNOLOGY LABORATORY   293
Head: Professor E. Stevens

LUNG FUNCTION LABORATORY I   294
Head: Professor K. Van de Woestÿne

LUNG FUNCTION LABORATORY II   295
Heads: Professor A. Gyselen, Professor M. Demedts

LUNG FUNCTION LABORATORY III   296
Heads: Professor L. Billiet, Professor L. Larcquet

NEPHROLOGY LABORATORY   297
Heads: Professor P. Michielsen, Professor R. Ver-
berkmoes

Pharmaceutical Sciences Department   298

Address: Farmaceutisch Instituut, Van Evenstraat 4,
B-3000 Leuven
Chairman: Professor H. Vanderhaeghe

ANALYTICAL CHEMISTRY   299
LABORATORY
Head: Professor C. De Ranter

CLINICAL CHEMISTRY LABORATORY   300
Head: Professor J. Claes

PHARMACEUTICAL CHEMISTRY   301
LABORATORY
Heads: Professor H. Vanderhaeghe, Professor P. Claes

PHARMACOGNOSY LABORATORY   302
Head: Professor J. Lemli

PRACTICAL AND INDUSTRIAL   303
PHARMACY LABORATORY
Address: Provisorium 2, Minderbroedersstraat 17-19,
B-3000 Leuven
Heads: Professor R. Kinget, Professor J. Polderman

TOXICOLOGY AND BROMATOLOGY   304
LABORATORY
Head: Professor P. Daenens

Physical Education Department   305

Address: Tervuursevest 101, B-3030 Heverlee
Chairman: Professor M. Ostyn

Public Health Department   306

Address: Vital Decosterstraat 102, B-3000 Leuven
Chairman: Professor H. Van de Voorde

EPIDEMIOLOGY DIVISION 307
Address: Kapucijnenvoer 35, B-3000 Leuven
Heads: Professor J.V. Joossens, Professor R. Boelaert, Professor A. Van Orshoven, Professor J. Heyrman

HEALTH ECOLOGY DIVISION 308
Address: Vital Decosterstraat 102, B-3000 Leuven
Heads: Professor H. Van de Boorde, Professor J. Schrijvers, Professor J. Bande-Knops, Professor G. Reybrouck, Professor J. Casselman

HOSPITAL SCIENCES CENTRE 309
Address: Vital Decosterstraat 102, B-3000 Leuven
Heads: Professor J. Blanpain, Professor A. Prims, Professor P. Quaethoven, Professor P. De Schouwer, Professor L. Groot, Professor G. Koehe, Professor L. Delesie, Professor R. Dewalsche, Professor M. Defever

OCCUPATIONAL AND INSURANCE 310
MEDICINE DIVISION
Address: Vital Decosterstraat 86, B-3000 Leuven
Heads: Professor H. De Geest, Professor D. Lahaye, Professor R. Masschelein, Professor R. Vanden Driessche, Professor R. Verwilghen, Professor J. Viaene

Stomatology and Dentistry 311
Department
Address: Academische Zickenhuis St-Rafael, Kapucijnenvoer 35, B-3000 Leuven
Chairman: Professor J. De Bondt
Heads: Professor J. De Bondt, Professor A. Reychler, Professor E. Fossion, Professor G. Vanherle, Professor M. Bossuyt, Professor M. Declercq, Professor D. Van Steenberphe

Surgical and Anaesthesiological 312
Sciences Department
Address: Academische Ziekenhuis St-Rafael, Kapucijnenveer 35, B-3000 Leuven
Chairman: Professor J. Van de Walle

ANAESTHESIOLOGY DIVISION 313
Heads: Professor J. Vandewalle, Professor H. Delooz, Professor P. Lauwers

CARDIOVASCULAR SURGERY 314
DIVISION
Head: Professor G. Stalpaert

GASTROENTEROLOGICAL SURGERY 315
DIVISION
Head: Professor R. Kerremans

ORTHOPAEDICS DIVISION 316
Heads: Professor J. Mulier, Professor M. Hoogmartens, Professor M. Martens, Professor J. Verstreken

UROLOGICAL SURGERY DIVISION 317
Heads: Professor H. Verduyn, Professor R. Vereecken

FACULTY OF SCIENCES 318
Address: Geel Huis, Kardinaal Mercierlaan 92, B-3000 Heverlee
Dean: Professor P. Mariens

Department of Biology 319
Chairman: Professor K. Buffel

ANIMAL SCIENCES 320
Address: Naamsestraat 59, B-3000 Leuven

Animal Physiology 321
Senior staff: Professor H. Koch

Endocrinology 322
Senior staff: Professor E. Kühn

Systematics 323
Senior staff: Professor J. Van Boven, Professor A. De Bont

PLANT SCIENCES 324
Address: Vaartstraat 24, B-3000 Leuven

Phytohydrobiology 325
Senior staff: Professor A. Louis

Plant Biochemistry 326
Senior staff: Professor A. Carlier

Plant Morphology and Systematic Botany 327
Senior staff: Professor F. Symons, Professor E. Petit

Plant Physiology 328
Senior staff: Professor K. Buffel, Professor J. Vendrig

Department of Chemistry 329
Chairman: Professor G. Hoornaert

ANALYTICAL AND INORGANIC 330
CHEMISTRY
Address: Celestijnenlaan 200F, B-3030 Heverlee
Head: Professor S. De Jaegere

BIOCHEMISTRY 331
Head: Professor R. Lontie

CHEMICAL AND BIOLOGICAL 332
DYNAMICS
Address: Celestijnenlaan 200F, B-3030 Heverlee
Head: Professor L. De Maeyer

GENERAL AND ORGANIC CHEMISTRY 333
Address: Naamsestraat 96, B-3000 Leuven
Head: Professor G. Hoornaert

INORGANIC CHEMISTRY 334
Address: Celestijnenlaan 200F, B-3030 Heverlee
Head: Professor W. D'Olieslager

MACROMOLECULAR AND ORGANIC 335
CHEMISTRY
Address: Celestijnenlaan 200F, B-3030 Heverlee
Head: Professor G. Smets

PHYSICO-CHEMISTRY AND KINETICS 336
Address: Celestijnenlaan 200D, B-3030 Heverlee
Head: Professor X. De Hemptinne

PHYSICO-CHEMISTRY AND 337
RADIATION CHEMISTRY
Head: Professor P. Huyskens

QUANTUM CHEMISTRY 338
Address: Celestijnenlaan 200F, B-3030 Heverlee
Head: L. Vanquickenborne

RADIOCHEMISTRY 339
Address: Celestijnenlaan 200F, B-3030 Heverlee
Head: Professor M. D'hont

Department of Geosciences 340

Chairman: Professor G. King

HISTORICAL GEOLOGY 341
Address: Redingenstraat 16 bis, B-3000 Leuven

Crystallography 342
Address: Redingenstraat 16 bis, B-3000 Leuven
Senior staff: Professor G. King

Palaeozoic Geology and Tectonics 343
Senior staff: Professor F. Geukens

Physico-Chemical Geology 344
Address: St Michielsstraat 6, B-3000 Leuven

Mineralogy 345
Senior staff: Professor W. Viaene

Petrology 346
Senior staff: Professor D. Vogel

Stratigraphical and Micropalaeontology 347
Senior staff: Professor J. Bouckaert, Professor P. Bultynck

Tertiary and Quaternary Geology 348
Senior staff: Professor F. Gullentops

PHYSICAL AND REGIONAL 349
GEOGRAPHY AND CARTOGRAPHY
Address: Redingenstraat 16 bis, B-3000 Leuven
Senior staff: Professor F. Gullentops, Professor J. De Ploey, Professor F. Depuydt, Professor P. Vermeersch, Professor J. Poppe

Department of Mathematics 350

Address: Celestijneniaan 200B, B-3030 Heverlee
Chairman: Professor P. Smeyers

ALGEBRA AND TOPOLOGY 351
Senior staff: Professor A. Warrinnier

ANALYSIS 352
Senior staff: Professor A. Van Daele

APPLIED MATHEMATICS 353
Senior staff: Professor H. Van de Vel, Professor J. Teugels

ASTRONOMY AND MECHANICS 354
Address: Naamsestraat 61, B-3000 Leuven
Head: Professor P. Smeyers

GEOMETRY 355
Senior staff: Professor L. Vanhecke

HISTORY OF MATHEMATICS 356
Senior staff: Professor A. Borgers

Department of Physics 357

Address: Celestijnenlaan 200D, B-3030 Heverlee
Chairman: Professor A. Dupré

ACOUSTICS AND HEAT 358
CONDUCTIVITY LABORATORY
Address: Celestijnenlaan 200D, B-3030 Heverlee
Acting Director: Professor H. Myncke
Activities: Research into acoustics and noise abatement; heat conductivity and thermal insulation; water vapour diffusion and related problems in building and insulating materials.

DIDACTIC PHYSICS 359
Address: Naamsestraat 61, B-3000 Leuven
Head: Professor K. De Clippeleir

LOW TEMPERATURES AND HIGH 360
MAGNETIC FIELDS
Senior staff: Professor A. Dupré

MOLECULAR PHYSICS 361
Senior staff: Professor W. Van Dael

NUCLEAR AND RADIATION PHYSICS 362
Senior staff: Professor P. Mariens

SOLID-STATE AND HIGH-PRESSURE 363
PHYSICS
Senior staff: Professor A. De Beck

SOLID-STATE PHYSICS AND MAGNETISM   364

Senior staff: Professor L. Van Gerven

THEORETICAL PHYSICS   365

Senior staff: Professor F. Cerulus

Koninklijke Maatschappij   366
voor Dierkunde van
Antwerpen

[Royal Zoological Society of Antwerp]
Address: Koningin Astridplein 26, B-2000 Antwerpen
Telephone: (031) 31 16 40
Director: J.F. Geeraerts
Sections: Laboratory, Dr W. De Meurichy; Museum of Natural History, G. Van Steenbergen
Graduate research staff: 5
Annual expenditure: £10 000-50 000
Activities: The Society is supported by the Province and City of Antwerp and by the Ministry of National Education and Culture. The Society's interests cover the whole zoological field.
Publications: Acta Zoologica et Pathologica Antverpiensa.

LABOFINA Société   367
Anonyme

Parent body: PETROFINA Société Anonyme

BRUSSELS BRANCH   368

Address: Chaussée de Vilvorde 100, B-1120 Bruxelles
Telephone: (02) 216 21 60
Telex: 23949
Managing Director: Dr G. Souillard
Sections: Motor fuels and lubricants, J. Vaerman; analysis, bitumen products and greases, J. Van Rijsselberge; industrial lubricants and special products, J. Bailleux; geochemistry, M. Leplat; antipollution products, A. Lepain; market research studies, I. Laznowski
Graduate research staff: 13
Annual expenditure: over £2m
Contract work: No

FELUY BRANCH   369

Address: Zone Industrielle, B-6520 Feluy
Telephone: (064) 556911
Telex: 57 919
Manager of research: Dr P. de Radzitzky

Sections: Polymers, W. Bracke; refining and petrochemical processes, J. Grootjans; paints, J. Bracken; catalysis, G. De Clippeleir
Graduate research staff: 24
Annual expenditure: over £2m
Activities: Polyolefins and styrenic polymers finished products; refining: hydrogenation, isomerization, denitrogenation of visbroken gasolines, extraction of aromatics; petrochemical processes: production of terephthalic acid and of ethylphenol, dearomatization of solvents.
Contract work: No
Publications: PETROFINA Technological Development.

Laboratoire Central/   370
Centraal Laboratorium

[Central Laboratory]
Address: 17 A Rue de la Senne, B-1000 Bruxelles
Telephone: (02) 511 77 69
Affiliation: Ministry of Economic Affairs
Director: Dr S.V. Vaeck
Departments: Food chemistry, Dr M. Bernaerts; Mineral products, L. Van Coillie; Textiles, detergents, Dr V. Merken
Graduate research staff: 9
Annual expenditure: £51 000-500 000
Activities: Methods of analysis and standard specifications for foods, petroleum products, minerals, textiles, detergents and consumer products.
Contract work: No

Landbouweconomisch   371
Instituut/Institut
Économique Agricole

[Agricultural Economics Institute]
Address: De Berlaimontlaan 78, B-1000 Bruxelles
Telephone: (02) 219 10 50
Affiliation: Ministry of Agriculture
Director: Ir R. Desutter
Departments: Macroeconomics and rural sociology, G. Pevenage; microeconomics and farm accounts, A. Villers
Graduate research staff: 30
Annual expenditure: over £2m
Activities: Agricultural statistics; sector planning; marketing; farm planning; typology; regional studies.
Contract work: No

Leuven Research & Development VZW* 372

Address: Groot Begijnhof, Benedenstraat 59, 3000 Leuven
Affiliation: Catholic University of Louvain
Governing council: F. Collin, G. Declercq, Professor Dr A. De Bock, Professor Dr Ir A. Deruyttere, Professor Dr W. Dumon Professor Dr Ir J. Uytterhoeven Professor Dr J. Vander Eecken
Directors: J. Bouckaert, Dr Ir H. Beke, L. Van Biervliet
Annual expenditure: BF36m (1979)
Activities: Leuven Research & Development, a nonprofit organization, has two objectives: to establish a service organization that gives the University better control over contract research, protection of research findings, and conclusion of licensing agreements; and thereby to enable University laboratories and research institutes to contribute to industrial innovation and the socioeconomic progress of the community. It offers the possibility of valorizing the existing University potential by promoting better contacts with industry, government, and socioeconomic organizations.

The university laboratories that are able to develop a project in a useful way in the framework of Leuven Research & Development are highly qualified and skilled in discovering new technologies. The firms that can profit from working with Leuven Research & Development must themselves have a sufficiently high technological level and potential. The market position of a company is an important factor. Only firms, large or small, that are active on world markets can afford to write off the investment and marketing costs of developing and merchandizing new technologies and products on the anticipated turnover.

During 1979, Leuven Research & Development took its first steps in direct industrial and commercial ventures. Examples of this are LISCO Inc which was established in Palo Alto, California, as a joint venture with individuals of Stanford University; the PROTEUS-Association, established with the NV Bekaert SA and the NV Metallurgie Hoboken-Overpelt; and Leuven Measurements & Systems PVBA. Leuven Research & Development participates in such ventures by subscribing to a portion of the capital and by concluding privileged association agreements that assure the further scientific and technological support of the ventures.
Contract work: Yes
Publications: Annual report.

BUILDING MATERIALS AND CONSTRUCTION DIVISION* 373

Head: Professor F. Mortelmans
Activities: Bridge reinforcement; measurement techniques that can be used in cryogenic situations such as string gauges; determination of the behaviour of sandwich constructions during explosions (explosion free tunnels); determination of real wind pressures caused by traffic on tunnel walls; determination of the characteristics of fibreglass-reinforced concrete; determination of temperatures and flows in frozen ground; construction of a cell that will provide calculation and draughting software for the construction industry.
Facilities: Drawing press equipped with cryogenic chamber; hydraulics laboratory for in situ measurements such as flow measurement in creeks, rivers and sewers; measurements in the laboratory, ie: calibration of flow and water meters, determination of pump characteristics and load losses, model studies of hydraulic engineering works; self-developed computer programs for: calculation of pipe network and sewer network characteristics, hydraulic studies, river pollution models.

COLLOIDS, SURFACES AND CATALYSIS DIVISION* 374

Head: Professor Dr Ir J.B. Uytterhoeven
Activities: Diffusion phenomena in clay.

GENETICS DIVISION* 375

Head: Professor H. Vandenberghe
Activities: Studies of pattern recognition systems and the use of digital electronics has led to original developments in the area of image processors and graphic terminals for which there is industrial interest.

INSTITUTE FOR URBAN AND ENVIRONMENTAL PLANNING* 376

Activities: The Institute has conducted a global traffic planning study for the City of Mechelen in which the relationship between traffic and the overall urban situation was central. Concrete proposals for a coherent traffic policy were formulated.

MECHANICAL ENGINEERING DIVISION* 377

Heads: Professor J. Peters, Professor R. Snoeys
Activities: The development and commercialization of high technological computer-controlled design, measurement, and production techniques in the areas of noise, vibration, and production control.

METALLURGY AND MATERIALS DIVISION*   378

Head: Professor Dr Ir A. Deruyttere
Activities: The PROTEUS Association was formalized as a research syndicate of Leuven Research & Development, NV Bekaert SA and the NV Metallurgie Hoboken-Overpelt. Their objective is the further development of the industrial and commercial potential of PROTEUS alloys. These copper alloys have remarkable characteristics, ie form memory; superelasticity; large vibration and noise damping capacity. The Association is particularly concerned with finding a solution to the technological problems that arise in the production and processing of these alloys.

MICROELECTRONICS INDUSTRIAL DIVISION*   379

Head: Professor R. Van Overstraeten
Activities: The development and commercial exploitation of software programs for the semiconductor industry. In 1977 a separate division was established for this purpose: LISCO (Leuven Industrial Software Company); the development and production of photovoltaic solar cells; the development of new technologies for the production of integrated circuits and the development of custom-designed integrated circuits for industrial clients; the programming of microprocessors for specific applications.

PROTEIN RESEARCH DIVISION*   380

Head: Professor M. Verstraete
Activities: Development, clinical evaluation and production of clinical biological reagents; production and commercial exploitation of antiserums.

REGA FOUNDATION*   381

Chairman: Professor P. De Somer
Activities: A new compound, developed at the University of Birmingham (UK) was tested by the Institute for its possible antiviral properties. In the initial clinical tests, it was found to be extremely active against certain herpes infections.

Limburgs Universitair Centrum   382

[Limburg University Centre]
Address: Universitaire Campus, B-3610 Diepenbeek
Rector: Professor Dr L. Verhaegen

FACULTY OF MEDICINE   383

Embryology, Histology and Anatomy Department   384

Director: Professor Dr J. Creemers
Senior staff: Professor W. Robberechts

Human and Social Sciences Department   385

Director: Professor Dr R.N. Bruynooghe

FACULTY OF NATURAL SCIENCES   386

Chemistry, Biology and Microbiology Department   387

Director: Professor Dr H. Teuchy
Senior staff: Professor H. Clijsters, Professor L. van Poucke
Research leaders: J. Billen, R. Carleer, C. Dambre, M. Thoelen

Mathematics, Physics and Physiology Department   388

Director: Professor Dr L. Stals
Senior staff: Professor M. Boutan, Professor H. Hendrickx, Professor P. Lambert
Research leaders: L. Bearden, C. Majchrowicz, J. Moens, D. Provoost, C. van Roost

Medisch Instituut St Barbara   389

[St Barbara Medical Institute]
Address: Bessemerstraat 478, B-3760 Lanaken
Telephone: (011) 714961
Director: Dr A. Minette
Sections: Clinical physiopathology, Dr M. Marcq; experimental physiopathology, Professor R. Serra
Graduate research staff: 1
Annual expenditure: BF75 000
Activities: Respiratory system and diseases; clinical pharmacology.
Contract work: Yes

Metallurgie Hoboken-Overpelt Société Anonyme   390

Address: A. Greinerstraat 14, B-2710 Hoboken
Telephone: (31) 28 10 00
Telex: 31443 MHO HOB
Research director: Dr C. Feneau
Graduate research staff: 40
Annual expenditure: over £2m
Activities: Extractive metallurgy of non-ferrous metals: smelting and refining processes; casting of ingots, billets, cakes and continuous rod; powders; materials for electronics and infrared optics.
Facilities: Research facilities are available in the Hoboken, Olen and Overpelt plants of the company.
Contract work No

Musée Royal de l'Afrique Centrale/Koninklijk Museum voor Midden-Afrika   391

[Royal Museum of Central Africa]
Address: Steenweg op Leuven 13, B-1980 Tervuren
Telephone: (02) 767 54 01
Affiliation: Ministries of National Education
Acting Director: D. Thys van den Audenaerde
Departments: Cultural anthropology, M. d'Hertefelt; geology, J. Klerkx; zoology, P. Benoit; history and general services, M. Luwel
Graduate research staff: 50
Annual expenditure: over £2m
Activities: The museum is an institute for scientific research on Africa with specialized research departments for cultural anthropology, geology and zoology. Research in cultural anthropology focuses on the peoples of Africa south of the Sahara with an extension, for comparative purposes, to America and Oceania. The geology programme includes the oceanic islands around Africa. The zoology department studies the terrestrial and aquatic fauna of the African mainland and of the neighbouring islands as well as the marine fauna of the continental fringe.
Contract work: Yes

Nationale Plantentuin van België/Jardin Botanique National de Belgique   392

[National Botanic Garden of Belgium]
Address: Domein van Bouchout, B-1860 Meise
Telephone: (02) 269 39 05
Affiliation: Ministry of Agriculture
Director: E. Petit
Sections: Bryophytes and Thallophytes Department, A. Bienfait; Spermatophytes and Pteridophytes Department, A. Lawalree; Documentation Service, R. Clarysse; Living Collections Service, E. Lammens
Graduate research staff: 10
Annual expenditure: £501 000-2m
Activities: Taxonomy and distribution especially of African and European plants, spermatophytes, pteridophytes, bryophytes, fungi and algae.
Facilities: Herbarium with over 2m specimens; library with about 200 000 volumes; living collections with about 19 000 species.
Contract work: No
Publications: Bulletin.

Opzoekingsstation van Gorsem   393

[Gorsem Research Station]
Address: Brede Akker 3, B-3800 Sint-Truiden
Telephone: (011) 682019
Telex: 39719 opzogo b
Affiliation: Instituut tot aanmoediging van het Wetenschappelijk Onderzoek in Nijverheid en Landbouw/Institut pour l'encouragement de la Recherche Scientifique dans l'Industrie et l'Agriculture
Director of research: Professor Dr Ir A. Soenen
Sections: Phytopathology, Ir C. Verheyden; phytotechnics, Ir W. Porreye; plant physiology, Dr R. Marcelle; entomology, G. Vanwetswinkel; phytovirology, Ir G. Gilles; Strawberry Department, Ir G. Gilles
Graduate research staff: 10
Annual expenditure: £51 000-500 000
Activities: Plant protection based not only on chemical and biological control of diseases and pests, but on production of healthy trees with a regular and high yield and taking into account all possible pomological, physiological, phytopathological, entomological and virological factors.
Contract work: No

Patscentre Benelux 394

Address: Avenue Albert Einstein, Local 6/20, B-1348
Louvain-la-Neuve
Telephone: (016) 41 80 85
Telex: 59188 Patsbx B
Research director: Dr P. Castle
Sections: Electronics, Dr P.W. Kitchin; physics, Dr
P.J. Bassett; applied sciences, Dr J.B. Peeters; mechanical sciences, C. Nazzer
Activities: Research and development in a wide variety
of fields for companies worldwide.
Contract work: Yes
See also: Patscentre International, UK; Patscentre
Scandinavia AB, Sweden

Philips Research Laboratory 395
Brussels

– PRLB
Address: Avenue E.H. Van Becelaere 2, B-1170 Bruxelles
Telephone: 673 41 90
Affiliation: NV Philips Gloeilampenfabrikken,
Netherlands
Director: V. Belevitch
Graduate research staff: 30
Annual expenditure: £501 000-2m
Activities: Exclusively theoretical research in applied
mathematics, computer science, circuit and system
theory of interest to Philips developments in computers
and wire communication.
Facilities: VAX computer.
Contract work: No

Rijkscentrum voor 396
Landbouwkundig
Onderzoek - Gent

[Government Agricultural Research Centre]
Address: Burgemeester van Gansberghelaan 96, 9220
Merelbeke
Telephone: (091) 52 20 81
Affiliation: Ministry of Agriculture
Director: A. Van Slycken
Annual expenditure: £501 000-2m
Activities: The research fields of the ten stations of the
Government Agricultural Research Centre at Ghent
comprise different sectors of vegetable and animal production.
Contract work: Yes

RIJKSSTATION VOOR KLEINVEETELT 397

[Government Research Station for Small Stock Husbandry]
Address: Burgemeester van Gansberghelaan 92, B-9220 Merelbeke
Telephone: (091) 51 19 71
Director: G. De Groote
Activities: Feeding, physiology, selection, housing and
product quality of small stock, especially poultry;
research on energy metabolism, blood groups and artificial insemination.

RIJKSSTATION VOOR 398
LANDBOUWTECHNIEK

[Government Research Station for Agricultural Engineering]
Address: Burgemeester Van Gansberghelaan 115, B-9220 Merelbeke
Telephone: (091) 52 18 21
Director: A. Maton
Activities: Application of technology in agriculture and
horticulture

RIJKSSTATION VOOR NEMATOLOGIE 399
EN ENTOMOLOGIE

**[Governmment Research Station for Nematology
and Entomology]**
Address: Burgemeester van Gansberhelaan 96, B-9220
Merelbeke
Telephone: (091) 52 20 85
Director: C.J. d'Herde
Activities: Distribution, host plants, biology,
pathogenicity and control of parasitic nematodes and
arthropods; beekeeping methods.

RIJKSSTATION VOOR 400
PLANTENVEREDELING

[Government Research Station for Plant Breeding]
Address: Burgemeester van Gansberghelaan 109, B-9220 Merelbeke
Telephone: (091) 52 19 81
Director: M. Rousseau
Activities: Phytotechnical, sociological and physiological research of grassland and green fodder crops.

RIJKSSTATION VOOR PLANTENZIEKTEN　401

[Government Research Station for Phytopathology]
Address: Burgemeester van Gansberghelaan 96, B-9220 Merelbeke
Telephone: (091) 52 20 83
Director: R. Veldeman
Activities: Applied phytopathology and control; ecology; physiology and paratism; research on verticillium.

RIJKSSTATION VOOR POPULIERENTEELT　402

[Government Research Station for Poplar Breeding]
Address: Gaverstraat 35, B-9500 Geraard
Telephone: (054) 41 44 97
Director: V. Steenackers

RIJKSSTATION VOOR SIERPLANTENTEELT　403

[Government Research Station for Ornamental Plant Growing]
Address: Caritasstraat 17, B-9230 Melle
Telephone: (091) 52 10 52
Director: J.G. Van Onsem
Activities: Flower crops and ornamental production methods and marketing.

RIJKSSTATION VOOR VEEVOEDING　404

[Government Research Station for Animal Nutrition]
Address: Scheldeweg 12, B-9231 Gontrode
or: Oosterzelesteenweg 86, B-9200 Wetteren
Telephone: (091) 52 26 01
Director: F. Buysse
Activities: Economical feeding of cattle and pigs; feeding techniques to increase productivity.

RIJKSSTATION VOOR ZEEVISSERIJ　405

[Government Research Station for Sea Fisheries]
Address: Ankerstraat 1, B-8400 Ostende
Telephone: (059) 320805
Director: P. Hovart
Sections: Biology, Dr F. Redant, Dr Ir R. Declerck; quality research, Dr Ir W. Vyncke; technology, Dr Ir W. Deschacht, Ir D. Declerck, Ir H. Devriendt; technical, Ir G. Vanden Broucke
Graduate research staff: 11
Annual expenditure: £51 000-500 000
Activities: Qualitative and quantitative improvement of catches; fish processing; rationalization of labour aboard fishing vessels.
Contract work: Yes

RIJKSZUIVELSTATION　406

[Government Station for Research in Dairying]
Address: Brusselsesteenweg 370, B-9230 Melle
Telephone: (091) 52 18 61
Director: M. Naudts
Activities: Problems arising from the transformation of milk into different dairy products.

Rijksuniversitair Centrum Antwerpen　407

[Antwerp State University Centre]
Address: Beukenlaan 12, B-2020 Antwerpen
Rector: Professor Dr M.A. de Groodt-Lasseel

FACULTY OF SCIENCES　408

Address: Groenenborgerlaan 171, B-2020 Antwerpen
Dean: Professor Dr W. Kuyk
Sections: Astronomy and geodesy, Professor Dr Albert Velghe
Biology, Professor Dr Frans Evens
Botany, Professor Dr Rogier Vanhoorne
Chemical technology, Professor Dr K. Van Lerberghe
Depth psychology, Professor Dr C. Lebaigue
Elementary mineralogy, geology and physical geography, Professor Dr William de Breuck
Experimental physics, Professor Dr Victor Vanhuyse
Genetics, Professor Dr Jules Leroy
Histology, Professor Dr Marie de Groodt-Lassel
Human anatomy, Professor Dr Lucien Vakaet
Human biochemistry, Professor Dr Wilfried Dierick
Human physiology, Professor Dr Dirk Brutsaert
Inorganic chemistry, Professor Dr Medard Herman
Organic chemistry, Professor Dr Frank Alderweireldt
Physics, Professor Dr S. Amelinckx
Psychology, Professor Dr P. Coetsier
Theoretical and mathematical physics, Professor Dr Piet Van Leuven
Theoretical mechanics, Professor Dr R. Gevers
Zoology, Professor Dr Walter Verheyen

Rijksuniversiteit-Gent　409

[State University of Ghent]
Address: Sint Pietersnieuwstraat 25, 9000 Gent
Telephone: (091) 23 38 21
Telex: 12754 RUGENT

Electric Machines 437

Head: Professor H. De Jong

Electricity 438

Head: Professor J. Willems

Electrometallurgy 439

Head: Professor F. Bosch

Electronics 440

Telephone: (091) 23 38 31
Head: Professor J. Colle

Electrotechnics 441

Heads: Professor J. Van Bladel, Professor M. Vanwormhoudt

Ferroconcrete Construction 442

Head: Professor F. Riessauw

Heat Techniques 443

Head: Professor R. Minne

Hydraulics 444

Director: Professor G. Tison

Industrial Management 445

Head: Professor H. Muller

Kinematics 446

Head: Professor R. Dechaene

Machines 447

Head: Professor H. Somerling

Maritime Techniques 448

Head: Professor J. Nibbering

Mathematical Analysis 449

Head: Professor F. Kuliasko

Mechanical Processes and Machine Components 450

Head: Professor C. De Koninck

Mining Engineering 451

Head: Professor H. Van Kerckhoven

Non-ferrous Metallurgy 452

Head: Professor A. Van Peteghem

Office of Shipbuilding 453

Address: Grote Steenweg Noord 12, B-9710 Zwijnaarde
Telephone: (091) 22 57 55
Head: Professor V. Ferdinande

Petrochemical Techniques 454

Head: Professor F. Froment

Textile Technology 455

Head: Professor G. Raes

Transport Techniques 456

Head: Professor C. Van Aken

FACULTY OF MEDICINE 457

Address: University Hospital, De Pintelaan 135, B-9000 Gent
Head: Professor A. De Schaspdrijver

Anaesthetics Service 458

Director: Professor G. Rolly

Cardiology Centre 459

Director: Professor R. Pannier

Dermatology Clinic 460

Director: Professor A. Kint

Dietetics and Internal Medicine 461

Head: Professor G. Verdonk

Embryology Laboratory 462

Address: Godshuizenlaan 4, B-9000 Gent
Director: Professor K. Dierickx

Gynaecology Clinic 463

Director: Professor D. Vandekerckhove

Higher Institute of Physical Education 464

Address: Watersportlaan 2, B-9000 Gent

PHYSICAL EDUCATION 465
Head: Professor W. Laporte

PHYSIOLOGICAL CHEMISTRY AND 466 GENERAL EXPERIMENTAL PHYSIOLOGY APPLIED TO PHYSICAL TRAINING
Head: Professor J. Stockx

PHYSIOLOGY AND BIOMETRICS 467 APPLIED TO PHYSICAL EDUCATION
Head: Professor J.-L. Pannier

Histology Laboratory 468

Address: K.L. Ledeganckstraat 35, B-9000 Gent
or: Godshuizenlaan 4, B-9000 Gent
Director: Professor M. Sebruyns

Human Physiology 469

Head: Professor E. Lacroix

Hygiene Laboratory 470

Director: Professor K. Vuylsteek

Internal Medicine Clinic 471

Director: Professor F. Barbier
Senior staff: S. Ringoir, M. Van Der Straeten, A. Vermeulen, R. Wieme

Invalid Psychopathology 472

Head: Professor A. Evrard

Medical Microbiology 473

Head: Professor E. Nihoul

Neuropsychology Clinic 474

Director: Professor H. Vander Eecken

Obstetrics Clinic 475

Director: Professor M. Thiery

Osteology, Arthrology, Myrology 476

Head: Professor J. Fautrez

Otorhinolaryngology Clinic 477

Director: Professor P. Kluyskens

Pathological Anatomy Laboratory 478

Director: Professor H. Roels

Pharmacology 479

Head: Professor A. De Schaepdrijver

Physics Applied to Medicine 480

Head: Professor O. Segaert

Physiological Chemistry and 481 Biochemistry Laboratory

Address: K.L. Ledeganckstraat 35, B-9000 Gent
Director: Professor L. Vandendriessche

Physiology and Pathology Laboratory 482

Director: Professor I. Leusen

Physiotherapy and Orthopaedics 483 Clinic

Director: Professor H. Claessens

Plastic Surgery Clinic 484

Director: Professor G. Matton

Psychiatry Clinic 485

Director: Professor E. Verbeek

Radiology Laboratory 486

Head: Professor E. Van De Velde

Radiotherapy Clinic 487

Head: Professor A. De Schrijver

Surgery Clinic 488

Head: Professor F. Derom

Theory and Analysis of Human 489 Movements Laboratory

Director: Professor R. Claeys

FACULTY OF PHARMACEUTICAL SCIENCES 490

Address: University Hospital, De Pintelaan 135, B-9000 Gent
Dean: Professor P. De Moerloose

Analytical Chemistry 491

Head: Professor A. Claeys

Pharmaceutical Chemistry 492

Head: Professor P. De Moerloose

Pharmaceutical Microbiology and Hygiene 493

Head: Professor J. Pijck

Pharmacognosy and Galenics 494

Head: Professor P. Braeckman

Toxicology 495

Head: Professor A. Heyndrickx

FACULTY OF SCIENCE 496

Dean: Professor P. Van Der Veken

Agrogeology 497

Head: Professor J. Ameryckx

Analytical Chemistry 498

Senior staff: Professor J. Hoste, Professor F. Verbeck

Analytical Geometry 499

Head: Professor J. Bilo

Applied Geology 500

Address: Geologisch Instituut R.U.G., Krijgslaan 271, B-9000 Gent
Telephone: (091) 22 57 15
Head: Professor W. De Breuck
Sections: Hydrogeology; geological mapping; geophysical survey and well logging; urban geology
Graduate research staff: 8
Annual expenditure: £10 000-50 000
Contract work: Yes

Astronomy, Geodesy, Probabilities Calculus 501

Head: Professor P. Dingens

Botanical Biochemistry 502

Head: Professor C. Van Sumere

Differential and Integral Calculus 503

Head: Professor F. Vanmassenhove

Ecology and General Biology 504

Head: Professor J. Huble

General Physics and the Study of Electric and Magnetic Properties of Matter 505

Head: Professor G. Robbrecht

Genetics 506

Head: Professor J. Schell

Geography 507

Head: Professor F. Snacken

Geology 508

Head: Professor R. Maréchal

Geometry and Combinatorics 509

Head: Professor J. Thas

Inorganic Chemistry 510

Head: Professor G. Van Der Kelen

Mathematical Physics 511

Senior staff: Professor P. Phariseau, C. Grosjean

Microbiology and Microbial Genetics 512

Head: Professor J. De Ley

Molecular Biology 513

Head: Professor W. Fiers

Morphology and Ecology of Plants, 514
Geobotany

Head: Professor P. Van Der Veken

Nuclear Physics 515

Head: Professor A. Deruytter

Organic Chemistry 516

Senior staff: Professor M. Antennis, M. Vandewalle
M. Verzele

Palaeontology 517

Head: Professor J. De Heinzelin De Braucourt

Physical Geography 518

Head: Professor R. Tavernier

Theoretical Mechanics 519

Head: Professor R. Mertens

Tropical Soil Science 520

Head: Professor C. Sys

Zoology 521

Head: Professor A. Coomans

FACULTY OF VETERINARY SCIENCE 522

Address: Casinoplein 24, B-9000 Gent
Dean: Professor M. Debackere

Ambulatory Clinic and Forensic 523
Medicine Department

Director: Professor F. Paredis

Animal Breeding and Veterinary 524
Science Experiment Station, and
Service of Animal Genetics and
Breeding

Address: Heidestraat 19, B-9220 Merelbeke

Animal Genetics and Breeding 525
Department

Director: Professor Y. Bonquet

Animal Nutrition Department 526

Director: vacant

Chemical Analysis of Food from 527
Animal Origin Department

Director: Professor R. Verbeke

Medicine of Large Animals 528
Department

Director: Professor W. Oyaert

Parasitology and Parasitic Diseases 529
Department

Director: vacant

Physiological Chemistry Department 530

Director: Professor R. Vercauteren

Poultry Pathology, Bacteriology and 531
Infectious Diseases Department

Director: Professor A. Devos

Reproduction and Obstetrics 532
Department

Director: Professor M. Vandeplassehe

Small Animal Medicine Department 533

Director: Professor D. Mattheeuws

Veterinary Anatomy Department 534

Director: Professor N. De Vos

Veterinary Food Hygiene Department 535

Director: Professor J. Van Hoof

Veterinary Pathology Department 536

Director: Professor J. Hoorens

Veterinary Pharmacology and 537
Toxicology Department

Director: Professor M. Debackere

Veterinary Physiology Department 538

Director: Professor G. Peeters

Veterinary Surgery Department 539

Director: Professor A. De Moor

INTERFACULTAIR CENTRUM VOOR 540 DE STUDIE VAN LUCHT-BODEM- EN WATERVERONTREINIGING

[Inter-Faculty Centre for the Study of Air, Soil and Water Pollution]
Address: Coupure Links 533, B-9000 Gent
President: Professor N. Schamp

INTERFACULTAIR CENTRUM VOOR 541 INFORMATION

[Inter-Faculty Centre for Informatics]
Address: Sint Pietersnieuwstraat 41, B-9000 Gent
President: Professor R. De Caluwe

INTERFACULTAIR CENTRUM VOOR 542 MANAGEMENT

[Inter-Faculty Centre for Management]
Address: Sint Pietersnieuwstraat 49, B-9000 Gent

INTERFACULTAIR STUDIE-EN 543 VORMINGSCENTRUM VOOR ONTWIKKELINGSSAMENWERKING

[Inter-Faculty Study and Training Centre for Developmental Cooperation]
Address: Universiteitstraat 4, B-9000 Gent
President: Professor R. Tavernier

Société Carbochimique 544 Société Anonyme

Address: Rue de la Carbo, B-7340 Tertre
Telephone: (065) 641321
Telex: 057 122
Research director: J. Cl. Maton
Sections: Fertilizers: polyethers for polyurethanes
Graduate research staff: 30
Activities: Ammonia, urea, ammonia and phosphate fertilizers; polyethers for polyurethanes.
Contract work: No

Société Intercommunale 545 Belge de Gaz et d'Electricité

– INTERCOM
[Belgian Cooperative Gas and Electricity Society]
Address: Place du Trône 1, B-1000 Bruxelles
Chairman: le Chevalier Albert Thys
Management Committee: Mariel Amorison, René Blareau, André Claude, Philippe Cols, Albert de Brouwer, Jean Demeure, Michel Dupuis, André Henskens, Pierre Masure, le Baron André Rolin, Fernand Rombouts, Jacques van der Schueren

CENTRE D'ÉTUDES ET DE 546 RECHERCHES GAZIèRES

– CERGA
[Gas Research and Study Centre]
Address: BP 11, B-1640 Rhode-Saint-Genèse
Telephone: (02) 358 35 25
Director: Paul Robert Helmann
Activities: Research on technical problems are studied. Properties and quality of gas; transport, distribution and utilization of gas energy in association with gas distributors and with the Association Royale des Gaziers Belges. Special attention is given to materials testing, with a view to supplying special materials for domestic and industrial users of natural gas, and for appliance manufacturers. The Centre participates in national and international committees for the purpose of research and exchange of information.

LABORATOIRE BELGE DE 547 L'INDUSTRIE ÉLECTRIQUE

– LABORELEC
[Belgian Electricity Industry Laboratory]
President: M.G. Blanchart
Director general: M.G. Lippeur
Sections: Power station and network problems, M.G. Hessrion, G. Dienne; electronics, H. Baleriaux, R. Wery; electric and photometric mensuration, M.M. Huberlaut, Ch. Vastrade; problems and mensuration in industrial physics and applied mechanics, M.Ch. Laire, M. Maljean; chemical and physical problems of the central power station, M.G. van Kuckhoven, A. Berger, J. Pirotte; materials study, M.F. Duelle, G. Darmont, Ch. Fontana, R. Wilputter; vibrations and acoustics, F. Maon, G. Pleeck; thermoelectricity and electrochemistry, M.J. Buls, Professor F. Pietermaat, M.B. Geeraat; mathematics, N. Germay
Activities: Scientific research and studies, and acquisition and dissemination of information on the numerous fields of the exploitation of electricity. Specific studies are concerned with the maintenance of an optimum level

of safety at nuclear power stations; problems resulting from the installation of nuclear stations on rivers; the use of Inconel 600 steel for steam generators for pressurized water reactor stations; degradation of solid insulation of alternators; emission of pollutants from thermal stations; reduction of noise emission; and dissipation of heat discharged from subterranean cables. Medium-term research is conducted, with the collaboration of the Institute for the Encouragement of Scientific Research in Industry and Agriculture (IRSIA), on the 'Descartes' project for the automation of the electric network, and on the 'Alpes' project for the application of programmed logic to electric stations. The activities of LABORLEC are divided between eight commissions which analyse results, propose working plans and research programmes, and fix budgets. There is also an additional mathematics service,

Facilities: SOFINA laboratories for materials study; central electricity laboratory of the Comité Électrotechnique Belge for developing electrometric and photometric means of measuring and testing electrotechnical materials; Central Laboratory INTER-ESCAUT specializing in the production and distribution of energy; national Belgian electrothermal and electrochemical laboratory.

Société Royale Belge de Géographie

548

[Royal Belgian Geographical Society]
Address: 194/1 Avenue Adolphe Buyl 87, B-1050 Bruxelles
Secretary-General: Jean-Pierre Grimmeau
Activities: Publication of 'Revue Belge de Géographie' (several times a year), which contains scientific papers on human, regional, physical and applied geography and geomorphology; organization of conferences on the same subjects. Research activities are coordinated with the Geographical Institute of the Free University of Brussels.

SOLVAY & Cie Société Anonyme

549

Address: 33 Rue du Prince Albert, B-1050 Bruxelles

CENTRAL LABORATORY

550

Address: 310 Rue de Ransbeek, B-1120 Bruxelles
Telephone: (02) 267 38 30
Telex: 26 619 SOLNOH B
Central research director: F. Bloyaert
Research director: J.P. De Wit
Divisions: Chemistry, A. Ryckaert; Services I, J, Petitjean; Vinyl Polymers, A. Oth; Polyolefins, R. Van Weynbergh; Plastics Fabrication, P. Bivort; Services II, F. Baugnies; Department of Materials Studies, L. Clerbois
Graduate research staff: 178
Annual expenditure: over £2m
Activities: Improvement of existing products and processes: sodium carbonate, sodium hydroxide and other sodium compounds; chlorine and derivatives; peroxygen compounds: hydrogen peroxide, persalts and organic peroxides; polymers: polyvinyl chloride and copolymers, polyolefins; fabricated plastic products for the building, packaging and automotive industries; development of new products aimed at solving the energy and raw materials crisis and increasing the technological content of their products through research into fine chemicals, biological products, technopolymers.
Contract work: No
See separate entry for: Duphar B.V.

Station de Recherches des Eaux et Forêts/Proefstation van Waters en Bossen

551

[Waters and Forests Research Station]
Address: Duboislaan 14, Groenendaal, B-1990 Hoeilaart
Telephone: (02) 657 03 86
Affiliation: Ministry of Agriculture
Director: J.A. Timmermans
Sections: Animal biology, J.A. Timmermans; forestry biology, J. Rogister
Graduate research staff: 7
Annual expenditure: £227 000
Activities: Forestry; forest genetics; forest pedology and cartography; forest biology; freshwater fishing; hydrobiology; hunting.
Contract work: No

Studiecentrum voor Kernenergie/Centre d'Étude de l'Énergie Nucléaire

552

– SCK/CEN
[Nuclear Energy Research Centre]
Address: Boeretang 200, B-2400 Mol
Telephone: (014) 311801
Telex: Atomol-31922
Affiliation: Ministry of Economic Affairs
Director: Severin Amelinckx
Sections: Materials science, Jozef Nihoul; waste treatment, Norbert Van de Voorde; nuclear fuels, Jean Flipot; applied electrochemistry, Gustaaf Spaepen; chemistry, Leon Baetsle; metallurgy, Jean-Jacques Huet; neutron physics, Marcel Neve de Mevergnies; reactor physics, José Debrue; safeguards Charles Beets; reactor safety, André Siebertz; technology and energy, Jacques Planquart; radiobiology, Jean Maisin
Graduate research staff: 300
Annual expenditure: £40m
Activities: Nuclear research into sodium cooled fast reactors; gas cooled reactors; light water reactors; fuel reprocessing; waste conditioning and disposal; fusion; safeguards; basic research in materials science, nuclear physics and radiobiology. Non-nuclear research into air pollution; pollution abatement and waste handling; the combination of a seawater desalination-regasification of a liquefied natural gas facility; production of drinking water; treatment of waste waters and sludges; electrolytic production of hydrogen; fuel cell power sources; general energy studies.
Facilities: Three reactors - one graphite moderated, air cooled, natural uranium fuelled, one a materials testing reactor of 100 MWe and one a 10 MWe pressurized water reactor.
Contract work: Yes
Publications: Annual report.

Studiecentrum voor Toegepaste Elektriciteit in Land- en Tuinbouw

553

[Agricultural and Horticultural Applications of Electricity Study Centre]
Address: Coupure Links 533, B-9000 Gent
Telephone: (091) 235 245
Affiliation: Instituut tot aanmoediging van het Wetenschappelijk Onderzoek in Nijverheid en Landbouw
Research director: Professor Dr ir M. Debruyckere
Graduate research staff: 1

Annual expenditure: £51 000-500 000
Activities: The use in horticulture of heat pumps; waste heat from power plants; artificial light; burning of litter from broiler-houses as an alternative energy-source; greenhouses: methods of energy saving; study of a mist-propagation system.
Contract work: No

Universitaire Instelling Antwerpen/Universiteit Antwerpen

554

[Antwerp University]
Address: Universiteitsplein 1, B-2610 Wilrijk
Telephone: (031) 28 25 28

FACULTY OF MEDICINE

555

Dean: W. Eylenbosch

Department of Medicine

556

Head: K. Van Camp
Graduate research staff: 139

Department of Pharmacy

557

Head: Professor A. Haemers
Graduate research staff: 15

FACULTY OF SCIENCES

558

Department of Biochemistry

559

Head: Professor P. Joos
Graduate research staff: 20

Department of Biology

560

Head: Professor F. De Vree
Graduate research staff: 13

Department of Chemistry

561

Head: Professor R. Gijbels
Graduate research staff: 27

Department of Mathematics

562

Head: Professor J. Haezendonck
Graduate research staff: 9

Department of Physics 563

Head: Professor D. Schoemaker
Graduate research staff: 22

Université Catholique de 564
Louvain

[Catholic University of Louvain]
Address: Place de l'Université 1, B-1348 Louvain-la-Neuve
Telephone: (010) 41 81 81
Telex: UCL B 59037
Rector: Monseigneur E. Massaux

FACULTY OF AGRICULTURAL 565
SCIENCES

Address: Place Croix du Sud 3, B-1348 Louvain-la-Neuve
Dean: Professor L. De Backer

Agricultural Engineering Unit 566

Address: Place Croix du Sud 3, B-1348 Louvain-la-Neuve
Head: Professor E. Persoons

Animal Nutrition Laboratory 567

Address: Place Croix du Sud 3, B-1348 Louvain-la-Neuve
Head: Professor M. Vanbelle

Brewing Laboratory 568

Address: Place Croix du Sud 3, B-1348 Louvain-la-Neuve
Head: Professor A. Devreux

Chemistry of Solids and Catalysis 569
Laboratory

Address: Place Croix du Sud 1, B-1348 Louvain-la-Neuve
Head: B. Delmon

General Pedology Laboratory 570

Address: Place Croix du Sud 2, B-1348 Louvain-la-Neuve
Head: Professor H. Laudelout

Genetics Laboratory 571

Address: Place Croix du Sud 2, B-1348 Louvain-la-Neuve
Head: F. Lints

Grassland Ecology Laboratory 572

Address: Place Croix du Sud 3, B-1348 Louvain-la-Neuve
Head: Professor J. Lambert

Microbial Biochemistry Laboratory 573

Address: Place Croix du Sud 3, B-1348 Louvain-la-Neuve
Head: Professor J. Mayaudon

Microbiological Chemistry Laboratory 574

Address: Place Croix du Sud 2, B-1348 Louvain-la-Neuve
Head: R. Lambert

Nutrition Biochemistry Laboratory 575

Address: Place Croix du Sud 3, B-1348 Louvain-la-Neuve
Head: Professor M. Vanbelle

Organo-Mineral Chemistry Laboratory 576

Address: Place Croix du Sud 1, B-1348 Louvain-la-Neuve
Head: P. Cloos

Physiological Biochemistry Laboratory 577

Address: Place Croix du Sud 2, B-1348 Louvain-la-Neuve
Head: A. Goffeau

Phytopathology Laboratory 578

Address: Place Croix du Sud 3, B-1348 Louvain-la-Neuve
Head: Professor J. Meyer

Rural Economics Research Centre 579

Address: Place Croix du Sud 3, B-1348 Louvain-la-Neuve
Head: Professor G. Bublot

Surface Physico-Chemistry Laboratory   580

Address: Place Croix du Sud 1, B-1348 Louvain-la-Neuve
Head: P. Rouxhet

Systematic and Applied Mycology Laboratory   581

Address: Place Croix du Sud 3, B-1348 Louvain-la-Neuve
Head: Professor G.L. Hennebert

Tropical and Subtropical Plant Husbandry Laboratory   582

Address: Place Croix du Sud 3, B-1348 Louvain-la-Neuve
Head: Professor R. Germain

Tropical Soils Research Centre   583

Address: Place Croix du Sud 2, B-1348 Louvain-la-Neuve
Head: R. Frankart

Waters and Forests Unit   584

Address: Place Croix du Sud 2, B-1348 Louvain-la-Neuve
Head: Professor R. Antoine

FACULTY OF APPLIED SCIENCES   585

Address: Rue Archimède 1, B-1348 Louvain-la-Neuve
Dean: Professor G. de Ghellinck

Applied Chemistry and Physics Group   586

CHEMICAL ENGINEERING LABORATORY   587
Address: Bâtiment Réaumur, Place Ste-Barbe 2, B-1348 Louvain-la-Neuve
Head: R. Leenaerts

CHEMISTRY AND PHYSICS OF HIGH POLYMERS LABORATORY   588
Address: Bâtiment Boltzmann, Place Croix du Sud 1, B-1348 Louvain-la-Neuve
Head: Professor J.P. Mercier

SOLID-STATE PHYSICO-CHEMISTRY AND PHYSICS LABORATORY   589
Address: Bâtiment Boltzmann, Place Croix du Sud 1, B-1348 Louvain-la-Neuve
Head: A. Martegani

Architecture and Construction Group   590

Address: Bâtiment Vinci, Place du Levant 1, B-1348 Louvain-la-Neuve
Sections: Architecture, Professor F. Simm; construction, Professor E. Lousberg

Electricity Group   591

Address: Bâtiment Maxwell, Place du Levant 3, B-1348 Louvain-la-Neuve
Sections: Strong currents, Professor G. Labbé; electronics, Professor P. Jespers; electromagnetism and hyperfrequencies, Professor A. Vander Voest

Industrial Management and Applied Mathematics Group   592

APPLIED MATHEMATICS UNIT   593
Address: Chemin du Cyclotron 2, B-1348 Louvain-la-Neuve
Head: Professor N. Rouche

INDUSTRIAL MANAGEMENT UNIT   594
Address: Voie du Roman Pays 34, B-1348 Louvain-la-Neuve
Head: Professor J.P. Vial

Mechanics Group   595

Address: Bâtiment Stevin, Place du Levant, B-1348 Louvain-la-Neuve
Sections: Applied mechanics, Professor M. Crochet; thermodynamics and turbo-machines, Professor P. Wauters; mechanical fabrications, Professor P.E. Lagasse; naval constructions, vacant

Metallurgy and Mining Group   596

MINERALOGY AND APPLIED GEOLOGY LABORATORY   597
Address: Bâtiment Mercator, Place L. Pasteur 3, B-1348 Louvain-la-Neuve
Head: vacant

ORE PROCESSING LABORATORY   598
Address: Bâtiment Réaumur, Place Ste-Barbe 2, B-1348 Louvain-la-Neuve
Head: Professor J. De Cuyper

PHYSICAL METALLURGY UNIT   599
Address: Bâtiment Réaumur, Place Ste-Barbe 2, B-1348 Louvain-la-Neuve
Head: Professor A. Lutts

FACULTY OF MEDICINE 600

Address: UCL 5020, Avenue E. Mounier 50, B-1200 Bruxelles
Dean: Professor G. Sokal

Occupational Medicine Group 601

Address: Clos Chapelle-aux-Champs 30, B-1200 Bruxelles

INDUSTRIAL TOXICOLOGY UNIT 602
Address: UCL 3054
Head: Dr R. Lauwerys

OCCUPATIONAL HYGIENE AND 603
MEDICINE UNIT
Address: UCL 3038
Head: Dr J. Malchaire

OCCUPATIONAL PHYSIOLOGY AND 604
CARDIOLOGY UNIT
Address: UCL 3035
Head: Professor L. Brasseur

PROFESSIONAL DERMATOLOGY UNIT 605
Address: UCL 3033
Head: Dr J.M. Lachapelle

School of Dental Medicine 606

Address: École de Médecine Dentaire, UCL 75.5732, B-1200 Bruxelles

DENTAL-FACIAL ORTHOPAEDICS UNIT 607
Head: Professor J. Dahan

DENTAL PROSTHETICS UNIT 608
Head: Professor A.O. Lejeune

PARADONTOLOGY UNIT 609
Head: vacant

PATHOLOGY AND DENTAL 610
THERAPEUTICS UNIT
Head: Professor A. Vermeersch

STOMATOLOGY AND MAXILLO- 611
FACIAL SURGERY UNIT
Head: Dr P. Lechien

School of Medicine 612

ANAESTHESIOLOGY GROUP 613
Address: Cliniques Universitaires St-Luc, Avenue Hippocrate 10, B-1200 Bruxelles
Head: Professor P. De Temmerman

ANATOMY, EMBRYOLOGY AND 614
HISTOLOGY GROUP
Address: UCL 5240, Avenue E. Mounier 52, B-1200 Bruxelles

Anatomy Unit 615
Address: UCL 5229, Avenue E. Mounier 52, B-1200 Bruxelles
Senior staff: Professor A. Dhem

Histology Unit 616
Senior staff: Professor S. Haumont

CARDIOVASCULAR AND THORACIC 617
SURGERY GROUP
Address: UCL 5570, B-1200 Bruxelles
Heads: Professor Ch.-H. Chalant, Professor R. Ponlot

DERMATOLOGY GROUP 618
Address: UCL 5259, Avenue E. Mounier 52, B-1200 Bruxelles
Head: Dr A. Bourlond

EXPERIMENTAL MEDICINE 619
DEPARTMENT
Address: UCL 7430, Avenue Hippocrate 74, B-1200 Bruxelles
Head: Professor P. Masson

GENERAL MICROBIOLOGY AND 620
MOLECULAR GENETICS GROUP
Address: UCL 7449, Avenue Hippocrate 74, B-1200 Bruxelles
Head: Professor C. Cocito

GENERAL PATHOLOGY LABORATORY 621
Address: UCL 7529, Avenue Hippocrate 75, B-1200 Bruxelles
Head: Professor M. De Visscher

GENERAL SURGERY GROUP 622
Address: UCL 5570, B-1200 Bruxelles
or: UCL 5460, B-1200 Bruxelles

Experimental Surgery Laboratory I 623
Senior staff: Professor J.J. Haxhe, Dr L. Lambotte

Experimental Surgery Laboratory II 624
Senior staff: Professor Ch. De Muylder

INTERNAL MEDICINE GROUP 625

Cardio-Pulmonary Physiopathology Research 626
Laboratory
Address: UCL 5550, B-1200 Bruxelles
Head: Professor L. Brasseur

Gastroenterology Unit 627
Address: UCL 5379, B-1200 Bruxelles
Head: Professor Ch. Dive

Haematology Unit   **628**
Address: UCL 3043, B-1200 Bruxelles
Head: Professor R. Masure

Nephrology Unit   **629**
Address: UCL 5450, Avenue Hippocrate 54, B-1200
Bruxelles
Head: Professor Ch. Van Ypersele de Strihou

Nuclear Medicine Centre   **630**
Address: UCL 5430 Avenue Hippocrate 54, B-1200
Bruxelles
Head: Professor C. Beckers

Nutrition and Endocrinology Unit   **631**
Address: UCL 5429, Avenue Hippocrate 54, B-1200
Bruxelles
Head: Professor J.J. Hoet

Rheumatology and Phospho-Calcium   **632**
Metabolism Unit
Address: UCL 5390 Avenue E. Mounier 53, B-1200
Bruxelles
Head: Professor Ch. Nagant de Deuxchaisnes

MEDICAL BIOCHEMISTRY GROUP   **633**

Hormonological and Pharmacognostic   **634**
Chemistry Unit
Address: UCL 5420, Avenue Hippocrate 54, B-1200
Bruxelles
Heads: Professor R. Devis, Professor M. Piraux

Medical Biochemistry Unit   **635**
Address: UCL 5340, Avenue E. Mounier 53, B-1200
Bruxelles
Head: Professor J. Sonnet

MEDICAL INFORMATION CENTRE   **636**
Address: UCL 1500, Avenue Hippocrate 10, B-1200
Bruxelles
Head: Professor J.J. Haxhe

MICROBIOLOGY GROUP   **637**
Address: Clos Chapelle-aux-Champs 30, B-1200 Bruxelles

Experimental Immunology Unit   **638**
Address: UCL 3056
Senior staff: Dr H. Bazin

Immunology Unit   **639**
Address: UCL 3056
Senior staff: Professor S. Stadtsbaeder

Microbiology Unit   **640**
Address: UCL 3058
Senior staff: Professor G. Bruynoghe

Virology Unit   **641**
Address: UCL 3055, Clos Chapelle-aux-Champs 300,
B-1200 Bruxelles
Head: M.-E. Lamy

NEUROLOGY GROUP   **642**

Clinical Neurophysiology Unit   **643**
Address: UCL 5433, Avenue Hippocrate 54, B-1200
Bruxelles
Head: Dr J. Bergmans

Experimental Neurology Unit   **644**
Address: Cliniques Universitaires St-Luc, Avenue Hip-
pocrate 10, B-1200 Bruxelles
Head: Professor A. Dereymaeker

Neurochemistry Unit   **645**
Address: UCL 5329, B-1200 Bruxelles
Head: Professor E.C. Laterre

Neurosurgery Unit   **646**
Address: UCL 5460, Avenue Hippocrate 54, B-1200
Bruxelles
Head: Dr G. Stroobandt

OBSTETRICS AND GYNAECOLOGY   **647**
GROUP
Address: UCL 5330, B-1200 Bruxelles
Head: Professor J. Ferin

OPHTHALMOLOGY GROUP   **648**
Address: UCL 5220, B-1200 Bruxelles
Head: Professor J. Michiels

ORTHOPAEDICS GROUP   **649**
Address: UCL 5388, B-1200 Bruxelles
Head: Professor A. Vincent

OTORHINOLARYNGOLOGY AND   **650**
AUDIO-PHONOLOGY GROUP
Address: Cliniques Universitaires St-Luc, Avenue Hip-
pocrate 10, B-1200 Bruxelles
Head: Professor J. Van Den Eeckhaut

PAEDIATRICS GROUP   **651**

Growth and Nutrition Unit   **652**
Address: UCL 5474, Avenue Hippocrate 54, B-1200
Bruxelles
Heads: Professor P. Malvaux
Professor A. Lambert

Paediatric Cardiology Unit   **653**
Address: Cliniques Universitaires St-Luc, Avenue Hip-
pocrate 10, B-1200 Bruxelles
Head: Professor A. Vliers

Teratology and Medical Genetics Unit   **654**
Address: UCL 5350, B-1200 Bruxelles
Head: Professor R. De Meyer

PATHOLOGICAL ANATOMY AND   **655**
NEUROPATHOLOGY GROUP
Address: UCL 5260, Avenue E. Mounier 52, B-1200
Bruxelles
Head: Professor J.M. Brucher

PHARMACOLOGY GROUP   **656**

Industrial and Medical Toxicology Unit   **657**
Address: UCL 3054, Avenue Chapelle-aux-Champs
30, B-1200 Bruxelles
Head: Dr R. Lauwerys

Medical Pharmacology and   **658**
Pharmacodynamics Unit
Address: Institut de Pharmacie, UCL 7350, Avenue E.
Mounier 73, B-1200 Bruxelles
Head: Professor Th. Godfraind

Pharmacotherapy Unit   **659**
Address: UCL 5349, Avenue E. Mounier 53, B-1200
Bruxelles
Head: Professor C. Harvengt

PHYSICAL MEDICINE AND   **660**
READAPTATION GROUP
Address: Cliniques Universitaires St-Luc, Avenue Hip-
pocrate 10, B-1200 Bruxelles
Head: Professor M. Soete

PHYSIOLOGICAL CHEMISTRY GROUP   **661**
Address: Laboratoire de Chimie Physiologique, UCL
7539, Avenue Hippocrate 75, B-1200 Bruxelles
Head: Professor C. De Duve

PHYSIOLOGY GROUP   **662**
Address: UCL 5540 Avenue Hippocrate 55, B-1200
Bruxelles

Endocrinology-Metabolism Unit   **663**
Address: UCL 5530, Avenue Hippocrate 55, B-1200
Bruxelles
Senior staff: Professor J. Crabbé

Muscle Physiology Unit   **664**
Senior staff: Professor X. Aubert

Neurophysiology Unit   **665**
Address: UCL 5449, Avenue Hippocrate 54, B-1200
Bruxelles
Senior staff: Professor M. Meulders

PNEUMOLOGY RESEARCH CENTRE   **666**
Address: Institut G. Thérasse, Godinne
Head: Professor J. Prignot

PSYCHO-MEDICAL-SOCIAL STUDY   **667**
CENTRE
Address: UCL 5389, Avenue E. Mounier 53, B-1200
Bruxelles
Head: Professor C. Mertens de Wilmars

PSYCHOPATHOLOGY-PSYCHIATRY   **668**
GROUP

Child Psychiatry Research Unit   **669**
Address: UCL 3049, Clos Chapelle-aux-Champs 30, B-
1200 Bruxelles
Head: Dr P.J. Fontaine

Clinical Psychiatric Research Unit   **670**
Address: Centre de Guidance, École de Santé Publi-
que, UCL 3049, Clos Chapelle-aux-Champs 30, B-1200
Bruxelles
Head: Professor L. Cassiers

Unit for Biological and   **671**
Psychopharmacological Research in
Psychiatry
Address: UCL 3049, B-1200 Bruxelles
Head: Professor P. Guilmot

RADIODIAGNOSIS GROUP   **672**
Address: Cliniques Universitaires St-Luc, Avenue Hip-
pocrate 10, B-1200 Bruxelles
Head: Professor P. Bodart

RADIOTHERAPY-CANCEROLOGY   **673**
GROUP
Address: Centre des Tumeurs, Cliniques Universitaires
St-Luc, Avenue Hippocrate 10, B-1200 Bruxelles
Head: Professor H. Maisin

Cancerology and Epidemiology of Cancer Unit   **674**
Address: UCL 5369, Avenue E. Mounier 53, B-1200
Bruxelles
Senior staff: Professor H. Maisin, Professor C.
Deckers

Experimental Neutron Therapy   **675**
Address: UCL 5469, Avenue Hippocrate 54, B-1200
Bruxelles
Senior staff: Professor A. Wambersie

Pathology and Cytology of Tumours Unit   **676**
Address: UCL 5249, Avenue E. Mounier 52, B-1200
Bruxelles
Senior Staff: Professor P. Maldague

SPECIAL PATHOLOGICAL ANATOMY   **677**
GROUP
Address: Laboratoires d'Anatomie Pathologique des
Cliniques Universitaires St-Luc, Avenue Hippocrate 10,
B-1200 Bruxelles
Head: Professor F. Meersseman

UROLOGY GROUP   **678**
Address: Cliniques Universitaires St-Luc, Avenue Hip-
pocrate 10, B-1200 Bruxelles
Head: Professor J. Brenez

Experimental Urology Unit   **679**
Senior staff: Professor P. Hennebert

School of Pharmacy   680

ANALYTICAL CHEMISTRY AND   681
THERAPEUTIC PHYSICO-CHEMISTRY
UNIT
Address: École de Pharmacie, UCL 7230 Avenue E.
Mounier 72, B-1200 Bruxelles
Head: Professor J. Rondelet

GALENIC, INDUSTRIAL AND   682
FORENSIC PHARMACY UNIT
Address: UCL 7320, Avenue E. Mounier 73, B-1200
Bruxelles
Head: Professor M. Roland

MEDICAL CHEMISTRY, TOXICOLOGY   683
AND BROMATOLOGY UNIT
Address: École de Pharmacie, UCL 5490, Avenue Hip-
pocrate 54, B-1200 Bruxelles
Head: Professor M. Mercier

PHARMACEUTICAL CHEMISTRY,   684
RADIOTOXOLOGY, AND DRUG
ANALYSIS UNIT
Address: École de Pharmacie, UCL 7340, Avenue E.
Mounier 73, B-1200 Bruxelles
Head: Professor P. Dumont

PHARMACOLOGY UNIT   685
Address: École de Pharmacie, UCL 7350, Avenue E.
Mounier 73, B-1200 Bruxelles
Head: Professor Th. Godfraind

School of Public Health   686

Address: École de Santé Publique, UCL 3030, Clos
Chapelle-aux-Champs 30, B-1200 Bruxelles

AUDIOPHONOLOGY CENTRE   687
Address: UCL 3040
Head: Professor J. Van Den Eeckhaut

BACTERIOLOGY AND ALIMENTARY   688
VIROLOGY UNIT
Address: UCL 3055
Head: vacant

EPIDEMIOLOGY UNIT   689
Address: UCL 3034
Head: Professor M.F. Lechat

GERONTOLOGY UNIT   690
Address: UCL 3036
Head: Professor A. Gommers

HAEMATOLOGY UNIT AND BLOOD   691
TRANSFUSION CENTRE
Address: UCL 3052
Head: Professor G. Sokal

MARITAL AND SEXUAL SCIENCES   692
UNIT
Address: UCL 3032
Head: G. Rucquoy

MEDICAL SOCIOLOGY UNIT   693
Address: UCL 3053
Head: J. Descy

NUTRITION UNIT   694
Address: UCL 3044
Head: vacant

PARASITOLOGY UNIT   695
Address: UCL 3046
Head: Professor J. Gillet

RADIOPROTECTION UNIT   696
Address: Chemin du Cyclotron 2, B-1348 Louvain-la-
Neuve
Head: vacant

SCHOOLS MEDICAL INSPECTION   697
UNIT
Address: UCL 3039
Head: A. Nöel

STUDENTS' PSYCHO-MEDICAL-SOCIAL   698
PROTECTION UNIT
Address: UCL 3048
Head: Professor R. Colon

FACULTY OF PSYCHOLOGY AND   699
EDUCATION

Address: Voie du Roman Pays 20, B-1348 Louvain-la-
Neuve
Dean: Professor J. Costermans

Child Psychopathology and   700
Orthopaedagogics Centre

Address: Voie du Roman Pays 20, B-1348 Louvain-la-
Neuve
Head: P.J. Fontaine

Criminology Research Unit   701

Address: Place Montesquieu 2, B-1348 Louvain-la-
Neuve
Head: Professor C. Debuyst

Differential and Clinical Psychology Centre   702

Address: Voie du Roman Pays 20, B-1348 Louvain-la-Neuve
Head: J. Schotte

Experimental and Comparative Psychology Centre   703

Address: Château à Pellenberg
Head: Professor G. Thinès

Experimental and Social Psychology Centre   704

Address: Tiensestraat 102, B-3000 Louvain-la-Neuve
Head: Professor J.P. Leyens

Genetic Psychology Laboratory   705

Address: Voie du Roman Pays 20, B-1348 Louvain-la-Neuve
Head: vacant

Pathological Psychology and Psychotherapy Research Centre   706

Address: Voie du Roman Pays 20, B-1348 Louvain-la-Neuve
Head: Professor R. Volcher

Psychodiagnostic Research and Psychological Consultation Centre 707

Address: Voie du Roman Pays 20, B-1348 Louvain-la-Neuve
Head: R. Depuydt-Berte

Psychometry Laboratory   708

Address: Voie du Roman Pays 20, B-1348 Louvain-la-Neuve
Head: Professor A. Bonboir

Psychophysiology Laboratory   709

Address: UCL 5449 Avenue Hippocrate 54, B-1200 Bruxelles
Head: Professor M. Meulders

FACULTY OF SCIENCES   710

Address: SC11, Place des Sciences 2, B-1348 Louvain-la-Neuve
Dean: Professor P. Berthet

Botany Group   711

Senior staff: Professor L. Waterkeyn

CYTOGENETICS UNIT   712
Address: Bâtiment Carnoy, Place Croix du Sud 4, B-1348 Louvain-la-Neuve
Head: Professor J. Bouharmont

CYTOLOGY AND PLANT MORPHOLOGY UNIT   713
Address: Bâtimant Carnoy, Place Croix du Sud 4, B-1348 Louvain-la-Neuve
Heads: Professor Waterkeyn Professor P. Moens

PALYNOLOGY AND PHYTOSOCIOLOGY UNIT   714
Address: Bâtiment Carnoy, Place Croix du Sud, B-1348 Louvain-la-Neuve
Head: Professor W. Mullenders

PLANT ECOLOGY UNIT   715
Address: Bâtiment Carnoy, Place Croix du Sud 4, B-1348 Louvain-la-Neuve
Head: Professor J. De Sloover

VEGETABLE PHYSIOLOGY UNIT   716
Address: Bâtiment Carnoy, Place Croix du Sud 4, B-1348 Louvain-la-Neuve
Head: C. Myttenaere

Chemistry Group   717

Senior staff: Professor A. Bruylants

GENERAL AND ORGANIC CHEMISTRY UNIT   718
Address: Bâtiment Lavoisier, Place L. Pasteur 1, B-1348 Louvain-la-Neuve
Head: Professor A. Bruylants

INORGANIC AND NUCLEAR CHEMISTRY UNIT   719
Address: Bâtiment SCl, Chemin du Cyclotron 2, B-1348 Louvain-la-Neuve
Head: Professor D. Apers

Biochemistry Unit   720
Senior staff: Professor R. Crichton

Chemical Kinetics Unit   721
Address: Bâtiment Lavoisier, Place L. Pasteur 1, B-1348 Louvain-la-Neuve
Head: Professor I. de Aguirre

Inorganic and Analytical Chemistry Unit   722
Senior staff: P. Claes

Organic Chemistry of Synthesis Unit   **723**
Address: Bâtiment Lavoisier, Place L. Pasteur 1, B-1348 Louvain-la-Neuve
Head: Professor L. Ghosez

Organic Chemistry Unit   **724**
Address: Bâtiment Lavoisier, Place L. Pasteur 1, B-1348 Louvain-la-Neuve
Head: Professor H.G. Viehe

Physical Chemistry and Crystallography Unit   **725**
Address: Bâtiment Lavoisier, Place L. Pasteur 1, B-1348 Louvain-la-Neuve
Head: Professor M. Van Meerssche

Physical Chemistry of Combustion Unit   **726**
Senior staff: P. Van Tiggelen

Quantitative Chemistry Unit   **727**
Address: Bâtiment Lavoisier, Place L. Pasteur 1, B-1348 Louvain-la-Neuve
Head: Professor G. Leroy

PRACTICAL WORKS UNITS   **728**
Address: Bâtiment Lavoisier, Place L. Pasteur 1, B-1348 Louvain-la-Neuve
Sections: General, organic and inorganic chemistry, Professor A. Bruylants, Professor L. Ghosez, Professor H. G. Viehe; analytical chemistry, vacant; physical chemistry, Professor M. Van Meerssche

Geology Group   729

Address: Bâtiment Mercator, Place L. Pasteur 3, B-1348 Louvain-la-Neuve
Senior staff: H. Martin

GENERAL GEOLOGY UNIT   **730**
Senior staff: Professor A. Lees

GEOCHEMISTRY UNIT   **731**
Senior staff: H. Martin

PALAEONTOLOGY UNIT   **732**
Senior staff: Professor R. Conil

PETROGRAPHY UNIT   **733**
Senior staff: Professor D. Laduxon

PHYSICAL GEOGRAPHY UNIT   **734**
Senior staff: G. Seret

Mathematics Group   735

Address: Bâtiment SCl, Chemin du Cyclotron 2, B-1348 Louvain-la-Neuve
Senior staff: Professor P. Hemard

MATHEMATICAL LOGIC UNIT   **736**
Senior staff: Th. Lucas

MECHANICS UNIT   **737**
Senior staff: Professor J. Roels

NUMERICAL ANALYSIS AND   **738**
PROGRAMMING UNIT
Senior staff: Professor J. Meinguet

PROBABILITY CALCULATION AND   **739**
STATISTICAL ANALYSIS UNIT
Senior staff: Professor J. Paris

PURE MATHEMATICS UNIT   **740**
Senior staff: Professor J. Mawhin

SPECIAL MATHEMATICAL   **741**
METHODOLOGY UNIT
Senior staff: Professor N. Rouche

Physics Group   742

Address: Bâtiment SCl, Chemin du Cyclotron 2, B-1348 Louvain-la-Neuve
Senior staff: Professor J. Deutsch

ASTRONOMY AND GEOPHYSICS UNIT   **743**
Senior staff: Professor A. Berger

ATOMIC AND MOLECULAR DYNAMICS   **744**
UNIT
Senior staff: Professor F. Brouillard

MOLECULAR SPECTROSCOPY UNIT   **745**
Senior staff: Professor A. Fayt

NUCLEAR PHYSICS UNIT   **746**
Senior staff: Professor P. Macq

SOLID-STATE PHYSICS UNIT   **747**
Senior staff: Professor A. Meessen

THEORETICAL AND MATHEMATICAL   **748**
PHYSICS UNIT
Senior staff: Professor J.P. Amtoine

Zoology Group   749

Address: Bâtiment Claude Bernard, Place Croix du Sud 5, B-1348 Louvain-la-Neuve
Senior staff: Professor Ph. Lebrun

ANIMAL ECOLOGY UNIT   **750**
Senior staff: Professor Ph. Lebrun, P. Berthet

ANIMAL MORPHOLOGY UNIT   **751**
Senior staff: Professor J. Demel

ANIMAL PHYSIOLOGY UNIT   **752**
Senior staff: F. Baguet

Domestic Animal Anatomy and Embryology 753
Unit
Senior staff: L. Henriet

Embryology, Comparative Anatomy and 754
Anthropology Unit
Senior staff: J. Picard

Molecular Genetics of Eucaryotes Unit 755
Senior staff: J. Delcour

INTERFACULTY RESEARCH CENTRES 756
AND INSTITUTES

Interfaculty Institute of Applied 757
Natural Sciences

Address: Place Croix du Sud 2, B-1348 Louvain-la-
Neuve
Senior staff: J. de Cuyper, A. Herbillon, Ph. Lebrun, J.
Demal

Interfaculty Institute of Family and Sex 758
Sciences

Address: Rue des Wallons 6, B-1348 Louvain-la-Neuve
Chairman: J.M. Jaspard

Interfaculty Institute of Pure and 759
Applied Mathematics

Address: Bâtiment SC1, Chemin du Cyclotron 2, B-
1348 Louvain-la-Neuve
Chairman: Professor J. Paris

Université de l'État à Mons   760

[Mons State University]
Address: Place Warocque 17, B-7000 Mons
Telephone: (065) 31 51 71
Telex: 57764 uemons b
Affiliation: Ministry of National Education and
French Culture

FACULTY OF PSYCHO- 761
EDUCATIONAL SCIENCES

Department of Psycho-Educational 762
Study and Research

Head: Professor J. Burion

Fundamental Psychology Laboratory 763

Head: Professor J. Dierkens

Psycho-Educational Guidance 764
Department

Head: Professor P. Georis

Psychopathology of Childhood, 765
Adolescence and Language

Head: Professor J. Cordier

FACULTY OF SCIENCES 766

Chemistry Institute 767

Heads: Professor J. Zanen, Professor R. Dagonnier

Mathematics Institute 768

Heads: Professor G. Lumer, Professor G. Noel

Physics Institute 769

Head: Professor J. Nuyts, Professor L. Laude

UNIVERSITY RESEARCH CENTRES 770

Computation and Informatics Centre 771

Head: Professor P. Thiry

Interdisciplinary Research Centre for 772
Economic, Educational and Social
Prospects

– CRIPES
Head: Professor E. Breuse

Research Centre for Organization, 773
Study, Development and Innovation in
the Public and Private Sector

Head: Professor L. Rousseau

Université de Liège 774

[Liège University]
Address: Place du Août, B-4000 Liège
Research council: Rector, Professor E.H. Betz; FNRS researcher, J.C. Dotreppa; Professor J.M. Ghuysen, Professor L. Habraken, Professor C. Houssier, Professor J. Humblet, R. Marcelle, P. Pastoret, Professor L. Pouplard, Professor C. Renard, Professor M. Tyssens, M. Voisin, P. Wathelet

APPLIED SCIENCE FACULTY 775

Dean: Professor G. Cantraine

Chemistry and Metallurgy Institute 776

Address: Rue A. Stévart, B-4000 Liège
Sections: Industrial organic chemistry, Professor A. Lefebvre; industrial inorganic chemistry, R. Mormont; applied organic chemistry, Professor H. Dieu; chemical engineering (reactors), Professor G. l'Homme; metallurgy, Professor P. Coheur; metallurgy of non-ferrous metals, Professor C. Ek; mineralogy and nuclear materials, Professor R. Collée

Civil Engineering Institute 777

Address: Quai Banning 6, B-4000 Liège
Sections: Hydraulic civil engineering constructions, Professor N.M. Dehousse; infrastructures, Professor A. Fagnoul; bridges and structures, Professor R. Baus; hydraulics, Professor A. Lejeune; civil engineering construction materials, Professor K. Gamski; material mechanics and construction stability, Professor Ch. Massonnet; mine working, Professor P. Stassen

Geology Institute 778

Address: Place du 20 Août 7, B-4000 Liège
Section: General and applied geology

Geology Institute 779

Address: Avenue des Tilleuls 45, B-4000 Liège
Sections: Applied geology; applied geology and geophysics, Professor P. Evrard; applied meteorology

Mechanics Institute 780

Address: Rue Ernest Solvay 21, B-4000 Liège
Sections: Machine construction, Professor J. Bozet; industrial production; methods of transport; mechanics of continuous media and aeronautical constructions, Professor G. Sander; thermic engines - aerospatial propulsion, A. Jamoulle; applied physics, thermodynamics and thermal machines, Professor G. Burney; water pumps and turbines, P. Sliosberg; technology and machine construction, Professor J. Wolper; thermotechnique, Professor J. Fafchamps; gas turbines, Professor S. Boudignes; chemical engineering, Professor L. Delvaux

Montefiore Electricity Institute 781

Address: Sart Tilman, B-4000 Liège
or: Rue Saint-Gilles 33, B-4000, Liège
Telephone: 562650; 562651
Sections: Acoustics - electrical acoustics, applied acoustics, Professor J. Dendal; systems and automation, Professor A. Danthine; automation, Professor L. van Mellaert; electric circuits, Professor M. Pavella; electric machine construction; theoretical electricity, Professor A. Calvaer; electric standards; transport and distribution of electricity, Professor E. Mean; electronics, Professor G. Cantraine; telecommunications, Professor A. Fawe; informatics, Professor D. Ribbens; electrotechnology, Professor J. Robert, Professor W. Legros

INTERFACULTY CENTRE FOR NUCLEAR SCIENCE 782

President: Professor J. Humblet

Nuclear Physics Institute 783

Address: Sart Tilman, B-4000 Liège
Section: Experimental nuclear physics, Professor L. Winnand

Radiochemistry Institute 784

Section: Nuclear chemistry, Professor J. Fuger

MEDICAL FACULTY 785

Dean: Professor R. Lambotte

Alfred Gilkinet Institute of Pharmacy   786

Address: Rue Fusch 3, B-4000 Liège
or: Rue Fusch 5, B-4000 Liège
Sections: Medicaments analysis, Professor J. Bosly;
analytical chemistry and pharmaceutical chemistry,
Professor Ch. L. Lapiere; legislation and dermatology,
E. Mesmaeker; Galenic pharmacy (pharmaceutical
technology) Professor F. Jaminet; pharmacognosy including phytochemistry, Professor L. Augenot

August Swaen Institute   787

Address: 20 Rue de Pitteurs, B-4020 Liège
Sections: Anatomy - systematic human anatomy and
neuronanatomy, Professor M. Gerebtzoff; anatomy -
topographic human anatomy and splanchnology,
Professor A. de Scoville; histology - embryology,
Professor R. Bassleer, Professor L. Simar; histology and
cytology, G. Goessens

Central Haematology Laboratory   788

Address: Boulevard de la Constitution 59, B-4020
Liège

Dermatology Clinic   789

Address: Hôpital de Bevière, Boulevard de la Constitution 66, B-4020 Liège
Section: Dermatology, Professor Ch. M. Lapière

Diabetes Laboratory   790

Address: Tour de Pathologie, Sart Tilman, B-4000
Liège

E. Malvoz Institute   791

Address: Quai du Barbon 4, B-4020 Liège
Sections: Clinical physiology, Professor J.M. Petit; medicine and social hygiene, Professor J.M. Petit

Experimental Surgery Laboratory   792

Address: Tour de Pathologie, Sart Tilman, B-4000
Liège

Hygiene and Social Medicine Institute   793

Address: Place Delcour 16, B-4020 Liège
Section: Applications of microbiology to hygiene,
Professor P. Frédéricq

Léon Frédéricq Institute   794

Address: Place Delcour 17, B-4020 Liége
Sections: Normal and pathological physiology,
Professor J. Lecomte; general and comparative
biochemistry, Professor E. Schoffeniels; psychophysiology and neurophysiology, Professor J. Faidherbe

Medical Institute   795

Address: Hôpital de Bavière, Boulevard la Constitu-
tion 66, B-4020 Liège
Sections: Medicine and medical pathology, Professor
H. van Cauwenberge; medicine and medical semiology,
Professor A. Nizet; outpatients, Professor P. Lefebvre

Medical Psychology Clinic   796

Address: Hôpital de Bavière, Boulevard de la Constitu-
tion 66, B-4020 Liège
Section: Psychosomatic medicine, medical psychology,
Professor D. Luminet

Ophthalmology Clinic   797

Address: Hôpital de Bavière, Boulevard de la Constitution 66, B-4020 Liège
Section: Ophthalmology, Professor R. Weekers

Otorhinolaryngology Clinic   798

Address: Hôpital de Bavière, Boulevard de la Constitution 66, B-4020 Liège

Paediatric Clinic   799

Address: Hôpital de Bavière, Boulevard de la Constitution 66, B-4020 Liège
Section: Paediatrics, Professor F. Geubelle

Pathological Anatomy Institute   800

Address: Rue des Bonnes Villes 1, B-4020 Liège
Section: Anatomy and pathological cytology,
Professor E.H. Betz

Pathology Institute   801

Address: Rue des Bennes Villes 1, B-4020 Liège
or: Sart Tilman, B-4000, Liege
Sections: Medical biochemistry, Professor C.
Heusghem; genetic biochemistry, Professor C. Lambotte; hygiene, Professor P. Frédéricq

Physiotherapy Institute   802

Address: Hopital de Baviere, Boulevard de la Constitution 66, B-4020 Liège
Section: Physical Medicine

Psychiatric Clinic   803

Address: Rue Saint-Laurent 58, B-4020 Liège
Section: Psychiatry, Professor J. Bobon

Radioimmunology Laboratory   804

Address: Tour de Pathologie, Sart Tilman, B-4000 Liège

Radiology Institute   805

Address: Hôpital de Bavière Boulevard de la Constitution 66, B-4020 Liège
Sections: X-ray diagnosis, Professor G. Leroux; neurosurgery, Professor J. Bonnal; radiology, Professor J. Closon

Stomatology Institute   806

Address: Hopital de Bavière, Boulevard de la Constitution 66, B-4020 Liège
Sections: Mouth and jaw surgery, Professor A. Steenebruggen; jaw and facial surgery, Professor A. Castermans; dental materials and bridges and crowns; dental pathology, surgical dentistry, parodontology, Professor J. Kohl; children's dental medicine and orthodontics, Professor A. Boniver; semiology, oral diagnosis and dental prosthesis, Professor R. Eisenring

Surgical Clinic   807

Address: Hôpital de Bavière, Boulevard de la Constitution 66, B-4020 Liège
Sections: Anaesthesia and resuscitation, Professor M. Lamy; general, cardiovascular, digestive and thoracic surgery, Professor D. Honoré; general surgery, traumatology, orthopaedics, renal transplants, muscular microsurgery, hand surgery, Professor G. Lejeune; plastic surgery, Professor A. Castermans

Urology Clinic   808

Address: Hôpital de Bavière, Boulevard de la Constitution 66, B-4020 Liège
Section: Urology, Professor Ch. Maquiney

SCIENCE FACULTY   809

Dean: Professor José A. Sporck

Astrophysics Institute   810

Address: Avenue de Cointe 5, B-4200 Cointe
Sections: Astronomy and theoretical astrophysics, Professor P. Ledoux; astronomy and geodesy, Professor P. Ledoux; astrophysics and spectroscopy, Professor L. Houziaux; electronics, optics and spectroscopy, Professor M. Migeotte; rational mechanics, Professor R. Simon

Botanical Institute   811

Address: Sart Tilman, B-4000 Liège
Sections: Plant biochemistry, Professor J. Aghion; biology and plant biology, Professor C. Sironvel; plant biology, Professor G. Bernier, Professor R. Bronchart, Professor J. Aghion; pharmaceutical botany and special systematics, Professor J. Ramaut; plant ecology; botanical garden, Professor J. Lambinon; plant morphology, Professor R. Bronchart; photobiology, Professor C. Sironval; plant physiology, Professor G. Bernier; bacterial biochemistry, Professor J.M. Ghuysen; molecular genetics, Professor L. Ledoux; systematic botany and phytogeography, Professor J. Lambinon

Chemistry Institute   812

Address: Sart Tilman, B-4000 Liège
Sections: Biochemistry, Professor W. Verly; muscular biochemistry, Professor G. Hamoir; general biology, vegetable and animal, Professor G. Hamoir; analytical chemistry, Professor G. Michel; inorganic chemistry, Professor P. Tarte; inorganic chemistry - physical chemistry of surfaces, Professor J. Mignolet; macromolecular chemistry and organic catalysis, Professor Ph. Teyssie; macromolecular chemistry and physical chemistry, Professor E. Fredericq; organic chemistry - chemistry of natural substances; organic chemistry - chemistry of natural substances of vegetable origin, Professor R. Huls; physical organic chemistry, Professor P. Laszlo; organic electrochemistry, I. Gillet; low temperature laboratory, R. Blanpain; electronic paramagnetic resonance laboratory, R. Hubin; organic chemistry - organic synthesis, Professor M. Renson; physical chemistry - study of ionization levels and quantitative chemistry, Professor J. Collin, Professor J.C. Lorquet; physical oceanography, Professor J. Nihoul; oceanology, Professor A. Disteche; mechanics of geophysical fluids irreversible phenomena, Professor J. Nihoul

Crystallography and Mineralogy Institute   813

Address: Place du 20 Août 9, B-4000 Liège
Section: Mineralogy, Professor P. Bourguignon

Geology Institute 814

Address: Sart Tilman, B-4000 Liège
Section: Geology, petrology, geochemistry, Professor J. Bellière

Geophysics Laboratory 815

Address: 6 Quai Banning, B-4000 Liège

Mathematics Institute 816

Address: Avenue des Tilleuls 15, B-4000 Liège
Sections: Functional analysis, Professor J. Schmets; mathematical and algebraic analysis, Professor H. Garnir; differential geometry, Professor M. de Wilde; advanced geometry, Professor F. Jongmans; mathematics, Professor J. Gobert; general mathematics, Professor J. Etienne; photoelasticity, graphic statics, pure and applied descriptive geometry; probabilities and mathematical statistics, Professor H. Breny; theory of mass, general algebra, mathematical methodology, mechanics, statistics, Professor L. Nollet; applied aerodynamics, Professor J. Smolderen; statistical methods and technical applications of probability calculus; applied statistics, Professor F. Monfort

Palaeontology Institute 817

Address: Place du 20 Août, B-4000 Liège
Sections: Palaeobotany and palaeopalynology, Professor M. Street; animal palaeontology, Professor G. Ubaghs

Physical Geography Institute 818

Address: Place du 20 Août 7, B-4000 Liège
Sections: Physical geography, Professor J. Alexandre; quaternary geomorphology and geology, Professor A. Pissart

Physics Institute 819

Address: Sart Tilman, B-4000 Liège
Sections: Physics methodology, Professor H. Sauvenier; physics of solids, Professor R. Evrard; experimental physics, Professor A. van de Vorst; general physics; theoretical nuclear physics, Professor J. Humblet; theoretical physics, Professor C. Mahaux; theoretical and mathematical physics; theoretical physics and solid-state physics, Professor J. Pirenne; structure of matter and molecular physics, Professor J. Duchesne; crystallography, Professor J. Toussaint

DIELECTRIC MATERIALS LABORATORY 820

Telephone: (041) 56 16 75
Research director: Professor K. Piotrowski
Activities: Electrical and dielectric properties of solid and liquid insulating materials submitted to high electrical strengths.

Zoology Institute 821

Address: Quai Van Beneden 22, B-4000 Liège
Sections: Marine biology, Professor J. Godeaux; marine ecology, Professor Ch. Jeuniaux; cellular biology, Professor H. Firket; general biology and animal biology, Professor J.C. Ruwet; general biology, Professor J. Godeaux; ethology and animal psychology, Professor J.C. Ruwet; functional morphology; morphology, systematics and animal ecology, Professor Ch. Jeuniaux; zoological museum and aquariums, Professor J.C. Ruwet; animal physiology, Professor R. Gilles

UNIVERSITY RESEARCH STATIONS 822

Station de Recherches Sons-Marines et 823 Océanographiques

– STARESCO
[Submarine and Oceanographic Research Station]
Address: BP 33, F-29260 Calvi, Corsica
Telephone: (95) 65 06 18
Head: Professor A. Distèche
Activities: Multidisciplinary approach to the sea, open to non-university and university researchers.

Station Scientifique des Hautes Fagnes 824

[Hautes Fagnes Scientific Station]
Address: Mont-Rigi, B-4898 Robertville
Telephone: (080) 44 61 82
Director: R. Schumacker
Activities: Multidisciplinary study of the environment, open to all those interested in natural history and related subjects.

VETERINARY MEDICINE FACULTY 825

Address: 45 Rue des Vétérinaires, B-1070 Bruxelles
Dean: Professor A. Lousse
Sections: Anatomy; bacteriology and the pathology of bacterial diseases, Professor A. Kaeckenbeeck; surgery and clinical pathology, Professor L. Lassoie; avian pathology and genetics, Professor R. Hanset; histology, parasitology and the pathology of parasites, Professor L. Pouplard; obstetrics, pathology of reproduction and medicine, Professor F. Ectors; general pathology, pathological anatomy and autopsies, Professor A.

Dewaele; medical and clinical pathology, Professor V. Bienfet; pharmacology, general therapeutics and toxicology; physiology and biochemistry, Professor A. Lousse; semiology and medicine of small animals; technology of food products of animal origin, Professor L. Fievez; virology and pathology of virus diseases; animal husbandry, Professor J.M. Bienfait

Université Libre de Bruxelles   826

[Free University of Brussels]
Address: Avenue Franklin Roosevelt 50, B-1050 Bruxelles
Telephone: (02) 6490030
Telex: 23069 unilib Brux

CENTRE SCIENTIFIQUE ET MÉDICALE   827
DE L'UNIVERSITé LIBRE DE
BRUXELLES EN AFRIQUE CENTRALE

– CEMUBAC
[Scientific and Medical Centre of the Free University of Brussels in Central Africa]
Address: 87 Avenue Adolphe Buyl, B-1050 Bruxelles
Chairman: Professor André Jaumotte
Secretary-General: Professor Pierre Feldheim
Activities: CEMUBAC is a non-profit establishment which aims to create centres of scientific research and education overseas.

FACULTY OF APPLIED SCIENCES   828

Address: Avenue Franklin D. Roosevelt 50, B-1050 Bruxelles
Dean: Professor Jean Nuyens

Aeronautics Institute   829

Director: Professor André Jaumotte

Chemistry Group   830

ANALYTICAL CHEMISTRY   831
DEPARTMENT
Director: Professor Claude Herbo
Senior staff: Paul Duvigneaud, Guy Schmitz

CHEMICAL ENGINEERING   832
DEPARTMENT
Director: Professor René Jottrand
Senior staff: Auguste Desmyter, Raymond Lhonneux, Guy Lhomme, Joseph Maréchal, Marcel Pahlavouni, Pierre Decroly, Luigi Forlano, Henri Masson

GENERAL CHEMISTRY AND   833
RADIOACTIVATION DEPARTMENT
Director: Professor René Cypres
Senior staff: Bernard Bettens, Colette Brackman-Danheux, Claude Delaunois

INDUSTRIAL CHEMISTRY AND   834
CHEMISTRY OF SOLIDS DEPARTMENT
Director: Professor René Cypres
Senior staff: Professor Émile Plumat, Professor Nemat Tenoutasse, Professor Meholi Ghodsi

ORGANIC CHEMISTRY DEPARTMENT   835
Director: Professor Jacques Reisse
Senior staff: Désiré Daloze, Robert Ottinger

PHYSICAL CHEMISTRY DEPARTMENT   836
Director: Professor Georges Thomaes
Senior staff: Jean-Claude Legros, Georges Petre

WATER TREATMENT AND POLLUTION   837
DEPARTMENT
Director: Professor Roland Wollast
Senior staff: Willy Masschelein

Civil Engineering Group   838

ARCHITECTURE DEPARTMENT   839
Director: Professor Pierre Guillissen
Senior staff: Professor José Vandevoorde

ARTERIAL ROADS DEPARTMENT   840
Senior staff: Professor Jean Vrebos, Professor Jacques Seyvert, Professor André Sterling, Professor Pierre Tielemans

CIVIL ENGINEERING DEPARTMENT   841
Senior staff: Professor André Homes, Professor André Winand, Professor Isidore Schiffman

SOIL MECHANICS DEPARTMENT   842
Director: Professor Jean Nuyens
Senior staff: Professor Albert Doyen, Professor Jean Reichert, Professor Victor Roisin, Professor Jean-Claude Verbrugge, Professor Roger Caignie

STRESS ANALYSIS DEPARTMENT   843
Director: Professor Jean Kestens
Senior staff: Professor Jean Ebbeni, Professor Pierre Halleux, Jacques Hougardy

TOWN PLANNING DEPARTMENT 844

Director: Professor Victor Martiny
Senior staff: Professor Jean Annaert, Professor Guy Ars, Professor Jean-Pierre Blondel, Professor Nicole Delruelle-Vosswinkel, Professor Robert Devleeshonwer, Professor Jean-Michel Favresse, Professor Marc Hustin, Professor Philippa Vanden Borre

Civil Engineering Institute 845

Director: Professor André Paduart

Electricity Group 846

AUTOMATION DEPARTMENT 847

Directors: Professor Richard Peretz
Senior staff: Professor Jean Charles, Professor Albert Foureau, Professor Paul Van der Grinten, Professor Paul Willems, Professor José Boland, Professor Claude Hubaut

ELECTRICAL ENGINEERING 848
DEPARTMENT

Director: Professor Robert Poncelet

ELECTROTECHNOLOGY DEPARTMENT 849

Director: Professor Robert Van den Damme

GENERAL ELECTRICITY DEPARTMENT 850

Director: Professor Oscar Beaufays
Senior staff: Professor Lida Rybowski-Lifschitz, Professor Robert Vanhauwermeiren, Marcel Dierickx, Serge Prohoroff

GENERAL ELECTRONICS AND RADIO- 851
ELECTRICITY DEPARTMENT

Director: Professor Paul Hontoy
Senior staff: Professor Christian Jauquet, Professor Jean Voge, Professor Yves Place, Professor Richard Grainson, Professor André Dumont, Professor André Herrent

INDUSTRIAL ELECTRONICS 852
DEPARTMENT

Director: Professor Jean-Louis Van Eck
Senior staff: Professor Gaston Maggetto

LOGICAL AND NUMERICAL SYSTEMS 853
DEPARTMENT

Director: Professor Jean Florine

Industrial Chemistry Institute 854

Management Committee: Professor Jacques Solvay, Professor René Mormont, Professor André Jaumotte, Professor René Jottrand

Industrial Management Group 855

INDUSTRIAL ACCOUNTANCY 856
DEPARTMENT

Director: Professor Simon Golstein

MANAGEMENT MATHEMATICS 857
DEPARTMENT

Director: Jean-Pierre Brans
Senior staff: Jean-Paul Grossart, Bernard Morelle, Christian Van Dorpe

SOCIAL AND POLITICAL ECONOMY 858
DEPARTMENT

Director: Professor Henri Vander Eycken
Senior staff: Jean-Michel Perrouty

Mathematics and Theoretical 859
Mechanics Group

ALGEBRA AND ANALYSIS 860
DEPARTMENT

Director: Professor Henri Bastin
Senior staff: Professor Monique Delchambre, Daniel Baye, Marcel Strasberg

ANALYTICAL MECHANICS 861
DEPARTMENT

Director: Professor Paul Janssens
Senior staff: Roland Sergysels

APPLIED MATHEMATICS 862
DEPARTMENT

Director: Professor Oscar Beaufays
Senior staff: Professor Michel Theys, Professor Alain Pirotte, Professor Philippe Janson

GEOMETRY DEPARTMENT 863

Director: Professor Roland De Groote

Mechanical Engineering Group 864

AERONAUTICS DEPARTMENT 865

Director: Professor André Jaumotte
Senior staff: Jean Ginoux, Professor Andrzej Kiedrzynski

APPLIED MECHANICS DEPARTMENT 866

Director: Professor André Jaumotte
Senior staff: Professor Marcel Barrère, Professor Jacques Bougard, Professor Daniel Deroux, Professor Andrzej Kiedrzynski, Professor Pierre Decak, Professor Jean-Louis Guiette

MACHINE DYNAMICS DEPARTMENT 867
Director: Professor Robert Jonckheere

Metallurgy and Materials Group 868

MATERIALS TESTING DEPARTMENT 869
Director: Professor Jean Kestens

METALLURGY AND 870
ELECTROCHEMISTRY DEPARTMENT
Director: Professor René Winand
Senior staff: Professor André Fontana

METALLURGY DEPARTMENT 871
Director: Professor Jacques Charlier
Senior staff: Professor Jean Lemoine, Jacqueline Hennaut-Diltour, Jacqueline Othmezouri-Decerf

PHYSICS OF SYNTHETIC MATERIALS 872
DEPARTMENT
Director: Professor Jean-Claude Bauwens
Senior staff: Colette Bauwens-Crowet, Jacqueline Othmezouri-Decerf

Mines, Geology and Topography 873
Group

EXPLOITATION OF MINES AND 874
MINERAL PREPARATION
DEPARTMENT
Director: Professor Georges Panou
Senior staff: Professor René Tille, Professor José Nicaise, René Derie

GEOLOGY AND APPLIED GEOLOGY 875
DEPARTMENT
Director: Professor Jacques Parent
Senior staff: Louis Doyen

TOPOGRAPHY AND 876
PHOTOGRAMMETRY DEPARTMENT
Director: Professor Robert Thonnard

Physics Group 877

ELECTRONIC PHYSICS DEPARTMENT 878
Director: Professor Georges Sylin

GENERAL PHYSICS DEPARTMENT 879
Director: Professor Robert Vanhauwermeiren
Senior staff: Nicole Verheulpen-Heymans, André Ponslet

NUCLEAR METROLOGY DEPARTMENT 880
Director: Professor Jacques Devooght
Senior staff: Stéphane Lejeune, Robert Beauwens, Pierre Govaerts, René Constant, Pierre Germain, Yves Goldschmidt, Pierre Marien, Jacques Planquart, Pierre Recht

NUCLEAR PHYSICS DEPARTMENT A 881
Director: Professor Marcel Demeur
Senior staff: Daniel Baye

NUCLEAR PHYSICS DEPARTMENT B 882
Senior staff: Robert Vanhauwermeiren

SEMICONDUCTORS DEPARTMENT 883
Director: Professor Bruno Batz

Telecommunications and Electronics 884
Institute
Director: Professor Paul Hontoy

Town Planning Institute 885
Director: Professor Victor Martiny

FACULTY OF MEDICINE AND 886
PHARMACY
Address: Rue Evers 2, B-1000 Bruxelles
Dean: Professor Jean-Lambert Pasteels

Building A 887
Address: 115 Boulevard de Waterloo, B-1000 Bruxelles

EXPERIMENTAL MEDICINE 888
LABORATORY
Director: Professor Willy Malaisse
Senior staff: Professor André Ermans, Professor Jacques Dumont

MICROBIOLOGY AND IMMUNOLOGY 889
LABORATORY
Director: Professor Lise Thiry
Sections: Bacteriology, Dr Jean-Pierre Gratia, Dr Bernard Vray; virology (Joseph Lemaire Laboratory), Dr Lise Thiry

PATHOLOGICAL CHEMISTRY 890
LABORATORY
Coordinator-Director: Professor Guy Graff
Senior staff: Christiane Gueuning, Raymond Lecocq

PHARMACODYNAMICS AND 891
THERAPEUTICS LABORATORY
Director: Professor Jean Reuse
Senior staff: André Herchuelz

PHYSIOLOGICAL CHEMISTRY 892
LABORATORY
Director: Professor Jean Christophe
Senior staff: Professor Jacques Winand

PHYSIOLOGY AND 893
PHYSIOPATHOLOGY LABORATORY
Coordinator: Professor Jean-Édouard Desmedt

Cardio-pulmonary Physiology Department 894
Director: Professor Henri Denolin
Senior staff: Serge Degré

General Physiology Department 895
Director: Professor Marcel Segers
Senior staff: Michel Kahn, Fernand Colin

Physiology and Physiopathology of the 896
Nervous System Department

　Brain Research Unit 897
　Director: Professor Jean-Édouard Desmedt
　Senior staff: Professor Karl Hainaut

　Metabolism Research Unit 898
　Director: Professor Victor Conard
　Senior staff: Eugenio Rasio, Étienne Brachet, Franz
　Legros

PHYSIOLOGY INSTITUTE 899
Director: Professor Pierre Rijlant

Building B 900

Address: 97 Rue aux Laines, B-1000 Bruxelles

ANATOMY AND HUMAN 901
EMBRYOLOGY LABORATORY
Director: Professor Jacques Mulnard
Senior staff: Professor Jacques Flamand

ELECTRON MICROSCOPY 902
LABORATORY
Director: Professor Pierre Dustin
Senior staff: Professor Jacqueline Flament-Durand,
Professor John-Olivier Perier

HISTOLOGY LABORATORY 903
Director: Professor Jean-Lambert Pasteels
Senior staff: Professor Jean Desclin

MEDICAL GENETICS LABORATORY 904
Senior staff: Hélène Lemaître-Galpérin

NEUROANATOMY LABORATORY 905
Director: Professor Jean-Olivier Perier

PATHOLOGICAL ANATOMY 906
LABORATORY
Director: Professor Pierre Dustin
Senior staff: Professor Raoul Parmentier

PRACTICAL WORK IN DENTAL 907
SCIENCE LABORATORY
Director: Professor Léon Charon

STOMATOLOGY RESEARCH 908
LABORATORY
Director: Professor Michel Pourtois

Building C 909

Address: 7 Rue Héger-Bordet, B-1000 Bruxelles

FORENSIC MEDICINE LABORATORY 910
Directors: Claudine Coopmans-Lambert, Professor
Raoul Parmentier

Forensic Medicine Unit 911
Director: Claudine Lambert

Thanatological Forensic Medicine Unit 912
Director: Professor Raoul Parmentier

SCIENTIFIC COMPUTATION 913
DEPARTMENT

Centre de Traumatologie et de 914
Réadaptation

[Traumatology and Rehabilitation Centre]
Address: Hôpital Universitaire Brugmann, Place Van
Gehuchten 4, B-1020 Bruxelles
Chairman: Professor André Jaumotte
Medical director: Dr Albert Tricot

ANAESTHESIOLOGY DEPARTMENT 915
Senior staff: Dr Marcelle Claereboudt, Colette Jenicot,
Marc-Henri Krior

NEUROLOGY DEPARTMENT 916
Senior staff: Dr Patrick Khoubesserian, Dr Paul
Dossin

PHYSIOTHERAPY DEPARTMENT 917
Head: Dr Josse Konings

SPINAL DEPARTMENT 918
Head: Dr André Heilporn

UROLOGY DEPARTMENT 919
Head: Dr E. Claereboudt

Hôpital Erasme 920
[Erasmus Hospital]
Medical director: Dr Alain de Wever
Managing director: Professor Stéphane Lejenne

ANAESTHESIOLOGY UNIT 921
Head: M. de Rood
Senior staff: M. Levarlet, J. Geens

ANATOMICAL PATHOLOGY LABORATORY 922
Head: A. Verhest
Senior staff: P. Ketelbant

BACTERIOLOGY LABORATORY 923
Head: E. Yourassowsky
Senior staff: E. Serruys-Schoutens

BIOLOGICAL CHEMISTRY LABORATORY 924
Head: H.-A. Ooms

DERMATOLOGY UNIT 925
Head: G. Achten
Senior staff: G. de Dobbeleer, M. Heenen

DIAGNOSIS BY ISOTOPES UNIT 926
Head: A. Schontens
Senior staff: M. Verhas

ENDOCRINOLOGY UNIT 927
Head: J. Mockel

HAEMATOLOGY LABORATORY 928
Heads: M. Wybran, M.P. Stryckmans

IMMUNOLOGY LABORATORY 929
Head: E. Dupont

INTENSIVE CARE UNIT 930
Head: R. Kahn
Senior staff: J.-P. Degaute

INTERNAL MEDICINE UNIT 931
Head: R. Bellens

MEDICAL CARDIOLOGY UNIT 932
Head: S. Degré
Senior staff: P. Vandermoten

MEDICAL GASTROENTEROLOGY UNIT 933
Head: M. Cremer

MEDICAL PNEUMONOLOGY UNIT 934
Head: J.-C. Yernault
Senior staff: A. de Troyer

NEONATAL UNIT 935
Heads: A. Pardou, D. Blum

NEONATOLOGY SECTION 936
Head: A. Pardou

NEPHROLOGY UNIT 937
Head: Ch. Toussaint
Sections: Renal transplants, P. Vereerstraeten; dialysis, J.-L. Vanherweghem; uraemic and transplant surgery, P. Kinnaert

NEUROLOGY UNIT 938
Head: J. Hildebrand
Senior staff: S. Borenstein

NURSING UNIT 939
Head: R. Askenasi

OBSTETRICS AND GYNAECOLOGY UNIT 940
Head: J. Schwers
Senior staff: F. Rodesch

OPHTHALMOLOGY UNIT 941
Head: A. Zanen

OTORHINOLARYNGOLOGY UNIT 942
Head: D. Hennebert
Senior staff: Y. Hanneuse

PSYCHIATRY UNIT 943
Head: J. Mendlewicz
Senior staff: P. Linkowski, C. Jadot

RADIOLOGY UNIT 944
Sections: General radiology, J. Struyven; alimentary radiology, L. Engelholm

REPARATIVE SURGERY UNIT 945
Head: Robert Ley

STOMATOLOGY UNIT 946
Head: R. Mayer
Senior staff: R. Rodembourg

SURGICAL GASTROENTEROLOGY UNIT 947
Head: J.P. Lambilliotte

THORACIC SURGERY UNIT 948
Head: P. Vanderhoeft
Senior staff: P. Rocmans

TRAUMATOLOGICAL AND ORTHOPAEDIC SURGERY UNIT 949
Head: P. Blaimont
Senior staff: F. Burny

UROLOGY UNIT 950
Head: C. Schulman

VASCULAR SURGERY UNIT 951
Head: J.-P. Dereume

Hôpital Universitaire Brugmann 952

[Brugmann University Hospital]
Address: Place Van Gehuchten 4, B-1020 Bruxelles

ANAESTHESIOLOGY DEPARTMENT 953
Head: Professor Jacqueline Primo-Dubois
Senior staff: Jacqueline Greens-Bastenier, Colette
Genicot, Alain d'Hollander, Mario Govaerts

CLINICAL BIOLOGY DEPARTMENT 954
Head: Professor Eugène Yourassowsky
Sections: Haematology, Henri Brauman; biochemis-
try, Jacqueline Brauman-Moreau de Melen

EXPERIMENTAL MEDICINE 955
LABORATORY
Director: Maurice Abramow
Senior staff: Francine Gregoire

GENERAL SURGERY DEPARTMENT 956
Head: Professor Jean Van Geertruyden
Sections: Bone surgery, Professor Robert de Marneffe;
cardiac surgery, Professor Georges Primo; vascular
surgery, Dr Robert Verost-Veroft; reparative surgery,
Dr Madeleine Lejour

GENERAL SURGERY RESEARCH 957
LABORATORY
Director: Professor Jean Van Geertruyden

GERIATRICS DEPARTMENT 958
Senior staff: Max Kunstler, Raymond Noel, Monique
Asiel

GYNAECOLOGICAL RESEARCH 959
LABORATORY
Director: Professor Roger Vokaer

INTERNAL MEDICINE DEPARTMENT 960
Director: Professor Jacques Corvilain
Sections: Neurology, Professor Christian Coërs;
haematology, Professor Jean-Pierre Naets; endocrinology, Dr Jacques Corvilain; cardiology, Dr Michel Teler-
man

MEDICAL PSYCHOLOGY LABORATORY 961
Director: Isidore Pelc
Assistant director: Serge Crahay

NEUROLOGICAL REHABILITATION 962
SERVICE
Head: Omer Demol
Senior staff: André Capon

OBSTETRICS AND GYNAECOLOGY 963
DEPARTMENT
Head: Professor Roger Vokaer
Sections: Diagnosis by ultrasound, Salvator Levi

PATHOLOGICAL ANATOMY 964
DEPARTMENT
Head: Professor Willy Gepts
Sections: Gynaecological pathological anatomy, Jean-
Pierre Cattoor

PSYCHIATRY DEPARTMENT 965
Head: Professor Jacques Flament
Senior staff: Serge Crahay, Pierre Van Reeth, René de
Buck

RADIOACTIVE ISOTOPES DIAGNOSIS 966
DEPARTMENT
Head: Professor André Schoutens
Senior staff: Michel Verhes, Pierre Bergmann

RADIOLOGY DEPARTMENT 967
Head: Professor Roland Potvliege
Senior staff: Nicole Dumont, Marc Rakofsky

Hôpital Universitaire Saint-Pierre 968

[St Pierre University Hospital]
Address: 322 Rue Haute, B-1000 Bruxelles

ADULT NURSING DEPARTMENT 969
Head: Professor Jacques Flamand

ANAESTHESIOLOGY DEPARTMENT 970
Head: Professor Paul Mundeleer
Senior staff: Jacqueline Besombe-Smets, Nadine
Jaspar-Sergysels

CARDIOLOGY RESEARCH 971
LABORATORY
Director: Professor Henri Denolin
Assistant director: Professor Marc Englert

GENERAL SURGERY DEPARTMENT 972
Head: Professor Antoine Bremer
Sections: Clinical research, Dr Jacques de Graef;
vascular surgery, Dr Maurice Goldstein

INFECTIOUS DISEASES UNIT   973
Telephone: (02) 25380614
Research director: Professor Jean-Paul Butzler
Graduate research staff: 6
Annual expenditure: £10 000-50 000
Activities: Infectious diseases; clinical microbiology; viral or bacterial intestinal infections; meningitis; venereal disease.

INTERNAL MEDICINE DEPARTMENT   974
Director: Professor Georges Copinschi
Sections: Cardiology, Professor Marc Englert; respiratory passages, Dr Armand de Coster; neurology, Professor Lucien Franken; endocrinology, Professor Georges Copinschi; gastroenterology, Dr René Platterborse

MEDICAL BIOLOGY DEPARTMENT   975
Director: Professor Jean-Paul Butzler
Sections: Medical chemistry, Professor J.-Marcel Franckson; microbiology, Professor Jean-Paul Butzler; haematology, Dr Pierre Fondu; immunology and blood transfusion; radioactive isotopes diagnosis, Professor André M. Ermans

OBSTETRICS AND GYNAECOLOGY   976
DEPARTMENT
Head: Professor Pierre-Olivier Hubinont
Sections: Sterility and infertility, Professor Pierre Rosa

PATHOLOGICAL ANATOMY   977
DEPARTMENT
Senior staff: Professor Raoul Parmentier, Professor Jacqueline Flament-Durand

PSYCHOSOMATIC MEDICINE   978
DEPARTMENT
Head: Professor Simone Duret-Cosyns

RADIOLOGY DEPARTMENT   979
Head: Professor André Bollaert
Sections: Paediatric radiology, Noémi Perlmutter

RHEUMATOLOGY AND PHYSICAL   980
MEDICINE DEPARTMENT
Head: Professor Jean-Pierre Famaey
Senior staff: Marie Vandermoten-Bauduin, Thierry Appelboom

Institut Bordet   981

[Bordet Institute]
Address: Rue Héger-Bordet 1, B-1000 Bruxelles
Scientific director: Professor Albert Claude

ANAESTHESIOLOGY DEPARTMENT   982
Head: Professor Henri Reinhold
Senior staff: Monique Mathieu-Hildebrand, Émile Mouawad

CLINICAL RESEARCH LABORATORY   983
Director: Jean-Claude Heuson
Senior staff: Guy Leclercq

EXPERIMENTAL NEUROSURGERY   984
LABORATORY
Director: Professor Jean Brihaye

GENERAL SURGERY DEPARTMENT   985
Head: Professor André Gerard
Sections: Cervical and facial cancer, Pierre Dor; reparative and reconstructive surgery, Madeleine Lejour

INTERNAL MEDICINE DEPARTMENT   986
Head: Professor Jean Klastersky
Senior staff: Jean-Claude Heuson, Pierre Stryckmans, Salomon Levin; anti-cancer chemotherapy, Yvon Kenis

NEUROSURGERY DEPARTMENT   987
Head: Professor Jean Brihaye
Senior staff: Jean Retif, Jacques Noterman

PATHOLOGICAL ANATOMY   988
DEPARTMENT
Head: Professor Claude Gompel
Senior staff: Rudolf Heimann

RADIO-RADIUM THERAPY   989
DEPARTMENT
Head: Professor Jacques Henry
Senior staff: Jacqueline Maréchal-Lustman

RADIOLOGY DEPARTMENT   990
Head: Professor Louis Jeanmart
Senior staff: Michel Osteaux, Danielle Waha-Baleriaux

Institute for Interdisciplinary Research 991
in Human and Nuclear Biology

Address: 20 Rue Evers, B-1000 Bruxelles
Activities: The Institute is under the joint control of Euratom, the Free University of Brussels, and the University of Pisa, Italy. It has permanent research units for research methodology; mathematical models, simulation, enzymology, cellular physiology, biology, metabolism, radio-immunology, and molecular biology.

BRUSSELS SECTION   992
Director: Professor Jacques Dumont
Assistant director: Claude Delcroix

Institute of Pharmacy 993

Address: Boulevard du Triomphe, B-1050 Bruxelles

ANALYTICAL CHEMISTRY, INORGANIC 994 PHARMACEUTICAL CHEMISTRY AND TOXICOLOGY LABORATORY
Director: Professor Léopold Molle
Senior staff: Professor Gaston Patriarche, Professor Michel Hanocq, Francine Lupant-André, Jean Vanden Balck

GALENIC PHARMACY AND 995 BIOPHARMACY LABORATORY
Director: Professor André Moës
Senior staff: Monique Hoton-Dorge

MEDICAL AND GENERAL 996 BIOCHEMISTRY LABORATORY
Director: Professor Claudine Fossoul
Senior staff: Yves Mardens

MICROBIOLOGY AND HYGIENE 997 LABORATORY
Director: Professor Jeanne Dong-Crotteux

ORGANIC PHARMACEUTICAL 998

CHEMISTRY AND BROMATOLOGY LABORATORY
Director: Professor Gaston Lagrange
Senior staff: Professor Colette Dorlet, Jacques Hoyois, Michel Gelbcke

PHARMACODYNAMICS AND 999 THERAPEUTICS LABORATORY
Director: Professor Jean Reuse
Senior staff: Jeannine Famaey-Fontaine

PHARMACOGNOSY LABORATORY 1000
Director: Professor Maurice Van Haelen
Senior staff: Renée Van Haelen-Fastre

PRACTICAL ANIMAL AND PLANT 1001 BIOLOGY
Director: Professor Paulette Van Gansen
Senior staff: Monique Boloukhere-Presburg

PRACTICAL BOTANY IN PREPARATION 1002 FOR PHARMACOGNOSY
Address: Jardins J. Massart, chaussée de Wavre 1850, Auderghem
Director: Professor Paul Duvigneaud
Senior staff: Simone Denaeyer-de Smet

PRACTICAL HUMAN ANATOMY AND 1003 PHYSIOLOGY
Director: Professor Marcel Segers

PRACTICAL PHYSICAL CHEMISTRY 1004 APPLIED TO PHARMACEUTICAL SCIENCE
Director: Professor Léopold Molle
Senior staff: Marc Van Damme

PRACTICAL PSYCHOLOGY 1005
Director: Professor Francine Robaye-Geelen

St Pierre and Brugmann University 1006 Hospitals Departments

CHILDREN'S MEDICINE DEPARTMENT 1007
Address: Rue Haute 322, B-1000 Bruxelles
Director: Professor Helmuth Loeb
Senior staff: Professor André Dachy, Professor Henri Vis; psychiatric medicine, Professor Nicole Dopchie; paediatric endocrinology, Dr Renée Wolter

Medico-psychological Centre 1008
Director: Professor Helmuth Loeb

CHILDREN'S SURGERY DEPARTMENT 1009
Address: Place Van Gehuchten 4, B-1020 Bruxelles
Head: Professor François Moyson
Senior staff: Frédéric Llittek; Madeleine Lejour

DERMATOLOGY AND VENEREOLOGY 1010 DEPARTMENT
Address: Rue Haute 322, B-1000 Bruxelles
Head: Professor Georges Achten
Senior staff: Marguerite Corbusier-Ledoux, Micheline Song-Denis

OPHTHALMOLOGY DEPARTMENT 1011
Head: Professor Pierre Danis
Senior staff: Daniel Toussaint

OTORHINOLARYNGOLOGY 1012 DEPARTMENT
Head: Professor Denis Hennebert
Senior staff: Michel Gerard

STOMATOLOGY DEPARTMENT 1013
Director: Professor Raymond Mayer
Senior staff: Professor Michel Pourtois, Jack Van Reck

UROLOGY DEPARTMENT 1014
Head: Dr Willy Gregoir
Senior staff: Michel Vandendris

School of Public Health   1015

Address: Campus Erasme, Route de Lennik 808, B-1070 Bruxelles
Telephone: (02) 568 31 11
Telex: 62546 Erasme B
Chairman: Professor André Heuse

ENVIRONMENTAL MICROBIOLOGY   1016
LABORATORY
Director: Professor Jacques Beumer
Senior staff: André Delmotte

EPIDEMIOLOGY AND SOCIAL   1017
MEDICINE LABORATORY
Director: Professor Ernst-Alfred Sand
Senior staff: Monique Asiel, Claude-Hector Thilly

MEDICAL STATISTICS LABORATORY   1018
Director: Professor Philippe Smets
Senior staff: Maurice Staquet

OCCUPATIONAL MEDICINE AND   1019
ENVIRONMENTAL HEALTH
LABORATORY
Senior staff: Professor André Heuse

University Laboratory of Cytology and 1020
Experimental Cancerology

Senior staff: Denise Bernaert

FACULTY OF SCIENCES   1021

Address: Avenue Franklin D. Roosevelt 50, B-1050 Bruxelles
Dean: Professor Georges Verhaegen

Astronomy and Astrophysics Institute 1022

Director: Professor Raymond Contrez

Botany   1023

President: Simone de Smet-Deraeyer

GENETICS OF HIGHER PLANT LIFE   1024
LABORATORY
Director: Professor Paul Duvigneaud
Senior staff: Claude Lefèbvre

PLANT MORPHOLOGY LABORATORY   1025
Director: Professor Jacques Homès
Senior staff: Van Huynh Long

PLANT PHYSIOLOGY LABORATORY   1026
Director: Professor Germaine Van Schoor-Homès
Senior staff: Professor Jacques Ansiaux, Professor Philippe Bourdeau, Professor Robert Lannoye, Thérèse Oedenkoven-Vandendriessche, Jacques Wouters

SYSTEMATIC BOTANY AND ECOLOGY 1027
LABORATORY
Director: Professor Paul Duvigneaud
Senior staff: André Galoux, Professor Jean Leonard

Centre Paul Brien   1028

Co-directors: Professor Jean Bouillon, Jean-Jacques Van Mol
Activities: Multidisciplinary research on environmental problems.

Chemistry   1029

President: Professor Émile Vander Donckt

GENERAL CHEMISTRY LABORATORY I 1030
Director: Professor José Leonis

GENERAL CHEMISTRY LABORATORY   1031
II
Directors: Professor Georges Geuskens, Professor Henri Hurwitz

INDUSTRIAL CHEMISTRY   1032
LABORATORY

MINERAL AND ANALYTICAL   1033
CHEMISTRY LABORATORY
Directors: Professor Lucien Gierst, Professor André Watillon, Professor Florent Bouillon
Senior staff: Professor Marcelle Offergeld-Jardinier

MOLECULAR PHYSICAL CHEMISTRY   1034
LABORATORY
Directors: Professor Réginald Colin, Professor Georges Verhaegen
Senior staff: Professor Charles Joachain

ORGANIC AND PHYSICAL ORGANIC   1035
CHEMISTRY LABORATORY
Director: Professor Jacques Nasielski
Senior staff: Professor Émile Vander Donckt, Professor Jacques Pecher, Professor Hubert Figeys

THERMODYNAMIC PHYSICAL   1036
CHEMISTRY LABORATORY
Director: Professor Ilya Progogine
Senior staff: Professor Françoise Henin-Jeener, Professor Victor Mathot, Professor Albert Sanfeld

Geography   1037
President: Professor Henri Nicolai

GEOMORPHOLOGY LABORATORY   1038
Director: Professor Roland Souchez
Senior staff: Michèle Lemmens-Souchez, Reginald Lorrain

HUMAN GEOGRAPHY LABORATORY   1039
Directors: Professor Henri Nicolai, Professor Robert André, Professor Jean Annaert
Senior staff: Christian Vandermotten

Geology   1040
President: Professor Edgard Picciotto

GEOCHEMISTRY LABORATORY   1041
Director: Professor Jacques Jedwab

**MINERALOGY AND PETROLOGY   1042
LABORATORY**
Directors: Professor Jean Michot, Professor Paul Dumont, Professor Alain Herbosch, Professor Roger Monteyne

**NUCLEAR GEOLOGY AND   1043
GEOCHEMISTRY LABORATORIES**
Director: Professor Edgard Picciotto

Mathematics   1044
President: Professor Guy Louchard

ACTUARIAL SCIENCES SEMINAR   1045
Directors: Professor Paul Gillis, Professor Jean Teghem

ALGEBRA SEMINAR   1046
Director: Professor Georges Papy
Senior staff: Professor Jean Drabbe, Anne-Marie Simon-Esser

ANALYTICAL MECHANICS SEMINAR   1047
Directors: Professor Robert Debever, Professor Raymond Coutrez, Professor Michel Cahen, Professor Georges Mayné
Senior staff: Alfred Quinet, Jules Leroy

ASTRONOMY SEMINAR   1048
Director: Professor Raymond Coutrez
Senior staff: André Koeckelenbergh

DIFFERENTIAL GEOMETRY SEMINAR   1049
Directors: Professor Michel Cahen, Professor Robert Debever
Senior staff: Monique Parker, Luc Lemaire

GENERAL MATHEMATICS SECTION   1050
Directors: Professor Michel Cahen, Professor André Gribaumont, Professor Roland De Groote

GEOMETRY SEMINAR   1051
Directors: Professor Francis Buekenhout, Professor Jean Doyen, Professor Xavier Hubaut

MATHEMATICAL ANALYSIS SEMINAR   1052
Directors: Professor Paul Gillis, Professor Lucien Waelbroeck

MATHEMATICAL STATISTICS SEMINAR 1053
Directors: Professor Paul Gillis, Professor Simone Huyberechts

PHYSICAL MATHEMATICS SEMINAR   1054
Director: Professor Robert Debever

**THEORETICAL COMPUTER SCIENCE   1055
LABORATORY**
Directors: Professor Guy Louchard, Professor André Gribaumont, Professor Claude Machgeels
Senior staff: Raymond Devillers

THEORY OF PROBABILITIES SEMINAR 1056
Director: Professor Jean Teghem
Senior staff: Robert Debry

Oceanography Laboratory   1057
Director: Professor Roland Wollast

Physics   1058
President: Professor Jean Jeener

ASTROPHYSICS DEPARTMENT   1059
Director: Professor Raymond Coutrez
Senior staff: André Koeckelenbergh

**CRYSTALLOGRAPHY DEPARTMENT   1060
AND LABORATORY**
Senior staff: Daniel Bariaux

**ELEMENTARY PARTICLE PHYSICS   1061
DEPARTMENT**
Senior staff: Professor Jean Reignier

**EXPERIMENTAL ELEMENTARY   1062
PARTICLE PHYSICS SECTION**
Director: Professor Jean Sacton

**FUNDAMENTAL INTERACTIONS   1063
DEPARTMENT**
Directors: Professor François Englert, Professor Robert Brout

GENERAL PHYSICS DEPARTMENT I   1064
Directors: Professor André Bellemans, Professor Jean De Prins, Professor François Englert, Professor Jean Jeener, Professor Marcel Lambert
Senior staff: Professor Robert Brout, Professor Grégoire Nicolis, Harry Stern

GENERAL PHYSICS DEPARTMENT II   1065
Directors: Professor Jean Jeener, Professor Robert Deltour, Professor Jean Florine, Professor Albert Art
Senior staff: Marie-Louise Lemmens

**LOW-TEMPERATURE PHYSICS   1066
DEPARTMENT**
Director: Professor Ilya Prigogine
Senior staff: Alkis Grecos, Fernand Mayné

**MACROSCOPIC PHYSICS   1067
DEPARTMENT**
Director: Professor Ilya Prigogine
Senior staff: Professor Radu Balescu

**STATISTICAL PHYSICS AND PLASMAS   1068
DEPARTMENT**
Director: Professor Ilya Prigogine
Senior staff: Professor André Bellemans, Professor Radu Balescu

**THEORETICAL AND MATHEMATICAL   1069
PHYSICS DEPARTMENT**
Directors: Professor Ilya Prigogine, Professor Marcel Demeur
Senior staff: Professor Radu Balescu, Professor Claude George

**THEORETICAL ATOMIC PHYSICS   1070
DEPARTMENT**
Director: Professor Charles Joachain
Senior staff: Professor Réginald Colin, Professor Georges Verhaegen

**THEORETICAL BIOPHYSICS   1071
DEPARTMENT**
Directors: Professor Ilya Prigogine, Professor Grégoire Nicolis

**THEORETICAL NUCLEAR PHYSICS   1072
DEPARTMENT**
Director: Professor Marcel Demeur

Zoology   1073

ANIMAL BIOLOGY DEPARTMENT   1074
President: Professor Jacques Pasteels

**Animal Biology and Comparative Histology   1075
Laboratory**
Senior staff: Jacqueline Naisse

Animal Parasitology Laboratory   1076
Senior staff: Jacqueline Coremans-Pelseneer

**Anthropology Laboratory-Anthropology   1077
Museum**
Senior staff: Rossine Orban-Segebarth

Cellular and Animal Biology Laboratory   1078
Coordinator: Professor Raymond Rasmont
Directors: Professor Raymond Rasmont, Professor Gysèle Van de Vijver, Professor Jacques Pasteels, Professor Jean Deligne

**Systematic Zoology and Zoo-ecology   1079
Laboratory**
Directors: Professor Jean-Jacques Van Mol, Professor Guy Josens

Zoology Laboratory   1080
Director: Professor Jean Bouillon
Senior staff: Professor Bernard Tursch, Guy Houvenaghel, Michel Jangoux

MOLECULAR BIOLOGY DEPARTMENT   1081
Address: Rue des Chevaux 67, B-1640 Rhode-Saint-Genèse
President: Professor Maurice Steinert

Animal Physiology Laboratory   1082
Director: Professor Jacques Urbain
Senior staff: Professor Marcelle Grenson, Georgette Vansanten-Urbain, Maurice Wikler

Biochemistry Laboratory   1083
Director: Professor Hubert Chantrenne
Senior staff: Professor André Sels, Henri Grosjean

Biophysics and Radiobiology Laboratory   1084
Director: Professor Maurice Errera
Senior staff: Miroslav Radman, Maximilienne Brunfaut

Cellular Biology Laboratory   1085
Director: Professor Raphaël Kram
Senior staff: Renée Tencer, Françoise Hanocq

Genetics Laboratory   1086
Director: Professor René Thomas
Senior staff: Albert Herzog, Christine Dambly-Chandière

Microbiology Laboratory   1087
Director: Professor Jean Wiame
Senior staff: Professor André Piérard, Robert Lavalle

**Molecular Cytology and Embryology   1088
Laboratory**
Directors: Professor Adrienne Ficq, Professor Maurice Steinert, Professor Paulette Van Gansen

Neurophysiology Laboratory 1089
Director: Professor Jean Cerf
Senior staff: Guy Carels

S.V. Veredelingsstation van 1090 Heverlee

[Plant Breeding Institute of Heverlee]
Address: 6 de Croylaan, B-3030 Leuven-Heverlee
Telephone: (016) 20 18 20
Affiliation: Belgian Farmers Association
Director: Ir J. Niclaes
Annual expenditure: BF10m
Activities: Breeding of cereals (wheat, rye, oats, barley).
Contract work: No
Publications: Annual report

Vrije Universiteit Brussel 1091

[Free University of Brussels]
Address: Pleinlaan 2, B-1050 Brussel
Telephone: (02) 648 55 40
Telex: 61051 VUBCO B
Vice-Chancellor: B. De Schutter

FACULTY OF APPLIED SCIENCES 1092

Dean: O. Steenhaut

Analytical Chemistry 1093

Head: Professor I. Elskens

Analytical Mechanics 1094

Head: Professor P. Janssens

Applied Continuum Mechanics and 1095 Physics

Head: Professor R. Van Geen
Activities: Numerical and experimental solution of the field equations of mechanics and electro-magnetism, including many applications, from civil engineering to medical emission and transmission tomography.

Chemical Engineering Techniques and 1096 Industrial Chemistry

Head: Professor S. Wajc
Senior staff: Professor A. Buekens
Activities: New type of catalyst for the post-combustion of gases and vapours; thermal methods of waste disposal: incineration, gasification and pyrolysis; assessment of various research projects in the United States of America, Japan and West Europe; patent study on grate designs in refuse incineration and fluidized bed incineration of sludge; market study of packaged refuse-fired boilers; incineration of hospital wastes; fundamental and applied studies on the gasification and pyrolysis of various plastic, rubber and agricultural wastes; recycling of wastes, such as plastics, rubber, lubricating and machining oils.

Electrical Engineering 1097

Head: Professor G. Maggetto
Activities: Electrical machines: new machine structures for application on variable speed drives; calculation method for induction machines fed by voltage or current inverters; power electronics: digital simulation of force commutated inverter; application of microprocessors to the control of inverters; choppers and inverters with power transistors; industrial applications: continuous anodizing system for aluminium coils associated with a colouring system; development of battery loaders based on the use of power transistors; electrical drives based on current-fed asynchronous machines for traction purposes.

Electronics and Computer Science 1098

Head: Professor O. Steenhaut
Activities: Biomedical signal processing: general health cardiograph; general health thermograph; electroencephalogram analysis; multiprocessor structures; microelectronics.

Fluid Mechanics 1099

Head: Processor C. Hirsch
Activities: International aerodynamics of turbines and compressors: computational fluid dynamics; experimental determination of three-dimensional flow structure; turbulence; wind effects on buildings - industrial aerodynamics; energy: solar and wind; energy conservation in industry.

Foundation Mechanics 1100

Head: Professor J. Nuyens

General and Organic Chemistry 1101

Head: Professor M. Gielen

General Electricity 1102

Head: Professor J. Renneboog
Activities: Fault localization on cables using digital techniques; electrical modelling of an electrochemical reaction; active antenna and optical fibres.

General Physics 1103

Head: Professor Ph. Ronsmans

Hydrology 1104

Head: Professor A. Van Der Beken

Materials Science 1105

Head: Professor J. Charlier

Mathematical Analysis 1106

Head: Professor L. Van Hamme

Mechanics 1107

Head: Professor R. Jonckheere

Mechanics and Acoustics 1108

Head: Professor R. Jonckheere

Metallurgy and Electrochemistry 1109

Head: Professor J. Vereecken
Activities: Surface treatments and methods of surface analysis; ecological modelling; including determination of the concentration of heavy metals in river water; extractive metallurgy: recovery of non-ferrous metals; bioelectrochemistry and biomedical engineering: inorganic and organic membranes; corrosion of biomaterials.

Physical Chemistry 1110

Head: Professor G. Huybrechts
Activities: Chemical kinetics: kinetics and stereochemistry of Diels-Alder reactions in the gas phase.

Vibration Mechanics and Sound Wave 1111 Transmission

Head: Professor R. Jonckheere

FACULTY OF MEDICINE AND 1112 PHARMACY

Dean: Professor Dr R. Vanden Driessche

Anaesthesiological Research 1113

Head: Professor F. Camu
Activities: Pharmacological, experimental and clinical evaluation of hypnotic, sedative and analgesic drugs for use in anaesthesia and intensive care; neurophysiological, cardiovascular and respiratory monitoring techniques and their application to anaesthesia and intensive care; measurement techniques in respiration physiology: application to evaluation of new ventilators.

Analytical Chemistry and Bromatology 1114

Head: Professor D. Massart

Biochemical Pathology 1115

Head: Professor A.D. Strosberg
Activities: Immunochemical studies; endocrinological studies; plant biochemistry. All these studies aim at a better understanding of molecular recognition mechanisms at the surface of the living cell.

Cell Biology and Histology 1116

Head: Professor E. Wisse
Activities: Structure and function of sinusoidal cells in the liver and their interaction with parenchymal cells using microscopical and biochemical techniques.

Children's Surgery 1117

Head: P. Deconinck

Clinical Microbiology and Ecology 1118

Head: Dr J.P. Butzler

Conservative Dentistry 1119

Head: P. Boute

Dental Prosthesis and Materials 1120 Research

Head: Professor W. Verlinden

Dentistry 1121

Head: W. Verlinden

Electron Microscopy 1122

Head: Professor E. Wisse

Epidemiology and Social Medicine 1123

Head: Professor R. Linz

Experimental Pathology and Pathological Anatomy 1124

Head: Professor W. Gepts

Experimental Surgery 1125

Head: Professor R. Keikens

Galenic and Magistral Pharmacy, Medical and Specific Biochemistry 1126

Head: Professor R. De Neve
Activities: Release of therapeutically active substances out of the dosage form, especially those dosage forms that provide the release over a longer period, and the parameters influencing adsorption of active principles onto macromolecules; lectins and the possible relationship between lectins and toxins.

Gastroenterological Research 1127

Head: G. Willems
Activities: Histophysiology and histopathology of gastrointestinal mucosa: mucin histochemistry of gastric mucosa; cell population kinetics in the stomach in man and in experimental animals; gall bladder; colon; experimental surgery on gastrointestinal tract, pancreas, bile ducts and liver in dogs.

Heart and Vascular Research 1128

Head: Professor F. Kornreich

Human Ecology 1129

Head: Professor Ch. Susanne

Human Physiology 1130

Head: S. Bekaert

Hygiene, Environmental Hygiene and Occupational Physiopathology 1131

Head: Professor S. Halter

Interdisciplinary Unit for Clinical Research 1132

Head: D. Pipeleers

Internal Medicine 1133

Head: R. Six

Medical Microbiology 1134

Head: Professor F. De Meuter

Medical Psychology 1135

Head: Professor A.W. Szafran

Medical Psychopathology 1136

Head: Professor S. Crahay

Metabolism 1137

Head: Professor D. Pipeleers
Activities: Intra-cellular analysis of the endocrine pancreas in health and disease, with particular reference to diabetes mellitus, obesity and certain gastrointestinal disorders; motility evaluation of human spermatozoa and its application in contraception and fertility.

Microbiology and Hygiene 1138

Head: Professor A. Boeye
Activities: Polio virus capsid polypeptides; relations between the spore antigens of different species of bacteria (genus Bacillus).

Neuro- and Psychophysiology 1139

Head: P. Visser

Obstetrics and Andrology 1140

Head: Professor R. Schoysman

Oncological Centre 1141

Head: Professor M. Van Rymenant
Senior staff: Dr J.L. Bernheim, Dr N. Naaktgeboren
Activities: Cell kinetics of in vitro immune response; relative contribution of endogenous and exogenous pathways to the thymidine triphosphate pool of lymphocytes and tumour cells.

Ophthalmology 1142

Head: Professor M. Van Geertruyden Brihaye

Otorhinolaryngology   1143

Head: P. Clement
Senior staff: Dr Decreton, Dr Bogaerts, Dr Clement, Dr Brondeel
Activities: Rhinology: scanning electronic microscopical aspect of the normal human nasal mucous membrane; cytology of nasal smears; rhinomanometrical apparatus for performing nose provocation tests in allergic diagnosis; fundamental research concerning the ventilation of the nose by passive anterior rhinomanometry and active anterior rhinomanometry; audiometry: brainstem evoked response audiometry, especially the assessment of the hearing threshold in children; vestibular studies: effect of otolith stimulation in rabbits; comparison of computer-assisted tomography scan findings and coronary sections of the human skull.

Paediatric Research   1144

Head: Professor H. Loeb
Senior staff: Dr A. Piepsz, Dr J. Otten, Dr I. Dab, Dr I. Liebaers
Activities: Radionuclides in paediatrics: renal, lung, gastrointestinal and heart studies; clinical applications of cell culture; relationship between lung function and atmospheric pressure; lysosomal storage diseases.

Pharmaceutical Chemistry and Drug   1145
Analysis

Head: Professor L. Dryon

Pharmacognosy, Phytochemistry and   1146
Toxicology

Head: Professor A. Vercruysse
Activities: Clinical biochemical determination (biochemical parameters in human diseases); clinical toxicological determinations (acute and chronic intoxications); drug abuse; plasma drug concentrations as therapeutic guides; quantitative and qualitative determination of toxics in biological material.

Pharmacology   1147

Head: Professor Dr R. Vanden Driessche

Physiology and Physiopathology   1148

Head: R. Bourgain
Activities: Arterial thrombosis: evaluation of antithrombotic drugs; atherogenesis; correlation of cortical somesthetic evoked potentials and anoxia and hypoxia; autoregulation in the brain; protective effect of a wide variety of drugs on neural function during either anoxia or hypoxia.

Physiopathology of the Nervous   1149
System

Head: Professor A. Lowenthal
Activities: Biochemical problems in neurological diseases: chemistry of humoral immunological reactions in cerebrospinal fluid, serum and brain tissues of patients with neurological diseases and mainly in multiple sclerosis and subacute sclerosing panencephalitis; determinations of trace metals in neurological material, mainly in the brain, together with studies on the topographical distribution of these metals; catecholamines; aphasia.

Radioimmunology   1150

Radiology   1151

Head: Professor P. Beeckman
Activities: The comparison of different imaging techniques in selected clinical situations; clinical evaluation of the respective value of nuclear medicine, ultrasound, conventional radiography, angiography and computerized axial tomography; basic research in the field of regional lung behaviour on the basis of conventional radiographs, transmission densitometry, nuclear medicine and computer-assisted tomography. Special attention is drawn to the standardization of technique and calculation of regional lung volumes, flow and lung expansion. In the field of breast diseases, factors enhancing mammography are studied.

Rheumatology   1152

Head: Professor S. Orloff

Stomatology and Dentistry   1153

Head: Professor R. Werelds

Stomatology and Maxillo-facial   1154
Surgery

Head: Professor R. Mayer

Surgical Clinic   1155

Head: Professor M. Van Der Ghinst

Urology   1156

Head: L. Denis
Activities: Basic research on cell functions and cell
cultures is performed with the support of the gastroenterology and cancer units. The clinical research is directed towards better patient care, better service to the
community and ways to provide this at less cost and with
less effort from the patient. Improved patient care relies
greatly on the advanced use of transrectal ultrasound to
provide exact diagnosis and staging of neoplastic diseases of the lower urinary tract by a noninvasive technique. Other advances in patient care are related to
multidisciplinary efforts in evaluating cancer
chemotherapy and evaluating infectious diseases in urology. In addition, cooperation with Antwerp 200 provides material for a long-term study of comparative
anatomy of the lower urinary tract in mammals.

FACULTY OF SCIENCES   1157

Dean: L. Neirinckx

Biology Department   1158

Chairman: Professor C. Susanne

ANATOMY   1159
Head: F. Roels
Activities: Cytological projects: cytochemical,
biochemical and electron microscopical study on
catalase and peroxidases; chromosome analysis:
mathematical analysis of human metaphase plates after
specific staining, and search for abnormal patterns in
individuals subjected to mutagens such as lead, mercury,
X-rays and certain drugs; cortico-vestibular and cortico-
nuclear projections in cat's cerebellum; origin of Kupffer
cells; cadaver analysis to investigate body composition.

ANIMAL PSYCHOLOGY AND ECOLOGY 1160
Head: P. Sevenster

BOTANICAL GENETICS   1161
Head: Professor M. Jacobs
Activities: Somatic cell genetics of the sugarbeet; expression of procaryotic genetic information in plant
cells; selection and characterization of mutants resistant
to amino acid analogues in three plants: barley, carrots,
Arabiodopsis; control mechanisms of enzyme activity
and enzyme polymorphism in plants.

ECOLOGY AND SYSTEMATIC BOTANY   1162
Head: Professor P. Polk
Activities: Phytoplankton; zooplankton; bacteriology;
population genetics on the Genus Tisbe (Harpacticoida);
distribution of sea-birds in relation with different marine
ecosystems; origin, distribution and development of fish-
eggs in plankton; evolution and accumulation of
pesticides in the food-web and the influence on the
thickness of bird egg shells; participation in international marine programmes and inter-calibration experiments.

GENERAL BIOLOGY   1163
Head: Professor R. Hamers

GENERAL BOTANY AND NATURE   1164
CONSERVATION
Head: Professor J.J. Symoens

GENETIC VIROLOGY   1165
Head: R. Hamers

INSTITUTE FOR MOLECULAR   1166
BIOLOGY
Director: R. Hamers
Activities: Regulation and structure of immunoglobulin allotypes; interference of pathogens with
the immune system and its bearing on immunosuppres-
sion in protozoan infections (malaria, trypanosomiasis);
structural analysis of the eukaryotic interphase genome.

MICROBIOLOGY   1167
Head: Professor N. Glansdorf
Activities: Mechanism and regulation of gene expression in procaryotic organisms (bacteria, mainly
Escherichia coli) and in lower eucaryotes; use of cellular
somatic genetics to improve nutritional quality of crop
plants.

PLANT PHYSIOLOGY   1168
Head: Professor L. Neirinckx

PROTEIN CHEMISTRY   1169
Head: Professor E. Kanarek

ZOOLOGY AND HUMAN GENETICS   1170
Head: Professor C. Susanne
Activities: Organization of the chromosomes in the
metaphase and in the interphase; mutagenesis; medical
genetics.

Chemistry   1171

Head: S. Wajc

ANALYTICAL CHEMISTRY 1172
Head: Professor I. Elskens
Activities: Chemical oceanography; sea-atmosphere pollutants; alternative sources of energy; geothermal systems.

ANALYTICAL CHEMISTRY AND FOOD 1173 ANALYSIS
Head: Professor D.L. Massart
Activities: Development of new methodology for chemical analysis: mathematical methods for data handling, mostly of chemical-analytical origin, but also, for instance, clinical data; role of trace elements in the life sciences.

BIOCHEMISTRY 1174
Head: Professor E. Schram

BIOCHEMISTRY AND NUTRITION 1175
Head: R. Crokaert

GENERAL AND ORGANIC CHEMISTRY; 1176 ORGANOMETALLIC CHEMISTRY
Head: Professor M. Gielen
Activities: Synthesis of chiral organotin compounds suitable for the stereochemical study of substitution reactions in tin; preparation and physico-chemical properties of organotin compounds with potential antitumour activity; group theoretical and experimental study of the dynamic stereochemistry of nonrigid molecules; organic syntheses via homogeneous catalytic and stoichiometric reactions of organic molecules with transition metal compounds; photoconversion processes on semiconductors of visible light into electrical or chemical energy.

GENERAL CHEMISTRY 1177
Head: L. Van Hove

ORGANIC CHEMISTRY 1178
Head: Professor G. Van Binst
Activities: Peptide chemistry; affinity labelling and drug-receptor interaction.
Facilities: 270 megahertz nuclear magnetic resonance spectrometer; MS902S mass spectrometer; two Finnigan 3200 GC/MS instruments linked to an INCOS data system.

PHYSICAL CHEMISTRY 1179
Senior staff: Professor J. Drowart
Activities: High-temperature chemistry: nature and thermodynamic properties of the gaseous species involved in vaporization and other processes; photo-ionization of inorganic molecules and vapours.

THEORETICAL PHYSICAL CHEMISTRY 1180
Head: Professor H. Lekkerkerker
Activities: The central theme of research is the investigation of forces, structures and motion in liquid crystals and suspensions. The emphasis lies on interrelated theoretical and experimental work with a view towards obtaining a coherent body of data that can be used effectively to further the knowledge of the systems involved.

THERMODYNAMICS 1181
Head: Professor V. Mathot

Earth and Mineral Sciences 1182
Head: R. Thonnard

GEOCHRONOLOGY 1183
Head: Professor P. Pasteels
Activities: Investigation of the suitability of the mineral glauconite in absolute dating with the rubidium-strontium and potassium-argon methods; volcanic activity associated with rifting in eastern Zaire, Rwanda, Burundi. In the Ruzizi Valley, dating of the lava flows interbedded with sediments may yield valuable information. A detailed investigation of an extinct volcano, the Karisimbi, will also be undertaken. This research, carried out jointly by the Koninklijk Museum voor Midden-Afrika, the Rijksuniversiteit Gent and the Koninklijk Meteorologisch Instituut, is complementary to a geological mapping programme.

HUMAN GEOGRAPHY 1184
Head: Professor Y. Verhasselt

PHYSICAL GEOGRAPHY 1185
Head: Professor L. Peeters

QUATERNARY GEOLOGY AND 1186 SEDIMENTOLOGY
Head: Professor R. Paepe
Activities: Continental and marine deposits of Belgium and North France; research programmes in Greece, Iraq and Brazil; laboratory work: sedimentology; palaeobotany (pollen analysis, diatoms); stratigraphy; palaeoclimatology.

SOIL MECHANICS AND 1187 GEOTECHNICAL MAPPING
Head: Professor J. Nuyens
Activities: The Brussels Geotechnical Mapping Centre is organized by the Soil Mechanics Department of the Free Brussels Universities. This centre elaborates engineering geological or geotechnical maps of the Brussels region which are part of an engineering geological atlas sponsored by the Belgian Committee on Geotechnical Mapping. The Soil Mechanics Laboratory also has a department for soil testing.

Mathematics Department 1188

Chairman: Professor F. Bingen

ALGEBRA 1189
Head: Professor F. Bingen

ALGEBRAIC TOPOLOGY 1190
Head: Professor G. Hirsch

ANALYSIS 1191
Head: I. Cnop

ASTRONOMY 1192
Head: Professor C. De Loore

Physics Department 1193

Chairman: W. Van Rensbergen

BIOPHYSICS 1194
Head: Professor C. Sybesma
Activities: Membrane potentials; the coupling factor-adenosine triphosphatease.

DIFFERENTIAL GEOMETRY 1195
Head: Professor G. Valette

ELEMENTARY PARTICLES 1196
Head: Professor J. Lemonne
Activities: The study of the weak and strong interactions of elementary particles.

FUNCTIONAL ANALYSIS 1197
Head: Professor N. De Grande-De Kimpe

GENERAL OPTICS 1198
Head: Professor R. Van Geen

GENERAL OPTICS, ASTROPHYSICAL 1199
INSTITUTE
Head: Professor C. De Loore
Activities: Evolution of massive single stars with mass loss; structure of the outer layers of luminous stars and the outflow of matter; evolution of massive close binaries; Wolf-rayet stars; evolutionary scenarios for the origin of binary X-ray sources; ultraviolet observations with Balloon Borne Ultraviolet Stellar Spectrograph; galactic evolution; peculiar A-stars.

LASER PHYSICS 1200
Head: Professor P. Ronsmans
Activities: Nd-YAG laser systems and their applications; properties of gaussian laser beams.

PRACTICAL PHYSICS 1201
Head: H. Eisendrath

PROJECTIVE AND COMBINATORY 1202
GEOMETRY
Head: Professor J.M. Van Buggenhaut

QUANTUM OPTICS 1203
Head: Professor H. Eisendrath

SOLID-STATE PHYSICS 1204
Head: Professor J. Jeener

STATISTICAL PHYSICS 1205
Head: Professor J. Philippot
Activities: Stochastic study of fluctuations in chemical and hydrodynamical systems; transport theory in plasmas; group theoretical study of nonrigid molecules.

STATISTICAL PLASMA MECHANICS 1206
Head: Professor G. Severne
Activities: Theoretical understanding of the statistical mechanics of gravitational systems: nature of the relaxation mechanism in gravitational systems; role of collective effects; effect of the coarse-graining inherent in the observational process.

STATISTICS 1207
Head: Professor J. Sonnenschein

THEORETICAL PHYSICS 1208
Head: Professor J. Reignier
Activities: Relativistic quark models of the hadrons; ee-physics; treatment of ill-posed problems; inverse potential scattering on the line and in three dimensions; axiomatic approach to quantum mechanics.

TOPOLOGY 1209
Head: Professor P. Wuyts

HIGHER INSTITUTE FOR PHYSICAL 1210
EDUCATION AND KINETIC THERAPY
Director: L. Bollaert

Experimental Physics 1211

Head: Professor M. Lemmens

General and Biological Chemistry 1212

Head: Professor André Barel

Human Biometry and Biomechanics   1213

Head: Professor M. Hebbelinck

Activities: Physical growth and motor development of children and adolescents; influence of ecological factors on physical and psychological growth, as well as on motor development of children; three dimensional cinematographic and computerized analysis of human movements in space; work and sports equipment.

Human Physiology and Special   1214
Physiology for Physical Education

Head: Professor J.J. S'Jongers

Massage and Kineotherapy   1215

Head: Professor A. Leduc

INTERFACULTY CENTRES AND   1216
PROGRAMMES

Centre for Industrial Plant Location   1217

Head: Professor J.P. Brans

Activities: Coordination of entrepreneurs and regional and state agencieswishing to attract new industries; location models for the public sector: modelling of location problems for public services, such as hospitals, fire stations and police stations; multiple criteria locational decisions: modelling and construction of algorithms; location of a coal valorization plant, bearing in mind the economic, social and ecological aspects.

Interfaculty Centre for   1218
Biomathematics

Head: E. Gussenhoven

Interuniversity Programme in   1219
Demography

Head: Professor J. Lesthaeghe

Activities: Intermediate fertility variables, such as post-partum taboos,and their responses to social and economic modernization; historical demography; economic demography.

The programme is an English language post-graduate programme of teaching and research in demography. It is a collaborative effort of four Belgian universities founded under the auspices of the Belgian National Science Foundation.

Waterbouwkundig   1220
Laboratorium, Ministerie
van Openbare Werken

[Hydraulics Research Laboratory, Ministry of Public Works]

Address: Berchemlei 115, B-2200 Borgerhout Antwerpen

Telephone: (031) 36 18 50

Director: Ir P. Roovers

Activities: Navigability conditions in the Western Scheldt and access to the port of Antwerp; the protection of the Scheldt basin against storm surges; water pollution; the seaward extension of the port of Zeebrugge; beach protection and amelioration of the east Belgian Coast; locks; wave phenomena in canals; urban hydrology; foreign studies within the framework of Belgian development cooperation.

BULGARIA

Bulgarian Academy of Sciences   1

Address: 7 Noemvri 1, 1040 Sofia
Telephone: 8 41 41
Telex: 22424 BAN SF BG
President: Academician Angel Balevski
Vice-Presidents: Academician Pantelej Zarev, Academician Dimităr Kosev, Academician Hristo Daskalov, Academician Georgi Brankov, Academician Ljubomir Željazkov, Corresponding Member Mako Dakov, Corresponding Member Blagovest Sendov
General Scientific Secretary: Academician George Bliznakov
Note: The Joint Centres for research are based on the integrated Academy units and the relevant faculties of Sofia University.
See separate entries for: Centre for Research in Biology
Centre for Research in Chemistry
Centre for Research in Earth Sciences
Centre for Research in Mathematics and Mechanics
Centre for Research in Physics
Research Association on Fundamental Problems of Technical Sciences
Scientific Units attached to the Praesidium:
Chief Department of Hydrology and Meteorology
National Natural Science Museum
Science of Science Museum.
Publications: Academy reference book, journals of the Praesidium, journals, subject series, periodical collections and serial publications.

Bulgarian Dermatological Society   2

Address: G. Sofiiski Boulevard 1, 1431 Sofia
Telephone: 53 21 448
Affiliation: Union of the Medical Societies

Research director: Professor P. Mikhailov
Clinics: Plovdiv, Professor I. Tolev; Varna, Dr Z. Penev; Pleven, Dr J. Tcheshmedjiev
Graduate research staff: 40
Activities: Climatotherapy of skin diseases, dermatoallergology, mycology, venereal diseases, non-gonococcal urethritis and prostatitis.
Contract work: Yes

Bulgarian Ship Hydrodynamics Centre   3

– BSHC
Address: 9003 Varna
Telephone: 77180; 77181
Telex: 77497 BSHC BG
Affiliation: Ministry of Machine Building State Economic Enterprise; Bulgarian Shipbuilding Industry
Director: Dr P. Bogdanov

Canning Research Institute   4

Address: Lenin Boulevard 21, 4000 Plovdiv
Affiliation: 'Bulgarplod' State Economic Organization
Director: B. Michov
Activities: Processing, storage, handling and packaging of fruit and vegetables. Technology of canned baby foods and dietetic products; canned and semifinished products for institutional feeding and semifinished products for further processing. Chemical and microbiological control in canneries, hygiene standards, and standardization of canned products. Process mechanization in the canning industry. Economics, organization, forecasting, and implementation of automatic management systems in the canning industry. Transport, grading and processing of mechanically harvested fruits and vegetables. Technology of handling and packaging of fresh fruit and vegetables for direct consumption.

Central Institute of Mechanical Engineering 5

– ZMI
Address: 12 Ho Chi Minh Boulevard, 1574 Sofia
Telephone: 720352
Telex: 22744 CNIMAX
Director-General: Pant ju Karapantev
Deputy Director: Doz Eng Angel Balashev
Sections: Computer-aided design and manufacture, T. Dzhonev; postgraduate training, G. Tavkov
Subsidiaries: Gabrovo, concerned with investigation, design and production of mechanization and automation of assembly and inspection (metrological) processes in the engineering industry. Machines are designed, and built on the unitizing principle.
Russe, computer-aided design and manufacture and CAPP problems.
Varna, investigation into technological processes, design and production of equipment for heat treatment, heating processes, corrosion, protection of metals and environmental protection.
Plovdiv, concerned with construction parts and metal cutting tools produced through PM methods.
Activities: Technological research and development in engineering. The Institute prepares articles for the State on important branches in the engineering industry as well as forecasts and recommendations for the evolution of metalworking techniques. Specific projects include: unified system for technical preparation of production; programme for implementation of engineering technologies for environmental protection. An Engineering Training Centre organizes and directs postgraduate training of engineers and technicians.
Contract work: Yes
Publications: Scientific Works of the Institute; information issues.

ENGINEERING INFORMATION CENTRE 6

Head: R. Bogdanov
Activities: To provide scientific and technical information to Bulgarian engineering industries.

ENGINEERING MATERIALS CENTRE 7

Head: D. Zegov
Activities: Research and development activities for technological processes and equipment related to the efficient use of materials in production engineering - forming, heat treatment, casting, non-destructive testing of materials, physical and mechanical testing of materials, parts, groups and machines, reliability tests on machines, chemical analysis.

ENGINEERING PRODUCTION ORGANIZATION AND MANAGEMENT DEPARTMENT 8

Head: I. Cholakov
Activities: Development of more efficient solutions for technological and design preparation of production. Data banks are created for billets, parts and machines. Catalogues are made for all standardized machine parts and groups being applied in the engineering industry. Projects include organization and management of machine building factories with manual or computerized data processing.

PRODUCTION TECHNOLOGY DEPARTMENT 9

Head: B. Makedonski
Activities: Investigation, development and implementation of efficient processes, tools and machines for metal cutting, grinding, finishing operations, electrochemical and electrophysical machining methods.

TECHNOLOGICAL PROJECT DESIGN DEPARTMENT 10

Activities: Problems of development and implementation in production of type and group technological processes; application of robots in engineering, development of projects for machine-building factories.

Centre for Research in Biology 11

Address: Academician Georgi Bončev Boulevard III, 1113 Sofia
Telephone: 71 31
Parent body: Bulgarian Academy of Sciences
Director: Academician Kiril Cočev Bratanov
Deputy directors: Professor Aleksandăr Atanasov Gidikov, Bogdan Vutov Bočev
Activities: Structure, biological functions and biosynthesis of proteins and nucleic acids; biophysics; regulation of the growth and development of plants; mechanism, control and self-regulation of plant organisms; raising forest productivity and effective management of the forest economy; biologically active substances of vegetable origin; development of methods of biological pest control; biology of malignant neoplasms; metabolism and biosynthesis in microorganisms and their regulation; ultrastructure, metabolism and function of the cell; photosynthesis; anthropological characteristics of Bulgaria's population; physiological mechanisms of control and self-regulation in animal and

human organisms; comparative morphology, metabolism and regeneration of the nervous system; morphological, biochemical and genetic aspects of immunity in normal and pathological states; heterosis of crop plants and its application in selection; relations between species and the law-governed regularities of inheritance and variability in distant plant hybridization; mechanism and chemistry of cell division, fertilization and embryogenesis in plants; genetic investigation into the resistance of plants to diseases and the virulence of their agents; nature and mechanism of the process of mutation, inducing and use of useful mutations in genetics and selection of plants; polyploids and aneuploids and their use in plant genetics and selection; biology and immunology of reproduction and development of organisms; effective utilization of forest resources; protection and restoration of forest ecosystems and the landscape; virus carcinogenesis and its molecular-biological aspects; measures for the protection and restoration of the environment; physiology, biochemistry and technology of the cultivation of microalgae and their practical utilization; cytogenetic and molecular mechanisms of ontogenesis.

CENTRAL LABORATORY OF BIOPHYSICS 12

Address: Academician Georgi Bončev Boulevard VI, 1113 Sofia
Telephone: 71 31
Director: Georgi Angelov Georgiev

CENTRAL LABORATORY OF HELMINTHOLOGY 13

Address: Academician Georgi Bončev Boulevard III, 1113 Sofia
Telephone: 71 31
Director: Ivan Vasilev Ivanov

CENTRAL LABORATORY ON THE PROBLEMS OF REGENERATION 14

Address: Zdrave 2, 1431 Sofia
Telephone: 52 12 72
Director: Georgi Petrov Gălăbov

EXPERIMENTAL AND BREEDING CENTRE FOR EXPERIMENTAL ANIMALS 15

Address: 2200 Slivnica
Telephone: 99 71 71
Director: Dr Pirin Vasilev Džambazor

FOREST INSTITUTE 16

Address: Želju vojvoda 62, 1080 Sofia
Telephone: 62 29 61
Director: Professor Marin Dimitrov Marinov

GEORGI UZUNOV CENTRAL LABORATORY FOR BRAIN RESEARCH 17

Address: Academician Georgi Bončev Boulevard II, 1113 Sofia
Telephone: 71 31
Director: Professor Ana Vărbanova Angelova

INSTITUTE OF BIOLOGY AND IMMUNOLOGY OF REPRODUCTION AND DEVELOPMENT OF ORGANISMS 18

Address: V.I. Lenin 73, 1113 Sofia
Telephone: 72 23 81
Director: Academician Kiril Cočev Bratanov

INSTITUTE OF BOTANY AND BOTANICAL GARDENS 19

Address: Academician Georgi Bončev Boulevard I, 1113 Sofia
Telephone: 71 31
Director: Professor Velco Ivanov Velčev

INSTITUTE OF GENERAL AND COMPARATIVE PATHOLOGY 20

Address: Academician Georgi Bončev Boulevard III, 1113 Sofia
Telephone: 71 31
Director: Zahari Mihajlov Mladenov

INSTITUTE OF GENETICS 21

Address: Plovdivsko Šose, 1113 Sofia
Telephone: 76 83 86
Director: Manol Josifov Stoilov

INSTITUTE OF MICROBIOLOGY 22

Address: Academician Georgi Bončev Boulevard III, 1113 Sofia
Telephone: 71 31
Director: Professor Milen Nikolov Beškov

INSTITUTE OF MOLECULAR BIOLOGY 23

Address: Academician Georgi Bončev Boulevard VI, 1113 Sofia
Telephone: 72 80 50
Director: Academician Rumen Georgiev Canev

INSTITUTE OF MORPHOLOGY 24

Address: Academician Georgi Bončev Boulevard III, 1113 Sofia
Telephone: 71 31
Director: Professor Ivan Trifonov Goranov

INSTITUTE OF PHYSIOLOGY 25

Address: Academician Georgi Bončev Boulevard VI, 1113 Sofia
Telephone: 71 31
Director: Professor Todor Georgiev Kadrev

RESEARCH AND APPLIED 26 LABORATORY FOR RAPID SPECTROSCOPY AND BIOPHYSICAL INVESTIGATIONS

Address: Academician Georgi Bončev Boulevard VIa, 1113 Sofia
Telephone: 71 31
Director: Julia Georgieva Vasileva

RESEARCH AND PRODUCTION 27 LABORATORY OF ALGOLOGY

Address: Academician Georgi Bončev Boulevard I, 1113 Sofia
Telephone: 71 31
Director: Hristo Vălkov Dilov

ZOOLOGICAL INSTITUTE 28

Address: Ruski 1, 1000 Sofia
Telephone: 88 51 15
Director: Professor Botju Atanasov Botev

Centre for Research in Chemistry 29

Address: Academician Georgi Bončev Boulevard V, 1113 Sofia
Telephone: 72 98 20
Parent body: Bulgarian Academy of Sciences

Director: Academician Bogdan Jordanov Kurtev
Deputy-director (research): Dimităr Georgiev Elenkov
Activities: Chemical kinetics, adsorption and catalysis; high-molecular compounds; theoretical foundations of chemical engineering; electrode processes (electrochemical power sources); electrocrystallization and corrosion; galvanic coatings; bio-organic chemistry (chemistry of natural and synthetic biologically active substances); structure and reactivity of organic compounds and development of methods of organic synthesis and of structural and functional organic analysis; structure of inorganic systems, formation of complexes, inorganic synthesis; analytical chemistry; physical solid-state chemistry; phase formation and crystal growth and solid-state photoprocesses; physical chemistry of surface phenomena and disperse systems; solid fuel chemistry; radiochemistry; methods and technical aids of training in chemistry.

CENTRAL LABORATORY FOR 30 THEORETICAL FOUNDATIONS OF CHEMICAL ENGINEERING

Address: Academician Georgi Bončev Boulevard V, 1113 Sofia
Telephone: 71 31
Director: Dimităr Georgiev Elenkov

CENTRAL LABORATORY OF 31 ELECTROCHEMICAL POWER SOURCES

Address: Academician Georgi Bončev Boulevard Va, 1113 Sofia
Telephone: 72 25 42
Director: Professor Evgeni Bogdanov Budevski

CENTRAL LABORATORY OF 32 PHOTOPROCESSES

Address: Academician Georgi Bončev Boulevard Vb, 1113 Sofia
Telephone: 71 31
Director: Professor Marin Mihajlov

INSTITUTE OF GENERAL AND 33 INORGANIC CHEMISTRY

Address: Academician Georgi Bončev Boulevard V, 1113 Sofia
Telephone: 71 31
Director: Academician Georgi Manuilov Bliznakov

INSTITUTE OF ORGANIC CHEMISTRY 34
WITH CENTRE FOR
PHYTOCHEMISTRY

Address: Academician Georgi Bončev Boulevard V,
1113 Sofia
Telephone: 71 31
Director: Academician Bogdan Jordanov Kurtev

INSTITUTE OF PHYSICAL CHEMISTRY 35

Address: Academician Georgi Bončev Boulevard V,
1113 Sofia
Telephone: 72 75 50
Director: Academician Rostilav Atanasov Kaišev

SPECIALIZED RESEARCH 36
LABORATORY OF CHEMICAL
REAGENTS AND PREPARATIONS

Address: Academician Georgi Bončev Boulevard V,
1113 Sofia
Telephone: 71 31
Director: Professor Dimităr Trendafelov Stojčev

Centre for Research in 37
Earth Sciences

Address: Academician Georgi Bončev Boulevard XIII,
1113 Sofia
Telephone: 87 40 53
Parent body: Bulgarian Academy of Sciences
Director: Kiril Mišev Ivanov
Deputy-director: Petăr Krušev Dragov
Activities: Formation and development of scientific
foundations for forecasting and all-round assessment of
natural mineral, power, water, agroclimatic, territorial
and recreational resources; study and forecasting of
adverse natural phenomena (earthquakes, landslides,
sinking of weak ground foundations, floods, droughts,
hailstorms, fog, etc) and elaboration of methods and
means of combating them; study of the chemical, physical, geological and other processes in the Black Sea and
elaboration of methods and means of utilizing its
resources and protecting it from pollution; study of the
composition, structure, dynamics and development of
the Earth and its crust: development of geophysical
methods of studying the Earth and its crust; research
into the tectonomagnetic cycles and petrology of magma
and metamorphic complexes; correlation of geological
phenomena and study of tectonic processes in the geo-
synclines; study of the sedimentary layer; investigation
into the morphostructure and movements of the Earth's
crust; complex study of the Danube in its Bulgarian
section; modern geodetic networks and parameters of
the Earth; physics and dynamics of the atmosphere;
formation and movement of air masses, improvement of
meteorological forecasting and development of means of
artificial control of atmospheric processes; space physics
and space instruments; remote aero and space methods
of surveying the Earth's resources; all-round study of the
natural socioeconomic territorial systems with a view to
the optimal distribution of the productive forces and
systems of towns and villages; protection and transformation of the environment and forecasting changes in it.
*Publications: Geologica Balcanica; Space Research in
Bulgaria.*

CENTRAL LABORATORY FOR SPACE 38
RESEARCH

Address: Ruski 1, 1000 Sofia
Telephone: 88 11 82
Director: Kiril Borisov Serafimov

CENTRAL LABORATORY OF HIGHER 39
GEODESY

Address: Academician Georgi Bončev Boulevard IV,
1113 Sofia
Telephone: 71 31
Director: N. Ivanov Georgiev

GEOLOGICAL INSTITUTE 40

Address: Academician Georgi Bončev Boulevard II,
1113 Sofia
Telephone: 71 31
Director: Academician Ivan Kostov Nikolov

INSTITUTE OF GEOGRAPHY 41

Address: Academician Georgi Bončev Boulevard XIII,
1113 Sofia
Telephone: 71 31
Director: Kiril Mišev Ivanov

INSTITUTE OF GEOPHYSICS 42

Address: Academician Georgi Bončev Boulevard XIII,
1113 Sofia
Telephone: 71 31
Deputy director: Dimităr Trapeev Samardžiev

INSTITUTE OF MARITIME RESEARCH 43
AND OCEANOLOGY

Address: Panagjuriste 17, POB 152, 9000 Varna
Telephone: (052) 7 72 00
Director: Zdravko Kirilov Belberov

LABORATORY FOR COMPLEX RESEARCH AND REINFORCEMENT OF WEAK GROUND FOUNDATIONS   44

Address: Academician Georgi Bončev Boulevard II, 1113 Sofia
Telephone: 71 31
Head: Professor Minko Slavčev Minkov

Experimental Branch   45

Address: 7000 Ruse
Telephone: (082) 2 40 42
Head: Petar Vasilev Dončev

LABORATORY FOR EXPERIMENTAL AND ENGINEERING MINERALOGY   46

Address: Ruski Boulevard 15, Kliment Ohridski University of Sofia, 1504 Sofia
Telephone: 85 81
Head: Mihal Najdenov Maleev

RESEARCH AND COORDINATION CENTRE FOR THE PROTECTION AND REPRODUCTION OF THE ENVIRONMENT   47

Address: J. Gagarin 2, 1113 Sofia
Telephone: 71 71 95
Director: Professor Simeon Todorov Nedjalkov

Centre for Research in Mathematics and Mechanics   48

Address: Academician Georgi Bončev Boulevard VIII, 1113 Sofia
Telephone: 71 31
Parent body: Bulgarian Academy of Sciences
Director: Academician Ljubomir Georgiev Iliev
Deputy-director: Petăr Hristov Bărnev
Activities: Mathematical structures: mathematical logic, topology, algebra, real and functional analysis, complex analysis, differential equations, geometry, mathematical programming, foundations of cybernetics and control theory; mathematical modelling studies of operations, probabilities and statistics; analytical mechanics, stability and control of mechanical systems, hydro-aero mechanics, deformable solid mechanics, infinite media mechanics, biomechanics.

INSTITUTE OF MATHEMATICS WITH COMPUTING CENTRE   49

Address: Academician Georgi Bončev Boulevard VIII, 1113 Sofia
Telephone: 71 31
Director: Academician Ljubomir Georgiev Iliev

INSTITUTE OF MECHANICS AND BIOMECHANICS   50

Address: Academician George Bončev Boulevard VIII, 1113 Sofia
Telephone: 71 31
Director: Academician Georgi Jordanov Brankov

Centre for Research in Philosophy and Sociology   51

Address: Patriarh Evtimij 6, 1000 Sofia
Telephone: 87 67 26
parent body: Bulgarian Academy of Sciences
Director: Professor Stefan Angelov Stefanov
Deputy-director (research): Professor Ivan Dimitrov Kalajkov
Activities: The socialist way of life: formation and development of the personality under socialism; atheistic education; psychological and pedagogical aspects of the development of the personality.

LABORATORY OF PSYCHOLOGY   52

Address: Benkovski 18, 1000 Sofia
Telephone: 87 83 07
Head: Professor Zdrava Borisova Ivanova

Centre for Research in Physics   53

Address: V.I. Lenin 72, 1113 Sofia
Telephone: 73 41
Parent body: Bulgarian Academy of Sciences
Director: Milko Borisov Ivanov
Deputy-director (research): Professor Paraskeva Dimitrova Simova
Activities: Condensed state physics: fundamental studies on the atomic and electron structure and dynamics of crystals, amorphous state bodies and other more complex systems; physics of systems of the metal-dielectric-semiconductor type; semiconductor, integrated and functional microelectronics; acoustic electronics and acoustic optics; thin layer and integral optics; new

media for magnetic and optical recording of information and for computer memories; liquid crystals; optical and photoelectric phenomena in semiconductors and dielectrics; physical problems of magnetic and superconducting materials and instruments; direct use of solar energy; physical electronics and radiophysics: plasma physics and plasma chemistry; new plasma, electron, ion and vacuum technologies; super-high-frequency physics and techniques. Quantum electronics and optics: development and mastering of new laser sources; use of lasers in various fields of the national economy; laser location and telemetry; holography and other methods of coherent optics; development of optical and optoelectrical devices for the requirements of computing engineering. Nuclear physics: physics of the atomic nucleus, high energies and elementary particles; nuclear-physical methods and devices; neutron physics; reactor physics and nuclear energetics. Astrophysics: physics and evolution of stars; extragalactic astronomy.

CENTRAL LABORATORY OF OPTICAL STORAGE AND PROCESSING OF INFORMATION   54

Address: Academician Georgi Bončev Boulevard Vb, 1113 Sofia
Telephone: 71 31
Director: Metodi Ivanov Kovačev

CENTRAL LABORATORY OF SOLAR ENERGY AND NEW ENERGY SOURCES   55

Address: V.I. Lenin 72, 1113 Sofia
Telephone: 73 41
Director: Professor Stefan Kănev Kănev

CENTRE FOR AUTOMATION OF SCIENTIFIC EXPERIMENTS   56

Address: V.I. Lenin 72, 1113 Sofia
Telephone: 73 41
Head: Ljubomir Jordanov Antonov

DEVELOPMENT AND TRANSFER CENTRE   57

Address: V.I. Lenin 72, 1113 Sofia
Telephone: 73 41
Head: Ivan Dimov Ivanov

INSTITUTE OF ELECTRONICS   58

Address: V.I. Lenin 72, 1113 Sofia
Telephone: 73 41
Director: Aleksandăr Jankov Spasov

INSTITUTE OF NUCLEAR RESEARCH AND NUCLEAR ENERGY   59

Address: V.I. Lenin 72, 1113 Sofia
Telephone: 73 41
Director: Academician Hristo Jankov Hristov

INSTITUTE OF SOLID-STATE PHYSICS   60

Address: V.I. Lenin 72, 1113 Sofia
Telephone: 73 41
Director: Milko Borisov Ivanov

SECTION OF ASTRONOMY AND NATIONAL OBSERVATORY   61

Address: V.I. Lenin 72, 1113 Sofia
Telephone: 73 41
Director: Kiril Borisov Serafimov

Chief Department of Hydrology and Meteorology   62

Address: V.I. Lenin 66, 1113 Sofia
Telephone: 72 22 71
Parent body: Bulgarian Academy of Sciences
Head: Kostadin Ivanov Stančev

INSTITUTE OF HYDROLOGY AND METEOROLOGY   63

Address: V.I. Lenin 66, 1113 Sofia
Telephone: 72 22 71
Director: Professor Petko Angelov Becinski
Activities: Climatology, synoptic and dynamic meteorology, study of avalanches, agrometeorology, hydrology, hydrogeology, water current processes, study of sediments, hydrometeorological aspects of air, water and soil pollution, active control of adverse atmospheric phenomena, etc.

Fishing Industry Institute *   64

Address: 3 Industrialna Strasse, 7000 Burgas
Director: V. Hitilov

Higher Institute of Architecture and Civil Engineering*

65

Address: Boulevard C. Smirnenski 2, Sofia
Telephone: 661771

FACULTY OF ARCHITECTURE*

66

FACULTY OF CIVIL ENGINEERING*

67

FACULTY OF GEODESY*

68

Head: Professor I. Stanev

FACULTY OF HYDROTECHNICAL ENGINEERING*

69

Head: Professor G. Ilčev

Higher Institute of Chemical Technology

70

Address: 8 Jelu Voivoda, Darvenitza, 56 Sofia
Telephone: 62 41 41
Rector: Professor M. Natov

FACULTY OF INORGANIC TECHNOLOGY

71

Dean: Professor R. Raytchev
Sections: Analytical chemistry, Professor V. Karadakov
Electrochemical processes, Professor I. Nenov
Heat engineering, Professor K. Doytchev
Inorganic compounds, Professor N. Videnov
Mineralogy and petrography, Professor I. Iliev
Mathematics, Professor D. Pirgov

FACULTY OF METALLURGY

72

Dean: Professor A. Avramov
Sections: Non-ferrous metals, Professor Chr. Vassilev
Metallurgy, Professor T. Nikolov
Semiconductor materials, Professor D. Dzhoglev
Mechanics, Professor K. Popov
Physics, Professor L. Hristov

FACULTY OF ORGANIC TECHNOLOGY

73

Dean: Professor G. Reev
Sections: Automation in organic technology, Professor I. Bozhov
Chemical engineering, Professor A. Aleksandrov
Chemical fibres and textile chemistry, Professor K. Dimov
Chemical technology (general), Professor D. Dimitrov
Chemical technology (wood), Professor D. Voltchev
Economics in chemical and metal production, Professor R. Gurov
Fuel technology, Professor A. Kaisev
Leather technology, Professor R. Tzvetkov
Organic chemistry, Professor B. Aleksiev
Organic synthesis, Professor A. Stoyanov
Physical chemistry, Professor S. Raitcheva
Plastics technology, Professor M. Natov
Rubber technology, Professor I. Tododrov

Higher Institute of Electrical and Mechanical Engineering*

74

Address: Kvartal Levski, PO 10, Varna
Telephone: 8 01 61

FACULTY OF ELECTRICAL ENGINEERING*

75

FACULTY OF MECHANICAL ENGINEERING*

76

FACULTY OF SHIPBUILDING*

77

Higher Institute of Food and Flavour Industries

78

Address: Lenin Boulevard 26, 4002 Plovdiv
Telephone: 4 18 11
Telex: 44669 vihvp
Affiliation: Ministry of Public Education
Rector: Professor Stoyan Tanchev
Vice-Rectors: Assistant Professor Tsvetan Obretenov, Assistant Professor Maria Baltadjieva, Assistant Professor Asen Konarev

Deans: Assistant Professor Boris Dimitrov, Assistant Professor Dimiter Tsankov
Research director: Professor Maria Baltadjieva
Sections: Fruit and vegetable canning technology, Professor S. Tanchev
Milk and dairy products technology, Assistant Professor M. Baltadjieva
Meat and fish technology, Professor E. Hristov
Technology of beer and soft drinks, Professor S. Manchev
Refrigeration technology and equipment, Assistant Professor M. Lalov
Tobacco and tobacco products technology, Professor L. Gyuzelev
Grain and baked products technology, Professor D. Shikrenov
Public catering products technology, Assistant Professor P. Peev
Microbiology, Professor M. Beshkov
Sugar and sugar products technology, Assistant Professor V. Vakrilov
Technology of wine and high-alcohol drinks, Professor T. Ivanov
Technology of vegetable fats and essential oils, Assistant Professor T. Hadjiyski
Automation of production, Assistant Professor I. Popov
Technology for food and flavour industries, Assistant Professor S. Ditchev
Higher mathematics, Assistant Professor G. Kirov
Mechanics, Professor I. Ivanov
Physics, Assistant Professor D. Hristozov
Processes and equipment, Assistant Professor K. Kolarov
Machine elements, Assistant Professor E. Zlatanova
Heat engineering, Assistant Professor G. Kimenov
Economics, organization and industrial construction, Professor K. Lukanov
Organic chemistry and biochemistry, Assistant Professor H. Kratchanov
Inorganic chemistry and physicochemistry, Professor Y. Popova
Analytical chemistry, Professor D. Maneva
Activities: Research related to the theory and practice of plant and animal raw materials and products; chemistry and technology of tobacco and tobacco products; chemistry and technology of essential oils, cosmetics and perfumery; chemistry and technology of food raw materials and products; organization and economics of tourism and recreation; chemistry and technology of yeasts, antibiotics, vitamins, aminoacids and other organic acids, steroids etc.
Contract work: Yes
Publications: Travaux Scientifiques de l'Institut Supérieur Technologique de l'Industrie Alimentaire.

Higher Institute of Mechanical and Electrical Engineering V.I. Lenin* 79

Address: Ulitsa 19 Fevruari 1, Sofia
Telephone: 88 43 51

FACULTY OF AUTOMATION* 80

Head: Professor D. Jordanov

FACULTY OF ELECTRICAL ENGINEERING* 81

Head: Professor V. Dinov

FACULTY OF ENERGY MACHINE CONSTRUCTION* 82

Head: Professor G. Mumžijan

FACULTY OF MACHINE BUILDING* 83

FACULTY OF MACHINE TECHNOLOGY* 84

FACULTY OF RADIOELECTRONICS* 85

FACULTY OF TRANSPORTATION* 86

Head: Professor S. Nedelčev

Higher Institute of Mining and Geology 87

Address: Darvenitza, 1156 Sofia
Telephone: 6 25 81
Rector: Professor R. Parashkevov
Deputy Rectors: Professor K. Bandov (Research); Professor N. Nenkov (Education); Professor St. Denev (Postgraduate Studies)
Graduate research staff: 95
Activities: Underground mining; open-pit mining; mineral processing; geological exploration.
Contract work: Yes
Publications: Annual of the Higher Institute of Mining and Geology, bibliographic index, anniversary publications.

FACULTY OF GEOLOGY   88

Dean: Assistant Professor M. Moev
Sections: Palaeontology, Professor B. Strashimirov
Structural geology, geological mapping, geology of
Bulgaria, Professor St. Zafirov
Geophysics, Professor T. Dobrev
Engineering geology, Professor An. Demirev
Exploration of mineral deposits, Professor B. Bogdanov
Oil and gas geology, Professor V. Troshanov
Physics of oil-bearing layers, Professor V. Balinov
Petrology, Professor I. Velinov
Mineralogy, crystallography, Professor S. Stoynov
Drilling, Professor N. Nenkov
Fluid dynamics, Professor S. Fildishev

FACULTY OF MINING   89

Dean: Assistant Professor Em. Dankov
Sections: Mine construction, Professor T. Chonkov
Underground ore mining, Professor St. Istatkov
Rock mechanics, Professor R. Parashkevov
Mine designing, Professor M. Velev
Mine transport, Professor K. Bandov
Mining machines, Professor K. Sheiretov
Mine hoisting, Professor V. Kovachev
Mine electrification, Professor D. Danailov
Automation of mining, Professor St. Irinkov
Physical methods in mineral processing, Professor St.
Stoev
Crushing, grinding and screening, Professor St. Denev
Flotation, Professor St. Gaidarjiev
Mineral processing plants, Professor K. Kovachev
Mine ventilation and occupational safety, Professor T.
Stefanov
Mine geometry, Professor I. Hristov
Higher geodesy, Professor N. Tzonkov
Mine surveying, Professor B. Stoyanov
Theoretical mechanics, strength of materials, con-
tinuous media mechanics, Professor I. Minchev
Strength of materials, Professor I. Dimov
Theoretical mechanics, Professor L. Kandov
Higher mathematics, Professor I. Ivanov
Theory of mechanisms, Professor D. Obreshkov

Institute for State Control of Drugs   90

Address: Vladimir Zaimov Boulevard 26, 1040 Sofia
Telephone: 44 65 66
Research director: Professor Radi Ovtcharov
Sections: Pharmacology, Professor R. Ovtcharov
Microbiology, Dr L. Danailova
Pharmacoanalysis, P. Zikolov
Antibiotics, Dr V. Angelova

Laboratory for expert analysis and methodical aid, A.
Petrov
Graduate research staff: 35
Activities: Research into the control and standardiza-
tion of drugs (pharmaceutical and microbiological pre-
parations); taxonomy of microorganisms; monitoring of
adverse drug reactions.
Contract work: No
Publications:'Izvestiya'.

Institute 'Niproruda'   91

Address: Al. Stambolijski Boulevard 205, 1309 Sofia
Telephone: 21 321
Telex: 22759
Affiliation: Ministry of Metallurgy and Mineral
Resources
Graduate research staff: 100
Activities: A complex scientific, research and design
Institute of mining and ore-dressing, it carries out scien-
tific, technological and building research for opencast
and underground mines and ore-dressing plants, and on
ores of ferrous, non-ferrous, rare and noble metals.
Departments deal with production, buildings, equipment, transport, mechanical, electrical, water and
energy supply, and communication problems, among
others. The Institute provides patent rights, supervises
and participates in the utilization of its own research and
development work, produces specific equipment of both
Bulgarian and foreign construction, and carries out
economic, technical and technological studies for mining and ore-dressing enterprises.
Publications: Year books and bulletins.

Institute of Fisheries   92

Address: 4 Chervenoarmeiska Street, 9000 Varna
Telephone: 2 25 86
Affiliation: State Economic Board
Director: Professor L. Ivanov
Sections: Ichthyology, J.M. Gheorghiev; hydrobiol-
ogy, Professor T. Marinov
Graduate research staff: 13
Annual expenditure: £51 000-500 000
Activities: Commercial fishery resources of the Black
Sea, littoral, lakes and Atlantic Ocean; aquaculture and
marine biology.
Contract work: Yes
Publications: Proceedings of the Institute, volumes 1 to
18.

Institute of Inland Water Fisheries* 93

Address: 66 Krai Strasse, 4003 Plovdiv
Director: A. Bojadžiev

Iron and Steel Research Institute 94

Address: Botunetz, 1770 Sofia
Telephone: 89 06 43
Telex: 022390
Affiliation: Ministry of Metallurgy and Mineral Resources
Director: Professor Boris Drakalyiski
Graduate research staff: 120
Activities: Preparation of raw materials and iron making; coke and chemicals; steelmaking; production of ferroalloys; rolling metals; steel products and tube making; heat technology and metallurgical furnaces; heat treatment; automation; analytical chemistry; fireproof production; air and water pollution control; economics; organization and management.
Contract work: Yes
Publications: Research reports.

Medical Academy* 95

Address: 1 George Sofijski Boulevard, Sofia 1431

HIGHER MEDICAL INSTITUTE AT PLEVEN* 96

Address: Karl Marx 1, Pleven

HIGHER MEDICAL INSTITUTE AT PLOVDIV* 97

Address: V. Aprilov 15A, Plovdiv

HIGHER MEDICAL INSTITUTE AT SOFIA* 98

Address: 1 George Sofijski Boulevard, Sofia

HIGHER MEDICAL INSTITUTE AT VARNA* 99

Address: M. Drinov 55, Varna

INSTITUTE OF ROENTGENOLOGY AND RADIOBIOLOGY* 100

Address: 8 Belo More Strasse, Sofia 1040

Laboratory of Clinical Dosimetry and Metrology of Ionizing Radiation 101

Address: 8 Belo More Street, Sofia 1040
Telephone: 4641
Head: D. Pentchev
Graduate research staff: 4
Annual expenditure: £10 000-50 000
Activities: Clinical dosimetry in telegamma and X-ray therapy; metrology of gamma and X-rays; radiation protection of staff and patients in nuclear medicine and in X-ray diagnostics.
Contract work: Yes

RESEARCH INSTITUTE FOR HYGIENE* 102

Address: 13 D. Nestorov Street, Sofia 1606
Director: Professor T. Tashev

Institute of Hygiene, Industrial Safety and Occupational Diseases* 103

Director: Professor F. Kaloyanova
Activities: Research in the fields of environmental pollution, industrial safety and health, occupational pathology, applied toxicology, and ergonomics.

RESEARCH INSTITUTE OF HAEMATOLOGY AND BLOOD TRANSFUSION 104

Address: Plovdivsko Pole 6, Sofia 1156
Director: Professor V. Serafimov-Dimitrov
Activities: The practical and scientific problems of clinical haematology and transfusiology. The fields of scientific investigations are mainly the epidemiology, pathogeneses, treatment and prophylaxis of the benign and the malignant haematological diseases; the transfusion and transplant haematology compatibility, kinetics and balance of blood components, plasmaphoreses and preparation of biological products.

RESEARCH INSTITUTE OF INFECTIOUS AND PARASITIC DISEASES* 105

– RIIPD
Address: 27 Boulevard Vl. Zaimov, Sofia
Director: Professor L. Shindarov

RESEARCH INSTITUTE OF OBSTETRICS AND GYNAECOLOGY 106

Address: Street Zdrave 2, Sofia 1431
Telephone: 53 - 60
Director of research: Professor Bozhil Vasilev
Sections: Department of Obstetrics, Assistant Professor Zhivko Andreev; Department of Gynaecology, Professor Karl Ornianov
Graduate research staff: 120
Annual expenditure: £200 000
Activities: Medico-biological and medico-social factors for increasing birth-rate and population growth (diagnosis, treatment and prophylactics of sterility; conservative and operative treatment of inflammatory genital diseases, prophylactics of endometrial cancer; hyperprolactinaemia in females).
Health care of pregnant women, the foetus and the newborn (prophylactics and management of premature deliveries, pain control in labour, birth infections). Bulgarian modern standards for the weight and length of the newborn.
Contract work: Yes

RESEARCH INSTITUTE OF ONCOLOGY* 107

Address: 6 Plovdivsko Pole, Sofia-Darvenica

RESEARCH INSTITUTE OF PAEDIATRICS* 108

Address: 11 D. Nestorov Street, Sofia 1606
Director: Professor Ninio Shimon
Activities: Physiology of motor reactions in early childhood; objective criteria for normal child development; creche environment and rational feeding in early childhood; organization of specialized paediatric medical care; control of morbidity and mortality in childhood - research in the fields of pathogenesis, respiratory diseases, cardiovascular diseases, renal diseases, gastrointestinal, metabolic and endocrine diseases, collagen diseases and allergies (especially drug allergy), puberty and development; blood diseases in childhood, and malignant diseases. All research is carried out in cooperation with related institutes of the Medical Academy.

RESEARCH INSTITUTE OF PNEUMOLOGY AND PHTHISIOLOGY* 109

Address: 17 D. Nestorov Street, Sofia 1606
Director: Professor R. Radanov

National Natural Science Museum 110

Address: Ruski 1, 1000 Sofia
Telephone: 88 51 15
Parent body: Bulgarian Academy of Sciences
Director: Academician Ivan Kostov Nikolov
Activities: Minerals in Bulgaria - special features, paragenetic interrelations, genetics, systematization; taxonomy, phylogeny and stratigraphic value of Lower Cretaceous ammonites; taxonomic and phylogenetic studies of the Tertiary mammal fauna in Bulgaria; natural and anthropogenic factors for the variability of natural grass associations; Bulgaria's fauna - species composition, distribution, taxonomy and autecology of land and freshwater crustacea, acarina, insects, fish and mammals; taxonomic revisions and descriptions of crustacea, arachnida and insects of the Palaeoarctic zoogeographic regions; preparation of displays for the geological, botanic and zoological departments in compliance with the present state of the particular sciences and the role of the Museum as a centre of dissemination of general and special knowledge on natural sciences.

NPO Selected Seeds and Planting Material 111

Address: Lenin Boulevard 125, Block 1, 1113 Sofia
Affiliation: Ministry of Agriculture and Food Industry
General director: Marin Petsanski
Activities: Scientific production of and research in alfalfa, etc; hybrid corn breeding, introduction, seed testing, seed maintenance and seed study. Production of selected seeds of cereals, forage crops, hybrid corn, vegetables and flower crops, potatoes, oil and technical cultivars, vine and fruit planting material and berries.

Plovdiv University Paisij Hilendarski* 112

Address: Car Asen 24, Plovdiv

FACULTY OF CHEMISTRY AND BIOLOGY* 113

FACULTY OF MATHEMATICS* 114

FACULTY OF PHYSICS* 115

Research Association on Fundamental Problems of Technical Sciences 116

Address: Academician Georgi Bončev Boulevard IV, 1113 Sofia
Telephone: 71 81 82
Parent body: Bulgarian Academy of Sciences
Director: Jordan Todorov Simeonov

CENTRAL LABORATORY OF PHYSICAL AND CHEMICAL MECHANICS 117

Address: Academician Georgi Bončev Boulevard IV, 1113 Sofia
Telephone: 72 47 20
Director: Jordan Todorov Simeonov
Activities: Rheology of structured dispersion systems; physical foundations of the strength and destruction of non-metallic composition materials; physical nature and mechanism of the deformations of non-metallic composition materials.

INSTITUTE OF ENGINEERING CYBERNETICS AND ROBOTICS 118

Address: Academician Georgi Bončev Boulevard XII, 1113 Sofia
Telephone: 7 14 01
Director: Angel Simeonov Angelov
Activities: Engineering cybernetics: cybernetic control systems, information, systematic research; industrial robots: elements and systems setting robots in motion; control of robots, robot systems.

INSTITUTE OF METAL SCIENCE AND TECHNOLOGY 119

Address: Čapaev 53, 1574 Sofia
Telephone: 72 34 25
Director: Academician Angel Tončev Balevski
Deputy-director: Ivan Dimov Nikolov
Activities: Development and application of the methods of processing materials under gas counter-pressure; development of the theoretical foundations of the methods of processing materials by gas counter-pressure; development of new materials (new alloys on a metal basis and new non-metallic materials); elaboration of special technologies for the production and working of new materials; elaboration of special technologies by the method of casting under counter-pressure for the casting of complex parts which cannot be cast by the methods known so far or which are worked by complicated and ineffective methods; development of machin-ery and equipment connected with the new materials and technologies.

INSTITUTE OF WATER PROBLEMS 120

Address: Academician Georgi Bončev Boulevard IV, 1113 Sofia
Telephone: 71 31
Director: Professor Petăr Dimitrov Ignatov
Activities: Optimization of long-term planning and management of water economic systems; run-off regulation and optimization of water economic balance; improvement of the water quality; water economics; theoretical and experimental studies of the static and dynamic behaviour and stability of hydroengineering installations and their foundations; optimization study of the structure of hydroengineering installations; multiphase motions, heterogeneous fluid motions, turbulence and mass-exchange processes; currents and filtration processes.

Road Research Institute 121

Address: 1739 Sofia
Telephone: 45 90 06
Research director: Bojčo Valčev
Graduate research staff: 30
Annual expenditure: £51 000-500 000
Activities: Research into planning, construction and maintenance of roads and bridges.
Contract work: Yes
Publications: Yearbook.

Science of Science Centre 122

Address: Serdika 4, 1000 Sofia
Telephone: 88 38 87
Parent body: Bulgarian Academy of Sciences
Director: Professor N. Kostadinov Stefanov
Activities: Organization and management of scientific research; potential of the scientific personnel (research on the main characteristics and tendencies of the scientific personnel of the Bulgarian Academy of Sciences and organization of labour in the field of science). Technologies connected with the optimization of the cycle 'research-elaboration-inmplementation' .

Shipbuilding Institute 123

Address: 128 D.Blagoev Boulevard, 9000 Varna
Telephone: 8 18 02
Telex: 077550
Affiliation: Bulgarian Shipbuilding Industry
Director of research: Dipl Eng G. Georgiev
Sections: Ship design and research; ship construction technology; design of ship machinery
Graduate research staff: 500
Annual expenditure: £501 000-2m
Activities: Designing tankers of 5000 dvt; river-sea,sea-going ships; container ships (500 TEU); multi-purpose carriers of 15000 dvt; bulkers of 25000, and 30000 dvt; product carriers of 6000 and 25000 dvt.
Contract work: Yes
Publications: Year book.

Sofia University* 124

Address: Boulevard Ruski 15, 1000 Sofia

FACULTY OF BIOLOGY* 125

Head: Professor G. Konstantinov

FACULTY OF CHEMISTRY* 126

FACULTY OF GEOLOGY AND GEOGRAPHY* 127

FACULTY OF MATHEMATICS* 128

Head: Professor R. Denčev

FACULTY OF PHYSICS* 129

Head: Professor C. Bončev

Textile Research Institute* 130

Address: 48 Vojvodina Mogila Street, 1619 Sofia
Director: Professor Dr K. Dzivanov
Activities: Analysis of textile raw materials for determination of their technological properties; development of and specific efficient methods for textile raw materials, semimanufactured articles, and goods testing; development of optimum technology for chemical textile raw materials processing; increase of textile productivity; mechanization, optimization and automation of machines and processes in the textile industry; evaluation of effectiveness of new machinery; organization of production, labour and managements; and improvement of working conditions in the textile industry.

Transport Medical Institute 131

Address: G. Dimitrov Boulevard 110, 1233 Sofia
Telephone: 31 51
Research director: Professor H. Zaprjanov
Sections: Physiology, labour psychology and transport ergonomics, Dr M. Wassileva
Labour hygiene in transport, Dr M. Dimitrov
Occupational diseases in transport, Dr Vl. Haralanov
Nutrition of transport workers, Dr N. Mitkova
Graduate research staff: 30
Activities: Founded in 1952, the Transport Medical Institute studies all aspects of on-the-job health hazards in transport and the transport industry: elimination or reduction of noxious fumes; studies on working and rest hours, in order to guarantee transport safety, working capacity; epidemiology and spread of diseases; rehabilitation after common diseases affecting transport workers; psycho-physiological methods of examination and fitness criteria assessment of workers in transport systems; occupational-protective nutrition of healthy and dietetic nutrition of sick transport workers.
Contract work: Yes
Publications: *Transport Medical News,* quarterly; research reports.

CYPRUS

Agricultural Research Institute
1

Address: Athalassa, Nicosia
Affiliation: Ministry of Agriculture and Natural Resources
Director: Dr V.D. Krentos
Sections: Agronomy, Dr A. Hadjichristodoulou; horticulture, C.V. Economides; plant protection, Dr C. Serghiou; soils and water use, Dr P.I. Orphanos; animal production, Dr S. Economides; agricultural economics, St. Papachristodoulou; chemistry, Dr D. Hadjidemetriou; Farm Manager, A. Tsingis
Publications: Annual report.

Ministry of Agriculture and Natural Resources
2

Address: Nicosia
Telephone: 40 2491
Director-General: Dr A. Papasolomontos
Graduate research staff: 200
Annual expenditure: over £2m
Contract work: No

DEPARTMENT OF AGRICULTURE
3

Director: A. Louca
Sections: Agricultural economics, P. Aristotelous; agronomy and seed production, E. Xenophontos; cattle and dairying, C. Constantinides; chemistry, S. Sophocleous; agricultural extension, G. Neocleous; fruit crops and nurseries, G. Agrotis; pastures and fodder, Th. Photiades; plant protection, J. Zyngas; poultry, A. Agrotis; sheep and goats, N. Neophytou; soils and plant nutrition, G. Grivas; swine and animal nutrition, L. Serghi; vegetables and flowers, A. Soteriadou; viticulture and oenology, Ch. Ypsarides; water use, P. Kalimeras
Publications: Annual report.

DEPARTMENT OF FISHERIES
4

Fisheries Officer: A. Demetropoulos
Publications: Annual report.

DEPARTMENT OF FORESTS
5

Director: E.D. Michaelides
Acting Assistant Director: L.I. Leontiades
Publications: Annual report.

DEPARTMENT OF GEOLOGICAL SURVEY
6

Director: C. Constantinou
Publications: Annual report.

DEPARTMENT OF METEOROLOGY
7

Meteorologist: Kleanthis Philaniotis
Publications: Annual report.

DEPARTMENT OF VETERINARY SERVICES
8

Director: K. Polydorou
Publications: Annual report.

DEPARTMENT OF WATER DEVELOPMENT 9

Director: C.S. Lytras
Assistant Director: K. Hassapis
Publications: Annual report.

Ministry of Health* 10

Address: 11 Byron Avenue, Nicosia
Activities: The Ministry is responsible for the planning and implementation of all plans and policies in the field of health, including development plans.

CZECHOSLOVAKIA

Astronomický ústav ČSAV   1

[Astronomical Institute]
Address: Budečská 6, 120 23 Praha 2
Telephone: 25 87 57
Parent body: Czechoslovak Academy of Sciences
Director: Václav Bumba
Deputies to the Director: Dr Miloslav Kopecký, Ing Vladimir Rajský
Activities: Astronomy and astrophysics, especially in the following respects: solar activity, effects of the Sun upon the Earth, structure and development of the stars and binaries, structure of the Galaxy, the meteors and interplanetary masses, the dynamics of the movement of artificial satellites and the bodies of the solar system, including the precise chronometry. The Institute also fulfils the tasks following agreements on multilateral cooperation among the socialist countries, in particular taking an active part in the cooperation among the socialist countries in research and exploitation of the cosmic space within the Interkosmos programme.

OBSERVATORY ONDŘEJOV   2

Address: 251 65 okres Praha-Východ
Telephone: 27 94 58
Sections: Solar Department, Dr Vojtěch Letfus
Department of Interplanetary Masses, Vladimír Guth
Computer Centre, Ing Vojtech Kaksa

Biofyzikální ústav ČSAV   3

[Biophysics Institute]
Address: Královopolská 135, 612 65 Brno
Telephone: 54 71 1
Parent body: Czechoslovak Academy of Sciences
Director: Assistant Professor Dr Zdeněk Karpfel
Deputy director: Dr Miloš Klímek

Activities: Research of radiation and molecular biophysics.

SECTOR OF MOLECULAR AND   4 CELLULAR BIOPHYSICS

Sections: Department of Biophysics of Macromolecules, Dr Jiří Pillich
Department of Cytogenetics, Assistant Professor Dr Věra Spurná
Department of Cellular Biophysics, Dr Jiří Soška
Department of General Biophysics, Professor Dr Ludvík Novák

SECTOR OF RADIATION BIOPHYSICS   5

Sections: Department of Radioisotopes, Dr Vladimír Drášil
Department of Biophysics of Bacteriophage, Assistant Professor Dr Zdena Hradečná
Department of Radiation and Applied Biophysics, Assistant Professor Dr Zdeněk Karpfel
Department of Radiation Injuries to the Cell, Assistant Professor Dr Miloslav Skalka
Department of Radiosensitivity of Mammals, Assistant Professor Dr Milan Pospíšil

Botanický ústav ČSAV   6

[Botanical Institute]
Address: Průhonice u Prahy čp 1, (zámek) 252 43 okres Praha-Západ
Telephone: 75 95 03
Parent body: Czechoslovak Academy of Sciences
Director: Slavomil Hejný
Deputy Director: Dr Pavel Tomšovic
Activities: The Institute comprises field units at Kvilda, Sudoměř, Lučnice n.L., Alběř, Dehtáře,

Klíčava, Kameničky, Lanžhot and Hlohovec, and develops basic research of plant communities - terrestrial and aquatic, from the points of view of their structure, production, development and relationship to the environment. The specific tasks of the Institute are aimed at the research of meadow ecosystems, synanthropic vegetation - weed and ruderal - and at important processes in the development cycle of the forest ecosystem.

BIOLOGY OF THE FOREST 7
DEPARTMENT

Address: Poříčí 3b, 603 00 Brno
Telephone: 33 11 59
Head: Vladimír Rypáček

BOTANICAL GARDEN 8

Address: Průhonice u Prahy čp 1, (zámek) 252 43 okres Praha-Západ
Head: Slavomil Hejný

ECOLOGY DEPARTMENT 9

Address: Stará 18, 662 61 Brno
Telephone: 67 63 44
Head: Dr Milena Rychnovská

GEOBOTANICAL DEPARTMENT 10

Address: Průhonice u Prahy čp 1, (zámek) 252 43 okres Praha-Západ
Head: Dr Jaroslav Moravec

HYDROBIOLOGICAL LABORATORY 11

Address: Vltavska 17, 151 05 Praha 5 - Smíchov
Telephone: 53 16 11
Head: Assistant Professor Jaroslav Hrbáček

HYDROBOTANICAL DEPARTMENT 12

Address: Dukelská 145, 379 82 okres Jindřichův Hradec
Head: Slavomil Hejný Třeboň

SYNANTHROPIC VEGETATION 13
DEPARTMENT

Address: Průhonice u Prahy čp 1, (zámek) 252 43 okres Praha-Západ
Head: Zdeněk Kropáč

TAXONOMY DEPARTMENT 14

Address: Průhonice u Prahy čp 1, (zámek) 252 43 okres Praha-Západ
Head: Dr Bohumil Slavík

České Vysoké učení 15
Technické v Praze*

[Prague Technical University]
Address: Zikova 4, Praha 6

FACULTY OF CIVIL ENGINEERING* 16

Dean: Professor Dr M. Holý

FACULTY OF ELECTRICAL 17
ENGINEERING*

Dean: Professor Z. Kotek

FACULTY OF MECHANICAL 18
ENGINEERING*

Dean: Professor J. Kamarád

FACULTY OF NUCLEAR PHYSICS* 19

Dean: I. Štoll

Československá akademie 20
věd

– ČSAV
[Czechoslovak Academy of Sciences]
Address: Národní třída 3, 111 42 Praha 1
Telephone: 24 34 419
Telex: 121 040 ACAD C
President: Academician Jaroslav Kožešník
Annual expenditure: over £2m
Activities: The Academy is the supreme national scientific institution in Czechoslovakia. Basic research programmes include: physical properties of matter and its microstructure (methods of contemporary mathematics); cosmic space, earth and the exploitation of its resources; theoretical fundamentals of technology; new chemical processes, their control and technology; structure and function of living matter; man and the biosphere; biological and medical foundations of the health development of man.
Contract work: Yes

Various research institutes and laboratories owe their allegiance to the Academy.

See separate entries for:
Astronomický ústav ČSAV
Biofyzikální ústav ČSAV
Botanický ústav ČSAV
Entomologický ústav ČSAV
Farmakologický ústav ČSAV
Fyzikální ústav ČSAV
Fyziologický ústav ČSAV
Geofyzikální ústav ČSAV
Geografický ústav ČSAV
Izotopová laboratoř biologických ústav ČSAV
Laboratoř radiologické dozimetrie ČSAV
Matematický ústav ČSAV
Mikrobiologický ústav ČSAV
Parazitologický ústav ČSAV
Psychologická laboratoř ČSAV
Psychologický ústav ČSAV
Společná laboratoř pro chemii a technologii silikátů ČSAV a VŠCHT
Ústav analytické chemie ČSAV
Ústav anorganické chemie ČSAV
Ústav experimentálnej biológie a ekológie ČSAV
Ústav experimentální botaniky ČSAV
Ústav experimentální medicíny ČSAV
Ústav fyzikální chemie a elektrochemie J. Heyrovskéko ČSAV
Ústav fyzikální metalurgie ČSAV
Ústav fyziky atmosféry ČSAV
Ústav fyziky plazmatu ČSAV
Ústav fyziologických regulací ČSAV
Ústav fyziologie a genetiky hospodářských zvířat ČSAV
Ústav jaderné fyziky
Ústav krajinné ekologie ČSAV
Ústav makromolekulární chemie ČSAV
Ústav molekulární genetiky ČSAV
Ústav organické chemie a biochemie ČSAV
Ústav přístrojové techniky ČSAV
Ústav pro elektrotechniku ČSAV
Ústav pro hydrodynamiku ČSAV
Ústav pro výzkum obratlovců ČSAV
Ústav radiotechniky a elektroniky ČSAV
Ústav teoretické a aplikované mechaniky ČSAV
Ústav teoretických základů chemické techniky ČSAV
Ústav teorie informace a automatizace ČSAV
Ústav termomechaniky ČSAV.

Československá Komise pro Atomovou Energii* 21

– ČKAE
[Czechoslovak Atomic Energy Agency]
Address: 9 Slezská, 120 29 Praha 2
Telephone: (02) 255551

Telex: 121 107 Fmt c
Chairman: Ing Jan Neumann
First Deputy Chairman: Ing Karel Barabas
Departments: Nuclear Energy, Ing Zdeněk Hatle; Nuclear Safety and Safeguards, Ing Jiří Beránek
Activities: Planning and coordination of the development of science and technique in the sphere of peaceful utilization of nuclear energy. Coordination and supervision of Czechoslovak institutions and institutes engaged in peaceful utilization of nuclear energy. Coordination of international relations in the sphere of nuclear energy and cooperation with international organizations.

Entomologický ústav ČSAV 22

[Entomology Institute]
Address: Viničná 7, 128 00 Praha 2
Telephone: 29 54 85
Parent body: Czechoslovak Academy of Sciences
Director: Vladimír Landa
Deputy director: Jaroslav Weiser
Sections: Department of Evolutionary Morphology, Vladimír Landa
Department of Insect Physiology, Dr Jaromír Pospíšil
Department of Insect Pathology, J. Weiser
Department of Insect Ecology, Dr Karel Novák
Department of Insect Toxicology, Assistant Professor Dr I. Hrdý
Activities: Study of the elementary regularities of the development and function of the insect organisms, the influence of physiologically active substances, the population dynamics, the relations within the communities, the resistance and diseases of insects; strives to achieve a synthesis of the obtained information.

Farmakologický ústav ČSAV 23

[Pharmacology Institute]
Address: Albertov 4, 128 00 Praha 2
Telephone: 29 46 13
Affiliation: Czechoslovak Academy of Sciences (ČSAV)
Director: Karel Mašek
Sections: Biochemical pharmacology, Dr K. Mašek; general pharmacology, Dr I. Janků; clinical pharmacology, Dr J. Elis; molecular pharmacology, Dr J. Seifert; psychopharmacology, Dr M. Kršiak
Graduate research staff: 14
Activities: Research in immunopharmacology (pharmacokinetic aspects, structure-action relationship and mechanism of action of immunomodulating compound), and neuropharmacology (biochemical aspects of

psychotropic drugs action and mechanisms involved in neurotransmitters synthesis and release).
Contract work: Yes
Publications: Pharmacology research reports.

Fyzikální ústav ČSAV   24

[Physics Institute]
Address: Na Slovance 2, 180 40 Praha 8
Telephone: 84 22 41
Parent body: Czechoslovak Academy of Sciences
Director: Ing Jaroslav Sedlák
Deputy director: Dr Jan Kaczér
Activities: Basic research in physics, ie in the physics of solids (magnetism, ferroelectrics, luminescence and other optical properties, the mechanical properties of solids), electric discharges in gases and the physics of elementary particles. Since 1964 the Institute has also been developing the field of applied optics.

DEPARTMENT OF APPLIED OPTICS   25

Address: Polská 26, Praha 2
Telephone: 25 33 07
Head: Dr Miroslav Malý

DEPARTMENT OF CHEMISTRY   26

Head: Ing Jiří Hejduk

DEPARTMENT OF CONSTRUCTION   27
AND MECHANICAL WORKSHOPS

Head: Bohumil Jehlička

DEPARTMENT OF DIELECTRICS   28

Head: Dr Jan Fousek

DEPARTMENT OF DISCHARGES IN   29
GASES

Head: Ing Václav Krejčí

DEPARTMENT OF ELECTRONICS   30

Head: Eduard Rechziegel

DEPARTMENT OF HIGH ENERGIES   31

Head: Dr Antonín Prokeš

DEPARTMENT OF LUMINESCENCE   32

Head: Miroslav Trlifaj

DEPARTMENT OF MAGNETISM   33

Head: Dr Zdeněk Frait

DEPARTMENT OF MECHANICAL   34
PROPERTIES OF SOLIDS

Head: Ing Bohdan Šesták

INSTITUTE OF SOLID-STATE PHYSICS   35

Address: Cukrovarnická 10, 162 53 Praha 6
Telephone: 35 42 41
Director: Ing Ladislav Štourač
Note: This was formerly a separate ČSAV Institute.

Fyziologický ústav ČSAV   36

[Physiology Institute]
Address: Budějovická 1083, 142 20 Praha 4 - Krč
Telephone: 49 11 57
Parent body: Czechoslovak Academy of Sciences
Director: Ladislav Vyklický
Deputy director: Assistant Professor Dr Stanislav Tuček
Sections: Department of Brain Research, Assistant Professor Dr Tomáš Radil
Department of the Physiology and Pathophysiology of the Neuromuscular System, Assistant Professor Dr Stanislav Tuček
Department of the Physiology and Pathophysiology of Metabolism, Dr Jiří Pařízek
Department of the Physiology and Pathophysiology of Ontogenesis, Assistant Professor Dr Jiří Jelínek
Activities: The physiology and pathophysiology of the nervous system concentrating on the general physiological problems of the nerve cell and the central nervous system, the questions of neuromuscular trophic relations, the mechanisms of locomotor functions, evolutionary physiology, and pathophysiology with special regard to the mechanisms of adaptation of the organism.

Geofyzikální ústav ČSAV   37

[Geophysical Institute]
Address: Boční II, č 1401,141 31 Praha 4
Telephone: 76 19 41
Parent body: Czechoslovak Academy of Sciences
Director: Václav Bucha

Deputy Director: Dr Oldřich Praus
Sections: Gravimetric Department, Dr Jan Pícha
Seismic Department, Dr Ludvík Waniek
Geomagnetic Department, Václav Bucha
Geoelectric Department, Dr Oldřich Praus
Ionospheric Department, Ing Pavel Tříska
Radiometry and geothermics group, Dr Vladimír Čermák
Activities: A comprehensive research of internal structure and the dynamics of the body of the Earth. In cooperation with other geophysical establishments the Institute renders more exact the data of the geophysical characteristics of the territory of Czechoslovakia. Within the framework of multilateral cooperation (KAPG - Commission for planetary geophysical research) the Institute tackles a number of tasks. It also ensures the operation of the affiliated geophysical observatories at Průhonice, Budkov, Kašperské Hory, Panská Ves, and the earth-tidal station in Příbram.

Geografický ústav ČSAV 38

[Geographical Institute]
Address: Mendelovo nám 1, 662 82 Brno
Telephone: 33 21 41
Parent body: Czechoslovak Academy of Sciences
Director: Assistant Professor Dr Jaromír Demek
Deputy Directors: Assistant Professor Dr Miroslav Macka, Jaroslav Slavíček
Activities: A centre of pursuits in research and science of the ČSAV in the areas of geography and living environment. The Institute has a multidisciplinary character, falling within the regions of natural and social sciences. It conducts research in relation to the systems of nature and the system of human society in space and time.

DEPARTMENT OF CARTOGRAPHY 39

Address: Na Příkopé 29, Praha
Telephone: 26 29 93
Head: Dr Zdeněk Hoffmann

DEPARTMENT OF ECONOMIC 40
GEOGRAPHY

Address: Mendelovo nám 1, 662 82 Brno
Head: Assistant Professor Dr Miroslav Macka

DEPARTMENT OF PHYSICAL 41
GEOGRAPHY

Address: Mendelovo nám 1, 662 82 Brno
Head: Assistant Professor Dr Jaromír Demek

DEPARTMENT OF THE COMECON 42

Address: Wenzigova 7, Praha 2
Head: Ing Vladimír Voráček

DEPARTMENT OF THE PROTECTION 43
OF ENVIRONMENT

Address: Mendelovo nám 1, 662 82 Brno
Telephone: 33 20 41
Head: Ing Antonín Buček

RESEARCH STATION SALMOVKA 44

Address: Moravian Karst, Skalní Mlýn Blansko
Telephone: 32 98

Geologický ústav Dionýza Štúra 45

[Geological Institute of Dionyz Stur]
Address: Mlynská dolina 1, 809 40 Bratislava
Telephone: 451 41-5
Director: Dr Ján Gašparik
Deputy director: Dr P. Reichwalder
Sections: Regional geology, Dr Ján Mello; economic geology, Dr Ján Ilavský; hydrogeology, Dr Vladimír Hanzel; geochemistry, Ing Stanislav Gazda; geochronology and isotopic geology, Ing Dr Jan Kantor
Graduate research staff: 100
Annual expenditure: over £2m
Activities: Regional geological mapping of West Carpathians (prospecting and geological research of mineral deposits; oil and gas prospecting, hydrogeological research, research of geothermal energy, biostratigraphy, sedimentology, engineering geology, geochemistry, geochronology, isotopic geology).
Contract work: No
Publications: Various journals.

Institut Hygieny a 46
Epidemiologie*

[Hygiene and Epidemiology Institute]
Address: Srobárova 48, 100 42 Praha 10
Activities: Guidance and monitoring of research into: hygiene, epidemiology, microbiology, occupational diseases, radiation hygiene, environmental hygiene, hygiene of children and adolescents, food hygiene.

Institut Klinicke a Experimentalni Mediciny*   47

– IKEM
[Clinical and Experimental Medicine Institute]
Address: Budějovická, 146 22 Praha 4
Affiliation: Czech Ministry of Health
Director: Professor Prokop Málek
Research centres: Cardiovascular, Professor Dr Libor Hejhal; Transplantation, Dr Vladimír Kočandrle; Clinical Pharmacology, Dr Zdeněk Modr; Metabolism and Nutrition, Professor Dr Josef Mašek
Activities: Cardiovascular diseases; organ transplantation.

EXPERIMENTAL LABORATORY*   48

Activities: Cardiovascular and transplantation experimental research.

MEDICAL ELECTRONICS DEPARTMENT*   49

Activities: Medical electronics in cardiovascular and transplantation research.

MEDICINE DEPARTMENT I*   50

Activities: Metabolic disturbances in relation to cardiovascular diseases and renal and hepatic insufficiency.

MEDICINE DEPARTMENT II*   51

Activities: Cardiology; angiology.

MEDICINE DEPARTMENT III*   52

Activities: Nephrology oriented to dialysis and renal transplantation.

NUCLEAR MEDICINE DEPARTMENT*   53

Activities: Radionuclide methods in cardiovascular and transplantation research.

PATHOLOGICAL ANATOMY DIVISION*   54

Activities: Postmortem and biopsy investigations and morphological research service.

SURGERY DEPARTMENT*   55

Activities: Cardiac, vascular and transplantation surgery.

THERAPEUTIC REHABILITATION DIVISION*   56

Activities: Therapeutic rehabilitation and special physical investigatory methods in cardiology and nephrology.

Izotopová laboratoř biologických ústav ČSAV   57

[Nuclear Biology and Radiochemistry Institute]
Address: Budějovická 1083, 142 20 Praha 4 - Krč
Telephone: 49 18 41
Parent body: Czechoslovak Academy of Sciences
Director: Ing Josef Benneš
Sections: Department of Synthesis of Labelled Organic Compounds, Ing Jan Hanuš
Department of Measurement of Radioactivity and Analysis of Radioactive Substances, Dr Arnošt Babický
Activities: Research of the preparation of organic metabolites labelled with radioactive isotopes, elaboration of methods for the measurement of radioactivity of organic compounds and for the measurement of activity of radionuclides in biological material. In cooperation with establishments engaging in biology, the Institute tackles tasks of basic research by applying isotope methods.

Laboratoř radiologické dozimetrie ČSAV   58

[Radiological Dosimetry Laboratory]
Address: Na Truhlářce 39/2a, 180 86 Praha 8 - Libeň
Telephone: 82 33 41
Parent body: Czechoslovak Academy of Sciences
Head: Ing Zdeněk Kovář
Sections: Physical and technical dosimetry, Ing František Cejnar; personal and environmental dosimetry, Assistant Professor Dr Zdeněk Spurný
Activities: Basic research in the regions of physical and personal dosimetry as well as in the study of dosimetric problems in the environs of nuclear installations.

Matematický ústav ČSAV 59

[Mathematics Institute]
Address: Žitná 25, 115 67 Praha 1 - Nové Město
Telephone: 22 66 01
Parent body: Czechoslovak Academy of Sciences
Director: Professor Jiří Fábera
Deputy director: Assistant Professor Alois Kufner
Activities: Basic research in mathematical analysis, (differential equations, numerical analysis, functional analysis), theory of probability and mathematical statistics, mathematical logic, topology, computer science, the graph theory and the theory of tuition of mathematics.

BRNO BRANCH 60

Address: Janáčkovo nám 2, Mendelovo nám 1, Brno
Telephone: 43 44 1
Head: Assistant Professor Ivan Kolář

DEPARTMENT OF CONSTRUCTIVE 61 METHODS OF MATHEMATICAL ANALYSIS

Address: Opletalova 45, Praha 1 - Nové Město
Telephone: 22 80 71
Head: Dr Milan Práger

DEPARTMENT OF NUMERICAL 62 ALGEBRA, GRAPH THEORY AND MATHEMATICAL LOGIC

Address: Žitná 28, Praha 2 - Nové Město
Telephone: 24 02 85
Head: Professor Miroslav Fiedler

DEPARTMENT OF THE THEORY OF 63 ORDINARY DIFFERENTIAL EQUATIONS

Address: Kladenská 60, Praha 6
Telephone: 36 13 36
Head: Jaroslav Kurzweil

DEPARTMENT OF THE THEORY OF 64 PARTIAL DIFFERENTIAL EQUATIONS

Address: Žitná 28, Praha 2 - Nové Město
or: Nové Mesto, Kratovská 10, Praha 1
Telephone: 24 02 85
Head: Assistant Professor Otto Vejvoda

DEPARTMENT OF THE THEORY OF 65 PROBABILITY AND MATHEMATICAL STATISTICS

Address: Žitná 25, 115 67 Praha 1 - Nové Město
Head: Dr František Zitek

DEPARTMENT OF TOPOLOGY AND 66 FUNCTIONAL ANALYSIS

Address: Žitná 28, Praha 2 - Nové Město
Telephone: 24 02 85
Head: Professor Vlastimil Pták

DIVISION FOR THE 67 MODERNIZATION OF THE TUITION OF MATHEMATICS

Address: Krakovská 10, Praha 1 - Nové Město
Telephone: 26 43 01
Head: Professor Jan Vysin

Mikrobiologický ústav 68 ČSAV

[Microbiology Institute]
Address: Budějovická 270/1083, 142 20 Praha 4 - Krč
Telephone: 49 18 41
Parent body: Czechoslovak Academy of Sciences
Director: Assistant Professor Ing Vladislav Zalabák
Deputy director: Dr Zdeněk Hošťálek
Activities: Basic research of the laws governing the growth and reproduction, the physiology, the biochemical activity and genetics of microorganisms and methodically close experimental models, the research of the relations among microorganisms, both among one another and with the external environment (soil macroorganism or the like); the obtained knowledge the Institute applies to the needs of the medical services, agriculture, nutrition and industry, in particular the fermentation industry.

BIOTECHNOLOGICAL LABORATORY 69

Address: Opatovický mlýn, Třeboň
Telephone: 22 04
Head: Dr Bohumil Prokeš

DEPARTMENT OF EVOLUTIONARY BIOLOGY   70

Address: Na Folimance 5, Praha 2 - Vinohrady
Telephone: 25 79 93
Head: Vladimír Novák

DEPARTMENT OF IMMUNOLOGY   71

Head: Dr Jaroslav Rejnek

DEPARTMENT OF MOLECULAR BIOLOGY AND GENETICS   72

Head: Karel Mikulík

DEPARTMENT OF SOIL MICROBIOLOGY   73

Head: Dr Vlastimil Vančura

DEPARTMENT OF TECHNICAL MICROBIOLOGY   74

Head: Dr Bohumil Sikyta

DEPARTMENT OF THE BIOGENESIS OF NATURAL SUBSTANCES   75

Head: Dr Zdenko Vaněk

GNOTOBIOLOGICAL LABORATORY   76

Address: okr Náchod, Nový Hrádek
Telephone: 75
Head: Dr František Kovářů

LABORATORY OF CELL-MEMBRANE TRANSPORT   77

Head: Arnošt Kotyk

Parazitologický ústav ČSAV   78

[Parasitological Institute]
Address: Flemingovo nám 2, 166 32 Praha 6 - Dejvice
Telephone: 32 01 41
Parent body: Czechoslovak Academy of Sciences
Director: Academician Bohumír Rosický
Deputy director: Dr Jan Prokopič
Activities: Research into the biological essence of parasitism aiming at the elucidation of evolutionary cycles, the ecology, histology and pathogeneity of important external and internal parasites of vertebrates; research aiming at the prevention of parasitoses; studies on the spatial structure and dynamics of the natural foci of infections of man and domestic animals in a cultivated landscape.

DEPARTMENT OF ARACHNOENTOMOLOGY AND NATURAL FOCALITY OF INFECTIONS   79

Head: Academician Bohumír Rosický

DEPARTMENT OF EXPERIMENTAL HELMINTHOLOGY   80

Head: Dr Jan Prokopič

DEPARTMENT OF HISTOLOGY AND PATHOLOGY   81

Head: Assistant Professor Dr Karel Blažek

DEPARTMENT OF PROTOZOOLOGY   82

Address: Viničná 7, Praha 2
Head: Dr Jiří Lom

Psychologická laboratoř ČSAV   83

[Psychology Laboratory]
Address: Mendelovo nám 1, 602 00 Brno
Telephone: 33 20 41
Parent body: Czechoslovak Academy of Sciences
Head: Assistant Professor Karel Hozman
Deputy to the head: Professor Robert Konečný
Sections: Department of Psychology of the Personality, Professor Robert Konečný
Department for the Comparative Study of the Similarities and Differences of Normal and Abnormal Mental Activity, Professor Robert Konečný
Department of Ontogenetic Psychology, Assistant Professor Josef Svančara
Central Laboratory, Assistant Professor Josef Svančara
Activities: Problems of the structure and the dynamics of the personality from the evolutionary viewpoint, from the angle of similarities and differences of normal and abnormal mental activity, and from the angle of creative activity.

Psychologický ústav ČSAV 84

[Psychological Institute]
Address: POD Vodárenskou Věži 4, 182 00 Praha 8
Telephone: 84 77 51
Affiliation: Czechoslovak Academy of Science
Director: Dr M. Kodým
Vice-Director: Dr S. Fraňková
Graduate research staff: 10
Activities: Basic research in psychology, general psychology, problem solving, creativity, thinking. Developmental psychology: personality formation, moral development. Comparative aspects: interaction between genotype and environment; influence of early malnutrition on behavioural development, animal model for the study of psychosomatic medicine. Pedagogical psychology: education, personality of the teacher, etc.
Contract work: Yes

Slovenská Vysoká Škola Technická Bratislava* 85

[Slovak Technical University in Bratislava]
Address: Gottwaldovo námestie 17, 880 43 Bratislava
Telephone: (07) 56 621

FACULTY OF CHEMICAL ENGINEERING* 86

Head: Professor A. Lodes

FACULTY OF CIVIL ENGINEERING* 87

Head: Professor M. Bielek

FACULTY OF ELECTRICAL ENGINEERING* 88

Head: Professor L. Hrušković

FACULTY OF MECHANICAL ENGINEERING* 89

Head: Professor S. Labuza

Společná laboratoř pro chemii a technologii silikátů ČSAV a VŠCHT 90

[Chemistry and Technology of Silicates Joint Laboratory]
Address: Suchbátarova 1905, 166 26 Praha 6 - Dejvice
Telephone: 332
Parent body: Czechoslovak Academy of Sciences
Head: Professor Ing Jaroslav Staněk
Deputy director and scientific secretary: Ing Jiří Götz
Sections: Department of Inorganic Glasses, Ing Jiří Götz
Department of Binding Materials, Assistant Professor Ing V. Šatava
Electron Microscopy Laboratory, Ing Václav Hulínský
Activities: Basic research in the field chemistry of silicates, primarily of inorganic glasses and certain types of binding materials.

Statni Ústav pro Kontrolu Leciv 91

[State Institute for Drug Control]
Address: Srobarova 48, 100 41 Praha 10
Telephone: 72 27 51
Director: J. Burianek
Activities: Governmental drug quality control and inspection.

Technickoekonomický Výzkumný Ústav Hutního Průmyslu 92

[Technical and Economic Research Institute of the Metallurgical Industry]
Address: Modřanská 18, 147 06 Praha 4 - Hodkovičky
Telephone: 46 30 41-49
Director: Josef Svatoš
Activities: Research of selected technological and economical problems for raising the efficiency of Czechoslovak ferrous metallurgy and ore mines.

Technický a skúšobný ústav stavebný 93

[Construction Engineering and Testing Institute]
Address: Lamačská, 809 42 Bratislava
Telephone: 42941
Director: Ing Ján Kováč
Graduate research staff: 50
Activities: Testing methods for building materials, elements and buildings. Research of these testing methods for industrial and on-site purposes as well as for standardization.
Contract work: Yes
Publications: Institute proceedings.

Univerzita J.E. Purkyně* 94

[Purkyně University]
Address: Arne nováka 1, 60177 Brno
Telephone: 59 711

FACULTY OF MEDICINE* 95

Dean: Professor Dr B. Bednářík

FACULTY OF NATURAL SCIENCES* 96

Dean: Professor Dr K. Hodák

Univerzita Karlova 97

[Charles University]
Address: Ovocný trh 5, 116 36 Praha 1
Telephone: 228 441
Rector: Professor Z. Češka

FACULTY OF HYGIENE 98

Dean: Professor V. Víšek

Anatomy Department 99

Head: Professor L. Puzanová

Forensic Medicine Department 100

Head: Professor S. Hájek

Gynaecology and Obstetrics Department 101

Head: Professor A. Novotný

Hygiene Department 102

Heads: Professor F. Janda, Professor K. Symon

Hygiene of Nutrition Department 103

Head: Professor A. Wolf

Internal Medicine Department 104

Head: Professor V. Vísek

Medical Organization Department 105

Head: Professor V. Bílek

Microbiology Department 106

Head: Professor V. Vacek

Neurology Department 107

Head: Professor V. Stýblova

Nuclear Medicine Department 108

Head: Professor J. Prokopec

Otorhinolaryngology Department 109

Head: Professor V. Chládek

Paediatrics Department 110

Head: Professor J. Ringel

Pathological Anatomy Department 111

Head: Professor M. Vorreith

Plastic Surgery Department 112

Head: Professor M. Fára

Professional Medicine Department 113

Head: Professor B. Svestka

Psychiatry Department 114

Head: Professor L. Hanzlícek

Roentgenology and Radiology Department 115

Head: Professor A. Sehr

Radiology Department 168

Head: Professor Z. Chudáček

Stomatology Department 169

Head: Professor B. Mejchar

Surgery Department 170

Head: Professor A. Podzimek

FACULTY OF NATURAL SCIENCES 171

Dean: Professor Ing F. Fabián

Analytical Chemistry Department 172

Heads: Professor J. Cíhalík, Professor J. Doležal, Professor J. Zýka

Applied Geophysics Department 173

Head: Professor L. Hradílek

Botany Department 174

Head: Professor R. Hendrych

Economic Geography Department 175

Head: Professor V. Häufler

Geology Department 176

Heads: Professor Z. Mísar, Professor M. Vaněček, Professor Z. Pouba

Geophysics Department 177

Head: Professor J. Gruntorád

Microbiology Department 178

Head: Professor O. Bendová

Mineralogy Department 179

Heads: Professor F. Cech, Professor Z. Pouba, Professor R. Rost

Organic Chemistry Department 180

Head: Professor J. Staněk, Professor A. Vystrčil

Palaeontology Department 181

Heads: Professor V. Pokorný, Professor Z. Špinar

Parasitology Department 182

Head: Professor B. Ryšavý

Petrography Department 183

Heads: Professor J. Konta, Professor F. Cech, Professor R. Rost

Petrology Department 184

Head: Professor F. Fediuk

Physical Chemistry Department 185

Head: Professor J. Dvorák

Physical Geography and Cartography 186
Department

Head: Professor V. Král

Soil Biology Department 187

Head: Professor J. Seifert

Zoology Department 188

Heads: Professor J. Doskočil, Professor F. Sládeček

FACULTY OF PAEDIATRICS 189

Dean: Professor J. Havlík

Gynaecology and Obstetrics 190
Department

Head: Professor A. Kotásek

Internal Medicine Department 191

Heads: Professor O. Gregor, Professor H. Havlík, Professor J. Svatý, Professor Z. Svoboda

Ophthalmology Department 192

Head: Professor H. Lomíčkova

Paediatrics Department 193

Heads: Professor Z. Hloušková, Professor J. Houštěk, Professor O. Hrodek, Professor O. Lesný

Pathology Department 194

Head: Professor V. Nahodil

Pharmacology Department 195

Head: Professor J. Vanéček

Physiotherapy Department 196

Head: Professor M. Máček

Surgery Department 197

Head: Professor J. Komínek

FACULTY OF PHARMACY 198

Address: ak Heyrovského 1203, 50027 Hradec Králové
Dean: Professor J. Květina

Chemistry Department 199

Head: Professor V. Jokl

Pharmacology Department 200

Heads: Professor J. Květina, Professor J. Solich

Univerzita Komenského Bratislava* 201

[Comenius University of Bratislava]
Address: Šafárikovo náestie 6, 885 45 Bratislava
Telephone: (07) 58 041

FACULTY OF MEDICINE AT BRATISLAVA* 202

Dean: Professor Dr G. Čatár

FACULTY OF MEDICINE AT MARTIN* 203

Dean: Professor Dr O. Hal'ák

FACULTY OF NATURAL SCIENCES* 204

Dean: Professor Dr S. Usačev

FACULTY OF PHARMACY* 205

Dean: Professor Dr M. Mandák

Univerzita Palackého v Olomouci* 206

[Palacký University]
Address: Křižkovského 10, 771 47 Olomouc
Telephone: (068) 22 441

FACULTY OF MEDICINE* 207

Dean: Professor Dr V. Švec

FACULTY OF NATURAL SCIENCES* 208

Dean: Professor Dr L. Sedláček

Univerzita Pavla Jozefa Šafárina* 209

[Safárik University]
Address: Srobárova 57, 040 00 Košice
Telephone: (095) 22 610

FACULTY OF MEDICINE* 210

Dean: Professor Dr J Lukáči

FACULTY OF NATURAL SCIENCES* 211

Dean: Professor Dr J. Daniel-Szabó

Ústav analytické chemie ČSAV 212

[Analytical Chemistry Institute]
Address: Leninova 82, 662 28 Brno
Telephone: 58 52 1
Parent body: Czechoslovak Academy of Sciences
Director: Assistant Professor Ing Jaroslav Janák
Sections: Department of Separation Methods, Ing Josef Novák
Department of Analysis of Gases, Ing Miloš Krejčí
Department of Electromigration Methods, Dr Petr Boček
Activities: Basic research of analytical micro to submicromethods, especially separation, further selected methods of structural analysis, as well as research of the corresponding instrumentation.

Ústav anorganické chemie ČSAV 213

[Inorganic Chemistry Institute]
Address: 250 68 Rez u Prahy
Telephone: 84 42 41
Parent body: Czechoslovak Academy of Sciences
Director: Ing Vladimír Zapletal
Deputy director: Assistant Professor Ing Vladimír Pour
Activities: Basic research in the areas of science of inorganic chemistry and technology and the regions related thereto, especially in the field of the synthesis of new and special inorganic compounds, as well as the research of their properties and kinetics, and the mechanism of inorganic reactions and the theoretical foundations of inorganic processes.

ESTABLISHMENT AT PRAHA 214

Address: Majakovského 24, Praha 6
Telephone: 32 58 34 - 6
Sections: Department of Homogeneous Kinetics and Catalysis, Ing Dr Josef Veprek-Šiška
Department of Theoretical Fundamentals of Inorganic Chemistry, Assistant Professor Ing Vladimír Pour
Department of Heterogeneous Reactions and Phase Transitions, Ing Ivo Sláma

Ústav experimentálnej biológie a ekológie ČSAV* 215

[Experimental Biology and Ecology Institute]
Address: Obrancov mieru 3, 88534 Bratislava
Affiliation: Czechoslovak Academy of Sciences

Ústav experimentálnej psychológie ČSAV* 216

[Experimental Psychology Institute]
Address: Kocelova 15, 80100 Bratislava
Affiliation: Czechoslovak Academy of Sciences

Ústav experimentální botaniky ČSAV 217

[Experimental Botany Institute]
Address: Na Karlovce 1, 160 00 Praha 6
Telephone: 32 57 85
Parent body: Czechoslovak Academy of Sciences
Director: Dr František Pospíšil
Deputy director: Jaroslav Kopta
Activities: Theoretical problems in the area of genetics, selection and breeding, physiology and pathology of plants.

DEPARTMENT OF GENETICS 218

Address: Na Pernikářce 59, Praha 6
Head: Dr Eva Klozová

DEPARTMENT OF PHYTOPATHOLOGY 219

Address: Na Karlovce 1, 160 00 Praha 6
Head: Dr Zdenko Polák

DEPARTMENT OF RADIOLOGY 220

Address: Ke dvoru 16/15, Praha 6 - Vokovice
Telephone: 36 86 04
Head: Ing Marie Králová

DEPARTMENT OF THE PHYSIOLOGY OF GROWTH AND DEVELOPMENT OF PLANTS 221

Address: Ke dvoru 16/15, Praha 6 - Vokovice
Telephone: 36 85 95
Head: Ing Ludovít Chvojka

DEPARTMENT OF THE PHYSIOLOGY OF NOURISHMENT OF PLANTS 222

Address: Na Karlovce 1, 160 00 Praha 6
Head: Dr František Pospíšil

DEPARTMENT OF THE PHYSIOLOGY OF PHOTOSYNTHESIS AND WATER RELATIONS OF PLANTS 223

Address: Flemingovo nám 2, Praha 6
Telephone: 32 83 41
Head: Dr Bohdan Slavík

DEPARTMENT OF THEORETICAL FOUNDATIONS OF BREEDING METHODS   224

Address: Sokolovská 6, Olomouc
Telephone: 09 86 14 3
Head: Dr Ing František J. Novák

Ústav experimentální medicíny ČSAV   225

[Experimental Medicine Institute]
Address: U nemocnice 2, 128 00 Praha 2
Telephone: 29 10 14
Parent body: Czechoslovak Academy of Sciences
Director: Vlastimil Kusák
Deputy director: Dr Milan Titlbach
Activities: The Institute has linked up the themes of medicine, otorhinolaryngology, plastic surgery, research of the ultrastructure of cells and tissues and ophthalmology that have previously been in hand in separate laboratories, in particular from the point of view of biological and medical research of the influence of external environment on the organism.

DEPARTMENT OF CHEMICAL CANCEROGENESIS   226

Address: Rzy v Orlických horách, Nový Hrádek
Telephone: 92 27 8
Head: Vlastimil Kusák Olešnice

DEPARTMENT OF IMMUNOLOGY   227

Address: U nemocnice 2, 128 00 Praha 2
Telephone: 29 29 41
Head: Dr Jiří Franěk

DEPARTMENT OF INNATE DEFECTS   228

Address: Šrobárova 50, Praha 10
Telephone: 73 44 51
Head: Professor Dr Václav Karfík

DEPARTMENT OF SENSORY ORGANS   229

Address: U nemocnice 2, 128 00 Praha 2
Telephone: 29 29 41
Head: Dr Luboš Voldřich

DEPARTMENT OF ULTRASTRUCTURE OF CELLS AND TISSUES   230

Address: Albertov 4, Praha 2
Telephone: 29 93 13
Head: Dr Milan Titlbach

Ústav fyzikální chemie a elektrochemie J. Heyrovského ČSAV   231

[J. Heyrovsky Physical Chemistry and Electrochemistry Institute]
Address: Maia Strana, Vlasska 9, 118 40 Praha 1
Telephone: 53 15 47
Affiliation: Czechoslovak Academy of Sciences
Director: Professor Dr A.A. Vlček
Deputy directors: Assistant Professor R. Kaldova, Assistant Professor D. Papoušek
Senior Officers: Cestmir Jech, Anton Fojtik
Sections: Chemical physics, Jan Vojtík; electrochemistry, Jiří Ríha; heterogeneous processes, Dr Ondřej Kadlec
Activities: The investigation of the structure and the reactivity of ions and molecules by means of quantum chemical, spectroscopic and other physical methods; the catalysis on the surfaces of metals, oxidation catalysis and homogeneous catalysis; electrochemistry; research of heterogeneous processes (sorption, kinetics and thermodynamics of heterogeneous processes, aerosols).

Ústav fyzikální metalurgie ČSAV   232

[Physical Metallurgy Institute]
Address: Žižkova 22, 616 62 Brno
Telephone: 58 11 1
Parent body: Czechoslovak Academy of Sciences
Director: Přemysl Ryš
Deputy director: Josef Čadek
Activities: Basic research on the properties of metals and alloys, particularly a study of the relations between the structure and the properties of alloys to improve the mechanical and the physical properties of metallic materials by means of systematic modifications of their structures, achieve higher use-values of metallic materials and a higher operational reliability of the elements made therefrom, under a simultaneous reduction of their weights.

DEPARTMENT OF ELECTRICAL AND MAGNETIC PROPERTIES   233

Address: Žižkova 22, 616 62 Brno
Head: Dr Tomáš Zemčík

DEPARTMENT OF HIGH-TEMPERATURE PROCESSES   234

Address: Žižkova 22, 616 62 Brno
Head: Josef Čadek

DEPARTMENT OF MECHANICAL PROPERTIES   235

Address: Žižkova 22, 616 62 Brno
Telephone: 59 28 7
Head: Professor Ing Mirko Klesnil

DEPARTMENT OF PHASE TRANSITIONS   236

Address: Žižkova 22, 616 62 Brno
Head: Dr Lubomír Karmazin

INSTITUTE OF THE THEORY OF METALLURGICAL PROCESSES OF THE ČSAV   237

Address: Místecká 17, Ostrava-Vítkovice
Telephone: 32 77 4
Head: Ing František Vyskup

PRAHA BRANCH   238

Address: Boční II, no 1401, Praha-Spořilov
Telephone: 76 25 45
Head: Dr Jaroslav Ježek

Ústav fyziky atmosféry ČSAV   239

[Atmospheric Physics Institute]
Address: Boční II čp 1401, 141 31 Praha 4 - Spořilov
Telephone: 76 19 41
Parent body: Czechoslovak Academy of Sciences
Director: Dr Vojtěch Vítek
Activities: Basic research in the areas of meteorology and physics of the atmosphere especially of the clouds, precipitations, and the meteorology of the boundary layer of the atmosphere, with application to the problem of air pollution.

DEPARTMENT OF ATMOSPHERIC AEROSOLS   240

Head: Dr F. Anýž

DEPARTMENT OF BOUNDARY LAYER OF THE ATMOSPHERE   241

Head: Dr J. Pretel
Sections: Observatories in Milesovka, p. Zalany, district Teplice v Cechach, and Kopisty u Mostu

DEPARTMENT OF CIRCULATION OF THE ATMOSPHERE   242

Head: Dr V. Vitek

DEPARTMENT OF PHASE TRANSITIONS IN THE ATMOSPHERE   243

Address: Husova 24, Hradec Králové 8
Telephone: 54 42 2
Head: V. Petera

Ústav fyziky plazmatu ČSAV   244

[Plasma Physics Institute]
Address: Nademlýnská 600, 180 69 Praha 9 - Hloubétín
Telephone: 86 21 12
Parent body: Czechoslovak Academy of Sciences
Director: Ing Jan Váňa
Activities: Basic physical research in the area of physics of plasma and the accelerators of electrons. In particular, research concentrates on the study of interaction of high-frequency waves and electron beams with plasma, with a view to using it for the heating of plasma to thermonuclear temperatures. In the field of accelerators the Institute is concerned with research and development of defectoscopic and medical betatrons.

DEPARTMENT OF ACCELERATORS   245

Head: Ing Karel Rytina

DEPARTMENT OF HIGH-TEMPERATURE PLASMA I   246

Head: Ing Pavel Šunka

DEPARTMENT OF HIGH-TEMPERATURE PLASMA II   247

Head: Dr Vladimir Kopecký

DEPARTMENT OF LOW-PRESSURE DISCHARGES   248

Address: U továren 261, Praha 10 - Hostivař
Telephone: 75 14 41
Head: Ing Emil Žizka

Ústav fyziologických regulací ČSAV   249

[Physiological Regulations Institute]
Address: Bulovka, wing 11, 180 85 Praha 8
Telephone: 82 15 06
Parent body: Czechoslovak Academy of Sciences
Director: Assistant Professor Dr Ctibor Dostálek
Sections: Research sector, Dr Jan Měšťan; clinical sector, Dr Jiří Neumann; technical sector, Ing Vladimír Novák
Activities: The study of the regulatory mechanisms of cardiac activity and the circulatory system at different levels - from the molecular level via the psychophysiological to the clinical level, making use of cybernetic approaches and modern computer methods.

Ústav fyziologie a genetiky hospodářských zvířat ČSAV   250

[Physiology and Genetics of Farm Animals Institute]
Address: Uhříněves, Pražká 560, 251 61 Praha 10
Telephone: 72 03 73
Parent body: Czechoslovak Academy of Sciences
Director: Jan Bílek
Deputy director: Ing Stanislav Bartoš
Activities: Physiology of the useful characteristics of farm animals and biochemical genetics.

DEPARTMENT OF BIOCHEMICAL GENETICS   251

Address: Rumburska 89, Liběchov near Mělník
Telephone: (9316) 3259
Head: Ing Miloslav Valenta

DEPARTMENT OF PHYSIOLOGY AT UHŘÍNĚVES   252

Head: Jan Bílek

Ústav jaderné fyziky   253

[Nuclear Physics Institute]
Address: Národní třída 3, 250 68 Řež
Telephone: 84 78 77
Telex: 122626 ujvc
Affiliation: Czechoslovak Academy of Sciences
Director: Josef Tuček
Departments: Theoretical Nuclear Physics, Dr Marian Gmitro, Dr Milan Vymazal
Nuclear Spectroscopy, Dr Jindřich Adam, Dr Josef Řízek, Dr Milan Honusek
Nuclear Reactions, Dr Vlastislav Presperín, Dr Pavel Bém
Neutron Physics, Dr Rudolf T. Michalec, Dr Zdeněk Kosina
Accelerators, Dr Václav Bejšovec, Dr Zdeněk Trejbal
Special Equipments, Dipl-Ing František Nový, Dipl-Ing Zdeněk Papež
Electronics, Dipl-Ing Josef Rousek, Dipl-Ing Jaromír Vícha

Ústav krajinné ekologie ČSAV   254

[Landscape Ecology Institute]
Address: 252 43 Průhonice
Telephone: 759 685
Affiliation: Czechoslovak Academy of Sciences
Research director: Dr Jaromír Pospíšil
Sections: Geoecology, Ing Jan Vaněk; plant and microbial ecology, Dr V. Mejstřík; animal ecology, Dr K. Šťastný; soil biology, Dr J. Rusek; hydrobiology, Dr J. Hrbáček
Graduate research staff: 90
Annual expenditure: £51 000-500 000
Activities: To promote a rational basis for inserting ecology into territorial planning and land use. The Institute is essentially multidisciplinary covering all important scientific approaches to landscape and to land use.
Contract work: No
Publications: Questiones Geobiologiceae.

HYDROBIOLOGICKÁ LABORATOŘ   255
ČSAV

[Hydrobiological Laboratory]
Address: Vltavská 17, 151 05 Praha 5
Telephone: 53 10 43
Head: Dr Jaroslav Hrbáček
Sections: Production processes, Dr J. Hrbáček; selfpurification processes, Dr V. Straškrabová; physiology of freshwater organism, Dr P. Blažka
Graduate research staff: 14
Annual expenditure: £10 000-50 000
Activities: Limnology of reservoirs from the level of monitoring and description of the distribution of organisms and abiotic parameters to the level of mathematical models (ie quantitative description of interactions) to quantify the processes and to pinpoint the critical inputs and/or processes within the system which are (or can be) influenced by man. A station at the Slapy Reservoir makes a continuous measurement of temperature stratification and meteorological parameters.
Contract work: No
Publications: Annual report; Hydrobiological studies 1-3.

Ústav makromolekulární   256
chemie ČSAV

[Macromolecular Chemistry Institute]
Address: Náměstí Heyrovského 2, 162 06 Praha 6
Telephone: 35 33 41
Parent body: Czechoslovak Academy of Sciences
Director: Karel Friml
Deputy directors: Professor Ing Jaroslav Kálal, Ing Jaroslav Hnídek
Sections: Department of Polymer Reactions, Ing Jiří Trekoval
Department of Special and Technical Polymers, Professor Ing Jaroslav Kálal
Department of Analytical and Spectral Methods in Macromolecular Chemistry, Ing Pavel Kratochvíl
Department of Physico-Chemical Properties of Macromolecular Compounds, Dr Miloslav Bohdanecký
Department of the Structure and Physical Properties of Macromolecular Compounds, Ing Karel Dušek
Computer centre, Dr Karel Huml
Activities: Scientific activity in the fields of macromolecular chemistry, macromolecular physical chemistry and macromolecular physics.

Ústav molekulární genetiky   257
ČSAV

[Molecular Genetics Institute]
Address: Flemingovo nám 2, 161 10 Praha 6 - Dejvice
Telephone: 32 01 41
Parent body: Czechoslovak Academy of Sciences
Director: Josef Říman
Sections: Department of Molecular Virology, Josef Říman
Department of Viral and Cellular Genetics, Dr Ivo Hložánek
Department of Tumour and Transplantation Immunology, Dr Jan Bubeník
Laboratory of Biochemistry and Viral Cancerogenesis, Dr Jindřich Kára
Department of Developmental Genetics, Alena Lengerová
Department of Immunogenetics, Dr Pavol Iványi
Activities: Basic research in the area of molecular biology and molecular genetics of the somatic cell, oriented at the study of the following: the properties and functional manifestations of onconoviruses and the control of activity of the genes responsible for cellular growth (with a special view to the onconogenic transformation of the cell); the properties of histocompatibility genes and the products of their activity, including the study of the mechanisms of gene expression and their effects.

Ústav organické chemie a   258
biochemie ČSAV

[Organic Chemistry and Biochemistry Institute]
Address: Flemingovo nám 2, 166 10 Praha 6 - Dejvice
Telephone: 32 01 41
Parent body: Czechoslovak Academy of Sciences
Director: Vlastimil Herout
Deputy directors: Ing Dr Karel Šebesta, Ing Otto Knessl
Activities: Basic research in the fields of organic chemistry, biochemistry and molecular biology. The trends of research are linked by interdisciplinary cooperation.

SECTOR OF BIOCHEMISTRY AND   259
MOLECULAR BIOLOGY

Sections: Department of Chemistry of Proteins, Ing V. Kostka
Department of Molecular Biology, Dr I. Rychlík

SECTOR OF ORGANIC CHEMISTRY 260

Sections: Department of Natural Substances, Dr L. Novotný
Department of Organic Synthesis, Ing J. Beránek
Service pilot plants at Lysolaje, Ing Dr J. Pliml

Ústav přístrojové techniky 261 ČSAV

[Scientific Instruments Institute]
Address: Královopolská 147, 612 64 Brno
Telephone: 54 31 1
Parent body: Czechoslovak Academy of Sciences
Director: Armin Delong
Deputy director: Professor Ing Vladimír Drahoš
Sections: Department of High-Frequency Spectroscopy, Ing Zenon Starčuk
Department of Quantum Radiation Generators, Ing Pratišek Petrů
Department of Electron Optics, Professor Ing Vladimír Drahoš
Activities: Research in the field of the methods and instruments of high-frequency spectroscopy, electron microscopy and the field of quantum radiation generators.

Ústav pro elektrotechniku 262 ČSAV

[Electrical Engineering Institute]
Address: Václavské nám 55, 116 90 Praha 1
Telephone: 26 59 45
Parent body: Czechoslovak Academy of Sciences
Director: Ing Miloš Štafl
Deputy director: Ing Dr Václav Hamata
Sections: Department of Physical Electrical Engineering, Ing Miloš Štafl
Department of Electromagnetic Field, Ing Jiří Kulda
Department of the Dynamics of Electric Machinery, Ing Dr Václav Hamata
Activities: The Institute with branches in Praha 1 - Staré Město, Praha 1 - Nové Město, Praha 3 - Vinohrady, and Rudná u Prahy, engages in basic research in heavy-current electrical engineering, especially in the area of the electromagnetic field and its application to electrical machinery and transformers, in the fields of dielectric strength, high voltages and the theory of dielectrics; concerned with the industrial applications of heavy-current electronics to the control of electric drives, as well as with the exploitation of the results of modern physics, to heavy-current electrical engineering.

Ústav pro hydrodynamiku 263 ČSAV

[Hydrodynamics Institute]
Address: Podbabská 13, 160 00 Praha 6 - Dejvice
Telephone: 32 90 51
Parent body: Czechoslovak Academy of Sciences
Director: Ing Anatas Curev
Deputy director: Assistant Professor Ing Alexandr Puzan
Sections: Flow of disperse systems, Ing Jaroslav Hrbek; transport phenomena in liquids and multiphase systems, Miroslav Rudiš; biomechanics, Assistant Professor Ing Alexandr Puzan; non-Newtonian liquids and rheology, Ing Jan Švec
Activities: Basic research in modern hydrodynamics and hydromechanics: the flow of non-Newtonian and Newtonian liquids and fluids, disperse and multiphase systems of organic and inorganic origins, their rheology, hydrodynamic part of biomechanics, hydrology and interdisciplinary problems of hydrodynamics. It investigates the most general problems of the mechanics of the continuum in the region of hydrodynamics.

Ústav pro výzkum 264 obratlovců ČSAV

[Vertebrate Zoology Institute]
Address: Květná 8, 603 65 Brno
Telephone: 33 11 43
Parent body: Czechoslovak Academy of Sciences
Director: Vlastimil Baruš
Activities: Basic research of vertebrates oriented towards economic and health service requirements, with a view to an active control of their population levels in order to protect field and forest crops, to protect stored materials, the health of man and of farm animals. Simultaneously, the Institute is concerned with a new conception of taxonomic units in biology, with the functional and evolutionary morphology of vertebrates, and investigates all ecological parameters, including the structure of the Central European fauna of vertebrates with respect to its origins.

EXPERIMENTAL-ECOLOGICAL 265 DEPARTMENT

Address: Studenec 122, p Koněšín, Třebíč
Telephone: 98 12 0

ICHTHYOLOGICAL DEPARTMENT 266

Head: Vlastimil Baruš

MORPHOLOGICAL DEPARTMENT 267

Head: Assistant Professor Oldřich Stěrba

ORNITHOLOGICAL DEPARTMENT 268

Head: Academician J. Kratochvíl

THERIOLOGICAL DEPARTMENT 269

Head: Assistant Professor Ing Jaroslav Pelikán

Ústav radiotechniky a elektroniky ČSAV 270

[Radio Engineering and Electronics Institute]
Address: Lumumbova 1, 180 88 Praha 8 - Kobylisy
Telephone: 84 37 41
Parent body: Czechoslovak Academy of Sciences
Director: Ing Václav Zima
Deputy director: Ing Ladislav Kratěna
Sections: Department of the Theory of Electronic Systems, Ing Václav Čížek
Depàrtment of Physical Problems of Optoelectronics, Ing Ján Mišek
Department of Optoelectronic Processing of Information, Ing František Hoff
Department of Microwave Electronics of Solids, Ing Anton Kuchar
Department of Electronics of Solids, Ing František Kubec
Department of Electronic Measurement Pulse Technique, Ing Jaroslav Šmíd
Department of Infrared Radiation, Ing Ladislav Kučera
Department of Precise Chronometry and Frequency, Ing Otokar Buzek
Activities: The theory of radioelectronic systems and physical problems of electronics and optoelectronics. The Institute's pursuits are primarily aimed at the research of electronic systems with a discrete processing of signals, at research of precise chronometry and frequency as well as the research of new physical phenomena suitable for exploitation in optoelectronics, microelectronics, microwave engineering and for optical transfer and processing of information.

Ústav teoretické a aplikované mechaniky ČSAV 271

[Theoretical and Applied Mechanics Institute]
Address: Vyšehradská 49, 128 49 Praha 2
Telephone: 29 64 51
Parent body: Czechoslovak Academy of Sciences

Director: Assistant Professor Ing Zdeněk Sobotka
Sections: Department of Non-Linear Mechanics, Assistant Professor Zdeněk Sobotka
Department of the Mechanics of Multi-Phase Media, Assistant Professor Ing Boris Kamenov
Department of the Mechanics of Non-Homogeneous Media, Assistant Professor Ing Jan Javornický
Department of Dynamics, Ing Jaroslav Šprinc
Department of Stability of Thin-Walled Bodies, Assistant Professor Ing Miroslav Škaloud
Activities: Basic and applied research in the area of the mechanics of plastic bodies and structures, particularly panels, shells, walls, networks and bridges. The Institute is primarily concerned with research into physically non-linear deformation processes including the influence of time; research into soils as multi-phase media with a special view to their rheological and structural properties; research into the dynamic problems of building and transportation structures, (to combine the phenomenological and the structural points of view).

Ústav teoretických základů chemické techniky ČSAV 272

[Chemical Process Fundamentals Institute]
Address: Rozvojová 135, 165 02 Praha 6 - Suchdol
Telephone: 32 94 41
Telex: 121339
Affiliation: Czechoslovak Academy of Sciences
Director: Dr J. Čermák
Departments: Separating processes, Dr V. Staněk
Chemical reactors, Dr J. Čermák
Heterogeneous reactions, Dr M. Kraus
Homogeneous reactions, Dr V. Chvalovský
Activities: The theory of chemical engineering, of which special attention is devoted to the hydrodynamics of single-phase and two-phase flows in chemical apparatus, extraction, column multi-stage chemical reactors, flow and mixing of non-Newtonian liquids, mechanics of loose materials, modelling and simulation of behaviour of chemical engineering systems, chemical thermodynamics of multiphase systems, kinetics of heterogeneously catalysed reactions, research of new types of catalysts and sorbents, selectivity of solid catalysts, the influence of structure on reactivity in homogeneous and heterogeneous catalytic reactions and the influence of the medium on the velocity and selectivity of the reactions in solutions.

Ústav teorie informace a automatizace ČSAV   273

[Theory of Information and Automation Institute]
Address: Pod vodárenskou věží 4, 180 76 Praha 8 - Libeň
Telephone: 84 77 51
Parent body: Czechoslovak Academy of Sciences
External Director: Academician Jaroslav Kožešník
Deputy director: Jiří Nedoma
Sections: Theory of automation, Professor Ing Vladimír Strejc; theory of information, Dr Otakar Sefl; operative research, Assistant Professor Ing Jiří Beneš; computer systems, Ing Karel Šmuk
Activities: Basic research in the areas of the theory of information, in the area of automation, in particular: the development of probability and statistical methods aimed at the applications in the region of industrial technology, biological cybernetics and the like; the theory of control of industrial and power-producing objects; development of special apparatus for investigating problems including the influence of random signals and processing the data for computers.

Ústav termomechaniky ČSAV   274

[Thermomechanics Institute]
Address: Puškinovo nám. č. 9, 160 00 Praha 6 - Bubeneč
Telephone: 32 60 41
Parent body: Czechoslovak Academy of Sciences
Director: Ing Miroslav Pichal
Deputy directors: Ing J. Kabelka, L. Půst
Sections: Thermodynamics and mechanics of fluid, Ing L. Tomanec; mechanics of solids, L. Půst
Activities: The basic responsibility of the Institute is research in the field of the mechanics of gases and rigid systems; thermomechanics of gases and solids, with special regard to conventional and non-conventional energy conversions and new technologies and procedures in the fields of engineering, metallurgy, and chemistry.
Publications: Research and technical reports.

Ústav zdravotní výchovy   275

[Health Education Institute]
Address: Třída Vítězného února 54, 121 39 Praha 2
Telephone: 292341
Director: Professor J. Holub
Research director: Professor A. Štaifová

Sections: Department of Young Generation, Professor A. Svobodová; Department of Adult Population, Professor S. Trča; Theoretical Group, Dr S. Huličník
Graduate research staff: 7
Annual expenditure: £10 000-50 000
Activities: Research into tasks of health education in the prevention of cardiovascular diseases; nutrition and prevention of cardiovascular diseases. Prevention of cardiovascular diseases in younger generation; school children and dependence involving substances. Health education and oncological programme. Socialist environment and its influence on healthy living; healthy living in developed socialist society. Health education possibilities and perspectives in mass media; possibilities of improving the preparation for conjugal life.
Contract work: No
Publications: Health Education (bulletin), *Actualities of health education* (journal).

Ústřední ústav geologický   276

[Geological Survey of Prague]
Address: Malostranské nám 19, 118 21 Praha 1
Director: Dr Jaroslav Vacek
Graduate research staff: 210
Annual expenditure: £501 000-2m
Activities: Basic and laboratory research, geological mapping, mineral resource prospecting activities, investigation of ore, non-metallic and oil deposits, geochemistry, hydrogeology.
Contract work: Yes
Publications: Journal of Geological Sciences, bulletin, geological and mineral deposit maps, monographs and bibliographies.

Výskumný ústav hutnictví železa dobrá   277

[Ferrous Metallurgy Research Institute]
Address: 739 51 Dobrá Okres Frýdek Místek
Telephone: 5421-5
Telex: 52691-2
Director: Karel Řericha
Vice Director: Vlastimil Lukeš
Sections: Ironmaking and steelmaking, Tasilo Prnka; electrosteel and materials, Miloš Karnovský; wire and screw production, Arnošt Bil
Activities: Scientific and technical development in the metallurgical technology field; ironmaking and steelmaking technology; properties of steel; development of new ferrous materials; metal forming; heat treatment; wire and screw production; automation of metallurgical processes.

Výskumný ústav lesného hospodárstva   278

[Forest Research Institute]
Address: 960 92 Zvolen
Telephone: 27 311
Telex: 72284 VÚLHZ C
Affiliation: Ministry of Forest and Water Management
Director: Igor Chudík
Vice-Director: J. Konôpka
Graduate research staff: 80
Annual expenditure: Kč24m
Activities: With six research stations, permanent and temporary research sites, and 3 000 research plots the main activity of the Institute is research work consisting of the solution of tasks resulting from the development of forestry to enable their highly effective use in forest operation; the application of research results in operational practice. Biology and improvement of forest tree species; silviculture; research of forest seed production; research of fast growing tree species; logging-technical research (classification of sites and forest stands, intermediate cutting and final cutting etc); development and construction (in transport at loading, at timber yards, forked devices for loaders, electrohydraulic devices used etc); research of forest road construction; building production; research of mathematical methods (for estimation of forest etc); research of the automated system of control; rationalization and work studies; ergonomical research; forest management; research of forest protection; game management; and ecological research. The Institute had substantially intensified its work in international scientific technical cooperation in utilization of timber, research of productivity, structure and functions of forest ecosystems, protection of forest ecosystems (geobiocenoses) and landscape, elaboration of methods for increasing forest productivity and intensification of forestry and finally in the programme-methodological bases of economical estimation of non-material forest functions, and has developed a wide cooperation with foreign partners on the basis of bilateral interbranch agreements with the USSR, Poland, German DR, Hungary, Bulgaria, Romania and Yugoslavia.
Contract work: No
Publications: Various reports and journals linked to research activity.

DEPARTMENT OF BIOLOGY AND SILVICULTURE   279

Head: A. Löffler
Activities: This Department is divided into four divisions which deal with the research of biology, improvement of forest tree species and silviculture.

Division of Biology and Improvement   280
of Forest Tree Species

Activities: Investigation of variability, selection and physiology of forest tree species; solving the care for improvement of forest genofunds.

Division of Fast Growing Tree Species   281

Activities: Improvement and cultivation of poplars, willows, acacias and other tree species, the foundation of lignicultures and other special wood plantations in lowland areas.

Division of Forest Seeds   282

Activities: Control and evidence of certified seed stands, elite trees, control and prognosis of seed collection, problems of seed storage and control and sowing, establishment of seed orchards, seed stands, establishment of forest orchards, etc.

Division of Silviculture   283

Activities: Problems of forest nurseries, afforestation, tending, regeneration, conversion, transformation and manuring of forests, simultaneously elaborating silvicultural measures according to groups of forest types.

DEPARTMENT OF ECONOMICS   284

Head: J. Gally
Activities: This Department comprises three scientific divisions dealing with the problems of forest economics, its control and the human factor in forest production.

Division of Enterprise and Branch   285
Economics

Activities: Methods of analyses and analyses of management at the level of forest enterprises, plants and branch.

Division of Ergonomics   286

Activities: Investigation of physical load and hygienics of labour, sociology of forest workers, humanization of labour in forests and improvement of care of forest workers.

Division of Mathematical Methods   287
and Management in Forestry

Activities: Methods of management, utilization of mathematical methods in management and especially with the possibilities of better utilization of the automation system of data processing and management.

DEPARTMENT OF FOREST MANAGEMENT, PROTECTION AND CREATION OF NATURAL ENVIRONMENT 288

Head: E. Sobocký
Activities: The Department consists of five divisions dealing with the problems of forest management, forestry amelioration, forest protection, game management, ecology of forests and natural environment.

Division of Forest Ecology and Natural Environment 289

Activities: Research of production, structure and functions of forest ecosystems and their relations to other ecosystems of landscape environment.

Division of Forest Management 290

Activities: Research of growth of forest stands, construction of growth, volume, assortment and other tables and new methods in forest management.

Division of Forest Protection 291

Activities: Research of biotic pests and abiotic causes of damage and protection against them. A separate group of workers is concerned with pest control and forecast, as well as with working out concrete instructions for protection against them.

Division of Forest-Technical Amelioration 292

Activities: Ameliorations of forest and landscape environment according to forest-technical methods, (the question of improving the atmosphere, water régime, soil, water courses and reservoirs).

Division of Game Management 293

Activities: Research of game, hunting grounds, methods of game keeping, its protection and protection of forest against game; methods of game management development.

TECHNICAL DEPARTMENT 294

Head: E. Kubašák
Activities: This Department also comprises four divisions which cover the technical problems in forestry.

Division of Development and Construction 295

Activities: Development, construction, production of functional models, mechanisms and their parts, testing of imported forest machines, adjustment of mechanisms produced in other branches of production and cooperation in the development and manufacture of mechanical equipment with engineering organizations.

Division of Development of Building Production 296

Activities: Elaborates geotechnical and hydrological basic material for forest road construction and other objects on the basis of investigation and it cooperates with the Division of Forest Buildings in the investigation of road construction with regard to the properties of the subsurface and kinds of building material.

Division of Forest Buildings 297

Activities: Investigation of technico-economical parameters of forest road construction, technologies of construction and maintenance of roads and other objects, simultaneously, evaluating machines used in forest road construction.

Division of Forest Technics 298

Activities: The problems of accessibility of stands, logging, skidding, transportation, storage, handling, loading, complex production technologies, measuring and evidence of timber and mechanization of silvicultural operations.

Výskumný ústav preventívneho lekárstva 299

[Preventive Medicine Research Institute]
Address: Limbová 14, 809 58 Bratislava
Telephone: 438 55 8
Telex: 92279
Director-General: Professor Juraj Červenka
Contract work: No
Note: The previous Institutes of Epidemiology and Microbiology, of Hygiene, and of Industrial Hygiene and Occupational Diseases, were integrated in August 1978 into the Institute of Preventive Medicine which is divided into four research centres.

EPIDEMIOLOGY AND MICROBIOLOGY CENTRE 300

Director: A. Milošovičová
Activities: Research in bacteriology, virology, epidemiology, parasitology and molecular biology.

HEALTH ADMINISTRATION CENTRE 301

Director: Dr J. Dejmek
Activities: Research in public health, and economy of health services.

HYGIENE CENTRE 302

Director: Professor L. Rosival
Activities: Research in general and environmental hygiene, hygiene of children and adolescents, food hygiene.

INDUSTRIAL HYGIENE AND OCCUPATIONAL DISEASES CENTRE 303

Director: Dr D. Líška
Activities: Research in industrial hygiene, physiology of work, radiation hygiene, occupational pathology.

Výskumný ústav rastlinnej výroby 304

[Plant Production Research Institute]
Address: Bratislavská cesta 122, 921 68 Piešťany
Telephone: 28-12,26-02
Affiliation: SLOVOSIVO, Scientific-Production Association for Plant Breeding and Seed Growing
Director: Ing Anton Piršel
Sections: Genetical engineering, Ing M. Užík; agricultural engineering, Ing S. Kubinec; agricultural systems, Ing J. Podoba; seed breeding, Ing T. Sinský
Graduate research staff: 125
Activities: Agrotechnics, genetics, plant nutrition, physiology, agricultural ecology, radiobiology, plant protection. Research into and breeding of cereals, forage plants, legumes and pulse crops. The Institute has eight affiliated breeding stations.
Contract work: No
Publications: Annual editions of scientific works (with summaries): Series A (forage plants), Series B (cereals and pulses).

Výskumný ústav tabakového priemyslu 305

[Tobacco Industry Research Institute]
Address: 951 34 Báb district Nitra
Telephone: 928 122
Research director: Ing František Serina
Sections: Plant breeding, Ing K. Škula; agrotechnics, Ing F. Majerník; technology of curing, Ing L. Hojer; protection of plants, Ing P. Uhrin; chemical technology, Ing E. Neščák; mechanization and automatization, Ing M. Griesbach
Graduate research staff: 4
Annual expenditure: Kč5.6m
Activities: Research on production of tobacco; breeding of new varieties, production of seeds, agrotechnics, protection of plants, diseases and insects, technology of priming and curing of tobacco; technology of fermentation, cutting, development of cigarette filters, development of cigarettes, automatic regulation of technological processes of production.
Contract work: Yes
Publications: Bulletin, and information sheets.

Výskumný ústav zváračský 306

– VUZ
[Welding Research Institute]
Address: Ulica Februárového vitazstva 71, 894 23 Bratislava
Telephone: 07 396
Telex: 093384 zvar c
Director: Ing Ján Skriniar
Research director: Ing Vladimír Uher
Head, Realization Department: Ing Marcel Sedlák
Sections: Physical metallurgy of welding processes, Ing Josef Vrbenský; weldability of structural steels, Ing Peter Ondrejček; weldability of high-alloy steels and alloys, Ing Koloman Malik; test methods and the research of properties of welded joints, Ing Karol Kálna; physics and technological development of welding methods, Ing Ladislav Lányi; welding machines and equipment, Ing Dušan Halabrín
Graduate research staff: 208
Annual expenditure: Kč42m
Activities: A member of the International Institute of Welding (IIW) and cooperates with East-European countries in the programme of the Council of Mutual Economic Aid, the Institute is a centrally directed research and development workplace in the sphere of welding in Czechoslovakia, solving problems in the field of new technological welding applications, develops systematically the physical metallurgy oriented to the weldability of structural materials and to the development of filler materials. It develops the research directed

to the reliability and functional safety of welded structures and appliances and renders valid modern scientific methods. The main tasks are: mechanization, automation, robotization of production; developing and applying unit type elements in constructions of welding machines and devices, applying ergonomics and hygienic modern design; investigating welding conditions and utilizing high-strength steels for welded structures; new applications of highly productive welding methods; developing filler materials (such as electrodes, fluxes, solders and metal powders) with special properties and a wide range of application; research of extreme state conditions resulting in failures of welded structures or devices from a stress viewpoint; research of physical and metallurgical welding conditions of structural materials; research of the work hygiene and safety in welding; analytical work for creating long term research and development programmes as well as predictions for welding development.

The Institute provides an advisory service to the industry, trains qualified welders and welding technologists, and manufactures special welding electrodes, fluxes, wires and solders in small quantities (pilot production), and is also responsible for standards, patents, and information services for welding in Czechoslovakia and has the following work places and branches to this end:

Branch workplace for scientific and technical development of welding

Branch department for patents and improvements

Branch centre for standardization

Branch department for scientific technical and economical information

State test board department and department of welders' education

Facilities: Thermorestor-W (welding thermal cycles simulator); electron microscopes JEOL and TESLA; scanning electron microprobes; neutron generator and full instrumentation for automatic activation analysis of metals; complete station for testing of model pressure vessels at ambient and low temperatures; testing machines and instruments for mechanical properties testing.

Contract work: Yes

Publications: Zvaračské správy (Welding News); *Zváranie* (Welding) in Slovak; research reports in Slovak; year book; seminar proceedings; catalogues of research results.

Vysoká škola báňská 307

[Mining and Metallurgy College]
Address: Třida Vitězněho února, 708 33 Ostrava-Poruba
Rector: Professor Oldřich Hajkr

FACULTY OF ECONOMY 308
Head: Professor Miloš Svoboda

FACULTY OF MECHANICAL AND 309 ELECTRICAL ENGINEERING
Head: Dr Ing Vladimír Podhorný

FACULTY OF METALLURGY 310
Head: Professor Karel Mazanec

FACULTY OF MINING ENGINEERING 311 AND GEOLOGY
Head: Professor Lubomír Šiška

Vysoká škola chemicko- 312 technologická

[Prague College of Chemical Technology]
Address: Suchbátarova 1905/5, 166 28 Praha 6 - Dejvice
Telephone: 341241,332
Telex: 122744-VSCH/C
Rector: Professor Jiří Mostecký
Vice-Rector: Professor Jaroslav Králíček
Faculty deans: Chemical technology, Associate Professor J. Matoušek
Fuel and water technology, Professor J. Pelikán
Foodstuffs and biochemical technology, Professor J. Davídek
Chemical engineering, Professor S. Valenta
Activities: Inorganic and organic materials development projects oriented towards pharmaceutical and medical applications as well as towards the areas of mechanical engineering, agriculture, electronics, etc; applied theory of catalytic processes; chemical reactors control theory; process optimization; kinetics, mechanisms, and thermodynamics of chemical and biochemical reactions.

Vysoká škola dopravy a 313 spojov v Žiline

[Žilina College of Transport and Communications]
Address: Moyzesova 20, 010 88 Žilina
Telephone: 238 03-5; 217 81-2
Rector: Professor Ing Jaroslav Jeřábek
Vice-Rector for Science, Research and Foreign Relations: Professor Ing Anton Puškár

FACULTY OF MECHANICAL AND ELECTRICAL ENGINEERING 314

Dean: Professor Ing Miroslav Zafka
Sub-Dean for Science, Research and Foreign Relations: Docent Ing Milan Kejzlar

Department of Communications 315

Head: Professor Oldřich Poupě

Department of Electrical Traction and Energetics 316

Head: Professor Ing Karel Horák

Department of Machining Technology and Bearing Production 317

Head: Professor Ing Bohuslav Matějka

Department of Mathematics 318

Head: Dr Pavol Grešák

Department of Mechanical Technology 319

Head: Professor Ing Jaromír Ponec

Department of Mechanics and Machine Elements 320

Head: Docent Ing Ladislav Málik

Department of Physical Training 321

Head: Docent Dr Bernard Šeffer

Department of Rolling Stock, Engines and Lifting Equipment 322

Head: Docent Ing Jaroslav Müller

Department of Rolling Stock Operation and Maintenance 323

Head: Docent Ing Dušan Habarda

Department of Technical Cybernetics 324

Head: Professor Ing Ladislav Skýva

Department of Technical Physics 325

Head: Docent Dr Ivan Baják

Department of Technological Management 326

Head: Ing Stanislav Kmet

Department of Telecommunications 327

Head: Docent Ing Karol Blunár

Department of Theoretical Electrotechnics and Electrical Machines 328

Head: Docent Ing Pavol Gerát

Department of Thermal and Hydraulic Machines 329

Head: Docent Ing Ferdinand Holeša

FACULTY OF OPERATION AND ECONOMY OF TRANSPORT AND COMMUNICATIONS 330

Dean: Docent Ing Ján Mikolaj
Sub-Dean for Science, Research and Foreign Relations: Docent Ing Ľudovít Šmál

Department of Air Transport 331

Head: Docent Ing Anton Slyško

Department of Communications 332

Head: Professor Ing Gabriela Mokošová

Department of Construction Planning and Ground Communication Reconstruction 333

Head: Docent Ing Michal Jacko

Department of Construction Planning and Railway Reconstruction 334

Head: Docent Ing Ján Hronský

Department of Engineering Structures and Bridges 335

Head: Docent Ing Ladislav Kapasný

Department of Geodesy and Geotechnology 336

Head: Ing Ivan Kubík

Department of Mathematical Methods 337

Head: Docent Marián Benický

Department of Mathematics 338

Head: Docent Dr František Púchovský

Department of Mechanics 339

Head: Docent Ing Václav Chyba

Department of Railway Transport and Traffic 340

Head: Docent Ing Bedřich Bureš

Department of Railway Transport Economy 341

Head: Professor Ing Bohumil Řezníček

Department of Road and City Transport 342

Head: Professor Ing Cyril Kubjatko

Vysoká Skola Lesnícka a Drevárska* 343

[Forestry and Wood Technology College]
Address: Šturova 4, Zvolen
Telephone: 23 271

FACULTY OF WOOD TECHNOLOGY* 344

Vysoká Skola Polnohospodá* 345

[Agricultural College]
Address: Nábrežie Mládeže, 949 76 Nitra
Telephone: (087) 26 241

FACULTY OF AGRICULTURAL ECONOMICS* 346

Dean: Professor J. Ševčík

FACULTY OF AGRONOMY* 347

Dean: Professor J. Benetín

FACULTY OF MECHANICS* 348

Dean: Professor P. Ducho

Vysoka Škola Technická v Košiciach* 349

[Košice Technical University]
Address: Svermova 9, Košice

FACULTY OF ELECTROTECHNICAL ENGINEERING* 350

Dean: Professor M. Rákoš

FACULTY OF ENGINEERING* 351

Dean: Professor J. Buda

FACULTY OF METALLURGY* 352

Dean: Professor J. Kocich

FACULTY OF MINING* 353

Dean: Professor J. Puzder

Vysoká škola veterinárska v Košiciach 354

[Košice College of Veterinary Sciences]
Address: Komenského 73, 041 81 Košice
Telephone: 321 11-15
Rector: Professor O.J. Vrtiak
Sections: Department of Veterinary Physiology, Histology and Anatomy, Professor P. Popesko
Department of Pathological Anatomy, Professor R. Škarda
Department of Pathological Physiology, Biochemistry and Toxicology, Professor K. Boďa
Department of Parasitology, Diseases of Fish, Bees and Game, Dr J. Hovorka
Department of Infectious Diseases, Biology and Tropical Diseases, Docent Dr A. Gdovinová
Department of Zootechnics and Veterinary Genetics, Professor Ing J. Gabriš

Department of Veterinary Dietetics and Nutrition, Professor J. Lazar
Department of Food Hygiene and Technology, Professor J. Pleva
Department of Internal Diseases of Ruminants and Swine, Professor L. Vrzgula
Department of Reproduction of Farm Animals, Professor P. Gamčík
Department of Diseases of Horses, Carnivores, Poultry, and Pharmocology, Professor K. Fried
Department of Surgery and Orthopaedics, Professor J. Šutta
Department of Veterinary Care, Postgraduate Education and Practice, Docent Dr S. Haladej
Department of Economics, Management and Organization of Agriculture, Professor Ing J. Šándor
Cabinet of the School Farm, Ing O. Žipaj
Central Laboratory of Electron Microscopy, Professor M. Belák
Annual expenditure: Kč6m

ÚSTAV EXPERIMENTÁLNEJ VETERINÁRNEJ MEDICÍNY 355

[Experimental Veterinary Medicine Institute]
Address: Duklianskych hrdinov 1, Košice
Telephone: 320 11
Telex: 77322
Director: Professor J.O. Vrtiak
Activities: Research into the essentials of animal health and diseases, reproduction and zoonoses.
Contract work: Yes

Vysoká škola zemědělská 356

[Agricultural College]
Address: Zemědělská 1, 662 65 Brno
Telephone: 05 604
Telex: 624 89
Rector: Professor Zdeněk Šteffl
Vice-Rectors: Professor Ing Jiří Ruprich, Professor Ing Jaroslav Krejčíř, Docent Ing Anton Matovič, Docent Ing Jiří Erbes, Docent Ing Jiří Žižlavský

FACULTY OF AGRICULTURAL ECONOMICS 357

Dean: Professor Ing Rudolf Kovář

Department of Agricultural Economics 358

Head: Professor Ing Alois Grolig
Activities: Planning and management of agriculture; internal farm management; expanded reproduction in agriculture; concentration, specialization, cooperation and integration in agricultural production.

Department of Agricultural Enterprise and Branch Economics 359

Head: Docent Ing Karel Vinohradský

Department of Energetics 360

Head: Professor Ing Rudolf Kovář

Department of Foundations of Technical Sciences 361

Head: Docent Ing Světmír Látal

Department of Interplant Mechanization and Electrification 362

Head: Docent Ing Cyril Kejík
Activities: Mechanization in cattle, pig and poultry breeding.

Department of Land Improvement and Agricultural Building 363

Head: Docent Ing Antonín Hrabal

Department of Law and Information Systems 364

Head: Docent Dr Stanislav Šuba

Department of Management in Agriculture 365

Head: Professor Ing Jan Truksa

Department of Mechanization of Plant Production 366

Head: Docent Ing Jaroslav Konupčík
Activities: Precise drilling of sugar-beet; potato and sugar-beet harvesting; combine harvesters.

Department of Operational Reliability of Machines and Engineering Technology 367

Head: Docent Ing Jan Satoria

Department of Organization of Agricultural Production 368

Head: Docent Ing Karel Novák
Activities: Management and planning in agricultural enterprises; organiz ational structure of agricultural enterprises, professional structure of agricultural managers; work studies in agriculture.

Department of Statistics and Mathematical Methods in Agriculture 369

Head: Docent Ing Jaroslav Dufek
Activities: General theory of statistics; agricultural statistics; biometry; scientific programming; production functions.

FACULTY OF AGRONOMY 370

Dean: Professor Ing Rudolf Vaculík

Department of Agricultural Chemistry, Plant Nutrition and Technology of Plant Products 371

Head: Docent Ing Bohumil Havelka
Activities: Effect of fertilization and agrotechnical measures on the formation of biomass, yield; content of nitrogen (protein or non-protein); quality of malting barley; fertility and chemical composition of floron sand.

Department of Agricultural Entomology and Phytopathology 372

Head: Docent Ing Zdeněk Čača
Activities: Occurrence and harmfulness of diseases in spring barley; health status of crops under irrigation; species of Drosophila gender in Czechoslovakia.

Department of Agricultural Practices 373

Head: Professor Ing Jaroslav Krejčíř
Activities: Agrotechnics of barley (place in crop rotation, straw utilization, weeds, nutrition, requirements on soil physical characteristics); requirements of legumes on soil physical characteristics, weed ecology in relation to concentration of different crops in crop rotation and to chemicalization; straw utilization for potato and sugarbeet.

Department of Botany and Plant Breeding 374

Head: Professor Ing Jiří Šebánek
Activities: Growth analysis and physiology of spring barley; study of the first growth stages of barley by means of film; control of dormancy in cereals; morphology and identification of spring barley varieties; weed flora of Moravia.

Department of Cattle, Horse and Sheep Breeding 375

Head: Docent Ing Jiří Zízlavsky
Activities: Increasing milk and meat performance of cattle; inbreeding of cattle; crossbreeding of domestic breeds of cattle; milk performance and early calving of heifers; large scale production technology of cattle.

Department of Chemistry and Biochemistry 376

Head: Docent Ing Lubor Vacek
Activities: Spectrophotometric and spectral determination of microelements; tanning matters in soil; analytical control of feedstuffs; distillation methods.

Department of Elements of Horticulture 377

Head: Docent Ing Jan Luzný
Activities: Effect of microelements on the performance of horticultural crops; influencing of plant growth with chemical substances; cultivation of selected varieties of vine in marginal areas; new technology of pot cultivation; utilization of plastics in horticulture.

Department of Farm Animal Nutrition and Feeding Technique 378

Head: Professor Ing Antonín Štěrba
Activities: Utilization of organic matter by pigs; feeding and breeding of rabbits; relations of nitrogen and energy metabolism of chickens; nutrition of hen and postnatal physiological state of the chick.

Department of Fisheries and Hydrobiology 379

Head: Docent Ing Jiří Jirásek
Activities: Plankton development; acclimatization of the coregonus family.

Department of Forage Crops and Feedstuffs Production 380

Head: Professor Ing Eduard Halva
Activities: Primary production in ecosystems of meadow communities; synecology and ecology of communities of forage plants; biology of growth and productivity of the most important feed legumes and grasses; mixtures for meadows and pastures; effectiveness of application of fertilizers in the second part of the growth season.

Department of General Animal Husbandry and Genetics 381

Head: Docent Ing Norbert Mašek
Activities: Selection effect of meat and milk production - construction of selection indices; changes in carcass quality of cattle; immunogenetic and physiological factors of poultry; polymorphism of milk protein fractions; protein polymorphism and enzyme activity of body liquids in cows.

Department of Morphology and Physiology of Farm Animals   382

Head: Professor Jan Podaný
Activities: Motility of digestive tract; frequency of food intake; energy metabolism in animals; zinc metabolism and animal physiology.

Department of Pig and Poultry Breeding   383

Head: Professor Ing František Špaček
Activities: Biological factors and meat performance of poultry; selection of meat type poultry; selection schemes in pig production; indices of meat performance; use of ultrasound for the determination of meat; fat ratio.

Department of Plant Production   384

Head: Docent Ing Josef Pflug
Activities: Productivity of the most important crops under conditions of South Moravia; study of transport of photosynthates in winter wheat; formation of biomass in dependence on agroecological conditions in spring barley; growth analysis in potato and sugarbeet; interrelations of root and shoot systems in fibre flax.

Department of Soil Science and Microbiology   385

Head: Professor Ing Rudolf Vaculík
Activities: Interrelations of microorganisms and plant roots; dynamics of chemical characteristics of soil within the complex of agrotechnical measures in spring barley; changes of soil character under irrigation; effect of fallout and exhalation on soil character.

Department of Zoohygiene and Technology of Animal Products   386

Head: Docent Ing Miloslav Novák
Activities: Milk quality and level of cows' performance; cooling of milk and its quality; evaluation of feed efficiency.

Department of Zoology and Small Farm Animal Breeding   387

Head: Professor František Tenora
Activities: Tropical insects and integrated methods of control; taxonomy of Central European members of the subfamily Iacrophaginae; parasitic worms of some vertebrates in Afghanistan; comparative and functional morphology of the tapeworm Cysticersus of the family Taenidae; density and dynamics of some economically important water birds.

Sub-Faculty of Horticulture   388

Address: 611 44 Lednice na Moravě

DEPARTMENT OF BIOCLIMATOLOGY AND LANDSCAPE ECOLOGY   389

Head: Docent Ing Vladimír Havícek
Activities: Microclimate of potato standing crop; radiation, climate and microclimate of foodplain forests; macrometeorological factors in relation to the formation of biomass in spring barley.

DEPARTMENT OF BIOTECHNICS OF LANDSCAPE VEGETATION   390

Head: Professor Ing Jan Jurča
Activities: Biotechnical changes of landscape by water management; organization of agricultural land resources within the framework of care of the landscape.

DEPARTMENT OF FRUIT GROWING AND VITICULTURE   391

Head: Professor Ing František Pospíšil
Activities: Determination of the optimal shape of the fruit tree; irrigation in fruit growing and viticulture; apricot varieties; rootstocks for vine; correlation of different parts of the vine plant; technology of wine production; yeast flora; history of agricultural education.

DEPARTMENT OF HORTICULTURAL TECHNOLOGY AND MECHANIZATION   392

Head: Professor Ing Zdeněk Šteffl
Activities: Dynamics of changes of material composition of fruit and vegetables during storage; mechanization of onion growing; post-harvest treatment of unstorable fruits and vegetables; study of the combination of mechanized and chemical soil tillage in vineyards.

DEPARTMENT OF LANDSCAPE GARDENING, AND ARCHITECTURE   393

Head: Professor Ing Bohdan Wágner
Activities: Formulating the principles of landscape formation in spa areas; normative values of species of trees important in landscape gardening; growing and breeding of lilies.

DEPARTMENT OF VEGETABLE CROP PRODUCTION   394

Head: Professor Ing Jaroslav Štambera
Activities: Ecosystems of selected vegetable species; agrotechnics of tomato and sweet pepper in South Moravia and under glass; flower biology of selected vegetable and ornamental species; breeding methods in Allium; agrotechnics of aromatic and curative plants; dormancy of vegetable fruits and seeds.

MENDELEUM EXPERIMENT STATION   395

Head: Docent Jan Vožda
Activities: Biometric and genetic analysis of quantitative traits and characters of plants; investigation and utilization of male sterility in Cucumis sativus; genetics of resistance of tomato to fungus diseases; development of a new synthetic variety of lucerne; maintenance breeding of hybrid maize.

FACULTY OF FORESTRY   396

Dean: Dr Ing Antonín Čihal

Department of Economics and   397
Management of Forestry

Head: Professor Ing Jiří Ruprich
Activities: Economics of multipurpose function of forests; reproduction process in forestry; systems of management and control in forestry; scientific programming in forestry; analysis of economic information in forestry; small size computers in forestry.

Department of Forest Botany and   398
Phytocoenology

Head: Professor Miroslav Penka
Activities: Physiology of nutrition; water relations; physiology of growth; cambial activity; taxonomy and ecology of the genus Salix; biogeocoenological units of Czechoslovakian forests; beech forests and their biogeocoenoses; biogeocoenoses of forest upper limit; transpiration of forest trees; relation of dormancy to water relations; primary productivity of lowland and highland forests; productivity of major field crops; photosynthesis and transpiration.

Department of Forest Engineering,   399
Reclamation and Torrent Training

Head: Docent Ing Jaroslav Beneš
Activities: Mechanical stability of forest stands; water balance of forest stands; watershed management; forest road network; erosion control; effect of forest cover percent on runoff; hydraulics of riperian stands; recreational function of forests; use of computers in forest road planning.

Department of Forest Establishing and   400
Tree Breeding

Head: Professor Ing Josef Kantor
Activities: Growth and regeneration capacity; genetics and physiology of reproductive organs; ageing of tree seeds; regeneration of germinated seedlings; breeding of Norway spruce, silver fir, poplar and willow; polyploidy.

Department of Forest Harvesting and   401
Wood Processing

Head: Professor Ing Jaroslav Dejmal
Activities: Non-destructive tests of wood; raw timber assortments; basic factors in logging and transport of timber; effect of tree spacing on rationalization of logging; ergonomics; work safety.

Department of Forest Management   402

Head: Docent Ing Lubomír Polák
Activities: Construction of yield tables; growth and increment of forest trees and stands; growth characteristics of typological units; regularities of changes of forest inventory quantities; methods of control and regulation of production; representative methods in forest inventories; methods of determination of management goals.

Department of Forest Mechanization   403
and Machinery Repair

Head: Professor Ing Vsevolod Petříček
Activities: Power chain saws; mechanization and automation of industrial log depots; mechanization of thinning; timber yard cross-cutting lines.

Department of Forest Protection   404

Head: Professor Ing Jaroslav Křístek
Activities: Insect pests of forest trees; effects of abiotic factors in floodplain forests; population dynamics of sawflies; predators of forest insects; fungus diseases of pine and oak; effect of mechanical injuries on infection by wood-destroying fungi; smoke pollutants; secondary pests in pine stands.

Department of Forest Soil Science and   405
Geology

Head: Dr Ing Emil Klimo
Activities: Water regime in forest soils; weathering and soil formation; clay minerals; manganese, cobalt and copper in forest soils; microbiology of forest soils; altitudinal soil zonality; podzolization; soils on drift sands.

Department of General and World   406
Forestry and Game Management

Head: Docent Ing Jaroslav Bergl
Activities: Regional assignment and production of main game species; criteria for allocation of hunting districts into quality classes; economics of game management; development and prognosis of forest resources in Czechoslovakia.

Vysoké Ucení Technické v Brne* 459

[Brno Technical University]
Address: Opletalova 6, 601 90 Brno
Telephone: (05) 25 83 13

FACULTY OF CIVIL ENGINEERING* 460

Dean: Professor M. Pokora

FACULTY OF ELECTRICAL ENGINEERING* 461

Dean: Professor Z. Ertinger

FACULTY OF MECHANICAL ENGINEERING* 462

Dean: Professor J. Žižka

FACULTY OF TECHNOLOGY* 463

Dean: Professor M. Mládek

Výzkrumná a vývojová 464 základna cukrovarnického průmyslu

[Sugar Industry Research and Development Institute]
Address: Komořanská 30, 143 19 Praha 4
Telephone: 46 87 41
Telex: 121791
Head: Ing Antonin Kovařik
Sections: Primary raw material, Ing L. Schmidt; technological research, Ing M. Friml; automatization, Dr Ing V. Valter; machinery research, Ing K. Duffek
Graduate research staff: 65
Activities: Processing of sugar beet, raw and white sugar; refining of raw sugar. Automatization of processes; analysis of sugar products.
Contract work: No

Výzkumný a vývojový 465 ústav dřevařský

[Timber Research and Development Institute]
Address: Pod plynojemem, 180 77 Praha 8
Telephone: 824841

Telex: 123 504
Affiliation: Board of management of the woodworking industry
Director: Ing Karel Pěnička
Graduate research staff: 77
Activities: Methods and machinery used in processing wood, timber and new materials.
Contract work: Yes

Výzkumný a zkušební 466 letecký ústav

[Aeronautical Research and Test Institute]
Address: 199 05 Praha 0 - Letňany 130
Director: Ing Josef Kurz
Activities: Wide activities applied to aeronautical research, development, testing, measuring and technology.

AEROSPACE INFORMATION 467 ANALYSIS AND DISSEMINATION CENTRE/ROS -VTEI VZLÚ

Address: 199 05 Praha 9 - Letňany 130
Head: Jiři Kůcera
Activities: Wide scope of aeronautical sciences, technology, and aeronautical SDI (selective dissemination of information) systems.

Výzkumný ústav chorob 468 revmatických

[Rheumatic Diseases Research Institute]
Address: Na slupi 4, 128 50 Praha 2
Telephone: 29 46 51
Director: Dr Alois Šusta
Sections: Clinical Department, C. Dostál; Laboratory Department, Dr J. Štěpán; rehabilitation, M. Králová
Activities: Degenerative diseases of joints and spine (pathophysiology of connective tissue; osteology; inflammatory rheumatic diseases; diffuse connective tissue diseases; clinical immunology; pharmacotherapeutical studies; surgery and rehabilitation; data processing and diagnostic modelling).
Contract work: No

Výzkumný ústav koželélný 469

[Shoe and Leather Research Institute]
Address: 762 65 Gottwaldov 2
Telephone: 067 231 51
Telex: 067 337 svit and 067 338 svit
Director: Ing Josef Horák
Sections: Technological Department of Footwear Production, Stanislav Kadlec; Research Department of New Shoemaking Materials, Eduard Mück
Graduate research staff: 110
Annual expenditure: Kč35m
Activities: Conservation of leather; new technologies of tanning; leather finishes; machines and equipment for the manufacture of new types of soft leathers, application of PUR in the shoemaking industry; processing of synthetic materials; shoemaking adhesives; new types of shoemaking machines and equipment; elimination of leather industry wastes with regard to environmental cleanliness.
Contract work: Yes
Publications: Bulletin.

Výzkumný ústav pro chemické využití uhlovodíků 470

[Hydrocarbon Chemical Utilization Research Institute]
Address: 436 70 Litvínov
Telephone: 035 294
Telex: Chemozavod Most 184278 or 184333
Affiliation: CHEMOPETROL, (Concern Enterprise Chemical Works of Czechoslovak-Soviet Friendship, Litvínov)
Director: Ing Milan Sýkora
Activities: Processes for the treatment of crude oil and petrochemistry, including development and evaluation of catalysts.

Výzkumný ústav pro práškovou metalurgii 471

[Powder Metallurgy Institute]
Address: 787 63 Šumperk
Director: Ing Karel Prokeš
Activities: Powder metallurgy of materials on the basis of metals, intermetallic compounds, cermets, including ferrites and superhard materials.

Výzkumný ústav rybářský a hydrobiologický 472

[Fisheries and Hydrobiology Research Institute]
Address: 389 25 Vodňany
Telephone: 905906
Affiliation: State Fishery
Director: Ing F. Kubů
Sections: Fish nutrition and protection, Ing V. Janeček; fish culture and biology, Ing J. Smíšek; natural waters and dam lakes, Ing J. Vostradovský; salmonid fish culture, Ing A. Komínek
Graduate research staff: 26
Activities: Research on fish culture, fisheries and hydrobiology, fish diseases, fish and water toxicology, fish culture economy, genetics, fish nutrition, optimalization of fish culture environment, utilization of heated effluents.
Facilities: Laboratories, experimental hatchery and rearing ponds; recirculating fish-culture system.
Contract work: No
Publications: Bulletin, papers, and bibliography.

DOL RESEARCH STATION 473

Address: 252 66 Libcice nad Vltavou Dol
Telephone: 896085-6
Head: Ing J. Vostradovský
Graduate research staff: 5
Activities: Research programme management of open waters (reservoirs and rivers in Bohemia) from the production and the sport fishing point of view, providing consultation and control services for optimization of ichthyofauna composition in dam reservoirs and rivers. Special interests are in specific fish stocks, management of the water supply reservoirs (drinking water); influence and support of predatory fishes, installation of new fish species, etc. Close contact is maintained with State Fishery, Anglers Union, and water management organizations.
Contract work: Yes
Publications: Bulletin.

Výzkumný ústav silnoproudě elektrotechniký 474

[Electrical Engineering Research Institute]
Address: 250 97 Praha 9 - Běchovice
Director: Dr Oldřich Hora
Activities: Theory of electrical machines and drives; physical problems in electrical engineering; power

electronics; switchgear technique; high-power testing laboratory; technical cybernetics; computer-aided design; analysis of development trends of electrical engineering.

Výzkumný ústav úpravy vod   475

– VUUV
[Water Treatment Research Institute]
Address: Pernerova 55, 186 06 Praha 8
Affiliation: CKD Dukla, National Enterprize
Director of the General Plant: Dr Pavel Jelínek
Director of Research: Dr Miloš Král
Activities: Technological research of water treatment processes for industrial and drinking purposes; development of apparatus, pilot scale examinations and conception proposals; consultant engineering; development of automatic photometric analyzers for automatic control of water treatment plants and stream pollution estimation.

Výzkumný Ústav Včelařský   476

[Apiculture Research Institute]
Address: Dol u, Libčic nad Vltavou
Director: Vladimir Veselý
Activities: Biology of bees and their protection from diseases; fodder bases, investigations in honey-bee products, economy and organization of beekeeping.

Výzkumný ústav veterinárního lékařství   477

[Veterinary Research Institute]
Address: Hudcova 70, 621 32 Brno
Telephone: 57811
Telex: 62475 vuvet

Affiliation: Ministry of Agriculture and Food
Director: Professor Antonín Holub
Sections: Infectious diseases, Dr V. Mádr; reproduction of farm animals, Dr V. Kummer; food hygiene, Dr J. Palásek; biophysics, Dr J. Hampl
Graduate research staff: 120
Activities: Physiology of young animals; control of infectious and parasitic diseases; control of reproduction (with special reference to intensive husbandry conditions). Health hazards associated with food of animal origin.
Contract work: No

Výzkumný ústav živočišne výroby   478

[Animal Production Research Institute]
Address: 251 61 Praha 10 - Uhřínéves
Telephone: 750 221
Telex: 121240
Director of Research: Dr Ing Miroslav Dvořáček
Sections: Genetics and farm animal improvement; technology of cattle breeding; technology of poultry breeding; nutrition and animal products evaluation; laboratory of farm animal physiology; group for research into and utilization of black and white cattle; coordination group
Activities: Rationalization of cattle breeding under large-scale production conditions; research into and working out of selection and hybridization programmes for farm animals; research into physiology of reproduction; research into nutrition including non-traditional feedstuffs utilization in farm animals; rationalization of poultry breeding under large-scale production conditions; working out of new technological systems for poultry breeding.
Contract work: Yes
Publications: Research reports.

DENMARK

Aalborg Universitetscenter   1

[Aalborg University Centre]
Address: Postbox 159, DK-9100 Aalborg
Telephone: (08) 15 91 11
Rector: Professor Sven Caspersen

FACULTY OF TECHNICAL AND   2
PHYSICAL SCIENCES

Dean: Jørgen Østergaard

Institute of Building Technology and   3
Structural Engineering

Head: E.J. Funch

Institute of Civil Engineering   4

Head: Torben Larsen

Institute of Development and Planning   5

Head: Jes Ryttersgaard

Institute of Electronic Systems   6

Head: Jørgen Nielsen

Institute of Industrial Construction   7
and Engineering Technology

Head: Knud Dalgaard-Jensen

Institute of Production and Production   8
Processes

Head: Poul Sveistrup

Abed Planteavlsstation   9

[Abed Plant Breeding Station]
Address: Abedvej 39, DK-4920 Søllested
Telephone: 03 911038
Director: Kurt Vive
Graduate research staff: 2
Annual expenditure: £51 000-500 000
Research activities: Plant breeding in spring barley and winter wheat.
Contract work: Yes

Akademiet for de Tekniske   10
Videnskaber

– ATV
[Danish Academy of Technical Sciences]
Address: Lundtoftevej 266, DK-2800 Lyngby
Telephone: (02) 88 13 11
Vice-President: Niels Gram
General-Secretary: Vibeke Q. Zeuthen
Activities: To further technical scientific research and the application of its results for the benefit of the Danish community and its industry and trade. ATV is responsible for general promotion work, establishing of new independent institutes and new research committees. It follows the trend of science andtechnology through the members of the Academy and through participation in international cooperation. The following committees within the ATV framework are at present in action:
Committee on Cooperation of Research, Development and Service
Committee on Indoor Climate
Committee on Industrial Research Education Programme
Committee on Computer Methods in Structural Mechanics

Committee on Development of Advanced Measuring Systems
See separate entries for:
Asfaltindustriens Oplysningskontor for Vejbygning
Asfaltindustriens Vejforskningslaboratorium
Bioteknisk Institut
BKF-Centralen
Danatom
Danfip
Danmedia
Dansk Automationsskelskab
Dansk Hydraulisk Institut
DDC
Elektronikcentralen
Emballageinstituttet
Fiskeriteknologisk Institut
Geoteknisk Institut
Korrosionscentralen ATV
Lydteknisk Laboratorium
Lysteknisk Laboratorium
Isotopcentralen
Medicoteknisk Institut
Optisk Laboratorium
Proteinkemisk Institut
Skibsteknisk Laboratorium
Skovteknisk Institut
Svejscentralen
Traeraadet
Vandkvalitetsinstituttet.
See also: Carbon 14 Centralen
Nordisk Forskningsinstitut for Maling og Trykfarver
which appear in the International Chapter of this book.

Arbejdsmiljøinstituttet 11

[Danish National Institute of Occupational Health]
Address: Baunegårdsvej 73, DK-2900 Hellerup
Telephone: (01) 68 28 68
Affiliation: Danish Labour Inspection Service
Director General: Dr Ib Andersen
Departments: Industrial hygiene/technical; Chemical-toxicological; Industrial medicine; Physiology/ergonomics; Industrialsociology/psychology; Technical/economical; Chemicals registration
Graduate research staff: 10
Activities: Occupational health, including industrial hygiene, medicine, toxicology. Research includes investigations of environmental hygiene in working places; air pollutants, microclimate, noise, ventilation; determination of toxic compounds in blood, urine.
Contract work: Yes

Århus Tandlaegehøjskole 12

[Royal Dental College, Århus]
Address: Vennelyst Boulevard 12, DK-8000 Århus C
Telephone: 06 132533
Dean: Professor Ole Fejerskov
Departments: Anatomy, Dr P.A. Knudsen
Bite Anatomy, Thor Troest
Conservative Dentistry, Dr Ole Fejerskov
Oral Diagnostics, Dr Steen Børglum Jensen
Oral Biology
Oral Histopathology, Dr H.P. Philipsen
Oral Surgery
Orthodontics, Dr Biete Melsen
Paedodontics, Dr Sven Poulsen
Periodontology, Dr Rolf Attstrom
Prosthetics, Ulrik Bertram
Public Health, Odd Lind
Technology
Graduate research staff: 50
Annual expenditure: over £2m

Århus Universitet 13

[Århus University]
Address: Ndr. Ringgade, DK-8000 Århus C
Telephone: (06) 13 43 11
Rector: Professor Carl F. Wandel
Pro-rector: Professor Ole Klindt-Jensen

FACULTY OF MEDICINE 14
Address: c/o Overlaege Palle Juul-Jensen, Neurology Department, Århus KommunehospitalNørrebrogade, DK-8000 Århus C
Telephone: (06) 12 55 55
Dean: Palle Juul-Jensen
Vice-Dean: Niels Ehlers
Scientific staff: 16

ANATOMY INSTITUTE A 15
Address: Wilhelm Meyers Allé, Universitetsparken, DK-8000 Århus C
Telephone: (06) 12 83 33
Head: Professor Arvid B. Maunsbach

ANATOMY INSTITUTE B 16
Address: Wilhelm Meyers Allé, Universitetsparken, DK-8000 Århus C
Telephone: (06) 12 80 66
Head: Professor Lennart Heimer

ANATOMY INSTITUTE C 17
Address: Wilhelm Meyers Allé, Universitetsparken, DK-8000 Århus C
Telephone: (06) 12 80 77
Head: Professor Andrus Viidik

BIOPHYSICS INSTITUTE 18
Address: Ole Worms Allé, Universitetsparken, DK-8000 Århus C
Telephone: (06) 12 95 88
Head: Irena Klodos

EXPERIMENTAL CLINICAL RESEARCH 19
INSTITUTE
Address: c/o Professor Erik Amdrup, Kirurgisk Afdeling L, Århus Komunehospital, DK-8000 Århus C
Telephone: (06) 12 55 55
Head: Professor Erik Amdrup

FORENSIC MEDICINE INSTITUTE 20
Address: Finsengade 15, DK-8000 Århus C
Telephone: (06) 12 56 77; 12 57 35
Head: Dr Markil Gregersen

GENERAL MEDICINE INSTITUTE 21
Address: Finsengade 10, DK-8000 Århus C
Telephone: (06) 12 24 98
Head: Erling Kjaerulff

HUMAN GENETICS INSTITUTE 22
Address: Bartholin Bygningen, Wilhelm Meyers Allé, Universitetsparken, DK-8000 Århus C
Telephone: (06) 13 97 11
Head: Dr Aage Juhl Therkelsen

HYGIENE INSTITUTE 23
Address: Ole Worms Allé, Universitetsparken, DK-8000 Århus C
Telephone: (06) 12 82 88
Head: F.B. Behrendt

MEDICAL BIOCHEMISTRY INSTITUTE 24
Address: Ole Worms Allé, Universitetsparken, DK-8000 Århus C
Telephone: (06) 12 93 99
Head: Dr Jesper Vuust Møller

MEDICAL MICROBIOLOGY INSTITUTE 25
Address: Bartholin Bygningen, Wilhelm Meyers Allé, Universitetsparken, DK-8000 Århus C
Telephone: (06) 13 97 11
Head: Claus Christensen

PHARMACOLOGY INSTITUTE 26
Address: Bartholin Bygningen, Wilhelm Meyers Allé, Universitetsparken, DK-8000 Århus C
Telephone: (06) 13 97 11
Head: Dr Folmer Nielsen-Kudsk

PHYSIOLOGY INSTITUTE 27
Address: Ole Worms Allé, Universitetsparken, DK-8000 Århus C
Telephone: (06) 12 99 55

SOCIAL MEDICINE INSTITUTE 28
Address: Vesterbro Torv 1-3,6, DK-8000 Århus C
Telephone: (06) 13 88 22
Head: Svend Sabroe

Hospitals 29

AALBORG SYGEHUS NORD 30
[Aalborg North Hospital]
Address: Reberbanegade, DK-9100 Aalborg
Telephone: (08) 13 11 11
Departments: Gynaecology-obstetrics; Paediatrics

ÅRHUS AMISSYGEHUS 31
[Århus County Hospital]
Address: Tage Hansensgade, DK-8000 Århus C
Telephone: (06) 12 68 66
Departments: Anaesthesiology; Surgical; Clinical Chemistry; Medical; Pathology Institute; Radiology

ÅRHUS KOMMUNEHOSPITAL 32
[Århus Municipal Hospital]
Address: Nørrebrogade, DK-8000 Århus C
Telephone: (06) 12 55 55
Departments: Anaesthesiology; Blood-bank and Tissue Type Laboratory; Gynaecology and Obstetrics; Clinical Chemistry Central Laboratory; Orthopaedic Surgery E; Urological Surgery K; Surgical L; Thoracic Surgery; Plastic Surgery 2; Medical C; Medical M Research; Cardiology; Neurology; Neurosurgery; Pathologic Anatomy; Paediatrics; Radiology; Ophthalmology; Otorhinolaryngology

ESBJERG CENTRALSYGEHUS 33
[Esbjerg Central Hospital]
Address: Østergade, DK-6700 Esbjerg
Telephone: (05) 12 82 33
Department: Paediatrics

HERNING CENTRALSYGEHUS 34
[Herning Central Hospital]
Address: DK-7400 Herning
Telephone: (07) 12 44 00
Department: Paediatrics

MARSELISBORG HOSPITAL 35
Address: P.P. Ørumsgade, DK-8000 Århus C
Telephone: (06) 14 27 77
Departments: Industrial Medicine Clinic; Dermatovenereological; Medical-epidemic A

ORTOPAEDISK HOSPITAL 36
[Orthopaedic Hospital]
Address: Randersvej 1, DK-8200 Århus N
Telephone: (06) 16 75 00

PSYKIATRISK HOSPITAL 37
[Psychiatric Hospital]
Address: Psykiatrisk Hospital ved Århus, Asylvej,
DK-8240 Risskov
Telephone: (06) 17 77 77

RANDERS CENTRALSYGEHUS 38
[Randers Central Hospital]
Address: Østervangsvej, DK-8900 Randers
Telephone: (06) 42 52 00
Departments: Anaesthesiology; Gynaecology-
obstetrics; Central Laboratory; Surgical; Medical;
Pathologic Anatomy; Paediatrics

ST JOSEPHS HOSPITAL 39
Address: Nørregade, DK-6700 Esbjerg
Telephone: (05) 12 93 11
Department: Gynaecology-obstetrics

SILKEBORG CENTRALSYGEHUS 40
[Silkeborg Central Hospital]
Address: Århusvej, DK-8600 Silkeborg
Telephone: (06) 82 16 00
Departments: Anaesthesiology; Gynaecology-
obstetrics; Surgical; Medical

FACULTY OF NATURAL SCIENCES 41
Dean: Dr Hans Henrik Andersen

Astronomy Institute 42
Address: Langelandsgade, Bygning 520, DK-8000
Århus C
Telephone: (06) 12 88 99
Head: Ole Møller
Scientific staff: 9

Botany Institute 43
Address: Nordlandsvej 68, DK-8240 Risskov
Telephone: (06) 21 06 77
Head: Benjamin Øllgaard
Scientific staff: 31

Chemistry Institute 44
Address: Langelandsgade, Bygning 510, DK-8000
Århus C
Telephone: (06) 12 46 43
Head: Jørgen Byberg
Scientific staff: 51

Exact Science History Institute 45
Address: Ny Munkegade, Bygning 521, DK-8000
Århus C
Telephone: (06) 12 71 88
Head: Kirsti Andersen
Scientific staff: 6

Genetics and Ecology Institute 46
Address: Ny Munkegade, Bygning 550, DK-8000
Telephone: (06) 12 71 88 (genetics, ecology); (06) 12 51
77 (palaeontology)
Scientific staff: 17

Geography Institute 47
Address: Vennelyst Boulevard 8, DK-8000 Århus C
Telephone: (06) 12 03 99
Head: Åke Micklander
Scientific staff: 12

Geology Institute 48
Address: Ole Worms Allé, Bygning 120, DK-8000
Århus C
Telephone: (06) 12 82 33
Head: Søren Rasmussen

ENDOGENETIC GEOLOGY 49
LABORATORY
Address: Ole Worms Allé, Bygning 120, DK-8000
Århus C
Telephone: (06) 12 82 33
Scientific staff: 11

EXOGENETIC GEOLOGY LABORATORY 50
Address: Ole Worms Allé, Bygning 120, DK-8000
Århus C
Telephone: (06) 12 82 33
Scientific staff: 6

GEOPHYSICS LABORATORY 51
Address: Finlandsgade 6-8, DK-8200 Århus N
Telephone: (06) 16 16 66
Scientific staff: 9

PALAEONTOLOGY AND 52
STRATIGRAPHY LABORATORY
Address: Ole Worms Allé, Bygning 120, DK-8000
Århus C
Telephone: (06) 12 82 33
Scientific staff: 4

PHYSICAL GEOGRAPHY LABORATORY   53

Address: c/o Fysiske Institut, Ny Munkegade, Bygning 521, DK-8000 Århus C
Telephone: (06) 12 88 99
Scientific staff: 8

Mathematics Institute   54

Address: Ny Munkegade 116, Bygning 530-40, DK-8000 Århus C
Telephone: (06) 12 71 88
Head: Professor Leif Kristensen

DATA DEPARTMENT   55

Address: Ny Munkegade 116, Bygning 540, DK-8000 Århus C
Telephone: (06) 12 83 55
Scientific staff: 22

MATHEMATICS DEPARTMENT   56

Address: Ny Munkegade 116, Bygning 530, DK-8000 Århus C
Telephone: (06) 12 71 88
Scientific staff: 34

THEORETICAL STATISTICS DEPARTMENT   57

Address: Ny Munkegade 116, Bygning 530, DK-8000 Århus C
Telephone: (06) 12 71 88
Scientific staff: 7

Molecular Biology and Plant Physiology Institute   58

Address: Ole Worms Allé, Bygning 130, DK 8000 Århus C
Telephone: (06) 12 51 77
Head: Ole S. Rasmussen
Scientific staff: 18

Physics Institute   59

Address: Ny Munkegade, Bygning 520, DK-8000 Århus C
Telephone: (06) 12 88 99
Head: Poul V. Thomsen
Scientific staff: 57

Social Geography Institute   60

Address: Vestergade 19, DK-8000 Århus C
Telephone: (06) 12 02 50
Head: Professor Johannes Humlum
Scientific staff: 2

Zoology and Zoo Physiology Institute   61

Address: c/o Zoologisk Laboratorium, Universitetsparken, Biologi III, Bygning 135, DK-8000 Århus C
Telephone: (06) 12 51 77
Head: Boy Overgaard Nielsen

ZOO PHYSIOLOGY LABORATORY   62

Address: Universitetsparken, Biologi II, Bygning 131, DK-8000 Århus C
Telephone: (06) 12 51 77
Scientific staff: 7

ZOOLOGICAL LABORATORY   63

Address: Universitetsparken, Biologi III, Bygning 135, DK-8000 Århus C
Telephone: (06) 12 51 77
Scientific staff: 12

FACULTY OF SOCIAL SCIENCES   64

Address: Ndr. Ringgade 1, Bygning 430, DK-8000 Århus C
Telephone: (06) 13 43 11
Dean: Niels Amstrup

Business Management Institute   65

Address: Bartholins Allé, Bygning 350, Universitetsparken, DK-8000 Århus C
Telephone: (06) 13 01 11
Head: Professor Chr. Andersen

Operations Analysis Institute   66

Address: c/o Matematisk Institut, Bygning 530, Ny Munkegade, DK-8000 Århus C
Telephone: (06) 12 71 88
Head: Kim Andersen

Psychology Institute   67

Address: Asylvej 4, DK-8240 Risskov
Telephone: (06) 17 55 11
Head: Knud Kielgast

Statistics Institute   68

Address: Bartholins Allé, Bygning 350, Universitetsparken, DK-8000 Århus C
Telephone: (06) 13 01 11
Head: Svend Terp

Asfaltindustriens Oplysningskontor for Vejbygning
69

[Danish Asphalt Industries' Information Office for Road Construction]
Address: Stamholmen 91, DK-2650 Hvidovre
Telephone: (01) 78 08 22
Affiliation: Akademiet for de Tekniske Videnskaber - ATV
Director of Research: J.M. Kirk
Activities: Consulting work for users of bituminous road materials; research is carried out through Danish Asphalt Industries' Laboratory for Road Construction.

Asfaltindustriens Vejforskningslaboratorium
70

[Danish Asphalt Industries' Laboratory for Road Construction]
Address: Stamholmen 91, DK-2650 Hvidovre
Affiliation: Akademiet for de Tekniske Videnskaber - ATV
Head: Jørgen la Cour

A/S C.E. Basts EFTF
71

Address: PO Box 3023,44 Ingerslevsgade, DK-1705 København V
Telephone: 451-313355
Telex: 22981 bast-dk
Director of Research: V. Jespersen
Deputy Director of Research: G. Kristensen
Graduate research staff: 3
Annual expenditure: £10 000-50 000
Activities: Research on consistency of fat blends; protein chemistry; biomedia; application of animal fats.
Contract work: No

Bioteknisk Institut
72

– BI
[Biotechnical Institute]
Address: Holbergsvej 10, DK-6000 Kolding
Telephone: (05) 52 04 33
Telex: 16 600 fotex dk attn Biotech Kolding
Affiliation: Akademiet for de Tekniske Videnskaber - ATV
Head: P. Sonne-Frederiksen
Activities: Chemical analysis and control of feeds, foods, technical finished and half-finished products. Development of advanced plants for industrial feed production, vegetable stores, straw processing plants, etc. Technical development within the processing and organic raw materials (grain, potatoes, straw, etc) with a view to limiting the pollution from industries and higher yield of finished goods. Chemical research in order to obtain more nutritive foods (animals and human beings). Research for public and private means when basic knowledge is needed for the above activities.

BKF-Centralen
73

[Danish Structural Research and Development Centre]
Address: Bygning 371, Elektrovej, DK-2800 Lyngby
Telephone: (02) 88 66 22
Affiliation: Akademiet for de Tekniske Videnskaber - ATV
Head: S. Øivind Olesen
Activities: The Centre has developed a tool for calculation and control of the hardening process in the production of concrete. Other activities includestrength and stiffness properties of building structures as well as concrete technology; theoretical and experimental testing, research and development projects, including tests on a 12 x 16 m span floor.

Carlsberg Forskningscenter
74

[Carlsberg Research Centre]
Address: Gammel Carlsbergvej 10, DK-2500 Valby København
Telephone: 01-221022
Affiliation: United Breweries Incorporated
Research directors: Professor Martin Ottesen, Professor Diter von Wettstein, B. Ahrenst Larsen, Lars Munck, ErikMernøe
Graduate research staff: 60
Annual expenditure: over £2m
Activities: Fundamental research within biochemistry and genetics; brewing chemistry; barley plant breeding; brewing technology; milling technology.
Contract work: No
Publications: Carlsberg Research Communications.

Carlsberg Laboratoriet
75

[Carlsberg Laboratory]
Address: Gammel Carlsbergvej 10, DK-2500 Valby København
Parent body: Carlsbergfondet

DEPARTMENT OF CHEMISTRY   76

Head: Professor Martin Ottesen
Activities: The molecular structure and function of proteins with emphasis on proteolytic enzymes.

DEPARTMENT OF PHYSIOLOGY   77

Head: Professor D. von Wettstein
Activities: Physiology and genetics with emphasis on barley and yeast.

Carlsbergfondet   78

[Carlsberg Foundation]
Address: H.C. Andersens Boulevard 35, DK-1553 København V
Telephone: 1-14 21 28
Chairman, Board of Directors: Professor Kristof Glamann
Directors: Professor C.J. Ballhausen, Professor HenrikGlahn, Professor Ebba Lund
Secretary-General: Niels Petri
Annual expenditure: £501 000-2m
Activities: The Foundation is required by its charter to own at least fifty-one per cent of United Breweries Limited. The five members of the Board are elected by the Danish Academy of Sciences and Letters from among its own membership. It grants funds to the Carlsberg Laboratory; supports the natural sciences, mathematics, philosophy, humanities and social sciences; maintains the Museum of Natural History, Frederiksborg Castle. Grants are not made for applied science.
Contract work: No
Publications: Annual reports, in Danish.
Note: See separate entries for Carlsbergfondets Biologiske Institut; Carlsberg Laboratoriet.

Carlsbergfondets Biologiske   79
Institut

[Biological Institute of the Carlsberg Foundation]
Address: 16 Tagensvej, DK-2200 København N
Telephone: 01-376715
Parent body: Carlsbergfondet
Acting Director: Dr Helge A. Andersen
Graduate research staff: 6
Annual expenditure: £51 000-500 000
Activities: Cancer research. The regulation of nucleic acid metabolism ineukaryote cells.
Contract work: No

A/S Cheminova   80

Address: PO Box 9, DK-7620 Lemvig
Telephone: (07) 83 41 00
Telex: 66514 Chemv DK
Director, Development and Research: Hans Rasmussen
Chemist: Per Dausell Klemmensen
Veterinarian: Erik Høgsbro Østergaard
Graduate research staff: 8
Annual expenditure: £501 000-2m
Activities: Research on activity of insect hormones and hormone mimics; activity of fungicides, especially industrial fungicides; intermediary products for pesticides, especially phosphorous compounds, carbamates and cyclopropane derivatives; phosphorous and carbamate insecticides; reaction kinetics, process design and unit operations in chemical engineering.
Contract work: No

Niels Clauson-Kaas   81
Chemical Research
Laboratory

Address: Rugmarken 28, DK-3520 Farum
Telephone: (02) 95 18 81
Telex: 37187 invent dk
Director: Niels Clauson-Kaas
Sections: Organic chemistry; contract research; custom synthesis
Graduate research staff: 10
Annual expenditure: £51 000-500 000
Activities: Laboratory research in order to prepare new molecules, or make new and cheaper production recipes for known compounds.
Facilities: Laboratory, pilot plant, library.
Contract work: Yes

Danatom   82

[Danish Association for Industrial Development of Atomic Energy]
Address: Allégade 2, PO Box 106, DK-3000 Helsingør
Telephone: (03) 36 00 22
Telex: 41110 SKIBYG
Affiliation: Akademiet for de Tekniske Videnskaber - ATV
General Secretary: Arne Jensen
Annual expenditure: £10 000-50 000
Activities: Established in 1956 to assist Danish industry and utility companies in technical and economical matters concerning nuclear power plants.
Contract work: No
Publications: Kort Nyt om Atomenergi.

Danfip 83

[Danish Federation for Information Processing]
Address: Kronprinsensgade 14, DK-1114 København K
Affiliation: Akademiet for de Tekniske Videnskaber - ATV
Secretary: Hans Kruger

Danfoss A/S 84

Address: DK-6430 Nordborg
Telephone: 45 4 45 2222
Telex: 50599
Research director: Jørgen Clausen
Research manager: Flemming Thorsøe
Sections: Industrial control and equipment, A.A. Højgaard; ultrasonics, B. Birker; energy and indoor climate, K. Hallgreen; solid-state physics, N. Lervad; ceramic technology, H. Ørum
Graduate research staff: 30
Annual expenditure: over £2m
Contract work: No

Danmarks Akvarium 85

[Denmark's Aquarium]
Address: Kavalergården 1, DK-2920 Charlottenlund
Telephone: 01-623283
Director: Dr Torben Wolff
Graduate research staff: 2
Activities: Artificial breeding of the European eel (Anguilla rostrata).
Contract work: No

Danmarks Apotekerforening 86

[Association of Danish Proprietor Pharmacists]
Address: Lergravsvej 59, DK-2300 København S
Director: Vibeke Waarst

DAK-LABORATORIET 87

[DAK Laboratories]
Telephone: 01-551188
Director: Hans Børsting
Sections: Pharmaceutical-technical, Thora Middelsen; chemical, Lis Smed; pharmacological, Aase Helles; microbiological, Lis Møhl
Graduate research staff: 11
Annual expenditure: £51 000-500 000
Activities: Development of pharmaceutical specialities for production andsale from Danish pharmacies.
Contract work: No

Danmarks Farmaceutiske Højskole* 88

[Pharmacy School of Denmark]
Address: 2 Universitetsparken, DK-2100 København O
Telephone: (045) 37 08 50
Head: Professor Dr Helmut Kofad
Activities: Pedology and research into pharmaceutical sciences in departments of chemistry, physics, pharmacy, pharmacognostics, microbiology, biology, and biochemistry.

Danmarks Fiskeri- og Havundersøgelser 89

[Danish Institute for Fisheries and Marine Research]
Address: Stormgade 2, DK-1470 København K
Telephone: (01) 62 85 50
Telex: 19960
Affiliation: Ministry of Fishery
Director: Jørgen Mødller Christensen
Graduate research staff: 38
Contract work: No
Publications: DANA, journal.

Danmarks Geologiske Undersøgelse   90

– DGU
[Geological Survey of Denmark]
Address: Thoravej 31, DK-2400 København NV
Telephone: 01-106600
Affiliation: National Agency for the Protection of Nature, Monuments and Sites, Ministry of the Environment
Research director: Ole Berthelsen
Departments: General Geology and Raw Materials, E. Heller; Geobotanical, Sv.Th. Andersen; Geochemical, H. Kristiansen; Subsurface Geology, O. Michelsen; Hydrocarbon; Stratigraphy Geology, L.B. Rasmussen; Hydrogeology, L.J. Andersen; Planning, N.V. Jessen
Graduate research staff: 50
Annual expenditure: £501 000-2m
Activities: Geological mapping; raw material research; vegetational history; water supply and geoelectrical research; geophysical research; oil and gas prospecting.
Contract work: Yes

Danmarks Ingeniørakademi   91

– DIA
[Engineering Academy of Denmark]
Address: Bygning 101, DK-2800 Lyngby
Telephone: 01-88 22 22
Rector: Professor E. Knuth-Winterfeldt

CHEMICAL ENGINEERING DEPARTMENT   92

Telephone: 01-88 56 00
Head: J.D. Morirad
Sections: Biochemistry and biochemical engineering, Uwe Nissen
Chemical engineering, L. Alfred Hansen
Electrical engineering,Otto Mortensen
Industrial chemistry, C. Jensen-Holm
Inorganic and physical chemistry, J. Potts
Management, Bent Hesse Rasmussen
Mathematics, J.D. Monrad
Mechanical engineering, E. Møller Andersen
Metallurgy, E. Maahn
Organic chemistry, Poul Sørensen
Physics, Peter Laut

CIVIL ENGINEERING DEPARTMENT   93

Telephone: 01-88 52 11
Head: N. Krebs Ovesen
Sections: Building materials, Anders Nielsen

Constructionengineering and management, Svend Borrit
Datalogy, O. Kayser
Design and construction of buildings, Henrik Nissen
Engineering drawing, F. Riemann
Heating and air conditioning, electrical and lighting engineering, P. Becher
Hydraulics and water engineering, vacant
Linear algebra and differential geometry, P. Printz
Mathematics, Ove Ditlevsen
Physics, Peter Laut
Road engineering, Morten Ludvigsen
Sanitary engineering, Ib Middelsen
Soil mechanics and foundation engineering, N. Krebs Ovesen
Structural design, N.J. Gimsing
Surveying, K. Engel Olsen
Theoretical and applied mechanics, Ervin Poulsen
Traffic and town planning, Vagn Lykke Pedersen

ELECTRICAL ENGINEERING DEPARTMENT   94

Telephone: 01-88 30 22
Head: Otto Mortensen
Sections: Electrical machines, E.W. Jensen
Electrical power systems, Jakob Lund
Electronics, Otto Mortensen
Electrotechnics, Erik Drag
Industrial economics, Svend Jensen
Industrial organization, Aage Tarp
Materials technology, Ulf Langer
Mathematics, Paul Edwin Kustaanheimo
Mechanical technology, J. Balle-Jensen
Physics, Hans Rahbek
Statics and strength of materials, J. Gerstoft
Theory of machines, Nis Rahr

MECHANICAL ENGINEERING DEPARTMENT   95

Telephone: 01-88 21 44
Head: Steen Laier
Sections: Chemistry and metallurgy, Niels Hansen
Economics, Jørgen Saabye
Electrical engineering, K.O.B. Jørgensen
Heating and ventilating, Georg Schmidt
Management and organization, Torben Stoubaek
Mathematics and mechanics, H.H. Hansen
Mechanical engineering, Andreas Andersen
Mechanical engineering and engineering drawing, Nis Rahr
Mechanical technology, E.H. Hertz
Physics, E. Winstrøm-Olsen
Strength of materials, Steen Laier

Danmedia 96

[Danish Research Society for Mass Media and Telecommunication]
Address: Anker Heegaards Gade 4, DK-1503 København V
Telephone: (01) 11 33 77
Affiliation: Akademiet for de Tekniske Videnskaber - ATV
Secretary-General: Mogens Boman
Graduate research staff: 2
Annual expenditure: £51 000-500 000
Activities: Mass media and telecommunication research concerning the impact of new technologies on society, trade and the individual.
Contract work: Yes

Dansk Automationsskelskab 97

[Danish Automation Society]
Address: Danmarks Tekniske Højskole, Bygning 229, DK-2800 Lyngby
Affiliation: Akademiet for de Tekniske Videnskaber - ATV
Secretary: Hakon Nielsen

Dansk Hydraulisk Institut 98

[Danish Hydraulic Institute]
Address: Agern Allé 5, DK-2970 Hørsholm
Telephone: (02) 86 80 33
Telex: 374O2dhicp dk
Affiliation: Akademiet for de Tekniske Videnskaber - ATV
Director: Torben Sørensen
Sections: Computational hydraulics centre, G.S. Rodenhuis; harbours and marine structures, J. Kirkegaard; transport processes, P. Mortensen; hydrology, T.J. Clausen
Graduate research staff: 10
Annual expenditure: £51 000-500 000
Activities: The Institute is engaged in field, laboratory and mathematical model studies of hydraulic and hydrologic problems in marine and civil engineering. The Institute has a wide range of instruments for field measurements of sub-bottom profiles, water depths, water levels, waves, currents, temperatures,salinities, tides, winds, iceberg profiles etc. Model basins and wave flumes for irregular wave and current studies are available, together with computers and software for the processing and statistical analysis of large quantities of data.

Advanced hydrodynamic models are developed and applied. The Institute alsodevelops field and laboratory equipment.
Contract work: Yes
Publications: Danish Hydraulics, a newsletter issued 2-3 times a year.

Dansk Rumforskningsinstitut 99

[Danish Space Research Institute]
Address: Lundtoftevej 7, DK-2800 Lyngby
Telephone: 02-882277
Telex: 37198 Danru
Affiliation: Ministry of Education
Research director: H.W. Schnopper
Graduate research staff: 21
Annual expenditure: £501 000-2m
Activities: Research on cosmic rays; ion-cyclotron waves; plasmas.
Contract work: Yes

Dansk Textil Institut 100

[Danish Textile Institute]
Address: Gregersensvej 5, DK-2630 Taastrup
Telephone: 02-99 88 22
Director: K. Sandahl Skov
Research director: Tormod Sørensen
Graduate research staff: 2
Annual expenditure: £51 000-500 000
Activities: Choice of suitable raw materials for production of textiles and clothing, reuse of dyehouse waste water, flammability of bedclothes, energy conservation in textile processing.
Contract work: Yes

Danske Hedeselskab 101

[Danish Land Development Service]
Address: Postboks 110, DK-8800 Viborg
Telephone: 06-626111
Telex: 66228 danla dk
Research director: Viggo Larsen
Sections: Soil improvement; drainage; irrigation;agro-hydrology; soil chemistry
Graduate research staff: 75 (forestry); 85 (engineering); 60 (agronomy)
Annual expenditure: £501 000-2m

Dataanalytisk Laboratorium 102

[Data Analysis Laboratory]
Address: Lottenborgvej 24, DK-2800 Lyngby
Telephone: (01) 87 06 31
Affiliation: Ministry of Agriculture, Danish Research Service for Plant and Soil Science
Head: Karl Sandvad
Sections: Experimental design and analysis of experimental data, Kristian Kristensen, Karen Dalbro; agricultural meteorology and climatology, Søren Aggergaard Middelsen
Graduate research staff: 4
Annual expenditure: £100 000
Activities: The Laboratory advises agricultural and horticultural institutes and experimental stations in matters concerning experimental design and analysis of experimental data by means of computers. Investigations into the relationships between climatological conditions and growth of agricultural crops.
Contract work: No

DDC 103

[Danish Datamatics Centre]
Address: Elektrovej, Bygning 341, DK-2800 Lyngby
Affiliation: Akademiet for de Tekniske Videnskaber - ATV
General Manager: Leif Rystrøm

DISA Elektronik A/S 104

Address: Mileparken 22, DK-2740 Skovlunde
Telephone: (02) 84 22 11
Telex: 3 53 49 disae dk
Parent body: Dansk Industri Syndikat A/S
Manager, Scientific Research Equipment: S.B. Jakobsson
Annual expenditure: £501 000-2m
Activities: To develop and produce scientific instrumentation for flow measurements (fluid mechanics), invasive (CTA), and optical (LDA laser). Medical:myographs, urodynamics.
Contract work: No
Publications: DISA Information.

Elektronikcentralen 105

[Danish Research Centre for Applied Electronics]
Address: Venlighedsvej 4, DK-2970 Hørsholm
Telephone: (02) 86 77 22
Telex: 37 121 elctr dk
Affiliation: Akademiet for de Tekniske Videnskaber - ATV
Head: Ove E. Petersen
Activities: Research, development, testing and consultative services for individual clients or on a multiclient basis. Main areas are: system engineering and circuit design; component and material technology; environmental engineering and testing. Participation in international projects ranging from feasibility studies to manufacturing programmes provides fundamental background in project management and quality assurance. Techniques aimed at a cost effective approach to research and development activities and pilot production.
Contractwork: Yes

Emballageinstituttet 106

[Danish Packaging Research Institute]
Address: Jemtelandsgade 1, DK-2300 København S
Telephone: (01) 54 00 22
Affiliation: Akademiet for de Tekniske Videnskaber - ATV
Research director: Kurt H. Garmin
Activities: Information and advisory services. Research on testing methods, mechanical and climatic environment, and general subjects. Confidential research is performed for organizations and firms in Denmark and abroad. Complete range of mechanical and climatic testing equipment. Laboratory simulation of transport and storage conditions in respect to handling, shunting, vibrations, stacking, humidity, high and low temperatures, and climate variations. Control of packaging and packaging materials according to international standards.

Finseninstitutet * 107

[Finsen Institute]
Address: Strandboulevarden 49, DK-2100 København
Telephone: (01) 26 08 50
Activities: Radiobiology; medical application of isotopes; health physics.

Fiskeriministeriets Forsøgslaboratorium 108

[Technological Laboratory, Ministry of Fisheries]
Address: Bygning 221 Lundtoftevej, DK-2800 Lyngby
Telephone: (02) 884066
Telex: 37529 DTHDIA DK
Affiliation: Ministry of Fisheries
Director: Poul Hansen
Annual expenditure: £10 000-50 000
Activities: Basic and applied research into the utilization and processing of fish and shellfish.
Contract work: No
Publications: Annual report.

Fiskeriteknologisk Institut 109

[Danish Institute of Fisheries Technology]
Address: Nordsøcentret, DK-9850 Hirtshals
Telephone: (08) 94 42 61
Affiliation: Akademiet for de Tekniske Videnskaber - ATV
Activities: The Institute implements research and development projects and offers all kinds of technological service within the areas of fisheries technology. In 1982 the Institute will take an advanced tank system into use for model research on the application of fishing tackle etc, and from 1983 the Institute will be able to carry through experiments and testings of the equipment, eg under the influence of extreme heat or cold, in its newly-built research premises and climate rooms.

Forskningssekretariatet 110

[Danish Research Administration]
Address: Holmens Kanal 7, DK-1060 København K
Telephone: 01-114300
Telex: 15652 FS
Affiliation: Ministry of Education
Research director: P.A. Koch
Graduate research staff: 400
Annual expenditure: £20m

DANDOK 111

[Danish Committee for Scientific and Technical Information and Documentation]
Chairman: Overbibliotekar Vibeke Ammundsen
Activities: Planning and coordination in scientific and technical information and documentation, advisory functions towards public authorities and institutions, Danish participation in the international cooperation in this field.

STATENS HUMANISTISKE FORSKNINGSRÅD 112

– SHF
[Danish Council for the Humanities]
Chairman: Professor Henning Spang-Hanssen

STATENS JORDBRUGS- OG VETERINAERUIDENSKABELIGE FORSKNINGSRÅD 113

– SJVF
[Danish Agricultural and Veterinary Research Council]
Chairman: Dr Birthe Palludan
Annual expenditure: £501 000-2m
Contract work: No

STATENS LAEGEVIDENSKABELIGE FORSKNINGSRÅD 114

– SLF
[Danish Medical Research Council]
Chairman: Professor Poul Kildeberg

STATENS NATURVIDENSKABELIGE FORSKNINGSRÅD 115

– SNF
[Danish Natural Science Research Council]
Chairman: Professor Henning Sørensen

STATENS SAMFUNDSVIDENSKABELIGE FORSKNINGSRÅD 116

– SSF
[Danish Social Science Research Council]
Chairman: Professor Ehrling B. Andersen

STATENS TEKNISK-VIDENSKABELIGE FORSKNINGSRÅD 117

– STVF
[Danish Council for Scientific and Industrial Research]
Chairman: Otto Gram Jeppesen

Forsøgsanlaeg Risø   118

[Risø National Laboratory]
Address: PO Box 49, DK-4000 Roskilde
Telephone: (02) 37 12 12
Telex: 43116 risoe dk
Affiliation: Ministry of Energy
Managing Director: Niels W. Holm
Assistant Directors: Niels E. Busch, Ingvard Rasmussen, Aksel Olsen
Sections: Accelerator Department, K. Sehested
Agricultural Research Department, Jens Sandfaer
Chemistry Department, B. Skytte Jensen
Computer Installation, Leif Hansson
Electronics Department, Jens Rasmussen
Energy Systems, Hans Larsen
Engineering Department, Christian Regenburg
Health Physics Department, H.L. Gjørup
Isotope Laboratory, Kaj Heydorn
Library, Eva Pedersen
Medical Service, M. Faber
Metallurgy Department, Niels Hansen
Safety Section, Klaus Iversen
Physics Department, H. Bjerrum Møller
Reactor DR 1, J. Olsen
Reactor DR3, H. Floto
Reactor Technology Department, B. Micheelsen
Waste Treatment Plant, Knud Brodersen
Graduate research staff: 250
Activities: Natural gas undergroundstorage; metal hydrides, lower weight, safer transport; solar collectors - higher efficiency, lower cost; biomass - bioconversion into liquid fuels; windmills - better performance of small mills, better materials for wings, longer life.Wind atlas for Denmark; batteries - solid-state lithium-iodide, higher capacity; engine research - Rankine cycle, low temperature waste heat; heat pumps - low temperature waste heat utilization; underground seasonal heat storage. Modelling of production and consumption for Danish energy planning.
Facilities: Test station for small windmills (six mills at the same time); underground seasonal heat storage in an aquifer (twenty miles from Risø).
Publications: Risø Reports.

Forsvarets   119
Forskningstjeneste

[Danish Defence Research Establishment]
Address: Staunings Plads 2, PO Box 2715, DK-2100 København Ø
Telephone: 01-425707
Telex: 22679 FLSKBH DK

Research director: V.M. Güntelberg
Sections: Physics; operations research; computer science
Graduate research staff: 12
Annual expenditure: £501 000-2m
Activities: Research activities are carried out in accordance with the demands from the Danish Defence Command and supported by the Defence Research Board, which acts as the consultative link to the Ministry of Defence. Work and results are normally of a classified nature, but often reflect the cooperation with the research community of North Atlantic Treaty Organization nations.
Contract work: No

Frøpatologisk Institut   120

[Seed Pathology for Developing Countries Institute]
Address: Ryvangs Allé 78, DK-2900 Hellerup
Telephone: 01-62 12 13
Affiliation: Ministry of Foreign Affairs; Danish International Development Agency
Director: Dr Paul Neergaard
Annual expenditure: £51 000-500 000
Activities: Research on seed borne diseases involves taxonomy and identification of seed borne organisms; to evolve routine seed health testing methods for the detection of bacteria, fungi and viruses; histopathology; transmission of pathogens from seed to plant and plant to seed; relationship between seed infection and disease incidence in the field, and control of seed borne diseases.
Facilities: Facilities available for carrying out major projects on seed borne diseases.
Contract work: No

Geodoetisk Institut   121

[Geodetic Institute]
Address: Rigsdagsgaarden 7, DK-1218 København K
Affiliation: Ministry of Defence
Director: Flemming Winblad
Graduate research staff: 15
Publications: Geodetic Institute Series: *Meddelelser; Skrifter;* internal reports.

GEODETIC DEPARTMENT 122

Address: Gamlehave Allé 2, DK-2920 Charlottenlund
Telephone: 01-631833
Telex: 15184 Seismo dk
Chief Geodesist: Elvin Kejlsø
Activities: Geodetic research in all geodetic fields especially on mathematical geodesy, determination of the earth's potential field, gravity, geodeticstatistics, levelling, geodetic edp (adjustment).
Contract work: No

SEISMIC DEPARTMENT 123

Address: Gamlehave Allé 2, DK-2920 Charlottenlund
Telephone: 01-631833
Telex: 15184 Seismo dk
State Geodesist: Jørgen Hjelme
Activities: Seismic research especially earthquake prediction, detection seismology, surface wave propagation, microseismic.
Contract work: No

Geoteknisk Institut 124

[Danish Geotechnical Institute]
Address: Maglebjergvej 1, DK-2800 Lyngby
Telephone: (02) 88 44 44
Telex: 37230 geotec dk
Affiliation: Akademiet for de Tekniske Videnskaber - ATV
Research director: Professor Bent Hansen
Graduate research staff: 5
Annual expenditure: £51 000-500 000
Activities: The Institute deals with all aspects of soil mechanics and foundation engineering, material prospection, and water wells and offers a comprehensive range of services within consulting and design, drilling and geophysical investigations, laboratory testing, research and development, running controlduring execution, in relation to all aspects of soil and rock mechanics, foundation engineering, water wells and ground water lowering systems, material prospecting, on land or sea. Research into strength and deformation properties of soils; failure problems in soil mechanics (especially theory of plasticity).
Contract work: Yes
Publications: DGI Bulletins.

Grønlands Fiskeriundersøgelser 125

[Greenland Fisheries Investigations]
Address: Jaegersborg Allé 1 B, DK-2920 Charlottenlund
Telephone: 01-629278
Affiliation: Ministry for Greenland
Research director: Sv.Aa. Horsted
Sections: Fishery biology, P. Kanneworff; marine mammals,F.O. Kapel; marine pollution, P. Johansen
Graduate research staff: 11
Annual expenditure: DKr6m
Research activities: Fishery biology, biological and physical oceanography, research on marine mammals and marine pollution.
Facilities: Research vessels: R/V Adolf Jensen; cutter Tornaq; R/V Dana at disposal about one to two months during the season.
Contract work: No

FISKERIBIOLOGISK LABORATORIUM 126

Address: Postbox 21, 3900 Godthåb, Greenland
Activities: Field laboratory.

Grønlands Geologiske Undersøgelse 127

[Geological Survey of Greenland]
Address: Øster Voldgade 10, DK-1350 København K
Telephone: 01-11 88 66
Telex: 19066 ggutel dk
Director: K. Ellitsgaard-Rasmussen
Sections: Geological mapping N. Henriksen; petroleum geology, F. Surlyk; glacio-hydrology, A. Weidick; mineral prospecting, B.L. Nielsen; geochemistry, F. Kalsbeek; geophysics, L.Thorning
Graduate research staff: 44
Annual expenditure: over £2m
Contract work: No
Publications: Bulletin: Grønlands Geologiske Undersøgelse; Rapporter: Grønlands Geologiske Undersøgelse; occasional publications; geological maps, various scales.

Havebrugscentret 128

[Horticulture Research Centre]
Affiliation: Ministry of Agriculture, Danish Research Service for Soil and Plant Sciences

INSTITUT FOR FRUGT OG BAER   129

[Pomology Institute]
Address: Blangsted Blangstedgaardsvej 133, DK-5220 Odense SØ
Telephone: (09) 15 90 46
Director: Erik Poulsen
Scientific staff: Pomology, J. Vittrup Christensen; growth regulators, J. Grauslund; physiology, P. Hansen; storage, P. Molls Rasmussen; nutrition; soil cultivation, O. Vang-Petersen
Graduate research staff: 7
Annual expenditure: £300 000
Activities: Varieties and clones of apple, pear, plum, cherry and bush fruit. Rootstock, pruning, planting, density, nutrition, growth regulators, harvesting, storage, quality and preservation.
Contract work: Yes

INSTITUT FOR GRØNSAGER   130

[Vegetables Institute]
Address: Kirstinebjergvej 6, DK-5792 Årslev
Telephone: (459) 99 17 66
Director: M. Blangstrup Jørgensen
Projects and scientific staff: Vegetables - maturity and post harvest physiology, H. Hansen; production systems, irrigation, plant establishment, K. Henriksen; vegetables - timing programmes, once-over-harvest problems, mechanized harvesting of vegetables, variety trials of perennial vegetables, J. Jensen; flower bulbs - field and forcing experiments, E. Rasmuss en; vegetables - storage, P. Molls Rasmussen; vegetables - nutrition and crop studies, T.N. Steen; breeding in small fruit and asparagus of ficinalis, crop studies in strawberries and perennial vegetables, lawn grasses, A. Thuesen; vegetables - variety trials of annual vegetables, run by the Joint Committee for Test-Growing Vegetables, E. Blankholm
Graduate research staff: 10
Activities: Field experiments, experiments in greenhouses and frames are carried out. Laboratories for plant breeding, for preservation of vegetables inconnection with growing experiments, and chemical laboratory, cold-stores for storage experiments for flower bulbs and vegetables etc. The institute utilizes1 740 m² greenhouse area and has a total area of 45 hectares at its disposal.
Contract work: Yes

INSTITUT FOR LANDSKABSPLANTER   131

[Landscaping Plants Institute]
Address: Hornum, DK-9600 Års
Telephone: (08) 66 13 33
Director: I. Groven
Sections: Ornamental trees and shrubs, P.E. Brander; container-grown plants, O. Bøvre; nursery nutrition, F. Knoblauch, propagation techniques and rose trials, O. Nymark Larsen; windbreaks, I. Groven
Activities: Nursery cultures; testing of trees and shrubs for recreation areas; propagation techniques; nursery nutrition and watering of nursery plants; plants grown in containers and inert media; storage of plants; windbreaks.

INSTITUT FOR   132
VAEKSTHUSKULTURER

[Glasshouse Crops Institute]
Address: Kirstinebjergvej 10, DK-5792 Årslev
Telephone: (459) 99 17 66
Director: V. Aa. Hallig
Projects and scientific staff: Variety trials of pot plants, V. Aa. Hallig; growth regulators for pot plants, E. Adriansen; glasshouseenvironment, energy saving, vegetables under glass, Dr M.G. Amsen; cutflowers: blueprint cropping, hypobaric storage and keeping quality, N. Bredmose; pot plants: production planning, variation of growth, nuclear stock,control of flowering, selection of clones, O. Voigt Christensen; propagation, hormones, dormancy, hypobaric storage of cuttings, rose cropping, Dr H.E. Kresten Jensen; electronics, process control, P. Konradsen; examination of new varieties of ornamental plants under glass, E. Rasmussen; substrates, water, nutrition, hydroponics, Dr J. Williamsen
Graduate research staff: 14
Facilities: At the Institute 4 000 m² are covered with glass, all glasshouses are detached, and most of them are divided into compartments with separate heat- and climatic-regulation outfit; phytotron with six daylight and eighteen darkroom facilities; propagation room; keepability room; growth chambers.
Contract work: Yes

Institut for   133
Fjerkraesygdomme

[Poultry Diseases Institute]
Address: Royal Veterinary and Agricultural University, DK-1870 København V
Telephone: (01) 37 77 77
Parent body: Ministry of Agriculture
Head: Professor H.E. Marthedal
Sub-branches: Langaa, Jutland, Dr G. Velling; Middelfart, Funen, P.B. Badstue
Graduate research staff: 10
Activities: Veterinary medicine.

Institut for Jordfysik og   134
Jordbearbejdning

[Soil Physics and Soil Tillage Institute]
Address: Siltoftvej 2, DK-6280 Højer
Affiliation: Ministry of Agriculture, Danish Research Service for Plant and Soil Sciences
Director: Lorens Hansen
Projects and scientific staff: Cultivation and liming, C. Nielsen; drainage, E. Frimodt Petersen; soil structure, P. Schjonning; soil tillage, K.J. Rasmussen
Graduate research staff: 5
Annual expenditure: £51 000-500 000
Activities: Marshland trials with drainage and cultivation of marshland, soil tillage in the field, and soil physics investigations in the laboratory. The station is situated on salt sea marsh.
Contract work: No

Isotopcentralen   135

[Danish Isotope Centre]
Address: Skelbaekgade 2, DK-1717 København V
Telephone: (01) 21 41 31
Telex: 16600 fotex DK attn isotopcent
Affiliation: Akademiet for de Tekniske Videnskaber - ATV
Head: Torben Sevel
Activities: Isotope techniques and similar methods form the background for all the Centre's activities covering consultancy, investigations, developmentand production of special instruments within: receiving water studies for planning or control of sewage outfalls to marine or fresh waters; environmental chemistry and ecology; trace element analysis by nuclear methods; nuclear gauging in industrial production; non-destructive testing in the industry and the building sector; measurements of flow, mixing, ventilation, wear etc; leak detectionin hidden pipes, tanks etc,

Jordbrugsøkonomisk   136
Institut

[Agricultural Economics Institute]
Address: Valby Langgade 19, DK-2500 Valby
Telephone: 01-30 45 22
Parent body: Ministry of Agriculture
Research director: Arne Larsen
Graduate research staff: 25
Annual expenditure: £51 000-500 000
Contract work: Yes

MACROECONOMIC DIVISION   137

Head: Walter Jørgensen
Activities: Economics of the agricultural sector or branches in relation to the Danish economy in general and in an international perspective. Apart from carrying out specific research projects, the aim is to provide sufficient general knowledge on the agricultural sector to be used in relation to agricultural economic and political questions.

MICROECONOMIC DIVISION   138

Head: Jhs. Christensen
Activities: The division is primarily concerned with research related to farm management and produces and extends information concerning the economic interrelations within the agricultural firm and within individual productions in order to support extension work and improve the basis for farm decisions. A considerable part of the work is carried out in connection with technical and biological research institutions.

STATISTICAL DIVISION   139

Head: T. Due Pedersen
Activities: To carry out statistical analyses on representative farm account samples in order to produce information on the economic conditions for agriculture and horticulture in general as well as for types of farms and horticulture firms; to furnish the Danish contribution to the European Economic Community farm accountancy data network. Price statistics for the farm sector and certain control functions for the Agricultural Ministry are also carried out.

Københavns Tandlaegehøjskole 140

[Royal Dental College, Copenhagen]
Address: Jagtvej 160, DK-2100 København Ø
Telephone: 01371700
Dean: Jan Jakobsen
Departments: Anatomy and Genetics, Tor Zelander
Stomatology and Dysfunction, Physiology, Eigild Möller
Biochemistry and Pharmacology, Knud Poulsen
Oral Surgery and Anaesthetics, Erik Hjörting-Hansen
Orthodontics, Arne Björk
Periodontology, Asger Frandsen
Oral Pathology and Medicine, Jens Jörgen Pindborg
Oral Diagnosis, Forensic Odontology, Erik Dabelsteen
Prosthetics, Antje Tallgren
Paedodontics, Erik Kisling
Cariology, Anders Thylstrup
Technology, Knud Dreyer Jörgensen
Community Dentistry, Sven Helm

Københavns Universitet 141

[Copenhagen University]
Address: Krystalgade 25-27, DK-1172 København K
Telephone: (01) 14 13 55
Principal: Professor Erik Skinhøj
Vice-Principal: ProfessorMogens Kortvedgaard

FACULTY OF MEDICINE 142

Address: Panum Instituttet, Blegdamsvej 3C, DK-2200 København N
Telephone: (01) 35 79 00
Dean: Olav Behnke

Anthropology Laboratory 143

Address: Nørre Allé 63, DK-2100 København Ø
Heads: Dr Jørgen Balslev-Jørgensen, Dr Ole Vagn Nielsen

Experimental Hormone Research Institute 144

Address: Nørre Allé 71, DK-2100 København Ø
Telephone: (01) 37 16 62
Head: Eigil Bojesen

Experimental Immunology Institute 145

Address: Nørre Allé 71, DK-2100 København Ø
Head: Professor Morten Simonsen

Experimental Medicine Institute 146

Address: Nørre Allé 71,3, DK-2100 København Ø
Telephone: (01) 37 16 65
Head: Dr P.P. Leyssac

Experimental Surgical Research Institute 147

Address: Nørre Allé 71, DK-2100 København Ø
Head: Ulla Sivertsen Weis-Fogh

Forensic Medicine Institute 148

Address: Frederik d. V's Vej, DK-2100 København Ø
Telephone: (01) 37 32 22
Head: Dr Hans Gürtler
Senior staff: Professor Jørgen A. Voigt
Departments: Forensic Anthropology, Dr Hans Gürtler; Forensic Chemistry; Forensic Pathology, Professor Jørgen A. Voigt; Forensic Serology

General Medicine Institute 149

Address: Juliane Maries Vej 20, Villaea, DK-2100 København Ø
Telephone: (01) 37 01 06
Head: Professor Paul Backer

GENERAL PRACTICE RESEARCH CENTRE 150

Telephone: (01) 37 02 12
Research head: Poul A. Pedersen

History of Medicine Museum 151

Address: Bredgade 62, DK-1260 København K
Telephone: (01) 15 25 01; (01) 15 45 31
Head: Jørgen Koch

Human Genetic Biology Institute 152

Address: Arvebiologisk Institut, Tagensvej 14, DK-2200 København N
Telephone: (01) 39 33 73
Head: Jørgen Hilden
Senior staff: Professor Jan Mohr

Hygiene Institute and Budde Laboratory 153

Address: Blegdamsvej 21, DK-2100 København Ø
Telephone: (01) 42 56 00
Head: Professor Bo Holma

Medical-Chemical Institute 154

Address: Rådmansgade 71, DK-2200 København N
Telephone: (01) 35 79 00
Head: Professor Arne E. Nielsen
Section heads: Fleming A. Andersen, Jens Toft

Neuropathological Institute 155

Address: Frederik d. V's Vej, DK-2100 København Ø
Telephone: (01) 37 32 22
Head: Dr Leif Klinken

Ophthalmology Institute 156

Address: Frederik d. V's Vej, DK-2lOO København Ø
Telephone: (01) 37 32 22
Head: Professor S. Ry Andersen

Panum Institute 157

Address: Blegdamsvej 3C, DK-2200 København N
Telephone: (01) 35 79 00
Head: J. Funder

BIOCHEMICAL DEPARTMENT A 158
Head: Svend Erik Hansen
Senior staff: Professor Dr Frank Lundquist
Section heads: Dr C.J. Hedeskov, Dr John Dich

BIOCHEMICAL DEPARTMENT B 159
Head and section leader: Dr Sune Frederiksen
Senior staff: Professor Dr Hans Klenow
Section head: Dr Ole Svensmark

BIOCHEMICAL DEPARTMENT C 160
Head: Inger Schousboe
Senior staff: Professor Dr Lars Josefsson

BIOPHYSICS DEPARTMENT 161
Head: Dr Jens Jensen-Holm
Senior staff: Professor Dr Ove Sten-Knudsen
Section heads: Dr Jens Jensen-Holm, Dr Jens Otto Wieth

MEDICAL-ANATOMICAL DEPARTMENT A 162
Head: Dr Kjeld Møllgård
Section heads: Dr Helge Andersen, Dr Martin Matthiessen

MEDICAL-ANATOMICAL DEPARTMENT B 163
Head: Morten Møller
Senior staff: Professor Jørgen Rostgaard
Section heads: Dr Frede Bro-Rasmussen, Dr Jørn Carstensen Egeberg

MEDICAL-ANATOMICAL DEPARTMENT C 164
Address: Universitetsparken 1, DK-2100, København Ø
or: Panum Institutet, Blegdamsvej 3C, DK-2200 København N
Telephone: (01) 35 79 00; 35 79 00

MEDICAL-PHYSIOLOGICAL DEPARTMENT A 165
Head: Dr Jørgen Funder
Senior staff: Professor Dr Christian Crone

MEDICAL-PHYSIOLOGICAL DEPARTMENT B 166
Head: Professor Dr Poul Kruhøffer

MEDICAL-PHYSIOLOGICAL DEPARTMENT C 167
Head: Professor Niels A. Thorn
Section head: Dr Joop Madsen

NEUROPHYSIOLOGICAL DEPARTMENT 168
Head: Professor Arne Mosfeldt Laursen
Senior staff: Professor Hans Hultborn

Pathological-Anatomical Institute 169

Address: Frederik d. V's Vej 11, DK-2100 København Ø
Telephone: (01) 37 32 22
Head: Folmer Elling
Senior staff: Professor Torben Schiødt, Professor Jakob Visfeldt

Pharmacology Institute 170

Address: Juliane Maries Vej 20, DK-2100 København Ø
Telephone: (01) 37 03 75
Head: Arne Geisler

Protein Laboratory 171

Address: Sigurdsgade 34, DK-2200 København N
Telephone: (01) 35 79 00
Head: Dr Elizabeth Bock

Psychochemical Institute 172

Address: Rigshospitalet, Blegdamsvej 9, DK-2100 København Ø
Telephone: (01) 37 30 90
Head: Professor Ole J. Rafaelson

Rockefeller Complex 173

Address: Juliane Maries Vej 26-36, DK-2100 København Ø
or: Henrik Harpestrengsvej 3-5, DK-2100 København Ø
Telephone: (01) 35 88 06; (01) 35 79 00

MEDICAL MICROBIOLOGY INSTITUTE 174
Telephone: (01) 39 44 66
Head: Professor Mogens Volkert

SOCIAL MEDICINE INSTITUTE 175
Telephone: (01) 39 44 44; (01) 39 44 54
Head: Professor Erik Holst

Joint Centre for Studies of Health Programs, 176 University of California at Los Angeles/ University of Copenhagen
American co-director: Professor Lester Breslow (School of Public Health, UCLA)
Danish co-director: Professor Erik Holst
Assistant director: Dr Patricia Sohl

FACULTY OF NATURAL SCIENCE 177

Address: Jagtvej 155 B, DK-2200 København N
Telephone: (01) 83 52 10
Dean: Bengt Saltin

Central Biology Institute 178

BIOLOGICAL CHEMISTRY INSTITUTE 179 A
Address: Universitetsparken 13, DK-2100 København Ø
Telephone: (01) 37 70 00
Head: Poul Kristensen
Senior staff: Professor H.H. Ussing
Section head: Dr Karl Zerahn

BIOLOGICAL CHEMISTRY INSTITUTE 180 B
Address: Sølvgade 83, DK-1307 København K
Telephone: (01) 11 10 23
Head: Per Nygaard
Senior staff: Professor Agnele Munch-Petersen

GENETICS INSTITUTE A 181
Address: Øster Farimagsgade 2 A, DK-1353 København K
Telephone: (01) 15 88 35
Head: E. Bahn
Senior staff: Professor Richard Egel
Section heads: Dr Albert Kahn, Dr Knud Sick

GENETICS INSTITUTE B 182 (BIOCHEMICAL GENETICS INSTITUTE)
Address: Øster Farimagsgade 2 A, DK-1353 København K
Telephone: (01) 15 88 42
Head: Professor Bent Foltmann

MICROBIOLOGY INSTITUTE 183
Address: Øster Farimagsgade 2 A, DK-1353 København K
Telephone: (01) 15 87 50
Head: Professor O. Maaløe

PLANT PHYSIOLOGY INSTITUTE 184
Address: Øster Farimagsgade 2 A, DK-1353 København K
Telephone: (01) 13 87 81
Head: Henning Frost-Christensen
Senior staff: Professor Erik G. Jorgensen

Central Botanical Institute 185

Address: Sølvgade 83, DK-1307 København K

BOTANICAL GARDEN 186
Address: Øster Farimagsgade 2 B, DK-1353 København K
Telephone: (01) 13 91 00
Head: Olaf Olsen

BOTANICAL MUSEUM 187
Address: Gothersgade 130, DK-1123 København K
Telephone: (01) 11 17 44
Head: J.B. Hansen
Senior staff: Professor Dr Rolf Dahlgren

COPENHAGEN UNIVERSITY'S ARCTIC 188 STATION
Address: Godhavn, DK-3953 Disko, Greenland
or: Institut for Plante-anatomi og Cytologi, Sølvgade 83, DK-1307 København K
Telephone: Greenland: Godhavn 47 294; (01) 13 91 16
Staff: Dr Bent Fredskild, Dr G. Høpner Petersen, Professor Niels Nielsen, Dr Henning Sørensen

ECOLOGICAL BOTANY INSTITUTE 189
Address: Øster Farimagsgade 2 D, DK-1353 København K
Telephone: (01) 15 86 59
Head: Peter Vestergaard
Senior staff: Professor Dr Mogens Køie

KRISTIANSMINDE OLD FORESTRY FARM 190
Address: Kristiansminde Gl. Skovridergård, Kristiansminde
Telephone: (01) 63 23 91
Head: Professor Morten Lange
Activities: Botanical field courses.

PLANT ANATOMY AND CYTOLOGY INSTITUTE 191
Address: Sølvgade 83, DK-1307 København K
Telephone: (01) 13 91 16
Head: Jette Dahl Møller

SPORE PLANTS INSTITUTE 192
Address: Øster Farimagsgade 2 D, DK-1353 København K
Telephone: (01) 14 61 81
Head: Aase Kristiansen

SYSTEMATIC BOTANY INSTITUTE 193
Address: Botanisk Laboratorium, Gothersgade 140, DK-1123 København K
Telephone: (01) 11 46 90
Head: Vilhelm Dalgaard
Senior staff: Professor Arne Strid

VORSØ ISLAND STATION 194
Address: Øen Vorsø, Horsens Fjord
or: Institut for Almen Zoologi, Universitetsparken 15, DK-2100 København Ø
Telephone: (01) 35 41 11
Heads: Professor Chr. Overgaard Nielsen, Professor Bent Christensen
Activities: Animal and plant sanctuary.

Central Chemistry Institute 195
Address: H.C. Ørsted Institutet, Universitetsparken 5, DK-2100 København Ø
Telephone: (01) 35 31 33
Head: Dr Aage E. Hansen

CHEMICAL LABORATORY I 196
(INORGANIC CHEMISTRY)
Telephone: (01) 35 31 33
Head: Peter Andersen
Senior staff: Professor Jannik Bjerrum

CHEMICAL LABORATORY II (GENERAL 197
ORGANIC CHEMISTRY)
Telephone: (01) 35 31 33
Head: Gustav Schroll
Senior staff: Professor Ole Buchardt, Professor K.A. Jensen (emeritus)

CHEMICAL LABORATORY III 198
(GENERAL AND THEORETICAL CHEMISTRY)
Telephone: (01) 35 31 33
Head: Professor Thor A. Bak

CHEMICAL LABORATORY IV 199
(PHYSICAL CHEMISTRY)
Head: Juul Møller
Senior staff: Professor C.J. Ballhausen

CHEMICAL LABORATORY V 200
(MOLECULAR SPECTROSCOPY)
Head: Flemming M. Nicolaisen
Senior staff: Professor Børge Bak

Central Geography Institute 201
Address: Haraldsgade 68, DK-2100 København Ø
or: Anneks: Øster Voldgade 7, DK-1350 København K
Telephone: (01) 29 30 88; (01) 13 21 05
Head: Hans Kuhlman
Senior staff: Professor Sofus Christiansen, Professor ViggoHansen, Professor N. Kingo Jacobsen, Professor Harald Svensson

Central Geology Institute 202
Address: Øster Voldgade 10, DK-1350 København K
Telephone: (01) 11 22 32
Head: Hans Jørgen Hansen

GENERAL GEOLOGY INSTITUTE 203
Address: Øster Voldgade 10, DK-1350 København K
Telephone: (01) 11 22 32
Head: Svend Petersen
Senior staff: Professor Asger Berthelsen

GEOLOGICAL MUSEUM 204
Address: Øster Voldgade 5-7, DK-1350 København K
Telephone: (01) 13 50 01
Head: Niels Hald
Senior staff: Professor David Bridgwater

HISTORICAL GEOLOGY AND 205
PALAEONTOLOGY INSTITUTE
Address: Øster Voldgade 10, DK-1350 København K
Telephone: (01) 11 22 32
Head: H.J. Hansen
Senior staff: Professor Tove Birkelund, Professor Valdemar Poulsen

MINERALOGY INSTITUTE 206
Address: Øster Voldgade 5-7, DK-1350 København K
Telephone: (01) 13 50 01
Head: Jørn Rønsbo
Senior staff: Professor Harry Micheelsen

PETROLOGY INSTITUTE 207
Address: Øster Voldgade 10, DK-1350 København K
Telephone: (01) 11 22 32
Head: Halldis J. Bollingberg
Senior staff: Professor Henning Sørensen

Central Mathematics Institute 208
Address: H.C. Ørsted Institutet, Universitetsparken 5, DK-2100 København Ø
Telephone: (01) 35 31 33

DATA INSTITUTE 209
Address: Sigurdsgade 41, DK-2200 København N
Telephone: (01) 83 64 66
Head: Jens Clausen
Senior staff: Professor Peter Johansen, Professor Peter Naur

MATHEMATICAL RESEARCH LABORATORY 210
Head: Professor Jan M. Hoem

MATHEMATICAL STATISTICS INSTITUTE 211
Head: Søren Tolver Jensen
Senior staff: Professor Hans Brøns, Professor Anders Hald

MATHEMATICS INSTITUTE 212
Head: Tage Gutmann Madsen
Senior staff: Professor Erik Sparre Andersen, Professor Thøger Bang, Professor Christian Berg, Professor Bent Fuglede, Professor Christian U. Jensen, Professor Gert Kjaergård Pedersen, Professor Olaf Schmidt, Professor Hans Tornehave

Central Physics Institute 213

ASTRONOMICAL OBSERVATORY 214
Address: Observatoriet i København, Øster Voldgade 3, DK-1350 København K
or: Observatoriet i Brorfelde, DK-4340 Tølløse
Telephone: (01) 14 17 90 (København); (03) 48 81 95 (Brorfelde)
Head: J.V. Clausen (Brorfelde)
Senior staff: Professor Anders Reiz (København)

GEOPHYSICAL ISOTOPE LABORATORY 215
Address: Haraldsgade 6, DK-2200 København N
Telephone: (01) 83 85 00
Head: Henrik B. Clausen
Senior staff: Professor Willi Dansgard

GEOPHYSICS INSTITUTE 216
Address: Haraldsgade 6, DK-2200 København N
Telephone: (01) 83 45 60
Head: Felix Träff

PHYSICAL OCEANOGRAPHY INSTITUTE 217
Address: Haraldsgade 6, DK-2200 København N
Telephone: (01) 83 39 92
Head: Henning Hundahl
Senior staff: Professor Gunnar Kullenberg

PHYSICS LABORATORY I 218
Address: H.C. Ørsted Institutet, Universitetsparken 5, DK-2100 København Ø
Telephone: (01) 35 31 33
Head: Kim Carneiro

PHYSICS LABORATORY II 219
Address: H.C. Ørsted Institutet, Universitetsparken 5, DK-2100 København Ø
Telephone: (01) 35 31 33
Head: Janus Staun Olsen

THEORETICAL METEOROLOGY INSTITUTE 220
Address: Haraldsgade 6, DK-2200 København N
Telephone: (01) 81 81 66; (01) 81 83 67
Head: Bennert Machenhauer
Senior staff: Professor Erik Eliassen

Central Zoo Physiology Institute 221
Address: August Krogh Institutet, Universitetsparken 13, DK-2100 København Ø
Telephone: (01) 37 70 00

GYMNASTIC THEORY LABORATORY A AND B 222
Head: Dr Bodil Nielsen

Gymnastic Theory Laboratory A 223
Head: Professor Gunnar Grimby

Gymnastic Theory Laboratory B 224
Head: Professor Bengt Saltin

ZOO PHYSIOLOGY LABORATORY A 225
Head: Professor C. Barker Jørgensen

ZOO PHYSIOLOGY LABORATORY B 226
Head: Bent Vestergaard-Bogind
Senior staff: Professor Ulrik Lassen

ZOO PHYSIOLOGY LABORATORY C 227
Head: Professor Svend O. Andersen

Central Zoology Institute 228

Head: Leif Lau Jeppesen

COMPARATIVE ANATOMY INSTITUTE 229
Address: Universitetsparken 15, DK-2100 København Ø
Telephone: (01) 35 41 11
Head: Jørgen Lützen
Senior staff: Professor K.G. Wingstrand

FRESHWATER BIOLOGY LABORATORY 230
Address: Helsingørsgade 49-51, Chr. IV's Vej 1 og 5, DK-3400 Hillerød
Telephone: (03) 26 76 00
Head: Kaj Sand Jensen
Senior staff: Professor Petur M. Jonasson

GENERAL ZOOLOGY INSTITUTE 231
Address: Universitetsparken 15, DK-2100 København Ø
Telephone: (01) 35 41 11
Head: Dr Jytte R. Nilsson
Senior staff: Professor Chr. Overgaard Nielsen

MARINE BIOLOGY LABORATORY 232
Address: Strandpromenaden, DK-3000 Helsingør
Telephone: (03) 21 33 44
Head: Hans Christensen

ZOOLOGICAL LABORATORY AND STUDY COLLECTION 233
Address: Universitetsparken 15, DK-2100 København Ø
Telephone: (01) 35 41 11
Head: Ole Stecher Tendal
Senior staff: Professor Bengt Christensen

ZOOLOGICAL MUSEUM 234
Address: Universitetsparken 15, DK-2100 København Ø
Telephone: (01) 35 41 11
Head: Dr Jørgen Nielsen

Isefjords Laboratory 235
Address: Vellerup Vig, DK-4200 Skibby
Telephone: (03) 32 92 05
Head: Dr Erik Rasmussen

Laesø Laboratory 236
Address: Lyngholt pr. Byrum, DK-9940 Byrum, Laesø
Telephone: (08) 49 81 00
Head: Professor Bent J. Muus

Ocean Biology Field Laboratory 237
Address: Kirkegade 8, DK-9900 Frederikshavn
Telephone: (08) 42 45 66
Head: Dr J.B. Kirkegaard

Niels Bohr Central Institute 238

NIELS BOHR INSTITUTE 239
Address: Blegdamsvej 17, DK-2100 København Ø
Telephone: (01) 42 16 16
Head: Professor Ove Nathan
Senior staff: Professor Aage Bohr, Professor Torben Huus, Professor Niels Ove Lassen, Professor Aage Winther

TANDEM ACCELERATOR LABORATORY 240
Address: Risø, DK-4000 Roskilde
Telephone: (02) 37 16 16
Senior staff: Professor Bent Elbek, Professor Ole Hansen
Department Head: Mogens Olesen

FACULTY OF SOCIAL SCIENCE 241

Dean: Leif Christensen
Vice-Dean: Jørgen Estrup

Economics Institute 242

Address: Studiegården, Studiestraede 6, DK-1455 København K
Telephone: (01) 15 21 66
Head: Professor Hector Estrup
Senior staff: Professor Ellen Andersen, Professor Sven Danø, Professor Birgit Grodal, Professor Svend Aage Hansen, Professor P. Nørregaard Rasmussen, Professor Niels Thygesen, Professor Karl Vind, Professor Anders Ølgaard

Statistics Institute 243

Address: Studiestraede 6, DK-1455 København K
Telephone: (01) 15 21 66
Head: Nils Kousgaard
Senior staff: Professor Erling B. Andersen, Professor P.C. Matthiessen

Københavns Vandforsyning 244

[Copenhagen Water Supply]
Address: 12 Axeltorv, DK-1609 København V
Telephone: 01-15 76 82
Director: J. Aage Husen
Annual expenditure: £10 000-50 000
Activities: Chemical and bacteriological control of untreated water; dissolved air and gases especially methane. Reduction of the content of trihalomethane formation by optimizing the treatment of surface water.
Contract work: No

Kongelige Akademi for de Skønne Kunster* 245

[Academy of Fine Arts]

LABORATORIET FOR BOLIGBYGGERI 246

[House Building Laboratory]
Address: P. Skramsgade 2, DK-1054 København K
Research director: Karen Zahle
Activities: Design and use of dwellings and housing estates.

Kongelige Danske Farvandsdirektoratet, Nautisk Afdeling 247

[Royal Danish Administration of Navigation and Hydrography]
Address: 19 Esplanaden, DK-1263 København K
Affiliation: Ministry of Defence
Hydrographer: K.S. Kaergaard
Activities: Hydrographic surveys and physical oceanography in Danish, Faroe and Greenland waters. Navigational safety including aids to navigation, pilotage and life boat service. Preparation and production of nautical charts and publications.

Kongelige Veterinaer- og Landbohøjskole 248

[Royal Veterinary and Agricultural University]
Address: Bülowsvej 13, DK-1870 København V
Telephone: (01) 35 17 88
Rector: Professor H.C. Asling
Pro-Rector: Dr Folke Rasmussen

FACULTY OF AGRICULTURAL SCIENCE 249

Agricultural Engineering Institute 250

Address: Agrovej 10, DK-2630 Tåstrup
or: Rolighedsvej 23, DK-1958 København V
Telephone: (02) 99 26 13; (01) 35 17 88
Head: Professor T. Tougaard Pedersen

Agricultural Plant Culture Department 251

Address: Thorvaldsenvej 40, DK-1871 København V
Telephone: (01) 35 17 88

Agricultural Research Department 252

Address: Forsøgsanlaeg Risø, DK-4000 Roskilde
Telephone: (03) 37 12 12
Superintendent: Dr Jens Sandfaer

Animal Husbandry Institute 253

Address: Rolighedsvej 23, DK-1958 København V
Telephone: (01) 35 17 88
Senior staff: Professor J. Fris Jensen, Professor A. Neimann-Sørensen, Professor H. Stein

Animal Physiology Department 254

Address: Rolighedsvej 25, DK-1958 København V
Telephone: (01) 35 81 00; (01) 35 17 88
Head: Professor P.E. Jakobsen

Economics Institute 255

Address: Thorvaldsenvej 40, DK-1871 København V
Telephone: (01) 35 17 88
Senior staff: Professor Søren Kjeldsen-Kragh, Professor Erik Kristensen, Professor Carl Chr. Thomsen

Hydrotechnics Laboratory and Climate Station 256

Address: Bülowsvej 23, DK-1870 København V
or: Højbakkegård, Agrovej 10, DK-2630 Tåstrup
Telephone: (01) 35 17 88; (02) 99 26 13
Head: Professor H.C. Aslyng

Plant Nutrition Department 257

Address: Thorvaldsenvej 40, DK-1871 København V
Telephone: (01) 35 17 88
Head: Professor Sigurd Larsen

Plant Pathology Department 258

Address: Thorvaldsenvej 40, DK-1871 København V
Telephone: (01) 35 17 88
Head: Professor J.E. Hermansen

Research Farm: Højbakkegård 259

Address: Agrovej 10, DK-2630 Tåstrup
Telephone: (02) 99 26 13

Research Farm: Rørrendegård 260

Address: Bartholinstraede 26, DK-2630 Tåstrup
Telephone: (02) 99 71 45; (02) 99 71 46

Research Farm: Snubbekorsgård 261

Address: Snubbekorsvej 1, DK-2630 Tåstrup
Telephone: (02) 99 36 86

FACULTY OF BASIC SCIENCE 262

Arboretum 263

Address: DK-2970 Hørsholm
Telephone: (02) 86 06 41

Botanical Institute 264

Address: Rolighedsvej 23, 1 sal, DK-1958 København V
Telephone: (01) 35 17 88
Senior staff: Professor Johan Lange, Professor Valdemar M. Mikkelsen, Professor Helge Vedel

Chemistry Institute 265

Address: Thorvaldsenvej 40, DK-1871 København V
Telephone: (01) 37 17 88
Senior staff: Professor A. Tovborg Jensen, Professor Peder Olesen Larsen, Professor Kjeld Rasmussen
Laboratories: Agricultural chemistry; organic chemistry; inorganic chemistry

General Genetics Department 266

Address: Bygning 1-6, Bülowsvej 13, DK-1870 København V
Telephone: (01) 35 17 88
Head: Professor Knud W. Henningsen

General Microbiology and Microbial Ecology Department 267

Address: Rolighedsvej 21, DK-1958 København V
Telephone: (01) 35 17 88
Head: Professor Vagn Jensen

Mathematics and Statistics Institute 268

Address: Thorvaldsenvej 40, DK-1871 København V
Telephone: (01) 31 17 88
Head: Svend E. Christiansen
Senior staff: Professor M. Flenstedt-Jensen, Professor Mats Rudemo

Physics Laboratory 269

Address: Thorvaldsenvej 40, DK-1871 København V
Telephone: (01) 35 17 88
Head: Professor K. Maack Bisgård

Physiological Botany Department 270

Address: Thorvaldsenvej 40, DK-1871 København V
Telephone: (01) 35 17 88
Head: Professor Raganatha Rajagopal

Zoology Institute 271

Address: Bülowsvej 13, DK-1870 København V
Telephone: (01) 35 17 88
Senior staff: Professor Niels Haarløv, Professor JørgenJørgensen

FACULTY OF DAIRY AND FOOD SCIENCE 272

Dairy Department 273

Address: Bülowsvej 13, DK-1870 København V
Telephone: (01) 35 17 88
Head: Professor E.-G. Samuelsson

Meat Technology Department 274

Address: Howitzvej 11, DK-2000 København F
Telephone: (01) 87 04 41; (01) 87 04 42

Milk Laboratory 275

Address: Bülowsvej 13, DK-1870 København V
Telephone: (01) 35 17 88
Head: Professor A. Jul Overby

Plant Food Technology Department 276

Address: Thorvaldsenvej 40, DK-1871 København V
Telephone: (01) 35 17 88
Head: Professor James M. Flink

FACULTY OF FORESTRY SCIENCE 277

Forestry Institute 278

Address: Thorvaldsenvej 57, DK-1871 København V
Telephone: (01) 35 17 88
Senior staff: Professor H.A. Henriksen, Professor P. Moltesen

Korrosionscentralen ATV　301

[Danish Corrosion Centre]
Address:　Park Allé 345, DK-2600 Glostrup
Telephone:　(02) 63 11 00
Telex:　333 88 SVC DK
Affiliation:　Akademiet for de Tekniske Videnskaber - ATV
Director:　Hans Arup
Departments:　Corrosion, Erik Nielsen; metallurgical, P.B. Ludwigsen
Graduate research staff:　17
Annual expenditure:　£70 000
Activities:　Corrosion research, including corrosion in sea water and corrosion of steel in concrete; failure analysis work, including fracture of metals. Dissemination of information. The Centre will act as consultants, give adviceon corrosion protection, investigate cases of corrosion, and undertake field inspections.
Contract work:　Yes
Publications: Steel in Concrete Newsletter, quarterly.

Landbrugscentret　302

[Agricultural Sciences Centre]
Affiliation:　Ministry of Agriculture, Danish Research Service for Plant and Soil Science

INSTITUT FOR GROVFODER　303

[Coarse Fodder Institute]
Address:　Amdrupvej 22, DK-8370 Hadsten
Telephone:　(06) 98 92 44
Director:　Kr.G. Mølle
Head of Laboratory:　E.J. Nørgaard
Sections:　Ensiling experiments, Norman Witte; pre-wilting, digestibility trials, ErikMøller; grass crops and haymaking experiments, Peter Winther; nursery crops and ley establishment, Svend Beck Hostrup; catch crops and management of field experiments, Mads Bisgaard
Graduate research staff:　7
Annual expenditure:　£51 000-500 000
Activities:　The main working programme includes experiments on growing and preservation of grass and forage, chemical treatments of forage and investigations on factors determining feed value. The station is provided with facilities for ensilage and hay experiments, ammonia treatment of straw, digestibility trials (sheep) and a chemical laboratory.
Contract work:　No

Statensforsøgsstation Silstrup　304

[State Experimental Station Silstrup]
Address:　Silstrup, DK-7700 Thisted
Telephone:　(07) 92 15 88
Head:　E. Bülow Skovborg
Activities:　The main working programme includes production of grass for silage and haymaking in practical scale experiments. The hay and silages are experimentally fed to dairy cows. The station is provided with large experimental silos, barn drying equipment, and about fifty dairy cows.

Landsforeningen til　305
Kraeftens Bekaempelse

[Danish Cancer Society]
Address:　Sølundsvej 1, DK-2100 København Ø
Telephone:　01-29 88 66
General Secretary:　K.H. Mygind
Contract work:　No
Publications:　Bulletin, twice yearly; annual report.

DANISH CANCER REGISTRY　306

Address:　Strandboulevarden 49, DK-2100 København Ø
Head:　Dr Ole Møller Jensen

FIBIGER-LABORATORIET　307

[Fibiger Laboratory]
Address:　Ndr Frihavnsgade 70,3, DK-2100 København
Telephone:　01-26 08 50
Director:　Dr Jørgen Kieler
Sections:　Environmental carcinogenesis, J. Kieler; virology, K. Ulrich; molecular virology, J. Forchhammer; endocrinology, experimental, P. Briand; endocrinology, clinical, S. Thorpe; experimental therapy, E. Langvad
Graduate research staff:　15
Annual expenditure:　DKrlOm
Contract work:　No
Publications:　Annual report.

KRAEFTFORSKNINGSINSTITUTTET I 308 ÅRHUS

[Århus Institute of Cancer Research]
Address: Radiumstationen, Nörrebrogade 44, DK-8000 Århus C
Telephone: (06) 12 55 55
Head: Dr Peter Ebbesen
Graduate research staff: 10
Annual expenditure: DKr6 410 000
Activities: Experimental and clinical studies of: colon cancer; ultraviolet light as a carcinogen; cancer treatment with heat; the relationship of Epstein-Barr virus to cancer.
Contract work: No
Publications: Danish Cancer Society Annual Report from the Institute of Cancer Research.

Lydteknisk Laboratorium 309

[Acoustical Laboratory]
Address: DTH, Bygning 352, DK-2800 Lyngby
Telephone: (02) 881622
Telex: 37529 dthdia dk
Affiliation: Akademiet for de Tekniske Videnskaber - ATV
Director: Professor Fritz Ingerslev
Sections: Building and architectural acoustics, Nic Michelsen; industrial and traffic noise, Jørgen Kragh; aircraft noise, Chr. Svane
Graduate research staff: 10
Annual expenditure: £51 000-500 000
Activities: Fundamental and applied research within the fields of acoustics, noise and vibration. Official testing of the acoustical characteristics of materials, constructions, equipment and machines. Acoustical and noise measurements of industry. Programming of noise abatement measures with the purpose of reducing the noise exposure of workers in industry; reducing the noise exposure in the environment from road and air traffic.
Contract work: Yes
Publications: Reports.

Lysteknisk Laboratorium 310

[Danish Illuminating Engineering Laboratory]
Address: Bygning 325, Lundtoftevej 100, DK-2800 Lyngby
Telephone: (02) 873911
Affiliation: Akademiet for de Tekniske Videnskaber - ATV
Director: Bjarne Nielsen
Graduate research staff: 10
Annual expenditure: £51 000-500 000
Activities: Research work on problems concerning interior lighting, daylight and energy, roadway lighting and light measurement. The Laboratory is authorized by The National Testing Board of Denmark to perform photometric testing of luminaires, light sources and signal lights and materials and to calibrate luminance and illuminance meters. Complex calculations are carried out using standard computer programs. Luminaire optics are developed as is measurement equipment based on light detection.
Contract work: Yes
Publications: Technical reports.

Medicoteknisk Institut 311

[Danish Medicotechnical Institute]
Address: Park Allé 345, DK-2600 Glostrup
Affiliation: Akademiet for de Tekniske Videnskaber - ATV
Head: A. Northeved

Nationalmuseets 312

[National Museum]

NATURVIDENSKABELIGE AFDELING 313

[Natural Science Department]
Address: Ny Vestergade 11, DK-1471 København K
Telephone: 01-13 44 11
Director: Dr J. Troels-Smith
Graduate research staff: 7
Annual expenditure: £51 000-500 000
Activities: Research in connection with archaeological examinations. Field work: soil determinations and sample collection at archaeological excavations. Laboratory work: dating by pollen analysis and dendrochronology, carbon-14 dating, wood- and macrofossil-determinations. Research in holocene vegetation development, especially human impact on vegetation.
Contract work: Yes

Naturhistorisk Museum 314

[Natural History Museum]
Address: DK-8000 Århus C
Director: Dr Anders Holm
Activities: Ecology, nature conservation, bio-acoustics, entomology, ornithology, mammalogy, and limnology.

MOLSLABORATORIET 315

[Mols Laboratory]
Address: Femmöller, DK-8400 Ebeltoft
Activities: Field laboratory.

Novo Industri A/S 316

Address: Novo Allé, DK-2880 Bagsvaerd
Telephone: (02) 98 23 33
Telex: 37173 novo dk
Research director: Professor Ulrik V. Lassen
Sections: Pharmaceuticals, Bertill Diamant; enzymes, M. Hilmer Nielsen; insulin, J. Schlichtkrull
Graduate research staff: 150
Annual expenditure: £10m
Activities: Diabetes, insulin, glucagen, other peptide hormones, heparin, antibiotics fermentation, enzyme fermentation, purificiation, immobilization etc.
Contract work: No

Odense Universitet 317

[Odense University]
Address: Campusvej 55, DK-5230 Odense M

FACULTY OF MEDICINE 318

Dean: Jøngen Ringsted

Anaesthesiology Department 319

Head: Professor Søren Jørgensen

Anatomy Department 320

Heads: Professor Leif Rasmussen, Professor Franz Bierring

Clinical Chemistry Department 321

Head: Professor Mogens Horder

Clinical Physiology Department 322

Head: Professor Jørgen Fabricius

Dermatology and Venereology Department 323

Head: Professor Henning Schmidt

Forensic Medicine Department 324

Head: Professor Jørn Simonsen

Genetic Pathology Department 325

Head: Professor Mogens Hauge

Hygiene Department 326

Head: Professor Morgens Unger

Medicine Department 327

Heads: Professor Bent Harvald, Professor Ejuind Kemp

Microbiology Department 328

Heads: Professor Knud Siboni, Professor Sven-Erik Svehag

Neuromedicine Department 329

Head: Professor Erik Hansen

Neurosurgery Department 330

Head: Professor Jørn Overgaard

Obstetrics and Gynaecology Department 331

Head: Professor Karl Kristoffersen

Ophthalmology Department 332

Head: Professor Ernst Goldschmit

Otorhinolaryngology Department 333

Head: Professor Poul Stoksted

Paediatrics Department 334

Head: Professor Poul Kildeberg

Pathology Department 335

Head: Professor Hans Ewald Christensen

Pharmacology and Toxicology Department 336

Heads: Professor Nirmal K. Chakravarty, Professor L.F. Gram

Physiology Department 337

Head: Professor Lars Garby

Psychiatry and Medical Psychology Department   338

Head: Professor Niels Juel-Nielsen

Radiology Department   339

Head: Poul E. Andersen

Radiotherapy Department   340

Head: Hans Brincker

Rheumatology Department   341

Head: P. Helby Petersen

Surgery Department   342

Head: Professor D. Andersen

FACULTY OF NATURAL SCIENCES   343

Dean: Carl Th. Petersen

Biochemistry Department   344

Head: Professor Per Schambye

Biology Department   345

Heads: Professor Ole Bjørn Karlog, Professor Axel Michelsen, Professor Roy Weber

Chemistry Department   346

Heads: Professor Per Mølgaard Boll, Professor Chr. Knakkergaard Møller

Mathematics Department   347

Head: Professor John Perram

Molecular Biology Department   348

Heads: Professor Paul Plesner, Professor Kurt Nordstrøm

Physics Department   349

Heads: Professor Ivan Balslev, Professor Hans Sigmund

Optisk Laboratorium   350

[Laboratory for Technical Optics]
Address: 100 Lundtoftevej, DK-2800 Lyngby
Telephone: (02) 883848
Affiliation: Akademiet for de Tekniske Videnskaber - ATV
Director: Werner Olsen
Sections: Optical design, W. Olsen; thin film optics, Ses. Schmitt; electro-optics
Graduate research staff: 5
Annual expenditure: £51 000-500 000
Activities: Research and development; imaging systems; thin film coatings, filters, mirrors; manufacture of thin film components; electro-optical systems design.
Contract work: Yes

Plantevaernscentret   351

[Crop Husbandry Centre]
Affiliation: Ministry of Agriculture, Danish Research Service for Soil and Plant Sciences

INSTITUT FOR PLANTEPATOLOGI   352

[Plant Pathology Institute]
Address: Lottenborgvej 2, DK-2800 Lyngby
Telephone: (02) 87 25 10
Director: H. Rønde Kristensen
Departments: Botany, Arne Jensen
Virology, H. Rønde Kristensen
Zoology K. Lindhardt
Advisory Service, O. Bagger,M.H. Dahl
Activities: Diseases and pests on horticultural and agricultural crops.
Facilities: Diagnosis laboratory for advisers.

INSTITUT FOR   353 UKRUDTSBEKAEMPELSE

[Weed Control Research Institute]
Address: Flakkebjerg, DK-4200 Slagelse
Telephone: (03) 58 63 00
Director: Søren Thorup
Activities: Study of weeds and weed control, mechanical and chemical.
Contract work: No

Polytekniske Laereanstalt - 354
Danmarks Tekniske
Højskole

[Technical University of Denmark]
Address: DK-2800 Lyngby
Telephone: (02) 88 22 22
Telex: 37529 DTH
Rector: Dr Peter Lawaetz

Acoustics Laboratory 355

Head: Professor Fritz Ingerslev

Applied Physics Laboratory 356

Senior staff: Professor G. Trumpy, Professor A. Lindegard Andersen, Professor A. Thölen

Biochemistry and Nutrition 357
Department

Head: Professor Robert Djurtoft

Building and Construction Engineering 358
Department

Head: Professor Aage Jespersen

Building Materials Laboratory 359

Head: Professor Torben C. Hansen

Building Technology Laboratory 360

Head: Professor T. Brøndum-Nielsen

Chemical Engineering Institute 361

Senior staff: Professor Knud Østergaard, Professor Aage Fredens Lund

Chemical Process Industries Institute 362

Head: Professor A. Björkman

Coastal Engineering Laboratory 363

Senior staff: Professor H. Lundgren, Professor F.A. Engelund

Combustion Engines Laboratory 364

Head: Professor Bjørn Quale

Communication Theory Laboratory 365

Senior staff: Professor Per G. Jensen, Professor Chr. Gram

Electromagnetic Theory Laboratory 366

Senior staff: Professor H. Lottrup Knudsen, Professor P. Gudmansen

Electronic Semiconductors Laboratory 367

Senior staff: Professor Georg Bruun, Professor N.I. Meyer

Electronics Laboratory 368

Head: Professor Georg Bruun

Electrophysics Laboratory 369

Senior staff: Professor V. Frank, Professor Asger Nielsen, Professor P.O. Øgaard

Fluid Mechanics Department 370

Head: Professor K. Refslund

Food Preservation Industry Laboratory 371

Head: Professor Frode Bramsnaes

Foundations and Geotechnics 372
Laboratory

Head: Professor Bent Hansen

General Electrotechnics Laboratory 373

Head: Professor Ulrik Krabbe

Heating and Air Conditioning 374
Laboratory

Head: Professor P.O. Fanger

Hydrodynamics and Hydraulic 375
Engineering Institute

Head: Professor J. Buhr Hansen

Industrial Electronics Laboratory 376

Head: H. Peülicke

Inorganic Chemistry Department 377
(Chemical Laboratory A)

Senior staff: Professor Flemming Woldbye, Professor JaromirRuzicka

Machine Elements Department 378

Head: Professor Eyvind Frederikson

Mathematical Statistics and 379
Operations Research Institute

Head: Professor Arne Jensen

Mathematics Institute 380

Senior staff: Professor K. Rander Buch, Professor H.E. Skovgaard

Mechanical Technology and 381
Production Planning Department

Senior staff: Professor C.H. Gundason, Professor Erik Trostmann

Metallurgy Institute 382

Head: Professor E.W. Lange

Microbiology Laboratory 383

Head: Professor Kaspar von Meyenburg

Mineralogy Institute 384

Head: Professor Hans Pauly

Naval Architecture Department 385

Head: Professor Sv. Aa. Harvald

Physical Chemistry Institute 386

Head: vacant

Physical Chemistry Laboratory 387
(Chemical Laboratory B)

Head: Professor Jens Peter Dahl

Physics Laboratory, Section I 388

Head: Professor K. Saermark

Physics Laboratory, Section II 389

Head: Professor T. Carlsen

Physics Laboratory, Section III 390

Head: Professor N.I. Meyer

Power Department 391

Head: J. Richard Hansen

Pulse and Digital Techniques 392
Laboratory

Head: Professor Per G. Jensen

Refrigeration Laboratory 393

Head: Professor P. Worsøe-Schmidt

Road and Railway Building and Town 394
Planning Laboratory

Senior staff: Professor N.O. Jørgensen, Professor Bent Thagesen

Sanitary Engineering Department 395

Head: Professor Poul Harremoës

Servo Laboratory 396

Head: Professor Jens Jensen

Solid-State Mechanics Laboratory 397

Head: Professor Frithioff Niordson

Structural Properties of Materials 398
Department

Head: Professor R.M. Cotterill

Surveying and Geodesy Laboratory 399

Head: Professor Ole Jacobi

Technical Biochemistry Department 400

Head: Professor Ole Bent Jørgensen

Technical Geology Institute 401

Head: vacant

Telegraphs and Telephones Laboratory 402

Senior staff: Professor Georg Bruun, Professor P.G. Jensen

Thermal Insulation Laboratory   403

Head: Professor Vagn Korsgaard

Proteinkemisk Institut   404

[Danish Institute of Protein Chemistry]
Address: Venlighedsvej 4, DK-2970 Hørsholm
Telephone: (02) 86 13 00
Affiliation: Akademiet for de Tekniske Videnskaber - ATV
Head: Kay Brunfeldt
Activities: Areas of research: instrumentation of organic chemical synthesis of peptides and oligonucleotides; synthesis of derivatized polyamino acids for energy research; synthesis of cyclic peptides for utilization in ion selective electrodes. Preparation of solid material for solid phase synthesis. Chromatographic fractionation in preparative scale. Synthesis of oligo- and polynucleotides. Genetic engineering. Determination of volatile and non-volatile nitrouscompounds. Sequence analysis of proteins.

Roskilde Universitetscenter   405

[Roskilde University Centre]
Address: Postbox 260, DK-4000 Roskilde
Telephone: (02) 75 77 11
Affiliation: Ministry of Education
Rector: Boel Jørgensen
Institutes: Institute of Biology and Chemistry
Institute of Mathematics and Physics
Institute of Geography, Social-economic analysis and Computer Science
Institute of Environment, Technologyand Society
Institute of Educational Research, Media Studies and Theory of Science
Institute of Social Economics and Planning
Institute of Social Sciences

Sadolin & Holmblad A.S.   406

Address: 4 Industrigrenen, DK-2635 Ishøj
Telephone: (02) 73 60 90
Telex: 33146 Sadogr dk
Research director: E.L.C. Smith-Petersen
Sections: Central coatings development, B. Hølvig Mikkelsen; printing ink, Palle Sørensen; adhesives, H.E. Andersen

Graduate research staff: 20
Annual expenditure: £501 000-2m
Activities: Research and development within coatings, printing inks, adhesives and related areas.
Facilities: Laboratories for research, development and analysis; application departments for coatings; test printing shop.
Contract work: No

Skibsteknisk Laboratorium   407

– SL
[Danish Ship Research Laboratory]
Address: Hjortekaersvej 99, DK-2800 Lyngby
Telephone: (02) 879325
Telex: 37223 shilab
Affiliation: Akademiet for de Tekniske Videnskaber - ATV
Director: M. Munk Nielsen
Head, R&D: Anders Bøgelund
Graduate research staff: 10
Annual expenditure: £51 000-500 000
Activities: Ship and ocean engineering: model basin tests; propulsion andmanoeuvring tests of vessels and offshore constructions with tests of seaworthiness; simulation of random vessels' penetration and access to ports - for educational purposes, for navigation personnel, pilots, and consultants. Wind engineering: wind forces and moments on floating offshore platforms; tests concerning nuisance connected with smoke from ship funnels and land based stacks; wind loading on buildings, structures etc, determined by wind tunnel tests; field measurements of wind turbines effect. Marine construction service: programs for direction of flame cutting machines, and computer programs for the calculation ofsafety requirements for ships and offshore structures. Approval tests for oil spill floating skimmers and oil spill containment and recovery.
Contract work: Yes

Skovteknisk Institut   408

– SI
[Danish Institute of Forest Technology]
Address: Amalievej 20, DK-1875 København
Telephone: (01) 24 42 66
Telex: 19765 dsh dk
Affiliation: Akademiet for de Tekniske Videnskaber - ATV
Director: Per Tutein Brenoe
Graduate research staff: 9
Annual expenditure: £51 000-500 000
Activities: Research and development projects include: harvest and transport of woods waste from forests,

hedges, parks, etc; improvement of the tractordriver's working conditions; development of forest equipment, and setting up aDanish industry of forest machinery; logging and transport; development of methods and equipment suited for work on small forest properties; silvicultural technique. Other projects will aim at: optimal exploitation of resources; increased forest production and improved quality of products; more flexible marketing of forest products; less hazardous investment in forest production.
Contract work: Yes

Slagteri- og Konserveslaboratoriet   409

[Meat Products Laboratory]
Address: Howitzvej 13, DK-2000 København F
Telephone: (01) 87 11 33
Telex: 16174 mealab dk
Parent body: Ministry of Agriculture
Research director: Mogens Jul
Sections: Chemical-technological, Knud Pedersen; microbiological, Sven Qvist
Graduate research staff: 8
Annual expenditure: £51 000-500 000
Activities: Development and testing of chemical and microbiological methods for food analysis; testing of shelf-life of meat and meat products includingpoultry meat; effect of nitrite in meat products stability of frozen meats.

Slagteriernes Forskningsinstitut   410

[Danish Meat Research Institute]
Address: Maglegårdsvej 2, DK-4000 Roskilde
Telephone: (02) 36 12 00
Director: Dr A. Toft Fensvig
Graduate research staff: 55
Annual expenditure: over £2m
Activities: The Institute promotes technological and economic progress through research on behalf of the Danish Meat Industry. It was founded by the Danish Bacon Factories Export Association and the Organization of Private Bacon Factories.
Contract work: No

SECTOR 1   411
Head: Svend Vahlun
Activities: Laboratories; pork quality; pig handling and transportation; stunning; pig slaughtering; bacon.

SECTOR 2   412
Head: Børge Sørensen
Activities: Pig disease prevention; cattle and beef; meat processing; inedible rendering; environmental matters.

SECTOR 3   413
Head: K.B. Madsen
Activities: Factory planning; technical development; industrial engineering; electronic automation.

SECTOR 4   414
Head: Steen Schneider
Activities: Patents and trade marks; publications; meetings and courses.

F.L. Smidth & Co A/S   415

– FLS
Address: 77 Vigerslev Allé, DK-2500 Valby København
Telephone: (01) 30 11 66
Telex: 270 40 flsco dk
Executive Vice-President and Technical Director: Ib Worning
Vice-President, and Director, Research and Development: N.E. Hastrup
Assistant to Director, Research and Development: Ernst Ellgaard
Departments: Development, F.E. Jensen; Chemical, A. Norholm; Process Technique, J. Touborg; Electrostatic Precipitator, K.B. Kjeldsen
Graduate research staff: 65
Annual expenditure: over £2m
Research activities: Cement: chemistry; production technology.
Facilities: Several pilot plants for the study of process techniques; semi-industrial and full scale test plants.
Contract work: No

Statens Byggeforskningsinstitut   416

[National Building Research Institute]
Address: Postbox 119, DK-2970 Hørsholm
Telephone: (02) 86 55 33
Director: Philip Arctamder
Divisions: Urban and Regional Planning, Svend Jensen
Building and Environmental Design, Tarja Cronberg
Building Physics, Georg Christensen
Building Services, Kaj Ovesen
Structural, Per Bredsdorff
Agricultural Building, Torben Huld
Economic, Dan Ove Pedersen
Indoor Climate, Erik Christophersen
Graduate research staff: 80
Annual expenditure: £3m
Activities: The building industry in the national economy; urban and regional planning; environmental and building design; building systems and components; indoor climate technology and energy economy; sanitary installation systems; urban renewal and building modernization.
Contract work: No

Statens Forsøgsstation, Roskilde   417

[National Experimental Station, Roskilde]
Address: Ledreborg Allé 100, DK-4000 Roskilde
Telephone: (02) 36 18 11
Affiliation: Ministry of Agriculture, Danish Research Service for Plant and Soil Sciences
Director: Poul Rasmussen
Projects and scientific staff: Crop husbandry on root crops, grain legumes and maize, S.P. Lyngby; variety testing of root crops and green fodder plants, including maize, K.E. Pedersen; storage experiments and laboratory, J.E. Augustinussen; vegetable experiments on peat soil, TheLammefjord, I. Jørgensen; variety testing of grain legumes and industrial plants and description of varieties (DUS-testing), P. Flengmark; seed production of herbage and vegetable crops, crop husbandry on industrial plants, A. Nordestgaard; bee experiments, pollination and bee poisoning, O. Svendsen
Graduate research staff: 8
Activities: Variety testing and crop husbandry experiments on root crops,grain legumes, green fodder crops and industrial plants. Seed production of grasses and vegetables. Storage experiments with beetroots and carrots. Experiments on vegetables on peat soil. The Lammefjord. Bee experiments.
Contract work: No

Statens Forsøgsstation, Tylstrup   418

[National Experimental Station, Tylstrup]
Address: Tylstrup, DK-9380 Vestbjerg
Telephone: (08) 26 13 99
Affiliation: Ministry of Agriculture, Danish Research Service for Plant and Soil Sciences
Director: Sv.E. Hansen
Scientific staff: Field experiments, Aa. Bach; laboratory, potato storage, S.P. Østergaard
Activities: Investigations on potato growing, including variety testing. Potato storage experiments in temperature and humidity regulated boxes. Varietytesting of grain, grass, roots etc.
Facilities: Forty three hectares land, of which five hectares are planted with potatoes.

Statens Forsøgsstation, Tystofte   419

[National Experimental Station, Tystofte]
Address: Tystofte, DK-4230 Skaelskør
Telephone: (03) 59 61 41
Affiliation: Ministry of Agriculture, Danish Research Service for Plant and Soil Sciences
Director: Jutta Rasmussen
Sections: Testing of cereal varieties, Jutta Rasmussen; testingof herbage varieties, Aksel Jensen; testing of disease resistance, C.Holm Nielsen
Graduate research staff: 3
Annual expenditure: DKr2m
Activities: Official testing of varieties of agricultural crops. The tests comprise: examination of distinctness, homogeneity and stability; examinationof agricultural value. The tests include evaluation of yield capacity, crop quality, disease resistance, etc.
Facilities: Laboratories and greenhouses for testing of disease resistance. Laboratory for testing varieties of wheatfor baking quality.
Contract work: No
Publications: List of varieties of agricultural crops.

Statens Forstlige Forsøgsvaesen   420

[National Forest Experiment Station]
Address: Springforbivej 4, DK-2930 Klampenborg
Telephone: 01-63 01 62
Parent body: Ministry of Agriculture
Director: Erik Holmsgaard
Sections: Growth and yield of stands; provenance studies; forest soils; forest pathology; forest recreation
Graduate research staff: 12
Annual expenditure: DKr4m
Contract work: No

Statens Husdyrbrugsforsøg   421

[National Institute of Animal Science]
Address: Rolighedsvej 25, DK-1958 København V
Telephone: 01-35 81 00
Parent body: Ministry of Agriculture
Directors: Research in cattle and sheep, Professor A. Neimann-Sørensen; research in pigs and horses, Professor Henning Staun; research in poultry and rabbits, Professor J. Fris Jensen; research in fur animals, Gunnar Jørgensen; animal physiology, biochemistry and analytical chemistry, Professor P.E. Jakobsen
Graduate research staff: 90
Annual expenditure: over £2m
Activities: Breeding, husbandry and nutrition experiment with cattle, sheep, pigs, poultry, rabbits and mink.
Contract work: Yes

Statens Jordbrugstekniske Forsøg   422

– SJF
[National Agricultural Engineering Institute]
Address: Bygholm, DK-8700 Horsens
Telephone: (05) 62 31 99
Parent body: Ministry of Agriculture
Sections: Work study; buildings and stall fixtures; barn and stall equipment; field machinery and equipment
Activities: Testing and investigating farming assets, including tractors,implements, field and barn machinery, equipment, farm buildings and fixtures. Carrying out tests with respect to strength, security, etc, requested by legal authorities. Developing new testing methods, testing new equipment and instrumentation; assisting in the development of new farm machinery, equipment and working methods. Carrying out work studies, including ergonomic studies, on farm operations.
Contract work: Yes

Publications: Research investigation bulletins; test reports; information sheets.
Note: The Institute was formerly called Statens Redskabsprøver.

Statens Øjenklinik   423

[National Eye Clinic for the Blind and Partially Sighted]
Address: 1 Rymarksvej, DK-2900 Hellerup
Telephone: (01) 62 41 00
Director: Dr Thomas Rosenberg
Annual expenditure: £51 000-500 000
Activities: National registration of blind and partially sighted childrenand young adults. Diagnostic examinations of hereditary and acquired eye diseases leading to blindness. Clinical research with nosographic, epidemiological, genetic and social aspects. Special department for optical aids including contact lenses.
Contract work: No

Statens Planteavls-Laboratorium   424

[National Laboratory for Soil and Crop Research]
Address: Lottenborgvej 24, DK-2800 Lyngby
Telephone: (02) 87 06 31
Affiliation: Ministry of Agriculture, Danish Research Service for Plant and Soil Sciences
Director: Aage Henriksen
Departments: Soil chemistry, Jens Jensen; microbiological, T. Vincents Nissen; agricultural chemistry, Chresten Sørensen
Graduate research staff: 12
Annual expenditure: £51 000-500 000
Activities: Nitrate reduction in soil; soil air; potassium, phosphorus and copper in soil; nitrogen mineralization in soil; general soil microbiology; biological degradation of pesticides; uptake of nutrients through leaves; nitrate reduction in plants; influence of nutrition on nitrogenous constituents in plants; development of methods for soil, water and plant analysis.
Contractwork: No

CENTRALANALYTISK AFDELING   425

[Central Analytical Department]
Address: Pedersholm, DK-7100 Vejle
Head: N.Kr. Sørensen

Statens Planteavlskontor 426

[National Crop Husbandry Committee]
Address: Kongevejen 83, DK-2800 Lyngby
Telephone: (02) 85 50 57
Affiliation: Ministry of Agriculture, Danish Research Service for Soil and Plant Sciences
Chief Administrative Officer: Halvor Skov
Administration Officer: E.H. Jensen
Activities: Administers establishments for the Danish Research Service for Soil and Plant Sciences.
Publications: Meddelelser fra Planteavlsforsøg, (Bulletins of the Danish State Research Service for Soil and Plant Sciences).

Statens Seruminstitut 427

[State Serum Institute]
Address: Amager Boulevard 80, DK-2300 København S
Telephone: (01) 95 28 17
Telex: 31316 Serum DK
Director: Ole Forsting
Scientific Director: J. Chr. Siim
Graduate research staff: 110
Contract work: Yes

ANIMAL DEPARTMENT 428

Head: Knud L. Fennestad
Activities: Supply of animal products, production, health and care of laboratory animals; diagnostic and consultative service; pyrogen test; room disinfection and pest infestation control.

Hvidesten Breeding Farm 429

Address: DK-3450 Allerød

Vansgård Breeding Farm 430

Address: DK-4690 Hasler

ANTIBIOTICS DEPARTMENT 431

Head: Dr Jørgen Bang
Activities: Determination of bacterial drug sensitivity. Diffusion problems; sensitivity testing methods; new antibiotics; serum levels of antibiotics; standardization of antibiotics in relation to disc production; measurement of antibiotics; clinical microbiology; chemotherapy.

BCG DEPARTMENT 432

Head: Kirsten Bunch-Christensen
Activities: Production and control of freeze-dried BCG vaccine; preparation of concentrated BCG vaccines for special purposes, scarification, cancer treatment, etc; collection by random sampling of registration forms of BCG vaccinations performed in Denmark; supply of histoplasmin and coccidioidin for diagnostic use in Denmark. Degradation studies on various BCG products; investigationson combined vaccination with BCG and toxoid antigens. WHO International Collaborating Centre for BCG Seed Lots and Control of EBC Products.

BIOLOGICAL CONTROL DEPARTMENT 433

Head: Dr Ebbe Ahrensburg Christensen
Activities: Tests for bacterial and mycotic contamination of vaccines andblood products; production of biological indicators for sterilization procedures; microbiological control of sterilization procedures in hospitals; tests forbacterial and mycotic contamination on medical products for hospitals, etc.

BIOLOGICAL STANDARDIZATION DEPARTMENT 434

Head: Dr Jørn Spaun
Activities: Custody and distribution of international standards and reference preparations (microbiological and immunological substances). Procurement and processing of materials for standards. Assays of immunity and toxicity relating to contagious diseases; processing technology. WHO International Laboratoryfor Biological Standards.

BIOPHYSICS DEPARTMENT 435

Heads: Aksel Birch-Andersen, Bendt Mansa
Activities: Electrophoresis (free and immuno-); ultracentrifugation (analytical and differential); quantitative immunochemical analysis; electron microscopy.

BIOSTATISTICAL DEPARTMENT 436

Head: Michael Weis Bentzon
Activities: Assistance to other departments in planning experiments and analyzing quantitative data, etc; general computer programs.

BLOOD BANK AND BLOOD GROUPING DEPARTMENT   437

Heads: Dr Jørgen Andersen, Dr Else Ehlert Knudsen, Dr Jørgen V. Spärck, Dr Klaus Lind
Activities: Administration of blood donor panel; collection of blood for transfusion and plasma fractionation; serological examination for Rh-immunization of pregnancy; investigation of blood transfusion problems, acquired haemolytic anaemia, and haemolytic disease of the newborn. Production of blood groupingtest sera, tissue typing sera and antiglobulin sera; plasmapheresis; serology of rheumatoid and autoimmune diseases; mycoplasmology; diagnosis of Mycoplasma pneumoniae infection. WHO National Blood Group Reference Laboratory.

BLOOD FRACTIONATION DEPARTMENT   438

Head: Dr Poul Hansen
Activities: Production of blood plasma for clinical and scientific purposes; estimation of human blood proteins and blood coagulation factors.

COLI DEPARTMENT   439

Heads: Dr Frits Ørskov, Dr Ida Ørskov
Activities: Serological typing of strains from Danish and foreign laboratories; preparation of diagnostic sera; custody of international Escherichia coli collection. WHO Collaborative Centre for Reference and Research on Escherichia.

DIAGNOSTIC BACTERIOLOGY DEPARTMENT   440

Heads: Dr Wilhelm Fredriksen, Dr Knud Gaarslev
Activities: Isolation and identification of pathogenic bacteria and fungifrom pathological material including enteric bacteriology and Widel tests. Postgraduate training in medical microbiology.

ENTEROVIRUS DEPARTMENT   441

Head: Dr Inger Petersen
Activities: Production and control of inactivated polio vaccine; diagnosis of enterovirus and other virus infections; preparation of cell cultures; titration of morbilli vaccine.

EPIDEMIOLOGY DEPARTMENT   442

Head: Dr Herdis von Magnus
Activities: Surveillance of communicable diseases; investigation of outbreaks and epidemics; organization of immunization programmes. WHO Collaborating Centre for Virus Reference and Research.

HORMONE DEPARTMENT   443

Head: Dr Svend G. Johnsen
Activities: Quantitative hormone analyses (gonadotrophic hormones, oestrogens, androgens, gestagens, corticosteroids, etc) in human blood and urine; pregnancy tests; investigations into physiology of reproduction.

HOSPITAL INFECTIONS DEPARTMENT   444

Head: Dr Kirsten Rosendal
Activities: Isolation, identification and phage typing of Staphylococcus aureus and coagulase-negative staphylococci; serological examination and phage typing of Pseudomonas seruginosa; hospital infections.

MEDIA DEPARTMENT   445

Head: Dr Vagn Møller
Activities: Preparation and development of media for routine and researchwork.

NATIONAL SALMONELLA CENTRE   446

Head: Dr Ida Orskov
Activities: Preparation of diagnostic sera and typing of strains from Danish laboratories.

NEISSERIA DEPARTMENT   447

Head: Dr Inga Lind
Activities: Bacteriological and serological diagnosis of gonorrhoea; drugsensitivity and determinations; identification of Neisseria species; serological grouping of Neisseria meningitidis; identification of Trichomonas vaginalis.

ORNITHOSIS DEPARTMENT 448

Head: Dr Carl-H. Mordhorst
Activities: Diagnosis of chlamydia and influenza virus infections; serodiagnosis of adenovirus, herpes simplex virus, morbilli virus, respiratory syncytial virus and tickborne encphalitis virus infections; Q-fever. WHO Collaborating Centre for chlamydiae. WHO National Influenza Centre.

RUBELLA DEPARTMENT 449

Head: Dr Jørgen Leerhøy
Activities: Rubella diagnosis; production of smallpox vaccine.

SERUM AND VACCINE DEPARTMENT 450

Head: Dr Poul Elo Christensen
Activities: Production of toxoid vaccines (diphtheria, tetanus) and bacterial vaccines (pertussis, typhoid, cholera, other vaccines); biological controlof vaccines and immunoglobulins. WHO Laboratory of Research and Reference Services for Certain Immunological Biological Products.

STREPTOCOCCAL DEPARTMENT 451

Head: Dr Jørgen Henrichsen
Activities: Bacteriological and serological examination of streptococci; serology of streptococcal diseases - antistreptolysis and antistreptococcalhyaluronidase; serology of mononucleoses (Paul Bunell) and staphylococcal infections (antistaphylolysin). Typing of pneumococci and preparation of diagnostic pneumococcal antisera; screening for phenylketonuria.

TOXOPLASMOSIS DEPARTMENT 452

Head: Dr Jørgen Chr. Siim
Activities: Protozoological and serological diagnosis of human and animaltoxoplasmosis; preparation of toxoplasma antigens, test sera and accessory factor; morphological diagnosis of malaria, leishmaniasis and schistosomiasis haematobii; serological diagnosis of invasive amoebiasis; culture of amoebae; Leishmania spp. and hookworm; serodiagnosis of mumps. FAO/WHO Collaborating Centre for Research and Reference on Toxoplasmosis.

TREPONEMATOSES DEPARTMENT 453

Head: Dr N. Axelsen
Activities: Serological examinations for syphilis; registration of syphilitic cases and non-syphilitic reactivities; examinations for leptospirosis. WHOCollaborating Centre for Reference and Research in Treponematoses.

TUBERCULIN DEPARTMENT 454

Head: Mogens Magnusson
Activities: Production of tuberculin and other sensitins; preparation of Freund's adjuvant; identification of mycobacteria and nocardiae; maintenance ofculture collection of mycobacteria and nocardiae.

TUBERCULOSIS DEPARTMENT 455

Head: Dr Hans Chr. Engbaek
Activities: Bacteriological examination for tuberculosis, including species designation and drug sensitivity determination; national register of tuberculosis cases.

Statens 456
Skadedyrlaboratorium

[National Pest Infestation Laboratory]
Address: Skovbrynet 14, DK-2800 Lyngby
Telephone: (02) 878055
Parent body: Ministry of Agriculture
Director: Preban Bang
Deputy Director: J. Keiding
Sections: Insect control, J. Keiding; insect biology, S. Rasmussen; mammals, M. Lund
Graduate research staff: 5
Annual expenditure: £51 000-500 000
Activities: Biology, ecology, and control of household and other domesticpests, pests of stored products, grain pest (mites), mites of public health importance (house dust mites); fleas; woodboring pests (hylotrupes); houseflies (insecticide resistance, behaviour); mosquitoes; rodents and moles (rodenticide resistance).
Facilities: Facilities for breeding insects and rodents, and for testing insecticides and rodenticides.
Contract work: Yes
Publications: Annual report.

Statens Veterinaere Institut 457 for Virusforskning

[National Veterinary Virus Research Institute]
Address: Lindholm, DK-4771 Kalvehave
Parent body: Ministry of Agriculture
Research director: M. Eskildsen
Activities: Production of vaccines and sera against foot-and-mouth disease; research on animal viral infections.

Statens Veterinaere Serum 458 Laboratory

[National Veterinary Serum Laboratory]
Address: Bülowsvej 27, DK-1870 København V
Parent body: Ministry of Agriculture
Research director: H.E. Ottosen
Activities: Bacteriological, serological and pathological diagnosis; production of biologicals.

Statsfrøkontrollen 459

[National Seed Testing Station]
Address: 20 Skovbrynet, DK-2800 Lyngby
Telephone: (02) 883366
Parent body: Ministry of Agriculture
Research director: P. Norup Pedersen
Section: Seed research, J. Jørgensen
Annual expenditure: £10 000-50 000
Activities: Research on methods of seed testing: purity, germination, vitality, variety and diseases.
Contract work: No

Sundhedsstyrelsens 460 Farmaceutiske Laboratorium

[Pharmaceutical Laboratory, National Board of Health of Denmark]
Address: Frederikssundsvej 378, DK-2700 Brønshøj
Telephone: (02) 94 37 73
Head: Steen Antonsen
Activities: Control unit for pharmaceutical specialities and pharmacy-produced drugs; development of analytical methods for these purposes. Research within analytical chemical techniques.
Contract work: No
Publications: Annual report, in Danish.

Svejsecentralen 461

[Danish Welding Institute]
Address: Park Allé 345, DK-2600 Glostrup
Telephone: (02) 96 88 00
Telex: 33388 svc dk
Affiliation: Akademiet for de Tekniske Videnskaber - ATV
Head: L.H. Larsen
Activities: The Institute provides expert assistance in a wide variety ofindustrial fields. New metal joining technologies; plasma, friction, and electron beam welding; adhesive bonding, automation and computer control of welding procedures; safety and working environment; measurement and analysis of noise and fumes; instruction and training in welding technology; quality control; radiographic and ultrasonic examinations; vacuum leak testing; offshore activities;inspection and supervision on site; safe design of welded structures; biomedical engineering; development of new and specialized equipment for medical applications.

Teknologisk Institut 462

[Technological Institute]
Address: Gregersensvej, DK-2630
Telephone: (02) 99 66 11
Telex: 33416
Director: Morten Knudsen
Sections: Production engineering, Aksel Nielsen; industrial metallurgy, Jan Lemkow; automotive engineering, Hans Bruun; industrial automation, Klaus Aarup; wood technology, Christian Boye;building technology, Jørgen Kelnaes; acoustics, noise, vibration control, Knud Skovgaard Nielsen; heating, ventilation, sanitary, energy, Hans Christian Sørensen; coatings technology, Poul Bastholm; chemical technology, Ulf Meyer Henius; leather technology, Ulf Meyer Henius; cleaning technology, Ulf Meyer Henius; plastics technology, Torben Knudsen; industrial psychology, Gert Graversen; educational technology, Benny Dylander; AV-centre, Benny Dylander; Danish invention centre, Bjørn Westphal Eriksen
Graduate research staff: 614
Activities: To develop, adapt and transfer new technology in support of trade and industry. The Institute is a polytechnical service centre whose resources and activities cover mechanical, civil, and chemical engineering as well asbusiness administration and economics. Assistance to trade and industry includes enquiry service, consultancy, testing, education, job training and research and development activities. Department activities are addressed to specific needs of certain trades - automotive, building, chemical, foundry, machine, plastics, tanning and woodworking industries. Problems of a

more general nature are also handled, such as automation, industrial pedagogics, management, materials testing, pollution control, product development, production engineering, surfacetreatment, and working conditions.
Contract work: Yes

Teleteknisk Forsknings Laboratorium 463

[Telecommunications Research Laboratory]
Address: Borups Allé 43, DK-2200 København N
Telephone: (01) 34 03 55
Telex: 15840 TELLAB DK
Affiliation: Danish Post Office, Concessional Telephone Company
Director: A. Kjerbye Nielsen
Graduate research staff: 15
Annual expenditure: £51 000-500 000
Activities: Telecommunications research.
Contract work: No

Ticra A/S* 464

Address: Kronprinsensgade 13, DK-1114 København K
Telephone: (01) 12 45 72
Telex: 16600 fotex dk
Research director: Dr N.C. Albertsen
Activities: Research and development into antennae, microwave techniques and other applications of electromagnetic theory.

Haldor Topsøe A/S 465

Address: Nymøllevej 55, PO Box 213, DK-2800 Lyngby
Telephone: (02) 878100
Telex: 37 444 HTAS DK
Chairman of the Board: Haldor F.A. Topsøe
Managing Director: R.M.Braca
Manager, Research and Development Division: Anders Nielsen
Sections: Energy research and syngas, J. Rostrup-Nielsen; gas purification, ammonia, methanol, I. Dybkjaer; hydroprocessing, A.C. Jacobsen; physical and analytical, J. Villadsen
Graduate research staff: 40
Activities: Heterogeneous catalysis for synthesis gas generation, oxidation, hydrogenation, gas conversion, ammonia synthesis, methanol synthesis, etc. Crystal structures (X-ray and electron diffraction, electron microscope and electron microprobe), radio isotopes, surface physics and associated fields, semiconductors and associated fields of solid-state physics; performance of catalytic converters, fractioning columns, absorption systems, heat exchange, etc; corrosion problems.
Facilities: Approximately one hundred catalytic reactors, electron microscopy, microprobe, X-ray diffraction, infrared chemisorbed molecules, XPS, UPS, AES, SIMS, microcalorimetry, Mössbauer spectroscopy. Research laboratories at Ravnholm, Lyngby.

Traeraadet 466

[Danish Wood Council]
Address: c/o Teknologisk Institut, Gregersensvej, DK-2630 Taastrup
Affiliation: Akademiet for de Tekniske Videnskaber - ATV
General Secretary: Chr. Boye
Activities: Coordination of development and research for those trades based on wood.

Vandkvalitetsinstituttet 467

– VKI
[Water Quality Institute]
Address: Agern Allé 11, DK-2970 Hørsholm
Telephone: (02) 86 52 11
Telex: 16600 fotex dk
Affiliation: Akademiet for de Tekniske Videnskaber - ATV
Director: P. Schjødtz Hansen
Departments: Aquaculture, K.I. Dahl-Madsen; Chemical Analysis (serving as National Reference Laboratory), Vibeke B. Jensen; Ecology and Hygiene, E. Gargas; Integrated Water Planning, J.F. Simonsen; Water Treatment Technology, P.E. Sørensen
Graduate research staff: 30
Annual expenditure: DKr 3m
Activities: Research and contract work in any kind of water quality problem (laboratory and field studies) eg, emission; water quality surveys and waterplanning; water and wastewater treatment technology; restoration and aquaculture; data processing and computation; ecology and hygiene.
Contract work: Yes

Vildtbiologisk Station* 468

[Game Biology Station]
Address: Kalø, 8410 Rønde
Affiliation: Game Foundation
Director: Dr H. Strandgård
Activities: Research is mainly carried out on the biology of mammals and birds.

Wolff og Kaaber 469

Address: Rugmarken 28, DK-3520 Farum
Telephone: (02) 95 16 61
Telex: 37187 invent dk
Directors: Per Wolff, Henning Kaaber
Graduate research staff: 10
Annual expenditure: £51 000-500 000
Activities: Polymer chemistry and technology; polymerization of vinyl compounds, co-polymers, graft-polymers, etc; organic and inorganic chemistry; custom synthesis.
Contract work: Yes

FINLAND

Åbo Akademi   1

[Swedish University of Åbo]
Address: Domkyrkotorget 3, SF-20500 Åbo 50
Telephone: 921-33 5133
Rector: Professor Dr Bill Widén

FACULTY OF CHEMICAL ENGINEERING   2

Dean: Professor Randolf von Schalien

Analytical Chemistry Institute   3

Head: Professor Erkki Verner Wänninen

Automatic Control Institute   4

Head: Professor Kurt Väinö Torolf Waller

Chemical Plant Engineering Institute   5

Head: Professor Bertel Johan Myréen

Heat Technology Institute   6

Head: Professor Sven Nils Randolf von Schalien

Inorganic Chemistry Institute   7

Head: Professor Kaj Hakan Karlsson

Polymer Chemistry Institute   8

Head: Professor Bengt Stenlund

Technical Chemistry Institute   9

Head: Professor Dr Leif Erik Ingmar Hummelstedt

Wood Chemistry and Chemical Technology Institute   10

Head: Professor Henrik Hugo Bruun

FACULTY OF MATHEMATICS AND NATURAL SCIENCES   11

Dean: Professor Bo-Jungar Wikgren

Biochemistry and Pharmacy Institute   12

Head: Professor Carl Gahmberg

Biology Institute   13

Head: Professor Bo-Jungar Wikgren

HUSÖ BIOLOGICAL RESEARCH STATION   14

Address: SF-22310 Pålsböle
Telephone: 928-37221
Director: Professor Erkki Leppäkoski

PARASITOLOGY INSTITUTE   15

Botany Department   16

Head: Docent Nils Henrik Skult

Geology and Mineralogy Department   17

Head: Professor Nils Holger Edelman

Information Processing Department   18

Head: Aimo Törn

Mathematics Institute   19

Head: Professor Karl Bertil Mathias Qvist

Organic Chemistry Institute   20

Head: Professor Göran Pensar

Physical Chemistry Institute   21

Head: Professor Ingvar Danielsson

Physics Institute   22

Head: Professor Marten Withmar Brenner

THEORETICAL PHYSICS   23
DEPARTMENT
Head: Professor Karl Jakob Gustav Fogel

Biokemiallinen   24
Tutkimuslaitos

[Biochemical Research Institute for the Finnish Cooperative Dairies' Association]
Address: 56B Kalevankatu, SF-00180 Helsinki 18
or: Laboratory, PO Box 176, SF-00181 Helsinki 18
Affiliation: Foundation for Nutrition Research
Director: Dr Kari Salminen
Section: Radioisotopes Department, Aino Rauramaa
Activities: Dairy and food science.
See also: Valion Laboratorio.

Eläinlääketieteellinen   25
Korkeakoulu

[Veterinary Medicine College]
Address: Hämeentie 57, SF-00550 Helsinki 55
or: PO Box 6, SF-00551 Helsinki 55
Telephone: 90 711 411
Telex: 123203 ELKK sf
Affiliation: Ministry of Education
President: Professor K.K. Kallela
Head of Administration: T.T. Ijäs
Sections: Department of Anatomy and Embryology, Professor S.I. Talanti
Department of Biochemistry, Professor P.O. Lindberg
Department of Food Hygiene, Professor T.J. Rekkanen
Department of Pharmacology and Toxicology, Professor M.W. Sandholm
Department of Physiology, Professor H.S.S. Sarajas
Department of Surgery, Professor S.K. Paatsama
Department of Animal Hygiene, Professor K.K. Kallela
Department of Microbiology and Epizootology, Professor J.T. Tvomi
Department of Obstetrics and Gynaecology, Professor K.P. Roine

Ambulatory Clinic, M.L.J. Alanko
Department of Pathology, Professor T.K. Rahko
Department of Medicine, Professor H.G.E. Oksanen
Laboratory of Electron Microscopy
Picture Laboratory
Central Laboratory
Tissue Culture Laboratory
Department of Roentgenology

Enso-Gutzeit Oy   26

Address: PO Box 309, SF-00101 Helsinki 10
Telephone: 90-16291
Telex: 124428 enso sf
Chairman, Board of Directors and Chief Executive Officer: O.J. Mattila
President and Chief Operating Officer: P. Salmi
Divisions: Paper Division, P. Larvio (Division Vice President)
Packaging Division, R. Korvenmaa (Division Vice President)
Wood Products Division, E. Linna (Division Vice President)
Engineering Division, S. Hirvonen (Division Vice President)
Forest Division, K. Viikama (Division Vice President)
Oy Finnlines Limited, J. Lanu (President)
Vaasanlaivat Oy, K. Tarnanen (President)
Annual expenditure: over £2m

RESEARCH INSTITUTE   27

Address: SF-55800 Imatra 80
Research centre manager: Matti Stén
Research director: J. Paronen
Activities: Pulp and paper, development work on new products, processes, machinery and pollution control. Resources are diverted, as required, into solving special problems encountered by the individual mill units, although the emphasis is on long-term projects, for example high yield chemi-mechanical wood pulp studies; the suitability of fibre raw materials of foreign origin; properties of multiply board; paper technology improvements in paper-coating techniques; development of X-ray instruments for measuring coating weight of coated paper; making newsprint paper from bagasse; development of processes for removing chlorinated phenols from waste waters.
Contract work: Yes

Geodeettinen Laitos 28

[Geodetic Institute of Finland]
Address: Ilmalankatu 1A, SF-00240 Helsinki 24
Affiliation: Ministry of Agriculture and Forestry
Director: Professor Juhani Kakkuri
Activities: First order triangulation and levelling; geodetic astronomy; satellite geodesy; gravity measurements; theoretical studies; photogrammetry.
Contract work: No
Publications: Research reports.

Geologinen Tutkimuslaitos 29

[Geological Survey of Finland]
Address: Kivimiehentie 1, SF-02150 Espoo 15
Telephone: 90 46 931
Telex: 123185 geolo sf
Affiliation: Ministry of Trade and Industry
Director: Professor Dr Kalevi Kauranne
Graduate research staff: 185
Annual expenditure: FMk69m
Activities: Geology, economic geology, marine geology, applied geophysics, crystallography, mineralogy, geochemistry, geochronology, airborne geophysical and quaternary deposits mapping, mineral exploration.
Contract work: No
Publications: Survey Bulletin; Report of investigation; Geological maps (with explanations) of pre-quaternary rocks and deposits in Finland; Geochemical maps; Annual reports.

DIVISION FOR MINERAL RESOURCES 30

Research Director: Lauri Hyvärinen

Exploration Department 31

Head: Timari Haapala
Activities: Mineral exploration and research, economic geology.

Geochemistry Department 32

Head: Alf Björklund
Activities: Geochemical research and mapping, development of sampling, analysis and statistical interpretation methods, chemical analyses of geological materials.

Geophysics Department 33

Head: Lauri Eskola
Activities: Airborne geophysical surveys, geophysical ground surveys, development and servicing of geophysical instruments.

DIVISION FOR PETROLOGY AND QUATERNARY GEOLOGY 34

Research director: Kauko Korpela

Petrological Department 35

Head: Atso Vorma
Activities: Geological mapping and research of the precambrian bedrock, geochronology, mineralogy, thematic studies.

Quaternary Geology Department 36

Head: Raimo Kujansuu
Activities: Geological mapping and research of quaternary deposits, hydrogeology, sand and gravel resources, marine geology, peat research, radiocarbon dating.

Hankkijan Kasvinjalostuslaitos 37

[Plant Breeding Institute of Hankkija]
Address: Anttila, SF-04300 Hyryla
Director: Professor Dr Erkki Kivi
Activities: Plant breeding (cereal crops, grasses, clovers, pea, oil plants).

Helsingin Teknillinen Korkeakoulu 38

[Helsinki University of Technology]
Address: Otakaari 1, SF-02150 Espoo 15
Telephone: 90 460 144
Telex: 12-1591 TKK sf
Rector: Professor Paul A. Wuori
Vice Rectors: Professor Jussi Hyyppä; Professor Hans Blomberg

DEPARTMENT OF ARCHITECTURE 39

Dean: Professor Bengt Lundsten

Institute of Architectural Research 40

Heads: Professor Bengt Lundsten, Professor Martti Jaatinen, Professor Osmo Lappo, Professor Jaakko Laapotti
Activities: All fields of architecture.

Institute of the History of Architecture 41

Head: Professor Henrik Lilius
Activities: History of the art of building.

Institute of Urban Planning   42

Head: Professor Ahti Korhonen
Activities: Urban and rural environment.

DEPARTMENT OF CHEMISTRY   43

Dean: Professor Pekka Linko

Biochemistry Laboratory   44

Head: Professor Veli Kauppinen
Activities: Enzymes, secondary metabolites, genetic engineering.

Chemical Engineering Laboratory   45

Head: Professor Harry V. Nordén
Activities: Process dynamics of distillation, calculation of multicomponent distillation, pulp washing, crystallization, investment cost estimation.

Food Technology Laboratory   46

Head: Professor Pekka Linko
Activities: Food process engineering, especially HTST-extrusion; enzyme engineering, especially immobilized biocatalyst technology, biotechnology, cereal, dairy, starch, and sugar technology.

Industrial Chemistry Laboratory   47

Telephone: 90 460 144
Telex: 2815
Head: Professor Johan B-son Bredenberg
Section: Materials projects, Associate Professor Viljo Tammela
Activities: Chemical reaction engineering, catalytic processes, polymers and petrochemicals.
Facilities: Extruder, injection moulding machine, and testing instruments for plastics.
Consultancy: No

Inorganic and Analytical Chemistry   48
Laboratory

Telephone: 90 460 177
Telex: 125161 htkk sf
Head: Professor Lauri Niinistö
Activities: Rare earth and uranyl compounds, trace element analysis by instrumental methods, X-ray crystallography; luminescence, thermal analysis.
Facilities: Trace element analytical facilities (MS, AAS, OES, XRD).
Publications: Annual report.

Organic Chemistry Laboratory   49

Head: Professor Mauri Lounasmaa
Activities: Natural products, especially alkaloids, their structure elucidation, synthesis and pharmacological activity.

Physical Chemistry Laboratory   50

Telephone: 90 460 144
Telex: 125161 htkk sf
Head: Professor Göran Sundholm
Section: Materials projects, Assistant Professor S. Liukkonen, P. Koukkari, K. Kontturi, P. Forssell, P. Saikkonen
Activities: Organic electrochemistry, electrolysis, transport in electrolytic solutions.

DEPARTMENT OF CIVIL   51
ENGINEERING

Dean: Professor Sulevi Lyly

Institute of General Construction   52
Engineering

BUILDING ECONOMICS LABORATORY   53
Head: vacant
Activities: Management of building projects (as owner), building cost models, information systems for building firms.

SOIL MECHANICS AND FOUNDATION   54
ENGINEERING LABORATORY
Head: Professor Kalle-Heikki Korhonen
Activities: Strength and deformation properties of soils.

Institute of Highway and Traffic   55
Engineering

HIGHWAY AND RAILWAY   56
LABORATORY
Head: Professor Jussi Hyyppä
Section: Materials projects, Dr Veijo Pelkonen
Activities: Geometric and structural design of roads, road construction, paving technology, airport technology, railroad engineering, maintenance of roads and railroads and street building.

TRAFFIC AND TRANSPORTATION   57
ENGINEERING LABORATORY
Head: Professor Sulevi Lyly
Activities: Economy level of service, safety and prognoses of traffic.

Institute of Structural Engineering   58

BRIDGE BUILDING LABORATORY   59
Head: Professor Heimo Paavola
Activities: Application of model technology in the analysis of bridge structures.

BUILDING TECHNOLOGY AND   60
MATERIALS LABORATORY
Head: Professor Pekka Kanerva
Activities: Short term and long term properties of building materials and structures.

STRUCTURAL MECHANICS   61
LABORATORY
Head: Professor Martti Mikkola
Activities: Analysis of non-linear structures, theory of stability, numerical and analytical methods of structural mechanics.

Institute of Water Engineering   62

HYDRAULIC ENGINEERING   63
LABORATORY
Head: Professor Harri Sistonen
Activities: Hydraulic model tests.

HYDROLOGY AND WATER RESOURCES   64
LABORATORY
Head: Professor Jussi Hooli
Activities: Hydrology, chemistry and biology of ground water and surface water.

WATER SUPPLY LABORATORY   65
Head: Professor Eero Kajosaari
Activities: Water supply and wastewater treatment.

DEPARTMENT OF ELECTRICAL   66
ENGINEERING

Dean: Professor Kauko Rahko

Institute of Electromagnetism   67

BASIC ELECTROMAGNETICS AND   68
MEASURING TECHNIQUES
LABORATORY
Head: vacant
Activities: Circuit theory and applications, electrical standards and measuring systems.

ELECTRON PHYSICS LABORATORY   69
Head: Professor Tor Stubb
Activities: Semiconductors, thin film techniques.

RADIO LABORATORY   70
Head: Professor Martti Tiuri
Activities: Development and design of microwave equipment, antennae and low-noise receivers.
See also: Metsahovi Radio Research Station.

DEPARTMENT OF FOREST   71
PRODUCTS

Dean: Professor Risto Juvonen

Mechanical Wood Technology   72
Laboratory
Head: Professor Risto Juvonen
Activities: Sawing operation and the manufacture of plywood, particle board and fibre-board.

Paper Technology Laboratory   73

Head: Professor Kari Ebeling
Activities: Mechanical pulping, beating and screening of pulp; structure of paper, stability of paper machine process.

Printing Technology Laboratory   74

Head: Professor Olavi Perilä
Sections: Materials projects, Dr Hannn Saarelma, Saija Ristimäk
Activities: Input, processing, and telecommunication systems of information, sewing and stitching processes, study and control of the variations in the reproduction in the various printing processes as they affect print quality, instrument control of printing itself.

Pulping Technology Laboratory   75

Head: Professor Risto Juvonen
Activities: Pulping and bleaching processes, chemical recovery, environmental protection.

Wood Chemistry Laboratory   76

Head: Professor Eero Sjöström
Activities: The reactions of carbohydrates during pulping and bleaching, chemical modification of cellulose, environmental problems in pulp industry, production of useful chemicals from pulping liquors and waste.

DEPARTMENT OF GENERAL   77
SCIENCES

Dean: Professor Matti A. Ranta

Institute of Economics 78

Head: Professor Osmo Jaskari
Activities: International economics.

Institute of Ecotechnics 79

Head: Associate Professor Pekka Haatanen
Activities: Industrial relations and industrial safety.

Institute of Mathematics 80

Head: Professor Harri Rikkonen
Activities: Functional analysis, stochastic processes, systems theory, iterative solution of non-linear equations, numerical integration of ordinary differential equations, finite-element methods for partial differential equations, integral equations, finite geometries and linear and tensor algebra.

LABORATORY OF PHYSICS 81

Head: vacant
Activities: X-ray physics.

Institute of Mechanics 82

Head: Professor Matti A. Ranta
Activities: Classical mechanics and its applications including numerical calculation methods.

DEPARTMENT OF MECHANICAL 83
ENGINEERING

Dean: Professor Valter Kostilainen

Institute of Industrial Economics 84

INDUSTRIAL ECONOMICS 85
LABORATORY

Head: Professor Tauno Olkkonen
Activities: Management and organization.

INDUSTRIAL PSYCHOLOGY 86
LABORATORY

Head: Professor Sauli Häkkinen
Activities: Problems connected with industrial and traffic psychology.

INFORMATION PROCESSING SCIENCE 87
LABORATORY

Head: Professor Reijo Sulonen
Activities: Software engineering and computer graphics.

Institute of Mechanical Engineering 88

AUTOMOTIVE ENGINEERING 89
LABORATORY

Head: Associate Professor Antti Saarialho
Activities: Tyre properties and manoeuvrability of cars; automobile design in arctic conditions.

HYDRAULIC MACHINES LABORATORY 90

Head: Professor Paul Wuori
Activities: Pumps, hydraulics and pneumatics.

INTERNAL COMBUSTION ENGINES 91
LABORATORY

Head: Professor Jorma Pitkänen
Activities: Diesel emissions, thermal loading problems, supercharging of medium speed and high speed diesel engines, future fuels.

MACHINE DESIGN LABORATORY 92

Head: Eino Matti Kleimola
Activities: Screw joints, springs, shaft vibrations, tribology, mechanisms.

MATERIALS SCIENCE LABORATORY 93

Head: Professor Juha Pietikäinen
Activities: Metal composites, fatigue and heat treatment of metals, metallography, welding and foundry technology.

METALS TECHNOLOGY LABORATORY 94

Head: vacant
Activities: Molten metals and their reactions with moulding materials, solidification processes, properties of cast alloys.

PRODUCTION ENGINEERING 95
LABORATORY

Head: Professor Veijo Kauppinen
Activities: Machining and forming of metals.

Institute of Naval Architecture and 96
Aircraft Engineering

AERODYNAMICS LABORATORY 97

Head: Professor Seppo Laine
Activities: Boundary layer flow, aerodynamics of aeroplanes.

LIGHT STRUCTURES LABORATORY 98

Telephone: 90 451 2709
Head: Professor Seppo Laine
Section: Materials projects, Ulv Mai; Olli Saarela
Activities: Plastics composites in aeroplane structures, optimal structural design.

SHIP DESIGN AND STRUCTURES LABORATORY   99
Head: Professor Ernst Enkvist
Activities: Basic ship design, structures, marine engineering and winter navigation technology.

SHIP HYDRODYNAMICS LABORATORY   100
Head: Professor Valter Kostilainen
Activities: Shallow water ship hydrodynamics, two-phase flow.

STRENGTH OF MATERIALS LABORATORY   101
Head: Professor Martti Kaila
Activities: Structural strength of machines, strength of materials, experimental stress analysis.

Institute of Thermal Engineering   102

HEATING, WATER AND AIR CONDITIONING LABORATORY   103
Telephone: 90 451 2683
Head: vacant
Section: Materials projects, Antti Majanen
Activities: Electrical heating, smoke and air pollution, heat transfer.

POWER GENERATION LABORATORY   104
Head: Professor Antero Jahkola
Activities: Power plants, energy supply and energy economics.

STEAM AND GAS DYNAMICS LABORATORY   105
Head: vacant
Activities: Supersonic and transonic gas dynamics.

THERMODYNAMICS AND APPLIED MECHANICS LABORATORY   106
Head: Associate Professor Nils-Erik Fagerholm
Activities: Thermal engineering and heat transfer.

DEPARTMENT OF MINING AND METALLURGY   107
Dean: Professor Martti Sulonen

Applied Physical Metallurgy Laboratory   108
Head: Professor Martti Sulonen
Activities: Metals processing and heat treatment.

Applied Process Metallurgy Laboratory 109
Head: Professor Kaj Lilius
Activities: Metallurgical processes, unit operations in metallurgical engineering.

Economic Geology and Applied   110
Geophysics Laboratory
Head: Professor Bengt Söderholm
Activities: Mining geology, structural geology, ore prospecting.

Mineral Dressing Laboratory   111
Head: Professor Toimi Lukkarinen
Activities: Comminution, concentration of ores and minerals.

Mining Engineering Laboratory   112
Head: Professor Raimo Matikainen
Activities: Rock mechanics.

Physical Metallurgy Laboratory   113
Head: Professor Veikko Lindroos
Activities: Dislocation theory and theory of phase transformations.

Process Metallurgy Laboratory   114
Head: Professor Lauri Holappa
Activities: Extraction metallurgy, pyrometallurgy, solid-state chemistry, electro-metallurgy, powder metallurgy, corrosion phenomena.

DEPARTMENT OF SURVEYING   115
Dean: Professor Erkki J. Hollo

Institute of Geodesy, Cartography and   116
Photogrammetry

LABORATORY OF GEODESY   117
Head: Professor Matti Martikainen
Activities: Calibration of geodetic instruments, analysis and optimization of networks, computer-aided cartography and geographical information systems.

LABORATORY OF PHOTOGRAMMETRY   118
Head: Professor Einari Kilpelä
Activities: Numerical photogrammetry, calibration of cameras and measuring instruments, non-topographic application of photogrammetry and remote sensing.

Institute of Real-Estate Techniques and Laws 119

Head: Professor Pekka V. Virtanen
Activities: Real-estate planning, administration and valuation, rural land use planning and techniques, urban real-estate techniques and also economic jurisprudence.

DEPARTMENT OF TECHNICAL PHYSICS 120

Dean: Professor Jorma Routti
Facilities: Triga research reactor.

Information Science Laboratory 121

Head: Professor Teuvo Kohonen
Activities: Automatic pattern recognition techniques, theory and applications of associative memory, information structures, digital signal processing, microprocessor systems.
Publications: Project reports, annual reports.

Materials Physics Laboratory 122

Head: Professor Eero Byckling
Activities: Materials research, laser technology, biomagnetism, theoretical physics.
Publications: Project reports, annual reports.

Nuclear Engineering Laboratory 123

Head: Professor Jorma Routti
Activities: Reactor analysis, positron physics, applied nuclear physics, solar energy, energy models.
Facilities: Triga research reactor.
Publications: Project reports, annual reports.

INSTITUTE OF COMMUNICATION ENGINEERING 124

Acoustic Laboratory 125

Head: Associate Professor Matti Karjalainen
Activities: Electro-acoustic instruments, analysis and synthesis of speech.

Applied Electronics Laboratory 126

Head: Professor Paavo Jääskeläinen
Activities: Display engineering, bioelectronics and industrial electronics.

Communication Transmission Laboratory 127

Head: Professor Seppo Halme
Activities: Optical fibre communications, digital radio systems, computer communications, lasers.

Control Engineering Laboratory 128

Head: Professor Antti Niemi
Activities: Digital real-time control systems for industrial processes.

Digital Systems Laboratory 129

Head: Professor Leo Ojala
Activities: Microprocessors, multiprocessor systems, theoretical computer science.

Electrical Machinery Laboratory 130

Head: Professor Tapani Jokinen
Activities: Development of rotary machine theories, electromechanical energy conversion in traction and ship propulsion systems, design and construction of electrical equipment.

Power Systems Laboratory 131

Head: Professor Jorma Mörsky
Activities: Network studies, reactive power compensation, high voltage testing techniques, insulation coordination.

Systems Theory Laboratory 132

Head: Professor Hans Blimberg
Activities: Methodology for systems modelling, control and optimization.

Telecommunication Switching Laboratory 133

Head: Professor Kauko Rahko
Activities: Transmission and switching systems for speech, image and data.

Use of Electrical Energy and Power Electronics 134

Head: Professor Yrjö Laiho
Activities: Static rectifiers, inverters and converters, lighting and electrical heating.

UNIVERSITY ASSOCIATED OR AFFILIATED INSTITUTIONS   135

Centre for Regional and Urban Planning   136

Head: Professor Olli Kivinen
Activities: A joint centre of fifteen universities in Finland for postgraduate training in rural and town planning.

Computing Centre   137

Head: Aarne Sipilä
Activities: Software development for the computers of the centre.
Facilities: Four computer systems, remote batch and display terminals for time-sharing.

Helsinki University of Technology Library   138

Librarian: Elin Törnudd
Activities: Functions as the National Central Library for Technology, research in information retrieval.

Low Temperature Laboratory   139

Head: Professor Olli Lounasmaa
Activities: Research at low and ultralow temperatures.

Helsingin Yliopisto   140

[Helsinki University]
Address: Hallituskatu 8, SF-00100 Helsinki 10
Telephone: 90 1911
Rector: Professor Nils Oker-Blom
Secretary-General: N.G. Fellman

FACULTY OF AGRICULTURE AND FORESTRY   141

Address: Viikki, SF-00710 Helsinki 71

AGRICULTURAL LIBRARY   142
Director: Professor Matti Antila

AGRICULTURAL MUSEUM   143
Director: Professor Eeva Tapio

CENTRE OF EXTENSION EDUCATION   144
Director: Professor Harri Westermarck

DEPARTMENT OF AGRICULTURAL CHEMISTRY   145
Director: Professor Armi Kaila
Activities: Soils and plant nutrients.

DEPARTMENT OF AGRICULTURAL ECONOMICS   146
Director: Professor Viljo Ryynänen

DEPARTMENT OF AGRICULTURAL ENGINEERING   147
Director: Professor Aarne Pehkonen

DEPARTMENT OF AGRICULTURAL POLICY   148
Director: Professor Risto Ihamoutila

DEPARTMENT OF ANIMAL BREEDING   149
Director: Professor Ulf Lindström

DEPARTMENT OF ANIMAL HUSBANDRY   150
Director: Professor Esko Poutiainen

DEPARTMENT OF APPLIED ZOOLOGY   151
Director: Professor Matti Nuorteva

DEPARTMENT OF DAIRY SCIENCE   152
Director: Professor Matti Antila
Activities: Milk and milk products.

DEPARTMENT OF ENVIRONMENTAL CONSERVATION   153
Director: Professor Pekka Nuorteva

DEPARTMENT OF FARM FORESTRY   154
Director: Professor Aarne Reunala

DEPARTMENT OF FOOD CHEMISTRY AND TECHNOLOGY   155
Director: Professor Pekka Koivistoinen

DEPARTMENT OF GENERAL BOTANY   156
Director: Professor Veikko Hintikka

DEPARTMENT OF GENERAL CHEMISTRY   157
Director: Professor Heikki Toivonen

DEPARTMENT OF HORTICULTURE   158
Director: Professor Erkki Kaukovirta

DEPARTMENT OF HOUSEHOLD ECONOMICS   159
Director: Professor Maire Honkanen

DEPARTMENT OF HOUSEHOLD   **160**
TECHNOLOGY
Director: Professor Aili Jokelainen

DEPARTMENT OF LAND USE   **161**
ECONOMICS
Director: Professor Kauko Hahtola

DEPARTMENT OF LIMNOLOGY   **162**
Director: Professor Reino Ryhänen

DEPARTMENT OF MEAT   **163**
TECHNOLOGY
Director: Professor Fritz Niinivaara

DEPARTMENT OF MICROBIOLOGY   **164**
Director: Professor Helge Gyllenberg
Activities: Basic research in general, agricultural and
food microbiology.

DEPARTMENT OF NUTRITION   **165**
Director: Antti Ahlström
Activities: Nutrition, biochemistry, foods and food pre-
paration.

DEPARTMENT OF PLANT BREEDING   **166**
Director: Professor Peter Tigerstedt

DEPARTMENT OF PLANT HUSBANDRY   **167**
Director: Professor Eero Varis

DEPARTMENT OF PLANT PATHOLOGY   **168**
Director: Professor Eeva Tapio

DEPARTMENT OF VETERINARY   **169**
SCIENCE
Director: Professor Eero Tanhuanpää

Forestry Departments   **170**
Address: Union Katu 40B, SF-00170 Helsinki 17

DEPARTMENT OF BUSINESS   **171**
ECONOMICS IN FORESTRY
Director: Professor Matti Keltikangas

DEPARTMENT OF FOREST   **172**
MENSURATION AND MANAGEMENT
Director: Professor Aarne Nyyssönen

DEPARTMENT OF FOREST PRODUCTS   **173**
MARKETING
Director: Professor Seppo Ervasti

DEPARTMENT OF FOREST   **174**
TECHNOLOGY
Director: Professor Kalle Putkisto
Activities: Forest products, their transport and pro-
cessing.

DEPARTMENT OF PEATLAND   **175**
FORESTRY

DEPARTMENT OF SILVICULTURE   **176**
Director: Professor Matti Leikola

DEPARTMENT OF SOCIAL   **177**
ECONOMICS OF FORESTRY
Director: Professor Päiviö Riihinen

FORESTRY LIBRARY   **178**
Director: Professor Matti Keltikangas

FORESTRY MUSEUM   **179**
Address: Viikki, SF-00710 Helsinki 71
Director: Professor Olli Makkonen

HYYTIÄLÄ FORESTRY STATION   **180**
Address: Hyytiälä, SF-35500 Korkeakoski
Telephone: 935 81911
Director: Rihko Haarlaa

ISOTOPE LABORATORY   **181**
Address: Viikki, SF-00710 Helsinki 71
Director: Professor Matti Antila

LABORATORY FOR EXPERIMENTAL   **182**
ANIMALS
Address: Viikki, SF-00710 Helsinki 71
Director: Professor Antti Ahlström

MUDDUSNIEMI EXPERIMENTAL FARM   **183**
Address: SF-99910 Kaamanen
Telephone: 717 99767
Director: Liisa Syrjälä

SUITIA EXPERIMENTAL FARM   **184**
Address: SF-02570 Siuntio kk
Director: Seppo Karttunen

VÄRRIÖ SUBARCTIC RESEARCH   **185**
STATION
Address: Ainijärvi, SF-98840 Ruuvaoja
Telephone: 992 44143
Director: Erkki Pulliainen

VIIKKI EXPERIMENTAL FARM   **186**
Address: SF-00710 Helsinki 71
Director: Pentti Kämäräinen

FACULTY OF MEDICINE   187

Address: Aura-talo, Tukholmankatu 2, SF-00250 Helsinki 25

Central Pathology Laboratory   188

Address: Haartmaninkatu 3, SF-00290 Helsinki 29
Director: Professor Lars Hjelt

Department and Museum for Medical   189
History

Address: Kasarmikatu 11-13, SF-00130 Helsinki 13
Director: Professor Harald Teir

Department of Anaesthesia   190

Address: Haartmaninkatu 4, SF-00290 Helsinki 29
Director: Professor Tapani Tammisto

Department of Anatomy   191

Address: Siltavuorenpenger 20, SF-00170 Helsinki 17
Director: Professor Olavi Eränkö

Department of Bacteriology and   192
Immunology

Address: Haartmaninkatu 3, SF-00290 Helsinki 29
Director: Professor Olli Mäkelä
Activities: Serological and bacteriological investigations.

Department of Biology   193

Address: Siltavuorenpenger 20B, SF-00170 Helsinki 17
Director: Professor Jorma Wartiovaara

Department of Clinical Chemistry   194

Address: Haartmaninkatu 4, SF-00290 Helsinki 29
Director: Professor Herman Adlercreutz

Department of Clinical Pharmacology 195

Address: Paasikivenkatu 4, SF-00290 Helsinki 29
Director: Professor Pentti Peltola

Department of Forensic Medicine   196

Address: Kytösuontie 11, SF-00280 Helsinki 28
Director: Professor Matti Möttönen
Activities: Forensic chemical toxicology; forensic analyses of pharmaceuticals and drugs; studies of intoxication.

Department of General Chemistry   197

Address: Siltavuorenpenger 10, SF-00170 Helsinki 17
Director: Professor Pauli Antikainen

Department of Medical Chemistry   198

Address: Siltavuorenpenger 10, SF-00170 Helsinki 17
Director: Professor Johan Järnefelt

Department of Medical Genetics   199

Address: Haartmaninkatu 3, SF-00290 Helsinki 29
Director: Professor Albert de la Chapelle

Department of Medical Physics   200

Address: Siltavuorenpenger 10, SF-00170 Helsinki 17
Director: Professor Peter Holmberg

Department of Pathology   201

Address: Haartmaninkatu 3, SF-00290 Helsinki 29
Director: Professor Erkki Saxén

Department of Pharmacology   202

Address: Siltavuorenpenger 10, SF-00170 Helsinki 17
Director: Professor Matti Paasonen

Department of Physiology   203

Address: Siltavuorenpenger 20, SF-00170 Helsinki 17
Director: Professor Matti Bergström

Department of Public Health Science 204

Address: Haartmaninkatu 3, SF-00290 Helsinki 29
Director: Professor Ilari Rantasalo

Department of Virology   205

Address: Haartmaninkatu 3, SF-00290 Helsinki 29
Director: Professor Kari Penttinen
Laboratory: Viral Immunopathology, Professor Kari Penttinen

Endocrine Research Laboratory   206

Address: Asematie 13, SF-02700 Kauniainen
Director: Professor Bror-Axel Lamberg

Institute of Dentistry 207

Address: Mannerheimintie 172, SF-00280 Helsinki 28
Director: Professor Johannes Haataja
Departments: Oral Surgery, Professor Valle Oikarinen; Cardiology, Professor Ilkka Paunio; Prosthetics, Professor Eino Mäkilä; Paedodontics and Orthodontics, Professor Keijo Mattila; Periodontology, Professor Jukka Ainamo; Oral Diagnosis and Treatment Planning, Matti Jokinen; Oral Pathology, Professor P.E.B. Calonius

Laboratory of Experimental Pathology 208

Address: Haartmaninkatu 3, SF-00290 Helsinki 29
Director: Professor Lauri Saxén

Unit of Educational Television 209

Address: Haartmaninkatu 4, SF-00290 Helsinki 29
Director and Head of Television Group: Osmo Visuri

FACULTY OF SCIENCE 210

Address: Fabianinkatu 33, SF-00170 Helsinki 17

Astrophysics Laboratory 211

Address: Tähtitorninmäki, SF-00130 Helsinki 13
Director: Professor Kalevi Mattila

Department of Biochemistry 212

Address: Unioninkatu 35, SF-00170 Helsinki 17
Director: Professor Juhani Jänne
Activities: Metabolic studies on plants and microorganisms, physiologically active peptides, structure studies on peptides and proteins, haemoproteins.

Department of Botany 213

Address: Unioninkatu 44, SF-00170 Helsinki 17
Director: Professor Jaakko Jalas
Sections: Botanical Museum, vacant; Botanical Garden, vacant

Department of Chemistry 214

Address: Wuorikatu 20, SF-00100 Helsinki 10
Director: Professor Pekka Hirsjärvi
Divisions: Analytical Chemistry, Professor Osmo Mäkitie; Inorganic Chemistry, Professor Aarne Pajunen; Physical Chemistry, Professor Jouko Koskikallio; Organic Chemistry, Professor Pekka Hirsjärvi
Activities: Chemical thermodynamics, reaction kinetics, complex compounds, structure of inorganic and organic compounds, alicyclic compounds, lignin, waste liquors from cellulose manufacture.

Department of Computer Science 215

Address: Tukholmankatu 2, SF-00250 Helsinki 25
Director: Professor Martti Tienari

Department of General Microbiology 216

Address: Mannerheimintie 172, SF-00280 Helsinki 28
Director: Professor Veronica Sundman

Department of Genetics 217

Address: P. Rautatiekatu 13, SF-00100 Helsinki 10
Director: Professor Olli Halkka

Department of Geography 218

Address: Hallituskatu 11-13, SF-00100 Helsinki 10
Director: Professor Kalevi Rikkinen

Department of Geology and Mineralogy 219

Address: Snellmaninkatu 5, SF-00170 Helsinki 17
Director: Professor Heikki V. Tuominen
Activities: Geology and mineralogy including geochemistry and mineral chemistry.

Department of Geology and Palaeontology 220

Address: Snellmaninkatu 5, SF-00170 Helsinki 17
Director: Professor Joakim Donner
Activities: Quaternary geology of Finland.

Department of Geophysics 221

Address: Vironkatu 7B, SF-00170 Helsinki 17
Director: Professor Juhani Virta

Department of Mathematics 222

Address: Hallituskatu 15, SF-00100 Helsinki 10
Director: Professor Lauri Myrberg

Department of Meteorology 223

Address: Hallituskatu 11-13, SF-00100 Helsinki 10
Director: Professor Eero Holopainen

Department of Nuclear Physics 224

Address: Siltavuorenpenger 20, SF-00170 Helsinki 17
Director: Professor Christofer Cronström

Department of Physics 225

Address: Siltavuorenpenger 20, SF-00170 Helsinki 17
Director: Professor Erik Spring
Laboratory: Accelerator Laboratory, Professor Folke Stenman
Activities: Physics, including resonance studies in light substances and excitation of atomic nuclei. Electron distribution studies by X-ray diffraction measurements. Nuclear spectroscopical studies on beta and gamma decay schemes, alphafine structure and low intensity alpha work. Calorimetry of ionic crystals.

Department of Radiochemistry 226

Address: Unioninkatu 35, SF-00170 Helsinki 17
Director: Professor Jorma Miettinen

Department of Theoretical Physics 227

Address: Siltavuorenpenger 20, SF-00170 Helsinki 17
Director: Professor Keijo Kajantie

Department of Wood and Polymer 228 Chemistry

Address: Meritullinkatu 1A, SF-00170 Helsinki 17
Director: Professor Johan Lindberg

Department of Zoology 229

Address: P. Rautatiekatu 13, SF-00100 Helsinki 10
Director: Professor Henrik Wallgren
Laboratories: Physiology, Professor Henrik Wallgren; Morphology and Ecology, Professor V. Ilmari Pajunen

Kilpisjärvi Biological Station 230

Address: SF-99490 Kilpisjärvi
Telephone: 996 713
Director: Professor Henrik Wallgren

Lammi Biological Station 231

Address: SF-16900 Lammi
Telephone: 917 32 501
Head: Professor Rauno Ruuhijärvi
Station Director: Dr Jaakko Syrjämäki
Sections: Lake ecosystem ecology, Dr I. Hakale; bog ecosystem ecology, Professor R. Ruuhijärvi
Graduate research staff: 6
Activities: Field base for instruction and research in biological, mainly ecological, and related sciences.
Facilities: Lecture rooms and teaching laboratories, laboratory instruments, hydrobiological and terrestrial research equipment for field research.
Contract work: No

Mineralogical Museum 232

Address: Snellmaninkatu 5, SF-00170 Helsinki 17
Director: Ossi Näykki

Observatory 233

Address: Tähtitorninmäki, SF-00130 Helsinki 13
Director: Professor Kalevi Mattila
Activities: Astronomical research covers star photography and spectrum photography. Theoretical work. Astrography.
Facilities: Instruments for spectrography and satellite observations.

School of Pharmacy 234

Address: Fabianinaktu 35, SF-00170 Helsinki 17
Director: Professor Max von Schantz
Laboratories: Pharmacognosy, Professor Max von Schantz; Pharmacology, Professor Liisa Ahtee; Pharmaceutical Chemistry, Professor Jaakko Halmekoski; Chemistry, Professor Antti Kivinen; Pharmaceutical Technology, Professor Eeva Kristoffersson; Microbiology, Professor Veli Kauppinen

Tvärminne Zoological Station 235

Address: SF-10850 Tvärminne
Telephone: 911 88161
Head: Professor Rolf Kristoffersson
Director: Jouko Sarvala

Zoological Museum 236

Address: P. Rautatiekatu 13, SF-00100 Helsinki 10
Director: Professor Walter Hackman
Divisions: General, Professor Göran Bergman; Entomology, Professor Walter Hackman

UNIVERSITY NON-FACULTY 237 DEPARTMENTS AND CENTRES

Central Medical Library 238

Address: Haartmaninkatu 4, SF-00290 Helsinki 29
Director: Professor Matti K. Paasonen

Centre for Studies of Developing 239 Countries

Address: Unioninkatu 40, SF-00170 Helsinki 17
Director: Professor Göran von Bonsdorff

Computing Centre 240

Address: Töölönkatu 11, SF-00100 Helsinki 10
Director: Lars Backström

Department of Electron Microscopy 241

Address: Malminkatu 20, SF-00100, Helsinki 10
Director: Dr Jorma Wartiovaara

Department of Seismology 242

Address: E. Hesperiankatu 4, SF-00100 Helsinki 10
Director: Dr Heikki Korhonen
See also: Nurmijärvi Geophysical Observatory,
Meteorological Institute of Finland.

Photographic Service Centre 243

Address: Snellmaninkatu 14, SF-00170 Helsinki 17
Director: Sakari Sorjonen
Activities: Scientific photography and cinematography.

Radiocarbon Dating Laboratory 244

Address: Snellmaninkatu 5, SF-00170 Helsinki 17
Director: Professor Joakim Donner

Research Institute for Theoretical 245
Physics

Address: Siltavuorenpenger 20, SF-00170 Helsinki 17
Director: Professor Stig Stenholm

University Library 246

Address: Unioninkatu 36, SF-00170 Helsinki 17
Director: Esko Häkli

Ilmatieteen Laitos 247

[Meteorological Institute of Finland]
Address: Vuorikatu 24, Box 503, SF-00101 Helsinki 10
Telephone: 90-171 922
Telex: 124436 efki sf
Affiliation: Ministry of Communications
Director General: Dr E. Jatila
Sections: Weather forecasting, Dr J. Rinne; climatology, Dr U.I. Helimäki; pollution, Dr A. Kulmala; earth magnetism, Dr C. Sucksdorff
Graduate research staff: 30
Annual expenditure: £501 000-2m
Activities: Meteorological fields (climatology, aerol-

ogy, synoptics) and geophysical fields (earth magnetism, ionospheric investigations, radioactivity of the air, aurora).
Contract work: Yes
Publications: Research reports, technical reports, climatological data, measurements and observations, *Meteorological Yearbook of Finland.*

GEOFYSIKAALINEN OBSERVATORIO 248

[Nurmijärvi Geophysical Observatory]
Address: SF-05130 Röykkä
Head: M. Kivinen
Activities: Geomagnetism, geomagnetic pulsations, ionospheric vertical sounding, oblique sweep-frequency recording, back scatter recording, riometer, aurora, seismology (main seismic station for the Department of Seismology, University of Helsinki).

Insinööri- Ja 249
Limnologitoimisto Oy
Vesitekniikka AB

Address: Terveystie 2, SF-15870 Salpakangas
Telephone: 918 803 525
Director of Research: Paavo Ristola
Sections: Limnology, Ansa Pilke; water chemistry, Lauri Waltari; water laboratory, Juhani Pilke
Graduate research staff: 4
Annual expenditure: £51 000-500 000
Activities: Engineering consultancy: water course investigations, pollution control, lake restoration, fishery research, biological monitoring, toxicity testing, wastewater characterization, drinking water studies, air pollution control.
Contract work: No

Invalidisäätiö 250

[Invalid Foundation of Finland]
Address: Tenholantie 10, SF-00280 Helsinki 28
Telephone: 90-418 155
Parent body: State National Board of Social Welfare
Director of Research: Anders Langenskiöld
Sections: Orthopaedic hospital research laboratories; Vocational training school; Vocational guidance unit
Graduate research staff: 2
Annual expenditure: £20 000
Activities: Methods of treatment of orthopaedic disabilities, testing capacity of work and rehabilitation therapy, new operative methods and techniques.
Facilities: Two and three year retraining courses and

workshops for invalids (metalwork, electrical, painting and upholstery, food management, fabrics, photographic).
Contract work: No

ORTHOPAEDICS APPLIANCES UNIT   251

Address: Tenholantie 9, SF-00280 Helsinki 28
Telephone: 90-418 224
Activities: Developing and testing new appliances.
Facilities: Demonstrations, model rooms and study meetings on rehabilitation, film loan on the use of appliances.

WORK CLINIC   252

Address: Sornaisten Rantatie 33D, SF-00500 Helsinki 50
Telephone: 90-739 288
Activities: Evaluating invalid's practical work capacity.
Facilities: Adaptability tests, mechanical aids.

Joensuun Korkeakoulu   253

[Joensuu University]
Address: PO Box 111, SF-80101 Joensuu 10
Telephone: 973-26 211
Telex: 46-137
Rector: Professor Heikki Kirkinen

DEPARTMENT OF CHEMISTRY AND BIOSCIENCES   254

Biology Section   255
Head: Professor Heikki Hyvärinen

Chemistry Section   256
Head: Professor Pentti Mälkönen

DEPARTMENT OF EDUCATION   257

Psychology Section   258
Head: Professor Yrjö-Paavo Häyrynen

Sociology Section   259
Head: Professor Ari Antikainen

DEPARTMENT OF HISTORY, GEOGRAPHY AND OTHER REGIONAL SCIENCES   260

Anthropology Section   261

Economics Section   262
Head: Professor Kyösti Pulliainen

Geography Section   263
Head: Professor Juhani Hult

Statistics Section   264

DEPARTMENT OF MATHEMATICS AND PHYSICS   265

Computing Science Section   266
Head: vacant

Mathematics Section   267
Head: Professor Ilpo Laine

Physics Section   268
Head: Professor Rauno Hämäläinen

Data Processing Centre   269

Karelian Research Institute   270
Activities: Study of Karelian culture and research advancing the economic development of Eastern Finland.

Mekrijärvi Research Station   271
Address: Mekrijärvi, SF-82900 Ilomantsi
Telephone: 974-48 105
Head: Professor Seppo Pasanen
Director: Jorma Aho
Activities: Research into natural sciences and ethnology.

Svomunjärvi Research Station   272
Address: Suomunjärvi, Lieksa
Activities: Research into natural sciences.

Jyväskylän Yliopisto* 273

[Jyväskylä University]
Address: Seminaarinkatu 15, SF-40100 Jyväskalä
Telephone: 941-10920

FACULTY OF MATHEMATICS AND 274
NATURAL SCIENCES*

Dean: Professor J. Eloranta

Kansanterveyslaboratorio 275

[Public Health Laboratory]
Address: Mannerheimintie 166, SF-00280 Helsinki 28
Telephone: 90-418 355
Director: Professor Jussi Huttunen
Deputy Director: Professor Veijo Raunio
Graduate research staff: 40
Annual expenditure: £501 000-2m
Activities: The Public Health Laboratory (comprising
the Central Laboratory in Helsinki and seven regional
laboratories) researches public health problems and advises central and local medical officers. Traditionally a
microbiological and serological laboratory, research into
alcohol and drugs, and surveillance of the chemical
environment has been included as part of future plans.
The regional laboratories are 'front line' laboratories in
the case of an epidemic, while the Central Laboratory
provides back-up diagnostic facilities.
Facilities: Centre for reference strains and diagnostic
reagent provision, epidemiological surveys and analyses;
toxicological and bacteriological services on drinking
water; specimen examination; diagnostic hospital work;
preparation andquality control of all vaccines used in
Finland.
Contract work: Yes

CENTRAL LABORATORY 276

Bacteriological Laboratory 277

Director: Professor P.H. Mäkelä
Divisions: General bacteriology, M. Sarvas; Enteric
pathogens, M. Jahkola, A. Siitonen; Mycobacteria, E.
Brander
Activities: Study of enteric diseases of bacterial origin.

Biochemical Laboratory 278

Director: Professor J. Pikkarainen
Divisons: Clinical chemistry, C.G. Gref; En-
docrinologicel laboratory examinations, E. Axelsson;
Special laboratory examinations, R. Schakir; Blood
alcohol determinations, R. Lindbohm.
Activities: Reference laboratory in field of clinical
chemistry; studies in methods of food analysis with
Nordic Committee on Food Analysis.

Epidemiological Research Unit 279

Director: Professor P. Puska
Activities: National applications of the epidemiological
methods and procedures developed within the North
Karelia project. Risk factors and health behaviour,
monitoring major non-infectious diseases (smoking and
nutritional issues), epidemiology of major infectious
diseases.

Immunobiological Laboratory 280

Director: Professor K. Aho
Divisions: General Serology, Dr I. Rostedt; blood
group serology, T. Palosvo; forensic serology, C.
Ehnholm.
Activities: Infections and immunopathological mechanisms in rheumatic andrenal diseases, study of lipoproteins in cardiovascular diseases, seroepidemiological surveys.

Production Department 281

Director: Professor L. Jannes
Divisions: Animal unit, L. Pyhälä; ampoulling and
packing, A. Holmström; central supply and control of
vaccines, I. Arponen; distribution of vaccines, M.
Nouro; media production, K. Sarviala; plasma fractionation, E. Vahvaselkä; production of vaccines,
Professor T. Kuronen.
Activities: Animal facilities, supply of microbiological
and cell culturemedia, plasma fraction and vaccine preparation, control, and distribution.

Virological Laboratory 282

Director: Professor K. Cantell
Divisions: General virology, Dr R. Pyhälä; enteric
viruses, K. Lapinleimu; tissue culture unit; production
of viral vaccines, M. Valle; virus serology, M. Kleemola.
Activities: Diagnostic services, study of plastic and
rubber products in cell cultures, epidemiological studies
and vaccine production and testing.
Facilities: The Laboratory acts as the National Influenza Centre and the National Enterovirus Centre of
the WHO in Finland.

REGIONAL LABORATORIES 283

Jyväskylä Laboratory 284
Address: Keskussairaalantie 19, SF-40620 Jyväskylä 62
Telephone: 941-211 663
Physician-in-charge: H. Arvilomni

Kuopio Laboratory 285
Address: Kasarmialue, rakennus 3, PL 267, SF-70101 Kuopio 10
Telephone: 971-127 633
Physician-in-charge: K. Kunnas

Lappeenranta Laboratory 286
Address: SF-53130 Lappeenranta 13
Telephone: 953-12 981
Physician-in-charge: K. Hällström

Oulu Laboratory 287
Address: Kajaanintie 46, SF-90100 Oulu 10
Telephone: 981-334 266
Physician-in-charge: E. Herva

Rovaniemi Laboratory 288
Address: Veitikantie 2, SF-90100 Rovaniemi 10
Telephone: 991-3303
Physician-in-charge: R. Sunila

Seinäjoki Laboratory 289
Address: Vapaudentie 26, SF-60100 Seinäjoki 10
Telephone: 964-22 442
Physician-in-charge: P. Uurasmaa

Turku Laboratory 290
Address: Künanmyllyn Katu 10, SF-20520 Turku 52
Telephone: 921-29 255
Physician-in-charge: S. Virtanen

Oy Kaukas Ab 291
Address: SF-53200 Lappeenranta 20
Telephone: 953 139 60
Telex: 58 211 kslpr sf
Research manager: Harri Holm
Sections: Paper, Juhani Pylkkö; pulp, Matti Saukkonen; chemical, Olle Schalin

Graduate research staff: 11
Annual expenditure: £51 000-500 000
Activities: LWC paper, pressure groundwood, pulping and bleaching, chemical by-products.
Contract work: No

Kemira Oy 292
Address: Box 330, SF-00101 Helsinki 10
Telephone: 90-694 2911
Telex: 12 3423 kekem
Director of Research: Dr Niilo Lounamaa
Graduate research staff: 100
Annual expenditure: over £2m
Activities: Development projects in organic and inorganic chemicals as well as biological fields; extraction and local production processes; trace element determinations; agricultural research and testing, covering man-made fibres.
Facilities: Experimental Farm, research and pilot plant laboratory services, industrial feasibility studies and technical management, supply of equipment and plant.
Contract work: Yes
Publications: Annual report.

ESPOO RESEARCH CENTRE 293
Address: Box 44, SF-02271 Espoo 27
Research director: Dr Ari Lokio

OULU RESEARCH LABORATORY 294
Address: Box 171, SF-90901 Oulu 10
Research director: Timo Mattila

Oy Keskuslaboratorio - Centrallaboratorium Ab 295
[Pulp and Paper Research Institute of Finland]
Address: PO Box 136, SF-00101 Helsinki 10
Telephone: 90-460 411
Telex: 12-1030 kcl sf
Managing Director: Dr Bo Mannström
Sections: Pulping processes, Ilpo Palenius; paper and board, Dr Lars Nordman; technical service, Jan-Erik Levlin
Graduate research staff: 85
Annual expenditure: £4.4m
Activities: Fundamental and applied technical and scientific research in the sphere of the pulp, paper and board industry including packaging, bleaching processes, the use of spent lacquers from pulping and

bleaching and the reduction of pollution. Participants in SCAN test and SCAN Forsk activities.
Facilities: Pilot plant, pulp and paper testing; chemical analysis; literature retrieval for the Finnish paper industry; international forum in research and standardization.
Contract work: Yes
Publications: Annual reports, research reports.

Kuopion Korkeakoulu 296

[Kuopio University]
Address: PO Box 138, SF-70101 Kuopio 10
Rector: Professor Tapani Vanha-Perttula

CLINICAL MEDICINE DEPARTMENT 297

Gynaecology and Obstetrics 298
Head: Professor Olli Castrén

Internal Medicine 299
Head: Professor Kalevi Pyörälä

Ophthalmology 300
Head: Professor Erkki Tuovinen

Otorhinolaryngology 301
Head: Professor Juhani Kärjä

Paediatrics 302
Head: Professor Kari Launiala

Psychiatry 303
Head: Professor Veikko Tähkä

Surgery 304
Heads: Professor Kauko Kettunen, Associate Professor Esko Alhava

CLINICAL THEORETICAL MEDICINE 305 DEPARTMENT

Clinical Microbiology 306
Head: Professor Rauno Mäntyjärvi

Pathology 307
Head: Professor Collan Yrjö

Pharmacology 308
Head: Professor Mauno Airaksinen

COMMUNITY HEALTH DEPARTMENT 309

Community Health 310
Head: Professor Hannu Vuori

Epidemiology 311
Head: Professor Olli Heinonen

Sociology 312
Head: Associate Professor Paavo Piepponen

DENTISTRY DEPARTMENT 313

Clinical Dentistry 314
Acting Head: Professor Yli-Urpo Antti

Oral Surgery 315
Head: Associate Professor Kotilainen Risto

Paradontology 316
Head: Associate Professor Matti Knuuttila

Preventive Dentistry 317
Head: Professor Heikki Luoma

ENVIRONMENTAL HYGIENE 318 DEPARTMENT

Chemico-Physical Analysis 319
Head: Professor Arvo Laamanen

Ecology 320
Head: Professor Lauri Kärenlampi

GENERAL BIOLOGY DEPARTMENT 321

Anatomy 322

Heads: Professor Tapani Vanha-Perttula, Associate Professor Heikki Helminen

Biochemistry 323

Head: Professor Pekka Mäenpää

Physiological Chemistry 324

Head: Professor Aarne Raina

Physiology 325

Heads: Professor Osmo Hänninen, Associate Professor Martti Hakumäki

Zoology 326

Head: Associate Professor Ossi Lindqvist

MATHEMATICS, PHYSICS AND 327 CHEMISTRY DEPARTMENT

Chemistry 328

Head: Professor Pentti Kauranen

Physics 329

Heads: Professor Lauri Patomäki, Associate Professor Pertti Puumalainen

PHARMACY DEPARTMENT 330

Pharmaceutical Chemistry 331

Head: Professor Carl-Johan Widen

Pharmaceutical Technology 332

Head: Professor Markku Juslin

Social Pharmacy 333

Head: Associate Professor Isoren Taisto

Kymi Kymmene Oy 334

Address: SF-45700 Kuusankoski
Telephone: 51-402 111
Telex: 5221 1 kymco sf

R&D Manager: Dr Pauli Paasonen
Graduate research staff: 10
Annual expenditure: £501 000-2m
Activities: Paper (cellulose and chemical); wood chemistry, organic chemistry, carbohydrate and extractive analysis; bleaching of groundwood, sulphite and sulphate pulps; manufacture of printing, writing, coated and self-copy papers; manufacture of bleaching chemicals and plasticisers.
Contract work: Yes

Lääketehdas Orion 335

Address: PO Box 19, SF-00101 Helsinki 10
Telephone: 90-717 411
Telex: 124721 orion sf
Affiliation: Orion Yhtyma Oy
Director R&D: Dr Antti Keränen
Sections: Ethical pharmaceuticals for human use, Dr Antti Keränen; pharmaceuticals for veterinary use, Dr Kauko Kauppinen
Graduate research staff: 80
Annual expenditure: £501 000-2m
Activities: Pharmaceuticals for human and veterinary uses; diagnostic aids; modern product development, active ingredients and pharmaceutical specialities; cardiovascular pharmacology and assessment of drug levels in biological materials.
Contract work: No
Publications: Various (topic lists available).

Lapin Tutkimusseura 336

[Research Society of Lapland]
Address: Hallituskatu 9, SF-96100 Rovaniemi 10
Telephone: 991-1007Y
Activities: All kinds of research on Lapland (scientific, technical and economical); research plans and the collection of all kinds of research reports on Lapland; the suggestion of investigation programmes for research workers; information on research concerning Lapland and the publication of research reports on Lapland.
Publications: Year book, bibliography.

Lappeenrannan Teknillinen 337 Korkeakoulu

[Lappeenranta University of Technology]
Address: Skinnarila, PO Box 20, SF-53851 Lappeenranta 85
Telephone: 953-27 570

DEPARTMENT OF CHEMICAL TECHNOLOGY   338

Head: Professor Seppo Wilska

DEPARTMENT OF INDUSTRIAL ENGINEERING AND MANAGEMENT   339

Head: Professor Veikko Orpana

DEPARTMENT OF MECHANICAL ENGINEERING   340

Head: Professor Erkki Niemi
Activities: Machine designing technology; steel structures; workshop technology; welding technology; strength and elasticity of materials; metal and plastics technology; mechanization and automation; transportation technology.

DEPARTMENT OF PHYSICS AND MATHEMATICS   341

Head: Assistant Professor Antti Luukko
Activities: Research supporting the vocational work of other departments.

DEPARTMENT OF POWER ENGINEERING   342

Head: Professor Pertti Sarkomaa
Activities: Heat and flow technology of nuclear reactors; power and energy economics; environmental protection technology; use of electricity; optimization of energy systems.

SPECIAL ADMINISTRATIVE UNITS   343

Computing Centre   344

Head: Antero Pajari

Language Centre   345

Head: Ola Berggren

Library   346

Head: Saara Raakkula

Lastentauntien Tutkimussäätiö *   347

[Paediatrics Research Foundation]
Address: 11 Stenbäckinkatu, SF-00290 Helsinki 29
Director: Professor N. Hallman
Activities: The Foundation conducts and supports basic and applied research in paediatrics.

Lihateollisuuden Tutkimuskeskus   348

[Meat Research Centre of Finland]
Address: Box 56, SF-13101 Hämeenlinna 10
Telephone: 917-215 51
Affiliation: Cooperative Slaughterhouses
Director: Mauno Kannari
Graduate research staff: 3
Activities: Planning of factories and machines, research and consultancy, quality control, hygiene control, training for the meat industry.
Contract work: No

Maatalouden Taloudellinen Tutkimuslaitos   349

[Agricultural Economics Research Institute]
Address: Rukkila, SF-00001 Helsinki 100
Telephone: 90-563 3 133
Affiliation: Ministry of Agriculture and Forestry
Director: Professor Matias Torvela
Sections: Farm management, Professor Matias Torvela; farm policy, Professor L. Kettunen; farm accounting, H. Järvelä
Graduate research staff: 15
Annual expenditure: £51 000-500 000
Activities: Farm management, marketing and accounting.
Contract work: No
Publications: Research reports.

Maatalouden Tutkimuskeskus   350

[Agricultural Research Centre]
Address: SF-31600 Jokioinen
Telephone: 916-13333
Affiliation: Ministry of Agriculture and Forestry
Director General: Professor Dr Juhani Paatela
Graduate research staff: 150

Annual expenditure: FMk43m
Activities: Improvement to and safeguarding of plant
and livestock production and prevention of the environ-
mental hazards of agriculture.
Facilities: Experimental stations, isotope laboratory,
computing and library centres.
Contract work: Yes
Publications: Statistical data bulletins, *Annales
Agriculturae Fenniae* (Scientific journal); *Kehittyvä
Maatalous* (Developments in Agriculture); *Koetoiminta
ja Käytäntö* (Experimentation and Practice) and *Tieto
Tuottamaan.*

INSTITUTE OF AGRICULTURAL 351
CHEMISTRY AND PHYSICS

Address: SF-31600 Jokioinen
Director: Professor Dr Paavo Elonen

INSTITUTE OF ANIMAL BREEDING 352

Address: SF-34600 Jokioinen
Director: Professor Dr Kalle Maijala

INSTITUTE OF ANIMAL HUSBANDRY 353

Address: SF-31600 Jokioinen
Director: Professor Dr Martti Lampila

INSTITUTE OF HORTICULTURE 354

Address: SF-21500 Piikkiö
Director: Professor Dr Jaakko Säkö

INSTITUTE OF PEST INVESTIGATION 355

Address: SF-01301 Vantaa 30
Director: Professor Dr Martti Markkula

INSTITUTE OF PLANT BREEDING 356

Address: SF-31600 Jokioinen
Director: Professor Dr Rolf Manner

INSTITUTE OF PLANT HUSBANDRY 357

Address: SF-31600 Jokioinen
Director: Professor Dr Jaakko Mukula

INSTITUTE OF PLANT PATHOLOGY 358

Address: SF-01301 Vantaa 30
Director: Professor Dr Aarre Ylimäki

INSTITUTE OF SOIL SCIENCES 359

Address: SF-31600 Jokioinen
Director: Professor Dr Mikko Sillanpää

RESEARCH AND EXPERIMENTAL 360
STATIONS AND UNITS

Central Finland Experimental Station 361

Address: SF-41370 Kuusa
Director: Paavo Simojoki

Central Pohjanmaa Experimental 362
Station

Address: SF-69310 Laitala
Director: Aulis Järvi

Häme Experimental Station 363

Address: SF-36600 Pälkäne
Director: Mauri Takala

Kainuu Research Station 364

Address: SF-92810 Pelsonsuo
Director: Martti Vuorinen

Kymenlaakso Experimental Station 365

Address: SF-46910 Anjala
Director: Kalevi Virri

Lapland Experimental Station 366

Address: Apukka Ppa 1, SF-97999 Rovaniemi
Director: Arvi Valmari

North Pohjanmaa Experimental Station 367

Address: SF-92400 Ruukki
Director: Heikki Hakkola

North Savo Experimental Station 368

Address: Halola, SF-71750 Maaninka
Director: Elsi Ettala

Sata-Häme Experimental Station 369

Address: SF-38460 Mouhijärvi
Director: Kalle Rinne

Satakunta Experimental Station 370

Address: SF-32810 Peipohja
Director: vacant

South Pohjanmaa Experimental Station 371

Address: SF-61400 Ylistaro
Director: Sirkka-Liisa Hiivola

South Savo Experimental Station 372

Address: Karila, SF-50600 Mikkeli 60
Director: Erkki Huokuna

South-West Finland Experimental Station 373

Address: SF-23140 Hietamäki
Director: Jaakko Köylijärvi

Swine Research Station 374

Address: SF-05840 Hyvinkää 4
Director: Timo Alaviuhkola

Bureau for Local Experiments 375

Address: SF-31600 Jokioinen
Director: Erkki Aura

Computing Service 376

Address: SF-31600 Jokioinen
Director: Jukka Ofversten

Isotope Laboratory 377

Address: SF-31600 Jokioinen
Director: Arja Paasikallio

Pesticide Regulation Unit 378

Address: SF-01301 Vantaa 30
Director: Professor Jaakko Mukula

Merentutkimuslaitos 379

[Marine Research Institute]
Address: PO Box 166, SF-00141 Helsinki 14
Telephone: 651 566
Telex: 12 4648
Affiliation: Ministry of Trade and Industry
Director: Dr Pentti Mälkki
Sections: Physical oceanography, Dr Jouko

Launiainen; chemical and biological oceanography, Dr Folke Koroleff; general oceanography, Dr Paavo Tulkki
Graduate research staff: 30
Annual expenditure: £501 000-2m
Activities: Physical, chemical and biological oceanographic and marine environmental studies, and monitoring research, particularly in the Baltic Sea, including ice research and other research for navigational purposes.
Contract work: Yes
Publications: *Finnish Marine Research*; *Meri*.

Metsähovin Radiotutkimusasema 380

[Radio Research Station Metsähovi]
Address: Metsähovi, SF-02540 Kylmälä
Telephone: 264 831
Telex: 122771 rorta sf
Affiliation: Helsinki: University of Technology Radio Laboratory
Research director: Professor M. Tiuri
Sections: Radioastronomy, microwave technology, remote sensing, Professor M. Tiuri; solar research, S. Urpo; radiometers, J.K. Peltonen; satellite communication, H. Sandell
Graduate research staff: 5
Activities: Radio research including remote sensing.
Facilities: Fourteen-metre radio telescope for 10-120 GHz, several radiometers and receivers for radioastronomy, microwave applications and satellite communications.
Contract work: Yes
Publications: Annual report.

Metsäntutkimuslaitos 381

[Forest Research Institute of Finland]
Address: Unioninkatu 40A, SF-00170 Helsinki 17
Telephone: 90-661401
Affiliation: Ministry of Agriculture and Forestry
Director: Professor Dr Olavi Huikari
Sections: Administrative Office, Kari Sohtanen
Graduate research staff: 160
Annual expenditure: FMk45m
Activities: Research and experiments to further the utilization of Finnish forestry, forest resources and forests.
Contract work: No.
Publications: Communicationes Instituti Forestalis Fenniae; Folio Forestalia; guidebooks on experimental areas; research reports of experimental stations.

DEPARTMENT OF FOREST ECONOMICS 382

Sections: Social economics, Professor Lauri Heikinheimo; business economics, Professor Jouko Hämäläinen
Activities: Estimating annual wood consumption and removal, comparisons with planned allowable cut; structural changes in forest ownership; studies and prognoses on forest labour force; profitability of different ways of producing forests (from nursery to final cutting); demand, supply and prices of raw wood.

DEPARTMENT OF FOREST GENETICS 383

Head: Professor Max Hagman
Activities: Studies on genetic structure of forest trees for breeding and regeneration.
Facilities: Tree breeding stations.

DEPARTMENT OF FOREST INVENTORIES 384

Sections: Forest inventories, Professor Kullervo Kuusela; yield studies, Professor Yrjö Vuokila
Activities: Continuous investigation of forest resources and their distribution; growth and yield improvements, effects of mechanized logging.

DEPARTMENT OF FOREST PROTECTION 385

Sections: Forest zoology, Professor Paavo Juutinen; forest pathology, Professor Tauno Kallio
Activities: Observations on damage caused to forests by animals and insects and fungi.
Facilities: Experimental station concentrating on studies of voles.

DEPARTMENT OF FOREST TECHNOLOGY 386

Sections: Forest operations, Professor Pentti Hakkila; wood research, Professor Matti Kärkkäinen
Activities: Structure and properties of wood, industrial use of wood, timber scaling, logging waste; ergonomics of forest work.

DEPARTMENT OF MATHEMATICS 387

Head: Professor Risto Seppälä
Activities: Develops and investigates statistical methods required by research; prepares yearly proposition for forest taxation.
Publications: Annual Yearbook of Forest Statistics.

DEPARTMENT OF PEATLAND FORESTRY 388

Head: Professor Eero Paavilainen
Activities: Utilization of peatland forests, basic factors, methods, techniques and realization of forest improvement; effects of ditching and fertilization.

DEPARTMENT OF SILVICULTURE 389

Head: Professor Erkki Lähde
Activities: Natural forest regeneration, forest tree seed crop and short-rotation cultivation.
Facilities: Experimental station for forest regeneration.

DEPARTMENT OF SOIL SCIENCE 390

Head: Professor Eino Mälkönen
Activities: Investigation into the physical, chemical and microbiological properties of mineral soils and their effect on fertility; the development of soils and methods of soil amelioration.

EXPERIMENTAL FOREST OFFICE 391

Head: Kauko Luoma
Activities: Experimental forests and conservation areas.

RESEARCH STATIONS 392

Kolariu Tutkimusasema 393

[Kolari Forest Research Station]
Address: SF-95900 Kolari
Telephone: 995-61401
Head: E. Numminen
Activities: Forest tree breeding in Lapland; ecological and hydrological problems in peatland forestry.

Parkanon Tutkimusasema 394

[Parkano Forest Research Station]
Address: SF-39700 Parkano
Telephone: 933-2912
Head: O. Laiho
Activities: Hydrological and ecological problems of peatland forestry; peatland forest regeneration; soil science and artificial regeneration.

Punkaharjun Jalostuskoeasema 395

[Punkaharju Forest Tree Breeding Station]
Address: SF-58450 Punkaharju
Telephone: 957-314142
Head: Professor M. Hagman
Note: This station is subordinated to the Department of Forest Genetics.

Pyhäkosken Tutkimusasema 396

[Pyhäkoski Forest Research Station]
Address: SF-91500 Muhos
Telephone: 981-431404
Head: J. Valtanen
Activities: Silviculture; peatland forestry; forest entomology and forest yield.

Rovaniemen Tutkimusasema 397

[Rovaniemi Forest Research Station]
Address: Eteläranta 55, SF-96300 Rovaniemi 30
Telephone: 991-15721
Head: E. Pohtila
Activities: Forest pathology; silviculture; forest economics; reafforestation in Lapland; multiple use of forests.

Ruotsinkylä Jalostuskoeasema 398

[Ruotsinkylä Forest Tree Breeding Station]
Address: SF-01590 Maisala
Telephone: 90-824420
Head: Professor M. Hagman
Director: K. Elo
Note: This station is subordinated to the Department of Forest Genetics.

Suonenjoken Metsänviljelyn Koeasema 399

[Suonenjoki Experiment Station for Reafforestation and Nursery]
Address: SF-77600 Suonenjoki
Telephone: 979-10771
Head: P. Pelkonen
Activities: Nursery and reafforestation studies; forest pathology; forest genetics.

Neste Oy 400

Address: Keilaniemi, SF-02150 Espoo 15
Telephone: 90 4501
Telex: 124 641
Assistant Vice President: Timo Karttunen
Laboratories: Oil refining; Lubricating oil; Engine research; Asphalt; Petrochemicals; Wood fibre and petrochemical composites; Analytical; Pilot plant
Graduate research staff: 40
Annual expenditure: over £2m
Activities: Research into whole range of refinery products (oil products, petrochemical products, plastics, bitumen, roofing felts); detection of faults; advice on new processes; product evaluation and development.
Facilities: Analytical laboratory equipment, pilot plant laboratory testing equipment and machinery.
Contract work: Yes

Oulu Osakeyhtiö 401

Address: Nuottasaari Mills, PO Box 196, SF-90101 Oulu 10
Telephone: 981-143 21
Telex: 3 2138 oulnssf; 121394 tl tx sf
Research and Development Director: Arvo Fredriksson
Graduate research staff: 4
Annual expenditure: £51 000-500 000
Activities: Research on organic industrial chemicals especially tall-oil and turpentine products and retention agents.
Contract work: No

Oulun Yliopisto 402

[Oulu University]
Address: PO Box 191, SF-90101 Oulu 10
Telephone: 981-222 700
Telex: 32375 oylin sf

FACULTY OF MEDICINE 403

Department of Anaesthesiology 404

Address: Yliopistollinen keskussairaala, Kajaanintie 50, SF-90220 Oulu 22
Head: Professor Arno Hollmén

Department of Anatomy 405

Address: Kajaanintie 52 A, SF-90220 Oulu 22
Head: Professor L. Kalevi Korhonen

Department of Clinical Chemistry 406

Address: Kajaanintie 50, SF-90220 Oulu 22
Head: Professor Reijo Vihko

Department of Dermatology 407

Address: Yliopistollinen keskussairaala, Kajaanintie 50, SF-90220 Oulu 22
Head: Professor Matti Hannuksela

Department of Diagnostic Radiology 408

Address: Yliopistollinen keskussairaala, Kajaanintie 50, SF-90220 Oulu 22
Head: Professor Pekka Vuoria

Department of Forensic Medicine 409

Address: Kajaanintie 52 D, SF-90220 Oulu 22
Head: Professor Jorma Hirvonen

Department of Internal Medicine 410

Address: Yliopistollinen keskussairaala, Kajaanintie 50, SF-90220 Oulu 22
Head: Professor W.J. Kaipainen

Department of Medical Biochemistry 411

Address: Kajaanintie 52 A, SF-90220 Oulu 22
Head: Professor Kari Kivirikko

Department of Medical Microbiology 412

Address: Kajaanintie 46 D, SF-90220 Oulu 22
Head: Professor Anja Tiilikainen

Department of Neurology 413

Address: Yliopistollinen keskussairaala, Kajaanintie 50, SF-90220 Oulu 22
Head: Professor Eero Hokkanen

Department of Neurosurgery 414

Address: Yliopistollinen keskussairaala, Kajaanintie 50, SF-90220 Oulu 22
Head: Professor Stig Nyström

Department of Obstetrics and Gynaecology 415

Address: Yliopistollinen keskussairaala, Kajaanintie 50, SF-90220 Oulu 22
Head: Professor Pentti A. Järvinen

Department of Ophthalmology 416

Address: Yliopistollinen keskussairaala, Kajaanintie 50, SF-90220 Oulu 22
Head: Professor Henrik Forsius

Department of Otorhinolaryngology 417

Address: Yliopistollinen keskussairaala, Kajaanintie 50, SF-90220 Oulu 22
Head: Professor Antti Palva

Department of Paediatrics 418

Address: Yliopistollinen keskussairaala, Kajaanintie 50, SF-90220 Oulu 22
Head: Professor Kauko Kouvalainen

Department of Pathological Anatomy 419

Address: Kajaanintie 52 D, SF-90220 Oulu 22
Head: Professor Kai Dammert

Department of Pharmacology 420

Address: Kajaanintie 52 E, SF-90220 Oulu 22
Head: Professor Niilo Kärki

Department of Physiology 421

Address: Kajaanintie 52 A, SF-90220 Oulu 22
Head: Professor Leo Hirvonen

Department of Psychiatry 422

Address: Oulunsuun sairaala, SF-90210 Oulu 21
Head: Professor Pekka Tienari

Department of Public Health Science 423

Address: Kajaanintie 46 D, SF-90220 Oulu 22
Head: Professor Onni Kari-Koskinen

Department of Radiotherapy 424

Address: Yliopistollinen keskussairaala, Kajaanintie 50, SF-90220 Oulu 22
Head: Professor Pentti J. Taskinen

Department of Surgery 425

Address: Yliopistollinen keskussairaala, Kajaanintie 50, SF-90220 Oulu 22
Head: Professor Teuvo Larmi

Institute of Dentistry 426

Address: Aapistie 3, SF-90220 Oulu 22
Head: Professor Markku Larmas

FACULTY OF SCIENCE 427

Applied Mathematics Department 428

Address: Linnanmaa, SF-90570 Oulu 57
Heads: Professor Elja Arjas, Assistant Professor Juha Tienari

Astronomy Department 429

Address: Linnanmaa, SF-90570 Oulu 57
Head: Professor Antero Hämeen-Anttila
Sections: Radioastronomy, Jorma Riihimaa; planetary astronomy, Professor Antero Hämeen-Anttila; lunar researches, Jouko Raitala
Graduate research staff: 6
Activities: Studies of lunar geology; theoretical work on statistical collisional systems; Jovian radio bursts.

Biochemistry Department 430

Address: Linnanmma, SF-90570 Oulu 57
Head: Professor Sakari Piha
Sections: Enzyme chemistry and molecular biology, Associate Professor Mauno J. Pyhtilä; clinical-analytical biochemistry, Assistant Professor Olli Jänne

Biophysics Department 431

Address: Linnanmaa, SF-90570 Oulu 57
Head: Professor Martti Mela

Botany Department 432

Head: Professor Paavo Havas
Sections: Ecology, Professor Paavo Havas, Assistant Professor Seppo Eurola; plant physiology, Professor Sirkka Kupila-Ahvenniemi; systematic botany and palaeobotany, Assistant Professor Yrjö Vasari; botanical garden, Assistant Professor Yrjö Vasari

Chemistry Department 433

Address: Linnanmaa, SF-90570 Oulu 57
Head: Professor Hans Krieger
Sections: Physical chemistry, Professor Olavi Virtanen, Assistant Professor Aulis Nissema; inorganic chemistry, Professor Lauri Lajunen; organic chemistry, Assistant Professor Erkki Pulkkinen; structure elucidation in chemistry, Professor Erkki Rahkamaa

Genetics Department 434

Address: Linnanmaa, SF-90570 Oulu 57
Head: Professor Seppo Lakovaara

Geography Department 435

Address: Linnanmaa, SF-90570 Oulu 57
Head: Professor Uuno Varjo
Sections: Geography, Professor Uuno Varjo; physical geography, Assistant Professor Paul Fogelberg; social geography, Assistant Professor Eino Siuruainen; cultural geography, Professor Arvo Naukkarinen

Geology Department 436

Address: Linnanmaa, SF-90570 Oulu 57
Head: Professor Risto Aario
Sections: Glaciology, Professor Risto Aario, Assistant Professor Matti Saarnisto; mineralogy, Professor Kauko Laajoki, Assistant Professor Tauno Piirainen

Geophysics Department 437

Address: Linnanmaa, SF-90570 Oulu 57
Head: Professor M.T. Porkka
Senior staff: Assistant Professor S.E. Hjelt

Mathematics Department 438

Address: Linnanmaa, SF-90570 Oulu 57
Head: Professor Yrjö Kilpi
Sections: Differential geometry, Professor Heikki Haahti; theory of automata and formal languages, Professor Paavo Turakainen; nonlinear analysis, Associate Professor Seppo Heikkilä; functional analysis, Associate Professor Vesa Mustonen; number theory, Associate Professor Keijo Väänänen

Oulu Biological Station 439

Address: Kiutaköngäs, SF-93850 Käylä
Telephone: 989-227 533
Head: Associate Professor Yrjö Vasari
Director: Juha Viramo

Physics Department 440

Address: Linnanmaa, SF-90570 Oulu 57
Head: Professor Pekka Tanskanen
Sections: Molecular physics, Assistant Professor Rauno Anttila; atomic physics, Assistant Professor Seppo Aksela; space physics, Professor Pekka Tanskanen, Assistant Professor J. Kangas; molecular physics, vacant

Physiological Zoology Department 441

Address: Aapistie 3, SF-90220 Oulu 22
Head: Professor Erkki Pulliainen
Sections: Zoophysiology, vacant; histology, Assistant Professor Raimo Hissa

Theoretical Physics Department 442

Address: Linnanmaa, SF-90570 Oulu 57
Head: Professor Alpo Kallio
Sections: Many body theory, Professor Alpo Kallio; elementary particles, Assistant Professor Esko Suhonen

Zoology Department 443

Address: Kasarmintie 8, SF-90100 Oulu 10
Head: Professor Erkki Pulliainen
Sections: Morphology and ecology, Professor Erkki Pulliainen, Assistant Professor Esko Lind, Assistant Professor Seppo Sulkava

FACULTY OF TECHNOLOGY 444

Architecture Department 445

Address: Aleksanterinkatu 6, SF-90100 Oulu 10
Head: Professor Jouko Mähönen
Senior staff: Professor Esko Järventaus, Professor Seppo Valjus, Professor Matti Mäkinen, Professor Osmo Mikkonen, Professor Paavo Huhtela

Electrical Engineering Department 446

Address: Linnanmaa, SF-90570 Oulu 57
Head: Professor Seppo Säynäjäkangas
Sections: Electrical engineering, Professor Matti Karras, Professor Juhani Oksman, Professor Antti Tauriainen, Professor Risto Myllylä, Professor Kalevi Kalliomäki, Professor Pentti Lappalainen; technical physics, Professor Eliel Lahteenkorva, Professor Seppo Leppävuori

Mechanical Engineering Department 447

Address: Linnanmaa, SF-90570 Oulu 57
Head: Professor Mauri Määttänen
Sections: Machine construction, Professor Uolevi Konttinen, Professor Teuvo Julkunen, Professor Raimo Parkkinen; mechanical technology, Professor Ilkka Honka; mechanics, Professor Mauri Määttänen, Professor Antti Pramila; physical metallurgy, Professor Markku Manerkoski, Professor Pentti Karjalainen

Process Technology Department 448

Address: Linnanmaa, SF-90570 Oulu 17
Head: Professor Sakari Kurronen
Sections: Chemical process technology, Professor Sakari Kurronen; heat and mass transfer, Professor Jorma Sohlo; control and systems engineering, Professor Paavo Uronen, Professor Aarne Halme

Structural Engineering Department 449

Address: Kasarmintie 8, SF-90100 Oulu 10
Head: Professor Aulis Ukkonen
Sections: Structural engineering, Professor A.I. Putkonen; construction of plates and shells, Professor P.A. Tupamäki; construction economics, Professor Juhani Kiiras; road construction, Professor Aulis Ukkonen; statics and bridge construction, Professor Esko Hyttinen; foundation engineering, Professor Jorma Hartikainen; hydraulic technology, Professor Lauri Helenius

Technical Mathematics Department 450

Address: Linnanmaa, SF-90570 Oulu 57
Heads: Professor Veikko Seppälä, Professor Juhani Nieminen

Perämeri Research Station* 451

Address: SF-90480 Hailuoto
Telephone: 981-409 478
Head: Professor Yrjö Vasari
Director: Tapaui Valtonen
Activities: Research centres on the Bothnian Bay and rivers flowing into it. Work is concentrated on brackish water and river biology and fisheries.

Outokumpu Oy 452

Address: PO Box 280, SF-00101 Helsinki 10

INSTITUTE OF PHYSICS 453

Address: PO Box 27, SF-02101 Espoo 10
Director of Research: Dr Pekka Rautala
Activities: Applied physics; design and construction of instruments for research and process control.

METALLURGICAL RESEARCH CENTRE 454

Address: PO Box 60, SF-28101 Pori 10
Director of Research: Esko Nermes
Activities: Pyro- and hydro-metallurgy; development of new metallurgical processes.

Panimolaboratorio Oy   455

[Brewing Laboratory]
Address: PO Box 192, SF-00121 Helsinki 12
Telephone: 90-464 472
Research director: Professor T.M. Enari
Annual expenditure: £51 000-500 000
Activities: Research projects concerned with quality of malting barley, improvement of malting, beer processes and beer quality. Research is sponsored at Valtion Teknillinen Tutkimuskeskus.
Contract work: No

Oy Partek Ab   456

Address: SF-21600 Pargas
Telephone: 921-744 422
Telex: 62220 pkpar sf
Vice President: Thor Brännback
Graduate research staff: 50
Annual expenditure: over £2m
Activities: Research on building materials and machinery, their manufacture and properties; mobile equipment and waste collection systems.
Contract work: No

Rautaruukki Oy,   457
Tutkimuslaitos

Address: SF-92170 Raahensalo
Telephone: 982 301
Telex: sf steel 32162
Director of Research and Development: Krister Relander
Manager of Research Centre: Dr Veikko Sjöberg
Sections: Research Department, Erkki Räsänen
Graduate research staff: 50
Annual expenditure: £501 000-2m
Activities: Iron and steel metallurgy including physical metallurgy and properties of steel, flat rolled products, steel pipes and tubes, ore benefications, processing of vanadium ores.
Contract work: No

Riista- Ja Kalatalouden   458
Tutkimuslaitos

[Game and Fisheries Research Institute of Finland]
Affiliation: Ministry of Agriculture and Forestry
Director: Professor Teppo Lämpio

FISHERIES DIVISION   459

Address: PO Box 193, SF-00131 Helsinki 13
Department Head: vacant
Activities: Fisheries in relation to the Baltic Sea and to Finnish lakes. Research on biology, production, utilization and management of fish and crayfish; economy of commercial and recreational fishing; fishery statistics; fish culture; effects of pollution on fisheries; toxicity tests with fish; fisheries improvement; assessment of fish populations and productivity of fish stocks; fishing techniques and technology.

Evon Kalastuskoeasema ja   460
Kalonviljelylaitos

[Evo Fish Testing and Cultivation Centre]
Address: SF-16970 Evo
Telephone: 917-35412
Head: K. Westman

Laukaan Keskuskalanviljelylaitos   461

[Laukaa Central Fish Cultivation Centre]
Address: SF-41360 Valkola
Telephone: 941-837521
Head: O. Sumari

Pohjois-Suomen   462
Keskuskalanviljelylaitos

[Northern Finland Central Fish Cultivation Centre]
Address: 658 Ohtaoja, SF-91999 Oulu
Telephone: 998-51811
Head: O. Simola

GAME DIVISION   463

Address: Pitkänsillanranta 3A, SF-00530 Helsinki 53
Telephone: 90-689180
Department Head: Teppo Lampio
Sections: Waterfowl, T. Lampio, M.K. Pirkola; tetraonids, P. Rajala, H. Lindén; moose, K. Nygrén; predatory mammals, E.S. Nyholm; reindeer, M. Nieminen; fur farming, P. Niemela
Graduate research staff: 8
Activities: Ecology of game species; abundance and structure of game populations, habitats and habitat improvement; game management techniques; effects of the industries on game population; methods for reducing damages caused by game; social importance of hunting; reindeer and reindeer management; fur farming.
Contract work: Yes
Publications: Riistatieteellisiä Julkaisuja and divisional bulletins.

Ahvenjärven Riistantutkimusasema 464

[Ahvenjärvi Game Research Station]
Address: SF-82950 Kuikkalampi
Telephone: 974-49121
Head: K. Nygrén
Director: Risto Komu

Evon Riistantutkimusasema 465

[Evo Game Research Station]
Address: SF-16970 Evo
Telephone: 917-35132
Head: M.K. Pirkola
Director: Heikki Koivunen

Meltauksen Riistantutkimusasema 466

[Meltans Game Research Station]
Address: SF-97310 Patokoski
Telephone: 991-761171
Head: P. Rajala
Director: A. Ylisuvanto

Söderskäriu Riistantutkimusasema 467

[Söderskär Game Research Station]
Head: O. Stenman
Director: M. Hario

Sähkötarkastuskeskus 468

[Electrical Inspectorate]
Address: PO Box 21, Särkiniementie 3, SF-00211
Helsinki 21
Telephone: 90-696 31
Telex: 122877 elins sf
Affiliation: Ministry of Trade and Industry
Managing Director: Erkki Yrjölä
Activities: Safety of electrical installations and equipment.
Contract work: No

Säteilyturvallisuuslaitos* 469

– STL
[Radiation Protection Institute]
Address: PO Box 268, SF-00101 Helsinki 10
Telephone: 90-61671
Telex: 122691 STL SF
Affiliation: Ministry of Health and Social Affairs
Director: Professor A. Isola
Graduate research staff: 100
Annual expenditure: FMk20m

Activities: Research in the general fields of radiation protection and reactor safety; analysis of the safety of nuclear installations; implementation of the control of construction and use of nuclear installations; examination of methods to control nuclear materials.
Publications: STL-A Reports.

G.A. Serlachius Oy 470

Address: SF-35800 Mänttä
Telephone: 934-4771
Telex: 22 122 Serla SF
Research Manager: Dr Ermo Kaila
Graduate research staff: 4
Activities: Research into the manufacturing properties of pulp and paper making and coating; economics and resources in wood processing industry; waste-waters in and new processes associated with the wood processing industry.
Contract work: No

Siipikarjanhoitajain Liitto 471
Ry

[Poultry Breeders Association]
Address: Kanakouluntie 1-3, SF-13100 Hämeenlinna
10
Telephone: 917-244 87
General Manager: Krister Eklund
Sections: RST station; Anita Eiskonen; development farm, vacant
Graduate research staff: 1
Activities: Research on laying hens hybrids; pure strains development; feed efficiency measuring and breeding experiments.
Contract work: No
Publications: Siipikarja, (monthly in Finnish).

Oy Sinebrychoff Ab 472

Address: PO Box 24, Sandviskajen 7, SF-00101
Helsinki 10
Telephone: 90-162 11
Telex: 122131
Research and Development Manager: Esko Pajunen
Head of Laboratory: K. Tääskelainen
Graduate research staff: 4
Annual expenditure: £10 000-50 000
Activities: Brewing and fermentation technology.

PORI BREWERY 473

Address: PO Box 49, Hallituskatu 18, SF-28101 Pori 10
Head of Laboratory: T. Härkönen

current problems, insulation materials, testing, developing.
Contract work: Yes
Publications: Stromberg News.

Sisäasiainministeriö- 474
Ympäristönsuojeluosasto

[Environmental Protection Department of the Ministry of the Interior]
Address: Hakaniemenkatu 2, SF-00530 Helsinki 53
Telephone: 90-1601
Affiliation: Ministry of the Interior
Deputy Director: Olli Paasivirta
Annual expenditure: £51 000-500 000
Activities: Responsibility for general planning, control and coordination of environmental protection; air pollution control, noise abatement, outdoor recreation, waste management and reuse and recycling of wastes.
Contract work: No

Suomalainen Tiedeakatemia 477

[Academy of Science and Letters]
Address: Snellmaninkatu 9-11, SF-00170 Helsinki 17
President: Professor Osmo Järvi
Secretary-General: Professor Lauri A. Vuorela
Activities: The Mathematics and Natural Sciences section is divided into eight groups: mathematics, physics, geophysics, chemistry, geology and geography, biology, agriculture and forestry, and medical sciences. The Humanities Section covers theology, philosophy, history and archaeology, linguistics and ethnography, jurisprudence and social sciences.

Sokerijuurikkaan 475
Tutkimuskeskus

[Sugar Beet Research Centre]
Address: SF-25170 Kotalato
Telephone: 924 6371
Director: Dr Kyösti Raininko
Sections: Weed and pest control, Nils Nuormala; fertilizing trials, Matti Erjala; feeds, Sirkka Raininko; laboratory, Marja Pelo; statistics, Hannu Kesävaara; machine trials, Juha Helle
Graduate research staff: 7
Annual expenditure: £51 000-500 000
Activities: Developing sugar beet cultivation techniques; machine trials, development of machinery and feeds; sugar beet quality research.
Contract work: No
Publications: Annual reports.

GEOFYSIIKAN OBSERVATORIO 478

[Geophysical Observatory of the Finnish Academy of Science and Letters]
Address: SF-99600 Sodankylä
Telephone: 993 12226
Telex: 37254 gefso sf
Director: Eero Kataja
Sections: Geomagnetism and magnetospheric physics, Eero Kataja; ionospheric physics, Tauno Turunen; ionospheric absorption, Hilkka Ranta; EISCAT, Tapani Äijänen; seismology, Airi Kataja; pole motion astronomy, Johannes Kultima
Graduate research staff: 10
Annual expenditure: £10 000-50 000
Activities: Geomagnetism and magnetospheric physics; statistics of geomagnetic activity; ionospheric physics; ionospheric absorption; aurora; seismology; measurement of pole variation.
Contract work: No
Publications: Monthly data bulletins.

Oy Strömberg Ab 476

Address: PO Box 69, SF-65101 Vaasa 10
Telephone: 61-258 222
Telex: 74211 strv sf
Research director: Dr Matti Karttunen
Graduate research staff: 100
Annual expenditure: over £2m
Activities: Research within heavy electrical industry: transformers, circuit-breakers; high-voltage and high-

Suomen Akatemia 479

[Academy of Finland]
Address: Ratamestarinkatu 12, SF-00520 Helsinki 52
Telephone: 90-141 611
Telex: 123416 Acad sf

CENTRAL BOARD OF THE ACADEMY 480

President: Professor Kai-Otto Donner
Secretary-General: Heikki Kallio
Research director: Dr Elisabeth Helander
Activities: Planning and coordinating research; acting as an organ for the formulation of science policy in Finland; preparing proposals for the consideration of the Ministry of Education and the Government in questions dealing with science policy and the distribution of funds; developing scientific publishing; bilateral exchange of scientists; arrangement of United Nations research programmes; participation in multilateral research cooperation subcommittees for EMBC, GARP, IHP, MAB, etc.

MEDICAL RESEARCH COUNCIL 481

Chairman: Professor Eino Heikkinen
Activities: Promoting research and making science policy in the fields of the medical sciences.

RESEARCH COUNCIL FOR 482
AGRICULTURE AND FORESTRY

Chairman: Professor Antti Ahlström
Sections: Agriculture, Professor Eeva Tapis; forestry, Professor Jouko Hämäläinen; nutrition, Professor Antti Ahlström
Activities: Promoting research and making science policy in the fields of agriculture and forestry.

RESEARCH COUNCIL FOR 483
TECHNOLOGY

Chairman: Professor Martti Kaila
Activities: Promoting research and making science policy in the fields of the technical sciences; subcommittee for NORDFORSK.

RESEARCH COUNCIL FOR THE 484
HUMANITIES

Chairman: Dr Olli Alho
Activities: Promoting research and making policy in the fields of humanities.

RESEARCH COUNCIL FOR THE 485
NATURAL SCIENCES

Chairman: Professor Gunnar Graeffe
Activities: Promoting research and making science policy in the fields of the natural sciences; subcommittee for EISCAT.

RESEARCH COUNCIL FOR THE 486
SOCIAL SCIENCES

Chairman: Professor Pertti Kettunen
Activities: Promoting research and making policy in the fields of social sciences.

Suomen Palontorjuntaliitto 487

[Fire Protection Association of Finland]
Address: Iso Roobertinkatu 7A 4, SF-00120 Helsinki 12
Telephone: 90-649 233
Director: P. Heikkonen
Section: Technical Section, P. Hallio
Graduate research staff: 4
Activities: Fire protection and prevention, provision of expert advice on technical fire problems and questions concerning fire safety in buildings; inspection of fire prevention and detector installations in Finland; standardization of firefighting equipment.
Contract work: Yes

Suomen Sokeri Oy 488

Address: Länsituulentie 7, SF-02101 Espoo 10
Telephone: 90-2985 131
Telex: 121076 supo sf
Graduate research staff: 14
Annual expenditure: FMk5.5m

RESEARCH CENTRE 489

Address: SF-02460 Kontvik
Director: Professor Asko Melaja
Activities: Sugar technology and carbohydrate chemistry, to improve production methods and usage and to develop new products and processes.

Suomen Syöpäyhdistys ry 490

[Cancer Society of Finland]
Address: Liisankatu 21B, SF-00170 Helsinki 17
Secretary-General: Niilo Voipio
Sections: President J.K. Paasikivi Foundation for Cancer Research, Ernst Palmén; Foundation for Cancer Research, Professor Lauri Rauramo
Activities: All aspects of cancer research. Both foundations grant awards and fellowships to scientists engaged in cancer research and also support organizations under the aegis of the Society.

Suomen Tiedeseura –   491
Finska Vetenskaps-
Societeten

[Finnish Society of Science and Letters]
Address: Snellmaninkatu 9-11, SF-00170 Helsinki 17
Telephone: 90-633005
Secretary-General: Professor Gösta Mickwitz
Activities: The Society finances publications and research activities by grants in various fields of research.
Contract work: No
Publications: Year book.

Tampereen Teknillinen   492
Korkeakoulu

[Tampere University of Technology]
Address: PO Box 527, SF-33101 Tampere 10
Telephone: 931-162111
Telex: 22-313 ttktr-sf
Rector: Professor Osmo Hassi
Graduate research staff: 100
Annual expenditure: £501 000-2m
Contract work: Yes

DEPARTMENT OF ARCHITECTURE   493

Institute of Architectural Theory   494

Head: Professor Helmer Stenros

Institute of Design of Buildings   495

Head: Olof Hansson

Institute of History of Architecture   496

Head: Associate Professor Pekka Laurila

Institute of Methods and Materials of   497
Building Construction

Head: Professor Erkki Helamaa

Institute of Urban Planning   498

Head: Professor Jere Maula

DEPARTMENT OF CIVIL   499
ENGINEERING

Geodesy and Photogrammetry   500

Head: Associate Professor Hannu Salmenperä

Institute of Building Construction   501

Head: Professor Lauri Mehto

Institute of Construction Economics   502

Head: Professor Raimo Salokangas

Institute of Road and Traffic   503
Engineering

Head: Professor Olli-Pekka Hartikainen

Institute of Soil Mechanics and   504
Foundation Engineering

Head: Professor Leo Keinonen

Institute of Theory of Structures   505

Head: Professor Herman Parland

Institute of Water Supply and Sewage   506

Head: Professor Matti Viitasaari

DEPARTMENT OF ELECTRICAL   507
ENGINEERING

Institute of Computer Engineering   508

Head: Professor Reino Kurki-Suonio

Institute of Control Engineering   509

Head: Professor Pauli Karttunen

Institute of Electrical Power   510
Engineering

Heads: Professor Juhani Käranä, Acting Professor Erkki Lakervi

Institute of Electronics   511

Head: Professor Yrjö Neuvo

Institute of Mathematics   512

Head: Professor Timo Lepistö

Institute of Measurement Engineering 513

Head: Professor Olli Aumala

Institute of Physics 514

Head: Professor Gunna Graeffe

DEPARTMENT OF MECHANICAL 515
ENGINEERING

Institute of Hydraulic Machines 516

Head: Professor Risto Keskinen

Institute of Industrial Economics 517

Head: Associate Professor Klaus Kerppola

Institute of Labour Protection 518

Head: Professor Jorma Saari

Institute of Machine Design 519

Head: Professor Kauko Aho

Institute of Materials Science 520

Head: Professor Pentti Kettunen
Sections: Non-metals, Professor P. Törmälä; deformation, amorphous, Dr T. Tiainen; corrosion, wear, Dr T. Mäntylä; fracture, Dr T. Lepisto
Annual expenditure: FMk1.5m
Activities: Mechanical and other constructional properties (strength, plasticity, strain hardening, fatigue, fracture, etc); development of the methods to test mechanical properties, reliability of the results; manufacturing properties (extrusion, joining, casting); selection of materials and development of new materials for certain purposes; surface studies; wear and erosion resistance; corrosion resistance; insulating properties; electrical properties; amorphous materials.

Institute of Production Engineering 521

Head: Professor Ilkka Lapinleimu

Institute of Refrigeration Engineering 522

Head: Professor Antero Aittomäki

Institute of Textile Technology 523

Heads: Professor Ahti Reijonen, Professor Jorma Sudquist
Graduate research staff: 6
Activities: Sizing, desizing and reuse of size; water, energy ahd chemicals - saving in chemical processes of textile industry; chemical pretreatments in textile industry.

Institute of Thermal Engineering 524

Head: Professor Ilmari Kurki-Suonio

Tampereen Yliopisto 525

[Tampere University]
Address: Kalevantie 4, SF-33100 Tampere 10
Telephone: 931-156111

DEPARTMENT OF BIOMEDICAL 526
SCIENCES

Address: Lääkärinkatu 3, SF-33520 Tampere 52
Telephone: 931-156111
Head: Associate Professor Pauli Leinikki
Sections: Anatomy, Professor P. Tuohimaa, Associate Professor Antti Hervonen
Medical Biochemistry, Professor T. Nikkari
Microbiology, Professor E. Jansson
Pathology, Professor K. Krohn
Physiology, Professor S. Oja
Pharmacology, Professor H. Vapaatalo
Virology, Associate Professor P. Leinikki
Activities: Research projects in neuroanatomy, neurobiology, reproduction biology and cell biology, mycoplasms, immunopathology, pharmacokinetics, brain metabolism, toxicology, immunobiology, viral diseases.

DEPARTMENT OF CLINICAL 527
SCIENCES

Address: Teiskantie 35, SF-33520 Tampere 52
Telephone: 931-156111
Head: Professor Amos Pasternack
Sections: Surgery, Professor P. Rokkanen
Internal Medicine, Professor A. Pasternack
Paediatrics, Professor J. Visakorpi
Gynaecology and Obstetrics, Professor P. Pystynen
Rheumatology, Professor O. Laitinen
Otorhinolaryngology, Professor P. Karma
Psychiatry, Professor P. Niskanen
Radiology, Professor E. Koivisto
Child Psychiatry, vacant

Neurology, Associate Professor M. Hyyppä
Dermatology, Associate Professor T. Reunala
Ophthalmology, Associate Professor M. Saari

DEPARTMENT OF LIBRARY AND   528 INFORMATION SCIENCES

Head: Professor Marjatta Okko
Graduate research staff: 15

DEPARTMENT OF MATHEMATICAL   529 SCIENCES

Address: PO Box 607, SF-33101 Tampere 10
Head: Professor Tarmo Pukkila
Sections: Computer Science, Professor P. Järvinen
Mathematics, Professor S. Hyyrö
Philosophy, Professor R. Kauppi
Statistics, Professor T. Pukkila

DEPARTMENT OF PUBLIC HEALTH   530

Address: PO Box 607, SF-33101 Tampere 10
Telephone: 931-156111
Telex: 22415 tayklsf
Head: Associate Professor Juhani Kirjonen
Sections: Social Psychiatry, Professor E. Anttinen
Epidemiology, Professor M. Hakama
Occupational Health, Professor J. Hasan
Primary Care, Professor M. Isokoski
Psychology and Sociology of Labour Protection, Associate Professor J. Kirjonen
Nutrition, Associate Professor L. Räsänen
Graduate research staff: 30

Teknillisten Tieteiden   531 Akatemia - Akademin för Tekniska Vetenskaper ry

[Finnish Academy of Technical Sciences]
Address: Kansakoulukatu 10A, SF-00100 Helsinki 10
Telephone: 90-694 4260
President: Professor Pentti Laasonen
Managing Director: Professor Olli Lokki
Activities: Promotion of research in technical sciences to further Finnish industry and the utilization of national resources. To this end, research results as well as textbooks on engineering are published, and international contacts are maintained. The Academy further acts as an advisory body in its field.

Turun Yliopisto*   532

[Turku University]
Address: SF-20500 Turku 50
Telephone: 921-335599

FACULTY OF MATHEMATICS AND   533 SCIENCES*

Dean: Professor U. Pursiheimo

FACULTY OF MEDICINE (INCLUDING   534 DENTISTRY)*

Dean: Professor P. Virtama

UNIVERSITY RESEARCH CENTRES*   535

Cardiovascular Research Unit*   536

Head: I. Välimäki

Saaristomeren tutkimuslaitos*   537

[Archipelago Research Institute]
Address: SF-21660 Navvo Seili
Telephone: 926-56110
Directors: T. Juusti, A. Petäjä

Tähtitieteellis-   538 Optillinentutkimusasema

[Turku Observatory]
Address: It. Pitkäkatu 1, SF-20520 Turku 52
Telephone: 921-431 863
Research director: Professor M. Valtonen
Sections: Astronomy, T. Korhonen; optics and geodesy, A. Niemi
Graduate research staff: 7
Annual expenditure: £10 000-50 000
Activities: Zenith tube and astrolabe observations; minor planet photography; photometric observations; objective prism spectroscopy; quasar variability surveys (optical and radio); celestial mechanics; astrophysics.
Contract work: No

Turun yliopiston Lapin tutkimuslaitos   539 Kevo

[Kevo Subarctic Research Institute]
Address: SF-99980 Utsjoki
Telephone: 997-72505
Telex: 37262
Director: Matti Sulkinoja
Activities: Natural sciences mainly in the botanical,

zoological, ecological and geographical field on different subarctic problems. Main research areas include: adaptation to thermal and light conditions; growth and productivity rates; occurence and ecology of terrestrial invertebrates; soil fauna; geomorphological studies; soil analysis; mapping of flora; fish population, subarctic passerine bird, and reindeer studies; environmental changes; socio-anthropological studies and aspects of Lapp culture.
Facilities: Meteorological and geophysical equipment, laboratory instruments, gas analysing laboratory.
Contract work: Yes
Publications: Reports from the Kevo Subarctic Research Station, (15 volumes, and annually), *Kevo Notes,* (5 volumes).

Wihuri Physical Laboratory*   540

Head: Professor L. Niemelä

Työterveyslaitos   541

[Occupational Health Institute]
Address: Haartmaninkatu 1, SF-00290 Helsinki 29
Telephone: 90-41 36 22
Director-General: Jorma Rantanen
Scientific Director: Sven Hernberg
Administrative Director: Martti Lehtokangas
Graduate research staff: 180 (including part-time staff)
Annual expenditure: FMk25-30m
Activities: Study of the interactions of work and health, providing authorities with information required to set norms and draft occupational health legislation, to create healthier, safer work conditions. The regional institutes concentrate on regional problems, industrial hygiene measurements, consultation services in occupational medicine, information and training, and ergonomics. They all possess mobile field clinics.
Contract work: Yes
Publications: Scandinavian Journal of Work, Environment and Health, quarterly; series: *Työterveyslaitoksen tutkimuksia, Työterveyslaitoksen julkaisuja;* periodical: *Työ Terveys Turvallisuus.*

DEPARTMENT OF EPIDEMIOLOGY   542
AND BIOMETRY

Activities: Sven Hernberg
Activities: Epidemiological research, sociological and sociomedical research, research data analysis.

DEPARTMENT OF INDUSTRIAL   543
HYGIENE AND TOXICOLOGY

Director: Harri Vainio
Activities: Chemical and physical industrial hygiene; toxicology, biological exposures.

DEPARTMENT OF OCCUPATIONAL   544
MEDICINE

Director: Vesa Vaaranen
Activities: Diagnosis and treatment of occupational diseases, assessment of work capacity, periodic health examinations, research and training.

DEPARTMENT OF OCCUPATIONAL   545
SAFETY

Director: vacant
Activities: Research on occupational accidents and their prevention; safety analysis.

DEPARTMENT OF PHYSIOLOGY   546

Director: Aarni Koskela
Activities: Ergonomics, occupational physiotherapy, work physiology, relationship between work-capacity and health, occupational safety, training and education.

DEPARTMENT OF PSYCHOLOGY   547

Director: Kari Lindström
Activities: Investigation of mental strain at work, mental effects of various environmental factors at work, mental health aspects of worklife and job satisfaction, research on aptitudes, clinical psychology examinations.

Kuopio Regional Institute   548

Director: Kaj Husman
Activities: National research tasks on agriculture and forestry.

Lappeenranta Regional Institute   549

Director: Raine Mäkinen
Activities: National research tasks on mechanical and chemical wood processing.

Oulu Regional Institute   550

Director: Juhani Hassi
Activities: National research tasks on mining and metallurgy.

Tampere Regional Institute 551

Director: Reino Laitinen

Turku Regional Institute 552

Director: Gustav Wickström
Activities: National research tasks on seafaring.

Uusimaa (Helsinki) Regional Institute 553

Director: Pentti U. Lehtinen

Valion Laboratorio 554

[Co-operative & Dairies' Association Laboratory]
Address: Kalevankatu 56B, SF-00180 Helsinki 18
Director: Dr Kari Salminen
Activities: Dairy chemistry.
See also: Biokemiallinen Tutkimuslaitos.

Valtion Eläinlääketieteellinen Laitos 555

[State Veterinary Medical Institute]
Address: Hämeentie 57, SF-00550 Helsinki 55
or: PO Box 368, SF-00101, Helsinki 10, Finland
Telephone: 90-736046
Director: Professor Esko Nurmi
Sections: Chemistry, Eeva Karppanan; food hygiene, Dr Jorma Hirn, Dr Leo Koiranen; pathology, Kurt Henriksson; production, Dr Eeva-Liisa Hintikka; serobacteriology, Dr Helvi Vasenius; virology, Erkki Neuvonen; Kuopio Laboratory, Dr Pekka Nurmio
Graduate research staff: 2
Annual expenditure: £51 000-500 000
Activities: The central laboratory for veterinary services in Finland and, with a regional laboratory at Kuopio, the main areas of work are: veterinary microbiology, immunology, virology, pathology, haematology, parasitology and chemistry; microbiology and control of the hygiene of food of animal origin; production, supply and quality control of veterinary biological and microbiological culture media; consultative field service, research and teaching.
Contract work: Yes
Publications: Annual report, research reports.

Valtion Maatalouskoneiden Tutkimuslaitos 556

[Research Institute for Engineering in Agriculture and Forestry]
Address: SF-03450 Olkkala
Telephone: 913-462 11
Research director: vacant
Activities: Machines, tools and implements used in agriculture, gardening, forestry, household work and home industries.

Valtion Maitotalouden Tutkimuslaitos 557

[State Institute for Dairy Research]
Address: SF-31600 Jokioinen
Telephone: 916-83500
Director: Professor Veijo Antila
Activities: Milk and milk products; the quality of milk; the developing of new dairy products; testing of dairy machinery.

Valtion Teknillinen Tutkimuskeskus 558

– VTT
[Technical Research Centre of Finland]
Address: Vuorimiehentie 5, SF-02150 Espoo 15
Telephone: 90-4561
Telex: 12 2972 vttin sf
Chairman: Counsellor Klaus Waris
Director-General: Professor Pekka Jauho
Graduate research staff: 1 000
Annual expenditure: £10m

General Division 559

Sections: Administration Office, Administration Director: Arto V. Klemola; Finance Office; Planning and Marketing Office; Computing Service Office, Jukka Kiwi

INSTRUMENT LABORATORY 560

Acting Director: Jukka Pesonen
Activities: Instrument development, planning and building of research equipment, machine shop work, central supply store, service of electronic equipment.

Technical Information Service   561

Director: Sauli Laitinen
Activities: Information service, library, technical archives, publications, Home Office of the Finnish Scientific Attachés.

BUILDING TECHNOLOGY AND   562
COMMUNITY DEVELOPMENT
DIVISION

Research Director: Professor Heikki Poijärvi

Building Economics Laboratory   563

Director: Professor Per-Olof Jarle
Activities: Research directed towards building and building planning, to clarify the choice solutions in the light of value and cost factors.

Building Laboratory   564

Acting Director: Timo Lounela
Activities: Research concerned with modernization, repair, management, maintenance, and administration problems of building construction, including economic investigations, and research of building materials, structures and methods required by the special conditions of Northern Finland.

Concrete and Silicate Laboratory   565

Director: Professor Asko Sarja
Activities: Research and development work on concrete and its constituents, mortars, masonry and other ceramic products, concrete structures and their reinforcements as well as masonry structures, and related production techniques.

Fire Technology Laboratory   566

Director: Professor Claes Holm
Activities: Research in fire safety properties of building materials, products, elements and buildings, including regional fire protection and fire extinguishing equipment and technology.

Forest Products Laboratory   567

Acting Director: Tuija Vihavainen
Activities: Structure and properties of wood and technology related to raw materials, manufacture, properties, further processing and use of forest products.

Geotechnical Laboratory   568

Director: Professor Markku Tammirinne
Activities: Research of building technological properties of the soil and rock and development of foundation methods for different structures and ground construction methods.

Heating and Ventilating Laboratory   569

Director: Professor Erkki Äikäs
Activities: Research and development of heating, ventilating and plumbing technology of buildings, acoustical research and testing, and questions related to air protection and municipal engineering in the field.

Land Use Laboratory   570

Director: Professor Pekka Raitanen
Activities: Research related to community planning, including land surveying, evaluating and real estate technology, community technology.

Road and Traffic Laboratory   571

Director: Professor Otto Wahlgren
Activities: Research and development of the technical and economic questions related to the design, construction, and maintenance of traffic routes and of traffic engineering, economics, and safety.

Structural Engineering Laboratory   572

Director: Professor Pauli Jumppanen
Activities: Research and development work concerned with physical properties and strength of structures, components, and building materials.

ELECTRICAL AND NUCLEAR   573
TECHNOLOGY DIVISION

Research Director: Professor Veikko Palva

Biomedical Engineering Laboratory   574

Director: Professor Pekka Ahonen
Activities: Research, development and testing of equipment and systems associated with hospital instrumentation and hospital automation.

Electrical Engineering Laboratory   575

Director: Professor Pekka Salminen
Activities: Electric power engineering, electric measurements, control and systems engineering and reliability analysis of technical systems.

Electronics Laboratory 576

Director: Professor Matti Otala
Activities: Research and development of industrial instrumentation, and other electronic research.

Nuclear Engineering Laboratory 577

Director: Professor Pekka Silvennoinen
Activities: Research on reactor core fuel management, reactor dynamics and safety.

Reactor Laboratory 578

Director: Professor Juhani Kuusi
Activities: Material, process and reactor physics research (based on the use of a FiR-1 reactor and radioactive isotopes), and development of measuring techniques.

Semiconductor Laboratory 579

Director: Professor Tor Stubb
Activities: Research of electrical and magnetic properties of semiconductor materials, and semiconductor technology.

Telecommunications Laboratory 580

Director: Professor Esko Heikkilä
Activities: Research and development work concerning electrical communications; data processing; radar techniques; testing of electronic equipment and components.

Work Safety Laboratory 581

Director: Professor Eero Siltanen
Activities: Research related to occupational safety and research of equipment and methods related to occupational health service.

MATERIALS AND PROCESSING 582 TECHNOLOGY DIVISION

Research Director: Professor Sakari Heiskanen
Total r&d staff : staff on materials projects: 1 918 : 380
Annual expenditure: Fmk35m

Biotechnical Laboratory 583

Director: Dr Veijo Mäkinen
Research Professor of the Finnish Academy: Professor Tor-Magnus Enari
Research Professor: Dr Matti Linko
Activities: Technology based upon biological processes.

Chemical Laboratory 584

Director: Professor Eero Avela
Research Professor: Dr Erkki Häsänen
Activities: Chemical analytics and technology, polymer chemistry, plastics and leather technology, environmental protection technology.

Domestic Fuel Laboratory 585

Acting Director: Dr Eino Kiukaanniemi
Activities: Production and utilization of domestic fuels and their environmental effects.

Food Research Laboratory 586

Director: Professor Yrjö Mälkki
Activities: Food analytics, technology, processing, hygiene and toxicology.

Fuel and Lubricant Laboratory 587

Director: Professor Veikko Rauhala
Activities: Processing of fuels, non-energy use of peat, lubricating technique and environmental effects.

Graphic Arts Laboratory 588

Director: Professor Simo Karttunen
Activities: Graphic technology.

Metallurgy and Mineral Engineering 589 Laboratory

Director: Professor Heikki Kleemola
Research Professor: Dr Tero Hakkarainen
Activities: Grinding and concentration of minerals, hydrometallurgy and pyrometallurgy, metal working and heat treatment, foundry technology and corrosion prevention.

Metals Laboratory 590

Director: Professor Jarl Forstén
Activities: Metallic materials, destructive and non-destructive testing, quality assurance, welding and machine shop and machine technology.

Ship Laboratory 591

Director: Professor Juhani Sukselainen
Activities: Hydrodynamics and aerodynamics, naval architecture and marine technology.

Textile Laboratory 592

Acting Director: Ben Malmström
Activities: Properties, manufacture and use of textile materials, textile products and their substitutes.

Vesientutkimuslaitos 593

[Water Research Institute]
Address: Vuorikatu 24, PO Box 250, SF-00101 Helsinki 10
Telephone: 90 171 922
Affiliation: National Board of Waters
Research director: Professor Seppo Mustonen
Sections: Hydrological Office, Risto Lemmelä
Water Research Office, Reino Laaksonen
Technical Research Office, Hannu Laikari
Research Laboratory, Kirsti Haapala
Graduate research staff: 50
Annual expenditure: £501 000-2m
Activities: Promotion and performance of water research, obtaining, collecting and issuing data on quantity, quality and use of national water resources, maintenance of a hydrological library; hydrological research (water levels, stream-flow precipitation, chemical analysis of rainwater, snow depth and ice thickness, soil frost penetration, water surface temperatures); research on water management and pollution control, treatment of sewage and effluents; geotechnical research and proposals regarding planning, construction, inspection and maintenance of hydraulic engineering works; work cooperation with IHP, OECD, COST and Nordforsk.
Contract work: No
Publications: Scientific papers, instructions, recommendations, and annual reports.

Viljavuuspalvelu Oy 594

Address: Vellikellontie 1, SF-00410 Helsinki 41
Director: Martti Kurki
Sections: Method and special studies, Leo Lappi; soil analysis, Esko Ylikylä; plant and water analysis, Aino Syrjäniemi; seed control, Markku Aaltonen
Graduate research staff: 10
Annual expenditure: £51 000-500 000
Activities: Research into the fertility of cultivated fields, gardens, orchards and forests; plant, water, animal tissue and other analyses in both field and laboratory, to give detailed instructions on soil improvement.
Contract work: Yes
Publications: Account of research findings, fertility maps, utilization booklets, research reports.

FRANCE

Applications de Recherches sur l'Énergie et la Société 1

– ARES
[Applied Research on Energy and Society]
Address: 39 rue Croix-Baragnou, 31000 Toulouse
Telephone: (061) 52 02 05
President: J.R. Mercier
Senior staff: Philippe Divet, Francis Dubourg, Maguy Durand, Pierre Dutoit, Monique Faure, Mariette Gerber, J.R. Mercier, Michel Mustin
Activities: ARES is consulted by French and foreign official organizations for research and commissions on: energy economy; renewable sources of energy; socioeconomic aspects and technologies. ARES is also consulted by agriculturalists when building new installations, by architects on the subject of solar and thermal buildings and by engineers on solar heating.

Association Scientifique des Médecins Acupuncteurs de France 2

– ASMAF
[Scientific Association of Acupuncture Doctors of France]
Address: 2 rue du Général-de-Larminat, 75015 Paris
Telephone: (01) 273 37 26
President: Dr Georges Cantoni
Activities: Development of acupuncture. The Association constitutes a centre for study, research and scientific propaganda.
Contract work: No
Publications: Meridiens, quarterly.

ÉCOLE FRANÇAIS D'ACUPUNCTURE 3

– EFA
[French College of Acupuncture]
Sections: Analgesic acupuncture, Dr Laval, Dr Mary; bioelectronics and medicine applied to acupuncture, Dr Georges Cantoni; experimental sphygmology, chronobiology, Dr Borsarello
Activities: The College was formed as an affiliation of ASMAF in 1977. It conducts teaching conferences for professionals and three-monthly meetings on specific topics.

Bertin & Cie 4

Address: BP 3, 78370 Plaisir
Telephone: (03) 050 25 00
Telex: 696231
Chairman and Director General: F. Chanrion
Directors-General: Michel Perineau, Georges Mordchelles
Sections: Automation, computerized control and optics; energy; structural and fluid mechanics; industrial processes and systems
Graduate research staff: 240
Annual expenditure: £51 000-500 000
Activities: Bertin & Cie's basic activity is research and development under contract to industry, either through the transfer of adaptable technologies existing in other industrial areas, or through the development of new technologies. The major areas of expertise are as follows: automation - electronics, electrotechniques, fluidics, hydraulics, pneumatics, optics, etc; special machines - for assembly, bottle dressing, packaging fragile products, machine tools, tropical food product processing, etc; manipulators - special manipulators, probes, sensors or actuators for robots, special computer programs, etc; rotating machines - compressors, circulators, centrifuges; laser technology; special furnaces - heat

transfer, insulation, heat generation, fluidized beds; cooling systems - especially in metallurgical industry and glass works; energy conservation; windmills - designed on Darrens principle for electricity production or direct water heating; biomass valorization - ethanol from vegetable wastes, methane from manure digestors, new process for production of furfural; noise reduction equipment; air cushion technology; high pressure water jets; carbon fibre technology; document coding and sorting; periscopes and borescopes; waste heat recovery turbogeneration; solar power plants; pollution monitoring; fog clearance systems.
Facilities: Anechoic chamber; hydraulic test tunnel; turbomachine test bench; Mach 5 Freon wind tunnel; clean room.
Contract work: Yes

REGIONAL OFFICES   5

Centre d'Automation d'Aix-en-Provence   6

Address: BP 22, 13290 Les Milles
Telephone: (042) 26 55 12
Telex: 420729

Centre de Bayonne   7

Address: BP 4, 40220 Tarnos
Telephone: (059) 55 05 10
Telex: 570026

Centre de Lyon   8

Address: 22 avenue Albert Einstein, 69100 Villeurbaune
Telephone: (078) 84 45 08
Telex: 340815

Bureau des Longitudes*   9

[Central Astronomy Office]
Address: 77 avenue Denfert-Rochereau, 75014 Paris
Telephone: (01) 320 12 10
Parent body: Ministère des Universités
Director: Dr B. Morando
Graduate research staff: 12
Annual expenditure: F500 000
Activities: Theoretical astronomy including relativity, astronomical ephemerides of the sun, moon, planets, Galilean satellites of Jupiter; nautical almanac; research in celestial mechanics applied to the solar system.

Centre Armoricain d'Étude Structurale des Socles*   10

[Brittany Centre for the Structural Study of Foundations]
Address: Institut de Géologie, BP 25A, 53031 Rennes Cedex
Affiliation: Centre National de la Recherche Scientifique
Director: Professor Jean Cogné

Centre d'Écologie de Camargue*   11

[Camargue Ecology Centre]
Address: 13200 Le Sambuc-Arles
Affiliation: Centre National de la Recherche Scientifique
Director: Pierre Heurteaux

Centre d'Étude des Phénomènes Aléatoires et Géophysiques   12

[Geophysical and Random Phenomena Study Centre]
Address: BP 15, 38040 Grenoble Cedex
Telephone: (076) 87 96 11
Affiliation: Institut National d'Astronomie et de Géophysique
Director: Jean-Louis Lacoume
Graduate research staff: 17
Activities: The laboratory's research is orientated towards the study of the magnetosphere, observations of the sun, thermodynamics of the ionosphere, measurement of plasma rays using the European Auroral Incoherent Scatter Facility. In the long term the laboratory's ionosphere-magnetosphere research will be used as part of the International Magnetic Study programme.

Centre d'Étude Spatiale des Rayonnements   13

– CESR
[Space Radiation Research Centre]
Address: 9 avenue du Colonel-Roche, BP 4346, 31029 Toulouse Cedex
Telephone: (061) 51 13 13
Affiliation: Institut National d'Astronomie et de Géophysique; Université Paul Sabatier (Toulouse III)

Director: Professor Francis Cambou
Graduate research staff: 45
Activities: The centre is involved in national and international research programmes among which the following subjects have been included: auroral phenomena; solar and interplanetary winds; nuclear astrophysics; detection of the earth's resources by satellite.

Centre d'Études Bioclimatiques* 14

[Bioclimatology Research Centre]
Address: 21 rue Becquerel, 67087 Strasbourg Cedex
Affiliation: Centre National de la Recherche Scientifique
Director: Professor Bernard Metz

Centre d'Études Biologiques des Animaux Sauvages* 15

[Biology of Wild Animals Research Centre]
Address: Forêt de Chizé, Villiers-en-Bois, 79360 Beauvoir sur Niort
Affiliation: Centre National de la Recherche Scientifique
Director: Jean-Claude Boissin

Centre d'Études d'Océanographie et de Biologie Marine* 16

[Oceanography and Marine Biology Research Centre]
Address: Station Biologique, place Georges-Teissier, 29211 Roscoff
Affiliation: Centre National de la Recherche Scientifique
Director: Professor Joseph Bergerard
Deputy Director: Louis Cabioch

Centre d'Études de Chimie Métallurgique* 17

[Metallurgical Chemistry Study Centre]
Address: 15 rue Georges-Urbain, 94400 Vitry
Affiliation: Centre National de la Recherche Scientifique
Director: Professor Michel Fayard
Deputy Director: Jean-Pierre Langeron

Centre d'Études de Géographie Tropicale* 18

[Tropical Geography Study Centre]
Address: CEGET, Domaine Universitaire, 33405 Talence
Affiliation: Centre National de la Recherche Scientifique
Director: Professor Guy Lasserre

Centre d'Études de l'Emploi 19

[Employment Research Centre]
Address: 51 rue de la Chaussée d'Antin, 75009 Paris
Telephone: (01) 285 72 07
Affiliation: Ministère du Travail et de la Participation
Director: Henri Chaffiotte
Sections: Employment structures and developments, M Ranchon; employment enterprises and markets, M Dumard; active population, Dr Rousselet
Graduate research staff: 30
Annual expenditure: Fl0m

Centre d'Études du Système Nerveux* 20

[Nervous System Study Centre]
Address: Laboratoire de Physiologie Nerveuse, 91190 Gif sur Yvette
Affiliation: Centre National de la Recherche Scientifique
Director: Robert Naquet

LABORATOIRE DE NEUROBIOLOGIE CELLULAIRE* 21

[Cellular Neurobiology Laboratory]
Address: 91190 Gif sur Yvette
Director: Ladislav Tauc

Centre d'Études et d'Expérimentation du Machinisme Agricole Tropical 22

– CEEMAT
[Tropical Agriculture Machinery Centre]
Address: Parc de Tourvoie, 92160 Antony

Telephone: (01) 668 61 02
Telex: 204565F
Research director: Claude Uzureau
Annual expenditure: £51 000-500 000
Activities: Research on agricultural machinery for tropical countries, in connection with French manufacturers. Technical and economic studies on animal-drawn, intermediate mechanization and motorization, including harvest and post-harvest.
Contract work: No
Publications: Machinisme Agricole Tropical, quarterly; newsletter, quarterly; bibliographical bulletin, monthly.

Centre d'Études et de Réalisations Cartographiques Géographiques*   23

[Geographical Cartography Centre]
Address: 191 rue Saint-Jacques, 75005 Paris
Affiliation: Centre National de la Recherche Scientifique
Director: Professor Fernand Joly

Centre d'Études et de Recherches de Chimie Organique Appliquée*   24

– CERCOA
[Applied Organic Chemistry Research and Study Centre]
Address: 2-8 rue Henri Dunant, BP 28, 94320 Thiais
Affiliation: Centre National de la Recherche Scientifique
Director: François le Gottic

Centre d'Études et de Recherches Géodynamiques et Astronomiques   25

– CERGA
[Geodynamics and Astronomics Research Centre]
Address: avenue Copernic, 06130 Grasse
Telephone: (093) 36 58 49
Telex: 470865
Affiliation: Institut National d'Astronomie et de Géophysique; Observatoire de Paris; Université de Franche-

Comté; Université de Bordeaux I; Université de Nice; Université de Strasbourg I
Director: Jean Kovalevsky
Sections: space dynamics, F. Barlier; moon, J. Kovalesky; interferometry, A. Labeyrie; astrometry, G. Billaud; Schmidt telescope, J.L. Heudier
Graduate research staff: 30
Annual expenditure: F4m
Activities: Research is concerned with movements in the earth-moon system, the solar system and star systems, as well as studies of the forces and parameters which govern these movements, in particular phenomena within the following framework: irregularities of the earth's rotation, movements of the pole and dynamics of man-made satellites; dynamics of the earth-moon system; movements of natural satellites of other planets; structure and assessment of infrared sources; catalogues of relative and semi-absolute stars; classification systems of astronomy.
Facilities: The centre has technical installations and an observatory on the Calern plateau at an altitude of 1 300 m, 25 km from Grasse, where its facilities include the following: Danjon astrolabe; Doppler receiver for Transit type satellites; laser telemeter for satellites; hororary and meteorology station; experimental clinometry station; infrared telescope (1 m) over 10 m; Schmidt type telescope 150-90 cm; infrared interferometer; lunar telemetry laser.
Contract work: No

Centre d'Études et Recherches des Charbonnages de France   26

– CERCHAR
[Coal-Mining Research Centre of France]
Address: BP 2, 60550 Verneuil en Halatte
Telephone: (04) 455 35 00
Telex: 140094 CERCHAR VERNH
Research director: J. Dangreaux
Sections: Mining techniques, C. Gagnière; mine safety and industrial safety, M. Giltaire; coal utilization, J. Desseine; pneumoconiosis, L. le Bouffant; coal carbonization, S. Delessard; chemistry, B. Lefrançois, L. Solaux
Graduate research staff: 160
Annual expenditure: over £2m
Activities: CERCHAR is France's only coal research and study centre. Its research work is in the following areas: mining techniques - strata control, stability of underground workings, mine ventilation and climate, dust control, emission of firedamp, mining machines, application of electronics; safety - explosions, mine fires, spontaneous combustion; approval of equipment, materials and explosives; pneumoconiosis; physiochemi-

cal analysis; coal utilization - combustion processes; coking; conversion of coal to synthetic fuels; coal by-products; liquefaction, ex- and in-situ gasification; fluidized bed combustion; fuel-coal mixtures; energy conservation; pollution control. It is also approved for carrying out measurements in the field of pollution: the fight against noise and examination of installations consuming thermal energy.
Contract work: Yes
Publications: Various reports.

LABORATOIRE DE MÉCANIQUE DES TERRAINS   27

[Strata Control Laboratory]
Address: École des Mines, 54042 Nancy Cedex
Telephone: (08) 355 04 79
Telex: 850 661
Affiliation: École Nationale Supérieure de la Métallurgie et de l'Industrie des Mines de Nancy
Research director: Professor C. Chambon
Head of Laboratory: M. Dejean
Graduate research staff: 9
Annual expenditure: £51 000-500 000
Activities: Stability of underground structures; ground subsidence; support structures; geotechnic and seismic studies.
Contract work: Yes

STATION EXPÉRIMENTALE DE MARIENAU   28

– SEM
[Marienau Experimental Centre]
Address: Houillères du Bassin de Lorraine, Usines de Marienau, 57600 Forbach
Telephone: (08) 785 88 22
Telex: 860244 HBL B MERLB
Affiliation: Institut de Recherche de la Sidérurgie
Director: Serge Delessard
Sections: Carbonization and thermatics, M Karboviac; industrial applications, M Puff
Graduate research staff: 9
Activities: Research and development in the following areas: coal technology (mainly carbonization); applications of fluidized bed (drying, preheating, crushing, combustion).
Contract work: No

Centre d'Études Nucléaires de Cadarache   29

[Cadarache Nuclear Research Centre]
Address: BP 1, 13115 Saint-Paul-lez-Durance Bouches du Rhône
Parent body: Commissariat à l'Énergie Atomique
Director: A. Junca
Activities: Theoretical research on rapid neutron reactors; critical state of rapid neutrons; mechanical and thermal research on rapid neutron reactors; analytical and applied chemistry; development of fuel elements; experimental research on radiological safety; electronics and instrumentation; medical and social sciences.

Centre d'Études Nucléaires de Fontenay aux Roses   30

[Fontenay aux Roses Nuclear Research Centre]
Address: BP 6, 92260 Fontenay aux Roses
Parent body: Commissariat à l'Énergie Atomique
Director: J. Asty
Activities: Chemical and analytical research; chemistry of irradiated fuels; plutonium; mining exploration and research; reactor exploitation; health protection; technical protection.

Centre d'Études Nucléaires de Grenoble   31

[Grenoble Nuclear Research Centre]
Address: BP 85, Centre de Tri, 38041 Grenoble Cedex
Parent body: Commissariat à l'Énergie Atomique
Director: P. Corbet
Activities: Accelerators; piles; solid-state physics magnetic resonance; nuclear physics; neutron diffraction; radiation metrology; biological analysis; plant and cellular biology; haematology; radiobiology; electronics and information technology.

Centre d'Études Nucléaires de Saclay   32

[Saclay Nuclear Research Centre]
Address: BP2, 91990 Gif sur Yvette
Telephone: (06) 908 50 41
Parent body: Commissariat à l'Énergie Atomique
Director: C. Chauvez
Activities: Reactor research; nuclear metallurgy;

nuclear chemistry; nuclear physics; biology; radioactive metrology; electronics; uranium isotopes separation; applications of radioelements.

ISOTOPIC SEPARATION DIVISION 33

Director: Claude Bernaud
Deputy Director: Jean-Hubert Coates
Departments: Isotopic engineering, Pierre Plurien (Saclay)
Tests and industrialization, Michel Gelee (Pierrelatte)
Chemistry and physics, Paul Rigny

REPROCESSING AND WASTE DIVISION 34

Director: Jean Megy
Deputy Director: Charles Fisher

Centre d'Études Phytosociologiques et Écologiques Louis-Emberger* 35

[Louis Emberger Phytosociological and Ecological Research Centre]
Address: route de Mende, BP 5051, 34033 Montpellier Cedex
Affiliation: Centre National de la Recherche Scientifique
Director: S. de Percevaux

Centre d'Études Techniques des Industries de l'Habillement 36

– CETIH
[Clothing Industry Technical Study and Research Centre]
Address: 14 rue des Reculettes, 75013 Paris
Telephone: (01) 535 24 01
Telex: 270019
Affiliation: CETIH is financed by a compulsory levy of French clothing manufacturers.
Research director: P. Langlois
Graduate research staff: 70
Annual expenditure: £51 000-500 000
Activities: Research into the quality of fabrics and trims including economy of raw materials; clothing production including techniques of pattern making and grading; the organization of production to improve competitiveness and working conditions; the better selection of equipment; production management for better use of resources through information flow systems.
Contract work: No
Publications: A monthly technical magazine.

Centre d'Études Vallourec 37

[Vallourec Research Centre]
Address: BP 1, 59620 Aulnoye-Aymeries
Telephone: (027) 62 99 00
Vice-President, Research and Development: Dr Jacques Dedieu
Head of Research: Dr A. Sulmont
Sections: Metallurgy, M Guntz; non-destructive testing, M Mondot; chemistry-corrosion, M Blanchard; statistics, M Ngo; technology, M Garnier
Graduate research staff: 18
Annual expenditure: F28m
Activities: Research on mechanical properties and anti-corrosion behaviour of tubes made of carbon, alloyed and stainless steels, nickel alloys and titanium; research on hot and cold transformations of these materials; studies of their weldability.
Contract work: No

Centre d'Hémotypologie 38

[Blood Typing Centre]
Address: BP 3210, CHU de Purpan, 31052 Toulouse
Telephone: (061) 49 60 80
Affiliation: Centre National de la Recherche Scientifique
Research Director: Professor Georges Larrouy
Sections: Erythrocyte immunology, J. Arnaud; immunoglobulins, M. Blanc; haemoglobins, P. Richard; cellular cultures, J.M. Dugoujon; enzymes; H. Vergnes; serum proteins, J. Constans.
Graduate research staff: 7
Annual expenditure: £10 000-50 000
Activities: Analysis of genetic markers in the human population; research on the biological importance of polymorphisms; correlations between polymorphisms and illnesses.
Contract work: No
Publications: Annual report.

Centre d'Immunologie 39

[Immunology Centre]
Address: 70 route Léon Lachamp, Case 906, 13288 Marseille Cedex 9
Telephone: (091) 41 01 33
Telex: 420579 RINGMA 248
Affiliation: Institut National de la Santé et de la Recherche Médicale; Centre National de la Recherche Scientifique
Director: François M. Kourilsky
Sections: T cell immunology, P. Golstein; T lymphocyte receptor, B. Rubin; H-2 restriction, A.-M. Schmitt-Verhulst; immunoglobulin genetics, M. Fougereau; human immunogenetics, C. Mawas; H-2 immunogenetics, F. Kourilsky; immunochemistry, Y. Manuel; molecular biology, B. Jordan
Graduate research staff: 55
Annual expenditure: £501 000-2m
Activities: Most scientific projects in the centre aim at explaining molecular mechanisms of the immune response, and imply a close collaboration between biochemists, molecular biologists, and cell biologists. Major scientific interests are cellular receptors for antigens (membrane immunoglobulins and T cell receptor); genetic and biochemical analysis of antigens of the major histocompatibility complex in mouse and man; analysis of effector mechanisms of immune response, especially T cell cytotoxicity; structure and genetics of mouse immunoglobulins; applications in the field of radioimmunoassays, hybridomas, liposomes, chemical manipulation of the antigens.
Contract work: No

Centre de Biochimie et de 40 Biologie Moléculaire

– CBM
[Biochemistry and Molecular Biology Centre]
Address: BP 71, 13277 Marseille Cedex 9
Telephone: (091) 71 90 42
Affiliation: Centre National de la Recherche Scientifique
Director: Professor Jacques Ricard
Sections: Plant biochemistry/molecular biology, G. Noat, J.C. Meunier, R. Miassod; lipase structure, M. Rovery; model membranes, R. Verger; protein nutrition, A. Puigserver; protein exportation, C. Lazdunski; biological membranes, S. Maroux
Graduate research staff: 40
Annual expenditure: F1946 000
Activities: Research interests in the following fields: chemistry and physical chemistry of protein structure and mechanisms; molecular biology of plant development; biochemistry of photosynthesis; biological membranes and model membranes; molecular biology of protein exportation in procaryotic and eucaryotic cells.
Contract work: Yes

Centre de Biophysique 41 Moléculaire

[Molecular Biophysics Centre]
Address: 1A avenue de la Recherche Scientifique, 45045 Orléans Cedex
Telephone: (038) 63 10 04
Telex: CNRS ORL 760351 F
Affiliation: Centre National de la Recherche Scientifique
Director: Professor Claude Hélene
Senior staff: B. Gallot, M. Leng, J.C. Maurizot, M. Monsigny, C. Nicolau, M. Ptak, G. Saint Ruf, G. Spach, Ph. Wahl
Graduate research staff: 30
Activities: Physicochemical study of biological systems on the molecular and supramolecular scale; structure of peptides, proteins and nucleic acids; interaction of cellular components, proteins, nucleic acids and phospholipids; membrane systems; transfer of genes with liposomes.
Facilities: Equipment for molecular and structural analysis of biopolymers.
Contract work: No

Centre de Calcul de 42 Strasbourg*

[Strasbourg Computing Centre]
Address: 23 rue du Loess, BP 20 CR, 67037 Strasbourg Cedex
Affiliation: Centre National de la Recherche Scientifique
Director: Professor Georges Monsonego
Sections: Theoretical physics; quantum chemistry; solid-state physics; crystallochemistry
Activities: Theoretical studies of structures and molecular interactions; crystallography; documentation and statistics; teleinformatics in the treatment of diseases; regional studies (geography, transport, etc); national and international health surveys; use and treatment of experimental results obtained on particle accelerators and bubble chambers.

Centre de Cooperation pour les Recherches Scientifiques Relative au Tabac

43

– CORESTA
[Centre for Cooperation in Scientific Research on Tobacco]
Address: 53 quai d'Orsay, 75340 Paris Cedex 07
General Secretary: Pierre Ray
Activities: Physics, chemistry, biochemistry, pharmacology, biology, genetics, breeding, agronomy, pathology, virology, and technology standardization related to tobacco.

Centre de Dépouillement des Clichés Astronomiques

44

– CDCA
[Astronomical Plate Measuring Centre]
Address: Observatoire de Nice, Le Mont Gros, 06300 Nice
Telephone: (093) 89 04 20
Affiliation: Institut National d'Astronomie et de Géophysique
Director: A. Bijaoui
Graduate research staff: 4
Activities: Management of a computer-controlled microphotometer; reception of foreign clients; setting up an information centre; processing and dissemination of information.
Facilities: PDS bidimensional microphotometer; astrometer; spectrographs.
Publications: CDCA Bulletin.

Centre de Génétique des Virus*

45

[Virus Genetics Centre]
Address: 91190 Gif sur Yvette
Affiliation: Centre National de la Recherche Scientifique
Director: Gilbert Brun

Centre de Génétique Moléculaire*

46

[Molecular Genetics Centre]
Address: 91419 Gif sur Yvette
Affiliation: Centre National de la Recherche Scientifique
Director: Professor Pierre Slonomski

Centre de Géomorphologie*

47

[Geomorphology Centre]
Address: Université de Caen, rue des Tilleuls, 14000 Caen
Affiliation: Centre National de la Recherche Scientifique; Université de Caen
Director: Professor André Journaux

Centre de Mécanique Ondulatoire Appliquée

48

[Applied Wave Mechanics Laboratory]
Address: 23 rue du Maroc, 75940 Paris Cedex 19
Telephone: (01) 200 11 44
Affiliation: Centre National de la Recherche Scientifique
Research director: Professor Raymond Daudel
Sections: Nuclear magnetic resonance, electron paramagnetic resonance, M Maruani; molecules trapped in matrix, M Allavena; quantum photochemistry, M Evleth, M Chalvet; phonons, photons, excitons, M Kottis; molecular electronic density, M Becker; quantum pharmacology, M Peradejordi
Graduate research staff: 35
Annual expenditure: F500 000
Activities: Wave mechanics applied to molecular physics, chemical physics, chemistry, biology and pharmacology.
Contract work: No

Centre de Morphologie Expérimentale*

49

[Experimental Morphology Centre]
Address: Institut de Biologie Animale, avenue des Facultés, 33400 Talence
Affiliation: Centre National de la Recherche Scientifique
Director: Professor André Haget

Centre de Neurochimie* 50

[Neurochemistry Centre]
Address: 5 rue Blaise Pascal, 67085 Strasbourg Cedex
Affiliation: Centre National de la Recherche Scientifique
Director: Professor Guy Vincendon

Centre de Pédologie Biologique* 51

[Biological Pedology Centre]
Address: 17 rue Notre Dame des Pauvres, BP 5, 54500 Vandoeuvre-les-Nancy
Affiliation: Centre National de la Recherche Scientifique
Director: Professor Bernard Souchier

Centre de Physique Théorique* 52

[Theoretical Physics Centre]
Affiliation: Centre National de la Recherche Scientifique
Director: Professor Jean-Marie Souriau

Centre de Recherche Agronomique d'Avignon* 53

[Avignon Agronomy Research Centre]
Affiliation: Institut National de la Recherche Agronomique

FOREST ZOOLOGY STATION 54

Address: avenue Vivaldi, 84000 Avignon
Telephone: (090) 89 33 25
Telex: INRAAVI 432 870 F
Director: Daniel Schvester
Graduate research staff: 6
Annual expenditure: £10 000-50 000
Contract work: No

VEGETABLE BREEDING STATION 55

Address: BP 94, 84140 Montfavet
Telephone: (090) 88 91 45
Telex: INRAAVI 432 870 F
Director: Pierre Pecaut
Graduate research staff: 10
Annual expenditure: £501 000-2m
Activities: Efficient creation of new vegetable varieties; breeding method studies; new variety selection.
Contract work: Yes

Centre de Recherche d'Antibes 56

– CRAA
[Antibes Research Centre]
Address: 62 boulevard du Cap, BP 78, 06602 Antibes
Telephone: (093) 61 55 60
Telex: INRAANT 46 1434 F
Affiliation: Institut National de la Recherche Agronomique
Activities: Research on flower cultivation, especially the rose and violet and on secondary economic products (anemones, mimosa, etc). At a regional level the Centre collaborates with other centres on the study of Mediterranean cultivars especially the olive and citrus fruits. At a third level it studies the problem of acclimatization. At a national level it is concerned with biological control using entomophagous insects, with nematode research and with the mineral nutrition of plants.

AGRONOMY AND PLANT PHYSIOLOGY STATION 57

Director: Denise Blanc
Sections: Substrates, H. Moulinier,R. Gras; mineral nutrition, D. Blanc; growth and development, A. Champeroux; soil and pesticides, J.C. Arvieu; agriculture and environment, A. Morisot; service activity

BOTANY AND PLANT PATHOLOGY STATION 58

Director: Jacques Ponchet
Sections: Phytopathology, A. Coleno; agronomy, L. Gachon; zoology, B. Hurpin; genetics and plant breeding, J. Huet
Graduate research staff: 61
Activities: Botany - forest protection and restoration; seaside protection; reconstitution of damaged areas.
Phytopathology - diseases of ornamentals; soil biology; pathogenicity; parasitism; tissue culture studies; vegetative reproduction; virology; serology; phytogenetics; epidemiology.

FLOWERING PLANT IMPROVEMENT STATION   59

Address: Domaine de la Gaudine, Fréjus
Activities: Adaptation, heredity, stability and reproduction of new species; hybrid development.

Seed and Variety Control Study Group   60

Address: Domaine de la Baronne, Saint Laurent du Var
Activities: Variety identification, biochemical and chromatographic studies.

NEMATODE RESEARCH STATION   61

Director: M. Ritter
Sections: Biochemistry, J.B. Berge; bacteriology and fungology, J.C. Cayrol; physiogenetics and virology, A. Dalmasso; taxonomy, G. de Guiran; insect parasitology, C. Laumond; general systematics and histopathology, M. Ritter; phytophage ecology and pathology, C. Scotto La Massese
Activities: Nematode taxonomy and systematics; plant-nematode relations; phytophage ecology; interaction between nematodes and other pathogenic agents; nematode-mushroom and nematode-bacteria interaction; nematodes as insect parasites; nematicides.

THURET GARDEN AND BOTANICAL SERVICE   62

Research director: J. Ponchet
Sections: Mycology, R. Tramier, P. Bonnet; virology, J.C. Devergne, A. Poupet
Activities: Protection and reconstitution of Mediterranean forests; seashore protection; vegetation reconstitution in degraded areas.

ZOOLOGY AND BIOLOGICAL CONTROL STATION   63

Address: 37 boulevard du Cap, BP 78, 06600 Antibes
Telephone: (093) 61-55 60
Director: Pierre Jourdheuil
Graduate research staff: 16
Activities: Parasite and predator-prey interactions; modelling; ecology; genetics; insect breeding; plant protection studies.

Centre de Recherche de Bordeaux*   64

[Bordeaux Research Centre]
Affiliation: Institut National de la Recherche Agronomique

ARBORICULTURE RESEARCH STATION   65

Address: Domain de la Grande Ferrade, 33140 Pont de la Maye
Telephone: (056) 87 84 84
Research director: René Bernhard
Graduate research staff: 12
Activities: Plant breeding; physiology; cultural technics; gene bank.

Centre de Recherche de Colmar   66

[Colmar Agricultural Research Centre]
Address: 28 rue d'Herrlisheim, BP 507, 68021 Colmar Cedex
Telephone: (089) 41 11 68
Telex: INRA COL 880657
Affiliation: Institut National de la Recherche Agronomique
Administrator: P.C. Robert

PLANT PATHOLOGY STATION   67

Director: C. Putz
Graduate research staff: 4
Activities: Plant protection; sugar beet and grapevine studies.

Centre de Recherche de Dijon*   68

[Dijon Research Centre]
Affiliation: Institut National de la Recherche Agronomique

SOIL MICROBIOLOGY LABORATORY   69

Address: 17 rue Sully, BV 1540, 21034 Dijon
Telephone: (080) 65 30 12
Telex: INRADIJ 350 507 F
Director: Gérard Catroux
Section: Soil science, J. Mamy
Graduate research staff: 9
Activities: Soil science; environmental studies.

WEED SCIENCE LABORATORY   70

Address: BV 1540, 21034 Dijon Cedex
Telephone: (080) 23 72 21
Director: G. Barralis
Graduate research staff: 6
Activities: Plant protection studies; taxonomy and biosystematics; ecological genetics; weed flora evolution; germination and competition studies.

Centre de Recherche de   71
Montpellier*

[Montpellier Research Centre]
Address: 9 place Viala, 34000 Montpellier
Affiliation: Institut National de la Recherche Agronomique

CEREALS TECHNOLOGY   72
LABORATORY

Address: 9 place Viala, 34000 Montpellier
Telephone: (067) 63 18 38
Telex: INRAMON 490 818 F
Director: Jean-Claude Autran
Sections: Biochemistry and genetics of technological quality, Jean-Claude Autran; durum wheat technology, Pierre Feillet
Graduate research staff: 8
Activities: Plant breeding; cereal technology and biochemistry.

Centre de Recherche de   73
Rennes*

[Rennes Research Centre]
Address: 65 rue de Saint Brieuc, 35042 Rennes Cedex
Affiliation: Institut National de la Recherche Agronomique; École Nationale Supérieure Agronomique

CIDER RESEARCH STATION   74

Address: Domaine de la Motte, 35650 Le Rheu
Telephone: (099) 60 71 92
Telex: INRARLR 740 060 F
Head: Jean-François Drilleau
Graduate research staff: 3
Activities: Food sciences; cider apple cultivation screening; quality control; microbiology; analytical method studies; fermentation technology.

DAIRY RESEARCH LABORATORY   75

Address: 65 rue de Saint-Brieuc, 35042 Rennes Cedex
Telephone: (099) 59 00 67
Telex: 730 866 F
Director: J.-L. Maubois
Graduate research staff: 13
Activities: Food science engineering and technology; ultrafiltration; electrodialysis; microfiltration; milk transformation and valorization studies.

PIG PRODUCTION RESEARCH   76
STATION

Address: l'Hermitage, 35590 Saint-Gilles
Telephone: (099) 64 62 63
Telex: INRARES 740 423
Director: Yves Henry
Activities: Animal production; pig husbandry and nutrition; productivity, feed and economic studies.
Publications: Journées de la Recherche Porcine en France, annually.

Monogastric Breeding Department   77

Address: Centre de Tours, BP 1, Nouzilly, 37380 Monnaie
Head: Jean Claude Blum
Graduate research staff: 16

PLANT IMPROVEMENT STATION   78

Address: BP 29, 35650 Le Rheu
Telephone: (099) 60 71 92
Telex: INRALR 740060 F
Director: Jacques Morice
Graduate research staff: 17
Activities: Plant breeding and genetics; selection; heterosis; sterility and self incompatibility; disease resistance; nutritional and technological quality studies.

RURAL ECONOMICS AND   79
SOCIOLOGY STATION

Address: 65 rue de Saint-Brieuc, 35042 Rennes Cedex
Telephone: (099) 59 29 52
Telex: INRARES 730 866 F
Director: C. Broussolle
Graduate research staff: 12
Activities: Agricultural economics and policy studies; rural sociology; production economics.
Publications: Annales Agronomiques, quarterly.

Agronomy and Plant Breeding Department 80

Address: 65 rue de Saint-Brieuc, 35042 Rennes Cedex
Telephone: (099) 59 02 40
Director: Professor J. Barloy
Sections: Agronomy, Professor J. Barloy; plant breeding, Y. Herve
Graduate research staff: 6

Biometry Department 81

Address: 65 rue de Saint-Brieuc, 35000 Rennes
or: 16 rue Claude Bernard, Paris 75005
Telephone: (099) 59 02 40
Heads: J.P. Masson (Rennes); R. Tomassone (Paris)

Chemistry Laboratory 82

Address: 65 rue de Saint-Brieuc, 35000 Rennes
Telephone: (099) 59 02 40
Director: Dr Philippe Lemarchal
Graduate research staff: 3
Activities: Animal metabolism studies - liver and adipose tissue unsaturated fatty acid metabolism, hormonal and nutritional regulation.
Publications: Annual report.

Dairy Cows Feeding and Management Research Laboratory 83

Address: l'Hermitage, 35590 Saint-Gilles
Telephone: (099) 64 62 63
Telex: 740 423
Research director: M. Journet
Graduate research staff: 8
Activities: Livestock husbandry and nutrition.

Fish Physiology Laboratory 84

Address: Campus de Beaulieu, 35042 Rennes Cedex
Telephone: (099) 63 18 88
Director: B. Jalabert
Graduate research staff: 15
Activities: Physiology, genetics and ethology of fish; natural population engineering; aquaculture and species domestication.

ZOOTECHNICAL RESEARCH STATION 85

Address: 65 rue de Saint-Brieuc, 35042 Rennes Cedex
Telephone: (099) 59 04 68
Telex: INRARES 730 866 F
Director: C.M. Mathieu
Research head: R. Toullec
Graduate research staff: 6
Activities: Livestock husbandry and nutrition.

Centre de Recherche de Toulouse* 86

[Toulouse Research Centre]
Address: chemin de Borderouge, BP 12, Auzeville, 31320 Castanet-Tolosan
Affiliation: Institut National de la Recherche Agronomique

ANIMAL GENETICS IMPROVEMENT STATION 87

Address: chemin de Borderouge, BP 12, Auzeville, 31320 Castanet-Tolosan
Telephone: (061) 73 81 75
Telex: INRATSE 520009 F
Chief scientist: G. Matheron
Section: F. Grosclaude
Graduate research staff: 7
Activities: Animal production; rabbits: genetic improvement and variability; increase of meat supply in poor countries.
Publications: Annual report.

CYTOGENETICS AND WILDLIFE LABORATORY 88

Director: François Spitz
Graduate research staff: 5
Activities: Plant rodent protection studies; game animal ecoethology; wild animal production management; animals in forest ecology.

FOOD ADDITIVES RESEARCH LABORATORY 89

Address: 180 chemin de Tournefeuille, 31300 Toulouse
Telephone: (061) 49 17 43
Director: Georges Bories
Graduate research staff: 6
Activities: Animal production; human consumer safety of animal products; feed contaminants, feed additives and veterinary drug studies.

OENOLOGY AND PLANT TECHNOLOGY STATION 90

Address: 11 boulevard du Général de Gaulle, BP 72, 11104 Narbonne Cedex
Telephone: (068) 32 04 86
Director: C. Jouret
Graduate research staff: 15
Activities: Research in food science.
Publications: Sciences des Aliments, triannual.

PÊCHE ROUGE EXPERIMENTAL FARM 91

Address: 11430 Gruissan, Aude
Telephone: (068) 31 81 44
Director: P. Bénard
Graduate research staff: 3
Activities: Food science studies; genetics, oenology.
Publications: Sciences des Aliments, triannual.

PLANT PRODUCTS TECHNOLOGY 92
LABORATORY

Address: chemin de Borderouge, BP 12, Auzeville, 31320 Castanet-Tolosan
Telephone: (061) 73 81 75
Telex: INRATSE 520009 F
Director: C. Jouret
Graduate research staff: 5
Activities: Food science studies.
Publications: Sciences des Aliments, triannual.

Centre de Recherche 93
Mécanique Appliquée au
Textile

– CERMAT
[Applied Mechanics Research Centre for Textiles]
Address: 11a rue Alfred Werner, 68093 Mulhouse Cedex
Telephone: (089) 43 20 62
Director: Michel Averous
Graduate research staff: 6
Annual expenditure: F800 000
Activities: Automation of textile machinery; improvement of materials; corrosion; study of the textile industry in order to improve working conditions: noise, safety, pollution, etc. Technical assistance in metallurgy tests and measurements of mechanical properties; analysis of steel structures.
Contract work: Yes
Publications: Information bulletin for members.

Centre de Recherche 94
Merrell International

[Merrell International Research Centre]
Address: 16 rue d'Ankara, 67084 Strasbourg Cedex
Telephone: (088) 61 48 89
Telex: MERRELL 890252F
Affiliation: Dow Chemical Company
Director of research planning and coordination: Dr David John Wilkins
Deputy director: Dr Jan Koch-Weser

Sections: Chemistry, Philippe Bey; biochemistry, Michel Jung; pharmacology, John Fozard; clinical research, Paul Schechter
Graduate research staff: 55
Annual expenditure: over £2m
Activities: The aim of the Centre is to discover new drugs, synthetic chemical entities or natural products, useful in the treatment or prevention of pathological disorders. Programmes are based upon a multidisciplinary fundamental research approach rather than the traditional synthesis and screening of vast numbers of analogues of known drugs.
Contract work: No

Centre de Recherche sur la 95
Synthèse et la Chimie des
Minéraux -

– CRSCM
[Mineral Synthesis and Chemistry Research Centre]
Address: 1A rue de la Férollerie, 45045 Orléans Cedex
Telephone: (038) 63 21 42
Telex: CNRS ORL 760351 F
Affiliation: Centre National de la Recherche Scientifique
Director: Z. Johan
Sections: Exchange equilibria, thermodynamics, J. Roux; crystal chemistry, J.L. Robert; sulphide minerals, C. Maurel; metallogenic processes, Z. Johan
Graduate research staff: 13
Annual expenditure: £51 000-500 000
Activities: CRSCM's research is intended to obtain thermodynamic parameters of coexisting minerals and their domains of stability and an understanding of the fundamentals of metal transport and deposition. The practical application of this research will be in the development of metal prospecting methods, mineral deposit evaluation, and the discovery of technologically interesting mineral properties.
Facilities: Scanning electron microscope; Mössbauer spectrometry; externally-heated pressure vessels for hydrothermal synthesis to 800°C; internally-heated pressure vessels to 1000°C; piston-cylinder system for mineral synthesis at high pressure.
Contract work: Yes
Publications: Liste des Publications.

Centre de Recherche sur les Mécanismes de la Croissance Cristalline   96

– CRMC2
[Crystal Growth Mechanisms Laboratory]
Address: Campus Luminy, Case 913, 13288 Marseille Cedex 2
Telephone: (091) 41 01 52
Affiliation: Centre National de la Recherche Scientifique; Université d'Aix-Marseille III
Director: Professor R. Kern
Sections: Epitaxy, R. Kern; interfaces, B. Mutaftschiev; field emission, M. Drechsler; solution growth, R. Boistelle; proteins, M. Frey
Graduate research staff: 50
Annual expenditure: F130 000
Activities: Crystal growth mechanisms are studied in the vapour phase, in solution either at normal pressure or hydrothermal melt growth. Surface problems, especially in connection with epitaxy are also considered.
Contract work: Yes
Publications: Rapport d'Activité Scientifique.

Centre de Recherche sur les Très Basses Températures*   97

[Very Low Temperature Research Centre]
Address: BP 166, 38042 Grenoble Cedex
Affiliation: Centre National de la Recherche Scientifique
Director: Robert Tournier

Centre de Recherches Agro-Alimentaires de Nantes   98

[Nantes Food Science and Industry Research Centre]
Address: chemin de la Géraudière, 44072 Nantes Cedex
Telephone: (040) 76 23 64
Telex: INRANTE 710074 F
Affiliation: Institut National de la Recherche Agronomique
Director: André Guilbot
Graduate research staff: 41
Annual expenditure: £501 000-2m
Contract work: Yes

ANIMAL FEED TECHNOLOGY LABORATORY   99
Head: J. Delort-Laval

ANIMAL FOOD PRODUCTS LABORATORY   100
Head: G. Goutefongea

FOOD BIOCHEMISTRY LABORATORY   101
Head: B. Godon

FOOD BIOPHYSICS LABORATORY   102
Head: J.L. Multon

FOOD INDUSTRY ECONOMICS LABORATORY   103
Head: F. Colson

HUMIDIFYING PROCESSES IN THE FOOD INDUSTRY LABORATORY   104
Head: A. Davin

Centre de Recherches Agronomiques du Sud-Est*   105

[South-East Agricultural Research Centre]
Address: Avignon
Affiliation: Institut National de la Recherche Agronomique

FOREST ZOOLOGY RESEARCH STATION*   106
Address: avenue A. Vivaldi, 84000 Avignon

MAURES FOREST EXPERIMENTAL STATION*   107
Address: Le Ruscas, 83230 Bormes-les-Mimosas

MEDITERRANEAN SILVICULTURE RESEARCH STATION 108

Address: avenue A. Vivaldi, 84000 Avignon
Telephone: (090) 89 33 25
Telex: 432870 F
Director: Pierre Delabraze
Sections: Protection; production
Graduate research staff: 2
Annual expenditure: £10 000-50 000
Activities: Forest fire protection - herbicide, pasture and mechanical studies.
Ecology - forest physiology, retimbering, tree adaptation, water utilization studies.
Production and management - natural regeneration.
Contract work: No

Centre de Recherches Agronomiques du Sud-Ouest* 109

[South West Agricultural Research Centre]
Address: Domaine de l'Hermitage Pierroton, 33610 Cestas Principal
Affiliation: Institut National de la Recherche Agronomique
Sections: Forest tree improvement; silviculture and pine ecology

Centre de Recherches Archéologiques 110

– CRA
[Archaeological Research Centre]
Address: Sophia Antipolis, 06565 Valbonne Cedex
Telephone: (093) 33 30 30
Affiliation: Centre National de la Recherche Scientifique
Director: Roland Martin
Assistant director: Bruno Helly
Sections: Osteology, J. Desse; palynology, M. Bui-Thi-Mai, M. Girard; petrology, mineralogy, M. Ricq; thermoluminescence, J.C. Ricq
Graduate research staff: 37
Annual expenditure: F2m
Activities: Experimentation on archaeological methods; scientific analysis of artefacts using physical, chemical and biological methods, osteology, palynology, mineralogy, ceramology, sedimentology and thermoluminescence.
The centre was founded in 1970 as the central laboratory for Unités de Recherches Archéologiques (URA).
Publications: Publications du Centre.

Centre de Recherches de Biochimie et de Génétique Cellulaires* 111

[Cellular Biochemistry and Genetics Research Centre]
Address: 118 route de Narbonne, 31077 Toulouse Cedex
Affiliation: Centre National de la Recherche Scientifique
Director: Professor Jean-Pierre Zalta

Centre de Recherches de Biochimie Macromoléculaire* 112

[Macromolecular Biochemistry Research Centre]
Address: route de Mende, BP 5051, 34033 Montpellier Cedex
Affiliation: Centre National de la Recherche Scientifique
Director: Professor Nguyen Van Thoai

Centre de Recherches de Microcalorimétrie et de Thérmochimie* 113

[Microcalorimetry and Thermochemistry Research Centre]
Address: 24 rue du 141e RIA, 13003 Marseille
Affiliation: Centre National de la Recherche Scientifique
Director: Jean-Claude Mathieu
Deputy Director: Jean Rouquerol

Centre de Recherches de Pont à Mousson 114

[Pont à Mousson Research Centre]
Address: BP 28, 54700 Pont à Mousson
Telephone: (08) 381 60 29
Telex: 961 330F
Affiliation: Groupe Saint Gobain - Pont à Mousson
Research director: Bernard Diot
Sections: Metallurgy, M Bellocci; pipelines, M Langenfeld; pipe fittings, M Thauvin; physics, M de Crevoisier; chemistry, M Miazga
Activities: Research and development in the following areas: improvement of quality for steels and cast-irons;

destructive and non-destructive tests; new products for pipelines and fittings; new methods in foundry technology; chemical analysis of materials and soils; study of building materials; problems of corrosion and water pollution.
Contract work: No

Centre de Recherches en Physique de l'Environnement Terrestre et Planétaire 115

– CRPE
[Earth and Planetary Environmental Physics Research Centre]
Address: avenue de la Recherche Scientifique, 45045 Orléans Cedex
or: 38-40 rue du Général-Leclerc, 92131 Issy-les-Moulineaux
Telephone: Orléans, (038) 63 00 86; Issy-les-que-Moulineaux, 645 44 44
Affiliation: Institut National d'Astronomie et de Géophysique; Centre National de la Recherche Scientifique; Centre National d'Études des Télécommunications
Director: James Hieblot
Graduate research staff: 64
Activities: Physical and chemical analysis of the factors which control the evolution of neutral and ionized planetary atmospheres. Research is mainly carried out into the high atmosphere, the ionosphere and the magnetosphere, using theoretical studies and modelling in the laboratory and geophysical observations using balloons, rockets, and satellites. Research is undertaken in cooperation with other organizations, in particular: European Space Research Organization using the European satellite GEOS; Laboratoire d'Astronomie, Meudon, using the ESRO-NASA satellite Mère-Fille; Centre d'Études Spatiales des Rayonnements, Toulouse, using the franco-soviet satellite ARCADE 3; and Max-Planck-Institut, Munich, using rocket probes (PORC'EPIC).

Centre de Recherches Forestières d'Orléans* 116

[Orleans Forestry Research Centre]
Address: Ardon, 45160 Olivet
Affiliation: Institut National de la Recherche Agronomique

FOREST AND ENVIRONMENT RESEARCH STATION* 117

FOREST TREE IMPROVEMENT RESEARCH STATION* 118

FOREST ZOOLOGY AND BIOGENETICS RESEARCH STATION* 119

Centre de Recherches Géophysiques 120

– CRG
[Geophysical Research Centre]
Address: CRG de Garchy, 58150 Pouilly sur Loire
Telephone: (086) 69 10 23
Affiliation: Centre National de la Recherche Scientifique; Institut National d'Astronomie et de Géophysique
Research director: Dr Jean-Paul Mosnier
Sections: Deep magnetic sounding, J. Mosnier; magnetotellurics, A. Dupis; archaeometry, A. Hesse
Graduate research staff: 6
Annual expenditure: £501 000-2m
Activities: Geophysical studies of deep or shallow structure by electric or electromagnetic methods.
Contract work: No

Centre de Recherches Hydrobiologiques* 121

[Hydrobiological Research Centre]
Affiliation: Institut National de la Recherche Agronomique

FISH ECOLOGY AND MANAGEMENT LABORATORY 122

Address: Saint Pée sur Nivelle, BP 3, 64310 Ascain
Telephone: (059) 54 10 54
Director: P. Davaine
Sections: Ecology, P. Davaine; ethology, M. Heland; genetics, J.M. Blanc
Graduate research staff: 7
Activities: Fresh-water fisheries studies; population and production assessment; production enhancement; management and efficiency; fish rearing for stocking natural environments; river rehabilitation.

FISH NUTRITION AND CULTURE LABORATORY   123

Address: Saint Pée sur Nivelle, BP 3, 64310 Ascain
Telephone: (059) 54 10 54
Director: Pierre Luquet
Graduate research staff: 10
Activities: Fish nutrition and husbandry; fresh-water fisheries studies.

MICROORGANISMS LABORATORY   124

Director: René Lesel
Graduate research staff: 1
Activities: Fish microbial ecology.

Centre de Recherches   125
Nucléaires de Strasbourg
Cronenbourg

[Strasbourg-Cronenbourg Nuclear Research Centre]
Address: BP 20 CR, 67037 Strasbourg Cedex
Affiliation: Centre National de la Recherche Scientifique
Director: Professor André Gallmann
Deputy Directors: J.-P. Coffin, M. Croissiaux, Professor R. Voltz
Divisions: Nuclear physics, J.-P. Coffin; High energy, M. Croissaux; Radiation chemistry and physics, R. Voltz
Activities: Nuclear physics - experimental and theoretical studies of the atom; the division collaborates regularly with CERN and the SATURNE National Laboratory in Saclay.
High energy - research is concentrated on particle physics and there are groups concerned with bubble and hydrogen chambers; heavy liquid chambers; counters; and high-energy theoretical physics.
Radiation physics and chemistry - research is mainly on different aspects of radiation- matter interaction and on materials science; there are groups concerned with radiation physics and nuclear electronics; nuclear chemistry; physics and the use of semiconductors.

Centre de Recherches   126
Pétrographiques et
Géochimiques

– CRPG
[Petrographic and Geochemical Research Centre]
Address: CO 1, 54500 Vandoeuvre les Nancy

Telephone: (08) 351 22 13
Telex: 960 431 F ADNANCY
Affiliation: Centre National de la Recherche Scientifique
Research director: S.M.F. Sheppard
Sections: Structures and transfers in the deep zones, P. leFort; balance between fluids and minerals, B. Poty, A. Weisbrod; isotopic geochemistry and geochronology, S. Sheppard, F. Albarede, J. Sonet; analysis of rocks and minerals, K. Govindaraju, ,M.Vernet, F. Lhote.
Graduate research staff: 34
Annual expenditure: £150 000
Activities: Petrography and geochemistry in the deep zones - the phenomena of high temperature and high pressure in the depths of the Earth's crust, their experimental reproduction, their products, the activity and circulation of fluid phases, the movements of matter, the formation of metallic concentrations, the measurement of age by radiometry; geochemical analysis - the quantities of principal and rare elements in materials, isotopic analysis, high performance quantitative analysis.
Publications: Geostandards Newsletter.

Centre de Recherches sur   127
la Chimie de la
Combustion et des Hautes
Températures*

[Combustion Chemistry and High Temperatures Research Centre]
Address: 1D avenue de la Recherche Scientifique, 45045 Orléans Cedex
Affiliation: Centre National de la Recherche Scientifique
Director: Ralph Delbourgo

Centre de Recherches sur   128
la Nutrition*

[Nutrition Research Centre]
Address: 9 rue Jules Hetzel, 92190 Meudon
Affiliation: Centre National de la Recherche Scientifique
Director: Alain Rerat
Deputy Director: Jean Peret

Centre de Recherches sur la Physico-Chimie des Surfaces Solides 129

[Physical Chemistry of Solid Surfaces Research Centre]
Address: 24 avenue du Président Kennedy, 68200 Mulhouse
Telephone: (089) 42 01 55
Affiliation: Centre National de la Recherche Scientifique
Director: Professor J.B. Donnet
Sections: Formation of solids, J. Lahaye; physical chemistry of silicates on large surfaces, B. Siffert; physical chemistry of carbons, J.B. Donnet, J. Lahaye; chemical modifications of surfaces, E. Papirer, J.B. Donnet; copolymers and polymerization through the opening of cycles, G. Riess; adhesion and cracking under stress, J. Schultz; solid lubrification, M. Brendle; valorization of recovered polymers, P. Goursot.
Graduate research staff: 50
Annual expenditure: £501 000-2
Activities: Research into: pigmentary and film solids; carbon black, fibres and composites, coal and coke; interactions between clays and organic compounds, catalytic properties of clays, dispersed systems and emulsions; chemical analysis of modified surfaces, grafting of molecules and macromolecules, use of modified solid surfaces; alternate copolymers, sequences and grafts; characterization of the surface of solids, adhesion phenomena, cracking of polymers under pressure in a liquid medium; gelification of liquids through powdery solids.
Contract work: Yes

Centre de Recherches sur la Physique des Hautes Températures* 130

[High Temperature Physics Research Centre]
Address: 1C avenue de la Recherche Scientifique, 45045 Orléans Cedex
Affiliation: Centre National de la Recherche Scientifique
Director: François Cabannes

Centre de Recherches sur les Macromolécules* 131

[Macromolecules Research Centre]
Address: 6 rue Boussingault, 67083 Strasbourg Cedex
Telephone: (088) 61 19 19
Affiliation: Centre National de la Recherche Scientifique; Université de Strasbourg I
Director: Professor Constant Wippler
Deputy Director: Jean-Pierre Roth
Sections:
Polymers in solution and in solid state, Professor H. Benoit
Macromolecular chemistry, P. Remp (Director), É. Franta, J. Herz (Heads), Professor J. Brossas
Synthesis and characterization of copolymer chains, Y. Gallot (Head)
Solid state, A. Kovacs (Director)
Radiation chemistry, J. Marchal (Director)
Mesomorphic state, A. Skoulios (Director)
Poyelectrolytes and ionic membranes, R. Varoqui (Head)
Molecular spectroscopy, Professor G. Weill
Rapid chemistry kinetics, R. Zana (Head)

Centre de Recherches sur les Macromolécules Végétales* 132

[Plant Macromolecules Research Centre]
Address: BP 53, 38041 Grenoble Cedex
Affiliation: Centre National de la Recherche Scientifique
Director: Professor Didier Gagnaire

Centre de Recherches sur les Solides à Organisation Cristalline Imparfaite 133

[Solids of Imperfect Crystal Formation Research Centre]
Address: 1B rue de la Férollerie, 45045 Orléans Cedex
Telephone: (038) 63 39 37
Affiliation: Centre National de la Recherche Scientifique
Director: Professor J.J. Fripiat
Senior staff: L. Gatineau, J. Conard, M.I. Cruz, J.J. Fripiat
Graduate research staff: 20
Annual expenditure: Flm
Activities: Research into relationships between struc-

ture defects and physical and surface properties of bidimensional lattices.
Contract work: No

Centre de Recherches Zootechniques et Vétérinaires de Theix 134

[Theix Animal Husbandry and Veterinary Research Centre]
Address: Theix, 63110 Beaumont
Telephone: (073) 92 42 63
Telex: Inratex 990 227 F
Affiliation: Institut National de la Recherche Agronomique
Activities: Research on feeding and management of cattle and sheep at a national level, and on the quality and conservation of their products. The Centre has twelve stations or laboratories.
Facilities: Four experimental farms comprising a total of 720 ha capable of supporting 1 000 head of cattle, 900 sheep and 50 horses.
Publications: Technical bulletin, three-monthly.

BREEDING ECONOMY LABORATORY 135

Director G. Liénard
Activities: Meat production and breeding economy studies.

ECOPATHOLOGY LABORATORY 136

Director: M. Brochart
Activities: Nutrition and fertility; immunity studies.

ENERGY METABOLISM RESEARCH LABORATORY 137

Director: M. Vermorel
Graduate research staff: 4
Activities: Farm animal nutrition; calf and lamb bioclimatology.

MEAT PRODUCTION LABORATORY 138

Director: C. Béranger
Activities: Quality studies; feed and butchering research.

MEAT RESEARCH STATION 139

Director: R. Boccard
Activities: Quality control of meat and meat products; zootechnical and biological influences; transport; refrigeration; muscle biology.

METABOLIC DISEASES LABORATORY 140

Director: P. Lavor
Activities: Endocrinology; nutrition; physiopathology; foetal development studies.

MICROBIOLOGY LABORATORY 141

Director: Ph. Gouet
Activities: Intestinal microflora; meat product microbiology.

NITROGEN METABOLISM RESEARCH LABORATORY 142

Director: R. Pion
Activities: Amino acid and protein studies; growth research.

NUTRITION LABORATORY 143

Director: C. Demarquilly
Activities: Feed studies, alimentary value.

NUTRITIONAL DISEASES LABORATORY 144

Director: M. Lamand
Activities: Nutrition and immunity studies; geography; analytic diagnosis studies.

RUMINANT BREEDING STATION 145

Director: R. Jarrige
Sections: Digestion, P. Thivend; ovine production, M. Thériez
Activities: Digestion - digestive utilization of foods; ovine production - productivity studies.

Milk Production Laboratory 146

Director: M. Journet
Activities: Research is focused on the feeding of dairy cows and its effect on the production and composition of milk.

Centre de Sédimentologie et de Géochimie de la Surface* 147

[Sedimentology and Surface Geochemistry Centre]
Address: 1 rue Blessig, 67084 Strasbourg Cedex
Affiliation: Centre National de la Recherche Scientifique
Director: Professor Georges Millot
Deputy Director: Professor Jacques Lucas
Activities: The Centre works in close collaboration with the Laboratory of Geology and Palaeontology and the Laboratory of Mineralogy, Petrography and Chemistry of Strasbourg University II. There are 3 laboratories and 12 research teams.
The principal themes of research are: structural geology and tectonic analysis; palaeoecology and palaeontology; geochemistry of soil alterations, palaeoalterations and palaeosoils; sedimentation and phosphate sediments on the continental margins; meteoric and sedimentary mineral layers; palynology and palaeoclimatology; isotopic geochronology and geochemistry; thermodynamic geochemistry; oceanology; petrography; mineralogy; crystallography.

Centre de Sélection et d'Élevage des Animaux de Laboratoire* 148

[Laboratory Animals Selection and Breeding Centre]
Address: 3B rue de la Férollerie, 45045 Orléans Cedex
Affiliation: Centre National de la Recherche Scientifique
Director: Michel Sabourdy

Centre de Spectrométrie Nucléaire et de Spectrométrie de Masse* 149

[Nuclear and Mass Spectrometry Centre]
Address: Bâtiment 104 CNRS Campus, 91406 Orsay
Affiliation: Centre National de la Recherche Scientifique
Director: Robert Klapisch

Centre des Faibles Radioactivités 150

– CFR
[Low Radioactivity Research Centre]
Address: Groupe des laboratoires du CNRS, 91190 Gif sur Yvette
Telephone: 907 78 28
Affiliation: Institut National d'Astronomie et de Géophysique; Centre National de la Recherche Scientifique; Commissariat à l'Énergie Atomique
Director: Jacques Labeyrie
Graduate research staff: 40
Activities: Research is centred on the application of nuclear methods to earth sciences (geology, geochemistry, geophysics, and oceanography), in particular: study of palaeoclimates, by means of foraminifera, diatoma, and marine levels; marine geochemistry; study of the interaction between oceanic atmosphere and atmospheric circulation; planetology.

Centre Expérimental de Recherches et d'Études du Bâtiment et des Travaux Publics 151

– CEBTP
[Building and Public Works Research Centre]
Address: 12 rue Brancion, 75737 Paris Cedex 15
Telephone: (01) 539 22 33
Telex: 250071 F
Research director: M Absi
Sections: Materials studies, M. Mamillan; large works and sites, J. Festa; secondary works and equipment, P. Dauphin; soil mechanics and roadways, A. Davis; instrumentation and measurement, C. Bonvalet; structures, M. Kavyrchine; interdisciplinary research, J. Paquet
Graduate research staff: 75
Annual expenditure: F30m
Activities: Research in civil engineering for the building industry and the National Federations of Building and Public Works, as well as for the nuclear and space industries.
The organization also has laboratories in Amiens, Bastia, Béziers, Besançon, Bordeaux, Caen, Clermont-Ferrand, Dijon, Grenoble, Lille, Limoges, Lyon, Marseilles, Montpellier, Nancy, Nantes, Nice, Niort, Orléans, Reims, Rennes, Rouen, Strasbourg, Toulouse and Tours.
Contract work: Yes

RESEARCH CENTRE   152

Address: Domaine de Saint-Paul, 78470 Saint-Rémy-les-Chevreuse
Telephone: 052 92 00
Facilities: Eight centres for applied research are located at this site, including: structures investigation centres where large testing rigs (such as a loading tunnel 42 m long, and a section bay approximately 7x7 m) make it possible to carry out tests on full-scale structural components; testing centre for external vertical surfaces, windows and shutters; noise and vibration laboratory, where sound can be measured along horizontal and vertical planes; soil mechanics experimental stations, two concerned with large-scale research on the bearing capacity of piles together with active and passive earth pressure and anchorage problems, and two devoted to pavement design and small-scale studies on soil; vertical laboratory for fluids, with 50 m tower building, used for investigation into hydraulic, thermal and acoustic problems; electronics laboratory, devoted to the design of new measuring devices and research methods making use of electric, electromagnetic and electronics techniques; experimental station for research on heat curing of concrete; equipment study centre for heating, ventilation and air-conditioning research.

Centre Français de   153
Recherches sur la
Gravitation

– CFRG
[French Gravitation Research Centre]
Address: 28 rue Saint-Suffren, 13006 Marseille
Telephone: (091) 37 64 30
Secretary-General: Charles Nahon
Activities: CFRG promotes, disseminates, develops and undertakes the study and research of the phenomena of gravitation.

Centre Géologique et   154
Géophysique de
Montpellier

[Montpellier Geology and Geophysics Centre]
Address: Université de Montpellier II, place Eugène-Bataillon, 34060 Montpellier Cedex
Telephone: (067) 63 49 83
Affiliation: Institut National d'Astronomie et de Géophysique; Centre National de la Recherche Scientifique
Director: Professor Pierre Louis
Graduate research staff: 17

Activities: Geological, geophysical and geochemical research into the arid zones of the earth. Work is based on Africa with a concentrated study of the pan-African chain, which makes a good subject for the study of plate tectonics. Comparative work in Brazil is planned.

Centre Inter-Régional de   155
Calcul Électronique*

[Interregional Electronic Computing Centre]
Address: Bâtiment 506 CNRS III Campus, 91405 Orsay
Affiliation: Centre National de la Recherche Scientifique
Director: Jeanine Connes
Deputy Director: Philippe Salzedo

Centre Interprofessionnel   156
Technique d'Études de la
Pollution Atmospherique

– CITEPA
[Atmospheric Pollution Technical Research Centre]
Address: 28 rue de la Source, 75016 Paris
Chairman: Jean-Paul Détrie
Director: Rémy Bouscaren
Activities: Research into all aspects of industrial and home atmospheric pollution, including dispersion and techniques of prevention.

Centre National d'Études   157
des Télécommunications*

– CNET
[National Centre for Telecommunication Studies]
Address: route de Tragastie, 22 Lannien Bretagne
Affiliation: Direction Générale de Télégraphe
Activities: CNET which has been conducting research into telecommunications since 1944 has a staff of 3 700. Its two main centres are at Issy-les-Moulineaux and Lannien.

Centre National d'Études Spatiales   158

– CNES
[National Centre for Space Studies]
Address: 129 rue de l'Université, 75007 Paris
Telephone: (01) 555 91 21
Telex: 204 627 CNESPAR
Chairman: Hubert Curien
Director General: Yves Sillard
Adjoint Director General, Research and Development: Pierre Morel
Director, Programmes and Planning: Jean Marie Luton
Sections: Applications, Gerard Brachet; European programmes, M. Lefevre; planning, Ph. Guerit; research and development, Michel Guionnet
Activities: CNES has been responsible for the conception and management of French space programmes since 1962. Today, CNES has at its disposal experienced teams of highly qualified engineers, technicians and scientists as well as the facilities necessary for the implementation of full-scale programmes: launching bases, tracking, telemetry and command network, technical centres, testing, control and computing facilities. Special areas of research interests include: study of remote sensing, biology, geodesy, astronomy, development of meteorological systems and telecommunications systems, and study of satellites and launchers, especially the heavy European launcher ARIANE.
Contract work: No
Publications: Annual report.

GUIANA SPACE CENTRE   159

Address: BP 6, 97310 Kourou, French Guiana
Director: Albert Vienne
Technical Assistant Director: P. Bescond

LAUNCHING DEPARTMENT   160

Address: boulevard de France, 91000 Erry
Director: Frederic d'Allest
Assistant Director: R. Deschamps

TOULOUSE SPACE CENTRE   161

Address: 18 avenue Edouard-Belin, 31000 Toulouse
Director: Jean-Claude Husson
Assistant Director: B. Estadieu
Sections: Projects and technical research, A. Remondière; operations and technical resources, R. Simon de Kergunic; industrial projects, J.-J. Sussel

Centre National de Coordination des Études et Recherches sur la Nutrition et l'Alimentation*   162

[National Centre for Coordination of Study and Research on Nutrition and Food]
Address: 72 rue des Sèvres, 75007 Paris
Affiliation: Centre National de la Recherche Scientifique
Director: André François

Centre National de la Recherche Scientifique   163

– CNRS
[National Scientific Research Centre]
Address: 15 quai Anatole-France, 75700 Paris
Telephone: (01) 555 92 25
Telex: 260 034
Affiliation: Ministère des Universités
President: Charles Thibault
Director-General: vacant
Scientific Directors: Nuclear and particle physics, Jean Yoccoz; mathematics and fundamental physics, Jacques Winter; physical sciences for engineers, Yves-André Rocher: chemistry, Raymond Maurel; earth and space sciences, Michel Petit; life sciences, Roger Monier; social sciences, Edmond Lisle; humanities, Jean Pouilloux; interdisciplinary research programme on the development of solar energy, Michel Rodot; external relations and information, Vladimir Mercouroff.
Graduate research staff: 8700 (in all CNRS establishments)
Annual expenditure: F3.1 billion
Activities: The main objects of the Centre are: to promote and coordinate scientific research; to make grants-in-aid to scientific establishments to enable them to carry out scientific research; and to set up and maintain laboratories for scientific research. The National Committee for Scientific Research, which is composed of forty-one sections each with twenty-six members, is the policy-forming body of the Centre.
Contract work: No

COMITÉ NATIONAL DE LA RECHERCHE SCIENTIFIQUE   164

[National Committee for Scientific Research]
Chairman: vacant
Sections: Mathematics and mathematical models; informatics, automation, systems analysis and treatment of signals; electronics, electrotechnics and optics;

mechanics and energetics; theoretical physics, nuclear and corpuscular physics; astronomy and planetary environment; atomic and molecular physics; molecular structure and dynamics and coordination chemistry; physico-chemistry of interfaces and interactions; chemistry and physico-chemistry of solid materials; solid-state physics - physics of solids; solid-state physics - crystallography; geophysics, internal geology and mineralogy; sedimentary geology and palaeontology; oceanography and atmospheric physics; organic synthesis and reactivity; biological organic chemistry and therapeutic chemistry; physico-chemistry of polymers and biological molecules; biochemistry; cellular biology; biology of cellular interactions; experimental and comparative pathology; experimental therapeutics and pharmacology; physiology; psychophysiology and psychology; plant biology and physiology; animal biology; ecology; anthropology, prehistory and ethnology; sociology and demography; geography, economic sciences, legal and political sciences; general linguistics and foreign languages and literature; French linguistics and literature and musicology; classical languages and civilizations; oriental languages and civilizations; national antiquities and mediaeval history; modern and contemporary history; philosophy, epistemology and history of sciences.

See separate entries for:
National Institutes:
Institut National de Physique Nucléaire et de Physique des Particules
Institut National d'Astronomie et de Géophysique
Laboratories and Scientific Departments:
I. Mathematics and Fundamental Physics -
Centre de Physique Théorique
Centre de Recherche sur les Mécanismes de la Croissance Cristalline
Centre de Recherches sur les Solides à Organisation Cristalline Imparfaite
Centre de Recherche sur les très Basses Températures
Laboratoire Aimé Cotton
Laboratoire d'Optique Électronique
Laboratoire d'Optique Quantique
Laboratoire de Cristallographie
Laboratoire de Magnétisme de Bellevue
Laboratoire de Photophysique Moléculaire
Laboratoire de Physique des Matériaux
Laboratoire de Physique du Solide
Laboratoire de Physique Théorique
Laboratoire des Intéractions Moleculaires et des Hautes Pressions
Laboratoire des Proprietés Mécaniques et Thermodynamiques des Matériaux
Laboratoire Léon Brillouin
Laboratoire Louis Néel
Laboratoire pour l'Utilisation du Rayonnement Électromagnétique
Service de Diffusion de la Technologie des Matériaux
Service National des Champs Intenses

II. Nuclear and Particle Physics -
Centre de Recherches Nucléaires de Strasbourg Cronenbourg
Centre de Spectrométrie Nucléaire et de Spectrométrie de Masse
Laboratoire d'Annecy-le-Vieux de Physique des Particles
III. Physical Sciences for Engineers -
Centre de Recherches sur la Physique des Hautes Températures
Laboratoire d'Aérothermique
Laboratoire d'Automatique et d'Analyse des Systèmes
Laboratoire d'Électrostatique
Laboratoire d'Energétique Solaire
Laboratoire d'Informatique pour la Mécanique et les Sciences de l'Ingénieur
Laboratoire de Mécanique et d'Acoustique
Laboratoire de Physique et Métrologie des Oscillateurs
Laboratoire des Signaux et Systèmes
Laboratoire des Verres
Computer Centres:
Centre de Calcul de Strasbourg
Centre Interrégional de Calcul Électronique
Centre Interuniversitaire de Calcul
IV. Chemistry -
Centre d'Études de Chimie Métallurgique
Centre d'Études et de Recherches de Chimie Organique Appliquée
Centre de Biophysique Moléculaire
Centre de Mécanique Ondulatoire Appliquée
Centre de Recherches de Microcalorimétrie et de Thermochimie
Centre de Recherches sur la Chimie de la Combustion et des Hautes Températures
Centre de Recherches sur la Physicochimie des Surfaces Solides
Centre de Recherches sur les Macromolécules
Centre de Recherches sur les Macromolécules Végétales
Groupe d'Étude et de Synthèse des Microstructures
Institut de Recherches sur la Catalyse
Laboratoire d'Analyse par Activation 'Pierre Sue'
Laboratoire de Chimie de Coordination
Laboratoire de Chimie du Solides
Laboratoire de Chimie Macromoléculaire Appliquée
Laboratoire de Recherches sur les Interactions Gaz-Solides 'Maurice Letort'
Laboratoire des Sciences du Génie Chimique
Laboratoire de Spectrochimie Infrarouge et Raman
Laboratoire des Ultra-Refractaires
Service Centrale d'Analyse
Service de Diffusion de la Technologie des Matériaux
V. Earth and Space Sciences -
Centre Armoricain d'Étude Structurale des Socles
Centre d'Études d'Océanographie et de Biologie Marine
Centre de Pédologie Biologique
Centre de Recherches en Physique de l'Environment Terrestre et Planétaire
Centre de Recherches Géophysiques

Centre de Recherches Pétrographiques et Géochimiques
Centre de Recherches sur la Synthèse et la Chimie des Minéraux
Centre de Sédimentologie et de Géochimie de la Surface
Centre des Faibles Radioactivités
Centre Géologique et Géophysique de Montpellier
Institut d'Astrophysique de Paris
Laboratoire d'Astronomie Spatiale
Laboratoire de Géologie du Quaternaire
Laboratoire de Glaciologie et de Géophysique de l'Environnement
Laboratoire de Météorologie Dynamique
Laboratoire de Physique Stellaire et Planetaire
Laboratoire Souterrain de Moulis
Observatoire de Haute-Provence
Service d'Aéronomie
VI. Life Sciences -
Centre d'Écologie de Carmargue
Centre d'Études Bioclimatiques
Centre d'Études Biologiques des Animaux Sauvages
Centre d'Études du Système Nerveux
Centre d'Études Phytosociologiques et Écologiques Louis-Emberger
Centre d'Hémotypologie
Centre d'Immunologie
Centre de Biochimie et de Biologie Moléculaire
Centre de Génétique des Virus
Centre de Génétique Moléculaire
Centre de Neurochimie
Centre de Morphologie Expérimentale
Centre de Recherches de Biochimie et de Génétique Cellulaires
Centre de Recherches de Biochimie Macromoléculaire
Centre de Recherches sur la Nutrition
Centre de Sélection et d'Élevage des Animaux de Laboratoire
Centre National de Coordination des Études et Recherches d'Animaux de Laboratoire
Institut d'Embryologie
Institut de Biologie Moléculaire et Cellulaire
Institut de Neurophysiologie et de Psychophysiologie
Institut de Recherches en Biologie Moléculaire
Institut de Recherches Scientifiques sur le Cancer
Instrumentation et Dynamique Cardiovasculaire
Laboratoire d'Enzymologie
Laboratoire de Biologie et de Génétique Evolutives
Laboratoire de Biologie et Technologie des Membranes
Laboratoire de Chimie Bactérienne
Laboratoire de Cytologie Expérimentale
Laboratoire de Cytophysiologie de la Photosynthèse
Laboratoire de Génétique et Physiologie de Développement des Plantes
Laboratoire de Pharmacologie et Toxicologie Fondamentales
Laboratoire de Photosynthèse
Laboratoire Physiologie Comparée des Régulations
Laboratoire de Physiologie des Organes Végétaux après Récolte

Laboratoire de Physiologie du Travail
Laboratoire de Physiologie Respiratoire
Laboratoire de Primatologie et d'Écologie des Forêts Équatoriales
Laboratoire du Phytotron
Service de la Carte de la Végétation
Service de Technologie Appliquée a la Microscopie Électronique
VII. Humanities -
Centre de Recherches Archéologiques
Centre de Géomorphologie
Centre d'Études de Géographie Tropicale
Centre d'Études et de Réalisations Cartographiques Géographiques
Laboratoire d'Information et de Documentation.

Centre National de Prévention et de Protection　165

– CNPP
[National Centre for Prevention and Protection]
Address: 5 rue Daunou, 72002 Paris
Telephone: (01) 261 57 61
Research director: Gérard Molière
Contract work: No
Publications: Face au risque, monthly review.

FIRE RESEARCH LABORATORY　166

Address: 65 avenue du Général de Gaulle, 77420 Champs sur Marne
Telephone: (01) 005 14 18
Activities: Research and development into prevention and protection against fire and burglary, in particular: automatic fire detection systems; fire extinguishers; carbon dioxide and halogenated extinguishing systems; intrusion detection systems; burglary protection devices (locks, doors, safes, vaults, etc).
Facilities: The Laboratory is equipped for testing automatic fire detection systems according to European standards.

Centre National de Recherche Agronomique*　167

[National Agricultural Research Centre]
Address: route de Saint-Cyr, Étoile de Choisy, 78000 Versailles
Telephone: (03) 950 75 22

PLANT PATHOLOGY STATION   168

Address: route de Saint-Cyr, Étoile de Choisy, 78000
Versailles
Telephone: (03) 950 75 22
Telex: INRAVER 695 269 F
Director: F. Rapilly
Section: Phytopathology, Professor A. Coleno
Graduate research staff: 25
Activities: Phytopathology and plant protection studies; mycology; bacteriology; virology; mycoplasmology.

Centre National de   169
Recherches Forestières

[National Centre for Forestry Research]
Address: Champenoux, 54280 Seichamps
Telephone: (08) 326 61 31
Telex: INRANCY 960 458 F
Affiliation: Institut National de la Recherche
Agronomique
Director: Pierre Bouvarel
Graduate research staff: 34
Annual expenditure: £501 000-2m
Activities: Forest production; genetics; entomology;
soil studies; bioclimatology; dendrometry; silviculture;
wood quality; parasitology; forest economy studies.
Contract work: No
Publications: Annual report.

BIOMETRY RESEARCH STATION   170

Activities: Numerical classification, multivariable
analysis, regional variation, modelling, cartographic studies.

CHALONS SUR MARNE SOIL   171
SCIENCE RESEARCH STATION

Address: route de Montmirail, Fagnières, 51000
Chalons sur Marne
Telephone: (026) 68 23 28
Activities: Calcareous soil studies; soil formation; cartography; drainage studies.

FOREST ECONOMY LABORATORY   172

Address: 14 rue Girardet, 54042 Nancy Cedex
Telephone: (083) 24 39 66
Activities: Forest productivity; product usage,
transport, marketing; forest politics.

FOREST PATHOLOGY LABORATORY   173

Director: C. Delatour
Graduate research staff: 5
Activities: Biology of forest tree pathogenic fungi; resistance mechanisms; breeding studies; silvicultural studies.

FOREST PHYTOECOLOGY   174
LABORATORY

Activities: Vegetation structure, phytosociology studies; ecology; regeneration; vegetation dynamics; urbanization studies.

FOREST PRODUCTS RESEARCH   175
LABORATORY

Activities: Regeneration, silviculture studies.

FOREST SOIL AND FERTILIZATION   176
RESEARCH STATION

Graduate research staff: 7
Activities: Physical, chemical and biological soil influence on forest production; soil fertility maintenance
studies.

FOREST TREE IMPROVEMENT   177
RESEARCH STATION

Activities: Species selection, genetic studies.

MIRECOURT EXPERIMENTAL FOREST   178

Address: BP 35, 88500 Mirecourt
Telephone: (029) 37 02 43
Activities: Vegetable and plant breeding; genetics,
development and nutrition studies.

SILVICULTURE AND PRODUCTION   179
RESEARCH STATION

Activities: The Station is especially concerned with
reafforestation (natural or artificial) and clearings.

Forest Bioclimatology Unit   180

Activities: Research on forest-climate interaction.

Weed Control Research Laboratory   181

Activities: Use of herbicides; characterization of 'undesirable' species.

WOOD QUALITY RESEARCH STATION 182

Activities: Factors influencing wood quality; genetics, environmental, insect studies; wood structure.

Centre National de Recherches Zootechniques* 183

[National Centre of Zootechnical Research]
Address: Domaine de Vilvert, 78350 Jouy-en-Josas
Affiliation: Institut National de la Recherche Agronomique

BIOMETRY LABORATORY 184

Address: Domaine de Vilvert, 78350 Jouy-en-Josas
Telephone: (03) 956 80 80
Telex: INRACRZ 695431 F
Director: Emmanuel Jolivet
Graduate research staff: 7
Activities: Applied mathematics in agronomy and biology; mathematical modelling of biological phenomena.

QUANTITATIVE AND APPLIED GENETICS STATION 185

Address: Domaine de Vilvert, 78350 Jouy-en-Josas
Telephone: (03) 956 80 80
Telex: INRACRZ 695431 F
Director: L. Ollivier
Graduate research staff: 12
Activities: Genetic improvement of animal production, using selection or crossing techniques (cattle, pigs and horses).

Centre National pour l'Exploitation des Océans 186

– CNEXO
[National Centre for the Exploitation of the Oceans]
Address: 66 avenue d'Iéna, 75116 Paris
Director General: Gérard Piketty
Sections: Programmes and coordination, Lucien Laubier; technology, Jean-Claude Pujol; international relations, Robert Leandri; information, Claude Benoit
Activities: The Centre examines and consults with Government departments on any matter of national interest concerning the exploitation and exploration of the oceans and cooperates in international projects in this field.
Publications: Annual report; *Bulletin d'information*, monthly.

MEDITERRANEAN OCEANOLOGY CENTRE 187

Address: Zone Portuaire de Brégaillon, BP 2, 83501 La Seyne Cedex
Director: Bruno Chomel de Varagnes

OCEANOLOGY CENTRE, BRITTANY 188

Address: BP 337, 29237 Brest Cedex
Director: Jean Vicariot

PACIFIC OCEANOLOGY CENTRE 189

Address: BP 7004, Taravao, Tahiti
Director: Jean de Chazeaux

Centre Régional d'Élevage et de Production d'Animaux de Laboratoire 190

– CREPAL
[Breeding and Production of Laboratory Animals Regional Centre]
Address: chemin Départemental 56, 13790 Rousset
Telephone: (042) 29 21 26
Affiliation: Centre National de la Recherche Scientifique
Director: Dr Pierre Lucciani
Annual expenditure: £10 000-50 000
Activities: Breeding and production of laboratory animals, especially cats, under conventional conditions; research on respiratory diseases of the young cat; genetic selection.
Contract work: No

Centre René Huguenin 191

[René Huguenin Centre]
Address: 35 rue Dailly, 92211 Saint Cloud
Telephone: 602 70 50
Telex: 204 167 F CRHSTCL
Director: Dr Jean Gest
Sections: Immuno-virology, Professor Andrée Desplaces; statistics and epidemiology, Dr Maurice Brunet; pathology, Dr Hélène Herbert; nuclear medi-

cine, Dr Gérard Delorme, Michèle Brière; information, M Zinger
Graduate research staff: 7
Annual expenditure: F800 000
Activities: Applied and clinical research into benign growths and cancer of the breast.
Contract work: No

Centre Technique de l'Industrie des Papiers Cartons et Celluloses   192

[Paper, Paperboard and Cellulose Industries Technical Centre]
Address: BP 7110, 38020 Grenoble Cedex
Telephone: (076) 44 82 36
Telex: 980642 F
Director General: Pierre Cognard
Research director: M Ducom
Sections: Pulp, M Monzie; paper, M Sauret; technology, M Ramaz
Graduate research staff: 30
Annual expenditure: over £2m
Activities: Research and development in the following areas: new processes of pulping; fibre modifications for papermaking; use of waste papers; research on liner board corrugating medium and corrugated board; automatization for paper machines; treatment processes for industrial effluents.

Centre Technique de l'Industrie du Décolletage   193

– CTDEC
[Bar-Turning Industry Technical Centre]
Address: Zone Industrielle des Grands Prés, BP 65, 74301 Cluses Cedex
Telephone: (050) 98 20 44
Director General: Roger Bonhomme
Head of Research and Study Department: M. Ragon
Activities: Research into automatic turning machines for cutting metals, measurement of effectiveness of lubricants on turning machines and efficiency of cutting utensils in the industry, noise and vibration.
Contract work: No
Publications: Bulletin d'information du CTDEC, quarterly.

Centre Technique de la Salaison de la Charcuterie et des Conserves de Viandes   194

[Pork Curing and Tinned Meat Technical Centre]
Address: MNE, 149 rue de Bercy, 75012 Paris Cedex 12
Telephone: (01) 346 12 20
Telex: ITP 670 035 F
Research director: Jean-Luc Vendeuvre
Activities: Quality control; analysis methods for meat products; meat technology.

Centre Technique de la Teinture et du Nettoyage   195

– CTTN
[Cleaning and Dyeing Technical Centre]
Address: route de Dardilly (chemin des Mouilles), BP 41, 69130 Ecully
Telephone: (078) 833 08 61
Research director: Marc Eglizeau
Sections: Technology, J.C. Salamond; trial laboratory, Jacky Constant
Graduate research staff: 6
Annual expenditure: £10 000-50 000
Activities: Research in the following areas: production methods; study of materials and textiles; care of clothes; water pollution by laundries; air pollution by cleaning fluids.
Contract work: No
Publications: Entretien des Textiles et du Nettoyage - ETN, monthly review.

Centre Technique des Industries de la Fonderie   196

– CTIF
[Foundry Industries Technical Centre]
Address: 12 avenue Raphaël, 75016 Paris
Telephone: (01) 504 72 50
General Manager: Pierre Brunschwig
Sections: Metallurgy and research laboratories, Claude Mascré; thermal investigations and moulding, Georges Ulmer; equipment and methods, Paul Falaise
Graduate research staff: 30
Annual expenditure: F14m
Activities: CTIF is the technical trade organization for the French foundry industry, its aim being to promote technical progress, participate in the improvement of output and guarantee quality within the industry.

In particular, research is undertaken into the following: foundry techniques, metallurgy, casting and laboratory methods of cast iron, steel castings, non-ferrous alloys and die-casting; thermal investigations; environmental studies; energy saving; working conditions.
Contract work: Yes
Publications: Fonderie; Fondeur d'aujourd'hui, both monthly.

CENTRAL LABORATORIES   197

Address: 44 avenue de la Division Leclerc, 92310 Sèvres
Telephone: (027) 27 54
Telex: CTIF - SÈVRE No 270 953
Facilities: Three air or vacuum emission spectrometers, two of which are equipped with a cathodoluminescent discharge for the chemical analysis of alloys; electron microprobe for point analysis; X-ray diffractometer for the identification of phases and inclusions; extensometers for recording curves of the tensile test with an amplification up to 2 000; machines for rapid fatigue testing; non-destructive test bench for magnetic inspection and non-destructive ultrasonic test equipment; equipment for impact and tensile testing at low temperature; equipment for tensile testing and strain gauge testing at high temperature; fixtures for oxygen, hydrogen and nitrogen determination in steel and cast-iron; vacuum heating plate for high-temperature micrographic examination; etc.
Experimental foundry for half-scale experimentation, equipped with a battery of fuel-oil or propane furnaces, medium-frequency air or vacuum induction furnaces and a pressure diecasting machine.
In the particular field of thermal examinations concerning household cooking and heating appliances as well as central heating equipment, the laboratories have: test benches for the testing of stoves and cookers working with solid or liquid fuels; a test section for gas cookers and radiators; a sealed test chamber for closed-circuit gas radiators; a special installation with an adjustable blower for testing balance flame terminal (sealed circuit) gas appliances; test benches for gas, fuel-oil and coal fired boilers.

Centre Technique des   198
Tuiles et Briques

– CTTB
[Tiles and Bricks Technical Centre]
Address: 17 rue Letellier, 75015 Paris
Telephone: (01) 578 65 00
Telex: 204 902 CTTB
Research director: Claude Abadie
Technical director: Lucien Alviset

Sections: Laboratory, C. Bardin, M. Albenque; buildings, H. Berbesson; scientific section, C. Huet; manufacturing, P. Rabuel; engineering, R. Hiebel
Graduate research staff: 15
Annual expenditure: F7500
Activities: Fundamental and applied research on manufacture, properties and uses of heavy clay products.
Contract work: No
Publications: Les Cahiers de la Terre Cuite.

Centre Technique du Bois   199

– CTB
[Wood Technical Centre]
Address: 10 avenue de Saint-Mandé, 75012 Paris
Telephone: (01) 344 06 20
Telex: 220064 F ETRAV EXT 9520
Director General: Blaise Quiquandon
Joint Director General: Pierre Malaval
Graduate research staff: 80
Activities: Research and development in the following areas: forest exploitation and sawmill industries; wood and wood products industries; wood properties, characteristics and uses in the furniture industries; wood preservation, glueing and finishing.
Contract work: No
Publications: Courrier de l'industriel du bois et de l'ameublement - CIBA; Bulletin d'informations techniques - BIT; Courrier de l'exploitation forestier et du scieur - CEFS, all quarterly.

COMMON SERVICE FOR RESEARCH   200
AND EXPERIMENTATION

Head: Walter D. Kauman
Divisions: Physics and mechanics, Michele Avale, Evelyne Cottereau; chemistry and preservation, Monique Roméis

TECHNICAL SERVICE FOR FORESTRY   201
AND INDUSTRY OF THE FIRST
CATEGORY

Head: François Mondy
Divisions: Forest exploitation, Jean-Michel Niérat; sawmills, André Hocquet; plywood, fibre board and chipboard, Jean-Louis Jaudon

TECHNICAL SERVICES FOR INDUSTRY OF THE SECOND CATEGORY 202

Head: Bernard Hochart
Divisions: Wood in construction, Philippe Loiseau; furniture, Pierre Parisot; development and new projects, Jean-Paul Lego

Centre Technique Forestier Tropical 203

– CTFT
[Tropical Forests Research Centre]
Address: 45 bis, avenue de la Belle-Gabrielle, 94130 Nogent sur Marne
Telephone: (01) 873 32 95
Telex: CTFT C/O UPIEX 220429F
Parent body: Groupement d'Études et de Recherches pour le Développement de l'Agronomie Tropicale - GERDAT
Director: M.H.L. Huguet
Research director, timber: M Cailliez
Research director, forestry and fisheries: M Bailly
Graduate research staff: 30
Activities: CTFT's research falls into three main areas: Study of tropical timber - anatomy and structure of tropical timbers, checking or defining their identity; use of tropical ligneous substances for the production of pulp and paper (setting up of paper manufacturing units in the tropical zone, the Gabon project for example); chemistry of tropical timbers with a view to carbonization or specific uses such as electrometallurgy and extraction of latex from the bark; physical and mechanical characteristics of tropical timbers, possible uses and particular features for conversion; improvement of sawing, slicing and peeling techniques; preservation of tropical timber from the forest to the conversion stage.
Forestry research - detection and assessment of damage caused to nurseries and plantations by insects and diseases, research into chemical, biological or silvicultural control methods and study of the biology of the main pests and parasites; formulation of soil conservation rules taking into account the rapidity and intensity of erosion and run-off phenomena under tropical climates, development of watershed management; forest inventories using statistical methods including photographic interpretation and ground sampling, drawing up of forest maps; planning of silviculture and management programmes for the development of dry zones and rain forests; tree felling and related operations, logging, stocking and handling, methods for measuring standing trees.
Fisheries and fish-farming - developing techniques and methods of breeding tropical species; studying the biology of fish species, developing the fish-breeding environ-ment in natural and man-made lakes; training professional and technical staff in the field.
Facilities: CTFT has research stations in Cameroon, Congo, Gabon, Ivory Coast, Niger, Senegal, Upper Volta, Madagascar, French Guiana and New Caledonia.
Contract work: No
Publications: Bois et Forêts des Tropiques, bi-monthly.

Centre Technique Industriel de la Construction Métallique 204

– CTICM
[Steel Construction Technical Centre]
Address: 20 rue Jean-Jaurès, 92807 Puteaux Cedex
Telephone: (01) 774 55 33
Telex: 611 677 F
Research director: Jacques Brozzetti
Sections: Project management, Yvon Lescouarc'h, Christian Soize; Fire Research Station, Paul Arnault
Graduate research staff: 30
Annual expenditure: £501 000-2m
Activities: The major research deals with: strength of materials and structural analysis; fire structural behaviour; fracture mechanics and fatigue; reliability and probabilistic mechanics; offshore platforms analysis under random waves and wind; structural and energy analysis of buildings; computer-aided design.
Contract work: No
Publications: Construction métallique, quarterly.

Centre Universitaire d'Avignon 205

[Avignon University Centre]
Address: 35 rue Joseph Vernet, 84000 Avignon
Telephone: (090) 82 68 10

FACULTY OF SCIENCE 206

Address: 33 rue Louis Pasteur, 84000 Avignon
Dean: Professor Jacques Nougier

Biology Department 207

Senior staff: Professor Coulomb, Professor Espagnac, Professor Reidenbach

Engineering Department 208

Head: Professor Vives

Geology Department 209

Senior staff: Professor Kraus, Professor Pavia, Professor Roggero

Mathematics Department 210

Senior staff: Professor Ballet, Professor Michel, Professor Pecaut, Professor di Guglielmo

Physics Department 211

Head: Professor Testard

CERIB - Centre d'Études et 212 de Recherches de l'Industrie du Béton Manufacturé

[Precast Concrete Technical Centre]
Address: BP 42, 28230 Epernon
Telephone: (037) 83 52 72
Affiliation: Ministère de l'Industrie et de la Recherche
General Director: Marcel Darcemont
Head of Research: F. Dutruel
Head of Quality: M. Valles
Graduate research staff: 30
Annual expenditure: £1m
Activities: The Centre has four main functions: it conducts research; it assembles and distributes technical information from and to industrialized countries; it is responsible for quality control and regulation, and it serves as a centre for administration and maintenance.
Main research activities include: different methods of concrete manufacture - raw materials, concrete formation, machines, hardening, handling, stocks; technical processes and automization; analyses of stress factors under different methods of manufacture; improvement of manufacturing processes; development of new products. Their 1980 programme covered various topics many of these long-term. These included:
Manufacturing processes - concrete preparation, concrete rheology; hardening accelerators; machine noise levels; machine resistance and auto-control.
Product use - pavements; shock resistance of encapsulating blocks; materials compatibility in concrete structures; military use and resistance to explosives; chutes.
Predevelopment - insulation and industrial needs.
Facilities: Modular testing machine for large structures; electrodynamic vibrating equipment; thermal properties testing chambers for measuring heat transfer across walls and floors.
Contract work: No
Publications: Research reports; annual report.

CIE 213

Address: 44 rue d'Alésia, 75014 Paris
Telephone: (01) 327 16 74
President: Jean-Louis Rossignol
Director General: Bernard Vuatrin
Adjoint Director General: G. Peyrard, Jean Larousse
Deputy Director General, scientific and technical: G. Noyelle
Activities: In 1968 the three organizations whose objectives covered all aspects of techniques of preserving foodstuffs: Centre Technique des Conserves de Produits Agricoles; Institut APPERT; and École de la Conserve, were, in the interest of efficiency, regrouped at a common address under the central organization of CIE. CTCPA is concerned with the standardization and control of products relevant to their expertise. APPERT is particularly responsible for the checking of canned foodstuffs in the laboratory, research and technical documentation. École de la Conserve is concerned with professional training. CIE's common services include: financial organization; relations with the canning industry; documentation and information; technical problems of interest to the three organizations, in particular research and assistance; maintenance of laboratories.

CENTRE TECHNIQUE DES 214 CONSERVES DE PRODUITS AGRICOLES

– CTCPA
[Canned Agricultural Products Technical Centre]
Telephone: (01) 327 66 80
Director: Bernard Vuatrin
Sections: Canned vegetables and related topics, Edouard de Metz Noblat; canned tomatoes and related topics, Gérard Bartholin
Graduate research staff: 10
Activities: Establishment of standards; testing of canned products; new testing and analysis methods; agricultural tests - varieties; weed-killer treatment, insecticide treatment, anti-parasite treatment on spinach, beans, peas, tomatoes; administration of experimental stations.
Contract work: No

d'Artiguères Experimental Station 215

Address: BP 68, 40002 Mont-de-Marsau
Activities: Research into the problems on canning foie gras.

Dury-les-Amiens Experimental Station   216

Address: avenue Paul-Claudel, Dury, 80480 Saleux
Telephone: (022) 95 32 84; 95 37 50
Activities: Experimental work on agricultural and industrial samples.

Puyricard Experimental Station   217

Address: 13450 Puyricard
Telephone: (042) 24 43 62; 24 41 91
Activities: Experimental work on agricultural and industrial samples.

INSTITUT APPERT   218
[Appert Institute]
Telephone: (01) 327 16 74
Director: Jean Larousse
Sections: Research laboratory, Léon Michiels
Graduate research staff: 3
Activities: The Institute is responsible for quality control on both the domestic and export markets; it also carries out chemical, bacteriological and histological analysis of new products from canneries. Appert has also set up a pilot plant for use by École de la Conserve for research work of interest to all canning industries. A large part of the work is devoted to studies of thermobacteriology.
Contract work: No
Publications: Bulletin Analytique, quarterly.

College de France   219

[College of France]
Address: 11 place Marcelin-Berthelot, 75231 Paris Cedex 05
Telephone: (01) 329 12 11
Affiliation: Ministère des Universités
President of the Assembly of Professors: Professor Yves La Porte

MATHEMATICS, PHYSICS AND   220
NATURAL SCIENCES

Algebra and Geometry Laboratory   221

Director: Professor Jean-Pierre Serre

Atomic and Molecular Physics   222
Laboratory

Director: Professor Claude Cohen-Tannoudji

Cellular Biochemistry Laboratory   223

Director: Professor François Gros

Cellular Communications Laboratory   224

Address: Institut Pasteur, 25 rue du Docteur-Roux, 75015 Paris
Director: Professor Jean-Pierre Changeux

Cellular Genetics Laboratory   225

Address: 28 rue du Docteur-Roux, 75015 Paris
Director: Professor François Jacob

Cellular Physiology Laboratory   226

Director: Professor François Morel

Corpuscular Physics Laboratory   227

Director: Professor Marcel Froissart

Developmental Neurophysiology   228
Laboratory

Director: Professor Julian de Ajuriaguerra

Developmental Physiology Laboratory   229

Director: Professor Alfred Jost

Experimental Surgery Station   230
(Voronoff Foundation)

Address: 4 avenue Gordon-Bennett, 75016 Paris
Director: Professor Jean Dausset

Group Theory Laboratory   231

Director: Professor Jacques Tits

Mathematical Analysis of Systems and   232
their Control Laboratory

Director: Professor Jacques-Louis Lions

Mathematical Physics Laboratory   233

Director: Professor André Lichnerowicz

Neurophysiology Laboratory   234

Director: Professor Yves Laporte

Nuclear Magnetism Laboratory   235

Director: Professor Anatole Abragam

Organic Chemistry of Hormones Laboratory   236

Director: vacant

Solid-State Physics Laboratory   237

Director: Professor Pierre-Gilles de Gennes

Theoretical Astrophysics Laboratory   238

Address: Institut d'Astrophysique, boulevard Arago 98 bis, 75014 Paris
Director: Professor Jean-Claude Pecker

Theoretical Physics of Elementary Particles Laboratory   239

Director: Professor Jacques Prentki

Comité Interprofessionnel   240
du Vin de Champagne

[Interprofessional Champagne Wine Comittee]
Address: 5 rue Henri-Martin, BP 135, 51204 Epernay Cedex
Telephone: (026) 51 40 47 and 54 45 61
Telex: CIVC 8305 16F
Director: Claude Badour
Sections: Oenology, M Moulin; chromatography, Mlle Ude; microbiology, M Valade; viticulture, M Richard
Graduate research staff: 8
Annual expenditure: F2.5m
Activities: Research and development in the following areas: vine cultivation (viticulture) - diseases and parasites of vineyards; cultural methods; tilling and fertilization of soils; vine plants selection; quality improvement; vine nursery; oenology - everything concerning the wine of Champagne, its components and elaboration.
Contract work: No
Publications: Le Vigneron Champenois.

Commissariat à l'Énergie   241
Atomique

– CEA
[Atomic Energy Commission]
Address: 31-33 rue de la Fédération, BP 510 75 752, Paris Cedex 15
Telephone: (01) 273 60 00
Telex: ENERGAT-PARIS 20 671
Affiliation: Ministère de l'Industrie

High Commissioner: J. Teillac
Administrator General: M. Pecqueur
Graduate research staff: 5600
Annual expenditure: £500m
Activities: General research is carried out by the Fundamental Research Institute. Research activities in the field of chemistry, metallurgy, thermal conductivity and electronics are carried out by teams operating within the different units but linked to the departments for applied research.
CEA research is divided into two parts: national research - elementary particle and nuclear physics; neutron flux; nuclear astrophysics; ionic bombardment; chemistry of fluorescent compounds; use of stable and radioactive isotopes in medicine, biology and agronomy; and the concentration of all these activities - study on controlled fission by magnetic containment.
The following four laboratories conducting research have separate entries:
Centre d'Études Nucléaires de Cadarache
Centre d'Études Nucléaires de Fontenay aux Roses
Centre d'Études Nucléaires de Grenoble
Centre d'Études Nucléaires de Saclay
See also entry for: Société Française pour la Gestion des Brevets d' Application Nucléaire.
Contract work: No
Publications: Annual report.

FUNDAMENTAL RESEARCH   242
INSTITUTE

Research director: Jules Horowitz
Sections: Division of Physics; Division of Controlled Fusion; Department of Biology; Department of Fundamental Research, Grenoble

MILITARY APPLICATIONS   243
DIRECTORATE

Address: 31-33 rue de la Fédération, 75015 Paris
Activities: Nuclear warheads and weapons: feasibility and security studies; developing nuclear weapons following the latest scientific advances; nuclear submarines.

Conservatoire National des   244
Arts et Métiers*

[National Conservatory of Arts and Manufacturing]
Address: 292 rue St Martin, 75141 Paris 3
Director: F. Cambou
Activities: The Conservatory provides professional and technical courses, and its institutes carry out some research and development.

Corning Europe Incorporated - Centre Européen de Recherche   260

Address: 7 bis avenue de Valvins, BP 3, 77211 Avon Cedex
Telephone: (06) 422 49 05
Telex: 600059
Director R&D: Jacques G. Lemoine
Sections: Biotechnology and materials, L. Dohan electrical and optical waveguides, R Jansen; optical, L. Bognar; consumer products A. Andrieu; engineering J.L. Pierucci; analytical and measurement services, D. Campbell
Graduate research staff: 60
Annual expenditure: over £2m
Activities: Research, development and engineering of products and/or processes related to Corning glass works' business.
Facilities: Pilot plant.
Contract work: No

Département d'Économie Medicale du CREDOC 261

[CREDOC Health Economics Department]
Address: 142 rue du Chevaleret, 75013 Paris
Telephone: (01) 584 97 59
Parent body: Centre de Recherche pour l'Étude et l'Observation des Conditions de Vie - CREDOC
Research directors: Arié Mizrahi, Andrée Mizrahi, Simone Sandier
Sections: Medical microeconomics, Arié Mizrahi, Andrée Mizrahi; medical macroeconomics, Simone Sandier
Graduate research staff: 12
Annual expenditure: F4.5m
Activities: Taking a census of social and economic data and supplying a method to analyze and plan health care.
Contract work: Yes

Dowell Schlumberger Research and Development Centre* 262

Address: BP 90, 42003 Saint Étienne Cedex
Activities: Oilfield service company specializing in cementing and simulation, and active in flow through porous media and fluid mechanics, applied geological mechanics, surfactant studies, chemistry of cement, advanced mathematical reservoir modelling techniques, and measurement of non-Newtonian fluids.

École Centrale de Lyon 263

– ECL
[Lyon Central College]
Address: 36 avenue Guy de Collongue, BP 163, 69130 Ecully
Telephone: (07) 833 27 00
Head of Research Secretariat: D. Letuvée
Graduate research staff: 185
Annual expenditure: F800 000
Contract work: Yes
Publications: Technica, bimonthly journal on research activities.

DEPARTMENT OF CONSTRUCTION TECHNOLOGY 264

Head: Professor Russier
Activities: Arm prosthetics; surgical equipment; tractor vehicles and tanks.

DEPARTMENT OF ELECTRONICS 265

Affiliation: Centre National de la Recherche Scientifique
Head: Professor J.J. Urgell
Activities: Research concentrates on electronics: fine electrical properties, synthesis of integral electronic functions. Research is based on four main aspects: semiconductor materials; manufacturing methods of integrated structures; physics of integrated compounds; synthesis of integrated functions.

DEPARTMENT OF ELECTROTECHNIQUES 266

Head: A. Foggia
Activities: Inductive motors of the non-sinusoidal type; linear inductive motors; inductive heating; transistor networks.

DEPARTMENT OF FLUID MECHANICS 267

Affiliation: Centre National de la Recherche Scientifique
Heads: Professor M.J. Mathieu, Professor G. Compte-Bellot
Sections: Turbulence, M Schon, M Charnay; mathematical models and modelling, M Brauner, M Gay, M Jeandel; acoustics, Professor G. Compte-Bellot, M Bataille, M Sunyach; turbomachinery, M Bois, M Leboeuf; prospective, M Bataille

DEPARTMENT OF MATHEMATICS AND COMPUTER SYSTEMS 268

Head: J.F. Maître
Activities: Partial equations and optimal control; informatics; theory of systems; calculus (finite element).

DEPARTMENT OF METALLURGY, PHYSICS AND MATERIALS 269

Head: Professor P. Guiraldenq
Activities: There are four main areas of research on solid-state metals and minerals: diffusion in solids; properties and behavioural mechanics; rust-proof materials, corrosion; metallic dental materials.

DEPARTMENT OF PHYSICS AND CHEMISTRY 270

Head: Professor Clechet
Laboratories: Chemistry; Physics
Activities: Chemistry - photoelectrochemistry based on semiconductors (solar energy conversion); measurement of metallic and non-metallic pollution in water by X-ray fluorescence and ion exchange.
Physics - wave propagation in a fluctuating environment.

DEPARTMENT OF SOLID-STATE MECHANICS 271

Head: F. Sidoroff
Activities: Vibration mechanics; materials resistance; soil mechanics.

DEPARTMENT OF SURFACE TECHNOLOGY 272

Affiliation: Centre National de la Recherche Scientifique
Head: Professor J.M. Georges
Activities: Research into: surface mechanics; lubricants and friction; surface analyses.

DEPARTMENT OF THERMAL MACHINERY 273

Head: A. Moiroux
Activities: The main areas of research concern alternative machinery for the production of energy or heat by: analyses, simulation and modelling; experimentation and testing; study and solution of new technological problems in order to reduce consumption, pollution, or to create new machinery.

École Centrale des Arts et Manufactures* 274

[Central School of Arts and Manufacturing]
Address: Grande Voie des Vignes, 92290 Chatenay-Malabry
Director: D. Gourisse
Laboratories: General Physics; Electronic Beams; Metal Physics; Corrosion; Solids Structure, Texture and Reactivity; Chemical Engineering and Data Processing; Solid-State Chemistry; Industrial Chemistry; Organic Chemistry; Nuclear Chemistry; Power Engineering; Mechanical Engineering; Mechanics of Continuous Media; Information Processing
Activities: Basic and applied research is carried out in the Physics and Metallurgy Institute, the Chemistry Institute and the Industrial, Power and Civil Engineering Institute.

École d'Électricité et Mécanique Industrielle (École Violet) 275

[Electricity and Industrial Mechanics College - École Violet]
Address: 115 avenue Émile-Zola, 75015 Paris
Telephone: (01) 575 62 98
Director: Marc Pichon

École National Vétérinaire d'Alfort 276

[Alfort National Veterinary College]
Address: 7 avenue du Général de Gaulle, 94704 Maisons-Alfort Cedex
Telephone: (01) 375 92 11
Telex: ECALFOR 213 863 F
Affiliation: Institut National de la Recherche Agronomique
Head: Professor Ch. Pilet
Graduate research staff: 58
Activities: Veterinary medicine.

ANIMAL AND COMPARATIVE IMMUNOLOGY INSTITUTE 277

Director: Professor Ch. Pilet
Graduate research staff: 5
Activities: Animal production, veterinary medicine; immunology; genetics.

École Nationale d'Ingénieurs de Saint-Étienne 278

[Saint-Étienne National Engineering College]
Address: 56-60 rue Jean-Parot, 42023 St Étienne Cedex
Telephone: (077) 25 71 40
Director: V. Martino
Sections: Metallurgy foundry, M. Paour; automation, M. Martin Calle; mechanics, J.C. Martin; soil mechanics, G. Chargelegue; manufacturing mechanics, M Larose
Graduate research staff: 5

Annual expenditure: £22 000
Activities:
Mechanics: trials of new composite materials and new materials of boron nitrate - special usage and numerical analysis: thermal motors; ultrasonics; biomechanics of lower limbs; calculation of structural finite elements; low-powered helicopters.
Automation: studies and realization of prosthetics of the shoulder taking into account the residual stump movement of an amputated arm; combined data acquisition.
Soil mechanics: studies on plastic analytical models of rheoelectric triaxial analogy; characcrization of geotextiles - smelting of spiroid graphite.
Foundry metallurgy: magnesium smelting.

École Nationale d'Ingénieurs de Tarbes 279

[National College of Engineers at Tarbes]
Address: chemin d'Azereix, BP 311, 65013 Tarbes Cedex
Telephone: (062) 93 98 21

DEPARTMENT OF MATERIALS ENGINEERING 280

Head: Professor J.A. Petit
Sections: Metallics and ceramics, P. Faure; polymers and composites, M. Boutoleau; applied chemical analysis, P. Lacaze
Graduate research staff: 4
Activities: Research in the following areas: mechanical behaviour and reactivity of metallic surfaces (wear and friction, corrosion, corrosion-abrasion, erosion, cavitation); durability of polymers and polymer composites (wear, degradation, weathering, stress cracking).

École Nationale des Ponts et Chaussées 281

– ENPC
[Bridges and Roads National College]
Address: 28 rue des Saints Pères, 75007 Paris
Telephone: (01) 260 34 13
Affiliation: Ministère de l'Environnement et du Cadre de Vie
Research director: Michel Deleau
Sections: Mechanics, J. Salençon; applied mathematics, M. Fremond; economics, S. Kolm
Graduate research staff: 23
Annual expenditure: £501 000-2m
Activities: The ENPC acts as a coordinating body for

various research centres and individuals. It also carries out research in the fields of:
Civil engineering - soil and foundation mechanics; pavements; materials (concretes, metals, soils, rocks); experimental analysis; numerical methods; marine structures; engineering geology.
Construction techniques - energy economy and new forms of energy for the home; export of products and transfer of technology; economic problems relating to materials, industrialization and management; building deterioration and construction methods.
Environmental techniques - sanitation; biological waste; environmental economy; impact studies; modelling of pollutant dispersal.
Facilities: Computing centre.
Contract work: No
See also entry for: Laboratoire de Mécanique des Solides.

APPLIED COMPUTER SCIENCES RESEARCH CENTRE 282

MANAGEMENT OF NATURAL RESOURCES AND THE ENVIRONMENT RESEARCH CENTRE 283

Address: 2 rue Alfred Fouillée, 75013 Paris
Telephone: (01) 585 53 97

SOIL MECHANICS RESEARCH CENTRE 284

Address: 2 rue Alfred Fouillée, 75013 Paris
Telephone: (01) 585 53 97
Research director: M Schlosser
Associate director: Ilan Juran
Graduate research staff: 10
Annual expenditure: F1m
Activities: The main research activities are related to: soil improvement - special techniques of preconsolidation of fine soils, constitutive laws for soils and particularly for partly saturated fine soil; in-situ testing with new electric piezocone penetrometers; multi tied back walls; soil reinforcement - reinforced earth and soil nailing.
The Centre has laboratory facilities and direct access to the computing centre of the École Nationale des Ponts et Chaussées.

École Nationale Supérieure Agronomique de Montpellier   285

– ENSAM
[Montpellier National Agricultural College]
Address: place Viala, 34060 Montpellier Cedex
Telephone: (067) 63 12 75
Telex: INRAMON 490 818 F
Affiliation: Ministère de l'Agriculture
Director: J.-F. Breton
Secretary General: Jean Granier
Activities: The research stations are linked to the National Institute of Agricultural Research and are especially concerned with the agro-alimentary chain and the position of the rural world within the socio-economic spectrum. The College looks at problems on production, processing and commerialization at all levels and cooperates on a technical and cultural level with various foreign institutes and universities, especially in the Mediterranean area.

AGRONOMIC SCIENCES UNIT   286

Fruit Arboriculture Department   287

Head: Professor J. Hugard
Senior staff: M Villemur
Activities: Genetic improvement of species: apricot, peach, olive, apple; orchard management and cultivation.

Phytotechnic Department   288

Senior staff: Professor Grignac, Professor Chery
Activities: Selection and creation of new varieties of cereals, forages and industrial plants.
Facilities: The experimental centres comprise: Lavalette at Montpellier (cereals, forages and industrial plants); one at Arles (rice); one annexed to St Martin de Hinx (maize).

Technology-Oenology Department   289

Head: Professor P. Bidan
Senior staff: M Olivieri, M Salgues
Activities: Nutrition   chemistry;   microbiology; enzymology.

Viticulture Department   290

Head: Professor D. Boubals
Senior staff: M Galet, M Bernard
Activities: Vine plant improvement (yield and quality); improvement of viticulture techniques; research on vine physiology.

Zootechnics Department   291

Head: Professor L. Dauzier
Senior staff: Professor Benevent, M Prud'hon, M Cordesse
Activities: Research is currently centred on lambs, rabbits and chickens in respect of their lipid, protein and nucleic metabolism and their hormonal control.
Note: The Department is linked to one of the animal physiology stations of INRA and carries out research on animal growth.

BIOLOGICAL SCIENCES UNIT   292

Animal Ecology-Agricultural Zoology   293 Department

Head: Professor Leclant
Senior staff: M Caremoli
Activities: Stinging   insects   and   vectors   of phytopathogenic organisms; carriers of plant diseases and predators.

Biochemistry and Vegetable   294 Physiology Department

Head: Professor L. Salsac
Senior staff: M Grignon, Mme Crouzet
Activities: Mechanisms of ionic absorption; vegetable ecology.

Genetics and Microbiology   295 Department

Head: Professor P. Galzy
Senior staff: M Arnaud, M Moulin
Activities: Genetic studies of microorganisms both in the area of biological manufacture (biomass and metabolite production), and in the area of cell structure; processing of agricultural waste with the aim of diminishing its nuisance value and re-using certain waste products.

Mathematics Department 296

Head: G. Vignau
Activities: Research activities are carried out in conjunction with the Centre Interuniversitaire de Traitement de l'Information de Montpellier.

Vegetable Ecology and Pathology Department 297

Head: Professor M. Signoret
Senior staff: M Chevassut, M Poinso
Activities: Viral diseases of graminae, soya, lucerne; soya and rice mycosis; mushroom ecology.

ECONOMIC AND SOCIAL SCIENCES UNIT 298

Rural Economics and Sociology Department 299

Head: Professor Ph. Lacombe
Senior staff: M Montagne, M Barthe, M Miclet
Activities: Analysis of the role of agriculture in today's society.

EQUIPMENT MANAGEMENT UNIT 300

Agricultural Engineering and Machines Department 301

Head: Professor F. de Chabaret
Senior staff: M Manière, M Luc
Activities: Mechanic viticulture (prototypes, new inventions); hydric capacity of soils.

Soil Sciences Department 302

Head: Professor E. Servat
Senior staff: M Moinereau, M Chamayou, M Herrmann
Activities: Study, characterization and cartography of soils, especially related to problems of soil production.

École Nationale Supérieure d'Arts et Métiers 303

– ENSAM
[Technical Skills National College]
Address: 151 boulevard de l'Hôpital, 75640 Paris Cedex 13
Telephone: (01) 336 49 55
Telex: 220 064 F ETRAV EXT 379

Scientific Director: J. Cliton
Sections: Electronics, electrotechnology and automation, M Soubie; production, M Lapujoulade; energetics, M Gublin; structures, M Barraco, M Gachon; materials metallurgy, M Maeder; polymers, M Chatain; photochemistry, M Verdu
Graduate research staff: 22
Annual expenditure: F3m
Activities: The accent is placed upon applied research (developed from pure research) taking into account economic and social considerations. Research is developing in relation with industry, especially in the field of mechanics which consists of: design techniques; methods and processes of production; energy generation/transformation devices; properties and uses of materials including plastics.
Contract work: No
Publications: Research reports.

École Nationale Supérieure de Biologie Appliquée à la Nutrition et l'Alimentation 304

[National College of Biology Applied to Nutrition and Food]
Address: Campus Universitaire, Montmuzard, 21000 Dijon
Telephone: (080) 30 82 57
Affiliation: Université de Dijon
Head: Professor Denise Simatos

APPLIED BIOCHEMISTRY 305

Director: Professor Christian Baron
Activities: Nutritional values of foods; organoleptic qualities; pesticide residues in food.

APPLIED BOTANY-MYCOLOGY 306

Director: Professor Pierre Henry
Activities: Yeasts, tannins; mycology; microbiology of food products.

CELLULAR BIOCHEMISTRY 307

Director: Professor Raymond Michel
Activities: Cell fraction; molecular biosynthesis; thyroid endocrinology; alimentary cells toxicology.

FERMENTATION 308

Director: Jacques Bergeret
Activities: Yeasts, wines.

MICROBIOLOGY 309

Director: Professor Victor Caumartin
Activities: Residual waters; methane fermentation; lactic fermentation; cheese lipolysis; disinfectants.

PHYSICOCHEMICAL BIOLOGY 310

Director: Professor Denise Simatos
Activities: Methodology of sensory evaluation; physical properties of water in food; flavours; physical properties of fats; freezing and defrosting.

PHYSIOLOGY OF NUTRITION 311

Director: Professor Jean Bezard
Activities: Lipid structure and use.

École Nationale Supérieure 312 de Ceramique Industrielle

[Industrial Ceramics National College]
Address: 47-73 rue Albert Thomas, 87065 Limoges Cedex
Telephone: (055) 79 34 80
Affiliation: Ministère des Universités
Director: Professor Philippe Boch
Activities: Engine research; new ceramic materials; batteries.

École Nationale Supérieure 313 de Chimie de Paris

[National College of Chemistry of Paris]
Address: rue Pierre et Marie Curie, 75231 Paris Cedex 05
Telephone: (01) 336 25 25
Director: Fernand Coussemant
Publications: Research reports; *Annales de la recherche.*

LABORATORY OF ANALYTICAL 314 CHEMISTRY AND ELECTROCHEMISTRY

Head: Professor B. Tremillon
Activities: Energy conversion; energy analysis and superacid media; electrochemical studies of metallic ions in ionized liquids.

LABORATORY OF BIOTECHNOLOGY 315

Head: Professor F. Le Goffic

LABORATORY OF CHEMICAL 316 ENGINEERING

Head: Professor J. Amouroux

LABORATORY OF CORROSION 317

Head: Professor J. Talbot

LABORATORY OF INDUSTRIAL 318 ORGANIC CHEMISTRY

Head: Professor Fernand Coussemant

LABORATORY OF METALLURGY 319

Head: Professor B. Dubois
Activities: Structure and mechanical properties of iron-chrome and copper-aluminium alloys.

LABORATORY OF ORGANIC 320 CHEMISTRY RESEARCH

Heads: Professor P. Cadiot, Professor P Cresson
Activities: The four main themes are: nuclear magnetic resonance; polar cyclo-additives; chiral derivatives; transition metal derivatives.

LABORATORY OF PHYSICAL 321 CHEMISTRY OF SOLUTIONS

Head: Professor R. Schaal
Activities: Synthesis and kinetic study of additive compounds derived from aromatic trifluoromethyl sulphates. This research is carried out in cooperation with the Research Institute of the Academy of Sciences of the USSR, Kiev.

LABORATORY OF PHYSICAL 322 ORGANIC CHEMISTRY

Head: Professor A. Casadevall
Activities: Carbocyclic compounds; in vivo study of the biochemical mechanisms of energy storing (enzymatic and biomimetic reactions).

LABORATORY OF SOLID-STATE CHEMISTRY 323

Head: Professor R. Collongues, Professor J. Livage
Activities: This is a newly-created laboratory which will be concentrating in the coming years on solid-state chemistry.

LABORATORY OF SURFACE AND PHYSICAL CHEMISTRY 324

Heads: Professor J. Bénard, Professor J. Oudar
Activities: Surface problems; surface compounds; effect of sulphur on metals.

École Nationale Supérieure des Arts et Industries de Strasbourg 325

[National College of Arts and Industries of Strasbourg]
Address: 24 boulevard de la Victoire, 67084 Strasbourg Cedex
Telephone: (088) 35 55 05
Director: J. Pichoir
Activities: Research in the following areas: public works, mechanical and electrical engineering, building equipment, topography, architecture.

École Nationale Supérieure des Industries Agricoles et Alimentaires 326

[Food and Agricultural Industries National College]
Address: 1 avenue des Olympiades, 91305 Massy
or: 105 rue de l'Université, 59509 Douai
Telephone: (06) 920 05 23; (027) 87 03 60
Telex: ENSIA 692 174 F; 12 0 582
Director: J.M. Clement

DEPARTMENT OF FOOD ENGINEERING 327

Head: Professor Bimbenet
Senior staff: Food engineering, Professor Bimbenet; sugar industry, M Guerin; food economy, M Treillon; mechanical, M Vasseur

DEPARTMENT OF FOOD SCIENCE 328

Head: Professor Scriban
Senior staff: Industrial microbiology, M Claveau, M Leveau, Mlle Bouix; malting and brewing industry, Professor Scriban; dairy industries, M Goursaud; fruit and vegetables industries, M Richard; sugar industry, M Roche; distilleries, M Mejane; microbial biochemistry, M Jakubczak

DEPARTMENT OF NUTRITION 329

Head: Professor Sandret
Senior staff: Food chemistry, H. Richard, Mme Berset, M Ducret; cereal industries, M Aunay, M Cuvelier; food economy, M Hossenlopp; meat industries, M Rosset

École Nationale Supérieure des Mines de Paris 330

– ENSMP
[National Mining College of Paris]
Address: 60 boulevard Saint-Michel, 75272 Paris Cedex 06
or: 35 rue Saint-Honoré, 77305 Fontainebleau, *or* Sophia-Antipolis, 06560 Valbonne
Telephone: (01) 329 21 05
Affiliation: Ministère de l'Industrie
Director: Pierre Lafitte
Research director: Jacques Lévy
Publications: Annual report.

SCHOOL OF APPLIED MATHEMATICS 331

Applied Mathematics Department 332

Head: Yves Rouchaleau

Automatic Control Research Centre 333

Head: Guy Cohen

Computer Science Research Centre 334

Head: Michel Lenci

Geostatistics and Mathematical Morphology Centre 335

Senior staff: Georges Matheron, Jean Serra

SCHOOL OF EARTH SCIENCES   336

Computing Geology and   337
Hydrogeology Centre
Head: Ghislain de Marsily

Engineering Geology Centre   338
Head: Marcel Arnold

General Mining and Geology Centre   339
Senior staff: Hubert Pélissonnier, Pierre de Graciansky

Mineralogy Centre   340
Senior staff: Claude Guilleman, Kieu-Duong Phan

Mines and Ground Organization   341
Centre
Senior staff: Edouard Tincelin, Jacques Fine, Michel Duchène

Natural Resources Research Centre   342
Head: Pierre-Noël Giraud

Remote Sensing Centre   343
Head: Jean-Marie Monget

SCHOOL OF ECONOMICS AND   344
SOCIAL SCIENCES

Scientific Management Centre   345
Head: Jean-Claude Moisdon

Sociology of Innovation Centre   346
Head: Lucien Karpik

SCHOOL OF MATERIALS SCIENCE   347
AND CHEMISTRY

Chemical Engineering Group   348
Head: H. Renon

Energetics Centre   349
Head: Paul Reboux

Irreversible Processes Research Group   350
Head: Francis Fer

Materials Research Centre   351
Address: BP 87, 91003 Evry Cedex
Telephone: (01) 078 80 11
Telex: CORAVIA 600 700
Head: Gilles Pomey
Senior staff: Powder metallurgy, Y. Bienvenu; ceramics, D. Broussand; composites, A.R. Bunsell; surfaces, M. Guttmann; corrosion, J.P. Henon; solidification, G. Lesoult; fracture and fatigue, A. Pineau; high-temperature fatigue, L. Remy; creep, J.L. Strudel
Graduate research staff: 65
Annual expenditure: £501 000-2m
Activities: Research falls into the following categories: mechanical properties - fatigue, thermal fatigue; fatigue-creep-oxidation interaction; creep; high-temperature plastic deformation, thermomechanical treatment, corrosion and oxidation, stress corrosion or oxidation, fracture and fracture mechanics, embrittlement segregation; manufacturing processes - solidification in foundry and precision casting, powder metallurgy of metals and ceramics, fibre composites, surface protection.
Contract work: Yes

Materials Shaping Centre   352
Head: Jean-Loup Chenot

École Nationale Supérieure   353
des Sciences Agronomiques
Appliquées

– ENSSAA
[National College of Applied Agricultural Sciences]
Address: 26 boulevard Docteur Petitjean, 21100 Dijon
Telephone: (080) 66 54 12
Affiliation: Ministère de l' Agriculture
Director: R. Merillon
Departments:
Vegetable products, Professor H. Laby, M. Richard, J.C. Fresse
Animal products, Professor J.L. Tisserand, Professor J.H. Teissier, J. Bonnemaire, C. Masson, M. Roux
Economic science, Professor M. Petit, P. Albert, J.B. Viallon, J.F. Soufflet, P. de la Vaissière
Information service, F. Francillon, D. Degueurce

Activities: The School is a centre of applications for the Institut National Agronomique Paris-Grignon and for the other Écoles Nationales Supérieures Agronomiques of Montpellier, Rennes, Nancy and Toulouse. Its aim is to train agronomy engineers for the Ministry of Agriculture but it will also train French and foreign civil engineers.

There is a laboratory attached to each of the three major departments and other specialist sections include Vegetable protection, Tropical agronomy, Agro-alimentary industries, Statistics.

École Nationale Vétérinaire de Lyon 354

[Lyon National Veterinary College]
Address: route de Sain-Bel, Marcy l'Étoile, 69260 Charbonnière-les-Bains
Telephone: (07) 887 00 84
Affiliation: Ministère de l'Agriculture
Secretary General: Michel Wolff
Graduate research staff: 55
Annual expenditure: F1 600 000
Contract work: No

DEPARTMENT OF ANATOMY 355

Head: Professor Barone
Activities: Comparative neuroanatomy; lung structure.

DEPARTMENT OF ANIMAL FOOD HYGIENE AND INDUSTRY 356

Head: Professor Chantegrelet
Activities: Epidemiology and public health (especially salmonella); animal products; microbiology - food composition and quality; new products, manufacturing accidents.

DEPARTMENT OF GENERAL PATHOLOGY AND MICROBIOLOGY 357

Head: Professor Oudar
Activities: Pathology of wild animals living in mountainous areas.

DEPARTMENT OF INFECTIOUS DISEASES 358

Head: Professor Joubert
Activities: Rabies and myxomatosis - epidemiology, vaccination; goat pathology; animal mycobacterium and transmission to humans, continual epidemiologic and immunologic surveillance of herds representative of various French regions; immunogenetics of Charolais cattle; enzootic epidemiology and diagnostics.

DEPARTMENT OF MEDICINE 359

Head: Professor Lapras
Activities: Clinical immunopathology, autoimmune diseases, Lupus; ethology and animal behaviour.

DEPARTMENT OF NUTRITION 360

Head: Professor Jean-Blain
Activities: Hepatic metabolism of isolated cells; lactoserum nutrition and pathology (pig and cow).

DEPARTMENT OF PARASITOLOGY 361

Head: Professor Euzeby
Activities: Helminthiasis in domestic and wild ruminants, therapeutics; control of Bilharzia carriers; prevention of babesiosis.

DEPARTMENT OF PATHOLOGICAL ANATOMY AND HISTOLOGY 362

Head: Professor Tisseur
Activities: Immunology of small ruminants.

DEPARTMENT OF PHARMACY AND TOXICOLOGY 363

Head: Professor Lorgue
Activities: Research into the doping of racehorses; human and veterinary medical pharmacokinetics; veterinary toxicology; rodent ethology and biology; rat poisons.

DEPARTMENT OF PHYSICS AND CHEMISTRY 364

Head: Professor Delatour
Activities: Endocrinology of experimental miscarriages in cattle and of carnivore endocrine glands; anthelminthic metabolism and toxicological analysis of their waste products.

DEPARTMENT OF PHYSIOLOGY   365

Head: Professor Bost
Activities: Physiology of the digestive system and nutrition of ruminants.

DEPARTMENT OF REPRODUCTION   366

Head: Professor Bertrand

DEPARTMENT OF SURGERY   367

Head: Professor Le Nihouannen
Activities: Application of videotechniques to veterinary studies.

DEPARTMENT OF SURGICAL   368
PATHOLOGY

Head: Professor Coulon
Activities: Experimental cardiovascular surgery; surgical reanimation; blood transfusions and substitute liquids; bone surgery and pathology of small species; muscular surgery and pathology of the calf.

DEPARTMENT OF ZOOTECHNICS   369

Head: Professor Froget
Activities: Normal and pathologic animal karyology.

École Normale Supérieure*   370

[Normal College]
Address: 45 rue d'Ulm, 75230 Paris Cedex 05
Telephone: (01) 329 12 25
Affiliation: Universités de Paris
Director: Jean Bosquet

LABORATORY OF CHEMISTRY   371

Address: 24 rue Lhomond, 25232 Paris Cedex 05
Telephone: (01) 329 12 25
Research director: Professor Marc Julia
Senior staff: Dr J.Y. Lallemand, Dr D. Mansuy, Professor J.C. Chottard, Professor J.C. Depezay, Dr S. Julia
Graduate research staff: 40
Annual expenditure: £51 000-500 000
Activities: Synthesis of natural products and new regulo- and stereoselective methods, especially with the aid of sulphones; biomimetic synthesis of terpenes; sulphonation; nuclear magnetic resonance: new ways of determining trace quantities; coordination chemistry

and antitumour action of drugs; study of enzymes active in the biotransformation of exogenous products; quantum chemistry.

École Supérieure   372
d'Agriculture de Purpan

– ESAP
[Purpan College of Agriculture]
Address: 271 avenue de Grande-Bretagne, 31076 Toulouse Cedex
Telephone: (061) 49 23 11
Affiliation: Institut Catholique de Toulouse
Director: Professor Robert Pinsdez
Activities: Research forms an integral part of the curriculum. The College assists the agricultural industry and professional organizations.
Contract work: No

LABORATORY OF AGRICULTURAL   373
RESEARCH

Head: Jean Magny
Activities: Agronomy - soil analysis, improvement of manures and animal feed; pure chemistry - pollution and toxicity in food, pesticides and herbicides, food quality and organoleptics, chemical products of wood.

LABORATORY OF COMPUTER   374
SCIENCES AND ECONOMIC
FINANCE

Head: Callixte Couffin
Activities: Budget control and planning. The Laboratory advises other countries on finance under the name Centre International de Contrôle Budgétaire Permanent (CIBP).

LABORATORY OF PLANT   375
PHYSIOLOGY

Head: Paul Cassagnes
Activities: Physiology of perennials and problems relating to fructification.

École Supérieure d'Électricité 376

– ESE
[Electricity College]
Address: Plateau du Moulon, 91190 Gif sur Yvette
or: avenue de la Boulais, 35510 Cesson-Sévigné
Telephone: (06) 941 80 40 and (099) 36 00 21
President: Alexis Dejou
Vice-President: Jacques Beghin
Activities: Research is closely linked to industry.

AUTOMATION DEPARTMENT 377

Head: D. Viault
Activities: Modelling, identification and process command; robotics; numerical command of machines and tools.

AUTOMATION DEPARTMENT - RENNES 378

Head: Y. Quenec'hdu
Activities: Automation; agroalimentary distribution processes; robotics; signalling; handicap aids.

ELECTROMAGNETICS DEPARTMENT 379

Head: Professor J.Ch. Bolomey
Activities: Numerical methodology for radiation and the diffraction of electromagnetic waves; microwave imagery, fixed measurements of near fields; electromagnetic diagnostics of non-homogenous media: biological and geological applications.

ELECTRONIC DEPARTMENT - RENNES 380

Head: J.P. Remblier
Activities: Technological procedures - phenomena (isolation by ionic implants), components (high resistance in monocrystalline and polycrystalline silicon), improvement of technological procedures, electric characterization; conception with the aid of computers - modelling, electric simulation, topology.

ELECTROTECHNICS AND INDUSTRIAL ELECTRONICS DEPARTMENT 381

Head: J. Renouard
Activities: The Department undertakes study, conception and application in collaboration with industry in: control of machine speeds; high performance or industrial converters; special machines.

INFORMATICS DEPARTMENT 382

Head: Dr J. Herbenstreit
Activities: Architecture of systems and distribution; basics; graphic interactive systems.

INFORMATICS DEPARTMENT - RENNES 383

Head: E. Fizzarotti
Activities: Teleinformatics; computer networks; local networks; telematics; office computer systems.

LANGUAGES AND COMMUNICATIONS DEPARTMENT 384

Head: Professor M. Savio

MEASUREMENT DEPARTMENT 385

Head: R. Duperdu
Activities: New measuring instruments; analogue electronic circuits; modelling of complex electronic compounds; study of measuring instruments which use microprocessors.

RADIOELECTRICITY AND ELECTRONICS DEPARTMENT 386

Head: A. Sorba
Activities: Treatment of signals, electronic logic and rapid electronics; high-frequency electronic instrumentation by base frequency numerical methods; characterization of high-frequency systems; optoelectronics.

École Supérieure de Fonderie 387

[Foundry Technology College]
Address: 280 avenue Aristide-Briand, 92220 Bagneux
Telephone: (01) 664 54 50
Director: J. Duflot

École Supérieure du Cuir et des Peintures Encres et Adhésifs 388

– ESCEPEA
[Leather, Paints, Inks and Adhesives Training Institute]
Address: 181/20 avenue Jean Jaurès, BP 7125, 69353 Lyon Cedex 2

Telephone: (07) 87 28 31
Activities: Parallel to its teaching and training, analysis and research is undertaken in the College's laboratories and workshops, especially through long-term contracts with large organizations, both governmental and industrial. The research is done essentially in the fields of leather, paint and plastics.
Note: The College was known formerly as the French School of Tannery.

Électricité de France*   389

– EdF
Address: 2 rue Louis Marat, 75008 Paris
Activities: This national power company is a public utility responsible for supplying electric power throughout France, by both conventional and nuclear systems.

OFFICE OF RESEARCH AND   390
DEVELOPMENT*

Address: 2 rue Louis Marat, 75008 Paris
Activities: This office coordinates research and development, is responsible for quality control, and provides operations assistance to conventional and nuclear power generating and transmiting systems in France. In 1981 it employed 2 300 staff members at five locations in the Paris area.

Chatou Laboratory*   391

Staff: 600 (1981)
Activities: Located on an island of the River Seine, Chatou houses EdF's hydraulic laboratories, carries out studies on nuclear steam generators and thermal machines, and concerns itself with automation and optimization of industrial energy-consuming processes.

ATMOSPHERE AND ENVIRONMENT   392
LABORATORY*
Address: 6 quai Wattier, 78400 Chatou

NATIONAL HYDRAULICS   393
LABORATORY*
Address: 6 quai Wattier, 78400 Chatou

Clamart-Fontenay Laboratories*   394

Address: BP 47, 92140 Clamart
Staff: 1 000 (1981)
Activities: Applications of electrotechnology are studied with respect to energy producing and transforming equipment; research into the planning of electricity transmission and distribution networks; the site houses

the acoustics and vibration laboratories; the laboratories house the computer which processes all EdF's scientific calculations.

Gennevilliers Laboratory*   395

Activities: Studies into the behaviour of steam, particularly in the expansion parts of plants.

Renardières Laboratories*   396

Staff: 500 (1981)
Activities: This laboratory devotes itself to electricity, production and uses, and materials testing and development. It incorporates two large electric laboratories which can produce 200 kA short-circuit currents for power testing, and can test devices under 400 and 800 kV.

Saint Dénis Laboratories*   397

Address: 1 quai de Saint Ouen, 93000 Saint Dénis
Staff: 110 (1981)
Activities: These laboratories develop the testing resources needed for measurement in generating plant.

THERMAL AND NUCLEAR STUDIES   398
AND PROJECTS DIVISION*

Address: Tour EDF-GDR, Défense Quartier Alsace, 92000 Courbevoie

Entreprise Minière et   399
Chimique

– EMC
[Opencast Mining and Chemistry Organization]
Address: 62 rue Jeanne d'Arc, 75646 Paris Cedex 13
Telephone: (01) 584 12 80
Telex: 200191
Director: M. Echard
Activities: Research in the fields of microbiology, biology and pedology as applied to the study of top soil.
Contract work: No

Etablissement Central de   400
l'Armement*

– ECA
[Central Armament Establishment]

Address: 16 bis avenue Prieur de la Côte d'Or, 94114 Arcueil

Fédération Nationale des Centres de Lutte Contre le Cancer   401

[French Federation of Anticancer Centres]
Address: 101 rue de Tolbiac, 75654 Paris Cedex 13
Telephone: (01) 584 11 49
Telex: 201123 F FEDCLCC
Research director: Professor F. Cabanne
Graduate research staff: 200
Annual expenditure: £185 000
Activities: The Federation promotes cooperation between centres, aids research programmes and organizes scientific meetings.
Contract work: No

CENTRE ALEXIS VAUTRIN*   402

Address: avenue de Bourgogne, RN 74 Brabois, 54500 Vandoeuvre les Nancy
Director: Professor C. Chardot

CENTRE ANTOINE LACASSAGNE*   403

Address: 36 voie Romaine, 06054 Nice Cedex
Director: Professor C. Lalanne

CENTRE CLAUDIUS RÉGAUD*   404

Address: 11 rue Piquemil, 31052 Toulouse Cedex
Director: Professor P.F. Combes

CENTRE EUGENE MARQUIS*   405

Address: Pontchaillou, 35011 Rennes Cedex
Head: Professor J.L. Richier

CENTRE FRANÇOIS BACLESSE*   406

Address: route de Lion sur Mer, BP 5026, 14021 Caen Cedex
Director: Professor J.S. Abbatucci

CENTRE GEORGES FRANÇOIS LECLERC*   407

Address: 1 rue du Professeur Marion, 21034 Dijon Cedex
Director: Professor F. Cabanne

CENTRE HENRI BECQUEREL*   408

Address: rue d'Amiens, 96038 Rouen Cedex
Director: Professor R. Laumonier

CENTRE JEAN PERRIN*   409

Address: 30 place Henri-Dunant, BP 392, 63011 Clermont Ferrand Cedex
Director: Professor G. Meyniel

CENTRE LÉON BÉRARD*   410

Address: 28 rue Laënnec, 69373 Lyon Cedex 2
Director: Professor M. Mayer

CENTRE OSCAR LAMBRET*   411

Address: rue Frédéric-Combemale, BP 307, 59020 Lille Cedex
Director: Professor A. Demaille

CENTRE PAUL LAMARQUE*   412

Address: Pavillon Curie - Cliniques St Eloi, avenue du Professeur Grasset, 34059 Montpellier
Director: Professor C. Romieu

CENTRE PAUL PAPIN*   413

Address: 2 rue Moll, 49036 Angers Cedex
Director: Professor F. Larra

CENTRE PAUL STRAUSS*   414

Address: 3 rue de la Porte de l'Hôpital, 67085 Strasbourg Cedex
Director: Professor G. Methlin

CENTRE RENÉ GAUDUCHEAU*   415

Address: quai Moncousu, 44035 Nantes Cedex
Director: Professor R. Guihard

CENTRE RENÉ HUGUENIN*   416

Address: 35 rue Dailly, 92211 Saint-Cloud Cedex
Director: Dr J. Gest

FONDATION BERGONIE*   417

Address: 180 rue de Saint-Genès, 33076 Bordeaux Cedex
Director: Professor C. Lagarde

INSTITUT J. PAOLI-I. CALMETTES* 418

[J. Paoli-I. Calmettes Institute]
Address: 232 boulevard de Sainte-Marguerite, 13273 Marseille Cedex 09
Director: Professor Y. Carcassonne

INSTITUT JEAN GODINOT* 419

[Jean Godinot Institute]
Address: 1 rue du Général Koenig, BP 171, 51056 Reims Cedex
Director: Professor A. Cattan

Fédération Universitaire et Polytechnique de Lille 420

[Lille University and Polytechnic Federation]
Address: 60 boulevard Vauban, 59046 Lille Cedex
Telephone: (020) 30 88 27
Telex: GEFIRN 120 369
Rector: M. Falise

FACULTY OF MEDICINE AND PHARMACY 421

Address: 56 rue du Port, 59046 Lille Cedex
Dean: Professor Jacques Liefooghe

Anatomy Department 422

Head: Professor Henri Batteur
Senior staff: Dr Pelerin

Bacteriology, Virology and Immunology Department 423

Head: Professor Marc Duhamel
Senior staff: Dr J.L. Demory; Noel Denis; J.C. Lemahieu

Biochemical Semeiology Department 424

Head: Professor J.L. Dhondt

Biochemistry Department 425

Head: Professor J.L. Dhondt

Cardiovascular Pathology Department 426

Senior staff: Professor Paul Giard, Professor Lucien Croccel, Professor Dutoit

Dermatology Department 427

Head: Professor Pierre De Beer

Digestive Tract and Nutrition Diseases Department 428

Senior staff: Professor B. Filoche, Professor Joseph Ampe, Professor Gustave Routier

Embryology Department 429

Head: Dr R. Fenart

Endocrine Diseases Department 430

Head: Professor Gustave Routier

General and Cellular Biology Department 431

Head: Professor L. Olivier
Senior staff: Dr Fenart

General and Organic Chemistry Department 432

Head: Bernard Van Bockstael

Gynaecology and Obstetrics Department 433

Senior staff: Professor Marcel Gaudefroy, Professor Louis Corette, Dr Coliche, Dr Delcroix

Haematology Department 434

Head: Professor Marc Duhamel
Senior staff: Dr J.L. Demory

Histology Department 435

Head: Professor Léon Olivier
Senior staff: Dr Jousserandot

Hygiene and Preventive Medicine Department 436

Senior staff: Professor Jacques Cousin, Dr Grimbelle, Dr Pettenati

Infectious Diseases Department 437

Senior staff: Professor Albert Fournier, Professor Anne Pauli, Professor Jacques Cousin

Locomotor Pathology Department 438

Senior staff: Rheumatology, Professor Georges Vincent, Dr Derreumaux; traumatology and orthopaedics, Professor Bertrand Vinchon

Medical Genetics Department 439

Head: Professor Jacques Cousin

Medical Semeiology Department 440

Head: Professor Philippe Choteau

Neurology and Psychiatry Department 441

Senior staff: Professor J.F. Dereux, Professor Jean Ernst, Professor Ph. Choteau

Ophthalmology Department 442

Head: Dr Philippe Leurent

Otorhinolaryngology Department 443

Head: Professor Van Nieuwenhuyse

Paediatrics Department 444

Senior staff: Professor Albert Fournier, Professor Anne Pauli, Professor Jacques Cousin, Professor Bayart

Parasitic Diseases and Exotic Pathology Department 445

Senior staff: Mme Vittu

Pathological Anatomy Department 446

Senior staff: Professor Jean Saout, Professor Creusy

Pharmacology Department 447

Head: Dr Michel Mathieu

Physics, Mathematics and Statistics Department 448

Senior staff: Professor Christian Vittu, Professor Dumoulin, M. Martin

Physiology Department 449

Head: Professor Jacques Liefooghe

Psychology Department 450

Senior staff: Professor Jean Ernst, Professor J.F. Dereux, Professor Ph. Choteau

Radiology Department 451

Head: Professor Empereur-Buisson

Reanimation and First Aid Department 452

Head: Professor Paul Langeron
Senior staff: Dr B. Lepoutre; Dr Prevost

Respiratory Pathology Department 453

Head: Professor Jacques Crinquette

Stomatology Department 454

Head: Dr Disclaire

Surgical Semeiology Department 455

Head: Professor Callens

Urology and Nephrology Department 456

Senior staff: Professor Henri Batteur, Professor Paul Giard

FACULTY OF SCIENCE 457

Address: 13 rue de Toul, 59046 Lille Cedex
Dean: Professor André Defebvre

Botany Department 458

Senior staff: Phytosociology and ecology, Professor Renée Lericq; vegetable physiology and phytopathology, Dr Joseph-Marie Richard; cellular biology, Irène Devos

MARINE BIOLOGY LABORATORY 459

Director: Irène Devos

Chemistry Department 460

Senior staff: Physical chemistry, Professor Gérard Lepoutre; organic synthesis, Professor Bernard Frémaux

Electrical Department 461

Director: Bernard Griffet
Senior staff: Machines, Bernard Griffet; power electronics, B. Verriez; measurement and control, Michel Vittu; automation, Jean Marie Grave

Electronics, Automatic Control and 462
Data Processing Department

Senior staff: Electronics, Professor Jean-Pierre Poupaert; automatic control, Professor Etienne Deffontaines; data processing, Professor Léon Carrez

Geology Laboratory 463

Senior staff: Devonian biostratigraphy (from brachiopoda of Afghanistan, France and the Arctic Islands), Professor Denise Brice; Devonian biostratigraphy (from stromato-poroids - Boulonnais F., Afghanistan), Bruno Mistiaen; Devonian biostratigraphy (from Rugosa), Jean-Claude Rohart

Mathematics Department 464

Senior staff: Variable functions, Professor Jean Delporte; special functions, Professor Bruno Sion

Physics Department 465

Director: Professor André Defebvre
Senior staff: Ultrasonic Laboratory, Professor André Defebvre; Solid-State Physics Laboratory, Michel Lannoo

Zoology Department 466

Head: Professor Jean Pierre Parent

POLYTECHNICUM DE LILLE 467

[Lille Polytechnic]

École des Hautes Études Industrielles 468

– HEI
[College of Advanced Industrial Studies]
Address: 13 rue de Toul, 59046, Lille Cedex
Telephone: (020) 30 83 14
Telex: GEFIRN 120 369
Director: Gerard Leroy
Research director: Bernard Griffet

ANALYTICAL AND INSTRUMENTAL 469
CHEMISTRY LABORATORY

Head: Christian Notteau
Graduate research staff: 6

AUTOMATION AND ELECTRONICS 470
LABORATORY

Head: Jean Marie Grave
Graduate research staff: 9

ELECTROTECHNICS AND POWER 471
ELECTRONICS LABORATORY

Head: Bernard Griffet
Graduate research staff: 5

ENERGETICS LABORATORY 472

Head: Professor Gérard Lepoutre
Graduate research staff: 4

MATHEMATICS OF STRUCTURES 473
LABORATORY

Head: Jean-Claude Debus
Graduate research staff: 5

ORGANIC SYNTHESIS LABORATORY 474

Head: Professor Bernard Frémaux
Graduate research staff: 5

Institut Supérieur d'Agriculture 475

– ISA
[Higher Institute of Agriculture]
Address: 39 bis rue du Port, 59046 Lille Cedex
Director: Professor René Dusautois

Institut Supérieur d'Électronique du 476
Nord

– ISEN
[Higher Electronics Institute of the North]
Address: 3 rue François Baës, 59046 Lille Ctdex
Director: Professor Gaston Vandecandelaere

Institut Technique Roubaisien 477

– ITR
[Roubaix Technical Institute]
Address: 37 rue du Collège, 59100 Roubaix
Director: Professor Bernard Avrin

ADVANCED TECHNOLOGY 478
DEPARTMENT

Activities: Textile mechanics and textile chemistry.

ENGINEERING DEPARTMENT 479

UNIVERSITY ATTACHED INSTITUTE 480

Institut Catholique d'Arts et Métiers 481

– ICAM
[Catholic Institute of Arts and Crafts]
Address: 6 rue Auber, 59046 Lille Cedex
Director: Professor Guy Carpier

Fenwick-Manutention 482

Address: 69 rue du Docteur Bauer, BP 190, 93404 Saint-Ouen Cedex
Telephone: (01) 252 81 80
Technical Director: P. Delesalle
Director, Manufacturing: J. Porry
Manager, Research: J.C. Van Dest
Activities: Research and development in the following: mechanical handling applications, especially for fork-lift trucks; pedestrian or rider-controlled electrical narrow-aisle trucks; and industrial tractors.

Fondation pour la Recherche Medicale 483

[Medical Research Foundation]
Address: 10 rue de Lisbonne, 75008 Paris
Telephone: (02) 292 14 40
Scientific Council President: Professor J.-F. Bach
Administrative Council President: Jacques de Fouchier
Activities: Promotion and coordination of all types of medical and scientific research and fundamental biology in relation to medicine.
Contract work: No
Publications: Recherche et Santé, three monthly.

Générale d'Aquiculture 484

Address: Ferme Aquicole Guerandaise, Saline Saint-Goustan, avenue Poincaré, 44490 Le Croisic
Affiliation: Compagnie Générale Maritime
Manager: Joseph Pedron
Activities: Breeding and selling living food for aquarium animals, such as 'artemia salina'.

Groupe d'Étude et de Synthèse des Microstructures* 485

[Microstructures Research and Synthesis Group]
Address: École Supérieure de Physique et Chimie In-dustrielle de la Ville de Paris, 10 rue Vauquelin, 75231 Paris Cedex
Affiliation: Centre National de la Recherche Scientifique
Director: Max Paulus

Groupement d'Études et de Recherches pour le Développement de l' Agronomie Tropicale 486

– GERDAT
[Tropical Agronomy Development Research and Study Group]
Address: 42 rue Scheffer, 75016 Paris
Telephone: (01) 704 32 15; 553 56 41
Scientific and Technical Director: Hervé Bichat
Graduate research staff: 1 323 (in all member institutes)
Annual expenditure: F400m
Activities: GERDAT is a group of tropical and subtropical orientated bodies which undertake work on research, development project study and development aid, within the framework of French scientific and technical cooperation with developing countries. The effectiveness of its operations depends upon the research carried out in the tropical zone, both in its own stations in the French Overseas Departments and Territories and also on foreign stations where its research teams provide assistance.
GERDAT has two main governing bodies: the Assembly of Members, a decision-making body consisting of representatives of the different ministries concerned with GERDAT's work, the Caisse Centrale de Cooperation Économique and member institutes; the Scientific and Technical Council, consisting of specially selected highly qualified people who examine the research programmes, see that they comply with the overall tropical agriculture research policies and submit the necessary options.
The eight member institutes are as follows (see also under their separate entries):
Centre Technique Forestier Tropical - CTFT
Institut d'Élevage de Médicine Vétérinaire des Pays Tropicaux - IEMVT
Institut Français du Café, du Cacao et autres Plantes Stimulantes - IFCC
Institut de Recherches Agronomiques Tropicales et des Cultures Vivrières - IRAT
Institut de Recherches sur le Caoutchouc - IRCA
Institut de Recherches du Coton et des Textiles Exotiques - IRCT
Institut de Recherches sur les Fruits et Agrumes - IRFA
Institut de Recherches pour les Huiles et Oléagineaux.

Other affiliated research centres (also with separate entries) are:
Centre d'Études et d'Expérimentation du Machinisme Agricole Tropicale - CEEMAT
Institut pour la Formation Agronomique et Rurale en Régions Chaudes - IFARC.
GERDAT's work involves all the plant and animal produce of the intertropical zone. Research however deals chiefly with the main resources such as: timber and forestry, freshwater fish-farming (CTFT); animal husbandry and zootechnology, animal vaccines, pastoralism (IEMVT); coffee, cocoa, tea, cola (IFCC); irrigated and upland rice, maize, wheat, sorghum, millet, food legumes, cassava and other tubers, market garden crops, fodder crops, sugar cane (IRAT); rubber (IRCA); cotton, sisal and other tropical fibres (IRCT); pineapple, banana, citrus fruit, avocado, mango, papaya and other tropical fruit (IRFA); oil palm, coconut, groundnut, soyabean (IRHO).
Apart from sectorial studies for each product, GERDAT also deals with general problems such as: soil and water conservation; irrigation methods and equipment; draught animals and motorized cultivation; general technological problems (crushing, fermenting, drying, preservation and stocking); cropping and production systems; integrated development of the natural environment; agricultural produce markets.
Contract work: Yes
Publications: AGRITROP, biennially, in French, English and Spanish.

MONTPELLIER RESEARCH CENTRE 487

Address: BP 5035, 34032 Montpellier Cedex
Telephone: (067) 63 91 70
Telex: 480 762 F
President: R. Huet
Activities: Applied research in tropical agriculture; technical support in development; training of specialized staff.
Facilities: 1 500 sq m of greenhouses.

Institut Catholique de Paris 488

[Catholic Institute of Paris]
Address: 21 rue d'Assas, 75270 Paris Cedex 06
Telephone: (01) 222 41 80
Rector: Mgr Paul Poupard
Vice-Rector: Michel Legrain
Note: The Colleges are linked to the Institute by an agreement to follow Catholic doctrines and which establishes their administrative and financial independence.

ÉCOLE DE FORMATION PSYCHO-PÉDAGOGIQUE 489

[College of Psycho-pedagogic Formation]
Address: 22 rue Cassette, 75006 Paris
Telephone: (01) 548 80 46
Director: Jean Ughetto

ÉCOLE DE PSYCHOLOGUES PRACTICIENS 490

[College of Practising Psychologists]
Telephone: (01) 548 17 75
Director: Jean Besson
Activities: Special emphasis is placed on pedagogic research and the College has a closed-circuit television with a magnetoscope.

ÉCOLE SUPÉRIEUR DE CHIMIE ORGANIQUE ET MINÉRALE 491

[Organic and Mineral Chemistry College]
Address: 12 rue Cassette, Paris 6
Telephone: (01) 548 87 43
Administrative Director: Pierre Mastagli

ÉCOLE SUPÉRIEURE DES SCIENCES ÉCONOMIQUES ET COMMERCIALES 492

– ESSEC
[Economic and Commercial Sciences College]
Address: BP 105, 95021 030 40 57
Director: Julien Coudy

INSTITUT GÉOLOGIQUE ALBERT DE LAPPARENT 493

[Albert de Lapparent Geology Institute]
Telephone: (01) 222 54 86
Director: Pierre Bordet

INSTITUT SUPÉRIEUR AGRICOLE DE BEAUVAIS 494

[Beauvais Institute of Agriculture]
Address: rue Pierre Wauguet, BP 313, 60026 Beauvais
Telephone: (04) 445 52 63
Director General: Jean Hurier

INSTITUT SUPÉRIEUR 495
D'ÉLECTRONIQUE DE PARIS

[Paris Institute of Electronics]
Telephone: (01) 548 24 87
Director General: l'Abbé Jean Vieillard
Activities: Industrial electronics; telecommunications; informatics.

Institut Curie 496

[Curie Institute]
Address: 26 rue d'Ulm, 75231 Paris Cedex 05
Telephone: (01) 329 12 42
Chairman: Professor F. Cabanne
Annual expenditure: over £2m
Activities: The Institute (formerly Foundation Curie-Institut du Radium) is devoted to the development of scientific research on radiation, in physics, biology and medicine. A large part of this research deals with cancer, from a fundamental point of view (carcinogenesis), as well as for practical medical applications (diagnosis, treatment, prevention).
Contract work: No

BIOLOGY SECTION 497

Director: Dr J.M. Lhoste
Graduate research staff: 100
Publications: Annual report.

MEDICAL AND HOSPITAL SECTION 498

Director: Dr R. Calle
Publications: Annual report.

PHYSICS AND CHEMISTRY SECTION 499

Director: Professor M. Duquesne
Graduate research staff: 40
Publications: Annual report.

Institut d'Astrophysique de 500
Paris

– IAP
[Astrophysics Institute of Paris]
Address: 98 boulevard Arago, 75014 Paris
Telephone: (01) 320 14 25
Affiliation: Centre National de la Recherche Scientifique; Institut National d' Astronomie et de Géophysique
Research director: Jean Audouze

Graduate research staff: 41
Activities: The main subjects of research concern the surroundings and atmosphere of stars and the sun.

Institut d'Élevage et de 501
Médecine Vétérinaire des
Pays Tropicaux

– IEMVT
[Institute of Animal Production and Veterinary Science for Tropical Countries]
Address: 10 rue Pierre Curie, 94700 Maisons-Alfort
Telephone: (01) 368 88 73
Parent body: Groupement d'Études et de Recherches pour le Développement de l'Agronomie Tropicale - GERDAT
General Manager: Alain Provost
Associate General Managers: Henri Serres, Georges Tacher
Activities: IEMVT's aim is to contribute to the development and improvement of livestock production and industries in hot countries and particularly in tropical and equatorial environments of Africa, Asia and South America. In order to fulfil this mission the Institute contributes to the training and further training of graduates and livestock assistants, circulates information, conducts research on animal products development (mammals, fowl, fish). IEMVT's areas of interest are the following: animal science, environment studies, range management, nutrition, livestock economics, animal and public health.
The Institute within agreements passed with organizations and governments, carries out permanent and temporary missions (setting up and management of laboratories and research stations), in Africa and in Asia (Thailand).
Research is concentrated in the following areas:
Protection of public and animal health - infectious diseases, zoonoses; epidemiological surveys; vaccine production; campaigns for disease prevention and treatment; vector eradication; health control of livestock; animal products for human consumption.
Planning and economics - socio-economic study of livestock; marketing of livestock and meat; abattoir management; small stock farming; livestock products and by-products, livestock industries; laboratory projects.
Animal production - biochemical genetics, biology; stock breeding surveys; selection of native breeds; crossbreeding and artificial insemination; livestock improvement; draught animals.
Environment and nutrition - botanical and ecological studies; survey and mapping of pastures; agropastoralism, stocking rate assessment; preservation, reclamation, improvement and management of pastures; intensifica-

tion of fodder production; ranching, animal nutrition; animal fattening; food science and agro-industrial by-products; wild life.
Contract work: Yes

Institut d'Embryologie* 502

[Embryology Institute]
Address: 49 bis avenue de la Belle-Gabrielle, 94130 Nogent sur Marne
Affiliation: Centre National de la Recherche Scientifique
Director: Professor Nicole Le Douarin

Institut d'Histochimie Médicale 503

[Medical Histochemistry Institute]
Address: 45 rue des Saints-Pères, 75270 Paris Cedex 06
Telephone: (01) 260 37 20
Parent body: Université Paris V
Research director: Professor Raymond J. Wegmann
Sections: GABA and brain, Professor F. Gonzáles-Ríos; fluorocarbons in placenta, Professor B. Vilala; triple densitometry, Professor M. Yamada; rymation (automatic quantitative multiple enzyme processor)
Annual expenditure: £50 000
Activities: Histo-enzymology (qualitative and quantitative), applied to medicine, pharmacology and industry; biophysical techniques applied to the cells and tissues: plasma atomic absorption; quantitative electron microscopes; X-rays; microprobes, electronic and ionic (EMMA, STEMMA, IMMA); laser Raman microprobe; nuclear magnetic resonance; electron spin resonance; circular dichroism.
Contract work: Yes

Institut de Biologie Moléculaire et Cellulaire* 504

[Molecular and Cellular Biology Institute]
Address: 15 rue René-Descartes, 67000 Strasbourg
Affiliation: Centre National de la Recherche Scientifique
Directors: Professor Jean-Pierre Ebel, Professor Léon Hirth
Departments:
Biochemistry, Professor J.P. Ebel, Professor G. Dirheimer, Professor J.H. Weil, Professor Y. Boulanger
Biophysics, Professor M. Daune
Physiological genetics, Professor F. Lacroute

Virology, Professor L. Hirth
Activities: RNA-DNA structures and interactions; chemical cancerogenesis; structure of chromatin histones; properties of nucleic acids, of ribosomes and of ribosomal proteins; biochemical genetics of yeasts; isometric viruses; mechanisms of virus combination; immunological study of viruses and viral proteins; viral genomes; replica enzymes of RNA viruses; biochemical study of the defense mechanisms of plants to viral infection; chromatine in higher plant life; cell differentiation in vegetables.

Institut de Neurophysiologie et de Psychophysiologie* 505

[Neurophysiology and Psychophysiology Institute]
Address: 31 chemin Joseph-Aiguier, 13274 Marseille Cedex 3
Affiliation: Centre National de la Recherche Scientifique
Director: Professor Jacques Paillard
Deputy Director: Noël Meï

Institut de Physique du Globe de Paris 506

[Paris Institute of Earth Physics]
Address: Tour 14,4 place Jussieu, 75230 Paris Cedex
Telephone: (01) 336 25 25 or 325 12 21
Affiliation: Institut National d'Astronomie et de Géophysique; Université Pierre et Marie Curie (Paris VI)
Director: Professor C.-J. Allegre
Graduate research staff: 96
Activities: The institute coordinates national and international fundamental research programmes; manages a permanent observation of natural phenomena in France and overseas; and operates individual observations of the earth, the sea, and space.
Among the programmes in which the institute participates are: aeromagnetic cartography of France and the western Mediterranean; deep magnetic soundings in the south of France; seismic surveying in western France, Massif Central, Rhône and Rhine valleys, Djibouti, Madeira and the Canaries, and the Atlantic ridge north of the Azores; chronology of basic and ultrabasic intrusions; analysis of Russian and American lunar samples; geophysical surveys in the Indian Ocean; establishing a seismological network of Djibouti; improvement of the seismological network around the Alboran Sea; ionospheric soundings using coherent radar.
Facilities: Saint-Maur Observatory; Chambon-la-Fo-

ret Observatory; observatories at Terre-Adélie, Kerguelen, Crozet, and Amsterdam; volcanological observatories at Guadeloupe and Martinique; seismological observatories at St Sauveur and Arta (Djibouti); seismological stations at Villiers-Adam and Moulis; facilities for magnetic cartography, geophysical prospection for archaeological prospection, experimental seismology and volcanology.

Institut de Physique du Globe de Strasbourg   507

[Strasbourg Institute of Earth Physics]
Address: 5 rue Descartes, 67084 Strasbourg Cedex
Telephone: (088) 61 48 20
Affiliation: Institut National d'Astronomie et de Géophysique; Université Louis Pasteur (Strasbourg I)
Research director: Roland Schlich
Graduate research staff: 32
Activities: Studies of the earth's crust and interior (gravimetry, geomagnetism, tides, and seismology), with particular emphasis on seismicity-localization of seismic zones and studies of their centres, and palaeomagnetism - reconstitution of gravitational fields and their application to the continental drift.
Facilities: Seismology stations at Strasbourg, Welschbruch and Sainte-Marie-aux-Mines; palaeomagnetic and gravimetric station at Griesham sur Souffel.

Institut de Recherche sur les Transports*   508

– IRT
[Transportation Research Institute]
Address: 2 avenue du Général Malleret Joinville, BP 28, 941 14 Arcueil
Activities: This government agency is particularly active in the field of fast inter-city links and short distance transport.

Institut de Recherches Agronomiques Tropicales et des Cultures Vivrières   509

– IRAT
[Tropical Agronomical Research Institute]
Address: 110 rue de l' Université, 75007 Paris
Telephone: (01) 550 32 10
Telex: 20039
Parent body: Groupement d'Études et de Recherches

pour le Developpement de l' Agronomie Tropicale - GERDAT
Research coordinator: Claude Dumont
Departments: Agronomy, R. Tourte; plant breeding and improvement, M. Tardieu; crop protection, J. Brenière
Graduate research staff: 200
Annual expenditure: over £2m
Activities: Research work on the following crops: upland rice; aquatic rice; maize; sorghum, millets; wheat, barley; sugar cane; sugar beet; soyabean; cassava, tuber crops; vegetable crops; with the following objectives: plant improvement - breeding, selection, seed production; plant physiology - drought resistance, mineral nutrition; crop protection - pest and disease control, weed control, storage; cultivation methods - rotations, tillage, mechanization; water management - water requirements of plants, drainage, irrigation; soil improvement - organic and mineral balances, fertilization; environmental study - soil survey, mapping, frequency analyses of climate; rural economy - analysis and simulation of production units; technology - nutritive qualities of cereals, industrial processing.
Other work is undertaken in close cooperation with agricultural development services on the following: evaluation of research innovations in the actual environment - test-farms and test-lands, experimental units; regional inventory of agricultural potentials; technical studies of development projects - improvement of traditional farming systems, farming systems for irrigated areas, agro-industrial complexes; support research - agro-economic analyses, preliminary experimentation of the projects, support for operations in progress.
In addition to the central establishment in France, IRAT is working in cooperation with various agricultural institutes in Brazil, Cameroon, Comoro Islands, French Guiana, Ivory Coast, Kenya, Madagascar, Mali, Martinique, Niger, Reunion, Senegal, Togo and Upper Volta.
Contract work: No
Publications: L'Agronomie Tropicale; annual report.

PROJECT STUDY DEPARTMENT   510

Address: 45 bis, avenue de la Belle Gabrielle, 94130 Nogent sur Marne
Telephone: (01) 873 58 66
Telex: 211937

SCIENTIFIC DEPARTMENT AND LABORATORIES   511

Address: avenue du Val de Montferrand, Montferrier sur Lèz, BP 5035, 34032 Montpellier
Telephone: (067) 63 91 70

Institut de Recherches du Coton et des Textiles Exotiques 512

– IRCT
[Cotton and Exotic Textile Research Institute]
Address: 34 rue des Renaudes, 75017 Paris
Telephone: (01) 622 54 26
Parent body: Groupement d'Études et de Recherches pour le Développement de l'Agronomie Tropicale - GERDAT
Director General: J. Dequecker
Research director: S. Cretenet
Sections: Entomology, R. Delattré; genetics, J.B. Roux; agronomy, L. Richard; technology, J. Gutknecht; agro-sociology, M. Braud; chemistry, J. Schwendiman; physiology, M. Cognée; phytopathology, J.C. Follin
Activities: Research in agronomy, genetics and plant protection (entomology, phytopathology, virology and biological control) for improving production and fibre quality of textile tropical plants (cotton, sisal and jute substitutes, etc); research on ginning techniques and fibre physical analysis; improving nutritional value of cottonseeds.
Contract work: No
Publications: Coton et Fibres Tropicales, quarterly.

Institut de Recherches en Biologie Moléculaire* 513

[Molecular Biology Research Institute]
Address: Université de Paris VII, 2 place Jussieu, tour 43, 75221 Paris Cedex 05
Affiliation: Centre National de la Recherche Scientifique; Université de Paris VII
Directors: Bernardi Georgis, François Chapeville

Institut de Recherches Hydrologiques 514

[Hydrological Research Institute]
Address: 10 rue Ernest Bichat, 54000 Nancy
Telephone: (08) 396 65 10
Scientific director: François Colin
Sections: Scientific, François Colin; technical, J.C. Boeglin
Graduate research staff: 7
Annual expenditure: £501 000-2m
Activities: Drinking and industrial water treatment; wastewater treatment; sludge and solid wastes treatment

and disposal; corrosion, scaling and fouling in industrial use of water.
Contract work: Yes

Institut de Recherches pour les Huiles et Oléagineaux 515

– IRHO
[Tropical Oil Crops Research Institute]
Address: 11 Square Pétrarque, 75016 Paris
Telephone: (01) 553 60 25
Telex: 630491
Parent body: Groupement d'Études et de Recherches pour le Développement de l'Agronomie Tropicale - GERDAT
Director: M.J. Fleury
Activities: Research and development in the following areas: adaptation of production techniques - economy of fertilizers, water and labour, combined with assessment of critical levels of mineral elements by leaf analysis; research into high-yielding varieties; crop protection - control of disease, pests and weeds; improvement of oil extraction techniques.
Publications: Oléagineaux, monthly.

SCIENTIFIC DEPARTMENTS AND LABORATORIES 516

Address: BP 5035, 34032 Montpellier Cedex
Telephone: (067) 63 91 70

Institut de Recherches Scientifiques sur le Cancer* 517

[Cancer Scientific Research Centre]
Address: 7 rue Guy Moquet, BP 8, 94800 Villejuif
Affiliation: Centre National de la Recherche Scientifique
Director: Roger Monier
Deputy Director: Pierre Burtin

Institut de Recherches sur la Catalyse* 518

[Catalysis Research Institute]
Address: 2 avenue Albert Einstein, 69626 Villeurbanne
Affiliation: Centre National de la Recherche Scientifique
Director: Boris Imelik
Deputy Directors: Louis de Mourgues, Pierre Gravelle

Institut de Recherches sur le Caoutchouc   519

– IRCA
[Rubber Research Institute]
Address: 42 rue Scheffer, 75016 Paris
Telephone: (01) 553 93 96
Telex: 620 871
Parent body: Groupement d'Études et de Recherches pour le Développement de l'Agronomie Tropicale - GERDAT
Chairman: M.R. de Padirac
General Manager: Jean Campaignolle
Senior staff: Director of technology, Jean Leveque; Head of agronomy, Paul Gener; Biochemistry division, Jean-Louis Jacob
Graduate research staff: 21
Annual expenditure: F24m (1981)
Activities: Research work is carried out under the supervision of a Committee made up of specialists from various disciplines and planters, the function of the Committee being to submit programmes to official government bodies empowered to take any relevant decisions.
Research is conducted in the following areas: raw materials derived from solar energy; morphogenetic study of heave, its production and cultivation; mineral nutrition; plant protection; improvements in exploitation techniques; degradation of rubber; work on developing new types of rubber (carried out in France through the Institut de Recherche Appliquée sur les Polymères). There are also research centres in the Ivory Coast and Cameroon working on new methods of processing and producing rubber, and collecting latex.
IRCA research workers assist in giving technical training in Third World countries; and the main services offered by IRCA are: pedological, agronomic, technological and economic studies; preparation of development projects for financing organizations; supplying of selected high-productivity planting material; technical advice on plantations; nutrition control; fertilization; phytosanitary control; formulation of industrial projects.
Facilities: 809 40 ha of experimental estates; pilot plant.
Publications: Annual report, half-yearly report.

LABORATOIRE *   520

Address: BP 5035, 34032 Montpellier Cedex

Institut de Recherches sur les Fruits et Agrumes   521

– IRFA
[Tropical Fruit Research Institute]
Address: 6 rue du Général Clergerie, 75116 Paris
Telephone: (01) 553 16 92
Parent body: Groupement d'Études et de Recherches pour le Développement de l'Agronomie Tropicale - GERDAT
Director: M.J. Cuille
Sections: Citrus fruit; pineapple; bananas; diversification; industrial technology
Activities: Research and development in the following areas: diseases of citrus fruits; control of banana parasites and pests; studies on tropical fruit for European markets including avocado, mango, lychee, mangosteen, pawpaw, cashew and passion fruit, and diversified cropping systems; agro-pedology, soil surveys, soil analysis; bioclimatology; biometry; entomology and nematology; plant pathology; plant nutrition, leaf analysis, mineral balances; research on essential oils and aromas; fruit juice analysis; bromeline research; new processing methods; definition of cropping systems, assessment of the economic value of innovations, agro-industrial projects; data collection on world fruit trade.

TECHNICAL DEPARTMENTS AND LABORATORIES   522

Address: BP 5035, 34032 Montpellier Cedex

Institut de Soudure   523

[Welding Institute]
Address: 32 boulevard de la Chapelle, 75880 Paris Cedex 18
Telephone: (01) 203 94 05
Telex: OFISOUD 210335 F
Research director: M Granjon
Sections: Welding technology, M Rosenzweig; fracture mechanics, M Bramat; metallurgy-weldability, M Dadian; hyperbaric welding, M Eliot
Graduate research staff: 10
Annual expenditure: £10 000-50 000
Activities: Research and development in the following areas: welding processes - parameters and applications; weldability of steels and nickel alloys; fatigue behaviour and mechanical characteristics of welded assemblies; health and safety of welders.
Contract work: No
Publications: Soudage et techniques connexés, (welding and allied processes).

Institut Des Corps Gras   524

[Fats and Oils Research Institute]
Address: 10A rue de la Paix, 75002 Paris
Telephone: (01) 296 50 29
Telex: 230905
General manager: Jean Pierre Wolff
Graduate research staff: 25
Annual expenditure: F6m
Activities: Technology and research on fats and their derivatives; methods, properties, applications in foodstuffs (oils, margarine) and in the chemical industry (soaps, detergents, paints, and lipid chemistry). Pilot plants for oil production and transformation; research laboratories for chemistry, biochemistry, catalysis, analytical research.
Contract work: No
Publications: Revue Français des Corps Gras.

Institut des Hautes Études   525
Cinematographiques

– IDHEC
[Cinematography Institute]
Address: 4 avenue de l'Europe, 94360 Bry sur Marne
Affiliation: Ministère de la Culture et de la Communication
President: Jean Delannoy
Activities: Teaching and research institute on all aspects of cinematographic and televisual arts.

Institut et Centre   526
d'Optométrie

– CEDOC-OPTO
[Optometry Institute and Centre]
Address: 134 route de Chartres, 91440 Bures sur Yvette
Telephone: (0336) 907 67 37
Founder-Director: Gérard-Charles Roosen
Departments:
Optometry, Gérard Guinhut, Catherine Thibault, Catherine Ravitsky, Odile L. Kienlin, Thérèse Thiébaut, Francine Duranton, J. Gresset, M. Pavillon, Jean-Paul Roosen, P. Roosen
Glasses, Henri Deveycx, Dominique Harel, Jean-Michel Jobard, Jacques Munck, Catherine Ravitsky, P. Roosen, Roger Soulier, Thierry Thomas
Activities: The aims of the Centre are to ensure the correct development in the teaching of ophthalmic optics and in the practice of optometry. It provides information on all subjects taught at the centre: optical physiology, ocular physiology, contact lenses, optometry, lense technology, etc. It is open for consultation and has facilities for research on certain topics.

Institut et Observatoire de   527
Physique du Globe du Puy-
de-Dôme

[Puy-de-Dôme Earth Physics Observatory and Institute]
Address: 12 avenue des Landais, 63001 Clermont-Ferrand Cedex
Telephone: (073) 92 57 19
Affiliation: Institut National d'Astronomie et de Géophysique; Université de Clermont-Ferrand II
Research director: P. Waltdeufel
Graduate research staff: 18
Activities: Research into: convective phenomena; atmospheric physics; geomagnetism.

Institut Français du Café,   528
du Cacao et autres Plantes
Stimulantes

– IFCC
[Institute of Coffee, Cocoa and other Stimulant Plants]
Address: 34 rue des Renaudes, 75017 Paris
Telephone: (01) 622 53 26
Telex: 270105F TXFRA/réf 758
Parent body: Groupement d'Études et de Recherches pour le Développement de l'Agronomie Tropicale - GERDAT
Director: René Coste
Sections: Genetics; agronomy; entomology; phytopathology; biometry; chemistry-technology
Graduate research staff: 80
Annual expenditure: F39 300 000
Activities: Design and implementation of all types of research on stimulant plants and their products, in liaison with producing and consuming countries, with the following aims: improvement of plant material and selection of cultivars suitable for each growing region; formulation of efficient agronomic methods depending on the environment and plant material used; study of diseases and parasites with a view to perfecting appropriate control methods; improvement of methods and techniques for processing harvested produce.
Contract work: Yes
Publications: Café Cacao Thé, quarterly; annual report.

Institut Français du Pétrole   529

[French Institute of Petroleum]
Address: 1 et 4, avenue de Bois-Préau, 92506 Rueil-Malmaison
Telephone: (01) 749 02 14
Telex: IPF 690666 F
General Director: Jean-Claude Balacéanu
Assistant General Director: Maurice Allègre
Director: Jean Favre
Director with the General Management: Jean Chapelle
Activities: The purpose of the Institute, with regard to petroleum and its derivatives and substitutes, is as follows: to instigate or carry out research and investigations of importance in furthering scientific knowledge and industrial technology; to train technical specialists, engineers and scientists, and technicians so as to render them capable of participating in the furthering, dissemination and effective application of new knowledge; to keep the Government, industry and technicians fully informed on scientific knowledge and industrial technology of importance to the nation's economy.

ÉCOLE NATIONALE SUPÉRIEURE DU   530
PÉTROLE ET DES MOTEURS

[Petroleum and Engines National College]
Telephone: (01) 967 11 10; 967 17 66
Director: Jean Limido
Head of research and development: Jean Favre
Sections: Exploration, Claude Sallé; reservoir engineering and production, Pierre Simandoux; industrial production systems, Jacques Delacour; refining and petrochemical processes, Clément Thonon; fine chemicals, Gabriel de Gaudemaris; energy, Bernard Salé
Information and documentation, Jacqueline Funck
Valorization of results, Gabriel Jacques
Economics and project evaluation, Pierre Leprince
Scientific management, Bernard Tissot
Foreign affairs, Hervé Lévi

SUBSIDIARY AND PARTICIPATING   531
CONCERNS

BEICIP, Bureau d'Études Industrielles   532
et de Coopération de l' Institut
Français du Pétrole

Address: 232 avenue Napoléon Bonaparte, 92505 Rueil-Malmaison
President: J. Favre
Activities: BEICIP is one of the leading engineering-consultancy companies in the petroleum sector for petroleum exploration, industrial projects and the establishment of training and research centres.

COFLEXIP   533

Address: 23 avenue de Neuilly, 75116 Paris
President: I. Behar
Activities: COFLEXIP is the world's leading manufacturer of high-performance and continuous-length flexible pipes mainly intended for subsea installations.

FLEXSERVICE   534
Activities: FLEXSERVICE specializes in the laying and connection of offshore flexible pipes.

PPT, PROGRESSIVE PRODUCTION   535
TECHNOLOGY
Activities: PPT promotes early production systems for offshore fields, which includes in particular the use of flexible pipes.

Compagnie Française d'Études et de   536
Construction

- TECHNIP
Address: Tour TECHNIP, La Défense 6, 92-090 Paris La Défense
President: J. Celerier
Managing Director: L. Pradère
Activities: TECHNIP is one of the leading European companies specializing in the engineering and construction of industrial units, in particular for the production and refining of oil, for the treatment and liquefaction of gas, and for petrochemicals and chemicals. Its activities also extend to the nuclear field, new energy sources, agronomic, cement and glass industries.

TECHNIP-GÉOPRODUCTION   537
Activities: Engineering for onshore or offshore hydrocarbon production installations.

Géomecanique   538
Address: 212 avenue Paul Doumer, 92508 Rueil-Malmaison
President: J. Leolésert
Activities: Géomecanique, a division of TECHNIP-Géoproduction, manufactures specific equipment for geophysical prospecting and petroleum laboratories.

FRANLAB, Bureau d'Études de   539
Gisements et d'Informatique
Pétrolière

Address: Sophia Antipolis, 06560 Valbonne
President: P. Jacquard
Activities: Hydrocarbon reservoir engineering; hydrology - general hydrogeology, numerical data processing, underground and surface hydraulics; mathematical, hydrodynamic, hydrological and economic models.

NAT, Nouvelles Applications Technologiques   540

Address: 370 avenue Napoléon Bonaparte, 92500 Rueil-Malmaison
Activities: NAT concentrates on engineering for small-size installations for associated gas processing and energy recovery.

PROCATALYSE   541

Address: rue Jean Goujon, 75360 Paris
Activities: PROCATALYSE is a large company for the manufacture of refining and petrochemical catalysts.

Institut Max Von Laue - Paul Langevin   542

– ILL
[Max Von Laue -Paul Langevin Institute]
Address: avenue des Martyrs, 156 X, 38042 Grenoble Cedex
Telephone: (076) 97 41 11
Telex: 320 621 F
Research director: Professor Dr T. Springer
Scientific Secretary: Dr B. Maier
Sections: Nuclear and fundamental physics, Dr Gönnenwein; solid-state physics, Dr Dorner, Dr Brown; biology, Dr Jacrot
Graduate research staff: 110
Annual expenditure: F16m
Activities: Experimental facilities are available to scientists from ILL member countries (France, German FR and the United Kingdom) to carry out approved experimental programmes. The aim of the organization is directed towards simplification in the use of its neutron beams and instruments and, the provision of advice and assistance in the running of experiments.
Facilities: High Flux Reactor and its special installations:
Neutron scattering facilities - three-axis, time of flight, backscattering and spin-echo spectrometers; powder diffractometers, single crystal and polarized neutron diffractometers; diffractometers for liquids; diffuse and small angle scattering instruments; neutron interferometer.
X-ray diffractometers and instruments for crystal testing - double crystal X-ray instrument, four-circle X-ray diffractometer; gamma diffractometer; two-circle neutron diffractometer.
Nuclear and fundamental physics - fission product mass separator; conversion electron, bent crystal gamma-ray, anti-compton, and pair formation spectrometers; ultra-cold neutron source; fission product mass separator; beam of cold polarized neutrons; in-beam nuclear magnetic resonance spectrometer.

The ILL is renewing its equipment and modernizing the conventional instruments. New instruments and techniques include: high resolution spectrometers; intensive and pure beams of polarized neutrons; a cold source with a neutron spectrum maximized at a shorter wavelength; ultra-cold neutrons.
Contract work: No
Publications: Annual report.

Institut National d'Astronomie et de Géophysique   543

– INAG
[National Institute of Astronomy and Geophysics]
Address: 77 avenue Denfert Rochereau, 75014 Paris
Telephone: (01) 320 13 30
Telex: 270070
Affiliation: Centre National de la Recherche Scientifique; Ministère des Universités
Research director: Michel Petit
Sections: Astronomy, Pierre Charvin; geophysics, Guy Aubert
Graduate research staff: 900 (in all the laboratories mentioned below)
Annual expenditure: F58 million
Activities: INAG was set up in 1967 with the purpose of facilitating research in astronomy and geophysics done in CNRS laboratories as well as in the astronomical observatories and earth physics institutes belonging to state universities. It coordinates research programmes in astronomy and geophysics, defines and carries out major national projects and manages research contracts especially in the case of the large industrial-type space programmes. INAG does not encroach upon the normal activities of the laboratories, which retain full responsibility and autonomy in matters of unprogrammed research, personnel, and operation of facilities. A twenty-member board of directors assists the director of INAG in defining and coordinating research programmes. In addition the Astronomy, Space, Physics, and Geophysics Sections of the CNRS national committee act as scientific advisers. To carry out major projects, INAG has created a technical division with a staff of approximately twenty engineers and technicians who, working in close association with potential users, design and develop prototypes, supervize construction and in certain cases manage the operation of research instruments.
The principal astronomy laboratories involved are: Laboratoire d'Astronomie Spatiale; Centre d'Études et de Recherches Géodynamiques et Astronomiques; Institut d'Astrophysique de Paris; Observatoire de Besançon; Observatoire de Bordeaux; Observatoire de Haute-Provence; Observatoire de Lyon; Observatoire de

Marseille; Observatoire de Nice; Centre de Dépouillement des Clichés Astronomiques; Observatoire de Paris; Observatoire de Strasbourg; Centre de Données Stellaires; Observatoire du Pic du Midi et de Toulouse; Laboratoire de Physique Stellaire et Planétaire.
Geophysics laboratories: Service d'Aéronomie; Centre Géologique et Géophysique de Montpellier; Laboratoire de Glaciologie et de Géophysique de l'Environnement; Centre de Recherches Géophysiques; Laboratoire de Météorologie Dynamique; Centre de Recherches en Physique de l'Environnement Terrestre et Planetaire; Centre d'Étude des Phénomènes Aléatoires et Géophysiques; Institut de Physique du Globe de Paris; Institut de Physique du Globe de Strasbourg; Centre d'Étude Spatiale des Rayonnements; Centre des Faibles Radioactivités.
INAG also participates in international projects, such as: 'Canada-France-Hawaii' 3.6 meter telescope; European Auroral Incoherent Scatter Facility - EISCAT; Concorde; and acts as technical adviser for various organizations such as the French national committee of the European Southern Observatory - ESO.
Publications: Annual report.

Institut National d'Études Démographiques   544

– INED
[National Demographic Research Institute]
Address: 27 rue du Commandeur, 75675 Paris Cedex 14
Telephone: (01) 320 13 45
Affiliation: Ministère du Travail et de la Participation
Research director: Gérard Calot
Scientific advisers: Louis Henry, Alain Girard, Louis Roussel
Graduate research staff: 42
Annual expenditure: F21m
Activities: The INED is a research body set up to study all aspects of demography, both pure and applied, and to diffuse the results of their research. It collects documentation, opens enquiries, carries out experiments, and follows those experiments carried out in other countries. The teams include: mathematicians, statisticians, historians, lawyers, sociologists, geographers and doctors, thus facilitating the collaboration between specialized researchers and the human sciences.
Contract work: No
Publications: Population, every three months; *Population et Sociétés*, monthly bulletin; various reports.

Economic Demography Unit   545

Head: Georges Tapinos

Economics and Population Unit   546

Head: Alfred Sauvy
Activities: World population structure; technological progress and employment; population growth and economic development.

Population Doctrines and Politics Unit   547

Head: Jacqueline Hecht

COOPERATION DEPARTMENT   548

Head: Robert Blanc
Activities: Especially concerned with demographic studies in the Third World.

GENERAL DEMOGRAPHY DEPARTMENT   549

Head: Daniel Courgeau
Sections: Urban demography and immigration, D. Courgeau; rural demography, Philippe Collomb

HISTORICAL AND MEDICAL DEMOGRAPHY DEPARTMENT   550

Head: Jean-Noël Biraben
Sections: Historical, Jacques Houdaille; mortality, Jacques Vallin; medical and biological, J.-N. Biraben

METHODS AND PROVISIONS DEPARTMENT   551

Head: Herve Le Bras
Activities: Methodological models; typological analyses; demographic projects.

POPULATION GENETICS DEPARTMENT   552

Head: Albert Jacquard
Activities: The evolution and transmission of genes of a particular group of living beings (human, animal, vegetable).

PSYCHO-SOCIOLOGY DEPARTMENT   553

Head: Henri Leridon
Activities: Research covers fecundity and families; contraceptives; careers for women; sociology.

SOCIAL DEMOGRAPHY DEPARTMENT   554

Head: Paul Paillat
Activities: Ageing; living conditions; sanitation.

Institut National de la   555
Recherche Agronomique

[National Institute of Agricultural Research]
Address: 149 rue de Grenelle, 75341 Paris Cedex 07
Telephone: (01) 550 32 00
Telex: INRAPAR 204719 F
President/Director General: Jacques Poly
Adjoint Scientific Director General: Roger Bouchet
Scientific directors: I Physical envirorment, R. Bouchet; II vegetable production, J. Marrou; III animal production, G. Jolivet; IV agricultural and food industries, G. Fauconneau; V social sciences, J.-C. Tirel
Research departments: Biometry, R. Tomassone
I, bioclimatology, P. Chartier; solar science, J. Mamy
II, agronomy, L. Gachon; plant management, M. Rives; plant physiology and biochemistry, J. Mossé; plant pathology and biology, A. Coleno; zoology, B. Hurpin; forestry research, P. Bouvarel; phytopharmacy and ecotoxicology, C. Descoins
III, animal genetics, B. Vissac; nutrition, A. Rerat; animal physiology, R. Ortavant; raising ruminants, R. Jarrige; raising monogastric animals, J.-C. Blum; animal pathology, P. Larvor; hydrobiology, cynegetics and wild fauna, J. Lecomte
IV, plant products technology, P. Dupuy; animal products technology, J. Hermier; consumption science, J. Flanzy
V, rural economy and sociology, vacant; agricultural systems and developments, B. Vissac
Graduate research staff: 1250
Annual expenditure: F1218m
Activities: INRA organizes and executes scientific research in the following areas: (i) the improvement of plant production and livestock involved in agriculture; (ii) optimal investment in agricultural enterprises; (iii) conservation and conversion of agricultural produce into foodstuffs; (iv) obtaining maximum use of agricultural by-products; (v) protection, and sensible use of natural resources; (vi) socioeconomic aspects and effects relevant to the agricultural world.
Organization: INRA has an Administrative Council which is responsible for examining and approving the management of the Institute and in defining its direction. The Scientific Committee interprets the objectives and sets specific programmes. INRA has a president/ director general and two adjoint director generals. There are five scientific directors.
INRA has a triple structure: (i) Research departments correspond to different groups of disciplines. (ii) Special-

ized commissions, comprising researchers, university representatives, and professionals, exist to enliven and coordinate research on an agricultural theme or by scientific discipline. In 1980 there were commissions in biochemistry, tropical research, agrometeorology, and biomass, and consultative councils in animal production and the agriculture/food industries. (iii) The centres of research follow general national objectives, but have an equivalent regional responsibility.
See also entries for:
Centre de Recherche Agronomique d'Avignon
Centre de Recherche d'Antibes
Centre de Recherche de Bordeaux
Centre de Recherche de Colmar
Centre de Recherche de Dijon
Centre de Recherche de Montpellier
Centre de Recherche de Nantes
Centre de Recherche de Rennes
Centre de Recherche de Toulouse
Centre de Recherches Agro-Alimentaires de Nantes
Centre de Recherches Forestières d'Orléans
Centre de Recherches Agronomiques du Sud-Est
Centre de Recherches Agronomiques du Sud-Ouest
Centre de Recherches Hydrobiologiques
Centre de Recherches Zootechniques et Vétérinaires
Centre National de Recherche Agronomique
Centre National de Recherches Forestières
Centre National de Recherches Zootechniques
École National Vétérinaire d'Alfort
Station d'Hydrobiologie Lacustre
Station de Recherches de Virologie et d'Immunologie.
Publications: Agronomie, monthly.

Institut National de la   556
Santé et de la Recherche
Medicale

– INSERM
[Health and Medical Research National Institute]
Address: 101 rue de Tolbiac, 75654 Paris Cedex 13
Telephone: (01) 584 14 41
Telex: 270 532
Director General: Dr Philippe Laudat
Graduate research staff: 1381
Annual expenditure: F640m
Activities: INSERM is a research institute which promotes, conducts and develops biomedical research, from molecular biology to public health, with predominant emphasis on pathology. The principal fields of research are: brain and mental health; biomedical and biomolecular engineering; food and nutrition; immunology; public health; reproduction and development.
Contract work: No
Publications: Série Santé Publique; Série Statistiques, Nomenclature; Collection Colloques INSERM; research reports.

RESEARCH UNITS AND GROUPS 557

1. Nutrition and Food Unit 558

Address: Hôpital Bichat, 170 boulevard Ney, 75877 Paris Cedex 18
Telephone: (01) 627 62 54
Director: Daniel Lemonnier
Activities: Physiopathology of unbalanced diets; obesity and thinness; calorie intake and energy use; diet balance; malnutrition in Africa; public research in nutrition.

2. Cardiovascular Pathology Unit 559

Address: Hôpital Léon Bernard, 94450 Limeil Brevannes
Telephone: (01) 569 32 26
Director: Professor Pierre-Yves Hatt
Activities: Experimental pathology; morphology (electronic microscope); metabolic biochemistry; contractile mechanics; arterial hypertension; renal physiology.

3. Neurophysiological Unit 560

Address: CHU, La Pitié-Salpêtrière, 47 boulevard de l'Hôpital, 75634 Paris Cedex 13
Telephone: (01) 584 57 54
Director: Professor Jean Scherrer
Activities: Experimental and human neurophysiology: synaptic transmission; cerebral electrophysiology; development neurophysiology; electrophysiology of nerve tissue; sleep and wakefulness; vestibulometry.

5. Osteoarticular Diseases Unit 561

Address: Hôpital Cochin Pavillon Hardy A, 27 rue du Faubourg Saint-Jacques, 75674 Paris Cedex 14
Telephone: (01) 320 12 40
Director: Professor B. Amor
Activities: Gout; experimental pathology of inflammatory rheumatisms; pathogenesis and treatment of bone decalcification.

6. Neurobiological Unit 562

Address: 280 boulevard Sainte-Marguerite, 13009 Marseille
Telephone: (091) 75 02 00
Director: Dr Suzanne Tyc-Dumont
Activities: Neuroanatomy; animal neurophysiology; neurochemistry; human neurophysiology.

7. Vascular and Renal Physiology and Pharmacology Unit 563

Address: Groupe Hospitalier Necker-Enfants Malades, 149/161 rue de Sèvres, 75730 Paris Cedex 15
Telephone: (01) 566 04 00
Director: Professor Philippe Meyer
Activities: Arterial pressure; cellular pharmacology of hormones and regulatory mediators of arterial pressure; action mechanism of corticosterones.

8. Cardiology Unit 564

Address: avenue du Haut Lévêque, 33600 Pessac
Telephone: (056) 45 40 13
Director: Professor Henri Bricaud
Activities: Research on the performance and functional value of the myocardium; study of adaptations to effort; influence of bioenergetics factors on the development of aortic atherosclerosis (experimental and human).

9. Hepatology Unit 565

Address: Centre de Recherches de l'INSERM, Hôpital Saint-Antoine, 184 rue du Faubourg Saint-Antoine, 75571 Paris Cedex 12
Telephone: (01) 344 11 10
Director: Dr Recaredo Infante
Activities: Metabolism of plasmatic lipoproteins and the molecular regulatory mechanisms of their renal and intestinal synthesis; enterohepatic circulation and biotransformation of bile acids in the different renal diseases; mechanisms of trans-membrane and cytoplasmatic transport of fatty acids in the liver; alterations in the hepatic and cerebral metabolism in comatose states resulting from acute hepatitis; study of haemofiltration and haemodialysis systems applicable to the treatment of comatose states as a result of renal failure.

10. Gastroenterology Unit 566

Address: Hôpital Bichat, 170 boulevard Ney, 75877 Paris Cedex 18
Telephone: (01) 627 54 44
Director: Professor Serge Bonfils
Activities: Physiology of stomach secretions; ulcers; cellular biology of gastric mucous membrane; endocrine morphophysiology of the digestive tube.

12. Medical Genetics Unit   567

Address: Hôpital des Enfants Malades, 149 rue de Sèvres, 75730 Paris Cedex 15
Telephone: (01) 555 92 80
Director: Professor Jean Frézal
Activities: Cell genetics; paediatric gastroenterology and nutrition; cartilage anomalies; experimental endocrinology.

13. Artificial Respiration Unit   568

Address: Hôpital Claude Bernard, 10 avenue de la Porte d'Aubervilliers, 75019 Paris
Telephone: (01) 203 36 44
Director: Jean-Jacques Pocidalo
Activities: Internal regulator mechanisms; effects of ventilation on the circulation; pulmonary oedemas; pulmonary-capillary permeability; cardiovascular pharmacology; antibiotic pharmacology; haemoglobinopathies and oxygen transport; biological effects of atmospheric pollution.

14. Respiratory Physiopathology Unit   569

Address: Centre de Recherches de l'INSERM, Plateau de Brabois, 54500 Vandoeuvre-les-Nancy
Telephone: (083) 55 02 24
Director: Professor Paul Sadoul
Activities: Respiratory functions and secretions; pulmonary diseases and treatment.

15. Molecular Pathology Unit   570

Address: Centre Universitaire Cochin-Port-Royal, 24 rue du Faubourg Saint-Jacques, 75014 Paris
Telephone: (01) 320 12 40
Director: Professor Georges Schapira
Activities: Normal and pathologic biosynthesis mechanisms of proteins; membranes; haemoglobins; prothrombins.

16. Protein Biochemistry Unit   571

Address: Place de Verdun, 59045 Lille Cedex
Telephone: (020) 97 26 15
Director: Professor Philippe Roussel
Activities: Isolation, purification, composition and study of structures of proteids: proteins and glucoproteins.

17. Experimental Hepatic Surgery Unit   572

Address: Hôpital Paul Brousse, 14 avenue Paul Vaillant Couturier, 94800 Villejuif
Director: Professor Henri Bismuth
Activities: Liver surgery (rat); consequences of portal deviation; hepatic transplants and grafts; hepatic cancer.

18. Phospho-calcium Metabolism Unit   573

Address: Centre André Lichtwitz, Hôpital Lariboisière, 6 rue Guy Patin, 75010 Paris
Telephone: (01) 285 26 89
Acting director: Livia Miravet
Activities: Rheumatic immunology; cartilage; phospho-calcium metabolism.

20. Immunobiology   574

Address: Hôpital Broussais, 96 rue Didot, 75674 Paris Cedex 14
Telephone: (01) 539 22 66
Director: Dr Panayotis Liacopoulos
Activities: Biology and action of immunostimulants; cell mechanisms and the formation of antibodies; immunologic defense mechanisms; immunopathology of the salivary glands.

21. Statistical Research   575

Address: 16 bis avenue Paul-Vaillant-Couturier, 94800 Villejuif
Telephone: 677 24 69
Director: Professor Daniel Schwartz
Sections: Biostatistics, A.J. Valleron; cancerology, R. Flamant; diabetes, E. Eschwege; fertility, reproduction (human), D. Schwartz
Graduate research staff: 15
Activities: Risk factors and diabetes; diagnostics and therapeutics of diabetes; cancers; perinatality, reproduction; biostatistics in cell biology.

22. Cell Physiology and Radiobiology,   576 and Cancer Unit

Address: Institut du Radium, Faculté des Sciences, Bâtiment 110, 91405 Orsay Cedex
Telephone: (0336) 907 64 67
Director: Dr François Zajdela
Activities: Cancer mechanisms of chemical and physical agents; physiopathology of muriform leukaemias; growth regulation of the rat's liver and effects of cancer.

23. Immunopathology and   577 Experimental Immunology Unit

Address: Centre de Recherches de l'INSERM, Hôpital Saint-Antoine, 184 rue du Faubourg Saint-Antoine, 75571 Paris Cedex 12
Telephone: (01) 344 15 52
Director: Dr Guy-André Voisin
Activities: Experimental and general immunology; immunity and transplants; immunopathology.

24. Hepatic Physiopathology Unit   578

Address: Hôpital Beaujon, 100 boulevard du Général Leclerc, 92118 Clichy Cedex 12
Director: Professor Jean-Pierre Benhamou
Activities: Hepatic physiology, physiopathology and applications to human hepatic pathology.

25. Nephrology Unit   579

Address: Hôpital Necker, 161 rue de Sèvres, 75015 Paris
Telephone: (01) 273 24 42
Director: Professor Jean Hamburger
Activities: Nephrology; transplants.

26. Experimental Toxicology Unit   580

Address: Hôpital Fernand Widal, 200 rue du Faubourg Saint-Denis, 75475 Paris Cedex 10
Telephone: (01) 202 95 20
Director: Professor Etienne Fournier
Activities: Experimental cytotoxicity; toxicology; experimental neurotoxicity; psychotropic drugs; allergies to chemical substances; toxinokinetics.

27. Arterial Hypertension Unit   581

Address: Centre Médico-chirurgical Foch, 42 rue Desbassayns de Richemond, 92150 Suresnes
Telephone: 772 15 88
Director: Dr Jacques Guedon
Activities: Arterial hypertension; respiratory physiopathology; hypoxia.

28. Renal and Vascular Pathology   582 Group

Address: Hôpital Broussais, 96 rue'Didot, 75674 Paris Cedex 14
Telephone: (01) 539 22 66
Director: Professor Jean Bariety
Activities: Renal immunopathology (human and experimental); vascular physiology and pathology.

29. Neonatal Development Biology   583 Unit

Address: Hôpital Port Royal, 123 boulevard de Port Royal, 75674 Paris Cedex 14
Telephone: (01) 326 14 97
Director: Professor Alexandre Minkowski
Activities: Study of the stages of development of the nervous system; retarded growth in the human and animal uterus; growth biochemistry of the foetus; relationship between premature birth and foetal suffering; physiology of the lamb foetus.

30. Infant Metabolic Diseases Unit   584

Address: Hôpital des Enfants-Malades, 149 rue de Sèvres, 75015 Paris
Telephone: (01) 555 92 80
Director: Professor P. Royer
Activities: Fundamental processes and physiopathologic anomalies in three sectors of organic metabolism during growth: cartilage, calcified tissues, renal regulation.

31. Digestive Pathology Unit   585

Address: 46 chemin de la Gaye, 13009 Marseille
Telephone: (091) 75 06 15
Director: Professor Henri Sarles
Activities: Protein biochemistry of the pancreas (human and animal); pancreatic cytology and physiology; lipid transport in the intestine; hepatic secretions; pathogenesis and therapeutic effects of bile lithia; informatic studies on pancreatic pathology.

32. Atherosclerosis Unit   586

Address: Hôpital Henri Mondor, 51 avenue du Maréchal de Lattre de Tassigny, 94010 Créteil
Telephone: 899 26 02
Director: Professor Jean-Louis Beaumont
Activities: Research of a clinical, biochemical, immunological and experimental nature in order to determine the causes, the mechanisms, manifestations and consequences of atherosclerosis.

33. Molecular Metabolism and Steroid   587 Physiopathology Unit

Address: Centre de Recherches de l'INSERM, Hôpital-Hospice de Bicêtre, 78 rue du Général Leclerc, 94270 Le Kremlin Bicêtre
Director: Professor Etienne Émile Baulieu
Activities: Metabolism, distribution and mode of action of steroid hormones, especially in relation to reproduction and the formation of hormone-sensitive tumours.

34. Infant Endocrinology and   588 Metabolism Unit

Address: Hôpital Debrousse, 29 rue Soeur Bouvier, 69322 Lyon Cedex 1
Telephone: (078) 25 18 08
Director: Professor Jean Bertrand
Activities: Experimental and physiopathologic research on hormonal control and sexual maturation; steroid synthesis.

35. Lipid Metabolism Group   589

Address: Hôpital Henri Mondor, 51 avenue du Maréchal de Lattre de Tassigny, 94010 Créteil
Telephone: 207 51 41
Director: Dr Marie-Hélène Laudat
Activities: Adipose tissue; serous lipoproteins.

36. Vascular Pathology and Renal   590
Endocrinology Unit

Address: 17 rue du Fer à Moulin, 75005 Paris
Telephone: (01) 336 47 35
Director: Professor P. Corvol
Activities: Experimental models (animal): congenital defects, renal endocrinology, hypertension.

37. Vascular Surgery and Organ   591
Transplants Unit

Address: 18 avenue du Doyen Lépine, 69500 Bron
Telephone: (078) 54 28 62
Director: Dr Marie-Rose Eloy
Activities: Heart transplant biology of the heart, lungs, and pancreas; physiopathology of haemostasis and thrombosis; vascular microsurgery; evaluation of prosthetic and biological materials.

38. Thyroid Physiopathology Group   592

Address: Faculté de Médecine, Laboratoire de Biochimie Médicale, 27 boulevard Jean Moulin, 13385 Marseille Cedex 4
Telephone: (091) 78 50 59
Director: Professor Serge Lissitzky
Activities: Action mechanism of thyroptropines; thyroid cell regulation and differentiation; thyroglobulin; molecular mechanism of conduction in excitable membranes.

40. Biology and Medical   593
Oceanography Group

Address: CERBOM, Parc de la Côte, 1 avenue Jean Lorrain, 06300 Nice
Telephone: (093) 89 72 49
Director: Dr Maurice Aubert
Activities: Studies on the problems of marine hygiene: bacteriologic, viral, chemical and physical ocean pollution; research on the pharmacological or nutritional uses of marine life.

42. Fungal and Parasitic Biology Group 594

Address: Domaine du CERTIA, 369 rue Jules Guesde, Fleurs-Bourg, 59650 Villeneuve d'Ascq
Telephone: (020) 91 15 12
Director: Professor Jean Biguet
Activities: Physiology and structure of yeasts of the Candida genus; mycotoxins; paludism and experimental trichinosis.

43. Viral Infections Unit   595

Address: Hôpital Saint-Vincent-de-Paul, 74 avenue Denfert Rochereau, 75674 Paris Cedex 14
Telephone: (01) 325 41 22
Activities: Interferon; cell hybridation; zoolectins.

44. Normal and Pathological   596
Neurochemistry Group

Address: Faculté de Médecine, 11 rue Humann, 67085 Strasbourg Cedex
Telephone: (088) 36 06 05
Director: Professor Guy Vincendon

45. Digestive Physiopathology Unit   597

Address: Hôpital Édouard Herriot, Pavillon H bis, 69374 Lyon Cedex 2
Telephone: (078) 53 81 11
Director: Professor René Lambert
Activities: Digestive immunology; physiological properties of gastrointestinal hormones; enteric membrane; intestinal cell renewal and calcium absorption; epidemiology of digestive cancers; immunopathology of viral hepatitis.

48. Cell Pathology Unit   598

Address: Hôpital de Bicêtre, 94270 Le Kremlin Bicêtre
Telephone: 588 61 95
Director: Professor M. Bessis
Activities: Red globule membrane; differentiation factors in blood cells; role of cellular organelles; chemotactility.

49. Hepatology Unit   599

Address: Hôpital de Pontchaillou, rue Henri le Guilloux, 35011 Rennes
Telephone: (099) 59 29 49
Director: Professor Michel Bourel
Activities: Hepatology; medical informatics.

50. Cancerology and Immunogenetics 600 Unit

Address: Hôpital Paul Brousse, 14/16 avenue Paul Vaillant Couturier, 94800 Villejuif
Telephone: 726 45 10
Director: Professor Georges Mathé
Activities: Studies on cancerous cells, reactions of the cancer patient and therapeutic action; evaluation study of the risk of cancer in the individual.

51. Fundamental and Applied Virology 601 Unit

Address: 1 place du Professeur Joseph Renaut, 69371 Lyon Cedex 2
Telephone: (078) 74 99 80
Director: Professor J. Huppert
Activities: Cellular interactions: tumour viruses and viruses with a slow development rate.

52. Experimental and Clinical 602 Neurophysiology Unit

Address: Experimental side, Université Claude-Bernard, 8 avenue Rockefeller, 69373 Lyon Cedex 2
or: Clinical side, Hôpital Neurologique, 59 boulevard Pinel, 69003 Lyon
Telephone: (078) 75 81 14; 53 81 81
Director: Professor Michel Jouvet
Activities: Neurobiological mechanisms of sleep and awakeness; anatomy and physiology of monoaminergic systems; sleep and dream problems.

53. Medical and Biological 603 Applications of Radioactive Isotopes Unit

Address: Domaine de Carreire, rue Camille Saint-Saëns, 33077 Bordeaux Cedex
Telephone: (056) 96 52 66
Director: Professor Paul Blanquet
Activities: Calcium and phosphorus metabolism; thyroid hormones, calcite interaction; new techniques in nuclear medicine; improvement of radioimmunologic treatments.

54. Physiopathology of the Digestive 604 System Unit

Address: Hôpital Saint Lazare, 107 rue du Faubourg Saint-Denis, 75475 Paris Cedex 10
Telephone: (01) 280 62 33
Director: Professor Jean-Jacques Bernier
Activities: Intestinal absorption in humans by profusion; intestinal absorption under the influence of different hormones (human and experimental); intestinal malabsorption; parenteral and enteral nutrition.

55. Diabetes and Radioimmunological 605 Studies of Proteic Hormones Unit

Address: Centre de Recherches de l'INSERM, Hôpital Saint-Antoine, 184 rue du Faubourg Saint-Antoine, 75571 Paris Cedex 12
Telephone: (01) 345 81 74
Director: Dr Gabriel Rosselin
Activities: Diabetes and nutrition; pancreatic hormone secretions; endocrine regulation of the intestinal cell; neonatal diabetes.

56. Infant Hepatology Unit 606

Address: Centre de Recherche de l'INSERM, Hôpital-Hospice de Bicêtre, 78 rue du Général Leclerc, 94270 Le Kremlin Bicêtre
Director: Professor Daniel Alagille
Activities: Congenital hepatic diseases; immunology of the foetus and the new-born infant; hepato-biliary malformations.

57. Atmospheric Pollution Unit 607

Address: BP 14, 31320 Vigoulet Auzil
Telephone: (061) 73 66 00
Director: Professor Pierre Bourbon
Activities: Physico-chemical approach to the study of the principal atmospheric pollutants; biological approach to the study of the effect of these pollutants on living organisms.

58. Steroid Biochemistry Unit 608

Address: Centre de Recherches de l'INSERM, 60 rue de Navacelles, 34100 Montpellier
Telephone: (067) 54 15 44
Director: Professor André Crastes de Paulet
Activities: Steroid hormones; cholesterol biosynthesis; prostaglandins; micellular catalysis.

59. Nutrition and Dietetics Group 609

Address: 40 rue Lionnois, 54000 Nancy
Telephone: (083) 37 38 26
Director: Professor Gérard Debry
Activities: Lipid metabolism; insulin and pro-insulin secretion under varying nutritional conditions and syndromes; quality of new sources of proteins; nutritional behaviour of different classes of the population; alimentary toxicology; vitamin E.

61. Experimental Surgery and Digestive Physiopathology Unit   610

Address: ZUP Hautepierre, 3 avenue Molière, 67200 Strasbourg Hautepierre
Telephone: (088) 30 58 68
Director: Professor Jacques F. Grenier
Activities: Intestinal enzymology; intestinal absorption, intestinal haemodynamics; intestinal motility; digestive short circuits; intestinal endocrinology; enzymatic secretions of the pancreas; pancreatic transplants.

63. Vascular Physiopathology Unit   611

Address: 22 avenue du Doyen Lépine, 69500 Bron
Telephone: (078) 54 30 73
Director: Serge Renaud
Activities: Hypercoagulability mechanisms and relationship with atherosclerosis; prevention of atherosclerosis and thrombosis by changes in nutrition; cell reaction to atherogenic agents (in vitro).

64. Normal and Pathological Nephrology Unit   612

Address: Centre de Recherches INSERM, Hôpital Tenon, 4 rue de la Chine, 75970 Paris Cedex 20
Telephone: (01) 361 39 58
Director: Professor Gabriel Richet
Activities: Physiology; pathology.

65. Bacteria-cell Interaction and Brucellosis Group   613

Address: Institut de Biologie, Faculté de Médecine, boulevard Henri IV, 34060 Montpellier Cedex
Telephone: (067) 72 49 31
Director: Professor Jacques Roux
Activities: Bacteria-host cell relationship; intracellular activity and antibiotics; study of brucellosis from a physiopathogenic, immunologic and epidemiologic viewpoint.

66. Clinical Radiobiology Group   614

Address: Institut Gustave Roussy-Paul Brousse, 16 bis avenue Paul Vaillant-Couturier, 94800 Villejuif
Telephone: 726 49 09
Director: Professor Maurice Tubiana
Activities: Improvement of diagnosis and treatment in man and animals based on ion radiation and radioactive isotopes.

68. Respiratory Physiopathology Unit   615

Address: Centre de Recherches INSERM, Hôpital Saint-Antoine, 184 rue du Faubourg Saint-Antoine, 75571 Paris Cedex 12
Telephone: (01) 559 49 09
Acting director: Claire Hatzfeld
Activities: Irreversible ventilation problems.

69. Mental Health of Children and Maladjusted Adolescents Group   616

Address: 1 rue du 11 novembre, 92120 Montrouge
Telephone: 735 80 89
Director: Dr Stanislaw Tomkiewicz
Activities: Mental deficiency epidemiology; economic and social consequences of acute handicaps in the first-born child; phenomenology, actiology and treatment of juvenile delinquency.

70. Maladjusted Children Unit   617

Address: 'Les Pins' Mas Prunet, 34000 Montpellier
Telephone: (067) 42 66 33
Director: Professor Jean-Pierre Visier
Activities: Behaviour of maladjusted children.

71. Marked Molecules Metabolism Unit   618

Address: rue Montalembert, BP 184, 63005 Clermont-Ferrand Cedex
Telephone: (073) 92 26 15
Director: Professor Gaston Meyniel
Activities: Synthesis and metabolic studies of molecules; radiobiology; biosynthesis of thyroid hormones.

72. Intermediate Metabolism Group   619

Address: UER Biomédicale des Saints-Pères, 45 rue des Saints-Pères, 75270 Paris Cedex 06
Telephone: (01) 260 95 58
Director: Professor Joseph Nordmann
Activities: Biochemical mechanisms of alcohol intoxication; biochemical pathogenesis of liver failure; regulatory mechanisms of lipids.

73. Prenatal Biology Group   620

Address: Centre International de l'Enfance, Château de Longchamp, 75016 Paris
Telephone: (01) 506 53 17
Director: Professor André Boué
Activities: Embryo-foetal effects of genetic and viral origin; critical study of diagnostic intra-uterine techniques, of chromosome abnormalities and of metabolic diseases.

74. Pathogenisis of Viral Infections Group   621

Address: Laboratoire de Virologie, 3 rue Koeberié, 67000 Strasbourg
Telephone: (088) 36 06 22
Director: Professor André Kirn
Activities: Study of the states of biosynthesis of viruses (DNA) in cytoplasmatic development; change in the metabolism of the host cell during a viral infection; pathogenic power of viruses during productive and non-productive infections.

75. Medical Enzymology Group   622

Address: CHU Necker, 156 rue de Vaugirard, 75730 Paris Cedex 15
Telephone: (01) 578 61 28
Director: Professor Pierre Cartier
Activities: Congenital enzymopathies; purines; enzyme deficiencies; neoglycogenesis regulation; use of dichloroacetate in the treatment of congenital lactic acidosis.

76. Blood Groups and Immunohaematology Group   623

Address: Centre National de Transfusion Sanguine, 53 boulevard Diderot, 75571 Paris Cedex 12
Telephone: (01) 344 78 90
Director: Professor Charles Salmon
Activities: Enzymopathy; purines; enzyme deficiencies.

77. Paediatric Pathology Group   624

Address: Groupe Hospitalier, Necker Enfants Malades, 149 rue de Sèvres, 75730 Paris Cedex 15
Telephone: (01) 555 92 80
Director: Professor Christian Nezelof
Activities: Infant morbidity and mortality; immuno-deficiency diseases in infants; tumours; reticulohistiocytosis.

78. Genetics of Human Protein Unit   625

Address: 543 chemin de la Bretèque, 76230 Bois-Guillaume
Telephone: (035) 60 02 60
Director: Professor Claude Ropartz
Activities: Immunology; immunogenetics; biochemistry; immunochemistry.

80. Metabolic and Renal Pathology Unit   626

Address: Hôpital Édouard Herriot, Pavillon P, 3 place d'Arsonval, 69003 Lyon
Telephone: (078) 54 82 41
Director: Professor Jules E. Traeger
Activities: Cellular immunology; experimental and clinical transplants; immunopathology of glomerulonephritis; ureic toxicity; nephrologic pharmacology; phospho-calcic metabolism in the kidney patient.

82. Pulmonary Interstitial Infiltratives Group   627

Address: Hôpital Bichat, 170 boulevard Ney, 75877 Paris Cedex 18
Telephone: (01) 627 42 44
Director: Dr Robert Georges
Activities: Pulmonary structure and biopathy; physiological processes.

83. Infant Diabetes and Nutrition Group   628

Address: Hôpital Herold, 7 place Rhin et Danube, 75935 Paris Cedex 19
Telephone: (01) 205 53 36
Director: Professor Henri Lestradet
Activities: Glycoenergetic and insulin metabolism in the normal child, the diabetic and hypoglycaemic patients.

84. Neuropsychology Group   629

Address: Hôpital de la Salpétrière, 47 boulevard de l'Hôpital, 75013 Paris
Telephone: (01) 584 14 12
Director: Professor F. Lhermitte
Activities: Role of the different nerve structures in human superior functions, ie memory, speech.

86. Ophthalmology Group   630

Address: Clinique Ophtalmologique, Hôtel Dieu, 1 place du parvis Notre Dame, 75004 Paris
Telephone: (01) 329 12 79
Director: Professor Yves Pouliquen
Activities: Biology of the cornea; ocular immunology; ocular barriers.

87. Toxicology of Food and Drink Group   631

Address: Université Paul Sabatier, 2 rue Françoise Magendie, 31400 Toulouse
Telephone: (061) 52 81 67
Director: Professor Roger Derache
Activities: Toxicity - methodology, nutrition, pollution.

88. Public Health and Socioeconomic Epidemiology Group   632

Address: CHU, Pitié Salpétrière, 91 boulevard de l'Hôpital, 75634 Paris Cedex 13
Telephone: (01) 783 82 40
Director: Professor François Gremy

90. Applications of Radioelements to Metabolic Diseases Unit   633

Address: Hôpital Necker, 161 rue de Sèvres, 75730 Paris Cedex 15
Telephone: (01) 566 04 58
Director: Professor Jean-Louis Funck-Brentano
Activities: Effect of PTH and vitamin D on the intestinal cell; haemodynamics and kidney structure; ureic toxaemia; prostaglandins.

91. Molecular Genetics and Haematology Unit   634

Address: Hôpital Henri Mondor, 51 avenue du Maréchal de Lattre de Tassigny, 94010 Créteil
Telephone: 899 27 08
Director: Professor Jean Rosa
Activities: Molecular biology and pathology of anaemias; haemapoietic normal and cancerous cells; erythrocyte antigens.

93. Immunogenetics of Human Transplants Group   635

Address: Institut de Recherches sur les Maladies du Sang, Hôpital Saint-Louis, 2 place du Docteur A. Fournier, 75475 Paris Cedex 10
Telephone: (01) 206 22 54
Director: Professor Jean Dausset
Activities: Serologic and genetic studies of antigens and their role in transplants.

94. Physiopathology of the Nervous System Unit   636

Address: Laboratoire de Neuropsychologie Expérimentale, 16 avenue du Doyen Lèpine, 69500 Bron
Telephone: (078) 54 65 78
Director: Professor Marc Jeannerod
Activities: Eye-hand coordination in the normal human; visual behaviour of the ape; visual information in the cat; visual behaviour of the kitten and new-born ape; residual vision in humans and animals with cortex lesions.

95. Experimental Cancerology and Radiobiology Unit   637

Address: Centre de Recherches de l'INSERM, Plateau de Brabois, 54500 Vandoeuvre-les-Nancy
Telephone: (083) 55 22 01
Director: vacant
Activities: Experimental cancerology; fundamental immunology; immunogenetics; membrane interaction.

96. Thyroid Gland and Hormonal Regulation Unit   638

Address: Centre de Recherches de l'INSERM, Hôpital de Bicêtre, 78 avenue du Général Leclerc, 94270 Le Kremlin Bicêtre
Telephone: 677 65 00
Director: Jacques Nunez
Activities: Thyroid hormonogenesis; thyroid mechanism and function.

97. Epilepsy Unit   639

Address: Centre Paul Broca de l'INSERM, rue d'Alésia, 75674 Paris Cedex 14
Telephone: (01) 589 53 07
Director: Dr Jean Bancaud
Activities: Clinical, neuroanatomical, stereotaxic and stereo-electroencephalographic studies; different forms of epilepsy; cerebral dysfunction; neurophysiologic, neuropharmacologic, neuroclinical and histologic studies of epileptogenic sources.

98. Chemical Pharmacology Unit   640

Address: 17 rue du Fer à Moulin, 75005 Paris
Telephone: (01) 337 66 39
Director: Richard Rips
Activities: Synthesis and action of compounds with psychotropic activity; animal behaviour under the influence of neuropeptides; molecular structure-biological action relationship.

99. Hepatic Pharmacology and Physiology Unit
641

Address: Hôpital Henri Mondor, 94010 Créteil
Telephone: 207 51 41
Acting director: Jacques Hanoune
Activities: Hepatic physiology; cellular mechanisms of hormonal action on the liver.

100. Immunology and Cytogenetics Unit
642

Address: CHU Purpan, 31052 Toulouse Cedex
Telephone: (061) 49 36 33
Director: Professor Jean Ducos
Activities: Different serological and cellular techniques; serum studies; cytogenetic and cytochemical studies of chromosomal malsegregation.

101. Lipid Biochemistry Unit
643

Address: Hôpital Purpan, 31052 Toulouse Cedex
Telephone: (061) 49 18 53
Director: Professor Louis Douste-Blazy
Activities: Phospholipases; biochemical studies of pulmonary surfactants; lipid metabolism.

103. Biomechanics Unit
644

Address: 395 avenue des Moulins, 34000 Montpellier
Telephone: (067) 63 27 48
Director: Professor Pierre Rabischong
Activities: Functions of the human hand compared to that of a robot's; artificial joints; vehicles for the handicapped.

104. Cellular Physiology and Immunology Unit
645

Address: Centre de Recherches de l'INSERM, Hôpital Saint-Antoine, 184 rue du Faubourg Saint-Antoine, 75571 Paris Cedex 12
Telephone: (01) 344 17 40
Director: Dr Roger Robineaux
Activities: Cytophysiology; plasmatic membrane; lysosomes; cytoimmunology; cytopathology.

106. Normal and Pathological Histology of the Nervous System Unit
646

Address: CMC Foch, 42 rue Desbassayns de Richemond, 92150 Suresnes
Telephone: 506 62 78
Director: Dr Constantino Sotelo
Activities: Functional neuroanatomy; neurocytology; nerve tissue culture; neuropathology.

107. Leukaemia Virology Unit
647

Address: Centre de Recherches de l'INSERM, Hôpital Saint-Louis, 12 bis rue de la Grange aux Belles, 75475 Paris Cedex 10
Telephone: (01) 209 33 50
Director: Professor Michel Boiron
Activities: Biology of retroviruses; aetiologic cancer agents; oncogenic viruses; type C viruses.

108. Immunochemistry and Immunopathology Unit
648

Address: Centre de Recherches de l'INSERM, Hôpital Saint-Louis, 12 bis rue de la Grange aux Belles, 75475 Paris Cedex 10
Telephone: (01) 209 33 50
Director: Professor Maxime Seligmann
Activities: Markers and antigens in the membrane of human lymphoid cells; serous immunoglobulins; primitive immunitary deficiencies; haemoglobin-haptoglobin interactions.

109. Neurobiology Unit
649

Address: Centre Paul Broca de l'INSERM, rue d'Alésia, 75014 Paris
Telephone: (01) 589 53 07
Director: Professor Jean-Charles Schwartz
Activities: Histamine and endorphines; cerebral neuromediators.

110. Epidemiology and Mental Troubles Unit
650

Address: Centre Paul Broca de l'INSERM, rue d'Alésia, 75014 Paris
Telephone: (01) 589 53 07
Director: Dr Raymond Sadoun
Activities: Standardization of epidemiologic evidence; morbidity in mental pathology; risk factors; evaluation of mental health; psychiatry and demographic differences.

111. Neuropsychological and Neurolinguistic Unit
651

Address: Centre Paul Broca de l'INSERM, rue d'Alésia, 75014 Paris
Telephone: (01) 589 53 07
Director: Professor Henry Hecaen
Activities: Pluridisciplinary research on verbal behaviour in patients with cerebral lesions; neurological, psychological, linguistic.

112. Role of Viruses in Cancer Genesis 652
Group

Address: Collège de France, 11 place Marcelin Berthelot, 75231 Paris Cedex 05
Telephone: (01) 326 80 97
Director: Dr François Haguenau
Activities: Study of oncogenic viruses or oncogenic potential.

113. Hormone Control of 653
Phosphocalcium Metabolism Group

Address: Service de Biophysique, Faculté de Médecine Saint-Antoine, 27 rue Chaligny, 75571 Paris Cedex 12
Telephone: (01) 344 33 33
Director: Professor Gérard Milhaud
Activities: Extraction, isolation, analysis and synthesis of polypetides with hormonal activity; radioimmunologic dosages; role and use of calcite; role of the thymus in bone renewal.

114. Neurobiology Group 654

Address: Collège de France, 11 place Marcelin Berthelot, 75231 Paris Cedex 05
Telephone: (01) 633 45 31
Director: J. Glowinski
Activities: In vivo and in vitro study of neurones and the effect of psychotropic drugs.

115. Medical Applications of Data 655
Processing Group

Address: Faculté de Médecine, avenue de la Forêt de Haye, BP 1080, 54019 Nancy Cedex
Telephone: (083) 55 81 72
Director: Professor Jean Martin
Director: J. Glowinski
Activities: Information retrieval and processing in hospitals; compartmental modelling and pharmacokinetics; dosimology; imaging in nuclear medicine.

116. Structure and Activity of Natural 656
Substances of Biological Interest
Group

Address: UER Biomédicale des Saints-Pères, 45 rue des Saints-Pères, 75270 Paris Cedex 06
Telephone: (01) 260 37 20
Director: Professor Pierre Jolles
Activities: Purification, structural studies, structure-action relations, kinetics and immunology of biologically-active proteins and glucoproteins.

117. Experimental Radiobiology and 657
Cancerology Unit

Address: Fondation Bergonié, 229 cours de l'Argonne, 33076 Bordeaux Cedex
Telephone: (056) 91 16 61
Director: Dr Jean-François Duplan
Activities: Action of ion radiation on cancer agents; virological studies on bovine leucocytes.

118. Gerontology Unit 658

Address: 29 rue Wilhem, 75016 Paris
Telephone: (01) 525 21 93
Director: Professor François Bourlière
Activities: Mechanisms of maturation and senescence of the organism.

119. Experimental Cancerology Unit 659

Address: 27 boulevard Lei Roure, 13009 Marseille
Telephone: (091) 75 49 86
Director: Dr Georges Meyer
Activities: Malignant transformations and genetic information; biological study of tumours in vivo and in vitro.

120. Hydromineral Metabolism Unit 660

Address: Centre de Recherches de l'INSERM, 44 chemin de Ronde, 78110 Le Vesinet
Telephone: 976 06 32
Director: Professor Henri Mathieu
Activities: Physiopathology of phosphocalcic metabolism during pre- and post-natal development.

121. Cardiac Electric Activity Group 661

Address: Hôpital Cardio-Vasculaire, 59 boulevard Pinel, BP Lyon-Montchat, 69394 Lyon Cedex 3
Telephone: (078) 53 81 81
Director: Dr Pierre Arnaud
Activities: Electrocardiographic machines; electrophysiology.

122. Mechanisms of Toxic Action of 662
Atmospheric Pollutants Group

Address: Laboratoire de Toxicologie, Université Paris-Sud, rue Jean-Baptiste Clément, 92290 Chatenay-Malabry
Telephone: 661 33 25
Director: Professor Claude Boudène
Activities: Toxic effects of a number of atmospheric pollutants.

123. Physiopathological Mechanisms 663
of Environmental Pollutants Unit

Address: Centre de Recherches de l'INSERM, 44 chemin de Ronde, 78110 Le Vesinet
Telephone: 976 48 18
Director: Dr Maurice Stupfel
Activities: Methodological and statistical approach of different parameters: physical, chemical, bio- and ethological; risk factors and 'nuisance' factors (alcohol, tobacco, etc) in mortality statistics; social and physical environments; genetic factors; circadian rhythms and other cycles.

124. Ultrastructural and Biochemical 664
Research on Normal and Cancerous
Cells Group

Address: Institut de Recherches sur le Cancer, BP 3567, 59020 Lille Cedex
Telephone: (020) 95 43 59
Director: Professor Gérard Biserte
Activities: Microcinematography and cytofluorometry of flux; normal and cancerous cells and membranes; macromolecular biophysics; experimental cancerology.

125. Genetic Research in Immunology 665
Group

Address: Institut du Radium, Section de Biologie, 26 rue d'Ulm, 75231 Paris Cedex 05
Director: Dr Guido Biozzi
Activities: Genetic control and immunologic response.

127. Heart and Valves Metabolism 666
Unit

Address: Centre de Recherches de l'INSERM, Hôpital Lariboisière, 41 boulevard de la Chapelle, 75010 Paris
Telephone: (01) 285 80 65
Director: Dr K. Schwartz
Activities: Biochemical characteristics of the human and animal heart muscle; genetic mechanism of antibodies; natural and artificial resistance to infections.

128. Cryobiology applied to the Study 667
of Metabolisms Group

Address: CNRS, BP 5051, 34033 Montpellier Cedex
Telephone: (067) 63 91 30
Director: Professor C. Balny
Activities: Research on the behaviour of biological compounds when subjected to cold conditions.

129. Pathological Enzymology Group 668

Address: Centre Universitaire Cochin-Port-Royal, 24 rue du Faubourg Saint-Jacques, 75014 Paris
Telephone: (01) 320 12 40
Director: Professor Jean-Claude Dreyfus
Activities: Genetic enzymopathy.

130. Lipid Transport Unit 669

Address: Centre de Recherches de l'INSERM, 10 avenue Viton, 13009 Marseille
Telephone: (091) 75 47 05
Director: Dr Jacques Christian Hauton
Activities: Bile lipoproteins and phospholipids.

131. Nephrology and 670
Immunopathology Unit

Address: 32 rue des Carnets, 92140 Clamart
Telephone: 632 12 08
Director: Professor Jean Dormont
Activities: Antibody-response in humans; antigen studies; immunology.

132. Immunopathology and Child 671
Rheumatology Group

Address: Hôpital Necker Enfants Malades, 149 rue de Sèvres, 75730 Paris Cedex 15
Telephone: (01) 555 92 80
Director: Professor Claude Griscelli
Activities: Study of the lymph system in relation to the digestive tract; immunopathology of immunitary deficiencies; leucocytes.

133. Renal Microcirculation Biology, 672
Pathology and Pharmacology Unit

Address: CHU, Hôpital de Rangueil, 31054 Toulouse Cedex
Telephone: (061) 52 14 09
Director: Professor Jean-Michel Suc
Activities: Glomerular structures; kidneys; intra-renal haemodynamics.

134. Experimental and Clinical 673
Neurobiology Group

Address: Hôpital de la Salpétrière, 47 boulevard de l'Hôpital, 75634 Paris Cedex 13
Telephone: (01) 331 61 68
Director: Dr Nicole Baumann
Activities: Myelin biology and diseases; biology of neurolipids, tumours and degenerative diseases of the nervous system.

135. Endocrine Biochemistry and Reproduction Group 674

Address: Hôpital de Bicêtre, 78 rue du Général Leclerc, 94270 Le Kremlin Bicêtre
Telephone: 677 81 77
Director: Professor Edwin Milgrom
Activities: Progesterone; glucocorticoids; proteins in uterine secretions; study and application of cancer-preventive methods of a hormone-dependent nature.

136. Tumour Immunology Unit 675

Address: Centre d'Immunologie INSERM/CNRS, de Marseille Luminy, 70 route Léon Lachamp, 13288 Marseille Cedex 2
Telephone: (091) 41 01 33
Director: François Kourilsky
Activities: Immunologic reactions: mechanisms and applications.

137. Molecular Biology of Animal Cells Group 676

Address: Centre Universitaire Cochin Port-Royal, 24 rue du Faubourg Saint-Jacques, 75014 Paris
Telephone: (01) 320 12 40
Director: Professor Jacques Kruh
Activities: Chromosomal proteins; glucocorticoid and thyroid hormones; iron metabolism.

138. Cardiocirculatory and Respiratory Physiology Group 677

Address: Hôpital Henri Mondor, 51 avenue du Maréchal de Lattre de Tassigny, 94010 Créteil
or: Faculté de Médecine, 6 rue du Général Sarrail, 94010 Créteil
Telephone: 205 51 41
Director: Professor Daniel Laurent
Activities: Cardiac physiology and function; respiratory physiology and technology.

139. Experimental and Human Glomerular Nephritis Group 678

Address: Hôpital Henri Mondor, 51 avenue du Maréchal de Lattre de Tassigny, 94010 Créteil
Telephone: 207 51 41
Director: Professor Gilbert Lagrue
Activities: Renal immunology; experimental and human glomerulonephritis.

140. Pharmacology of Anticancer Drugs Group 679

Address: Institut Gustave-Roussy, 16 bis avenue Paul Vaillant Couturier, 94800 Villejuif
Telephone: 726 49 09
Director: Professor Claude Paoletti
Activities: Biochemistry and biophysics of DNA; pharmacokinetics of drugs used in cancer chemotherapy.

141. Physiology applied to Cardiac Reanimation Unit 680

Address: Centre de Recherches de l'INSERM, Hôpital Lariboisière, 41 boulevard de la Chapelle, 75010 Paris
Telephone: (01) 285 86 72
Director: Dr Rémi Saumont
Activities: Arterial walls and haemodynamics; cardiac fibrillation and defibrillation; haemodynamic criteria in severe heart attacks.

142. Child Endocrine Physiology Group 681

Address: Hôpital Trousseau, 26 avenue du Docteur Arnold Netter, 75012 Paris
Telephone: (01) 346 13 90
Director: Dr Michel Binoux
Activities: Growth hormone regulation; hypophysical physiology.

143. Physiopathology of Haemostasis and Thrombosis Group 682

Address: Institut de Pathologie Cellulaire, Hôpital de Bicêtre, 94270 Le Kremlin Bicêtre
Telephone: 588 61 95
Director: Professor Marie-Josette Larrieu
Activities: Biological and immunological study of fibrinogen and its derivatives and of anti-haemophiliac factors; Willebrand factor - blood platelet interaction.

144. Child Practical and Theoretical Psychopathology Group 683

Address: Hôpital Henri Rousselle, 1 rue Cabanis, 75674 Paris Cedex 14
Telephone: (01) 581 11 20
Director: Dr Gabrielle C. Lairy
Activities: Clinical, electrophysiological studies; informatics.

145. Polypeptide Hormones and Endocrine Physiopathology Group   684

Address: Faculté de Médecine, chemin de Vallombrose, 06034 Nice Cedex
Telephone: (093) 85 16 54
Director: Dr Pierre Freychet
Activities: Polypeptide hormones, especially insulin.

146. Microbe Ecotoxicology Unit   685

Address: Domaine du CERTIA, 369 rue Jules Guesde, 59650 Villeneuve d'Ascq
Telephone: (020) 95 43 59
Director: Professor Henri Leclerc
Activities: Epidemiology; ecology and taxonomy; toxicology; automatic methodology.

148. Cellular and Molecular Endocrinology Unit   686

Address: Centre de Recherches de l'INSERM, 60 rue de Navacelles, 34100 Montpellier
Telephone: (067) 54 15 44
Director: Professor Henri Rochefort
Activities: Steroid hormones: their mechanism and their role in cancers.

149. Mother and Child Epidemiology Group   687

Address: Centre de Recherches de l'INSERM, 44 chemin de Ronde, BP 34, 78110 Le Vesinet
Telephone: 976 33 33
Director: Dr Claude Rumeau-Rouquette
Activities: The role of exogenous factors in obesity; aetiology of sterility; perinatal pathology; evaluation of health programmes.

150. Experimental Thrombosis and Haemostasis Unit   688

Address: Centre André Lichtwitz, Hôpital Lariboisière, 6,8 rue Guy Patin, 75010 Paris
Telephone: (01) 280 02 54
Director: Professor Jacques Caen
Activities: Biochemistry, physiology and pathology of blood platelets; plasmatic proteins - Willebrand factor; epidemiology of thrombosis.

151. Digestive Biology and Pathology Group   689

Address: CHU Rangueil, chemin du Vallon, 31400 Toulouse
Telephone: (061) 25 21 52
Director: Professor André Ribet
Activities: Physiology; biochemistry; histopathology; clinical research.

152. Tumour Immunology and Virology Group   690

Address: Hôpital Cochin, 27 rue du Faubourg Saint-Jacques, 75674 Paris Cedex 14
Telephone: (01) 320 12 40
Director: Professor Jean-Paul Lévy
Activities: Cellular immunity; antigens; genetics and immunology; cancer agents.

153. Neuromuscular Biology and Pathology of Myopathies Unit   691

Address: Bâtiment INSERM, 17 rue du Fer à Moulin, 75005 Paris
Telephone: (01) 336 46 31
Director: Dr Michel Fardeau
Activities: Neuromuscular pathology; myogenesis and neuromuscular synopsis; human neuropathology.

154. Development and Pathology of the Nervous System and Muscles of a Child Group   692

Address: Hôpital Saint-Vincent-de-Paul, 74 avenue Denfert-Rochereau, 75674 Paris Cedex 14
Telephone: (01) 325 22 51
Director: Dr Edith Farkas
Activities: Enzyme maturation in the cerebral cortex; development of the nervous system; effect of malnutrition; studies on the foetal muscles and nervous system and their diseases.

155. Epidemiological Genetics Group   693

Address: Château de Longchamp, Bois de Boulogne, 75016 Paris
Telephone: (01) 772 77 91
Director: Dr Josué Feingold
Activities: Formal genetics of hereditary diseases; genetics of human populations; statistics applied to genetics.

156. Hypothalmic Control of   694 Prehypophysial Gonadotrophic Activity Unit

Address: Laboratoire d'Histologie, Faculté de Médecine, place de Verdun, 59045 Lille Cedex
Telephone: (020) 96 92 31
Director: Professor Julien Barry
Activities: Immunocytochemistry and histophysiology of hypothalmic neurones.

157. Odontology Group   695

Address: Faculté de Chirurgie Dentaire, 4 rue de Kirschleger, 67000 Strasbourg
Telephone: (088) 36 25 26
Director: Professor Robert Frank
Activities: Prevention of dental caries; bucco-dental epidemiology; physiology and pathology of calcified tissues.

158. Problems Related to the Sick   696 Child Group

Address: Pavillon Méry, Hôpital des Enfants Malades, 149 rue de Sèvres, 75015 Paris
Telephone: (01) 567 08 11
Director: Dr Ginette Raimbault
Activities: Psychological aspects of renal transplants and artificial nutrition; psycho-social study of mother-child relationships; value of medical information given to a diabetic and his acceptance of his condition; sociological study of human weaknesses.

159. Neuroendocrinology Unit   697

Address: Centre Paul Broca de l'INSERM, rue d'Alésia, 75014 Paris
Telephone: (01) 589 53 07
Director: Claude Kordon
Activities: Neurotransmitter - neuropeptide interaction in hypophysial functions; peptide biosynthesis and degradation.

160. Enzymology of the Blood Cells   698 Unit

Address: Hôpital Beaujon, 100 boulevard du Général Leclerc, 92118 Clichy Cedex
Telephone: 739 33 40
Director: Professor Pierre Boivin
Activities: Purification and characterization of normal human blood cells; protein composition of erythrocytic membranes in normal and diseased humans; phagocytosis.

161. Pharmacological Neurophysiology   699 Unit

Address: 2 rue d'Alésia, 75014 Paris
Telephone: (01) 589 36 62
Director: Jean-Marie Besson
Activities: Pluridisciplinary research on the physiology of pain and the effects of analgesics.

162. Hormonal Control of Cell Activity   700 Unit

Address: Hôpital Debrousse, 29 rue Soeur Bouvier, 69322 Lyon Cedex 1
Telephone: (078) 25 18 08
Director: Dr José M. Saez
Activities: Role of adrenocorticotrophic hormone in the renal system; role of gonadotrophins in hormone regulation.

163. Recombinant and Expression   701 Genetics Group

Address: Institut Pasteur, 25 rue du Docteur Roux, 75015 Paris
Telephone: (01) 541 52 66
Director: vacant
Activities: Recombination genetics, in vivo and in vitro; cloning of eukaryotic genes; genetic fusion; hybrid proteins.

164. Health, Health Care Systems and   702 Prevention Evaluation Unit

Address: Centre de Recherches de l'INSERM, 44 chemin de Ronde, BP 34, 78110 Le Vesinet
Telephone: 976 33 33
Director: Dr François Hatton
Activities: General morbidity and mortality; evaluation of care and prevention systems.

165. Infectious Diseases and Toxic   703 Accidents Unit

Address: Centre de Recherches de l'INSERM, 44 chemin de Ronde, BP 34, 78110 Le Vesinet
Telephone: 976 05 08
Director: Dr Gilbert Martin-Bouyer
Activities: Infectious diseases - epidemiologic surveillance and surveys of morbidity; toxic accidents.

166. Reproduction Endocrinology Group 704

Address: Maternité de Port Royal, 123 boulevard de Port Royal, 75014 Paris
Director: Dr Lise Cedard
Activities: New types of plasmatic hormones dosages; steroid hormone synthesis.

167. Parasite Immunology and Biology Group 705

Address: CIBP Institut Pasteur, 20 boulevard Louis XIV, 59000 Lille
Telephone: (020) 52 33 33
Director: Professor André Capron
Activities: Immunitary response to parasitic diseases; bilharziasis, trypanosomiasis and filariasis; immunochemistry; immunopathology.

168. Obstetrical Physiology and Perinatal Pharmacology Group 706

Address: Hôpital de la Grave, 31052 Toulouse Cedex
Telephone: (061) 42 33 33
Director: Professor Georges Pontonnier
Activities: Physiology and physiopathology of the foetus during pregnancy; bio- and medical engineering; sexual steroids; thyroid synthesis regulation by means of insulin.

169. Statistical and Epidemiological Methods and their Application to the Study of Diseases Unit 707

Address: Institut Gustave Roussy, 16 bis avenue Paul Vaillant-Couturier, 94800 Villejuif
Telephone: 677 24 69
Director: Joseph Lellouch
Activities: Research on statistical and epidemiological studies in medicine, especially in relation to cardiac diseases and environmental factors.

170. Environment and Health Epidemiology and Statistics Unit 708

Address: Institut Gustave Roussy, 16 bis avenue Paul Vaillant-Couturier, 94800 Villejuif
Telephone: 726 51 27
Director: Philippe Lazar
Activities: Study of the environment in relation to epidemiological and statistical methodology. Fields of particular interest are: health - the quality of human reproduction; environment - work factors and quality of the drinking water.

171. Functional Neurochemistry Group 709

Address: Université Claude Bernard, 8 avenue Rockefeller, 69373 Lyon Cedex 2
Telephone: (078) 75 81 14
Director: Dr Jean-François Pujol
Activities: Regulatory mechanism of central monoaminergic neurones; anatomical, biochemical and neurophysiological control mechanisms; regulatory mechanism models.

172. Chemistry and Mode of Action of Animal Toxins Group 710

Address: Laboratoire de Biochimie, Faculté de Médecine Secteur Nord, boulevard Pierre-Dramard, 13326 Marseille Cedex 3
Telephone: (091) 51 90 01
Director: Professor Hervé Rochat
Activities: Animal poisons, (scorpions and serpents) and antidotes.

173. Human and Comparative Cytogenetics Unit 711

Address: Hôpital des Enfants Malades, Clinique de Génétique Médicale, 149 rue de Sèvres, 75730 Paris Cedex 15
Telephone: (01) 555 92 80
Director: Dr Jean de Grouchy
Activities: Chromosomal aberrations in congenital malformations; mental weakness and sexual development in humans; chromosomal phylogenesis in primates.

174. Asthma Physiopathology and Obstructive Syndromes Unit 712

Address: Centre de Recherches de l'INSERM, 10 avenue Viton, 13009 Marseille
Telephone: (091) 74 23 40
Director: Professor Jacques Charpin
Activities: Respiratory physiopathology and immunology; atmospheric allergens.

175. Experimental Cardiology Unit 713

Address: Centre de Recherches de l'INSERM, 10 avenue Viton, 13009 Marseille
Telephone: (091) 74 00 95
Director: Professor Jean Torresani
Activities: Haemodynamics; vasoactive drugs; cardiac failure; cardiocirculatory aid.

176. Neurobiology of Behaviour Unit   714

Address: Domaine de Carreire, rue Camille St-Saëns, 33077 Bordeaux Cedex
Telephone: (056) 96 52 66
Director: Professor J.-D. Vincent
Activities: Subcellular mechanics of neurosecretions; hydro-mineral balance, motor functions and elementary behaviour (hunger, thirst); arterial pressure in primates; reproduction regulatory system in rabbits and primates.

177. Nutrition Physiopathology Group   715

Address: Institut Biomédical des Cordeliers, 15-21 rue de l'École de Médecine, 75270 Paris Cedex 06
Telephone: (01) 329 21 77
Director: Pierre De Gasquet
Activities: Glucose-lipid metabolism; aetiology of experimental obesity; genetic factors in human obesity.

178. Differentiation Immunology   716
Group

Address: Hôpital Broussais, 96 rue Didot, 75674 Paris Cedex 14
Telephone: (01) 539 22 66
Director: Dr Alain Zweibaum
Activities: Regulatory factors in glycogenesis; the role of hormones in skin-graft rejections; neuro-retinal and cerebellar cells and oncogenic viruses.

179. Epidemiology and Socioeconomic   717
Aspects of Tuberculosis and
Respiratory Diseases Unit

Address: Centre de Recherches de l'INSERM, 44 chemin de Ronde, BP 34, 78110 Le Vesinet
Director: vacant
Activities: Epidemiological surveillance, especially in relation to tubercular incidences; epidemiology of respiratory diseases; cost-effective studies of respiratory diseases; prevention measures and public behaviour.

180. Molecular Biology and Pathology   718
of Glycoproteins Group

Address: UER Biomédicale des Saints-Pères, 45 rue des Saints-Pères, 75006 Paris
Telephone: (01) 260 37 20
Director: Professor Y. Goussault
Activities: Glycoconjugates secreted by the urinary system; membrane glycoproteins; plasma membranes; physico-chemical interaction of saccharide lectins and ligands.

181. Glycoconjugated and Extracellular   719
Membrane Structure Group

Address: Laboratoire de Biochimie Médicale, Faculté de Médecine Saint-Antoine, 27 rue de Chaligny, 75571 Paris Cedex 12
Director: Professor Jacques Picard
Activities: Role, structure, metabolism, antigen properties of glycoproteins and proteoglycins; serum and urinary mucopolysaccharides.

182. Cerebrovascular Physiology and   720
Physiopathology Group

Address: UER Lariboisière-Saint-Louis, 10 avenue du Verdun, BP 110-10, 75463 Paris Cedex 10
Telephone: (01) 203 94 26
Director: Jacques Seylaz
Activities: Regulation of blood-flow to the brain; cerebral damage; developments in cerebral technology.

183. Physiopathology of Cell   721
Organisms Group

Address: Institut Biomédical des Cordeliers, 21 rue de l'École de Médecine, 75270 Paris Cedex 06
Telephone: (01) 329 21 77
Director: Dr Michel Bouteille
Activities: Nuclear medicine; comparison between laboratory and outside viruses.

184. Molecular Biology and Genetic   722
Engineering Group

Address: Faculté de Médecine, Institut de Chimie Biologique, 11 rue Humann, 67085 Strasbourg Cedex
Telephone: (088) 36 56 70
Director: Professor Pierre Chambon
Activities: Genetic engineering; genetic information in eukaryotic cells.

185. Sociopathy Unit   723

Address: Centre de Recherches de l'INSERM, 44 chemin de Ronde, BP 34, 78110 Le Vesinet
Director: Dr François Davidson
Activities: Morbid interactions between the individual and his social environment; infant sociopathology; deviant behaviour in the adolescent (alcoholism, suicide, etc).

186. Oncolological Research Unit   724

Address: 15 rue Camille Guérin, 59019 Lille
Telephone: (020) 52 33 33
Director: D. Stehelin

187. Human Reproduction Physiology and Psychology Unit 725

Address: Hôpital Antoine Béclère, 92140 Clamart
Director: Dr E. Papiernik

188. Growth Research Unit 726

Address: 74 avenue Denfert Rochereau, 75014 Paris
Telephone: (01) 320 14 74
Director: Professor J.-C. Job

189. Glycoconjugate Biology and Pathology Unit 727

Address: Laboratoire de Biochimie, Faculté de Médecine - Lyon Sud, chemin de Petit Revoyet, 69600 Oullins
Telephone: (078) 51 08 26
Director: Professor Pierre Louisot
Activities: Normal and pathological metabolism of glycoconjugates.

190. Skin Virus and Cancer Unit 728

Address: 25 rue du Dr Roux, 75015 Paris
Telephone: (01) 306 19 19
Director: G. Orth

191. Cell Energy Research Unit 729

Address: 85 avenue des Martyrs, 38041 Grenoble
Telephone: (076) 97 41 11
Director: Professor P. Vignais

192. Paediatric Nephrology Unit 730

Address: 149 rue de Sèvres, 75730 Paris
Telephone: (01) 783 90 16
Director: Dr R. Habib

193. Myopathy Research Unit 731

Address: 12 rue Louis Braille, 77100 Meaux
Telephone: (01) 009 24 69
Director: Dr J. Demos

194. Medical Informatics and Statistics Unit 732

Address: 91 boulevard de L'Hôpital, 75634 Paris
Telephone: (01) 586 19 49
Director: Professor J.-F. Boisvieux

195. Cardiovascular Pharmacology Research Unit 733

Address: place Henri Dunant, 63001 Clermont Ferrand
Telephone: (073) 26 56 75
Director: Dr P. Duchene Marullaz

196. Interferon Research Unit 734

Address: 26 rue d'Ulm, 75231 Paris
Telephone: (01) 329 12 42
Director: Dr E. Falcoff

197. Endocrine Physiopathology Research Unit 735

Address: rue Guillaume Paradin, 69008 Lyon
Telephone: (07) 874 85 89
Director: Professor R. Mornex

198. Hormone Biochemistry and Regulation Research Unit 736

Address: route de Dole, 25000 Besançon Chateaufarine
Telephone: (081) 52 33 00
Director: Professor G. Adessi

199. Enterobacteria Research Unit 737

Address: 25 rue du Docteur Roux, 75724 Paris
Telephone: (01) 306 19 19

200. Allergy Immunopharmacology Research Unit 738

Address: 32 rue des Carnets, 92140 Clamart
Telephone: (01) 632 12 07
Director: Dr J. Benveniste

201. Molecular and Cellular Photobiological Processes Research Unit 739

Address: 61 rue Buffon, 75005 Paris
Telephone: (01) 535 23 89
Director: Professor C. Hélène

202. Immunochemistry and Molecular Biology Unit 740

Address: Institut Biomédical des Cordeliers, 15 rue de l'École de Médecine, 75270 Paris Cedex 06
Telephone: (01) 329 21 77
Director: Professor Lucien Hartmann
Activities: Human and animal physiopathology; gas-liquid chromatography.

203. Immunopharmacology Unit   741

Address: Laboratoire de Pathologie Expérimentale, Faculté Necker-Enfants Malades, 156 rue de Vaugirard, 75730 Paris Cedex 15
Telephone: (01) 578 61 28
Director: Dr Claude Burtin
Activities: Reactions and allergies caused by medicines.

204. Cellular Kinetics in Haematology   742
and Cancerology Unit

Address: Hôpital Saint-Louis, 2 place du Docteur A. Fournier, 75475 Paris Cedex 10
Telephone: (01) 205 83 10
Director: Professor Yves Najean
Activities: These focus on the kinetics of cell populations in haematology and cancerology; study of isotopic methods in vivo and in vitro.

205. Chemical Pharmacology and   743
Biochemistry of New Antimetabolites
Unit

Address: Institut National des Sciences Appliquées de Lyon, Laboratoire de Chimie Biologique, 20 avenue Albert Einstein, 69621 Villeurbanne Cedex
Telephone: (078) 68 81 12
Director: Professor Henri Pacheco
Activities: Different and new molecular types; studies in humans and animals of the effect of diverse medicines on the cholesterol metabolism.

206. Vascular Pharmacology Unit   744

Address: Institut de Pharmacologie et de Médecine Expérimentale, 11 rue Humann, 67000 Strasbourg
Telephone: (088) 36 06 91
Director: Professor Jean Schwartz
Activities: Vasomotors; alpha-adrenergic receptors; intrarenal activity; hypertension.

208. Biochemical Differentiation of   745
Eukaryotic Cells and Experimental
Cancerogenesis Unit

Address: Faculté de Médecine, 7 boulevard Jeanne d'Arc, 21033 Dijon
Telephone: (080) 65 23 23
Director: Professor Prudent Padieu
Activities: Biochemical differentiation of eukaryotic cells in culture.

210. Differentiation Marker Antigens   746
Unit

Address: UER de Médecine, chemin de Vallombrose, 06034 Nice Cedex
Telephone: (093) 81 71 25
Director: Professor René Masseyeff
Activities: Alpha-foetoprotein and other tumour markers.

211. Cell Interactions in Cancers Unit   747

Address: UER de Médecine et CRLC de Nantes, quai Moncousu, 44035 Nantes Cedex
Telephone: (040) 47 40 01
Director: Professor B. P. Le Mevel
Activities: Cell interactions; isolation and characteristics of cytoplasmatic membranes.

212. Dermatology and Immunology   748
Unit

Address: Fondation Ophthalmologique A. de Rothschild, 25-29 rue Manin, 75019 Paris
Telephone: (01) 203 96 96
Director: Professor Michel Prunieras

213. Growth Control of Craniofacial   749
Cartilage and Bones Unit

Address: Institut de Physiologie de la Faculté de Médecine, 4 rue Kirschleger, 67085 Strasbourg Cedex
Telephone: (088) 36 06 91
Director: Dr Alexandre Petrovic
Activities: Growth mechanisms of primary and secondary cartilage of the craniofacial skeleton.

214. Respiratory System Antibody   750
Defences Unit

Address: Clinique de Pneumo Phtisiologie, Hôpital Laënnec, 42 rue de Sèvres, 75007 Paris
Telephone: (01) 548 48 05
Director: Professor Jacques Chrétien
Activities: Lung disorders and purification.

215. Neurological Handicap and   751
Growth Unit

Address: Hôpital Raymond Poincaré, 92380 Garches
Telephone: 970 67 70
Director: Dr Catherine Tardieu
Activities: Understanding and therapeutics of the major problems affecting neurologically handicapped patients; comparison with the normal child.

216. Marine Chemistry and 752 Biochemistry for the Study of Trace Metals Unit

Address: Laboratoire de Physique et de Chimie Marines, Station Marine de Villefranche sur Mer, La Darse, 06230 Villefranche sur Mer
Telephone: (093) 55 56 56
Director: Professor Paul Bougis
Activities: Study of the balance between trace metals and organic substances in a marine environment; substances produced by phytoplankton, especially those of therapeutic interest.

217. Plasmatic Proteins Unit 753

Address: Laboratoire d'Hématologie, Département de Recherche Fondamentale, Centre d'Études Nucléaires, 85 X 38041 Grenoble Cedex
Telephone: (076) 97 41 11
Director: M. Suscillon
Activities: Study of the diverse factors in blood coagulation.

218. Experimental Immunology and 754 Cancerology Unit

Address: Centre Léon Bérard, 28 rue Laënnec, 69373 Lyon Cedex 2
Telephone: (078) 74 04 36
Director: Dr Jean-François Doré
Activities: Markers of human lymphocytes; antigens associated with tumours in man; immunological host-tumour relations.

219. Molecular Biophysics Unit 755

Address: Institut Curie - Section de Biologie, Laboratoire 112 - Centre Universitaire, 91405 Orsay
Director: Dr Jean-Marc Lhoste
Activities: Molecular biophysics and electronic and magnetic spectroscopy.

220. Imagery and Detector Methods 756 Unit

Address: Laboratoire de Biophysique des Rayonnements et de Méthodologie, Université Louis Pasteur - Faculté de Médecine, 11 rue Humann, 67085 Strasbourg Cedex
Telephone: (088) 36 06 91
Director: Roger Rechenmann
Activities: Ionographic and autoradiographic methods; nuclear medicine and radiobiology.

221. Study of Biological Structures 757 Unit

Address: UER Biomédicale des Saints-Pères, 45 rue des Saints-Pères, 75006 Paris
Telephone: (01) 260 37 20
Director: Dr Annette Alfsen
Activities: Study of proteins in solutions; study of the membrane structure.

222. Regulatory Functions of 758 Biological Membranes Unit

Address: Laboratoire de Physiologie Cellulaire, Collège de France, 11 place Marcelin-Berthelot, 75231 Paris Cedex 05
Telephone: (01) 329 12 11
Director: Professor Serge Jard
Activities: Neurohypophysial peptide cell mechanisms; modification in hormonal receptivity.

223. Physiopathology of the 759 Hypophysis Unit

Address: CHU Pitié Salpétrière, 105 boulevard de l'Hôpital, 75634 Paris Cedex 13
Telephone: (01) 707 67 79
Director: Dr François Peillon

224. Comparative Biology of 760 Molecular Interactions Unit

Address: Laboratoire de Biochimie, UER Biomédicale des Saints-Pères, 45 rue des Saints-Péres, 75270 Paris Cedex 06
Telephone: (01) 260 37 20
Director: Professor Emmanuel Nunez
Activities: Biological study of macromolecular interaction and macromolecular-ligand interaction in the endocrine system in the normal and neoplastic development of various animal species; study in vivo and in vitro of the biological interactions of alpha 1.

225. Calcified Tissue Unit 761

Address: Faculté de Chirurgie Dentaire, place Alexis Ricordeau, 44042 Nantes
Telephone: (040) 47 48 66
Director: Professor Bertrand Kerebel
Activities: Structural, ultrastructural, crystallographic, and biochemistry of calcified dental tissue and of the alveolar bone; effects of calcium, magnesium, and vitamin D deficiencies in the alveolar bone; study of biological appetites and the role of fluoride ions.

226. Mechanisms of Respiratory 762 Malfunctions Unit

Address: Laboratoire de Physiopathologie Respiratoire et de Morpho-immunologie, Hôpital Beaujon, 100 boulevard du Général Leclerc, 92110 Clichy
Telephone: 739 33 40
Director: Professor René Pariente
Activities: Pulmonary malfunctions: structure, function and epidemiology.

227. Physiopathology of Arterial 763 Hypertension Unit

Address: Hôpital St-Charles, 34059 Montpellier Cedex
Telephone: (067) 63 91 64
Director: Professor Paul Barjon
Activities: Interaction of vasoactive intrarenal systems; renal haemodynamics; renal neurotransmitters; arterial hypertension.

228. Cardiovascular 764 Neuropharmacology Unit

Address: Département de Pharmacologie, Faculté de Médecine Paris-Broussais, 15 rue de l'École de Médecine, 75006 Paris
Telephone: (01) 329 21 77
Director: Professor Henri-Lucien Schmitt
Activities: Pharmacological study of alpha-presynaptic receptors; action of neuromediators on the central cardiovascular system; effects of morphinomimetic substances on the central nervous system.

229. Experimental Audiology Unit 765

Address: Laboratoire d'Audiologie Expérimentale, Hôpital Pellegrin, place Amélie-Raba-Léon, 33076 Bordeaux Cedex
Telephone: (056) 96 83 83
Director: Jean-Marie Aran
Activities: Study of the internal ear by means of electrophysiological and histological means; electrophysiological evaluation of the function of the auditory tract in humans; artificial audio stimulation for the deaf.

230. Haemodynamics and Cerebral 766 Energy Unit

Address: Service de Neurologie, CHU Purpan, 31052 Toulouse Cedex
Telephone: (061) 49 11 33
Director: Professor J.-P. Marc-Vergnes
Activities: Development of methods to explore the cerebral circulation in humans by means of radiotracers, angiography and tomodensitometry; cerebral tumours; cerebral ischaemia.

231. Cholesterol Biodynamics Unit 767

Address: Laboratoire de Physiologie de la Nutrition, Université Paris XI, 91405 Orsay Cedex
Telephone: 941 67 50
Director: Professor François Chevallier
Activities: Description of the cholesterol system of the rat and of man.

232. Chemotherapy of Malignant 768 Diseases Unit

Address: Hôpital de la Salpétrière, 42 boulevard de l'Hôpital, 75634 Paris Cedex
Telephone: (01) 584 14 12
Director: Claude Jacquillat
Activities: Research on the amelioration and prolongation of life of patients with malignant diseases.

233. Molecular Virology Unit 769

Address: Centre de Recherches INSERM à Lille, Cité Hospitalière, place de Verdun, 59045 Lille Cedex
Telephone: (020) 57 51 22
Director: Professor Pierre Boulanger

234. Pathology of Calcified Tissues 770 Unit

Address: Faculté Alexis Carrel, 8 rue Guillaume Paradin, 69008 Lyon
Telephone: (078) 74 85 89
Director: Professor Pierre Meunier

235. Retina Diseases Unit 771

Address: Laboratoire de Recherches sur les Maladies de la Rétina, Hôpital Cochin, 27 rue du Faubourg Saint-Jacques, 75674 Paris Cedex 14
Telephone: (01) 329 21 21
Director: Professor François Regnault

236. Tumour Immunopharmacology 772 Unit

Address: Laboratoire d'Immuno-pharmacologie des Tumeurs, Centre Paul Lamarque, Hôpital Saint-Eloi, BP 5054, 34033 Montpellier Cedex
Telephone: (067) 63 28 73
Director: Dr Bernard Serrou

237. Pathological Role of Proteases 773 Unit

Address: Faculté de Pharmacie, 74 route du Rhin, 67400 Illkirch-Graffenstaden
Telephone: (088) 66 90 77
Director: Joseph Bieth

238. Immunochemistry Unit   774

Address: Département de Recherche Fondamentale, Centre d'Études Nucléaires, avenue des Martyrs, 38000 Grenoble
Telephone: (076) 97 41 11
Director: Professor Maurice Colomb

239. Biology and Physiology of   775
Digestive Cells Unit

Address: Faculté de Médecine Xavier Bichat, 16 rue Henri Huchard, 75018 Paris
Telephone: (01) 263 84 20
Director: Professor François Potet

240. Risk Evaluation and Prevention   776
Unit

Address: Centre d'Études Nucléaires, BP 48, 60-68 avenue du Général Leclerc, 92260 Fontenay aux Roses
Director: Francis Fagnani

241. Cardiac Cell Physiology Unit   777

Address: Laboratoire de Physiologie Comparée, Campus Universitaire, 91405 Orsay
Director: Guy Vassort

242. Chromosomal Physiopathology   778
Unit

Address: Centre de Génétique Médicale, Hôpital d'Énfants du Groupe Hospitalier de la Timone, 13385 Marseille Cedex 04
Telephone: (075) 49 90 48
Director: Francis Giraud

243. Pharmacology of Vascular and   779
Bronchial Muscles Unit

Address: Laboratoire de Pharmacodynamie, Faculté de Pharmacie, 70 route du Rhin, Illkirch-Graffenstaden
Telephone: (088) 66 90 77
Director: Professor Jean-Claude Stoclet

244. Cell Mechanism of Humoral   780
Effectors Unit

Address: Centre d'Études et de Recherches sur les Macromolécules Organisées - CERMO, Université Scientifique et Médicale de Grenoble, Domaine Universitaire, BM 53 X, 38041 Grenoble Cedex
Director: Professor E. Chambaz

245. Molecular Biology of the   781
Interferon System Unit

Address: Institut de Biologie Physico-chimique, 13 rue Pierre et Marie Curie, 75005 Paris
Telephone: (01) 325 26 09
Director: Minh Nguy Thang

246. Nephric Physiology and   782
Pathology Research Unit

Address: BP2, Gif sur Yvette
Director: Dr J.-P. Bonvalet

247. Normal and Cancerous Cell   783
Radiobiology Research Unit

Address: rue Camille Desmoulins, Villejuif
Telephone: (01) 559 49 09
Director: Dr E.-P. Malaise

249. Contractile Systems Biochemistry 784
Research Unit

Address: boulevard Henri IV, BP 5015, 34033 Montpellier
Telephone: (067) 63 91 30
Director: Professor J. Demaille

250. Cell Kinetics Research Unit   785

Address: rue Camille Desmoulins, 94805 Villejuif
Telephone: (01) 559 49 09
Director: Dr E. Frindel

Institut National de   786
Recherche Chimique
Appliquée

– IRCHA
[National Institute of Applied Chemical Research]
Address: 18 bis boulevard de la Bastille, 75012 Paris
Affiliation: Ministère de l'Industrie

RESEARCH CENTRE*   787

Address: BP No 1, 91710 Vert-le-Petit
Telephone: (06) 493 24 75
Telex: 800 820 F IRCHA
Graduate research staff: 50
Annual expenditure: F56m (1980)
Activities: Research is carried out on a contract basis for private companies or public organizations, and covers the following subjects:
Chemistry - organic chemistry, including: fluorine

chemistry; organophosphorus (mainly heterocyclic) chemistry; transition metal complexes; scaling-up and development at pilot level of the synthesis of organic compounds; custom-made fine chemicals at the ton-level; hydrometallurgy: mechanistic study of the extraction of transition metals; screening of newer extractants; pilot-scale study of extraction processes in various media; study and development of perm selective membranes forreverse osmosis, ultrafiltration (electrochemical application); dry lubricants and self-lubricating plastic-based materials for use in various environments; composite materials - filled and fibre-reinforced thermo plastic and thermosetting materials, reuse of mixed plastic wastes.

Biochemistry-biology: biotechnologies - liquid-phase fermentation, solid-phase fermentation, application to protein enrichment of natural products, production of enzymes, biogas technology; identification of microorganisms; screening and formulation of insecticides, fungicides, bactericides and herbicides; treatment of biological corrosion.

Ecology-environment - ecology: impact assessment studies, especially for industrial projects; ecotoxicity - degradation, metabolization, bioaccumulation, biomagnification of toxic substances in soils and waters; standardization and study of newer ecotoxicity tests; water pollution: detection, identification and measurement of pollutants; development of relevant analytical techniques; physico-chemical and biological treatment of domestic and industrial used waters; treatment of hydrocarbons by dispersants; microbiology of water, study and treatmentof biological corrosion of materials; survey of natural waters; sampling and testing industrial effluents; design of water-treatment units; - air pollution: pilot station activity with the European air control network (acidic fallout, long-range pollution, atmospheric oxidants, etc); development of improved detection and measurement for air pollutants; evaluation of air control equipment; modelling of dispersion of air pollutants; on-site testing of pollutants and emissions; - solid wastes: recycling of industrial plastic wastes via newer technologies.

Facilities: These include molecular spectroscopy, nuclear magnetic resonance, electron microscopy, etc.

Contract work: Yes

Regional Laboratory   788

Address: rue de la Chanterelle, BP 46, Flers-Bourg, 59651 Villeneuve-d'Ascq
Telephone: (020) 91 03 20

Institut National des Sciences Appliquées de Lyon   789

– INSA
[National Institute of Applied Sciences of Lyon]
Address: 20 avenue Albert Einstein, 69621 Villeurbanne Cedex
Telephone: (07) 893 81 12
Telex: INSALYN 380 856 F
Director: Jean Pradal
Graduate research staff: 300
Annual expenditure: £4m
Contract work: No
Publications: Annual report.

DEPARTMENT OF BIOCHEMISTRY   790

Head: L. Cronenberger

Biochemistry Laboratory   791

Head: H. Pacheco
Senior staff: L. Cronenberger
Activities: Isolation and purification of enzymes, enzyme function and inhibition; structure and synthesis of nucleasides and nucleotides, non-natural compounds; cholesterol biosynthesis.

Biology Laboratory   792

Head: P. Laviolette
Activities: Insect nutritional physiology, genetics and endocrinology; gametes and embryo studies; melanogenesis; uses of the APIZYM method.

Microbiology Laboratory   793

Head: F. Stoeber
Activities: Bacterial genetics, genetic engineering and biomedical and industrial applications; bacterial periplasmic space studies; membrane active transport and energy exchange; genetic biochemistry.

Organic Chemistry Laboratory   794

Head: R. Gelin
Activities: Organic synthesis of heterocyclic molecules; development of relations with INRA.

Physiology and Pharmacology Laboratory 795

Head: E. Brard
Activities: Oestrogen action mechanisms; cardiovascular, reproductive and digestive physiopathology; electrophysiological studies; central nervous system pharmacology; biological effects of microwaves and high frequencies; biomaterial and biomechanical studies.

DEPARTMENT OF CIVIL ENGINEERING AND TOWN PLANNING 796

Head: H. Botta

Concretes and Structures Laboratory 797

Head: J.C. Cybaud
Senior staff: J.F. Jullien
Activities: Materials, new materials, basic components, hydraulic elasticity studies, fibrous and filamentous reinforcement; material mechanics, elasticity, material rupture, acoustic emission studies; calculation methods and theories, structural stability; experimental analysis of constraints; reinforced and prestressed concrete structures.

Geotechnics Laboratory 798

Head: P. Lareal
Senior staff: J. Gielly, N. Mongereau
Activities: Regional geotechnical and geotechnical survey studies; foundations and ground stabilization; support and excavation.

Habitat Equipment Laboratory 799

Head: M. Gery
Activities: Thermophysical properties of building materials; thermal behaviour of buildings; underground energy stockage and destockage.

Methods Laboratory 800

Head: H. Botta
Activities: Building, design and function; water sanitation, management of urban, peri-urban and rural areas.

DEPARTMENT OF ELECTRICAL ENGINEERING 801

Head: H. Kleimann

Electrical Engineering and Ferroelectricity Laboratory 802

Senior staff: Y. Fetiveau H. Kleimann
Activities: Thermodynamics and ferroelectricity; electroacoustics and scientific instrumentation; industrial electricity and energetics; industrial and medical, mini- and micro-information.

Material Studies Laboratory 803

Head: M. Chevreton
Activities: Electronic properties of metallic interphases; transport and magnetic properties of sulphur, selenium and tellurium compounds of iron and chromium; structural studies; nuclear industry studies.

Mineral Thermochemistry Laboratory 804

Head: J. Bousquet
Senior staff: G. Perachon
Activities: Material energetics; calorimetry and thermodynamics; thermochemical constant determination.

Signal and Ultrasonic Treatment Laboratory 805

Head: R. Goutte
Senior staff: C. Guillard
Activities: Development of ultrasonic analysis methods and control; numerical treatment of signals and images, non-destructive material control, biological engineering and medical applications.

DEPARTMENT OF ENGINEERING ENERGETICS 806

Head: B. Claudel

Applied Physical Chemistry and Environment 807

Head: J. Veron
Senior Staff: M. Murat, M. Peyron
Activities: Atmospheric pollution problems of industries, municipalities and government organizations; measurement, control, energy-economics relationships; industrial waste analysis, treatment and recovery; primary materials; agricultural wastes.

Energetics and Automation 808

Head: R. Reynaud
Senior staff: M. Richard
Activities: Automation - physical system modelling and optimization; multivariable system identification and control.
Energetics - development and improvement of thermodynamic and thermic energy systems and non-conventional energy sources; combustion, thermic transfer.

Kinetics and Chemical Engineering 809

Head: B. Claudel
Activities: Kinetics and photochemical reactions; liquid phase catalysis and photocatalysis; 'new' energies and energy economics in chemical procedures.

DEPARTMENT OF INFORMATICS 810

Head: R. Arnal

Applied Informatics Laboratory 811

Head: R. Arnal *Senior staff:* J. Favet, Y. Martinez, P. Prevot
Activities: Management information - decision aiding systems; organization systems and information systems architecture; urban systems; automatic control analysis of continuous complex systems, industrial processes and natural systems; industrial automation and microprocessors; logical engineering - applications in biological and medical engineering.

DEPARTMENT OF MECHANICAL 812
CONSTRUCTION ENGINEERING

Head: J. Bahaud

Gas Hydraulics and Dynamics 813
Laboratory

Head: E. Rieutord
Activities: Transitory direction flows; rapid relaxation and compression of gas, shock waves; thermic transfers.

Industrial Automation Laboratory 814

Head: A. Jutard
Activities: Modelling of physical phenomena; biomedical robotics; industrial robotics, electrohydraulic systems, industrial task analysis; shape recognition; numerical command.

Manufacturing Processes Laboratory 815

Head: C. Bedrin
Senior staff: C. Marty
Activities: Mechanical action processes - tool cutting, stamping, rolling; non-conventional processes - electroerosion, electrochemistry.

Mechanics of Solids Laboratory 816

Head: J. Bahaud
Senior staff: M. Boirin
Activities: Fatigue, rupture, plasticity; biomedical engineering - osteosynthetic plate development, prosthesis use, effect of microwaves on osteogenesis, podoscope development.

Metallurgy and Thermic Treatment 817
Laboratory

Head: M. Theolier
Activities: Mechanical and structural relationships of industrial materials; internal stress; fatigue mechanisms; properties of superficial layers; plastic deformations.

Vibration and Acoustics Laboratory 818

Head: C. Lesueur
Activities: Acoustic radiance of machines and structures; vibration and noise transmission by assembled structures; noise level reduction using different materials and techniques, particularly composite and multilayer materials.

DEPARTMENT OF MECHANICAL 819
DEVELOPMENT ENGINEERING

Head: M. Godet

Contact Mechanics Laboratory 820

Head: M. Godet
Senior staff: D. Berthe
Activities: Surface damage - fatigue, sticking, contact corrosion; mechanism studies - dryness and lubrication levels, abutments, rotation, gears, brakes, clutches, variators; lubrication rheology; fundamental aspects of tribology; conception assistance and optimization.

Structural Mechanics Laboratory 821

Head: M. Lalanne
Activities: Structural calculation; non-linear and vibration mechanics; bending machine dynamics; deadening; mechanics of sports vibration materials; application to turbines, compressors, ski design.

DEPARTMENT OF PHYSICAL MATERIAL ENGINEERING   822

Head: P. Gobin

Electronics Application to Surface Physics Laboratory   823

Head: C. Guittard
Activities: Surface observation and simultaneous measurement of local potential variation; microinformation; electron microscope studies; base energy electron diffraction theory.

Industrial Physico-Chemistry Laboratory   824

Head: G. Monnier
Senior staff: M. Rolin, J. Robin
Activities: Refractory steels - paraffin cracking; cokage and carburation resistance; electrochemical and physicochemical measurements in salt solutions; vapour phase deposits, metal oxidation and corrosion; plasma spectrochemistry.

Industrial Physics Laboratory   825

Head: P. Pinard
Activities: Thermics - thermophysical properties of isolation and stockage materials; impulse head exchanges in solid-solid contacts; surface temperature measurements; heat exchange between fluids and surfaces.
Electronic spectroscopy and corpuscular optics - instrumentation; physico-chemical studies of materials, particularly semiconductors; electrostatic systems.

Macromolecular Materials Laboratory   826

Head: J. Gole
Activities: Polymer-model preparation - polymerization and copolymerization mechanisms; linear polycondensations and tridimensional chemical modification of polymers; method analysis.
Solid-state polymer properties - static and dynamic viscoelasticity, mechanical and physical properties, composites, interface studies, instrumentation.

Metallurgical Physics and Material Physics Study Group   827

Head: F. Gobin
Senior staff: E. Pernoux, J. Perez, R. Rivière
Activities: Micromechanical and mechanical properties of solids defects; solid-state phase transformation; solid solution instability.
Inorganic and organic forms - visco-elastic and viscoplastic deformation, vitreous transition temperatures.
Refractories - oxides, carbides, nitrides; high-temperature microscopic deformation.
Glass - micromechanical properties and structural faults.
Dislocation - default interaction, material fatigue.
Acoustic emission - dynamic microplasticity of materials; non-destructive control, plastification, rupture, fatigue, composite materials.
Precipitation - solid solutions; equilibrium diagrams; mechanical properties of biphase alloys.
Phase transition - nucleation of martensitic transformations by ultrasonic propagation; electron microscope studies; monocrystal studies; martensite matrix interface, propagation of rapid resistance and acoustic emission.

Physics of Materials Laboratory   828

Head: P. Pinard
Activities: Physical studies and fault characterization in semiconductors - optoelectronic and optical telecommunication materials; semi-isolant and integral circuit materials; photovoltaic conversion materials - electron bombardment, thin layer polycrystalline silicons.

Institut National Polytechnique   829

[Polytechnical National Institute]
Address: place des Hauts Murats, BP 354, 31006 Toulouse Cedex
Telephone: (061) 52 21 37
Annual expenditure: £400 000
Contract work: No

ÉCOLE NATIONALE SUPÉRIEURE AGRONOMIQUE DE TOULOUSE   830

[Toulouse National Agricultural College]
Address: 145 avenue de Muret, 31076 Toulouse Cedex 03
Telephone: (061) 42 83 98
Director: Professor P. Raynaud
Activities: Animal husbandry - nutrition and reproduction; ichthyology - fish farming and water pollution; plant genetics; plant nutrition; pest control - entomology, phytopathology, chemical dynamics of pesticides; food processing; soil science and land development; solar biotechnology; microbiology.

ÉCOLE NATIONALE SUPÉRIEURE 831 D'ÉLECTROTECHNIQUE, D'ÉLECTRONIQUE, D'INFORMATIQUE ET D'HYDRAULIQUE DE TOULOUSE

[Toulouse National College of Electrotechnics, Electronics, Computer Sciences and Hydraulics]
Address: 2 rue Charles-Camichel, 31071 Toulouse Cedex
Telephone: (061) 62 10 10
Director: Professor Crestin

Electrical Engineering and Industrial 832 Electronics Laboratory

Research director: B. Trannoy
Sections: Static convertors, M Foch; automatic circuit machines, M Lajoie-Mazenc; electric drive, M de Fornel
Graduate research staff: 15
Annual expenditure: F800 000
Activities: Thyristor and power transistor static convertors; magnetic and magnetoresistant electronic commutative devices; numerical command, regulation and control of semiconductor systems.
Facilities: World numeric simulator (SACSO); semiconductor simulator (CASSIS); electromagnetic calculus programme (DFIMEDI).
Contract work: Yes

ÉCOLE NATIONALE SUPÉRIEURE DE 833 CHIMIE DE TOULOUSE

[Toulouse National College of Chemistry]
Address: 111 rue de Narbonne, 31077 Toulouse Cedex
Director: Professor Lattes

INSTITUT DE GÉNIE CHIMIQUE DE 834 TOULOUSE

[Toulouse Chemical Engineering Institute]
Address: chemin de la Loge, 31078 Toulouse Cedex
Director: Professor Gardy

Institut National 835 Polytechnique de Grenoble

[National Polytechnic Institute of Grenoble]
Address: 46 avenue Félix Viallet, 38031 Grenoble Cedex
Telephone: (076) 47 98 55
President: Professor Philippe Traynard
Vice-President: Professor René Pauthenet
Graduate research staff: 440
Annual expenditure: F10m

Activities: Research is based on three main areas: materials study and characterization; energy; treatment of information and telecommunications.

ÉCOLE FRANÇAISE DE PAPETERIE 836

[French Pulp and Paper College]
Address: Domaine Universitaire, BP 3, 38400 Saint-Martin d'Hères
Telephone: (076) 42 01 27
Telex: CETEPAP 980 642 attention EFP
Director: Claude Foulard
Joint director: Professor R. Charuel
Activities: Chemistry of cellulose and other plant materials; morphology of fibres; applied physics - pulp and paper; structural study of paper; chemistry of pulp and paper process; chemical engineering applied to pulp and paper process.
Contract work: Yes
Publications: Research reports.

Department of Paper Chemistry 837

Head: A. Robert
Activities: Research is orientated towards plant fibres: lignin - macromolecular properties, biosynthesis, topochemistry, treatment; polysaccharides.

Department of Paper Engineering 838

Heads: Professor R. Charuel, M. Renaud
Activities: Study of operations in the manufacture of paper, from paste to papers and cardboards, in order to improve the quality, means of production and investment costs.

Department of Paper Physics 839

Head: J. Silvy
Activities: The main aspects of research into the usage of paper and cardboard are as follows: transfer properties of light rays; transfer properties of liquid fluids and gas; mechanical properties; electrical properties in terms of isolation.

Department of Polymer Chemistry 840

Head: H. Cheradame
Activities: There are two main areas of research: synthesis and study of macromolecular materials in the paper industry; use of materials with special properties and structure - property relationship.

ÉCOLE NATIONALE SUPÉRIEURE D'ÉLECTROCHIMIE ET D'ÉLECTROMÉTALLURGIE 841

[Electrochemistry and Electrometallurgy National College]
Address: BP 44, 38401 Saint-Martin d'Hères
Telephone: (076) 54 41 27
Director: Professor Jean-Charles Pariaud
Director of Studies: F. Durand

Laboratory of Adsorption and Solid-State Gas Reaction 842

Head: Professor L. Bonnetain
Senior staff: J. Besson
Graduate research staff: 24

Laboratory of Analysis and Chemical Testing 843

Head: Professor H. Bozon

Laboratory of Electrochemistry 844

Head: Professor C. Deporters
Senior staff: J.C. Pariaud, M.J. Barbier, J. Guitton, J.C. Sohm, J.J. Rameau
Graduate research staff: 54

Laboratory of Thermodynamics and Metallurgical Physical Chemistry 845

Head: Professor E. Bonnier
Senior staff: P. Desre, F. Durand, P. Guyot, M Peffen; J. Driole, I. Ansara, P. Hicter
Graduate research staff: 62

ÉCOLE NATIONALE SUPÉRIEURE D'ÉLECTRONIQUE ET DE RADIOÉLECTRICITÉ 846

[Electronics and Radio-Electricity National College]
Address: avenue des Martyrs, 38031 Grenoble Cedex
Director: Professor Buyle-Bodin

Laboratory of Electromagnetism 847

Head: Professor A. Coumes

Laboratory of Electronics 848

Head: Professor Kamarinos
Activities: Compounds physics; semiconductors.

Laboratory of Vocal Communication and Metrology Instrumentation 849

Head: Professor R. Lancie

ÉCOLE NATIONALE SUPÉRIEURE D'HYDRAULIQUE 850

[Hydraulics National College]
Address: Domaine Universitaire, centre de Tri, BP 53, 38041 Grenoble Cedex
Director: Professor Philippe LeRoy

ÉCOLE NATIONALE SUPÉRIEURE D'INFORMATIQUE ET DE MATHÉMATIQUES APPLIQUÉES 851

[Data Processing and Applied Mathematics National College]
Address: Domaine Universitaire, centre de Tri, BP 53, 38041 Grenoble Cedex
Director: Professor Gérard Veillon

Laboratory of Computer Sciences and Applied Mathematics 852

Head: Professor Sakarovitch

ÉCOLE NATIONALE SUPÉRIEURE D'INGENIEURS ÉLECTRICIENS DE GRENOBLE 853

[Electrical Engineering National College of Grenoble]
Address: BP 45, 38402 Saint-Martin d'Hères
Director: Professor Daniel Bloch

Centre of Hazardous Phenomena and Geophysics Research 854

Head: Professor Jean-Pierre Lacoume

Laboratory of Automation 855

Head: Professor R. Perret

Laboratory of Electrotechnics 856

Head: Professor P. Brissonneau

Laboratory of Materials Structure 857

Head: Professor Fruchart

Laboratory of Physical Engineering 858

Head: Professor Joubert

STUDY AND RESEARCH UNIT OF   859
CELLULOSE MATERIAL AND
PAPERMAKING

Address: 46 avenue Félix Viallet, 38031 Grenoble
Cedex
Director: Professor Claude Foulard

Department of Molecular Physics   860
Chemistry

Head: H. Cheradame

Institut National   861
Polytechnique de Lorraine*

[Lorraine National Polytechnic Institute]
Address: Porte de la Craffe, BP 3308, 54014 Nancy
Cedex
Telephone: (083) 36 46 25
President: Claude Pair

ÉCOLE NATIONALE SUPÉRIEURE   862
D'AGRONOMIE ET DES INDUSTRIES
ALIMENTAIRES

– ENSAIA
[Agronomy and Food Industries National College]
Address: 38 rue Sainte Catherine, 54000 Nancy
Telephone: (08) 332 93 94
Director: Professor Fernand Jacquin
Activities: Improvement of agricultural products
through the application of soil sciences, fertilization and
correct cultural techniques; selection of suitable animal
breeds and plant varieties; efficient product preservation
techniques; food transformation and processing through
basic research, particularly in fermentation technology;
applied ecology through the rational improvement and
protection of natural and cultivated areas.

Laboratory of Bio-Agrotechnology   863

Sections: Chemistry and biochemistry, M Barthel; soil
sciences, M Jacquin; physico-chemistry and data processing, M Barthel; plant protection and ecology, M
Cachan; economics, M Coujard; crop farming, M
Guckert; animal husbandry, M Vignon

Laboratory of Food Sciences and   864
Technology

Sections: Physics (electronics and automation), M
Chollot; microbiology, Mme Veillet, M Germain;
mycology, M Payen; dairy technology, M Weber; food
chemistry, Mme Novak; food industrial engineering, M
Engasser

ÉCOLE NATIONALE SUPÉRIEURE   865
D'ÉLECTRICITÉ ET DE MÉCANIQUE*

[Electricity and Mechanics National College]
Address: 2 rue de la Citadelle, BP 850, 54014 Nancy
Cedex
Director: Professor M. Lucius

ECOLE NATIONALE SUPÉRIEURE DE   866
GÉOLOGIE APPLIQUÉE ET DE
PROSPECTION MINIÈRE*

[Applied Geology and Mine Prospecting National
College]
Address: 94 avenue de Lattre de Tassigny, BP 452,
54001 Nancy Cedex
Director: Professor P. Blazy

Raw Materials Beneficiation Research   867
Centre

Address: BP 452, 54500 Vandoeuvre
Telephone: (08) 351 43 71
Telex: Nancy F 850 078
Affiliation: Centre National de la Recherche Scientifi-
que
Director: Professor Pierre Blazy
Sections: Useful materials, Professor Y. Champetier;
applied geophysics, Professor M. Pham; physico-
chemistry of surface minerals, Professor J. Cases;
hydrometallurgy, Professor P. Blazy, Professor J. Be-
sière; processes, Professor R. Houot; industrial circuits
automation, Professor M. Aubrun, Professor Humbert
Graduate research staff: 45
Annual expenditure: £501 000-2m
Activities: Fundamental and applied research in physical chemistry, ore dressing and extractive metallurgy of
metals and industrial minerals; mining exploration and
applied geophysics. The Centre also helps to set up
mining installations.
Contract work: Yes

ÉCOLE NATIONALE SUPÉRIEURE DE   868
LA MÉTALLURGIE ET DE L'INDUSTRIE
DES MINES *

[Metallurgy and the Mining Industry National
College]
Address: Parc de Saurupt, 54000 Nancy
Director: Professor B. Deviot

ÉCOLE NATIONALE SUPÉRIEURE DES   869
INDUSTRIES CHIMIQUE*

[Industrial Chemistry National College]
Address: 1 rue Grandville, 54000 Nancy
Director: Professor J. Bordet

Institut National Supérieur   870
de Chimie Industrielle de
Rouen - Institut Émile
Blondel

**[Rouen National Institute of Industrial Chemistry -
Émile Blondel Institute]**
Address: Place Émile Blondel, BP 08, 76130 Mont
Saint Aignan
Telephone: (046) 71 71 41
Affiliation: Ministère des Universités
Director: Professor R. Darrigo
Sections: Chemical Engineering Laboratory, R. Dar-
rigo; Metallurgical Research Laboratory, R. Graf;
Organic Chemistry Laboratory, G. Queguiner, M.
Devaud, N. Collignon, H. Garreau; Physics and
Spectroscopy Laboratory, M. Lenglet, P. Laforie

Institut Pasteur*   871

[Pasteur Institute]
Address: 25 rue du Docteur Roux, 75024 Paris 15
President: P. Royer
Director: Professor F. Gros
Deputy Directors: Professor L. Chambon, Professor B.
Viriat, Professor E. Wollman
Scientific Director: M Goldberg
Applied Research and Development: J. De Rosnay
Activities: This is a private foundation now partly supported by government funds, carrying out fundamental
and applied research in microbiology, virology, immunology, cellular and molecular biology. Medical
research includes medical aspects of bacteriology, virology, immunology, and epidemiology of transmissible
diseases. The Institute plays an important role as a
centre of reference, expertise, and documentation as well
as being a centre of postgraduate teaching. Institutes are
at Paris, Lyon, Lille, four are in French overseas territories, and thirteen in other overseas territories.

BACTERIOLOGY DEPARTMENT*   872

Activities: Anaerobes; enterobacteria; medical
microbiology; systematic bacteriology and culture collection; tuberculosis and mycobacteria.

BIOCHEMISTRY AND MICROBIAL   873
PHYSIOLOGY DEPARTMENT*

Activities: Cell biochemistry and cell physiology;
microbial physiology; protein chemistry; enzymology;
genetic engineering; soil microbiology.

ECOLOGY DEPARTMENT*   874

Activities: Biological control of insects; cholera and
vibrios; histopathology; leptospirosis; mycology; pests
and related agents; experimental parasitology.

EXPERIMENTAL PHYSIOPATHOLOGY   875
AND MEDICAL IMMUNOLOGY
DEPARTMENT*

Activities: Immuno-allergy, immunohaematology and
immunopathology; experimental immunotherapy; pharmacology and toxicology; analytical radioimmunology;
tuberculins; bacterial vaccines and venoms.

IMMUNOLOGY DEPARTMENT*   876

Activities: Analytical immunochemistry; antigens
biochemistry; bacterial antigens; cell immunology;
microbial immunology; physiopathology of immunity;
protein immunochemistry.

MOLECULAR BIOLOGY   877
DEPARTMENT*

Activities: Biochemistry; cell differentiation; cell genetics and cell immunophysiology; electron microscopy;
experimental cytogenetics; immunocytochemistry;
molecular genetics; molecular neurobiology; oncogenic
viruses; physical chemistry of biological
macromolecules.

PASTEUR INSTITUTE, LILLE*   878

Address: 20 boulevard Louis XIV, 59000 Lille
Director: Professor J. Samaille
Laboratories: Mycobacteria; General Bacteriology; In-
fant Nutrition Laboratory and Phenylketonuria Centre;
Virology; RespiratoryPathology and Pollution; Lipid
Metabolism Physiopathology; Electron Microscopy;
Histology; Regional Lactarium; Pasteur Department;
Product Production and Laboratory Reagents Centre

PASTEUR INSTITUTE, LYON* 879

Address: 77 rue Pasteur, 69365 Lyon 2
Director: Professor M Carraz
Laboratories: General Microbiology; Immunology; Mycobacterial Research; Serology; Nelson Tests; Applied Hygiene; Biochemistry; Cytogenetics; Microbiological Estimation of Vitamins and Amino Acids; Virology; Pathological Anatomy; Haematology; Haemocytology; Protein Biochemistry; Rabies

VIROLOGY DEPARTMENT* 880

Activities: Animal microbiology; antirabies centre; medical and vaccine virology; rabies and rhabdovirus; rickets; dignosis; viral ecology; viral oncology.

Institut pour le Management de l'Information 881

– IMI
[Information Management Institute]
Address: 35 boulevard de Sebastopol, 75001 Paris
Telephone: (01) 2333 71 91
Affiliation: Ministère de l'Industrie; Ministère des Universités
Research director: Jean Louis Peaucelle
Graduate research staff: 5
Annual expenditure: F500 000
Activities: Analysis of information needs; information systems.
Contract work: Yes

Institut Scientifique et Technique des Pêches Maritimes* 882

– ISTPM
[Marine Fisheries Scientific and Technical Institute]
Address: La Noe, route de la Jonelière, BP 1049, 44037 Nantes
Affiliation: Direction Général de la Marine Marchande
Scientific and Technical Director: R. Letaconnoux
Research director: L. Faure

EXTERNAL CENTRES AND LABORATORIES:* 883

Arcachon Laboratory* 884

Address: 63 boulevard Deganne, 33120 Arcachon
Head: M Deltreil

Boulogne sur Mer Laboratory* 885

Address: 150 quai Gambetta, 62200 Boulogne sur Mer
Head: M Maucorps
Activities: Biology of marine species; herrings; population dynamics; fishing tackle technology.

La Rochelle Research Centre* 886

Address: 74 allée du Mail, 17000 La Rochelle
Director: M Dardignac
Laboratories: Oceanography and Fisheries; Conchological Biology
Activities: Biology of hake, tuna and sardines; biology of molluscs.

La Tremblade Research Centre* 887

Address: 37 rue du Maréchal-Leclerc, 17390 La Tremblade
Director: M Gras
Laboratory: Conchological Biology
Activities: Research on oysters and mussels; study of oyster beds and waters.

Lorient Laboratory* 888

Address: rue François-Toullec, 56100 Lorient
Head: M Guéguen

Marine Biology Station* 889

Address: 29211 Roscoff
Head: Jacques Andouin
Activities: Ecology; restocking and methods of fishing.

Saint Gilles Croix de Vie Laboratory* 890

Address: 12 rue Pasteur, 85800 Saint Gilles Croix de Vie
Head: M Moreau

Sète Research Laboratory* 891

Address: 1 rue Jean-Vilar, 34200 Sète
Head: M Comps

Trinité sur Mer Research Centre*   892

Address: 12 rue des Résistants, 56470 Trinité sur Mer
Director: M Marin
Activities: Ecology of Morbihan oysters; species of Lamellibranchiata; study of the composition of breeding grounds.

MEDITERRANEAN AND TROPICAL   893
OCEANOGRAPHY, FISHERIES AND
MARINE CULTURES DEPARTMENT*

Director: Charles Allain

Sète Research Centre (Oceanography   894
Department)*

Address: 1 rue Jean-Vilar, 34200 Sète
Director: M Favel
Laboratories: Oceanography and Fisheries; Conchological Biology

NORTH ATLANTIC   895
OCEANOGRAPHY, FISHERIES AND
MARINE CULTURES DEPARTMENT*

Director: G. Kurc
Sections: Demersal fishes; marine cultures; Clupeidae Laboratory; Tuna Laboratory; Experimental Fish Laboratory; Plankton Laboratory; Algology Laboratory

TECHNOLOGY AND INSPECTION   896
DEPARTMENT*

Address: rue de l'Ile d'Yeu, BP 1049, 44037 Nantes
Sections: Mollusc culture and conchological inspection; pollution; refrigeration; processing of marine products; Chemistry Laboratory

Conchological Bacteriology   897
Laboratories*

Note: There are laboratories at Boulogne sur Mer, Lac sur Mer, Saint Servan, Trinité sur Mer, Saint Gilles Croix de Vie, La Rochelle, La Tremblade, Arcachon and Sète.

Institut Technique de la   898
Pomme de Terre

[Potato Technical Institute]
Address: Saint-Rémy-L'Honoré, 78690 Les Essarts-le-Roi
Telephone: 874 36 03

Research director: Jean-Claude Crosnier
Activities: Applied research for the improvement of potato growing and utilization.

Institut Textile de France*   899

– ITF
[Textile Institute of France]
Address: 35 rue des Abondances, 92100 Boulogne sur Seine
Telephone: (021) 825 18 90
Telex: 25940
Activities: Structure of fibrous materials; relationships between structure and physico-chemical properties; imparting new properties to existing materials; research on new products. Textile postgraduate school; textile training; testing facilities; textile machinery experiments and evaluation.

CENTRAL LABORATORY*   900

Address: 35 rue des Abondances, 93100 Boulogne sur Seine
Director: J. Jacquemart

INDUSTRIAL TESTING, CONTROL,   901
ANALYSIS AND RESEARCH
LABORATORY*

Address: rue de Bradford, 81200 Mazamet

ITF-LYON*   902

Address: chemin des Mouilles, 69130 Ecully
Director: P. Rochas

ITF-MAILLE - KNITTED GOODS   903
RESEARCH CENTRE*

Address: 270 rue du Faubourg Croncels, 10042 Troyes

ITF-NORD*   904

Address: rue de la Recherche, BP 37, 59650 Villeneuve d'Ascq-Flers
Director: G. Mazingue

TECHNICAL ASSOCIATION FOR THE   905
PRODUCTION AND USE OF FLAX
AND OTHER BEST FIBRES*

Address: Lagny le Sec, 60330 Le Plessis-Belleville

Instrumentation et Dynamique Cardiovasculaire

906

[Instrumentation and Cardiovascular Dynamics Group]
Address: Hôpital Broussais, 96 rue Didot, 75674 Paris Cedex 14
Telephone: (01) 542 37 93
Affiliation: Centre National de la Recherche Scientifique
Director: P. Peronneau
Sections: Electronics, A. Herment, M. Vaysse, J.P. Guglielmi; biophysics, M. Nakache; physiology, J.P. Moutet; clinical investigations, J.L. Guermonprez, L. Guize, M. Safar
Graduate research staff: 12
Activities: Making instruments for examinations by ultrasonic process; the cardiovascular system, blood circulation, cardiac mechanism, cardiac electrophysiology; cardiology, hypertension, vascular medicine.
Contract work: No

Laboratoire Aimé Cotton

907

[Aimé Cotton Laboratory]
Address: CNRS II - Bâtiment 505, Campus d'Orsay, 91405 Orsay Cedex
Telephone: (06) 907 60 50
Telex: 692 166 F
Affiliation: Centre National de la Recherche Scientifique; Université Paris-Sud
Research director: Professor Serge Feneuille
Assistant director: Claude Morillon
Graduate research staff: 43
Annual expenditure: F12 600 000
Activities: Theory of atomic structure, classification of complex atomic spectra; the Rydberg state of atoms; nuclear effects of hyperfine spectroscopy on radioactive isotopes of alkaline atoms; atomic collisions - spectral profiles, radiative collisions, reactional dynamics; intense electromagnetic fields - superradiance; spectroscopy of paramagnetic ions in crystals; recording and analysing molecular spectra.
Contract work: No

Laboratoire Central des Industries Électriques

908

– LCIE
[Electrical Industries' Central Laboratory]
Address: BP No 8, 92260 Fontenay aux Roses
Telephone: (01) 645 21 84
Telex: LABELEC 250080 F
Director General: J. Oswald
Chief Engineer: Gérard Wind
Sections: Insulation, B. Fallou; contacts, J. Galand
Activities: Research and development in the following areas: electrical metrology; characteristics of materials; behaviour of insulations; instrumentation; electric contacts phenomena; dielectric properties; automatic regulation and control equipment; electromedical equipment; electrical energy transformers; applications of microelectronics; contacts and measurement equipment; methods and equipment for inspection and testing.
Publications: LCIE Informations, quarterly; annual report.

Laboratoire Central des Ponts et Chaussées

909

– LCPC
[Road and Bridge Central Laboratory]
Address: 58 boulevard Lefèbvre, 75732 Paris Cedex 15
Telephone: (01) 532 31 79
Telex: LCPARI 200361 F
Affiliation: Ministère de l'Urbanisme et du Logement
Director: Jean-Claude Parriaud
Director of Research, Control and Information: Alain Bonnet
Director of Programmes and Applications: Ch. Parey
Sections: Pavements, J. Bonnot; structures and bridges, Cl. Bois; geotechnics, M. Panet; concrete and metals, M. Brachet; soils and foundations, F. Baguelin
Graduate research staff: 165
Annual expenditure: F110m
Activities: The scientific and technical research activities of the LCPC involve several fields which are of interest for external services depending on the Ministry of the Environment and Quality of Life and the Ministry of Transport. The fields dealt with are: materials (aggregates, hydraulic and hydrocarboned binders, road materials, concrete, steels); transport infrastructures (alignment, earthworks, bridges, pavements, retaining structures); environment and urbanism (environmental surveys, water pollution, noises and vibrations).
Specific subjects of research are as follows: aggregates and road material deposits; concrete and hydraulic binders; bituminous binders and coated material; steels; plastic materials; pavement design; compacting; soil

stabilization; road building equipment; road surface characteristics; engineering structures; use of waste products; water quality; noise problems; mathematical calculation; measuring methods; radio-elements applications; chemical analysis.

LCPC also operates: sixteen regional laboratories, most of which are incorporated in its seven Equipment Technical Study Centres which are located at Lille, Rouen, Metz, Nantes, Bordeaux, Lyon, and Aix-en-Provence; two Prototype Design and Building centres at Angers and Rouen; and a Road Testing Centre at Rouen.

Contract work: Yes
Publications: Bulletin de Liaison des Laboratoires des Ponts et Chaussées (Interlaboratory Bulletin); research reports; technical information notices; test procedures; general activity report.

NANTES-BOUGUENAIS CENTRE 910

Address: BP 19, 44340 Bouguenais
Telephone: (40) 65 14 88
Telex: LCNANTE 710805 F
Research director: P. Autret
Sections: Water and environment, J.-L. Olié; methods and materials, R. Baroux; structures and characteristics of roadways, P. Autret

Laboratoire d'Aérothermique 911

[Aerothermics Laboratory]
Address: 4ter route des Gardes, 92190 Meudon
Telephone: 534 75 50
Telex: LABOBEL 204 135F
Affiliation: Centre National de la Recherche Scientifique
Research director: Professor J.J. Bernard
Sections: Heat and mass transfer; fluid mechanics; rarefied gases; kinetic chemistry (plasma combustion)
Graduate research staff: 20
Activities: Dynamics of rarefied gases, with their expansion in kinetic chemistry at low pressures and temperatures; behaviour of interfaces and the propagation of a frozen surface in dispersed mediums, with very varied applications ranging from the shattering of rocks and building materials by freezing to the treatment of foodstuffs; study of the stability of thermo-convective movements, of mixed flows, of thermal disturbance, and, most recently, of the oscillations of fluid mediums in spatial weightlessness; energy problems: fluid movements associated with electrostatic phenomena and phase changes, energy storage and thermal exchange with a great diversity of applications bearing on solar energy as well as medical diagnosis.
Contract work: No

Laboratoire d'Analyse par 912
Activation 'Pierre Sue'*

['Pierre Sue' Activation Analysis Laboratory]
Address: BP 2, 91190 Gif sur Yvette
Affiliation: Centre National de la Recherche Scientifique; Commissariat d' Énergie Atomique
Director: Gilles Revel
Deputy Director: Norbert Deschamps

Laboratoire d'Annecy-le- 913
Vieux de Physique des
Particules*

[Particle Physics Laboratory of Annecy]
Address: BP 909, 74019 Annecy-le-Vieux Cedex
Affiliation: Centre National de la Recherche Scientifique
Director: Marcel Vivargent

Laboratoire d'Astronomie 914
Spatiale

[Astronomy Laboratory]
Address: allée Peiresc, Les Trois Lucs, 13012 Marseille
Telephone: (091) 66 08 32
Affiliation: Centre National de la Recherche Scientifique; Institut National d'Astronomie et de Géophysique
Director: Georges Courtès
Graduate research staff: 13
Activities: Scientific research in the field of astronomy based on the utilization of space vehicles outside dense atmosphere. The laboratory studies stars and nebulae with the aid of stratospheric balloons, rocket probes, and satellites. These studies lead to research into the development of optical, mechanical, and electronic instruments, and studies of component instruments of the powerful telescopes of Canada-France-Hawaii and European Southern Observatory.
Facilities: La Foux d'Allos observation station; siderostat; monochromators; collimators; technology of optics laboratory; electronic, mechanical and optical measuring equipment.

Laboratoire d'Automatique   915
et d'Analyse des Systèmes*

[Automation and Systems Analysis Laboratory]
Address: LAAS, Complex Aérospatial de Toulouse, Lespinet, 7 avenue Colonel Roche, 31400 Toulouse Cedex
Affiliation: Centre National de la Recherche Scientifique
Director: Professor Georges Grateloup

Laboratoire d'Électronique   916
et d'Automatique du Nord
de la France

– LEANORD
[Electronics and Automation Laboratory of Northern France]
Address: 236 rue Sadi Carnot, 59320 Haubourdin
Telephone: (020) 07 30 55
Telex: 810910 F
Affiliation: Creusot-Loire ISA
Director: Bernard Pronier
Technical Manager: Claude Stach
Sections: Electronics, M N'Guyen; computer, C. Barbot; telecommunications, J. Jongler; physics, M Clique
Graduate research staff: 10
Annual expenditure: £51 000-500 000
Activities: Research and development in the field of industrial controls including: data acquisition on magnetic tapes; minicomputers; microcomputers; eddy currents and acoustic emission as non-destructive testing methods.
Contract work: No

Laboratoire d'Électronique   917
et d'Informatique
Dauphinois

– LEAD
Address: 43 rue du 11 Novembre 1918, 94700 Maisons-Alfort
Telephone: (01) 893 44 44
Telex: 230 455 F
Affiliation: LEAD - USA
President: Dr Ferdy Mayer
Sections: Electric components; automotive electronics
Graduate research staff: 4
Annual expenditure: £51 000-500 000
Activities: Major fields of interest and expertise are related to the following subjects:

Electromagnetic compatibility - industrial RFI suppression cables; low pass cables; low transfer impedance cables; common mode suppression cables; brute force filters; dielectromagnetic filters; suppressor ignition cables; filters plugs; electronic ignition systems; RFI-based remote measurement and control; automotive EMC-systems (EMCA); multiplex (RECAP).
Automotive electronics - man-machine interface systems (driver behaviour and electronic incentives) (CADAC); automotive electronic systems; diagnosis (RETAP); gas-mileage optimizer (ASPLIC); interface-flasher (MAI); deceleration, pressure, skid, measurement and control.
Instrumentation and control - displays (ALADIN-COLOR); high-accuracy comparator and instrumentation; system-oriented transducers; sensors and modifiers; VHF and UHF measurement techniques; remote measurements (oil research); industrial measurements and control.
Mechanism, electromechanisms - contacts and connectors; sensitive relays - SSR; circuit breaker control; differential circuit breaker and interruptors - GFCI; variable speed motors and control; actuators.
Materials and components - electronic composite materials; lines and cables (low loss, controlled loss); dielectromagnetics; extruded components; electronic glasses and amorphous materials; fuses and controlled fuses.
In addition, LEAD has made many studies on management systems, under government contracts. More especially, original techniques have been developed for corporate planning research and development management, technology forecasting and technology transfer in peculiar sociocultural environments.
Contract work: Yes

Laboratoire   918
d'Électrostatique*

[Electrostatics Laboratory]
Address: BP 166X, 38042 Grenoble Cedex
Affiliation: Centre National de la Recherche Scientifique
Director: Professor Noël Felici

Laboratoire d'Énergétique   919
Solaire*

[Solar Energy Laboratory]
Address: BP 5, Odeillo-Via, 66120 Font-Romeu
Affiliation: Centre National de la Recherche Scientifique
Director: André Vialaron

Laboratoire d'Enzymologie* 920

[Enzymology Laboratory]
Address: 91190 Gif sur Yvette
Affiliation: Centre National de la Recherche Scientifique
Director: Jékisiel Szulmajster

Laboratoire d'Information et de Documentation en Géographie Intergéo* 921

[Geographical Information and Documentation Laboratory]
Address: 191 rue Saint-Jacques, 75005 Paris
Affiliation: Centre National de la Recherche Scientifique
Director: Professor Roger Brunet

Laboratoire d'Informatique pour la Mécanique et les Sciences de l'Ingénieur* 922

[Informatics Laboratory for Mechanics and Engineering Sciences]
Address: Université de Paris XI, BP 30, 91405 Orsay
Affiliation: Centre National de la Recherche Scientifique
Director: Guy Renard

Laboratoire d'Optique Électronique* 923

[Electronic Optics Laboratory]
Address: 29 rue Jeanne-Marvig, BP 4347, 31055 Toulouse Cedex
Affiliation: Centre National de la Recherche Scientifique
Director: Bernard Jouffrey
Deputy Director: Professor Jacques Trinquier

Laboratoire d'Optique Quantique* 924

[Quantum Optics Laboratory]
Address: Laboratoire de l'École Polytechnique, route de Saclay, 91120 Palaiseau
Affiliation: Centre National de la Recherche Scientifique
Director: Christos Flytzonis

Laboratoire de Biologie et de Génétique Évolutives* 925

[Evolutionary Biology and Genetics Laboratory]
Address: 91190 Gif sur Yvette
Affiliation: Centre National de la Recherche Scientifique
Director: Professor Jean David

Laboratoire de Biologie et Technologie des Membranes* 926

[Membrane Biology and Technology Laboratory]
Address: 43 boulevard du 11 novembre 1918, 69621 Villeurbanne
Affiliation: Centre National de la Recherche Scientifique
Director: Professor Danielle Gautheron

Laboratoire de Chimie Bactérienne 927

[Bacterial Chemistry Laboratory]
Address: 13277 Marseille Cedex 9
Telephone: (091) 71 90 42 or (091) 71 16 96
Telex: 430 225 F CNRSMAR
Affiliation: Centre National de la Recherche Scientifique
Director: Professor Jacques C. Senez
Sections: Bacterial genetics and physiology, Professor J.C. Senez; electron transfer, Dr M. Bruschi; cellulolytic bacteria, Dr J. Cattanéo; bioenergetics and methanogenesis, Professor J.P. Belaich
Graduate research staff: 28
Annual expenditure: £200 000
Activities: Research into the following: Structure and function of cytochromes and non-heminic electron carriers in bacteria; bacterial cellulose metabolism; bacterial methanogenesis; bioenergetics; bacterial membranes.

Laboratoire de Chimie de   928
Coordination

[Coordination Chemistry Laboratory]
Address: 205 route de Narbonne, 31400 Toulouse
Telephone: (061) 52 11 66
Affiliation: Centre National de la Recherche Scientifique
Director: Professor René Poilblanc
Senior staff: Professor J.J. Bonnet, Professor Y. Dartiguenave, J. Galy, Professor D. Gervais, J.P. Laurent, Professor Ph. de Loth, P. Cassoux
Graduate research staff: 60
Activities: Development of research in the molecular chemistry of metallic elements particularly the transition elements, concentrating on compounds of synthesis and organic catalysis, the synthesis and study of materials with unusual physical and physico-chemical properties and the study and application of phenomena of metallic ion compounds in biology.
Contract work: No

Laboratoire de Chimie   929
Macromoléculaire
Appliquée*

[Applied Macromolecular Chemistry Laboratory]
Address: 2-8 rue Henri Dunant, BP 28, 94320 Thiais
Affiliation: Centre National de la Recherche Scientifique
Director: Adolphe Chapiro

Laboratoire de   930
Cristallographie

[Crystallography Laboratory]
Address: 166X, 38042 Grenoble Cedex
Telephone: (76) 96 98 37
Telex: 320254 CNRSALP GRENO
Affiliation: Centre National de la Recherche Scientifique
Director: E.F. Bertaut
Sections: Solid-state physics and magnetism, D. Fruchart; structure and physical properties of fluorides, S. Aléonard; physics of crystals, F. de Bergevin; condensed phosphates, A. Durif; hydrothermal synthesis and high pressures, J.C. Joubert
Graduate research staff: 15
Annual expenditure: F1198 980
Activities: The laboratory was founded in 1943. Research involves the systematization of structural mineral chemistry; structure and physical properties

(especially magnetism and conductability). Achievements include the discovery of ferromagnetic garnets.
Contract work: Yes
Publications: Liste des Publications.

Laboratoire de Cytologie   931
Expérimentale*

[Experimental Cytology Laboratory]
Address: 67 rue Maurice Günsbourg, 94200 Ivry
Affiliation: Centre National de la Recherche Scientifique
Director: Professor Pierre Favard

Laboratoire de   932
Cytophysiologie de la
Photosynthèse

[Cytophysiology of Photosynthesis Laboratory]
Address: 91190 Gif sur Yvette
Telephone: 907 78 28
Telex: 691 137 F CNRS - GIF
Affiliation: Centre National de la Recherche Scientifique
Research director: Professor M. Lefort-Tran
Graduate research staff: 11
Annual expenditure: £10 000-50 000
Activities: Research is being carried out on the following topics: vitamin B_{12} starvation in euglena - cortical and nuclear events during cell cycle blockage and release (histone post synthetic modifications); functional and structural organization of chloroplastic membranes - (a) properties of system II photosynthetic units in the developing thylakoids of euglena, (b) triple layered envelope of euglena chloroplast and the transfer of proteins; genetic control of membrane fusion in exocytosis in paramecium; signal and recognition between membranes in paramecium endosymbiosis.
Contract work: No

Laboratoire de Dynamique   933
et Microphysique de
l'Atmosphère

[Dynamics and Microphysics of the Atmosphere Laboratory]
Address: Complex Scientifique des Céseaux, avenue de Landais, 63170 Aubière
Telephone: (073) 92 22 26

Affiliation: Institut National d'Astronomie et de Géophysique
Director: René Soulage
Graduate research staff: 10
Activities: The laboratory studies dynamic and microphysical aspects of atmospheric convective phenomena in three categories: solar atmosphere; planetary atmosphere; and free atmosphere.

Laboratoire de Génétique et Physiologie du Développement des Plantes* 934

[Genetics and Physiology of Plant Development Laboratory]
Address: 91190 Gif sur Yvette
Affiliation: Centre National de la Recherche Scientifique
Director: Jean Pernes

Laboratoire de Géochronologie et Volcanologie 935

[Geochronology and Volcanology Laboratory]
Address: 5 rue Kessler, 63038 Clermont-Ferrand Cedex
Telephone: (073) 93 35 71
Affiliation: Institut National d'Astronomie et de Géophysique; Université de Clermont-Ferrand II
Director: Maurice Roques
Graduate research staff: 18
Activities: Chronology of phases of metamorphism, granitization, folding, faulting, distension, and lifting in the formation of Hercynian and Precambrian crystalline shelves; origin, formation, and rise of volcanic magmas; structure of volcanic formations; chronology of eruptions; geothermy.

Laboratoire de Géologie du Quaternaire 936

[Quaternary Geology Laboratory]
Address: CNRS - Luminy, Case 907, 13288 Marseille Cedex 2
Telephone: (091) 41 01 90
Telex: CNRSMAR 430 225 F

Affiliation: Centre National de la Recherche Scientifique
Research directors: Professor Hugues Faure; H. Alimen
Sections: Geology, prehistory, E. Bonifay; palynology, R. Bonnefille; palaeoecology, Sahara, N. Petit-Maire; palaeontology, F. Bonifay; nuclear geology, C. Gaven; quaternary pedology, geochemistry, M. Icole; geology, sedimentology, neotectonics, Ethiopian rifts, M. Taieb
Graduate research staff: 20
Annual expenditure: F650 000
Activities: Subjects of research include the following: climatic changes in the intertropical zone; aridification of the Sahelian zone; palaeolimnology; palynology sedimentation and continental change; changes in ranges and shorelines and quantitative neotectonics; tectonic and magnetic evolution in the Quaternary period; the evolution of man and early industry.
Contract work: Yes
Publications: Rapport d'Activité.

Laboratoire de Glaciologie et de Géophysique de l'Environnement 937

[Glaciology and Environmental Geophysics Laboratory]
Address: 2 rue Très-Cloîtres, 38031 Grenoble Cedex
Telephone: (076) 87 65 65 and 66
Affiliation: Institut National d'Astronomie et de Géophysique; Centre National de la Recherche Scientifique
Director: Professor Louis Lliboutry
Graduate research staff: 20
Activities: Research into the following subjects: polar geochemistry (as part of the International Antarctic Glaciological Programme); glacier dynamics; mass/energy ratio of a glacier; physics and mechanics of snow and ice; physics of precipitation.

Laboratoire de Magnétisme de Bellevue* 938

[Bellevue Magnetism Laboratory]
Address: 1 place Aristide-Briand, 92190 Meudon
Affiliation: Centre National de la Recherche Scientifique
Director: M Boccara

Laboratoire de Mécanique des Solides 939

[Solid Mechanics Laboratory]
Address: École Polytechnique, 91128 Palaiseau Cedex
Telephone: (06) 941 82 00
Telex: ECOLEX 691596 E
Affiliation: École Polytechnique; École Nationale des Ponts et Chaussées; École Nationale Supérieure des Mines (Paris); Centre National de la Recherche Scientifique
Director: Professor Pierre Habib
Sections: Constraint, Professor D. Radenkovic; behaviour, Professor J. Zarka; soil mechanics, Professor J. Salençon; rock mechanics, Professor P. Habib; fracture mechanics, Professor H.D. Bui
Graduate research staff: 28
Annual expenditure: F10m
Activities: Plasticity; viscoelasticity; thermoviscoplasticity; fracture mechanics; fatigue; flow; soil and rock mechanics; behaviour.
Contract work: Yes

Laboratoire de Mécanique et d'Acoustique* 940

[Mechanics and Acoustics Laboratory]
Address: 31 chemin Joseph-Aiguier, 13274 Marseille Cedex 2
Affiliation: Centre National de la Recherche Scientifique
Director: Professor Bernard Nayroles

Laboratoire de Météorologie Dynamique 941

[Dynamic Meteorology Laboratory]
Address: École Polytechnique, route D 36, 91120 Palaiseau
or: École Normale Supérieure, 24 rue Lhomond, 75231 Paris
Telephone: Palaiseau 941 81 60; Paris 331 72 73
Affiliation: Institut National d'Astronomie et de Géophysique; Centre National de la Recherche Scientifique
Director: Professor André Berroir
Graduate research staff: 18
Activities: The laboratory's research comes under three main headings: dynamic meteorology (including work with the Global Atmospheric Research Programme); infrared radiometry (with ESSOR in liaison with the Centre National d'Études Spatiales); numerical modelling of atmospheric circulation, currently pertaining to the earth's atmosphere but eventually to those of Mars and Venus.

Laboratoire de Pharmacologie et Toxicologie Fondamentales* 942

[Fundamental Pharmacology and Toxicology Laboratory]
Address: 205 route de Narbonne, 31078 Toulouse Cedex
Affiliation: Centre National de la Recherche Scientifique
Director: Professor Claude Paoletti

Laboratoire de Photophysique Moléculaire* 943

[Molecular Photophysics Laboratory]
Address: Université de Paris XI, Bâtiment 213, 91405 Orsay
Affiliation: Centre National de la Recherche Scientifique
Director: Sydney Leach

Laboratoire de Photosynthèse* 944

[Photosynthesis Laboratory]
Address: 91190 Gif sur Yvette
Affiliation: Centre National de la Recherche Scientifique
Director: Jean Lavorel

Laboratoire de Physiologie Comparée des Régulations* 945

[Comparative Physiology Laboratory]
Address: 23 rue du Loess, BP 20 CR, 67037 Strasbourg Cedex
Affiliation: Centre National de la Recherche Scientifique

Director: Professor Jean-Henri Vivien
Deputy Director: Professor Raymond Kirsch
Activities: The main topic of research is the exchange of water and electrolytes in fish and some invertebrates within the physico-chemical limits of their environment.

Laboratoire de Physiologie 946 des Organes Végétaux après Récolte

[Physiology of Plant Organs after Harvesting Laboratory]
Address: 4ter route des Gardes, 92190 Meudon
Telephone: (01) 534 75 50
Telex: 204135 LABOBEL
Affiliation: Centre National de la Recherche Scientifique
Director: Professor Daniel Come
Sections: Fruits, P. Marcellin, C. Leblond; cut flowers, A. Paulin; plant propagative organs, P. Soudain; freezing, J. Philippon; plant proteins, J. Daussant; seeds, D. Come
Graduate research staff: 20
Annual expenditure: £51 000-500 000
Activities: Research is carried out in the following areas: postharvest physiology and preservation of fruits and vegetables; fruit ripening; low temperature survival and storage by refrigeration; freezing temperatures, industrial freezing; seed physiology, germination, and dormancies; physiology of plant propagative organs, flowers and survival of cut flowers; plant proteins and enzymes.
Contract work: No

Laboratoire de Physiologie 947 du Travail

[Work Physiology Laboratory]
Address: 91 Boulevard de l'Hôpital, 75634 Paris Cedex 13
Telephone: (01) 331 85 29
Affiliation: Centre National de la Recherche Scientifique
Director: Professor Hugues Monod
Sections: Physiology of movement, B. Maton; muscle work capacity, H. Monod; muscle fatigue, J. Sanchez; sport physiology, G. Peres; ergonomics, P. Logeay; mental activity, F. Lille
Graduate research staff: 20
Annual expenditure: £40 000
Activities: Research into physiology of movement, muscle work capacity, muscle fatigue, sport physiology, ergonomics, and mental activity.
Contract work: No
Publications: Liste des Publications.

Laboratoire de Physiologie 948 Respiratoire

[Respiratory Physiology Laboratory]
Address: 23 rue Becquerel, 67087 Strasbourg Cedex
Telephone: (088) 29 13 29
Affiliation: Centre National de la Recherche Scientifique
Director: Dr P. Dejours
Graduate research staff: 8
Activities: The laboratory mainly deals with work in comparative respiratory physiology: O_2 and CO_2 exchanges between the body compartments, between the body fluids and the cells in all conditions of natural life, and in various ambient conditions (humidity, heat, cold) and ambient pressures. The aim is to study respiratory and circulatory adaptations, from morphological and physiological points of view, in either hypobaric or hperbaric maintained conditions.
Facilities: Altitude chamber
Contract work: No

Laboratoire de Physique 949 des Matériaux*

[Materials Physics Laboratory]
Address: 1 place Aristide-Briand, 92190 Meudon
Affiliation: Centre National de la Recherche Scientifique
Director: Professor Jean Philibert

Laboratoire de Physique du 950 Solide*

[Solid-State Physics Laboratory]
Address: 1 place Aristide-Briand, 92190 Meudon
Affiliation: Centre National de la Recherche Scientifique
Director: Yves Marfaing

Laboratoire de Physique et 951 Métrologie des Oscillateurs

– LPMO
[Physics and Metrology of Oscillators Laboratory]
Address: 32 avenue de l'Observatoire, 25000 Besançon
Telephone: (081) 50 39 67
Affiliation: Centre National de la Recherche Scientifique
Director: Jean-Jacques Gagnepain

Sections: Non-linear propagation of elastic and electromagnetic waves; physics of oscillators and noise; quantum electronics and microwave oscillators; metrology of frequencies.
Graduate research staff: 15
Annual expenditure: F4m
Activities: Studies of physical principles leading to the production of sources of very stable frequencies; application of frequency standards and oscillators for aerospace use; effects of bulk, surface, and microwave oscillators on quartz; development of systems of measurement of frequency, stability, and spectral purity; technology of surface-wave apparatus and hybrid circuits.
Contract work: No

Laboratoire de Physique Stellaire et Planetaire 952

[Stellar and Planetary Physics Laboratory]
Address: BP 10, 91370 Verrières-le-Buisson
Telephone: 920 10 60
Affiliation: Institut National d'Astronomie et de Géophysique; Centre National de la Recherche Scientifique; Centre National d'Études Spatiales
Director: Roger-Maurice Bonnet
Graduate research staff: 17
Activities: High resolution study of the surface and atmosphere of the sun by means of spectroheliometers and spectrometers launched in balloons, rockets, and satellites. Two important satellite projects are: D2B - a study of solar activity and the vertical distribution of chemical components of the earth's atmosphere; OSO-1 - working in cooperation with the Centre National d'Études Spatiales and the US National Aeronautics and Space Administration to study the ultraviolet spectra of the sun.

Laboratoire de Physique Théorique* 953

[Theoretical Physics Laboratory]
Address: École Normale Supérieure, 24 rue Lhomond, 75231 Paris Cedex 05
Affiliation: Centre National de la Recherche Scientifique
Research director: Jean-Louis Gervais

Laboratoire de Primatologie et d'Écologie des Forêts Équatoriales* 954

[Equatorial Forests Primatology and Ecology Laboratory]
Address: 4 avenue du Petit-Château, 91800 Brunoy
Affiliation: Centre National de la Recherche Scientifique
Director: André Brosset
Note: The field laboratory is at Makokou, Gabon.

Laboratoire de Recherches Balistiques et Aérodynamiques 955

[Ballistics and Aerodynamic Research Laboratory]
Address: BP 914, 27207 Vernon Cedex
Telephone: (032) 21 0740
Telex: 77 817
Affiliation: Ministère de la Defense
Chief Engineer: F. Simon
Sections: Inertial guidance; aerodynamics; electronic missile equipment; environmental testing
Contract work: No

Laboratoire de Recherches et de Contrôle du Caoutchouc 956

– LRCC
[Rubber Research and Control Laboratory]
Address: 12 rue Carvès, 92120 Montrouge
Telephone: 655 71 11
Telex: 202 963 F
Affiliation: Syndicat National du Caoutchouc et des Plastiques
Director General: Pierre Martinon
Graduate research staff: 8
Annual expenditure: £51 000-500 000
Activities: LRCC has the scientific and technical means to carry out research, testing and standards control for the rubber and plastic industry and deals with both the raw materials and the finished product. Special attention is paid to rubber techniques - new products; behaviour; energy and raw materials economics; new machinery or manufacturing methods.
Publications: Technical reports.

DEPARTMENT OF ANALYTICAL STUDIES 957

Activities: Identification and measurement of the main materials used in rubber manufacture; quality control; polymer structure.
Facilities: Chromatography; gas phase testing; thin film analysis; spectrography, etc.

DEPARTMENT OF MATERIALS AND TESTING 958

Activities: Measuring the properties of raw and vulcanized rubber mixtures and plastics; dynamic testing; testing of the finished product.
Facilities: Rheometer; viscosimeter; plastometer; injectometer; temperature testing; abrasion testing; relaxometer.

DEPARTMENT OF TECHNOLOGY 959

Activities: Transformation of rubbers.
Facilities: All the equipment needed to simulate laboratory and industrial conditions for the above purpose.

Laboratoire de Recherches sur les Interactions Gaz-Solides 'Maurice Letort' 960

['Maurice Letort' Laboratory for Gas-Solid Interactions Research]
Address: route de Vandoeuvre, BP 104, 54600 Villers-les-Nancy
Telephone: 327 60 10
Affiliation: Centre National de la Recherche Scientifique
Research director: A. Cassuto
Sections: Physisorption, X. Duval, Λ. Thomy
Graduate research staff: 25
Annual expenditure: F100 000
Activities: Research into techniques of introducing gas to solid surfaces. Utilization of modern techniques for analyzing the surfaces allowing measurement of concentrations near the surface and identification of adsorbent types.
Contract work: No

Laboratoire de Spectrochimie Infrarouge et Raman 961

[Infrared and Raman Spectrochemistry Laboratory]
Address: 2 rue Henri Dunant, 94320 Thiais
Telephone: 687 33 55
Affiliation: Centre National de la Recherche Scientifique
Director: Professor Michel Delhaye
Graduate research staff: 50
Annual expenditure: £51 000-500 000
Activities: Spectrochemistry: structural analysis of molecular crystals, of interactions in solution by using infrared, Raman and nuclear magnetic resonance instrumentation in Raman-laser spectrometry.
Contract work: No

Laboratoire des Intéractions Moléculaires et des Hautes Pressions* 962

[Molecular Interactions and High Pressure Laboratory]
Address: rue Jean Baptiste-Clément, 93430 Villetaneuse
Affiliation: Centre National de la Recherche Scientifique
Director: Jacques Romand

Laboratoire des Propriétés Mécaniques et Thermodynamics des Matériaux* 963

[Mechanical and Thermodynamic Properties of Materials Laboratory]
Address: Université de Paris-Nord, avenue J.-B. Clément, 93430 Villetaneuse
Affiliation: Centre National de la Recherche Scientifique
Director: Professor Georges Saada

Laboratoire des Sciences du Génie Chimique   964

– LSGC
[Chemical Engineering Science Laboratory]
Address: 1 rue Grandville, 54042 Nancy Cedex
Telephone: (08) 336 66 23
Affiliation: Centre National de la Recherche Scientifique
Director: Professor Jean-Claude Charpentier
Research director: Jacques Villermaux
Sections: Electrochemical engineering and fluidization, A. Storck; separation methods, D. Tondeur; chemical engineering applied to the environment, Professor C. Prost; gas-liquid reactors and polyphases, J.-C. Charpentier; reaction chemistry engineering, Professor J. Villermaux; living systems chemical engineering, Professor J.M. Engasser; automatic handling of chemical information, Professor J. Bordet, Professor J.L. Greffe; energetics of industrial operations, Professor P. Le Goff
Graduate research staff: 46
Annual expenditure: £51 000–500 000
Activities: Electrochemical engineering procedures; percolation, separation and reaction in a transition state in porous mediums; hydrodynamics and transfers in gas-liquid reactors; study and simulation in industrial gas-liquid reactors; engineering of rapid reactions at high temperatures - solar chemical reactors; micromixing phenomena in continuous stirred reactors; engineering of biological compositions; polymerization; chemical reactor modelling; energetics; microprocessors and chemical engineering; energy economics, conversion and optimization.
Contract work: No
Publications: Various reports.

Laboratoire des Signaux et Systèmes*   965

[Signals and Systems Laboratory]
Address: École Supérieure d'Électricité, le Plateau du Moulon, 91190 Gif sur Yvette
Affiliation: Centre National de la Recherche Scientifique
Director: Professor Bernard Picinbino
Deputy Director: Pierre Bertrand

Laboratoire des Ultra-Réfractaires*   966

[Ultra-Refractories Laboratory]
Address: BP 5, Odeillo-Via, 66120 Font-Romeu
Affiliation: Centre National de la Recherche Scientifique
Director: Georges Urbain

Laboratoire des Verres*   967

[Glass Laboratory]
Address: Université de Montpellier II, place Eugène-Bataillon, 34060 Montpellier Cedex
Affiliation: Centre National de la Recherche Scientifique
Director: Professor Jersy Zarzicki

Laboratoire du Phytotron*   968

[Phytotron Laboratory]
Address: 91419 Gif sur Yvette
Affiliation: Centre National de la Recherche Scientifique
Director: Roger Jacques

Laboratoire Léon Brillouin   969

[Léon Brillouin Laboratory]
Address: Centre d'Etudes Nucléaires de Saclay, BP2, 91190 Gif sur Yvette Cedex
Telephone: 908 52 22
Telex: 690641 F
Affiliation: Centre National de la Recherche Scientifique; Commissariat à l'Energie Atomique
Research directors: Dr Daniel Cribier; Professor M. Lambert
Sections: theory of incommensurate phases, S. Aubry; crystalline structures and magnetism, P. Meriel; liquids and amorphs, G. Tourand; metallurgy, H. Gilder; polymers, G. Jannink; magnetic excitations, B. Hennion; phonons - molecular movements, G. Pepy; electronic properties of alloys - diffuse scattering, G. Parette; pseudo-magnetism and antiferromagnetism, P. Meriel; high pressures, D. Debray
Graduate research staff: 39
Activities: Fundamental research with some applied research. Principal fields of research are: magnetism; nuclear magnetism; structures and dynamics of the

condensed matter and phase transitions in crystals; liquid crystals, liquid and amorphous polymers.
Facilities: The laboratory acts as a national centre for researchers needing to use neutron diffraction or neutron spectrometry.
Contract work: No
Publications: Rapport d'Activité.

Laboratoire Louis Néel 970

[Louis Néel Laboratory]
Address: 166X, 38042 Grenoble Cedex
Telephone: (076) 96 98 37
Telex: 320254
Affiliation: Centre National de la Recherche Scientifique
Research director: M. Schlenker
Sections: Rare-earth intermetallics, R. Lemaire; anisotropy, G. Aubert; theory, M. Cyrot; magnetic insulators, M. Guillot; magnetization processes, R. Vergne, J.L. Porteseil; pressure and strain effects in magnetism, D. Bloch
Graduate research staff: 50
Contract work: Yes
Note: This laboratory was formerly named Laboratoire de Magnétisme de Grenoble.

Laboratoire National de la Santé 971

[National Health Laboratory]
Address: 25 boulevard Saint-Jacques, 75680 Paris Cedex 14
Telephone: (01) 707 45 69
Affiliation: Ministère de la Santé et de la Securité Sociale
Director General: Dr Robert Netter
Departments: Medicine control, Professor Bon, Professor Puech; vaccine control, Dr Chippaux, Dr Huet; virus epidemiology, Professor Aymard, Professor Fleurette; hydrology, Dr Ninard; toxicology, Mlle Beaulaton
Graduate research staff: 50
Activities: Research on: sulphur in mineral water; mutagenesis test in animal cells; legionellosis; gastroenteritis; antiseptic activity evaluation; hepatitis; emetine and derivatives; compatibility between drugs and plastic vials.
Contract work: Yes

Laboratoire pour l'Utilisation du Rayonnement Électromagnétique 972

– LURE
[Utilization of Electromagnetic Radiation Laboratory]
Address: bâtiment 209C, Faculté des Sciences, 91405 Orsay
Telephone: 941 82 70
Affiliation: Centre National de la Recherche Scientifique; Université de Paris-Sud
Research director: Dr Yves Petroff
Sections: Atomic physics, Dr Francois Wuilleumer; molecular physics, Dr Irene Nenner; solid-state physics, Dr Jean Lecante; Extended X-ray Absorption Fine Structure Studies (EXAFS), Dr Pierre Lagarde; biophysics, Dr Roger Fourme; structures (crystallography), Dr Claudine Williams; X-ray topography, Dr Michele Sauvage; applied physics, Marc Lemonnier.
Graduate research staff: 50
Annual expenditure: F710 000 000
Activities: LURE is the Frencn Synchrotron Radiation Centre using ultra violet light emitted by an ACO electron storage ring and the X-ray beam delivered by a DCI electron storage ring. Various types of research both fundamental and applied, are carried on using these sources.
Contract work: Yes
Publications: Rapport d'Activité (annual).

Laboratoire Souterrain de Moulis* 973

[Moulis Underground Laboratory]
Address: 09410 Moulis
Affiliation: Centre National de la Recherche Scientifique
Director: Professor Claude Drogue
Deputy Director: Christian Juberthie

Laboratoires ARIA 974

Address: 65 quai de la Gare, 75013 Paris
Telephone: (01) 584 11 90; 583 98 37
Telex: Paris 21 838
Parent body: Grands Moulins de Paris
Director: Alain Colas
Sections: Biochemistry of early wheats, A. Colas; gluten/starch separation, baking-extrusion, M. Munier
Graduate research staff: 2

Annual expenditure: £10 000-50 000
Activities: Research in the following areas: valorization of early wheats (study of varieties) - identification of varieties by electrophoresis; study of new types of flour for specific usages; separation of gluten and starch by moisturization; baking-extrusion.
Contract work: No

Laboratoires d'Électronique et de Physique Appliquée 975

– LEP
Address: 3 Avenue Descartes, BP 15, 94450, Limeil-Brévannes
Telephone: (0) 5699610
Telex: LEPARIS 203475 F
Research director: Dr J. Bonnerot

Laboratoires de Marcoussis 976 - Centre de Recherches

[Marcoussis Laboratories - Research Centre]
Address: route de Nozay, 91460 Marcoussis
Telephone: (06) 449 10 00
Telex: LABMARC 692 415
Parent body: Compagnie Générale d'Électricité
General Manager: L. Citti
Divisions: Energy, P. Dubois; electrochemistry, R. Vic; lasers, M. Etiènne; materials, P. Dumas; electronics and optics, P. Engler
Graduate research staff: 180
Annual expenditure: over £2m
Activities: Research in the following areas: telecommunications; electronic components; fibre optics; computer science; artificial intelligence; office automation; tele-informatics; lasers - high-power and energy lasers, isotopic separation, semiconductor lasers; single crystals; ceramics; solar generators; biomass; very-high-voltage insulation; cryoelectricity; batteries; hydrogen.

LCC-CICE 977

Address: 36 avenue Galliéni, 93170 Bagnolet
Technical Manager: Y.L.E. Duriau
Activities: Research and development in the following areas: dielectrics (ceramic and others); semiconductive ceramics; piezo ceramics; soft ferrites.

Le Carbone Lorraine 978

Address: Tour Manhattan - Cedex 21, 92087 Paris La Défense 2
Telephone: (01) 773 34 56
Telex: LCLFR 630 090
Activities: Research and development in the following areas: preparation and properties of carbon and graphite; carbonization and heat treatment; crystalline state; electromagnetic and mechanical properties; porosity; permeability; activity.

Lesieur Cotelle et Associés 979

Address: 122 avenue du Général Leclerc, 92103 Boulogne Billancourt
Telephone: (021) 604 81 40
Telex: 27 931
Research director, food products: Jean-Paul Helme
Sections: Laboratories, F. Zwobada; documentation and patents, P. Marquand; food sciences department, P. Pabst; detergents, J.P. Steiner
Graduate research staff: 75
Annual expenditure: £501 000-2m
Activities: Research and development in the following areas: new processes and products in food sciences fields; nutrition and toxicology; influence of the technologies on the quality of the products.
Contract work: Yes

COUDEKERQUE LABORATORY 980

Address: route de Bourbourg, 59000 Coudekerque-Branche
Head: F. Zwobada
Activities: Research into edible oils, soaps, meat and poultry products.

IVRY LABORATORY 981

Address: 78 avenue de Verdun, 94000 Ivry
Head: J.P. Steiner
Activities: Research into detergents, cleaning products and cosmetics.

Musée Nationale d'Histoire Naturelle 982

[National Museum of Natural History]
Address: 57 rue Cuvier, 75231 Paris Cedex 05
Telephone: (01) 336 14 41
Affiliation: Ministère des Universités
Director: Professor Jean Doist

ALPINE GARDEN 983

Address: La Jaysina, 74340 Samoéns
Director: Professor J.L. Hamel

ANTHROPOLOGY LABORATORY 984

Address: Musée de l'Homme, Palais de Chaillot, place du Trocadéro, 75116 Paris
Director: Professor Y. Coppens

APPLIED PLANT BIOLOGY LABORATORY 985

Address: 61 rue de Buffon, 75231 Paris Cedex 05
Director: Professor J.L. Hamel

AQUATIC POPULATION DYNAMICS LABORATORY 986

Address: 57 rue Cuvier, 75231 Paris Cedex 05
Director: Professor J. Daget

BIOLOGICAL APPLICATIONS OF CHEMISTRY LABORATORY 987

Address: 63 rue de Buffon, 75231 Paris Cedex 05
Director: Professor D. Molho

BIOPHYSICS LABORATORY 988

Address: 61 rue de Buffon, 75231 Paris Cedex 05
Director: Professor C. Hélène

COMPARATIVE ANATOMY LABORATORY 989

Address: 55 rue de Buffon, 75231 Paris Cedex 05
Director: Professor J. Anthony

CROPS LABORATORY 990

Address: 43 rue de Buffon, 75231 Paris Cedex 05
Director: vacant

CRYPTOGAMY LABORATORY 991

Address: 12 rue de Buffon, 75231 Paris Cedex 05
Director: Professor S. Jovet

ENTOMOLOGY LABORATORY 992

Address: Harmas de Fabre, Sérignan, Vaucluse
Director: Professor J. Carayon

ETHNOBOTANICAL LABORATORY 993

Address: 57 rue Cuvier, 75231 Paris Cedex 05
Director: vacant

ETHNOLOGY LABORATORY 994

Address: Musée de l'Homme, Palais de Chaillot, place de Trocadéro, 75116 Paris
Director: Professor J. Guiart

ETHOLOGY OF WILD ANIMALS LABORATORY 995

Address: 53 avenue de Saint-Maurice, 75012 Paris
Director: Professor F. Doumenge

EVOLUTION OF NATURAL AND MODIFIED SYSTEMS LABORATORY 996

Address: 36 rue Geoffroy St Hilaire, 75005 Paris
Director: Professor J.C. Lefeuvre

FAUNA AND FLORA SECRETARIAT 997

Address: 57 rue Cuvier, 75231 Paris Cedex
Director: François de Beaufort

GENERAL AND APPLIED ENTOMOLOGY LABORATORY 998

Address: 45 bis rue de Buffon, 75231 Paris Cedex 05
Director: Professor J. Carayon

GENERAL AND COMPARATIVE PHYSIOLOGY LABORATORY 999

Address: 7 rue Cuvier, 75231 Paris Cedex 05
Director: Professor Y.A. Fontaine

GENERAL ECOLOGY LABORATORY 1000

Address: 4 avenue du Petit-Château, 91800 Brunoy
Director: Professor C. Delamare Deboutteville

GEOLOGY LABORATORY 1001

Address: 61 rue de Buffon, 75231 Paris Cedex 05
Director: Professor L. Leclaire

MARINE INVERTEBRATES BIOLOGY AND MALACOLOGY LABORATORY — 1002

Address: 57 rue Cuvier, 75231 Paris Cedex 05
or: 55 rue de Buffon, 75231 Paris Cedex 05
Director: Professor C. Lévi

MARINE LABORATORY — 1003

Address: 17 avenue George V, 35800 Dinard
Director: Professor C. Lévi

MENAGERIE OF THE NATURAL HISTORY MUSEUM — 1004

Address: 57 rue Cuvier, 75231 Paris Cedex 05
or: Parc Zoologique de Bois de Vincennes, 53 avenue de Saint-Maurice, 75012 Paris
Director: Professor F. Doumenge

MINERALOGY LABORATORY — 1005

Address: 61 rue de Buffon, 75231 Paris Cedex 05
Director: Professor J. Fabriès

NATURE CONSERVATION SERVICE — 1006

Address: 36 rue Geoffroy Saint Hilaire, 75005 Paris Cedex 05
Director: Georges Tendron

PALAEONTOLOGY LABORATORY — 1007

Address: 8 rue de Buffon, 75231 Paris Cedex 05
Director: Professor J.P. Lehman

PHANEROGAMY LABORATORY — 1008

Address: 16 rue de Buffon, 75231 Paris Cedex 05
Director: Professor J.F. Leroy

PHYSICAL OCEANOGRAPHY LABORATORY — 1009

Address: 57 rue Cuvier, 75231 Paris Cedex 05
Director: Professor H. Lacombe

PHYSICS APPLIED TO NATURAL SCIENCES LABORATORY — 1010

Address: 57 rue Cuvier, 75231 Paris Cedex 05
Director: Professor P. Douzou

PREHISTORY LABORATORY — 1011

Address: Musée de l'Homme, Palais de Chaillot, place du Trocadéro, 75116 Paris
or: 1 rue René-Panhard, 75013 Paris
Director: Professor H. De Lumley

ZOOLOGY OF ARTHROPODS LABORATORY — 1012

Address: 61 rue de Buffon, 75231 Paris Cedex 05
Director: Professor Y. Coineau

ZOOLOGY OF GRUBS AND LARVAE LABORATORY — 1013

Address: 57 rue Cuvier, 75231 Paris Cedex 05
Director: Professor A. Chabaud

ZOOLOGY OF MAMMALS AND BIRDS LABORATORY — 1014

Address: 55 rue de Buffon, 75231, Paris Cedex 05
Director: Professor Jean Dorst

ZOOLOGY OF REPTILES AND FISHES LABORATORY — 1015

Address: 57 rue Cuvier, 75231 Paris Cedex 05
Director: Professor E.R. Brygoo

Neyrpic — 1016

Address: Centre de Tri, BP 75, 38041 Grenoble Cedex
Telephone: (076) 96 48 30
Telex: 320750 Grenoble
Affiliation: CREUSOT - Loire SA
Technical Manager: S. Casacci
Sections: Calculus, structure and thermics, M Huffenus; hydraulics, M Boussuges
Graduate research staff: 30
Annual expenditure: £10 000-50 000
Activities: Flow optimization in turbomachinery; vibrations in vacuo and in fluid media; calculus and programme structures; piston cross-heads; hydrodynamics; lubrication; elasticity shells; hydro- and thermo-elasticity; feedback control, mainly hydraulic and pneumatic systems.
Contract work: No

Observatoire de Besançon 1017

[Besançon Observatory]
Address: 41 avenue de l'Observatoire, 2500 Besançon
Telephone: (081) 80 03 30
Affiliation: Institut National d'Astronomie et de Géophysique; Université de Franche-Comté
Director: Michel Crézé
Graduate research staff: 14
Activities: Recent theoretical research includes: stellar and galactic dynamics; theory of signals - study of models of the optimum atmospheric conditions for the transmission of photons; neutral atmospheric models (above altitude 200km) for the study of trajectories of man-made satellites. Astronomical and geodynamic observations on: rotation of the earth; movement of the moon.

Observatoire de Bordeaux 1018

[Bordeaux Observatory]
Address: 33270 Floirac
Telephone: (056) 86 43 30
Affiliation: Institut National d'Astronomie et de Géophysique; Université de Bordeaux I
Director: Fernand Poumeyrol
Graduate research staff: 18
Activities: Studies of positions of stars and their terrestrial movements; satellite measurements by theodolite - characteristics of very high atmosphere and the effects of the earth's gravity; radioastronomy; study of the spectra of planetary nebulae and H II regions.
Facilities: Millimetric inferometer.

Observatoire de Haute Provence 1019

[Haute Provence Observatory]
Address: Saint Michel l'Observatoire, 04300 Forcalquier
Telephone: (092) 76 73 68
Telex: OHP 410690F
Affiliation: Centre National de la Recherche Scientifique; Institut National d'Astronomie et de Géophysique
Director: Professor Charles Fehrenbach
Sections: Astronomy, C. Fehrenbach, Yvette Andrillat; electronics, J.P. Berger; informatics, A. Vin
Graduate research staff: 2
Annual expenditure: £501 000-2m
Activities: Stellar, galactic and extragalactic astrophysics; photographic spectrography; spectral classification - measurement of radial velocity; study of stars, comets, novae and the structure of the galaxy; study of quasars; aeronomy.
Facilities: 1.9m telescope working to Newtonian, cassegranian and Loudé focus; 1.52m unique Loudé telescope; 60-90 cm Schmidt telescope.
Contract work: No
Publications: Rapport d'activité (annual) *Publication de la Clichothèque* (quarterly).

Observatoire de Lyon 1020

[Lyon Observatory]
Address: avenue Charles-André, 69230 Saint-Genis-Laval
Telephone: (078) 56 07 05
Affiliation: Institut National d'Astronomie et de Géophysique; Université Claude-Bernard (Lyon I)
Director: Guy Monnet
Graduate research staff: 19
Activities: Photometric, photographic, and photoelectric methods are used for: determination of interstellar adsorption, calibration of star magnitude, searching for new stars, study of regions where stars are formed, study of spectra of planetary nebulae; spectrophotometric studies of stellar atmospheres; extragalactic studies - structure of the Large Magellanic Cloud, stellar population of galaxies in relation to their structure, theoretic work on the reddening of galaxies, optic and radio measurements of galaxies.
Facilities: 1 m telescope; measuring apparatus - photometers, polarimeters, monochrometers, etc. Major observations are carried out at the Observatoire de Haute-Provence and the European Southern Observatory.

Observatoire de Marseille 1021

[Marseilles Observatory]
Address: 2 place Le Verrier, 13004 Marseille
Telephone: (091) 50 07 03 or (091) 50 05 29
Affiliation: Institut National d'Astronomie et de Géophysique; Université d'Aix-Marseille I
Director: Yvon Georgelin
Graduate research staff: 38
Activities: Measurement of radial speeds; stellar and solar spectrography; studies of interstellar gases; space research.

Observatoire de Nice   1022

[Nice Observatory]
Address: Le Mont Gros, 06300 Nice
Telephone: (093) 89 04 20
Affiliation: Institut National d'Astronomie et de Géophysique; Université de Nice
Director: J.P. Zahn
Graduate research staff: 40
Activities: Solar physics - solar activity, photosphere, chromosphere, corona; stellar physics - internal structure of stars, their atmospheres and evolution, variable stars; stellar dynamics; equatorial astrometry; astrography of asteroids and man-made satellites.
Facilities: Equatorial coude Patry telescope with 40 cm aperture; equatorial Bischoffsheim telescope with 76 cm aperture and 18 m focal length.

LABORATOIRE D'ASTROPHYSIQUE   1023

[Astrophysics Laboratory]
Address: Parc-Valrose, 06304 Nice Cedex
Telephone: (093) 84 60 29

Observatoire de Paris   1024

[Paris Observatory]
Address: 61 avenue de l'Observatoire, 75014 Paris
Telephone: (01) 326 06 44
Affiliation: Institut National d'Astronomie et de Géophysique
Director: J. Boulon
Sections: Stellar and galactic physics; solar and planetary astronomy; fundamental astronomy; fundamental astrophysics; radio astronomy; space research; optics and photometry.
Graduate research staff: 240
Activities: The organization operates from three centres - the observatories at Paris and Meudon and the radioastronomy station at Nançay. The facilities offered by national or international observatories situated near Paris-Meudon - at Haute-Provence, Pic du Midi, and the Southern European Observatory - are essential to the work of the Parisian researchers. Space research is conducted with Centre National d'Études Spatiales and the European Space Research Organization as part of their work in cooperation with the USA and USSR.
Apart from astronomical research the observatory develops certain branches of theoretical or experimental physics particularly relevant to astrophysics: plasmas; atomic and mollecular physics; and physics of collisions.

OBSERVATOIRE DE MEUDON   1025

[Meudon Observatory]
Address: 5 place Jules-Janssen, 92190 Meudon
Telephone: 626 16 30 or 626 28 20
Activities: Surveillance of the sun's activities; optical observation of the level of the photosphere and the chromosphere; detailed mapping of magnetic fields and the movements of matter in the centres of activity.

STATION DE RADIOASTRONOMIE   1026
DE NANÇAY

[Nançay Radioastronomy Station]
Address: 18330 Nançay sur Barangeon
Telephone: (036) 51 62 41
Activities: Study of solar emissions; intensity, locality, source and spectra of radiation; extragalactic research; galactic origins; interstellar matter; and the solar system. Work with the large radiotelescope has led to the following notable achievements in the past few years: the discovery of immense clouds of neutral hydrogen surrounding certain groups of galaxies; the measurement of the spiral structure of galaxy M 31 in the hydrogen spectrum at 21 cm; the discovery of neutral hydrogen in abundance in certain galaxies and the establishment of laws relating their diffuse hydrogen content to the structures of the galaxies; measurement of distances of pulsars by study of absorption of interstellar hydrogen - the same method obtained estimates of the distance of a source of stellar X-rays; a project in collaboration with Russian scientists on the emission of the molecule OH from cold stars enabled identification of a new class of stellar objects.
Facilities: Radioheliograph; large radiotelescope with two reflectors - one flat, north facing, 200 metres long and 40 metres high, the other, is curved, south facing, 300 metres long and 70 metres high, concentrating energy from an aerial situated 280 metres away.

Observatoire de Strasbourg 1027

[Strasbourg Observatory]
Address: 11 rue de l'Université, 6700 Strasbourg
Telephone: (088) 35 43 00
Affiliation: Institut National d'Astronomie et de Géophysique; Université Louis Pasteur (Strasbourg I)
Director: Alphonse Florsch
Graduate research staff: 12
Activities: Spectrophotometric studies of radial speeds, stars and nebulae; astrometry; space measurements.
Facilities: Schmidt telescope.

CENTRE DE DONNÉES STELLAIRES   1028

[Stellar Data Centre]
Activities: The aim of the centre is the cataloguing, conservation and dissemination of all that is known about stars - their position, usual movement, radial speeds, size, colour, spectral classification, spectral details, speed of rotation, etc, with a view to setting up a bibliographic service for individual stars. The centre works in collaboration with national and foreign organizations, particularly the observatories at Paris, Marseille, Lausanne, Geneva, and Heidelberg.

Observatoire du Pic du   1029
Midi et de Toulouse

[Pic du Midi and Toulouse Observatory]
Address: 9 rue du Point de la Moulette, 65200 Bagnères de Bigorre
or: Observatoire de Toulouse, 1 avenue Camille-Flammarion, 31500 Toulouse
Telephone: Bagnèrres de Bigorre (062) 95 00 69; Toulouse, (061) 48 58 78; summit of Pic du Midi station, (062) 93 30 30
Affiliation: Institut National d'Astronomie et de Géophysique; Université Paul Sabatier (Toulouse III)
Director: Professor Jean Rösch
Graduate research staff: 26
Facilities: Two metre diameter telescope.

Office de la Recherche   1030
Scientifique et Technique
Outre-Mer

– ORSTOM
[Overseas Scientific and Technical Research Bureau]
Address: 24 rue Bayard, 75008 Paris
Telephone: (01) 225 31 52
Telex: ORSTOM 640 295 F
Affiliation: Ministère de la Coopération; Ministère des Universités
Head, Scientific Programming: Roger Fauck
Research director: Professor Guy Camus
Sections: Geophysics, J. Dubois; geology, H. Faure; pedology, N. Leneuf; hydrology, J. Rodier; oceanography and hydrobiology, A. Crosnier; soil biology, J. Senez; botany and plant biology, C. Lioret; phytopathology and applied zoology, L. Hirth; biology and improvement of useful plants, J. Pernes; agronomy, F. Fournier; microbiology, parasitology, medical entomology, J. Mouchet; nutrition, A. François; sociology and psychosociology, J. Lombard; economy and demography, M. Rochefort; geography, P. Pelissier; anthropology, J. Garanger
Annual expenditure: F375m
Activities: ORSTOM's main functions are: to contribute towards development and research in non-temperate zones in the areas of earth and water sciences, biological sciences, human sciences; to train researchers and technicians for its own research programmes and to meet the demands of those countries where work is being carried out; to supply data on their work and to publish results.
Contract work: No
Publications: Maps; various annual reports on projects.

Office National d'Études et   1031
de Recherches
Aérospatiales

– ONERA
[National Aerospace Research Office]
Address: 29 avenue la Division Leclerc, 92320 Châtillon
Director-General: André Auriol
Secretary-General: Robert Masson
Research director: Marcel Barrère
Planning director: Maurice El Gammal
Activities: Aerodynamics; energetics; flight mechanics; aeroelasticity and dynamics of structures; metallic and organic materials; optics, acoustics, and electronics; flight experiments. Basic research. Conception and experimentation in methods and new equipment. Technical assistance. There are experiment centres at Mondane, Fauga-Mauzac (near Toulouse), Chalais-Meudon, Palaiseau, Le Bouchet, and Satory.

CENTRE D'ÉTUDES ET DE   1032
RECHERCHES DE TOULOUSE

– ONERA-CERT
[Toulouse Study and Research Centre]
Address: 2 avenue Edouard Belin, 31055 Toulouse Cedex
Director: Marc Pélegrin

Organisme National de   1033
Securité Routière

– ONSER
[National Council for Road Safety]
Address: 2 avenue du Général Malleret-Joinville, BP 34, 94114 Arcueil Cedex

Telephone: 581 12 12
Telex: 270768 ONSER
Director: Jean Moreau de Saint-Martin
Graduate research staff: 55
Annual expenditure: F3lm
Activities: Research into all aspects of road accidents and their prevention, particularly concentrating on drivers, vehicles, roads and regulations.
Contract work: No
Publications: Bulletin; study documents.

ACCIDENT AND BIOMECHANICS LABORATORY 1034

Address: 109 avenue Salvador Allende, 69500 Bron
Telephone: (078) 26 14 18
Head: M Leroy
Activities: Development of road safety equipment, medical engineering accident studies; simulation techniques; mathematical modelling; studies of existing road safety systems; the results of these studies influence the choice of safety systems used on French roads.

EVALUATION CENTRE 1035

Head: M Bluet
Activities: Evaluation of road safety measures in terms of numbers of accident victims, cost and public opinion studies.

PSYCHOLOGY OF DRIVING LABORATORY 1036

Address: autodrome de Linas-Montlhéry, 91310 Montlhéry
Telephone: 901 61 50
Director: M Chich
Activities: Training of drivers and public safety standards; analysis of driving standards to determine risk factors.

Papeteries Bolloré SA 1037

Address: BP 2, 29111 Scaer
Telephone: (098) 59 40 38
Telex: 940 171 ISOLE SCAER
Research director: J.J. Courtet
Senior staff: Paper chemistry, P. Breux; polypropylene, M. Cloarec; metallized products, A. Liziard
Graduate research staff: 7
Annual expenditure: £51 000-500 000
Activities: Physico-chemical and dielectric studies on

thin insulating papers and plastic films - applications to capacitor and cable industry.
Contract work: Yes

Pechiney Ugine Kuhlmann 1038

– PUK
Address: 23 rue Balzac, BP 787 08, 75360 Paris Cedex 08
Telephone: (01) 561 61 61
Telex: 290 503
Research director: Michel Wintenberger
Sections: DCRD, Voreppe, M. Plateau; CTAL, Paris, Robert Gauvry
Graduate research staff: 525
Activities: Research and development in the following areas: light metals and alloys; alloyed steels; titanium; zirconium; tungsten; carbon and graphite electrodes; polyvinyl chloride; polyesters; halocarbons; pharmaceuticals; dyes; inks.

CENTRE TECHNIQUE DE L'ALUMINIUM 1039

[Aluminium Technical Centre]
Address: 87 boulevard de Grenelle, 75015 Paris
Telephone: (01) 783 47 70
Telex: CTAI 204359 F
Research director: Robert Gauvry
Graduate research staff: 16
Activities: Research into technical applications of aluminium.
Contract work: Yes

Protection des Plantes et Environnement - Centre d'Études et d'Informations 1040

– PPE
[Plant Protection and Environment Information Centre]
Address: 1 rue Gambetta, 92100 Boulogne
Telephone: (021) 825 09 81
Chairman: J.F. Breton
Manager: J.C. Lamontagne
Activities: Studying, within the framework of public health and nature conservation, all plant and crop protection problems, and informing all those concerned about these problems and their solutions.
Note: Non-profit information centre directed by agricultural and farming associations, pesticides manufacturers and distributors, and food organizations.

Pyromeca   1041

Address: chemin de la Roquette, 83000 Toulon
Telephone: (094) 41 28 77
Telex: ODISE 400287 F. Poste 803 P
Affiliation: Leafields Engineering Limited, Corsham, Wiltshire SN13 9SS, UK
Technical director: Roger Gouallec
Senior staff: Jean-Pierre Gouallec
Graduate research staff: 5
Annual expenditure: £20 000
Activities: Design and manufacturing of pyrotechnically operated devices; remote control of mechanisms (actuators, cable cutters, valves) with low energy input signal and high energy output.
Contract work: No

Roussel Uclaf   1042

Address: 35 boulevard des Invalides, BP 12007, 75323 Paris Cedex 07
Telephone: (01) 555 91 55
Telex: 200675 F
Affiliation: Hoechst
Research director: Dr E. Sakiz
Senior staff: Pharmaceuticals, Professor J. Boissier; non-pharmaceutical, G. Nomine
Graduate research staff: 400
Annual expenditure: £501 000-2m
Activities: Research and development in the following areas: antibiotics such as cephalosporins and those concerned with the central nervous system; chemical and biochemical processes designed for competitive industrial use; chemical and biochemical development - improvement of new processes in order to adapt them to industrial requirements; biochemical fermentation and multistage synthesis - applications in medicine, veterinary science and agriculture; agriculture - industrial preparation of pyrethroids, insecticides which are non-toxic for man and the environment.
Roussel Uclaf has laboratories at Romainville near Paris, Marseille, Osny, Neuville sur Seine, Vertolaye, as well as at Swindon in the UK, Milan in Italy, and Rio de Janeiro in Brazil.
Contract work: No

Service Centrale   1043
d'Analyse*

[Central Analysis Department]
Address: BP 22, autoroute Lyon-Vienne, Échangeur de Solaize, 69390 Vernaison
Affiliation: Centre National de la Recherche Scientifique
Director: Alain Lamotte

Service d'Aéronomie   1044

[Aeronomy Department]
Address: Fort Verrières BP 3, 91370 Verrières-le-Buisson
Telephone: 920 10 60
Affiliation: Institut National d'Astronomie et de Géophysique; Centre National de la Recherche Scientifique
Director: Professor Jacques Émile Blamont
Graduate research staff: 29
Activities: Studies of the composition, structure, and movements of the earth's atmosphere in relation to solar and geophysical phenomena.

Service de Diffusion de la   1045
Technologie des
Matériaux*

[Materials Technology Diffusion Department]
Address: Université de Paris XI, Bâtiment 490, 91405 Orsay
Affiliation: Centre National de la Recherche Scientifique
Director: Professor Jean-Pierre Chapelle

LABORATOIRE DE CHIMIE DU   1046
SOLIDE

[Solid-State Chemistry Laboratory]
Address: Université de Bordeaux I, 351 cours de la Libération, 33405 Talence Cedex
Telephone: (056) 80 84 50
Affiliation: Centre National de la Recherche Scientifique
Director: Professor Paul Hagenmuller
Senior staff: J. Claverie, G. le Flem, J.M. Reau, C. Cros, R. Naslain, B. Tanguy, G. Demazeau, M. Onillon, A. Tressaud, J. Etourneau, J. Portier, C. Fouassier, M. Pouchard, J. Grannec, J. Ravez
Annual expenditure: $1m
Activities: Research is largely oriented towards the

relationships between the properties of materials (usually physical or mechanical) and their structure and composition. The main research activities include: magnetic properties: dimensionality studies, magnetic clusters, ferri- or ferromagnetic fluorides, new magnetic semiconductors, chromium dioxide derivative materials; insulator-metal transitions mechanisms in different materials in collaboration with solid-state physics laboratories in France or in foreign countries; thermoemissive materials in connection with industrial laboratories; optical properties of materials; high performance dielectric materials and non-linear properties as applied to devices; composite materials; energy conversion and storage problems; chemical bonding problems; problems related to the preparation and elaboration of classical or advanced materials.

Collaboration with many laboratories of solid-state chemistry, of material science, of solid-state physics, of chemical thermodynamics and of electrochemistry, and with many foreign laboratories, in particular in countries such as: United States, Japan, Canada, Argentina, Great Britain, German FR, Sweden, Netherlands, Belgium, Switzerland, Spain, Yugoslavia, USSR, Poland, Czechoslovakia, Bulgaria, German DR, China, India, Vietnam, Morocco. This collaboration concerns not only the important university or academic laboratories, but the industrial research centres (Bell Telephone, GE, Philips, Hitachi, etc) as well.

Publications: Various reports.

LABORATOIRE DE PHYSIQUE CRISTALLINE* 1047

[Crystalline Physics Laboratory]
Address: Université de Paris XI, Bâtiment 490, 91405 Orsay
Director: Professor Jean-Pierre Chapelle

Service de la Carte de la Végétation* 1048

[Vegetation Mapping Department]
Address: 29 rue Jeanne-Marvig, BP 4009, 31055 Toulouse Cedex
Affiliation: Centre National de la Recherche Scientifique
Director: Professor Paul Rey
Deputy Director: Henri Decamps

Service de Technologie Appliquée à la Microscopie Électronique* 1049

[Department of Technology applied to Electron Microscopy]
Address: 105 boulevard Raspail, 75272 Paris Cedex 06
Affiliation: Centre National de la Recherche Scientifique
Director: Jacques Escaig

Service du Cyclotron 1050

[Cyclotron Department]
Address: 3A rue de la Férollerie, 45045 Orléans Cedex
Affiliation: Centre National de la Recherche Scientifique
Director: Roland Muxart
Activities: The Service du Cyclotron is a laboratory whose principal role is to provide facilities for research and development within the medium of charged particles produced by cyclotrons. The Service has among its users chemists, biologists, doctors and dentists, but mostly physicists.

Service National des Champs Intenses* 1051

[National Department of Intense Fields]
Address: BP 166X, 38042 Grenoble Cedex
Affiliation: Centre National de la Recherche Scientifique
Director: Professor Guy Aubert

Shell Recherche Société Anonyme 1052

Address: 29 rue de Berri, 75397 Paris Cedex 08
Affiliation: Royal Dutch/Shell

GRAND COURONNE RESEARCH CENTRE 1053

Address: 76 Grand Couronne
Director: A. Marmin
Activities: Oil products and processes.

Société Européenne de Propulsion   1054

– SEP
[European Propulsion Society]
Address: tour Roussel-Nobel, Cedex 3 92080 Paris La Defense
Telephone: (01) 778 15 15
Telex: 630 906 F
Chairman and Director-General: Pierre Soufflet
Secretary General: Ph. Simionesco
Graduate research staff: 440
Annual expenditure: over £2m
Activities: Research and development into: solid and liquid propellant rocket motors; weapons systems; satellite components; receiving stations for signals transmitted from satellites; resolution image reconstruction unit; composite materials - carbon, carbon composite materials, structural composite materials; active magnetic bearings; pressure transducers; equipment and operating systems for offshore oil-field operations.
Publications: SEP 5.

Société Française de Ceramique   1055

[French Ceramic Society]
Address: 23 rue de Cronstadt, 75015 Paris
Affiliation: National Study Centre for Ceramic Research
Director General: André Baudran
Activities: Chemical analysis, physical and hot testing, technical and industrial research; research is aimed to encourage technical progress in the ceramics industry.

Societé Française pour la Gestion des Brevets d'Application Nucléaire   1056

– BREVATOME
[Nuclear Patents French Society]
Address: 25 rue de Ponthieu, 75008 Paris
Telephone: (01) 225 17 80
Telex: SPIBREV 660028 F
Parent body: Commissariat à l'Énergie Atomique
Director General: Pierre Pottier
Research director: Ing André Mongrédien
Sections: Patents; law
Graduate research staff: 10
Activities: Filing and defence of patents in all countries; negotiation of licences and agreements. In 1974 BREVATOME created a subsidiary: Société de Protection

des Inventions (Society for the Protection of Inventions).
Contract work: No

Société Nationale d'Exploitation Industrielle des Tabacs et Allumettes   1057

– SEITA
Address: 53 quai d'Orsay, 75340 Paris Cedex 07
Telephone: (01) 555 9 50
Telex: SEITABA 250 604
Director: Pierre Ledez
Sections: Mutagenesis, genotoxicity; neuropsychology, Dr Camille Izard; fundamental chemistry
Graduate research staff: 7
Annual expenditure: 501 000-2m
Activities: Chemical composition of tobacco smoke, analysis and identification; biological effects of smoking, mutagenesis, cancerogenesis, and neuropsychology.
Contract work: No
Publications: Annales du Tabac.

CENTRE FOR EXPERIMENTAL RESEARCH ON TOBACCO   1058

Address: 4 rue André Dessaux, BP 2, 45401 Fleury-les-Aubrais
Telephone: (038) 88 68 25
Telex: SEITALA 760084
Director: M Pietrucci
Sections: Chemistry, M Viart; studies and experimental products, M Buisson; studies and experimental procedures, M Palmade; materials and development, M Berthou
Graduate research staff: 14
Annual expenditure: £2m
Activities: Research on tobacco and technology of cigarette and cigar manufacture.
Contract work: No

INSTITUT EXPERIMENTAL DU TABAC 1059

[Tobacco Experimental Institute]
Address: domaine de la Tour, BP 168, 24108 Bergerac
Telephone: (053) 57 47 88
Telex: SEITABAG 570 220
Director: Jacques Chouteau
Sections: Genetics, biology and vegetable pathology, Pierre Schiltz; dessication, fermentation, Jean-Pierre Albo; agronomy and vegetable physiology, Jacques Tancogne; experimental culture, Roger Arrestier
Graduate research staff: 8
Annual expenditure: £501 000-2m
Activities: Fundamental research on the tobacco plant

and raw materials; vegetable genetics and pathology; selection and creation of new varieties of plants, adaptation to climatic conditions; improvement of cultivation techniques and treatment after harvest; analysis of raw or transformed agricultural products; tobacco protein studies.
Contract work: Yes

Société Nationale des Chemins de Fer Français　　1060

– SNCF
[French National Railways]
Address: 88 rue Saint Lazare, 75436 Paris Cedex 09
Telephone: (01) 285 60 00
Telex: 290936 SNCF D.G. PARIS

GENERAL STUDIES AND RESEARCH　1061 DEPARTMENT

Head: R. Monnet

MATERIALS DEPARTMENT　　　　　1062

Address: 20 rue de Rome, 75008 Paris
Head: J. Bouley

PERMANENT WAY DEPARTMENT　　1063

Address: 17 rue d'Amsterdam, 75008 Paris
Head: J. Alias

TRANSPORT DEPARTMENT　　　　　1064

Address: 20 rue de Rome, 75008 Paris
Head: R. Gerin

Société Nationale des　　　　1065 Pétroles d'Aquitaine*

– SNPA
Address: 7 rue Nelaton, 75739 Paris 15
Scientific and Technical Research Director: B. Delapalme
Deputy Scientific and Technical Research Director: J. Berthelot
Activities: Exploration, production, refining and distribution of petrochemicals; organic chemicals; large molecular weight polymers; hydrocarbon and sulphur-containing organic compound research. There are five main centres for research: at Boussens, which employs

about 20 graduates, research is carried out into exploration and production techniques; at Chambourcy, which employs about 10 graduates, geological and seismic calculations are carried out; at Solaize, which employs about 52 graduates, studies into refining petrochemicals and their distribution is carried out; more basic research is carried out at Lacq and Pau.

LACQ RESEARCH CENTRE*　　　　1066

Address: BP 34, Lacq 64170 Artix
Activities: Sulphur organic chemistry; organic chemistry (oxidation and catalysis processes); high polymers.

PAU RESEARCH CENTRE*　　　　　1067

Address: avenue du Président Angst, 64000 Pau
Activities: Technique regarding petroleum exploration and production; physics; theoretical chemical engineering.

Station Biologique de la　　　1068 Tour du Valat

[Tour du Valat Biological Research Station]
Address: Le Sambuc, 13200 Arles
Telephone: (090) 98 90 13
Telex: F 410 804 TOURVAL SAMBU
Scientific Director: Dr L. Hoffmann
Sections: Mammals, Dr Patrick Duncan; aquatic invertebrates, Dr Robert Britton; birds, Dr Luc Hoffmann
Graduate research staff: 12
Annual expenditure: £300 000 (1980)
Activities: Research on wetland ecology and on scientific background for conservation and management of freshwater marshes, mainly of the Carmargue, with special attention to wetland birds.
Facilities: 5 000 acre estate of freshwater and salt marshes.
Contract work: Yes
Publications: Biennial report.

Station d'Hydrobiologie　　　1069 Lacustre

[Lacustrine Hydrobiology Station]
Address: 75 avenue de Corzent, 74203 Thonon-les-Bains
Telephone: (050) 71 49 55
Affiliation: Institut National de la Recherche Agronomique
Director: P.J. Laurent

Sections: Macrophytes, J.P. Dubois; zoology, G. Balvay; algology, J.P. Pelletier, J. Feuillade; lake restoration, G. Barroin
Graduate research staff: 10
Annual expenditure: £10 000-50 000
Activities: Lake biology and management studies.
Contract work: Yes

Station de Recherches de Virologie et d'Immunologie   1070

[Virology and Immunology Research Station]
Address: route de Thiverval, 78850 Thiverval-Grignon
Telephone: 056 45 45
Affiliation: Institut National de la Recherche Agronomique
Director: Dr Alain Paraf
Sections: Virology, Dr R. Scherrer; immunology, Dr P. Pery; ichthyopathology, Dr P. De Kinkelin; porcine pathology, Dr J.M. Aynaud; membranes and adjuvants of immunity, Dr A. Paraf
Graduate research staff: 35
Annual expenditure: £501 000-2m
Activities: Research into virology and immunology of cattle, pigs and fish. Special studies on Rotavirus, Coronavirus, Rhabdovirus and Herpes virus. Among the parasites studied are Haemonchus contortus in sheep and trout Furunculosis.
Publications: Annual report.
Contract work: Yes

Station Expérimentale de l'Endive   1071

[Endive Experimental Station]
Address: rue Pierre Waguet, 60000 Beauvais
Telephone: (04) 445 29 10
Affiliation: Centre Technique Interprofessionnel des Fruits et Légumes (CTIFL); Fédération Nationale des Producteurs d'Endives (FNPE)
Research director: J.P. Cochet
Annual expenditure: £10 000-50 000
Activities: Improvement of cultural techniques, particularly accurate sowing, chemical cleaning, and comparison between different forcing techniques.

Syndicat pour l'Amélioration des Sols et des Cultures   1072

– SAS
[Soils and Crops-Improvement Syndicate]
Address: 1 avenue Victor Hugo, 78440 Gargenville, Yvelines
Telephone: (03) 093 60 71
Director: C. Lesire

Télémécanique Électrique SA   1073

Address: 33 bis avenue du Maréchal-Joffre, 92002 Nanterre Cedex
Telephone: 725 96 08

RESEARCH AND DEVELOPMENT DEPARTMENT   1074

Director: L. Fechant
Activities: Research and development into electricity, electromagnetism and electronics.

Thomson CSF   1075

Address: 73 boulevard Haussmann, BP 700-08, 75360 Paris Cedex 08

CENTRAL RESEARCH LABORATORY   1076

Address: Domaine de Corbeville, BP 10, 91401 Orsay
Telephone: (0336) 941 82 40
Telex: TCSF 204780 F
Director: Dr Erich Spitz
Graduate research staff: 150
Activities: Materials - single crystals, epitaxial techniques, dielectrics, liquid crystals, ceramics, ferrites; components - microwave components, ultra high-speed logic circuits, light emitting and detecting diodes, lasers diodes, optical fibres, optical connections, integrated optics, electro-acoustic components; liquid crystal displays; holography; video recording; theory of programming languages.
Contract work: No

PROFESSIONAL ELECTRONIC EQUIPMENT BRANCH 1077

Address: 23 rue de Courcelles, BP 96-08, 75362 Paris Cedex 08

Union Technique de l'Automobile, du Motocycle et du Cycle 1078

– UTAC
[Automobile, Motorcycle and Cycle Technical Union]
Address: 157-159 rue Lecourbe, 75015 Paris
Director General: Louis-Christian Michelet
Technical Director: Edouard Chapoux
Activities: Testing of standards and specifications in the automobile field; vehicle safety, air pollution, noise abatement.
See also entry for the Psychology of Driving Laboratory under: Organisme National de Securité Routière.

Université d'Aix Marseille I (Provence)* 1079

[Provence University]
Address: 3 place Victor Hugo, 13331 Marseille 3
Telephone: (091) 95 90 71
See also entry for: Observatoire de Marseille.

INSTITUTE OF MECHANICS OF TURBULENCE* 1080

INSTITUTE OF PETROLEUM CHEMISTRY AND INDUSTRIAL ORGANIC SYNTHESIS* 1081

UNIT OF CHEMISTRY* 1082

UNIT OF MATHEMATICS* 1083

Head: Professor F. Borel

UNIT OF MEDITERRANEAN STUDIES* 1084

Head: Professor A. Machin

UNIT OF NATURAL SCIENCES* 1085

Head: Professor A. Machin

UNIT OF PHYSICS* 1086

Head: Professor J. Pantaloni

Université d'Aix-Marseille II 1087

[Aix-Marseille University II]
Address: Jardin Émile Duclaux, 58 boulevard Charles Livon, 13007 Marseille
Telephone: (091) 52 90 34
President: G. Serratrice

FACULTY OF DENTAL SURGERY 1088

Address: 27 boulevard Jean Moulin, 13385 Marseille Cedex 4
Head: Professor J. Garbarino
Activities: Histology; embryology; cytology; microradiography; metal techniques.

FACULTY OF MEDICINE 1089

Address: 27 boulevard Jean Moulin, 13385 Marseille Cedex 4

Biochemistry 1090

LABORATORY OF BIOCHEMISTRY 1091

Head: G. Laurent
Activities: Structure and physiology of carbonic anhydrites.

Cardiovascular System 1092

LABORATORY OF EXPERIMENTAL CARDIOLOGY 1093

Address: Groupe Hospitalier de la Timone, 13385 Melle Cedex 4
Head: Professor Gerard

LABORATORY OF EXPERIMENTAL SURGERY 1094

Head: Professor Monties
Activities: Experimental surgery; artificial heart.

LABORATORY OF PHYSIOLOGY 1095
Address: Secteur Nord, boulevard P. Dramard, 13015 Melle
Head: Professor Zwirn
Activities: Cardiovascular physiology.

Digestive System 1096

DIGESTIVE SURGERY TEAM 1097
Address: 46 chemin de la Gaye, 13009 Melle
Head: Professor J.C. Sarles
Activities: Sphincter and rectal electrophysiology.

LABORATORY OF EXPERIMENTAL 1098
SURGERY
Address: Hôpital Nord, chemin Bourrely, 13015 Melle
Head: Professor Dalmas
Activities: Liver; pancreas.

LABORATORY OF PHOSPHO-CALCIC 1099
METABOLISM
Address: Groupe Hospitalier de la Timone, 13385 Melle Cedex 4
Head: Professor Simonin
Activities: Immuno-reactive calcitonen; Vitamin D.

Genetics - Paediatrics 1100

LABORATORY OF CLINICAL 1101
OBSTETRICS
Address: 144 rue Saint Pierre, 13005 Melle
Head: Professor Serment
Activities: Perinatal studies.

LABORATORY OF EMBRYOLOGY 1102
Head: Professor Cotte
Activities: Cytogenetics.

PAEDIATRICS INSTITUTE 1103
Address: 21 rue Virgile Marron, 13005 Melle
Head: Professor Orsini
Activities: Study of haemoglobins and erythrocytic enzymopathies; toxiplasmosomes.

Haematology 1104

LABORATORY OF HAEMATOLOGY 1105
Head: Professor Muratore
Activities: Blood cytology.

Hormonology 1106

LABORATORY OF BIOLOGICAL 1107
CHEMISTRY
Head: Professor Rolland
Activities: Proteins; thyro-globulin; thyroid hormonogenesis and proteins.

LABORATORY OF CLINICAL 1108
ENDOCRINOLOGY
Address: Groupe Hospitalier de la Timone, 13385 Melle Cedex 4
Head: Professor J. Vague
Activities: Diabetes.

LABORATORY OF ENDOCRINOLOGY 1109
Head: Professor Boyer
Activities: Lipids; steroid hormones and polypeptides; enzymes.

LABORATORY OF HORMONE 1110
RECEPTORS
Address: Secteur Nord, boulevard P. Dramard, 13015 Melle
Head: Dr R. Martin
Activities: Oncologic hormonology.

LABORATORY OF 1111
NEUROENDOCRINOLOGY
Address: Secteur Nord, boulevard P. Dramard, 13015 Melle
Head: Dr C. Oliver
Activities: Hypothalamo-hypophyseal encephalins.

LABORATORY OF PROTEIN 1112
HORMONES
Head: Professor Lissitky

Neurology 1113

LABORATORY OF MEDICAL 1114
PHARMACOLOGY
Head: Professor P. Bouyard
Activities: Chronopharmacology.

LABORATORY OF NEUROMUSCULAR 1115
DISORDERS
Address: Groupe Hospitalier de la Timone, rue Saint Pierre, 13385 Melle Cedex 4
Head: Professor G. Serratrice
Activities: Degenerative diseases of the nervous system.

LABORATORY OF NEUROPHYSIOLOGY 1116
Address: Groupe Hospitalier de la Timone, rue Saint Pierre, 13385 Melle Cedex 4
Head: Professor Poneet

LABORATORY OF PATHOLOGICAL ANATOMY 1117
Head: Professor Toga
Activities: Cerebral ageing; cerebral hormone receptors.

LABORATORY OF PHYSIOLOGY 1118
Head: Professor J. Corriol
Activities: Neurophysiology; neurochemistry.

LABORATORY OF PSYCHOLOGY 1119
Address: Groupe Hospitalier de la Timone, rue Saint Pierre, 13385 Melle Cedex 4
Head: H. Luccioni
Activities: Clinical psychology.

LABORATORY OF VIROLOGY 1120
Address: Groupe Hospitalier de la Timone, rue Saint Pierre, 13385 Melle Cedex 4
Head: Professor Tamalet
Activities: Slow viral infections; nervous system disorders.

Respiratory System 1121

LABORATORY OF EXPERIMENTAL MEDICINE 1122
Head: Professor Grimaud
Activities: Respiratory physiology and physiopathology; bronchomatricity.

LABORATORY OF PATHOLOGICAL ANATOMY 1123
Head: Professor Payan
Activities: Thoracic pathology.

PNEUMOPHTHISIOLOGY STUDY AND RESEARCH 1124
Address: 84 rue de Lodi, 13006 Melle
Head: Professor Laval
Activities: Respiratory physiopathology.

ELECTRORADIOLOGY CENTRAL SERVICE 1125
Address: Groupe Hospitalier de la Timone, 13385 Melle Cedex 4
Head: Professor Chevrot
Activities: Radiocinematography; tomodensitometry.

LABORATORY OF ANATOMY 1126
Address: Secteur Nord, boulevard P. Dramard, 13015 Melle
Head: Professor Farisse
Activities: Traumatology.

LABORATORY OF ANATOMY 1127
Head: Professor Gambarelli
Activities: Dissection; anatomy and tomodensitometry; biomechanics.

LABORATORY OF BACTERIOLOGY 1128
Head: Professor Peloux
Activities: Anaerobics - dental flora.

LABORATORY OF CELL BIOLOGY AND HISTOLOGY 1129
Head: Professor Seite
Activities: Cell nuclei.

LABORATORY OF HISTOLOGY AND EMBRYOLOGY I 1130
Head: Professor Vitry
Activities: Cytology; experimental ultrastructures.

LABORATORY OF HYGIENE AND SOCIAL MEDICINE 1131
Head: Professor Gevaudan
Activities: Epidemiology; public health; environment.

LABORATORY OF IMMUNOLOGY 1132
Head: Professor Depieds
Activities: Auto-immunodiseases; immunological functions of macrophages.

LABORATORY OF INFORMATICS 1133
Head: Professor M. Roux
Activities: Epidemiologic statistics; automation in clinical research.

LABORATORY OF LEGAL AND OCCUPATIONAL MEDICINE 1134
Head: Professor Jullien
Activities: Pharmacokinetic study of alcohol.

LABORATORY OF NEPHROLOGY 1135
Address: Hôpital Sainte Marguerite, Melle
Head: Professor Muriscaco
Activities: Molecules.

LABORATORY OF NEUROSURGERY 1136
Address: Groupe Hospitalier de la Timone, 13385 Melle Cedex 4
Head: Professor Sedan
Activities: Cerebral stereotaxis.

LABORATORY OF PARASITOLOGY 1137
Address: Secteur Nord, boulevard P. Dramard, 13015 Melle
Head: Professor Nicoli
Activities: Organisms living within human cavities, especially the genito-urinary tract.

LABORATORY OF PARASITOLOGY 1138

Head: Professor Ranque
Activities: Parasitic immunity.

**LABORATORY OF PATHOLOGIC 1139
ANATOMY**

Address: Secteur Nord, boulevard P. Dramard, 13015
Melle
Head: Professor Lebreuil
Activities: Nephroblastomy; sympathetic blastomy.

**LABORATORY OF PHYSICAL 1140
MEDICINE**

Head: Professor Kaphan
Activities: Biophysics - nuclear medicine and
radioprotection.

LABORATORY OF PHYSICS 1141

Address: Secteur Nord, boulevard P. Dramard, 13015
Melle
Head: Professor P.J. Bernard
Activities: Cell electrophysiology.

TROPICAL HEALTH CENTRE 1142

Address: 416 chemin de la Madrague Ville, 13015 Marseille
Head: Professor Pene
Activities: Epidemiology and tropical health; health
economics in tropical zones.

**VESICULAR-URETHRAL EXPLORATION 1143
UNIT**

Address: Groupe Hospitalier de la Timone, 13385
Melle Cedex 4
Head: Professor Padovani
Activities: Radiological electromanometric and
electromyographic exploration of an infant's urinary
tract.

FACULTY OF PHARMACY 1144

Address: 27 boulevard Jean Moulin, 13005 Marseille

Laboratory of Analytical Chemistry 1145

Head: Professor J. Pastor
Activities: Automatic analysis.

Laboratory of Biological Chemistry 1146

Head: Professor J. Reynaud
Activities: Molecular hydrodynamics.

Laboratory of Biophysics 1147

Head: Professor A. Crevat
Activities: Protein-ligand interaction; uraemic
molecules.

Laboratory of Botany and Cryptogamy 1148

Head: Professor P. Regli
Activities: Antifungal substances.

Laboratory of Bromatology 1149

Head: Professor A. Gayte-Sorbier
Activities: Bromatology - analysis of medicines.

**Laboratory of Chemical Pharmacy and 1150
Legislation**

Head: Professor B. Cristau
Activities: Structure of medicines; pharmaceutical law.

**Laboratory of Galenic Pharmacy and 1151
Materia Medica**

Head: Professor P. Bernard
Activities: Plant chemistry.

Laboratory of General Chemistry 1152

Head: Professor R. Baret
Activities: Thermodynamics of ternary alloys.

**Laboratory of General Toxicology and 1153
Biotoxicology**

Head: Professor A. Viala
Activities: Biotoxicology and pharmacokinetics of
atomospheric pollution.

Laboratory of Human Biology 1154

Head: Professor M. Lanza
Activities: Reproduction biology; experimental
physiopathology.

**Laboratory of Hygiene, Microbiology, 1155
Parasitology and Zoology**

Head: Professor Ch. Grebus
Activities: Acariasis.

**Laboratory of Microbiology and 1156
Microbial Hygiene**

Head: Professor A. Cremieux
Activities: Antimicrobes; industrial fermentation.

Laboratory of Mineral Chemistry — 1157

Head: Professor J. Barbe
Activities: Treatment of molecules with therapeutic potential.

Laboratory of Mineral Chemistry and Hydrology — 1158

Head: Professor A. Arnoux
Activities: Continental and marine hydrology; littoral pollution; mineral chemistry.

Laboratory of Organic Chemistry — 1159

Head: Professor C. Ghiglione
Activities: Humus compounds.

Laboratory of Pharmaceutical Physics — 1160

Head: Professor Cl. Briand
Activities: Molecular pharmacology; radiochemistry; physico-chemical control of medicines.

Laboratory of Pharmaco- and Toxicokinetics — 1161

Head: Professor J.P. Cano
Activities: Pharmacokinetic study of medicines.

Laboratory of Pharmacodynamics — 1162

Head: Professor J. Mercier
Activities: Study of psychotropic drugs.

FACULTY OF SCIENCE, LUMINAY — 1163

Address: 70 route Léon Lachamp, case 901, 13288 Marseille Cedex 2

Department of Chemistry — 1164

LABORATORY OF BIOCHEMISTRY — 1165
Head: M Rosset
Activities: Nervous system; cerebral electrical activity.

LABORATORY OF MINERAL AND MACROMOLECULAR PHYSICAL CHEMISTRY — 1166
Head: Mme Carbonnel
Activities: Identification of chemical species by phase diagrams.

LABORATORY OF ORGANIC CHEMISTRY — 1167
Head: M Savidan
Activities: Study of chemical degradation of polychloride vinyl; terpenephenol condensation.

LABORATORY OF PHYSICAL CHEMISTRY — 1168
Head: M Peneloux
Activities: Methodology and practice of thermodynamic determinations; properties of polyphase fluid systems under high pressure - applications in petrol fluids.

Department of Information Mathematics — 1169

ARTIFICIAL INTELLIGENCE GROUP — 1170
Head: M Colmerauer
Activities: Natural languages; word recognition; logic and programming; robotics.

FUNCTIONAL ANALYSIS TEAM — 1171
Head: M Billard

LABORATORY OF INFORMATION THEORY — 1172
Head: M Bianco
Activities: Theory and practice of compilation; specialized programming language.

LABORATORY OF LOGICAL ANALYSIS — 1173
Head: Mme Preller-Ellison
Activities: Universal algebra; demonstration theory.

LABORATORY OF MATHEMATICS - INFORMATICS — 1174
Head: M Zeller-Meier
Activities: Operator and algebra in Hilbert space.

LABORATORY OF MATHEMATICS, MARSEILLE — 1175
Head: M Carmona
Activities: Lie groups and analysis applications.

LABORATORY OF NUMERICAL ANALYSIS — 1176
Head: M Morel
Activities: Analysis and information; partial equations; topology and algorithms.

LABORATORY OF THEORY OF NUMBERS — 1177
Head: M Rauzy
Activities: Risk process simulation.

Department of Molecular and Cell Biology   1178

INSTITUTE OF CYTOLOGY AND CELL BIOLOGY   1179
Head: M Buvat
Activities: Cytology and biochemistry of cell differences.

LABORATORY OF BIOMEMBRANE STRUCTURE AND FUNCTION   1180
Head: M Azoulay
Activities: Microbe physiology from an energetic aspect.

LABORATORY OF CELL PHYSIOLOGY   1181
Head: M Ducet
Activities: Plant bioenergetics.

LABORATORY OF HISTOLOGY AND ANIMAL MORPHOGENESIS   1182
Affiliation: Centre National de la Recherche Scientifique
Head: M Thouveny
Activities: Gene action in development and regeneration.

LABORATORY OF PLANT BIOCHEMISTRY   1183
Affiliation: Centre National de la Recherche Scientifique
Head: M Ricard
Activities: Regulation of the CALVIN cycle; aromatic compound degradation.

LABORATORY OF PLANT FUNCTIONS   1184
Head: M Peauol-Lenoel
Activities: Biology and molecular biology; plant physiology.

Department of Physics   1185

LABORATORY OF INFORMATICS AND MUSICAL ACOUSTICS   1186
Head: M Risset
Activities: Analysis and synthesis of musical sounds; musical acoustics and psycho-acoustics.

LABORATORY OF SOLID-STATE PHYSICS   1187
Head: M Hanus
Activities: Electronic structure of crystal-molecular-metal interfaces; modelling and biological systems.

LABORATORY OF SURFACES - INTERFACES   1188
Head: M Bienfait
Activities: Metallic semiconductor and metal-oxide semiconductor interfaces; phase changes in two dimensions.

LABORATORY OF THEORETICAL PHYSICS   1189
Head: M Mebkhout
Activities: Mathematical physics; physics of elementary particles.

PARTICLE PHYSICS CENTRE, MARSEILLE   1190
Head: M Aubert
Activities: Muon physics.

Department of Sea and Environmental Sciences   1191

ENDOUME MARINE STATION AND OCEANOGRAPHY CENTRE   1192
Address: rue de la Batterie des Lions, 13007 Marseille
Telephone: (091) 52 73 29
Affiliation: Centre National de la Recherche Scientifique
Director: Professor J.-M. Peres
Associate Director:
Ecophysiology of marine invertebrates - distribution in the pelagial; production in the pelagial; pollution and protection of the marine environment; hard substrates - bioconstruction, biodegradation; coral reefs and neighbouring environments; benthic production; microbiology and protophytes; marine biochemistry; physiology of crustaceans and shrimp farming; physiology of fishes and fish farming; biology of marine invertebrates; marine geology and sedimentology
Annual expenditure: £51 000-500 000
Activities: Both research and teaching, the principal laboratory activity being biological oceanography.
Facilities: The laboratories consist of two main buildings, at the Marine Station itself and on the University campus. Laboratories are well equipped, the library specializes in marine science. Four vessels allow work on shelf and upper slope areas: they are 18 m, 16 m with diving support, 9 m, and 6.5 m; a Boston whaler is also available. The station provides facilities for visiting investigators, especially encouraged to work in cooperation with one of the groups upon its permanent research programme.
Contract work: Yes

LABORATORY OF INVERTEBRATE 1193
MARINE BIOLOGY

Affiliation: Centre National de la Recherche Scientifique
Head: M Vitiello
Activities: Study of meiobenthos in the abyssal zones and the continental shelf.

LABORATORY OF MARINE GEOLOGY 1194
AND APPLIED SEDIMENTOLOGY

Affiliation: Centre National de la Recherche Scientifique
Head: J.J. Blanc
Activities: Marine and coastal geology; marine sedimentology; sedimentary petrology; applied sedimentary palaeoecology; cartography; geological remote sensing and photography.

LABORATORY OF MARINE 1195
HYDROBIOLOGY

Affiliation: Centre National de la Recherche Scientifique
Head: A. Bourdillon
Activities: Pollution: urban, domestic, thermic.

LABORATORY OF PLANT BIOLOGY 1196

Affiliation: Centre National de la Recherche Scientifique
Head: M Molinier
Activities: Phytosociology.

LABORATORY OF QUATERNARY 1197
GEOLOGY

Affiliation: Centre National de la Recherche Scientifique
Head: M Faure
Activities: Environmental evolution.

UNIT OF GEOGRAPHY 1198

Address: 29 avenue Robert Schumann, 13100 Aix-en-Provence
Head: Professor De Reparaz

Mediterranean Geography 1199

Head: Professor De Reparaz
Activities: Social and economic geography of the Mediterranean.

Physical Geography 1200

Senior staff: Professor Vaudour, Professor Nicod
Activities: Neotectonics; karstology; cartography; soil formation.

Fluid Mechanics Institute 1201

Address: 1 bis rue Honorat, 13003 Marseille
Activities: M Chauvin
Activities: Subsonic aerodynamics; supersonic biomechanics; energy.

Statistical Mechanics of Turbulence 1202
Institute

Address: 12 avenue Général Leclerc, 13003 Marseille
Head: Professor A. Favre
Activities: Turbulence flow; atmosphere-ocean interaction; wave generation.

Université d'Aix-Marseille 1203
III - Université de Droit, d'Économie et des Sciences

[Aix Marseille III University - Law, Economics and Sciences University]
Address: 3 avenue Robert Schumann, Aix-en-Provence
Telephone: (042) 59 99 20
Note: Two facilities are devoted to law and political sciences and to applied economics. Scientific units are listed below.

CENTRE SCIENTIFIQUE DE SAINT 1204
JÉRÔME

[Saint Jérôme Scientific Centre]
Address: 13397 Marseille Cedex 04
Telephone: (091) 98 90 10
Director: Professor Michel Dussardier
Graduate research staff: 100
Annual expenditure: F4 360 000
Contract work: Yes
Publications: Annual report.

Faculty of Science and Technology* 1205

Address: rue Henri Poincaré, 13397 Marseille Cedex 13
Dean: Professor Jean-Claude Maire

UNIT OF BASIC SCIENCES* 1206

Director: Professor Roger Coulon

UNIT OF SCIENTIFIC AND TECHNICAL 1207
RESEARCH

Department of Biology and Physiology 1208
Head: Professor Michel Dussardier
Activities: Neurophysiology.

Department of Earth Sciences 1209
Head: Professor J. Sougy
Activities: Structural geology; petrology; sedimentology; mineralogy.

Department of Organic Chemistry 1210
Head: Professor J. Metzger
Activities: Organic synthesis; oil chemistry; lipochemistry.

Department of Physics (Materials Science) 1211
Head: Professor J. Kern
Activities: Materials science - crystallography; metallurgy; photoelectricity; thin films; optics.

UNIT OF SCIENTIFIC AND TECHNICAL 1212
TRAINING*

Laboratory of Crystals Physics 1213
Telephone: (042) 98 90 10
Head: Professor L. Capella
Sections: Applied electron microscopy, Professor C. Boulesteix; electron microscopy and electron diffraction, Professor E. Gillet, Professor M. Gillet; physics of dislocations in metals, Professor F. Minari
Annual expenditure: $600 000
Activities: Surface and interface studies - structure and growth mechanisms of metallic crystals on various substrates (main materials: gold, palladium, platinum, nickel, silver - possible applications to catalysis problems in the case of very small particles of palladium); role of growth conditions on the stability of the liquid-solid interface during the unidirectional solidification of dilute binary alloys (copper-lead).
Mechanical properties - structure of mechanical twins in rare earth oxides; behaviour of dislocations in highly perfect metal crystals (copper, silver-tin, gallium) under controlled stresses.
Facilities: Transmission electron microscope; scanning electron microscope; electron microprobe; auger spectroscopy; X-ray topographic cameras.

Laboratory of Photoelectricity 1214
Telephone: (042) 98 90 10
Head: Professor J.P. David
Sections: Polycrystalline and thin film semiconductors, Professor S. Martinuzzi; amorphous semiconductors, Professor H. Carchano
Annual expenditure: $100 000
Activities: Thin film transistors and insulators; photodiodes; solar cells.
Facilities: Light-induced current and photovoltage scannings; measurements of diffusion length and lifetime in semiconductors.

Université d'Angers 1215

[Angers University]
Address: 30 rue des Arènes, BP 3532, 49035 Angers Cedex
Telephone: (041) 88 58 43
President: J.-C. Remy
Activities: The policy of the University in matters of research is: to create a number of units or laboratories based on competence and actual results; to regroup the available potential of the University round a certain number of chosen themes which fall within the curriculum; to create a Centre of Cooperative Research associated to innovative workshops (this would be especially valuable to industries); to create a number of common service centres with equipment for research. These centres can be used by other public or private establishments and the five current ones are listed below.

Faculty of Letters and Sciences 1216

Address: 30 rue Mégevand, 25030 Besançon Cedex
Telephone: (081) 82 25 01

Faculty of Medicine and Pharmacy 1217

Address: place Saint Jacques, 25030 Besançon Cedex
Telephone: (081) 81 11 45
Dean: Professor Jacques Berthelay

DEPARTMENT OF MATHEMATICS, 1218
INFORMATICS, STATISTICS
Head: M.D. Bozon
Activities: Mathematical analysis in biology; classification methods; multidimensional series.
Contract work: Yes

DEPARTMENT OF 1219
OTORHINOLARYNGOLOGY AND
AUDIOPHONOLOGY
Senior staff: J.Cl. Lafon, J. Guichard, M.A. Menegaux
Activities: Deafness; neonatal motor responses; education of deaf children; noise and learning; audiology; pathology and noise.
Contract work: Yes
Publications: Bulletin d'Audiophonologie, quarterly.

LABORATORY OF ANATOMY AND 1220
ORGANOGENESIS
Head: Professor Henri Duvernay
Activities: Vascular system in the human brain; biomechanical studies of the sciatic nerve; arthrology.

LABORATORY OF BACTERIOLOGY, 1221
VIROLOGY, PARASITOLOGY
Head: Professor Yvon Michel-Briand
Activities: Bacterial adaptation (especially in an antibiotic environment and dealing with the resistance mechanisms); study of the human bacterial environment.
Contract work: Yes

LABORATORY OF BIOCHEMISTRY 1222
Head: Professor Jean Charles Henry
Activities: Lipid-protein interactions; role of enzymes in metabolic activity; enzyme biosynthesis; biochemical study of the heart; protein and enzyme composition of the gonad.
Contract work: Yes

LABORATORY OF BIOPHYSICS AND 1223
NUCLEAR MEDICINE
Address: CHU, place Saint Jacques, 25030 Besançon Cedex
Telephone: (081) 82 80 23
Head: Professor Roland Bidet
Activities: Radioelement exploration of skin and kidneys; scintigraphic images for hepatic examinations; information microprocessors.
Contract work: Yes

LABORATORY OF CHEMICAL 1224
PHARMACY
Heads: Professor J.J. Panouse, Professor J.F. Robert
Activities: Synthesis of molecules with medicinal properties; structure-action relations in biology; analytical chemistry and bromatology - chromatography; aromatic substances; cheese; pesticides in dairy produce; statistical studies of wine analyses.
Contract work: Yes

LABORATORY OF CLINICAL 1225
DERMATOLOGY
Address: CHU, place Saint Jacques, 25030 Besançon Cedex
Telephone: (081) 82 80 23
Head: Professor Pierre Agache
Activities: Skin photosensitivity; solar radiation; psoriasis; sebaceous secretions; viral papilloma.
Contract work: Yes

LABORATORY OF EXPERIMENTAL 1226
ANAESTHESIOLOGY
Heads: Professor F. Barale, Professor A. Niedhardt
Activities: Electrical anaesthesia; extra-corporal oxygenation; effect of cardiac drugs on an inadequate respiratory system.
Contract work: Yes

LABORATORY OF EXPERIMENTAL 1227
MEDICINE
Head: Professor Jean-Pierre Maurat
Activities: Study of the effect of phenytoin on the rat's metabolism; experimental laboratory work on drugs and cardiac conditions.

LABORATORY OF EXPERIMENTAL 1228
STUDY
Address: Clinique Universitaire de Gynécologie et d'Obstétrique, CHU, Rond Point du Pont Carot, 25030 Besançon Cedex
Telephone: (081) 82 80 89
Head: Professor Claude Colette
Activities: Social attitudes to adolescents and sex; biology of adolescent growth, reproductive system and genitalia; surgical treatment for female sterility.
Contract work: Yes

LABORATORY OF EXPERIMENTAL 1229
SURGERY
Address: CHU, place Saint Jacques, 25030 Besançon Cedex
Telephone: (081) 82 80 23
Head: Professor P. Milleret
Activities: Work on the ligatures of the rat's inferior vena cava; anastomosis in the rat's portal vein.

LABORATORY OF GALENIC 1230
PHARMACY
Head: J. Millet
Activities: Capsule formulae; powder dissolution; capsule manufacture; bacteriostatics; bacterial or anti-fungal agents of natural origin.

LABORATORY OF HISTOLOGY, 1231
EMBRYOLOGY, CYTOGENETICS
Head: Professor Claude Bugnon
Activities: Glandular neuroendocrinology and cytophysiology in humans and other mammals and non-mammalian vertebrates. Human cytogenetics - chromosomal aberrations; prenatal chromosome aberrations; fibroblast culture. Male sterility and spermology; cytoimmunology.
Contract work: Yes

LABORATORY OF HUMAN 1232
PHYSIOLOGY
Head: Professor Jacques Berthelay
Activities: Study of the use of glucose and fatty acids during muscular activity and the evolution of the hormonal system during these activities. Homeostatic control mechanisms: hypertension; hormonal adaptation in the obese; parathyroid activity in the formation of hypercalcaemia.

LABORATORY OF IMMUNOLOGY AND   1233
HAEMATOLOGY
Head: Professor André Peters
Activities: Immunology-transplants;   cryobiology;
rheology of red corpuscles and platelets.

LABORATORY OF MEDICAL   1234
MATERIALS
Head: Professor M. Leboeuf
Activities: The study of medicinal plants in overseas
areas and French African countries.
Publications: Research reports.

LABORATORY OF PATHOLOGICAL   1235
ANATOMY
Address: CHU, place Saint Jacques, 25030 Besançon
Cedex
Telephone: (081) 82 80 23
Head: Professor André Oppermann
Activities: Cancer of the uterus and steroid hormones
in the rat; cell cultures and caryotypes applied to human
tumours; non-tumour pathology. Scientific cooperation
with the Ministry of Foreign Affairs.

LABORATORY OF PHARMACEUTICAL   1236
MICROBIOLOGY
Head: Jacques Panouse
Activities: Immunologically active substances; electron
microscopic studies of ultrastructure which affect the
hepatitis virus, and immunity; lecithin-cholesterol compositions.

LABORATORY OF PHARMACEUTICAL   1237
PHYSIOLOGY
Head: D. Durand
Activities: Role of the central neurotransmitters in the
secretion of the growth hormone in the non-
anaesthetized rat.
Contract work: Yes

LABORATORY OF ZOOLOGY AND   1238
PARASITOLOGY
Head: Professor Pierre Tran Ba Loc
Activities: Cancer immunochemotherapy; oncogenic
viruses.
Publications: Research reports.

Clinical Pharmacology Service   1239
Address: CHU, place Saint Jacques, 25030 Besançon
Cedex
Telephone: (081) 82 80 23
Heads: Professor Pierre Bechtel, Professor Bernard
Vandel
Activities: Studies on the correlation between the
plasmatic concentration of antidepressants and their
clinical effects; interaction between amitriptyline and
phenothiazine in man; biotransformation of hepatic

drugs in man; effects of 2-3 DHP drugs in heart conditions; biotransformation of phenazone in diabetic diseases.

Hepatology and Gastroenterology Service   1240
Address: CHU, place Saint Jacques, 25030 Besançon
Cedex
Telephone: (081) 82 80 23
Head: Pierre Carayon
Activities: Clinical pharmacology - appreciation in vivo
and in vitro of the hepatic biotransformation of medi-
cines in humans; medicinal enzymatic induction;
hepatoxicity of xenobiotics. Medical pedagogy; digestive
cancer; gastric secretions; viral hepatitis.
Publications: Research reports.

Neurology and Psychiatry Clinic   1241
Address: CHU, place Saint Jacques, 25030 Besançon
Cedex
Telephone: (081) 82 80 23
Heads: Professor Pierre Volmat, Dr Gérard Allers
Activities: Psychopharmacology; psychopathology of
non-verbal communication; clinical psychiatry; clinical
psychology.

Neurosurgery Service   1242
Head: Professor Raoul Stelmle
Activities: Micro-sutures and intercranial anastomosis;
microsurgery and intercranial aneuyisms; cancer pains.

Ophthalmology Service   1243
Address: CHU, place Saint Jacques, 25030 Besançon
Cedex
Telephone: (081) 82 80 23
Heads: Professor Jean Royer, Professor André Roth
Activities: Physiopathology of visual perception; ocu-
lar microcirculation and pigment distribution; ocular
surgical techniques especially new instruments and
biocompatibility; documentation; lacrimal duct.

Paediatrics Clinic   1244
Heads: Professor André Raffi, Professor André Noir
Activities: Research is currently concentrated on infant
pathology: nervous system; metabolic disorders; respiratory, circulatory, urinary, renal problems; infectious
diseases; neonatalogy; genetics.

Pneumonology Service   1245
Address: CHU, place Saint Jacques, 25030 Besançon
Cedex
Head: Professor André Depierre
Activities: Research on therapeutic treatment for
cancer of the lungs.

Radiology Central Service   1246
Address: CHU, place Saint Jacques, 25030 Besançon
Cedex
Telephone: (081) 82 80 23
Head: S. Schraub
Activities: Fundamental research is carried out on
radiation dosages used in gynaecological therapy. Other

subjects of research include: intestinal tolerance after radiation treatment; chemotherapy and radiotherapy to treat cancer of the rectum and other cancers; epidemiologic research; cancer patient rehabilitation; new drugs.

Radiology Service 1247

Address: CHU, place Saint Jacques, 25030 Besançon Cedex
Telephone: (081) 82 80 23
Head: Professor F. Weill
Activities: The use of echotomography to study the digestive system, especially hepatopancreatic activity.
Publications: Research reports.

Urology Service 1248

Address: CHU, place Saint Jacques, 25030 Besançon Cedex
Telephone: (081) 82 80 23
Head: Professor M. Bittard
Activities: Cancer studies - determining population risks of obtaining urinary cancer; urinary cancer statistics; bowel and prostate cancers; regional chemotherapy. Incontinence; transplants; male sterility; hyperparathyroidism; medical diagnosis in urology; mathematical analysis of urinary cancers; renal calculi detection by means other than X-ray.

Faculty of Science and Technology 1249

Address: route de Gray, 25030 Besançon Cedex
Telephone: (081) 53 81 22
Dean: Professor Jean Bulabois

LABORATORY OF ANIMAL 1250 PHYSIOLOGY

Address: place Leclerc, 25042 Besançon Cedex
Telephone: (081) 80 32 67
Head: Professor Jean Ripplinger
Activities: Comparative research on the control mechanisms and regulatory processes of contractile activity.

LABORATORY OF APPLIED 1251 MECHANICS

Head: Professor Raymond Chaleat
Activities: Linear and non-linear structural vibrations; theoretical and experimental studies of materials and continuous mediums; mechanism and microtechnology.
Contract work: Yes

LABORATORY OF ASTRONOMY 1252

Address: Observatoire, 41 bis, avenue de l'Observatoire, 25000 Besançon
Telephone: (081) 50 30 88
Head: Professor G. Moreels
Activities: Physics of the planets' atmospheres; galactic dynamics; Spacelab; space research in collaboration with other countries, ie Canada, USSR.

LABORATORY OF BIOCHEMISTRY 1253

Head: Professor Yves Gaudemer
Activities: Oestrogen metabolism and activity; prostaglandin metabolism and activity; ontogenesis of the communication system and renal physiology of the young child.

LABORATORY OF BIOLOGY AND 1254 ANIMAL ECOLOGY

Head: Professor Pierre Real
Activities: After several years of collecting ecological observations the research field has been narrowed down to the study of ecophysiological and ethological problems.
Contract work: Yes

LABORATORY OF BOTANY 1255

Address: place Leclerc, 25042 Besançon Cedex
Telephone: (081) 80 32 67
Head: Professor B. Millet
Activities: Recurrent phenomena in growth and development; response mechanisms.
Contract work: Yes

LABORATORY OF CRYSTALLOGRAPHY 1256 AND MINERAL SYNTHESIS

Head: Professor Henri Merigoux
Activities: Crystal growing; radiocrystallography.
Contract work: Yes

LABORATORY OF 1257 ELECTROCHEMISTRY

Head: Professor Robert Guy
Activities: Vitrified and crystallized mineral polymers - preparation, structure, chemical properties, electric and electronic chemistry; thin film technology and electrochromatic properties; solid-liquid interaction in a dispersive medium.
Contract work: Yes

LABORATORY OF EXPERIMENTAL 1258 TAXONOMY AND PHYTOSOCIOLOGY

Head: Professor M. Bidault
Activities: Current research is centred on phytosociology and ecology of the Jura using numerical analysis. Laboratory work is concentrated on management, nature protection, complete studies of ecosystems, ie structure and function.
Contract work: Yes

LABORATORY OF GENERAL 1259 CHEMISTRY

Head: Professor Claude Devin
Activities: Synthesis and physico-chemical studies of coordinated compounds; metallic compounds; catalytic activity; mineral synthesis.

LABORATORY OF HERZIAN 1260
SPECTROSCOPY AND ELECTRONICS
Head: Professor J. Gérard Theobald
Activities: Electron resonance; molecular structure and frequency.

LABORATORY OF HISTORIC GEOLOGY 1261
AND PALAEONTOLOGY
Address: place Leclerc, 25042 Besançon Cedex
Telephone: (081) 80 32 67
Head: Professor Yves Rangheard
? *Activities:* Stratigraphic and structural studies in the Mediterranean and Indo-Madagascan areas; palaeoecologic evolution through the study of post-palaeozoic sediments; palaeontology; cartography; hydrogeology; soil management.
Contract work: Yes

LABORATORY OF HYDROBIOLOGY 1262
AND HYDROECOLOGY
Address: place Leclerc, 25042 Besançon Cedex
Telephone: (081) 80 32 67
Head: Dr J. Verneaux
Activities: Biology of aquatic systems; comparative bio-coenosis; relationships between species and habitats; experimental ecology.
Contract work: Yes

LABORATORY OF MATHEMATICS 1263
Groups: Non-linear analysis, Professor Ph. Benilan, Professor Jacques Robert; numerical theory, Professor Robert Bantegnie, Professor G. Gras, Professor J. Cougnard

LABORATORY OF MOLECULAR 1264
PHYSICS
Heads: Professor Louis Galatry, Professor Daniel Robert
Activities: Research is concentrated on potential inter-molecular energy and its effect on absorption or diffusion.
Publications: Research reports.

LABORATORY OF NUMERICAL 1265
ANALYSIS AND INFORMATICS
Groups: Numerical analysis, Professor Jean Claude Miellou, Professor Pierre Lesoint; informatics, Professor M. Trehel, A. Jaurat
Activities: Numerical analysis - resolution of numerical problems in engineering and physics; finite-element techniques; algorithms; stability of systems; approximate integration; multiprocessors. Informatics - parallel calculus; language programming.

LABORATORY OF OPTICS 1266
Head: Professor Jean-Charles Viénot
Activities: Optical-digital treatment of images; spatio-temporal optics; surface metrology and structure formation; technology and instrumentation.
Contract work: Yes
Publications: Research reports.

LABORATORY OF ORGANIC 1267
CHEMISTRY
Head: Professor Bernard Laude
Activities: Dipolar cycloadditions; reaction of ninhydrins to aromatic substances; isolation, synthesis and properties of indolic derivatives as applied to plant growth.

LABORATORY OF PETROGRAPHY AND 1268
MINERALOGY
Heads: Professor J. Thiebaut, Professor J.P. Karche
Activities: Petrology - magmatic evolution and metamorphosis; clay minerals in tertiary and quaternary formations in the Jura. Applied geology - materials exploitation.
Contract work: Yes

LABORATORY OF PLANT ECOLOGY 1269
AND PEDOLOGY
Address: place Leclerc, 25042 Besançon Cedex
Telephone: (081) 80 32 67
Head: Professor S. Bruckert
Activities: Properties of the soil in relation to vegetation and climate in the Jura mountains.
Contract work: Yes
Publications: General reports.

LABORATORY OF 1270
PSYCHOPHYSIOLOGY
Head: Professor Hubert Montagner
Activities: Communication systems in insect societies; communication systems in hibernating mammals; communication systems and biological rhythms in infants.

LABORATORY OF STRUCTURAL AND 1271
APPLIED GEOLOGY
Address: place Leclerc, 25042 Besançon Cedex
Telephone: (081) 80 32 67
Heads: Professor Pierre Chauve, Professor Pierre Broquet
Activities: Structural studies in the Mediterranean area; geology of the Jura mountains; hydrogeology; road construction; fuels; secondary sources of energy; petrological studies.
Contract work: Yes

LABORATORY OF THEORETICAL MECHANICS
1272

Heads: Professor Pierre Capodanno, Lucette Losco
Activities: Hydrodynamics; analytical mechanics; celestial mechanics.

LABORATORY OF THEORETICAL PHYSICS
1273

Head: Professor Philippe Pluvinage
Activities: Studies on Rydberg states of an atom with thin film potential; the reformulation of the bases of physics in view of modern logical needs in the teaching of mathematics; didactic-paedagogic relations in education.

LABORATORY OF ZOOLOGY AND EMBRYOLOGY
1274

Address: place Leclerc, 25042 Besançon Cedex
Telephone: (081) 80 32 67
Head: Professor Lucien Gomot
Activities: Sexual differentiation and reproductive system of the Helix aspersa; heart structure and function in amphibians.
Note: The Centre Universitaire d'Héliciculture was set up in 1978 to study means of increasing the species of edible snails and to consider problems of import.
Contract work: Yes

EXACT AND NATURAL SCIENCES UNIT
1275

Address: boulevard Lavoisier, Belle-Beille, 49045 Angers Cedex
Telephone: (041) 48 32 24
Dean: Professor Lucien Gouin

Algebra and Geometry
1276

Head: Professor A. Beauville
Activities: Algebraic geometry; Fano variations; algebraic surfaces.

Applied Statistics
1277

Head: J. Bayer
Activities: Statistics; analysis; perception; environment; music.

Differential and Relative Geometry
1278

Head: Professor C. Latremolière
Activities: Differential variations and their application to theoretical physics: general relativity.

Informatics Applied to Physics
1279

Head: Professor J. Moret Bailly
Activities: Thermic problems in informatic programmes (FORTRAN).

LEIMDL
1280

Head: Professor M. Thibeau
Activities: Raleigh and Raman diffusion; integral intensities; correlations of orientation and density.

Metallic Vapours
1281

Head: Professor Y. Leycuras
Activities: Spectroscopic study of metallic atoms.

MEDICAL AND PHARMACEUTICAL SCIENCES UNIT
1282

Address: Medical Section, rue Haute de Reculée, 49000 Angers
or: Pharmacy Section, 16 boulevard Daviers, 49000 Angers
Telephone: (041) 48 04 22; 48 14 22
Dean: Honorary Professor Jean Émile

Department of Clinical Sciences
1283

Address: CHU 1, avenue de l'Hôtel-Dieu, 49040 Angers Cedex
Telephone: (041) 88 69 51

CHRONIC ILLNESS A
1284

Head: Professor R. Bonniot
Activities: Atherosclerosis prevention; occupational medicine: hygiene and nutrition.

CLINICAL OBSTETRICS AND GYNAECOLOGY
1285

Head: Professor P. Grosieux
Activities: Ultrasonic exploration; foetal surveillance; urodynamic exploration; ovary tubes microsurgery.

DERMATOVENEREAL DISEASES
1286

Head: J.-L. Verret
Activities: Photobiology, electronic microscopy and dermatosis.

DIABETIC NUTRITION
1287

Head: Dr J. Bøyer
Activities: C-peptide dosages in diabetes.

GENERAL MEDICINE C
1288

Head: J.-C. Bigorgne
Activities: Autoimmunity and hypophysical pathology.
Contract work: Yes

GENETICS AND BIOCHEMISTRY   1289
Address: Genetics, 1 avenue de l'Hôtel-Dieu, 49040 Angers Cedex
or: Biochemistry, boulevard Daviers, 49040 Angers Cedex
Telephone: (041) 88 69 51; 48 14 22
Head, Genetics: Professor L. Larget-Piet
Head, Biochemistry: Professor A. Desjobert
Activities: Prenatal diagnosis of genetic diseases; serum analysis of the neural tract during pregnancy; myoglobin dosages in the amniotic cavity as a means of diagnosing myopathy during pregnancy; metabolic diseases during the neonatal period; hyperthyroid conditions during the neonatal period.
Contract work: Yes

MEDICAL CLINIC B   1290
Heads: Professor Fresneau, Dr Fressinaud
Activities: Arterial hypertension; role of hypertension.

MICROSURGICAL STUDIES   1291
Head: Honorary Professor J. Desnos
Activities: Venal grafts on the arteries of young rats.
Contract work: Yes

NEUROLOGY   1292
Senior staff: J.-L. Truelle, Honorary Professor J. Émile, J.-M. De Bray
Activities: Frontal-lobe syndromes; involuntary movements; Parkinson's disease; vertebro-basilar circulation, Doppler effect; bismuth encephalopathy.
Contract work: Yes

OPHTHALMOLOGY   1293
Head: A. Bechetoille
Activities: Microsurgical experiments on glaucoma; role of prostaglandins; haemato-ocular barrier; microinformatics in ophthalmology.
Contract work: Yes

ORTHOPAEDIC SURGERY AND REPAIR 1294
Head: L. Piolhorz
Activities: Strength of the femur after fracture; prevention of phlebothrombosis; homografts in the treatment of osteitis.

PNEUMOPHTHISIOLOGY   1295
Senior staff: E. Tuchais, J.-L. Racineux
Activities: Analysis of whistling sounds in the lung; bronchial asthma.
Facilities: Magnetophone; sonometer; pneumatograph.
Contract work: Yes

PSYCHIATRY   1296
Address: Psychotherapeutic Centre, BP 3607, 49036 Angers Cedex
Telephone: (041) 66 79 08
Head: Honorary Professor R. Wartel
Activities: Clinical pharmacology of mental diseases.

RADIOLOGY   1297
Senior staff: C. Caron-Poitreau, Professor J. Caron
Activities: Tomography: renal lesions and cancers; lumbar cancers.

RHEUMATOLOGY   1298
Head: Professor J.-C. Renier
Senior staff: Dr M. Bernat, Dr M. Audran
Activities: Vitamin D; osteomalacia; osteoporosis; idiopathic calculus.
Contract work: Yes

UROLOGY   1299
Head: Professor L. Rognon
Activities: Incontinence; cancer of the prostate gland.

Department of Fundamental Sciences   1300

ANATOMY   1301
Address: 1 rue Haute de Reculée, 49000 Angers
Telephone: (041) 48 04 22
Heads: Professor J. Pillet, P. Albarct
Activities: Artery and vein vascular systems.

BACTERIOLOGY   1302
Address: CHU, avenue de l'Hôtel-Dieu, 49040 Angers Cedex
Telephone: (041) 88 69 51
Head: B. Carbonnelle
Activities: Human infections and their relation to bacteria in the environment.

HAEMATOLOGY AND   1303
IMMUNOPATHOLOGY
Address: CHU, 1 avenue de l'Hôtel-Dieu, 49040 Angers Cedex
Telephone: (041) 88 69 51
Senior staff: Honorary Professor D. Hurez
Activities: Frequency of abnormalities in monoclonal immunoglobulins; autoimmunity in endocrine glands; myelodysplasia and acute secondary leukaemia.
Contract work: Yes

HISTOLOGY-EMBRYOLOGY   1304
Address: 1 rue Haute de Reculée, 49000 Angers Cedex
Telephone: (041) 88 69 51
Head: Professor A. Rebel
Senior staff: M. Basle
Activities: Study of the cell structure of the bone tissue

in Paget's disease and the meaning of cytologic anomalies in osteoclasts; origins of osteoclasts; the application of ultrastructural techniques and histomorphometry to bone diseases.
Contract work: Yes

IMMUNOALLERGENICS 1305

Address: CHU, 1 avenue de l'Hôtel-Dieu, 49040 Angers Cedex
Telephone: (041) 88 69 51
Head: A. Sabbah
Activities: Allergy immunopathology; lymphoblast transformations; cells and mediators of immediate hypersensitivity.

MATHEMATICAL BIOLOGY 1306

Address: 1 rue Haute de Reculée, 49000 Angers Cedex
Telephone: (041) 48 04 22
Head: G. Chauvet
Activities: Mathematical models in theoretical biology; ventilation mechanics; electrophysiology; cell biology; auto-organization of molecular systems and regulatory mechanisms.
Contract work: Yes

MEDICAL BIOCHEMISTRY 1307

Address: 1 rue Haute de Reculée, 49000 Angers Cedex
Telephone: (041) 48 04 22
Head: Professor M. Girault
Senior staff: J. Marcais, A. Girault
Activities: Molecular pathology; amniotic fluids; proteins of a chymotripsic nature; endocrine disorders caused by cirrhosis of the liver; aldosterone dosages.

MEDICAL BIOPHYSICS 1308

Address: 1 rue Haute de Reculée, 49000 Angers Cedex
Telephone: (041) 48 04 22
Head: Professor P. Jallet
Senior staff: Dr P. Laget
Activities: Membrane biology.
Contract work: Yes

MICROBIOLOGY 1309

Head: Professor J.-C. Darbord
Activities: Antibacteria; spores; radio-sterilization; antiseptics; disinfectants; sterilization.

NEUROPHYSIOLOGY 1310

Address: 1 rue Haute de Reculée, 49000 Angers Cedex
Telephone: (041) 88 04 22
Head: J. Chanelet
Activities: Neurophysiology and neuropharmacology of the spine marrow; neuropharmacology of the synaptic structure.
Contract work: Yes

PARASITOLOGY, ZOOLOGY, 1311
MYCOLOGY

Head: Professor J.-M. Senet
Activities: Parasite immunology and fungi; substances possessing anti-fungal and anti-parasitic properties.
Contract work: Yes

PATHOLOGICAL ANATOMY 1312

Address: CHU, avenue de l'Hôtel-Dieu, 49040 Angers Cedex
Telephone: (041) 88 69 51
Head: Professor C. Simard
Activities: Various fields of histology especially through the use of a fluorescent microscope.

PHARMACODYNAMIC PHYSIOLOGY 1313

Head: Professor M. Prelot
Activities: Growth hormone and phospho-calcic metabolism; cell mechanism of the renal hypophosphoric action of the growth hormone; hormonal and nutritional factors in the control of the cyclic secretion of growth hormones.

PHARMACOLOGY 1314

Address: CHU, 1 avenue de l'Hôtel Dieu, 49040 Angers Cedex
Telephone: (041) 88 69 51
Head: Honorary Professor P. Allain
Activities: Pharmacology and metabolism of oligo-elements; study of the metabolism of various medicines and their toxins and mediums.
Contract work: Yes

PHYSIOLOGY 1315

Address: CHU, 1 avenue de l'Hôtel-Dieu, 49040 Angers Cedex
Telephone: (041) 88 69 51
Head: Professor D. Coullaud
Activities: Pulmonary transfer of carbon oxide in both a normal condition and in apnoea.

PLANT MEDICINE STUDY CENTRE 1316

Head: Professor J. Bruneton
Activities: The Centre's role is to improve the quality of existing information on plants with a view to their exploitation in diverse areas: therapeutic, pharmaceutical, agro-alimentary industry. It conducts research with industry and acts as a technical and scientific advisory body for the production industry in terms of quality control and improvement.

RADIOBIOLOGY   1317
Address: Centre Paul-Papin, 2 rue Moll, 49000 Angers Cedex
Telephone: (041) 48 10 66
Head: Honorary Professor F. Larra
Activities: Cell kinetics; radiotherapy; carcino-embryonic antigens; beta microglobulin.
Contract work: Yes

Department of Pharmaceutical   1318
Sciences
Address: 16 boulevard Daviers, 49000 Angers Cedex
Telephone: (041) 48 14 22

ANALYTICAL CHEMISTRY   1319
Head: Professor J. Jolivet
Activities: Medicinal plants: cultivation, picking, drying, storing; pesticides and herbicides.

BOTANY AND CELL BIOLOGY   1320
Head: Professor C. Pareyre
Activities: Cell physiology; ultrastructural cytology; cytotoxicology; cell kinetics.

ORGANIC CHEMISTRY   1321
Head: Professor L. Gomes-Mavoungu
Activities: Study of the furan group especially in relation to pharmacology.
Contract work: Yes

RAW MATERIALS AND MEDICINE OF   1322
NATURAL ORIGINS
Head: Professor J. Bruneton
Activities: Chemical structure; secondary metabolites; alkaloids; synthesis of structural analogues.

SCIENCE AND TECHNOLOGY UNIT   1323
Address: boulevard Lavoisier, Belle-Beille, 49045 Angers Cedex
Telephone: (041) 48 46 12

Animal Biology   1324
Head: Professor G. Matz
Activities: Cytopathology (tumours), immunology and embryology of insects.
Contract work: Yes

Animal Physiology and Biochemistry   1325
Head: Professor J. Schwander
Activities: Effect of pesticides on the physiology of organisms; cell physiology of the nerve system; ornithological studies.

Bioorganic Chemistry   1326
Head: Professor J. Fournier
Activities: Biological structures and activities.
Contract work: Yes

Energetics   1327
Head: Professor André Roux
Activities: Restoration of high temperatures in materials subjected to neutron radiation by thermic cycles.

Geology   1328
Head: R. Brossé
Activities: Sedimentology; sedimentary petrography.

Mineral and Thermodynamic   1329
Physicochemistry
Heads: Professor J.-C. Remy, Y. Pauleau
Activities: Study of materials in thin layers: physical chemistry; electric properties; electronic microscopy.
Facilities: Spectrometer; calorimeters.

Molecular Structure   1330
Head: Professor B. Taravel
Activities: Area of coordination of heavy atoms in mineral and organic complexes with the aid of molecular spectroscopy.

Natural Sciences and Biology   1331
Heads: Professor A. Diara, Professor J. Roger
Activities: Biology; transformation; evolution; living matter; heredity; chemistry.

Non-linear Optics   1332
Head: Professor G. Rivoire
Activities: High-powered lasers; molecular physics; information.

Organic Chemistry   1333
Sections: Theme 1, Professor Lucien Gouin; Theme 2, R. Mornet; Theme 3, J. Cousseau
Activities: Reaction of acetylene compositions to additives; ethanoyl trisubstitutes; chemistry of hormones derived from waste matter; utilization of ion complexes.
Contract work: Yes

Plant Biology   1334

Head: Professor M. Astie
Activities: Physiology and morphogenesis of reproduction; germination inhibition; reproduction in vitro.
Facilities: Reichert microscope; climatic chambers; culture chambers.

Solar Energy   1335

Head: Professor J. Hladik
Activities: Mathematical modelling of energetic phenomena in direct and indirect isolation.
Contract work: Yes

Ultrasonic Physics   1336

Head: Professor C. Magnien
Activities: Acoustic spectroscopy; marine plankton.

Zoology   1337

Head: Professor A. Gabriel
Activities: Biochemical studies of the regeneration of Turbellaria in fresh waters.

UNIVERSITY INSTITUTE OF   1338
TECHNOLOGY, BELFORT

Address: rue Engel Gros, 90016 Belfort
Telephone: (081) 21 01 00

Laboratory of Electrical Engineering   1339

Head: Professor Jean-Marie Kauffmann
Activities: Electromechanic converters associated with non-linear devices.
Contract work: Yes

ARTIFICIAL INTELLIGENCE   1340
Head: Professor G. Stamon
Activities: Choice of relevant characteristics; improvement of biomedical imaging; automatic diagnosis (medical applications).
Contract work: Yes

MATERIALS RHEOLOGY AND FLUID   1341
MECHANICS
Heads: Professor Claude Olknine, Professor Gérard Mandret
Activities: Heat transfer in porous media; rheology of the blood in microcirculation.
Contract work: Yes

OPTICAL RESEARCH   1342
Head: Professor Jean Pierre Prenel
Activities: Ocular microsurgery; visualization and measurement of supersonic emissions.

Université de Bordeaux I*   1343

[Bordeaux University I]
Address: 351 cours de la Libération, 33405 Talence
Telephone: (056) 80 69 50
See also entry for: Observatoire de Bordeaux.

LIPIDS RESEARCH INSTITUTE*   1344
Director: J. Valade

MARINE BIOLOGY INSTITUTE*   1345

MATHEMATICS RESEARCH   1346
INSTITUTE*

METAL ASSAYING LABORATORY*   1347
Director: R. Naslain

PINE RESEARCH INSTITUTE*   1348
Director: J. Valade

SCHOOL OF CHEMICAL   1349
ENGINEERING*

SCHOOL OF ELECTRONICS AND   1350
RADIOELECTRICAL ENGINEERING*
Head: Professor G. Bousseau

UNIT OF BIOLOGY*   1351
Head: Professor Chaperon

UNIT OF CHEMISTRY*   1352
Head: Professor Gasparrou

UNIT OF GEOLOGICAL STUDIES IN AQUITAINE* 1353

Head: Professor Klingebiel

UNIT OF MATHEMATICS AND DATA PROCESSING* 1354

Head: Professor M. Garandel

UNIT OF PHYSICS* 1355

Head: Professor Charru

UNIT OF SCIENCES* 1356

Head: Professor M. Pinot

UNIVERSITY INSTITUTE OF TECHNOLOGY* 1357

Director: Professor P. Descaurion

Université de Bordeaux II* 1358

[Bordeaux University II]
Address: 146 rue Léo Saignat, 33076 Bordeaux
Telephone: (056) 90 91 24

AFFILIATED RESEARCH INSTITUTES* 1359

Centre for Biological Studies of Wild Animals* 1360

Address: Villiers en Bois, 79360 Beauvoir sur Niort
Head: Dr M. Boissin

Research Group on Hormone Behaviour and Neurobiology* 1361

Address: 24 rue Paul-Broca, Bordeaux
Head: Professor J.D. Vincent

Research Unit on Cardiology* 1362

Address: Hôpital du Tondu, Bordeaux
Head: Professor H. Bricaud

Research Unit on Experimental Radiology and Cancerology* 1363

Address: Fondation Bergonié, 180 rue de Saint-Genès, Bordeaux
Head: Dr Duplan

Research Unit on Immunology of Parasitic Diseases* 1364

Address: Domaine de Carreire, rue Camille Saint-Saens, Bordeaux
Head: Professor R. Pautrizal

Research Unit on the use of Radioactive Isotopes in Medicine and Biology* 1365

Address: Domaine de Carreire, rue Camille Saint-Saens, Bordeaux
Head: Professor P. Blanquet

UNIT OF BIOCHEMISTRY AND CELLULAR BIOLOGY* 1366

Director: Professor Begueret

UNIT OF DENTISTRY* 1367

Director: Professor Fourteau

UNIT OF ENVIRONMENTAL BIOLOGY AND PHYSIOPATHOLOGY* 1368

Director: Professor Varene

UNIT OF MEDICAL SCIENCES I* 1369

Director: Professor J.-D. Vincent

UNIT OF MEDICAL SCIENCES II* 1370

Director: Professor J. Tavernier

UNIT OF MEDICAL SCIENCES III* 1371

Director: Professor Quinton

UNIT OF PHARMACEUTICAL SCIENCES* 1372

Director: Professor Crockett

UNIT OF PSYCHIATRY*   1373

Director: Professor Bourgeois

UNIT OF SOCIAL AND   1374
PSYCHOLOGICAL SCIENCE*

Director: Professor Artemenko

Centre of Industrial Psychology*   1375

Institute of Applied Human Sciences* 1376

Director: Professor Saingolet

Institute of Industrial Medicine*   1377

Institute of Industrial Pharmacy*   1378

Institute of Oenology*   1379

Director: Professor J. Ribéreau-Gayon

Institute of Surgical Research*   1380

UNIT OF TROPICAL MEDICINE AND   1381
HYGIENE UNIT*

Director: Professor G. Moretti

Université de Bretagne   1382
Occidentale

[University of Western Brittany]
Address: rue des Archives, BP 137, 29269 Brest Cedex
Telephone: (098) 03 24 83
President: Professor Michel Quesnel

FACULTY OF DENTISTRY   1383

Address: avenue Camille Desmoulins, BP 815, 29279
Brest Cedex
Director: Christiane Castel Dupont

FACULTY OF MEDICINE   1384

Address: rue Camille Desmoulins, BP 815, 29000 Brest
Cedex
Dean: Professor Gabriel Le Menn

FACULTY OF SCIENCE AND   1385
TECHNOLOGY

Address: 6 avenue Victor le Gorgeu, 29000 Brest
Cedex
Director: M Le Bihau

UNIVERSITY INSTITUTE OF   1386
TECHNOLOGY, BREST

Address: Plateau du Bouguen, 29000 Brest Cedex
Director: Professor Guglielmetti

Applied Biology (Environmental   1387
Health) Department

Business Administration Department   1388

Electrical Engineering Department   1389

Mechanical Engineering Department   1390

UNIVERSITY INSTITUTE OF   1391
TECHNOLOGY, LORIENT

Address: rue Jean Zay, 56100 Lorient
Director: Professor Jean-Jacques Quéméner

Heat Engineering Department   1392

Hygiene and Safety Department   1393

UNIVERSITY INSTITUTE OF   1394
TECHNOLOGY, QUIMPER

Address: rue de l' Université, 29000 S-Quimper-
Penhars
Director: Professor Lucien Le Cam

Applied Biology (Food Sciences)   1395
Department

Business Administration Department   1396

Commercial Techniques Department   1397

Transport and Logistics Department   1398

Université de Caen*   1399

[Caen University]
Address: Esplanade de la Paix, 14032 Caen
Telephone: (031) 94 81 61

SCHOOL OF CHEMICAL   1400
ENGINEERING*

UNIT OF FOOD TECHNOLOGY AND 1401
NUTRITION*

Head: Professor P. Boivinet

UNIT OF HUMAN SCIENCES AND   1402
DATA PROCESSING*

Head: Professor J. Guglielmi

UNIT OF LIFE SCIENCES*   1403

Head: Professor G. Prunus

UNIT OF MEDICINE*   1404

Head: Professor R. Villey

UNIT OF PHARMACEUTICAL   1405
SCIENCES*

Head: Professor J.-V. Le Talaer

UNIT OF SCIENCES*   1406

Head: Professor M. Ebel

UNIT OF SOIL SCIENCES AND   1407
REGIONAL DEVELOPMENT*

Head: Professor F. Dore

UNIVERSITY INSTITUTE OF   1408
TECHNOLOGY (PHYSICS AND
APPLIED BIOLOGY)*

Address: boulevard Maréchal Juin, 14032 Caen
Head: Professor J.-P. Leroux

Université de Clermont-   1409
Ferrand II

[Clermont-Ferrand University II]
Address: UER de Recherche Scientifique et Technique, 24 avenue des Landais, BP 45, 63170 Aubière
Telephone: (078) 26 41 10
President: Pierre Cabanes
Activities: Research plays a large part in the University's programme: the Observatory is entirely geared
towards research, the School of Chemistry and the Unit
of Exact and Natural Sciences have each developed their
own research programme. Since its foundation the
University has improved the quality of its research in
terms of interdisciplinary studies, and outside relationships especially with other universities and with industry. The science and technology laboratories receive the
aid of the CNRS.
Contract work: Yes
See separate entry for:
Institut et Observatoire de Physique du Globe du Puy-
de-Dôme
Laboratoire de Géochronologie et Volcanologie.

Unit of Exact and Natural Sciences   1410

Address: Ensemble Scientifique des Cézeaux, BP 45,
63170 Aubière
Telephone: (078) 26 41 10
Research director: Professor Alain Kergomard
Annual expenditure: F981 000 (1980)
Activities: The Unit plays a large role in developing the
research potential of the whole region. Of the 29
research groups, 12 are linked to the CNRS, 18 have
contacts with public or private organizations. Its policy
is to concentrate on the practical aspects within the
national and regional economy.
Publications: Research reports.

ANIMAL BIOLOGY AND EMBRYO   1411
TOXICOLOGY
Head: Professor Hubert Lutz
Activities: Pesticides; sexuality; pineal gland.

ANIMAL PHYSIOLOGY   1412
Head: Professor Paul Delost
Activities: Androgenous hormones; androgens and en-
docrine cycles.

APPLIED MATHEMATICS   1413
Head: Jean-Pierre Crouzeix
Activities: Probability and functional analysis; numerical analysis and optimization; probability calculus; applied informatics; didactics.

BIOCHEMISTRY AND GENETIC ENGINEERING 1414
Head: Roger Durand
Activities: Biochemistry of mitochondrial membranes; mitochondria and cardiac metabolism; biochemical engineering.

BIOLOGY AND PLANT PHYSIOLOGY 1415
Head: Jean Claude Fondeville
Activities: Biological rhythms and irritability; applied microbiology; meristem organization and activity; photoreception and plant movements; Tuberales; dormancy.

CELL BIOLOGY AND GENETICS 1416
Head: Honorary Professor Jean-Pierre Dufaure
Activities: Cytogenetics; cytophysiology; genetics.

CHEMISTRY AND BIOCHEMISTRY OF RAW MATERIALS 1417
Head: Jean-Claude Gramain
Activities: Chemical and photochemical synthesis of nitrogenous substances; chromatography of gaseous states.

CIVIL ENGINEERING 1418
Head: Maurice Lemaire
Activities: Granular materials and structures.

CORPUSCULAR PHYSICS 1419
Head: P. Bertin
Activities: Theoretical analysis; nuclear physics; hadron scattering; photon-photon diffusion; heavy ions; applied nuclear physics; photon-atom interaction, nuclear spectrometry.

CRYSTALLOGRAPHY AND PHYSICS OF CONDENSED PHASES 1420
Head: Robert Cadoret
Activities: Growth parameters in gas vapour phases; vapour growth of HgI_2 in sealed ampoules.

ELECTRONICS AND MAGNETIC RESONANCE 1421
Head: Professor Ginette Berthet
Activities: Semi-and organic conductors; liquid crystals; instrumentation.

MATERIALS PHYSICS 1422
Head: Professor Jean Roche
Activities: Dielectrics, magnetoelectric effects; electric arc; crystallography and physical chemistry of materials.

MINERAL CHEMISTRY 1423
Head: Professor Robert Kohlmuller
Activities: Crystalline growth; synthesis and properties of rhodites.

ORGANIC BIOCHEMISTRY 1424
Head: Professor Alain Kergomard
Activities: Ionophoric antibiotics; bioconversions; organic synthesis.

ORGANIC CHEMISTRY 1425
Head: Professor Roger Vessière
Activities: Epoxide and episulphur reduction and synthesis; carbon-carbon nucleophile reactions; acetylene and allenic synthesis and reduction; aziridines; vinyl-cyclopropanes.

ORGANIC ELECTROCHEMISTRY 1426
Head: Jacques Simonet
Activities: Electrochemical reduction; coordination chemistry; graphite as a cathode material; sulphones; epoxides.

ORGANIC SPECTROSCOPY 1427
Head: Daniel Besserre
Activities: Magnetic resonance study of structures; molecular movements of organophosphorous compounds, especially in relation to biology.

PETROLOGY 1428
Address: 5 rue Kessler, 63000 Clermont-Ferrand
Telephone: (073) 93 35 71
Head: Honorary Professor Jacques Kornprobst
Activities: Volcanology and hydrothermics; geochronology; metamorphic strata and granitoids; mineralogy; mathematical analysis; mass spectrography; atomic absorbtion spectrometry; experimental petrography.

PHYSICAL CHEMISTRY 1429
Head: Jean-Pierre Morel
Activities: Thermodynamics and kinetic chemistry; thermodynamics of binary liquid mixtures; photochemistry.

PHYSICAL METEOROLOGY 1430
Head: Professor R.G. Soulage
Activities: Dynamic and thermodynamic atmospheric parameters; convective cloud formations; physics of the environment and its modification; radiosonde; cloud microphysics and photogrammetry; photography; synoptic meteorology; atmospheric chemistry.

PURE MATHEMATICS 1431
Head: Professor Françoise Hennequin
Activities: Algebra; mathematics; mathematical physics; logic; differential geometry.

RADIOELECTRONICS AND THEORY OF 1432 SOLIDS

Head: Professor G. Raoult
Activities: Cross-relaxation studies; microwaves and materials; Herzian polarimetry; microwave propagation; spin correlation.

SOLID-STATE CHEMISTRY   1433

Head: Professor Jean-Claude Cousseins
Activities: Physical properties of fluorous and oxyfluorous compounds of metallic elements; photoluminescence; electrical and magnetic properties.

WAVE PHYSICS   1434

Head: Professor René Combe
Activities: Guided propagation of acoustic and electromagnetic waves; electromagnetic theory of open resonators.

Biology Station, Besse en Chandesse   1435

Address: 63610 Besse en Chandesse
Telephone: 79 50 20
Sections: Botany, Professor J.E. Loiseau; Animal Biology, Professor P. de Puytorac
Activities: Plant life and habitat in the Loire and the Allier valleys; phytosociology and pedology of the Clermont region; Sahelian vegetation.

ZOOLOGY AND PROTISTOLOGY   1436

Head: vacant
Activities: Permeability and excitability of the Paramecium membrane; ruminant biology and microorganisms; biology and comparative cytophysiology of flagellate Protista; regional hydrobiology and ecology; insect cytophysiology; insecticides and protozoaic parasite transmission.

Unit of Technology   1437

Address: rue des Meuniers, BP 48, 63170 Aubière
Director: Professor Jacques Fontaine

BIOLOGICAL ENGINEERING   1438
DEPARTMENT

CIVIL ENGINEERING DEPARTMENT   1439

ELECTRICAL ENGINEERING   1440
DEPARTMENT

INFORMATION PROCESSING FOR   1441
MANAGEMENT DEPARTMENT

PHYSICAL ENGINEERING   1442
(INSTRUMENTATION) DEPARTMENT

ÉCOLE NATIONALE SUPERIEURE DE   1443 CHIMIE

[National College of Chemistry]
Address: Ensemble Scientifique des Cézeaux, BP 71, 63170 Aubière
Director: Professor Roger Vessière

Laboratory of Photochemistry   1444

Head: Professor J. Lemaire
Activities: Polyolefine degradation; photochemical evolution of water pollutants; photochemistry of azo compounds.

Laboratory of Solid-State Chemistry   1445

Head: Professor Jean-Claude Cousseins
Activities: Luminescence; energy transfer.

MONTLUÇON UNIVERSITY   1446
INSTITUTE OF TECHNOLOGY

Address: avenue Aristide Briand, 03107 Montluçon
Director: Professor Michel Mercier

Electrical Engineering Department   1447

Mechanical Engineering Department   1448

Computation Centre   1449

Address: BP 45, 63170 Aubière
Telephone: (073) 26 41 10
Director: P. Lambey
Activities: The Centre caters for the teaching and research needs of the University by providing personnel and facilities.

Regional Centre of Measurement   1450

Address: Ensemble Scientifique des Cézeaux, BP 45, 63170 Aubière
Telephone: (073) 26 41 10
Head: Professor J. Lemaire
Activities: The Centre provides facilities for the University and the public and private laboratories in the field of: electron microscopy; radioactive beta rays; infrared spectrophotometry; nuclear magnetic resonance; radiocrystallography.

Université de Dijon   1451

[Dijon University]
Address: Campus Universitaire de Montmuzard, BP
138, 21004 Dijon Cedex
Telephone: (080) 66 64 13
Telex: 350188 F DIJUNIV
Chancellor: J. Lambert-Faivre
President: Jacques Vaudiaux
Activities: The University pursues a coherent and concerted research policy designed to instigate the formation of teams on common topics. It is linked to other major research centres, handles research contracts and organizes scientific conferences.
Contract work: Yes
Publications: Annual report.
See separate entry for: École National Supérieure de Biologie Appliquée à la Nutrition et à l'Alimentation.

EARTH SCIENCES UNIT   1452

Address: 6 boulevard Gabriel, 21000 Dijon
Dean: Professor Pierre Feuillée

Palaeobiological Research   1453

Director: Professor Henri Tintant
Activities: Jurassic Cephalopoda and Brachiopoda.

Quaternary Palaeoecology   1454

Director: Jean Chaline
Activities: Evolution of small mammals; the application of the results to prehistoric chronology and quaternary ecology; quaternary stratigraphy.

Sedimentary Geodynamics   1455

Director: Professor Pierre Rat
Activities: Sediments in orogenic areas, in stabilized areas, in tertiary areas; origin and evolution of detrital minerals; characterization of sedimentary layers.

LIFE AND ENVIRONMENTAL   1456
SCIENCES UNIT

Dean: J. Pagès

Applied Botany   1457

Director: Professor Roger Bessis
Activities: Research is centred on the vine, especially plant morphogenesis, reproduction and growth. Work is carried out in laboratories and in the field. The laboratory seeks to further relations with those in the wine-growing industry and will accept offers of collaboration even if these fall outside its immediate area of research.

Applied Psychophysiology   1458

Director: Professor Jean Parrot
Activities: Effects of noise on man, acquisition of, and recovery from aural fatigue; noise-muscular work interaction; effects of urban noise.

Biochemistry of Cell Interactions 1459

Director: Professor Bernard Maume
Activities: Cell cultivation without animal organs; biosynthetic regulation of steroid hormones and cholesterol by the kidney; regulation of the steroid hormone metabolism by the liver; application of cell culture to biochemical engineering by steroid synthesis.

Botany and Ecology   1460

Director: Professor François Bugnon
Activities: Morphology of plant organs; structure and function of meristems; embryogenesis; phytogeography and regional ecology.

Cellular and Plant Biology   1461

Director: Michel Guyot
Activities: Plant epidermis; cytophysiology of stomata.

General and Animal Biology   1462

Directors: Professor Jean Chaudonneret, Professor François Graf
Activities: Biology, anatomy and histophysiology of arthropods: biology, ecology and histophysiology of Peracarida crustaceans; anatomical morphology and evolution; biology and ecology of Myriapoda.

General Biochemistry   1463

Director: Professor Christian Baron
Activities: Biochemistry of the human skin; cellular biochemistry of prokaryotids; gibberellins and cytokinines.

Mineral Nutrition of Plants   1464

Director: Renée Strauss
Activities: Resistance of aquatic organisms to strong concentrations of ions in their environment; nutritional behaviour of algae which are able to live equally well in salt or sweet waters.

Plant Physiology 1465

Director: Professor Jeannine Monin
Activities: Physiology and biochemistry of plants in the higher kingdom: analysis of the respective roles played by genetic and physical factors; study of hormones and climate in dormancy; behaviour control of the embryo by means of its surroundings.

MATHEMATICAL, INFORMATION, 1466 PHYSICAL AND CHEMICAL SCIENCES UNIT

Dean: Maurice Person

Analytical and Applied Chemistry 1467

Director: Professor Maurice Person
Activities: Organic electrochemistry; analytical chemistry.
Facilities: Equipment for electrochemical analyses; Hewlett Packard 98-25A calculator.

Coordination Chemistry 1468

Director: Honorary Professor Michel Pâris
Activities: Stability of compounds in analytical and biological chemistry; compounds formed by polyelectrolytes and metallic ions, and their application in marine chemistry.

Crystal Optics 1469

Directors: Professor Étienne Coquet, Professor Michel Remoissenet
Activities: Theory and spectroscopy of elementary linear and non-linear excitations in crystals.

Electronics 1470

Director: Professor Pierre Cachon
Activities: Dispersion of the permittivity complex of dielectrics in terms of frequency.

Mathematical Physics 1471

Director: Professor Moshe Flato
Activities: Theory of mathematics and the application of such theories to fundamental physics, mechanical statistics and particle physics.

Molecular Spectrometry 1472

Director: Jacques Moret-Bailly
Activities: Vibration-rotation spectroscopy of molecules.
Facilities: Raman spectrometer; CARS spectrometer.

Numerical Analysis and Informatics 1473

Director: Pierre Loridan
Activities: Numerical analysis: theoretical and practical studies of convex and non-convex optimization; applications in the field of economy, systems control and biomathematics; informatics: artificial intelligence, form recognition.

Oenology 1474

Director: Professor Michel Feuillat
Activities: Wine colloids and their enzymatic decomposition: studies on fermentation, clarification and stabilization of wines; yeasts.

Organometallic Synthesis and 1475 Electrosynthesis

Director: Professor Jean Tirouflet
Activities: Organometallic compounds; heterocyclic chemistry; electrochemistry.

Probability 1476

Director: vacant
Activities: Dynamic systems in ergonomics.

Solid Reagents 1477

Director: Professor Pierre Barret
Activities: Equations in heterogenous kinetics; oxygen-ferrite interactions; oxy-hydrogen interactions; separation and adsorption on monocrystalline metallic surfaces in contact with hydrogen; oxy-metallic interactions; kinetics and mechanisms of hydration; corrosion; decomposition of crystal structures; solid-gas interfaces.

Solid-State Physics 1478

Directors: Professor Lucien Godefroy, Professor Pierre Vernier
Activities: Absorption and photoemission; photoelectron analyses; characterization of materials; photo-ferroelectric effects; network analysis; semiconductor surfaces.
Facilities: Helium liquifier; Raman spectrometer; lasers; X-ray diffractors; optical ammeter; angular spectrograph for photoelectrons; infrared spectrometer.

Theory of Physics 1479

Director: Guy Burdet
Activities: Classic mechanics, quantity mechanics, theory of Jauge; differential geometry.

Topology 1480

Director: Professor Robert Moussu
Activities: Singularities in differential and analytical geometry.

MEDICINE UNIT 1481

Address: 7 boulevard Jean d'Arc, 21000 Dijon
Dean: Professor J. Guerrin

Anaesthesiology 1482

Director: Professor Bernard Caillard
Co-director: Professor Michel Wilkening
Activities: Local-regional analgesics; post-operative and traumatic diets; operational research on the organization and foundation of a department of anaesthesia-reanimation.

Biophysics 1483

Director: Dr Jean-Louis Pelletier
Activities: Biophysical methods used in the exploration of the hypothalamus; algorithms and their use in tomography.

Burgundy Register of Digestive 1484 Cancers

Director: Professor Claude Klepping
Activities: Systematic registration of cases of digestive cancer in the Côte d'Or Département since January 1976. Among the activities of the Registry are: the study of those factors influencing the development of digestive cancers; research on the possibilities of prevention; comparison with the results produced by other Registries and also an analysis of the results in the different geographical sections of the Côte d'Or.

Carcinology 1485

Director: Professor Ferdinand Cabanne
Activities: Gonadic tumours; tumours of the mammary gland; malignant lymphoma of the lymphatic ganglions; pathological anatomy; therapeutic tests.

Cardiology 1486

Director: Professor Jean Bouhey
Activities: Clinical and pharmacological studies of antiarrhythmia; role of cholesterol in atherosclerosis.

Clinical Biology Research Group 1487

Activities: Physiopathology and immunology of transplantation; alterations to the immune response provoked by plasma exchange.

LABORATORY OF BACTERIOLOGY- 1488 VIROLOGY
Head: A. Kazmierczak

LABORATORY OF HAEMATOLOGY 1489
Head: J. Bonhomme

LABORATORY OF HYGIENE 1490
Head: Honorary Professor M. Caron

LABORATORY OF NEPHROLOGY AND 1491 TRANSPLANT IMMUNOLOGY
Head: G. Rifle

LABORATORY OF PARASITOLOGY AND 1492 MYCOLOGY
Head: P. Camerlynck

LABORATORY OF PHARMACOLOGY 1493
Head: A. Escousse

Clinical Gynaecology and Obstetrics 1494

Director: Professor Jean Jahier
Activities: Oncology; infectious diseases of the genitalia; prevention of premature birth.

Digestive Tumours Immunology and 1495 Biology

Director: Professor François Martin
Activities: Immunology and biology of digestive cancers in humans.

Experimental Surgery 1496

Director: Professor Camille Ferry
Activities: Vascular microsurgery on rats; arthrotomy of the knee; vascular malformations of the colon.

Functional Reeducation 1497

Director: Professor Jean-Pierre Didier
Activities: Energy use in the physically handicapped; artificial joints; ischaemic-heart metabolism.

Histology, Embryology, Cytogenetics 1498

Director: Professor Jean-Pierre Zahnd
Activities: Cytogenetics - chromosomal variations in man; Fanconi anaemia; carcinogenesis.

Infectious Diseases Laboratory 1499

Director: Professor Ferdinand Destaing
Activities: Antibiotic pharmacokinetics; antibiotic metabolism and concentrations in the blood; antibiotics in bile, bones and pleura.

Medical Biochemistry 1500

Director: Professor Prudent Padieu
Activities: Cell culture; regulation of steroid-hormone metabolism in vivo and in vitro in the perinatal period in man; metabolic process of cholesterol transfer in plasma lipoproteins; the effects of medicine on cancers.

Medical Informatics 1501

Director: Dr Liliane Dusserre
Activities: Mathematical models and their use in medicine; multidimensional statistics to aid medical decisions.

Neurosurgery Laboratory 1502

Director: André Thierry
Activities: Vascular surgery of small blood vessels; experimental studies on aneurysm.

Normal Anatomy 1503

Director: Professor Pierre Barry
Activities: Paediatrics; foetal anatomy and teratology; angiology; biomechanics.

Orthopaedic Traumatology Laboratory 1504

Director: Paul Grammont
Activities: Pressures on the knee; musculature of the shoulder; cancer prosthesis.

Paediatric Clinic 1505

Director: Professor Michel Alison
Activities: Statistical and epidemiological study of methods of care of the premature baby; caffeine blood levels in the premature baby; vitamin E in anaemia in premature infants; puerperal fever and renal complications in the new-born; congenital malformations.

Paediatrics II 1506

Director: Professor Jean-Louis Nivelon
Activities: Clinical and biological studies on neonatal paediatrics, medical genetics, and general paediatry.

Pathological Anatomy 1507

Director: Professor Robert Michiels
Activities: Experimental and human digestive carcinogenesis; statistical study of tumours in the Burgundy area; clinical-anatomical research on various subjects.

Physiology 1508

Director: Professor Jacques Klepping
Activities: Nutrition; myocardial biology and function; muscular physiology.

Pneumophthisis 1509

Director: Louis Jeannin
Activities: Study of the bronchia; kinetics of antibiotics in the pleura; radiotherapy in lung cancer.

Rheumatology Service 1510

Director: Professor Jean Strauss

Stomatology and Maxillo-Facial Surgery 1511

Director: Gabriel Malka
Activities: Cranio-facial congenital malformations; vascular surgery; odontology; prosthetic rehabilitation in cancer patients; facial surgery.

Surgery III 1512

Director: Professor G. Piganiol
Activities: Road injuries; accidents and protective measures; safety helmets and cyclists.

Surgical Clinic 1513

Director: Professor Henri Viard
Activities: Vascular pathology - juvenile arthritis, Raynaud syndrome; encysted tumours. Digestive pathology - gastro-oesophagus reflux; oesophagus dyskinesia; surgical treatment of digestive haemorrhage.

Urology 1514

Director: Professor Serge Briet

NUTRITION UNIT 1515

Address: Campus Universitaire, 21000 Dijon
Head: Professor Jean Bezzard

Animal Physiology and Nutrition 1516

Directors: Jean Bezzard, J. Clement
Activities: Lipid metabolism in the animal kingdom, especially in the rat.

Zoology 1517

Director: Charles Noirot
Activities: Research is concentrated on insects: biological development; chemistry of communication; cell biology.

PHARMACY UNIT 1518

Address: boulevard Jean d'Arc, 21000 Dijon Cedex
Dean: Professor Anne Zoll

Biophysics 1519

Director: Jean-Pierre Schreiber
Activities: Fluorometric methods in the study of molecular interactions.

Botany and Cryptogamy 1520

Director: Professor Alain Delcourt
Activities: Toxic action of metallic ions on algae and fungal cells.

Galenic Pharmacy and Industrial 1521
Technology

Directors: Professor Gabriel Nouvel, Professor Y. Pourcelot-Roubeau
Activities: Oral solids: powders, granules, jellies, capsules - pulverization, rheologic aptitude and mechanism; influence of methods of formulation and manufacture.

Legal Pharmacognosy 1522

Sole researcher: Sylvette Huichard
Activities: Pharmaceutical labelling.

Organic Chemistry and Chemical 1523
Pharmacy

Director: Professor Paul-Louis Compagnon
Activities: Analysis and study of medicinal metabolism; synthesis and radiochemical purity of marked molecules.

Pharmaceutical Biochemistry, 1524
Analytical Chemistry, Bromatology

Directors: Professor Nicole Autissier, Professor Roger Truchot
Activities: Biochemistry: enzyme induction by medicine in relation to nutritional and hormonal factors; analytical chemistry.

Pharmaceutical Physiology 1525

Director: Professor Jean Bralet
Activities: Metabolism and function in the renewal of chemical mediators in the nervous system, their regulatory mechanism and their modification in certain physiopathological situations; study of substances which affect the cardiovascular system.

Pharmacodynamics 1526

Director: Professor Jean-Robert Rapin
Activities: Pharmacokinetics of molecular formulae in a therapeutic and radio-diagnostic sense; cerebrovascular molecules in encephalographic models.

Pharmacognosy 1527

Director: Professor Anne Zoll
Activities: Flavones - extraction, separative chromatography, spectrophotometry.

Toxicology 1528

Director: Professor Marc Thevenin
Activities: Hepatotoxicity - action of toxics on the metabolism of lipids and proteins.

Université de Franche- 1529
Comté - Besançon

[Franche-Comte University]
Address: 30 avenue de l'Observatoire, 25030 Besançon Cedex
Telephone: (081) 50 81 21
President: Professor Pierre Lévêque *Vice-President and Head of Research:* Professor Jacques Robert
Activities: The University has structured its research activities around nine main themes: social attitudes; communication; mathematical, informatic andoptical methods applied to humanities and economics; regional studies; clinical pharmacology; reproduction and genetics biology; microtechnology; mathematicsand general physics; physical chemistry and biological functions of natural substances and of synthesis.
The University's scientific long- and short-term plans, and financial requirements are all based on the choice of these themes.
Publications: Annual report.
See separate entry for: Observatoire de Besançon.

ÉCOLE NATIONALE SUPÉRIEURE DE MÉCANIQUE ET DES MICROTECHNOLOGIES 1530

[Mechanics and Microtechnology National College]
Address: route de Gray, 25030 Besançon Cedex
Telephone: (081) 50 36 55
Director: Professor Raymond Chaleat

Laboratory of Automation 1531

Head: Professor François Lhote
Activities: Robots; vocal communication; parallel calculus; ultrasonic detection; assembly-line conduit systems.
Contract work: Yes

Laboratory of Chronometry and Piezoelectrics 1532

Head: Professor R. Besson
Activities: Resonators; wave volume; microtechniques; high-frequency waves.
Contract work: Yes

INSTITUTE OF CHEMISTRY 1533

Address: 32 rue Mégevand, 25030 Besançon Cedex
Telephone: (081) 81 36 78
Director: Professor Ernest Cerutti

Laboratory of Applied Chemistry 1534

Head: Ernest Cerutti
Activities: Organic synthesis and molecules.
Contract work: Yes

Laboratory of General Chemistry 1535

Head: Professor R. Perrot
Activities: Electrochemistry; physico-chemical composition of metals.
Contract work: Yes

Laboratory of Physical Chemistry 1536

Head: Professor J. Bernard
Activities: Work centres on the study of surfaces; structure of antimony and arsenic.
Contract work: Yes

Laboratory of Water Analysis 1537

Head: F. Remy
Activities: Analytical determination of phenol traces in industrial waters; of toxic minerals in waters by atomic absorption; the nature of solid pollutants in the air; pollutants in industrial effluents.
Publications: Pollution de l'Air, annual report.

UNIT FOR BIOLOGICAL AND MEDICAL RESEARCH AND FEEDING 1538

Address: place Saint Jacques, 25030 Besançon Cedex
Telephone: (081) 81 11 45
Director: Professor Jean-Pierre Maurat
Activities: The Unit is open to all those carrying out research in the Faculty of Medicine and Pharmacy, in addition to which, their equipment is made available to anyone carrying out research in the other faculties. The laboratories within the Unit are as follows:
Medicine and Pharmacy:
Pathological Anatomy
Bacteriology, Virology, Parasitology
Dermatology
Haematology (Blood Transfusion Centre)
Histology, Embryology, Cytogenetics
Zoology and Parasitology
Science and Technology:
Botany
Electrochemistry
Structural and Applied Geology
Animal Physiology
Psychophysiology
Zoology and Embryology.

Université de Haute Alsace 1539

[Haute Alsace University]
Address: 61 rue Albert Camus, 68093 Mulhouse Cedex
Telephone: (089) 42 68 82
President: Jean-Baptiste Donnet
Secretary-General: Bernard Schub
Annual expenditure: Flm
Activities: About 270 research staff work on private and public research in more than 20 laboratories. Emphasis is placed on socioeconomic needs but a balance is maintained between general and applied research. The University has several links with other countries as a result of contracts and congresses.
Publications: Annual report; various research publications.
See also: Centre de Recherches sur la Physico-Chimie des Surfaces Solides.

ÉCOLE NATIONALE SUPÉRIEURE DE 1540 CHIMIE DE MULHOUSE

[Mulhouse National College of Chemistry]
Address: 3 rue Alfred Werner, 68200 Mulhouse
Telephone: (089) 42 70 20
Director: J.P. Fleury

Laboratory of Applied Mineral 1541 Chemistry

Affiliation: Centre National de la Recherche Scientifique
Director: Professor J. Hatterer
Graduate research staff: 9
Activities: Physical chemistry of metal alkalines; physical chemistry of solid oxyderived alkalines: study, theory, applied research.
Contract work: Yes
Publications: Research reports.

Laboratory of General Mineral 1542 Chemistry

Director: Professor R. Wey
Graduate research staff: 4
Activities: All research is on silicates.
Contract work: Yes
Publications: Research reports.

Laboratory of General Photochemistry 1543

Director: J.P. Fouassier
Senior staff: Professor M. Rohmer
Graduate research staff: 18
Activities: Molecular photochemistry and photophysics; photochemical and photophysical processes in polymer mediums; applied photopolymerization; techniques development.
Contract work: Yes
Publications: Research reports.

Laboratory of Interface Physical 1544 Chemistry

Director: Professor J. Schultz
Graduate research staff: 15
Activities: Characterization of solid phase surfaces; polymer fission in a liquid state.
Contract work: Yes
Publications: Research reports.

Laboratory of Macromolecular 1545 Chemistry

Affiliation: Centre National de la Recherche Scientifique
Director: Professor G. Riess
Graduate research staff: 10
Activities: Synthesis and characterization of copolymers; solid-liquid phase copolymers; copolymer applications in colloidal chemistry; polymerization; subaquatic paints.
Contract work: Yes
Publications: Research reports.

Laboratory of Physical Chemistry of 1546 Solids

Director: J.M. Chezeau
Graduate research staff: 1
Activities: Diffusion in molecular crystals; interface molecular movements.

Laboratory of Synthesis and Organic 1547 Photochemistry

Affiliation: Centre National de la Recherche Scientifique
Director: Professor J. Streith
Graduate research staff: 9
Activities: Synthesis of poly-functional molecules thermic and photochemical behaviour.
Contract work: Yes
Publications: Research reports.

Laboratory of Textile Chemistry 1548

Director: Professor R. Freytag
Graduate research staff: 7
Activities: Hydrophilization of polyester fibres; ultraviolet whitening of cottons; use of liquid ammonia for treating cellulose to avoid pollution; hydrogen oxygen whitening of cottons; use of high frequency rays to improve textile quality.
Contract work: Yes
Publications: Research reports.

ÉCOLE NATIONALE SUPÉRIEURE DES 1549 INDUSTRIES TEXTILES DE MULHOUSE

[Mulhouse National College of Textile Industry]
Address: 11 rue Alfred Werner, 68200 Mulhouse
Telephone: (089) 42 100 11
Director: Professor R. Schulz

Laboratory of Mechanics and Rheology 1550

Director: Professor C. Wolff
Graduate research staff: 2
Activities: Noise pollution in the textile industry; hydro- and aerodynamic mechanisms in the textile industry; industrial filters; polymer rheology problems and their solutions.
Contract work: Yes
Publications: Research reports.

Laboratory of Physics and Textile Chemistry 1551

Director: Dr R. Schutz
Graduate research staff: 19
Activities: An original feature of this laboratory is the creation of a group involved in teaching, research and industry called 'Modèle Mulhousien'. The main areas of research concern the optimal use of raw materials; improving the processing cycle in terms of energy use and techniques; energy economy and antipollution.
Publications: Research reports.

INSTITUT INTERNATIONAL DE TRANSPORT 1552

[International Transport Institute]
Address: 12 rue d'Alsace, 68200 Mulhouse
Director: Professor Wackermann

INSTITUTE OF EXACT AND APPLIED SCIENCES 1553

Address: 4 rue des Frères Lumière, 68093 Mulhouse Cedex
Telephone: (089) 42 52 22
Director: André Jung

Laboratory of Electronics and Instrumentation 1554

Senior staff: Digital electronics, information sciences, Professor G. Metzger; linear electronics, automation, Professor F.M. Schmitt; nuclear physics, Professor R. Stein
Graduate research staff: 30
Activities: Systems modelling in particle physics; industrial automation; industrial computer sciences; signalling; medico-biological instrumentation.
Contract work: Yes
Publications: Research reports.

Laboratory of Information Sciences 1555

Director: Professor J.C. Spehner
Graduate research staff: 1
Activities: Study of various algorithms related to the theory of codes; isomorphism problems in graphs.
Contract work: Yes
Publications: Research reports.

Laboratory of Mathematics 1556

Director: Professor R. Lutz
Graduate research staff: 13
Activities: Research centres on the idea of transformation groups applied to the study of structures.
Publications: Research reports.

Laboratory of Physics and Electronic Spectroscopy 1557

Senior staff: Professor A. Jaegle, Professor A. Kalt, Professor R. Riedinger
Graduate research staff: 15
Activities: Surface and interface electronic structures; amorphic semiconductors; magnetic properties; theory of electronic structures; silicons and silicates; photoelectron spectroscopy.
Contract work: Yes
Publications: Research reports.

Laboratory of Solid-State Electronic Physics 1558

Address: 24 avenue Kennedy, 68200 Mulhouse
Telephone: (089) 42 01 55
Affiliation: Centre National de la Recherche Scientifique
Director: Professor R. Manquenouille
Graduate research staff: 4
Activities: Electric and electronic properties of metallic semiconductor interfaces.

UNIVERSITY INSTITUTE OF TECHNOLOGY 1559

Address: 61 rue A. Camus, 68093 Mulhouse Cedex
or: place du 2 Février, 68000 Colmar
Acting director: Professor R. Stein
Activities: Mulhouse - electrical and mechanical engineering; enterprise and administration management. Colmar - juridical and judiciary careers; commercialization techniques.

Electrical Engineering Department 1560

Head: Professor J. Gresser

Mechanical Department   1561

Head: Professor Robert Manquenouille

Université de Lille III - Sciences Humaines, Lettres et Arts   1562

[Lille University III - Human Sciences, Letters and Arts]
Address: Domaine Universitaire Littéraire et Juridique, Pont de Bois, BP 149, 59653 Villeneuve d'Ascq Cedex
President: Professor Jean Celeyrette

UNIT OF MATHEMATICS AND SOCIAL SCIENCES   1563

Director: M Mazet

UNIT OF REHABILITATION TECHNIQUES   1564

Director: M Frackowiac

UNIVERSITY INSTITUTE OF TECHNOLOGY   1565

Director: M Lancial

Université de Limoges*   1566

[Limoges University]
Address: allée André Maurois, 87065 Limoges Cedex
Telephone: (055) 01 60 55
President: R. Julien

CERAMICS RESEARCH CENTRE   1567

Affiliation: Centre National de la Recherche Scientifique
Director: Professor Michel Billy
Sections: Sintering and processing, P. Goursat; reactivity at high temperature, J. Desmaison; thermophysical properties, P. Fauchais; mechanical properties, P. Boch; structural studies, B. Frit
Graduate research staff: 35
Annual expenditure: £51 000-500 000
Activities: Nitrogen and special ceramics for high temperature applications.
Contract work: Yes

UNIT OF MEDICINE AND PHARMACY*   1568

Address: 2 rue du Dr Marcland, 87100 Limoges
Director: Professor M. Caix

UNIT OF SCIENCES*   1569

Address: 123 avenue Albert Thomas, 87060 Limoges Cedex
Telephone: (055) 79 46 22
Director: J.-L. Teyssier
Activities: Mathematics, physics, biochemistry, chemistry, physiology, plant biology, biology and animal ecology, geology.

UNIVERSITY INSTITUTE OF TECHNOLOGY*   1570

Address: allée André Maurois, 87065 Limoges Cedex
Director: J. Mexmain

Université de Metz   1571

[Metz University]
Address: Ile du Saulcy, 57000 Metz
Telephone: (087) 30 15 25
Affiliation: Académie de Nancy-Metz
Chairman: Professor Jean David

FACULTY OF EXACT AND NATURAL SCIENCES   1572

Dean: Professor Dominique Durand

Laboratory of Mechanical Reliability   1573

Telephone: (08) 730 58 40
Head: Professor G. Pluvinage
Senior staff: Fatigue Crack Propagation Division, C. Robin; Fracture of Wood Division, M Jodin; Low-cycle Fatigue Division, M Lebienvenu
Activities: Materials research - mechanical properties, plasticity, elasticity, fatigue, and rupture.
Facilities: Fatigue testing machines (S - 200T); split Hopkinson pressure bars; LAMMA.

Laboratory of Physics and Technology of Materials CRGPM   1574

Telephone: (08) 730 58 40
Head: Professor Bernard Baudelet
Senior staff: Superplasticity and rheocasting, M. Suery; sheet metal forming, J.M. Jalinier

Annual expenditure: F400 000
Activities: Areas of research include: superplasticity - fundamentals and industrial applications of copper-zinc alloys, copper-aluminium alloys and titanium alloys; sheetmetal forming - damage, rheology and plastic instability of aluminium alloys and steels; rheocasting - mechanical properties of semi-solid alloys and applications to forming operations.
Facilities: Scanning electron microscope; transmission electron microscope; uniaxial and biaxial testing apparatus; density measurements.
Publications: Annual report.

Physical Engineering Laboratory   1575

Telephone: (08) 730 15 25
Head: Professor C. Carabatos
Senior staff: Transition metal oxides lattice dynamics, G. Kugel; transition metal oxides band structure, J. Hugel; phase transitions in peroxides, M. Fontana; ferroelastics, D. Durand; automatic manufacturing, B. Mutel
Activities: Areas of research include: lattice dynamics and spin waves; phase transitions; electronic and optical properties of oxides; automatic manufacturing and classification. The laboratory plans to develop research on superconducting new materials such as Nb_3Ge, in collaboration with other laboratories.
Facilities: Raman scattering as a function of temperature; holography (up to 1 m² holograms); conductivity (electronic and ionic, AC or DC) and photoconductivity; computers.

UNIT OF ECOLOGY   1576

Address: 1 rue des Récollets, 57000 Metz
Director: Professor Jean Claude Pihan

UNIVERSITY INSTITUTE OF   1577
TECHNOLOGY

Telephone: (087) 30 15 25
Director: Professor Raymond Baro

Laboratory of Structural Metallurgy   1578

Telephone: (087) 30 58 40
Head: Professor Raymond Baro
Senior staff: Iron oxides reactivity, Professor J.J. Heizmann; crystallographic textures, Dr D. Ruer, Dr C. Eshing
Activities: Subjects of research include: theoretic and experimental methods for the determination of crystallographic textures; chemical reactivity sintering. The Laboratory has built an automatic pole figures recorder called TEXTUREX, which is now being marketed by Siemens; a new device is being developed.

Facilities: Thermogravimetric, specific area and porosity apparatus; automatic X-ray goniometers for texture analysis; scanning electron microscope.

Université de Montpellier I*   1579

[Montpellier University I]
Address: 39 rue de l'Université, 34060 Montpellier
Telephone: (067) 72 22 22

EUROPEAN INSTITUTE OF   1580
INDUSTRIAL PHARMACY*

UNIT OF ALIMENTARY AND   1581
BIOLOGICAL STUDIES*

Head: Professor S. Brun

UNIT OF DENTISTRY*   1582

Head: Professor L. Gourgas

UNIT OF INDUSTRIAL PHARMACY*   1583

Head: Professor H. Delenca

UNIT OF MEDICINE*   1584

Head: Professor P. Rabischong

UNIT OF PHARMACY*   1585

Dean: Professor J. Castel

Université de Nancy I   1586

[Nancy University I]
Address: BP 3137, 54013 Nancy Cedex
Telephone: (08) 332 81 81
Telex: NANCY I 960 646
President: Professor Michel Boulangé
Scientific Council: Professor Jean Protas

DENTAL SURGERY RESEARCH UNIT   1587

Director: Professor Vadot

Bacterio-odontology Department   1588

Head: Professor Marguerite

Dento-facial Orthopaedics   1589
Department

Head: Professor Heck

Experimental Surgery Department   1590

Head: Professor Durivaux

Neurophysiology Department   1591

Head: Professor Jacquart

Paedodontics Department   1592

Head: Professor Vadot

Parodontal Research Department   1593

Head: Professor Abt

Radiology Department   1594

Head: Professor Cresson

EARTH SCIENCES, METALLURGY   1595
AND INORGANIC CHEMISTRY
RESEARCH UNIT

Director: Professor Hertz

Applied Hydraulics and Civil   1596
Engineering Department

Head: Professor Durand

Applied Inorganic Chemistry   1597
Department

Head: Professor Herold

Metallurgical Thermodynamics   1598
Department

Head: Professor Hertz

Mineral Chemistry Department   1599

Affiliation: Centre National de la Recherche Scientifique
Head: Professor Roques

Mineralogy and Crystallography   1600
Department

Head: Professor Protas
Senior staff: Professor Becker

Pedology Department   1601

Head: Professor Souchier

Petrology and Geochemistry   1602
Department

Senior staff: Professor Rocci, Professor Brown

Physics of Metallic Deposits   1603
Department

Head: Professor Flechon

Regional Geology Department   1604

Head: Professor Gagny

Sedimentary and Structural Geology   1605
Department

Head: Professor Haguenauer

Sedimentology Department   1606

Head: Professor Hilly

Solid-State Physics Department   1607

Senior staff: Professor Gerl, Professor Janot

ENGINEERING SCIENCES INSTITUTE   1608

Director: Professor Mari

Automation and Applied Research   1609
Department

Head: Professor Humbert

Corrosion and Materials Protection   1610
Department

Head: Professor Germain

Fluid Mechanics and Energetics   1611
Department

Head: Professor Braun

Kinetic Chemistry and Applied   1612
Research Department

Head: Professor Mari

Mössbauer Spectrometry Department   1613

Head: Professor Genin

Spectroscopy and Molecular Structure 1614
Department

Head: Professor Grange

FOOD AND NUTRITION SCIENCE   1615
RESEARCH UNIT

Director: Professor Bonaly

Applied Biology Department   1616

Head: Professor Georges

Biochemistry Department   1617

Head: Professor Siest

Biological Chemistry Department   1618

Head: Professor Chapon

Botany Department   1619

Head: Professor Hayon

Centre d'Analyse des Milieux   1620
Alimentaires

[Alimentary Research Centre]
Affiliation: Centre National de la Recherche Scientifique
Head: M Thouvenot

Cryptogamy Department   1621

Head: Professor Lectard

Health Research Department   1622

Head: Professor Senault

Medical Biochemistry Department   1623

Head: Professor Nicolas

Medicine Department D   1624

Head: Professor Grilliat

Microbial Biochemistry Department   1625

Head: Professor Bonaly

Microbiology Department   1626

Head: Professor Schwartzbrod

Neonatal Medicine Department   1627

Head: Professor Vert

Nutrition and Metabolic Diseases   1628
Department

Head: Professor Debry

Organic Chemistry Department   1629

Head: Professor Loppinet

Paediatrics Department   1630

Head: Professor Pierson

Pharmacognosy Department   1631

Head: Professor Mortier

Public Health and Hygiene Research   1632
Department

Head: Professor Foliquet

Surgical Research Department   1633

Head: Professor Gaucher-Bigard

MATERIALS SCIENCE RESEARCH   1634
UNIT

Director: Professor Rocci

Analytic Chemistry and   1635
Electrochemistry Department

Head: Professor Bessière

Applied Photochemistry Department   1636

Head: Professor Deglise

Automation and Applied Research 1637
Department

Head: Professor Aubrun

Automation and Electricity 1638
Department

Head: Professor Frühhing

Biophysics Department 1639

Head: Professor Horn

Electronics and Physics of Interfaces 1640
Department

Head: Professor Ravalet

Experimental Physics Department 1641

Head: Professor Suhner

Heterogeneous Catalysis and Kinetics 1642
Department

Senior staff: Professor Duval, Professor Amariglio

Infrared Optics Department 1643

Head: Professor Hadni

Laboratoire de Recherches sur les 1644
Interactions Gas-Solides 'Maurice
Letort'

See separate entry.

Mechanical Physics Department 1645

Head: Professor Pujol

Organic Chemistry Department I 1646

Head: Professor Caubeve

Organic Chemistry Department II 1647

Head: Professor Castro

Organic Chemistry Department III 1648

Head: Professor Gross

Organic Physical Chemistry 1649
Department

Head: Professor Delpuech

Physical Chemistry and Petrochemistry 1650
Department

Senior staff: Professor Come, Professor Martin

Physics of Ionized Media Department 1651

Head: Professor Felden

Quantum Physics Department 1652

Head: Professor Weishinger

Spectroscopy and Microwave 1653
Technology Department

Affiliation: Centre National de la Recherche Scientifique

Head: M Roussy

Theoretical and Applied Electronics 1654
and Mechanics Department

Head: Professor Lebouche

Theoretical Chemistry Department 1655

Head: Professor Rivail

Theoretical Physics Department 1656

Head: Professor Baumann

Thermomagnetism Department 1657

Senior staff: Professor Mainard, Professor Fousse

MATHEMATICAL SCIENCE RESEARCH 1658
UNIT

Director: Professor Noverraz

Complex Analysis Department 1659

Head: Professor Noverraz
Senior staff: Professor Barlet

Computer Science Department 1660

Senior staff: Professor Derniame, Professor Haton

Elie Cartan Institute 1661

Head: Professor Noverraz

Equations with Incomplete Derived Functions Department   1662

Senior staff: Professor Lumer, Professor Huet

Functional Analysis Department   1663

Head: Professor Ferrier

Geometry Department   1664

Head: Professor Morlet

Harmonic Analysis and Group Theory Department   1665

Senior staff: Professor Eymard, Professor Rausseau, Professor Takahash, Professor Clere

Management Computer Science Department   1666

Senior staff: Professor Legras, Mme Rolland

Numerical Theory Department   1667

Head: Professor Legrens

Probability and Statistics Department   1668

Senior staff: Professor Depaix, Professor Schreiber

Scientific Computer Science Department   1669

Head: Professor Legras

Theory of Numbers Department   1670

Head: Professor Kaplan

Topology and Analysis Department   1671

Senior staff: Professor Berard-Bergery, Professor Ferrier, Professor Morlet, Professor Lannes

MEDICAL SCIENCE RESEARCH UNIT   1672

Adult Psychiatry Department   1673

Head: Professor Lexenaire

Anatomy Department A   1674

Head: Professor Cayotte

Anatomy Department B   1675

Head: Professor Borrely

Bacteriology Department   1676

Head: Professor Burdin

Biophysics Department   1677

Head: Professor Bertrand

Cancerology Department   1678

Head: Professor Chardot

Cardiology Department   1679

Senior staff: Professor Faivre, Professor Gilgenkrantz

Chemistry Department   1680

Head: Professor Burnel

Child Psychiatry Department   1681

Head: Professor Tridon

Child Surgery Clinic   1682

Senior staff: Professor Beau, Professor Prevot

Dermato-venereology Clinic   1683

Head: Professor Beury

Endocrinology Department   1684

Head: Professor Hartemann

Experimental Medicine Department   1685

Head: Professor Lacoste

Experimental Nephrology Clinic   1686

Head: Professor Cross

Experimental Neuroanatomy and Surgery Department   1687

Head: Professor Renard

Experimental Neuroradiology Department   1688

Head: Professor Luc Picard

Functional Rehabilitation and   **1689**
Reeducation Department

Head: Professor André

General Surgery Clinic   **1690**

Senior staff: Professor Grosdidier, Professor Frisch, Professor Lochard

Genetic Paediatrics Department   **1691**

Senior staff: Professor Neimann, Professor Pierson

Gynaecology and Obstetrics Clinic   **1692**

Senior staff: Professor Richon, Professor Ribon

Haematology Department A   **1693**

Head: Professor Herbeuval

Haematology Department B   **1694**

Head: Professor Streiff

Haemostasis Department   **1695**

Head: Professor Alexandré

Haemotheology Department   **1696**

Head: Professor Larcan

Hepatology and Gastroenterology   **1697**
Department

Head: Professor Heully

Immunology Department   **1698**

Head: Professor Duheille

Industrial Medicine Department   **1699**

Head: Professor Pernot

Infectious Diseases Department   **1700**

Head: Professor Dureux

Internal Medicine Department   **1701**

Senior staff: Professor Herbeuval, Professor Cuny, Professor Kissel, Professor Duc, Professor Schmitt

Legal Medicine Department   **1702**

Head: Professor De Ren

Medical Biochemistry Department   **1703**

Head: Professor Paysant

Medical Biology Department   **1704**

Head: Professor Crignon

Medical Computer Science   **1705**
Department

Head: Professor Martin

Microbiology Department   **1706**

Head: Professor De Lavergne

Nephrology Department   **1707**

Head: Professor Huriet

Neurology Clinic   **1708**

Head: Professor Arnould

Neurosurgery Clinic   **1709**

Senior staff: Professor Montant, Professor Lepoire

Ophthalmology Department   **1710**

Senior staff: Professor Thomas, Professor Cordier

Orthopaedics and Traumatology   **1711**
Department

Head: Professor Gosserez

Otorhinolaryngology Clinic   **1712**

Head: Professor Wayoff

Parasitology and Mycology   **1713**
Department

Head: Professor Percebois

Pathological Anatomy Department A   **1714**

Senior staff: Professor Duprez, Professor Rauber

Pathological Anatomy Department B   **1715**

Head: Professor Floquet

Pharmacology Department 1716

Head: Professor Lamarche

Pharmacology Department 1717

Head: Professor Royer

Physiology Department 1718

Head: Professor Arnould

Physiology of Sport Department 1719

Head: Professor Boura

Physiopathology Department 1720

Head: Professor Polu

Plastic and Reconstructive Surgery and 1721
Stomatology Department

Head: Professor Sommelet

Pneumology-Phthisiology Clinic 1722

Senior staff: Professor Lamy, Professor Anthoine

Radiology Department 1723

Senior staff: Professor Roussel, Professor Bernadac, Professor Treheux

Radiology Department 1724

Head: Professor Hoeffel

Readaptation Department 1725

Head: Professor Pierquin

Reanimation Department 1726

Head: Professor Larcan

Renal Physiopathology Department 1727

Head: Professor Maillie

Respiratory Physiopathology 1728
Department

Head: Professor Sadow

Rheumatology Department 1729

Head: Professor Gaucher

St Charles Hospital Research Centre 1730

Head: Professor Guerci

Thoracic Surgery and Cardiovascular 1731
Clinic

Head: Professor Chalnot

Urology Department 1732

Head: Professor Guillemin

PHARMACEUTICAL AND 1733
BIOLOGICAL SCIENCES RESEARCH
UNIT

Analytical Chemistry and Toxicology 1734
Department

Head: Professor Mirjolet

Bacteriology and Virology Laboratory 1735

Head: Professor Schwartzbrod

Biochemistry Department 1736

Head: Professor Siest

Biological Chemistry Department 1737

Head: Professor Pierfitte

Biological Sciences Applied to 1738
Pharmacy Department

Head: Professor Vigneron

Botany Department 1739

Head: Professor Haydon

Cryptogamy Department 1740

Head: Professor Lectard

Galenic Pharmacy Laboratory 1741

Head: Professor Hoffmann

Hygiene Department 1742

Head: Professor Girard

Inorganic Chemistry Department 1743

Head: Professor Martin

Mathematics Laboratory 1744

Head: Professor Dixneuf

Microbial Biochemistry Laboratory 1745

Head: Professor Bonahy

Microbiology Department 1746

Head: Professor Schwartzbrod

Organic Chemistry Department 1747

Head: Professor Loppiner

Pharmaceutical Law Department 1748

Head: Professor Lemay

Pharmacodynamics Department 1749

Head: Professor Besson

Pharmacodynamics Laboratory 1750

Head: Professor Jacque

Pharmacognosy Department 1751

Head: Dr Mortier

Toxicology Laboratory 1752

Head: Professor Rudler

PHYSICS, CHEMISTRY AND BIOLOGY RESEARCH UNIT 1753

Animal Biology Department 1754

Head: Professor Frentz

Applied Biochemistry Department 1755

Head: Professor Alais

Applied Biology Department 1756

Head: Professor Divies

Biological Behaviour Department 1757

Head: Professor Krafft

Biological Chemistry Department 1758

Head: Professor Gay

Biology of Insects Department 1759

Head: Professor Bareth

Botany and Microbiology Department 1760

Head: Professor Mangenot

Botany Department 1761

Head: Professor Dexheimer

Electronics Department 1762

Head: Professor Tosser

Experimental Cancerology and Radiology Department 1763

Head: Professor Burg

Experimental Surgery Department 1764

Head: Professor Frisch

General Physiology Department I 1765

Head: Professor Gayet

General Physiology Department II 1766

Head: Professor Davrainville

General Zoology Department 1767

Senior staff: Mme Professor Stephan, Professor Stephan

Histology Department 1768

Head: Professor Legait
Senior staff: Professor Burlet

Medical Biochemistry Department 1769

Senior staff: Professor Nabet, Professor Nabet-Belleville

Medical Biophysics Department 1770

Head: M Robert

Physiology Department I 1771

Head: Professor Boulangé

Physiology Department II 1772

Head: M Crancé

Phytopathology Department 1773

Head: Professor Goujon

Plant and Agricultural Physiology Department 1774

Head: Professor Garnier

Plant Biology Department 1775

Head: Professor Gadal

Plant Cytogenetics Department 1776

Head: Professor Kammacher

Psychophysiology Department 1777

Head: Professor Vuillaume

Surgery Department D 1778

Head: Professor Michon

Surgical Research Department (CHU Brabois) 1779

Head: Professor Benichoux

Zoological Investigation Department 1780

Head: Professor Condé

UNIVERSITY ATTACHED INSTITUTE 1781

Centre de Recherche en Informatique de Nancy 1782

[Computer Science Research Centre]
Address: CO 140, 54037 Nancy
Telephone: (08) 328 93 93
Telex: 960 646 F
Affiliation: Centre National de la Recherche Scientifique

Research directors: Professor Claude Pair, Professor Jean-Paul Haton
Senior staff: Language theory, compilation, M. Griffiths; software engineering, C. Pair, J.C. Derniame; pattern recognition and artificial intelligence, J.-P. Haton; information systems, data bases, M. Crehange; natural language processing, D. Coulon
Graduate research staff: 30
Annual expenditure: £51 000-500 000
Contract work: No

Université de Nantes 1783

[Nantes University]
Address: 1 quai de Tourville, BP 1026, 44035 Nantes Cedex
Telephone: (040) 89 73 16
President: Jacques Vilaine
Vice President, Research: Bruno Wojtkowiak
Publications: Annual report.

HIGHER NATIONAL COLLEGE OF MECHANICAL ENGINEERING 1784

Address: 1 rue de la Noë, 44072 Nantes, Cedex
Telephone: (040) 74 79 76
Director: Professor M. Pironneau
Activities: Mechanical structures and their conception, manufacture and exploitation.

Laboratory of Automation 1785

Affiliation: Centre National de la Recherche Scientifique
Head: Professor R. Mezencev
Activities: Identification; filtration; command of multivariable processes; repeating systems; numerical stimulation; image recognition.

Laboratory of Civil Engineering 1786

Head: Professor J. Vilaine
Activities: Construction materials mechanics; rheology; soil dynamics; oceanic engineering.

Laboratory of Diphasic Flow Dynamics 1787

Head: J.M. Fitremann
Activities: Diphasic flow; stratified flow; bubble studies; fluid mechanics; aeroacoustics.

Laboratory of Energetics   1788

Head: Professor R. Pointeau
Senior staff: Professor P. Le Lec
Activities: Metal corrosion mechanisms; electrochemistry; transfer and separation of materials in solution.

Laboratory of Marine Hydrodynamics   1789

Head: Professor P. Guevel
Activities: Marine and offshore industry; wave resistance, turbulence; numerical modelling; pollution.

Laboratory of Mathematics   1790

Affiliation: Centre National de le Recherche Scientifique
Head: Professor M. Larneau
Activities: Elastic and elastoplastic stability; continuous medium evolution dynamics; marine hydrodynamics; quantum mechanics.

Laboratory of Metal Physics   1791

Head: Professor S. Offret
Sections: Dynamic plasticity, Professor M. Leroy; surface and interface, Professor M. Cailler; new materials, Professor C. Becle
Activities: Electromagnetics; electrohydraulics, plasticity, deformation; materials; mathematical modelling.
Surfaces and interfaces in relation to mechanical behaviour; materials studies; spectroscopy.
Crystalline and mechanical properties; electron microscope studies.

Laboratory of Production Techniques   1792 and Technology

Head: Professor F. Lemaitre
Senior staff: Professor Ch. Bouchy
Activities: Factory techniques; metallurgy and metal welding; motor and mechanism studies.

Laboratory of Structural Mechanics   1793

Director: Professor Y. Pironneau
Sections: structural mechanics, Professor O. Debordes, Professor S. Dubigeon; materials resistance, Professor P. Vaussy
Activities: Vibrations mechanics - structure resistance and stability, study of structures and their role in the environment, biomechanics; materials resistance - rupture mechanics, photoelastimetry, automatic calculation.

UNIT OF CHEMISTRY   1794

Address: 2 rue de la Houssinière, 44072 Nantes Cedex
Telephone: (040) 75 50 70
Director: M. Chabanel

Laboratory of Ion Spectrochemistry   1795

Head: Professor M. Chabanel
Activities: Identification of ionic associations in solution; spectrometry studies.

Laboratory of Molecular Physical   1796 Chemistry and Organic Physical Chemistry

Affiliation: Centre National de la Recherche Scientifique
Head: Professor G. Martin, Professor M.L. Martin
Activities: Application of nuclear magnetic resonance to chemical reactivity and the structures of biological materials.

Laboratory of Molecular   1797 Spectrochemistry

Heads: Professor B. Wojtkowiak, Professor C. Laurence
Activities: Spectroscopic studies; research on aromatic and aliphatic substances.

Laboratory of Organic Chemistry I   1798

Head: Professor Y. Graff
Activities: Natural marine substances; lactone and pheromone studies.

Laboratory of Organic Chemistry II   1799

Head: Professor H. Quiniou
Activities: Organic synthesis; analytical chemistry; industrial chemistry; spectrometry studies.

Laboratory of Physical Chemical   1800 Molecular Biology

Head: Professor J. Pieri
Activities: Enzymatic and structural membrane studies; protein screening.

Laboratory of Solid-State Chemistry   1801

Affiliation: Centre National de la Recherche Scientifique
Head: Professor J. Rouxel
Sections: Electrode materials; intercalation chemistry; properties of low-dimension materials
Graduate research staff: 25

Annual expenditure: £51 000-500 000
Activities: Physics and chemistry of low dimensional materials; new compound synthesis; ionic and molecular intercalation chemistry; chemistry of low-temperature metastable phases.
Contract work: No

UNIT OF GEOGRAPHY   1802

Address: chemin de la Sensive du Tertre, 44036 Nantes Cedex
Telephone: (040) 74 74 01
Director: Professor J.P. Pinot

Agrarian and Rural Geography   1803

Head: J. Renard
Activities: Agricultural industrialization; redistribution of wooded areas; accelerated transformation of French rural regions.

Nantais Research Centre for Regional   1804
Management

Heads: Professor A. Vigarie, Professor J. Renard
Activities: Urban and rural management; tourism; environments in relation to human needs.

Oceanography   1805

Head: Professor J.P. Pinot
Activities: Cartography;   teledetection;   littoral dynamics; studies of the continental shelf

Physical and Regional Geography of   1806
the French Littoral

Head: Professor J. Gras
Senior staff: Professor B. Bousquet, Professor J.M. Palierne
Activities: Environmental geography; methodology; continental and littoral physical geography.

Urban Geography and Transport   1807
Research Group

Head: Professor A. Vigarie
Activities: Town and regional planning; management; social geography; transport and circulation.

UNIT OF INDUSTRIAL ENGINEERING 1808

Address: 2 rue de la Houssinière, 44072 Nantes Cedex
Telephone: (040) 74 88 11
Director: Professor Y. De Roeck-Holtzhauer
Activities: The Unit coordinates applied research carried out by universities, industry and education on the subjects of: pollution, environmental hazards, food engineering.

Industrial Pharmacy   1809

Head: Professor Y. De Roeck-Holtzhauer
Activities: Sterilization; agro-alimentary studies.

UNIT OF MATHEMATICS   1810

Address: 2 rue de la Houssinière, 44072 Nantes Cedex
Telephone: (040) 74 50 70
Director: Pham The Lai

Algebra Research Centre   1811

Head: Professor J. Petresco
Activities: Group theory; module and ring theories.

Analysis Research Centre   1812

Head: Pham The Lai
Activities: Differential   operators,   spectral   theory; abstract   measurement   and   probability;   funtional analysis.

Information and Mathematical   1813
Applications Research Centre

Heads: Professor M. Lucas, Professor Pham The Lai
Activities: Numerical   analysis;   graphic   techniques; programme methodology.

Institute of Mathematical Teaching   1814
Research

Head: Professor Jean-Pierre Letourneux
Activities: Mathematics history; education.

Study of Scientific Activities   1815

Heads: Professor J. Dhombres, Professor J.L. Gardies
Activities: Science and mathematics history; scientific politics and development.

Topology and Geometry Research Centre 1816

Heads: Professor J. Barge, Professor H. Ibisch, Professor D. Leborgne, Professor P. Vogel
Activities: Geometric and algebraic topology; algebraic and analytical method studies.

UNIT OF MEDICINE AND MEDICAL TECHNIQUES 1817

Address: 1 rue Gaston Veil, 44035 Nantes Cedex
Telephone: (040) 47 60 06
Director: M. Malvy
Activities: Studies of living structures, biology, pathology, and immunology, electronmicroscope studies; adaptation and physiopathology of major functions, nervous system, digestive system and cardiovascular system.

Child Medicine Clinic 1818

Address: Pavillon Mère et Enfant, CHU, 44035 Nantes Cedex
Telephone: (040) 48 33 33
Activities: General paediatrics, prematurity, infantile reanimation, medical genetics, paediatric nephrology.

Dermatology Clinic 1819

Address: Hôtel Dieu, Place Alexis Ricordeau, 44035 Nantes Cedex
Telephone: (040) 48 33 33
Head: Professor H. Barrière
Activities: Clinical dermatological research; immunological techniques; electron microscope studies; dermatological and general pathology; immunofluorescence; cancer research; ultraviolet radiation studies.

Laboratory of Anaesthesiology and Reanimation 1820

Head: Professor F. Nicolas
Activities: Haemodynamics; hyperthermia; shock; isochemical cardiopathy; anaesthetics; circulation; hypertension control.

Laboratory of Applied Physiology, Biology and Sport Medicine 1821

Head: Professor J. Ginet
Senior staff: Biology, P. Guiheneuc; cardiology, M. Potiron; neuropsychiatry, F. Vecchierini; pharmacy, B. Lucas
Activities: Nervous system; sport biology and medicine; cardiology; respiration.

Laboratory of Cancerology 1822

Head: Professor B. Le Mevel
Activities: Cancer research; plasmic membrane, enzyme studies; myelomonocytic differentiation; pharmacology; lignanes.

Laboratory of Clinical and Experimental Biology 1823

Heads: Professor S. Cottin, Professsor J. Mussini-Montpellier
Activities: Bone and cartilage studies, metabolism, anatomy, ageing, inflammation, development, mineral activity, hormone action.

Laboratory of Experimental Neurology and Neuro-Muscular Pathology 1824

Heads: Professor J.R. Feve, Professor J. Mussini-Montpellier
Activities: Human intoxication; muscular dystrophy studies; muscular maturation.

Laboratory of Gynaecology, Obstetrics and Human Reproduction Biology 1825

Head: Professor M.F. Lerat
Activities: Muscular cell ultrastructure; parturition; female sterility.

Laboratory of Histology, Embryology and Cytogenetics 1826

Heads: Professor G. Lefranc, Professor J. André
Activities: Endocrine cell studies, histochemistry, morphology; cytogenetics; fluorescence, electron microscope studies; immunocytochemistry, autohistoradiography.

Laboratory of Molecular Microbiology 1827

Head: Professor A. Courtieu
Activities: Bacteriology, taxonomy, antibiotic action, anaerobic studies; virology; electron microscope studies.

Laboratory of Nephrology and Medical Pathology 1828

Head: Professor J. Guenel
Activities: Nephrology; immunology; haemodialysis; transplantation.

Laboratory of Parasitology and Exotic 1829 Pathology

Head: Professor C. Vermeil
Activities: Cellular and microorganism interactions; mycology; helminthology; entomology; parasitic pathology.

Laboratory of Pathological Anatomy 1830

Heads: Professor J.P. Kerneis, Professor J. Mussini-Montpellier, Professor Y. Lenne
Activities: This laboratory is divided into two sections: Hôpital Saint Jacques - cosmetopathology, general pathology, digestive pathology, haematological pathology, bone pathology.
Hôtel-Dieu - ovary studies, glandular parenchyma, general cancerology, neuropathology, paediatrics, nephro-urology, eclampsia, heart and pulmonary pathology.

Laboratory of Pharmacology 1831

Head: Professor C. Larousse
Activities: Microsomal enzyme studies; enzyme induction in animals and man; pharmacokinetics; medicament metabolism; medicinal psychotrope studies.

Laboratory of Pneumophthisiology I 1832

Address: Hôpital Laënnec, rue Paul Bert, 44035 Nantes Cedex
Telephone: (040) 48 38 21
Head: Professor C. Moigneteau
Activities: Chronic respiratory insufficiency; tuberculosis; asbestosis.

Laboratory of Pneumophthisiology II 1833

Address: Hôpital Laënnec, rue Paul Bert, 44035 Nantes Cedex
Telephone: (040) 48 38 21
Head: Professor J. Corroller
Activities: Cancer; alveolar macrophage characterization; pulmonary immune reactions.

Medical Clinic 1834

ENDOCRINE AND METABOLIC 1835 DISEASES LABORATORY

Activities: Prostaglandin studies; immunology; hormone function and liverdiseases; lipid and apoprotein metabolism; diabetes research.

LIVER AND DIGESTIVE TRACT 1836 DISEASES LABORATORY

Activities: Gastroenterology and laser use; endocrine and digestive tractstudies.

Medical History Centre 1837

Dean: J.P. Kerneis
Activities: Documentation research.

Neurosurgical Clinic 1838

Address: Hôtel Dieu, Place Alexis Ricordeau, 44035 Nantes Cedex
Telephone: (040) 48 31 89
Head: Professor P. Descuns
Activities: Peripheral nervous system; cerebral circulation; paediatric neurosurgery; neurosurgical oncology; anatomy and anthropology.

Ophthalmology University Clinic 1839

Address: Hôtel Dieu, Place Alexis Ricordeau, 44035 Nantes Cedex
Telephone: (040) 48 33 33
Head: Professor M.A. Quere

DEPARTMENT OF OCULAR 1840 HISTOPATHOLOGY

Head: Professor F. Hervouet
Activities: Ocular histopathology studies.

DEPARTMENT OF OCULAR 1841 MICROSURGERY

Head: P. Sourdille
Activities: Crystalline implant studies, lacrymal gland studies.

DEPARTMENT OF OCULAR-SENSORY 1842 MOTRICITY

Head: Professor M.A. Quere
Activities: Electro-oculographic studies, oculomotor irregularity.

Orthopaedic Clinic 1843

Address: Hôpital Saint-Jacques, 85 rue Saint-Jacques, 44035 Nantes Cedex
Telephone: (040) 48 37 36
Head: Professor J.V. Bainvel
Activities: Orthopaedic infection; experimental and applied microsurgery; hip pathology; applied neuro-orthopaedic pathology.

Stomatology Clinic   1844

Address: Hôtel Dieu, Place Alexis Ricordeau, 44035 Nantes Cedex
Telephone: (040) 73 42 59
Head: Professor J. Delaire
Activities: Cranio-facial growth, orthopaedic and surgical treatment of congenital malformations of and growths on the face.

Surgical Clinic   1845

Head: Professor P. Malvy
Activities: Use of lasers in gastric pathology; conservation of skin grafts by freezing; microsurgical artery and vein suture permeability, micrografting.

Traumatology Clinic   1846

Head: Professor J. Sourdille
Activities: Articular fractures, prosthetic replacement; polytraumas.

Urology Clinic   1847

Telephone: (040) 48 31 86
Heads: Professor J. Auvigne, Professor J.M. Buzelin
Activities: Urinary apparatus; diagnosis, disfunction; laser studies.

UNIT OF NATURAL SCIENCES   1848

Address: 2 rue de la Houssinière, 44072 Nantes Cedex
Telephone: (040) 74 50 70
Director: J.P. Margerel

Laboratory of Animal and Cell   1849
Physiology

Head: Professor G. Le Douarin
Activities: Functional differentiation of the heart; neuromuscular and synaptic differentiation.

Laboratory of Cell Differentiation   1850
Physiology

Head: Professor D. Renaud
Activities: Neuromuscular synaptogenesis; functional cardiac differentiation.

Laboratory of Developmental Biology   1851

Head: Professor R. Ferrand
Activities: Haematopoietic organ ontogenesis; endocrine system studies.

Laboratory of Ecology and   1852
Phytogeography

Head: Professor P. Dupont
Activities: Flora and vegetation of the Atlantic and Mediterranean regions; floral mapping; systematics and evolution; electron microscope studies.

Laboratory of Historic Geology   1853

Head: Professor P. Cavet
Activities: Structural analysis; stratigraphy; sedimentology; tectonics; micropalaeontology; faunal studies.

Laboratory of Marine and Applied   1854
Geology

Head: Professor F. Ottmann
Activities: Geomorphology; sedimentology; geophysics; cartography; evolution; water supplies; pollution; natural material studies.

Laboratory of Marine Biology   1855

Head: Professor Y. Saudray
Activities: Ecology of the Loire estuary and adjacent areas: productivity, pollution, population and energy flow studies.

Laboratory of Mineralogy and   1856
Petrology

Head: Professor F.H. Forestier
Activities: Mineralogy; petrography; cartography; applied geology.

Laboratory of Plant Biology and   1857
Cytophysiology

Head: Professor J.N. Hallet
Activities: Cytology; morphogenesis; metabolism; microspectrophotometry, autoradiography and electron microscope studies.

Laboratory of Plant Cytopathology   1858

Head: Professor S. Renaudin
Activities: Cytology; parasitism and symbiosis; tumour development; meristematic organ development; electron microscope and spectrophotometry studies.

Laboratory of Psychophysiology   1859

Head: Professor L. Amouriq
Activities: Relationship between nerve structure and behaviour; genetics; biochemistry; physiology; cytophotometry; electron microscope studies.

Laboratory of Social Insects Endocrinology 1860

Head: Professor D. Lebrun
Activities: Termite studies: caste determination, reproduction, sexual biology; electron microscope studies.

Laboratory of Tectonophysics 1861

Affiliation: Centre National de la Recherche Scientifique
Head: Professor A. Nicolas
Senior staff: Natural deformation, F. Boudier, J.L. Bouchez; experimental deformation, Y. Gueguen; simulation of deformation, J.L. Vigneresse
Graduate research staff: 6
Annual expenditure: £10 000-50 000
Activities: Experimental and theoretical rock and mineral deformation mechanisms; natural deformation, mantle flow, oceanic crust and mantle modelling, crustal deformation, mineral resources.
Contract work: No

Laboratory of Zoology 1862

Head: Professor R. Sellier
Activities: Insects: evolution, hydrobiology, ecology, electron microscope studies.

UNIT OF ODONTOLOGY 1863

Address: 1 Place Alexis Ricordeau, 44042 Nantes Cedex
Telephone: (040) 48 33 33
Director: H. Hamel

Laboratory of Biology and Fundamental Materials 1864

Head: Professor S. Clergeau-Guerithault
Senior staff: Professor J. Pouëzat
Activities: Histology, cytology, embryology, anatomy, pathology, electron microscope studies.

Laboratory of Inflammation Research 1865

Head: Professor A. Daniel
Activities: Inflammation; buccal cavity studies; stereological analysis.

Laboratory of Materials Research 1866

Head: Professor J. Lemounier
Activities: Dental materials; plaque bacteria; dental prosthesis.

UNIT OF PHARMACEUTICAL SCIENCES 1867

Address: 1 rue Gaston Veil, 44035 Nantes, Cedex
Telephone: (040) 47 76 90
Director: A. Foucaud

Laboratory of Analytical Hydrological Chemistry 1868

Head: vacant
Activities: Trace elements; water quality.

Laboratory of Botany and Cryptogamy 1869

Heads: Professor H.P. Reveillère, Professor A. Foucaud
Activities: Toxic moulds; macromycetes taxonomy; medicinal plants, toxic plants studies; pharmacy.

Laboratory of Cosmetology and Industrial Pharmacy 1870

Address: 68 boulevard Eugène Orieux, Nantes Cedex
Telephone: (040) 74 23 22
Head: Professor Y. De Roeck-Holtzhauer
Activities: Cosmetology; industrial and hospital pharmacology.

Laboratory of Galenic Pharmacy and Pharmacotechnics 1871

Head: Professor M. Rouzet
Activities: Aromatic materials; chromatographic and spectroscopic studies; dermobiochemistry.

Laboratory of General and Applied Biochemistry 1872

Head: Professor B. Bousquet
Activities: Medical biochemistry; clinical biology.

Laboratory of Materia Medica 1873

Head: Professor J.F. Verbist
Activities: Natural substances; marine algae; pharmacological substances.

Laboratory of Mineral Chemistry 1874

Head: vacant

Laboratory of Pharmacodynamics 1875

Head: Professor L. Welin
Activities: Therapeutic chemistry, anti-inflammatory studies; marine algae pharmacodynamics; experimental hypoxia.

Laboratory of Physics   1876

Head: Professor P. Arnaud
Activities: Spectrophotometry studies.

Laboratory of Physiology   1877

Head: Professor A. Combre
Activities: Environmental action on skin ageing; ultraviolet ray studies; radioisotopic studies.

Laboratory of Therapeutic and   1878
Organic Chemistry

Heads: Professor J. Ploquin, Professor L. Sparfel
Activities: Therapeutic chemistry; anticancer pharmacology; antifungal and antibacterial studies; natural substance chemistry.

Laboratory of Toxicology and   1879
Industrial Hygiene

Head: Professor H.L. Boiteau
Activities: Relationship between trace elements and cardiovascular, nervous and renal disease; anti-inflammatory action studies.

Laboratory of Trace Element Dosages 1880

Head: Professor H.L. Boiteau
Activities: Spectrometry and atomic absorption studies; renal transplantation; detergent and nickel allergy.

UNIT OF PHYSICS   1881

Address: 2 rue de la Houssinière, 44072 Nantes Cedex
Telephone: (040) 74 50 70
Director: Guy Goureaux
Contract work: Yes

Laboratory of Corpuscular Physics   1882

Heads: Professor L.H. Collet, Professor B. Grolleau
Activities: Cathode pulverization of plasmas; plasma reaction under high frequency electrical discharges; ion-solid surface interaction.

Laboratory of Experimental Physics   1883

Head: Professor A. Boulloud
Activities: Electrical discharges into vacuum and gases; phenomena in intense space.

Laboratory of Materials Physics and 1884
Electronic Components

Affiliation: Centre National de la Recherche Scientifique
Head: Professor G. Goureaux
Activities: Materials physics and electronic components; experimental and theoretical studies; ionic implantation; interface and electrode studies.

Laboratory of Mathematical Physics   1885

Head: Professor W. Laskar
Activities: Mathematical analysis of particles; energy physics; theoretical nuclear physics; energy exchange in solids.

Laboratory of Nuclear Spectroscopy   1886

Heads: Professor P. Avignon, Professor L.H. Rosier
Activities: Nuclear physics: heavy ion studies; reaction mechanisms.

Laboratory of Quantum Electronics   1887

Head: Professor R. Le Naour
Activities: Spectroscopy and polarization studies; magneto-optics; optic resonators; laser studies.

Laboratory of Solid-State Physics   1888

Head: Professor S. Minn
Activities: Thin film (amorphous, metallic); dielectric crystal studies.

Laboratory of Surface Physics   1889

Affiliation: Centre National de la Recherche Scientifique
Head: Professor R. Le Bihan
Activities: Surfaces of solids; spectrometry and electron microscope studies; thin layer studies; new mineral compounds.

Laboratory of Theoretical Physics   1890

Heads: Professor P. Loncke, Professor R. Le Maitre
Activities: Nuclear physics theory; solid-state theory; quantum physics and mathematics; numerical problems.

Laboratory of Thermodynamics   1891

Head: Professor H. Mouton
Activities: Heat and mass transfer studies; natural and forced convection; transfer couples; heliothermics.

Laboratory of Thermokinetics 1892

Affiliation: Centre National de la Recherche Scientifique
Head: Professor J.P. Bardon
Activities: Heat transfer at solid-solid and solid-liquid interfaces.

Université de Nice 1893

[Nice University]
Address: Parc Valrose, 06034 Nice Cedex
Telephone: (093) 51 91 00
President: Marcel Azzaro
See also entry for: Observatoire de Nice.

FACULTY OF DENTISTRY 1894

Director: Professor P. Ciosi

Biology and Fundamental Materials 1895
Laboratory

Head: Professor Monteil

Operational Dentistry Laboratory 1896

Head: Professor Heos

Orthopaedic and Facial Dentistry 1897
Laboratory

Head: Professor Affia

Parodontology Laboratory 1898

Head: Professor P. Ciosi

Preventive Paedodontics Laboratory 1899

Head: Professor Jesmin

Prosthesis and Occlusive Dentistry 1900
Laboratory

Senior staff: Professor Exbrayat, Professor Pallenca

Therapeutic Pathology Laboratory 1901

Head: Professor Guidicelli

FACULTY OF SCIENCE AND 1902
TECHNOLOGY

Director: M Laheou

Animal Biology and Cytology 1903
Laboratory

Director: M Greuet

Atomic and Molecular Optics 1904
Laboratory

Director: M Stringat

Atomic and Structural Chemistry 1905
Laboratory

Director: M Ythier

Biochemistry Laboratory 1906

Director: M Lazdunski

Botanical Laboratory 1907

Director: M Lapraz

Comparative Physiology Laboratory 1908

Director: M Lahlou

Electricity Laboratory 1909

Director: M Lalangue

Electronics Laboratory 1910

Director: M Rivier

Experimental Physics Laboratory 1911

Director: M Keller

Geology and Sedimentology 1912
Laboratory

Director: M Mangin

Marine Zoology and Protistology 1913
Laboratory

Telephone: (093) 55 56 56
Director: M Cachon

Micropalaeontology Research Centre 1914

Director: M Moullade

Neurophysiology Laboratory 1915

Director: M Godet

Petrology and Mineralogy Laboratory   1916

Director: M Turco

Plant Biology Laboratory   1917

Director: M Rigaud

Plant Physiology Laboratory   1918

Director: Mlle Bulard

Psychophysiology Laboratory   1919

Director: M Gottesmann

Radiochemistry Laboratory   1920

Director: M Ardisson

Structural Geology Laboratory   1921

Director: M Dars

INSTITUTE OF MATHEMATICS AND   1922
PHYSICAL SCIENCES

Director: F. Rocca

Astrophysics Laboratory   1923

Director: M Roddier

Computer Science Laboratory   1924

Director: M Boussard

DYMOR Laboratory   1925

Director: M Sixou

Electro-Optics Laboratory   1926

Directors: M Richard, M Ostrowsky

Mathematics Laboratory   1927

Director: M Piriou

Mechanical Statistics Laboratory   1928

Director: M Coste, M Peyraud

Molecular Mineral Chemistry   1929
Laboratory

Director: M Riess

Organic Chemistry of Fluorine   1930
Laboratory

Director: M Cambon

Organic Structural Chemistry   1931
Laboratory

Director: M Guedj

Physical Chemistry Laboratory   1932

Director: M Guion

Physics of Condensed Materials   1933
Laboratory

Director: M Peyraud

Physics of Liquids Laboratory   1934

Director: M Brot

Physics of Solids Laboratory   1935

Director: M Laheurte

Signals and Systems Laboratory   1936

Director: M Boeri

Theoretical Physics Laboratory   1937

Director: M Le Bellar

LITERATURE AND HUMAN SCIENCE   1938
UNIT

Address: 98 boulevard Edouard Herriot, 06034 Nice
Cedex

Geography Department   1939

QUANTITATIVE AND APPLIED SPATIAL   1940
ANALYSIS RESEARCH CENTRE
Head: M Dauphine

RAOLD BLANCHARD GEOGRAPHY   1941
LABORATORY
Head: M Miege

TROPICAL GEOGRAPHY CENTRE   1942
Head: Mme Le Bourdiec

Psychology Department   1943

CLINICAL AND GENETIC   **1944**
PSYCHOLOGY RESEARCH GROUP
Head: M Sieye

DIFFERENTIAL AND APPLIED   **1945**
GENERAL PSYCHOLOGY LABORATORY
Head: M Raymondis

EXPERIMENTAL AND COMPARATIVE   **1946**
PSYCHOLOGY LABORATORY
Head: M Flores

SOCIAL AND CLINICAL PSYCHOLOGY   **1947**
LABORATORY
Head: Mme Ancelin-Schutzen-Berger

MEDICAL RESEARCH UNIT   **1948**
Director: Professor H. Richelme

Adult Psychiatry Laboratory   **1949**
Head: Professor G. Darcourt

Anaesthesiology Laboratory   **1950**
Head: Professor P. Maestrecci

Bacteriology-Virology Laboratory   **1951**
Head: Professor M. Vandekerkove

Biochemistry Laboratory   **1952**
Head: Professor P. Sudaka

Biophysics Laboratory   **1953**
Head: Professor F. Lapalus

Cancerology Laboratory   **1954**
Head: Professor M. Schneider

Cardiology Laboratory   **1955**
Head: Professor P. Morand

Child Psychiatry Laboratory   **1956**
Head: Professor M. Myquel

CRECEC Laboratory   **1957**
Head: Dr A. Varenne

Dermatology-Venereology Laboratory   **1958**
Senior staff: Dr Aarety, Professor J.P. Ortonne

Endocrinology Laboratory   **1959**
Head: Professor M. Harter

Experimental Medicine and INSERM   **1960**
U145 Laboratory
Head: Professor P. Freychet

General Surgery Laboratory I   **1961**
Head: Professor J.A. Inglesakis

General Surgery Laboratory III   **1962**
Head: Professor J. Mouiel

Genetic Paediatrics Laboratory   **1963**
Head: Professor R. Mariani

Gynaecology and Obstetrics   **1964**
Laboratory
Head: Professor J.Y. Gillet

Hepatogastroenterology Laboratory   **1965**
Head: Professor J. Delmont

Histology Laboratory   **1966**
Head: Professor N. Ayraud

Immunology and INSERM Laboratory   **1967**
Head: Professor R. Masseyeff

Infectious Diseases Laboratory   **1968**
Head: Professor M. Bocquet

Internal Medicine Laboratory I   **1969**
Head: Professor M. Gazaix

Internal Medicine Laboratory II   **1970**
Head: Professor P. Dujardin

Legal Medicine Laboratory   **1971**
Head: Professor A. Ollier

Medical and Surgical Anatomy   1972
Laboratory

Head: Professor H. Richelme

Medical Clinic I   1973

Head: Professor P. Audoly

Medical Clinic II   1974

Head: Professor P. Babeau

Nephrology Clinic   1975

Head: Professor H. Duplay

Neurology Laboratory   1976

Head: Professor P. Martin

Neurosurgery Laboratory   1977

Head: Professor J. Duplay

Orthopaedic Surgery and   1978
Traumatology Laboratory

Head: Professor C. Argenson

Otorhinolaryngology Laboratory   1979

Head: Professor F. Demard

Parasitology Laboratory   1980

Head: Dr Y. Le Fichoux

Pathological Anatomy Laboratory I   1981

Head: Professor J. Kermarec

Pathological Anatomy Laboratory II   1982

Head: Professor R. Loubière

Pharmacology Laboratory   1983

Head: Professor E. Savini

Physiology and Functional Exploration   1984
of Respiration Laboratory

Head: Professor J.L. Ardisson

Pneumophthisiology Laboratory   1985

Head: Professor B. Blaive

Preventive Medicine, Public Health   1986
and Hygiene Laboratory

Head: Professor J.P. Bocquet

Radio Diagnostics Laboratory I   1987

Head: Professor J.J. Serres

Radio Diagnostics Laboratory II   1988

Head: Professor A. Coussement

Radiotherapy Laboratory   1989

Head: Professor C.M. Lalanne

Rheumatology Laboratory   1990

Head: Professor G. Ziegler

Surgery Clinic   1991

Head: Professor P. Le Bas

Therapeutics, Medical Rehabilitation,   1992
Fundamental Reeducation and
Hydrology Laboratory

Head: Professor M. Mattei

Thoracic and Cardiovascular Surgery   1993
Laboratory

Head: Professor V. Dor

Urology Laboratory   1994

Head: Dr Raymond
Senior staff: Professor J. Toubol

MEDITERRANEAN POLYTECHNICAL   1995
INSTITUTE

Director: M Rouillard

Biological Oceanography Laboratory   1996

Director: M Fredj

Biophysics Laboratory   1997

Director: M Vasilescu

Dynamic and Applied Geology   1998
Laboratory

Director: M Polveche

Ecology of Arid Regions Laboratory 1999

Director: M Barry

Electricity Laboratory 2000

Director: M Renucci

Experimental Thermodynamics 2001
Laboratory

Director: M Elegant

Geography Laboratory 2002

Director: M Julian

Marine Biology and Ecology 2003
Laboratory

Director: M Vaissière

Mediterranean Geology Research 2004
Centre

Director: M Guardia

Organic Chemistry Laboratory 2005

Director: M Luft

Physical Organic Chemistry Laboratory 2006

Director: M Azzaro

Université de Paris V - 2007
Université René Descartes

[Paris V University - René Descartes University]
Address: 12 rue de l'École de Médecine, 25270 Paris
Cedex 06
Telephone: (01) 329 21 77
Note: The Conseil Supérieur de la Recherche has 70
members throughout the six colleges. Its main aim is the
promotion of biomedical research.
See also: Institut d'Histochimie Médicale.

HUMANITIES 2008

Address: 12 rue Cujas, 75230 Paris Cedex 05
Vice-president: Professor M. Barbut

Institute of Psychology 2009

Address: 28 rue Serpente, 75270 Paris Cedex 06
Telephone: (01) 329 12 12
Director: Professor Claude Levy-Leboyer

LABORATORY OF INTERCULTURAL 2010
PSYCHOLOGY
Director: Professor C. Camilleri

PERSONALITY PATHOLOGY CENTRE 2011
Directors: Professor R. Doron, Professor D.
Widlocher

PROJECTIVE PSYCHOLOGY GROUP 2012
Director: Professor N. Rausch de Traubenbery

Unit of Mathematics, Formal Logic 2013
and Informatics

Address: 12 rue Cujas, 75230 Paris Cedex 05
Telephone: (01) 329 12 13
Director: Professor M. Barbut
Activities: The Unit is associated to various research
programmes in the university, among them there is a
Laboratory of Methods and Techniques of Sociology
and a mathematics and psychology team.

Unit of Psychology 2014

Address: 28 rue Serpente, 75270 Paris Cedex 06
Telephone: (01) 329 12 13
Director: Professor Colette Chiland

LABORATORY OF CLINICAL 2015
PSYCHOLOGY
Director: Professor C. Chiland

LABORATORY OF DIFFERENTIAL 2016
PSYCHOLOGY
Address: 41 rue Gay-Lussac, Paris
Director: Professor M. Reuchlin

LABORATORY OF EXPERIMENTAL 2017
PSYCHOLOGY
Director: Professor G. Noizet

LABORATORY OF GENERAL AND 2018
COMPARATIVE PSYCHOLOGY
Director: Professor G. Simondon

LABORATORY OF GENETIC 2019
PSYCHOLOGY
Address: 46 rue Saint-Jacques, Paris
Director: Professor P. Oleron

LABORATORY OF PATHOLOGIC   **2020**
PSYCHOLOGY
Director: Dr H. Faure

LABORATORY OF SOCIAL   **2021**
PSYCHOLOGY
Directors: Professor G. Durandin, Professor G. Montmollin

MEDICINE   2022

Faculty of Medicine Cochin Port-Royal 2023

Address: 24 rue du Faubourg Saint-Jacques, 75674 Paris Cedex 14
Telephone: (01) 320 12 40
Dean: G. Cremer
Activities: Human biology: immunopathology and immunogenetics; mathematical models in medicine; energy biology (circulation, respiration, heat); medical psychology.

LABORATORY OF ANATOMY   **2024**
Head: Professor Cl. Aaron

LABORATORY OF BACTERIOLOGY   **2025**
Head: Professor P. Nevot

LABORATORY OF BIOPHYSICS   **2026**
Head: Professor J.Cl. Roucayrol

LABORATORY OF CARDIOVASCULAR   **2027**
AND HAEMODYNAMIC RESEARCH
Head: Professor M. Degeorges

LABORATORY OF CLINICAL   **2028**
OBSTETRICS
Head: Professor C. Sureau

LABORATORY OF CLINICAL UROLOGY   **2029**
Head: Professor A. Steg

LABORATORY OF CYTOGENETIC   **2030**
HISTOEMBRYOLOGY
Head: Professor A. Salesses

LABORATORY OF DERMATOLOGY   **2031**
Head: Professor J. Hewitt

LABORATORY OF HISTOEMBRYOLOGY 2032
Head: Professor B. Schramm

LABORATORY OF IMMUNOLOGY   **2033**
Head: Professor M. Renoux

LABORATORY OF OPHTHALMOLOGY   **2034**
Head: Professor H. Hamard

LABORATORY OF PARASITOLOGY   **2035**
Head: Professor J. Lapierre

LABORATORY OF PERINATAL   **2036**
PHARMACOLOGY
Head: G. Olive

LABORATORY OF PHARMACOLOGY   **2037**
Head: J.P. Giroud

LABORATORY OF   **2038**
PHARMACOVIGILANCE
Head: Professor H. Pequignot

LABORATORY OF PHYSIOLOGY   **2039**
Head: Professor E. Florentin

LABORATORY OF   **2040**
PNEUMOPHTHISIOLOGY
Head: Professor B. Kreis

LABORATORY OF RESEARCH ON   **2041**
POLYVALENT REANIMATION
Head: Professor J. Monsallier

LONGJUMEAU GENERAL HOSPITAL   **2042**
Laboratory of Biochemistry   **2043**
Head: Professor P. Pin

Laboratory of Pathologic Anatomy **2044**
Head: Professor Ph. Galian

Service of Internal Medicine   **2045**
Head: J.P. Ancelle

Service of Surgery   **2046**
Head: J.P. Lenriot

RESEARCH ON MEDICAL ULTRASONIC 2047
IMAGERY
Head: Professor J. Perrin

SAINT-ANNE PSYCHIATRY CENTRE   **2048**
Laboratory of Biological Psychiatry   **2049**
Head: Professor P. Deniker

Laboratory of Human Cerebral Tumours **2050**
Head: Professor Cl. Vedrenne

Laboratory of Medical Psychology **2051**
Head: Professor P. Pichot

Research Centre on Clinical Pharmacology   **2052**
Head: A. Soulairac

Service of Neurology   **2053**
Head: Professor P. Rondot

Service of Neurosurgery   **2054**
Head: G. Mazars

SAINT-VINCENT-DE-PAUL HOSPITAL   **2055**

Laboratory of Histopathology and   **2056**
Histochemistry of the Nervous System
Head: E. Farkas

Laboratory of Pathological Anatomy on   **2057**
Infant Mortality
Head: Professor Tran Vinh Hien

Laboratory of Research on Growth   **2058**
Head: Professor J.C. Job

Laboratory of Research on Paediatric   **2059**
Immunology
Head: J. Badoual

SERVICE OF ANAESTHESIOLOGY   **2060**
Head: Professor J. Lassner

SERVICE OF   **2061**
ELECTROCARDIOGRAPHY
Head: Professor G. Pallardy

SERVICE OF ENDOCRINE AND   **2062**
METABOLIC DISORDERS
Head: Professor H. Bricaire

SERVICE OF GASTROENTEROLOGY   **2063**
Head: Professor J. Guerre

SERVICE OF PATHOLOGICAL   **2064**
ANATOMY
Head: Professor R. Abelanet

Faculty of Medicine Necker-Enfants-   **2065**
Malades

Address: 156 rue de Vaugirard, 75015 Paris
Telephone: (01) 783 33 03
Dean: Professor J. Rey

LABORATORY OF ANAESTHESIOLOGY   **2066**
Head: Professor M. Cara

LABORATORY OF ANATOMY   **2067**
Head: Professor J. Hureau

LABORATORY OF BIOCHEMISTRY   **2068**
Head: Professor H. Jerome

LABORATORY OF BIOPHYSICS   **2069**
Head: Professor C. Kellershohn

LABORATORY OF   **2070**
ELECTRORADIOLOGY
Head: Professor J. Frézal

LABORATORY OF EXPERIMENTAL   **2071**
PATHOLOGY
Head: Professor J. Paupe

LABORATORY OF EXPERIMENTAL   **2072**
SURGERY
Head: Professor M. Arsac

LABORATORY OF HAEMATOLOGY   **2073**
Head: Professor F. Josso

LABORATORY OF HISTOLOGY-   **2074**
EMBRYOLOGY
Head: C. Da Lage

LABORATORY OF INFANT RENAL   **2075**
METABOLISM AND DISEASES
Head: Professor P. Royer

LABORATORY OF INFANT SURGERY   **2076**
Head: Professor D. Pellerin

LABORATORY OF MEDICAL   **2077**
INFORMATICS
Head: Professor H. Ducrot

LABORATORY OF MICROBIOLOGY   **2078**
Head: Professor L. Le Minor

LABORATORY OF PARASITOLOGY   **2079**
Head: Professor Ho Thi Sang

LABORATORY OF PHYSIOLOGY   **2080**
Head: Professor C. Sachs

LABORATORY OF UROLOGY   **2081**
Head: Professor J. Cukier

Faculty of Medicine Paris-Ouest   **2082**

Address: 104 boulevard Raymond-Poincaré, 92380
Garches
Dean: Professor C. Betourne

LABORATORY OF ANAESTHESIOLOGY 2083
Address: 15 rue de l'École-de-Médecine, 75270 Paris
Cedex 06
Head: Professor G. Vourc'h

LABORATORY OF BIOCHEMISTRY   **2084**
Head: Professor J. Nordmann

LABORATORY OF EXPERIMENTAL AND 2085
CARDIOVASCULAR SURGERY
Address: Centre Médico-Chirurgical Foch, 40 rue
Worth, 92150 Suresnes
Head: D. Guilmet

LABORATORY OF HAEMATOLOGY   2086
Address: Ambroise-Paré, 9 avenue du Général-de-Gaulle, 92100 Boulogne
Head: A. Goguel

LABORATORY OF INFANT   2087
NEUROLOGY
Address: Raymond-Poincaré, 104 boulevard Raymond-Poincaré, 92380 Garches
Head: Professor Ph. Lacert

LABORATORY OF NEUROLOGIC   2088
REHABILITATION
Address: Raymond-Poincaré, 104 boulevard Raymond-Poincaré, 92380 Garches
Head: Professor J.P. Held

LABORATORY OF PATHOLOGICAL   2089
ANATOMY
Head: Professor J. Mignot

LABORATORY OF REANIMATION   2090
Address: Raymond-Poincaré, 104 boulevard Raymond-Poincaré, 92380 Garches
Head: Professor M. Goulon

LABORATORY OF TRAUMATIC   2091
SURGERY
Address: Raymond Poincaré, 104 boulevard Raymond-Poincaré, 92380 Garches
Head: Professor A. Patel

Unit of Biomedical Research Saints-   2092
Pères

Address: 45 rue des Saints-Pères, 75270 Paris Cedex 06
Telex: (01) 260 37 20
Director: Professor A. Coblentz

LABORATORY OF ANATOMY   2093
Head: Professor A. Hureou

LABORATORY OF BIOCHEMISTRY   2094
Head: Professor M. Engler

LABORATORY OF BIOPHYSICS   2095
Head: Professor M.M. Hanss

LABORATORY OF EMBRYOLOGY   2096
Head: Professor Cl. Roussel

LABORATORY OF HISTOLOGY   2097
Head: Professor J.-P. Dadoune

LABORATORY OF PHYSIOLOGY   2098
Head: Professor M. Martineaud

Unit of Medical and Biological Studies 2099
Address: 45 rue des Saints-Pères, 75270 Cedex 06
Telephone: (01) 260 37 20
Director: Professor Madeleine Jaffrain

ODONTOLOGY   2100

Unit of Odontology   2101
Address: 1 rue Maurice-Arnoux, 92120 Montrouge
Dean: Professor B. Tuest
Senior staff: Dental orthopaedics, Professor P. Demoge, Professor E. Klingler; biology, Professor M. Gaspard; surgical dentistry, Professor A. Limoge, Professor R. Weill; prosthetics, Professor H. Sahel

PHARMACY   2102

Unit of Human and Experimental 2103
Biology

Address: 4 avenue de l'Observatoire, 75006 Paris
Director: Professor J. Savel
Sections: Biochemistry and physiopathology of energy and growth hormones, Professor R. Michel; biochemical structure and metabolism of the normal and diseased cell, Professor F. Percheron; metabolic examination and clinical and experimental biochemistry, Professor C. Dreux; hydrology and the public water supply, Professor R. Vilagines; cell physiopathology, Professor Savel
Activities: The Unit organizes and developes scientific cooperation at a national and international level through its techniques, publications, seminars, congresses and symposiums.

Unit of the Mechanisms of Action of 2104
Medicines and Toxins

Address: 4 avenue de l'Observatoire, 75006 Paris
Director: Professor R. Boulu
Sections: Therapeutic chemistry, Professor P. Delaveau; pharmacodynamics, Professor R. Boulu; pharmacokinetics, Professor R. Bourdon; biological control, Professor A. Desuignes; pharmacodynamics and biological tests on medicines, Professor P. Rossignol; toxicology, Professor G. LeMoan
Activities: Research is concentrated on the mechanisms of medicines and toxins in relation to living organisms: tissue, cell, molecule and organelle.

Université de Paris VI - Pierre et Marie Curie   2105

[Paris VI University - Pierre and Marie Curie]
Address: 4 place Jussieu, 75230 Paris Cedex 05
Telephone: (01) 336 25 25; 329 12 21
Telex: UPMC6 200 145
Educational establishment with r&d capability
President: Professor Jean Dry
See also entry for: Institut de Physique du Globe de Paris.

MEDICAL STUDY AND RESEARCH UNITS   2106

Faculty of Medicine Broussais-Hôtel-Dieu   2107

Address: 15 rue de l'École-de-Médecine, Paris
Telephone: (01) 329 21 77
Director: Professor Jacques Diebold

ANATOMY DEPARTMENT   2108
Head: Professor V. Meininger

BIOCHEMISTRY DEPARTMENT   2109
Head: Professor R. Engler

BIOPHYSICS DEPARTMENT   2110
Head: Professor Coursaget

FORENSIC MEDICINE DEPARTMENT   2111
Head: Professor Proteau

GENERAL PATHOLOGY DEPARTMENT   2112
Head: Professor Housset

HISTOLOGY DEPARTMENT   2113
Head: Professor Daoloune

MICROBIOLOGY DEPARTMENT   2114
Head: Professor Acar

PARASITOLOGY DEPARTMENT   2115
Head: Professor Picot

PATHOLOGICAL ANATOMY DEPARTMENT   2116
Head: Professor J. Diebold

PHARMACOLOGY DEPARTMENT   2117
Head: Professor Schmitt

PHYSIOLOGY DEPARTMENT   2118
Head: Professor Baillet

Antoine-Chantin Hospital   2119
Address: 38 rue Antoine-Chantin, Paris
Telephone: (01) 828 18 21

Broussais-la-Charité Hospital   2120
Address: 96 rue Didot, 75014 Paris
Telephone: (01) 828 37 62

Anaesthesiology Department   2121
Head: Dr Passelecq

Cardiology and Arterial Hypertension Department   2122
Head: Professor P. Maurice

Cardiovascular Surgery Department   2123
Head: Professor Dubost

Gastroenterology Department   2124
Head: Professor Petite

General Radiology Department   2125
Head: Mme Plainfossé

General Surgery Department   2126
Head: Professor J.H. Alexandre

Nephrology Department   2127
Head: Professor Milliez

Otorhinolaryngology Department   2128
Head: Professor Demaldent

Stomatology Department   2129
Head: Professor Descrozailles

Vascular Diseases Department   2130
Head: Professor Housset

Vascular Radiology Department   2131
Head: Professor Gaux

Hôtel-Dieu Hospital   2132
Address: 1 place du Parvis-Notre-Dame, Paris
Telephone: (01) 326 07 79

Faculty of Medicine Pitié-Salpêtrière   2133

Address: 91 boulevard de l'Hôpital, 75634 Paris Cedex 13
Telephone: (01) 584 11 84
Director: Professor J.C. Legrand

CHARLES-FOIX-JEAN-ROSTAND HOSPITAL GROUP   2134
Address: 7 avenue de la République, 94200 Ivry
Telephone: (01) 670 15 92

PITIÉ HOSPITAL   2135
Address: 83 boulevard de l'Hôpital, Paris
Telephone: (01) 336 04 56

SALPÊTRIÈRE HOSPITAL 2136

Address: 47 boulevard de l'Hôpital, Paris
Telephone: (01) 336 04 56

Faculty of Medicine Saint-Antoine 2137

Address: 27 rue de Chaligny, 75571 Paris Cedex 05
Telephone: (01) 341 71 00
Director: Professor Picard
Note: The Unit consists of a centre and the following
four hospitals:

ROTHSCHILD HOSPITAL 2138

Address: 11 rue de Santerre, Paris
Telephone: (01) 343 61 52

SAINT-ANTOINE HOSPITAL 2139

Address: 184 rue du Faubourg-Saint-Antoine, Paris
Telephone: (01) 344 33 33

TENON HOSPITAL 2140

Address: 4 rue de la Chine, Paris
Telephone: (01) 636 88 40

TROUSSEAU HOSPITAL 2141

Address: 36 rue du Docteur-Arnold-Netter, Paris
Telephone: (01) 343 96 71

Stomatology Institute 2142

Address: 47 boulevard de l'Hôpital, 75634 Paris
Director: Professor J.M. Vaillant

SCIENTIFIC STUDY AND RESEARCH 2143
UNITS

Analytical Mathematics Unit 2144

Director: Professor Priouret

Animal Physiology Unit 2145

Director: Professor Albe-Fressard

Applied Physics Unit 2146

Director: Professor Garnier

Biochemistry Unit 2147

Director: Professor Le Pecq

Computer Sciences and Statistics Unit 2148

Director: Professor Robinet

Earth Sciences Unit 2149

Director: Professor Poignant

Genetics Unit 2150

Director: Professor Favard

Inorganic Chemistry Unit 2151

Telephone: (01) 336 25 25
Director: Professor Herpin
Activities: Preparation of new materials and studies of
their properties.

Optics and Atomic Physics, Molecular 2152
and Crystal Physics Unit

Director: Professor Abelès

Organic Chemistry Unit 2153

Director: Professor Casadevall

Physical Chemistry Unit 2154

Director: Professor Chemla

Plant Biology Unit 2155

Director: Professor Lejal-Nicol

Pure and Applied Mathematics Unit 2156

Director: Professor Vauthler

Solid-State Physics Unit 2157

Director: Professor Authier

Statistics Institute 2158

Director: Professor Dugue

Theoretical and Applied Mechanics 2159
Unit

Director: Professor Duvaut

Theoretical and Corpuscular Physics 2160
Unit

Director: Professor Briand

Zoology Unit 2161

Director: Professor Raccaud

HENRI POINCARÉ INSTITUTE   2162

Address: 11 rue Pierre et Marie Curie, 75231 Paris Cedex 05
Telephone: (01) 354 42 10
Research director: Roger Descombes
Sections: Pure and applied mathematics; history of mathematics; theoretical physics
Annual expenditure: £10 000-50 000
Contract work: No

LABORATORY OF SOLID-STATE   2163
ELECTRONIC PHYSICS

Address: 4 place Jussieu, 75230 Paris Cedex 05
Telephone: (01) 329 12 21
Research director: Professeur Henri Benoit
Senior staff: W. Ghidalia, J.-P. Legrand
Activities: Magnetic properties and magnetic structures through magnetic resonance in the microwave range at pumped He_4 and He_3 temperatures. The materials studied are hydrated salts of transition elements and nonconducting spin glasses.
Facilities: Microwave equipment between 9.5 and 40 GHz.

LABORATORY OF ULTRASONICS   2164

Address: 4 place Jussieu, 75230 Paris Cedex 05
Telephone: (01) 336 25 25
Affiliation: Centre National de la Recherche Scientifique
Annual expenditure: F200 000
Activities: Elastic and electrical properties of amorphous materials and insulators; crystal growth - ferroelectrics.
Facilities: Apparatus for emission and detection of ultrasonic waves from audio-frequency to 36 GHz.
Consultancy: No

PHYSICS OF LIQUIDS AND   2165
INTERFACIAL ELECTROCHEMISTRY
CNRS RESEARCH GROUP

Address: 4 place Jussieu, 75230 Paris Cedex 05
Telephone: (01) 336 25 25
Affiliation: Centre National de la Recherche Scientifique
Senior staff: Solid-liquid interface structure, A. Defrain, L. Bosio, J.C. Lestrade, J.P. Badiali; electrochemical kinetics, M. Garreau, M. Keddam; electrocrystallization and corrosion of metals, M. Froment, R. Wiart, A. Hugot-Le Goff
Annual expenditure: F1 500 000
Activities: Electrical, optical properties; surface studies; corrosion resistance; electrochemical batteries.
Facilities: X-ray diffraction and analysis; scanning transmission electron microscopy; electrochemical impedance measurements.

VILLEFRANCHE SUR MER MARINE   2166
STATION

Address: 06230 Villefranche sur Mer
Telephone: (093) 55 55 56
Affiliation: Centre National de la Recherche Scientifique
Research director: Professor Paul Bougis
Sections: Marine biology, zooplankton, Professor Paul Bougis; physical and chemical oceanography, Professor A. Morel; geodynamics, Professor G. Boillot
Graduate research staff: 30
Annual expenditure: £51 000-500 000
Activities: A wide range of research activities from animal physiology to ocean geology, among them ecology of marine plankton; marine biology and physiology, physics and chemistry; oceanography.
Facilities: Two research vessels.
Contract work: No
Publications: Research reports.

Université de Paris VII   2167

[Paris University VII]
Address: 2 place Jussieu, 75221 Paris Cedex 05
Chairman: Professor Yves Le Corre

DEPARTMENT OF EARTH SCIENCES   2168

Address: 2 place Jussieu, 75221 Paris Cedex 05
Director: Professor Courtillet

Laboratory of Geochemistry and   2169
Cosmochemistry

Head: Professor Claude Allègre

Laboratory of Geochemistry of Stable   2170
Isotopes

Head: Dr Marc Javoy

Laboratory of Lithosphere Dynamics   2171

Head: Dr Jean Andrieux

Laboratory of Pedology   2172

Head: Dr Gérard Bocquier

FACULTY OF DENTAL SURGERY   2173

Address: 5 rue Garancière, 75006 Paris
Director: Professor Guy Penne

Laboratory of Basic Dentistry and Histology   2174

Head: Professor Roger Monteil

Laboratory of Basic Dentistry and Special Physiology   2175

Head: Professor Julien Philippe
Section: Special physiology, Professor L. Lejoyeux

Laboratory of Biomechanics and Physiology   2176

Heads: Professor Samuel Kleinfinger, Professor Richard Ogolnik

Laboratory of Ceramics   2177

Head: Professor Robert Dupont

Laboratory of Dental Pathology, Therapeutics and Radiography   2178

Heads: Professor Clément Vialatel, Professor Alain Mouille
Sections: Therapeutics, Professor F. Gory; pathology, Professor Clément Vialatel; radiology, Professor Alain Mouille

Laboratory of Dento-Facial Orthopaedics   2179

Head: Professor Roger O'Meyer

Laboratory of Epidemiology, Prophylaxis and Dental Hygiene   2180

Head: Professor Jean-Pierre Cavaillon

Laboratory of Maxillo-Facial Prosthesis   2181

Head: Professor Pierre Voreaux

Laboratory of Operational Dentistry   2182

Head: Professor Robert Rolland
Senior staff: Professor M.T. Drue, Professor V. Gauval, Professor H. Herbert, Professor E. Macler, Professor M. Maringe, Professor R. Ogolnik, Professor C. Sebban

Laboratory of Paradontology   2183

Head: Professor Jean-Jacques Barelle
Senior staff: Professor L. Marcus

Laboratory of Prosthesis (Adjoint)   2184

Head: Professor Joseph Lejoyeux

Laboratory of Prosthesis (Conjoint)   2185

Heads: Professor Albert A. Clément, Professor Albert Jeanmonod

FACULTY OF MEDICINE LARIBOISIÈRE-SAINT-LOUIS   2186

Address: Hôpital Saint-Lazare, 107 rue du Faubourg-Saint-Denis, 75010 Paris
Dean: Professor Raymond Houdart

Cancer Study and Research Group   2187

Head: Professor Lucien Israël

Central Laboratory of Microbiology   2188

Address: Hôpital Saint-Louis, 2 place Alfred-Fournier, 75010 Paris
Head: Dr Yvonne Perol

Clinic of Infectious Diseases   2189

Address: Hôpital Claude-Bernard, 10 avenue de la Porte d'Aubervilliers, 75019 Paris
Head: Professor André Domart

Clinic of Otorhinolaryngology   2190

Address: Hôpital Lariboisière, 2 rue Ambroise-Paré, 75010 Paris

Department of Biophysics and Bioelectronics   2191

Address: Faculté de Médecine, 45 rue des Saints-Pères, 75006 Paris
Head: Professor Michel Burgeat

Laboratory of Cardiac Physiopathology Research   2192

Address: Hôpital Lariboisière, 2 rue Ambroise-Paré, 75010 Paris
Head: Professor Yves Bouvrain

Laboratory of Electron Microscopy   2193

Address: Hôpital Fernand-Widal, 200 rue du Faubourg-Saint-Denis, 75010 Paris
Head: Professor Jean Bescal-Liversac

Laboratory of Gynaecology, Obstetrics 2194 and Obstetric Physiology

Address: Hôpital Lariboisière, 2 rue Ambroise-Paré, 75010 Paris
Head: Professor Paul Morin

Research on Dermatology, 2195 Immunology and Mycology

Address: Hôpital Saint-Louis, 2 place Alfred-Fournier, 75010 Paris
Head: Professor Robert Degas

Research Unit of Digestive 2196 Physiopathology

Head: Professor Jean-Jacques Bernier

Research Unit on Anaesthesiology 2197

Address: Hôpital Lariboisière, 2 rue Ambroise-Paré, 75010 Paris
Head: Dr Ernest Echter

Research Unit on Applied Biophysics 2198

Address: Hôpital Fernand-Widal, 200 rue du Faubourg Saint-Denis, 75010 Paris
Head: Professor Claude Dubost
Section: Gas exchanges, Professor A. Celerier

Research Unit on Biophysics 2199

Address: Hôpital Fernand-Widal, 200 rue du Faubourg Saint-Denis, 75010 Paris
Head: Dr Michel Duvelleroy

Research Unit on Cardiology 2200

Address: Hôpital Fernand-Widal, 200 rue du Faubourg-Saint-Denis, 75010 Paris
Head: Professor Jean-Jacques Welti

Research Unit on Child Diabetes and 2201 Nutrition

Address: Hôpital Hérold, 2 place Rhin-et-Danube, 75019 Paris
Head: Professor Henri Lestradet

Research Unit on Experimental 2202 Pathology

Address: rue de l'École-de-Médicine, 75006 Paris
Head: Professor François Cottenot
Activities: Dermato-immunology.

Research Unit on Experimental 2203 Surgery

Address: Hôpital Saint-Louis, 2 place Alfred-Fournier, 75010 Paris
Head: Professor Claude Dufourmentel

Research Unit on Functional 2204 Exploration of Nutrition - Endocrinology

Address: Hôpital Saint-Louis, 2 place Alfred-Fournier, 75010 Paris
Head: Professor Jean Canivet

Research Unit on General Medicine 2205

Address: Hôpital Saint-Louis, 2 place Alfred-Fournier, 75010 Paris
Head: Dr M. Pestel
Activities: Atheroma studies.

Research Unit on Histology, 2206 Embryology and Pathological Anatomy

Address: Hôptil Fernand-Widal, 200 rue du Faubourg-Saint-Denis, 75010 Paris
Head: Dr Michel Maillet

Research Unit on Human Physiology 2207

Address: 45 rue des Saints-Pères, 75270 Paris Cedex
Heads: Professor Jean-Paul Martineaud, Professor Andréa Teillac

Research Unit on Human Skin 2208 Tumours

Address: Fondation Rothschild, 29 rue Manin, 75019 Paris
Head: Dr M. Prunieras

Research Unit on Ophthalmology 2209

Address: Fondation Rothschild, 29 rue Manin, 75019 Paris
Head: Professor Paul Payraud

Research Unit on Physiology and 2210 Chronobiology

Address: Fondation Rothschild, 29 rue Manin, 75019 Paris

Research Unit on Toxicomania 2211

Address: Hôpital Fernand-Widal, 200 rue du Faubourg-Saint-Denis, 75010 Paris
Head: Professor Etienne Fournier

Therapeutic Clinic 2212

Head: Professor Michel Lamotte

Unit of Analytical Toxicology Research 2213

Address: Hôpital Fernand-Widal, 200 rue du Faubourg-Saint-Denis, 75010 Paris
Head: Professor R. Bourdon
Note: Associated with the Biochemistry and Toxicology Unit of Université de Paris V.

Unit of Biochemistry Research 2214

Address: Faculté de Médecine, 45 rue des Saints-Pères, 75006 Paris
Head: Professor Roland Bourrillon
Activities: Centre of protein research.

Unit of Experimental Toxicology 2215
Research

Address: Hôpital Fernand-Widal, 200 rue du Faubourg-Saint-Denis, 75010 Paris
Heads: Professor Etienne Fournier, Professor Michel Gaultier

Unit on Physiology and 2216
Neurophysiology

Address: Hôpital Lariboisière, 2 rue Ambroise-Paré, 75010 Paris
Head: Professor Hubert Marno

FACULTY OF MEDICINE XAVIER- 2217
BICHAT

Address: Hôpital Beaujon, 100 boulevard du Général Leclerc, 92110 Clichy
Dean: Professor François Bonnet De Pailleret

Clinic of Infectious Diseases 2218

Address: Hôpital Claude Bernard, 10 avenue de la Porte d'Aubervilliers, 75018 Paris
Head: Professor Raymond Bastin

Department of Haematology 2219

Head: Professor Pierre Boivin

Laboratory of Respiratory Pathology 2220

Address: Hôspital Bichat, 170 boulevard Ney, 75018 Paris
Head: Professor Toussaint J. Turiaf

Laboratory of the Louis-Mourier 2221
Hospital

Address: Hôpital Louis-Mourier, 92700 Colombes
Head: Dr Jean-Pierre Hardouin

Research Unit on Applied 2222
Neurophysiology

Head: Professor Jean Cambier

Research Unit on Erythrocyte and 2223
Leucocyte Biochemistry

Head: Professor Pierre Boivin

Research Unit on Gastroenterology 2224

Address: Hôpital Bichat, 170 boulevard Ney, 75877 Paris Cedex
Head: Professor Serge Bonfils

Research Unit on Haematology and 2225
Immunology

Address: Hôpital Louis-Mourier, 92700 Colombes
Heads: Professor Jean-Noël Maillard, Dr François Teillet

Research Unit on Haemostasis and 2226
Immunology

Head: Dr Doris Ménaché

Research Unit on Hepatic 2227
Physiopathology

Head: Professor Jean-Pierre Benhamou
Sections: Biliary secretions, Dr Serge Erlinger; hepatic ultrastructure, Dr Gérard Feldmann; hepatic haemodynamics, Professor Jean-Pierre Benhamou; hepatic encephalopathy, Dr Christian Sicot; enzymlogy, Professor Pierre Boivin

Research Unit on Human Nutrition 2228
and Dietetics

Address: Hôpital Bichat, 170 boulevard Ney, 75018 Paris

Research Unit on Hydro-Mineral Metabolism 2229

Address: Hôpital Bretonneau, 2 rue Carpeaux, 75877 Paris Cedex 18
Head: Professor Henri Mathieu

Research Unit on Microbiology 2230

Head: Dr Philippe Goullet

Research Unit on Neonatal Pathology 2231

Address: Hôpital Louis-Mourier, 92700 Colombes
Head: Dr Yves Nordmann

Research Unit on Nuclear Biophysics 2232

Address: 45 rue des Saints-Pères, 75006 Paris
Head: Dr Michèle Vulpillat

Research Unit on Physiology 2233

Address: Service d'Explorations Fonctionnelles, Hôpital Louis-Mourier, 92700 Colombes
Head: Professor Claude Amiel

Research Unit on Reanimation 2234

Address: Hôpital Claude-Bernard, 10 avenue de la Porte d'Aubervilliers, 75018 Paris
Head: Dr Jean-Jacques Pocidalo

RESEARCH GROUP FOR ENVIRONMENTAL STUDIES 2235

Address: 2 place Jussieu, 75221 Paris Cedex 05
Head: Dr Jacques Vigneron

UNIT OF BIOCHEMISTRY 2236

Address: 2 place Jussieu, 75221 Paris Cedex 05
Director: Geneviève Treboul
Chairman of Scientific Council: Professor Jean-Paul Aubert

Institute of Molecular Biology 2237

Directors: G. Bernardi, F. Chapeville

LABORATORY OF BIOCHEMICAL GENETICS 2238

Head: Professor Jean Tavlitzki

LABORATORY OF BIOLOGICAL PHYSICS 2239

Head: Professor René Cohen

LABORATORY OF BIOMEMBRANES 2240

Head: Professor Adam Képès

LABORATORY OF BIOMOLECULAR SPECTROSCOPY 2241

Head: Professor Jeorge Brahms

LABORATORY OF CELLULAR BIOCHEMISTRY 2242

Head: Professor Raymond Dedonder

LABORATORY OF CELLULAR GENETICS 2243

Head: Professor Gérard Buttin

LABORATORY OF DEVELOPMENTAL BIOLOGY 2244

Head: François Chapeville

LABORATORY OF ELECTRON MICROSCOPY 2245

Head: Professor Ennio-Lucio Benedetti

LABORATORY OF IMMUNODIFFERENTIATION 2246

Head: Professor Jean-Marie Dubert

LABORATORY OF MICROBIAL GENETICS 2247

Head: Professor Michel Yarmolinsky

LABORATORY OF MOLECULAR GENETICS 2248

Head: Professor G. Bernardi

Laboratory of Cellular Physiology 2249

Address: Institut Pasteur, 25 rue du Docteur-Roux, 75015 Paris
Head: Professor Jean-Paul Aubert

Laboratory of Metabolism of Enzymes of Sulphur Amino Acids 2250

Address: 96 boulevard Raspail, 75006 Paris
Head: Professor Fernande Chatagner

Laboratory of Physical Chemistry of Proteins 2251

Address: Institut Pasteur, 25 rue du Docteur-Roux, 75015 Paris
Head: Professor Michel Goldberg

Laboratory of Porphyrine Biochemistry 2252

Head: Professor Pierre Labbe

Laboratory of Virus Physiology 2253

Address: Institut Pasteur, 25 rue du Docteur-Roux, 75015 Paris
Head: Professor Marc Girard

UNIT OF BIOLOGY AND GENETICS 2254

Address: 2 place Jussieu, 75221 Paris Cedex 05
Director: Professor J. Schaeverbete
Chairman of Scientific Council: Professor Luc Picon

Laboratory of Biological Anthropology 2255

Head: Professor Albert Ducras
Section: Human adaptability, Professor A. Carli

Laboratory of Biological Membranes 2256

Head: Professor Marianne Lévy

Laboratory of Biological Sciences 2257
Teaching

Head: Professor Jacques Fiszer

Laboratory of Biostatistics 2258

Head: Dr Alain J. Valleron

Laboratory of Cellular Differentiation 2259
Physiology

Head: Professor Ariès Kovoor

Laboratory of Comparative 2260
Neuroanatomy

Head: Professor Roland Bauchot

Laboratory of Developmental Biology 2261

Head: Professor Charles Devillers
Section: Morphogenesis, Professor J. Rosenberg

Laboratory of Developmental 2262
Physiology of Foetal and Newborn
Mammals

Head: Professor Luc Picon

Laboratory of Differentiation 2263
Physiology

Address: 12 rue Cuvier, 75005 Paris
Head: Professor Jean Schaeverbete

Laboratory of Experimental 2264
Neuroembryology

Head: Professor Pierre Clairambault

Laboratory of Functional 2265
Differentiation of the Kidney and
Stomach of Mammals

Head: Professor Jean-Pierre Geloso

Laboratory of General and Applied 2266
Ecology

Head: Professor Jorge Vieira da Silva

Laboratory of Human Ecology 2267

Head: Professor J. Hiernaux

Laboratory of Invertebrate Biology 2268

Address: 7 quai Saint-Bernard, 75005 Paris
Head: Professor Alexis Grjebine

Laboratory of Invertebrate Hard 2269
Organs

Head: Professor Monique Chetail

Laboratory of Neurobiology 2270

Address: ENS, 46 rue d'Ulm, 75005 Paris
Head: Professor Claude Bergman

Laboratory of Neurophysiopathology 2271

Address: 2ter rue d'Alésia, 75014 Paris
Head: Professor Michel Lamarche

Laboratory of Plant Cellular Biology 2272

Head: Professor Simone Puiseux-Dao

Laboratory of Plant Cellular 2273
Physiology

Head: Professor Robert Esnault

Laboratory of Plant Cytology 2274

Head: Professor Jacqueline Vazart

Laboratory of Plant Physiology 2275

Head: Professor René Heller

Laboratory of Plant Reproduction and Differentiation 2276

Head: Professor Henri Camefort

Laboratory of Population Genetics 2277

Head: Professor Claudine Petit

Laboratory of Psychophysiology 2278

Head: Professor Jean Delacour

Laboratory of Skeletal Structures 2279

Address: 7 quai Saint-Bernard, 75005 Paris
Head: Professor Yves François

UNIT OF CHEMISTRY 2280

Address: 2 place Jussieu, 75221 Paris Cedex 05
Director: Professor Gérard Lapluye
Chairman of Scientific Council: Professor Jean-Pierre Doucet

Institute of Systems Topology and Dynamics 2281

Address: 1 rue Guy-de-la-Brasse, 75005 Paris
Head: Professor Jacques-Emile Dubois

Laboratory of Electrochemistry 2282

Head: Professor Jean-Michel Saveant

Laboratory of Hydrogeochemistry 2283

Head: Professor Gilles Michard

UNIT OF CLINICAL HUMAN SCIENCES 2284

Address: 13 rue de Santeuil, 75005 Paris
Director: Professor Pierre Fedida

Laboratory of Individual and Social Clinical Psychology 2285

Head: Professor Claude Revault-d'Allonnes
Senior staff: Professor J. Favez-Boutonier, Professor A.-M. Rocheblave

Laboratory of Pathological Psychology and Psychoanalysis 2286

Head: Professor Jean Laplanche
Sections: Blind children, Professor Jacques Postel
Psychiatric, Professor Jacques Postel
Psychoanalysis, Dr Ginette Michaud
Child psychosomatics, Dr Philippe Gutton
Pharmacological effects of drugs on the aged, Dr Jean-Claude Arbousse-Bastide

UNIT OF GEOGRAPHY AND SOCIAL SCIENCES 2287

Address: 2 place Jussieu, 75221 Paris Cedex 05
Director: Professor Jean Nicolas

Automatic Cartography 2288

Head: Dr Marie-Thérèse Gambin

Department of Physical Geography 2289

Head: Professor Fernand Joly

Department of Spatial Analysis of Geographical Data 2290

Head: Professor Etienne Dalmasso

Inequalities of Development in the Third World 2291

Address: Institut de Géographie, 191 rue Saint-Jacques, 75005 Paris
Heads: Professor Olivier Dollfus, Professor Jean Dresch

Structure of Rural Areas in Western Europe 2292

Head: Dr Claude Moindrot

UNIT OF HAEMATOLOGY 2293

Address: Hôpital Saint-Louis, 2 place Alfred-Fournier, 75010 Paris
Director: Professor Jean Bernard

Department of Blood Separation 2294

Head: Dr Annette Bussel

Department of Electron Microscopy 2295

Head: Professor Georges Flandrin

Laboratory of Animal Experimentation 2296

Head: Dr Georges Mahouy

Laboratory of Biochemistry 2297

Head: Dr Constantin Mihaesco

Laboratory of Chemotherapy 2298

Head: Dr Claude Jacquillat

Laboratory of Clinical Research 2299

Head: Dr Jeannine Dumont

Laboratory of Experimental 2300 Haematology

Head: Professor Michel Boiron

Laboratory of Graphical Haematology 2301

Head: Professor Jean Bernard

Laboratory of Haemostasis and 2302 Experimental Thrombosis

Head: Dr Jacques Caen

Laboratory of Immunochemistry 2303

Head: Professor Maxim Seligmann

Laboratory of Immunohaematology 2304

Head: Professor Jean Dausset

Laboratory of Nuclear Medicine 2305

Head: Professor Yves Najean

Laboratory of Tumour Immunology 2306

Heads: Dr François Kourilsky, Dr Jean-Paul Lévy

UNIT OF MATHEMATICS 2307

Address: 2 place Jussieu, 75221 Paris Cedex 05
Director: Professor François Norguet

Analysis Group 2308

Heads: Professor Bernard Maurey, Professor Laurent Schawrtz

Arithmetic Group 2309

Head: Professor Yvette Amice

Department of Geometric Theories 2310

Head: Professor Marcel Berger
Sections: Geometry, Professor M. Karoubi, Professor Verdier, Professor P. Libermann, Professor F. Norguet, Professor M. Zisman
Logic, Professor D. Lacombe
Theory of Lie Groups, Professor F. Bruhat, Professor R. Godement, Professor M. Lazard, Professor Paul Gerardin, Professor M. Duflo

Department of Information Theory 2311

Heads: Professor Maurice Nivat, Professor Louis Nolin, Professor Marcel Schutzenberger

UNIT OF PHYSICS 2312

Address: 2 place Jussieu, 75221 Paris Cedex 05
Director: Professor Jean Klein

Laboratory of Bio-Rheology and 2313 Physiological Hydrodynamics

Head: Professor Daniel Quémada

Laboratory of High Energy 2314 Experimental Physics

Head: Professor Bernard Grossetête

Laboratory of High Energy Theoretical 2315 Physics

Head: Professor Bernard Diu

Laboratory of Physical Sciences and 2316 Technology Teaching

Head: Professor Goery Delacote

Laboratory of Surface Magnetism 2317

Head: Professor Jean-Loup Motchane

Laboratory of Theoretical Automation 2318

Head: Professor Augustin Blaquière

Laboratory of Theoretical Physics and 2319 Mathematics

Head: Professor Guy Rideau

Laboratory of Thermodynamics of   **2320**
Ionic and Biological Media

Head: Professor Jacques Chanu

Physics of Solids Group   **2321**

Head: Professor Michel Schott
Senior staff: Professor P. Baruch, Professor J. Bok,
Professor M. Hulin, Professor D. Saint-James

Université de Paris IX -   2322
Université de Paris-
Dauphine

[Paris University IX - Paris-Dauphine University]
Address: place de-Lattré-de-Tassigny, 75775 Paris
Cedex 16
Chairman: Professor Henri Tezenas du Montiel
Note: The Paris-Dauphine University is mainly con-
cerned with management and organization sciences.

UNIT OF MANAGEMENT DATA   **2323**
PROCESSING

Director: Gérard Levy

UNIT OF MATHEMATICS   **2324**

Director: Professor Hervé Moulin

Université de Paris XI -   2325
Université de Paris-Sud

[Paris University XI - Paris-South University]
Address: 15 rue Georges Clémenceau, 91405 Orsay
Cedex
Telephone: (0336) 941 67 50
Telex: 69 21 66 F

CHANTENAY-MALABRY   **2326**
PHARMACEUTICAL CENTRE

Vice-Chairman and Director: Yves Cohen

Research laboratories   **2327**

DEPARTMENT OF MICROBIOLOGY   **2328**
Heads: A. German, A.M. Quéro, P. Bourlioux

LABORATORY OF ANALYTICAL   **2329**
CHEMISTRY I
Heads: M. Guernet, Fernand Pellerin

LABORATORY OF ANALYTICAL   **2330**
CHEMISTRY II
Heads: M. Hamon, G. Mahuzier

LABORATORY OF APPLIED ANIMAL   **2331**
BIOLOGY
Head: P. Binet

LABORATORY OF APPLIED   **2332**
BIOCHEMISTRY
Head: A. Lemonnier

LABORATORY OF BOTANY AND PLANT 2333
BIOLOGY
Head: J.L. Guignard

LABORATORY OF CELL BIOLOGY   **2334**
Head: J.C. Mestre

LABORATORY OF CHEMISTRY OF   **2335**
THERAPEUTIC NATURAL SUBSTANCES
Head: J. Poisson

LABORATORY OF CYCLIC   **2336**
NUCLEOTIDES
Head: G. Cehovic

LABORATORY OF GALENIC   **2337**
PHARMACY
Heads: A. Mangeot, F. Puisieux, D. Duchene

LABORATORY OF GENERAL AND   **2338**
MINERAL CHEMISTRY I
Head: P. Khodadad

LABORATORY OF GENERAL AND   **2339**
MINERAL CHEMISTRY II
Head: C. Souleau

LABORATORY OF GENERAL   **2340**
BIOCHEMISTRY
Head: J. Agneray

LABORATORY OF HAEMATOLOGY   **2341**
Head: M. Leclerc

LABORATORY OF HYDROLOGY   **2342**
Head: R. Laugier

LABORATORY OF HYGIENE   **2343**
Head: P. Bourrinet

LABORATORY OF MATERIA MEDICA   **2344**
Heads: A. Cave, M. Leboeuf, M. Paris

LABORATORY OF MATHEMATICS AND 2345
STATISTICS
Head: J.R. Didry

LABORATORY OF MINERAL 2346
CHEMISTRY III
Head: N. Rodier

LABORATORY OF NUTRITION AND 2347
CELL KINETICS
Head: R. Valencia

LABORATORY OF ORGANIC 2348
CHEMISTRY I
Head: M. Mioque

LABORATORY OF ORGANIC 2349
CHEMISTRY II
Head: C. Combet-Farnoux

LABORATORY OF PARASITOLOGY 2350
Head: Ph. Gayrol

LABORATORY OF PHARMACEUTICAL 2351
AND THERAPEUTIC CHEMISTRY
Heads: P. Reynaud, S. Kirkiacharian

LABORATORY OF PHARMACEUTICAL 2352
CHEMISTRY II
Head: M. Plat

LABORATORY OF PHARMACEUTICAL 2353
LAW AND DEONTOLOGY
Head: M Tisseyre

LABORATORY OF 2354
PHARMACODYNAMICS
Heads: Y. Cohen, J. Wepierre, C. Jacquot

LABORATORY OF PHYSICS 2355
Head: M. Bailly

LABORATORY OF PHYSICS AND 2356
BIOPHYSICS
Head: H. Renault

LABORATORY OF PHYSICS IN 2357
MEDICINE
Head: G. Hazebroucq

LABORATORY OF PHYSIOLOGY 2358
Heads: J.C. Gounelle, P. Mynard

LABORATORY OF TOXICOLOGY 2359
Head: C. Boudene

Unit of Hygiene and the Protection of 2360
Man and his Environment
Head: Jean-Charles Mestre

Unit of Pharmaceutical and Biological 2361
Sciences
Head: Yves Cohen

Unit of Therapeutic Chemistry 2362
Head: Fernand Pellerin

KREMLIN-BICÊTRE MEDICAL CENTRE 2363 - UNIT OF MEDICINE

Address: Centre Universitaire de Kremlin-Bicêtre, 63 rue Gabriel-Péri, 94270 Le Kremlin-Bicêtre
Telephone: 670 11 85
Vice-Chairman and Director: Jean Dormont
Annual expenditure: Fl 333 000 (1980)
Activities: The Paris-Sud Medical University together with the administrative department in Paris form the Kremlin-Bicêtre Medical Centre. This contains three hospitals which are dependents of the Paris Hospital itself: Hôpital de Bicêtre, Hôpital Paul-Brousse and Hôpital Antoine-Béclère. It also has links with other hospitals.
The main areas of research concern: cancerology and immunology; reproduction biology; fundamental cytology; normal and pathological haemostasis; experimental surgery; epidemiology and medical statistics.
Another of the Centre's functions is to provide assistance to those research groups which do not have any major sponsors in the fields of: fundamental and clinical pharmacology; respiratory physiology and physiopathology; morphological and ultrastructural investigations; nuclear medicine; normal and pathological infant development.
Contract work: No

Biophysics and Nuclear Medicine 2364 Service

Address: Hôpital de Bicêtre, 78 rue du Général Leclerc, 94270 Le Kremlin-Bicêtre
Telephone: 677 81 77
Head: Professor Alex Desgrez
Activities: Biophysics; radioactivity; velocimetry; ultrasonic techniques.

Central Laboratory of Pathological Anatomy 2365

Address: Hôpital Paul-Brousse, 14 avenue Paul Vaillant-Couturier, 94800 Villejuif
Telephone: 726 50 00
Head: Professor Jean Berger
Activities: Renal immunology; morphological study of experimental hepatic lesions.

Department of Human Physiology 2366

Address: Centre Chirurgical Marie Lannelongue, 133 avenue de la Résistance, 92350 Le Plessis-Robinson
Telephone: 630 21 33
Head: Professor Jacques Durand
Activities: Human ecophysiology.

Department of Human Physiology 2367

Address: Hôpital de Bicêtre, 78 rue du Général Leclerc, 94270 Le Kremlin-Bicêtre
Telephone: 222 00 71
Head: Professor Gabriel Barres
Activities: Physiology; ventilation; respiratory control.

Institute of Paediatrics 2368

Address: Institut Gustave Roussy, 16 bis avenue Paul Vaillant-Couturier, 94800 Villejuif
Telephone: 726 49 09
Head: Odile Schweisguth
Activities: Clinical research on tumours in infants and their treatment.

Laboratory of Hepatic Surgery 2369

Address: Hôpital Paul-Brousse, 14 avenue Paul Vaillant-Couturier, 94800 Villejuif
Telephone: 726 50 00
Head: Professor Henri Bismuth
Activities: Liver; encephalopathy; hepatectomy; regeneration; experimental cirrhosis.

Laboratory of Histoembryology and Cytogenetics 2370

Address: Hôpital de Bicêtre, 78 rue du Général Leclerc, 94270 Le Kremlin-Bicêtre
Telephone: 677 81 77
Head: Professor Georges David
Activities: Histoembryology; cytogenetics; sperm; reproduction; central nervous system.

Laboratory of Microbiology 2371

Address: Hôpital de Bicêtre, 78 rue du Général Leclerc, 94270 Le Kremlin-Bicêtre
Telephone: 677 81 77
Head: Professor Paul Tournier
Activities: New diagnostic techniques in bacteriology and virology.

Laboratory of Multidisciplinary Research 2372

Address: Hôpital de Bicêtre, 78 rue du Général Leclerc, 94270 Le Kremlin-Bicêtre
Telephone: 677 68 85
Head: Professor Philippe Auzepy
Activities: Experimental study of acute intoxication by glycol diethyline; experimental study of shock.

Laboratory of Nephrology and Renal Transplants 2373

Address: Hôpital Paul-Brousse, 14 avenue Paul Vaillant-Couturier, 94800 Villejuif
Telephone: 725 50 00
Head: Professor Daniel Fries
Activities: Immunology of urinary infections; renal transplants in the dog.

Laboratory of Neuropathology 2374

Address: Hôpital de Bicêtre, 78 rue du Général Leclerc, 94270 Le Kremlin-Bicêtre
Telephone: 677 81 77
Head: Professor Jean Lapresle
Activities: Anatomo-clinical correlations; neuropathology; neuromuscular pathology.

Laboratory of Personality Genetics 2375

Address: Fondation Vallée, 7 rue Bénérade, 94250 Gentilly
Telephone: 581 11 35
Heads: Professor Roger Mises, Roger Perron
Activities: Development of the personality and its problems; the infant and institutions.

Laboratory of Pharmacology 2376

Address: Hôpital de Bicêtre, 78 rue du Général Leclerc, 94270 Le Kremlin-Bicêtre
Telephone: 329 21 77
Head: Professor Jean-François Giudicelli
Activities: Pharmacology; heart and lungs; hypertension; angina pectoris.

Laboratory of Physiology and Human 2377 Reproduction

Address: Hôpital Antoine-Béclère, 157 rue de la Porte-de-Trivaux, 92140 Clamart
Telephone: 630 21 22
Heads: Professor Émile Papiernik, Ondinet Bomsel-Helmreich
Activities: Normal and pathologic ovulation in the woman and the rabbit; foetal hypotrophy; new-born infants.

Laboratory of Pulmonary 2378 Ultrastructure

Address: Hôpital Antoine-Béclère, 157 rue de la Porte-de-Trivaux, 92140 Clamart
Telephone: 630 21 22
Head: Professor René Pariente
Activities: Lung ultrastructure and pathology; structure-function relations; clinical immunology.

Laboratory of Surgery 2379

Address: Centre Chirurgical Marie-Lannelongue, 133 avenue de la Résistance, 92350 Le Plessis-Robinson
Telephone: 630 21 33
Director: Michel Weiss
Activities: Experimental surgery; heart; lungs; transplants; hypothermia.

Research Group on Physiopathology 2380 of Haemostasis and Thrombosis

Address: Hôpital de Bicêtre, 78 rue du Général Leclerc, 94270 Le Kremlin-Bicêtre
Telephone: 588 61 95
Head: Professor Marie-Josette Larrieu
Activities: Haemostasis; thrombosis; Factor VIII; Willebrand factor; Factor IX; fibrinogenes.

Research Groups for Neonatal 2381 Pathology

Address: Hôpital Antoine-Béclère, 157 rue de la Porte-de-Trivaux, 92140 Clamart
Telephone: 630 21 22
Head: Professor Jean-Claude Gabilan
Activities: Paediatrics; new-born infants; respiratory disorders; neonatal icterus; thigh dislocation.

Research Laboratory for Hepatology 2382 and Digestive Pathology

Address: Hôpital Antoine-Béclère, 157 rue de la Porte-de-Trivaux, 92140 Clamart
Telephone: 630 21 22
Head: Professor Jean-Pierre Étienne
Activities: Hepatology; liver; immunology; alcohol; digestive tract; pharmacokinetics.

Research Laboratory for Surgery and 2383 Digestive Physiology

Address: Hôpital Antoine-Béclère, 157 rue de la Porte-de-Trivaux, 92140 Clamart
Telephone: 630 21 22
Head: Professor Hubert Larrieu
Activities: Digestive electromyography; experimental prevention of ulcers; protection of colon sutures.

Research Unit on Molecular 2384 Metabolism and Steroid Physiopathology

Address: Hôpital de Bicêtre, 78 rue du Général Leclerc, 94270 Le Kremlin-Bicêtre
Telephone: 677 65 00
Head: Professor Étienne Baulieu
Activities: Biochemistry; steroids; hormones; transport proteins.

Unit of Statistics Applied to Medical 2385 Research

Address: Institut Gustave Roussy, 16 bis avenue Paul Vaillant-Couturier, 94800 Villejuif
Telephone: 677 24 69
Head: Professor Robert Flamant
Activities: Methodology of therapeutic tests; epidemiological studies; prognostics and diagnostics.

ORSAY SCIENTIFIC CENTRE 2386

Vice-Chairman: Hubert Coudanne

Institute of Nuclear Physics 2387

Director: Xavier Tarrago

Laboratory of Linear Accelerators 2388

Director: Jean Perez y Jorba

Unit of the Third Cycle and of 2389 Research

Director: Gabriel Ruget

BIOLOGY - BIOPHYSICS 2390

Biology and Agronomy Experimental Centre 2391
Affiliation: Centre National de la Recherche Scientifique
Head: Emmanuel Picard

Institute of Biochemistry 2392
Director: Dr Bernard Rossignol
Groups: Biochemistry of cell transport, Dr Bernard Rossignol
Endocrinology and cell regulation, Simone Harbon
Peptides, Evanghélos Bricas, Jean Heijenoort
Lipopolysaccharide bacterial physico-chemistry, Ladislas Szabo
Energy metabolism and regulation, Pierre Volfin
Immunostimulants of bacterial origin, Jean-François Petit
Structure and reactivity of proteins, Julio Pudles
Genetic information and development, Professor Michel Jacquet
Metabolism and biosynthesis of aromatic amino acids, Robert Azerad

Institute of Experimental Biology 2393
Director: Philippe Vigier
Groups: Cell biology and genetics, Professor Jean-Luc Rossignol
General biology, Professor Jean-Claude Mounolou
Biology and molecular genetics, Michel Guerineau
Genetics I, Professor Denise Marcou
Genetics II, Professor Philippe Vigier
Ribosomes, Professor Marguerite Bennoun

Institute of Microbiology 2394
Groups: Biochemistry of nucleic acid, Professor Jean Legault-Demarc
Pro- and eukaryotic regulation, Professor Jean-Claude Patte

Laboratory of Animal Biology 2395
Head: Professor Théodore Lender

Laboratory of Biomembranes 2396
Head: Professor Emanuel Shechter

Laboratory of Biophysics 2397
Head: vacant

Laboratory of Botany II 2398
Head: Professor René Nozeran

Laboratory of Cell Biology IV 2399
Head: Professor Jean André

Laboratory of Cell Biology V 2400
Head: Professor Jean Mousseau

Laboratory of Comparative Physiology 2401
Head: Professor Edouard Coraboeuf

Laboratory of Cryptogamy 2402
Head: Professor Jean Chevaugeon

Laboratory of Endocrinology 2403
Head: Professor Jacques Roffi

Laboratory of Entomology 2404
Head: Professor Yves Gillou

Laboratory of General Zoology 2405
Head: Professor François Ramade

Laboratory of Genetics and Physiology of Plant Development 2406
Head: Professor Jean Pernes

Laboratory of Heart Cell Physiology 2407
Head of research: Guy Vassort

Laboratory of Insect Biology 2408
Head of research: Suzel Fuzeau-Breasch

Laboratory of Insect Reproduction and Development 2409
Head: Professor Ginette Lauge

Laboratory of Marine Ecophysiology 2410
Head: Professor Joseph Bergerard

Laboratory of Molecular Plant Biology 2411
Head: Professor François Quetier

Laboratory of Movement Physiology 2412
Affiliation: Centre National de la Recherche Scientifique
Head: Professor Simon Bouisset

Laboratory of Nutrition Physiology 2413
Head: Professor François Chevallier
Senior staff: Professor Claude Lutton

Laboratory of Photosynthesis and Metabolism 2414
Head: M.L. Champigny

Laboratory of Physical Biochemistry 2415
Research director: Jean Garnier

Laboratory of Physico-Chemical Enzymology 2416
Research director: Jeannine Yon-Kahn

Laboratory of Plant Biology B 2417
Head: Professor Alain Lacoste

Laboratory of Plant Biology C 2418
Head: Professor Robert Gorenflot

Laboratory of Plant Ecology 2419
Head: Professor Bernard Saugier

Laboratory of Plant Improvement 2420
Head: Professor Yves Demarly

Laboratory of Plant Physiology 2421
Head: vacant

Laboratory of Psychophysiology 2422
Head: Professor Vincent Bloch

Laboratory of Sensory Physiology 2423
Head: vacant

Laboratory of Structure and Metabolism 2424
Head: Professor Robert Bourdu

Laboratory of Tissue Culture 2425
Head: Professor Claude Lioret

Laboratory of Vertebrate Biology 2426
Head: Professor André Beaumont
Group: Cytophysiology of fish nutrition, Professor Jean-Marie Vernier

Laboratory of Zoology II 2427
Head: Professor Jean Genermont

CHEMISTRY 2428

Laboratory of Amorphous Materials Physical 2429
Chemistry
Head: Professor Michel Ghelfenstein

Laboratory of Applied Chemistry 2430
Head: Professor Alexandre Revcolevschi

Laboratory of Asymmetric Synthesis 2431
Head: Professor Henri Kagan

Laboratory of Atomic and Molecular 2432
Collisions
Research director: Michel Barat

Laboratory of Biological Organic Chemistry 2433
Head: Professor Michel Vilkas

Laboratory of Bioorganic Coordination 2434
Head: Professor Alain Gaudemer

Laboratory of Carbocyclic Chemistry 2435
Head: Professor Jean-Marie Conia

Laboratory of Corrosion 2436
Head: Professor Jacques Galland

Laboratory of Gas in Metals 2437
Head: Professor Jacques Plusquellec

Laboratory of Ionic and Electronic Resonance 2438
Head: Professor Rose Marx

Laboratory of Metallic Materials Structure 2439
Head: Professor Georges Cizeron

Laboratory of Mineral Physico-Chemistry 2440
Head: Charles Mazières

Laboratory of Multifunctional Organic 2441
Chemistry
Head: Professor Serge David

Laboratory of Non-Stoichiometric Compounds 2442
Head: Professor Paul Gerdanian

Laboratory of Organic Materials Chemistry 2443
Head: Professor Hubert Coudanne

Laboratory of Organic Synthesis 2444
Head: Professor Michel Golfier

Laboratory of Organometallic Chemistry 2445
Head: Professor Erica Henry-Basch

Laboratory of Photophysical Chemistry 2446
Research director: Annette Bernas

Laboratory of Physical Metallurgy 2447
Head: vacant

Laboratory of Reaction Intermediates 2448
Head: Professor Jean Faure

Laboratory of Spectrochemistry of Transition 2449
Elements
Head: Professor Olivier Kahn

Laboratory of Structural Organic Chemistry 2450
Head: Professor Jean Jullien

Laboratory of Theoretical Chemistry 2451
Research director: Nguyen Trong Anh

COMPUTER SCIENCES 2452

Laboratory of Computer Science for 2453
Mechanics and Engineering
Research director: Guy Renard

Laboratory of Research in Computer Sciences 2454
Head: Professor Jean Vuillemin

EARTH SCIENCES 2455

Laboratory of Cartography and African 2456
Geology
Head: Professor Anne Faure-Muret

Laboratory of Geophysics and Geodynamics 2457
of Active Coastlines
Head: Jacques Dubois

Laboratory of Hydrology and Isotope 2458
Geochemistry
Head: Professor Jean-Charles Fontes

Laboratory of Internal Dynamic Geology 2459
Head: Professor Jacques Mercier

Laboratory of Internal Geophysics 2460
Head: Professor Claude Froidevaux

Laboratory of Petrography and 2461
Volcanography
Head: Professor Robert Brousse

Laboratory of Sedimentary Petrology and 2462
Palaeontology
Heads: Professor Bruce Purser, Professor Jean-Pierre Cuif

Laboratory of Sedimentary Rock 2463
Geochemistry
Head: Professor Michel Steinberg

Laboratory of Structural and Applied Geology 2464
Head: Professor François Ellenberger

MATHEMATICS 2465

Laboratory of Mathematics 2466
Director: François Laudenbach
Sections: Harmonic analysis, Professor Jean-Pierre Kahane, Professor Yves Meyer
Numerical and functional analysis, Professor Roger Temam
Arithmetic and algebraic geometry, Professor Michel Raynaud
Applied statistics, Professor D. Dacunha-Castelle
Differential topology, Jean Cerf (Research director)
Mathematics library, Professor Georges Poitou, Françoise Emery

Didactics of Physical Sciences 2467
Head: Georges Soussau

Interdisciplinary Centre for the Study of the 2468
Evolution of Ideas and Science Techniques
Director: E.M. Laperrousaz

Université de Paris XII – 2469
Université Paris-Val de Marne

[Paris University XII - Paris-Val de Marne University]
Address: avenue du Général de Gaulle, 94010 Créteil Cedex
Telephone: 898 91 44
President: Professor Michel Guillou
Activities: In addition to the departments which conduct research there are a number of research institutes which were set up in order to develop multidisciplinary research activities. One of the special projects at the moment involving these institutes is the study of man and his environment.
Multidisciplinary centres: Computer sciences; audiovisual aids.

INSTITUTE OF TOWN PLANNING 2470

Address: avenue du Général de Gaulle, 94010 Créteil Cedex
Telephone: 989 91 44
Head: Professor Gabriel Dupuy
Activities: Principal research themes include: the environment - economic, socioeconomic research, ecology and pollution; urban technology - infrastructure; town planning and design in the Third World; reconstruction of ancient habitats and new habitats.

Laboratory of Environmental Physical 2471
Chemistry
Head: Gérard Toupanée
Activities: Terrestrial and planetary environments.

Spatial Analysis Group 2472
Head: Professor Jean-Louis Guigou
Activities: Soil appropriation and use; regionalization; spatial solidarity.

UNIT OF MEDICINE 2473
Address: 6 avenue du Général Sarrail, 94000 Créteil
Facilities: Animal centre; microanalysis centre.

Centre for Surgical Research 2474
Telephone: 207 51 41
Affiliation: Centre National de la Recherche Scientifique
Head: Professor Jean Paul Cachera
Activities: Mechanical assistance for the left ventricle; implant prosthetics; microsurgery; urinary prosthetics; study of biomaterials; organ transplants.

Department of Anaesthesia and 2475
Reanimation
Address: Hôpital Henri-Mondor, 51 avenue du Maréchal de Lattre de Tassigny, 94010 Créteil
Telephone: 207 51 41
Heads: Christian Debras, Professor Pierre Huguenard
Activities: Clinical and fundamental research; health economics; study of medical instruments; ergonomics. Reanimation and anaesthesia; shock; alcohol.

Department of Anatomy 2476
Telephone: 207 51 41
Head: Professor Claude Kenesi
Activities: Prosthetics; bone deformities.

Department of Bacteriology and 2477
Virology
Address: Hôpital Henri-Mondor, 51 avenue du Maréchal de Lattre de Tassigny, 94010 Créteil
Telephone: 207 51 41
Head: Professor Jean Roger Duval
Activities: Antibacterial agents and pharmacokinetics; epidemiology; anaerobic bacteria.

Department of Biochemistry 2478

Address: Hôpital Henri-Mondor, 51 avenue du Maréchal de Lattre de Tassigny, 94010 Créteil
Telephone: 207 51 41
Head: Professor Pierre Gonnard
Activities: Neurochemistry.

Department of Biological 2479 Haematology

Address: Hôpital Henri-Mondor, 51 avenue du Maréchal de Lattre de Tassigny, 94010 Créteil
Telephone: 207 51 41
Head: Claude Sultan
Activities: Malignant lymphs; myelofibrosis; dysmelia; Menetrier's disease; interrelationship between folates, vitamin B_{12} and DNA synthesis; detection of antibodies harmful to DNA by immunofluorescence means using Crithidra luciliae.

Department of Biophysics 2480

Address: Hôpital Henri-Mondor, 51 avenue du Maréchal de Lattre de Tassigny, 94010 Créteil
Telephone: 207 51 41
Head: Professor Pierre Galle
Activities: Ultrastructure; intra-cellular analysis; nuclear medicine.

Department of Cardiology 2481

Address: Hôpital Henri-Mondor, 51 avenue du Maréchal de Lattre de Tassigny, 94010 Créteil
Head: Professor Pierre Vernant
Activities: Heart attacks; atherosclerosis.

Department of Dermatology 2482

Address: Hôpital Henri-Mondor, 51 avenue du Maréchal de Lattre de Tassigny, 94010 Créteil
Telephone: 207 51 41
Head: Professor René Touralne
Activities: Skin inflammation and medicines; photoactive molecules.

Department of Endocrinology and 2483 Nutrition Diseases

Address: Hôpital Henri-Mondor, 51 avenue du Maréchal de Lattre de Tassigny, 94010 Créteil
Telephone: 207 51 41
Head: Professor Jean Hazard
Activities: Surgery for hypothyroid patients; obesity.

Department of Facial Surgery 2484

Address: Hôpital Henri-Mondor, 51 avenue du Maréchal de Lattre de Tassigny, 94010 Créteil
Head: Professor Maurice Grellet
Activities: Use of the scanner in facial pathology.

Department of Gastroenterology 2485

Address: Hôpital Albert Chenevier, 40 rue Mesly, 94010 Créteil
Telephone: 898 92 90
Head: Paul Fouet
Activities: Nutrition for cirrhosis victims; digestive manometrics.

Department of General Surgery 2486

Address: Hôpital Henri-Mondor, 51 avenue du Maréchal de Lattre de Tassigny, 94010 Créteil
Telephone: 207 51 41
Head: Professor André Germain
Activities: Study of veins after arterial surgery; arterial reconstruction; thyroid cancers; hypothyroid - medicosurgical treatment.

Department of Gynaecology and 2487 Obstetrics

Address: Hôpital Henri-Mondor, 51 avenue du Maréchal de Lattre de Tassigny, 94010 Créteil
Telephone: 207 51 41
Head: Professor Jean Pierre Gautray
Activities: Effect of Dopamine on the gonadotrophic function; alteration of maternal hormones on childbirth; study of uterine collagen in pregnancy.

Department of Hepatology and 2488 Gastroenterology

Address: Hôpital Intercommunal, 40 allée de la Source, 94190 Villeneuve St-Georges
Telephone: 925 10 90
Head: Daniel Cattan
Activities: Metabolism of folates and vitamin B_{12} in human epithelial cells; use of scanner and ectomography for jaundice diagnosis; epidemiological studies of cirrhosis of the liver.

Department of Histology, Embryology 2489 and Cytogenetics

Telephone: 207 51 41
Head: Professor Jean Chevreau
Activities: Tumours in the human central nervous system; embryo nerve cells in tissue culture; immunology study of the human lungs; mechanisms of metallic impregnations.

Department of Internal Medicine 2490

Address: Hôpital Henri-Mondor, 51 avenue du Maréchal de Lattre de Tassigny, 94010 Créteil
Telephone: 207 51 41
Head: Professor Jean-Louis Portos
Activities: Depression in internal medicine.

Department of Medical Reanimation 2491

Address: Hôpital Henri-Mondor, 51 avenue du Maréchal de Lattre de Tassigny, 94010 Créteil
Telephone: 207 51 41
Head: Professor Maurice Rapin
Activities: Immunological, haemodynamic and respiratory study of septic shock; medical pharmacokinetics related to shock; acute respiratory malfunction; reanimation surveillance; economic study of reanimation.

Department of Neurology 2492

Address: Hôpital Albert Chenevier, 40 rue Mesly, 94010 Créteil
Telephone: 989 92 90
Head: Professor Jean Paul Gautier
Activities: Cause, prevention and treatment of cerebral vascular accidents; Parkinson's disease.

Department of Neurosurgery 2493

Address: Hôpital Henri-Mondor, 51 avenue du Maréchal de Lattre de Tassigny, 94010 Créteil
Telephone: 207 51 41
Head: Professor Jean Pierre Caron
Activities: Aneurisms; experiments with radioisotopes in surgery.

Department of Ophthalmology 2494

Address: Hôpital Intercommunal de Créteil, 40 avenue de Verdun, 94010 Créteil
Telephone: 898 91 80
Head: Gabriel Coscas
Activities: Macular deterioration; retinal occlusions; retinal anomalies in the diabetic.

Department of Orthopaedic Surgery 2495 and Traumatology

Address: Hôpital Intercommunal, 40 allée de la Source, 94190 Villeneuve St-Georges
Telephone: 925 39 40
Head: Professor Marcel Bombart
Activities: Fracture osteosynthesis; treatment of rickets; pathology of amputated stumps.

Department of Orthopaedics and 2496 Traumatology

Address: Hôpital Henri-Mondor, 51 avenue du Maréchal de Lattre de Tassigny, 94010 Créteil
Telephone: 207 51 41
Head: Professor Daniel Goutallier
Activities: Clinical research.

Department of Parasitology 2497

Telephone: 207 51 41
Head: Professor René Houin
Activities: Bilharzia in Madagascar; transmission of leishmaniosis in Corsica and Brazil.

Department of Pathological Anatomy 2498

Address: Hôpital Henri-Mondor, 51 avenue du Maréchal de Lattre de Tassigny, 94010 Créteil
Telephone: 207 51 41
Head: Yvon Pinaudeau
Activities: Hormones; pulmonary emphysema; subcutaneous conjunctive tissue; diabetes and hypertension.

Department of Pharmacology 2499

Telephone: 207 51 41
Head: Jean Paul Tillement
Activities: Tissue liaison between medicines; pharmacokinetics and pharmaco-immunology of medicines.

Department of Psychiatry 2500

Address: Hôpital Albert Chenevier, 40 rue Mesly, 94010 Créteil
Telephone: 898 92 90
Head: Professor André Bourgignon
Activities: Relationship between infant traumas and later psychopathology; family structure and infant mortality; post-obstetrical traumas; psychopathy and delinquency in institutionalized children.

Department of Radiology 2501

Address: Hôpital Henri-Mondor, 51 avenue du Maréchal de Lattre de Tassigny, 94010 Créteil
Telephone: 207 51 41
Head: Professor Jean Ferrane
Activities: Use of tomodensitometry in haematology, pancreatic pathology, cardiac pathology, orthopaedics.

Department of Reeducation and Communication　2502

Address: Hôpital Henri-Mondor, 51 avenue du Maréchal de Lattre de Tassigny, 94010 Créteil
Telephone: 207 51 41
Head: Professor Claude Hamonet
Activities: Orthopaedics; handicap aids; prosthetics; integration of handicapped patients in urban communities; artificial limb control.

Laboratory of Protein Pathology　2503

Address: Hôpital Henri-Mondor, 51 avenue du Maréchal de Lattre de Tassigny, 94010 Créteil
Telephone: 899 27 09
Head: Professor Jean Rosa
Activities: Molecular pathology of red blood cells (genetic study).

Research Laboratory for Biological Engineering and Applied Medicine　2504

Head: Georges Cannet
Activities: Ventilation mechanics; obstetrical mechanics; muscular biomechanics; oculography.

UNIT OF SCIENCES　2505

Address: avenue du Général de Gaulle, 94010 Créteil Cedex
Telephone: 989 92 24
Facilities: Radiocrystallography; microspectrophotometry.

Laboratory of Animal Biology　2506

Head: Albert Le Moigne
Activities: Traumatic regeneration in invertebrates; modes of tissue reparation.

Laboratory of Biopolymer Physical Chemistry　2507

Head: Professor Bernard Sebille
Activities: Protein interactions; polymer reagents; polymers and metallic ions in non-aqueous media.

Laboratory of Cell Biology　2508

Head: Professor Philippe Chevaillier
Activities: Structure and physiology of eukaryotic chromates.

Laboratory of Electrochemical Energy and Biochemistry　2509

Head: Professor René Buvet
Activities: Bioelectrochemical energetics; primordial chemical evolution; biosphere energetics; ecological bioelectrochemistry.

Laboratory of General Physiology　2510

Head: Professor Jean Mambrini
Activities: Synapsis.

Laboratory of Organic Electrochemistry　2511

Head: Professor Jacques Perichon
Activities: Mechanism of electrochemical reduction in solid-state materials used for lithium batteries; electrochemical study of metal compounds used on catalysts for organic reactions; electrochemical study of mineral catalysts.

Laboratory of Physical Chemistry and Bioelectromagnetism　2512

Head: Professor Alfred Caristan
Graduate research staff: 3
Activities: Influence of magnetic fields and waves on antibody-antigen complexes; liberation of hydrogen peroxide by peritoneal cells in parasitology.
Contract work: No

Laboratory of Plant Biology and Applied Microbiology　2513

Head: Richard Moreau
Activities: Microbiology of French and tropical forest soils; microbiology of fresh- and marine waters.

Laboratory of Plant Physiology and Applied Plant Ecophysiology　2514

Head: Professor Philippe Louguet
Activities: Metabolism of organic acids in folic epidermis; analysis of stomata ultrastructure; enzymology study of stomata cells; microspectrophotometry. Applied research on: stomata and pollution; soya bean stomata; drought resistance and stomata.

Laboratory of Structural Physical Chemistry　2515

Sections: Crystallography, Professor Michel Renaud; molecular spectroscopy, Roger Fourme
Activities: Structure of molecular crystals and crystalline polymorphism; structure of enzymes; three-

dimensional structure of biological macromolecules by X-ray; oxygen fixation in cobalt-protein compounds; high-accuracy X-ray measurements.

UNIVERSITY INSTITUTE OF TECHNOLOGY   2516

Address: avenue du Général de Gaulle, 94010 Créteil Cedex
Telephone: 989 92 24
Head: Professor Maurice Gaudaire
Activities: Image reconnaissance; medical instrumentation.

Department of Commercial Techniques   2517

Head: Professor Bernard Dizambourg
Activities: Market analysis; distribution; investments; commercial study of regions; worker education and its role in the economy.

Laboratory of Physical Metrology   2518

Head: Professor Bernard Chappey
Activities: New measurement systems; systems modelling.

Laboratory of Physiology and Pharmacology   2519

Head: Professor Raymond Boulouard
Activities: Metabolism of different substances with pharmacological properties; interaction between electric stimulus in encephalography and the administration of neuroleptics.

Laboratory of Thermodynamics and Electrochemistry of Materials   2520

Head: Professor Michel Guillou
Activities: Energy properties of materials.

UNIVERSITY INSTITUTES FOR RESEARCH   2521

Institute of Energetics and Dynamics of Complex Systems   2522

Address: avenue du Général de Gaulle, 94000 Créteil
Telephone: 898 92 24
Director: Professor Michel Guillou
Activities: Production and decentralization of energy; energy demands; technological developments and their social impact.

Institute of Medical Engineering   2523

Address: avenue du Général de Gaulle, 94000 Créteil
Telephone: 898 92 24
Director: Professor Maurice Gaudaire
Departments: Surgical techniques; Artificial organs; Analysis systems

Institute of the Environment   2524

Address: avenue du Général de Gaulle, 94000 Créteil
Telephone: 898 92 24
Director: Professor Jean-Louis Guigou
Activities: Health and the environment; human sciences and the environment; natural sciences and the environment.

Université de Paris XIII - Université de Paris-Nord*   2525

[Paris University XIII - Paris North University]
Address: avenue J.-B. Clément, 93430 Villetaneuse
Telephone: (01) 831 61 70
President: Professor Maurice Nisard
First Vice-President: Pierre Joisson

SCIENTIFIC AND POLYTECHNIC CENTRE   2526

Address: avenue J.-B. Clément, 93430 Villetaneuse
Telephone: (01) 821 61 70
Director: Michel Glass

Applied Theoretical Mathematics Group   2527

Affiliation: Centre National de la Recherche Scientifique
Activities: Applied and theoretical mathematics.

Calculus Centre   2528

Activities: Computer studies; numerical analysis; applied mathematics.

Laser Physics Laboratory   2529

Affiliation: Centre National de la Recherche Scientifique

Macromolecular Research Group   2530

Affiliation: Centre National de la Recherche Scientifique

UNIVERSITY INSTITUTE OF   2533
TECHNOLOGY, SAINT-DENIS*

Address: place du 8 Mai 1945, Saint Denis
Director: Jacques Bodin

Department of Mechanical   2534
Engineering*

Activities: Mathematics; mechanics; materials resistance; energetics; metallurgy; construction; manufacture; industrial organization.

Department of Physical Mensuration* 2535

Activities: Physics; electronics; physical chemistry: mensuration in research laboratories or industry; installation servicing.

UNIVERSITY INSTITUTE OF   2536
TECHNOLOGY, VILLETANEUSE*

Address: avenue J.-B. Clément, 93430 Villetaneuse
Telephone: (01) 821 61 70
Director: Henri Charpentier
Activities: Computer sciences; data processing.

Université de Pau et des   2537
Pays de l'Adour

[University of Pau and the Adour Region]
Address: 68 rue Montpensier, BP 576, 64010 Pau Cedex
Telephone: (059) 32 56 47
Affiliation: Académie de Bordeaux
Chairman: Professor Daniel Levier
Vice-Chairman: Professor Michel Capdeville

FACULTY OF EXACT AND NATURAL   2538
SCIENCES

Address: avenue Philippon, 64000 Pau
Dean: Dr P. Xans

Chemistry Department   2539

Mathematics Department   2540

Natural Sciences Department   2541

Physics Department   2542

FACULTY OF LETTERS AND HUMAN   2543
SCIENCES

Address: avenue du Doyen Poplawski, 64000 Pau
Dean: M Manso

Geography Department   2544

UNIVERSITY INSTITUTE OF   2545
SCIENTIFIC RESEARCH

Address: avenue Philippon, 64000 Pau
Director: J. Delfand

Chemistry Department   2546

Mathematics Department   2547

Physics Department   2548

UNIVERSITY INSTITUTE OF   2549
TECHNOLOGY OF THE ADOUR
REGION

Address: 29 cours du Compte de Cabarrus, 64100 Bayonne
Dean: Dr Verdun

Université de Picardie   2550

[Picardy University]
Address: rue Salomon Malhanghu Campus, 80025 Amiens Cedex
Telephone: (022) 95 13 14
President: Professor Bernard Rousset
Note: The University consists of twelve Units for Teaching and Research (UER), the following being devoted to scientific disciplines:

SAINT-QUENTIN UNIT 2551

Address: 48 rue Raspail, 02109 Saint-Quentin Cedex
Director: Professor Bauer

UNIT OF EXACT AND NATURAL SCIENCES 2552

Address: 33 rue Saint-Leu, 80039 Amiens Cedex
Director: Professor Paul Personne

UNIT OF MATHEMATICS 2553

Address: 33 rue Saint-Leu, 80039 Amiens Cedex
Director: Professor A. Chevalier

UNIT OF MEDICINE 2554

Address: 12 rue Frédéric-Petit, 80000 Amiens Cedex
Director: Professor Bernasconi

UNIT OF PHARMACY 2555

Address: 3 place Louis-Dewailly, 80037 Amiens Cedex
Director: Professor Perdu

UNIVERSITY INSTITUTE OF TECHNOLOGY 2556

Address: avenue des Facultés, le Bailly, 80044 Amiens Cedex
Director: Professor Tudo

Civil Engineering Department 2557

Head: Professor Meriaux

Commercial Techniques Department 2558

Head: Professor Bruillon

Mechanical Engineering Department 2559

Head: Professor Abbar

Université de Poitiers 2560

[Poitiers University]
Address: 15 rue de Blossac, 86034 Poitiers Cedex
Telephone: (049) 88 26 32
Telex: 790563
Chairman: Professor Raymond Legeais

BASIC AND APPLIED SCIENCE RESEARCH UNIT 2561

Address: 40 avenue du Recteur Pineau, 86022 Poitiers
Telephone: (049) 46 26 30
Director: Professor Jacques Borzeix

Botany Department 2562

Senior staff: Plant biology and physiology, Professor Jean-Louis Bonnemain; microbiology and oyster and marine biology, Professor Philippe Daste; phyco-ecology and plant biology, Dr Pierre Dupuy, Dr François Grossin, Dr Gérard Trotet; ecophysiology, Dr Claude-Charles Mathon

Chemistry Department 2563

Senior staff: Mineral chemistry and chemical kinetics, Professor Michel-Louis Bernard; organic catalysis, Professor Michel Blanchard, Professor Michel Guisnet, Professor Raymond Maurel; physical chemistry, Professor André Cointot; organic synthesis, Professor Mme Leone Miginiac; mineral crystallo-chemistry, Professor Antoine Hardy; organometallic chemistry, Professor Philippe Miginiac; organic chemistry, Professor Jean-Claude Jacquésy; dielectric physico-chemistry, Professor Maurice Gomel

Civil and Maritime Engineering Department 2564

Address: IUT, rue de Roux, 17026 La Rochelle Cedex
Head: Professor Michel Veyssière
Senior staff: Professor Y. Tcheng

Earth Science Department 2565

Senior staff: Geology and mineralogy, Professor Colchen; sedimentary geology and palaeobiology, Professor Jean Gabilly; vertebrate and human palaeontology, Professor De Bonis; pedology, Professor Jacques Dupis; sedimentology, Professor Jean Pimienta

Mathematics Department 2566

Senior staff: Mathematics, Professor Pierre Bernat, Professor Simone Dolbeault, Professor Jacques Fort, Professor Alain Guichardet, Professor Daniel Lazard, Professor Annie Page, Professor Mustapha Rais, Professor Guy Renault, Professor Francis Sergeraert; numerical analysis, Professor Jacques Ezra; computer science, Professor A. Arnold

Mechanics Department 2567

Senior staff: General mechanics, Professor Jean Boscher, Professor Claude Mathurin, Professor Liviu Solomon, Professor René Souchet; mechanics of solids, Professor Alexis Lagarde, Professor Jean Frène, Professor Gamby, Professor Guinot; mechanics of fluids, Professor Joseph Bourot

Physics Department 2568

Senior staff: Electronics and mass spectroscopy, Professor René Vauthier; luminescence, Professor Huges Payen De La Garanderie; physical metallurgy, Professor Jules Caisso, Professor Jean Grilhe, Professor Pierre Moine, Professor Desoyer, Professor Junqua; molecular optics, Professor Alain Le Roy, quantum optics, Professor Abraham Rachman; opto-electronics, Professor Gilles Batailler, Professor Pierre Bugnet; high atmospheric physics, Professor René Rivault, Professor Yvonne Corcuff; fluid physics and mechanics, Professor Jacques Borzeix, Professor Paul Dumargue; molecular physics, Professor Elie Gray

Physiology Department 2569

Senior staff: Animal physiology and cellular physiology of contractile structures, Professor Yves-Michel Gargouil, Professor Claude Bernard, Professor Jean Delèze, Professor Lenfant, Professor Walden; neurophysiology and psychophysiology, Professor Gérard Galand, biochemistry, Professor Bernard Lubochinsky, Professor Karst

Zoology and Animal Biology Department 2570

Senior staff: Zoology and cellular biology, Professor Joseph Schrevel, Professor Jean-Pierre Collin; animal biology (crustacean physiology and genetics), Professor Jean-Jacques Legrand, Professor Emmannuelle Legrand

APPLIED BIOCHEMISTRY AND MICROBIOLOGY 2571

Address: IUT, rue de Roux, 17026 La Rochelle Cedex
Head: Professor Jean-Louis Larrouquère

MARINE BIOLOGY AND BIOCHEMISTRY 2572

Address: IUT, rue de Roux, 17026 La Rochelle Cedex
Head: Professor Jean Tardy

ÉCOLE NATIONALE SUPÉRIEURE DE 2573 MÉCANIQUE ET D'AÉROTECHNIQUE

[Mechanics and Aeronautical Engineering School]
Address: 20 rue Guillaume VII, 86034 Poitiers Cedex
Director: Professor Jacques De Fouquet
Deputy Director: Jean Coirier

Aerodynamics Laboratory 2574

Affiliation: Centre National de la Recherche Scientifique
Head: Professor Raymond Goethals
Activities: Areas of research include: supersonic and hypersonic flows; shock-wave-boundary layer interaction for turbomachinery; research in large wind tunnel at low speed on buildings, chimneys, airfoils and rotors; Aeolian energy.

Energetics and Detonation Laboratory 2575

Affiliation: Centre National de la Recherche Scientifique
Activities: Research in the following areas: gaseous, liquids and solids detonation; shock waves in condensed media; unconfined and confined flame propagation and related explosion phenomena; combustion in turbulent flow.

Heat Laboratory 2576

Heads: Professor Henri Cordier, Professor Jean Coutanceau, Professor Jean Martinet
Activities: Research in the following subjects: heat conduction and heat phenomena caused by friction; heat convection; radiation of solids and gases; influence of radiation on surface conditions.

Heat Transfer Laboratory 2577

Affiliation: Centre National de la Recherche Scientifique
Heads: Professor Henri Cordier, Professor Jean Coutanceau, Professor Jean Martinet
Activities: Topics of research include: heat conduction and heat phenomena caused by friction; heat convection; heat pipes; thermal modelling; properties of semi-transparent materials.

Mechanics and Materials Physics Laboratory 2578

Affiliation: Centre National de la Recherche Scientifique
Heads: Professor Paul Laurent, Professor Jacques De Fouquet
Activities: Research on mechanical properties of solids

in relation to their structural state (plastic deformation processes, fatigue processes, fracture mechanics, internal friction).

EXACT AND NATURAL SCIENCE RESEARCH UNIT 2579

Address: 40 avenue du Recteur Pineau, 86022 Poitiers
Telephone: (049) 46 26 30
Director: Professor Guy Renault

MEDICINE AND PHARMACY RESEARCH UNIT 2580

Address: 34 rue du Jardin des Plantes, 86034 Poitiers Cedex
Director: Professor Dominique Patté

Anaesthesiology Department 2581

Head: Professor Pierre Desforges-Meriel

Anatomy Department 2582

Senior staff: Professor Robert Odano, Professor Yves Rideau, Professor Pierre Kamina

Bacteriology Department 2583

Senior staff: Professor Yves De Rautlin De La Roy, Professor Monique Castets

Biochemistry Department 2584

Senior staff: Professor Daniel Reiss, Professor Jacques Gombert

Biophysics Department 2585

Senior staff: Professor Régis Dutheil, Professor François Begon

Botany Department 2586

Head: Professor Jacqueline Rousseau

Cardiology Department 2587

Senior staff: Professor Georges Rousseau, Professor Jean Demange, Professor Robert Barraine

Chemistry Department 2588

Senior staff: Professor Michel Vierfond, Professor Danièle Barthes, Professor J. Jacques Giraud, Professor Jean-Bernard Fourtillan

Dermatology Department 2589

Head: Professor Marc Larregue

Galenic Pharmacy Department 2590

Head: Professor Christian Merle

Haematology Department 2591

Head: Professor Joseph Tanzer

Histology and Embryology Department 2592

Head: Professor Pierre Burin

Internal Medicine Department 2593

Head: Professor Yves Sudre

Materia Medica Department 2594

Head: Professor Jean-Louis Pousset

Medical and Gastroenterology Clinic 2595

Head: Professor Claude Matuchansky

Nephrology and Reanimation Department 2596

Head: Professor Dominique Patté

Neurology Department 2597

Senior staff: Professor Jean-Paul Lefèvre, Professor Roger Gil

Neurophysiology Department 2598

Head: Professor Albert Marillaud

Neurosurgery Department 2599

Head: Professor Maurice Salles

Obstetrics Clinic 2600

Senior staff: Professor Henri De Nas De Tourris, Professor Jean-Robert Giraud

Orthopaedics Department 2601

Head: Professor Jean-Pierre Clarac

Paediatrics Department 2602

Senior staff: Professor Alexandre Hoppeler, Professor Alain Main De Boissière

Parasitology Department 2603

Head: Professor Jean-Louis Jacquemin

Pathological Anatomy Department 2604

Senior staff: Professor Jean Payen, Professor Philippe Babin

Pharmacodynamics Department 2605

Head: Professor Philippe Courtois

Physiology Department 2606

Head: Professor Michel Baudry

Pneumophthisiology Department 2607

Senior staff: Professor Françoise Patté

Radiology Department 2608

Senior staff: Professor Christian Gasquet, Professor Henri Morin, Professor Alain Daban

Respiratory Physiology Department 2609

Head: Professor Paul Potocky

Rheumatology Department 2610

Head: Professor Daniel Bontoux

Surgical Clinic 2611

Head: Professor Jacques Frailong

Urology Department 2612

Head: Professor Jacques Aubert

Visceral and Vascular Surgery Department 2613

Senior staff: Professor Jacques Barbier, Professor Patrick Bloch

UNIVERSITY INSTITUTE OF TECHNOLOGY 2614

Address: avenue Jacques Coeur, 86034 Poitiers Cedex
Director: Professor Claude Gasc

Department of Chemistry 2615

Senior staff: Professor Jacques Barbier, Professor Jean-Claude Jacquesy, Professor Alain Junqua

Department of Electrical Engineering 2616

Senior staff: Professor Gilles Batailler, Professor Pierre Bugnet

Department of Mechanical Engineering (Angoulême) 2617

Senior staff: Professor Paul Dumargue, Professor Denys Gamby

Department of Mechanical Engineering (Poitiers) 2618

Senior staff: Professor Claude Gasc, Professor Liviu Solomon

Department of Thermic Engineering 2619

Senior staff: Professor Jean Coutanceau, Professor René Henry

UNIVERSITY INSTITUTE OF TECHNOLOGY AT LA ROCHELLE 2620

Address: rue de Roux, 17026 La Rochelle Cedex
Director: Professor André Ballage

Department of Applied Biology 2621

Head: Professor Jean Larrouquère

Department of Civil Engineering 2622

Head: Professor Michel Veyssière

Department of Commercial Techniques 2623

Head: Professor Alain Benoit

Université de Reims 2624

[Reims University]
Address: 23 rue Boulard, 51100 Reims
Telephone: (026) 40 04 98
President: Professor L. Bernard
Vice-Presidents: J. Bur, J.-C. Étienne

UNIT OF EXACT AND NATURAL SCIENCES · 2625

Address: Moulin de la Housse, BP 347, 51062 Reims Cedex
Telephone: (026) 85 16 68
Dean: B. Gastambide

Department of Biological and Natural Sciences · 2626

CENTRE OF DIFFERENTIATION STUDIES AND MODULATION · 2627

Laboratory of Animal Biology · 2628
Director: Professor Mellinger
Activities: Cytologic, physiologic and biochemical studies of the Scyliorhinus caniculus egg.

Laboratory of Animal Physiology · 2629
Affiliation: Centre National de la Recherche Scientifique
Directors: Professor Jacquot, M Nagel
Activities: Hormonal intervention in maturation phenomena; foetal and new-born physiology; studies of the organism, the organ and the cell.

Laboratory of Biochemistry · 2630
Affiliation: Centre National de la Recherche Scientifique
Director: Professor Jacquemin
Activities: Study of hormonal activity and regulation.

Laboratory of Cell and General Biology · 2631
Affiliation: Centre National de la Recherche Scientifique
Directors: Mlle Gontcharoff, M Bierne
Activities: Cell differentiation in embryogenesis and regeneration; cell regulatory mechanism; invertebrate endocrinology and immunology.

INDEPENDENT LABORATORIES · 2632

Laboratory of Biology and Plant Physiology · 2633
Director: M Chardard
Activities: Infrastructural study of diverse plant cells (normal and modified); protoplast production and cell fusion.

Laboratory of Botany · 2634
Director: Professor Favere-Ducharte
Activities: Cytology and biology of higher plant life.

Laboratory of Earth Sciences · 2635
Sections: Palaeoentomology and evolution palaeontology, Professor Laurentiaux; Geological study group, M Fourquin
Activities: Geodynamics; paleontology, palaeoecology; regional studies - Champagne-Ardenne.

Laboratory of Oenology · 2636
Director: M Feuillet
Activities: Nitrogenous compounds in wine; new analytical methods.

Laboratory of Zoology · 2637
Director: Professor Gaumont
Activities: Physiology of Ciliata in the stomach of ruminants; Plannipennia anatomy and biology; Hymenoptera physiology; biological balances; vineyard insects; vine aphids.

Department of Mathematics · 2638

LABORATORY OF ALGEBRA AND THE THEORY OF NUMBERS · 2639

Senior staff: Mlle Callais, M David, M Legrange
Activities: Involution and ordinate structures in the theory of radicals; non-commutative algebra, homology, finite groups, Galois theory; arithmetic functions, approximate integrations, square root decompositions.

LABORATORY OF FUNCTIONAL ANALYSIS AND PARTIAL EQUATIONS · 2640

Senior staff: Professor Authier, Mme Unterberger, M Unterberger
Activities: Differential equations; pseudo-differential operations and Fourier systems; limit problems.

LABORATORY OF MECHANICS · 2641

Senior staff: Professor Levy-Bruhl, Mme Rigolot
Activities: Elasticity - plasticity; hyperelasticity; integral equations in solid-state mechanics.

LABORATORY OF THEORETICAL PHYSICS · 2642

Senior staff: Professor Payen
Activities: Probability and quantum mechanics.

Department of Physics and Chemistry · 2643

CENTRE OF MICROANALYSIS OF CONDUCTED MATTER · 2644

Laboratory of Electricity and Electron Microscopy · 2645
Director: Professor Laberrigue
Activities: High resolution and electron microscopy; contrast phase electron microscopy; high-tension electron microscopy; study of low-temperature objects; electron diffraction applied to crystals; creep in steels.

Laboratory of Electron Spectroscopy · 2646
Director: M Gazaux
Activities: Study of medium energy electron condensed matter interaction; microanalysis apparatus.

Laboratory of Electronics and X-ray Analysis 2647
Director: Professor Despujols
Activities: Fundamental mechanisms determining conductivity in amorphous dielectric thin seams; characterization of interfacial electronic states; luminous and electronic emission in thin seams; X-ray study of materials; surface characterization by diffraction analysis and electronic emission.

Laboratory of Materials Science   2648
Director: M Collot
Activities: Research is geared towards the structural study of different types of materials and the improving of their mechanical behaviour. There are two main areas of research: physical chemistry of metallic materials; materials used in civil engineering.

**CENTRE OF MOLECULAR   2649
SPECTROSCOPY**
Note: There are about 70 research staff in the seven laboratories.

Laboratory of Coordination Chemistry   2650
Director: Mlle Fromage
Activities: Development of physico-chemical methods to study coordinated compounds in solid-state and in solution.

Laboratory of Mineral Chemistry   2651
Director: Professor Hugel
Activities: Research on the coordination compounds of transition metals: study of their structure by physico-chemical methods; study of their thermodynamic stability in aqueous and non-aqueous solution by spectrophotometry, potentiometry, polarography, colorimetry; reaction study.

Laboratory of Molecular Optics   2652
Director: M Rousset
Activities: Study of inter-molecular energy transfer in solution or in mixed crystal; photo- and thermoluminescence of compounds of type II and VI (zinc sulphide, copper, cobalt).

Laboratory of Optical Research   2653
Director: Professor Bernard
Activities: Raman effects of resonance; force measurements; Raman spectroscopy studies of molecules of biological interest; crystals; matter-radiation interaction.

Laboratory of Organic Physics   2654
Affiliation: Centre National de la Recherche Scientifique
Director: Professor Chuche
Activities: Thermal isomerization; nuclear magnetic resonance.

Laboratory of Photochemistry   2655
Affiliation: Centre National de la Recherche Scientifique
Director: Professor Pete
Activities: Study of the action of light on organic compounds; reaction synthesis induced by radiation.

**Laboratory of Physical Chemistry - Molecular 2656
Structure and Spectroscopy**
Director: Professor Guenebaut
Activities: Electronic spectroscopy of di- and tri-atomic molecules.

**ENERGY TRANSFER CHARGE STUDY   2657
GROUP**

Laboratory of Applied Wave Dynamics   2658
Director: Professor Lafargue
Activities: Condensed phase molecular structure; electrochemical processes.

Laboratory of Electrochemistry   2659
Head: Mme Lafargue
Activities: Magnetoelectric effects of electrolytes; photoelectrochemistry.

Laboratory of Organic Chemistry   2660
Director: Professor Gastambide
Activities: Research is mainly in the area of chemical and physical properties of cyclic organic compounds.

Laboratory of Structural Chemistry   2661
Director: Professor Nguyen-Quang Trinh
Activities: Theoretical and experimental study of inter-molecular associations; polar and conformational analysis of molecules in dicyclic and heterocyclic series.

Independent Laboratories   2662

**LABORATORY OF MOLECULAR   2663
PHYSICS**
Director: Professor Jouve
Activities: High resolution spectroscopy of asymmetric molecule and mineral elements in the atmosphere; study of atmospheric layers by laser; interaction between a power laser and double and mixed frequency crystals.

**LABORATORY OF ORGANIC   2664
SYNTHESIS**
Director: Professor Anatol
Activities: Synthesis of natural compounds and analogous structures with a therapeutic effect.

LABORATORY OF PARTICLE PHYSICS 2665
Director: M Lacombe
Activities: Theory of the hadronic processes: dynamics and phenomenology.

LABORATORY OF QUANTUM MECHANICS   2666

Director: Professor Schachter
Activities: General approach to quantum mechanics. probability, logic, and information studies.

Thermomechanic Group   2667

Director: M Padet
Activities: Quantum mechanics; classic mechanics and thermal exchange: heat transfer and fluid mechanics; information studies.

UNIT OF MEDICINE   2668

Address: 51 rue Cognacq Jay, 51095 Reims Cedex
Telephone: (026) 06 26 13
Dean: Professor Kochman
Contract work: Yes

Anaesthesiology   2669

Head: Professor J. Rendoing
Activities: Electromedical anaesthesia - experimentation with dogs; neurosurgery.

Anatomy   2670

Head: Professor Quereux
Activities: Morphology and topography of abdominal viruses; plexus distortion; mastication and hearing system.

Biophysics and Nuclear Medicine   2671

Head: Professor Valeyre
Activities: Research is mainly in the area of nuclear medicine.

Cancerology   2672

Head: Professor Cattan
Activities: Metastatic diffusion and haemostasis; pharmacokinetics; cancer chemotherapy; comparative analysis of different treatments for human cancers; prognosis, especially in breast cancer. Research is conducted in collaboration with various French or European organizations.

Cardiology   2673

Head: Professor Bajolet
Activities: Rhythmic disorders; pacemakers; use of Holter technique in the study of cardiac cycles; coronary spasms; angiographic studies of the heart; echocardiography; automated analysis; use of isotopes in acute coronary malfunction; clinical pharmacology of anti-arrhythmia and antihypertension devices; documenta-tion of pacemakers and haemodynamics; audiovisual teaching project.

Clinic for Respiratory Disorders   2674

Head: Professor J.M. Dubois de Montreynaud
Activities: Medical pedagogy; physiopathology of bronchial cancer.

Electroradiology   2675

Head: Professor B. Menanteau
Activities: Research is orientated towards anatomy and pathologic echography and angiography used in pathological studies of the abdomen and the extremities.

Functional Exploration Service and   2676
Readaptation with Locomotor Apparatus

Head: Professor J.C. Étienne
Activities: Interdisciplinary study of collagen; articular and peri-articular calcic crystalline deposits; clinical research on neurogenic arthropathies, vertebral pathology, synovial osteochondriosis.

Gastroenterology   2677

Head: Professor P. Zeitoun
Activities: Treatment of pathologic digestive denaturation; digestive cell morphology.

General Medicine Service B   2678

Heads: Professor Luetenegger, Professor J. Caron
Activities: Study of subjects with metabolic and vascular risk factors; analysis of the results of long-term treatment of the diabetic; study of diabetic haemoglobin, micro-angiopathy, erythrocytosis and platelets in the diabetic; metabolic studies with the aid of an artificial pancreas.

General Psychiatry Service   2679

Head: Professor G. Pascalis
Activities: Epidemiology and treatment of depression in the Champagne-Ardenne region; handling of psychiatric emergencies; psychopharmacology of medicines.

General Surgery Service C   2680

Head: Professor J.C. Levasseur
Activities: Properties of reabsorbable synthetic prosthesis in visual surgery; surgical techniques; microsurgery.

Haematology   2681

Head: Professor G. Potron
Activities: Haematologic cytology; haemostasis.

Laboratory of Experimental Pathology 2682

Head: Professor Kochman
Activities: Exploration of the respiratory system; allergies.

Laboratory of Respiratory System   2683
Exploration

Head: Professor J.M. Dubois de Montreynaud
Activities: Simple pulmonary exploration for use in the clinic.

Medical Biochemistry   2684

Head: Professor Borel
Activities: Biochemistry of conjunctive tissue; biochemistry and physiopathology of glucoside haemoglobins.

Medical Clinic A   2685

Heads: Professor P. Coudoux, Dr P. Collery
Activities: Research is on the disturbances in the magnesium metabolism and haemostasis during cancer.

Microbiology, Bacteriology, Virology, 2686
Immunology

Head: Professor Dropsy
Activities: Cell immunology; immunology to perinatal viruses; plasmic resistance to tetracyclines; antibiotherapy in hospital infections; resistance to cephalosporins.

Nephrology Service and Laboratory of 2687
Radioimmunology

Head: Professor Jacques Chanard
Activities: Renal exploration; water, and phosphor-calcium metabolism; endocrine function of the kidney; external purification systems (ie haemodialysis); kidney transplants.

Neurology Service and Laboratory for 2688
the Exploration of the Central Nervous
System

Head: Professor Morice
Activities: Study of cerebral rheo-encephalography; its application in cerebral circulatory malfunctions and vascular headaches.

Neurosurgery Service   2689

Head: Professor Guyot
Activities: Neurosurgical treatment of cerebral oedema; role of Pecinian corpuscles.

Orthopaedic and Traumatology Clinic 2690

Head: Professor Gérard
Activities: Hip orthoplastics; osteitis treatment; complete shoulder prosthesis.

Orthopaedics and Traumatology   2691
Surgical Service

Head: Professor P. Ségal
Activities: Surgery of traumatic ligament lesions of the knee.

Otorhinolaryngology, Craniofacial   2692
Surgery and Auditory Service

Head: Professor M. Legros
Activities: Cancer treatment in collaboration with the Jean Godinot Institute; facial fractures; otitis; reeducation of the deaf child; ageing of the nasal, buccal and pharyngeal mucous membrane; auditory potential of the cerebral trunk.

Paediatrics and Puerilism Service   2693

Head: Professor Fandre
Activities: Detection of congenital metabolic disorders, especially of the central nervous system; congenital cardiopathies in the newborn and in infants; syndromes of digestive malabsorption; nephro-urologic disorders.

Pathologic Anatomy and Cytology   2694

Head: Professor Caulet
Activities: Ultrastructural studies and cyto-enzymology of lymphoid malignant tumours; cytochemical and electronic study of inter-cellular modifications in pathology; modifications of the hepatic cell and fibroblasts; electronic study of neuromuscular disorders; pulmonary parenchyma.

Pharmacology   2695

Head: Professor Choisy
Activities: Effect of medicines on alcohol metabolism; action of cardiotropic medicines on mycocardial cells; acute and chronic toxicity, pharmacokinetics, macrovigilance.

Radiology Service   2696

Head: Professor P. Lacour
Activities: Articular radiography; endovascular treatment of carotid fistula.

Rheumatology Clinic   2697

Head: Professor R. Gougeon

Surgical Clinic   2698

Head: Professor Rives
Activities: Biliary and pancreatic pathology.

Urology Service   2699

Head: Professor B. Lardennois
Activities: Functional and neuro-uro-dynamic exploration; urologic microsurgery.

Vascular Surgery Service   2700

Head: Professor H. Nicaise
Activities: Vascular functional exploration; cardiovascular surgical techniques; pathology.

UNIT OF ODONTOLOGY   2701

Address: 2 rue du Général Koenig, 51100 Reims
Telephone: (026) 40 55 40
Director: Professor Ducrot
Activities: Development of dental enamel after the removal of braces; photopolymerization of Bowen resin by ultraviolet rays; prosthesis; destruction mechanism of paradontal tissue; morphologic and electronic microscopy studies of cement alterations.

Department of Biophysics and Materials   2702

Senior staff: Dr Severin

Department of Prevention and Buccal Biology   2703

Senior staff: Professor Clerc

UNIT OF PHARMACY   2704

Address: 51 rue Cognacq Jay, 51096 Reims Cedex
Telephone: (026) 06 26 13
Director: Professor Jean Levy

Department of Biology   2705

Activities: Interaction of natural or synthetic substances; cancer studies.

LABORATORY OF BIOCHEMISTRY   2706

LABORATORY OF BOTANY   2707

LABORATORY OF CELL PHYSIOLOGY   2708

LABORATORY OF HYGIENE   2709

LABORATORY OF MICROBIOLOGY   2710

LABORATORY OF PARASITOLOGY   2711

LABORATORY OF PHARMACODYNAMICS   2712

LABORATORY OF PHARMACOKINETICS   2713

Department of Physical Chemistry   2714

Affiliation: Centre National de la Recherche Scientifique
Activities: Isolation of natural substances and study of their structure; synthesis in collaboration with the laboratories dealing with therapeutic substances; preparation of pharmaceutical compounds and their control.

LABORATORY OF ANALYTICAL CHEMISTRY   2715

LABORATORY OF CHEMICAL TRANSFORMATIONS AND SYNTHESIS   2716

LABORATORY OF EXTRACT CHEMISTRY   2717

LABORATORY OF PHARMACOTECHNICS   2718

LABORATORY OF STRUCTURAL CHEMISTRY   2719

LABORATORY OF THERAPEUTIC CHEMISTRY   2720

SPECTROSCOPY SERVICE   2721

Université de Rennes I* 2722

[Rennes University I]
Address: 2 rue du Thabor, 35000 Rennes
Telephone: (099) 36 28 54

SCHOOL OF CHEMICAL ENGINEERING* 2723

UNIT OF BEHAVIOURAL AND ENVIRONMENTAL SCIENCES* 2724

Head: Professor M. Trehen

UNIT OF BIOLOGICAL SCIENCES* 2725

Head: Professor P. Razet

UNIT OF CLINICAL AND THERAPEUTIC MEDICINE* 2726

Head: Professor J. Gouffault

Laboratory of Material Technology and Joint Prosthetics 2727

Director: Professor B. Joniot
Senior staff: Professor A. Roditti, Professor J. Verge
Activities: Dental material technology, mechanics and biophysics; prosthetics; metrology; mastication physiology.
Contract work: Yes

UNIT OF DENTISTRY* 2728

Head: Professor C. Bigarre

UNIT OF MATERIALS SCIENCE* 2729

Address: Campus de Beaulieu, 35042 Rennes Cedex
Telephone: (099) 36 48 15

Laboratory of Mineral Chemistry C 2730

Affiliation: Centre National de la Recherche Scientifique
Head: Professor J. Lang
Sections: Preparation study, R. Marchand; structures, Y. Laurent

UNIT OF MATHEMATICS AND DATA PROCESSING* 2731

Head: Professor G. Boulaye

UNIT OF MEDICAMENTS* 2732

Head: Professor P.-L. Biget

UNIT OF ODONTOLOGY* 2733

Head: M Bigarre

UNIT OF PHYSICAL CHEMISTRY AND APPLIED BIOLOGY* 2734

Head: Professor F. Picard

UNIT OF PUBLIC HEALTH* 2735

UNIT OF STRUCTURE AND PROPERTIES OF MATTER* 2736

Head: Professor J.-M. Hameurt

UNIVERSITY INSTITUTE OF TECHNOLOGY (LANNION) 2737

Address: route de Perros Guirrec, BP 112, 22302 Lannion
Head: Professor J. Le Bot

UNIVERSITY INSTITUTE OF TECHNOLOGY (RENNES) 2738

Address: rue de Clos Courtel, Buttes de Coësmes, 35000 Rennes
Head: Professor J. Le Bot

Université de Rouen (Haute-Bretagne Normandié)* 2739

[Rouen University]
Address: rue Thomas Becket, 76130 Mont-Saint-Aignan
Telephone: (035) 74 03 32

INSTITUTE OF SCIENTIFIC RESEARCH* 2740

Head: Professor P. Granger

NATIONAL INSTITUTE OF CHEMISTRY* 2741

Address: place Émile Blondel, 76000 Mont-Saint-Aignon
Director: Dr R. Darrigo

UNIT OF BEHAVIOURAL SCIENCES AND EDUCATION* 2742

Head: Professor H. Le Halle

UNIT OF MEDICINE AND PHARMACY* 2743

Dean: Professor H. Piguet

UNIT OF SCIENCE AND TECHNOLOGY* 2744

Address: place Émile Blondel, 76000 Mont-Saint-Aignon
Head: Professor J. Gallot
Activities: Chemistry, mathematics, physics, plant biology, animal biology, animal physiology, geology, electronics.

UNIT OF SCIENCE AND TECHNOLOGY (LE HAVRE)* 2745

Head: Professor J. Lagpue

UNIVERSITY INSTITUTE OF TECHNOLOGY (LE HAVRE)* 2746

Head: Professor J. Ripoche

UNIVERSITY INSTITUTE OF TECHNOLOGY (ROUEN)* 2747

Head: Professor J. Gouault

Université de Saint-Étienne 2748

[Saint-Etienne University]
Address: 34 rue Francis Baulier, 42023 Saint-Étienne Cedex
Telephone: (077) 25 22 02
President: C. Forestier

MEDICAL RESEARCH LABORATORIES 2749

Address: UER de Médicine, 30 rue Ferdinand Gambon, 42100 Saint-Étienne Cedex
Activities Apart from the work of the laboratories listed below, research is carried out on a smaller scale in the following subjects: paediatrics; neurology; parasitology; dermatology; pharmacology; haematology; pathological anatomy; biological and medical engineering; digestive and vascular surgery.

Anatomy Laboratory 2750

Biochemistry of Collagen Laboratory 2751

Director: Professor J. Frey
Graduate research staff: 5

Biology of Bone Tissue Laboratory 2752

Biomedical Automation Research Group 2753

Directors: Professor J.C. Healy, Professor J.L. Laurent
Graduate research staff: 8

Human Glomerulonephritis Research Group 2754

Directors: Professor O.G. Gaudin, Professor F. Berthoux
Graduate research staff: 4

Physiology Laboratory 2755

SCIENTIFIC RESEARCH LABORATORIES 2756

Address: UER de Sciences, 23 rue du Docteur Paul Michelon, 42023 Saint-Étienne Cedex

Applied Mathematics Laboratory 2757

Director: Professor Carmona
Graduate research staff: 19

Biology Laboratory	2758

Geology Unit	2759

Ionics and Molecular Spectrometry Laboratory	2760

Macromolecular Chemistry Laboratory 2761

Directors: Professor May, Professor Montheard, Professor Vergnaud
Graduate research staff: 12

Signals and Instrumentation Laboratory	2762

Director: Professor J.N. Massot
Graduate research staff: 13

Université de Strasbourg I - 2763
Université Louis Pasteur

[Strasbourg University I - Louis Pasteur University]
Address: 4 rue Blaise Pascal, 67000 Strasbourg Cedex
Telephone: (088) 61 48 30
Rector: Pierre Magnin
Head, Research Division: Bernard Kaempf
Activities: In terms of research the University is linked to the major centres of scientific research in France and also promotes and encourages international relationships with other universities and scientific organizations. Research is centred in the various institutes, each of which is administered by a Council for the Research Unit. There is also a special administrative division whose sole concern is research.
A specialized area of research concerns 'Man and the quality of life' and four transdisciplinary groups have been formed to deal with this subject:
Research Group on Biomedical Instrumentation
Strasbourg Study Group on Osteoarticular Biology
Research and Testing Group on Applied Photonics
Department of Permanent Education.
They undertake research on: water resources and the constraints relative to their use, phytoecology, faunal distribution, soil occupation; ecological cartography; subterranean waters; formation of fog on the Rhine plain; plant ecology; radiometric teledetection.
Facilities: Mass spectrometry centre; electron microscopy service; physical measurements; image treatment; biochemical spectroscopy; electronic microscopy; audiovisual service; tissue culture; helium liquifier; statistics centre.
See separate entry for: Observatoire de Strasbourg.

UNIT OF ATMOSPHERIC AND EARTH SCIENCES	2764

Institute of Earth Sciences	2765

Address: 1 rue Blessig, 67084 Strasbourg Cedex
Telephone: (088) 35 66 03

LABORATORY OF GEOLOGY AND PALAEONTOLOGY 2766
Head: Professor Georges Millot
Senior staff: Professor Jacques Lucas, Professor Gilbert Dunoyer de Segonzac
Activities: Structural geology and tectonic analysis; palaeoecology and palaeontology.

LABORATORY OF MINERALOGY AND PETROGRAPHY 2767
Head: Professor Jean-Pierre Eberhart
Senior staff: Professor Thierry Juteau
Activities: Petrography; mineralogy; crystallography.

LABORATORY OF STRUCTURAL GEOLOGY 2768
Head: Professor André Michard

Institute of Geophysics 2769

Address: rue René Descartes, 67084 Strasbourg Cedex
Telephone: (088) 61 48 20
Research director: Roland Schlich
Activities: Palaeomagnetism; terrestrial magnetism; geochronology; geothermics; seismology; gravimetry and marine geophysics.
Facilities: Magnetics observatory; seismology observatory; seismic surveillance; Euro-Mediterranean seismology centre; climatology service.

LABORATORY OF MARINE GEOPHYSICS 2770
Research director: Roland Schlich
Senior staff: Professor Jean Bonnin

LABORATORY OF PALAEOMAGNETISM, MAGNETISM, GEOCHRONOLOGY AND GEOTHERMICS 2771
Head: Professor Alexandre Roche

LABORATORY OF SEISMOLOGY 2772
Head: Professor Bernard Bourrouilh

LABORATORY OF SEISMOLOGY AND GRAVIMETRY 2773
Research director: Roland Schlich

UNIT OF BIOMEDICAL SCIENCES   2774

Address: 14 rue Kirschleger, 67085 Strasbourg Cedex
Telephone: (088) 36 06 91
Director: Professor André Kirn

Cardiology Clinic   2775

Address: Hôpital de Hautepierre, avenue Molière, 67098 Strasbourg Cedex
Telephone: (088) 28 90 00
Head: Professor Raymond Voegtlin

Centre for Epidemiological Research   2776
on Tuberculosis and Respiratory Diseases

Address: Hôpital Saint-François, 10 rue David Richard, 67000 Strasbourg
Telephone: (088) 31 18 44
Head: Professor Guy Burghard

Institute of Biological Chemistry   2777

Address: 11 rue Humann, 67000 Strasbourg
Telephone: (088) 36 06 91
Head: Professor Pierre Chambon
Senior staff: Professor Jules Kempf, Professor Guy Vincendon

LABORATORY OF EUKARYOTIC   2778
MOLECULAR GENETICS

Heads: Professor Pierre Chambon, Monique Jacob

Institute of Biological Physics   2779

Address: 1 place de l'Hôpital, 67000 Strasbourg
Telephone: (088) 36 11 44
Head: Professor Jacques Chambron
Senior staff: Professor Gérard Methlin

Institute of Haematology   2780

Address: Hôpital de Hautepierre, avenue Molière, 67098 Strasbourg Cedex
Telephone: (088) 28 90 00
Head: Professor Simone Mayer
Senior staff: Professor Francis Oberling

Institute of Hygiene and Preventive   2781
Medicine

Address: 1 place de l'Hôpital, 67000 Strasbourg
Telephone: (088) 36 71 11
Head: Professor Jean La Villaureix

Institute of Normal Anatomy   2782

Address: 1 place de l'Hôpital, 67000 Strasbourg
Telephone: (088) 36 71 11
Head: Professor Jean-Georges Koritke
Senior staff: Professor Henri Sick, Professor Norbert Aprosio

Institute of Parasitology and Tropical   2783
Pathology

Address: 3 rue Koeberlé, 67000 Strasbourg
Telephone: (088) 35 35 55
Head: Professor Michel Kremer
Senior staff: Professor Thai Kien-Truong

Laboratory of Anaesthesiology   2784

Address: 1 place de l'Hôpital, 67000 Strasbourg
Telephone: (088) 36 71 11
Head: Professor Pierre Gauthier-Lafaye
Senior staff: Professor Jean-Claude Otteni

Laboratory of Applied Physiology   2785

Address: 21 rue Becquerel, 67200 Strasbourg
Telephone: (088) 30 30 65
Head: Professor Bernard Metz

Laboratory of Audiology and   2786
Phonology

Address: 1 place de l'Hôpital, 67000 Strasbourg
Telephone: (088) 36 71 11
Head: Professor Claude Conraux

Laboratory of Bacteriology and   2787
General Immunology

Address: 3 rue Koeberlé, 67000 Strasbourg
Telephone: (088) 36 06 22
Head: Professor Raymond Minck
Senior staff: Professor Charles Nauciel

Laboratory of Biochemistry   2788

Address: Hôpital de Hautepierre, avenue Molière, 67098 Strasbourg Cedex
Telephone: (088) 28 90 00
Head: Jean Mark

Laboratory of Clinical Gynaecology   **2789**
and Obstetrics I

Address: Hôpital de Hautepierre, avenue Molière, 67098 Strasbourg Cedex
Telephone: (088) 28 90 00
Head: Professor Robert Gandar
Senior staff: Professor B. Keller

Laboratory of Clinical Gynaecology   **2790**
and Obstetrics II

Address: 1 place de l'Hôpital, 67000 Strasbourg
Telephone: (088) 36 71 11
Head: Professor Pierre Muller
Senior staff: Professor Pierre Dellenbach

Laboratory of Clinical Ophthalmology   **2791**

Address: 1 place de l'Hôpital, 67000 Strasbourg
Telephone: (088) 36 71 11
Heads: Albert Bronner, Professor Alfred Brini
Senior staff: Professor Jean-Pierre Gerhard

Laboratory of Clinical Psychiatry   **2792**

Address: 1 place de l'Hôpital, 67000 Strasbourg
Telephone: (088) 36 71 11
Head: Professor Léonard Singer

Laboratory of Dermato-Chemistry   **2793**

Address: Clinique Dermatologique, 1 place de l'Hôpital, 67000 Strasbourg
Telephone: (088) 36 02 44
Head: Professor Claude Benezra

Laboratory of Electromyography and   **2794**
Functional Reeducation

Address: Hôpital de Hautepierre, avenue Molière, 67098 Strasbourg Cedex
Telephone: (088) 28 90 00
Head: Professor François Isch
Senior staff: Professor Michel Jesel

Laboratory of Electroradiology   **2795**

Address: 11 rue Humann, 67085 Strasbourg Cedex
Telephone: (088) 36 06 91
Head: Professor Auguste Wackenheim

Laboratory of Embryology   **2796**

Address: 11 rue Humann, 67085 Strasbourg Cedex
Telephone: (088) 36 06 91
Head: Professor Jean Clavert

Laboratory of Endocrine and Bone   **2797**
Cytophysiology

Research director: Alexandre Petrovic

Laboratory of Experimental   **2798**
Nephrology

Address: 1 place de l'Hôpital, 67000 Strasbourg
Telephone: (088) 36 71 11
Head: Professor Henri Jahn

Laboratory of Functional Exploration   **2799**
of the Nervous System

Address: Hôpital de Hautepierre, avenue Molière, 67098 Strasbourg Cedex
Telephone: (088) 28 90 00
Head: Professor Daniel Kurtz

Laboratory of Functional Exploration   **2800**
of Vestibular Pathology

Address: 1 place de l'Hôpital, 67000 Strasbourg
Telephone: (088) 36 71 11
Heads: Professor Claude Conraux, Maurice Collard

Laboratory of General and   **2801**
Experimental Pathology

Address: 1 place de l'Hôpital, 67000 Strasbourg
Telephone: (088) 36 71 11
Head: Professor Frédéric Stephan
Senior staff: Professor Philippe Reville

Laboratory of General Pathological   **2802**
Anatomy

Address: Hôpital de Hautepierre, avenue Molière, 67098 Strasbourg Cedex
Telephone: (088) 28 90 00
Head: Professor André Batzenschlager

Laboratory of General Pathology   **2803**

Address: 1 place de l'Hôpital, 67000 Strasbourg
Telephone: (088) 36 71 11
Head: Professor Julien Warter
Senior staff: Professor Daniel Storck, Professor Léopold Asch

Laboratory of General Surgery   **2804**

Address: Hôpital Pasteur, 68000 Colmar
Telephone: (089) 41 16 00
Head: Professor Philippe Reys

Laboratory of Geriatric Medicine   2805

Address: Pavillon Schutzenberger, rue Himmerich, 67000 Strasbourg
Telephone: (088) 31 08 62
Head: Professor Francis Kuntzmann

Laboratory of Histology   2806

Telephone: (088) 36 07 40
Head: Professor Claude Aron
Senior staff: Professor Michel Fabre, Professor Jean Marescaux, Professor Michel Roos

Laboratory of Infant Surgery   2807

Address: Hôpital de Hautepierre, avenue Molière, 67098 Strasbourg
Telephone: (088) 29 90 00
Head: Professor Paul Buck
Senior staff: Professor Paul Sauvage

Laboratory of Internal and   2808
Experimental Pathology

Address: 1 place de l'Hôpital, 67000 Strasbourg
Telephone: (088) 36 71 11
Head: Professor Marc Dorner
Senior staff: Professor René Bockel, Professor Louis Fincker, Professor Jean-Marie Brogard, Professor Marc Imler

Laboratory of Medical Biology   2809

Address: Hôpital de Hautepierre, avenue Molière, 67098 Strasbourg Cedex
Telephone: (088) 28 90 00
Head: Professor Jean-Victor Ruch

Laboratory of Neurochemistry   2810

Address: 11 rue Humann, 67085 Strasbourg Cedex
Telephone: (088) 36 06 91
Head: Albert Waksmann

Laboratory of Neurophysiology   2811

Address: 11 rue Humann, 67085 Strasbourg Cedex
Telephone: (088) 36 06 91
Head: Professor Pierre Karli

Laboratory of Neurosurgery   2812

Address: 1 place de l'Hôpital, 67000 Strasbourg
Telephone: (088) 36 71 11
Head: Professor Fernand Buchheit

Laboratory of Orthopaedic Surgery   2813
and Traumatology

Address: Centre de Traumatologie, allée Baumann, 67400 Illkirch-Graffenstaden
Telephone: 66 90 00
Head: Professor Ivan Kempf
Senior staff: Professor Maxime Champy

Laboratory of Paediatrics   2814

Address: Hôpital de Hautepierre, avenue Molière, 67098 Strasbourg Cedex
Telephone: (088) 28 90 00
Head: Professor Jean Juif
Senior staff: Professor Daniel Willard, Jean Geisert

Laboratory of Pathological Anatomy   2815

Address: Hôpital de Hautepierre, avenue Molière, 67098 Strasbourg Cedex
Telephone: (088) 28 90 00
Heads: Professor Yvon Legal, Professor André Batzenschlager
Senior staff: Professor Émile Philippe

Laboratory of Pharmacology   2816

Address: 11 rue Humann, 67000 Strasbourg
Telephone: (088) 36 06 91
Head: Professor Jean Schwartz
Senior staff: Professor Roger Bloch, Professor Jean-Louis Imbs

Laboratory of Physiology   2817

Head: Professor Charles Marx
Senior staff: Professor Pascal Haberey, Professor Georges Schaff

Laboratory of Pneumophthisiology   2818

Address: Pavillon Laennec, 1 place de l'Hôpital, 67000 Strasbourg
Telephone: (088) 36 71 11
Head: Professor Emile Roegel

Laboratory of Psychiatry III   2819

Address: 1 place de l'Hôpital, 67000 Strasbourg
Telephone: (088) 36 71 11
Head: Professor Lucien Israel

Laboratory of Psychotherapeutics for 2820 Children and Adolescents

Address: 1 place de l'Hôpital, 67000 Strasbourg
Telephone: (088) 36 71 11
Head: Professor René Ebtinger

Laboratory of Respiratory Functional 2821 Exploration

Address: Hôpital de Hautepierre, avenue Molière, 67098 Strasbourg Cedex
Telephone: (088) 28 90 00
Head: Jean-Paul Schieber

Laboratory of Skin and Allergies 2822 Research

Address: Clinique Dermatologique, 1 place de l'Hôpital, 67000 Strasbourg
Telephone: (088) 36 71 11
Head: Professor André Basset
Senior staff: Professor Edouard Grosshans

Laboratory of Stomatology and 2823 Maxillofacial Surgery

Address: 1 place de l'Hôpital, 67000 Strasbourg
Telephone: (088) 36 71 11
Head: Professor Maxime Champy

Laboratory of Toxicology and 2824 Professional Haematology

Address: 11 rue Humann, 67085 Strasbourg Cedex
Telephone: (088) 36 06 91
Head: Professor André Chaumont

Laboratory of Virology 2825

Address: 3 rue Koeberlé, 67000 Strasbourg
Telephone: (088) 36 06 22
Head: Professor André Kirn

Laboratory of X-ray Biophysics and 2826 Methodology

Address: 11 rue Humann, 67000 Strasbourg
Telephone: (088) 36 06 05
Head: Roger Rechenmann

L.M. Paturier Laboratory 2827

Address: Hôpital Civil, 67000 Strasbourg
Telephone: (088) 36 71 11
Head: Professor Jacques Grenier

Medical Reanimation and Anti-Poison 2828 Centre

Address: 1 place de l'Hôpital, 67000 Strasbourg
Telephone: (088) 36 71 11
Head: Professor Albert Jaeger
Senior staff: Professor Jean-Daniel Tempe

Neurological Clinic 2829

Address: 1 place de l'Hôpital, 67000 Strasbourg
Telephone: (088) 36 71 11
Head: Professor Francis Rohmer
Senior staff: Professor Maurice Collard

Psychiatric Clinic 2830

Address: 1 place de l'Hôpital, 67000 Strasbourg
Telephone: (088) 36 71 11
Head: Professor Théophile Kammerei

Raymond Poincaré Surgical Research 2831 Centre

Address: Pavillon Poincaré, Hôpital Civil, 67000 Strasbourg
Telephone: (088) 36 71 11

René Leriche Surgical Research 2832 Laboratory

Address: Pavillon Poincaré, Hôpital Civil, 67000 Strasbourg
Telephone: (088) 36 71 11
Head: Professor Claude Bollack
Senior staff: Professor Jean Geisert

UNIT OF CHEMISTRY 2833

École Nationale Supérieure de Chimie 2834 de Strasbourg

– ENSCS
[Strasbourg National College of Chemistry]
Address: 1 rue Blaise Pascal, 67008 Strasbourg Cedex
Telephone: (088) 61 48 02
Director: Professor Marc Daire

DEPARTMENT OF MATERIALS 2835 SCIENCE

Head: Paul Paix
Senior staff: Professor Jean-Claude Bernier, Professor Marc Daire
Activities: The main area of research is in the chemistry of solids: metals, refractory and abrasive materials, crystallochemistry, physical properties and reactions, structural analyses.

DEPARTMENT OF MATERIALS SCIENCE (METALS)   2836
Head: Professor Auguste Clauss

LABORATORY OF MINERAL CHEMISTRY   2837
Head: Professor Mauride Leroy

LABORATORY OF ORGANIC CHEMISTRY   2838
Head: Professor Guy Solladie
Activities: Synthesis and fine organic chemistry; recent work on liquid crystals.

LABORATORY OF PHYSICAL CHEMISTRY   2839
Head: Professor Marie-José Schwing

LABORATORY OF PHYSICAL CHEMISTRY AND ELECTROANALYSIS   2840
Head: Professor Jean-Paul Schwing

Institute of Chemistry   2841

Address: 1 rue Blaise Pascal, 67008 Strasbourg Cedex
Telephone: (088) 61 48 02

LABORATORY OF APPLIED ORGANIC CHEMISTRY   2842
Head: Professor Antonin Brini
Sections: Organic synthesis, Professor Mathilde Brini
Applied organic chemistry, Professor Charles Tanielian

LABORATORY OF HYDROCARBON PHYSICAL CHEMISTRY   2843
Head: Professor Jean Sommer

LABORATORY OF ORGANIC CHEMISTRY   2844
Head: Professor Jean-Jacques Riehl

LABORATORY OF ORGANIC CHEMISTRY OF NATURAL SUBSTANCES   2845
Head: Professor Guy Ourisson
Sections: Geochemistry, Pierre Albrecht
Dermatochemistry, Professor Claude Benezra
Biological organic chemistry, Jean-François Biellmann (Research director)
Organic chemistry, Henri Jacques Callot
Mass spectrometry, Robert Wolff
Biochemical research, Francis Schuber
Activities: Research on organic geochemistry; dermatochemistry; neurochemistry.

LABORATORY OF PHYSICAL ORGANIC CHEMISTRY I   2846
Head: Professor Paul Federlin
Activities: Research on stereoelectronic effects and reactions of molecular receptors.

LABORATORY OF SYNTHETIC ORGANIC CHEMISTRY   2847
Head: Michel Franck-Neumann
Activities: Research on the possibilities offered by systems with a high energy content (tension and polymaturation) and carbonyl metals for the synthesis of organic compounds (ie insecticides, pheromones).

UNIT OF GEOGRAPHY   2848

Address: 43 rue Goethe, 67000 Strasbourg
Telephone: (088) 35 43 00
Affiliation: Centre National de la Recherche Scientifique
Director: Professor P. Michel

Centre of Applied Geography   2849

Director: J. Tricart
Sections: Natural Resources Division
Laboratory for the Study of Dry Zones
Laboratory for the Study of Tropical Countries, Professor P. Michel
Activities: Research on natural habitats and the relationship between living beings and the geographical environment; research into the organizational process of human societies in their envirorment.

Laboratory of Physical Geography in Temperate Zones   2850

Head: H. Vogt
Activities: Research on: the geomorphology of the south-west Rhenish border; quantitative integration of ecological, hydryological, pedological and geomorphological phenomena; interrelationship between ecology, agronomic techniques, sociology and economy in order to determine overall managerial problems; erosion of agricultural soils in northern Alsace.

UNIT OF LIFE SCIENCES   2851

Activities: Research for medicine, agronomy and oceanology; technology - bio- and medical engineering, pharmacy, agriculture and biotechnics.

Institute of Botany 2852

Address: 28 rue Goethe, 67083 Strasbourg Cedex
Telephone: (088) 35 25 53
Activities: Systematics; floristics (inventory of the regional flora).

DEPARTMENT OF CECIDOLOGY 2853

Research director: Jean Meyer
Activities: Morphological study of gall-midge tissue; morphological change after gall has been effected by gall-midges.

DEPARTMENT OF PHYTOGENETICS 2854

Head: Professor Alice Gagnieu
Activities: Cytology; genetics.

DEPARTMENT OF PLANT BIOCHEMISTRY 2855

Head: Pierre Benveniste
Activities: Cell biochemistry; biosynthesis regulation by sterols.

DEPARTMENT OF PLANT ECOLOGY 2856

Head: Professor Michel Gounot
Activities: Field, forest and regional ecology.

DEPARTMENT OF PLANT MORPHOLOGY 2857

Head: Professor Jacques Roux
Activities: Descriptive and experimental research: causal morphology; use of tissue cultures for cultivated plants.

DEPARTMENT OF PLANT PHYSIOLOGY 2858

Head: Professor Henri Duranton
Activities: Research on plastids; primary structure of proteins in terms of viral morphogenesis; modulation of the enzymatic action of cells under the influence of external agents (light, pesticides).

Institute of Physiology and Biological Chemistry 2859

Affiliation: Centre National de la Recherche Scientifique
Note: Most of the research is linked to work carried out by the CNRS.

LABORATORY OF COMPARATIVE NEUROENDOCRINOLOGY 2860

Director: Professor Ph. Richard
Activities: Multidisciplinary study of the hypothalamic-hypophyseal regulation mechanism.

PANCREATIC HORMONES RESEARCH GROUP 2861

Director: Professor P. Mialhe
Activities: Endocrine action in the liver and intestine - application of the results to both the diabetic and the obese.

Institute of Zoology and General Biology 2862

LABORATORY OF ZOOLOGY AND EXPERIMENTAL EMBRYOLOGY 2863

Affiliation: Centre National de la Recherche Scientifique
Head: Professor Jean-Henri Vivien
Senior staff: Jean-Jacques Thiebold, Professor Raymond Kirsch
Activities: Morphogenesis and functional variation in the genital tract of amniotic vertebrates; endocrinology and neuro-endocrinology poikilothermic vertebrates; ecophysiology of primitive types of insects (Collembola).

Laboratory of Microbial Biochemistry 2864

Address: Institut Le Bel, 4 rue Blaise Pascal, 67070 Strasbourg Cedex
Telephone: (088) 61 48 30
Director: Professor Benoit Wurtz
Activities: Microbiology in the field of agriculture: conservation of animal feeds.

UNIT OF MATERIALS SCIENCE 2865

Note: This Unit concentrates on teaching rather than on research except in the case of the Applied Polymer Science College.

École d'Application des Hauts Polymères 2866

[Applied Polymer Science College]

Telephone: (088) 61 34 67
Director: Professor Morand Lambla
Sections: Polymer chemistry, Professor M. Lambla; polymer physics, Professor D. Froelich; polymer processing, Professor J. Terrisse
Graduate research staff: 20
Annual expenditure: F2m
Activities: Properties and processing of polymers - synthesis, characterization, transformation; new developments of polymer composites.
Facilities: Bringing together in the same building specialists and equipment of polymer science, from chemistry to manufacturing.

UNIT OF MATHEMATICS 2867

Research Institute on Advanced Mathematics 2868

Address: 10 rue du Général Zimmer, 67084 Strasbourg Cedex
Telephone: (088) 61 48 22
Director: Professor Raymond Gerard
Activities: Probability; differential equations; analytical geometry; geometry-topology-trajectories; algebra-topology-trajectories; statistics; advice centre; computer studies.

Research Institute on the Teaching of Mathematics 2869

Address: 10 rue du Général Zimmer, 67084 Strasbourg Cedex
Telephone: (088) 61 48 22
Director: Professor Jean Martinet
Activities: Research into the teaching of advanced mathematics; documentation on the teaching of mathematics.

UNIT OF ODONTOLOGY 2870

Odontological Research Centre 2871

Address: 1 place de l'Hôpital, 67085 Strasbourg Cedex
Telephone: (088) 36 15 55
Director: Professor Robert Frank
Activities: Research is orientated towards a better understanding of buccodental diseases in terms of their frequency, aetiopathogenesis and prevention. This is achieved by a multidisciplinary approach in the fields of epidemiology, ultrastructural studies, biochemistry, microbiology, immunology and biophysics.

UNIT OF PHARMACEUTICAL SCIENCES 2872

Address: 74 route du Rhin, 67400 Illkirch-Graffenstaden
Telephone: 66 90 70
Director: Professor Pierre Metais
Activities: Research concerns life mechanisms; origin of pathological disturbances in man and their remedy.

Laboratory of Analytical Chemistry 2873

Head: Professor Michel Hasselmann
Senior staff: Professor Paul Laugel

Laboratory of Applied Biochemistry 2874

Head: Professor Georges Ferard

Laboratory of Bacteriology and Cryptogamy 2875

Head: Professor Dominique Vidon

Laboratory of Biological Chemistry 2876

Address: Centre de Traumatologie, avenue Baumann, 67400 Illkirch-Graffenstaden
Telephone: 66 90 00
Head: Professor Pierre Metais

Laboratory of Botany 2877

Head: Professor Roland Carbiener

Laboratory of Bromatology and Nutrition Research 2878

Address: chemin du Routoir, 67400 Illkirch-Graffenstaden
Telephone: 66 48 96
Head: Professor Michel Hasselmann

Laboratory of Enzymology 2879

Head: Jean Bieth

Laboratory of Galenic Pharmacy 2880

Head: Professor Claude Mathis
Senior staff: Professor André Stamm

Laboratory of General and Mineral Chemistry 2881

Head: Professor Charles Lapp

Laboratory of Immunology 2882

Head: Professor Jacques Malgras

Laboratory of Materia Medica 2883

Head: Professor Robert Anton

Laboratory of Mathematics 2884

Head: Professor Hans Lami

Laboratory of Organic Chemistry 2885

Heads: Professor Jean Schreiber, Professor Camille Wermuth

Laboratory of Pharmaceutical Biochemistry 2886

Head: Professor André Stahl

Laboratory of Pharmaceutical Chemistry 2887

Head: Professor Louis Jung

Laboratory of Pharmacodynamics 2888

Head: Professor Jean-Claude Stoclet

Laboratory of Pharmacology 2889

Head: Professor Yves Landry

Laboratory of Physics 2890

Head: Professor Gilbert Laustriat

Laboratory of Physiology 2891

Head: Professor Alexis Gairard

Laboratory of Toxicology and Molecular Biology 2892

Head: Professor Guy Dirheimer

Laboratory of Virology 2893

Head: Professor Philippe Poindron

Laboratory of Water Analysis 2894

Address: 74 route du Rhin, 67400 Illkirch-Graffenstaden
Head: Professor Jean Schreiber

Laboratory of Zoology and Parasitology 2895

Head: Bernard Pesson

UNIT OF PHYSICS 2896

Activities: Fundamental and applied physics. Research in nuclear and particle physics depends entirely on the work being carried out by the Institut National de Physique Nucléaire et de Physique des Particules at the Centre de Recherches Nucléaires at Strasbourg-Cronenbourg.

Institute of Fluid Mechanics 2897

Address: 2 rue Boussingault, 67000 Strasbourg
Telephone: (088) 61 43 00
Director: Professor Jean-José Fried
Activities: Fundamental and applied research are closely linked. The main areas of research concern: hydrodynamics and porous media; biomechanics; non-Newtonian fluids; aerothermodynamics.

LABORATORY OF BIOMECHANICS 2898
Head: René Feidt

LABORATORY OF HYDRODYNAMICS OF POROUS MEDIA 2899
Head: Lothaire Zilliox

LABORATORY OF NON-NEWTONIAN FLUID FLOW 2900
Head: Claude Gebel

LABORATORY OF TURBULENCE IN NON-NEWTONIAN FLUIDS 2901
Head: Olivier Scrivener
Senior staff: Professor Henri Burnage

Institute of Physical Technology 2902

Address: 7 rue de l'Université, 67000 Strasbourg
Telephone: (088) 35 51 50
Director: Professor Gilbert Sulter

Institute of Physics 2903

Address: 3-5 rue de l'Université, 67084 Strasbourg Cedex
Telephone: (088) 36 35 32
Activities: Research concerns surface and solid-state physics (electronic structures, magnetism, optoelectrical properties of different materials); molecular acoustics; biomedicine and teledetection of natural resources.

LABORATORY OF MAGNETISM 2904
Head: Professor Jules Wucher
Activities: Physics of solids and surfaces (electronic and magnetic structure).

LABORATORY OF SOLID-STATE SPECTROSCOPY AND OPTICS 2905
Head: Jean-Bernard Grun
Activities: Interaction between light and condensed matter.

Le Bel Institute 2906

Address: 4 rue Blaise Pascal, 67070 Strasbourg Cedex
Telephone: (088) 61 48 30

LABORATORY OF MOLECULAR ACOUSTICS   2907

Head: Professor Roger Cerf
Activities: Hydrodynamics and viscoelastic properties of polymers in solutions and of polymeric gels; dynamics of biological molecules; properties of liquid crystals.

LABORATORY OF THE ELECTRONIC STRUCTURE OF SOLIDS   2908

Head: Professor François Gautier
Senior staff: Professor Emile Daniel, Professor Claude Robert
Activities: Joint research with the Laboratory of Magnetism.

Université de Strasbourg III*   2909

[Strasbourg University III]
Address: Place d'Athènes, 67084 Strasbourg Cedex
Telephone: (088) 61 18 18
President: Jean-Marc Bischoff

UNIT FOR APPLIED RESEARCH AND TECHNOLOGY*   2910

Director: M Soguel
Activities: Applied research in computer studies financial management and conversion systems; conversion systems on microordinators. Applied research in civil engineering - cements, structures and methods.

Université de Technologie de Compiègne   2911

[Compiègne University of Technology]
Address: rue Roger Couttolenc, BP 233, 60206 Compiègne
Telephone: (04) 420 99 77
Telex: UNITECH 150110F
Chairman: Guy Denielou
Sections:
Mechanical Engineering Department, Professor Domique François
Bioengineering Department, Professor Georges Broun
Chemical Engineering Department, Professor Maurice Gelus
Computing and Applied Mathematics Department, Professor Robert Colcombet
Institute of Data Processing and Management, Pierre Mathelot

Université de Toulon   2912

[Toulon University]
Address: avenue de l'Université, 83130 La Garde
Telephone: (094) 75 90 50
Telex: O.DI.SE 400 287
Chairman: Professor Pierre Broche
Secretary General: Guy Slawy

SCIENCE AND TECHNOLOGY RESEARCH UNIT   2913

Director: Professor Jean-François Cavassilas

Applied Chemistry Laboratory   2914

Head: Professor Jean-Louis Vernet

Applied Geophysics Laboratory   2915

Head: Professor Regis Ballestracci

Applied Mathematics Laboratory   2916

Senior staff: Professor Marie-Claude Pelissier, Professor Patrick Penel

Automatic and Applied Informatics Laboratory   2917

Head: Professor Gilles Enea

Electromagnetic Soundings of the Terrestrial Environment Laboratory   2918

Senior staff: Professor Michel Crochet, Professor Pierre Broche

Materials Research Laboratory   2919

Head: Professor Henri Bartholin

Organometallic Chemistry Laboratory   2920

Head: Professor Jean-Yves Benaim

Physics-Mathematics Laboratory   2921

Head: Professor Jean-Michel Combes

Signals and Systems Laboratory   2922

Head: Professor Georges Bonnet

UNIVERSITY INSTITUTE OF TECHNOLOGY 2923

Director: Professor Jean-Louis Vernet

Department of Commercial Technology 2924

Head: Hervé Terlier

Department of Electrical Engineering 2925

Head: Pierre Loubet

Department of Mechanical Engineering 2926

Head: Jean-Marie Piton

Université de Valenciennes 2927 et du Hainaut-Cambrésis

[Valenciennes and Hainaut-Cambrésis University]
Address: le Mont Houy, 59326 Valenciennes Cedex
Telephone: (027) 46 66 08
Chairman: Professor N. Malvanche

FACULTY OF SCIENCE 2928

Dean: M Le Ray

Laboratory of Hydrodynamics, Aerodynamics and Energy 2929

Head: M Le Ray
Graduate research staff: 15

Laboratory of Plastic Deformation of Metals 2930

Head: M Oudin
Graduate research staff: 2

Laboratory of Pure and Applied Mathematics 2931

Head: M Barre
Graduate research staff: 13

Laboratory of Science of Communication 2932

Head: M Martinache
Graduate research staff: 13

Laboratory of Thermoenergy 2933

Head: G. Matton
Graduate research staff: 4

NATIONAL COLLEGE OF ENGINEERING 2934

Head: M Torguet

UNIVERSITY INSTITUTE OF TECHNOLOGY 2935

Head: Mme Moriamez

Laboratory of Chemistry and Metallurgy 2936

Head: Pierre Lecocq
Graduate research staff: 2

Laboratory of Computer Science, Artificial Intelligence and Pattern Recognition 2937

Head: M Bourton
Graduate research staff: 17

Laboratory of Crystallography and Metallurgy 2938

Head: Mme Moriamez
Graduate research staff: 6

Laboratory of Crystals Chemistry 2939

Head: D.J. Thomas
Graduate research staff: 10

Laboratory of Cybernetics and Man-Machine Systems 2940

Head: M Malvache
Graduate research staff: 22

Laboratory of Fluid Mechanics 2941

Head: M Tournier
Graduate research staff: 14

Laboratory of Optical and Acoustical Electronics 2942

Head: M Marcou
Graduate research staff: 24

Université des Sciences et Techniques de Lille 2943

[Lille University of Sciences and Technology]
Address: Cellule Recherche, 59655 Villeneuve d'Ascq Cedex
Telephone: (020) 91 92 22
Telex: EUNOR 131 339 F/300/A-10

UNIT OF AGRICULTURAL SCIENCES 2944

Laboratory of Applied Physiology and Zootechnics 2945

Head: Professor Rousseau
Activities: Physiology of reproduction in domestic animals; uterine motricity in sheep; ovary duct motricity in rabbits.

Laboratory of Seed Testing and Analysis 2946

Head: Professor R. Bouriquet
Activities: Wheat gluten in relation to its baking value; plant micropropagation.
Contract work: Yes

UNIT OF BIOLOGY 2947

Laboratory of Algology 2948

Head: Professor Bodard
Activities: Red algae - morphogenesis; practical uses.
Contract work: Yes

Laboratory of Applied Biology 2949

Head: Professor Montuelle
Activities: Bacterial ecology and organic compounds of the soil.

Laboratory of Applied Microbiology 2950

Head: Professor J. Guillaume
Senior staff: Professor Tailliez

Laboratory of Biological Chemistry 2951

Affiliation: Centre National de la Recherche Scientifique
Head: Professor J. Montreuil
Activities: Molecular biology of glycoconjugates - molecular pathology of those compounds, medicines for treatment, nutrition.
Contract work: Yes

Laboratory of Comparative and Invertebrate Endocrinology 2952

Affiliation: Centre National de la Recherche Scientifique
Head: Professor M. Durchon
Sections: Annelide and molluscan endocrinology, Professor M. Durchon; arthropod endocrinology, M Joly
Contract work: Yes

Laboratory of Cryptogamy 2953

Head: Professor Lacoste
Activities: Biology and ecophysiology; photopathology.
Contract work: Yes

Laboratory of Cytogenetics and Ecology 2954

Head: vacant
Activities: Analysis of fertilization mechanisms in higher plants; karyological analysis of ecotypes in extreme geographical situations (littoral, mountains, etc); evaluation of natural sites in view of pre-management studies.
Contract work: Yes

Laboratory of Experimental Morphogenesis 2955

Head: Professor Bart

Laboratory of Microbiology 2956

Head: Professor J. Guillaume
Senior staff: Professor Derieux
Activities: Genetic study and phylogeny of rhizobium and its energy metabolism; relationship between leguminous plants and rhizobium.
Contract work: Yes

Laboratory of Physiology and **2957** Psychophysiology

Affiliation: Centre National de la Recherche Scientifique
Head: Professor Rousseau
Sections: Functional neurobiology, M Delorme; plant neurophysiology, Professor Rousseau; cell physiology, M Guilbault; neuromuscular physiology, M Pertuzon; psychophysiology I, M Coquery; psychophysiology II, M Roy
Contract work: Yes

Laboratory of Plant Physiology   **2958**

Head: Professor R. Bouriguet
Senior staff: Mlle Paupardin
Activities: Cell proliferation and differentiation of tissues and cultivated plant cells (in vitro); formation of secondary metabolites by cultivated plant tissues (in vitro).
Contract work: Yes

Laboratory of Protistology and   **2959** Electron Microscopy

Affiliation: Centre National de la Recherche Scientifique
Head: Professor E. Vivier
Activities: Freshwater ecology and Ciliata; protozoic parasites.
Contract work: Yes

UNIT OF CALCULUS AND   **2960** INFORMATION SCIENCE

Laboratory of Applied Computer   **2961** Science

Affiliation: Centre National de la Recherche Scientifique
Head: Professor V. Cordonnier
Activities: New methods of architecture: information treatment; projects OMPHALE, MAUD and SAUGE; S-machines; parallel processors; associative processors; graphic interactive informatics.
Contract work: Yes

Laboratory of Automation   **2962**

Head: Professor P. Vidal
Sections: Biological and medical engineering, Professor P. Vidal, M Toulotte; analysis and command of complex systems, M Staroswiecki; industrial logic, M Toulotte; industrial processes - conduits, M Povy, M Soenen, M Toulotte

Activities: Research is orientated towards the use of microprocessors in industry and medicine.
Contract work: Yes

Laboratory of Computer Sciences   **2963**

Head: Professor Jacob
Sections: Theory of languages, M Latteux; theory of trees, M Dauchet; systems algebra, Professor Jacob
Contract work: Yes

Laboratory of Data Analysis and   **2964** Computer Science

Head: Professor Losfeld
Activities: Statistical analysis of data; analysis by graphic interactive informatics.

Laboratory of Electromechanic   **2965** Systems

Head: Professor Maizières
Activities: Analogue and numeric simulations of static converters and associated machines; variation and regulation speed by static converters; description and synthesis of logic commands adapted to microelectronics.

Laboratory of Electrotechnology   **2966**

Head: Professor G. Seguier
Activities: Static converters; machines fed by converters; high performance machines.
Contract work: Yes

Laboratory of Graph Theory and   **2967** Combinatorics

Head: Professor Sterboll
Activities: Theory of graphs and combinatorics.

Laboratory of Numerical Analysis and   **2968** Optimization

Head: Professor Brezinski
Sections: Applied analysis, M Mignot; numerical analysis, Professor Brezinski; optimization, M Huard de la Mare
Contract work: Yes

Laboratory of Radiopropagation and   **2969** Electronics

Affiliation: Centre National de la Recherche Scientifique
Head: Professor R. Gabillard
Sections: Electromagnetic soil surveys, M Cautermann; theoretical and experimental study of foundation

examinations by radar, M Degauque; electronics, Professor Gabillard, M Louage
Contract work: Yes

Laboratory of Solid-State Spectrometry 2970

Head: Professor Lebrun
Activities: Study of the properties of porous bodies; study of electric and infrared properties; instruments for measuring in situ humidity.
Contract work: Yes

Laboratory of Systematics 2971

Head: Professor Laurent
Activities: Large-scale systems; process commands; modelling and simulation.

Semiconductor and High Frequency 2972 Centre

Affiliation: Centre National de la Recherche Scientifique
Head: Professor Constant
Senior staff: Professor Leroy, Professor Raczy, Professor Salmer
Activities: Instrumentation; propagation and circuits; dielectrics; hyperfrequency active components; semiconductors.
Contract work: Yes

UNIT OF CHEMISTRY 2973

Laboratory of Applied Mineral 2974 Chemistry

Head: Professor G. Tridot
Activities: Study and interpretation of ternary diagrams; study of uranium sulphur and transition metals.

Laboratory of Crystallochemistry 2975

Head: Professor Thomas
Activities: Solid-state electrolytes; triad oxides; non-linear materials.
Contract work: Yes

Laboratory of Heterogeneous and 2976 Homogeneous Catalysis

Affiliation: Centre National de la Recherche Scientifique
Head: Professor Bonnelle
Senior staff: Professor Petit
Activities: Heterogenetic catalysis; electrosynthesis; homogenetic and supported catalysis.
Contract work: Yes

Laboratory of Infrared and Raman 2977 Spectroscopy

Head: Professor Delhaye
Activities: Instrumentation and new techniques; study of physicochemical problems by vibration spectroscopy.
Contract work: Yes

Laboratory of Kinetics and 2978 Combustion Chemistry

Head: Professor Lucquin
Sections: Combustion spectrochemistry, M Sochet; combustion spectrochemistry and aerodynamics, M Sawerysyn; macromolecular and heterogeneous combustion, M Delfosse; amino- and halogenated additives in combustion, M Antonik; nitrated additives and simulation in combustion, M Dechaux, M Perche
Contract work: Yes

Laboratory of Macromolecular 2979 Chemistry

Head: Professor Loucheux
Activities: Macromolecular reactions; synthetic peptides and polypeptides; photochemistry of polymers.
Contract work: Yes

Laboratory of Metallurgy 2980

Head: Professor Bonte
Activities: Study of the strength and the mechanics of fracture in metals under the influence of metallurgical, mechanical and electrochemical factors.

Laboratory of Mineral Chemistry and 2981 Analytic Methology

Head: Professor Vandorpe
Activities: Mineral and analytical chemistry.
Contract work: Yes

Laboratory of Mineral Chemistry I   2982

Head: Professor J. Heubel
Sections: Synthesis and fundamental study of ox-yfluoride or graphite compounds by spectroscopy, M Vast; activation of agents by sulphonation, nitration and electrochemical means, M Wartel; synthesis and study of oligomers and polymers by spectroscopy, M Legrand, M De Jaeger; synthesis and study of non-linear materials, M Barbier
Contract work: Yes

Laboratory of Mineral Chemistry II   2983

Head: Professor Devrainne
Activities: Crystallization.

Laboratory of Organic Chemistry II   2984

Head: Professor Sliwa
Sections: Molecules of biological interest, M Blondeau; molecules of industrial interest, M Picavet
Contract work: Yes

Laboratory of Organic Synthesis   2985

Head: Professor Couturier
Sections: Synthesis of oligosaccharide sugars with biochemical applications, M Venot; synthesis and stereochemical study of cyclo-azide carbons, M Hasiak
Contract work: Yes

Laboratory of Physical and   2986
Thermochemical Metallurgy

Head: Professor Foct
Senior staff: Professor Perrot
Activities: Metallurgical thermochemistry; physical metallurgy; mechanical metallurgy.
Contract work: Yes

Laboratory of Physical Chemistry of   2987
Agitated Molecules and Free Radicals

Head: Professor Goudmand
Sections: Ultraviolet spectroscopy of weak interactions, M Vidal; elementary reactions of atomic nitrogen and triple molecular nitrogen, Mlle Dessaux; industrial prototypes for the destruction of nitrogen oxides in the nutrition industry and in pollution industries, Mlle Dessaux; photo- and thermo-decomposition of water, Professor Goudmand
Contract work: Yes

Laboratory of Spectroscopy and   2988
Organic Systems Reactions

Affiliation: Centre National de la Recherche Scientifique
Head: Professor Lablache-Combier
Senior staff: Professor Lhomme
Activities: Organic photochemistry, synthesis; elimination reactions of solids support in conditions of light thermolysis; polymer photochemistry; synthesis and properties of molecules of biological interest; chemistry of natural substances.
Contract work: Yes

UNIT OF EARTH SCIENCES   2989

Laboratory of Applied Geology   2990

Head: Professor J. Paquet
Sections: Tectonic physics, Professor J. Paquet; hydrogeology, M Crampon, M Mania; Ostracoda palaeontology, M Lethiers; palaeosedimentology in the eastern Mediterranean, M Hoyez
Contract work: Yes

Laboratory of Dynamic Geology   2991

Affiliation: Centre National de la Recherche Scientifique
Head: Professor P. Celet
Activities: Geological research in the Alpines; marine geology in collaboration with CNEXO; geological studies in Japan; cartography and regional hydrogeology; regional pedological studies.
Contract work: Yes

Laboratory of Mineralogy   2992

Head: Professor J. Prouvost
Activities: Crystal formation; experimental study of sulphate crystallization; use of Raman molecular microwaves to study crystals; preparation of aggregates with high coefficients; conversion of concretes and clays.

Laboratory of Palaeobotany and   2993
Palaeontology

Head: Professor J.-P. Laveine
Activities: Carboniferous biostratigraphy; study of Devonian and Carboniferous series in Boulogne, Ardenne, the Armorican Massif and the Iberian peninsula; comparative palaeozoic palynology in Europe and Africa; stratigraphic palaeontology; Ordovician, Silurian, Devonian and Carboniferous comparative studies in France, Canada and Afghanistan.
Contract work: Yes

Laboratory of Regional and Fundamental Geology 2994

Head: Professor C. Delattre
Senior staff: M Waterlot, Mme Corsin
Activities: Mining petrography (coal); mesozoic palaeobotany; palaeozoic geology.

Laboratory of Sedimentology and Geochemistry 2995

Affiliation: Centre National de la Recherche Scientifique
Head: Professor Chamley
Senior staff: Professor Debrabant
Activities: Continental palaeoenvironments through deep sea drilling; influence of the oceans in ancient Atlantic ocean sediments; tectonic-sedimentary relationships in the Mediterranean sea, and Atlantic and western Pacific oceans; clay sediments and pollutants; stratigraphy and geodynamics in the region of Gibraltar.
Contract work: Yes

UNIT OF FUNDAMENTAL PHYSICS 2996

Laboratory of Acoustics 2997

Head: Professor Deprez
Activities: Propagation of acoustic waves in construction materials; characterization of the absorbing properties of foam.

Laboratory of Anisotropic Physics 2998

Affiliation: Centre National de la Recherche Scientifique
Head: Professor Billard
Activities: Study of electromagnetic waves in voids and mesophases; study of the physical properties of mesophases; elaboration, characterization and classification of discophases.
Contract work: Yes

Laboratory of Atomospheric Optics 2999

Affiliation: Centre National de la Recherche Scientifique
Head: Professor Lenoble
Sections: Study of planetary atmospherics by photometry and polarimetry, M Herman; teledetection and oceanography, M Deschamps; climatology, M Fouquart
Contract work: Yes

Laboratory of Crystallography 3000

Affiliation: Centre National de la Recherche Scientifique
Head: Professor R. Fouret
Activities: Crystal dynamics; transition phases; structure of plastic crystals, surgical materials and biological compounds.

Laboratory of Hertzian Spectroscopy 3001

Affiliation: Centre National de la Recherche Scientifique
Head: Professor R. Wertheimer
Sections: Energy levels and identification of lasers and mass molecules, M Bellet, M Demaison; physics and ray-molecule and molecule-molecule interactions, quantum optics, M Macke; instrumentation, M Journel; study of the structure of impurity bands in semiconductors III-V, M Dubois
Contract work: Yes

Laboratory of Molecular Spectroscopy 3002

Affiliation: Centre National de la Recherche Scientifique
Head: Professor Becart
Senior staff: Professor Schamps
Activities: Electronic structure and means of liaison of diatomic compounds and transition metals; resolute laser spectroscopy; spectroscopic study of high vibration levels of acid hydrides.
Contract work: Yes

Laboratory of Solid-State Physics 3003

Affiliation: University College of Engineering, Lille; Centre National de la Recherche Scientifique
Head: Professor Escaig
Sections: Plasticity of solid polymers, M Rietsch, Professor Escaig; tectonic physics, M Paquet; physical metallurgy of minerals, M Doukhan; crystalline plasticity, Professor Escaig; crystalline electronic structure and flaws, M Lenglart, M Farvacque
Contract work: Yes

Laboratory of Theoretical Physics 3004

Senior staff: Professor Cortois, Professor Locqueneux, Professor Tillieu
Activities: Fadeev equations, n body problems, secondary quantification, collisions theory; non-linear optical problems in molecules and crystals; Hartree-Fock equations.

UNIT OF GEOGRAPHY AND RURAL PLANNING   3005

Laboratory of Climatology and Hydrology   3006

Head: Professor P. Biays
Activities: Climate and climatic change in temperate and cold zones; hydrological survey.
Contract work: Yes

Laboratory of Geomorphology and Quaternary Studies   3007

Head: Professor Somme
Senior staff: Professor Llenaff
Activities: Geomorphology, neotectonics and quaternary studies of southern France; prehistory and environment of palaeolithic man; quaternary stratigraphy and palaeogeography of north-west Europe; north-west Europe palaeoclimatology; geomorphology of the continental margins of the north Atlantic and of calcareous regions; dynamic geomorphology; morphogenesis and neotectonics of western and central Mediterranean, Yugoslavia and Italy.
Contract work: Yes

Laboratory of North-West Europe Population Dynamics   3008

Affiliation: Centre National de la Recherche Scientifique
Head: Professor Lentacker
Activities: Movements and commercial installations in north-west Europe; migration patterns in northern France.
Contract work: Yes

Laboratory of Tropical Geography   3009

Head: Professor Nguyen-Van-Chi
Activities: Modernization of the fishing industry, the craft industry and tourism in Senegal; role of women in Brazzaville; diamond craft industry in central Africa; agro-industrial complex of the N'Kayi in the Congo; the souks in the area west of Morocco.

Laboratory of Urban, Industrial and Population Geography   3010

Head: Professor Bruyelle
Activities: Economic mutations in the old industrial areas of north-west Europe; regional urban planning in north-west Europe; demo-geography of the area.
Contract work: Yes

UNIT OF PURE AND APPLIED MATHEMATICS   3011

Laboratory of Differential Geometry and Topology   3012

Affiliation: Centre National de la Recherche Scientifique
Head: Professor Lehmann
Sections: Rational homotopy and characteristic classes, Professor Lehmann; thin section geometry, M Hector; singularity and monodromy, M Schwartz; K theory, M Mohammed

Laboratory of Mechanics   3013

Head: Professor R. Zeytounian
Senior staff: Professor Parsy

Laboratory of Probability and Statistics   3014

Head: Professor Boscq
Activities: Functional statistics; density studies, Gaussian convergence; measurement representation; information theory and qualitative probability.

Laboratory of Pure Mathematics   3015

Head: Professor G. Coeure
Senior staff: M Antoine, M De Paris

Mechanics Service - Aerodynamics   3016

Head: Professor Dyment
Activities: Quasi-horizontal free surfacc flow; flow movement between rotational solid bodies; influence of cavities on flow and parietal pressure; use of velocimetric measurements in aerodynamics; inter-stationary rapid variable flow.
Contract work: Yes

Research Institute on Teaching Mathematics   3017

Head: Professor Tison
Activities: Audiovisual research; analysis; informatics; mathematics and economics; mathematics and interdisciplinary applications; history of science; pedagogic use of programmable pocket calculators.

Lille College of Chemistry   3018

LABORATORY OF CATALYSIS AND   3019
PHYSICAL CHEMISTRY OF SOLIDS
Head: Professor Leroy
Sections: Catalysis, M Baussart; materials, corrosion,
M Bavay

Materials Science and Construction   3020
Techniques Research Centre

Head: Professor Lebrun
Sections: Propagation of sound waves in materials, M
Deprez; thermics, M Thery; modelling and instrumenta-
tion, M Dubus; mensuration and automation, Professor
Lebrun
Activities: Current work is centred on: energy
economics; buildings instrumentation; microinformatics
in construction and in industry.
Contract work: Yes

University College of Engineering, Lille 3021

See under: Laboratory of Solid-State Physics.

Wimereux Institute of Marine and   3022
Regional Biology

Address: BP 41, 69230 Wimereux
Director: Professor M. Durchon
Senior staff: M Richard
Activities: Cephalopoda; marine ecology; molysmol-
ogy.
Contract work: Yes

MEASUREMENT CENTRE   3023
Sections:
High frequency components and circuits, Professor
Raczy
Micro informatics, vacant
Automated diffractometer, Professor R. Fouret
Cryogenic centre, Professor Biskupski
Materials testing and electrohydraulics, Professor
Escaig, Professor Foct
RIBERMAG spectrometer, Professor Lablache-Com-
bier
BECKMANN spectrometer, Professor Goudmand,
Professor Vidal
Molecular microprobe, Professor Dhamelincourt
Electronic paramagnetic resonance, Professor Sochet
Rapid kinetics, Professor Loucheux
Nuclear magnetic resonance, Professor Bonelle,
Professor Lhomme
Quadripolar analysis, Professor Lucquin, Professor
Sawerysyn
Infrared spectrometer, Professor Wallart

Magnetometer, Professor Leroy
CAMEBAX electronic microprobe, Professor Foct
Animal house, Professor Rousseau
Electronic microscope, Professor Dhainaut, Professor
J.-P. Laveine
High pressure and high temperature chamber, Professor
J. Paquet
Cambridge Stereoscan Type 96 113 Mark BA, Professor
Vivier
JEOL U3 electron microscope, Professor Doukhan

Université du Maine   3024

[Le Mans University]
Address: route de Laval, BP 535, 72017 Le Mans
Cedex
Telephone: (043) 24 70 37
President: Professor Philip

FACULTY OF SCIENCES   3025

Address: Vaurouzé, route de Laval, BP 535, 72017 Le
Mans Cedex
Dean: M Reyx

Chemistry Department   3026

Head: Professor Bouchet
Sections: Organic chemistry, Professor Rouessac,
Professor Brown
Organic macromolecular chemistry, Professor Pinazzi
Physical and photochemistry, Professor Casals
Macromolecular physical chemistry, Professor Bruneau
Solid-state chemistry, Professor De Pape
Materials sciences, Professor Cupcic
Natural sciences, biology, Professor Lejuez
Earth sciences, Professor Gelard
Computer sciences, Professor Moret-Bailly

Mathematics Department   3027

Head: vacant

Physics Department   3028

Head: Professor R. Lehmann

UNIVERSITY INSTITUTE OF   3029
TECHNOLOGY

Address: route de Laval, BP 535, 72017 Le Mans
Cedex
Director: Professor R. Lehmann

Chemistry Department 3030

Head: Professor Sauvage

Industrial Administration Department 3031

Head: Professor Thomas

Mechanical Engineering Department 3032

Head: Professor Lalos

Université François Rabelais - Université de Tours 3033

[François Rabelais University - Tours University]
Address: 3 rue des Tanneurs, 37041 Tours Cedex
Telephone: (047) 20 47 62
Chairman: Professor M. Maillet

EXACT AND NATURAL SCIENCES RESEARCH UNIT 3034

Address: Pare de Grandmont, 37200 Tours

Algebra and Geometry Laboratory 3035

Head: Dr Gramain

Animal Physiology Laboratory 3036

Head: Dr D. Garnier

Applied Analyses and Mathematics Laboratory 3037

Head: Dr Sibony

Chemical Energetics, Electrochemistry and Heterogeneous Kinetics Laboratory 3038

Head: Professor P. Belin

Comparative Physiology Laboratory 3039

Head: Professor A. Peyre

Electronic Molecular Spectroscopy Laboratory 3040

Head: Professor L. Marsigny
Senior staff: Dr Lebreton

Ethology and Psychophysiology Laboratory 3041

Head: Professor Henri Verron

Geology and Geomorphology Laboratory 3042

Head: Dr L. Rasplus

Institute for Experimental Biocoenosis of Agricultural Systems 3043

DYAMICS OF PLANT POPULATIONS 3044
Head: Dr J. Boscher

DYNAMICS AND EVOLUTION OF INSECT POPULATIONS 3045
Head: Professor V. Labeyrie

ECOPHYSIOLOGY OF INSECT REPRODUCTION 3046
Head: Dr J. Huignard

SENSORIAL PHYSIOLOGY AND BEHAVIOUR OF INSECTS 3047
Head: J. Pouzat

Kinetics of Organic and Biological Reactions Laboratory 3048

Head: Dr S. Langlois

Organic and Biological Chemistry Laboratory 3049

Head: H. Zamarlik

Organic Physical Chemistry Laboratory 3050

Head: J. Guenzet

Physics of Solid Materials Laboratory 3051

Head: Dr J.P. Loup

Plant Biology and Physiology Laboratory 3052

Head: Professor R. Duperon
Senior staff: Dr A. Guillot

Quantum Physics and Electronic Optics Laboratory 3053

Head: Professor Phan Van Loc

Theoretical Physics Laboratory   **3054**
(Relativity-Electromagnetism)

Head: Professor J. Henry

MEDICAL SCIENCE RESEARCH UNIT   **3055**

Address: 2 bis boulevard Tonnellé, 37032 Tours Cedex

Anatomy Laboratory   **3056**

Head: Professor A. Gouaze

Bacteriology-Virology Department   **3057**

Head: Professor A. Audurier

Biochemistry of Glycoproteins of the   **3058**
Basal Vascular Membranes Laboratory

Head: Dr J.P. Muh

Biochemistry of Plasmic Proteins   **3059**
Laboratory

Head: Professor H. Mouray

Cancerology Department   **3060**

Head: Professor J.P. Lamagnère

Child Psychiatry Department   **3061**

Head: Professor D. Sauvage

Conditioned Neurophysiology and   **3062**
Sensory Psychopathology Laboratory

Head: Professor G. Lelord

Digestive Physiology and   **3063**
Electromyography Laboratory

Head: Professor J. Bertrand

Electronic Microscopy Laboratory   **3064**

Head: Professor M. Maillet

Electrophysiology and   **3065**
Physiopathology Research Institute

Head: Dr A. Martin

Embryology Laboratory   **3066**

Head: Professor M. Tharanne

Experimental Cardiology Laboratory   **3067**

Head: Professor J.P. Fauchier

Experimental Surgery Laboratory   **3068**

Head: Professor J. Barsotti

Experimental Surgery Laboratory   **3069**
(Digestive Physiopathology)

Head: Professor J. Murat

General Surgery Department   **3070**

Head: Professor B. Tomieux

Haematology Department   **3071**

Head: Professor J. Leroy

Haematology Laboratory   **3072**

Head: Professor M. Leroux

Histology Department   **3073**

Head: Professor Cl. Moraine

Immunology Laboratory   **3074**

Head: Professor G. Renoux

Infantile Surgery Department   **3075**

Head: Professor M. Robert

Medical and Reanimation Clinic   **3076**

Head: Professor F. Lamisse

Medical Biophysics Laboratory   **3077**

Senior staff: Professor J.C. Besnard, Professor L. Pourcelot, Professor R. Itti

Microbial Ecology in the Newborn   **3078**
Laboratory (Perinatology)

Head: Professor J. Laugier
Senior staff: Dr J.C. Borderon

Microbiology Laboratory   **3079**

Head: Professor R. Vargues

Neuropathology Laboratory   3080

Head: Professor A. Autret

Ocular Sensory-Motor   3081
Physiopathology Laboratory

Head: Professor A. Larmande

Orthopaedic Surgery Clinic   3082

Head: Professor J. Castaing

Pathological Anatomy Department   3083

Head: Professor A. Benatre

Pathological Anatomy Laboratory   3084

Head: Professor P. Jobard

Pharmacology Laboratory   3085

Head: Professor M. Bieteau

Physiological Mechanism and Early   3086
Detection of Alcoholism Laboratory

Head: Professor J. Weill

Physiology Laboratory   3087

Head: Professor J. Thouvenot

Pneumophthisiology Department   3088

Head: Professor M. Lavandier

Research and Applied Study Centre   3089
for Treatment of Sterility and Control
of Fecundity

Address: CHR Bretonneau, 37032 Tours Cedex
Director: Professor J. Soutoul

Respiratory Physiopathology   3090
Laboratory

Head: Professor J. Moline

Surgical and Digestive   3091
Physiopathology Research Group

Head: Professor J. Murat

Zoology-Parasitology Department   3092

Head: Professor Combescot

PHARMACEUTICAL SCIENCE   3093
RESEARCH UNIT

Address: 2 bis boulevard Tonnellé, 37032 Tours Cedex
Telephone: (047) 64 16 91

Analytical Chemistry Laboratory   3094

Head: Professor P. Levillain

Biochemistry Laboratory   3095

Head: Professor J. Lamy

Chemical Pharmacy and Chemistry of   3096
Natural Substances Laboratory

Head: Professor R. Lacroix

Galenic Pharmacy Laboratory   3097

Head: Professor J. Baumert-Paris

Hygiene-Toxicology Laboratory   3098

Head: Professor G. Narcisse

Materia Medica Laboratory   3099

Head: Professor M. Durand

Mineral Chemistry and Hydrology   3100
Laboratory

Senior staff: Professor F. Clanet, Professor R. Ceolin

Parasitology and Tropical Medicine   3101
Laboratory

Head: Professor C. Combescot

Pharmaceutical Physics and Biophysics   3102
Laboratory

Senior staff: Professor G. Crouzat-Reynes, Professor
M. Lecureuil

Pharmacodynamics Laboratory   3103

Head: Professor O. Foussard-Blanpin

Physiology and Nutrition Laboratory   3104

Head: Professor A. Rougereau

Plant Cell Culture Biotechnology and 3105
Phytochemistry Group

Head: Professor J.C. Chenieux

Prevention of Infections and 3106
Oncogenic Process by Active
Immunization Laboratory

Senior staff: Professor Ph. Maupasse, Professor J.P. Chirot

Therapeutic Organic Chemistry 3107
Laboratory

Head: Professor P. Nivière

Université Lyon I - Claude 3108
Bernard

[Lyon I University - Claude Bernard]
Address: 86 rue Pasteur, 69007 Lyon Cedex 2
Telephone: (07) 858 05 46
President: D. Germain
See also entry for: Observatoire de Lyon.

Alexis-Carrel Medicine Unit 3109

Address: rue Guillaume Paradin, 69008 Lyon
Telephone: (07) 875 81 14
Director: Professor René Mornex

LABORATORY OF ANATOMY 3110
Head: Professor A. Bouchet

LABORATORY OF BACTERIOLOGY - 3111
VIROLOGY
Head: Professor J. Fleurette

LABORATORY OF BIOLOGICAL 3112
CHEMISTRY AND MEDICAL
BIOCHEMISTRY
Head: vacant

LABORATORY OF CANCER VIROLOGY 3113
AND EPIDEMIOLOGY
Head: B. De The

LABORATORY OF EXPERIMENTAL 3114
MEDICINE
Head: Professor René Mornex

LABORATORY OF EXPERIMENTAL 3115
OTOLOGY
Head: Professor H. Martin

LABORATORY OF HAEMOBIOLOGY 3116
Head: M Dechavanne

LABORATORY OF HISTOLOGY AND 3117
CYTOGENETIC EMBRYOLOGY
Head: Professor Girod

LABORATORY OF INFANTILE 3118
METABOLISM AND ENDOCRINE
SYSTEM
Head: Mme Rui Hon
Senior staff: Professor R. François

LABORATORY OF LEGAL MEDICINE 3119
AND TOXICOLOGY
Head: Professor Rochel

LABORATORY OF MEDICAL 3120
PSYCHOLOGY
Head: Professor Guyotat

LABORATORY OF METABOLIC AND 3121
RENAL PHYSIOLOGY
Head: Professor M. Pellet

LABORATORY OF NEUROPATHOLOGY 3122
Head: Professor M. Tommasi

LABORATORY OF NUCLEAR MEDICINE 3123
Head: Professor M. Berger
Senior staff: Professor Ch. A. Bizollan

LABORATORY OF OCCUPATIONAL 3124
MEDICINE
Head: Professor Tolot
Senior staff: Professor Bourret

LABORATORY OF 3125
OTORHINOLARYNGOLOGY
Head: Professor Martin
Senior staff: H. Lafon

LABORATORY OF PHARMACOLOGY 3126
Head: J.C. Evreux

LABORATORY OF PREVENTIVE 3127
MEDICINE
Head: Professor J.C. Monier

LABORATORY OF STRUCTURAL 3128
BIOCHEMISTRY
Head: Professor C. Nofre

Grange-Blanche Medicine Unit 3129

Address: 8 avenue Rockefeller, 69373 Lyon Cedex 2
Telephone: (07) 875 81 14
Director: Professor Paul Zech

ALEXANDRE LACASSAGNE INSTITUTE 3130
OF LEGAL AND CRIMINAL MEDICINE
Address: 12 avenue Rockefeller, 69373 Lyon Cedex 2
Head: Professor M. Colin

LABORATORY OF AUDIOPHONOLOGY 3131
Head: Professor A. Morgon

LABORATORY OF BACTERIOLOGY - 3132
VIROLOGY
Head: A. Aymard

LABORATORY OF BIOLOGICAL 3133
CHEMISTRY
Head: Professor R. Creyssel
Senior staff: Professor J. Delaunay

LABORATORY OF BIOPHYSICS 3134
Head: Professor Peyrin

LABORATORY OF BONE AND 3135
CARTILAGE HISTOLOGY
Head: Professor Vignon
Senior staff: P. Meunier

LABORATORY OF CLINICAL 3136
CRIMINOLOGY
Head: Professor M. Colin

LABORATORY OF CYTOGENETIC 3137
HAEMATOLOGY
Head: Professor D. Germain

LABORATORY OF DIGESTIVE 3138
PHYSIOPATHOLOGY
Head: Professor R. Lambert

LABORATORY OF EXPERIMENTAL 3139
RADIOLOGY
Head: M Amiel

LABORATORY OF GENERAL ANATOMY 3140
Head: L.P. Fischer
Senior staff: A. Morin

LABORATORY OF GENERAL 3141
PATHOLOGY
Head: Professor M. Jouvet

LABORATORY OF HISTOLOGY - 3142
EMBRYOLOGY
Head: Professor J.C. Czyba
Senior staff: H. Pellet

LABORATORY OF 3143
IMMUNOPATHOLOGY AND
DERMATOLOGICAL RESEARCH
Head: Professor J. Thivolet

LABORATORY OF MEDICAL 3144
PHARMACOLOGY
Head: Professor G. Faucon

LABORATORY OF PALAEOPATHOLOGY 3145
Head: R. Perrot
Senior staff: A. Morin

LABORATORY OF PARASITOLOGY AND 3146
EXOTIC PATHOLOGY
Head: Professor J. Coudert

LABORATORY OF PATHOLOGICAL 3147
ANATOMY
Head: Professor J. Feroldi

LABORATORY OF PHYSIOLOGY 3148
Head: Professor J.F. Cier

LABORATORY OF RENAL DISORDERS 3149
Head: Professor Paul Zech

NEONATAL SERVICE 3150
Head: Professor B. Salle

Lyon Nord Medicine Unit 3151
Address: 8 avenue Rockefeller, 69374 Lyon Cedex 2
Telephone: (07) 875 81 14
Director: Professor Yves Minaire

LABORATORY OF BIOPHYSICS 3152
Head: B.E. Lahneche

LABORATORY OF CARDIOVASCULAR 3153
HAEMODYNAMICS
Head: Professor J. Delaye

LABORATORY OF CARDIOVASCULAR 3154
RESEARCH
Head: Professor P. Marion

LABORATORY OF CLINICAL 3155
OBSTETRICS
Head: Professor M. Dumont

LABORATORY OF DIGESTIVE 3156
THERAPEUTICS
Head: Professor Bel

LABORATORY OF ENDOCRINE 3157
BIOCHEMISTRY
Head: J. André

LABORATORY OF ENDOCRINOLOGY 3158
Head: Professor J. Tourniaire

LABORATORY OF GENERAL ANATOMY 3159
Head: J.P. Neidhart

LABORATORY OF HEPATOLOGY 3160
Head: Professor R. Brette

LABORATORY OF HISTO- 3161
HAEMATOLOGY AND ELECTRONIC
MICROSCOPY
Head: P.A. Bryon

LABORATORY OF HISTOLOGY, 3162
EMBRYOLOGY, CYTOGENETICS
Head: N. Moreau

LABORATORY OF HORMONAL 3163
CONTROL OF CELLULAR ACTIVITY
Head: M Saez

LABORATORY OF MEDICAL 3164
BIOCHEMISTRY
Head: Professor J.P. Reboud

LABORATORY OF MEDICAL BIOLOGY 3165
AND PHARMACODYNAMICS
Head: Professor A. Frédérich

LABORATORY OF MEDICAL 3166
PSYCHOLOGY
Head: M.J. Hochmann

LABORATORY OF MICROBIOLOGY 3167
Head: Professor P. Vincent

LABORATORY OF NEPHROLOGY AND 3168
METABOLIC DISORDERS
Head: Professor J. Traeger

LABORATORY OF NEUROCHEMISTRY 3169
Head: M Pujol

LABORATORY OF OCCUPATIONAL 3170
MEDICINE
Head: G. Prost

LABORATORY OF 3171
OTORHINOLARYNGOLOGY
Head: Professor J. Gaillard

LABORATORY OF PARASITOLOGY AND 3172
TROPICAL PATHOLOGY
Head: Professor J.P. Garin

LABORATORY OF PATHOLOGICAL 3173
ANATOMY
Head: Professor J.C. Vauzelle

LABORATORY OF PHYSIOLOGY 3174
Heads: Professor J. Chatonnet, Professor Yves
Minaire

LABORATORY OF PLEURO- 3175
PULMONARY DISEASES
Head: Professor J.C. Kalb
Senior staff: J.C. Guerin

LABORATORY OF PREVENTIVE 3176
MEDICINE AND PUBLIC HEALTH
Head: Professor M. Sepetjan

LABORATORY OF THERAPEUTICS 3177
Head: Professor E. Lejeune

NEUROLOGY SERVICE 3178
Head: Professor J. Courjon

Lyon Sud Medicine Unit 3179

Address: chemin du Petit Revoyet, BP12, 69600
Oullins
Telephone: 851 08 26
Director: Professor Jean Normand

CARDIOLOGY SERVICE 3180
Head: Professor J. Normand

DERMATOLOGY SERVICE 3181
Head: Professor D. Colomb

INSTITUTE OF CARDIOVASCULAR 3182
RESEARCH
Head: Professor Termet

LABORATORY OF APPLIED 3183
BIOCHEMISTRY
Head: vacant

LABORATORY OF BACTERIOLOGY 3184
Head: vacant

LABORATORY OF CANCER RESEARCH 3185
Head: Professor Mayer
Senior staff: P. Noel

LABORATORY OF CLINICAL 3186
ELECTROPHYSIOLOGY
Head: Professor Touboul

LABORATORY OF CLINICAL 3187
NEUROLOGY RESEARCH
Head: Professor Aimard

LABORATORY OF DERMATOLOGY AND 3188
VENEREOLOGY
Head: Professor D. Colomb

LABORATORY OF ENDOCRINOLOGY   3189
Head: Professor Mollard

LABORATORY OF EXPERIMENTAL   3190
NEUROPSYCHOLOGY
Head: M Jeannerod

LABORATORY OF EXPERIMENTAL   3191
OPHTHALMOLOGY
Head: Professor M. Bonnet

LABORATORY OF GENERAL ANATOMY   3192
Head: Professor Braillon

LABORATORY OF GENERAL   3193
BIOCHEMISTRY
Head: Professor Louisot

LABORATORY OF GENETICS   3194
Head: Professor J.M. Robert

LABORATORY OF HAEMOPATHOLOGY   3195
Head: Professor R. Tete

LABORATORY OF HEPATIC AND   3196
PANCREATIC PATHOLOGY
Head: Professor Ph. Berard

LABORATORY OF HISTOLOGY AND   3197
EMBRYOLOGY
Head: Professor P. Dubois

LABORATORY OF IMMUNOLOGY   3198
Head: Professor Revilland

LABORATORY OF INFANTILE   3199
MEDICINE
Head: Professor Gilly

LABORATORY OF MEDICAL   3200
INFORMATION SCIENCES
Head: Professor Site

LABORATORY OF   3201
MICRORADIOGRAPHY
Head: Professor F. Pinet
Senior staff: Dr Clermont

LABORATORY OF NEUROMUSCULAR   3202
PATHOLOGY
Head: Professor Trillet

LABORATORY OF OBSTETRICS   3203
Head: Professor Toulon

LABORATORY OF   3204
OTORHINOLARYNGOLOGY
Head: Professor Haguenauer

LABORATORY OF   3205
PSYCHOPHYSIOLOGY
Head: Professor M. Cabanac

LABORATORY OF RADIOBIOLOGY   3206
AND CANCEROLOGY
Head: Professor J.P. Gerard

LABORATORY OF SENSORY   3207
NEUROPHYSIOLOGY
Head: Dr R. Duclaux

LABORATORY OF UROLOGY   3208
Head: Professor Archimbaud

CHEMISTRY AND BIOCHEMISTRY   3209
UNIT

Address: 43 boulevard du 11 Novembre 1918, 69622
Villeurbanne
Telephone: (07) 852 07 04
Director: Professor Annick Varagnat

Laboratory of Analytical Chemistry I   3210
Head: Professor J.C. Merlin

Laboratory of Analytical Chemistry II 3211
Head: Professor G. Thomas-David

Laboratory of Analytical Chemistry III 3212
Head: Professor M. Porthault

Laboratory of Applied Biochemistry   3213
Head: Professor A. Ville

Laboratory of Applied Chemistry and   3214
Chemical Engineering
Head: Professor C. Eyraud

Laboratory of Applied Chemistry II   3215
Head: Professor G. Siclet

Laboratory of Biological Chemistry   3216
Head: Professor J. Chopin

Laboratory of Chemistry   3217
Head: Professor P. Clechet

Laboratory of Dynamic Biochemistry 3218

Affiliation: Centre National de la Recherche Scientifique
Head: Professor D. Gautheron

Laboratory of Industrial Chemistry 3219

Head: Professor R. Perrin

Laboratory of Membrane Biochemistry 3220

Head: Professor R. Got

Laboratory of Microbial Biochemistry 3221

Head: Professor G. Michel

Laboratory of Mineral Chemistry I 3222

Head: Professor R. Paris
Senior staff: J.P. Scharff

Laboratory of Mineral Chemistry III 3223

Head: Professor J. Paris

Laboratory of Mineral Physical Chemistry I 3224

Head: Professor J. Bouix

Laboratory of Mineral Physical Chemistry II 3225

Head: Professor R. Cohen-Adad

Laboratory of Mineral Physical Chemistry III 3226

Head: Professor A. Tranquard

Laboratory of Mineral Synthesis 3227

Head: Professor J. Gauthier

Laboratory of Molecular Biology 3228

Head: Professor A.J. Cozzone

Laboratory of Molecular Physical Chemistry 3229

Head: Professor C. Chapelet-Letourneux

Laboratory of Nuclear Chemistry 3230

Head: Professor J. Tousset
Note: This laboratory also belongs to the Nuclear Physics Unit.

Laboratory of Organic Catalysis 3231

Head: Professor J.E. Germain

Laboratory of Organic Chemistry and Physics 3232

Head: Professor M. Chastrette

Laboratory of Organic Chemistry I 3233

Head: Professor J. Gore

Laboratory of Organic Chemistry II 3234

Head: Professor G. Descotes

Laboratory of Organic Chemistry III 3235

Head: Professor A.L. Laurent

Laboratory of Organic Chemistry IV 3236

Head: Professor J. Huet

Laboratory of Photochemistry I 3237

Head: Professor B. Pouyet

Laboratory of Photochemistry II 3238

Head: Professor P. Meallier

Laboratory of Photoelectron Spectroscopy 3239

Head: Professor Tran Minh Duc

Laboratory of Plastic Materials 3240

Head: Professor G. Vallet

Laboratory of Synthesis and Applied Organic Chemistry 3241

Head: Professor J. Dreux
Senior staff: Professor R. Longersy

Laboratory of Thermodynamics and Kinetic Chemistry 3242

Head: Professor S.T. Teichner

Metallurgical Service 3243

Head: Professor P. Guiraldenq

HUMAN BIOLOGY UNIT 3244

Address: 8 avenue Rockefeller, 69373 Lyon Cedex 2
Telephone: (07) 875 81 14
Director: J.P. Revillard

MATHEMATICS UNIT 3245

Address: 43 boulevard du 11 Novembre 1918, 69622
Villeurbanne
Telephone: (07) 852 07 04
Director: Professor Philippe Picard

Institute of Mathematics 3246

Address: 43 boulevard du 11 Novembre 1918, 69622
Villeurbanne
Telephone: (07) 889 81 24
Director: M Braemer

Laboratory of Algebra 3247

Head: Professor G. Maury
Senior staff: Professor E. Coromiras

Laboratory of Algebra and Geometry 3248
Analysis

Head: Professor J. Braconnier
Senior staff: Professor E. Combet

Laboratory of Computer Science I 3249

Head: Professor J. Kouloumdjian

Laboratory of Computer Science II 3250

Head: Professor A. Dussauchoy
Senior staff: Professor D. Vandorpe

Laboratory of Documentation 3251

Head: Professor F. Bouche

Laboratory of Functional Analysis and 3252
Topology

Head: Professor H. Buchwalter

Laboratory of Logic 3253

Head: Professor J.F. Pabion
Senior staff: D. Ponasse

Laboratory of Numerical Analysis and 3254
Information Science

Head: Professor J. Baranger

Laboratory of Probability-Density 3255

Head: Professor R. Feron

Laboratory of Rational Mechanics 3256

Head: Professor G. Malecot

MECHANICS UNIT 3257

Address: 36 route de Dardilly, 69130 Ecully
Telephone: 833 27 00
Director: Professor G. Compte-Bellot

Laboratory of Fluid Mechanics 3258

Affiliation: Centre National de la Recherche Scientifi-
que
Head: Professor J. Mathieu
Senior staff: Professor G. Compte-Bellot

Laboratory of Surface Technology 3259

Head: Professor J.M. Georges

Laboratory of Thermic Machinery 3260

Head: Professor A. Moiroux

NATURAL SCIENCES UNIT 3261

Address: 43 boulevard du 11 Novembre 1918, 69622
Villeurbanne
Telephone: (07) 852 07 04
Director: Professor Yves Lemoigne

Animal Biology and Zoology 3262
Department

Sections: Population statistics and dynamics, M. Bour-
naud; subterranean biology, Professor R. Ginet; population ecology and dynamics, Professor A.L. Roux; freshwater ecology, Professor E. Pattée; limnology, J. Juget;
rhythms and behaviour, Professor L. Caillère

Earth Sciences Department 3263

Sections: Petrography, mining geology, Professor M.
Chenevoy; petrology and magma geochemistry,
Professor M. Girod; sedimentology, Professor P.
Cotillon; general palaeontology, Professor L. David;
western Sahara and applied geology, Professor P. Gevin;

tertiary geology, Professor G. Demarcq; jurassic geology, Professor R. Enay; quaternary geology, Professor P. Elouard; geotechnics, Professor J. Gielly; jurassic-mesozoic, professor S. Elmi; biostratigraphy - palaeoecology and palaeo-biogeography, P. Donze

General and Applied Biology Department   3264

Sections: Cell difference, Professor V. Nigon; cell difference and transformation, Professor J. Daillie; genetic physiology and nematology, Professor J. Brun; biometry, Professor J.M. Legay; results analysis, Professor J. Pontier; insect physiology, Professor J. Fourche; molecular evolution, Professor R. Grantham; thalassic genetics, Professor J. Godet; insect population biology and genetics, M. Bouletreau

Histology and Tissue Biology Group   3265

Sections: Histology, Professor M. Pavans de Ceccaty; cytology and neurobiology, G. Nicaise

Plant Biology Department   3266

Sections: Compatibility, Professor P. Terra; experimental mycotaxonomy, Professor J. Boidin; hymenopteran biotaxonomy, Professor D. Lamoure; phytochemistry and phytophysiology, Professor Ph. Lebreton; ascomycete biology and phytopathology, Professor P. Berthet; plant physiology, Professor G. Manachère; microbe ecology, Professor A.M. Gounot; soil biology, Professor R. Bardin; plant waste his tophysiology, M. Rougier; plant physiopathology, Professor M. Gabriel; mycochemistry and physiology, N. Arpin; palaeobotany, Professor Y. Lemoigne

NUCLEAR PHYSICS UNIT   3267

Address: 43 boulevard du 11 Novembre 1918, 69622 Villeurbanne
Telephone: (07) 852 07 04
Head: Professor M.M. Gusakow

Laboratory of Atomic Collisions in Solids   3268

Head: Professor M.J. Gaillard
Senior staff: J.C. Poizat, J. Remillieux

Laboratory of High-Energy Physics   3269

Head: Professor J.P. Burg
Senior staff: Professor M. Lambert

Laboratory of Neutron Studies   3270

Head: Professor J. Depraz

Laboratory of Nuclear Physics   3271

Head: Professor J.R. Pizzi
Senior staff: Professor M. Gusakow

Laboratory of Nuclear Reactions   3272

Head: A. Chevarier
Senior staff: A. Demeyer

Laboratory of Nuclear Spectrometry   3273

Head: Professor I. Berkes
Senior staff: Professor R. Chery

Laboratory of Theoretical Nuclear Physics   3274

Head: Professor M. Ericson

Laboratory of Theoretical Nuclear Physics   3275

Head: Professor E. Elbaz

Laboratory of Theoretical Physics   3276

Head: Professor J. Lafourcrière

ODONTOLOGY UNIT   3277

Address: bâtiment Universitaire de la Buire, rue Guillame Paradin, 69008 Lyon
Telephone: (07) 874 88 59
Director: Professor Jean Parret

Department of Periodontology   3278

Head: Professor G. Perdrix

Laboratory of Biomaterials   3279

Head: Professor J. Brugirard

Laboratory of Bucco-dental Biology   3280

Head: Professor Jean Parret
Senior staff: Salivary physiopathology, Professor J. Parret; microbiology, Professor J. Dumont; conjunctive tissue and collagen, Professor M. Magloire

PHARMACY UNIT　　　　　　　3281

Address:　8 avenue Rockefeller, 69373 Lyon Cedex 2
Telephone:　(07) 875 81 14
Director:　Professor Charles-Albert Bizollan

Department of Biophysical　　3282
Pharmaceutics, Mathematics and
Information Sciences

Head:　Professor Charles-Albert Bizollan
Senior staff:　Professor R. Bador, Professor C. Paultre

Department of Public Health and　3283
Immunology

Head:　Professor M. Carraz

Laboratory of Analytical Biochemistry　3284
and Physiopathology

Head:　Professor R. Mallein

Laboratory of Analytical Chemistry　3285

Head:　Professor C. Quincy
Senior staff:　Professor J.J. Vallon, Professor H. Pinatel

Laboratory of Biochemical　　3286
Pharmaceutics

Head:　Professor J. Gras

Laboratory of Cell Botany and Biology　3287

Head:　Professor J. Raynaud

Laboratory of Chemical Pharmacy　3288

Head:　Professor M. Cussac

Laboratory of Cryptogamy and　3289
Phytopharmacy

Head:　Professor L. Oddoux

Laboratory of Endocrine and　3290
Metabolic Biochemistry

Head:　Professor A. Revol

Laboratory of Hygiene and Pollution　3291

Head:　Professor C. Collombel

Laboratory of Immunology　　3292

Head:　Professor J.P. Bringuier

Laboratory of Industrial Galenic　3293
Pharmacy

Head:　Professor M. Rollet

Laboratory of Industrial Pharmacy and 3294
Applied Dermatology

Head:　Professor J. Cotte

Laboratory of Organic Chemistry　3295

Head:　Professor A. Daudon

Laboratory of Parasitology and　3296
Medical Mycology

Head:　Professor A.F. Petavy

Laboratory of Pharmacognosy and　3297
Legal Pharmaceutics

Head:　Professor S. Ferry

Laboratory of Physiology and Clinical　3298
Pharmacology

Head:　Professor J. Sassard
Senior staff:　Professor B. Renaud

Laboratory of Toxicology and　3299
Industrial Hygiene

Head:　Professor P. Chambon

PHYSICS UNIT　　　　　　　3300

Address:　43 boulevard du 11 Novembre 1918, 69622
Villeurbanne
Telephone:　(07) 852 07 04
Director:　Professor Jean Delmau

Energetics - Solar Energy　　3301

LABORATORY OF HIGH FREQUENCY　3302
AND MICROWAVES
Head:　Professor J.P. Pelissier

LABORATORY OF SOLAR AND　3303
THERMIC STUDIES
Head:　Professor G. Menguy

Information - Automation *　　3304

LABORATORY OF AUTOMATION	3305

Head: Professor G. Gilles

LABORATORY OF ELECTRICITY 3306
Head: Professor G. Asch

LABORATORY OF ELECTRONIC 3307
PHYSICS I
Head: Professor G. Mesnard

LABORATORY OF MEDICAL AND 3308
BIOENGINEERING
Head: Professor J.P. Girard

Materials Physics 3309

DEPARTMENT OF MATERIALS 3310
PHYSICS
Head: Professor R. Uzan

LABORATORY OF ELECTRONIC 3311
PHYSICS II
Head: Professor M. Maitrot

LABORATORY OF ELECTRONIC 3312
PHYSICS III
Head: F.M. Michel-Calendini

LABORATORY OF ELECTRONIC 3313
PHYSICS IV
Head: J. Fornazero

LABORATORY OF MICROPHYSICAL 3314
TREATMENT OF METALS
Head: P. Poncet
Senior staff: J. Rousseau

LABORATORY OF MINERALOGY - 3315
CRYSTALLOGRAPHY
Head: Professor P. Michel

Molecular and Ionic Atomic Physics 3316

LABORATORY OF ELECTRONIC 3317
PARAMAGNETIC RESONANCE AND
SPECTROSCOPY
Head: Professor A. Erbeiz

LABORATORY OF EXPERIMENTAL 3318
PHYSICS
Head: Professor F. Gaume

LABORATORY OF HERTZIAN 3319
SPECTROSCOPY
Head: Professor J. Delmau

LABORATORY OF IONIC AND 3320
MOLECULAR SPECTROMETERY
Head: Professor M. Dufay
Senior staff: Professor J. D'Incan

LABORATORY OF RADIATION 3321
Head: Professor R. Schmitt

LABORATORY OF THEORETIC 3322
SPECTROSCOPY
Head: Professor G. Bessis

PHYSICAL CHEMISTRY OF 3323
LUMINESCENT MATERIALS GROUP
Head: Professor E. Duval
Senior staff: Mme F. Gaume

PHYSIOLOGICAL SCIENCES UNIT 3324

Address: 43 boulevard du 11 Novembre 1918, 69622
Villeurbanne
Telephone: (07) 852 07 04
Head: Professor J.F. Worbe

Laboratoire Maritime de Physiologie - 3325
Institut Michel Pacha

[Marine Laboratory of Physiology - Michel Pacha
Institute]
Address: 1337 corniche de Tamaris, 83500 Tamaris sur
Mer
Telephone: (094) 94 82 02
Director: Professor G. Pérès
Sections: Digestion and metabolism of fish, Professor
G. Pérès; lipid metabolism of fish, G. Brichon; pollution,
Professor G. Pérès
Graduate research staff: 8
Activities: Research is centred on general and applied
fish physiology - metabolic regulation; digestive process;
ecology; pollution.
Contract work: Yes
Publications: Annales de l'Institut Michel Pacha.

Laboratory of Cell Physiology 3326
Head: Professor M. Buclon

Laboratory of Communication 3327
Ethology
Head: Professor J. Cosnier

Laboratory of Electrophysiology 3328
Head: Professor A. Holley

Laboratory of Excitable Elements Physiology 3329

Head: Professor O. Raugier

Laboratory of Experimental Ethology 3330

Head: Professor L. Leguelte

Laboratory of General and Comparative Physiology 3331

Head: Professor G. Pérès

Laboratory of Metabolic Physiology 3332

Head: Professor J.F. Worbe

Laboratory of Physiology 3333

Head: Professor Cl. Bacques

Laboratory of Psychophysiology 3334

Head: Professor J. Chanel

Laboratory of Regulatory Physiology 3335

Head: Professor C. Bange

READAPTATION TECHNIQUES UNIT 3336

Address: 8 avenue Rockefeller, 69373 Lyon Cedex 2
Telephone: (07) 875 81 14
Director: Professor A. Morgon

Department of Audioprosthetics, Audiometry 3337

Department of Kinetic and Occupational Therapy 3338

Department of Orthophony 3339

Department of Orthoptics 3340

Department of Psychomotricity 3341

UNIVERSITY INSTITUTE OF TECHNOLOGY I 3342

Address: 43 boulevard du 11 Novembre 1918, 69622 Villeurbanne
Telephone: (07) 868 03 27
Director: Albert Ville
Departments: Chemistry; Applied biology; Civil engineering; Computer sciences

UNIVERSITY INSTITUTE OF TECHNOLOGY II 3343

Address: 17 rue de France, 69100 Villeurbanne
Telephone: (07) 868 21 81
Director: J. Gallet
Departments: Mechanical engineering I; Mechanical engineering II; Electrical engineering

UNIVERSITY INSTITUTES 3344

Institute of Audiophonology 3345

Address: Hôpital Edouard Herriot, 5 place d'Arsonval, 69003 Lyon
Telephone: (07) 853 81 11
Head: Professor Morgon

Institute of Cardiology 3346

Address: 8 avenue Rockefeller, 69373 Lyon Cedex 2
Telephone: (07) 875 81 14
Director: Professor P. Marion

Institute of Hydrology and Climatology 3347

Address: 8 avenue Rockefeller, 69373 Lyon Cedex 2
Telephone: (07) 875 81 14
Director: Professor G. Vignon

Institute of Industrial Pharmacy 3348

Address: 8 avenue Rockefeller, 69373 Lyon Cedex 2
Telephone: (07) 875 81 14
Head: Professor J. Cotte

Institute of Medicine and Tropical Hygiene 3349

Address: 8 avenue Rockefeller, 69373 Lyon Cedex 2
Telephone: (07) 875 81 14
Director: Professor J. Coudert

Institute of Meteorology and Climatic Sciences   3350

Address: 43 boulevard du 11 Novembre 1918, 69622 Villeurbane
Telephone: (07) 889 81 24
Director: vacant

Institute of Stomatology   3351

Address: Hôpital Edouard Herriot, 5 place d'Arsonval, 69003 Lyon
Telephone: (07) 853 81 11
Director: Professor P. Dumas

Pierre Mazel Institute of Occupational Medicine   3352

Address: 8 avenue Rockefeller, 69373 Lyon Cedex 2
Telephone: (07) 875 81 14
Director: Professor Tolot

UNIVERSITY MEASUREMENT AND ANALYSIS CENTRES   3353

Centre of Analysis and Image Dissection   3354

Head: Robert Goutte

Centre of Automated Diffractometry   3355

Head: G. Thomas-David

Centre of Electronic Microanalysis   3356

Head: Pierre Guiraldenq

Centre of Electronic Microscopy and Auger Microanalysis   3357

Head: Gérard Fontaine

Centre of Electronic Microscopy for Biology and Geology   3358

Head: R. Garrone

Centre of Isotope Analysis   3359

Head: Jacques Evin

Centre of Mass Spectrometry for Organic and Biological Molecular Analysis   3360

Head: Roger Guilluy

Centre of Nuclear Magnetic Resonance   3361

Head: Jean Delmau

Centre of Photoelectron Spectroscopy   3362

Head: Professor Tran Minh Duc

Centre of Quantum Physics   3363

Head: Catherine Sauchier

Centre of Topography and X-ray Studies of Defects in Solids   3364

Head: Christian Mai

Production of Cryogenic Fluids Service   3365

Head: Eugène Duval

Université Scientifique et Médicale (Grenoble I)*   3366

[Grenoble University I]
Address: BP 53, 38041 Grenoble
Telephone: (076) 54 81 52

INSTITUTE OF ADVANCED MATHEMATICS*   3367

Director: Professor H. Raynaud

INSTITUTE OF NUCLEAR SCIENCES*   3368

Director: Professor J.-P. Longequeue

UNIT OF BIOLOGICAL AND MEDICAL SCIENCES (CYCLE I)*   3369

Head: Professor M. Tanche

UNIT OF BIOLOGICAL AND MEDICAL SCIENCES (CYCLE II, III)*   3370

Head: Professor M. Geindre

UNIT OF BIOMEDICAL AND PHARMACEUTICAL RESEARCH*   3371

Head: Professor J. Lacharme

UNIT OF CHEMISTRY AND ORGANIC PHYSICAL CHEMISTRY*   3372

Head: Professor M. Rinaudo

UNIT OF CHEMISTRY OF MATERIALS*   3373

Head: Professor G. Cauquits

UNIT OF EARTH SCIENCES*   3374

Head: Professor J. Perriaux

UNIT OF EXACT AND NATURAL SCIENCES (CYCLE I)*   3375

Head: Professor J.-F. Dulac

UNIT OF MECHANICAL ENGINEERING*   3376

Head: Professor P. Le Roy

UNIT OF PHARMACEUTICAL SCIENCES*   3377

Head: Professor G. Carraz

UNIT OF PHYSIOLOGICAL BIOLOGY AND ECOLOGY*   3378

Head: Professor P. Sengel

UNIT OF PLASMA PHYSICS*   3379

Head: Professor A. Poggi

UNIT OF SOLID PHYSICS AND THERMODYNAMICS*   3380

Head: Professor M. Cyrot

UNIT OF SPECTROMETRY AND CRYSTALLOGRAPHY*   3381

Head: Professor J.-C. Pebay-Peroula

UNIVERSITY INSTITUTE OF TECHNOLOGY*   3382

Director: Professor R. Sibille

Université Toulouse III –   3383
Université Paul Sabatier

[Toulouse III University - Paul Sabatier University]
Address: 118 route de Narbonne, 31062 Toulouse Cedex
Telephone: (061) 53 11 20
Telex: UNIPSAB 52 1880 F
Secretary-General: Jean-Pierre Prinau
Activities: The policy of this University is to encourage cooperation between its research groups, recognizing that small teams working in cooperation tend to function most efficiently.
See separate entry for: Observatoire du Pic du Midi et de Toulouse.

FACULTY OF DENTAL SURGERY   3384

Address: route de Narbonne, Toulouse
Activities: Biology of buccal and dental tissues; dental materials research.

Laboratory of Biology, Fundamental   3385
Materials and Biomaterials

Director: Professor J.Ph. Lodter
Senior staff: Professor D. Duffaut, Professor G. Brunel
Activities: Histology, buccal histopathology; tissue culture research; facial electromyography; bacteriology; cytology; antibiotic studies, crystallography and electron microscope studies.
Contract work: No

Laboratory of Conservative   3386
Odontology

Director: Professor A. Clauzade
Senior staff: Professor L. Daudibertières, Professor F. Manas, Professor A. Maurette
Activities: Antiseptics in endodontics; anaerobic flora and toxicity studies; biomaterials; tissue antibody studies; immunofluorescence; radiological techniques; electron microscope and chromatographic studies.
Contract work: No

Laboratory of Dental Prosthesis,   3387
Maxillo-Facial and Occlusodontal

Director: Professor A. Lubespère
Senior staff: Professor A. Rotenberg, Professor H. Soulet
Activities: Prosthetic retention studies; nuclear medicine; metal microstructures; buccal cavity functional morphology.
Contract work: Yes

Laboratory of Paradontology   3388

Director: Professor E.P. Benque
Activities: Bone lesion studies; dental implant and orthodontic movement research; electromyography; gum studies.
Contract work: No

Laboratory of Pathology and Bucco-   3389
Dental Therapeutics

Director: Professor J. Lagarrigue
Senior staff: Professor Ph. Guiraud, Professor P. Reynes
Activities: Bucco-dental pathology; saliva and calcification studies; cancer research; bone and metabolic research.
Contract work: No

FACULTY OF MEDICINE - TOULOUSE 3390
PURPURAN

Dean: B. Guiraud-Chaumeil
Note: Much of the research undertaken in the laboratories is carried out in collaboration with the Centre National de la Recherche Scientifique and the Institut National de la Santé et de la Recherche Médicale.

Centre of Geriatric Medicine   3391

Address: 170 chemin de Casselardit, 31300 Toulouse Purpuran
Telephone: (061) 49 11 33
Director: Professor J.L. Albarede
Senior staff: Professor L. Pous
Activities: Medical and medico-social studies of dependence in the aged; sanitary protection service studies.
Contract work: Yes

Laboratory of Anaesthetics and   3392
Reanimation

Address: place Baylac, 31052 Toulouse Cedex
Telephone: (061) 49 11 33
Director: Professor L. Lareng
Senior staff: Professor Ch. Virenque, Professor B. Cathala
Activities: Respiratory functions; mass spectrometry.
Contract work: Yes

Laboratory of Anatomy and   3393
Organogenesis

Address: 133 route de Narbonne, Toulouse
Director: Professor G. Bastide

Laboratory of Applied Physiology and 3394
Pharmacology

Address: 37 allées Jules Guesde, Toulouse
Telephone: (061) 53 03 53
Director: Professor P. Montastruc
Activities: Pharmacology of arterial hypertension, bone circulation and obesity; pharmacology and physiology of antidiuretic hormones.
Contract work: No

Laboratory of Bacteriology-Virology   3395

Address: 37 allées Jules Guesde, 31077 Toulouse
Telephone: (061) 53 03 53
Affiliation: Centre National de la Recherche Scientifique
Director: Professor M.B. Lareng
Activities: Genetics; genital and urinary infection studies; antibiotics; immunology; electron microscope studies.
Contract work: No

Laboratory of Biophysics and Nuclear 3396
Medicine

Address: 133 route de Narbonne, Toulouse
Director: Professor R. Guiraud
Senior staff: Professor R. Auvergnat
Activities: Images in nuclear medicine; pharmacokinetics; radioisotope circulation studies.
Contract work: Yes

Laboratory of Carcinological Research 3397

Address: Centre C. Régaud, 11 rue Piquemil, 31052 Toulouse Cedex
Telephone: (061) 42 32 22
Director: Professor P.F. Combes
Senior staff: Professor E. Cabarrot, Professor M. Carton, Professor Ph. Courrière, Professor J.F. David, Professor G. Soula
Activities: Cancer epidemiology; bioclinical research; pharmacokinetics; cell culture; irradiation studies.
Contract work: No

Laboratory of Clinical Psychiatry   3398

Address: Hôpital de la Grave, place Lange, 31052 Toulouse
Director: Professor L. Gayral
Senior staff: Professor M. Escande; Professor R. Huron
Activities: Psychopharmacology; depression and aggression studies; medical psychology.
Contract work: Yes

Laboratory of Cytogenetics   3399

Address: Hôpital Purpuran, 31052 Toulouse Cedex
Telephone: (061) 49 35 55
Director: Professor P. Colombies
Activities: Neonatal genetics; cytochemistry and pathology; cancer research.
Contract work: Yes

Laboratory of Experimental Medicine   3400 and Endocrinology

Address: 37 allées Jules Guesde, 31077 Toulouse
Director: Professor C. Boulard
Senior staff: Professor J.P. Louvet
Activities: Reproduction biology; endocrinology; clinical therapeutics.
Contract work: Yes

Laboratory of Functional Exploration   3401 in Occupational Medicine

Address: Hôtel-Dieu, Pont Neuf, Toulouse
Directors: Professor R. Ballinelli, Y. Rouch
Activities: Epidemiology; respiratory problems; industrial pollution studies.
Contract work: Yes

Laboratory of Gastroenterology   3402

Address: Hôpital Purpuran, 31052 Toulouse Cedex
Telephone: (061) 49 11 33
Director: Professor J.P. Pascal
Activities: Digestive haemorrhage studies; cancer research; physiopathology.
Contract work: Yes

Laboratory of Haemostasis   3403

Address: Hôpital Purpuran, 31052 Toulouse Cedex
Telephone: (061) 49 35 55
Director: B. Boneu
Activities: Thrombosis research; spectrophotometry; electrophoresis; fluoresence studies.
Contract work: Yes

Laboratory of Hydrology and Nutrition 3404 Service

Address: Hôtel Dieu, Pont Neuf, Toulouse
Director: Professor Y. Denard
Activities: Therapeutic action of thermal cures; meteoropathology; nutritional diseases; diabetes research.
Contract work: No

Laboratory of Hygiene and Social   3405 Medicine, and Blood Diseases Department

Address: 37 allées Jules Guesde, 31077 Toulouse
Telephone: (061) 53 03 53
Director: Professor J. Monnier
Senior staff: Professor J. Pous
Activities: Antibiotic pharmacokinetics; economic and educational studies.
Contract work: Yes

Laboratory of Immunology   3406

Address: Hôpital Purpuran, 31052 Toulouse Cedex
Telephone: (061) 49 35 55
Affiliations: Centre National de la Recherche Scientifique
Director: Professor J. Ducos
Senior staff: Professor E. Ohayon
Activities: Renal transplant studies; immunopathology; autoimmunity; his tocompatibility; immunofluorescence and spectrophotometry studies.
Contract work: Yes

Laboratory of Informatics and Medical 3407 Statistics

Address: 133 route de Narbonne, Toulouse
Director: P. Fernet
Activities: Preventive medicine and epidemiology; medical teaching studies.
Contract work: No

Laboratory of Medical Biology and   3408 Spatial Biology Research Group

Address: 37 allées Jules Guesde, 31077 Toulouse
Activities: Biological effects of ionizing radiation; cosmic rays and ultraviolet radiation; cancer research; electron microscope studies.
Contract work: No

Laboratory of Ophthalmic Research   3409

Address: Hôpital Purpuran, 31052 Toulouse Cedex
Telephone: (061) 49 11 33
Director: Professor J.L. Arnet, Professor P. Bec

Laboratory of Orthopaedics and   3410 Traumatology

Address: Hôpital Purpuran, 31052 Toulouse Cedex
Telephone: (061) 49 11 33
Director: Professor G. Utheza
Activities: Thoracic surgery; prophylaxy; post-operative studies.
Contract work: No

Laboratory of Osteo-Articular Disease 3411 Research

Address: Hôpital Purpuran, 31052 Toulouse Cedex
Telephone: (061) 42 33 33
Director: Professor A. Fournie
Senior staff: Professor M. Mansat
Activities: Immunopathology; enzymology; microbiology; rheology; kinetic electrophysiology; biomaterial and calcified structure studies.
Contract work: Yes

Laboratory of Pathological Anatomy 3412

Address: 37 allées Jules Guesde, 31077 Toulouse
Telephone: (061) 53 03 53
Director: Professor J. Fabre
Senior staff: Professor G. Delsol
Activities: Morphology; histo-enzymology; immunology; biomaterial compatability; cancer research; electron microscope studies.
Contract work: No

Laboratory of Physiology 3413

Address: 133 route de Narbonne, Toulouse
Telephone: (061) 53 23 13
Affiliation: Centre Nationale de la Recherche Scientifique
Director: Professor J.P. Bessou
Senior staff: Professor B. Pages
Activities: Command and control of somatic motricity; equilibration in man; limb plethysmography.
Contract work: Yes

Laboratory of Plastic Surgery 3414

Address: CHU de Rangueil, 31054 Toulouse Cedex
Director: Professor M. Costagliola di Polidori

Laboratory of Renal Immunopathology 3415

Address: Hôpital Purpuran, 31052 Toulouse Cedex
Telephone: (061) 49 11 33
Director: Professor J.J. Conte
Activities: Physiopathology; immunology; cancer research; spectrophotometry.
Contract work: Yes

Laboratory of Surgical 3416 Physiopathology

Address: Hôpital Purpuran, 31052 Toulouse Cedex
Telephone: (061) 49 11 33
Director: Professor A. Gedeon
Senior staff: Professor J.L. Gouzi, Professor A. Barret
Activities: Metabolism and nutritional studies; limb surgery.
Contract work: No

Laboratory of the Centre for Study 3417 and Detection of Infant Metabolic Diseases, and Infantile Medical Clinic A

Address: Hôpital Purpuran, 31052 Toulouse Cedex
Director: Professor J. Ghisolfi
Activities: Nutrition studies; atomic absorption and chromatography research.
Contract work: No

Laboratory of the Cutaneous and 3418 Syphilitic Diseases Clinic

Address: Hôpital Purpuran, 31052 Toulouse Cedex
Telephone: (061) 49 15 03
Director: A. Dupre
Activities: Photobiology; cutaneous physiology; electron microscopy.
Contract work: Yes

Laboratory of the Infantile Medical 3419 Clinic B

Address: Hôpital Purpuran, 31052 Toulouse Cedex
Telephone: (061) 44 11 33
Director: Professor C. Regnier
Senior staff: Professor M. Rolland
Activities: Epidemiology; perinatal mortality, morbidity and development; malformation studies; socioeconomic and sociocultural studies.
Contract work: No

Laboratory of the Infectious and 3420 Tropical Diseases Clinic

Address: Hôpital Purpuran, 31052 Toulouse Cedex
Telephone: (061) 49 11 33
Director: Professor M. Armengaud
Activities: Pharmacokinetics; epidemiology; meningitis research.
Contract work: No

Laboratory of Urodynamics (CECOS)   3421

Address: Hôpital de la Grave, place Lange, 31052 Toulouse Cedex
Telephone: (061) 42 96 45
Director: Professor F. Pontonnier
Activities: Masculine hyper-fertility research; electron microscope studies.
Contract work: No

FACULTY OF MEDICINE-TOULOUSE   3422 RANGUEIL

Address: CHU de Rangueil, 31054 Toulouse Cedex
Telephone: (061) 53 11 33
Dean: P. Puel

Laboratory of Applied Anatomy   3423

Address: 133 route de Narbonne, Toulouse
Director: Professor S. Juskiewenski
Senior staff: Professor J. Becue, Professor Ph. Vaysse
Activities: Anatomy of congenital malformations; urinary surgical and functional anatomy; visceral vascularization; locomotor anatomy.
Contract work: No

Laboratory of Applied Physiology and   3424 Pharmacology

Director: Professor P. Montastruc
Senior staff: Professor J. Cotonat
Activities: Hypertension research; anaesthetics and reanimation; lymphatic system pharmacology.
Contract work: No

Laboratory of Bacteriology-Virology   3425

Telephone: (061) 25 21 53
Director: Professor L. Enjalbert
Senior staff: Professor J. Didier
Activities: Bacterial and viral pathogenicity; electron microscope studies; immunology; clinical research.
Contract work: Yes

Laboratory of Biochemistry   3426

Telephone: (061) 25 21 53
Director: Professor P. Valdiguie
Activities: Clinical chemistry information systems development; renal diseases and dialysis treatment; phthalic toxicity studies.
Contract work: Yes

Laboratory of Cancerology   3427

Address: Centre C. Régaud, 11 rue Piquemil, 31052 Toulouse Cedex
Telephone: (061) 43 32 22
Director: Professor M. Carton
Activities: Effects of ionizing radiation on metabolism; epidemiology; information and automatic techniques; chemotherapy and radiotherapy studies.
Contract work: Yes

Laboratory of Cardiovascular Surgery   3428 Research

Director: Professor A. Enjalbert
Senior staff: Professor P. Puel, Professor A. Cerene
Activities: Haemodynamics; vascular exploration; cardiac surgery studies.
Contract work: Yes

Laboratory of Clinical and   3429 Experimental Cardiology

Director: Professor J.P. Bounhoure
Senior staff: Professor J.M. Fauvel
Activities: Heart disease: diagnosis, treatment, cause, and rehabilitation studies.
Contract work: No

Laboratory of Clinical Haemodynamics 3430 and Cardiology

Director: Professor P. Bernadet

Laboratory of Dermatology   3431

Director: Professor A. Dupre
Activities: Congenital and transmissible ectodermic disease studies; genetic research.
Contract work: Yes

Laboratory of Digestive Tract Diseases 3432

Telephone: (061) 52 14 07
Affiliation: Institut National de la Santé et de la Recherche Médicale
Director: Professor A. Ribet
Senior staff: Professor D. Balas, Professor J. Frexinos
Activities: Neuro-hormonal correlations; digestive tract peptides, secretions and histophysiology; cancer research, chromatography.
Contract work: Yes

Laboratory of Experimental Endocrinology   3433

Director: Professor F. Bayard
Activities: Reproduction biology; tissue culture; steroid hormone studies.
Contract work: Yes

Laboratory of Experimental Surgery   3434

Director: Professor P. Puel
Activities: Cardiac and plastic surgery; urogenital microsurgery; circulation physiopathology; vasodilator action and valve prosthesis studies.
Contract work: Yes

Laboratory of Functional Exploration in Neurology   3435

Director: Professor L. Arbus

Laboratory of General Surgery   3436

Director: Professor M. Grimoud

Laboratory of Haematology   3437

Director: Professor R. Bierme
Senior staff: Professor J. Corberand
Activities: Circulatory system; effects of smoking; nutrition studies.
Contract work: Yes

Laboratory of Histology and Cytology   3438

Address: 133 route de Narbonne, Toulouse
Director: Professor A. Guilhem
Senior staff: Professor Ch. Bimes
Activities: Histology, histochemistry and biometric studies of gonads, cell population development, embryonic organ development; thymus hormone studies, electron microscopy.
Contract work: No

Laboratory of Histology and Embryology   3439

Address: 133 route de Narbonne, Toulouse
Director: Professor J.F. David
Activities: Cell culture and hormone action research; cancer cyto-diagnosis; histo-cytology; electron microscope studies.
Contract work: No

Laboratory of Immunology   3440

Address: Hôpital Purpuran, 31052 Toulouse Cedex
Telephone: (061) 49 35 55
Director: Professor E. Ohayon
Senior staff: Professor J. Ducos
Activities: Renal transplant studies; human histocompatibility; auto-immunity; skin disease immuno-pathology; genetics; immunofluorescence and spectrophotometry studies.
Contract work: Yes

Laboratory of Infantile and Orthopaedic Surgery   3441

Address: Hôpital Purpuran, 31052 Toulouse Cedex
Director: Professor J. Gaubert
Activities: Cartilage traumas and unequal limb studies; radiography and histology.
Contract work: No

Laboratory of Infantile Endocrinology and Growth Diseases   3442

Director: Radioimmunological foetal growth studies; thyroid research; immunology and persistent infections.
Contract work: Yes

Laboratory of Infectious and Tropical Diseases   3443

Address: Hôpital Purpuran, 31052 Toulouse Cedex
Telephone: (061) 49 11 33
Director: Professor J.Ch. Auvergnat
Activities: Meningitis research; antibiotic pharmacokinetics.
Contract work: No

Laboratory of Medical Psychology   3444

Director: Professor P. Moron
Activities: Infant psychology; surgical psychology; audio-psycho-phonological techniques; anti-depressant dosage studies; videography.
Contract work: Yes

Laboratory of Nephrology   3445

Affiliation: Institut National de la Santé et de la Recherche Médicale
Director: Professor J.M. Suc
Senior staff: Professor D. Durand, Professor J.L. Ader
Activities: Kidney structure, electron microscope studies; circulation and hypertension research.
Contract work: Yes

Laboratory of Neurology 3446

Telephone: (061) 52 13 22
Director: Professor A. Bes
Senior staff: Professor G. Geraud
Activities: Circulation studies; physiopathology; physiology of man in space; ultrasonic studies.
Contract work: Yes

Laboratory of Neuroradiology 3447

Director: Professor C. Manelpe
Activities: Embolism; cerebral therapeutics; angiographic studies.
Contract work: No

Laboratory of Neurosurgery 3448

Director: Professor G. Lazorthes
Activities: Cerebral blood loss measurement; morphine pharmacokinetics; cerebral stimulation studies.
Contract work: No

Laboratory of Nuclear Medicine 3449

Telephone: (061) 25 21 53
Director: Professor A. Bru
Senior staff: Professor H. Regis
Activities: Radioimmunology; cancer research; circulatory system, endocrine system, digestive system studies; rheology.
Contract work: Yes

Laboratory of Obstetrics and 3450 Gynaecology

Address: Hôpital de la Grave, place Lange, 31052 Toulouse Cedex
Affiliation: Institut National de la Santé et de la Recherche Médicale
Director: Professor G. Pontonnier
Senior staff: Professor J. Cros, Professor J.M. Reme
Activities: Obstetrical physiology and physiopathology; foetal vitality and perinatal pharmacology; biological and medical genetics.
Contract work: Yes

Laboratory of Osteo-Articular Diseases 3451

Address: 133 route de Narbonne, Toulouse
Directors: Professor J. Arlet, Professor P. Ficat
Activities: Electron microscope studies; biochemistry; histology; physiopathology; histo-pathological research; cartilage degeneration, bone and articular lesion studies.
Contract work: Yes

Laboratory of Otorhinolaryngology 3452 Research

Address: Hôpital Purpuran, 31052 Toulouse Cedex
Telephone: (061) 49 11 33
Director: Professor Y. Lacomme
Activities: Hearing - threshold determination, lesions, infant development studies; toxaemia and trauma research.
Contract work: No

Laboratory of Parasitology and 3453 Mycology

Telephone: (061) 25 21 53
Director: Professor J.P. Seguela
Activities: Toxoplasmosis and pregnancy studies; immunology research.
Contract work: Yes

Laboratory of Pathological Anatomy 3454

Director: Professor H. Bouissou
Activities: Atherogenesis; membrane and circulatory studies; ageing; immunofluorescence and electron microscopy.
Contract work: Yes

Laboratory of Physiology 3455

Address: 133 route de Narbonne, Toulouse
Director: Professor J.L. Ader
Senior staff: Professor J.P. Besombes
Activities: Physiology and pharmacology of renal circulation; hyperbaric oxygen therapy and endocrinology; respiratory studies.
Contract work: Yes

Laboratory of Radiology 3456

Director: Professor J. Roulleau
Activities: Radiodiagnosis, dosage determination studies.
Contract work: No

Laboratory of Respiratory Diseases 3457

Director: Professor J. Miguères
Senior staff: Professor A. Jover
Activities: Oxygenotherapy; muscular, enzymatic, cardio-respiratory and psychological studies; respiratory virus diseases.
Contract work: No

Laboratory of Stomatology and 3458
Maxillo-Facial Surgery

Telephone: (061) 52 14 72
Director: Professor H. Cadenat
Senior staff: Professor R. Combelles
Activities: Facial vascular system, musculature and orthopaedics; facial surgery.
Contract work: No

FACULTY OF PHARMACEUTICAL 3459
SCIENCES

Address: 31 allées Jules Guesde, 31077 Toulouse
Telephone: (061) 52 89 34
Dean: J. Cros

Laboratory of Analytical Chemistry 3460
and Bromatology

Director: Professor G. Pitet
Activities: Element spectral analysis and biopharmaceutical applications; synthesis, structural analysis and activity of medicines; spectrographic studies.
Contract work: Yes

Laboratory of Applied Zoology and 3461
Parasitology

Director: Professor P. Gayrel
Senior staff: Professor R. Ecalle
Activities: Parasitology and diagnosis; antiparasitic and antimycosic agent medicine studies; pharmacological cell cycle control; cardiovascular system studies.
Contract work: No

Laboratory of Biochemistry 3462

Director: Professor G. Soula
Activities: Lipid metabolism in arterial walls, cholesterol studies; cancerological biochemistry, drug pharmacokinetics, anti-inflammatory and anti-cancer drug studies, clinical cancerology, pathology, enzyme and antigen studies, chromatography.
Contract work: Yes

Laboratory of Botany and Cryptogamy 3463

Director: Professor S. Lascombes
Senior staff: Professor P. Rouge
Activities: Lecithin - action, synthesis, localization, evolution and degradation in plants; lecithin interactions in man; fungal lipid studies metabolism, comparative physiology, morphology, ultrastructure and phylogeny; electrophoresis studies.
Contract work: Yes

Laboratory of Chemical Pharmacy 3464

Director: Professor Y. Adam
Senior staff: Professor P. Coutourier, Professor P. Loiseau
Activities: Chromatographic and spectrometric studies.
Contract work: No

Laboratory of Galenic Pharmacy 3465

Director: Professor R. Rouffiac
Activities: Medicine production and bioavailability; dissolution and reabsorption devices; mathematical modelling; anti-inflammatory and alkaloid studies.
Contract work: No

Laboratory of Industrial Microbiology 3466
and Virology

Director: Professor G. Michel
Activities: Antimicrobial medicines; screening studies; antibacterial resistance to antibiotics and antiseptics; pharmacology, lymphatic system studies.
Contract work: No

Laboratory of Materia Medica 3467

Director: Professor E. Stanislas
Activities: Spectrophotometry; pharmacology and phytochemistry of anti-hypertensive medicines; molecular studies of medicines.
Contract work: No

Laboratory of Microbiology and 3468
Immunology

Director: Professor J. Breuillaud
Activities: Immune response research; bacterial taxonomy; immunoserum preparation; immunological characterization; clinical and statistical studies.
Contract work: Yes

Laboratory of Pharmaceutical 3469
Chemistry

Director: Professor M. Payard
Senior staff: Professor G. Saqui-Sannes
Activities: Phosphorus nitrogen compounds; methylation, heterocyclic aromatic amines.
Contract work: No

Laboratory of Pharmacodynamics I 3470

Director: Professor D. Caujolle
Activities: Antibiotic toxicology and pharmacology; medicines research.
Contract work: Yes

Laboratory of Pharmacodynamics II   3471

Director: Professor J. Cros
Activities: Pharmacology of morphine analgesics, en-
domorphine physiopathology; clinical studies;
spectrometry.
Contract work: Yes

Laboratory of Physics   3472

Director: Professor J. Oustrin
Senior staff: Professor P. Courriere
Activities: Pharmacokinetic and metabolic studies;
atomic physics; electron transport studies; chronophar-
macokinetics; spectrometry studies.
Contract work: No

Laboratory of Physiology and   3473
Pharmaceutic Haematology

Director: Professor G. Roux
Senior Staff: Professor J.C. Dumas
Activities: Nutritional physiology; metabolic regulation studies; hepatic physiology and histology; endocrinology; haematology and circulatory system
research; biological effects of microorganisms.
Contract work: No

UNIT OF MATHEMATICS,   3474
INFORMATION SCIENCE AND
MANAGEMENT

Director: R. Cuppens

Centre of Information   3475

Director: Professor M. Laudet
Senior staff: Professor R. Laudet-Lapeyre
Activities: Biomathematical models; data analysis;
language; programming; microprocessor development;
data bases; error propagation; finite elements; system
control; non-linear problems.
Contract work: Yes

Laboratory of Algebra and   3476
Combinatorics

Director: Professor Frasnay
Senior staff: Logic, Professor Frasnay; combinatorics,
Professor Guerin; algebra, Professor Desq; arithmetic,
Professor Terjanian
Contract work: No

Laboratory of Business Cybernetics,   3477
Image Recognition and Artificial
Intelligence

Affiliation: Centre National de la Recherche Scientifique
Directors: Professor G. Perennou, Professor S. Castan
Senior staff: Group A, Professor G. Perennou; Group
B, Professor S. Castan; Group C, Professor J. Luguet
Activities: Group A - Image recognition; speech
synthesis, recognition and compression; acoustics and
phonetics; data bases; linguistic applications; multi-
microprocessor systems.
Group B - Image recognition; man-machine com-
munications; logic.
Group C - Automatic information systems; data bases;
organization theories; bureaucracy.
Contract work: Yes

Laboratory of Functional and Complex 3478
Analysis

Director: Professor P. Lalague
Senior staff: Professor Mascart, Professor Nguyen,
Professor Pommiez, Professor Stoka
Activities: Analytical functions; nuclear spaces and
holomorph functions; polynomial approximation; topol-
ogy; geometric probability; composition equations.
Contract work: No

Laboratory of Language and   3479
Information Systems

Affiliation: Centre National de la Recherche Scientifi-
que
Director: Professor R. Beaufils
Senior staff: Professor Betourne, Professor Bruel,
Professor Galinier, Professor Vignolle
Activities: Information system architecture; operator
systems logic; numerical image treatment; languages
and programming; information theory.
Contract work: Yes

Laboratory of Mechanics   3480

Director: Professor J. Mauss
Senior staff: Professor P. Calvet, Professor R.L. Clerc,
Professor I. Gumowski, Professor C. Hartmann,
Professor R. Thibault
Activities: Aerothermics;   rheology;   non-linear
dynamic systems and applications.
Contract work: Yes

Laboratory of Numerical Analysis 3481

Director: Professor M. Atteia
Senior staff: Professor J. Audounet, Professor J. Couot
Activities: Approximation; optimization; variational methods and mathematical physics; stationary solution studies.
Contract work: Yes

Laboratory of Statistics and Probability 3482

Affiliation: Centre National de la Recherche Scientifique
Director: Professor H. Caussinus
Senior staff: Professor R. Cuppens, Professor J. Dauxois, Professor P. Ettinger, Professor J.R. Hait, Professor R. Huron, Professor B. Lacaze, Professor G. Letac, Professor A. Pousse
Activities: Probability; inferential statistics, linear models, chronological series; data analysis, mathematical models, descriptive statistics; logic and assisted production.
Contract work: No

Laboratory of Variance Analysis 3483

Director: Professor A. Crumeyrolle
Senior staff: Professor Ch. Barbance, Professor D. Bancel
Activities: General relativity and quantum field theory; variance studies.
Contract work: No

UNIT OF NATURAL SCIENCES 3484

Graduate research staff: 250
Activities: Research at molecular, cellular, organism and population levels; geological and mineral studies.

Centre of Plant Physiology 3485

Affiliation: Centre National de la Recherche Scientifique
Senior staff: Microorganisms - plant interactions, Professor A. Touze; metabolism and function of phenol compounds, Professor A.M. Boudet; metabolism and productivity, photorespiration studies, Professor G. Cavalie
Activities: Plant-microorganism interactions - symbiosis and pathogenesis; economically important disease studies; plant defence mechanisms and immunization. Metabolism and function of phenol compounds - biosynthesis, vacuole studies, vegetable growth. Metabolism and productivity - photosynthesis and photorespiration studies; regulation and product usage.
Contract work: Yes

Laboratory of Animal Physiology 3486

Director: Professor R. Agid
Activities: Metabolism research; nutrition; pharmacology; genetics; hibernation studies.
Contract work: Yes

Laboratory of Botany and Biogeography 3487

Director: Professor A. Baudière
Activities: Forest dynamics and regeneration; evolution studies; atmospheric pollen and allergy research; ionizing radiation effects.
Contract work: No

Laboratory of Botany and Forestry 3488

Director: Professor Y. De Ferre
Activities: Vascular plant morphology and biosystematics; parasitism; electron microscope studies.
Contract work: Yes

Laboratory of Cell Biology 3489

Address: 38 rue des 36 Ponts, 31078 Toulouse Cedex
Telephone: (061) 53 35 33
Affiliation: Institut National de la Santé et de la Recherche Médicale
Director: Professor E. Hollande
Activities: Endocrinology; immunocytochemistry; radioimmunology; cell culture; electron microscope studies; heavy metal toxicity.
Contract work: Yes

Laboratory of Cell Biology and Phytopathology 3490

Director: Professor A. Schneider
Activities: Ultrastructure, biochemistry and systematics of fungi; parasitology; phytopathogenic studies.
Contract work: No

Laboratory of Cryptogamy 3491

Director: Professor Ch. Montant
Activities: Fungal physiology; cytodifferentiation; morphogenesis; biosynthesis.
Contract work: No

Laboratory of Crystallographic Mineralogy 3492

Address: 39 allées Jules Guesde, 31400 Toulouse
Telephone: (061) 53 02 35
Affiliation: Centre National de la Recherche Scientifique
Director: Professor M. Orliac

Senior staff: Professor R. Perami, Professor R. Pulou
Activities: Mineralogy; mineral ecology; metallo-engineering; geochemistry; thermodiffusion; fluorescence; materials and geotechnical studies.
Contract work: Yes

Laboratory of Digestion and Nutritional Physiology 3493

Director: Professor P. Raynaud
Activities: Agro-alimentary nutrition; digestive tract microorganism studies; protein source studies; prevention of nutritional illness.
Contract work: No

Laboratory of Entomology (Toulouse) 3494 and Forest Entomology (Artigues)

Director: Professor A. Ledoux
Senior staff: Professor P. Colombel
Activities: Ecological, phasic and social insect polymorphism; biology of mountain forest insects; electron microscope and electrophoresis studies.
Contract work: No

Laboratory of Fish Ecophysiology 3495

Director: Y. Creach
Activities: Ecology; physiology; nutrition and metabolism studies.
Contract work: Yes

Laboratory of General Biology 3496

Director: Professor J.C. Beetschen
Senior staff: Professor P. Deparis Professor A. Jaylet
Activities: Amphibian development and differentiation; embryonic determination; genetic markers and enzymatic differentiation; metamorphosis; biochemical criteria in species determination.
Contract work: Yes

Laboratory of Genetics and Chromosome Replication 3497

Affiliation: Centre National de la Recherche Scientifique
Director: Professor J.M. Louarn
Activities: Bacterial cell cycle studies; chromosome replication and cell synthesis; mutation; chromosome map studies.
Contract work: Yes

Laboratory of Geology 3498

Director: Professor P. Souquet
Senior staff: Professor J. Rey
Activities: Sedimentology; tectonics; micropalaeontology; palaeoecology; regional geology of the Pyrenees and Iberian peninsula.
Contract work: Yes

Laboratory of Geology and Geochronology 3499

Director: Professor Y. Gourinard
Activities: Geological management; stratigraphic and radiometric studies.
Contract work: Yes

Laboratory of Geophysics 3500

Director: Professor Rosch

Laboratory of Hydrobiology and Oredon Biological Station 3501

Director: Professor E. Angelier
Senior staff: Professor Cl. Berthelemy
Activities: Consequences of human action on continental waters; canals, hydroelectricity, pollution.
Contract work: Yes

Laboratory of Insect Biology 3502

Director: Professor J. Bitsch
Activities: Insect reproduction, physiology and general biology; electron microscope studies.
Contract work: No

Laboratory of Mediterranean and Pyrenean Geology 3503

Affiliation: Centre National de la Recherche Scientifique
Director: Professor M. Durand-Delga
Activities: Structural geology; sedimentology; geodynamic evolution; cartography; geological decomposition and geometric structure studies.
Contract work: No

Laboratory of Membrane Biochemistry 3504

Director: Professor J. Asselineau

Laboratory of Neuroethology 3505

Director: Professor R. Campan
Activities: Vertebrate etho-ecology; insect behaviour; electrophysiology.
Contract work: No

Laboratory of Pedology and 3506
Geochemistry

Address: 31078 Toulouse
Telephone: (061) 53 35 33
Director: Professor Y. Tardy
Senior staff: Professor F. Bourgeat
Activities: Pedogenesis and soil evolution; geothermics and reservoir diogenesis; metallo-engineering; irrigation; geochemistry; thermodynamics.
Contract work: Yes

Laboratory of Petroleum Geology 3507

Director: Professor M. Lelubre
Senior staff: Professor R. Mirouse
Activities: Stratigraphy; sedimentology; palaeontology; petrology; metamorphism and metallo-engineering; tectogenesis; diffraction, fluorescence and thermic analysis.
Contract work: Yes

Laboratory of Phytogeography 3508

Director: Professor P. Legris

Laboratory of Plant Biology 3509

Director: Professor C. Leredde
Activities: Ecology and systematics; morphology and structural anatomy; cytophysiology; ethnobotany; reproduction biology.
Contract work: No

Laboratory of Plant Ecology 3510

Address: 39 allées Jules Guesde, 31400 Toulouse
Telephone: (061) 53 02 35
Director: Professor P. Rey
Activities: Pollution studies; ecosystem ecophysiology; teledetection, cartography and biogeography; spectrophotometry and chromatography studies.
Contract work: Yes

Laboratory of Protistology (Zoology) 3511

Director: Professor J. Lecal
Activities: Invertebrate evolution; ultrastructural morphology; ecosystem studies; adaptive and evolutive physiology; electron microscope studies.
Contract work: No

Laboratory of Psychophysiology 3512

Director: Professor J. Medioni
Activities: Genetics and behaviour; physiological determinants of animal behaviour; behavioural studies of man at work.
Contract work: Yes

Laboratory of Quantitative Biology 3513

Director: Professor L. Bonnet
Activities: Natural population and ecosystem studies; ecology; palaeoecology; biological indicator studies; ultrastructure research; bioavailability.
Contract work: Yes

Laboratory of Tectonophysics 3514

Address: 38 rue des 36 Ponts, 31078 Toulouse
Telephone: (061) 53 35 33
Director: Professor P. Sirieys
Activities: Rock deformation studies; rock anisotropy.
Contract work: No

Laboratory of Zoology and Terrestrial 3515
Invertebrate Ecology

Director: Professor P. Cassagnau
Activities: Systematics; ecology; evolution; biogeography; population polymorphism; genetics; reproduction biology.
Contract work: No

UNIT OF PHYSICS, CHEMISTRY AND 3516
AUTOMATION

Director: Professor D. Blanc

Centre for Space Research 3517

Director: Professor F. Cambou

Centre of Atomic Physics 3518

Affiliation: Centre National de la Recherche Scientifique
Director: Professor D. Blanc
Senior staff: Professor J. Fontan, Professor P. Benoit-Cattin, Professor J.L. Teyssier
Activities: Discharges in gases; atomic collision studies; radiological physics; aerosol physics and atmospheric changes.
Contract work: Yes

Centre of Atomic Physics, Laboratory 3519
of Aerosol Physics and Atmospheric
Changes

Director: Professor J. Fontan
Activities: Planetary layer dynamics; ozone layer studies; tropospheric studies.
Contract work: Yes

Institute of Geotechnical Civil Engineering   3520

Address: avenue de Rangueil, Toulouse
Telephone: (061) 25 21 13
Director: Professor B. Thenoz
Senior staff: Professor C. Legrand Professor J. Grandet
Activities: Material physicohemistry; material mechanics; soil mechanics and rheology; structural mechanics; building thermics; solar energy studies.
Contract work: No

Laboratory of Astronomy   3521

Director: Professor R. Bouigue
Activities: Relativity; spectroscopic and spectrophotometric studies.
Contract work: Yes

Laboratory of Atmospheric Physics   3522

Director: Professor R. Picca
Activities: Lightning research; cloud studies; storm modelling.
Contract work: Yes

Laboratory of Atmospheric Physics (Radiometry)   3523

Director: Professor R. Saporte
Activities: Atmospheric aerosol action; radiometric and optic studies; infrared thermography of combustion; convection studies.
Contract work: Yes

Laboratory of Bioinorganic Chemistry   3524

Address: 38 rue des 36 Ponts, 31400 Toulouse
Telephone: (061) 53 35 33
Director: Professor M. Massol
Activities: Paramagnetic metallic ion complexes, biochemical and pharmacological applications; biosynthesis; cell biology; biomedicine; pharmacology.
Contract work: Yes

Laboratory of Biological and Medical Engineering   3525

Affiliation: Institut National de la Santé et de la Recherche Médicale
Director: Professor J.P. Morucci
Activities: Circulation studies; ergonomics; biomechanics; physiological signals; laser nephelometry.
Contract work: Yes

Laboratory of Electrical Engineering   3526

Affiliation: Centre National de la Recherche Scientifique
Director: Ai Bui
Senior staff: Professor C. Huraux, Professor R. Lacoste
Activities: Insulated surface-discharge interactions; solid insulators; electrical properties of ceramics, circuit studies.
Contract work: Yes

Laboratory of Electron Microscopy and Optoelectronics   3527

Director: Professor J. Trinquier
Activities: Electron microscopy; optoelectronics; holographic interferometry; solar energy studies; aerial photography; mass and heat transfer.
Contract work: No

Laboratory of Electronic and Ionic Physics   3528

Director: Professor A. Degeilh
Senior staff: Professor P. Larroque, Professor P. Pilod, Professor P. Verdier
Activities: Ion-matter and electron-matter interaction, transmission phenomena; electronic emission; solar energy studies.
Contract work: Yes

Laboratory of Electronic Physics-Metal Studies   3529

Director: Professor P. Coulomb
Activities: Plastic deformation of metals and alloys; deformation texture studies.
Contract work: Yes

Laboratory of Energy Research   3530

Director: Professor J.P. Traverse
Activities: Energy conversion; energy economics; solar energy research; thermo-optics, thermochemistry and photoelectrolysis.
Contract work: Yes

Laboratory of Experimental Physics   3531

Director: Professor A. Pagani
Senior staff: Professor Y. Gourinard
Activities: Elementary surface excitations; geochronology; mass spectrometry; water pollution.
Contract work: No

Laboratory of Ionized Media Physics 3532

Director: Professor J.M. Rocard
Activities: Spectroscopy; autonomic discharge and solar energy studies.
Contract work: No

Laboratory of Magnetism and 3533 Quantum Electronics

Address: 39 allées Jules Guesde, 31078 Toulouse Cedex
Telephone: (061) 53 02 35
Director: Professor J. Pescia
Activities: Spin relaxation studies; spectrometry; magnetism.
Contract work: No

Laboratory of Materials Chemistry 3534

Director: Professor A. Rousset
Activities: Phase studies; electrical and magnetic properties; catalysis.
Contract work: Yes

Laboratory of Mathematics for the 3535 Physical Sciences and Random Phenomena

Director: Professor J. Meric
Activities: Spectral analysis; aerial circulation.
Contract work: No

Laboratory of Metrology, Acoustics 3536 and Instrumentation

Address: 38 rue des 36 Ponts, 31077 Toulouse Cedex
Telephone: (061) 53 22 35
Director: Professor P. Josserand
Activities: Metrology; environmental acoustics; signal treatment; microprocessor studies; instrumentation; biological and medical engineering; pedagogic studies of teaching machines.
Contract work: Yes

Laboratory of Organic Applied 3537 Chemistry

Director: Professor J. Sotiropoulos

Laboratory of Organo-Mineral 3538 Chemistry

Director: Professor J. Satge
Activities: Organometallic derivatives; photoelectron and spectrometry studies; pharmacological and radiopharmacological applications.
Contract work: Yes

Laboratory of Organometallics 3539

Director: P. Mazerolles
Senior staff: Professor M. Lesbre
Activities: Organometallic stereo modelling; photochemistry; cyclic derivative and intermediate reaction studies.
Contract work: No

Laboratory of Phosphorus and 3540 Nitrogen Heterocycles

Directors: Professor J. Barrans, Professor F. Mathis
Activities: Synthesis, reactivity and spectral properties of phosphorus heterocycles.
Contract work: Yes

Laboratory of Physicochemistry and 3541 Electrochemistry

Affiliation: Centre National de la Recherche Scientifique
Director: Professor J. Mahenc
Senior staff: Professor M. Comtat
Activities: Chemical aspects, electrochemistry and hydrodynamics of interface and membrane transport; membrane and fibre studies; applications in biological engineering, medicine and industry.
Contract work: Yes

Laboratory of Polyfunctional 3542 Nitrogenous Compounds

Director: Professor A. Lattes
Senior staff: Professor J.J. Perie; Professor M. Rivière
Activities: Organometallic studies; photochemistry; amphipathetic studies; bio-organic chemistry; organic synthesis; carboxylation.
USE 31

Laboratory of Pyrones and Pyridines 3543

Affiliation: Centre National de la Recherche Scientifique
Director: Professor V. Herault
Activities: Agro-alimentary and chemotherapeutic studies; cardiovascular and central nervous system studies.
Contract work: Yes

Laboratory of Quantum Physics 3544

Director: Professor Ph. Durand
Activities: Electronic structure of atoms and molecules; statistical quantum mechanics.
Contract work: No

Laboratory of Solid-State and High Pressure Chemistry 3545

Address: 38 rue des 36 Ponts, 31400 Toulouse
Telephone: (061) 53 35 33
Director: Professor G. Bonel
Activities: Mineral phosphate structure, synthesis and properties; calcified tissue studies.
Contract work: No

Laboratory of Solid-State Physics 3546

Affiliation: Centre National de la Recherche Scientifique
Director: F. Pradal
Senior staff: Professor P. Carrara, Professor J. Dugas, Professor C. Fert, Professor P. Gautier, Professor J.P. Cottu, Professor S. Askenazy, Professor M. Brousseau, Professor P. Groh, Professor J.C. Portal, Professor C. Levade
Activities: Electronic structure of solids; magnetism; molecular movement; electronic excitation; recombination studies; metal physics, calcified tissue research; solar energy studies.
Contract work: Yes

Laboratory of Structural Organic Chemistry 3547

Director: Professor P. Mauret
Activities: Polarity; transition metal organometallic derivative studies; catalysis; corrosion, corrosion prevention; humidity studies; chromatography.
Contract work: Yes

Laboratory of Structural Physics 3548

Affiliation: Centre National de la Recherche Scientifique
Director: Professor L. Lafourrade
Senior staff: Professor P. Larroque, Professor G. Collette
Activities: Thin layer studies, crystallochemistry, physicochemistry, physical properties; metastable phase studies; plastic deformation; biocrystallochemistry; electron microscope studies.
Contract work: Yes

Laboratory of Structure and Life 3549

Director: J.F. Labarre
Activities: Inorganic cycles; anti-tumour activity; quantum chemistry; chemotherapy; cancerology.
Contract work: Yes

Laboratory of Synthesis and Organic Physicochemistry 3550

Director: Professor P. Maroni
Activities: Organic heterocycles; structure and nucleophile reactivity of functional metal derivatives.
Contract work: No

Laboratory of Terpene Chemistry and Applied Organic Chemistry 3551

Director: Professor C. Bertrand
Senior staff: Professor J. Sotiropoulos, Professor P. Bedos
Activities: Synthesis of terpene derivatives, optical properties and structural relationships; synthesis, structure and application of new organic substances; spectropolarimetry studies.
Contract work: No

Valeo 3552

Address: 4 rue Gambetta, 93406 Saint-Ouen
Telephone: 264 50 00
Telex: 280 086 F
Adjoint Director, Central Research and Studies: Roland H. Lindas
Research director: R. Filderman
Senior staff: Materials, Pierre Léroy; electronic hydromechanics, C. Jubal; physics, M. Ricco; mathematics, data processing, P. Molinier
Graduate research staff: 30
Annual expenditure: over £2m
Activities: Research and development in the following areas: friction linings and composite materials; thermodynamics; aerodynamics; acoustics; mechanical engineering; mathematics.
Facilities: Road simulation rig.
Contract work: No

GERMAN DEMOCRATIC REPUBLIC

Akademie der Landwirtschaftswissenschaften der Deutschen Demokratischen Republik
1

[Academy of Agricultural Sciences of the German Democratic Republic]
Address: Krausenstrasse 38/39, Postfach 1295, DDR-1086 Berlin
Telephone: (02) 00 04 61
Telex: 11 26 86
President: Professor Dr E. Rübensam
Vice-President: Professor Dr D. Spaar
Activities: Soil fertility; animal production; plant production; plant protection; fertilization; mechanization; veterinary science.
Contract work: No
Publications: Handbücherei der Sozialistischen Landwirtschaft.
Archives: Beiträge zur Entomologie; Archiv für Gartenbau; Archiv für Acker- und Pflanzenbau und Bodenkunde; Archiv für Tierzucht; Archiv für Naturschutz und Landschaftsforschung; Archiv für Phytopathologie und Pflanzenschutz; Archiv für Züchtungsforschung; Archiv für Experimentelle Veterinärmedizin;
Periodicals: Gartenbau; Nachrichtenblatt für den Pflanzenschutz in der DDR; Feldwirtschaft; Tierzucht; Standardisierung Land-,Forst- und Nahrungsgüterwirtschaft.

FORSCHUNGSZENTRUM FÜR BODENFRUCHTBARKEIT MÜNCHEBERG
2

[Soil Fertility Research Centre]
Address: Wilhelm-Pieck-Strasse 72, DDR-1278 Müncheberg

FORSCHUNGSZENTRUM FÜR MECHANISIERUNG DER LANDWIRTSCHAFT SCHLIEBEN-BORNIM
3

[Agriculture Mechanization Research Centre]
Address: DDR-7912 Schlieben

FORSCHUNGSZENTRUM FÜR TIERPRODUKTION DUMMERSTORF-ROSTOCK
4

[Animal Production Research Centre]
Address: DDR-2551 Dummerstorf Kreis Rostock

FRIEDRICH-LOEFFLER-INSTITUT FÜR TIERSEUCHENFORSCHUNG INSEL RIEMS
5

[Friedrich-Loeffler Institute for Animal Epidemic Research]
Address: DDR-2202 Insel Riems

INSTITUT FÜR AGRARGESCHICHTE UND INTERNATIONALE LANDWIRTSCHAFT
6

[Rural History and International Agriculture Institute]
Address: Joseph-Nawrocki-Strasse 10, DDR-1162 Berlin

INSTITUT FÜR BAKTERIELLE TIERSEUCHENFORSCHUNG JENA
7

[Bacterial Epizootics Institute]
Address: Naumburger Strasse 96a, DDR-6900 Jena Zwätzen

INSTITUT FÜR 8
DÜNGUNGSFORSCHUNG LEIPZIG-POTSDAM

[Fertilization Research Institute]
Address: Gustav-Kühn-Strasse 8, DDR-7022 Leipzig

INSTITUT FÜR FUTTERPRODUKTION 9
PAULINENAUE

[Forage Production Institute]
Address: DDR-1551 Paulinenaue

INSTITUT FÜR 10
GEMÜSEPRODUKTION GROSSBEEREN

[Vegetable Production Institute]
Address: Theodor-Echtermeyer-Weg,   DDR-1722 Grossbeeren

INSTITUT FÜR 11
GETREIDEFORSCHUNG BERNBURG-HADMERSLEBEN

[Cereal Research Institute]
Address: Mitschurinstrasse 22, DDR-4351 Bernburg Strenzfeld

INSTITUT FÜR IMPFSTOFFE DESSAU 12

[Vaccines Institute]
Address: Jahnstrasse 8, DDR-4500 Dessau

INSTITUT FÜR 13
KARTOFFELFORSCHUNG GROSS LÜSEWITZ

[Potato Research Institute]
Address: DDR-2551 Gross Lüsewitz

INSTITUT FÜR 14
LANDSCHAFTSFORSCHUNG UND NATURSCHUTZ HALLE

[Landscape Research and Nature Management]
Address: Neuwerk 4, DDR-4020 Halle Saale

INSTITUT FÜR 15
LANDWIRTSCHAFTLICHE INFORMATION UND DOKUMENTATION

[Agricultural Information and Documentation Institute]
Address: Krausenstrasse 38, DDR-1086 Berlin

INSTITUT FÜR OBSTFORSCHUNG 16
DRESDEN-PILLNITZ

[Fruit Research Institute]
Address: Pillnitzer Platz 2, DDR-8057 Dresden

INSTITUT FÜR 17
PFLANZENERNÄHRUNG JENA

[Plant Nutrition Institute]
Address: Naumburger Strasse 96a, DDR-6900 Jena Zwätzen

INSTITUT FÜR 18
PFLANZENSCHUTZFORSCHUNG KLEINMACHNOW

[Plant Protection Research Institute]
Address: Stahnsdorfer Damm 81, DDR-1532 Kleinmachnow

INSTITUT FÜR PFLANZENZÜCHTUNG 19
GÜLZOW-GÜSTROW

[Plant Breeding Institute]
Address: DDR-2601 Gülzow -Güstrow

INSTITUT FÜR PHYTOPATHOLOGIE 20
ASCHERSLEBEN

[Phytopathology Institute]
Address: Theodor-Roemer-Weg   4,   DDR-4320 Aschersleben

INSTITUT FÜR RINDERPRODUKTION 21
IDEN-ROHRBECK

[Cattle Production Institute]
Address: DDR-3541 Iden

INSTITUT FÜR RÜBENFORSCHUNG KLEINWANZLEBEN   22

[Beet Research Institute]
Address: DDR-3105 Kleinwanzleben

INSTITUT FÜR ZÜCHTUNGSFORSCHUNG QUEDLINBURG   23

[Breeding Research Institute]
Address: Ethel- und Julius-Rosenberg-Strasse 22-23, DDR-4300 Quedlinburg

Akademie der Wissenschaften der Deutschen Demokratischen Republik   24

[Academy of Sciences of the German Democratic Republic]
Address: Otto-Nuschke-Strasse 22/23, DDR-1080 Berlin
Telephone: (02) 20 0316
Telex: 011 2456

CHEMICAL RESEARCH   25

Address: Rudower Chaussee 5, DDR-1199 Berlin Adlershof
Telephone: (02) 67 02 841
Director: Professor Dr Gerhard Keil

Forschungsinstitut für Aufbereitung   26

[Processing Research Institute]
Address: Strasse des Friedens 40, DDR-9200 Freiberg
Telephone: 700
Director: Professor Dr Edelhard Töpfer

Forschungsstelle für Chemische Toxikologie   27

[Chemical Toxicology Research Centre]
Address: Permoserstrasse 15, DDR-7050 Leipzig
Telephone: (041) 68 61 321
Director: Professor Dr Karlheinz Lohs

Institut für Chemische Technologie   28

[Institute for Chemical Technology]
Address: Rudower Chaussee 5, DDR-1199 Dresden
Telephone: (051) 67 02 841
Director: Professor Dr Gerhard Keil

Institut für Polymerenchemie   29

[Institute for Polymer Chemistry]
Address: Kantstrasse 55, DDR-1530 Teltow Seehof
Telephone: 4831
Director: Professor Dr Burkart Philipp

Institut für Technische Chemie   30

[Institute for Technical Chemistry]
Address: Permoserstrasse 15, DDR-7050 Leipzig
Telephone: (041) 68 61 225
Director: Professor Dr Manfred Ringpfeil

Institut für Technologie der Fasern   31

[Institute for Technology of Fibres]
Address: Hohe Strasse 6, DDR-8010 Dresden
Telephone: (051) 46 58 220
Director: Professor Wolfgang Bobeth

Zentralinstitut für Anorganische Chemie   32

[Central Institute for Inorganic Chemistry]
Address: Rudower Chaussee 5, DDR-1199 Berlin Adlershof
Telephone: (02) 67 02 841
Director: Professor Dr Lothar Kolditz

Zentralinstitut für Organische Chemie   33

[Central Institute for Organic Chemistry]
Address: Rudower Chaussee 5, DDR-1199 Berlin Adlershof
Telephone: (02) 67 02 841
Director: Professor Dr Siegfried Nowak

Zentralinstitut für Physikalische Chemie   34

[Central Institute for Physical Chemistry]
Address: Rudower Chaussee 5, DDR-1199 Berlin Adlershof
Director: Professor Dr Wolfgang Schirmer

GEOLOGICAL AND SPACE RESEARCH   35

Address: Telegrafenberg, DDR-1500 Potsdam
Telephone: (033) 4551

Institut für Elektronik   36

[Institute for Electronics]
Address: Rudower Chaussee 5, DDR-1199 Berlin Adlershof
Telephone: (02) 67 02 841

Institut für Geographie und Geoökologie 37

[Institute for Geography and Geo-ecology]
Address: Georgi-Dimitroff-Platz 1, DDR-7010 Leipzig
Telephone: (041) 34 531
Director: Professor Dr Heinz Lüdemann

Institut für Meereskunde 38

[Institute for Oceanography]
Address: Seestrasse 15, DDR-2530 Warnemünde
Telephone: 58 288
Director: Professor Dr Klaus Voigt

Zentralinstitut für Astrophysik 39

[Central Institute for Astrophysics]
Address: Rosa-Luxemburg-Strasse 17a, DDR-1502 Potsdam Babelsberg
Telephone: (033) 76 2225

Zentralinstitut für Physik der Erde 40

[Central Institute for Physics of the Earth]
Address: Telegrafenberg, DDR-1500 Potsdam
Telephone: (033) 4551

Zentralinstitut für Solar-terrestrische Physik 41

[Central Institute for Solar-Terrestrial Physics]
Address: Rudower Strasse 5, DDR-1199 Berlin Adlershof
Telephone: (02) 67 02 841
Director: Professor Dr Jens Traubenheim

MATHEMATICS AND CYBERNETICS RESEARCH 42

Address: Rudower Chaussee 5, DDR-1199 Berlin Adlershof
Telephone: (02) 67 02 871
Director: Professor Dr Manfred Peschel

Zentralinstitut für Kybernetik und Informationsprozesse 43

[Central Institute for Cybernetics and Information Processing]
Address: Rudower Chaussee 5, DDR-1199 Berlin Adlershof
Telephone: (02) 67 02 841
Director: Professor Dr Volker Kempe

Zentralinstitut für Mathematik und Mechanik 44

[Central Institute for Mathematics and Mechanics]
Address: Mohrenstrasse 39, DDR-1080 Berlin
Telephone: (02) 20 00 561
Director: Professor Dr Klaus Matthes

Zentrum für Rechentechnik 45

[Computer Technology Centre]
Address: Rudower Chaussee 5, DDR-1199 Berlin Adlershof
Telephone: (02) 67 02 841
Director: Professor Dr Hermann Meier

MOLECULAR BIOLOGY AND MEDICINE RESEARCH 46

Address: Lindenberger Weg 70, DDR-1199 Berlin Buch
Telephone: (02) 56 97 851
Director: Professor Dr Günter Pasternak

Forschungsstelle für Wirbeltierforschung (im Berliner Tierpark) 47

[Vertebrate Research Centre]
Address: Am Tierpark 125, DDR-1136 Berlin Friedrichsfelde
Telephone: (02) 52 030
Director: Professor Dr Heinrich Dathe

Institut für Biochemie der Pflanzen, Forschungszentrum für Molekularbiologie 48

[Institute of Plant Biochemistry and Research Centre for Molecular Biology and Medicine]
Address: Weinberg 3, Postfach 250, DDR-4020 Halle Saale
Telephone: (046) 601312
Telex: 04263
Research director: Professor Dr Klaus Schreiber
Departments: Plant Hormones and Plant Growth Substances, Professor Dr Günther Sembdner; Mechanisms of Regulation of Plant Growth and Development Processes, Professor Dr Benno Parthier; Regulation of Secondary Metabolism, Professor Dr Detlef Gröger; Natural Products Chemistry, Professor Dr Günter Adam
Activities: Long-term basic research work in the fields of molecular biology, biochemistry, and physiology of plants, phytopharmacology, and natural products chemistry; investigation of the occurrence, chemistry, metabolism, mode, and mechanism of action of plant

hormones, and other hormone-like compounds of plant origin; investigation of the regulation and control of selected processes of growth, development, and metabolism in plants; development of new synthetic plant growth substances and of new drugs for therapeutical application; studies on the metabolism and mode of action of new synthetic plant growth substances; investigation of the specific processes of the nucleic acid and protein metabolism in plants, and their regulation under special consideration of the chloroplast biogenesis; research to investigate processes of cell differentiation and cell specialization, especially during ergot alkaloid biosynthesis as well as production, transformation, and accumulation of biological active substances by cell cultivation of higher plants; isolation, structural elucidation, synthesis, and biochemistry of new biological active plant constituents, for example alkaloids and terpenoids: application of physical methods for structural investigations (IR, UV, NMR, MS, ORD/CD, X-ray crystal structural analysis).

Institut für Wirkstofforschung   49

[Institute for Hormone Research]
Address: Alfred-Kowalke-Strasse 4, DDR-1136 Berlin

Zentralinstitut für Ernährung   50

[Central Institute for Nutrition]
Address: Arthur-Scheunert-Allee 114-116, DDR-1505 Potsdam Renbrücke
Telephone: (033) 321
Director: Professor Dr Helmut Haenel

Zentralinstitut für Genetik und   51
Kulturpflanzenforschung

[Central Institute for Genetics and Research on Cultivated Plants]
Address: Corrensstrasse 3, DDR-4325 Gatersleben
Telephone: 5 220
Director: Professor Dr Helmut Böhme

Zentralinstitut für Herz- und Kreislauf-   52
Regulationsforschung

[Central Institute for Heart and Blood Circulation Control Research]
Address: Wiltbergstrasse 50, DDR-1115 Berlin Buch
Telephone: (02) 56 97 821
Director: Professor Dr Horst Heine

Zentralinstitut für Krebsforschung   53

[Central Institute for Cancer Research]
Address: Lindenberger Weg 70, DDR-1199 Berlin Buch
Telephone: (02) 56 97 851

Zentralinstitut für Mikrobiologie und   54
Experimentelle Therapie

[Central Institute for Microbiology and Experimental Therapy]
Address: Beuthenbergstrasse 11, DDR-6900 Jena
Telephone: (078) 88 56 14
Director: Professor Dr Odo Taubeneck

Zentralinstitut für Molekularbiologie   55

[Central Institute for Molecular Biology]
Address: Linderberger Weg 70, DDR-1115 Berlin Buch
Telephone: (02) 56 97 851

PHYSICS, NUCLEAR SCIENCES AND   56
MATERIALS RESEARCH

Address: Rudower Chaussee 5, DDR-1199 Berlin Adlershof
Telephone: (02) 67 02 841
Director: Professor Dr Günter Albrecht

Institut für Festkörperphysik und   57
Elektronenmikroskopie

[Solid-State Physics and Electron Microscopy Institute]
Address: Am Weinberg 2, DDR-4010 Halle
Telephone: (046) 60 13 12
Director: Professor Dr Heinz Bethge

Institut für Hochenergiephysik   58

[High-Energy Physics Institute]
Address: Platanenallee 6, DDR-1615 Zeuthen
Telephone: 67 58 001
Director: Professor Dr Karl Lanius

Institut für Physik der   59
Werkstoffbearbeitung

[Institute for the Physics of Materials Processing]
Address: Seestrasse 82, DDR-1166 Berlin Rahnsdorf
Telephone: (02) 65 89 671

Zentralinstitut für Elektronenphysik   60

[Central Institute for Electron Physics]
Address: Mohrenstrasse 40-41, DDR-1080 Berlin
Telephone: (02) 20 00 561
Director: Professor Dr Karl Friedrich

Zentralinstitut für Festkörperphysik   **61**
und Werkstofforschung

[Central Institute for Solid-State Physics and
Materials Research]
Address: Helmholtzstrasse 20, DDR-8027 Dresden
Telephone: (051) 46 59 380
Director: Professor Dr Otto Henkel

Zentralinstitut für Isotopen- und   **62**
Strahlenforschung

[Central Institute for Isotope and Radiation
Research]
Address: Permoserstrasse 15, DDR-7050 Leipzig
Telephone: (041) 08 61 308
Director: Professor Dr Klaus Wetzel

Zentralinstitut für Kernforschung   **63**

[Central Institute for Nuclear Research]
Address: Postfach 19, DDR-8051 Dresden
Telephone: (051) 59 12 350
Director: Professor Dr Günter Flach

Zentralinstitut für Optik und   **64**
Spektroskopie

[Central Institute for Optics and Spectroscopy]
Address: Rudower Chausse 5, DDR-1199 Berlin
Adlershof
Telephone: (02) 67 02 841
Director: Professor Dr Klaus Junge

Zentrum für Wissenschaftlichen   **65**
Gerätebau

[Centre for Scientific Instrument Making]
Address: Rudower Chaussee 5, DDR-1199 Berlin
Adlershof
Telephone: (02) 67 02 841
Director: Dr Norbert Langhoff

SOCIAL SCIENCES RESEARCH   **66**

Address: Otto-Nuschke-Strasse 10/11, DDR-1080 Berlin
Telephone: (02) 22 08 673
Director: Professor Dr Werner Kalweit

Berg-Akademie Freiberg*   67

[Freiberg Mining Academy]
Address: Akademiestrasse 6, 82 Freiberg

CHEMISTRY DEPARTMENT*   **68**

DEEP SEA DRILLING TECHNOLOGY   **69**
DEPARTMENT*

EARTH SCIENCES DEPARTMENT*   **70**

GEOLOGY AND MINING   **71**
DEPARTMENT*

MATHEMATICS DEPARTMENT*   **72**

METALLURGY AND MATERIALS   **73**
ENGINEERING DEPARTMENT*

PHYSICS DEPARTMENT*   **74**

POWER AND MECHANICAL   **75**
ENGINEERING DEPARTMENT*

PROCESSING TECHNOLOGY AND   **76**
SILICATE INDUSTRY DEPARTMENT*

Ernst-Moritz-Arndt   77
Universität Greifswald*

[Ernst-Moritz-Arndt University of Greifswald]
Address: Domstrasse 11, DDR-2200 Greifswald

BIOLOGY DEPARTMENT*   **78**

CHEMISTRY DEPARTMENT*   **79**

GEOLOGY DEPARTMENT*   **80**

MATHEMATICS DEPARTMENT*   **81**

MEDICINE DEPARTMENT * 82

PHARMACY DEPARTMENT * 83

PHYSICS AND ELECTRONICS DEPARTMENT * 84

Forschungsinstitut für Balneologie und Kurortwissenschaft Bad Elster 85

[Scientific Research Institute for Balneology and Spa Treatment]
Address: Karl-Marx-Strasse 5, DDR-9933 Bad Elster
Telephone: 7/328
Research director: Professor Dr Herbert Jordan
Graduate research staff: 15
Activities: Research into the treatment of cardiological and rheumatic diseases at the spa; investigation of the adaptive effects of non-specific therapies, the biological chronology of the course of recovery, and the mode of operation of natural therapies.
Contract work: No
Publications: Wissenschaftliche Informationen; Informationsdienst Rheumatologie; Mitteilungen für rheumatologisch tätige Ärete in der DDR.

Forschungsinstitut Manfred von Ardenne * 86

[Manfred von Ardenne Research Institute]
Address: Zeppelinstrasse 7, 8051 Dresden
Telephone: (051) 37151
Telex: 2158
Head: Professor Dr Manfred Von Ardenne
Activities: Radiochemistry using electron-beam generators; development and use of duoplasmatron ion sources.

Forschungszentrum des Werkzeugmaschinenbaus 87

[Machine Tools Research Centre]
Address: Postfach 1061, DDR-9010 Karl-Marx-Stadt
Telephone: (071) 6520
Telex: 07-253
Affiliation: VEB Werkzeugmaschinenkombinat 'Fritz Heckert'
Research director: Dipl-Ing M. Speck
Senior staff: Professor Dr Russig
Graduate research staff: 700
Annual expenditure: over £2m
Activities: Research and development in the fields of metal-cutting machine tools, production-technological and cutting processes, as well as rationalization of the technical preparation of manufacture in the machine-tool building industry.
Contract work: Yes
Publications: WMW - Katalog für Rationalisierungslösungen; Bibliographie 'Werkzeugmasduinen- und Werkzeugbau'.

Friedrich-Schiller-Universität Jena * 88

[Friedrich-Schiller University Jena]
Address: Goetheallee 1, 68 Jena

BIOLOGY SECTION * 89

CHEMISTRY SECTION * 90

INSTRUMENT TECHNOLOGY SECTION * 91

MATHEMATICS SECTION * 92

MEDICINE DEPARTMENT * 93

PHYSICS SECTION * 94

Hochschule für Landwirtschaft und Nahrungsgüterwirtschaft Bernburg* 　95

[Agriculture and Food Technology College]
Address:　Mitschurinstrasse 28, 435 Bernburg

Hochschule für Verkehrswesen 'Friedrich List'* 　96

[Friedrich List Transportation and Communication College]
Address:　Friedrich-List-Platz 1, 801 Dresden

HIGHWAY AND RAILWAY ENGINEERING SECTION* 　97

MATHEMATICS, COMPUTER TECHNOLOGY AND NATURAL SCIENCES SECTION* 　98

TRANSPORT CYBERNETICS SECTION* 　99

VEHICLE TECHNOLOGY SECTION* 　100

Humboldt-Universität zu Berlin* 　101

[Humboldt University of Berlin]
Address:　Unter den Linden 6, DDR-1086 Berlin
Telephone:　(02) 2030

ANIMAL HUSBANDRY AND VETERINARY MEDICINE SECTION* 　102

BIOLOGY SECTION* 　103

CHEMISTRY SECTION* 　104

ELECTRONICS SECTION* 　105

HORTICULTURE SECTION* 　106

MATHEMATICS SECTION* 　107

MEDICINE SECTION* 　108

NUTRITION AND FOOD TECHNOLOGY SECTION* 　109

PHYSICS SECTION* 　110

PLANT PRODUCTION SECTION* 　111

Karl-Marx-Universität Leipzig* 　112

[Karl-Marx University Leipzig]
Address:　Karl-Marx Plantz, 701 Leipzig

ANIMAL HUSBANDRY AND VETERINARY MEDICINE SECTION* 　113

BIOLOGY SECTION* 　114

CHEMISTRY SECTION* 　115

GEOPHYSICAL INSTITUTE* 　116

Collm Geophysical Observatory* 　117

Address:　7261 Collm
Telephone:　(0405) 2120
Director:　Dr Rudolf Schminder
Activities:　Ground-based high-atmosphere wind observations in the upper mesopause region (90-100 km) over central Europe deduced from ionospheric drift measurements in the low frequency range.

Martin-Luther-Universität Halle-Wittenberg*   121

[Martin-Luther University of Halle-Wittenberg]
Address: Universitätsplatz 10, DDR-4020 Halle

Medizinische Akademie 'Carl Gustav Carus' Dresden*   129

[Carl Gustav Carus Medical Academy of Dresden]
Address: Fetscherstrasse 74, DDR-8019 Dresden
Rector: Professor Dr H.G. Knoch

Medizinische Akademie Erfurt*   132

[Medical Academy, Erfurt]
Address: Nordhäuser Strasse 74, DDR-50 Erfurt
Rector: Professor Dr W. Usbeck

Medizinische Akademie Magdeburg*   133

[Medical Academy, Magdeburg]
Address: Leipziger Strasse 44, DDR-3014 Magdeburg
Rector: Professor Dr R.D. Koch

Nationales Komitee der DDR zur Bekämpfung und Erforschung der Poliomyelitis und Verwandter Erkrankungen   134

[National Committee for Research on Poliomyelitis and Similar Diseases]
Address: Britzer Strasse 1-3, DDR-1190 Berlin
Secretary: Dr Barbara Böthig
Activities: Scientific problems of control and surveillance of poliomyelitis, enteroviruses, measles and mumps - especially vaccinations; aetiology of viral diseases of the central nervous system.

Sächsische Akademie der Wissenschaften zu Leipzig   135

– SAW
[Saxon Academy of Sciences at Leipzig]
Address: Goethestrasse 3-5, DDR-7010 Leipzig
Telephone: (041) 292886
President: Professor Dr Werner Bahner
Vice-President: Professor Dr Edgar Lehmann
Graduate research staff: 60
Activities: The Academy is a research association without its own institutes: in the Mathematics and Natural Sciences section, research work is conducted at the Universities of Jena, Dresden, Leipzig, Freiberg and, Halle.
Contract work: No
Publications: Jahrbuch der Sächsische Akademie der Wissenschaften; Berichte der Sächsische Akademie der Wissenschaften; Abhandlungen der Sächsische Akademie der Wissenschaften.

MATHEMATICS AND NATURAL SCIENCES SECTION 136

Secretary: Professor Dr Herbert Beckert

Commission for Special Environmental Problems 137

Director: Professor Dr Klaus Dörter

WORKING GROUP FOR INVESTIGATION OF THE OPERATION OF NEUROHORMONES 138

Address: Erbertstrasse 1, DDR-6900 Jena
Telephone: (078) 27122
Head: Professor Dr Manfred Gersch
Activities: Biochemical investigation of hormonal effects on cell metabolism, particularly on the promotion and inhibition of cancer.

WORKING GROUP FOR INVESTIGATION OF THE STRUCTURAL AND ENVIRONMENTAL PROBLEMS OF WATER 139

Address: Bernhard-von-Cotta-Strasse 4, DDR-9200 Freiberg, Sachsen
Telephone: 512 592
Heads: Professor Dr Wolfgang Bucheim, Professor Dr Herbert Jordan, Professor Dr Adolf Watznauer
Activities: Physico-chemical investigation of water, particularly of therapeutically-useful waters of the springs in the south of the German DR; geoscientific and biochemical studies of the environmental influences of water.

WORKING GROUP FOR THE INVESTIGATION OF NATURAL HABITATS AND LOCAL ENVIRONMENT 140

Address: Zellescher Weg 19, DDR-8027 Dresden
Telephone: (051) 46 33 275 and 49 33 87
Head: Professor Dr Ernst Neef
Activities: Monitoring and recording the Dresden countryside, including ecological, botanical, hydrological, and economic surverys for landscape planning.

WORKING GROUP FOR THE INVESTIGATION OF THE EFFECTS OF CARNITINE ON THE PHYSIOLOGICAL AND PATHOLOGICAL METABOLISM, AND ON TUMOUR METABOLISM 141

Address: Liebigstrasse 16, DDR-7010 Leipzig
Telephone: (041) 7164479
Head: Professor Dr Erich Strack
Activities: Research into the chemical and biological compositon and properties of carnitine, and its therapeutic effects on animal metabolism.

WORKING GROUP FOR THE LIMNOLOGY OF RESERVOIRS 142

Address: Zellescher Weg 40, DDR-8027 Dresden
Telephone: (051) 46 34 946
Head: Professor Dr Dietrich Uhlmann
Activities: Chemical, biochemical and zoological study of freshwaters, in particular reservoirs; investigation of phytoplankton ecology.

WORKING GROUP FOR THE PSYCHOLOGICAL INVESTIGATION OF MANAGEMENT ACTIVITY AS AN ENVIRONMENTAL HEALTH FACTOR ON THE PSYCHOLOGICAL STABILITY OF THE WORKER 143

Address: Universitätshochhaus, Schiller-Strasse, DDR-6900 Jena
Telephone: (078) 83 48 43
Head: Professor Dr Hans Hiebsch
Activities: Investigation of the possible determining factors of psychological health and social wellbeing of the worker in socialist industry, as they are influenced by different styles of management. This project is being carried out in conjunction with the Psychology Department of the Friedrich-Schille University, Jena.

WORKING GROUP FOR THE PURIFICATION OF WASTE WATER BY MEANS OF ABSORPTION 144

Address: Schlossberg 2, DDR-4020 Halle Saale
Telephone: (046) 21 191
Head: Professor Dr Friedrich Wolf
Activities: Research into the purification of waste waters by non-ionic copolymerization under gas pressure and by ionic exchange with acidic and alkaline cleansing agents, and investigation of high and low pressure purification methods.

WORKING GROUP ON THE INFLUENCES ON ENZYMATIC BREAKDOWN OF EGG WHITE BY ENVIRONMENTAL AGENCIES 145

Address: Hollystrasse 1, DDR-4020 Saale, Sachsen
Telephone: (046) 29261
Heads: Professor Dr Horst Hanson, Professor Dr Harald Aurich

Technische Hochschule 'Carl Schorlemmer' Leuna-Merseburg* 146

[Carl Schorlemmer Technical University Leuna-Merseburg]
Address: Geusaer Strasse, 42 Merseburg

CHEMICAL ENGINEERING SECTION* 147

MATERIALS ENGINEERING SECTION* 148

MATHEMATICS AND COMPUTER 149
SCIENCES SECTION*

PHYSICS SECTION* 150

PROCESS TECHNOLOGY SECTION* 151

Technische Hochschule 152
Ilmenau*

[Ilmenau Technical University]
Address: Postschliessfach 327, 63 Ilmenau

BASIC SCIENCES SECTION* 153

Activities: Mathematics, physics, chemistry, general
and theoretical electrical engineering.

LOW-VOLTAGE ENGINEERING 154
SECTION*

Activities: High-frequency engineering, microwave
technology, and electronics.

PRECISION MECHANICS AND 155
OPTICS SECTION*

PRODUCTION TECHNOLOGY 156
SECTION*

Activities: Materials sciences, production engineering
and mechanical engineering.

Technische Hochschule 157
Karl-Marx-Stadt*

[Karl-Marx-Stadt Technical University]
Address: Strasse der Nationen 62, 90 Karl-Marx-Stadt

CHEMISTRY AND MATERIALS 158
TECHNOLOGY SECTION*

MACHINE AND COMPONENT 159
ENGINEERING SECTION*

MATHEMATICS SECTION* 160

METAL CUTTING AND INDUSTRIAL 161
METAL PROCESSING TECHNOLOGY
SECTION*

METAL PRODUCTION ENGINEERING 162
SECTION*

PHYSICS AND ELECTRONIC 163
ENGINEERING SECTION*

PROCESSING TECHNOLOGY 164
SECTION*

Technische Hochschule 165
Leipzig*

[Leipzig Technical University]
Address: Karl Leibknecht-Strasse 132, 703 Leipzig

AUTOMATION SECTION* 166

CONSTRUCTIONAL ENGINEERING 167
SECTION*

ELECTRICAL ENGINEERING SYSTEMS 168
SECTION*

MATHEMATICS AND COMPUTER 169
TECHNOLOGY SECTION*

Technische Hochschule 'Otto von Guericke' Magdeburg*   170

[Otto von Guericke Technical University, Magdeburg]
Address: Boleslaw-Bierut-Platz 5, 301 Magdeburg

COMPUTER TECHNOLOGY AND DATA PROCESSING SECTION*   171

MATHEMATICS AND PHYSICS SECTION*   172

MECHANICAL ENGINEERING SECTION*   173

Technische Universität Dresden*   174

[Dresden Technical University]
Address: Mommenstrasse 13, 8027 Dresden

AUTOMOTIVE, AGRICULTURAL AND TRANSPORT ENGINEERING SECTION*   175

BASIC MECHANICAL ENGINEERING SECTION*   176

CHEMISTRY SECTION*   177

CONSTRUCTION ENGINEERING SECTION*   178

ELECTRICAL ENGINEERING SECTION*   179

ELECTRONICS AND PRECISION APPARATUS ENGINEERING SECTION*   180

ENERGY TRANSFORMATION SECTION*   181

FORESTRY SECTION*   182

HYDRAULIC ENGINEERING SECTION*   183

MANUFACTURING AND PROCESSING SECTION*   184

MATHEMATICS SECTION*   185

PHYSICS SECTION*   186

Head: Professor Dr V. Schuricht

PRODUCTION TECHNIQUES AND MACHINE TOOLS SECTION*   187

SURVEYING AND CARTOGRAPHY SECTION*   188

Veb Carl Zeiss Jena*   189

Address: Carl-Zeiss-Strasse 1, DDR-69 Jena
Activities: Development and manufacture of microscopes, analytical instruments, medical instruments, and optical instruments.

VEB Wissenschaftlich-Technisches Zentrum der Holzverarbeitenden Industrie   190

[Scientific-technical Centre of the Woodworking Industry]
Address: Winckelmannstrasse 9, DDR-8010 Dresden
Research director: W. Jacobi
Activities: Furniture development; test techniques; production engineering; materials development; surface techniques; fundamental physical, chemical and biological research; information and documentation; standardization.

Zentralinstitut für Arbeitsmedizin der Deutschen Demokratischen Republik   201

[Central Institute for Occupational Medicine of the German Democratic Republic]
Address: Nöldnerstrasse 40-42, DDR-1134 Berlin
Affiliation: Ministry of Health
Director: Professor Dr Hans-Günther Häublein
Research director: W. Bachmann
Leader of scientific department: Dr Blau
Activities: Industrial hygiene; industrial toxicology; industrial hygiene standardization; industrial physiology; industrial psychology; industrial medicine; occupational diseases; occupational health service; industrial medical performance and functions' analysis.

GERMAN FEDERAL REPUBLIC

AEG Telefunken Aktiengesellschaft   1

Address: Theodor-Stern-Kai 1, D-6000 Frankfurt am Main 70
Telephone: (0611) 600 1
Telex: 411 076
Graduate research staff: about 4000
Annual expenditure: over £2m
Activities: AEG-Telefunken produces telecommunications technology, equipment such as modems and displays, and semiconductor components. Its subsidiaries Olympia, Telefunken, AEG-Kable, ATM Computer, and Telefonbau and Normalzeit produce office systems, consumer electronics, and cable, computer and switching technologies.

Research and development is conducted not only into individual products of the various sectors, but also into coordinated systems of components enabling new communication and information systems to be constructed. This research is intended for application in the following fields: in industrial production, from the supervision of materials flow to systems for fully-automated production; in the transport industry; in offices, for documentation and storage of speech, written text and data; in the home, for entertainment, information and monitoring of various household systems, and also for interchange of information with banks, public authorities, and shops.

Research is particularly concerned with the development of a digital communication network which can be used equally for picture, speech, data, and text transmission; and also with communication between user and machine, that is display terminals, and automatic writing and speech recognition.
Contract work: No

BERLIN RESEARCH INSTITUTE   2

Address: Holländerstrasse 31-34, D-1000 Berlin 51
Telephone: (030) 4501334
Telex: 1 81 748
Research director: Dr Ing W. Jentsch
Sections: Energy systems, Dr Ing J. Nestler; inverter drive systems, Dipl-Ing P. Grumbrecht; system engineering, Dipl-Ing P. Mehring
Graduate research staff: 40
Contract work: Yes

FRANKFURT RESEARCH INSTITUTE   3

Address: Goldsteinstrasse 235, D-6000 Frankfurt Niederrad
Telephone: (0611) 6679212
Telex: 414474
Research director: Dr F. Schneider
Sections: General physics, Dr H. Voigt; solid-state physics, Dr R. Zeyfang; electronics, Dr Feldmann
Graduate research staff: 46
Annual expenditure: over £2m
Contract work: No

ULM RESEARCH INSTITUTE   4

Address: Sedanstrasse 10, D-7900 Ulm Donau
Telephone: (0731) 192 3267
Telex: 7 12 723
Research director: Dr Stefan Maslowski
Graduate research staff: 100
Contract work: No

Agrarsoziale Gesellschaft eV

5

– ASG

[Agrarian Social Society]

Address: Kurze Geismarstrasse 23-25, Postfach 667, D-3400 Göttingen
Telephone: (0551) 59797/59778
Research director: Professor Dr Friedrich-Karl Riemann
Graduate research staff: 13
Annual expenditure: £51 000-500 000
Activities: Research into the affairs of rural communities, and infrastructure and the reorganization of rural communities; land settlement policy; social security of agricultural workers; labour research in agriculture.
Contract work: Yes
Publications: Schriftenreihe für ländliche Sozialfragen; ASG-Materialsammlung; ASG-Kleine Reihe; Rundbrief der Agrarsozialen Gesellschaft.

Akademie der Wissenschaften und der Literatur Mainz

6

[Mainz Academy of Sciences and Letters]

Address: 2 Geschwister-Scholl-Strasse, D-6500 Mainz 1
President: Professor Dr Heinrich Otten
Activities: The Academy has three major working groups: mathematics and natural sciences; humanities and social sciences; literature.

MATHEMATICS AND NATURAL SCIENCES DIVISION

7

Vice-President: Professor Dr Gerhard Thews

Commission for Biochemistry and Macromolecular Chemistry

8

Chairman Professor Dr H.H. Inhoffen
Members: Professor Dr F. Patat, Professor Dr H. Ringsdorf, Professor Dr K.G. Zimmer
Activities: Research on dicyano-cobyrinacid-heptamethylester (derivative of Vitamin B_{12}).

Commission for Biological Cybernetics

9

Chairman: Professor Dr M. Lindauer
Members: Professor Dr H. Hartmann, Professor Dr R. Jung, Professor Dr W. Nachtigall, Professor Dr W. Reichardt, Professor Dr G. Thews, Professor Dr R. Wehner, Professor Dr K. Wezler, Professor Dr R.K. Zahn
Activities: Perception mechanism of the honey bee for weak magnetic fields; daily variations of earth's magnetic field and gravitation as an external time indicator for bees; transfer of information through the sense of smell; generalization and invariant formation in the learning process of the honey bee; caste differentiation of the honey bee; terrestrial and astronomic navigation of insects.

Commission for Botanical Research

10

Chairman: Professor Dr W. Rauh
Members: Professor Dr P.S. Vogel, Professor Dr F. Weberling
Activities: Patterns of growth and vegetation elements; evolutionary shifts from attraction to camouflage in pollen-bearing flowers.

Commission for Earth Sciences

11

Chairman: Professor Dr W. Lauer
Members: Professor Dr J. Büdel, Professor Dr H.K. Erben, Professor Dr W. Rauh, Professor Dr E. Seibold, Professor Dr K.H. Wedepohl
Activities: Three-dimensional geography and landscape ecology of the earth; geochemistry of the earth's crust; marine geology; Holo-evolutionistic view of fossil and contemporary man, and problems of evolution theory; geobotanical studies; geography of the Pleistocene and Holocene periods; preglacial geomorphology of the Alps.

Commission for Gerontology

12

Chairman: Professor Dr J.W. Rohen
Members: Professor Dr E. Barany, Professor Dr H. Bredt, Professor Dr G. Dhom, Professor Dr G. Haberland, Professor Dr P. Schölmerich, Professor Dr B.L. Strehler, Professor Dr F. Thews, Professor Dr K. Wezler, Professor Dr R.K. Zahn
Activities: Research into age-dependent changes in protein biosynthesis; in vitro tests on age-dependent changes of glycosaminoglycan synthesis and the phagocytose activity of human fibroblasts and cells of the trabecular network of the primate eye; structural changes of the accommodation apparatus of the primate by ageing; medical experiments on blood-vessel changes.

Commission for Human Research   13

Chairman: Professor Dr G. Thews
Members: Professor Dr H. Bredt, Professor Dr A. Dabelow, Professor Dr G.L. Haberland, Professor Dr R. Jung, Professor Dr W. Lenz, Professor Dr D.W. Lübbers, Professor Dr J.W. Rohen, Professor Dr K. Wezler, Professor Dr R.K. Zahn
Activities: Analysis of pulmonary gas exchange; regulation of cerebral oxygen supply; cerebral blood flow regulation under the conditions of arterial hypoxia.

Commission for Mathematics and   14
Astronomy

Chairman: Professor Dr J. Ehlers
Members: Professor Dr F. Becker, Professor Dr D.M. Deuring, Professor Dr G.L. Hachenberg, Professor Dr O. Haupt, Professor Dr G. Ludwig

Commission for Molecular Biology   15

Chairman: Professor Dr R.K. Zahn
Members: Professor Dr H. Bredt, Professor Dr F. Patat, Professor Dr J.W. Rohen, Professor Dr K.G. Zimmer
Activities: DNA-confirmation in solution and on interfaces; effects of microbial products on nuclear DNA-synthesizing enzyme systems; the significance of cellular and herpes-virus polymerases for chemotherapy; DNA-replication complex; biological effects of low-level detergent pollution; detection of mutagen Xenobiotica in water samples; cell-cell reciprocation; aggregation of sponge cells.

Commission for Palaeobiological   16
Research

Chairman: Professor Dr H.K. Erben
Members: Professor Dr H. Bredt, Professor Dr C. Gregoire, Professor Dr F. Patat, Professor Dr J.W. Rohen, Professor Dr E. Seibold, Professor Dr K. Wezler
Activities: Palaeobiological ultrastructures; palaeobiological and isotopic studies of eggshells from a declining dinosaur species compared with eggshells from extant reptiles and birds; biorhythmic growth periods and their dependence on external environmental factors.

Commission for Technical Physics   17
Research

Chairman: Professor Dr G. Lautz
Members: Professor Dr H. Ehrenberg, Professor Dr O. Hachenberg, Professor Dr E. Justi, Professor Dr K. Lingenberg
Activities: Utilization of solar energy by water electrolysis and storage of electrolysis gases; optimization of high-duty hydrogen anodes for alkaline fuel cells; efficiency loss of terrestrial solar cells due to increase in their operating temperature through solar heating (Quasi-Carnot-Processes).

Commission for Zoology   18

Chairman: Professor Dr P. Ax
Members: Professor Dr T. Karling, Professor Dr M. Lindauer
Activities: Research on seabed microfauna (Galapagos project); biology of sand microfauna of the German North Sea coast and other coasts; ultrastructures of cells, tissues and elements of microorganisms of the sea sand.

Albert-Ludwigs-Universität   19
Freiburg im Breisgau

[Freiburg in Breisgau University]
Address: Werthmannplatz, D-7800 Freiburg im Breisgau
Rector: Professor Dr Bernhard Stoeckle

FACULTY OF BIOLOGY   20

Dean: Professor Dr Günter Feix

Biology Institute I (Zoology)   21

Address: Katharinenstrasse 20, D-7800 Freiburg im Breisgau
Directors: Professor Dr Bernhard Hassenstein, Professor Dr Günther Osche, Professor Dr Klaus Sander

Biology Institute II   22

Address: Schänzlestrasse 1, D-7800 Freiburg im Breisgau
Director: Professor Dr Peter Schopfer

BOTANICAL GARDEN   23
Head: Professor Dr Dieter Vogellehner

BOTANY DEPARTMENT   24
Head: Professor Dr H. Mohr

CELL BIOLOGY DEPARTMENT   25
Head: Professor Dr P. Sitte

EARTH BOTANY DEPARTMENT   26
Head: Professor Dr Ottilie Wilmanns

Geography Institute II   47

Address: Werderring 4, D-7800 Freiburg im Breisgau
Directors: Professor Dr Wolf-Dieter Sick, Professor Dr
Walther Manshard, Professor Dr Rudolf Ullmann,
Professor Dr Jörg Stedelbauer

Geology and Palaeontology Institute   48

Address: Albertstrasse 236, D-7800 Freiburg im
Breisgau
Director: Professor Dr Reinhard Pflug

Meteorology Institute   49

Address: Werderring 10, D-7800 Freiburg im Breisgau
Director: Professor Dr Albrecht Kessler

Mineralogy Institute   50

Address: Albertstrasse 236, D-7800 Freiburg im
Breisgau
Director: Professor Dr Wolfhard Wimmenauer

FACULTY OF FORESTRY   51

Dean: Professor Dr Erwin Niesslein

Environmental Management Institute   52

Address: Bertoldstrasse 17, D-7800 Freiburg im
Breisgau
Director: Professor Dr Hansjörg Steinlin

Forest Biology and Wood Biology   53
Institute

Address: Bertoldstrasse 17, D-7800 Freiburg im
Breisgau
Director: Professor Dr Helmut J. Braun

Forest Biometry Department   54

Address: Holstmarktplatz 6, D-7800 Freiburg im
Breisgau
Director: Professor Dr Dieter R. Pelz

Forest Labour Research Institute   55

Address: Bertoldstrasse 17, D-7800 Freiburg im
Breisgau
Director: Professor Dr Rolf Grammel

Forest Organization and Management   56
Institute

Address: Bertoldstrasse 17, D-7800 Freiburg im
Breisgau
Director: Professor Dr Gerhard Speidel

Forest Production Institute   57

Address: Bertoldstrasse 17, D-7800 Freiburg im
Breisgau
Director: Professor Dr Peter Abetz

Forest Wood Industry Policy Institute   58

Address: Bertoldstrasse 17, D-7800 Freiburg im
Breisgau
Director: Professor Dr Erwin Niesslein

MARKET RESEARCH DEPARTMENT   59

Forest Zoology Institute   60

Address: Bertoldstrasse 17, D-7800 Freiburg im
Breisgau
Director: Professor Dr Jean Pierre Vité

Forestry Institute   61

Address: Bertoldstrasse 17, D-7800 Freiburg im
Breisgau
Director: Professor Dr Helmut Schmidt-Vogt

Research Station for Landscape   62
Ecology

Address: Belfortstrasse 18-20, D-7800 Freiburg im
Breisgau
Director: Professor Dr Jörg Barner

Soil Science Institute   63

Address: Bertoldstrasse 17, D-7800 Freiburg im
Breisgau
Director: Professor Dr Heinz Zottl

Wood Pathology and Wood Protection   64
Department

Address: Holzmarktplatz 4, D-7800 Freiburg im
Breisgau
Head: Professor Dr Horst Courtois

FACULTY OF MATHEMATICS   65

Dean: Professor Dr Otto H. Kegel

Applied Mathematics Institute 66

Address: Hermann-Herder-Strasse 10, D-7800 Freiburg im Breisgau
Directors: Professor Dr Karl Nickel, Professor Dr Joachim Nitsche

Mathematical Stochastics Institute 67

Address: Hermann-Herder-Strasse 10, D-7800 Freiburg im Breisgau
Director: Professor Dr Hermann Witting

Mathematics Institute 68

Address: Albertstrasse 236, D-7800 Freiburg im Breisgau
Directors: Professor Dr Helmut Klingen, Professor Dr Martin Barner, Professor Dr Otto H. Kegel, Professor Dr Rolf Schneider, Professor Dr Jürgen Spilkes, Professor Dr Rolf Wallisser, Professor Dr Dieter Wolke

ELEMENTARY MATHEMATICS DEPARTMENT 69

Head: Professor Dr Friedrich Flohr

MATHEMATICAL LOGIC DEPARTMENT 70

Head: Professor Dr Ronald B. Jensen

FACULTY OF MEDICINE 71

Dean: Professor Dr med Eduard Seidler

Clinical Medicine 72

ANAESTHESIOLOGY INSTITUTE 73

Address: Hugstetter Strasse 55, D-7800 Freiburg im Breisgau
Director: Professor Dr Kurt Wiemers

CHILDREN'S CLINIC 74

Address: Mathildenstrasse 1, D-7800 Freiburg im Breisgau
Directors: Professor Dr Wilhelm Künzer, Professor Dr Robert Beckmann

CLINICAL RADIOLOGY INSTITUTE 75

Address: Hugstetter Strasse 55, D-7800 Freiburg im Breisgau
Directors: Professor Dr med Werner Wenz, Professor Dr Dr Michael Kammenmacher, Professor Dr Günter Hoffmann

DENTAL AND JAW CLINIC 76

Address: Hugstetter Strasse 55, D-7800 Freiburg im Breisgau
Directors: Professor Dr Dr Werner Reither, Professor Dr Wilfried Schilli, Professor Dr Thomas Rakosi, Professor Dr Dr Wolfgang Fötze

DERMATOLOGY CLINIC 77

Address: Hauptstrasse 7, D-7800 Freiburg im Breisgau
Director: Professor Dr Erwin Schöpf

EAR, NOSE AND THROAT CLINIC 78

Address: Killianstrasse (Hochhaus), D-7800 Freiburg im Breisgau
Director: Professor Dr Chlodwig Beck

EYE CLINIC 79

Address: Killianstrasse (Hochhaus), D-7800 Freiburg im Breisgau
Directors: Professor Dr Günter Meckensen, Professor Dr Güntram Kommebele

MEDICAL CLINIC 80

Address: Hugstetter Strasse 55, D-7800 Freiburg im Breisgau
Directors: Professor Wolfgang Gerok, Professor Georg-Wilhelm Löhr, Professor Dr Lothar Kerp, Professor Dr Hansjörg Jüst, Professor Dr Heinrich Matthys, Professor Dr Peter Schollmeyer, Professor Dr Dieter Maas, Professor Dr Josef Keul

NEUROSURGERY CLINIC 81

Address: Hugstetter Strasse 55, D-7800 Freiburg im Breisgau
Directors: Professor Dr Wolfgang Seeger, Professor Dr Fritz Mundinger

OBSTETRICS AND GYNAECOLOGY CLINIC 82

Address: Hugstetter Strasse 55, D-7800 Freiburg im Breisgau
Directors: Professor Dr Hans-G. Hillemanns, Professor Dr Albrecht Pfleiderer, Professor Dr Meinert Breckwoldt, Professor Dr Hans-Adolf Ladner

PNEUMONOLOGY DEPARTMENT 83

Address: Hugstetter Strasse 55, D-7800 Freiburg im Breisgau
Telephone: (0761) 2703806
Research director: Professor Dr med H. Matthys
Graduate research staff: 4
Annual expenditure: £51 000-500 000
Activities: Data processing and biomedical engineering in clinical pneumonology and nuclear medicine.
Contract work: Yes

PSYCHIATRY AND NERVE CLINIC   84
Address: Hauptstrasse 5, D-7800 Freiburg im Breisgau
Director: Professor Dr Rudolf Degkwitz
Senior staff: Professor Dr Johannes Cremerius, Professor Dr Peter Strunk

SURGICAL CLINIC   85
Address: Hugstetter Strasse 55, D-7800 Freiburg im Breisgau
Director: Professor Dr Eduard Ferthmann
Senior staff: Professor Dr Eugen Kuner, Professor Dr Volker Schlosser, Professor Dr Wilhelm Wolfart, Professor Dr Horst Sommerkamp, Professor Dr Achim Reichelt

THERAPEUTIC GYMNASTIC SCHOOL   86
OF THE UNIVERSITY CLINIC
Address: Fehrenbachallee 8, D-7800 Freiburg im Breisgau
Head: Professor Dr Alexander Puff

Theoretical Medicine   87

ANATOMY INSTITUTE FREIBURG   88
Address: Albertstrasse 17, D-7800 Freiburg im Breisgau
Directors: Professor Dr Jochen Staubesand, Professor Dr Dietrich Wittekind, Professor Dr Dieter Sasse

BALNEOLOGY AND CLIMATE   89
PHYSIOLOGY INSTITUTE
Address: Hermann-Herder-Strasse 7, D-7800 Freiburg im Breisgau
Director: Professor Dr med Eberhard Bassenge

BIOCHEMISTRY INSTITUTE   90
Address: Hermann-Herder-Strasse 7, D-7800 Freiburg im Breisgau
Directors: Professor Dr Karl Decker, Professor Dr Helmut Holzer

BIOPHYSICS AND RADIOBIOLOGY   91
INSTITUTE
Address: Albertstrasse 23, D-7800 Freiburg im Breisgau
Director: Professor Dr Werner Kreutz

FORENSIC MEDICINE INSTITUTE   92
Address: Albertstrasse 9, D-7800 Freiburg im Breisgau
Director: Professor Dr med Balduin Forster

HISTORY OF MEDICINE INSTITUTE   93
Address: Stefan-Meier-Strasse 26, D-7800 Freiburg im Breisgau
Director: Professor Dr med Eduard Seidler

HUMAN GENETICS AND   94
ANTHROPOLOGY INSTITUTE
Address: Albertstrasse 11, D-7800 Freiburg im Breisgau
Director: Professor Dr med Ulrich Wolf

HYGIENE INSTITUTE   95
Address: Hermann-Herder-Strasse 11, D-7800 Freiburg im Breisgau
Directors: Professor Dr med Arnold Vogt, Professor Dr Wolfgang Bredt, Professor Dr Konrad Hummel, Professor Dr Harald zur Hausen

IMMUNOBIOLOGY INSTITUTE   96
Address: Stefan-Meier-Strasse 8, D-7800 Freiburg im Breisgau
Director: Professor Dr Dr Sabine Freifrau von Kleist

MEDICAL PSYCHOLOGY INSTITUTE   97
Address: Stefan-Meier-Strasse 17, D-7800 Freiburg im Breisgau
Director: Professor Dr med Sebastian Goeppert

MEDICAL SOCIOLOGY INSTITUTE   98
Address: Stefan-Meier-Strasse 17, D-7800 Freiburg im Breisgau
Director: Professor Dr Jürgen von Troschke

MEDICAL STATISTICS AND   99
DOCUMENTATION INSTITUTE
Address: Stefan-Meier-Strasse 26, D-7800 Freiburg im Breisgau
Director: Professor Dr Dr Edward Walter

PATHOLOGY INSTITUTE (LUDWIG-   100
ASCHOFF-HANS)
Address: Albertstrasse 19, D-7800 Freiburg im Breisgau
Directors: Professor Dr med Walter Sandritter, Professor Dr Wolfgang Gehlert, Professor Dr Paul Kleihues, Professor Dr Otto von Deimling

PHARMACOLOGY INSTITUTE   101
Address: Katharinenstrasse 29, D-7800 Freiburg im Breisgau
Directors: Professor Dr Georg Hertting, Professor Dr Klaus Starke

PHYSIOLOGICAL INSTITUTE   102
Address: Hermann-Herder-Strasse 7, D-7800 Freiburg im Breisgau
Directors: Professor Dr Albrecht Fleckenstein, Professor Dr Hermann Antoni

FACULTY OF PHYSICS 103

Address: Hermann-Herder-Strasse 3, D-7800 Freiburg im Breisgau
Dean: Professor Dr Klaus Pohlmeyer
Directors: Professor Dr John Stuart Briggs, Professor Dr Josef Hohnerkamp, Professor Dr Hartmann Römer, Professor Dr Konradin Westpfahl, Professor Dr Andreas Barnberger, Professor Dr Rüdiger Brems, Professor Dr Hellmut Haberland, Professor Dr Volker Kempter, Professor Dr Hartmut Röppke, Professor Dr Hans Schmitt, Professor Dr Werner Mehlhorn, Professor Dr Otto Osberghans, Professor Dr Helmut G. Reik, Professor Dr Erwin Rössle, Professor Dr Kay Runge, Professor Dr Christoph Schlier, Professor Dr Hans-Erhart Stier

Alexander von Humboldt Stiftung 104

[Alexander von Humboldt Foundation]
Address: Schillerstrasse 12, D-5300 Bonn 2 (Bad Godesberg)
President: Professor Dr Wolfgang Paul
Secretary General: Dr Heinrich Pfeiffer
Activities: The Humboldt Foundation offers post-doctoral research fellowships to scholars of foreign nationality up to the age of forty years, to carry out research projects of their own choice in the Federal Republic of Germany for a period of six months to two years.

Alfred-Wegener-Institut für Polarforschung 105

[Alfred Wegener Institute for Polar Research]
Address: Columbuszentrum, Bürgermeister-Smidt-Strasse 20, D-2850 Bremerhaven
Parent body: Bundesministerium für Forschung und Technologie
Activities: The Alfred Wegener Institute was established in 1980 as part of the Antarctic Research Programme of the Federal Republic of Germany, a large-scale programme sponsored jointly by various federal and regional ministries, the German Research Society, the universities, institutes of federal and regional government, the Max Planck Society, and German industry. With a budget of approximately DM380m for the period 1979-83, the programme provides for the construction of a German research station in Antarctica, the building of a polar research ship, the foundation of the Alfred Wegener Institute at Bremerhaven, and an extensive programme of field research.

The research programme will cover the following areas: biological sciences, including particular study of the polar food chain and the interaction between the supplies of krill and phytoplankton, as well as the biochemical bases of cold adaptation; geodesy, cartography and remote sensing; geosciences, including tectonics of the Eastern Antarctic shield and the Western Antarctic mountains; glaciology, including detailed analysis of ice core and sediments as palaeoclimatological evidence, and chemistry of ice masses and their place in the world CO_2 system; meteorology and oceanography, including research into the dynamics of the troposphere, the ice-water balance of the Weddell Sea, the circumpolar current system, trace gas behaviour, heavy metal content of polar waters, and the formation and spread of bottom waters; upper atmosphere and extraterrestrial physics, including study of micrometeorites and cosmic dust, plasma processes in the magnetosphere, and low frequency radio emissions and terrestrial magnetic pulsations of the polar regions; polar engineering and shipbuilding technology.

The functions of the Alfred Wegener Institute consist of logistical coordination and support for the above-mentioned programmes, and analysis and evaluation of data gathered in the Antarctic.

Annawerk Keramische Betriebe GmbH 106

Address: Postfach 1144, D-8633 Rödental
Telephone: (09563) 911
Telex: 06 63226

CERANOX DIVISION 107

Research director: Professor Dr Ernst Guegel
Senior staff: Dipl Ing W. Engel, Dr G. Leimer, Dipl Ing D. Steinmann
Graduate research staff: 5
Annual expenditure: £501 000-2m
Activities: Ceramics research, particularly on silicon nitride and silicon carbide in all known dense and porous forms, in the following areas: mechanical properties (bending, strength, elasticity, resistance to wear, creep, thermal fatigue, thermal shock behaviour, duration of life, critical stress) and the correlation between these properties; manufacturing properties (the results of fabrication, extrusion, casting, pressing, hot pressing, machining, shaping methods, grinding, sintering); insulating and thermal properties; surface studies; and resistance to corrosion.

The objective of this research is the development of ceramic materials of higher efficiency for application in the field of high-temperature engineering, for example,

gas turbine and conventional automotive engines; to decrease wear and abrasion in sliding seals; and for other applications in the chemical, metallurgical, and electrical industries.
Contract work: No

Aral Aktiengesellschaft   108

Address: Querenburger Strasse 46, D-4630 Bochum 1
Telephone: (0234) 315 2232
Telex: 825841 08H
Research director: Dipl-Ing G.H. Seidel
Sections: Testing and development, Dr Dipl chem H. Gondermann
Graduate research staff: 11
Activities: Research into fuels and lubricants for automotive and industrial application.
Facilities: Chemical laboratory; engine test benches; climatized chassis dynamometer.
Contract work: Yes

Arbeitsgemeinschaft   109
Industrieller
Forschungsvereinigungen
eV

– AIF
[Working Party of Industrial Research Associations]
Address: 23 Bayenthalguertel, D-5000 Köln 51
Telephone: (0221) 37 20 91
Telex: 8881101
President: C.-O. Bauer
Managing Director: Dr Ing H. Klein
Activities: AIF is an organization of private trade and industry for the promotion of research and development. It represents the interests of the industrial research associations and at the same time looks after the interests of the smaller and medium-sized companies carrying out research and development. It furthers research for the Federal Government and is an agent for the Foundation for Promoting Research for Trade and Industry.
At present 87 research associations are members of the AIF from 32 different industries with 63 research institutes dedicated to particular technologies. There are a further 150 institutes each year which carry out joint research programmes with AIF. Separate entries for active research associations will be found elsewhere in this chapter.
In 1980 the total expenditure was about DM500m with 4821 industrial companies engaged in research projects.

Arbeitsgemeinschaft   110
Versuchsreaktor GmbH

– AVR
Address: 105 Luisenstrasse, Postfach 14 11, D-4000 Düsseldorf
Telephone: (0211) 821 4490
Telex: 08582907 c/o Stadtwerke Düsseldorf
Research director: Dr rer nat Chrysanth Marnet
Departments: Research and experimental, Günther Ivens; Technical, Ing Egon Ziermann
Graduate research staff: 30
Annual expenditure: over £2m
Activities: AVR is the erector and operator of a high-temperature experimental nuclear power station (15 MWe, 950°C gas outlet temperature), characterized by a pebble bed core consisting of spherical fuel elements. Scientific, technical, and economic knowledge and experience will be gained in cooperation with the research centre (Kernforschungsanlage), universities, and the industry, for the erection and operation of a commercially sized high-temperature reactor. Main activities in the field of high-temperature technology are: fuel element-tests and -behaviour, fission product release; test of components.
Contract work: No

Astronomisches Rechen-   111
Institut *

[Astronomical Institute]
Address: Mönchhofstrasse 12-14, D-6900 Heidelberg 1
Telephone: (06221) 49026
Activities: Fundamental astronomical constants; fundamental astrometry; dynamics of the planetary system; kinematics and dynamics of stellar systems near stars.
Publications: Astronomy and Astrophysics Abstracts, annual.

Baden-Württembergische   112
Forstliche Versuchs- und
Forschungsanstalt

[Baden-Württemberg Forestry Research Centre]
Address: Sternwaldstrasse 16, D-7800 Freiburg-im-Breisgau 1
Parent body: Bundesministerium für Ernährung, Landwirtschaft, Umwelt und Forsten, Baden-Württemberg
Research director: Professor Dr Hans-Ulrich Moosmayer

Activities: Botany; forestry vegetation; soil research; fertilization; phytopathology; biometry; forest influences and water management.

BASF Aktiengesellschaft   113

Address: D-6700 Ludwigshafen
Telephone: (0621) 60-1
Telex: 464811 basf d
President: Bernhard Timm
Chairman of the Board: Matthias Seefelder
Research Director: Professor Dr-Ing Horst Pommer
Activities: BASF has four scientific laboratories at Ludwigshafen: the Main Laboratory (organic intermediates, fine chemicals, bioactive agents (for pharmaceuticals and for plant protection and pest control), vitamins, and inorganic chemistry); the Ammonia Laboratory (petrochemistry, auxiliaries, organic intermediates, catalysts, and chemical engineering); the Plastics Laboratory (macromolecular science); and the Dye Research Laboratory (dyes and pigments). To these laboratories are affiliated two large analytical laboratories and a measuring and testing laboratory. Medical and biological laboratories are responsible for the pharmacological and toxicological testing. In addition, the various production departments have their own research facilities for development connected more directly with their own work. Apart from this, most of the subsidiary and associated companies carry out their own research activities connected with their special areas, particularly those closely related to marketing.

Battelle-Institut eV   114

Address: Am Römerhof 35, Postbus 900160, D-6000 Frankfurt am Main 90
Telephone: (0611) 79080
Telex: 0411966 biffm
Affiliation: Battelle Memorial Institute, Columbus, Ohio, USA
Managing director: Dr Horst Haeske
Director, research and technology: Dr Gerd Sandstede
Graduate research staff: 400
Annual expenditure: over £2m
Activities: Materials behaviour - acoustic emission analysis, mechanical properties, reliability, corrosion; materials engineering - manufacturing processes, substitutes for dangerous and strategic materials, energy saving; ceramics - hot isostatic pressing, high-temperature materials; building materials - composite materials, asbestos and substitutes; recycling - waste treatment for recycling and deposition; surface technology - vapour deposition, galvano-techniques, laser treatment, plating,

polymers, adhesive properties, plasma and flame spraying; solid-state physics - photovoltaic solar cells, electrical, thermal, optical and insulating properties; biomaterials - polymers, ceramics, composites.
Note: Battelle Frankfurt operates as a contracting research institute with industrial and governmental sponsors. The work includes specialized activities in the fields of nuclear, military, space, medical and industrial research.
Facilities: Laboratories equipped for materials behaviour testing (including experiments with animals); a mobile laboratory for acoustic emission analysis and analytical chemistry; high-power lasers; test facilities for explosive impact.
Publications: Battelle Today (worldwide); *Battelle aktuel* (Germany); annual report.

CHEMISTRY AND BIOLOGY   115
DEPARTMENT

Head: Dr R. Reiner
Sections: Applied chemistry, Dr W. Kruger; process engineering, W. Schuster; spectroscopy and analytical chemistry, Dr D. Pruggmayer; toxicology, Dr R. Reiner, acting; applied biology, Dr H. Puchinger
Activities: Fields of capability include applied chemistry, including polymer chemistry and membrane technology, biochemistry and medical engineering, organic synthesis; process engineering, including process and product development, and process and product research; spectroscopy and analytical chemistry, including active principal determination and trace analysis, physical chemistry, and photochemistry; toxicology, including pharmacokinetics, physiology, endoprosthetics; applied biology, including microbiology and biotechnology, medical engineering, ecology.

ECONOMICS AND SOCIAL SCIENCES   116
DEPARTMENT

Head: Dr B. Ante
Sections: Industrial economics, B. Weidlich; business planning, Dr M. Geschka; technical economics, Dr B. Pilz; environmental and transportation policy analysis, Dr G. Krampe; social sciences, Dr J. Scharioth
Activities: Fields of capability include industrial economics, including construction, energy economics, capital goods marketing; business planning, including innovative planning, banking research, strategic corporate planning; technical economics, including econometrics, infrastructure planning, planning information systems, raw materials and mining, labour market research; environmental and transportation policy analysis, including urban and transportation research; environmental planning, early warning systems for corporate planning; social sciences, includ-

ing social assessment of new technologies, communication and social behaviour, social and labour market policy.

ENERGY AND TRANSPORTATION SYSTEMS DEPARTMENT 117

Head: B. Rüdiger
Sections: Thermal engineering, Dr J. Spitzer; experimental facilities, B. Mölzer; automotive engineering, Dr K.-J. Melzer
Activities: Fields of capability include thermal engineering, including safety of nuclear plants, reactor technology, energy conservation, fluid-dynamic experiments, fluidmechanic computer codes; experimental facilities, including experimental techniques, requisition and processing of process data, process control, transducer technology; automotive engineering, including drive systems and vehicle components, vehicle systems, transportation and operating systems, safety and accident research, civil engineering.

INFORMATION PROCESSING DEPARTMENT 118

Head: H. Herweling
Sections: Communications, Dr K. Schwandtner; applied computer sciences, Dr A. Braig; technical computer sciences, G. Mörler; electronics, P. Kauschka
Activities: Fields of capability include communications, including communications systems, communications technology, image processing; applied computer sciences, including software engineering, data base systems, techno-scientific data processing applications; technical computer sciences, including computer-aided automation, operating software, computer graphics; electronics, including electronic systems, microelectronics applications, and equipment for position-finding and navigation.

MATERIALS TECHNOLOGY DEPARTMENT 119

Head: Dr W. Dupold
Sections: Materials behaviour, Dr J. Eisenblätter; materials engineering, Dr G. Walter; physical engineering, Dr W. Geiger; ceramic and building materials, U. Hoffmann; materials structure and dynamics, Dr E. Schäpermeier
Activities: Fields of capability include materials behaviour, including evaluation of materials, metals and composites; materials engineering, including surface technology, measuring procedures and structural analysis; ceramic and building materials, including technical mineralogy, building materials and builders,

raw materials, waste disposal, recycling; materials and structure dynamics.

PHYSICS DEPARTMENT 120

Head: Dr H. Rabenhorst
Sections: Solid-state physics, Dr D. Bonnet; laser and optics, Professor Dr K. Gürs; technical physics, Dr M. Sellers; acoustics, Dr W. Burgtorf; techno-scientific studies, Dr B. Oberbacher
Activities: Fields of capability include solid-state physics, including thin film technology and solar cells, infrared detectors and systems, imaging and display, and information storage; laser and optics, including laser development, laser systems, laser spectroscopy and laser chemistry, coherence optics and general optics; technical physics, including electrostatics, surface treatment and coating, physical apparatus and methods, sensors, physicochemical processes; acoustics, including ultrasonic processes in technology, medicine and materials evaluation, primary and secondary noise control, and acoustic information and signal processing; techno-scientific studies, including risk analysis, theoretical physics, and atmospheric physics.

Bayer AG - Research and Development* 121

Address: 509 Leverkusen
Telephone: (0214) 301
Telex: 8510881
Head: Professor K.-H. Büchel
Activities: Basic chemical, physical and engineering research with over 1 000 graduates employed in research and development at the corporate research laboratories and the product divisions.

Bayerische Akademie der Wissenschaften 122

[Bavarian Academy of Sciences]
Address: Marstallplatz 8, D-8000 München 22
Telephone: (089) 228271
Telex: 5213550 dgfid
President: Professor Dr Herbert Franke
Graduate research staff: 160
Annual expenditure: over £2m
Activities: The Academy conducts long-term research programmes mainly in the field of humanities (special-

ized dictionaries and rare editions), but also in the field of natural and technical sciences.
Contract work: No
Publications: Yearbook.

COMMISSION FOR GERMAN GEODESY 123

German Geodetic Research Institute 124
Department I: Theoretical Geodesy

Research director: Dr Ing Christoph Reigber
Graduate research staff: 15
Annual expenditure: £51 000-500 000
Activities: The drawing-up and correction of continental and intercontinental triangulation networks and grids; stellar triangulation and azimuth-fixing using geodetic sounding balloons; observation and analysis of the tidal deformation of the earth's crust, and other geodynamic effects, at the Berchtesgaden Tectonic Station; geological models and plate tectonics; determination of global and regional gravitational fields; satellite geodesy, including trajectory analysis and experiments measuring gravitation fields and polar movement, at the Wettzell satellite station.

COMMISSION FOR GLACIOLOGY 125

Activities: The Commission has a complex research programme concentrating on water and mass balances in glaciers, particularly glaciers of the eastern Alps; two meteorological stations and the Flow Measurement Station on the Vernagtbach collect data for snow and rainfall and for melting ice and snow drainage, enabling the build-up of a complete climatological profile of an area of the Ötztal of 11.4 km^2 with 82 per cent ice cover. The Commission also publishes glacier maps, and acts as an advisor to the national Antarctic research programme.

COMMISSION FOR INFORMATION PROCESSING 126

Leibniz Computer Centre 127

Address: Barerstrasse, D-8000 München
Activities: The Leibniz Computer Centre is the principal computer installation serving both Munich universities, the Academy, and the Munich and Rosenheim technical colleges; it supplies programming and systems advice and technology, and provides data processing facilities for all areas of scientific research.

COMMISSION FOR INTERNATIONAL GEODESY 128

Activities: Astronomical and satellite geodesy, classical geodesy.
Publications: Astronomisch-geodätische Arbeiten.

COMMISSION FOR LOW-TEMPERATURE RESEARCH 129

Activities: Physical and physico-chemical experiments at low temperature and absolute zero.

Bayerische Forstliche Versuchs- und Forschungsanstalt 130

[Bavarian Forestry Research and Testing Station]
Address: Schellingstrasse 14, D-8000 München 40
Telephone: (089) 21801
Parent body: Bayerisches Staatsministerium für Ernährung, Landwirtschaft und Forsten
Director: Dr Hanskarl Goettling
Sections:
Habitat and countryside conservation, Dr Rudolf Hüser
Production and planning, Dr Eckhard Kennel
Wood utilization and technology, vacant
Forest policy and management, Peter Zang
Forest conservation and seed testing, Dr Günter Braun
Graduate research staff: 20
Annual expenditure: £500 000-2m
Activities: Conservation of forest land, including soil and habitat studies, climatology, biology, hydrology, forest vegetation, fertilization and nutrition studies, and investigations into the possible use of forest lands as sites for natural waste disposal; forest production and planning, including biometry, wildlife and hunting studies, and replanting methods; forest exploitation processes and technology; forestry and forest management; influences of pollution on plant and animal species; seed testing.
Contract work: Yes
Publications: Forschungsberichte der Forstliche Forschungsanstalt München.

Bayerische Julius-Maximilians-Universität Würzburg

131

[Julius-Maximilians University Würzburg]
Address: Sanderring 2, D-8700 Würzburg
Telephone: (0931) 311
Telex: 06 8 671
President: Professor Dr phil Theodor Berchem
Facilities: Computer centre.

FACULTY OF BIOLOGY

132

Address: Röntgenring 10, D-8700 Würzburg
Telephone: (0931) 31-649
Dean: Professor Dr Helmut Wilhelm Sauer

Botany and Pharmaceutical Biology Institute and Botanical Gardens

133

Address: Mittlerer Dallenbergweg 64, D-8700 Würzburg
Directors: Professor Dr Ulrich Heber, Professor Dr Otto Ludwig Lange, Professor Dr Franz-Christian Czygan

Genetics and Microbiology Institute

134

Address: Röntgenring 11, D-8700 Wurzburg
Directors: Professor Dr Martin Heisenberg, Professor Dr Werner Goebel

Zoology Institute

135

Address: Röntgenring 10-11, Koellikerstrasse 2, D-8700 Würzburg
Directors: Professor Dr Martin Lindauer, Professor Dr Helmut Wilhelm Sauer, Professor Dr Karl Eduard Linsenmair

FACULTY OF CHEMISTRY AND PHARMACY

136

Address: Am Hubland, D-8700 Würzburg
Telephone: (0931) 888 364/5
Dean: Professor Dr Ing Siegfried Hünig

Biochemistry Institute

137

Address: Röntgenring 11, D-8700 Würzburg
Director: Professor Dr Hans Joachim Gross

Inorganic Chemistry Institute

138

Directors: Professor Dr Max Schmidt, Professor Dr Helmut Werner

Organic Chemistry Institute

139

Directors: Professor Dr Siegfried Hünig, Professor Dr Waldemar Adam

Pharmacy and Food Chemistry Institute

140

Directors: Professor Dr Carl Heinz Brieskorn, Professor Dr Josef Riehl, Professor Dr Peter Schreier

Physical Chemistry Institute

141

Address: Marcusstrasse 9-11, D-8700 Würzburg
Directors: Professor Dr Friedemann Schneider, Professor Dr Walter Strohmeier

FACULTY OF GEOSCIENCES

142

Address: Pleicherwall 1, D-8700 Würzburg
Telephone: (0931) 31-561
Dean: Professor Dr Horst-Günter Wagner

Geography Institute

143

Address: Am Hubland, D-8700 Würzburg
Directors: Professor Dr Horst Hagedorn, Professor Dr Helmut Jäger, Professor Dr Horst-Günter Wagner, Professor Dr Dieter Böhn

Geology Institute

144

Director: Professor Dr Walter Schnitzer

Mineralogy and Crystallography Institute

145

Address: Am Hubland, D-8700 Würzburg
Directors: Professor Dr Siegfried Matthes, Professor Dr Willi Lindemann

Palaeontology Institute

146

Director: Professor Dr Klaus Sdzuy

FACULTY OF MATHEMATICS

147

Address: Am Hubland, D-8700 Würzburg
Telephone: (0931) 888 5021
Dean: Professor Dr Hans Wilhelm Knobloch

Applied Mathematics and Statistics Institute — 148

Directors: Professor Dr Waldemar Velte, Professor Dr Josef Stoer, Professor Dr Werner Uhlmann

Mathematics Institute — 149

Directors: Professor Dr Hermann Heineken, Professor Dr Hans Wilhelm Knobloch, Professor Dr Woldemar Barthel, Professor Dr Stephan Ruscheweyh, Professor Dr Hans-Joachim Vollrath

FACULTY OF MEDICINE — 150

Address: Josef-Schneider-Strasse 2, D-8700 Würzburg
Telephone: (0931) 201 3583
Dean: Professor Dr Karl-Heinrich Wulf

Anaesthesiology Institute — 151

Director: Professor Dr Karl Heinz Weis

Anatomy Institute — 152

Address: Koellikerstrasse 6, D-8700 Würzburg
Directors: Professor Dr Theodor Heinrich Schiebler, Professor Dr Johannes Lang

Child Psychiatry Clinic and Polyclinic — 153

Director: Professor Dr Gerhardt Nissen

Dermatology and Venereology Clinic and Outpatients Clinic — 154

Director: Professor Dr Helmut Röckl

Forensic Medicine Institute — 155

Address: Versbacher Strasse 3, D-8700 Würzburg
Director: Professor Dr Wolfgang Schwerd

Human Genetics Institute — 156

Address: Koellikerstrasse 2, D-8700 Würzburg
Director: Professor Dr Holger Höhn

Hygiene and Microbiology Institute — 157

Director: Professor Dr Heinz Seeliger

Medical Clinic — 158

Director: Professor Dr Kurt Kochsiek
Sections: Clinical experimental nephrology, Professor Dr August Heidland

X-RAY DIAGNOSIS DEPARTMENT — 159

Head: Professor Dr Heribert Braun

Medical Outpatients Clinic — 160

Address: Klinikstrasse 8, D-8700 Würzburg
Director: Professor Dr Hans Franke

Medical Radiation Institute — 161

Address: Versbacher Strasse 5, D-8700 Würzburg
Director: Professor Dr Albrecht M. Kellerer

Neurology Clinic and Outpatients Clinic — 162

Address: Josef-Schneider-Strasse 11, D-8700 Würzburg
Director: Professor Dr Hans-Georg Mertens

Neuroradiology Department of the Head Clinic — 163

Address: Josef-Schneider-Strasse 11, D-8700 Würzburg
Head: Professor Dr Maschallah Nadjmi

Neurosurgery Clinic and Outpatients Clinic — 164

Address: Kopfkliniken, Josef-Schneider-Strasse, D-8700 Würzburg
Director: Professor Dr Karl-August Bushe
Sections: Neuroendocrinology, Dr Eckard Halves
Paediatric neurosurgery, Dr Niels Sörensen
Stereotaxy and functional neurosurgery, Professor Dr Harm Spuler

Nuclear Medicine Department — 165

Head: Professor Dr Wilhelm Börner

Obstetrics and Gynaecology Clinic and Outpatients Clinic — 166

Address: Josef-Schneider-Strasse 4, D-8700 Würzburg
Director: Professor Dr Karl-Heinrich Wulf
Section: Gynaecological urology and nephrology, Professor Dr Horst Kremling

Ophthalmology Clinic and Outpatients Clinic — 167

Address: Josef-Schneider-Strasse 11, D-8700 Würzburg
Director: Professor Dr Wolfgang Leydhecker

Physics Institute 187

Directors: Professor Dr Max Scheer, Professor Dr Wolfgang Hink, Professor Dr Gottfried Landwehr, Professor Dr Hans-Georg Häfele, Professor Dr Helmut Steinwedel, Professor Dr Dieter Heuer

SPECIAL RESEARCH PROJECTS: 188

Note: Würzburg University conducts the following Special Research Projects, which are partly funded by federal and regional government through the Deutsche Forschungsgemeinschaft.

Cytological Bases of Experimental 189 Biology

Address: Versbacher Strasse 5, D-8700 Würzburg
Telephone: (0931) 201 3385
Director: Professor Dr Eberhard Wecker

Oral Cavity Biology 190

Address: Pleicherwall 2, D-8700 Würzburg
Telephone: (0931) 31-812
Director: Professor Dr Günther Siebert

Sensory Perception 191

Address: Zoologisches Institut, Röntgenring 10, D-8700 Würzburg
Director: Professor Dr Karl Eduard Linsenmair
Activities: Structure adaptation and mechanism.

Structural and Biological Analysis of 192 Macromolecules by X-Ray

Address: Am Hubland, D-8700 Wurzburg
Telephone: (0931) 888-1
Director: Dr Manfred Bühner

Bayerische Landesanstalt 193 für Fischerei

[Bavarian Research Centre for Fishery]
Address: Weilheimer Strasse 8a, D-8130 Starnberg
Telephone: (08151) 12674
Parent body: Bayerische Staatsministerium für Ernährung, Landwirtschaft und Forsten
Director: Dr Mathias von Lakowicz
Sections:
Trout culture, Dr H. Bayrle
Carp culture, Dr C. Proske
Lake and river fishery, M. Klein
Recreational fishing, F. Jahn

Graduate research staff: 7
Annual expenditure: £10 000-50 000
Activities: Management of lakes and rivers; population dynamics and fishing intensity of open waters; reproduction of fish; fish production in traditional and modern aquaculture systems.
Contract work: No
Publications: Annual report.

Bayerische Landesanstalt 194 fur Tierzucht

[Bavarian Research Centre for Animal Husbandry]
Address: Professor-Dürrwaechter-Platz 1, D-8011 Grub bei München
Telephone: (089) 9093-1
Parent body: Bayerisches Staatsministerium für Ernährung, Landwirtschaft und Forsten
Director: Professor Dr H. Bogner
Sections:
Cattle production, Dr A. Gottschalf
Pig production, Dr H. Blendl
Sheep production, Dr M. Burgkart
Poultry production, Dr R. Abelein
Animal nutrition, Dr P. Hofmann
Animal housing and stable construction, Dr G. Koller
Graduate research staff: 30
Annual expenditure: £51 000-500 000
Activities: Applied research, teaching and services, both at Grub and at seven other independent state-owned experimental farms, is conducted in the following areas: animal breeding, including performance value, evaluation of phenotypic and genetic parameters, breeding value and cross-breeding experiments; animal nutrition, including the influence of feedstuffs and feeding methods on animal health and food value, fattening processes, silage making and chemical fodder treatments; production techniques, including milking machines, halothane stress-testing, X-ray and ultrasonic veterinary techniques; animal housing, including open barns, slatted and perforated floors, and the effects of housing conditions on animal behaviour.
Contract work: No
Publications: Annual report.

Bayerische Landesanstalt für Weinbau und Gartenbau 195

[Bavarian Research Centre for Viticulture and Horticulture]
Address: Residenzplatz 3, D-8700 Würzburg 11
Telephone: (0931) 50701
Parent body: Bayerisches Staatsministerium für Ernährung, Landwirtschaft und Forsten
President: Dr Georg Scheuerpflug
Sections:
Horticulture, W. Müller-Haslach
Viticulture, K. Geiger
Oenology, Dr A. Schmitt
Vine breeding, Dr I. Benda
Graduate research staff: 16
Activities: Applied research in horticulture and viticulture.
Contract work: No

Bayerisches Geologisches Landesamt 196

[Bavarian Geological Survey]
Address: 28 Prinzregentenstrasse, D-8000 München 22
Telephone: (089) 2162-2532
President: Professor Dr Helmut Vidal
Graduate research staff: 45
Activities: Preparation and revision of the geological, hydrogeological and pedological maps of Bavaria; engineering geology; geophysics; geochemistry; earth sciences data bank.
Contract work: Yes
Publications: *Geologica Bavarica*, geological, hydrogeological and pedological maps of Bavaria and commentaries.

Bergbau-Berufsgenossenschaft 197

SILIKOSE-FORSCHUNGSINSTITUT 198
– SFI
[Silicosis Research Institute]
Address: Hunscheidtstrasse 12, D-4630 Bochum
Telephone: (0234) 316 1
Affiliation: Mutual Accident Insurance Association for the mining industry
General Director: Dr Brandts

Sections: Technical and natural sciences research, Dr Ing H.D. Bauer; medical and clinical research, Dr med W.T. Ulmer
Activities: Development of devices and methods for dust suppression; testing of dust suppression installations and methods in the mining industry; development and testing of dust measuring instruments; research on dust limit values and dust measuring methods; pneumoconiosis research, lung function tests, animal experiments.

Bergbau-Forschung GmbH – Forschungsinstitut des Steinkohlenbergbauvereins 199

[Brown Coal Mining Association Research Institute]
Address: Postfach 130 140, 61 Franz-Fischer-Weg, D-4300 Essen 13, Kray
Telephone: (0201) 1051
Telex: 857830 bergb d
Affiliation: Arbeitsgemeinschaft Industrieller Forschungsvereinigungen eV
Scientific Director: Professor Dr W. Peters
Scientific staff: 170
Activities: Dust control; prevention of pneumoconiosis; atmospheric conditions in mines; prevention of rock falling; traction methods; mining and conveyer techniques.

Biologische Anstalt Helgoland 200

[Biological Institute Heligoland]
Address: Palmaille 9, D-2000 Hamburg 50
Telephone: (040) 381601
Telex: 02 14 911
Parent body: Bundesministerium für Forschung und Technologie
Director: Professor O. Zinne
Assistant Director: Professor H.-P. Bulnheim
Sections: Marine Zoology Department, Professor H.-P. Bulnheim; Marine Botany Department, Dr K. Lüning; Biological Oceanography Department, Professor M. Gillbricht; Experimental Ecology Department, Dr G. Uhlig; Marine Microbiology Department, Dr W. Gunkel; Taxonomic Working Group, Dr K. Hülsemann
Graduate research staff: 42
Activities: Marine biological research, including studies of the essential structures, functions and dynamics of marine ecosystems; analysis of the responses of marine organisms to variations in environmental factors;

investigations on the effects of pollutants on marine organisms and on protection of life in oceans and coastal waters; exploration of the methodological and biological background required for the successful cultivation of marine organisms (including commercial aquaculture).
Facilities: Three research vessels; nineteen guest laboratories at Heligoland and Sylt for the use of visiting scientists.
Publications: Jahresbericht; Helgoländer Wissenschaft-liche Meeresuntersuchungen.

Isotope Laboratory 201

Address: Wüstland 2, D-2000 Hamburg 55
Telephone: (040) 871020

LITTORAL STATION 202

Address: D-2282 List/Sylt
Telephone: (04652) 428
Activities: Studies on sandy beach communities and coastal protection projects.

MARINE STATION 203

Address: D-2129 Helgoland
Telephone: (04725) 791
Telex: 02 32 1 18
Activities: Cultivation of sensitive marine organisms, ecosystem analysis, and applied environmental research.

Biologische Bundesanstalt 204 für Land- und Forstwirtschaft

[Federal Biological Research Centre for Agriculture and Forestry]
Parent body: Bundesministerium fur Ernährung, Landwirtschaft und Forsten
President: Professor Dr Schumann
Graduate research staff: 150
Annual expenditure: over £2m
Contract work: No
Publications: Nachrichtenblatt des Deutschen Pflanzenschutzdienstes; Mitteilungen ans der Biologischen Bundesanstalt für Land- und Forst-wirtschaft; Amtliche Pflanzenschutzbestimmungen; Jahresbericht der Biologischen Bundesanstalt; Jahresberichte des Deutschen Pflanzenschutzdienstes.

INSTITUTES AT BERLIN-DAHLEM 205

Address: Königin-Luise-Strasse 19, D-1000 Berlin 33
Telephone: (030) 8 30 41

Bacteriology Institute 206

Activities: Research on plant pathogenic bacteria and mycoplasms, and diseases caused by these organisms; diagnostic and taxonomic studies; host-parasite studies; cytological, histological, and physiological investigations of plant resistance.
Facilities: Transmission electron microscope, scanning electron microscope.

Diseases for Ornamental Plants 207 Institutes

Activities: Investigating diseases and pests of ornamental plants, and developing control methods.

Mycology Institute 208

Activities: Investigation of plant diseases caused by fungi; diseases of unknown aetiology; mycological methods for isolating, cultivating, and preserving phytopathogenic fungi.

Non-Parasitic Plant Diseases Institute 209

Activities: Investigation of all non-parasitic diseases of plants, caused by climatic factors, physical and chemical properties of soils, misapplication of chemical treatments, wrong rotation of crops, and toxic agents in air and soil.

Pesticide Research Institute 210

Activities: Problems of residue analysis, mode of action, and metabolic effects of chemicals used in plant protection; structure of metabolites, and their influence on enzyme systems, side effects and incompatibilities.

Stored Products Protection Institute 211

Activities: Protection of plant and animal products against insect damage in long-term storage, including biological, ecological, and epidemiological investigations.

Zoology Institute   212

Activities: Development of non-polluting control methods for animal pests in agriculture, horticulture and forestry, including the sterile partner method for the control of aphid species, the use of optic, acoustic, odorous or taste effects to interfere with the sense-perception of pest insects, and the application of hormones and synthetic analogues.

INSTITUTES AT BRAUNSCHWEIG   213

Address: Messeweg 11/12, D-3300 Braunschweig 33
Telephone: (0531) 39 91

Agricultural Virus Research Institute   214

Director: Professor Dr H.L. Paul
Sections:
Physico-chemical properties of viruses, Dr H.L. Paul
Serological methods and viruses of fruit plants, Dr R. Casper
Preparation of sera, Dr R. Bartels
Cereal and grass virology, Dr W. Huth
Ornamental plants and vegetable virology, Dr R. Koenig
Electron microscope diagnosis and cytology, Dr D.-E. Lesemann
Hops and vegetable virology, epidemiology and chemotherapy, Dr H. Rohloff
Potato virology, virus carriers, resistance tests, Dr H.-L. Weidemann
Activities: Research into virus diseases of cultivated plants, and development of control measures; the development of rapid tests for virus indexing, virus transmission; the biology and ecology of vectors, and disease epidemiology; morphological characteristics and virus classification.

Biochemistry Institute   215

Director: Professor Dr H. Stegemann
Sections:
Biochemical processes for the determination of virus resistance, Dr H. Stegemann
Biochemical potato morphology, Dr V. Loeschke
Chemotherapy, Dr B. Lerch
Activities: The analysis by biochemical means of the natural response of plants and cultivars to pathogens and to environmental challenges; disease resistance; investigation of macromolecules, proteins and enzymes.

Field and Grass Crops Protection   216
Institute

Director: Professor Dr F. Schütte
Sections:
Disease resistance, Dr J. Ulrich
Cereal rust, Dr E. Fuchs
Leaf and ear diseases of cereals, Dr G. Bartels
Tuber diseases of the potato, Dr E. Langerfeld
Leaf and dry rot, Dr B. Schöber
Graduate research staff: 12
Annual expenditure: £501 000-2m
Activities: The Institute carries out research on biology, occurrence, spread, and economic significance of pathogens and pests of agricultural crop plants, and on the possible methods of controlling them.

KITZEBERG SUBSTATION   217

Address: Schlosskoppelweg 8, D-2305 Heikendorf Kitzeberg
Telephone: (0431) 2 34 95
Director: Dr W. Krüger
Sections:
Diseases of cereals, Dr H. Mielke
Diseases of rape and maize, Dr W. Krüger
Diseases of grass and forage crops, Dr A. Tenteberg
Cereals pests, Dr T. Basedow
Fireblight of orchard and ornamental crops, Dr W. Zeller
Annual expenditure: £10 000-50 000
Activities: Studies on the resistance of cereals, maize and rape varieties to root rot, leaf, ear and stem diseases; studies on the epidemiology of pathogens and the development of methods for disease control and the reduction of damage; research on the population dynamics of animal pests in agricultural crops for the purpose of developing prognoses on their occurrence and integrated methods of control; identification of fungal pathogens of fodder and lawn grasses and forage plants, as well as determination of the economic significance of these fungi; studies of epidemiology and control of fireblight of orchard and ornamental plants.
Contract work: No

Pesticides and Plant Protection   218
Division

Director: Professor Dr T. Voss

APPLICATION TECHNIQUES   219
INSTITUTE
Sections:
Applications technology, Dr Ing H. Kohsiek
Plant protection testing, Dipl-Ing S. Rietz
Activities: Tests and investigations of plant protection equipment and stored plant products.

BOTANICAL PESTICIDE TESTING INSTITUTE 220
Director: Dr H. Lyre
Sections:
Plant treatments for vine cultivation, Dr H. Lyre
Toxic treatments and fungicides, Dr H. Ehle
Fungicides and herbicides, Dr J. Martin
Herbicides, Dr W.G. Heidler
Growth regulation, Dr H.T. Laermann
Activities: Tests of fungicides and herbicides.

CHEMICAL PESTICIDE TESTING INSTITUTE 221
Director: Professor Dr W. Weinemann
Sections:
Physical and chemical data, Dr W.Dobrat
Residual effects of insecticides, acaricides, and nematicides, Dr A. Röpsth
Residual effects of fungicides, Dr H. Parnemann
Residual effects of herbicides, Dr J.R. Lundehn
Chemical tests, Dr K. Claussen
Soil and water residues, Dr K. Schinkel
Data processing, Dr Ing W.D. Schwartz
Analysis of residual effects, Dr H.G. Nolting
Activities: Determination of the chemical composition of pesticides, residues left in crops, tolerance levels and waiting periods.

ZOOLOGICAL PESTICIDE TESTING INSTITUTE 222
Director: Dr W. Herfs
Sections:
Ecotoxicology, Dr H. Becker
Nematicides and molluscicides, Dr H. Rothert
Insecticides and acaricides, Dr F. Riepert
Forest protection, M. Grasblum
Ecotoxicology (plant treatments), Dr E. Wolf
Bee protection, Dr D. Brasse
Investigations of bee poisoning, Dr Ing I. Kaufmann
Activities: Tests of insecticides and pesticides.

Virus Serology Institute 223
Activities: Serological diagnosis of plant viruses and serological methods; special treatments of viruses of potatoes, fruit trees, vines, and ornamental plants.

Weed Research Institute 224
Director: Dr G. Maas
Sections:
Weed control in vegetable crops, Dr G. Maas
Weed control in cereal crops, Dr P. Niemann
Biology, ecology and spread of weeds, and biological weed control, Dr T. Eggers
Influence of herbicides on the microflora of the soil, Dr H.P. Malkomes
Ecological effects of herbicides, Dr W. Pestemer

Activities: Investigation of the biology of weeds, and procedures of mechanical, chemical and biological weed control; absorption, mode of action, residual effects and efficiency of herbicides, the importance of weeds as hosts of pests and plant diseases.

INSTITUTES IN OTHER LOCATIONS 225

Biological Pest Control Institute 226
Address: Heinrichstrasse 243, D-6300 Darmstadt
Telephone: (0615) 4 40 61
Activities: Investigation of insect population dynamics and natural enemies of pest insects, including pathogens, predators, and parasites; introduction, acclimatization and mass production of beneficial insects in conjunction with chemical methods.

Diseases in Fruit Plants Institute 227
Address: Schwabenheimerstrasse, D-6901 Dossenheim
Telephone: (06221) 8 52 38
Director: Professor Dr A. Schmidle
Sections:
Virology of pome and stone fruits, Dr Kunze
Virology of berry fruits and vectors, Dr Drczal
Mycology of pome and stone fruits, Professor Dr A. Schmidle
Mycology and histology of berry fruits, Dr Seemüller
Entomology, Dr Dickler
Graduate research staff: 5
Annual expenditure: £51 000-500 000
Activities: Investigation of diseases and pests of pome, stone, and berry fruits, and the development of methods of detection and control.
Contract work: No

Diseases of Forest Plants Institute 228
Address: Kasselerstrasse 22, D-3510 Hannover Münden
Telephone: (05541) 42 54
Activities: Investigation of pests and diseases of forest plants, especially trees and timber, including the symptoms of the host, biology, morphology and taxonomy of disease-causing organisms; testing of pesticides for forestry; taxonomy of timber-discolouring fungi.

Root Crops Diseases and Nematology 229 Institute

Address: Toppheideweg 88, D-4400 Münster
Telephone: (0251) 5 15 32
Activities: The study of plant parasitic nematodes and the development of control methods, and the study of virus diseases of beets; the interrotation of crop rotation, cultural practices, and population dynamics of parasitic nematodes.

Vegetable Diseases Institute 230

Address: Marktweg 60, D-5035 Fischenich Köln
Telephone: (02233) 7 28 56
Activities: Investigation of pests and diseases of vegetable crops; the interactions between ecological factors, epidemiology, and cultural practices; fungal pathogens of damping off diseases of beans, peas and broad beans; the prevention of seed-transmission of fungal and bacterial pathogens.

Vine Diseases Institute 231

Address: Brüningstrasse 84, D-5550 Bernkastel Kues
Telephone: (06531) 3 64
Activities: Investigation of non-parasitic disease, viruses, mycoplasmic disease, bacteria, fungi, and pests of grape vines, and the development of control methods; humus-depletion, nutritional disturbances, and the accumulation of phytotoxic substances in the soil.

Bodensee - 232 Wasserversorgung

[Lake Constance Water Supply Authority]
Address: D-7770 Überlingen Süssenmühle
Telephone: (07551) 4086
Research director: Dr D. Maier
Graduate research staff: 2
Annual expenditure: £10 000-50 000
Activities: Water analysis and treatment; hydrobiology and bacteriology.
Contract work: Yes

Robert Bosch GmbH 233

Address: Postfach 50, D-7000 Stuttgart 1
Telephone: (0711) 8111
Telex: 72 37 34

CENTRAL RESEARCH DEPARTMENT 234

Research director: Dr Heinrich Düker
Sections: Chemistry and materials, Dr Hermann Ziener; mechanics and instruments, Professor Dr Kurt Melcher; physics, Dr Wolfgang Heinz
Graduate research staff: 80
Annual expenditure: over £2m
Activities: New technologies in the automotive and electrical fields, for example antipollution systems, fuel injection, traffic control systems, optical and electrical application of thin films, laser applications, electrochemistry, ceramics, permanent magnets, powder metallurgy, physical and chemical analysis, tribology, technical mathematics.
Contract work: No
Publications: Bosch Technische Berichte.

Botanischer Garten und 235 Botanisches Museum Berlin-Dahlem

[Botanical Garden and Museum, Berlin-Dahlem]
Address: Königin-Luise-Strasse 6-8, D-1000 Berlin 33
Telephone: (030) 8314041
Research director: Professor Dr Werner Greuter
Graduate research staff: 17
Annual expenditure: £51 000-500 000
Activities: Research in plant taxonomy and phytogeography.
Facilities: Botanical garden with about 18 000 living plant species (outdoors and in greenhouses); worldwide herbarium with about 2m specimens; library with about 50 000 volumes, specializing in floristics, plant taxonomy and phytogeography.
Contract work: No
Publications: Willdenowia; Englera; OPTIMA-Newsletter, OPTIMA leaflets.

BOTANICAL GARDEN 236

Head: Professor Dr H. Ern

CRYPTOGAMS DEPARTMENT 237

Head: Professor Dr W. Schultze-Motel

DOCUMENTATION DEPARTMENT 238

Head: Professor Dr H. Scholz

PHANEROGAMS DEPARTMENT 239

Head: Professor Dr P. Hiepko

PUBLIC MUSEUM 240

Head: Professor Dr E. Potztal

Brown, Boveri & Cie 241

– BBC

CENTRAL RESEARCH LABORATORY 242

Address: Eppelheimer Strasse 82, D-6900 Heidelberg
Telephone: 06221/701-1
Telex: 461 827 stko d
Research director: Dr Franz Gross
Sections: Chemical physics, Dr R. Langpape; heat transfer and storage, Dr H. Birnbreier; material technology, Dr F. Gross; surface physics and coatings, Dr G. Wahl
Graduate research staff: 40
Annual expenditure: over £2m
Activities: Energy conversion and systems; high temperature batteries; heat transfer and storage; solar energy; high temperature coatings; material science and technology; physical and chemical analysis.
Contract work: For Bundesminister für Forschung und Technologie, only.
See also: Brown Boveri Forschungszentrum, Switzerland

Bundesanstalt für 243
Fettforschung

[Federal Centre for Lipid Research]
Address: Piusallee 68-76, D-4400 Münster
Telephone: (0251) 4 35 10 and 5 75 97
Parent body: Bundesministerium für Ernährung, Landwirtschaft und Forsten
Directors: Professor Dr A. Scher, Professor Dr H.-K. Mangold
Graduate research staff: 25
Annual expenditure: £501 000-2m
Activities: Scientific and technological problems related to oil seeds, oil-bearing fruits and extracted dietary fats; research on chemical, physical and biological properties of fats and oils, their constituents and minor components; the influence of processing on biochemical and nutritional properties; the development and evaluation of methods of investigation and processing of

vegetable and animal fats, marine oils, oilseed residues and other lipids.
Contract work: No

BIOCHEMISTRY AND TECHNOLOGY 244
INSTITUTE

Director: Professor Dr K.-K. Mangold
Activities: The development of new processes for the production of fats and oils from oil-bearing plants and raw materials; characterization of hidden fats; lipid-based biological pest control, and harmless methods of plant protection and production; biological production of fats and protein.

GENERAL AND ANALYTICAL 245
CHEMISTRY INSTITUTE

Director: Professor Dr A. Seher
Activities: Research into the composition and properties of dietary fats, frying fats, emulsifiers, fat additives, and fat-bearing raw materials; methods for the detection and control of processing treatments, such as refining and interesterification.

Bundesanstalt für 246
Fleischforschung

[Federal Centre for Meat Research]
Address: E.-C.-Baumann-Strasse 20, D-8650 Kulmbach, Bayern
Parent body: Bundesministerium für Ernährung, Landwirtschaft und Forsten
Director: Professor Dr Fritz Wirth
Activities: Bacteriology, microbiology, histology, chemistry and physics of meat and meat products.

CHEMISTRY AND PHYSICS 247
INSTITUTE

Director: Professor Dr Reiner Hamm
Activities: Influence of temperature and freezing rate on the quality of beef and sausage-meats, lead concentration studies.

MEAT PRODUCTION INSTITUTE 248

Director: Professor Dr Lothar Schön
Activities: Physiology of meat-producing animals, including analysis of muscle and fatty tissue distribution.

MICROBIOLOGY, TOXICOLOGY AND HISTOLOGY INSTITUTE   249

Director: Professor Dr Lothar Leistner
Activities: Investigation of bacteriological activity in stored meats.

TECHNOLOGY INSTITUTE   250

Director: Professor Dr Fritz Wirth
Activities: Processing technologies, including vacuum and low-temperature packing, smoking techniques, and chemical methods of meat preservation.

Bundesanstalt für Geowissenschaften und Rohstoffe   251

– BGR
[Federal Institute for Geosciences and Natural Resources]
Address: Stilleweg 2, Postfach 51 01 53, D-3000 Hannover 51
Telephone: (0511) 64681
Telex: 923730 bfb(bgr) ha d
Parent body: Bundesminister für Wirtschaft
President: Professor Dr Friedrich Bender
Sections: Economic geology, Professor Dr Martin Kürsten; general and technical geology, Professor Dr Helmut Venzlaff; geophysics, Professor Dr Hans-Joachim; geochemistry and mineralogy, Professor Dr Wolfgang Stahl
Graduate research staff: 300
Annual expenditure: DM80m
Activities: Energy resources, including geothermal resources, nuclear fuel, coal and oil shale; mineral resources (water and soil) including irrigation, land development, waste disposal, soil conservation and hydraulic engineering geology; geotechnical safety and establishment of nuclear waste depots; environmental protection; international geoscientific cooperation.
Contract work: Yes
Publications: Yearbook.

Bundesanstalt für Gewässerkunde   252

[Federal Centre for Hydrology]
Address: Kaiserin-Augusta-Anlagen 15-17, Postfach 309, D-5400 Koblenz
Telephone: (0261) 12431
Telex: 8-62 499

Parent body: Bundesministerium für Verkehr
Sections:
Department M - quantity and morphology of inland and coastal waters
Department G - geology and groundwater
Department N - physics, chemistry, and biology
Department T - radiology and technology
Department V - surveying
Graduate research staff: 40
Activities: The Centre is active in all areas of hydrological research and development, in order to provide scientific bases for federal policy-making; pollution control and radioactivity measurement; waterways levelling and maintenance; data collection and processing, publications and information dissemination.
Facilities: Chemical, biological, and isotope laboratories; a bedload and suspended load research laboratory; groundwater laboratory; hydrological library.
Contract work: No
Publications: Deutsche Gewässerkundliche Mitteilungen, bimonthly.

Bundesanstalt für Materialprüfung   253

– BAM
[Federal Institute for Materials Testing]
Address: Unter den Eichen 87, D-1000 Berlin 45
Telephone: (030) 81 041
Telex: 01-83261 bamb d
Parent body: Bundesminister für Wirtschaft
Research director: Professor Dr G.W. Becker
Sections: Metals and structures of metals, Professor Dr D. Aurich; building, Professor Dr A. Plank; organic materials, Professor Dr H. Feuerberg; chemical safety engineering, Professor Dr J. Zehr; special fields of materials testing, Professor Dr H. Czichos; methods independent of the type of material, Professor Dr E. Mundry
Graduate research staff: 270
Annual expenditure: over £2m
Activities: Problems of materials and materials testing for metals, construction materials and organics; physical, chemical and biological testing; chemical safety engineering; development of new materials and of methods for non-destructive testing; special topics such as tribology, colour metrics, welding, nuclear power.
Contract work: Yes
Publications: Annual report.

Bundesanstalt für Strassenwesen 254

[Federal Highway Research Centre]
Address: Brühler Strasse 1, Postfach 51 05 30, D-5000 Köln 51
Telephone: (0221) 3702-1
Telex: 088 82 189 bas d
Parent body: Bundesministerium für Verkehr
Director: Professor Dr Ing Heinrich Praxenthaler
Sections:
Department B - road construction techniques, Professor Dipl-Ing Egil Nakkel
Department V - traffic engineering techniques, Professor Dr Ing Karl Krell
Department U - accident research, Professor Dr Ing Karl-Heinz Lenz
Department Z - central services, Professor Dipl-Ing Peter Camosois
Graduate research staff: 116
Annual expenditure: over £2m
Activities: Road construction, including earthworks, drainage, geosciences, foundations research, concrete and bitumen constructions, road surface technology, civil engineering, bridges and tunnels science; traffic engineering, including flow and exhaust measurements, highway network design and analysis, traffic flow regulation; accident research, including prevention, medical treatments, statistics and sociology; computer sciences and information dissemination.
Facilities: Internal drum testing machine, crash test facilities, soil and material testing laboratories, electronic testing laboratory, and computer centre.
Contract work: Yes
Publications: Three year report.

Bundesanstalt für Wasserbau 255

– BAW
[Federal Centre for Waterway Engineering]
Address: Kussmaulstrasse 17, D-7500 Karlsruhe 21
Parent body: Bundesministerium für Verkehr
Director: Professor Dr Ing Heinz Graewe
Activities: Fluvial and maritime hydraulics; soil mechanics and foundations; structures (locks, weirs); river training and canalization; morphology of rivers and estuaries; mechanics of material transport (bed load and suspended sediment); interaction between ships and beds (river or canal); bank and coastal protection; effect of inlets and outlets on navigation; harbours; geology (coastal geology, tectonic, petrography); flow in porous media and groundwater; material testing (soil, steel, concrete, synthetic products); protection from corro-

sion; equipment for model and field measurements; use of computers. Theoretical studies as well as model investigations (mathematical, hydraulic) and field tests are carried out.

DEPARTMENT OF COASTAL ENGINEERING* 256

Address: Moorweidenstrasse 14, D-2000 Hamburg 13
Head: Dr Ing Hans Rohde

Bundesbahn-Versuchsanstalt Minden 257

[Federal Railways Research Institute Minden]
Address: Pionierstrasse 10, D-4950 Minden 2
Telephone: (0571) 393222
Director: Dipl-Ing W. Westerkamp
Scientific and technical staff: 200
Contract work: Yes

DEPARTMENT OF BRAKE SYSTEMS 258

Telephone: (0571) 393222
Head: Dr Ing W. Hendrichs
Activities: Regulation and control techniques; mechanical brake components; brake evaluation; braking dynamics and load shock analysis.

DEPARTMENT OF DYNAMICS AND VIBRATION 259

Telephone: (0571) 393583
Head: Dipl-Ing E. Scheunemann
Activities: Interactions between rails and wheels and its effect on position stability of the track base.

DEPARTMENT OF MECHANICS 260

Telephone: (0571) 393308
Head: Dipl-Phys K. Egelkraut
Activities: Mechanical experiments, eg servo-hydraulic testing of vibration characteristics of large train components; ultrasonic testing of wheel axles and rails.

DEPARTMENT OF THERMODYNAMICS AND HEAT TRANSFER 261

Telephone: (0571) 393581
Head: Dipl-Ing J. Kauschke
Activities: Efficiency tests of new steam boilers and drinking water separating plants; thermodynamic

measurements of steam turbines in railway power stations, utilization of waste materials and more economical fuels.

DEPARTMENT OF WELDING TECHNOLOGY   262

Address: 41 Leinhäuser Weg, D-3000 Hannover 21
Telephone: (0511) 1983228
Head: Dr Ing E. Pahl
Activities: Welding of metallic and non-metallic materials; thermal separation system; acceptance testing; quality control.

Bundesforschungsanstalt   263
für Ernährung

[Federal Research Centre for Food and Nutrition]
Address: Engesserstrasse 20, D-7500 Karlsruhe
Parent body: Bundesministerium fur Ernährung, Landwirtschaft und Forsten
Director: Professor Dr H.K. Frank
Activities: Research in the field of nutrition, food science and food technology (especially food preservation).

BIOCHEMISTRY INSTITUTE   264

Director: Professor Dr J.F. Diehl
Activities: Research into the mutagenic effects of colouring substances, sweetening substances, and irradiated food; investigation into the addition of bran to wholewheat breads.

BIOLOGY INSTITUTE   265

Director: Professor Dr H.K. Frank
Activities: The determination of biological quality control criteria.

FOOD CHEMISTRY INSTITUTE   266

Director: Professor Dr A. Fricker
Activities: Heat-sterilization techniques; blanching and freezing.

HOME ECONOMICS INSTITUTE   267

Director: Professor Dr E. Stübler
Activities: Consumer protection; microwave cooking methods.

PROCESS ENGINEERING INSTITUTE   268

Director: Professor Dr H. Schubert
Activities: Freezing technologies, protein concentrates, powdered foods.

Bundesforschungsanstalt   269
für Fischerei

[Federal Research Centre for Fisheries]
Address: Palmaille 9, D-2000 Hamburg 50
Telephone: (040) 38 16 01
Parent body: Bundesministerium für Ernährung, Landwirtschaft und Forsten
Research director: Professor Dr W. Schreiber

BIOCHEMISTRY AND TECHNOLOGY   270
INSTITUTE

Director: Professor Dr Wolfgang Schreiber
Deputy director: Professor Dr W. Flechtenmacher
Sections:
Analysis of fishery products, legal definitions, Dr N. Antonacopoulos, Dr J. Oehlenschläger
Under-utilized species, Dr A. Birnbaum, Dr K.P. Wirtz
Freezing, cooling and processing techniques, Professor Dr W. Flechtenmacher
Microbiology of fish and fish products, Dr G. Karnop
Protein and enzyme chemistry, Dr H. Rehbein, Professor Dr W. Schreiber
Krill processing and technology, Dr O. Christians, M. Martheg, Dr A. Birnbaum
Product development, Dr Horst Kart

COASTAL AND FRESHWATER   271
FISHERIES INSTITUTE

Director: Professor Dr Klaus Tiews
Deputy director: Dr G. Rauck
Activities: Investigation of the effects of commercial exploitation and industrial pollution on coastal fish populations; fish farming, especially of oysters and eels.

Ahrensburg Laboratory   272

Head: Professor Dr C. Meshe

Coastal Fisheries in the North Sea and   273
Baltic Sea

Director: Professor Dr Klaus Tiews
Sections:
North Sea fishery, Professor Dr Klaus Tiews
Baltic and salmon fisheries, Professor Dr F. Thurow

Flatfish fisheries, Dr G. Rauek, Dr W. Weber
Cod and other North Sea fisheries, Dr F. Lamp
Shellfish fisheries, Dr R. Meixner, T. Neudecker
Exploratory fishing, Dr G. Kühlmorgen-Hille
Benthos and Baltic fishery, Dr G. Kühlmorgen-Hille
Electrical fishing, electrophysiology, pollution, Dr E. Halsband
Freshwater fisheries and fish diseases, H. Koops, Dr V. Hilge
Aquaculture, Professor Dr C. Meske, Dr V. Hilge, H. Koops, Dr M. Kuhlmann
Marine pollution, Dr E. Huschenbeth, Dr V. Dethlefsen

Cuxhaven Laboratory 274

Head: Dr W. Weber
Section:
Toxicological laboratory, Dr V. Dethlefsen

Kiel Laboratory 275

Head: Professor Dr F. Thurow

Langballigan Laboratory 276

Head: T. Neudecker

FISHING TECHNIQUES INSTITUTE 277

Director: Professor Dr Rolf Steinberg
Deputy director: Professor Dr H. Bohl
Sections:
Catching methods, Professor Dr R. Steinberg, Dr E. Dahm, H. von Seidlitz, Dr H.G. Klug, W. Kelle
Electronics, Dr T. Mentjes, Ing W. Horn, M. Kruger
Selection of fishing gear, Professor Dr H. Bohl
Fish behaviour, Dr H. Mohr, Dr W. Fischer
Ship and gear noise, Dr G. Freytag
Naval architecture, K. Lange
Activities: Energy-saving alternatives to trawl-fishing.

ISOTOPE LABORATORY 278

Director: Professor Werner Feldt
Deputy director: Dr H. Bühringer
Sections:
Fishery biology, radiation biology, Dr H. Bühringer, M. Vobach
Radiochemistry, R. Lauer
Chemistry of trace elements, Dr U. Harms
Nuclear radiation techniques, G. Kanisch
Applied isotope techniques, neutron activation, Professor W. Feldt, H.-J. Kellermann
Electronics and computer techniques, Ing G. Nagel

SEA FISHERIES INSTITUTE 279

Director: Professor Dr Dietrich Sahrhage
Deputy director: Professor Dr A. Schumacher
Activities: Biological monitoring of fish species; promotion of international cooperation on fisheries management.

Bremmerhaven Substation 280

Director: Dr J. Messtorff

ATLANTIC FISHERIES 281
Section:
Ichthyology, Dr A. Post, Dr K. Stehmann

NORTHWEST AND NORTHEAST 282
ATLANTIC FISHERIES
Director: Dr J. Messtorff
Sections:
Haddock and cod, G. Wagner
Redfish biology, Dr K. Kosswig
Coalfish biology, Dr H.H. Reinsch
Hake biology, Dr F. Mombeck
Population dynamics, Professor Dr A. Schumacher
Herring biology, Professor Dr A. Schumacher, Dr H. Dornheim
Plankton, benthos, Dr H. Schutz
Tagging, haddock, whiting, G. Wagner
Fisheries statistics, H.-P. Cornus
New fishing grounds and species, Dr S. Ehrich, K.-H. Kock, F. Nast, Professor Dr D. Sahrhage, R. Schöne, V. Siegel
Fisheries hydrography, M. Stein, P. Cornus, C. Wegner

WORLD FISHERIES 283
Director: Professor Dr Dietrich Sahrhage

Bundesforschungsanstalt 284
für Forst- und
Holzwirtschaft

[Federal Research Centre for Forestry and Forest Products]
Address: Leuschnerstrasse 91, Postfach 80 01 10, D-2050 Hamburg 80
Telephone: (040) 73 91 91
Parent body: Bundesministerium für Ernährung, Landwirtschaft und Forsten
Research director: Professor Dr G. Eisenhauer
Graduate research staff: 55
Annual expenditure: over £2m
Activities: Conservation of forests and improvement of their wood production to ensure sufficient raw material supply, environmental benefits, and recreational poten-

tial; conservation, improvement and standardization of the properties of timber and wood products; development and rationalization of techniques for treatment and processing of wood, and the promotion of technologies which are less harmful to the environment; investigation of properties and use/potential of lesser-used wood species, especially of tropical and subtropical areas; observation of market conditions.

Contract work: No

Publications: Mitteilungen der Bundesforschungsanstalt für Forst- und Holzwirtschaft; Weltforstatlas; Silvae Genetica; BFH-Nachrichten, quarterly.

FOREST GENETICS AND FOREST TREE BREEDING INSTITUTE   285

Director: Professor Dr G.H. Melchior

WOOD BIOLOGY AND WOOD PROTECTION INSTITUTE   286

Director: Professor Dr W. Liese

WOOD CHEMISTRY AND CHEMICAL WOOD TECHNOLOGY INSTITUTE   287

Director: vacant

WOOD PHYSICS AND MECHANICAL WOOD TECHNOLOGY INSTITUTE   288

Director: Professor Dr D. Noack

WORK SCIENCE INSTITUTE   289

Director: Professor Dr G. Eisenhauer

WORLD FORESTRY INSTITUTE   290

Director: Professor Dr C. Wiebecke

Bundesforschungsanstalt für Gartenbauliche Pflanzenzüchtung   291

[Federal Research Centre for Horticultural Plant Breeding]
Address: Bornkampsweg, D-2070 Ahrensburg
Telephone: (04102) 5 11 21
Parent body: Bundesministerium für Ernährung, Landwirtschaft und Forsten
Director: Professor Dr R. Reimann-Philipp

Sections:
Cytogenetics, Professor Dr R. Reimann-Philipp, Professor Dr F. Walther, Dr H. Schmidt
Plant breeding, S. Handke, E. Wende, C. Jordan
Plant physiology, Dr W. Preil, Dr H. Junge
Phytopathology, F. Persiel, Dr J. Krüger
Graduate research staff: 10
Annual expenditure: £501 000-2m
Activities: Horticultural plant breeding and cytogenetics, for the selection of resistance, quality, and low adaptation.
Contract work: No
Publications: Annual report.

Bundesforschungsanstalt für Getreide- und Kartoffelverarbeitung   292

[Federal Research Centre for Cereal and Potato Processing]
Address: Postfach 23, Schützenberg 12, D-4930 Detmold
Telephone: (05231) 2 34 51
Telex: 09-35851
Parent body: Bundesministerium für Ernährung, Landwirtschaft und Forsten
Director: Professor Dr Hans Bolling
Graduate research staff: 26
Annual expenditure: over £2m
Activities: The Institute conducts basic research into cereal and potato processing, the development of new processing technologies, investigation and quality control of raw materials and end products; the findings are made available to industry and the ministries as scientific bases for policy making in the fields of nutrition, food law, and environmental protection.
Contract work: No
Publications: Getreide, Mehl und Brot; Die Stärke/Starch, periodicals; annual report.

BAKING TECHNOLOGY INSTITUTE   293

Director: Professor Dr W. Seibel
Activities: Research into bread and small baked goods, flour confectionery and biscuits, pasta, and extruded products; chemical, rheological and microbiological analysis of raw materials, ingredients and additives, processed materials and end products.

BIOCHEMISTRY AND ANALYTICS INSTITUTE 294

Director: Professor Dr H.-D. Ocker
Activities: Research into contaminants, proteins and protein complexes, carbohydrates, and enzymes, using chemical, biochemical, physical and tracer techniques.

MILLING TECHNOLOGY INSTITUTE 295

Director: Professor Dr H. Bolling
Activities: Research into bread making and other cereals; storage and processing techniques, including flour milling of wheat, durum, rye, maize, and hulling of barley, oats, rice and sorghum; quality surveying of wheat and rye varities; humidity and viscosity studies of doughs and stored grains.

STARCH AND POTATO TECHNOLOGY INSTITUTE 296

Director: Professor Dr W. Kempf
Activities: Research into starch-containing materials, starch production, and starch derivatives; application technology and saccharification; dried, fried, and wet potato products.

Bundesforschungsanstalt 297 für Landeskunde und Raumordnung

[Federal Research Institute for Regional Geography and Regional Planning]
Address: Am Michaelshof 8, Postfach 200130, D-5300 Bonn 2
Telephone: (02221) 8261
Affiliation: Ministry of Regional Planning, Building and Urban Development
Sections: Research, Dr F. Spreer; information, Dr K. Türke
Graduate research staff: 35
Annual expenditure: £10 000-50 000
Activities: The Institute conducts research in the sectors of urban and regional planning. It is concerned with research into spatial structure as well as planning. The aim of the research projects is to provide information and aid the political decision-making of the Ministry of Regional Planning, Building and Urban Development, hence research is usually restricted to the area of the Federal Republic of Germany. At the same time the Institute is a focal point for research in the above-mentioned disciplines within the framework of the European Economic Community.
Contract work: Yes

Bundesforschungsanstalt 298 für Landwirtschaft Braunschweig-Völkenrode

– FAL
[Federal Research Centre for Agriculture Braunschweig-Völkenrode]
Address: Bundesallee 50, D-3300 Braunschweig
Telephone: (0531) 5961
Parent body: Bundesministerium für Ernährung, Landwirtschaft und Forsten
President: elected every two years
Graduate research staff: 180
Contract work: No
Publications: Landbauforschung Völkenrode, annually and special issues.

AGRICULTURAL MARKET RESEARCH INSTITUTE 299

Director: Professor Dr E. Buchholz
Activities: Prediction of markets and production trends.

ANIMAL HUSBANDRY AND ANIMAL BEHAVIOUR RESEARCH INSTITUTE 300

Director: Professor Dr Dr D. Smidt
Activities: Physiological and ethological effects of housing conditions.

ANIMAL NUTRITION RESEARCH INSTITUTE 301

Director: Professor Dr H.J. Olsage
Activities: Effects of protein and mineral balance in the fattening of pigs; calf fattening.

CROP SCIENCE AND PLANT BREEDING RESEARCH INSTITUTE 302

Director: Professor Dr M. Dambroth
Activities: Plant breeding for increased digestibility.

FARM BUILDING RESEARCH INSTITUTE 303

Director: Professor Dr J. Piotrowski
Activities: Research into cost-efficiency of farm buildings.

FARM MANAGEMENT RESEARCH INSTITUTE 304

Director: Professor Dr K. Meinhold
Activities: Economics, including profitability studies.

FARM MECHANIZATION AND MANAGEMENT RESEARCH INSTITUTE 305

Director: Professor Dr H. Schön

FUNDAMENTALS OF AGRICULTURAL ENGINEERING RESEARCH INSTITUTE 306

Director: Professor Dr W. Batel
Activities: Labour and environmental protection, including pollution, noise and odour controls in working conditions; energy, research, including conservation and new sources.

GRASSLAND AND FORAGE RESEARCH INSTITUTE 307

Director: Professor Dr E. Zimmer
Activities: Forage production and conservation technology; protein metabolism of silage.

PLANT NUTRITION AND SOIL SCIENCE RESEARCH INSTITUTE 308

Director: Professor Dr D. Sauerbeck
Activities: Analysis of organic compounds and herbicide residues in soils, and their influence on plant metabolism.

POULTRY AND SMALL ANIMAL RESEARCH INSTITUTE 309

Address: Dömbergstrasse 25-27, D-3100 Calle
Telephone: (05141) 31031/2
Director: Professor Dr Rose-Marie Wegner
Sections:
Breeding and reproduction, Dr W. Hartmann
Feeding, Dr H. Vogt
Husbandry and behaviour, Professor Dr R.-M. Wegner
Hygiene and diseases, Professor Dr H.-C. Löliger
Graduate research staff: 16
Annual expenditure: £51 000-500 000
Activities: Poultry and rabbit production, including breeding and reproduction, feeding, management, animal behaviour and health. Research objectives include the following: production of animal protein food products of high quality at economically acceptable prices; improving the efficiency of conversion of feedstuffs into

animal products; adapting industrialized production methods to the requirements of animal welfare and environmental protection; establishing scientific bases for legislation in the areas of food production, animal welfare, and environmental protection.
Contract work: Yes

SOIL BIOLOGY RESEARCH INSTITUTE 310

Director: Professor Dr K.H. Domsch
Activities: Microbial biomass analysis; soil inoculation; biological waste recycling.

STRUCTURAL RESEARCH INSTITUTE 311

Director: Professor Dr E. Neander
Activities: Analysis of farmland prices and rents; comparative price studies in urban and rural communities.

TECHNOLOGY RESEARCH INSTITUTE 312

Director: Professor Dr Ing W. Baader
Activities: Biogas processes, and solar energy exploitation.

Bundesforschungsanstalt für Milchforschung 313

[Federal Research Centre for Dairy Products]
Address: Hermann-Weigmann-Strasse 1-27, D-2300 Kiel
Telephone: (0431) 609-1
Telex: 29 29 66 mifo d
Parent body: Bundesministerium für Ernährung, Landwirtschaft und Forsten
Head: Professor Dr H.W. Kay
Research director: Professor Dr A. Tolle
Graduate research staff: 60
Annual expenditure: over £2m
Activities: The Centre conducts basic research on milk production, treatment and processing of milk, marketing of milk and milk products and their use for human nutrition. The findings are made available for the dairy industry and the ministries in decision-making for nutritional, agricultural, and consumer policies.
Facilities: Documentation department and experimental farm.
Contract work: No
Publications: Kieler Milchwirtschaftliche Forschungsberichte; Milchwissenschaft (Milk Science International); annual report.

CHEMISTRY AND PHYSICS INSTITUTE 314

Director: Professor Dr Dr W. Kaufmann

DATA PROCESSING AND INFORMATION INSTITUTE 315

Director: Professor Dr H.W. Kay

ECONOMICS AND MARKET RESEARCH INSTITUTE 316

Director: vacant

HYGIENE INSTITUTE 317

Director: Professor Dr A. Tolle

MICROBIOLOGY INSTITUTE 318

Director: Professor Dr M. Teuber

MILK PRODUCTION INSTITUTE 319

Director: Professor Dr H.O. Gravert

PHYSIOLOGY AND BIOCHEMISTRY OF NUTRITION INSTITUTE 320

Director: vacant

PROCESS ENGINEERING INSTITUTE 321

Director: Professor Dr H. Reuter

Bundesforschungsanstalt für Naturschutz und Landschaftsökologie 322

[Federal Research Centre for Nature Conservation and Landscape Ecology]
Address: Konstantinstrasse 110, D-5300 Bonn
Telephone: (0228) 33 00 41
Parent body: Bundesministerium für Ernährung, Landwirtschaft und Forsten
Director: Professor Dr W. Trautmann
Graduate research staff: 26
Activities: Research into vegetation ecology, nature conservation, animal ecology, landscape management, landscape and recreational planning, and related fields.
Contract work: No

LANDSCAPE MANAGEMENT AND LANDSCAPE ECOLOGY INSTITUTE 323

Director: Professor Dr Mrass
Activities: The Institute is engaged in basic research for the application of landscape management and landscape ecology to the landscape planning process, and also in developing methods for surveying and assessing the carrying capacity of the landscape, and the effects of different types of use, especially on the natural balance and on the landscape itself.

NATURE CONSERVATION AND ANIMAL ECOLOGY INSTITUTE 324

Director: Professor Dr Erz
Activities: The objective of the Institute is to provide scientific information for nature conservation (especially for habitat conservation and wildlife conservation), to be integrated into relevant legislation concerning nature conservation, physical planning, hunting, fisheries, and to provide the basis for practical conservation measures. The main activities in the field of original research are concerned with zooecological analysis of ecosystems; the compilation of criteria for the establishment of an ecological system of reserves covering the diversity of fauna and vegetation, and the variety of habitats of the Federal Republic of Germany.

PLANT ECOLOGY INSTITUTE 325

Director: Professor Dr W. Trautmann
Activities: The objective of the Institute is to process scientific information on the flora and vegetation of the Federal Republic of Germany, and to study the practical application of nature preservation and landscape planning. Emphasis is being placed on the following subjects: investigation of endangered plants, plant communities, and habitats as a basis for protective regulations and programmes; examination of the plant cover as a bioindicator of site quality and environmental impact; investigation of vegetation succession in natural forest areas as models of ecosystems without human influence and investigation of the consequences of fallow land-use and new land-use techniques for the plant cover and landscape equilibrium; mapping the vegetation of the Federal Republic of Germany as an aid for landscape classification on an ecological basis and for setting up a representative system of protected areas; testing the suitability of plant species for the purpose of protecting river banks against erosion and studying seed mixtures suitable for motorway turfs requiring little maintenance.

Centre for Agricultural Documentation 326 and Information

Activities: Agricultural documentation and information services; supplying and compiling national and international publications; cartography; record centres for nature reserves and wetlands, endangered species, nature parks, and national parks.

Bundesforschungsanstalt 327 für Rebenzüchtung Geilweilerhof

[Federal Research Centre for Vine Breeding at Geilweilerhof]
Address: D-6741 Siebeldlingen
Telephone: (06345) 445
Parent body: Bundesministerium für Ernährung, Landwirtschaft und Forsten
Director: Professor Dr G. Alleweldt
Sections:
Breeding research, Professor Dr G. Alleweldt
Genetics and cytology, Dr Blaich
Biochemistry, Dr Rapp
Graduate research staff: 13
Annual expenditure: £501 000-2m
Activities: The Institute's responsibility covers the field of breeding research on grapes and the breeding of new grapevine varieties. The main breeding efforts are directed towards the development of new varieties which are resistant against fungus diseases and phylloxera. The breeding programme also includes the improvement of Vitis vinifera by intraspecific crossings, and investigations into cold hardiness, drought tolerance, chlorosis resistance, and the physiological, biochemical and genetic causes of parasite resistance. Further phenotypic and character analyses are carried out with the aim of finding better and earlier ways of selecting seedlings with a high sugar content, an efficient interaction between scion and rootstock, and a high capability of absorbing nutrients. The analysis of aroma components in musts and wines is performed to characterize grapevine cultivars for early diagnosis of undesired compounds.
Contract work: No
Publications: Vitis.

Bundesforschungsanstalt 328 für Viruskrankheiten der Tiere

[Federal Research Institute for Animal Virus Diseases]
Address: Paul-Ehrlich-Strasse 28, D-7400 Tübingen
Telephone: (07071) 6031
Telex: 07 262846
Parent body: Bundesministerium für Ernährung, Landwirtschaft und Forsten
Director: Dr M. Mussgay
Sections:
Microbiology, Dr M. Mussgay
Immunology, Dr U. Koszinowski
Vaccines, Dr G. Wittmann
Graduate research staff: 28
Annual expenditure: £501 000-2m
Activities: Research on animal virus diseases, and development of vaccines and diagnostic procedures; testing of foot and mouth disease vaccines; immune response in viral infections; pathogenesis of viral infections; electron microscopy.
Contract work: No
Publications: Arbeiten aus der Bundesforschungsanstalt für Viruskrankheiten der Tiere, annually.

Bundesgesundheitsamt 329

[Federal Health Office]
Address: Thielallee 88-92, Postfach 33 00 13, D-1000 Berlin 33
Telephone: (030) 8308 741
Telex: 01 84 016
Vice-President: Werner S. Kierski
Activities: The Federal Health Office comprises seven scientific institutes and central services such as a Central Laboratory Animals Unit and a Central Unit for Data Processing. Interdisciplinary collaboration between the institutes aims at the improvement of the protection of health, reduction of environmental hazards and control of diseases. The terms of reference of the Federal Health Office include the performance of research projects and commissions in all fields of public health, scientific consultant functions on behalf of the Federal Government and the Länder, scientific advice to various international bodies, and tasks of approval and monitoring, particularly in the fields of narcotics and drugs legislation.
Publications: Journal.
See separate entry for:
Institut für Arzneimittel
Insitut für Sozialmedizin und Epidemiologie
Institut für Strahlenhygiene

Institut für Veterinärmedizin
Institut für Wasser-, Boden- und Lufthygiene
Max von Pettenkofer-Institut
Robert Koch-Institut.

CENTRAL LABORATORY ANIMALS UNIT 330

Head: Dr med vet Wolfgang Scharmann

CENTRAL UNIT: AUTOMATIC DATA PROCESSING, DOCUMENTATION AND STATISTICS 331

Head: Joachim Zeiler

CENTRE FOR SURVEILLANCE AND HEALTH EVALUATION OF ENVIRONMENTAL CHEMICALS 332

Head: Dr med vet Peter Weigert
Activities: FAO/WHO collaborating centre on Food Contamination Monitoring.

OCCUPATIONAL HEALTH 333

Head: Professor Dr Giselher Von Nieding

OCCUPATIONAL SAFETY 334

Head: Erwin Dentzer

Bundesinstitut für Berufsbildung 335

– BIBB
[Federal Institute of Vocational Training]
Address: Fehrbelliner Platz 3, D-1000 Berlin 31
Telephone: (030) 86831
Parent body: Bundesministerium für Bildung und Wissenschaft
Activities: The Institute is chiefly concerned with vocational training, and legislative provisions for education and research in science, medicine, agriculture and engineering.

Bundesministerium des Innern 336

[Federal Ministry of the Interior]
Address: 198 Graurheindorfer Strasse, Postfach, D-5300 Bonn 1
Telephone: (0228) 6811
Telex: 8-86664; 8-86896
Activities: The research and development programme initiated by the Ministry of the Interior is carried out by scientists in university institutes, independent research institutes and industrial research laboratories, under the organization of Umweltbundesamt (see below).
The programme for 1980 consisted of 888 single projects making up 109 different subject programme areas.

UMWELTBUNDESAMT 337

[Federal Office for Environment]
Address: 1 Bismarckplatz, D-1000 Berlin 33

Division of Environmental Issues 338

Head: Herr Menke-Glückert

DEPARTMENT OF BASIC ENVIRONMENTAL ISSUES 339
Head: Herr Herfeld
Activities: Environmental planning; ecology.

DEPARTMENT OF WATER MANAGEMENT, WASTE MANAGEMENT, AIR POLLUTION CONTROL, NOISE ABATEMENT 340
Head: Dr Feldhaus
Activities: Water management: development and testing of mathematical models for water-economy planning purposes; improvement of water storage including ground water accumulation; optimization of drinking water purification by industrial process technology; biological quality determination of ocean waters; flow distributions and effects of specified waste materials in water (evaluation, burden and sanitation concepts); reduction of phosphor content in washing and cleaning agents with view to entire elimination of the phosphor content; development and standardization of analysis and measuring techniques and instruments; development of water-economy control systems; development of waste water purification techniques and optimization of conventional methods; treatment of industrial waste water; natural waste water purification and waste avoidance; storage and transport of potentially water foiling materials.
Waste management: economics, energy and raw material yield from waste products; improved utilization of sludge; control of incineration of dangerous waste

material on open sea; improvement and further development of conventional methods of waste incineration; new methods of thermal waste treatment; energy extraction from waste material; safety, sanitation and recultivation of stored wastes; reduction of pollution from wastes of titanium dioxide production; recovery of secondary raw materials from communal waste products; utilization of industrial by-products especially in the building industry; utilization of secondary raw materials, for example waste paper; measures for reduction, avoidance or use of production-specific waste materials.

Air pollution control: further understanding of the physico-chemical reactions of air pollution; reduction of fine dust particle emissions and health-hazard dust particles; reduction of particularly health-hazard organic compound emissions; reduction of inorganic gaseous air pollution; reduction of trace emissions; reduction of waste material of motorcars; improvement and further development of exhaust gas testing methods; investigations into ecological effects and further development of cooling methods; detection, evaluation and regulation of the thermal burden of the atmosphere.

Noise abatement: measurement and control techniques; sound-diffusing obstructions and meteorological influence; reduction of noise from building contractors plant and other mobile equipment; reduction of noise from large plant and stationary equipment; reduction of noise from domestic sources, eg lawn mowers and heat pumps; reduction of traffic noise, air and rail.

Environmental chemicals/effects of pollutants: early recognition of biological reactions for chemical products; experimental investigations into gaseous air pollution, biozides; toxic dust particles, environmental carcinogens; effects on plants and animals.

Division of Nuclear Reactor Safety, 341 Safety of other Nuclear Installations, Radiation Protection

Head: Herr Sahl

DEPARTMENT OF RADIATION 342 PROTECTION

Head: Professor Dr Hösel
Activities: Radiation protection technology, radioecology; medicine and radiation protection.

DEPARTMENT OF SAFETY FOR 343 NUCLEAR INSTALLATIONS

Head: Herr Pfaffelhuber
Activities: Investigations into problems of safety for nuclear plants.

Bundesministerium für 344 Bildung und Wissenschaft

[Federal Ministry of Education and Science]
Address: Heinemaunstrasse 2, Postfach 200108, D-5300 Bonn
Telephone: (0228) 571-1
Telex: 8 85 666
Activities: All matters concerning education in schools, high schools, universities and colleges of further education as far as the Federal Government is involved. The Ministry is also concerned with basic research in universities and with the German Research Society (Deutsche Forschungsgemeinschaft - DFG), as well as with other institutions supporting or conducting fundamental research.
See separate entry for:
Bundesinstitut für Berufsbildung.

Bundesministerium für 345 Ernährung, Landwirtschaft und Forsten

[Federal Ministry of Food, Agriculture and Forestry]
Address: Postfach 14 02 70, D-5300 Bonn 1
Telephone: (0228) 529-1
Telex: 886844; 886612
Graduate research staff: 639
Annual expenditure: over £2m
Activities: The Federal Ministry maintains 13 Federal Research Centres which are responsible for providing scientific bases for decisions to be taken by policymakers in the fields of food, agricultural, forestry and consumer policies, and for extending scientific knowledge in these fields for the benefit of the general public.

Their research is concentrated on the following areas: maintenance and improvement of the quality of agricultural produce, and of the products of the food industry; development of safe, pollution-free production and processing methods in agriculture and in the food industry; rationalization of production and marketing in agriculture and forestry, structural improvements in the rural area; conservation and exploitation of biological resources, environmental protection, conservation of nature, landscape preservation, protection of animals; improvement of the world food situation and external agricultural relations.
Contract work: Yes
See separate entry for:
Biologische Bundesanstalt für Land und Forstwirtschaft
Bundesanstalt für Fleischforschung
Bundesforschungsanstalt für Ernährung

Bundesforschungsanstalt für Fettforschung
Bundesforschungsanstalt für Fischerei
Bundesforschungsanstalt für Forst- und Holzwirtschaft
Bundesforschungsanstalt für Gartenbauliche Pflanzen-züchtung
Bundesforschungsanstalt für Getreide- und Kar-toffelverarbeitung
Bundesforschungsanstalt für Landwirtschaft Braunsch-weig-Völkenrode
Bundesforschungsanstalt für Milchforschung
Bundesforschungsanstalt für Naturschutz und Lands-chaftsökologie
Bundesforschungsanstalt für Rebenzüchtung Geil-weilerhof
Bundesforschungsanstalt für Viruskrankheiten der Tiere
Deutsche Wissenschaftliche Kommission für Meeresforschung.

Bundesministerium für Forschung und Technologie   346

– BMFT
[Federal Ministry of Research and Technology]
Address: Heinmannstrasse 2, Postfach 200706, D-5300 Bonn 2
Telephone: (0228) 591
Telex: 885674
Parliamentary State-Secretary: Erwin Stahl
State Secretary: Hans-Hilger Haunschild
Annual expenditure: DM5.8m
Activities: The Federal Ministry for Research and Technology was established in 1972 to take re-sponsibility for applied research and development and for financial support of industrial research and technol-ogy.
See separate entry for:
Alfred-Wegener-Institut für Polarforschung
Biologische Anstalt Helgoland.

DIRECTORATE GENERAL I   347

Director-General: Dr Friedrich Bischoff
Sections: Directorate 11: Administration and Orga-nization;
Directorate 12: Research Policy, Finance;
Group 12a: Planning

DIRECTORATE GENERAL II   348

Director-General: Dr Günter Lehr
Sections: Directorate 21: General Research Support, Research Coordination;
Directorate 22: International and Intra-German Cooperation

DIRECTORATE GENERAL III   349

Director-General: Dr Wolf Schmidt-Küster
Sections: Directorate 31: Energy Research and Energy Technology;
Group 32: Safety Research and Environmental Research;
Group 33: Raw Materials and Geosciences

DIRECTORATE GENERAL IV   350

Director-General: Dr Fritz-Rudolf Güntsch
Sections: Directorate 41: Information Technology and Specialized Information;
Directorate 42: Manufacturing Technology, Electronics, Humanization of the Working Environment

DIRECTORATE GENERAL V   351

Director-General: Dr Wolfgang Finke
Sections: Directorate 51: Aeronautics and Space;
Directorate 52: Building and Transport, Medicine, Biol-ogy, Marine Research

Carl Zeiss   352

Address: Postbus 1369/1380, D-7082 Oberkochen
Telephone: (07364) 201
Telex: 07-1375155
Director: Professor Dr W. Schmidt
Departments: Research, Professor Dr W. Schmidt;
Development, Dr R. Grosskopf
Graduate research staff: 140
Annual expenditure: DM75m
Activities: Related to technology in the field of optics, optoelectronics, precision mechanics; and to the development of optical instruments including micro-scopes and electron microscopes, image processing units, ophthalmic instruments, computer-aided optical and precision mechanical measuring, surveying, astronomic and photogrammetric instruments, holographic gratings, lenses for photography and microlithography.
Contract work: No

Carolo-Wilhelmina Technische Universität Braunschweig

353

[Carolo-Wilhelmina Technical University of Brunswick]
Address: Pockelsstrasse 14, D-3300 Braunschweig
Telephone: (0531) 3911
Telex: 09 52 526
President: Professor Dr agr Gerhard Schaffer

FACULTY OF CONSTRUCTION ENGINEERING

354

Department of Architecture

355

Address: Pockelsstrasse 4, D-3300 Braunschweig
Dean: Professor Dr F. Stracke

AGRICULTURAL BUILDINGS DEPARTMENT

356

Address: Mühlenpfordtstrasse 22-23, D-3300 Braunschweig
Head: Professor Dr R. Guldager

ARCHITECTURAL DRAWING DEPARTMENT

357

Address: Mühlenpfordtstrasse 22-23, D-3300 Braunschweig
Head: Professor H. Röcke

BUILDING AND ELEVATION SYSTEMS DEPARTMENT A

358

Head: Professor M. von Gerkan

BUILDING AND ELEVATION SYSTEMS DEPARTMENT B

359

Head: Professor G. Wagner

BUILDING AND ELEVATION SYSTEMS DEPARTMENT C

360

Head: Professor R. Ostertag

BUILDING CONSTRUCTION AND DESIGN PRINCIPLES DEPARTMENT

361

Address: Pockelsstrasse 4, Trakt Schleinitzstrasse, D-3300 Braunschweig
Head: Professor G. Auer

BUILDING CONSTRUCTION DEPARTMENT

362

Address: Schleinitzstrasse, Steinbaracke, D-3300 Braunschweig
Head: Professor Dr J. Herrenberger

BUILDING MATERIALS AND REINFORCED CONCRETE DEPARTMENT

363

Address: Beethovenstrasse 52, D-3300 Braunschweig
Head: Professor Dr K. Kordina

BUILDING STATICS DEPARTMENT

364

Address: Pockelsstrasse 4, D-3300 Braunschweig
Head: Professor Dr R. Grimme

ELEMENTARY SHAPES DEPARTMENT

365

Address: Uhlenpatt, D-3300 Braunschweig
Head: Professor Jürgen Weber

INDUSTRIAL BUILDINGS INSTITUTE

366

Head: Professor Dr W. Henn

TECHNICAL EXPANSION DEPARTMENT

367

Address: Rebenring 18, D-3300 Braunschweig
Head: Professor Dr B. Gockell

TOWN, REGIONAL AND COUNTRY PLANNING INSTITUTE

368

Address: Mühlerpfordstrasse 22-23, D-3300 Braunschweig
Head: Professor Dr F. Stracke

Department of Construction Engineering and Surveying

369

Address: Pockelsstrasse 4, D-3300 Braunschweig
Dean: Professor Dr Ing Günther Garbrecht

BUILDING CONSTRUCTION AND PREFABRICATION DEPARTMENT

370

Address: Schleinitzstrasse, Steinbaracke, D-3300 Braunschweig
Head: Professor Dr H. Paschen

BUILDING ECONOMICS AND MANAGEMENT DEPARTMENT

371

Address: Pockelsstrasse 4, D-3300 Braunschweig
Head: Professor K. Simons

FOUNDATIONS AND SOIL MECHANICS DEPARTMENT

372

Address: Gaussstrasse 2, D-3300 Braunschweig
Head: Professor Dr H. Simons

HIGHWAYS, SOIL AND FOUNDATION ENGINEERING DEPARTMENT

373

Address: Pockelsstrasse 4, D-3300 Braunschweig
Head: Professor Dr W. Arand

LEICHTWEISS INSTITUTE FOR HYDRAULIC ENGINEERING

374

Head: Professor Dr G. Garbrecht

Hydrodynamics and Coastal Hydraulic   375
Engineering Department
Address: Beethovenstrasse 51a, D-3300 Braunschweig
Head: Professor Dr A. Führböter

Water Supply and Engineering Department   376
Address: Beethovenstrasse 51a, D-3300 Braunschweig
Head: Professor Dr S. Falk
Head: Professor Dr Ing Günther Garbrecht

MECHANICS AND STABILITY   377
DEPARTMENT
Address: Abt-Jerusalem-Strasse 7, D-3300 Braunschweig
Head: Professor Dr S. Falk

PHOTOGRAMMETRY AND   378
CARTOGRAPHY DEPARTMENT
Address: Gaussstrasse 22, D-3300 Braunschweig
Director: Professor Dr Ing Günter Weimann

REINFORCED CONCRETE AND HEAVY   379
CONSTRUCTIONS DEPARTMENT
Address: Pockelsstrasse 4, D-3300 Braunschweig
Head: Professor Dr K. Kordina

STATICS INSTITUTE (MECHANICS   380
CENTRE)
Address: Beethovenstrasse 51, D-3300 Braunschweig
Director: Professor Dr H. Duddeck

STEEL CONSTRUCTIONS INSTITUTE   381
Address: Beethovenstrasse 51, D-3300 Braunschweig
Director: Professor Dr J. Scheer

STRUCTURAL MATERIALS, CONCRETE   382
CONSTRUCTION AND FIRE
PROTECTION INSTITUTE
Address: Beethovenstrasse 52, D-3300 Braunschweig
Director: Ferdinand S. Rostasy

SURVEYING INSTITUTE   383
Address: Pockelsstrasse 4, D-3300 Braunschweig
Director: Professor Dr D. Möller

TOWN BUILDINGS INSTITUTE   384
Address: Pockelsstrasse 4, D-3300 Braunschweig
Director: Professor Dr W. Ruske
Note: The Institute also studies street and underground construction.

TRAFFIC, RAILWAYS AND ROAD   385
SAFETY INSTITUTE
Address: Pockelsstrasse 4, D-3300 Braunschweig
Director: Professor Dr K. Pierick

Electrical Communications and High   386
Frequency Engineering
Head: vacant

FACULTY OF MECHANICAL AND   387
ELECTRICAL ENGINEERING
Address: Pockelsstrasse 14, D-3300 Braunschweig
Dean: Professor Dr rer nat Walter Schultz

Department of Electrical Engineering   388
Dean: Professor Dr Ing Eduard Schwartz

COMMUNICATION ENGINEERING   389
INSTITUTE
Address: Schleinitzstrasse 23, D-3300 Braunschweig
Director: Professor Dr Ing Helmut Schönfelder

COMMUNICATION SYSTEMS   390
DEPARTMENT
Address: Hans-Sommer-Strasse 66, D-3300 Braunschweig
Head: Professor Dr Ing Harro-Lothar Hartmann

CONTROL ENGINEERING INSTITUTE   391
Address: Hans-Sommer-Strasse 66, D-3300 Braunschweig
Director: Professor Dr Ing Werner Leonhard

DATA PROCESSING INSTITUTE   392
Address: Hans-Sommer-Strasse 66, D-3300 Braunschweig
Director: Professor Dr Ing Hans-Otto Leilich

ELECTRICAL MACHINES, DRIVES AND   393
RAILWAYS INSTITUTE
Address: Hans-Sommer-Strasse 66, D-3300 Braunschweig
Director: Professor Dr Ing Herbert Weh

ELECTRICAL POWER INSTITUTE   394
Address: Pockelstrasse 4, D-3300 Braunschweig
Director: Professor Dr Ing Adil Erk

ELECTRONICS INSTITUTE   395
Address: Hans-Sommer-Strasse 66, D-3300 Braunschweig
Director: Professor Dr Walter Schultz

ELECTROPHYSICS INSTITUTE   396
Address: Hans-Sommer-Strasse 66, D-3300 Braunschweig
Director: Professor Dr Ing Günter Lautz

FOUNDATIONS OF ELECTRICAL   **397**
ENGINEERING AND ELECTRICAL
METROLOGY INSTITUTE
Address: Hans-Sommer-Strasse 65-66, D-3300 Braunschweig
Director: vacant

GENERAL ELECTRICAL ENGINEERING   **398**
DEPARTMENT
Address: Langer Kamp 19c, D-3300 Braunschweig
Head: Professor Dr Ing Eduard Schwartz

HIGH-FREQUENCY ENGINEERING   **399**
INSTITUTE
Address: Schleinitzstrasse 23, D-3300 Braunschweig
Director: Professor Dr Ing Hans-Georg Unger

HIGH-VOLTAGE ENGINEERING   **400**
INSTITUTE
Address: Pockelsstrasse 4, D-3300 Braunschweig
Director: Professor Dr Ing Hermann Karner

WOOD TECHNOLOGY INSTITUTE   **401**
Address: Bienroderweg 54e, D-3300 Braunschweig
Director: Professor Dr Ing Gert Kossatz

Department of Mechanical   **402**
Engineering

Dean: Professor Dr Ing Franz Gustav Kollmann

AGRICULTURAL MACHINERY   **403**
INSTITUTE
Address: Langer Kamp 19a, D-3300 Braunschweig
Director: Professor Dr Ing Hans-Jürgen Matthies

AIRCRAFT CONSTRUCTION INSTITUTE   **404**
Address: Langer Kamp 19a, D-3300 Braunschweig
Director: Professor Dr Ing Horst Kossira

AIRCRAFT CONTROL INSTITUTE   **405**
Address: Hans-Sommer-Strasse 66, D-3300 Braunschweig
Director: Professor Dr Ing Karl Heinrich Doetsch

CONSTRUCTION, MACHINES AND   **406**
PRECISION PRINCIPLES INSTITUTE
Address: Langer Kamp 8, D-3300 Braunschweig
Director: Professor Dr Ing Karlheinz Roth

FACTORY MANAGEMENT AND   **407**
DEVELOPMENT DEPARTMENT
Address: Katharinenstrasse 3, D-3300 Braunschweig
Head: Professor Dr Ing Ulrich Berr

FLUID MECHANICS INSTITUTE   **408**
Address: Bienroder Weg 3, D-3300 Braunschweig
Director: Professor Dr Ing Boris Laschka

HEAT AND FUEL TECHNOLOGY   **409**
INSTITUTE
Address: Franz-Liszt-Strasse 35, D-3300 Braunschweig
Acting director: Professor Dr Ing Jörg Schwedes

INTERNAL COMBUSTION ENGINES   **410**
INSTITUTE
Address: Langer Kamp 6, D-3300 Braunschweig
Director: Professor Dr Ing Alfred Urlaub

MACHINE ELEMENTS AND   **411**
CONVEYORS INSTITUTE
Address: Langer Kamp 19b, D-3300 Braunschweig
Director: Professor Dr Ing Franz Gustav Kollmann

MACHINE TOOLS AND PRODUCTION   **412**
ENGINEERING INSTITUTE
Address: Langer Kamp 19b, D-3300 Braunschweig
Director: Professor Dr Ing Ernst Saljé

MATERIALS AND MANUFACTURING   **413**
PROCESSES INSTITUTE
Address: Langer Kamp 8, D-3300 Braunschweig
Director: Professor Dr Frank Haessner

MECHANICAL PROCESS   **414**
ENGINEERING DEPARTMENT
Address: Volkmaroder Strasse 4-5, D-3300 Braunschweig
Director: Professor Dr Ing Hans-Jiörg Schwedes

METROLOGY AND REPLACEMENT   **415**
UNITS INSTITUTE
Address: Langer Kamp 19b, D-3300 Braunschweig
Director: Professor Dr Ing Klaus Horn

PFLEIDERER INSTITUTE FOR FLUID   **416**
MACHINES
Address: Langer Kamp 6, D-3300 Braunschweig
Director: Professor Dr Ing Hartwig Petermann

PRECISION AND CONTROL   **417**
ENGINEERING INSTITUTE
Address: Langer Kamp 8, D-3300 Braunschweig
Director: Professor Dr Ing Hans Schier

PROCESS AND NUCLEAR   **418**
ENGINEERING DEPARTMENT
Address: Langer Kamp 7, D-3300 Braunschweig
Director: Professor Dr Ing Matthias Bohnet

SPACECRAFT ENGINEERING AND   **419**
REACTOR THEORY DEPARTMENT
Address: Hans-Sommer-Strasse 5, D-3300 Braunsch-weig
Head: Professor Dr Werner Oldekop

TECHNICAL MECHANICS INSTITUTE   **420**
(MECHANICS CENTRE)
Address: Spielmannstrasse 11, D-3300 Braunschweig
Director: Professor Dr Ing Eberhard Brommundt

Aircraft Mechanics Department   **421**
Address: Rebenring 18, D-3300 Braunschweig
Head: Professor Dr Ing Gunther Schanzer

Mechanics Department B   **422**
Address: Gaussstrasse 14, D-3300 Braunschweig
Head: Professor Dr Ing Elmar Steck

Mechanics Department C   **423**
Address: Gaussstrasse 17, D-3300 Braunschweig
Head: Professor Dr Jürgen Stickforth

THERMODYNAMICS INSTITUTE   **424**
Address: Hans-Sommer-Strasse 5, D-3300 Braunsch-weig
Director: Professor Dr Ing Hans-Jürgen Löffler

TRANSMISSION AND MACHINE   **425**
DYNAMICS INSTITUTE (MECHANICS
CENTRE)
Address: Gaussstrasse 17, D-3300 Braunschweig
Director: Professor Dr Ing Bekir Dizioglu

VEHICLE ENGINEERING INSTITUTE   **426**
Address: Hans-Sommer-Strasse 4, D-3300 Braunsch-weig
Director: Professor Dr Ing Manfred Mitschke

WELDING AND MATERIALS   **427**
TECHNOLOGY INSTITUTE
Address: Langer Kamp 8, D-3300 Braunschweig
Director: Professor Dr Ing Jürgen Ruge

WÖHLER INSTITUTE FOR STABILITY   **428**
AND VIBRATIONS RESEARCH
Address: Langer Kamp 8, D-3300 Braunschweig
Directors: Professor Dr Ing Jürgen Ruge, Professor Dr Frank Haessner

FACULTY OF NATURAL SCIENCES   429

Dean: Professor Dr phil nat Claus Führer

Department of Anthropological   **430**
Geography
Address: Langer Kamp 19c, D-3300 Braunschweig
Head: Professor Dr Arnold Beuermann

Department of Chemistry, Pharmacy   **431**
and Life Sciences
Dean: Professor Dr rer nat Thomas Hartmann

AGRICULTURAL TECHNOLOGY AND   **432**
SUGAR INDUSTRY INSTITUTE
Address: Langer Kamp 5, D-3300 Braunschweig
Director: Professor Dr Erich Reinefeld

ANTHROPOLOGY INSTITUTE   **433**
Address: Konstantin-Unde-Strasse 3, D-3300 Braun-schweig
Head: Professor Dr Egon Renèr

BIOCHEMISTRY AND   **434**
BIOTECHNOLOGY DEPARTMENT
Address: Mascheroder Weg 1, D-3301 Stöckheim
Head: Professor Fritz Wagner

BOTANY INSTITUTE AND BOTANICAL   **435**
GARDEN
Address: Humboldtstrasse 1, D-3300 Braunschweig
Director: Professor Dr Gottfried Galling

CHEMICAL TECHNOLOGY INSTITUTE   **436**
Address: Hans-Sommer-Strasse 10, D-3300 Braunsch-weig
Director: Professor Dr Joachim Klein

FOOD CHEMISTRY INSTITUTE   **437**
Address: Fasanenstrasse 3, D-3300 Braunschweig
Director: Professor Dr Hans-Gerhard Maier

HUMAN AND CYTOGENETICS   **438**
INSTITUTE
Address: Gaussstrasse 17, D-3300 Braunschweig
Head: Professor Dr Paul Eberle

INORGANIC CHEMISTRY INSTITUTE A   **439**
Address: Pockelsstrasse 4, D-3300 Braunschweig
Director: Professor Dr Ulrich Wannagat

INORGANIC CHEMISTRY INSTITUTE B   **440**
Address: Pockelsstrasse 4, D-3300 Braunschweig
Director: Professor Dr Reinhard Schmutzler

MICROBIOLOGY DEPARTMENT   **441**
Address: Gaussstrasse 7, D-3300 Braunschweig
Head: Professor Dr Rolf Näveke

**ORGANIC CHEMISTRY DEPARTMENT   442
B**
Address: Pockelsstrasse 4, D-3300 Braunschweig
Head: Professor Dr Peter Boldt

**ORGANIC CHEMISTRY INSTITUTE   443
AND ORGANIC CHEMISTRY
DEPARTMENT A**
Address: Pockelsstrasse 4, D-3300 Braunschweig
Director: Professor Dr Henning Hopf

**PHARMACEUTICAL CHEMISTRY   444
INSTITUTE**
Address: Beethovenstrasse 55, D-3300 Braunschweig
Director: Professor Dr Gerwalt Zinner

**PHARMACEUTICAL TECHNOLOGY   445
INSTITUTE**
Address: Pockelsstrasse 4, D-3300 Braunschweig
Director: Professor Dr Claus Führer

**PHARMACOGNOSY AND BIOLOGY   446
INSTITUTE**
Address: Pockelsstrasse 4, D-3300 Braunschweig
Director: Professor Dr Thomas Hartmann

**PHARMACOLOGY AND TOXICOLOGY   447
INSTITUTE**
Address: Bultenweg 17, D-3300 Braunschweig
Director: Professor Dr Erich Heeg

**PHYSICAL CHEMISTRY DEPARTMENT   448
B**
Address: Hans-Sommer-Strasse 10, D-3300 Braunsch-
weig
Head: Professor Dr Herbert Dreeskamp

**PHYSICAL CHEMISTRY INSTITUTE   449
AND PHYSICAL CHEMISTRY
DEPARTMENT A**
Address: Hans-Sommer-Strasse 10, D-3300 Braunsch-
weig
Director: Professor Dr Rolf Lacmann

PSYCHOLOGY INSTITUTE   450

Psychology Department A   451
Address: Spielmannstrasse 19, D-3300 Braunschweig
Head: Professor Dr Karl Friedrich Wender

Psychology Department B   452
Address: Spielmannstrasse 12a, D-3300 Braunschweig
Head: Professor Dr Hans Christoph Micko

SPORT SCIENCES DEPARTMENT   453
Address: Franz-Liszt-Strasse 34, D-3300 Braunsch-
weig
Head: Professor Dr K.H. Leist

ZOOLOGY INSTITUTE   454
Address: Pockelsstrasse 10a, D-3300 Braunschweig
Director: Professor Dr Carl Hauenschild

Department of Industrial Management   455
Address: Abt-Jerusalem-Strasse 4, D-3300 Braunsch-
weig
Director: Professor Dr Hans-Joachim Engeleiter

**Department of Mathematics and   456
Computer Sciences**
Dean: Professor Dr rer nat Ernst Henze

APPLIED MATHEMATICS INSTITUTE   457
Address: Pockelsstrasse 14, D-3300 Braunschweig
Director: Professor Dr Ernst Henze

COMPUTER ENGINEERING INSTITUTE   458
Address: Pockelsstrasse 14, D-3300 Braunschweig
Director: Professor Dr Manfred Feilmeier

Informatics Department A   459
Address: Gaussstrasse 12, D-3300 Braunschweig
Head: Professor Dr Klaus Alber

Informatics Department B   460
Address: Gaussstrasse 12, D-3300 Braunschweig
Acting head: Professor Dr Vladimir Cherniavsky

Informatics Department C   461
Address: Gaussstrasse 11, D-3300 Braunschweig
Head: Professor Dr Roland Vollmar

Informatics Department D   462
Address: Gaussstrasse 11, D-3300 Braunschweig
Head: Professor Dr Günther Stiege

MATHEMATICS INSTITUTE A   463
Address: Pockelsstrasse 14, D-3300 Braunschweig
Director: Professor Dr Joachim Jaenicke

MATHEMATICS INSTITUTE B   464
Address: Pockelsstrasse 14, D-3300 Braunschweig
Director: vacant

MATHEMATICS INSTITUTE C   465
Address: Pockelsstrasse 14, D-3300 Braunschweig
Director: Professor Dr Hans-Joachim Kowalsky

MATHEMATICS INSTITUTE D   466
Address: Pockelsstrasse 14, D-3300 Braunschweig
Director: Professor Dr Udo Ott

MATHEMATICS INSTITUTE E   467
Address: Pockelsstrasse 14, D-3300 Braunschweig
Director: Professor Dr Helmut Brass

Department of Physical Geography　468

Address: Langer Kamp 19c, D-3300 Braunschweig
Head: Professor Dr Heinrich Rohdenborg

Department of Physics and Earth　469
Sciences

Dean: Professor Dr rer nat Herbert Brömer

GEOGRAPHY INSTITUTE　470
Address: Langer Kamp 19c, D-3300 Braunschweig
Director: Professor Dr Arnold Beuermann

GEOLOGY AND PALAEONTOLOGY　471
INSTITUTE
Address: Pockelsstrasse 4, D-3300 Braunschweig
Director: Professor Dr Wolfgang Krebs

GEOPHYSICS AND METEOROLOGY　472
INSTITUTE
Address: Mendelssohnstrasse 1, D-3300 Braunschweig
Director: Professor Dr Walter Kertz

MINERALOGY AND PETROGRAPHY　473
INSTITUTE
Address: Gaussstrasse 29, D-3300 Braunschweig
Director: Professor Dr Martin Okrusch

PHYSICS INSTITUTE A　474
Address: Mendelssohnstrasse 1, D-3300 Braunschweig
Director: Professor Dr Christoph Schwink

PHYSICS INSTITUTE B　475
Address: Pockelsstrasse 4, D-3300 Braunschweig
Director: Professor Dr Franz Rudolf Kessler

TECHNICAL PHYSICS INSTITUTE　476
Address: Mendelssohnstrasse 1, D-3300 Braunschweig
Director: Professor Dr Wolfgang Grey

THEORETICAL PHYSICS INSTITUTE A　477
Address: Mendelssohnstrasse 1, D-3300 Braunschweig
Director: Professor Dr Gerhard Simon

THEORETICAL PHYSICS INSTITUTE B　478
Address: Mendelssohnstrasse 1, D-3300 Braunschweig
Director: Professor Dr Egon Richter

Department of Political Economy and　479
Economics Institute

Address: Pockelsstrasse 14, D-3300 Braunschweig
Director: Professor Dr Herbert Wilhelm

Department of Statistics and　480
Econometrics

Address: Abt-Jerusalem-Strasse 4, D-3300 Braunschweig
Head: Professor Dr Jochen Schwarze

Celamerck GmbH & Co KG　481

– CM
Address: Binger Strasse, D-6507 Ingelheim am Rhein
Telephone: 06132/771
Telex: 04187130; 04187137
Research director: Dr Klaus Brückner
Sections: Chemical research, Dr Walter Ost; biological research, Dr Franz-Peter Schicke; biological, Dr Hermann Körner
Graduate research staff: 38
Annual expenditure: over £2m
Activities: Synthesis of new chemical compounds, development of pesticides and similar products. Research activities cover all related fields, for instance, chemistry, screening, biochemistry, toxicology, ecology, etc. Celamerck possesses a number of laboratories, and experimental stations in Germany and Colombia.
Contract work No

Christian-Albrechts-　482
Universität Kiel

[Christian-Albrechts University Kiel]
Address: Olshausenstrasse 40-60, D-2300 Kiel
Telephone: (0431) 8801
President: Professor Dr Gerd Griesser

FACULTY OF AGRICULTURE　483

Agricultural Labour and Management　484
Institute

Address: Neue Universität, Haus N 2a/b, D-2300 Kiel
Chairman: Professor Dr Cay Langbehn
Sections: Farming economics, Professor Dr Claus-Hennig Hanf; applied agricultural management, Professor Dr Cay Langbehn, Professor Dr Klaus Riebe

Agricultural Policy and Marketing Institute 485

Address: Neue Universität, Haus N 2, D-2300 Kiel
Chairman: Professor Dr Wilhelm Scheper
Sections: Agricultural policy, Professor Dr Wilhelm Scheper; marketing, Professor Dr Ulrich Koester; market research and international food economics, Professor Dr Adolf Weber

Agricultural Techniques Institute 486

Address: Neue Universität, Haus N 23, D-2300 Kiel
Chairman: Professor Dr Edmund Isensee

Animal Husbandry and Behaviour Institute 487

Address: Neue Universität, Haus S 20c, D-2300 Kiel
Chairman: Professor Dr Ernst Kalm
Senior staff: Professor Dr Ekkehard Ernst

Animal Nutrition and Fodder Science Institute 488

Address: Neue Universität, Haus S 24c, D-2300 Kiel
Chairman: Professor Dr Kraft Drepper
Senior staff: Professor Dr Helmut Henkel

Federal Institute of Dairy Research 489

Address: Hermann-Weigmann-Strasse 1-27, D-2300 Kiel
Director: Professor Dr Hans-Otto Gravert
Departments: Hygiene, Professor Dr Adolf Tolle, Professor Dr Walther Heeschen; Virus research and experimental medicine, Professor Dr Michael Teuber; Chemistry, vacant; Physics, Professor Dr Ernst Knoop; Management and market research, Professor Dr Neitzk; Dairy techniques, Professor Dr Helmut Reuter
Note: This is a cooperative institute.

Human Nutrition and Food Science Institute 490

Address: Düsternbrooker Weg 17/19, D-2300 Kiel
Chairman: Professor Dr Walter Feldheim
Senior staff: Professor Dr Helmut Ebersdobler

Nutrition, Economics and Consumption Institute 491

Address: Düsternbrooker Weg 17/19, D-2300 Kiel
Chairman: vacant
Senior staff: Professor Dr Klaus Hesse, Professor Dr Hans Stamer

Plant Cultivation and Breeding Institute 492

Address: Neue Universität, Haus S 20a, D-2300 Kiel
Chairman: Professor Dr Gerhard Geisler
Sections: Plant cultivation and breeding, Professor Dr Gerhard Geisler, Professor Dr Manfred Hühn; general plant cultivation, Professor Dr Herbert Hanus

Plant Nutrition and Soil Science Institute 493

Address: Neue Universität, Haus S 20a, D-2300 Kiel
Chairman: Professor Dr Wenzel Hoffmann
Sections: Plant nutrition, Professor Dr Arnold Finck, Professor Wenzel Hoffmann; soil sciences, Professor Dr Gerhard Brümmer, Professor Dr Diedrich Schroeder

Plant Pathology Institute 494

Address: Neue Universität, Haus S 24c, D-2300 Kiel
Chairman: Professor Dr Horst Börner

Water Economics and Landscape Ecology Institute 495

Address: Neue Universität, Haus S 24c, D-2300 Kiel
Chairman: Professor Dr Norbert Knauer
Senior staff: Professor Dr Peter Widmoser

FACULTY OF MATHEMATICS AND NATURAL SCIENCES 496

Anthropology Institute 497

Address: Neue Universität, Haus S 12a, D-2300 Kiel
Chairman: Professor Dr Hans W. Jürgens

Applied Physics Institute 498

Address: Neue Universität, Haus N 61a, D-2300 Kiel
Chairman: Professor Dr Hans Hinkelmann
Senior staff: Professor Dr Kurt Vanselow, Professor Dr Erich O. Schulz-Dubois

Botanical Institute and Botanical Garden 499

Address: Neue Universität, Gebäude N 41, D-2300 Kiel
Chairman: Professor Dr Rainer Kollmann
Senior staff: Professor Dr Horst Binding, Professor Dr Klaus Dierssen, Professor Dr Rainer Kollmann, Professor Dr Hansjörg Rudolph, Professor Dr Jörg Sauter, Professor Dr Herbert Straka

Domestic Animal Sciences Institute 500

Address: Neue Universität, Haus S 20c, D-2300 Kiel
Chairman: Professor Dr Herwart Bohlken
Senior staff: Professor Dr Eberhard Haase, Professor
Dr Wolfhart Schultz

Experimental Physics Institute 501

Address: Neue Universität, Haus N 61d, D-2300 Kiel
Chairman: Professor Dr Johannes Richter
Senior staff: Professor Dr Frithjof Karstensen,
Professor Dr Reimer Lincke, Professor Dr Michael
Skibowski, Professor Dr Ruprecht Haensel

General Microbiology Institute 502

Address: Neue Universität, Biologiezentrum, D-2300
Kiel
Chairman: Professor Dr Peter Hirsch

Geographical Institute 503

Address: Neue Universität, Haus S 13c, D-2300 Kiel
Chairman: Professor Dr Jürgen Bähr
Senior staff: Professor Dr Hermann Achenbach,
Professor Dr Dietrich Bartels, Professor Dr Klaus Hor-
mann, Professor Dr Reinhard Stewig

Geology and Palaeontology Institute 504
and Museum

Address: Neue Universität, Haus S 13a, D-2300 Kiel
Chairman: Professor Dr Horst Böger
Senior staff: Professor Dr Klaus Duphorn, Professor
Dr Rolf Köster, Professor Dr Johann M. Sarnthein-
Lotichius, Professor Dr Eugen Seibold, Professor Dr
Gerhard F. Lutze, Professor Dr Georg Matthess,
Professor Dr Eckart Walger

Geophysics Institute 505

Address: Neue Universität, Haus S 61c, D-2300 Kiel
Chairman: Professor Dr Rudolf Meissner
Senior staff: Professor Dr Jochen Zschau

Information Sciences and Practical 506
Mathematics Institute and Computer
Centre

Address: Neue Universität, Haus S 12a, D-2300 Kiel
Chairman: Professor Dr Bodo Schlender
Senior staff: Professor Dr Peter Kandzia, Professor Dr
Hans Langmaack, Professor Dr Alfons Jammel,
Professor Dr Gerhard Zimmermann

Inorganic Chemistry Institute 507

Address: Neue Universität, Haus N 13a, D-2300 Kiel
Chairman: Professor Dr Gerhard Lagaly
Senior staff: Professor Dr Wilhelm Preetz, Professor
Hanskarl Müller-Buschbaum

Mathematics Seminar 508

Address: Neue Universität, Haus S 12a, D-2300 Kiel
Chairman: Professor Dr Helmut Bender
Senior staff: Professor Dr Joachim Ahrens, Professor
Dr Dieter Betten, Professor Dr Klaus Floret, Professor
Dr Wolfgang Gaschütz, Professor Dr Martin Götzky,
Professor Dr Hans Günzler, Professor Dr Roland
Schmidt, Professor Dr Peter Kosmol, Professor Dr
Joseph Wloka, Professor Dr Hilger Wolff

Mineralogy and Petrography Institute 509
and Museum

Address: Neue Universität, Haus S 13a, D-2300 Kiel
Chairman: Professor Dr Paul Hörmann
Senior staff: Professor Dr Hartmut Kern, Professor Dr
Horst Küppers, Professor Dr Friedrich Liebau,
Professor Dr Friedrich Seifert, Professor Dr Michael
Raith

Museum and Zoological Institute 510

Address: Hegewisch Strasse 3, D-2300 Kiel
Chairman: Professor Dr Hans-Dieter Jankowsky
Senior staff: Professor Dr Klaus Böttger, Professor Dr
Berndt Heydemann, Professor Dr Helmut Laudien,
Professor Dr Wolfram Noodt, Professor Dr Hubert
Pschorn-Walcher, Professor Dr Fritz-Helmut Ullerich,
Professor Dr Wolf Wünnenberg, Professor Dr Katesa
Schlosser

Organic Chemistry Institute 511

Address: Neue Universität, Haus N 21, D-2300 Kiel
Chairman: Professor Dr Werner Tochtermann
Senior staff: Professor Dr Günter-Paulus Schiemenz,
Professor Dr Erich Vorwonkel

Pharmaceutical Biology Institute 512

Address: Grasweg 9, D-2300 Kiel
Chairman: Professor Dr Peter Pohl
Senior staff: Professor Dr Dietrich Frohne, Professor
Dr Ferdinand Amelunxen

Pharmaceutical Institute   513

Address: Gutenbergstrasse 76-78, D-2300 Kiel
Chairman: Professor Dr Rolf Haller
Senior staff: Professor Dr Jörg Schnekenburger,
Professor Dr Bernd Müller

Physical Chemistry Institute   514

Address: Neue Universität, Haus S 12c, D-2300 Kiel
Chairman: Professor Dr Antonio Guanieri
Senior staff: Professor Dr Horst Brodowsky, Professor
Dr Helmut Dreizler, Professor Dr Ralf Schindler

Pure and Applied Nuclear Physics   515
Institute

Address: Neue Universität, Haus N 20a, D-2300 Kiel
Chairman: Professor Dr Klaus-Oswald Thielheim
Senior staff: Professor Dr Otto-Claus Allkofer,
Professor Dr Gerd Wibberenz

Theoretical Physics Institute and   516
Astronomical Observatory

Address: Neue Universität, Haus N 61c, D-2300 Kiel
Chairman: Professor Dr Volker Weidemann
Senior staff: Professor Dr Kurt Hunger, Professor Dr
Heinz Koppe, Professor Dr Hartmut Holweger,
Professor Dr Dieter Schluter

University Affiliated Institutes   517

OCEANOGRAPHY INSTITUTE   518
Address: Düsternbrooker Weg 20, D-2300 Kiel
Director: Professor Dr Bernt Zeitzschel
Departments: Regional oceanography, Professor Dr
John Woods; Theoretical oceanography, Professor Dr
Wolfgang Krauss; Marine physics, Professor Dr Gerold
Siedler; Maritime meteorology, Professor Dr Lutz
Hasse; Marine chemistry, Professor Dr Klaus
Grasshoff; Fishery biology, Professor Dr Gotthilf
Hempel; Marine zoology, Professor Dr Dieter Adelung;
Marine botany, vacant; Marine planktonology,
Professor Dr Bernt Zeitzschel; Marine microbiology,
Professor Dr Gerhard Rheinheimer

THEORY OF PHYSICAL SCIENCE   519
INSTITUTE
Address: Olshausenstrasse 40-60, D-2300 Kiel
Chairman: Professor Dr Karl Frey

FACULTY OF MEDICINE   520
Address: Olshausenstrasse 40-60, D-2300 Kiel

Anatomical Institute   521

Chairman: Professor Dr Helmut Leonhardt
Senior staff: Professor Dr Ulrich Welsch, Professor Dr
Fritz-Wilhelm Pehlemann, Professor Dr Bernhard Til-
lmann, Professor Dr Karl Zilles

Applied Physiology and Medical   522
Climatology Institute

Chairman: Professor Dr Erich Witzleb
Deputy Chairman: Professor Dr Uwe Jessel

Biochemical Institute   523

Chairman: Professor Dr Bent Havsteen
Senior staff: Professor Dr Friedrich Klink

Clinical Centres   524

Address: Hospitalstrasse 21-23, D-2300 Kiel
Chairman: Professor Dr Gustav Schimmelpenning
Deputy Chairman: Professor Dr Arnold Bernsmeier

Clinical Theoretical Medicine Centre I   525

Director: Professor Dr Karl Lennert

CHILD PATHOLOGY DEPARTMENT   526
Address: Hospitalstrasse 42, D-2300 Kiel
Head: Professor Dr Dieter Harms

CYTOPATHOLOGY DEPARTMENT   527
Address: Hospitalstrasse 42, D-2300 Kiel
Head: Professor Dr Ernst Sprenger

GENERAL PATHOLOGY AND   528
PATHOLOGICAL ANATOMY
DEPARTMENT
Address: Hospitalstrasse 42, D-2300 Kiel
Head: Professor Dr Karl Lennert
Deputy Head: Professor Dr Hans-Jochen Stutte

HYGIENE, SOCIAL HYGIENE AND   529
HEALTH DEPARTMENT
Address: Brunswiker Strasse 2-6, D-2300 Kiel
Head: Professor Dr Knut-Olaf Gundermann

IMMUNOLOGY DEPARTMENT   530
Address: Brunswiker Strasse 2-6, D-2300 Kiel
Head: Professor Dr Wolfgang Müller-Ruchholtz

MEDICAL MICROBIOLOGY   531
DEPARTMENT
Address: Brunswiker Strasse 2-6, D-2300 Kiel
Head: Professor Dr Uwe Ullmann

Clinical Theoretical Medicine Centre II 532

Director: Professor Dr Oskar Grüner

GENERAL FORENSIC MEDICINE 533
DEPARTMENT
Address: Hospitalstrasse 17-19, D-2300 Kiel
Head: Professor Dr Oskar Grüner
Sections: State Blood Alcohol Office, Professor Dr Oskar Grüner; Sexual Medicine Research and Consultation Office, Professor Dr Reinhard Wille

PHARMACOLOGY DEPARTMENT 534
Address: Hospitalstrasse 4-6, D-2300 Kiel
Head: Professor Dr Heinz Lüllmann

SPECIAL FORENSIC MEDICINE 535
DEPARTMENT
Address: Hospitalstrasse 17-19, D-2300 Kiel
Head: vacant

TOXICOLOGY DEPARTMENT 536
Address: Hospitalstrasse 4-6, D-2300 Kiel
Head: Professor Dr Otmar Wassermann

Conservative Medicine Centre I 537

Director: Professor Dr Arnold Bernsmeier

DERMATOLOGY AND VENEREOLOGY 538
DEPARTMENT
Address: Schittenhelmstrasse 7, D-2300 Kiel
Head: Professor Dr Enno Christophers

GENERAL INTERNAL MEDICINE 539
DEPARTMENT
Address: Schittenhelmstrasse 12, D-2300 Kiel
Head: Professor Dr Arnold Bernsmeier
Deputy Head: Professor Dr Fred Hartmann

NERVOUS DISEASES CENTRE 540
Address: Niemannsweg 147, D-2300 Kiel
Director: Professor Dr G.W. Schimmelpenning

Child and Adolescent Psychiatry Department 541
Head: vacant

Neurology Department 542
Head: Professor Dr Dieter Soyka
Deputy Head: Dr Klaus Christiani

Psychiatry Department 543
Head: Professor Dr G.W. Schimmelpenning
Deputy Head: Professor Dr Hans Grahmann

**Psychotherapy and Psychosomatics 544
Department**
Head: Professor Dr Heinrich Völkel

SPECIAL CARDIOLOGY DEPARTMENT 545
Address: Schittenhelmstrasse 12, D-2300 Kiel
Head: Professor Dr Jochen Schaefer

SPECIAL NEPHROLOGY AND DIALYSIS 546
DEPARTMENT
Address: Schittenhelmstrasse 12, D-2300 Kiel
Head: Professor Dr Walter Niedermayer

Conservative Medicine Centre II 547

Address: Schwanenweg 18-26, D-2300 Kiel
Director: Professor Dr Paul Heintzen

GENERAL PAEDIATRICS DEPARTMENT 548
Head: Professor Dr Jüngen Schaub
Sections: Infectious diseases and clinical microbiology, Professor Dr Claus Simon; cytogenetics, Professor Dr Maria-Elisabeth Tolksdorf

HUMAN GENETICS DEPARTMENT 549
Head: Professor Dr Werner Grote
Deputy Head: Professor Dr Horst Behnke

PAEDIATRIC CARDIOLOGY 550
DEPARTMENT
Head: Professor Dr Paul Heintzen

PAEDIATRIC NEUROLOGY 551
DEPARTMENT
Head: Professor Dr Hermann Doose

History of Medicine and Pharmacy 552
Institute

Address: Brunswiker Strasse 2a, D-2300 Kiel
Chairman: Professor Dr Fridolf Kudlien
Deputy Chairman: Professor Dr Gerhard Rudolph

Interdisciplinary Centre 553

Director: Professor Dr Helmut Gremmel

ANAESTHESIOLOGY DEPARTMENT 554
Address: Schwanenweg 21, D-2300 Kiel
Head: Professor Dr Jürgen Wawersik
Deputy Head: Dr Klaus-J. Fischer

BLOOD TRANSFUSION DEPARTMENT 555
Address: Klaus-Groth-Platz 2, D-2300 Kiel
Head: Professor Dr Volkmar Sachs

MEDICAL STATISTICS AND 556
DOCUMENTATION DEPARTMENT
Address: Brunswiker Strasse 2a, D-2300 Kiel
Head: Professor Dr Karl Sauter

RADIOLOGY DEPARTMENT   557
Address: Arnold-Heller-Strasse 9, D-2300 Kiel
Head: Professor Dr Helmut Gremmel
Deputy Head: Professor Dr Hans Werner

Operative Medicine Centre I   558
Director: Professor Dr Kurt Semm

CARDIOVASCULAR SURGERY   559
DEPARTMENT
Address: Hospitalstrasse 40, D-2300 Kiel
Head: Professor Dr Alexander Bernhard

GENERAL SURGERY DEPARTMENT   560
Address: Hospitalstrasse 40, D-2300 Kiel
Head: Professor Dr Horst Hamelmann
Deputy Head: Dr Hans Troidl

OBSTETRICS AND GYNAECOLOGY   561
DEPARTMENT
Address: Hegewischstrasse 4, D-2300 Kiel
Head: Professor Dr Kurt Semm

UROLOGY DEPARTMENT   562
Address: Hospitalstrasse 40, D-2300 Kiel
Head: Professor Dr Heribert Wand

Operative Medicine Centre II   563
Director: Professor Dr Hans-Peter Jensen

EAR, NOSE AND THROAT   564
DEPARTMENT
Address: Hospitalstrasse 20, D-2300 Kiel
Head: Professor Dr Heinrich Rudert

NEUROSURGERY DEPARTMENT   565
Address: Wiemarer Strasse 8, D-2300 Kiel
Head: Professor Dr Hans-Peter Jensen

OPHTHALMOLOGY DEPARTMENT   566
Address: Hegewischstrasse 2, D-2300 Kiel
Head: Professor Dr Wilhelm Böke
Deputy Head: Professor Dr Hans-J. Thiel

ORTHOPAEDICS DEPARTMENT   567
Address: Klaus-Groth-Platz 4, D-2300 Kiel
Head: Professor Dr Walter Blauth
Deputy Head: Dr Peter Hippe

ORTHOPTICS AND PLEOPTICS   568
DEPARTMENT
Address: Hegewischstrasse 2, D-2300 Kiel
Head: Professor Dr Wilfried de Decker

Physiological Institute   569
Chairman: Professor Dr Miklos Mályusz
Senior staff: Professor Dr Robert Schmidt, Professor
Dr Werner Ulbricht

Tooth, Mouth and Jaw Centre   570
Address: Arnold-Heller-Strasse, D-2300 Kiel
Director: Professor Dr Karlheinz Körber

CONSERVATIVE DENTISTRY   571
DEPARTMENT
Head: Professor Dr Wolfgang Hoppe
Section: Paradontology, Professor Dr Hans-C. Plagmann

DENTAL SURGERY DEPARTMENT   572
Head: Professor Dr Franz Härle
Deputy Head: Professor Dr Rolf Ewers

ORTHODONTICS DEPARTMENT   573
Acting head: Professor Dr Karlheinz Körber

PROSTHESIS DEPARTMENT   574
Head: Professor Dr Karlheinz Körber

DECHEMA-Institut (Karl-   575
Winnacker-Institut)

[DECHEMA German Association for Chemical
Engineering]
Address: Theodor-Heuss-Allee 25, Postfach 970146,
D-6000 Frankfurt-am-Main 97
Telephone: (0611) 75641
Telex: 412490 dchma d
President: Professor Dr Heinz-Gerhard Franck
Research director: Professor Dr Dieter Behrens
Activities: The Institute is concerned with research and
teaching in industrial chemistry, process engineering
and materials sciences, and the scientific fundamentals
of chemical engineering. Experimental courses under
practical conditions are organized for practising scientists and engineers from the chemical industry, chemical
plant manufacturers, and engineering firms.
In the research sector the Industrial Chemistry Department investigates problems of chemical reaction and
process engineering, industrial biochemistry, physical
measurement and instrumentation, and the analysis of
emissions.
The Materials and Corrosion Department is engaged in
research projects covering the strength of materials and
components, design problems and fracture toughness of
materials, electrochemistry, high-temperature corrosion, and corrosion testing.
Contract work: Yes

INDUSTRIAL CHEMISTRY DEPARTMENT 576

Head: Professor Dr Kurt Kirchner
Sections: Chemical reactions and process engineering, K. Kirchner; technical biochemistry, K. Buchholz; physical measurement, V.G. Gundelach; applied emissions analysis, K.H. Bergert

MATERIALS AND CORROSION DEPARTMENT 577

Heads: Professor Dr Ing C.-M. von Meysenbug, E. Heitz
Sections: Materials behaviour, C.-M. von Meysenbug, H.-E. Buhler; corrosion, E. Heitz; high-temperature corrosion, A. Rahmel; electrochemistry, G. Kreysa; applied corrosion testing, H.-E. Buhler; exhaust gas measurement, K.-H. Bergert

Degussa AG 578

Address: Postfach 26 44, D-6000 Frankfurt am Main 1
Telephone: (0611) 218-1
Telex: 41222-0 dg d
Research Directors: Metals, Professor Dr Bernhard Liebmann; chemicals, Dr Heribert Offermanns; pharmaceuticals, Dr Heribert Offermanns
Sections: Metals research, Dr Hans-H. Beyer; chemicals research, Dr Heribert Offermanns; pharmaceuticals research, Dr Ansgar von Schlichtegroll
Graduate research staff: 250
Annual expenditure: over £2m
Activities: Metals, especially precious metals, dental alloys, materials for electrical contacts, brazing alloys, electrical thermometers, heat treatment and surface coatings. Chemistry of silicas, carbon blacks, hydrogen peroxide, peroxy compounds, hydrogen cyanide, amino acids, acrolein, (meth)acrylates, catalysts, pigments and glazes. Heart, circulatory, respiratory, gastro-intestinal, cancer and virus diseases.
Contract work: No

Deutsche Babcock Aktiengesellschaft 579

Address: Duisburger Strasse 375, D-4200 Oberhausen 1
Telephone: (0208) 833 1
Telex: 856951 DBAB
Note: Through its many subsidiaries, Deutsche Babcock produces plant and technology in the following major areas: power generation and thermal engineering;

general mechanical engineering; environmental engineering; textile engineering; process engineering; ventilation and air conditioning; piping, steelwork and vessels; civil engineering; industrial services and supplies.

RESEARCH AND DEVELOPMENT DIVISION 580

Research director: Dipl-Ing Rudolf Willach
Sections: Boiler engineering; firing systems; process engineering
Graduate research staff: 60
Annual expenditure: over £2m
Activities: Firing systems: study of fuel properties; fuel desulphurization, systems for the combustion of oil, gas and solid fuels including fluidized bed firing systems; flue gas flows; flue gas desulphurization; flue gas analyses.
Boiler engineering: heat transfer; applied fluid dynamics; metallurgy; problems of mechanical strength; mathematical methods of calculation for steam generators; chemical composition of metals; phase break; fluid mechanics.
Process engineering: pyrolysis; noxious matter absorption; non-ferrous metal winning; black liquor treatment.
Contract work: No
Publications: Babcock-Mitteilungen.

Deutsche Forschungs- und Versuchsanstalt für Luft- und Raumfahrt eV 581

– DFVLR
[German Aerospace Research Establishment]
Address: Linder Höhe, Postfach 90 60 58, D-5000 Köln 90
Telephone: (02203) 6011
Telex: 08 874410 dfvw d
Chairman: Professor Dr rer nat Hermann L. Jordan
Graduate research staff: 1 000
Annual expenditure: £501 000-2m
Activities: DFVLR is the largest research establishment dealing with engineering sciences in the Federal Republic of Germany. Its research centres are located in Braunschweig, Göttingen, Köln-Porz, Stuttgart, and Oberpfaffenhofen near Munich. Research is mainly in aerospace and the results are also applied to a certain extent in other fields; such as the development of advanced transportation and communication systems, non-nuclear energetics and improvement of living conditions.
Facilities: Wind tunnels for subsonic to hypersonic speeds; test stands for aircraft and rocket engines;

spacecraft data receiving and command stations, plus mobile launch equipment for sounding rockets; space simulation chambers of different sizes; test bed and experimental aircraft as well as ground and airborne simulators.
Contract work: Yes
Publications: DFVLR-Nachrichten; DFVLR Guide (in English).

COMMUNICATIONS TECHNOLOGY 582 AND REMOTE SENSING RESEARCH DEPARTMENT

Address: Oberpfaffenhofen, D-8031 Wessling
Telephone: (08153) 281
Telex: 526419 (dvlop d)
Activities: Communication and data transmission via satellites from earth to earth and from earth to ship; satellite experiments; remote sensing of the earth from aircraft and satellite by camera and line scanner in the visible, infrared, and microwave range; development of sensors in the visible, infrared, and microwave range.
Contract work: Yes

Institute for Atmospheric Physics 583

Head: Dr rer nat M.E. Reinhardt
Activities: Atmospheric measurement techniques; atmospheric influences within the programme of target recognition and reconnaissance; measurement of man-made pollution in the atmospheric environment; theoretical-meteorological system simulation.

Institute for Optoelectronics 584

Head: Professor Dr F. Lanzl
Activities: User-oriented missions of remote-sensing techniques: electromagnetic properties, spectral emission and reflection of natural and artificial surfaces in the range of visible and infrared wave lengths are utilized for object recognition and identification; definition of the sensor payload part of future space missions, especially Spacelab.

Institute for Radio Frequency 585 Technology

Head: Dr W. Keydel
Activities: Electromagnetic wave fields; aerials and sensors; high frequency components and circuits; high frequency measuring technology; radio voice and data transmission; radar procedures; microwave radiometry; radio frequency systems.

Institute for Telecommunications 586

Head: Dr H. Häberle
Activities: Development of applicable techniques in telecommunications, communications theory, digital image processing and circuit technology.

ENERGETICS RESEARCH 587 DEPARTMENT

Address: Pfaffenwaldring 38-40, D-7000 Stuttgart 80
Telephone: (0711) 78321
Telex: 7 255 689 (dfvs d)
Head: Dr Ing C.-J. Winter
Activities: Systems studies for future non-nuclear energy systems; utilization of solar energy; hydrogen technology; technical combustion processes; gas- and plasma-dynamic high-energy lasers; thermionic energy conversion; lubrication systems; missile propulsion; electric thruster; chemical rocket propulsion.

Institute for Chemical Propulsion and 588 Chemical Engineering

Address: Lampoldshausen, D-7101 Hardthausen/Kocker
Telephone: (06289) 5011
Telex: 4 66 797
Head: Professor Dr phil R.E. Lo
Activities: Energy and process technology; defence technology; space technology; test of equipment and components for process technology, especially with high energy transfer; test of missile propulsion systems, especially solid-fuel systems; test of space propulsion systems.

Institute for Physical Chemistry of 589 Combustion

Head: Dr rer nat Th. Just
Activities: Reduction of emission of pollutants in technical combustion processes by exact investigation of chemical mechanisms leading to the production of pollutants in the flame; optical methods for service-free long-term monitoring of air cleanliness and of the pollutant concentrations in exhaust gases.

Institute for Physical Technology 590

Head: Professor Dr rer nat Th. Peters
Acting head: Dr Ing U. Fischer
Activities: Energy system techniques; utilization of solar energy; hydrogen as secondary energy system; thermiomic energy conversion and high-temperature technology; gas-dynamic laser systems; recombination laser systems; use of gas lasers in material processing;

projects for Spacelab experiments; qualification and physics of electric space propulsion systems.

FLIGHT MECHANICS - GUIDANCE AND CONTROL RESEARCH DEPARTMENT 591

Address: Airport, D-3300 Braunschweig
Telephone: (0531) 3951
Telex: 952800 (dfvlr d)
Head: Professor Dr Ing F. Thomas
Activities: Vehicle movement: dynamics, control and guidance; project and systems analysis, optimization and control; flight medicine; human engineering; environment protection.

Air Transport Science Division 592

Address: Linder Höhe, D-5000 Köln 90
Telephone: (02203) 6011
Telex: 08 874 410 (dfvw d)
Head: Dr Ing H.-G. Nüsser
Activities: Applied transportation research problems, primarily those relating to demand forecasts, optimization of operations and impacts anticipated in connection with the introduction of new transport technologies.

Institute for Aerospace Medicine 593

Address: Linder Höhe, D-5000 Köln 90
Telephone: (02203) 6011
Telex: 08 874 410 (dfvw d)
Director: Dr K.E. Klein
Sections: Aerospace physiology and psychology, Dr Steininger; space medicine and biology, Dr Briegleb; environmental and underwater medicine, Dr Vogt; biophysics, Professor Dr Bücker
Graduate research staff: 35
Annual expenditure: £501 000-2m
Activities: Space medicine: selection and training of spacelab payload specialists; space related research on the adaptation of the circulatory system and the vestibular organ of man to zero gravity; effects of reduced gravity, space radiation and vacuum on biological material. Aerospace physiology and psychology: effect of mental and physical stress on system operators and flight safety; circadian rhythm studies, modelling of the biodynamic response of the human body. Underwater medicine: effects of pressure changes on divers; toxicity of oxygen; development of decompression tables.
Facilities: Human centrifuge, man rated and other chambers (low and high pressure vacuum, radiation), diving simulator.
Contract work: Yes

Institute for Flight Guidance 594

Head: Dr rer nat H. Winter
Activities: On-board systems for flight guidance; ground systems and procedures for air traffic control.

Institute for Flight Mechanics 595

Head: Dr Ing P. Hamel
Activities: Flight mechanics of manned fixed-wing and rotary-wing aircraft; flight mechanics of unmanned flight vehicles; rescue and recovery systems; mathematical methods for the identification, analysis and evaluation of systems which are relevant to flight mechanics.

Institute for Flight Systems Dynamics 596

Address: Oberpfaffenhofen, D-8031 Wessling
Telephone: (08153) 281
Telex: 5 26 419 (dvlop d)
Head: Dr Ing J. Ackermann
Activities: Dynamics, guidance and control of technical aerospace and ground transport systems.

FLUID MECHANICS RESEARCH DEPARTMENT 597

Address: Bunsenstrasse 10, D-3400 Göttingen
Telephone: (0551) 7091
Telex: 96839 (avagoe d)
Acting head: Professor Dr rer nat H.L. Jordan
Activities: External design of aircraft and space components; internal design of turbo engines and their integration into complete systems; minimization of environmental pollution.

Division for Technical Acoustics 598

Address: Bienroder Weg 53, D-3300 Braunschweig
Telephone: (0531) 350021
Telex: 952 800 (dfvlr d)
Head: Dr Ing H. Heller
Activities: Propeller, rotor and airframe noise research, with the general objectives of improving noise prediction accuracies and developing advanced noise reduction technologies.

Institute for Design Aerodynamics 599

Address: Airport, D-3300 Braunschweig
Telephone: (0531) 3951
Telex: 052 800 (dfvlr d)
Acting head: Dr Ing H. Körner
Activities: Processing of knowledge available from research into fluid mechanics in such a way as to make it directly applicable to the design of new, efficient aircraft and vehicles.

Institute for Experimental Fluid Mechanics   600

Head: Professor Dr rer nat W. Wuest
Acting head: Professor Dr rer nat H. Ludwieg
Activities: Experimental research and description of the physics of flow behaviour in the field of subsonic, transonic/supersonic and rarefied gas flows. The work is to provide user-oriented solutions to problems of aerospace, general transport and process technology.

Institute for Propulsion Technology   601

Address: Linder Höhe, D-5000 Köln 90
Telephone: (02203) 6011
Telex: 8 874 410 (dfvw d)
Head: Professor Dr Ing G. Winterfeld
Activities: Advanced internal combustion machines, especially gas turbines, and turbomachinery, with regard to air transport and heavy engineering in general.

Institute for Theoretical Fluid Mechanics   602

Acting head: Professor Dr Rues
Activities: Theoretical research of physical problems associated with fluid mechanics; application of this research to aerospace problems and problems of general transport and process technologies.

MATERIALS AND STRUCTURES RESEARCH DEPARTMENT   603

Address: Pfaffenwaldring 38-40, D-7000 Stuttgart 80
Telephone: (0711) 78321
Telex: 7 255 689 (dfvs d)
Head: Dr Ing C.-J. Winter
Activities: Safety of structures, at minimum weight, high strength, required quality of surface finish, and reasonable production cost; advanced materials for future turbine systems, with the objective of improved efficiency and reduced pollutive emission; interactions between structures and the ambient flow medium; non-destructive materials testing and component testing; work procedures and experimental techniques in space with human assistance.

Institute for Aeroelasticity   604

Address: Bunsenstrasse 10, D-3400 Göttingen
Telephone: (0551) 7091
Telex: 96 839 (avagoe d)
Head: Professor Dr Ing H. Försching
Activities: Aeroelastic stability of aircraft and high buildings.

Institute for Materials Research   605

Address: Linder Höhe, D-5000 Köln 90
Telephone: (02203) 6011
Telex: 8 874 410 (dfvw d)
Head: Professor Dr rer nat W. Bunk
Activities: Improvement of conventional lightweight materials; development of new high-strength and high-temperature composites; damage analysis; testing methods.

Institute for Space Simulation   606

Address: Linder Höhe, D-5000 Köln 90
Telephone: (02203) 6011
Telex: 8 874 410 (dfvw d)
Acting head: Dr Ing C.-J. Winter
Activities: Research work for experiments and experimental techniques used in space; simulation of conditions during space flight; use of solar energy.

Institute for Structural Design and Technology Research   607

Address: Pfaffenwaldring 38-40, D-7000 Stuttgart 80
Telephone: (0711) 78321
Telex: 7 255 689 (dfvs d)
Head: Dr Ing G. Grüninger
Activities: Optimum weight applications of fibre-reinforced composites in lightweight aerospace structures; wind energy utilization; design of a ceramic turbine for motor vehicles.

Institute for Structural Mechanics   608

Address: Airport, D-3300 Braunschweig
Telephone: (0531) 3951
Telex: 952800 (dfvw d)
Head: Dr Ing H.W. Bergmann
Activities: Static and dynamic behaviour of conventional and fibre-reinforced structures and of bonded hybrid components; new material concepts; non-destructive inspection methods; filament-winding techniques; testing of airframe components; development of analysis methods for improvement of design processes and reduction of test requirements; damage mechanics of fibre-reinforced structures.

PROJECT MANAGEMENT DEPARTMENT   609

Address: Linder Höhe, D-5000 Köln 90
Telephone: (02203) 6011
Telex: 8 874 410 (dfvw d)
Head: Dipl-Ing H. Schreiber
Activities: The department is responsible for all tasks resulting from the appointment of DFVLR to manage

projects in federally funded programmes, and acts on behalf of the Federal Ministry of Research and Technology, awarding contracts and allocating funds to industrial firms and scientific organizations. The fields covered include large-scale projects, medicine, biotechnology, materials research, and process engineering.

SCIENTIFIC-TECHNICAL FACILITIES DEPARTMENT   610

Address: Oberpfaffenhofen, D-8031 Wessling
Telephone: (08153) 281
Telex: 526 419 (dvlop d)
Head: Dr Ing J.W. Beck
Activities: The department combines the test facilities of the following divisions below. In addition to ensuring the economical, user-oriented and safe operation of the available installations, the department plays a major part in engineering and consultancy on user problems and in conceiving and designing new test facilities. These requirements are met by making available operating teams and systems-technology oriented work teams in the individual main divisions.

German-Dutch Wind Tunnel   611

– DNW
Address: Postbus 175, 8300 AD Emmeloord, Netherlands
Telephone: (00 31-52 74) 30 55
Telex: 42 175 (dnw nl)
Directors: Professor Dr Ing J. Barche, F. Jaarsma
Activities: This is the largest and most versatile new wind tunnel project in Europe, established and operated jointly by DFVLR and NLR (National Lucht-en Ruimtevaartlaboratorium, Netherlands).

German Space Operations Centre   612

Head: Dipl-Ing W. Markwitz
Activities: Planning and realization of engineering tasks and operational missions in the fields of data management, data acquisition, and systems technology, with the principal target of supporting space missions and their users.

Main Division Computing Centre   613

Address: Oberpfaffenhofen, D-8031 Wessling
Telephone: (08153) 281
Telex: 526 419 (dvlop d)
Head: Dipl-Math Dr rer nat H.M. Wacker
Activities: Provision of scientific, systems, technological, and operational services in all fields of data processing and information technology.

Main Division for Research Flight Operations   614

Telephone: (08153) 281
Telex: 526 419 (dvlop d)
Head: Dipl-Ing J.F. Schatt
Activities: Research on aircraft, the investigations and tests being originated by the research departments on flight mechanics/flight guidance and fluid mechanics, and handled by the Braunschweig-based flight division; research where aircraft are used as carriers for different experiments resulting in particular from work done by the communications technology/remote sensing research department.

Main Division Low-Speed Wind Tunnels   615

Address: Airport, D-3300 Braunschweig
Telephone: (0531) 3951
Telex: 952 800
Head: Dr Ing G. Kausche
Activities: The division operates three low-speed wind tunnels, most of the work being done in close cooperation with the aerospace industry. Investigations done for non-aerospace projects include the aerodynamics of buildings, antennas, and smoke and exhaust problems.

TECHNICAL SERVICES DEPARTMENT   616

Address: Linder Höhe, D-5000 Köln 90
Telephone: (02203) 6011
Telex: 8 874 410 (dfvw d)
Head: Dr Ing H. Luks
Activities: Produces test equipment and carries out construction for DFVLR.

Deutsche Forschungsgemeinschaft   617

– DFG
[German Research Society]
Address: Kennedyallee 40, D-5300 Bonn 2
Telephone: (0221) 8851
Telex: 885 420 wzd
President: Professor Dr Eugen Seibold
General Secretary: Dr Carl Heinz Schiel
Annual expenditure: DM755.5m (1979)
Activities: DFG supports all branches of science by financial contributions to research projects with special attention to the advancement of young scientists. In many scientific disciplines DFG has accepted responsibility for strengthening cooperation between researchers, for the coordination of basic research and for its collaboration with research promotion from

government departments. It advises the government on scientific matters and ensures a close correlation between science and the economy. Special emphasis is placed upon close cooperation between German scientists and foreign researchers.

Expenditure in 1979 was divided along the following lines: the humanities and social sciences received 17.6 per cent; biomedical sciences 38.1 per cent; natural sciences 22.7 per cent; and engineering sciences 22.1 per cent.

Members of the DFG are as follows: universities and other research institutions of general importance; academies that are members of the Conference of the Academies of Sciences; scientific associations of general importance.

Some major research projects recently supported by the DFG: biopolymer and biomechanics of connective tissue systems; biology of ageing; physiology and pathophysiology of the immune system; neural mechanism of behaviour; biochemistry of the nervous system; deep-sea drilling project; transferability of material characteristics; operational behaviour of dynamically-loaded machines; embryonal development and differentiation; endocrinology; medical molecular biology and biochemistry; teratological research and rehabilitation of the multiple handicapped; molecular biology of the cell; biological membrane and specificity; solid-state body reactions in solids and surface; ocean research (impulse, energy and material transport in the ocean system); interaction between sea and sea-bottom; flight control; processing technology - flexible processing systems; thermal power station; water research in coastal areas.

Contract work: No

Deutsche Gesellschaft für 618 Holzforschung eV

– DGFH

[German Association for Wood Research]
Address: 9 Prannenstrasse, D-8000 München 2
Telephone: (089) 29 94 65
Affiliation: Arbeitsgemeinschaft Industrieller Forschungsvereinigungen eV
Managing Director: H. Freiherr Von Bodman
Activities: Promotion and coordination of wood research, production and processing, treatment and utilization of wood and wood materials; wood protection and evaluation of results for the economy.

Deutsche Gesellschaft für 619 Mineralölwissenschaft und Kohlechemie eV

Address: Nordkanalstrasse 28, D-2000 Hamburg 1
Telephone: (040) 2802277
Telex: 0211446 dgmk
Directors: Chairman and committee elected annually
Research leaders: Dr G.A. Schulze, Dr Rieckmann, R. Fiala
Activities: In 1980 DM5 672 659 was spent on research projects. In the area of exploration, extraction and underground storage or petroleum and natural gas, projects were initiated and continued into geophysics, geochemistry, bore techniques, and storage techniques. Interests in processing and environment range through work into toxicology, noise studies, petrochemistry, water and effluent waters, transport studies. Several projects are being carried out into the development of analytical techniques, especially for secondary metals. In the area of applications, projects are being undertaken into fuel development, inflammables, and lubricants. Work is being carried out into coal chemistry.
Liaison: The following foreign organizations have been involved with one or more of the company's research projects: European Petroleum Technical Cooperation; Association Française des Techniciens du Pétrole; CAMPSA; CONCAWE; Danish Petroleum Industry Association; Finnish Petroleum Federation; Koninklijk Instituut van Ingenieurs; Norsk Petroleum Institutt; Österreichische Gesellschaft für Erdölwissenschaften; Schweizerische Erdölvereinigung; Société Belge pour l'Étude du Pétrola; Svenska Petroleum Institutet; Institute of Petroleum; Unione Petrolifera.
Publications: Annual report.

Deutsche 620 Wissenschaftliche Kommission für Meeresforschung

[German Scientific Comission for Oceanographic Research]
Address: 11 Palmaille 9, D-2000 Hamburg 50
Parent body: Bundesministerium für Ernährung, Landwirtschaft und Forsten
Chairman: Professor Dr D. Sahzhage
Secretary: Professor Dr K. Tiews
Activities: Fisheries biology and related marine research interests.
See also entry under: Bundesforschungsanstalt für Fischerei.

Deutscher Beton-Verein eV 621

[German Concrete Association]
Address: Postfach 2126, 61 Bahnhofstrasse, D-6200 Wiesbaden
Telephone: (06121) 37 20 71
Affiliation: Arbeitsgemeinschaft Industrieller Forschungsvereinigungen eV
Managing Director: Dr Ing H. Seiler
Activities: Promotion and development of scientific and technical basis for concrete and reinforced concrete construction by research of material properties, theoretical investigations and experiments.

Deutscher Braunkohlen-Industrie-Verein eV 622

[German Brown Coal Industry Association]
Address: Postfach 100 446, 1-3 Laurenplatz, D-5000 Köln 1
Telephone: (0221) 23 56 82
Telex: 8883013/014 rhv d
Affiliation: Arbeitsgemeinschaft Industrieller Forschungsvereinigungen eV
Managing Director: H. Sondermann
Activities: Research and research promotion of technical developments in brown coal (lignite) mining.
Publications: Journal.

Deutscher Bundestag 623

[Federal Diet]
Address: Bundeshaus, D-5300 Bonn 12
Telephone: (0228) 162861

COMMITTEE FOR RESEARCH AND TECHNOLOGY 624

Chairman: Dr Albert Probst
Counsellor: Dr Dr Peter Lichtenberg
Activities: Research policy, domestic and international; technology; nuclear technology and research; ocean research; technical sciences.

Deutscher Krebsgesellschaft* 625

[German Cancer Society]
Address: Hufelandstrasse 55, D-43 Essen

Deutscher Wetterdienst* 626

[German Meteorological Service]
Address: Frankfurter Strasse 135, D-6050 Offenbach Main
Activities: The Deutscher Wetterdienst has divisions of synoptic meteorology, climatology, agricultural meteorology, and research. There are two observatories.

AGRARMETEOROLOGISCHE BERATUNGS- UND FORSCHUNGSSTELLE GEISENHEIM RHEIN 627

[Agrometeorological Advice and Research Station Geisenheim/Rhein]
Address: Kreuzweg 25, D-6222 Geisenheim
Telephone: (06722) 83 72
Telex: 42111ghdwd
Graduate research staff: 4
Annual expenditure: £51 000-500 000
Activities: Meteorological research for agriculture and viticulture; weather and growing; climate, weather and quality of plants; climatology.
Contract work: Yes
Publications: Reports.

METEOROLOGISCHES OBSERVATORIUM HAMBURG* 628

[Hamburg Meteorological Observatory]
Address: Frahmredder 95, D-2000 Hamburg 65
Telephone: (040) 601 79 24
Telex: 02162912 DWSA D
Activities: The Hamburg Meteorological Observatory is responsible for research, development and consulting in the following fields: atmospheric trace substances as dependent on meteorological parameters and processes; radiation andoptics of the atmosphere including the duties of a national radiation centre; atmospheric exchange especially in the planetary boundary layer.

METEOROLOGISCHES OBSERVATORIUM HOHENPEISSENBERG* 629

[Hohenpeissenberg Meteorological Observatory]
Address: Albin-Schwaiger-Weg 10, 8126 Hohenpeissenberg Kreis-Schongau

Deutsches Elektronen-Synchroton   630

– DESY
[German Electron-Accelerator]
Address: 85 Notkestrasse, D-2000 Hamburg 52
Telephone: (040) 89 69 81
Telex: 215124
Chairman of the Board: Professor Dr H. Schopper
Staff: 1100
Activities: High-energy physics with elementary particles; utilization of synchrotron radiation by acceleration of electrons and positrons for experiments in surface and solid-state physics and molecular biology.

Deutsches Hydrographisches Institut   631

[German Hydrographic Institute]
Address: Bernhard-Nocht-Strasse 78, Postfach 200, D-2000 Hamburg 4
Parent body: Bundesministerium für Verkehr
Director: Professor Dr Gerhard Zickwolff
Activities: Oceanography, tides and currents, geomagnetism, gravimetry, time service, nautical technology, navigation methods, hydrographic surveys and nautical geodesy, bathymetry, seabed geology, pollution control, ice information service, nautical charts and publications, library and hydrographic information service.

Deutsches Krankenhausinstitut   632

– DKI
[German Hospitals Institute]
Address: Tersteegenstrasse 9, D-4000 Düsseldorf 30
Telephone: (0211) 434422
Telex: 08584240 vlk d
Affiliation: Universität Düsseldorf
Research directors: Professor Dr Siegfried Eichhorn, Dr Karl Jeute, Professor Dr Hans-Werner Moller, Richard-Joachim Sahl
Graduate research staff: 12
Annual expenditure: £51 000-500 000
Activities: The research programme of the DKI is divided into the following areas: the development of hospital and health services; the requirements, demands and organization of medical services, especially hospital services; the planning, organization and control of hospital operations, and other institutions of the medical

services; information and communication in the field of health and hospital services.
Contract work: Yes

Deutsches Kunststoff-Institut   633

– DKI
[German Plastics Institute]
Address: Schlossgartenstrasse 6 R, D-6100 Darmstadt
Telephone: (06151) 162104
Affiliation: Trägervereinigung:
Forschungsgesellschaft Kunststoffe eV
Research director: Professor Dr Dietrich Braun
Sections: Chemistry, Professor Dr Dietrich Braun; physics, Dr Joachim H. Wendorff; technology, Dr Ing Günter Mennig; documentation, Jutta Wierer
Graduate research staff: 45
Annual expenditure: £501 000-2m
Activities: Research into the structure and material properties of plastics; development of new materials; documentation of plastics, rubber, and fibres; production technology and testing.
Contract work: Yes
Publications: Mitteilungen aus dem Deutschen Kunststoff-Institut, Darmstadt, biannual report.

Deutsches Textilforschungs-Zentrum Nord-West eV   634

– DTNW
[German Textile Research Centre North-West]
Address: Frankenring 2, D-4150 Krefeld
Telephone: (02151) 770018
Telex: 0853864 tfad
Graduate research staff: 15
Annual expenditure: £51 000-500 000
Activities: DTNW serves the whole field of textile appliances from textile production to textile care. Its members derive from the concerned industries, trade groups to commercial laundries, dry-cleaners and consumers. The main fields of activity are fundamental and applied research, teaching and training in the field of textile processing, textile quality control, testing and textile care. This work is done in three institutes with different main topics, and the institutes cooperate with the Öffentliche Prüfstelle und Textilinstitut für Vertragsforschung eV, which carries out testing and contract research.
Contract work: Yes

INSTITUT FÜR TEXTILE MESSTECHNIK 635 MÜNCHENGLADBACH

[Textile Metrology Institute]
Address: Voltastrasse 2, D-4050 Münchengladbach
Telephone: (02161) 23458
Head: Dr W. Stein
Activities: Testing methods for continuous synthetic filaments, especially textured yarns; influence of climatic conditions on the mechanical properties of textiles; lubricants for textile yarns; textile body armour; micro dust problems in textile processes.

TEXTILFORSCHUNGSANSTALT 636 KREFELD

[Textile Research Institute]
Head: Dr G. Heidemann
Sections: Textile production, Dr J. Berndt; textile finishing, E. Schollmeyer
Activities: Influences of material and process parameters on end-use properties; simple technical tests for practical use; thermosetting (polyesters, polyamides, acrylics) during texturing, setting-up and finishing.

Department of Textile Chemistry 637

Sections: Pretreatment; dyeing and printing; finishing

Department of Textile Technology 638

Sections: Textile production; clothing technology; machinery for the dye house

WÄSCHEREIFORSCHUNG KREFELD 639 (INSTITUT FÜR TEXTILPFLEGE)

[Laundry Research Institute (Institute for Textile Care)]
Address: Adlerstrasse 44, D-4150 Krefeld
Telephone: (02151) 770072
Head: Dr H. Krüssmann
Activities: The objective of the Institute is production-oriented research on chemical, physico-chemical and technological steps of fabric care process including washing, dry cleaning and carpet cleaning.

Deutsches Wollforschungsinstitut an der TH Aachen eV 640

[German Wood Research Institute at the Technical University Aachen]
Address: 8 Veltmanplatz, D-5100 Aachen
Telephone: (0241) 399 21
Telex: 832829
Affiliation: Arbeitsgemeinschaft Industrieller Forschungsvereinigungen eV
Scientific Director: Professor Dr H. Zahn
Activities: Refinement of wood containing fibres; thermoanalysis of keratin fibres; chemical modification of wool and collagen, methodical investigations into synthesis of proteins, especially insulin, experiments of pro-insulin synthesis; chemical and physical research on untreated and treated human hair.

Dornier System GmbH 641

Address: Postfach 1360, D-7990 Friedrichshafen 1
Telephone: (07545) 8-1
Telex: 073210 - 0
Parent body: Dornier GmbH
Chairman of the Board: Dipl Ing SilviusDornier
Managing Directors: Dr Karl-Wilhelm Schäfer; Dr Bernhard Schmidt; Dipl-Kaufmann Klaus Peter Thomé; Dr Helmut Ulke
Research Director: Dr Helmut Ulke
Graduate research staff: 650
Activities: Research, development and production; space technologies; special electronics; management and engineering consulting; integral safety systems and organization. New technologies: environmental; transport; marine; energy; nuclear; medical; bearing and power systems; applied research; special technological programmes.
Contract work: Yes
Publications: Dornier GmbH Geschäftsbericht.

Eberhard-Earle-Universität Tübingen* 642

[Tübingen University]
Address: Wilhelmstrasse 7, D-7400 Tübingen

Elektroschmelzwerk Kempten GmbH 643

Address: Herzog Wilhelm Strasse 16, Postfach 609, D-8000 München 33
Telephone: (089) 51201
Telex: 0522749
Research and development director: Dr Alfred Lipp
Senior staff: Dr K. Reinmuth, Dr K.A. Schwetz, H.J. Lukschandel
Activities: Research into the production of non-oxide ceramics for use as abrasives and corrosion- and wear-resistant materials, at normal and high temperatures.

Elektrowärme-Institut Essen eV 644

[Electric Heating Institute Essen]
Address: 9 Nünningstrasse, D-4300 Essen 1
Telephone: (0201) 298 71
Affiliation: Arbeitsgemeinschaft Industrieller Forschungsvereinigungen eV
Managing Director: Dr Ing J. Pautz
Scientific staff: 8
Activities: Electric heating; air-conditioning and waste heat recovery.

Enka AG 645

Address: Postfach 10 01 49, Enka-Hans Kasinostrasse, D-5600 Wuppertal 1
Telephone: (0202) 32 27 88
Telex: 8 592 755
Parent body: AKZO

OBERNBERG RESEARCH INSTITUTE 646

Address: D-8753 Obernberg
Research director: Dr Ostertag
Activities: Synthetic and cellulosic fibres, membranes and related products.

Fachhochschule Hamburg* 647

[Hamburg Technical College]
Address: Winterhuder Weg 29, D-2000 Hamburg 76
Telephone: (040) 29188/1

EXPORT PACKAGING INSTITUTE 648

Address: Lohbrügger Kirchstrasse 65-A1N, D-2050 Hamburg 80
Telephone: (040) 72 52 27 56
Director: Professor Dipl-Ing R. Eschlee
Graduate research staff: 2
Annual expenditure: £10 000-50 000
Activities: Prevention of corrosion with volatile corrosion inhibitors; construction of wooden boxes.
Contract work: Yes

Fernmeldetechnisches Zentralamt 649

– FTZ
[Telecommunications Engineering Centre]
Address: Am Kavalleriesand 3, Postfach 5000, D-6100 Darmstadt
Telephone: (06151) 831
Telex: 419511 ftzd
Affiliation: Deutsche Bundespost
Research director: Professor Richard Meisel
Sections:
Information processing, Professor Gallenkamp
Transmission systems and physical media, Professor Dr Ing Mahr
Antennae and electromagnetic wave propagation, Dr Ing Kuhn
Solid-state electronics, Professor Dr Ing Hesse
Switching systems and networks, vacant
Graduate research staff: 190
Annual expenditure: over £2m
Activities: General telecommunications engineering; modes of transmission (optical fibre links under test); wave propagation (satellite test station). Solid-state electronics (molecular beam epitaxy-MBE); hyperfrequency engineering (anechoic test chamber); documentation and information centre; speech recognition and synthesis; processing of digital television and high quality sound signals; mathematical (computer) service in fields of research and science.
Contract work: No

Fonds der Chemischen Industrie 650

[Chemical Industry Fund]
Address: Karlstrasse 21, D-6000 Frankfurt am Main 2
Telephone: (0611) 2556481
Affiliation: Chemischen Industrie Verein
Executive director: Dr Burchard Ording

Graduate research staff: 4
Annual expenditure: DM8m
Activities: The Chemical Industry Fund channels financial support from the West-German chemical industry to students and chemistry teachers throughout the country's high schools, technical colleges and universities. It awards annual cash prizes in certain fields of chemical excellence, compiles data and publishes a variety of literature.
Contract work: No

Forschungkreis der Ernährungsindustrie eV 651

[Nutrition Industry Research Association]
Address: 3 Heinrich-Kümmel-Strasse, D-3000 Hannover
Telephone: (0511) 88 76 22
Affiliation: Arbeitsgemeinschaft Industrieller Forschungsvereinigungen eV
Managing Director: Dr Mindemann
Activities: Analytical research and experiments on raw materials, additives, finished products in the confectionery industry; flour contents, especially proteins with respect to baking properties; sugar technology; waste water separation and waste water disposal in the sugar industry; metallic packaging and containers including coating and lacquers and their interaction with food; fruit and vegetable preservation; jams and fruit syrups; microbiology of tins; general food analysis; chemical and technical problems in the food sciences, especially coffee, tea and dietary products.

Forschungs- und Materialprüfungsanstalt Baden-Württemberg* 652

[Research and Material Testing Centre Baden-Württemberg]
Address: Kaiserstrasse 12, D-7500 Karlsruhe
Affiliation: Universität Fridericiana Karlsruhe - Technische Hochschule
Director: K.-H. Breckenfelder

SPECIAL RESEARCH PROGRAMMES* 653

Current Dispersion and Transport Processes 654

Chairman: Professor Dr E. Plate

Stress and Stress Changes in the Lithosphere* 655

Chairman: Professor Dr K. Fuchs
Activities: Stress and strain in the upper lithosphere; structure and deformation of the lower lithosphere.

Technical Principles of Processes for Water and Gas Purification* 656

Chairman: Professor Dr K. Hedden
Activities: Water purification; impulse exchange in polyphase currents; gas purification.

Forschungsanstalt der Bundeswehr für Wasserschall- und Geophysik 657

[Hydroacoustics and Geophysics Defence Research Institute]
Address: Klausdorfer Weg 2-24, D-2300 Kiel 14
Telephone: (0431) 726070
Affiliation: Federal Ministry of Defence
Head: Professor Dr Ing Günter H. Ziehm
Activities: Shallow water research; hydroacoustics; sound propagation; acoustics of sediment; oceanography; sea waves bottom properties.

Forschungsgemeinschaft der Deutschen Kalkindustrie eV 658

[German Lime Industry Research Association]
Address: 67-71 Annastrasse, D-5000 Köln 51
Telephone: (0221) 38 05 28
Affiliation: Arbeitsgemeinschaft Industrieller Forschungsvereinigungen eV
Managing Director: Dr N. Rogmann
Activities: Research and finance of production and utilization of lime, limestone and dolomite.

Forschungsgemeinschaft Explorations-Geophysik eV 659

[Exploration Geophysics Research Association]
Address: 9 Theodor-Fontane-Strasse, D-3007 Gehrden
Telephone: (05108) 4211
Affiliation Arbeitsgemeinschaft Industrieller Forschungsvereinigungen eV

Managing Director: Dr W. Döderlein

Activities: Development of measuring techniques of applied geophysics for locating ore and other mining deposits; geological/tectonic problems of salt mining; regional geophysical investigations into problems of potash, mineral salt and ore mining.

Forschungsgemeinschaft 660 für Hochspannungs-, und Hochstromtechnik eV

– FGH
[High Voltage and Peak Current Technology Research Association]
Address: Postfach 810169, Hallenweg, D-6800 Mannheim 81
Telephone: (0621) 89 50 51
Telex: 462279 fgh d
Affiliation: Arbeitsgemeinschaft Industrieller Forschungsvereinigungen eV
Chairman: Professor Dr K.-H. Schneider
Activities: Problems of voltage and current loads with electrical transfer and distribution networks; reduction of space requirements for this plant; increase of operating voltage and short-circuit power; modification of transfer systems; new materials; maximum utilization of equipment; reduction of faults.

Forschungsgemeinschaft 661 für Technisches Glas eV

[Technical Glass Research Association]
Address: Postfach 96, 25 Bismarckstrasse, D-6980 Wertheim 1
Telephone: (09342) 6591
Affiliation: Arbeitsgemeinschaft Industrieller Forschungsvereinigungen eV
Managing Director: K. Lantzsch
Activities: Promotion of chemical, physical and technical research on raw glass and finished glass products; new glass processing technology; research and development of machines and instruments.

Forschungsgemeinschaft 662 ZINK eV

[Zinc Research Association]
Address: 37-39 Friedrich-Ebert-Strasse, D-4000 Düsseldorf 1
Telephone: (0211) 350867

Affiliation: Zinkberatung eV
Chairman: H. Maczek
Director: Dr H. Johnen
Annual expenditure: £51 000-500 000
Activities: Promoting the use of zinc in many new different areas, working in close collaboration with university institutes and industry.
Contract work: No

Forschungsgesellschaft 663 Druckmaschinen eV

[Printing Machines Research Association]
Address: Postfach 710 109, 18 Lyoner Strasse, D-6000 Frankfurt am Main-Niederrad 71
Telephone: (0611) 660 34 51
Affiliation: Arbeitsgemeinschaft Industrieller Forschungsvereinigungen eV
Managing Director: S. Holderried
Activities: Machines and instruments for the printing industry.

Forschungsgesellschaft für 664 Agrarpolitik und Agrarsoziologie eV

[Society for Research on Agricultural Policy and Agricultural Sociology]
Address: Meckenheimer Allee 125, D-5300 Bonn 1
Telephone: (02221) 634781
Research director: Dr Richard Struff
Graduate research staff: 10
Annual expenditure: £51 000-500 000
Activities: Agrarian politics and rural sociology; rural and developing regions; rural and agricultural population.
Contract work: Yes

Forschungsgesellschaft 665 Steinzeugindustrie eV

[Clay Pipe Industry Research Association]
Address: Max-Planck-Strasse 6, Postfach 400547, D-5000 Cologne 40 (Marsdorf)
Telephone: (02234) 507 1
Telex: 889118 stg d
Research director: Dipl-Ing Wolfgang Zäschke
Activities: Research development and testing in the field of clay sewer pipes and joints.

Forschungsinstitut Borstel 666

[Borstel Research Institute]
Address: Parkallee 1-40, 2061 Borstel
Telephone: (04537) 293
Affiliation: Borstel Foundation
Director: Professor Dr H.-D. Flad
Graduate research staff: 45
Activities: Biology and immunology of infection; microbiology; chemotherapy.
Contract work: No

Forschungsinstitut der 667 Feuerfest-Industrie

[Refractory Industry Research Institute]
Address: An der Elisabethkirche 27, D-5300 Bonn
Telephone: (0228) 21 10 51
Telex: 886533 FF BN D
Research director: Professor Dr Ing Aleksander Majdic
Graduate research staff: 8
Annual expenditure: £51 000-500 000
Activities: Research and testing on all kinds of refractory raw materials and refractories. Facilities for: X-ray fluorescence analysis, X-ray diffractometers, infrared spectrometer, electron microprobe analysis, high-temperature testing, thermal conductivity, testing of unshaped refractory materials, acoustic emission, vibration and isostatic press.
Contract work: Yes

Forschungsinstitut der 668 Forschungsgemeinschaft Eisenhüttenschlacken

[Research Institute of the Research Association for Ironworks Slagging]
Address: 62 Bliersheimer Strasse, D-4100 Duisburg 14, Rheinhausen
Telephone: (02135) 470 86
Affiliation: Arbeitsgemeinschaft Industrieller Forschungsvereinigungen eV
Director: Professor Dr G. Blunk
Scientific staff: 9
Activities: Slags as raw materials, components and fertilizers made of slags (ironworks concrete, light and heavy concrete aggregates, roadworks materials, fertilizers and insulating materials; application possibilities and utilization-behaviour of slag products; new fields of application and processing.

Forschungsinstitut der 669 Forschungsgesellschaft für Uhren- und Feingerätetechnik

[Horology and Precision Engineering Research Association]
See entry under: Universität Stuttgart, Horology and Precision Engineering Institute.

Forschungsinstitut der 670 Zementindustrie

[Cement Industry Research Institute]
Address: Tannenstrasse 2-4, D-4000 Düsseldorf 30
Telephone: (0211) 4578-1
Telex: 08/584 867
Affiliation: Verein Deutscher Zementwerke eV
Research director: Professor Dr Ing Gerd Wischers
Departments: Concrete, Professor Dr Ing J. Bonzel; cement, Professor Dr F.W. Locher
Graduate research staff: 30
Annual expenditure: over £2m
Activities: Cement and concrete research and technology; cement chemistry and mineralogy; cement manufacturing processes; environmental protection and works safety; safeguarding of the quality of cement.
Contract work: No
Publications: Schriftenreihe der Zementindustrie; Betontechnische Berichte; Zement-Taschenbuch; Tätigkeitsbericht; Verfahrenstechnik der Zementherstellung.

Forschungsinstitut für 671 Edelmetalle und Metallchemie

[Precious Metals and Metal Chemistry Research Institute]
Address: 17 Katharinenstrasse, D-7070 Schwäbisch Gmünd
Telephone: (07171) 620 54
Affiliation: Arbeitsgemeinschaft Industrieller Forschungsvereinigungen eV
Scientific Director: Dr Ch.J. Raub
Scientific staff: 11
Activities: Alloying of high melting and less common metals; low-temperature properties; two and multi-component alloying precious metals; electrolytic separation of metals and alloys; anodic oxidation.

Forschungsinstitut für Pigmente und Lacke eV   672

[Paint and Pigment Technology Research Institute]
Address: Wiederholdstrasse 10-1, D-7000 Stuttgart 1
Telephone: (0711) 29 75 49
Research director: Professor Dr Lothar Dulog
Graduate research staff: 7
Annual expenditure: £501 000-2m
Activities: Chemical, physical and technological research on coatings, their components and interactions (pigments, binders), corrosion protection, characteristics, test procedures.
Facilities: Electron microscope; scanning electron microscope; infrared-, ultraviolet- and visible spectrophotometers; gas chromatographs; thermomechanical analysis instruments; colour measurements; corrosion measurements; various viscometric measurements; standard test procedures.
Contract work: Yes
Publications: Research results are published in scientific and/or technical periodicals; biannual institute report.

APPLIED TECHNOLOGY SECTION   673

Head: Dr Helmut Haagen
Activities: Applied technology of coatings; behaviour of coatings on substrates; advice on painting problems; investigations of paint failures; expert advice.

Forschungsinstitut und Naturmuseum Senckenberg   674

[Senckenberg Research Institute and Nature Museum]
Address: Senckenberganlage 25, D-6000 Frankfurt am Main 1
Telephone: (0611) 75421
Telex: 413129 sng
Affiliation: Senckenbergische Naturforschende Gesellschaft, Frankfurt am Main
Director: Professor Dr Willi Ziegler
Contract work: Yes
Publications: Senckenbergiana biologica; Senckenbergiana lethaea; Senckenbergiana maritima; Natur und Museum, Kleine Senckenberg-Reihe; Courier Forschung Institut Senckenberg; Abhandlungen der Senckenburgishen Naturforschenden Gesellschaft; Aufsätze und Reden; Archiv für Molluskenkunde.

SENCKENBERG INSTITUTE FOR MARINE GEOLOGY AND BIOLOGY   675

Address: Schlensenstrasse 39a, D-2940 Wilhelmshafen
Director: Professor Dr Hans-Erich Reineck
Activities: Marine geology, palaeontology, sedimentology and biology. Investigations of primary physical structures, trace and body fossils, sedimentary textures and heavy minerals, macrobenthic organisms and pollution of different marine environments and sedimentary deposits.

SENCKENBERG RESEARCH INSTITUTE, FRANKFURT AM MAIN   676

Research director: Professor Dr Willi Ziegler
Sections: Vertebrate zoology, Dr W. Klausewitz; invertebrate zoology, Dr G. Richter; geology and palaeontology, including micropalaeontology, Dr W. Struve; botany and palaeobotany, Dr H.-J. Conertt
Graduate research staff: 40
Annual expenditure: over £2m
Activities: General and applied research in systematics, taxonomy, morphology, ecology and evolution of recent and fossil animals and plants; physical palaeoanthropology, stratigraphic and historic geology; marine geology, biology and ecology.

Lochmühle Research Station   677

Address: D-6465 Biebergemünd 3
Head: Dr D. Mollenhauer
Activities: Regional biology and ecology.

Forschungsrat Kältetechnik eV   678

[Refrigeration Technology Research Council]
Address: Postfach 710 109, 18 Lyoner Strasse, D-6000 Frankfurt am Main 71
Telephone: (0611) 660 31
Affiliation: Arbeitsgemeinschaft Industrieller Forschungsvereinigungen eV
Managing Director: Dr W. Kühnel
Activities: Promotion of research into refrigeration and applications.

Forschungsstelle für Insel- 679 und Küstenschutz Norderney

[Norderney Research Station for Island and Coast Protection]
Address: Ander Mühle 5, D-2982 Norderney
Telephone: (04932) 517 1518
Affiliation: Niedersächsische Wasserwirtschaftsverwaltung
Research director: Dr Ing Luck
Sections: Geology and soil mechanics, Dipl-Ing Ragutzki; morphological investigations, Dipl-Ing Stephan; survey and cartography, Ing Kowalski; hydrometrics, Dipl-Ing Niemeyer; ecology, Dr Michaelis
Graduate research staff: 9
Annual expenditure: £51 000-500 000
Activities: Investigations of basic data for the functional planning of island and coast protection; ecological investigations (marine biology).
Contract work: Yes

Forschungsverein der 680 Gipsindustrie eV

[Plaster Industry Association]
Address: 13 Birkenweg, D-6100 Darmstadt
Telephone: (06151) 843 10
Affiliation: Arbeitsgemeinschaft Industrieller Forschungsvereinigungen eV
Managing Director: Dipl-Ing K. Volkart
Activities: Promotion of scientific research and development of plaster products and application.

Forschungsvereinigung der 681 Deutschen Asphaltindustrie eV

[Research Association for the German Asphalt Industry]
Address: 105 Geleitstrasse, D-6050 Offenbach am Main
Telephone: (0611) 88 33 05
Affiliation: Arbeitsgemeinschaft Industrieller Forschungsvereinigungen eV
Managing Director: Dr W. Jösch
Activities: Cooperative research in the fields of production technology of tar and asphalt mixing materials; application techniques for construction; energy saving and environmental protection.

Forschungsvereinigung 682 Verbrennungskraft- maschinen eV

[Combustion Engines Research Association]
Address: Lyoner Strasse 18, D-6000 Frankfurt am Main 71
Telephone: (0611) 660 31
Telex: 411321 VDMA
President: Dr Ing Dinger
Secretary: Dipl-Ing Vettermann
Activities: General problems of scientific aspects in the field of internal combustion engines and gas turbines.

Fraunhofer-Gesellschaft zur 683 Förderung der Angewandten Forschung eV

– FLG
[Fraunhofer Society for the Promotion of Applied Research]
Address: Leonrodstrasse 54, D-8000 München 19
Telephone: (089) 1205-1
Telex: 05-215 382
President: Dr Heinz Keller
Research director: Dr H.H. Jung
Graduate research staff: 850 (in all institutes)
Annual expenditure: DM260m (1981)
Activities: The Society carries out research and development in areas of the natural and engineering sciences by contracts from industry and public services. These projects are of direct economic and social significance. The individual research units of the Society assist in turning the results of basic research into practice. The promotion of the Society by state funds enables them also to work on self-generated research projects and constantly to observe new technological developments. Since 1969 the Society has been supported by state funds as the main organization for applied research in the Federal Republic of Germany. At present it has 26 research units, 2 documentation centres and 1 patent centre.
See also entries for:
Envirormental research and technology:
Fraunhofer-Institut für Atmosphärische Umweltforschung
Fraunhofer-Institut für Hydroakustik
Fraunhofer-Institut für Toxikologie und Aerosolforschung
Materials in structures and plants:
Fraunhofer-Institut für Angewandte Materialsforschung

Fraunhofer-Institut für Betriebsfestigkeit

Fraunhofer-Institut für Kurzzeitdynamik - Ernst-Mach-Institut

Fraunhofer-Institut für Silicatforschung

Fraunhofer-Institut für Werkstoffmechanik

Fraunhofer-Institut für Zerstörungsfreie Prüfverfahren

Production engineering:

Fraunhofer-Institut für Arbeitswirtschaft und Organisation

Fraunhofer-Institut für Grenzflächen- und Bioverfahrenstechnik

Fraunhofer-Institut für Lebensmitteltechnologie und Verpackung

Fraunhofer-Institut für Produktionsanlagen und Konstruktionstechnik

Fraunhofer-Institut für Produktionstechnik und Automatisierung

Fraunhofer-Institut für Produktionstechnologie

Fraunhofer-Institut für Transporttechnik und Warendistribution

Fraunhofer-Institut für Treib- und Explosivstoffe

Solid-state electronics and information processing:

Fraunhofer-Institut für Angewandte Festkörperphysik

Fraunhofer-Institut für Festkörpertechnologie

Fraunhofer-Institut für Informations- und Datenverarbeitung

Fraunhofer-Institut für Physikalische Messtechnik

Fraunhofer-Institut für Solare Energiesysteme

Structural engineering and wood technology:

Fraunhofer-Institut für Bauphysik

Fraunhofer-Institut für Holzforschung - Wilhelm-Klauditz-Institut

Systems analysis and technology transfer:

Fraunhofer-Institut für Naturwissenschaftlich-Technische Trendanalysen

Fraunhofer-Institut für Systemtechnik und Innovationsforschung

Contract work: Yes

Publications: Jahresbericht, annual report; *Forschungsplan,* annually.

Fraunhofer-Institut für Angewandte Festkörperphysik   684

[Fraunhofer Institute for Applied Solid-State Physics]

Address: 4 Eckerstrasse, D-7800 Freiburg

Affiliation: Fraunhofer-Gesellschaft zur Förderung der Anwandten Forschung eV

Director: Professor Dr A. Goetzberger

Graduate research staff: 51

Annual expenditure: DM8.9m

Activities: Solid-state, in particular semiconductor research; new materials for application in solid-state electronics and optics; physics and technology of in frared and microwave devices; displays (ie, liquid crystals).

Specific projects include: 'Gunn oscillators' for low-noise-level millimetre wave reception systems; plasma etching of fine structures; a new intensive hypersonic source for technical application.

Publications: Annual report.

Fraunhofer-Institut für Angewandte Materialsforschung   685

[Fraunhofer Institute for Applied Materials Research]

Address: 36 Lesumer Heerstrasse, D-2820 Bremen-Lesum

Affiliation: Fraunhofer-Gesellschaft zur Förderung der Angewandten Forschung eV

Director: Professor Dr H.D. Kunze

Graduate research staff: 25

Annual expenditure: DM6.1m

Activities: Materials sciences with processing technology for surface coating; powder metallurgy and high-strength materials; material characteristics; load and stress analysis, guarantee of quality; corrosion chemistry; joining techniques and adhesion research on structural and compound materials.

Specific projects include: acoustic emission analysis for detection of faults in welded joints; thermoshock testing equipment.

Fraunhofer-Institut für Arbeitswirtschaft und Organisation   686

[Fraunhofer Institute for Ergonomics]

Address: 17 Holzgartenstrasse, D-7000 Stuttgart 1

Affiliation: Fraunhofer-Gesellschaft zur Förderung der Angewandten Forschung eV

Director: Professor Dr H.J. Warnecke

Graduate research staff: 35

Annual expenditure: DM7.4m

Activities: Automation and rationalization of working processes; personnel training and organization development in production and administration.

Publications: Annual report.

Fraunhofer-Institut für Atmosphärische Umweltforschung 687

[Fraunhofer Institute for Atmospheric Environmental Research]
Address: 19 Kreuzeckbahnstrasse, D-8100 Garmisch-Partenkirchen
Affiliation: Fraunhofer-Gesellschaft zur Förderung der Angewandten Forschung eV
Director: Dr R. Reiter
Graduate research staff: 10
Annual expenditure: DM2.8m
Activities: Research and development in the following areas: physics and chemistry of the atmosphere; exchange and transport in the stratosphere and troposphere; formation, behaviour and decomposition of aerosols and trace gases; bioclimatology; atmospheric electricity and radioactivity; development of measuring and analytical techniques.
Publications: Annual report.

Fraunhofer-Institut für Bauphysik 688

[Fraunhofer Institute for Structural Physics]
Address: Königstrasse 74, D-7000 Stuttgart 70
Telephone: (0711) 76 50 08
Affiliation: Fraunhofer-Gesellschaft zur Förderung der Angewandten Forschung eV
Director: Professor Dr F.P. Mechel
Sections: Heat transfer problems, Dr Kupke; weather exposure of material, H. Künzel; building acoustics, Dr R. Schumacher; technical acoustics, Dr Fuchs; development of structural material and components, Dr Bertsch
Graduate research staff: 25
Annual expenditure: DM6m
Activities: Research and development in the following areas: acoustics of buildings and noise control (traffic and industrial noise); thermal insulation and moisture problems in buildings; heating-energy-saving, air-conditioning, and weathering of buildings; development and testing of building constructions and components.
Contract work: Yes
Publications: Annual report.

Fraunhofer-Institut für Betriebsfestigkeit 689

– IBF
[Fraunhofer Institute for Structural Fatigue Strength]
Address: Bartningstrasse 47, D-6100 Darmstadt-Kranichstein
Telephone: (06151) 357 1
Telex: 04 192031 bfd
Affiliation: Fraunhofer-Gesellschaft zur Förderung der Angewandten Forschung eV
Director: Professor Dr Ing O. Buxbaum
Sections: Analysis of operational loads, Dr Ing J.M. Zaschel; stress analysis and strength evaluation, Dr Ing V. Grubic; mathematical methods and systems behaviour, Dr Ing H.P. Lehrke; fatigue behaviour of materials, Dipl-Ing H. Ostermann; optimization and proof testing, W. Lipp; fatigue life prediction and fracture mechanics, Dr Ing D. Schütz
Graduate research staff: 40
Annual expenditure: DM9m
Activities: Fatigue life and safety assessments of structures; measurement, analysis and simulation of service loads; stress analysis; influence of design, material and production on fatigue strength.
Specific projects include: investigations into the effects of resonant vibrations on drilling platforms in deep-water; failure-proof turbine rotors by research on corrosion vibration of applied materials.
Contract work: Yes
Publications: Annual report.

Fraunhofer-Institut für Festkörpertechnologie 690

[Fraunhofer Institute for Solid-State Technology]
Address: 42 Paul-Gerhardt-Allee, D-8000 München 60
Affiliation: Fraunhofer-Gesellschaft zur Förderung der Angewandten Forschung eV
Director: Professor Dr I. Ruge
Graduate research staff: 45
Annual expenditure: DM12.3m
Activities: Development of new technology for the fabrication of semiconductor devices; development and production of devices for special fields of application; failure analysis of components; material characterization; medical electronics.
Specific projects include: ion radiation lithography for highly integrated electronic components; microprocessor-controlled monitoring systems; process stimulation for optimizing semiconductor components.
Publications: Annual report.

Fraunhofer-Institut für 691 Grenzflächen- und Bioverfahrenstechnik

[Fraunhofer Institute for Interfacial and Bio-Process Engineering]
Address: 12 Nobelstrasse, D-7000 Stuttgart 80
Affiliation: Fraunhofer-Gesellschaft zur Förderung der Angewandten Forschung eV
Director: Professor Dr H. Chmiel
Graduate research staff: 24
Annual expenditure: DM5.3m
Activities: Research and development in the following areas: problems in interfacial science, particularly adsorption processes; low-temperature preservation; medical measuring technique, biorheology, biotechnology; research on a smaller, transportable artificial kidney.
Publications: Annual report.

Fraunhofer-Institut für 692 Holzforschung - Wilhelm-Klauditz-Institut

[Fraunhofer Institute for Wood Research - Wilhelm-Klauditz Institute]
Address: Bienroder Weg 54e, D-3300 Braunschweig
Telephone: (0531) 350098-99
Telex: 952942 wkibs d
Affiliation: Fraunhofer-Gesellschaft zur Förderung der Angewandten Forschung eV
Director: Professor Dr Ing Gert Kossatz
Sections: Automation, L. Mehlhorn; technology of wood-based panel products, C. Harbs; chemical technology, pollution control, Dr R. Marutzky; raw materials, surface coating, Dr P. Böttcher
Graduate research staff: 20
Annual expenditure: DM4.4m
Activities: Research and development in the following areas: utilization of small-sized woods; upgrading of wood wastes; combination of wood or wood-based panels with other construction material; optimization of the technology to produce wood-based panel products by computer control; analogue or digital circuit design; automation techniques; chemical processes for the production of wood-based panels; further development of structural wood material; problems of coating.
Facilities: Large workshop for making wood-based panels; testing-machines with on-line computer processing; double climatic chamber for testing of wall-elements in life-size; chemical laboratories with the following analytical equipment - IR, UV-Vis, AAS, HPLC, gas

chromatograph (capillary-technique), nitrogen-analyser, sugar-analyser; paper laboratory.
Contract work: Yes
Publications: Annual report.

Fraunhofer-Institut für 693 Hydroakustik

[Fraunhofer Institute for Hydroacoustics]
Address: 41 Waldparkstrasse, D-8012 Ottobrunn bei München
Affiliation: Fraunhofer-Gesellschaft zur Förderung der Angewandten Forschung eV
Director: Dr H. Merbt
Graduate research staff: 9
Annual expenditure: DM2.8m
Activities: Research and development in the following areas: generation, propagation and reduction of machinery noise, propeller noise, and flow noise in and around naval vessels; inception of hydrodynamic cavitation; documentation centre for ship and underwater acoustics.
Publications: Annual report.

Fraunhofer-Institut für 694 Informations- und Datenverarbeitung

[Fraunhofer Institute for Information and Data Processing]
Address: Sebastian-Kneipp-Strasse 12-14, D-7500 Karlsruhe 1
Telephone: (0721) 6091-1
Telex: 07-825931 iitb
Affiliation: Fraunhofer-Gesellschaft zur Förderung der Angewandten Forschung eV
Directors: Dr A. Schief, Professor Dr M. Syrbe
Assistant directors: Dr K. Ossenberg, Dr H. Steusloff
Graduate research staff: 90
Annual expenditure: DM15.6m
Activities: Research and development in the following areas: optical and acoustic signal processing, pattern recognition, ergonomics; sensors and man-machine interfaces in production, defence, testing, medicine, information, traffic and control technologies; automation systems; computer-aided design, cybernetics, man-computer, computer-computer communication, association/correlation storage, artificial intelligence.
Specific projects include: data connection system for wide-meshed-distributed dataflow; fault-tolerant com-

puter systems; picture-processing systems for process and quality control.
Contract work: Yes
Publications: Annual report.

Fraunhofer-Institut für Kurzzeitdynamik - Ernst-Mach-Institut

695

[Fraunhofer Institute for High-Speed Dynamics - Ernst-Mach Institute]
Address: Eckerstrasse 4, D-7800 Freiburg im Breisgau
Telephone: (0761) 2714-1
Telex: 772510
Affiliation: Fraunhofer-Gesellschaft zur Förderung der Angewandten Forschung eV
Directors: Dr H. Reichenbach, Dr G.A. Schröder
Sections: Fluid dynamics, ballistics, shock and blast
Graduate research staff: 38
Annual expenditure: DM9.3m
Activities: Unsteady gas dynamics, impact studies; structural dynamics; protective structures technology; blast and shock simulation; high-speed measuring techniques; internal and muzzle ballistics, terminal ballistics and ballistics of shrapnel, explosive physics.
Specific projects include: reinforced concrete for protective structures and reactor buildings; vibration characteristics of an arch dam with blast wave loads; research into highly resistant material for protection of armoured tanks against the impact of explosive weapons.
Facilities: Shock tubes; light gas guns; aeroballistic ranges; blast simulators; X-ray flash equipment; visar interferometer.
Contract work: Yes
Publications: Annual report.

BALLISTICS DEPARTMENT

696

Address: 18 Hauptstrasse, D-7858 Weil am Rhein

Fraunhofer-Institut für Lebensmitteltechnologie und Verpackung

697

[Fraunhofer Institute for Food Technology and Packaging]
Address: 35 Schragenhofstrasse, D-8000 München 50
Affiliation: Fraunhofer-Gesellschaft zur Förderung der Angewandten Forschung eV
Directors: Dr G. Schricker, Dr L. Robinson
Graduate research staff: 20
Annual expenditure: DM4.5m

Activities: Food technology (chemical, physical, microbiological processes); quality maintenance of food by packaging; techniques of packaging (mechanical processing of packaging materials, optimization of transported packages).
Specific projects include: selective ion chromatography; investigations into the efficiency of tube-bag-machines of the type 'transwrap 125 H'.
Publications: Annual report.

Fraunhofer-Institut für Naturwissenschaftlich-Technische Trendanalysen

698

[Fraunhofer Institute for Scientific-Technical Trend Analysis]
Address: 2 Appelsgarten, D-5350 Euskirchen
Affiliation: Fraunhofer-Gesellschaft zur Förderung der Angewandten Forschung eV
Director: vacant
Activities: Applied physical research in military engineering; forecasts as to defence techniques; scientific aspects of security policy; analysis of non-conventional weapons and assessment of potential counter measures.

Fraunhofer-Institut für Physikalische Messtechnik

699

[Fraunhofer Institute for Physical Measurement]
Address: 8 Heidenhofstrasse, D-7800 Freiburg
Affiliation: Fraunhofer-Gesellschaft zur Förderung der Angewandten Forschung eV
Director: Professor Dr J. Hesse
Graduate research staff: 27
Annual expenditure: DM5.7m
Activities: Development of new measuring processes and systems in combination with optics, electronics and data processing on the basis of advanced sensor principles (ie laser spectroscopy, fibre optics) and evaluation processes (microprocessors).
Publications: Annual report.

Fraunhofer-Institut für Produktionsanlagen und Konstruktionstechnik

700

[Fraunhofer Institute for Production Plants and Construction Technology]
Address: 23-26 Kleiststrasse, D-1000 Berlin 30

Affiliation: Fraunhofer-Gesellschaft zur Förderung der Angewandten Forschung eV
Director: Professor Dr G. Spur
Graduate research staff: 66
Annual expenditure: DM9.1m
Activities: Research and development in the following areas: automation in construction and manufacture; computer-aided design and planning; development and control of production plants; numerical control; microelectronics for production; new structures in production techniques; quality data processing; innovation technology.
Specific projects include: software for a 6-axle point-control; CNC control with integrated programme and tool measuring system.
Publications: Annual report.

Fraunhofer-Institut für Produktionstechnik und Automatisierung

701

– IPA
[Fraunhofer Institute for Production Engineering and Automation]
Address: 17 Holzgartenstrasse, Postfach 951, D-7000 Stuttgart 1
Telephone: (0711) 226017
Affiliation: Fraunhofer-Gesellschaft zur Förderung der Angewandten Forschung eV
Director: Professor Dr H.J. Warnecke
Sections: Factory planning, Professor Dr H.J. Bullinger; production technology, Dr Ing K. Zerweck; automation, Dr Ing R.D. Schraft
Graduate research staff: 150
Annual expenditure: DM14.3m
Activities: Industrial engineering; production planning and control; factory planning; automation of material flow; DV in production control; automatic handling and assembly, production measuring technique; galvanic and lacquer technique; visual testing; sensors.
Specific projects include: fully automatic assembly-line for seat-belt blocking systems with integrated testing machines; working system for efficient assembly of electric motors.
Contract work: Yes
Publications: Annual report.

Fraunhofer-Institut für Produktionstechnologie

702

[Fraunhofer Institute for Production Technology]
Address: 53B Arnold-Sommerfeld-Strasse, D-5100 Aachen
Affiliation: Fraunhofer-Gesellschaft zur Förderung der Angewandten Forschung eV
Director: Professor Dr W. König
Graduate research staff: 18
Annual expenditure: DM2.7m
Activities: Process technology: laser and water jet processing, glass and ceramics processing, high-speed processing; production machines: process control, dynamic behaviour; production measuring technique: laser measuring technique, operational testing, sensors.
Publications: Annual report.

Fraunhofer-Institut für Silicatforschung

703

[Fraunhofer Institute for Silicate Research]
Address: Neunerplatz 2, D-8700 Würzburg
Telephone: (0931) 42014
Affiliation: Fraunhofer-Gesellschaft zur Förderung der Angewandten Forschung eV
Director: Professor Dr H. Scholze
Sections: Ceramics, glass, silicate, Dr H. Schmidt; glass, ceramics, gypsum, Dr Ing H. Engelke
Graduate research staff: 15
Annual expenditure: DM4m
Activities: Development and improvement of non-metallic inorganic materials (glass, ceramic, cement, lime, gypsum, organic-modified silicates) and their technologies; behaviour of the materials during production and application; environmentally acceptable processes.
Contract work: Yes
Publications: Annual report.

Fraunhofer-Institut für Solare Energiesysteme

704

[Fraunhofer Institute for Solar Energy Systems]
Address: Oltmannsstrasse 22, D-7800 Freiburg
Telephone: (0761) 405046
Telex: 0772510
Affiliation: Fraunhofer-Gesellschaft zur Förderung der Angewandten Forschung eV
Director: Professor Dr A. Goetzberger
Sections: Collectors, Dr V. Wittwer; energy storage, Dr E. Hollax; solar cells, B. Voss; materials research, Dr

A. Räuber; regulation and control technology, Dr J. Schmid
Graduate research staff: 9
Annual expenditure: DM3.2m
Activities: Research and development in the following areas: electrical and thermal solar collectors, especially fluorescent collectors; semiconductor materials for solar cells; thermal and electrochemical energy storage; regulation and control techniques for small-scale energy supply (heating and air-conditioning for buildings).
Contract work: Yes
Publications: Annual report.

Fraunhofer-Institut für Systemtechnik und Innovationsforschung   705

– ISI
[Fraunhofer Institute for Systems-Analysis and Innovation Research]
Address: Sebastian-Kneipp-Strasse 12-14, D-7500 Karlsruhe 1
Telephone: (0721) 60911
Telex: 07-825-931 iitb d
Affiliation: Fraunhofer-Gesellschaft zur Förderung der Angewandten Forschung eV
Director: Professor Dr Ing Helmar Krupp
Sections: Systems analysis, Dr Ing Eberhard Jochem; innovation research, Dr Günther Schäfer; technology transfer, Dr Siegfried Lange
Graduate research staff: 40
Annual expenditure: DM6.8m
Activities: Research and development in the following areas:
Systems analysis - condensing, integrating and systematizing information for planning, forecasting and technology assessment; computer-aided simulation of complex systems.
Innovation research - investigation and evaluation of programmes to encourage innovations; demonstration projects.
Technology transfer - planning and management in research, technology and innovation.
Contract work: Yes
Publications: Annual report.

Fraunhofer-Institut für Toxikologie und Aerosolforschung   706

[Fraunhofer Institute for Toxicology and Aerosol Research]
Address: D-5948 Schmallenberg
Telephone: (02972) 494-96
Telex: 841520
Affiliation: Fraunhofer-Gesellschaft zur Förderung der Angewandten Forschung eV
Directors: Dr Hubert Oldiges, Professor Werner Stöber
Sections: Biology, Dr Otto; chemistry, Dr Schoene; physics, Dr Hochrainer; physical chemistry, Professor Spurny; inhalation and toxicology, Dr Heinrich
Graduate research staff: 45
Annual expenditure: DM12.2m
Activities: Assessment of biological impact of air pollutants; toxicology of biocides; physico-chemical analysis and biochemistry of harmful airborne material (gases, aerosols); protective measures against environmental pollutants; dust measuring technique.
Specific projects include: development of a rat liver-cell system for testing its biochemical functional efficiency; impulse cytophotometry to be used for fertility tests.
Contract work: Yes
Publications: Annual report.

Fraunhofer-Institut für Transporttechnik und Warendistribution   707

[Fraunhofer Institute for Transport Technology and Goods Distribution]
Address: Postfach 50 05 00, D-4600 Dortmund 50
Affiliation: Fraunhofer-Gesellschaft zur Förderung der Angewandten Forschung eV
Director: Professor Dr R. Jünemann
Graduate research staff: 15
Annual expenditure: DM2.8m
Activities: Research and development in the following areas: material flow-planning, simulation, automation; construction and development, testing, reliability tests of conveying and handling machines; new technologies and development of new structures; sensors, conductivity; disposal, packaging and loading.
Publications: Annual report.

Fraunhofer-Institut für   708
Treib- und Explosivstoffe

– ICT
[Fraunhofer Institute for Propellants and Explosives]
Address: Institutsstrasse, Postfach 1240, D-7507 Pfinztal-Berghausen
Telephone: (0721) 46101
Telex: 07826909
Affiliation: Fraunhofer-Gesellschaft zur Förderung der Angewandten Forschung eV
Director: Dr Hiltmar A.O. Schubert
Graduate research staff: 26
Annual expenditure: DM12m
Activities: Chemistry, physics, process and applied engineering of propellants, explosives and pyrotechnics; safety technology of explosive systems, combustion processes; environmental simulation and transport loads; energy conversion.
Specific projects include: production of a chemically-stable polyvinyl nitrate with the required purity for technical application purposes; munition without cartridges with a high thermal and mechanical stability for 4.7 mm calibre.
Contract work: Yes
Publications: Annual report.

Fraunhofer-Institut für   709
Werkstoffmechanik

– IWM
[Fraunhofer Institute for Materials and Mechanics]
Address: Rosastrasse 9, D-7800 Freiburg
Telephone: (0761) 35374
Telex: 772510
Affiliation: Fraunhofer-Gesellschaft zur Förderung der Angewandten Forschung eV
Director: Dr E. Sommer
Sections: Strength of metallic materials, Dr J.G. Blauel; strength of non-metallic materials, Dr W. Döll; experimental stress-strain analysis, Dr J.F. Kalthoff; theoretical numerical analysis, W. Schmitt; surface properties, Dr R. Prümmer
Graduate research staff: 25
Annual expenditure: DM4.9m
Activities: Investigation of fracture processes - experimental and numerical stress-strain analysis in specimens, structural members with or without cracks and defects under static and dynamic loading conditions; analysis of material and strength properties - physical-mechanical investigations of fracture related processes

in materials such as metals, polymers, glass, and ceramics.
Contract work: Yes
Publications: Annual report.

Fraunhofer-Institut für   710
Zerstörungsfreie Prüfverfahren

– IzfP
[Fraunhofer Institute for Non-destructive Test Methods]
Address: Gebäude 37 - Universität, D-6600 Saarbrücken 11
Telephone: (0681) 3023800; 3023801
Telex: 04-421328
Affiliation: Fraunhofer-Gesellschaft zur Förderung der Angewandten Forschung eV
Director: Professor Dr P. Höller
Section heads: Dr G. Deuster, Dr G. Dobmann, Dr K. Goebbels, Dr V. Schmitz
Graduate research staff: 37
Annual expenditure: DM12.7m
Activities: Methods for non-destructive testing for examination of materials, semi-finished products, components, and plant, with regard to properties and flaws (basic research, development, and application in quality control during production process and in reactor safety).
Specific projects include: ultrasonic sound generation, without coupling agent and contactless, tested and further developed by superimposing magnetic fields and eddy current patterns; use of ultrasonic sound-phased arrays for non-destructive material testing for production control of components and testing of primary enclosure of nuclear plant (pressure vessel, pipeline systems).
Contract work: Yes
Publications: Annual report.

Freie Universität Berlin   711

[Free University of Berlin]
Address: Altensteinstrasse 40, D-1000 Berlin 33
Telephone: (030) 798 83 81
Telex: 018 40 19 fublnd
President: Professor Dr Eberhard Lämmert

CHARLOTTENBURG UNIVERSITY CLINIC 712

Address: Spandauer Damm 130, D-1000 Berlin 19
Telephone: (030) 35 22 02
Medical Director: Professor Dr Karl-Hermann Meyer zum Büschenfelde

Ear, Nose and Throat Hospital 713

Address: Spandauer Damm 130, D-1000 Berlin 19
Telephone: (030) 356 92
Director: Professor Dr Ernst Kastenbauer

Eye Hospital 714

Address: Spandauer Damm 130, D-1000 Berlin 19
Telephone: (030) 356 19
Director: Professor Dr Josef Wollensak

Gynaecology Hospital Charlottenburg 715

Address: Pulsstrasse 4-14, D-1000 Berlin 19
Telephone: (030) 320 31
Director: Professor Dr Günther Kindermann
Departments: Gynaecology and obstetrics, Professor Dr Günther Kindermann; gynaecological endocrinology, Professor Dr Josef Nevinny-Stickel

Medical Hospital 716

Address: Spandauer Damm 130, D-1000 Berlin 19
Telephone: (030) 356 21
Director: Professor Dr Meta Alexander
Departments: Gastroenterology, Professor Dr Klaus Erich Hampel; haematology, Professor Dr Heinrich Gerhartz; infectious diseases, Professor Dr Meta Alexander; nephrology, Professor Dr Michael Kessel; cardiology and pulmonology, Professor Dr Horst Schmutzler; artificial respiration, Professor Dr Karla Ibe

Neurosurgical-Neurological Hospital 717

Address: Spandauer Damm 130, D-1000 Berlin 19
Telephone: (030) 35 22 90
Director: Professor Dr Stanislaw Kubicki
Departments: Neurosurgery, Professor Dr Ekkehard Kazner; neurology, Professor Dr Dieter Janz; clinical neurophysiology, Professor Dr Stanislaw Kubicki

Orthopaedic Hospital 718

Address: Clayallee 229, D-1000 Berlin 33
Telephone: (030) 81 30 11
Director: Professor Dr Günther Kindermann

Paediatric Hospital 719

Address: Heubnerweg 6, D-1000 Berlin 19
Telephone: (030) 320 31
Director: Professor Dr Hans Helge
Departments: Psychosomatic, vacant; neonatology and intensive care, Professor Dr Leonore Ballowitz; paediatric cardiology, Professor Dr Georg Bein; paediatric endocrinology and metabolism, Professor Dr Hans Helge; paediatric neurology, Professor Dr Folker Hanefeld; paediatric radiology, Professor Dr Herbert J. Kaufmann; paediatric haematology, Professor Dr Hansjörg Riehm

Psychiatric Hospital 720

Address: Eschenallee 3, D-1000 Berlin 19
Telephone: (030) 300 31
Director: Professor Dr Hanfried Helmchen

Psychiatry and Neurology Hospital 721

Address: Nussbaumallee 36, D-1000 Berlin 19
Director: vacant

Skin Hospital 722

Address: Augustenburger Platz 1, D-1000 Berlin 65
Telephone: (030) 450 51
Director: Professor Dr Günther Stüttgen
Department: Clinical immunology, Professor Gert Kunkel

Surgical Hospital 723

Address: Spandauer Damm 130, D-1000 Berlin 19
Telephone: (030) 356 31
Director: Professor Dr Emil-Sebastian Bücherl

Urological Hospital 724

Address: Spandauer Damm 130, D-1000 Berlin 19
Telephone: (030) 356 94
Director: Professor Dr Reinhard Nagel

X-ray Hospital 725

Address: Spandauer Damm 130, D-1000 Berlin 19
Telephone: (030) 356 70
Director: Professor Dr Ulrich Haubold
Departments: Radiology, Professor Dr Roland Felix; paediatric radiology, Professor Dr Herbert J. Kaufmann

CLINICAL AND EXPERIMENTAL PLASMOPROTEIN RESEARCH 726

Address: Bitterstrasse 14, D-1000 Berlin 33
Head: Professor Dr Martin Siegert

INSTITUTE OF ANAESTHESIOLOGY 727
Address: Spandauer Damm 130, D-1000 Berlin 19
Telephone: (030) 355 04
Director: Professor Dr Hans-Joachim Eberlein
Departments: Clinical anaesthesiology, Professor Dr Hans-Joachim Eberlein; experimental anaesthesiology working group, Professor Dr Hans-Wolfgang Reinhardt; circulatory research working group, Professor Dr Jürgen B. Brückner.

INSTITUTE OF FORENSIC PSYCHIATRY 728
Address: Limonenstrasse 27, D-1000 Berlin 45
Telephone: (030) 832 70 14
Director: Professor Dr Wilfried Rasch

INSTITUTE OF HUMAN GENETICS 729
Address: Heubnerweg 6, D-1000 Berlin 19
Telephone: (030) 320 33 76
Directors: Professor Joachim Klose, Professor Karl Sperling

INSTITUTE OF PATHOLOGY 730
Address: Spandauer Damm 130, D-1000 Berlin 19
Telephone: (030) 356 75
Director: Professor Dr Sigurd Blümcke

INSTITUTE OF PHARMACOLOGY 731
Address: Thielallee 69-73, D-1000 Berlin 33
Telephone: (030) 838 33 70
Director: Professor Dr Hans Herken

INSTITUTE OF TOXICOLOGY AND 732
EMBRYOPHARMACOLOGY
Address: Garystrasse 9, D-1000 Berlin 33
Telephone: (030) 838 31 92
Director: vacant

FACULTY OF BIOLOGY 733
Address: Grunewaldstrasse 34a, D-1000 Berlin 41
Head: Professor Dr Randolf Menzel

Institute of Animal Physiology and 734
Applied Zoology
Director: Professor Dr K. Graszynski

Institute of Applied Genetics (Heredity 735
and Breeding Research)
Address: Albrecht-Thaer-Weg 6, D-1000 Berlin 33
Director: Professor Dr K.-D. Krolow

Institute of Biochemistry and 736
Molecular Biology
Address: Ehrenbergstrasse 26-28, D-1000 Berlin 33
Director: Professor Ernst-Randolf Lochmann

Institute of Genetics 737
Address: Arnimallee 5-7, D-1000 Berlin 33
Director: Professor Dr I. Lamprecht
Departments: Anthropology and human biology, Professor Carsten Niemitz; biophysics and radiobiology, Professor Dr I. Lamprecht, Professor Wolfgang Laskowski

Institute of Plant Physiology and Cell 738
Biology
Address: Königin-Luise-Strasse 12-16a, D-1000 Berlin 33
Director: Professor Dr H. Paradies

Institute of Systematic Botany and 739
Plant Geography
Address: Altensteinerstrasse 6, D-1000 Berlin 33
Director: Professor Dr U. Geissler

Institute of Zoology 740
Address: Königin-Luise-Strasse 1-3, D-1000 Berlin 33
Director: Professor Dr H.-D. Pfannenstiel

FACULTY OF CHEMISTRY 741
Address: Takustrasse 3, D-1000 Berlin 33
Head: Professor Dr Jürgen Simon

Institute of Biochemistry 742
Address: Ostpreussendamm 111, D-1000 Berlin 45
Telephone: (030) 712 10 07
Director: Professor Dr Ferdinand Hucho

Institute of Crystallography 743
Address: Takustrasse 6, D-1000 Berlin 33
Director: Professor Dr Hans Bradaczeck

Institute of Inorganic and Analytical 744
Chemistry
Address: Fabeckstrasse 34-36, D-1000 Berlin 33
Director: Professor Dr Roman Frydrych

Institute of Mineralogy 745

Address: Takustrasse 6, D-1000 Berlin 33
Director: Professor Dr Wilhelm Büsch

Institute of Organic Chemistry 746

Address: Takustrasse 3, D-1000 Berlin 33
Director: Professor Dr Georg Manecke

Institute of Physical Chemistry and 747 Quantum Chemistry

Address: Takustrasse 3, D-1000 Berlin 33
Director: Professor Dr Wolfgang Hirschwald

Institute of Quantum Chemistry 748

Address: Holbeinstrasse 48, D-1000 Berlin 45
Telephone: (030) 833 62 19
Director: Professor Dr Ernst Ruch

FACULTY OF DENTAL SCIENCES 749

Address: Apmannhauser Strasse 4-6, D-1000 Berlin 33
Head: Professor Dr Dieter Hermann

Dental Hospital including Jaw and 750 Face Surgery

Director: Professor Dr Baldur Kempfle
Departments: Jaw and plastic facial surgery, Universitätsklinikum Steglitz, Professor Dr Rudolf Stellmach

Institute of Clinical and Theoretical 751 Dental Sciences

Director: Professor Dr Joachim Viohl

FACULTY OF GEOSCIENCES 752

Address: Patschkauer Weg 38, D-1000 Berlin 33
Head: Professor Dr Gerhard Stäblein

Institute of Anthropogeography, 753 Applied Geography and Cartography

Address: Grunewaldstrasse 35, D-1000 Berlin 41
Director: Professor Dr Frido Bader

Institute of Applied Geology 754

Address: Wichernstrasse 16, D-1000 Berlin 33
Director: Professor Dr Hanskarl Brühl

Institute of Geology 755

Address: Altensteinerstrasse 34a, D-1000 Berlin 33
Director: Professor Dr Volker Jaconshagen

Institute of Geophysical Sciences 756

Director: Professor Dr Peter Giese

Institute of Meteorology 757

Address: Podbielskiallee 62, D-1000 Berlin 33
Telephone: (030) 832 85 18
Director: Professor Dr Gert Hoffmann
Departments: Radioactivity, vacant; radiation, Professor Dr Bernhard Lindenbein; technical meteorology, Professor Dr Gert Hoffmann; weather forecasting, Leopold Klauser; synoptic diagnosis and climatology, Professor Dr Manfred Gebb; local weather forecast research, Professor Horst Malmberg; stratospheric research, Professor Dr Karin Labitzke; meteorological satellite research, Professor Dr Ingrid Haupt; hydro and tropics meterology, Professor Dr Klaus Fraedich

Institute of Palaeontology 758

Address: Schwendenerstrasse 8, D-1000 Berlin 33
Director: Professor Dr Gundolf Ernst

Institute of Physical Geography 759

Address: Grunewaldstrasse 35, D-1000 Berlin 41
Secretary: Anne Beck

GEOMORPHOLOGICAL LABORATORY 760
Address: Altensteinstrasse 19, D-1000 Berlin 33
Director: Professor Dr Karlheinz Kaiser
Departments: Institute of Eastern European Geography, Professor Peter Rostankowski, Professor Wilhelm Wöhlke; John F.-Kennedy Institute for Geography, Professor Karl Lenz

FACULTY OF MEDICINE 761

Address: Gustav-Meyer Strasse 7, D-1000 Berlin 33
Head: Professor Dr Rolf Winau

Institute of Anatomy 762

Address: Königin-Luise-Strasse 15, D-1000 Berlin 33
Director: Professor Dr Hans-Joachim Merker

Institute of Molecular Biology and 763 Biochemistry

Address: Arnimallee 22, D-1000 Berlin 33
Director: Professor Dr Friedrich Körber

Institute of Physiology   764

Address: Arnimallee 22, D-1000 Berlin 33
Director: Professor Dr Ekkehard Zerbst

Preventive Medicine   765

Address: Hindenburgdamm 27, D-1000 Berlin 45
Telephone: (030) 798 36 04
Director: vacant

FACULTY OF PHARMACOLOGY   766

Address: Schweinfurthstrasse 82, D-1000 Berlin 33
Head: Professor Dr Rudolf Hänsel

Institute of Pharmacognosy and   767
Phytochemistry

Address: Königin-Luise-Strasse 2-4, D-1000 Berlin 33
Director: Professor Dr Rudolf Hansel

Institute of Pharmacology   768

Address: Königin-Luise-Strasse 2-4, D-1000 Berlin 33
or: Kelchstrasse 31, D-1000 Berlin 41
Director: Professor Dr Peter Nickel

FACULTY OF PHYSICS   769

Address: Hüninger Strasse 44, D-1000 Berlin 33
Head: Professor Dr Eckart Matthias

Institute of Astronomy and   770
Astrophysics

Address: Ernst-Reuter-Platz 7, D-1000 Berlin 10
Director: Professor Dr Roland Wielen

Institute of Molecular Physics   771

Address: Boltzmannstrasse 20, D-1000 Berlin 33
Director: Professor Dr K. Möbius

Institute of Nuclear and Solid-State   772
Physics

Address: Boltzmannstrasse 20, D-1000 Berlin 33
Director: Professor Dr Dieter Quitmann

Institute of Nuclear Physics   773

Address: Glienicker Strasse 100, D-1000 Berlin 39
Director: Professor Dr G. Vogl

Institute of Theory of Condensed   774
Matter

Address: Arnimallee 3, D-1000 Berlin 33
Director: Professor Dr K.D. Schotte

Institute of Theory of Elementary   775
Particles

Address: Arnimallee 3, D-1000 Berlin 33
Director: Professor Dr W. Theis

FACULTY OF VETERINARY MEDICINE   776

Address: Ehrenbergstrasse 17, D-1000 Berlin 33
Head: Professor Dr Gerhard Böhme

Clinic for Clawed Animals and   777
Reproduction Science

Address: Königsweg 65, D-1000 Berlin 37

Clinic for Horse Diseases and General   778
Surgery

Address: Oertzenweg 19 B, D-1000 Berlin 37
Director: Professor Dr Hanns-Jürgen Wintzer

Clinic for Small Domestic Animals   779

Address: Oertzenweg 19 B, D-1000 Berlin 37
Director: Professor Dr Lukas Felix Müller

Institute of Animal Breeding and   780
Animal Nutrition

Address: Brümmerstrasse 34, D-1000 Berlin 33
Director: Professor Dr Kurt Bronsch

Institute of Food Hygiene, Meat   781
Hygiene and Meat Technology

Director: Professor Dr Hans-Jürgen Sinell

Institute of Laboratory Animal Science 782
and Diseases

Address: Tietzenweg 85-87, D-1000 Berlin 45
Director: Professor Dr Norbert-Christian Juhr

Institute of Microbiology, Poultry   783
Diseases, Electron Microscopy and
Animal Hygiene

Director: Professor Dr Gerhard Monreal

Institute of Parasitology and Tropical Veterinary Medicine 784

Director: Professor Dr Franz Hörchner

Institute of Veterinary Anatomy, Histology and Embryology 785

Address: Koserstrasse 20, D-1000 Berlin 33
Director: Professor Dr Klaus-Dieter Budras

Institute of Veterinary Pathology 786

Address: Drosselweg 1-3, D-1000 Berlin 33
Director: Professor Dr Horst Loppnow

Institute of Veterinary Physiology, Biochemistry, Pharmacology and Toxicology 787

Address: Koserstrasse 20, D-1000 Berlin 33
Director: Professor Dr Hansdieter Krzywanek

UNIVERSITÄTSKLINIKUM STEGLITZ 788

Address: Hindenburgdamm 30, D-1000 Berlin 45
Telephone: (030) 798 33 21
Medical Director: Professor Dr Dietmar Zühlke

Ear, Nose and Throat Hospital 789

Address: Hindenburgdamm 30, D-1000 Berlin 45
Telephone: (030) 798 24 31
Director: Professor Dr Dietmar Zühlke
Departments: Ear, nose and throat diseases, Professor Dr Dietmar Zühlke; audiology and phoniometry, Professor Dr Odo von Arentsschild

Eye Hospital 790

Address: Hindenburgdamm 30, D-1000 Berlin 45
Telephone: (030) 798 23 31
Director: Professor Dr Hugo Hager

Gynaecology Hospital 791

Address: Hindenburgdamm 30, D-1000 Berlin 45
Telephone: (030) 798 24 57
Director: Professor Dr Georg Hörmann
Departments: Gynaecology and obstetrics, Professor Dr Georg Hörmann; gynaecological endocrinology, sterility and family planning, Professor Dr Jürgen Hammerstein

Medical Hospital 792

Address: Hindenburgdamm 30, D-1000 Berlin 45
Telephone: (030) 798 23 43
Director: Professor Dr Ernst-Otto Riecken
Departments: Endocrinology, Professor Dr Horst Schleusener; gastroenterology, Professor Dr Ernst-Otto Riecken; haematology and oncology, Professor Dr Horst Brücher; pulmonology and cardiology, Professor Dr Rolf Schröder

Neurosurgical and Neurological Hospital 793

Address: Hindenburgdamm 30, D-1000 Berlin 45
Director: Professor Dr Max Straschill
Departments: Neurosurgery, Professor Dr Mario Brock; neurology, Professor Dr Roland Schiffter; clinical neurophysiology, Professor Dr Max Straschill

Radiology, Nuclear Medicine and Physical Therapy Hospital 794

Address: Hindenburgdamm 30, D-1000 Berlin 45
Telephone: (030) 798 30 51
Director: Professor Dr Helmut Ernst
Departments: Diagnostic radiology, Professor Dr Roland Felix; radiation therapy, Professor Dr Helmut Ernst; nuclear medicine, Professor Dr Karl Oeff

Skin Hospital 795

Address: Hindenburgdamm 30, D-1000 Berlin 45
Telephone: (030) 798 22 92
Director: Professor Dr Constantin Orfanos

Surgical Hospital 796

Address: Hindenburgdamm 30, D-1000 Berlin 45
Telephone: (030) 798 25 41
Director: Professor Dr Rudolf Häring
Departments: General surgery I, Professor Dr Rudolf Häring; general surgery II with plastic surgery, Professor Dr Rahim Rahmanzadeh; paediatric surgery, Professor Dr Jürgen Waldschmidt

Urological Hospital 797

Address: Hindenburgdamm 30, D-1000 Berlin 45
Telephone: (030) 798 25 75
Director: Professor Dr Wilhelm Brosig

INSTITUTE OF ANAESTHESIOLOGY 798
Address: Hindenburgdamm 30, D-1000 Berlin 45
Telephone: (030) 798 27 31
Director: Professor Dr Klaus Eyrich

INSTITUTE OF CLINICAL CHEMISTRY 799
AND CLINICAL BIOCHEMISTRY
Address: Hindenburgdamm 30, D-1000 Berlin 45
Telephone: (030) 798 25 55
Director: Professor Dr Hans-Joachim Dulce

INSTITUTE OF CLINICAL 800
PHARMACOLOGY
Address: Hindenburgdamm 30, D-1000 Berlin 45
Telephone: (030) 798 22 79
Director: Professor Dr Helmut Kewitz

INSTITUTE OF CLINICAL 801
PHYSIOLOGY
Address: Hindenburgdamm 30, D-1000 Berlin 45
Telephone: (030) 798 25 34
Director: Professor Dr Klaus Hierholzer

INSTITUTE OF NEUROPATHOLOGY 802
Address: Hindenburgdamm 30, D-1000 Berlin 45
Telephone: (030) 798 23 39
Director: Professor Dr Jorge Cervós-Navarro

INSTITUTE OF PATHOLOGY 803
Address: Hindenburgdamm 30, D-1000 Berlin 45
Telephone: (030) 798 22 95
Director: Professor Dr Eberhard Altenähr

Friedrich Alexander 804
Universität Erlangen-
Nürnberg

[Friedrich Alexander Erlangen-Nuremberg University]
Address: Schlossplatz 4, D-8520 Erlangen
Telephone: (09131) 851

FACULTY OF MEDICINE 805

Anaesthesiology Institute 806

Address: Maximilliansplatz 1, D-8520 Erlangen
Head: Professor Dr E. Rügheimer

Anatomy Institute 807

Address: Krankenhausstrasse 9, D-8520 Erlangen
Head: Professor Dr J.W. Rohen

Clinic and Outpatients Department for 808
Ear, Nose and Throat

Address: Waldstrasse 1, D-8520 Erlangen
Head: Professor Dr M.E. Wigand

SPEECH AND VOICE DISORDERS 809
DEPARTMENT

Clinical and Outpatients Department 810
for Tooth, Mouth, and Jaw Disorders

Address: Glückstrasse 11, D-8520 Erlangen
Heads: Professor Dr M. Hoffmann, Professor Dr A. Kröncke, Professor Dr A. Fleischer-Peters, Professor Dr E. Steinhäuser

Clinical Immunology and 811
Rheumatology Institute and
Outpatients Department

Address: Krankenhausstrasse 12, D-8520 Erlangen
Head: Professor Dr J.R. Kalden

Clinical Microbiology and Infectious 812
Diseases Institute

Address: Wasserturmstrasse 3, D-8520 Erlangen
Head: Professor Dr W. Knapp

Clinical Virology Institute 813

Address: Loschgestrasse 7, D-8520 Erlangen
Head: Professor Dr B. Fleckenstein

Dermatological Clinic and Outpatients 814
Department

Address: Hartmannstrasse 14, D-8520 Erlangen
Head: Professor Dr O. Hornstein

Environmental Hygiene and Preventive 815
Medicine Institute

Address: Wasserturmstrasse 5, D-8520 Erlangen
Head: Professor Dr Dr W. Gräf

Eye Clinic and Outpatients 816
Department

Address: Schwabachanlage 6, D-8520 Erlangen
Head: Professor Dr G.O.H. Naumann

Forensic Medicine Institute 817

Address: Universitätsstrasse 22, D-8520 Erlangen
Head: Professor Dr H.B. Wümerling

Gerontology Institute 818

Address: Heimerichstrasse 58, D-8500 Nürnberg
Head: Professor Dr D. Platt

Gynaecological Clinic and Outpatients 819
Department

Address: Universitätsstrasse 21-23, D-8520 Erlangen
Head: Professor Dr K.G. Ober

MIDWIFERY DEPARTMENT 820

Human Genetics and Anthropology 821
Institute

Address: Bismarckstrasse 10, D-8520 Erlangen
Head: Professor Dr R.A. Pfeiffer

Industrial and Social Medicine 822
Institute

Address: Schillerstrasse 25, D-8520 Erlangen
Head: Professor Dr H. Valentin

Medical Clinic and Outpatients 823
Department

Address: Krankenhausstrasse 12, D-8520 Erlangen
Head: Professor Dr L. Demling

Medical Outpatients Department 824

Address: Ostliche Stadtmauerstrasse 29, D-8520 Erlangen
Head: Professor Dr K. Bachmann

Medical Radiology Institute 825

Address: Krankenhausstrasse 12, D-8520 Erlangen
Head: Professor Dr Dr H. Pauly

NUCLEAR MEDICINE DEPARTMENT 826
Head: Professor Dr F. Wolf

RADIATION THERAPY CLINIC AND 827
OUTPATIENTS DEPARTMENT
Address: Krankenhausstrasse 12, D-8520 Erlangen
Head: Professor Dr R. Sauer

Medical Statistics and Documentation 828
Institute

Address: Waldstrasse 6, D-8520 Erlangen
Head: Professor Dr L. Horbach

Nerve Clinic and Outpatients 829
Department

Address: Schwabachanlage 6, D-8520 Erlangen
Head: vacant

Neurosurgical Clinic and Outpatients 830
Department

Address: Schwabachanlage 6, D-8520 Erlangen
Head: vacant

Orthopaedic Clinic and Outpatients 831
Department

Address: Waldkrankenhaus St Marien, Rathsberger-strasse 57, D-8520 Erlangen
Head: Professor Dr D. Hohmann

Paediatric Clinic and Outpatients 832
Department

Address: Loschgestrasse 15, D-8520 Erlangen
Head: Professor Dr K. Stehr

Pathology and Pathological Anatomy 833
Institute

Address: Krankenhausstrasse 8-10, D-8520 Erlangen
Head: Professor Dr Volker Becker

Pharmacology Institute 834

Address: Universitätsstrasse 22, D-8520 Erlangen
Head: Professor Dr C.-J. Estler

Physiological Chemistry Institute 835

Address: Fahrstrasse 17, D-8520 Erlangen
Heads: Professor Dr W. Kersten; Professor Dr K. Brand

Physiology Institute I 836

Address: Universitätsstrasse 17, D-8520 Erlangen
Head: Professor Dr W.D. Keidel

Physiology Institute II 837

Address: Waldstrasse 6, D-8520 Erlangen
Head: Professor Dr M. Kessler

Surgical Clinic and Outpatients 838
Department

Address: Maximilliansplatz 1, D-8520 Erlangen
Head: Professor Dr F.P. Gall

Urological Clinic and Outpatients Department   839

Address: Maximilliansplatz 1, D-8520 Erlangen
Head: Professor Dr A. Sigel

FACULTY OF NATURAL SCIENCES   840

Applied Chemistry Institute   841

Address: Schuhstrasse 19, D-8520 Erlangen
Heads: Professor Dr O. Dann, Professor Dr E. Nürnberg

Applied Physics Institute   842

Address: Glückstrasse 9, D-8520 Erlangen
Heads: Professor Dr H. Burzlaff, Professor Dr K. Müller, Professor Dr M. Schulz

Botany Institute and Botanical Gardens   843

Address: Schlossgarten 4, D-8520 Erlangen
Head: Professor Dr W. Haupt
Senior staff: Professor Dr E. Kessler

Crystallography Institute   844

Address: Loewenichstrasse 22, D-8520 Erlangen
Head: Professor Dr H. Burzlaff

Geographical Institute   845

Address: Kochstrasse 4, D-8520 Erlangen
Heads: Professor Dr F. Tichy, Professor Dr W.-D. Hütteroth

Geology Institute   846

Address: Schlossgarten 5, D-8520 Erlangen
Head: Professor Dr W. Schwann

APPLIED GEOLOGY DEPARTMENT   847
Head: Professor Dr G. Lüttig

PALAEONTOLOGY DEPARTMENT   848
Head: Professor Dr E. Flügel

Inorganic Chemistry Institute   849

Address: Egerlandstrasse 1, D-8520 Erlangen
Heads: Professor Dr phil K. Brodersen, Professor Dr D. Sellmann

Karl Remeis Observatory, Institute of Astronomy   850

Address: Sternwartstrasse 7, D-8600 Bamburg
Heads: Professor Dr I. Bues, Professor Dr J. Rahe

Mathematics Institute   851

Address: Bismarckstrasse 1, D-8520 Erlangen
Senior staff: Professor Dr Heinz Bauer, Professor Dr K. Jacobs, Professor Dr D. Kölzow, Professor Dr W.P. Barth, Professor Dr W.-D. Geyer, Professor Dr K. Strambach, Professor Dr H. Berens, Professor Dr E.-D. Geyer

Microbiological and Biochemical Institute   852

Address: Friedrichstrasse 33, D-8520 Erlangen
Heads: Professor Dr W. Heumann, Professor Dr E. Schweizer

Mineralogy Institute   853

Address: Schlossgarten 5, D-8520 Erlangen
Head: Professor Dr H.-J. Kuzel

Organic Chemistry Institute   854

Address: Henkestrasse 42, D-8520 Erlangen
Heads: Professor Dr H.J. Bestmann, Professor Dr P. von R. Schleyer

Physical Chemistry Institute I   855

Address: Egerlandstrasse 3, D-8520 Erlangen
Head: Professor Dr W. Jaenicke

Physical Chemistry Institute II   856

Address: Egerlandstrasse 3, D-8520 Erlangen
Head: Professor Dr G. Wedler

Physics Institute   857

Address: Glückstrasse 6, D-8520 Erlangen
Senior staff: Professor Dr J. Christiansen, Professor Dr N. Fibiger, Professor Dr E. Finckle, Professor Dr A. Hofmann, Professor Dr W. Kreische, Professor Dr A. Lohmann, Professor Dr G. Saemann-Ischenko, Professor Dr H. Wegener

Theoretical Chemistry Institute   858

Address: Egerlandstrasse 3, D-8520 Erlangen
Head: Professor Dr J. Ladik

Theoretical Physics Institute   859

Address: Glückstrasse 6, D-8520 Erlangen
Heads: Professor Dr S. Hess, Professor Dr G.M. Huber, Professor Dr A. Hüller
Senior staff: Professor Dr L. Waldmann, Professor Dr M.G. Huber

Zoology Institute I   860

Address: Universitätsstrasse 19, D-8520 Erlangen
Head: Professor Dr R. Siewing

Zoology Institute II   861

Address: Bismarckstrasse 8-10, D-8520 Erlangen
Head: Professor Dr O.V. Helversen

FACULTY OF TECHNOLOGY   862

Applied Mathematics Institute I   863

Address: Martensstrasse 3, D-8520 Erlangen
Head: Professor Dr Weinitschke

Applied Mathematics Institute II   864

Address: Martensstrasse 3, D-8520 Erlangen
Head: Professor Dr B. Dejon

Communications Institute   865

Address: Canerstrasse 7, D-8520 Erlangen
Head: Professor Dr Ing W. Schüssler

Control Engineering Institute   866

Address: Canerstrasse 7, D-8520 Erlangen
Head: Professor Dr H. Schlitt

General and Theoretical Electrical   867
Engineering Institute

Address: Canerstrasse 7, D-8520 Erlangen
Head: Professor Dr R. Unbehauen

High-Frequency Engineering Institute   868

Address: Canerstrasse 9, D-8520 Erlangen
Head: Professor Dr Ing H. Brand

Materials Science Institute I (General   869
Materials Science)

Address: Martensstrasse 5, D-8520 Erlangen
Head: Professor Dr B. Ilschner

Materials Science Institute II (Metal   870
Materials Technology)

Address: Martensstrasse 5, D-8520 Erlangen
Head: Professor Dr U. Zwicker

Materials Science Institute III (Glass   871
and Ceramics)

Address: Martensstrasse 5, D-8520 Erlangen
Head: Professor Dr H.J. Oel

Materials Science Institute IV   872
(Corrosion and Surface Treatment)

Address: Martensstrasse 7, D-8520 Erlangen
Head: Professor Dr H. Kaesche

Mathematical Machines and Data   873
Processing Institute

Address: Martensstrasse 3, D-8520 Erlangen
Head: Professor Dr W. Händler

Mechanical Process Engineering   874
Institute

Address: Martensstrasse 9, D-8520 Erlangen
Head: Professor Dr Ing O. Molerus

Technical Chemistry Institute I   875

Address: Egerlandstrasse 3, D-8520 Erlangen
Head: Professor Dr H. Hofmann

Technical Chemistry Institute II   876

Address: Egerlandstrasse 5, D-8520 Erlangen
Head: Professor Dr S. Peter

Technical Electronics Institute   877

Address: Canerstrasse 9, D-8520 Erlangen
Head: Professor Dr Ing D. Seitzer

Fritsch GmbH   878
Laborgeraetebau

Address: Hauptstrasse 542, D-6580 Idaroberstein 1
Telephone: (06781) 27092
Telex: 426203 frits d
Director: Willi Fritsch

LABORATORY OF APPLIED TECHNICS 879

Research director: Dipl phys Götz von Bernuth
Sections: Development, Ing Heinz Kessler; Applied technics, Dipl chem Ulrich Gerber
Graduate research staff: 8
Annual expenditure: £51 000-500 000
Activities: The development of ranges of laboratory apparatus for comminution, particle sizing and classification, and auxiliary processes.
Contract work: Yes

Gaswärme-Institut Essen eV 880

[Gas Heating Institute Essen]
Address: 101 Hafenstrasse, D-4300 Essen-Borbeck
Telephone: (0201) 34 10 23
Affiliation: Arbeitsgemeinschaft Industrieller Forschungsvereinigungen eV
Scientific Director: Professor Dr H. Kremer
Scientific staff: 5
Activities: Use of gas and heat generated by fuel; fuel and pyrotechnical properties of energy carrying materials and combustion processes; burners; combustion chambers and control plant of gas and fuel-heated equipment and fireplaces.

Geologisches Landesamt Baden-Württemberg 881

[Geological Survey of Baden-Württemberg]
Address: Albertstrasse 5, D-7800 Freiburg im Breisgau
Telephone: (0781) 204 1
President: Professor Dr Kurt Sauer
Sections: Geological mapping, Dr Schreiner; hydrogeology, Dr Werner; engineering geology, Dr Eissele
Graduate research staff: 30
Annual expenditure: £51 000-500 000
Contract work: No
Publications: Jahreshefte und Abhandlungen des Geologischen Landesamts Baden-Württemberg.

Geologisches Landesamt des Saarlandes 882

[Saarland Geological Survey]
Address: Am Tummelplatz 7, D-6600 Saarbrücken
Telephone: (0681) 53729
Activities: Geological research in the Saarland: stratigraphy, petrology, mainly in triassic, lower permian and carboniferous series, also research in hydrogeology and engineering geology; geological maps and scientific publications; information to public and private investigators in all regional geological questions.

Geologisches Landesamt Hamburg 883

[Geological Survey of Hamburg]
Address: Oberstrasse 88, D-2000 Hamburg 13
Director: Dr Friedrich Grube
Activities: Applied geology; engineering geology; hydrogeology; quaternary geology; geology of Hamburg and its surroundings; geology of shore shifts.

Geologisches Landesamt Nordrhein-Westfalen 884

[Geological Survey of North Rhine-Westphalia]
Address: De-Greiff-Strasse 195, D-4150 Krefeld
Telephone: (02151) 8970
Parent body: Ministerium für Wirtschaft, Mittelstand und Verkehr des Landes Nordrhein-Westfalen
President: Dipl-Ing Eckart Reiche
Sections: Geological sciences laboratory, Dr Brelie; geology, hydrogeology and stratigraphy, Dr H. Kuhn-Volten; soil science, Dr G. Heide; geological engineering, Dr Wolters
Graduate research staff: 108
Annual expenditure: over £2m
Activities: Geology, economic geology, hydrogeology, soil science, engineering geology and geophysics; surveying, consulting services and documentation in these fields for the territory of North Rhine-Westphalia.
Contract work: Yes
Publications: Annual report.

Geologisches Landesamt   885
Rheinland-Pfalz

[Geological Survey of Rhineland-Palatinate]
Address: Postfach 2045, D-6500 Mainz
Managing director: Dr Wolfgang Dillmann
Deputy managing director: Professor Dr Volker Sonne
Activities: Geological, hydrological and pedological
cartography, and publications; geological and pedologi-
cal tests; geological research and investigation of mineral
deposits; consulting and surveying activities; establish-
ment of archives and collections.
Publications: Mainzer geowissenschaftliche Mitteilungen.

Georg-August-Universität   886
Göttingen

[Göttingen University]
Address: Wilhelmsplatz 1, D-3400 Göttingen
Telephone: (0551) 394330
Telex: 96703

FACULTY OF AGRICULTURE   887

Dean: Professor Dr Horst S.H. Seifert

Agricultural Machinery Department   888

Address: Gutenbergstrasse 33, D-3400 Göttingen
Head: Professor Dr Ing Franz Wieneke

Animal Breeding and Domestic Animal 889
Genetics Department

Address: Albrecht-Thaer-Weg 1, D-3400 Göttingen
Head: Professor Dr Hans-Jürgen Langholz
Senior staff: Professor Dr P. Glodek, Professor Dr W.
Holtz

Animal Physiology and Nutrition   890
Department

Address: Oskar-Kellner-Weg 6, D-3400 Göttingen
Head: Professor Dr Klaus-Dietrich Günther

FOOD UTILIZATION DIVISION   891
Head: Professor Dr Johannes Otto Gutte

Farm Management Department   892

Address: Nikolausberger Weg 11, D-3400 Göttingen
Head: Professor Dr G. Schmitt
Senior staff: Professor Dr W. Brandes, Professor Dr
W. Grosskopf, Professor Dr H. de Haen, Professor Dr
M. Köhne, Professor Dr H. Lauensteinn, Professor Dr
Leserer, Professor Dr S. Tangermann

HOLTENSEN FARM MANAGEMENT   893
EXPERIMENTAL STATION
Head: Professor Dr M. Köhne

Overseas Agriculture Department   894

Address: D-3400 Göttingen
Head: Professor Dr Frithjof Kuhnen

STUDY CENTRE FOR TROPICAL AND   895
SUBTROPICAL AGRICULTURE AND
FORESTRY
Senior staff: Professor Dr Sigmund Rehm, Professor
Dr Hans Lamprecht, Professor Dr F. Kuhnen

Plant Cultivation and Breeding   896
Department

Senior staff: Plant cultivation, Professor Dr Kord
Baeumer; plant breeding, Professor Dr Gerhard Röb-
belen; cytogenetics, Professor Dr Gerd Kobabe

PLANT CULTIVATION AND BREEDING   897
EXPERIMENTAL STATION
Address: F. Norten-Hardenberg 352, D-3400 Göt-
tingen
Head: Professor Dr Kord Baeumer

Plant Pathology and Protection   898
Department

Address: Griesbachstrasse 6, D-3400 Göttingen
Head: Professor Dr Rudolf Heitefuss

ENTOMOLOGY DIVISION   899
Head: Professor Dr Hubert Wilbert

Soil Science Department   900

Address: Von-Siebold-Strasse 8, D-3400 Göttingen
Head: Professor Dr Brunk Meyer

Sugar Beet Research Department   901

Address: Holtenser Landstrasse 77, D-3400 Göttingen
Head: Dr C. Winner

Tropical and Subtropical Plant Cultivation Department   902

Address: Griesbachstrasse 6, D-3400 Göttingen
Head: Professor Dr Wolfram Achtnich

Veterinary Department   903

Address: Groner Landstrasse 2, D-3400 Göttingen
Head: Professor Dr Horst-Hermann Schimmelpfennig

FACULTY OF FORESTRY   904

Address: Büsgenweg 5, D-3400 Göttingen
Dean: Professor Dr Ernst Röhrig

Forest Botany Department   905

Address: Büsgenweg 2, D-3400 Göttingen

FOREST BOTANICAL GARDEN   906
Head: Professor Dr W. Eschrich

Forest Exploitation Department - Wood Research and Wood Cutting   907

Address: Büsgenweg 4, D-3400 Göttingen
Head: Professor Dr Wolfgang Knigge

Forest Genetics and Plant Breeding Department   908

Address: Büsgenweg 2, D-3400 Göttingen
Heads: Professor Dr Hans-Heinrich Hattemer, Dr Jochen Kleinschmit

Forest Labour and Machinery Department   909

Address: Büsgenweg 6, D-3400 Göttingen
Head: Professor Dr Siegfried Häberle

Forest Management Department   910

Head: Professor Dr H. Kramer

Forest Organization and Production Department   911

Head: Professor Dr H. Kramer

Forest Policy, Wood Marketing, Forest History and Nature Conservation Department   912

Head: Professor Dr Rolf Zundel

Forest Zoology Department   913

Address: Büsgenweg 3, D-3400 Göttingen
Head: Professor Dr Siegfried Bombosch

Forestry Department   914

Address: Büsgenweg 1, D-3400 Göttingen
Head: Professor Dr Ernst Röhrig

Game and Hunting Department   915

Address: Büsgenweg 3, D-3400 Göttingen
Head: Professor A. Festetics

Soil Science and Forest Nutrition Department   916

Address: Büsgenweg 2, D-3400 Göttingen
Head: Professor Dr Bernhard Ulrich

FACULTY OF MATHEMATICS AND NATURAL SCIENCES   917

Dean: Professor Dr H. Grauert

Biology Department   918

MICROBIOLOGY DIVISION   919
Address: Griesbachstrasse 8, D-3400 Göttingen
Telephone: (0551) 39 37 71
Heads: Professor Dr H.G. Schlegel, Professor Dr G. Gottschalk
Graduate research staff: 20
Annual expenditure: £10 000-50 000
Activities: Basic research concentrates on photosynthetic, chemolithoautotrophic and anaerobic bacteria. Physiology and comparative biochemistry are the main fields of interest: citrate formation and degradation; fermentative metabolism of clostridia; physiology of hydrogen bacteria; regulation of biosynthetic pathways. A special biotechnological programme aims at the production of protozoa protein on the basis of hydrogen bacteria and of hydrogen and carbon dioxide as raw materials. The microbial degradation of chlorinated and sulphonated aromatic compounds is studied as a model system of the decomposition of environmental chemicals.
Contract work: Yes

Earth Sciences Department   920

Chairman: Professor Dr O.-H. Walliser

GEOCHEMISTRY DIVISION   921
Address: Goldschmidtstrasse 1, D-3400 Göttingen
Head: Professor Dr Hans Wedepohl

GEOGRAPHY DIVISION   922
Address: Goldschmidtstrasse 5, D-3400 Göttingen
Head: Professor Dr Jürgen Hagedorn
Senior staff: Professor Dr Jürgen Hövermann,
Professor Dr H.-J. Nitz

GEOLOGY-PALAEONTOLOGY   923
DIVISION
Address: Goldschmidtstrasse 3, D-3400 Göttingen
Heads: Professor Dr Henno Martin, Professor Dr
Otto-Heinrich Walliser

MINERALOGY-CRYSTALLOGRAPHY   924
DIVISION
Address: Goldschmidtstrasse 1, D-3400 Göttingen
Head: Professor Dr Vladimir Kupćic

MINERALOGY-PETROLOGY DIVISION   925
Address: Goldschmidtstrasse 1, D-3400 Göttingen
Head: vacant

SEDIMENTOLOGY-PETROGRAPHY   926
DIVISION
Address: Goldschmidtstrasse 1, D-3400 Göttingen
Head: Professor Dr Hermann Harder

Mathematics Department   927
Chairman: Professor Dr R. Schaback

MATHEMATICAL AND ECONOMIC   928
STATISTICS DIVISION
Address: Lotzestrasse 13, D-3400 Göttingen
Head: Professor Dr U. Krengel

MATHEMATICS DIVISION   929
Address: Bunsenstrasse 3-5, D-3400 Göttingen
Senior staff: Professor Dr E. Heinz, Professor Dr H.
Grauert, Professor Dr M. Kneser, Professor Dr S.J.
Patterson

NUMERICAL AND APPLIED   930
MATHEMATICS DIVISION
Address: Lotzestrasse 16/18, D-3400 Göttingen
Head: Professor Dr R. Kress

FACULTY OF MEDICINE   931
Address: Wilhelmsplatz 2, D-3400 Göttingen
Dean: Professor Dr D. Kettler

Germanischer Lloyd   932

Address: Postfach 11 16 06, D-2000 Hamburg 11
Telephone: (040) 36 14 91
Telex: 21 28 28a glhh d
Managing director: Dipl-Ing Reinhard Mau
Sections: Naval architecture, Dr Payer; mechanical
engineering, Mr Agena
Graduate research staff: 15
Activities: The development of safety standards and
systems technology, and the analysis of stress and vibrations in the field of marine engineering; offshore,
hydraulic and mechanical engineering and technologies.
Recent research areas include: hull strength; ship safety;
marine engineering; electrotechnology; new ship construction and renewal.
Note: In its capacity as a project-assisting institution to
the Federal Ministry of Research and Technology, Ger-
manischer Lloyd attended in the course of a year to
almost 60 research and development projects in the
marine and offshore technology fields promoted by the
said Ministry.

Gesamthochschule Kassel   933

[Kassel University]
Address: Mönchebergstrasse 19, D-3500 Kassel
Telephone: (0561) 80 41
Telex: 99572 ghkks d
Vice President: Professor Dr Teichler

DEPARTMENT OF AGRICULTURE   934

Address: Nordbahnhofstrasse 1a, D-3430 Witzen-
hausen
Head: Professor Dr Bernd Wirthgen
Sections: Animal production, Professor Dr Günter
Biedermann, Professor Dr Engelhard Boehncke,
Professor Dr Ernst Granz
Agricultural economy, Professor Dr Ralf Bokermann,
Professor Dr Franz Leiber
Agricultural policy, Professor Wilhelm Niebuer
Agricultural engineering, Professor Dr Werner
Rückmann
Chemistry, Professor Dr Reinhold Kickhut
Chemistry of agriculture, Professor Dr Christian Rich-
ter
Ecology of agriculture, Professor Dr Helge Schmeisky
Mathematics for agriculture, Professor Siegfried Ren-
nebarth
Biology, Professor Dr Peter Rzepka
Plant production, Professor Dr Walter Kühbauch,
Professor Dr Konrad Scheffer
Soil science and geology, Professor Volkmar Seifert

DEPARTMENT OF BIOLOGY AND   935
CHEMISTRY

Address: Heinrich-Plett-Strasse 40, AVZ, D-3500 Kassel
Head: Professor Dr Luise Stange
Sections: Human biology, Professor Dr Anton Castenholz
Biology, Professor Dr Vjekoslav Glavác
Morphology, Professor Dr Helmut Freitag
Chemistry, Professor Dr Peter Ludwig
Inorganic chemistry, Professor Dr Hans Joachim Seifert
Organic chemistry, Professor Dr Jürgen Gosselck
Technical chemistry, Professor Dr Klaus Harigel
Physiology of plants, Professor Dr Rüdiger Grotha
Zoology, Professor Dr Hans-Wilhelm Borchers, Professor Dr Jörg-Peter Ewert, Professor Dr H.-O. Hofer, Professor Dr Werner Meinel
Activities: Thermal analysis; chemical thermodynamics; organic-sulphuric compounds for the development of synthones; reactivity of organic compounds in and at aluminium-layer silicates of the type Montmovillonit; investigations into correlation between ozone, nitrous oxide and hydrocarbon concentrations in the air and of microclimatic parameters, carried out in the medium-sized city of Kassel and the surrounding clean air areas.

DEPARTMENT OF CIVIL   936
ENGINEERING

Address: Wilhelmshöher Allee 71, D-3500 Kassel
Sections: Reinforced concrete structures, Professor Dipl-Ing F. Benthaus, Professor Dr Ing D. Haberland, Professor Dipl-Ing L. Klindt
Social and economic conditions with civil engineering, Professor Dr Hanns-Peter Ekardt
Road building, Professor Dipl-Ing Karl Heinz Gastmeyer
Railway construction, Professor Dipl-Ing Herbert Henking
Steel Structures, Professor Dipl-Ing Reinhold Hohmann, Professor Dipl-Ing Friedrich Walter
Building management, Dr Ing Wolfram Keil
Industrial production, Professor Dr Ing Helmut Körner
Light building, Dr Ing Michael Link
Limnology, Professor Dr Ing Wolfgang Pürschel
Basic building, Dr Ing Heinrich Sommer
Data orientated civil engineering, Professor Dipl-Ing Bernd Stolzenberg

DEPARTMENT OF ELECTRICAL   937
ENGINEERING

Address: Wilhelmshöher Allee, D-3500 Kassel
Head: Professor Dr Ing Walter Hofmann
Sections: Materials science of electrotechnics, Professor Dipl-Phys Werner Blume
Electrical engineering, Professor Dipl-Ing Richard Bopp, Professor Dr Ing Horst Moser
Electrotechnics, Dr Michael Dietrich
High-frequency engineering, Professor Dr Ing Henning Früchtin, Professor Dipl-Ing J. Petermann
Electrical machines, Professor Dipl-Ing Otto Haack
Electromechanical construction, Professor Dr Ing Dieter Hars
Communication, Professor Dipl-Ing Klaus Hueter
Energy electronics, Professor Dr Ing Werner Kleinkauf
Control engineering, Professor Dipl-Ing Menno Koopmann
Metrology, Professor Dipl-Ing Ernst Mekiffer
Impulse technology, Professor Dipl-Ing Werner Meyer
Transmission, Professor Dr Ing Erich Sinemus, Professor Dipl-Ing Helmut Todebusch
Power plant technology, Professor Dipl-Ing Helmut Thüre
Heavy current engineering, Professor Dipl-Ing Martin Würz

DEPARTMENT OF INTERNATIONAL   938
AGRICULTURE

Address: Steinstrasse 19, D-3430 Witzenhausen
Head: Professor Dr Eckhard Baum
Sections: Environmental production, Professor Dr Heinz Bliss
Animal production, Professor Dr Ekkehart Feist
Agricultural cooperation, Professor Dr Hans-J. Glauner
Tropical plant cultivation and protection, Professor Dr Carl Hoeppe
Soil science, plant nutrition, fertilizers, Professor Dr Werner Kramer
Agricultural machines and implements, Professor Dr Franz Lorenz
Communications, Professor Hartmut Matzat
Development policy, Professor Dr Franz-H. Riebel
Agricultural botany and genetics, Professor Dr M. Rommel
Agricultural engineering and technology, Professor Dr Walter
Agricultural policy, Professor Dr Johannes Wörz
Climatology and meteorology, Professor Dr Peter Wolff

DEPARTMENT OF MATHEMATICS 939

Address: Heinrich-Plett-Strasse 40, AVZ, D-3500 Kassel
Head: Professor Dr Heinz Griesel
Senior staff: Professor Dr Klaus Barner, Professor Dr Werner Blum, Professor Dr Bruno Bosbach, Professor Dr Ing Hartmut Bossel, Professor Dr Clemens Burg, Professor Dipl-Hdl Uwe Dahlke, Professor Dr Hilmar Drygas, Professor Dipl-Ing Roland Ernst, Professor Stephan Freiger, Professor Dr Heinz Griesel, Professor Dr Herbert Haf, Professor Dr Josef Hainzl, Professor Dr Rita Jeltsch Fricker, Professor Dr Arnold Kirsch, Professor Dr Peter Krauss, Professor Dipl-Ing Dietrich Kreft, Professor Dipl-Ing Norbert Meckelein, Professor Dr G. Merz, Professor Helmut Postel, Professor Dr Siegfried Seyfferth, Professor Dr W. Sippel, Professor Karl Spies, Professor Dr Heinrich Werner, Dr Peter Wildenauer, Professor Dr Friedrich Wille, Professor Dr Herbert Ziezold
Activities: Mathematics; statistics; mathematics for technical sciences.

DEPARTMENT OF MECHANICAL ENGINEERING 940

Address: Wilhelmshöher Allee 73, D-3500 Kassel
Head: Professor Dr Helmut Wohlfahrt
Sections: Technical mechanics, Professor Dr Ing O.T. Bruhns, Professor Dr Ing Burkhard Schultz-Jander
Materials science, artificial substances, Professor Dr Ing Gottfried Ehrenstein
Control engineering, Professor Dr Ing Helmut Giesler
Thermodynamics, Professor Dr Ing Helmut Hausenblas, Professor Dipl-Ing Hubertus Schurian, Professor Dr Ing Wolfried Wissmann
Measuring, Professor Dr Ing Wolfgang Holzapfel
Materials science, Professor Dipl-Ing Helmut Klosner, Professor Dr Ing Horst Hentze, Professor Dr Ing Günter Kirschling
Motor vehicles, Professor Dipl-Ing Otto Uwe Liegniez
Tool Machines, Professor Dr Ing Eberhard Paucksch, Professor Dipl-Ing Hans-Werner Stange
Construction, Professor Dr Ing Alfred Puck, Professor Dipl-Ing Erich Siemon
Production systems, Professor Dipl-Ing Adolf Reinhardt
Drives and gears, Professor Dipl-Ing Dieter Richter
Factory organization, Professor Dipl-Kfm Gerhard Rossmann
Experimental construction, Professor Dr Ing Wolfgang Steinchen
Mechanics and machine parts, Professor Dipl-Ing H. Trinter
Transformation, Professor Dr Ing Hans-W. Wagener
Machine tools, Professor Dr Ing Joachim Dietrich
Activities: Polymeric materials, eg fibre reinforcement and mechanical joining; non-linear problems of continuous mechanical processes; further development of fibre composite materials; improvement of conventional wheelchairs; cold mass formation, eg cold pressing of steel and titanium materials; synthesis of control systems.

DEPARTMENT OF PHYSICS 941

Address: Heinrich-Plett-Strasse 40, AVZ, D-3500 Kassel
Head: Professor Dr Klaus Schäfer
Senior staff: Professor Wilfrid Balk, Professor Dr Otto Böttger, Professor Dr Heinrich Deuling, Professor Dr Ing Karl-Joachim Euler, Professor Dr Burkhard, Professor Dr Helmut Gärtner, Professor Dr Josef Hölzl, Professor Dr Dietmar Kolb Dr Tihomir Morovíc
Activities: Space charge influence on electrical behaviour of polyethylene; elastic and non-elastic electron diffusion in reflection and transmission; thermo-emission and electron re-emission of ferro- and paramagnetics; thermo forces of oxides; temperature and pressure dependence of iron, nickel and silver powder; photo effects; silver electrode measurements; freezing of water from powder mixtures; numeric solution to Dirac equation in 2-atomic molecules; numeric solution of Poisson equation.

INTERDISCIPLINARY RESEARCH GROUP ON TECHNOLOGY 942

Activities: Biogas plant for small-scale farming; plant-water purificatinn systems; loam processing methods; self-constructed solar system; simplified wheelchair, ie Kasseler wheelchair.

Gesamthochschule Wuppertal 943

[Wuppertal University]
Address: Gausstrasse 20, D-5600 Wuppertal
Telephone: (0202) 439 21 31
Telex: 8592262
President: Professor Dr Rainer Gruenter
Annual expenditure: £501 000-2m

FACULTY OF CHEMISTRY AND BIOLOGY 944

Telephone: (0202) 439 24 95
Dean: Professor Dr Hans Gotthardt

FACULTY OF ELECTRICAL ENGINEERING   945

Telephone: (0202) 439 29 56
Dean: Professor Ewald Forner

FACULTY OF MATHEMATICS   946

Telephone: (0202) 439 26 57
Dean: Professor Dr Michael Reeken

FACULTY OF MECHANICAL ENGINEERING   947

Telephone: (0202) 439 20 44
Dean: Professor Dr Rolf Seybold

FACULTY OF PHYSICS   948

Telephone: (0202) 439 2621
Dean: Professor Dr Jurgen Drees

Gesellschaft für   949
Epilepsieforschung eV

[Epilepsy Research Association]
Address: Königsweg 3, D-4800 Bielefeld 13
Telephone: (0521) 1443514
Chairman: Pastor Johannes Busch
Research director: Helmut Schütz
Sections: Biochemistry, Dr Bernhard Ramvecj; neurophysiology, vacant; clinical department, Dr Stenzel, Dr Boenigk; neuropathology, Professor Dr Gerhard Veith; serology-immunology, Professor Dr Siegfried Heinrith; EEG, Professor Dr Degen
Graduate research staff: 5
Annual expenditure: £51 000-500 000
Activities: Research into the various forms of epilepsy; development of the appropriate means of treatment.
Contract work: No

Gesellschaft für   950
Mathematik und
Datenverarbeitung mbH

[Mathematics and Data Processing Association]
Address: Schloss Birlinghoven, Postfach 1240, D-5205 St Augustin 1
Telephone: (02241) 14 22 45
Scientific director: Professor Dr rer nat Fritz Krückeberg

Graduate research staff: 240
Annual expenditure: over £2m
Activities: Computer science for organizational fields within government administration; mathematics for computer application, especially planning models.
Contract work: Yes

Gesellschaft für   951
naturwissenschaftlich-
technische Dienste mbH

– NATEC
[Society for Scientific-Technical Services]
Address: 154 Behringstrasse, D-2000 Hamburg 50
Telephone: (040) 882 77 50
Director: Professor Dr K.-F. Gander
Scientific staff: 200
Activities: Analysis and trace analysis; synthesis; radiochemistry; microbiology; metabolisms; physical investigations; packaging research and technology; development of scientific equipment; environmental research.

Gesellschaft für Praktische   952
Energiekunde eV

[Association for Practical Energy Science]
Address: 71 Am Blütenanger, D-8000 München 50
Telephone: (089) 150 20 77
Affiliation: Arbeitsgemeinschaft Industrieller Forschungsvereinigungen eV
Scientific Director: Professor Dr H. Schaefer
Scientific staff: 12
Activities: Connection between energy requirements and effects; analysis and project planning of energy-economical developments; technical and economic problems in energy; energy-economics of plant, machines and equipment.

Gesellschaft für   953
Reaktorsicherheit mbH

– GRS
Address: Glockengasse 2, D-5000 Köln 1
Telephone: (0221) 206 81
Telex: 8881807 grs d
General managers: Professor Dr A. Birkhofer, Dipl-Ing O. Kellermann
Activities: GRS is engaged in research and development in the fields of nuclear engineering, the fuel cycle,

radiological and environmental protection, and related safety engineering.

Gesellschaft für Schwerionenforschung

954

– GSI
[Heavy Ion Research Laboratory]
Address: Postfach 110541, D-6100 Darmstadt 11
Telephone: (06151) 359 648/649
Telex: 0419593
Research director: Professor Gisbert zu Putlitz
Sections: Nuclear physics with heavy ions; atomic physics with heavy ions; applied physics with heavy ions
Graduate research staff: 100
Annual expenditure: over £2m
Activities: GSI is a research centre devoted to fundamental research with energetic atomic nuclei called heavy ions; research is conducted using a Universal Linear Accelerator (UNILAC) for heavy ions, along with the corresponding experimental research facilities. To date about 400 scientists from German universities, research centres, and industry have been attracted to the centre to work with in-house GSI teams; there is also collaboration with foreign laboratories and universities. The majority of heavy ion experiments are set up in the large experimental hall, where the beam is available at all energies between 2 and 13 MeV per projectile nucleon. All experiments investigate the interaction of heavy ions with target materials hit by the beam. Research is focused on processes such as nuclear scattering, nuclear transmutations by means of mass transfer between target and projectile, nuclear fusion and fission, and many other reactions that change the matter structure of individual nuclei.

The nature of such processes is studied through the investigation of the final products of different types of reaction: single particles or reaction fragments can be identified by their mass, charge, quantal internal state, emission momentum, and time correlations. These observable features are recorded by a range of specialized detection equipment, integrated both spatially and by means of computers.

In the small experimental hall a fixed energy beam of 1.4 MeV per projectile nucleon is used to study the atomic physics of inner atomic shells, electron rearrangements and excitations, and electron emission as induced by ion-atom-collision, using X-ray and electron spectrometers to monitor the experiments. Research is also conducted into the interreaction of energetic ions in extended media, such as special solid-state materials which undergo structural change, or biological tissue where metabolic or membrane changes and damage-repair reactions are induced by heavy ion bombardment.
Facilities: Electronic, chemical, and special laboratories are available for the preparation and support of experiments; the detector laboratory designs detectors for heavy ion reaction products. A system of linked computers is available for the task of recording a large number of experimental parameters at high rates which are typical for heavy ion experiments.
Contract work: No
Publications: *Wissenschaftlicher Jahresbericht; Forschungs- und Entwicklungsprogram; GSI-Nachrichten.*

Gesellschaft für Strahlen- und Umweltforschung mbH

955

– GSF
[Radiation and Environmental Research Society]
Address: Ingolstädter Landstrasse 1, D-8042 Neuherberg
Telephone: (089) 3874-0
Telex: 523125 strahl d
Director: Professor Dr Rudolf Wittenzellner
Graduate research staff: 333
Annual expenditure: DM100m
Activities: The research work of the GSF concerns the solution of problems in the public interest in the areas of environmental research and of health care. The work is directed towards the protection of man and his environment against harmful influences, and towards the utilization of scientific and technical knowledge for the improvement of public health.
GSF consists of the institutes and departments entered below.
Contract work: Yes
Publications: Annual report.

INSTITUTE OF APPLIED PHYSICS

956

Director: W. Westphal

Department of Applied Optics

957

Head: Professor Dr W. Waidelich
Graduate research staff: 14
Activities: Optical information processing for medical diagnosis; laser optical methods for biomedicine and biology; laser light therapy.

Department of Ecological Physics 958

Address: Herrenhäuserstrasse 2, D-3000 Hannover
Head: Professor Dr H. Glubrecht
Graduate research staff: 10
Activities: Studies on physical factors determining the balance of substances in the ecosphere and the behaviour of environmental substances; binding kinetics of psoralenes with DNA; photodynamic decomposition of NADH; quantitative microscopy and fluorescence analysis; determinations of the iodine-129 content in bovine thyroid glands (EURATOM contract).

Department of Technological Physics 959

Head: W. Westphal
Graduate research staff: 20
Activities: Research and development in the following areas: investigation of the quality of ion beams by measurement of the current density profiles at focus point; relative isotopic abundances of calcium and iron in chemically-processed human blood; mechanisms of secondary ion emission; importance of trace elements in life sciences (ie their incorporation, distribution, metabolism and mutual interaction with enzyme systems).

INSTITUTE OF BIOLOGY 960

Director: Professor Dr U. Hagen

Department of Biophysical Radiation 961
Research

Address: Paul-Ehrlich-Strasse 15 und 20, D-6000 Frankfurt am Main
Head: Professor Dr W. Pohlit
Graduate research staff: 14
Activities: Research and development in the following areas: cell cybernetics, cascade accelerator; basic problems for improving radiation therapy of cancer, especially by the use of dense ionizing particles; metabolism kinetics; clinical problems in the metabolism of trace elements; aerosol biophysics; a newly developed whole-body counter for measurements of the regional deposition of particles in the human lung.

Department of Joint Equipment - 962
Applied Physics

Head: O. Balk
Graduate research staff: 4
Activities: Irradiation techniques in body irradiation and electrophysiological problems.

Department of Nuclear Biology 963

Head: Professor Dr H. Kriegel
Graduate research staff: 12
Activities: Tests of radioactive substances for their possible application in nuclear medical localization and functional diagnosis; animal experiments for the control of the efficacy of therapeutic measures in malignant tumours; biokinetics of radiopharmaceuticals; synergistic effects of ionizing radiation and chemical compounds on prenatal and postnatal development.

Department of Pathology 964

Head: Professor Dr W. Gössner
Graduate research staff: 11
Activities: Research in radiotoxicity; pathogenesis of radiation-induced osteosarcoma; morphological investigations into the early stages of the radium-224-induced osteosarcoma of mice; virological-immunological studies.

Department of Physiology 965

Head: Professor Dr H. Müller-Mohnssen
Activities: Investigation into mechanisms controlling the passive transport of substances through different types of biological boundary structures, through the cell membrane, taking nerve membranes as an example, and through cellular layers such as the arterial intima.

Department of Radiobiology 966

Head: Professor Dr U. Hagen
Graduate research staff: 17
Activities: Research in the following areas: primary reactions and molecular mechanisms; cell damage; studies on intact animals; experimental tumour therapy.

Station for the Breeding and Upkeep 967
of Laboratory Animals

Head: Dr M. Nüssel
Graduate research staff: 2

INSTITUTE OF GENETICS 968

Director: Dr U.H. Ehling

Department of Mammalian Genetics 969

Head: Dr U.H. Ehling
Graduate research staff: 8
Activities: Research in the following areas: determination of genetic damage induced by environmental chemicals; proving the mutagenicity of a compound; potential risk of the chemical mutagen; the tolerable level of risk.

Department of Molecular Genetics 970

Address: Griesebachstrasse 8, D-3400 Göttingen-Weende
Head: Professor Dr H. Prell
Activities: Studies of the mechanisms involved in regulating gene expression; functioning of a new type of regulatory protein, the antirepressor, and regulation of antirepressor synthesis.

Department of Plant Genetics 971

Head: Professor Dr G. Fischbeck
Graduate research staff: 7
Activities: Studies on induced mutations with regard to their significance for general genetics and the improvement in plant breeding; interactions between genotype and environmental factors.

INSTITUTE OF HAEMATOLOGY 972

Address: Landwehrstrasse 61, D-8000 München 2
Head: Professor Dr P. Dörmer

Department of Clinical Haematology 973

Address: Marchionstrasse 15, D-8000 München 70
Head: Professor Dr W. Wilmanns
Graduate research staff: 13
Activities: Stem cell kinetics; biochemical principles of cytostatic therapy of leukaemias and malignant tumours; testing resistance of carcinomas; porphyrin biochemistry; enzyme-immunohistochemistry of lymphocytes; investigations on how to improve supralethal whole body irradiation; transplantation of cryopreserved autologous bone marrow.

Department of Experimental Haematology 974

Head: Professor Dr P. Dörmer
Graduate research staff: 9
Activities: Instrumental and preparative developments for diagnosis of blood and bone marrow cells; characterization of normal and diseased haematopoieses in man; recognition and analysis of bone marrow lesions by cytotoxic agents such as environmental factors, irradiation or cytostatic cancer treatment.

Department of Haematomorphology 975

Address: Ziemssenstrasse 1, D-8000 München 2
Head: Professor Dr R. Burkhardt
Graduate research staff: 4
Activities: Morphological evaluation of the haematopoietic cells and tissues in the human, and especially of their interactions in situ during the course of morbid changes due to external or internal causes; the main attention is focused on the human bone marrow.

Department of Immunology 976

Head: Professor Dr S. Thierfelder
Activities: Transplantation of bone marrow to lethally irradiated mammals; methods of overcoming immunological complications of transplantation; immunodiagnosis of leukaemias; development of methods for early diagnosis and therapy control; new methods and techniques of transfusion and transplantation haematology.

INSTITUTE OF MEDICAL INFORMATICS AND HEALTH SERVICES RESEARCH 977

Address: Arabellastrasse 4, D-8000 München 81
Director: Professor Dr W. van Eimeren
Graduate research staff: 41
Activities: The Institute's five fields of research are as follows:
Effective and efficient strategies of prevention and early detection of diseases for large-scale application (eg cancer and coronary artery diseases).
Utilization of computers as a supporting and integrated technological tool for large-scale medical application (eg automatic analysis of electrocardiographs and electroencephalographs, radiographs, scintigrams and sonographic pictures).
Design and implementation of efficient information systems and software for statistical evaluation.
Methods to assess performance in the health sector (eg health indicators).
Development of methods for systems analysis of health care (eg models for planning health care facilities).

INSTITUTE OF TOXICOLOGY AND BIOCHEMISTRY 978

Director: Professor Dr J. Berndt

Department of Cell Chemistry 979

Head: Professor Dr J. Berndt
Graduate research staff: 8
Activities: Areas of research include: effect of c-AMP on the induction of detoxicating enzymes; effect of pesticides on the cell membrane; regulation of cholesterol biosynthesis, serum lipids.

Department of Enzyme Chemistry   980

Head: Professor Dr H. Holzer
Graduate research staff: 7
Activities: Studies of the effect of sulphur dioxide and other air polluting materials; enzymes for health care and therapy.

Department of Pharmacology   981

Head: Professor Dr M. Reiter
Graduate research staff: 4
Activities: Areas of research include: effects of the organometallic mercury compound on the intact papillary muscle of the guinea-pig; intracellular effects of manganese; calcium exchange between myocardial tissue and the incubation medium.

Department of Toxicology   982

Head: Professor Dr H. Greim
Graduate research staff: 39
Activities: Subjects of research include: the effects and persistence of environmental chemicals in experimental animals; the effect of foreign substances on non-human primates; the development, standardization and application of test systems to assess toxic, mutagenic and carcinogenic effects on cells.

GKSS-Forschungszentrum   983
Geesthacht GmbH

[GKSS-Research Centre Geesthacht]
Address: Reaktorstrasse 7-9, D-2054 Geesthacht Tesperhude
Telephone: (04152) 12 1
Telex: 0218712gkssg
Scientific Technical Director: Dr Erich Schröder
Deputy Technical Manager: Dipl-Ing Hermann Schmidt
Graduate research staff: 115
Annual expenditure: over £2m
Activities: The Centre conducts pre-industrial research and development. The programme reflects the research goals of the Federal Republic of Germany. The activities encompass basic research and the development of new technologies, as well as the construction and operation of pilot plants. The results of the research and development programme are published.
The research and development programme includes the following areas; nuclear ships; reactor safety; environmental research; water desalination/marine chemistry; marine technology.
Facilities: Research reactors FRG 1 (5 MW), and FRG 2 (21 MW), including irradiation facilities; hot cells for

the treatment and investigation of radioactive material; test facility for pressure suppression systems; test field for reactor pumps; ship movements simulator; test facilities for water desalination; deep diving simulator.
Contract work: Yes
Publications: Annual report.

Hahn-Meitner-Institut für   984
Kernforschung Berlin
GmbH

[Hahn-Meitner-Institute for Nuclear Research in Berlin]
Address: Glienicker Strasse 100, D-1000 Berlin 39
Telephone: (030) 8009 1
Telex: 0185763 hmi sm
Scientific and technical director: Professor Dr H.W. Levi
Departments: Nuclear and radiation physics, Professor Dr W. von Oertzen; Radiation chemistry, Professor Dr K.D. Asmus; Nuclear chemistry, Professor Dr H. Dachs; Data processing and electronics, Professor Dr K. Zander
Graduate research staff: 300
Annual expenditure: DM70m
Activities: Solid-state and material research; low energy nuclear physics and heavy ion research; atomic physics; radiation chemistry; trace elements research in biological and medical problems and in raw material technology; data processing and electronics.
Facilities: 5 MW swimming-pool reactor BER II; 400 MW heavy ions accelerator machinery VICKSI; 4 MW electronic accelerator ELBENA, which can be pulsed in the field of nanoseconds; central data processing equipment.
Contract work: No
Publications: Annual report.

Hamburger Sternwarte   985

[Hamburg Observatory]
Address: Gojenbergsweg 112, D-2050 Hamburg 80
Telephone: (040) 7252-4112
Telex: 217 884-hamst d
Affiliation: Universität Hamburg
Research director: Professor A. Weigert
Graduate research staff: 16
Activities: Theoretical astrophysics, optical astronomy, radioastronomy.
Contract work: No
Publications: Abhandlungen der Hamburger Sternwarte.

Hamburgische Gartenbau- 986
Versuchsanstalt Fünfhausen

[Hamburg-Fünfhausen Experimental Centre for
Horticultural Science]
Address: Ochsenwerder Landscheideweg 277, D-2050
Hamburg 80
Telephone: (040) 737 2310
Affiliation: Behörde für Wirtschaft, Verkehr und
Landwirtschaft des Senates der Freien und Hansestadt
Hamburg
Research director: U. Schmoldt
Sections: Flowers, T. Miske; vegetables, J. Weitzel
Graduate research staff: 4
Annual expenditure: £51 000-500 000
Activities: Experiments to improve the economics of
horticultural practice, including lower costs for heating;
development of controlled horticulture and higher
quality; testing of new varieties; testing of new fertilizers
and plant protection.
Contract work: No
Publications: Annual report.

Hamburgische Schiffbau- 987
Versuchungsanstalt GmbH

– HSVA
Address: 164 Bramfelder Strasse, D-2000 Hamburg 60
Telephone: (040) 61 75 51
Telex: 2174236
Director: Professor Dr O. Krappinger
Scientific staff: 120
Activities: Resistance and propulsion of ships on open
sea and ice; manoeuvre technology; propeller cavitation;
hydro-acoustics; sea-going behaviour of ships; behaviour
and strain of offshore buildings on open sea and ice;
measuring techniques (for example laser-anemometry).

Henkel KGaA 988

Address: Henkelstrasse 67, D-4000 Düsseldorf 1
Telephone: (0211) 797 1
Telex: 085817-0
Research director: Dr J. Conrad
Sections: Organic chemistry, Dr Schnegelberger; in-
organic chemistry, Dr Worms; fat and oil chemistry, Dr
Baumann; physical chemistry, Dr Schwuger;
macromolecular chemistry, Dr Budnowski; biotechnol-
ogy, Dr Schmid
Annual expenditure: over £2m
Contract work: No

Hessische Forstliche 989
Versuchsanstalt

[Hessian Forest Research Station]
Address: Professor Oelkers-Strasse 6, Postfach 1308,
D-3510 Hann Münden 1
Telephone: (05541) 1032
Parent body: Hessian Ministry of Land Development,
Environment, Agriculture and Forestry
Director: Dr E.J. Gärtner
Graduate research staff: 11
Contract work: Yes
Publications: Annual report.

FAST GROWING TREES INSTITUTE 990

Telephone: (05541) 1034
Director: Dr Horst Weisgerber
Graduate research staff: 5
Activities: Provenance tests; progeny tests; tree breeding, especially spruce, pine, larch, Douglas fir and popu-
lars; vegetative propagation; poplar research; resistance
breeding.

FOREST HYDROLOGY INSTITUTE 991

Director: Dr H.M. Brechtel
Activities: Analysis of watershed management
problem, of forest watersheds; investigations on
possibilities of increasing water yield by special forest
management techniques; preservation of evidence for
ground water utilization projects.

FOREST PRODUCTION INSTITUTE 992

Director: Dr L. Dimitri
Activities: Forest tree planting techniques; stand-tend-
ing; thinning methods; protection against biotic and
abiotic damage; fertilization; environmental aspects of
forest management.

Hessische 993
Landwirtschaftliche
Versuchsanstalt

[Hessian Agricultural Research and Experimental
Station]
Address: Am Versuchsfeld 13, D-3500 Kassel-
Harleshausen
or: Rheinstrasse 91, D-6100 Darmstadt
Telephone: (0561) 88141 (Kassel); (06151) 81091
(Darmstadt)

Parent body: Hessian Ministry of Land Development, Environment, Agriculture and Forestry
Director: Dr H. Brüne
Darmstadt section: Dr H. Schlüter
Graduate research staff: 14
Annual expenditure: DM1 500 000
Activities: Soil science; plant nutrition; fertilizers; quality analysis; mycotoxin; heavy metals in feedstuffs.
Contract work: Yes

Hochschule der Bundeswehr Hamburg 994

[Technical University of the Federal Defence Forces]
Address: 85 Holstenhofweg, D-2000 Hamburg 70
Telephone: (040) 654 11

FACULTY OF ELECTROTECHNOLOGY 995

Research staff: 51
Activities: Applied research and development in communications technology; energy supply; high frequency technology; laser technology; automatic control technology.

Institute for Control Technology 996

Head: Professor Dr D. Franke

Institute for Electronics and Data Processing 997

Head: Professor Dr B. Morgenstern

Institute for Energy Supply 998

Head: Professor Dr K. Heuck

Institute for Experimental Physics 999

Head: Professor Dr G. Guthöhrlein

Institute for Fundamentals of Electrotechnology 1000

Head: Professor Dr Loocke

Institute for General Communications 1001 Technology

Head: Professor Dr Vom Stein

Institute for High-Frequency Technology 1002

Head: Professor Dr H. Wässerling

Institute for Laser Technology 1003

Head: Professor Dr H. Harde

Institute for Measurement Technology 1004

Head: Professor Dr H. Trinks

Institute for Theoretical Electrotechnology-High Voltage Technology 1005

Head: Professor Dr H. Singer

Laboratory for Electrical Machines and Drives 1006

Head: Professor Dr F. Taegen

FACULTY OF MATERIALS TECHNOLOGY 1007

Inorganic Chemistry Department 1008

Head: Professor Dr T. Petzel
Scientific staff: 3
Activities: Evaporation thermodynamics and kinetics of heavy-volatile inorganic material systems; phase studies and high temperature by thermal analysis and X-ray diffraction methods; chemical transport reactions; thermal properties of organic lubricants.

FACULTY OF MECHANICAL ENGINEERING 1009

Graduate research staff: 78
Activities: Research and development of automation technology; construction and finishing technology; conveyer technology; materials technology.

Institute for Automation Technology 1010

Head: Professor Dr Lunderstädt

Institute for Construction and Processing Technology 1011

Head: Professor Dr A. Behrens

Institute for Machine Components and 1012 Conveyer Technology

Head: Professor Dr Bechtloff

Institute for Materials Technology- 1013 Metal Science

Head: Professor Dr H. Kreye

Institute for Mechanics 1014

Head: Professor Dr H. Rothert

Institute for Mechanics and Vibration 1015

Head: Professor Dr H. Witfeld

Institute for Motor Transport and 1016 Piston Engines

Head: Professor Dr Schmid

Institute for Thermodynamics-Heat 1017 Transfer

Heads: Professor Dr H.D. Baehr, Professor Dr W. Roetzel

Laboratory for Hydrostatic Drives and 1018 Controls

Head: Professor Dr H. Nikolaus

Laboratory for Materials Science and 1019 Welding Technology

Head: Professor Dr H. Hoffmeister

Hoechst Aktiengesellschaft 1020

Address: Postfach 80 03 20, D-6230 Frankfurt am Main 80
Telephone: (0611) 305-1
Telex: 41234 hoeag d
Vice President and Director of Corporate Research and Development: Professor Dr Klaus Weissermel
Graduate research staff: 2100 (worldwide)
Annual expenditure: over £2m
Activities: Hoechst AG conducts business activities and research in the following divisions: inorganic chemicals; organic chemicals; agriculture; dyes and pigments; tensides and auxiliaries; fibres; resins; plastics and waxes; films and sheetings; reprography; pharmaceuticals; cosmetics; paints; plant engineering; welding technology, and industrial gases.

All research disciplines are represented, from fundamental research to research on application techniques as well as all necessary service groups.
Facilities: Hoechst AG has research departments at the plants in: Frankfurt am Main; Bobingen; Gendorf; Gersthofe; Knapsack; Marburg; Wiesbaden and Wuppertal. In addition, overseas research laboratories are situated in Austria, France, Great Britain, India, Japan and USA.
Contract work: No
See also entry for: Union Rheinische Braunkohlen Kraftstoff Aktiengesellschaft.

GENDORF PLANT 1021

Address: D-8261 Gendorf
Telephone: (08679) 7258
Telex: 56932 hoegd d
Research director: Dr Ulrich Schwenk
Sections: PVC, Dr Engelmann; PTFE, Dr Kuhls; analytics, Dr Puschmann; tensides, Dr Billenstein; organic intermediates, Dr Ulm
Graduate research staff: 24
Annual expenditure: over £2m
Activities: Polyvinyl chloride, polytetrafluorethylene, tensides, fluorine chemistry, ethelyne-oxide chemistry.
Contract work: No

Howaldtswerke-Deutsche 1022 Werft Aktiengesellschaft Hamburg und Kiel

– HDW
Address: Postfach 6309, D-2300 Kiel 14
Telephone: (0431) 23000 1
Telex: 0299883 hdwk
Affiliation: Salzgitter Group
Director: W. Ilchmann
Graduate research staff: 8
Annual expenditure: £501 000-2m
Activities: Development of sea transport systems; resistance, propulsion, vibration, strength of ships; computer-aided ship design; fuel saving engine plant conceptions.
Facilities: Centralized navigational and ship control station; main engine remote control systems; electronic cable failure measuring techniques.
Contract work: No

Hüttentechnische Vereinigung der Deutschen Glasindustrie eV   1023

[Metallurgical Association for the German Glass Industry]
Address: 75-77 Mendelssohnstrasse, D-6000 Frankfurt am Main
Telephone: (0611) 74 90 88
Affiliation: Arbeitsgemeinschaft Industrieller Forschungsvereinigungen eV
Managing Director: Professor Dr W. Trier
Activities: Glass properties; technology of glass manufacture and glass processing; application of various glass products.

Hygiene-Institut des Ruhrgebiets   1024

[Hygiene Institute of the Ruhr District]
Address: Rotthauser Strasse 19, Postfach 1040, D-4650 Gelsenkirchen
Telephone: (0209) 15251
Research directors: Professor Dr med C.A. Primavesi, Professor Dr med H. Althaus
Graduate research staff: 8
Annual expenditure: £51 000-500 000
Activities: Bacteriology; virology; air pollution, sewage pollution, and pollution of drinking and domestic water supplies.
Contract work: Yes

Hygienisches Institut   1025

[Hygiene Institute]
Address: Gorch-Fock-Wall 15-17, D-2000 Hamburg 36
Telephone: (040) 34971
Parent body: Gesundheitsbehörde, Freie und Hansestadt Hamburg
Director: Professor Dr J. Bockemühl
Activities: Problems of occupational and preventive medicine; applied medical microbiology (serology of treponematosis; epidemiology and pathogenesis of bacterial intestinal disease; National Reference Centre for Salmonella).
Contract work: No

CENTRAL INSTITUTE FOR OCCUPATIONAL MEDICINE   1026

Director: Professor Dr G. Lehnert

CHEMICAL AND FOOD INVESTIGATION INSTITUTE   1027

Director: vacant

MEDICAL INVESTIGATION INSTITUTE   1028

Director: Professor Dr J. Bockemühl

IFRA   1029

[Inca Fiej Research Association]
Address: Washingtonplatz 1, D-6100 Darmstadt
Telephone: (06151) 76057
Telex: 0419273
Research director: Nils Enlund
Annual expenditure: £10 000-50 000
Activities: IFRA does not do actual research but initiates, funds and coordinates research activities in other research organizations. These research activities are mainly concerned with methods of improving newspaper production methods, and developing new methods of processing and distributing news information.
Contract work: No

Institut der Deutschen Forschungsgesellschaft für Druck- und Reproduktions-tecknik eV   1030

[Institute of the German Research Association for Printing and Reproduction Technology]
Address: Postfach 800 469, 19 Streitfeldstrasse, D-8000 München 80
Telephone: (089) 43 40 06
Affiliation: Arbeitsgemeinschaft Industrieller Forschungsvereinigungen eV
Scientific Director: Dr P. Scheidt
Scientific staff: 15
Activities: High-intensity book printing; high-intensity newspaper printing; continuous forms printing; flat printing; printing paper; printing ink; reproduction techniques; surface chemistry; graphic electronics.

Institut für Angewandte Geodäsie 1031

– HAG
[Institut for Applied Geodesy]
Address: Richard-Strauss-Allee 11, D-6000 Frankfurt-am-Main 70
Telephone: (0611) 638091/96
Telex: ifag-d 0413592
Parent body: Bundesministerium des Innern
Director: Dr W. Satzinger
Graduate research staff: 27
Annual expenditure: DM9.5m
Activities: Scientific research in all fields of geodesy, cartography, photogrammetry, and the processing of research results for practical application.
Note: The Institute is a federal research institute under the Ministry of the Interior, it is also affiliated to the German Geodetic Research Institute, a division of the Bavarian Academy of Sciences.
See separate entry under: Bayerische Akademie der Wissenschaften.
Contract work: No
Publications: Mitteilungen des Instituts für Angewandte Geodäsie; Nachrichten aus dem Karten und Vermessungswesen; Various maps series.

CARTOGRAPHIC RESEARCH DIVISION 1032

Activities: Studies on the introduction of modern techniques for the compilation, production, and revision of official map series: analysis of the relations between the overall design of a map and the information content; analysis of the processes in the generalization of map features, and application of mathematic methods for automatic data processing; digital acquisition and processing of line, raster, and text data as well as data storage in cartographic data banks; data reproduction by means of precise drawing table, raster plotter, and phototypesetter.

GEODETIC RESEARCH DIVISION 1033

Activities: Laser distance measurements to satellites and to the moon in order to investigate, geodynamic problems; Doppler measurements to satellites in order to investigate the determination of position, the definition of paramount reference systems, and the determination of polar motion; application of satellite altimetry for geoid determination; astronomic precision observations for the standardization of the central European net of longitudes and for the determination of deflections of the vertical; astro-gravimetric geoid determinations in the German FR; investigations on the improvement of the primary triangulation net; cooperation in the determina-

tion of a new primary gravity network; precision gravity measurements for the investigation of tectonic phenomena; earth tide research by means of gravimetric long-term recordings; development of an instrumental system for an absolute gravity measurement.
The activities in the field of satellite geodesy are part of Special Research Project 78 'Satellite Geodesy', at Munich Technical University; satellite observations are carried out at the satellite observation station at Wettzell in the Bavarian Forest.
See separate entry under: Bayerische Akademie der Wissenschaften.

PHOTOGRAMMETRIC RESEARCH DIVISION 1034

Activities: Investigations on data acquisition techniques for aerial and space imagery; research on the physical factors influencing the data acquisition; application of remote sensing; studies and tests on the overall design, production, and reproduction of photomaps; photo interpretation for the production of topographic and thematic maps; investigation on the instrumental and operational rationalization of photogrammetry by automation in connection with analogue correlation, orthophoto technique, numerical data acquisition, and digital terrain models; research and experimental studies on the technology and application of digital image processing of aerial and space imagery with special emphasis on cartographic problems, areas of special research activity include digital correlation, pattern recognition, and geometric image corrections; activities in the field of development and application of computer-assisted plotting instruments.

Institut für Arzneimittel 1035

[Institute for Drugs]
Address: Stauffenbergstrasse 13, D-1000 Berlin 30
Telephone: (030) 2637-1
Telex: 0 183 310
Parent body: Bundesgesundheitsamt
Head: Dr med Bernhard Schnieders
Activities: Drug approval; drug toxicology; experimental and clinical pharmacology; manufacture, distribution and sale of drugs; narcotic drugs (Federal Opium Board); pharmaceutical chemistry, biology and technology.

Institut für Diabetesforschung 1036

[Diabetes Research Institute]
Address: 1 Kölner Platz, D-8000 München 40
Heads: Professor Dr H. Mehnert, Professor Dr O. Wieland
Annual expenditure: DM20.2m
Activities: Research into diabetes mellitus.

Institut für Erdölforschung 1037

[Petroleum Research Institute]
Address: Am Kleinen Felde 30, D-3000 Hannover 1
Telephone: (0511) 712347
Vice-director: Dr H.J. Neumann
Departments: Chemistry, Professor Dr H.J. Neumann; analysis, Dr D. Severing; physics, Dr H. Killesreiter; lubrication, E. Wedepohl
Graduate research staff: 20
Annual expenditure: £501 000-2m
Activities: Petroleum recovery, especially by chemical flooding; petroleum physics; petroleum refining and petroleum products, especially lubricants and lubrication, and analysis of petroleum and its products.
Contract work: Yes
Publications: Annual report in German.

Institut für Gewerbliche Wasserwirtschaft und Luftreinhaltung eV 1038

[Institute for Wastewater Management and Air Pollution Control]
Address: Oberländer Ufer 84-88, D-5000 Köln 51
Telephone: (0221) 3708 1
Technical director: Dr Edgar Heckel
Departments: Air pollution, Dr Breuer; Water and waste management, Dr Dittrich
Graduate research staff: 5
Annual expenditure: £51 000-500 000
Activities: All ecology relevant to the fields of water and air pollution; including mechanical and chemical analytical procedures.
Contract work: Yes
Publications: Mostly reports to government agencies.

Institut für Kunststoffverarbeitung in Industrie und Handwerk an der Rheinisch-Westfälischen Technischen Hochschule Aachen 1039

– IKV
[Institute for Plastic Processing in Industry and Trade at the Rheinisch-Westfälischen Technical University Aachen]
Address: 49 Pontstrasse, D-5100 Aachen
Telephone: (0241) 80 38 06
Affiliation: Arbeitsgemeinschaft Industrieller Forschungsvereinigungen eV
Scientific Director: Professor Dr G. Menges
Scientific staff: 71
Activities: Extrusion; injection moulding of thermoplastic materials; injection moulding of structural foam components; computer control processing of difficult materials; foaming; pressure-free polyurethane foaming; reinforcing of plastics; wrapping of complicated components; jointing; finishing and transforming.

Institut für Landes- und Stadtentwicklungsforschung des Landes Nordrhein-Westfalen 1040

[Institute for Research of Regional and Urban Development of the North Rhine-Westphalia Region]
Address: Königswall 38-40, Postfach 12 11, D-4600 Dortmund 1
Telephone: (0231) 14 23 51
Director: Dr V. Von Malchus
Research director: Dr G. Boeddinghaus
Sections: Statistics, Dr H. Dürholt; regional research, Dr R. Gruber; land-use planning, Dipl-Soz W. Zühlke; municipal building, Dr G. Boeddinghaus; municipal building research, Dipl-Ing H. Dix
Graduate research staff: 25
Annual expenditure: £501 000-2m
Activities: The Institute's main task consists in elaborating the fundamentals and decision aids for the planning of regional and urban development, taking an active part in the coordination of research of spatial relevance within the North Rhine-Westphalia region, in keeping up a scientific exchange of experiences at home and abroad and in informing the authorities engaged in problems of regional and urban development on the results of research. The Institute works on the basis of

medium-term and annually planned research assignments, and appertains to the portfolio of the Prime Minister of North Rhine-Westphalia.
Contract work: Yes
Publications: Annual research programme; annual progress report.

Institut für Meeresforschung   1041

[Marine Research Institute]
Address: Am Handelshafen 12, D-2850 Bremerhaven 1
Telephone: (0971) 20641
Affiliation: Council for Education, Science and Arts, Bremen
Research director: Professor Dr Sebastian Gerlach
Sections: Zoology, Professor Gerlach; hydrography, Professor Krause; chemistry, Dr Ernst; botany, Dr Gaertner; microbiology, Dr Weyland
Graduate research staff: 30
Annual expenditure: over £2m
Activities: Marine botany (particularly mycology and diatoms); marine zoology; bacteriology; hydrochemistry and coastal sedimentology; chemistry (particularly organic chemistry).
Contract work: No

Institut für Motorenbau   1042
Professor Huber eV

[Professor Huber Combustion Engine Institute]
Address: 104 Eggenfeldener Strasse, D-8000 München 81
Telephone: (089) 93 60 93
Director: Dr Ing K. Prescher
Sections: MOT I, Dipl-Ing R. Decker; MOT II, Dipl-Ing Th. Koller; MOT III, Dr Ing G. Heinrich; theory and measurement, Dr Ing W. Schley
Graduate research staff: 16
Annual expenditure: £51 000-500 000
Activities: Research into mixture formation and combustion by schlieren photography; theoretical and experimental investigations into reaction kinetic processes; fuel jet injection equipment for diesel engines; physical conditions for calculating the performance of combustion engines; reduction of exhaust emission of combustion engines; test data transfer from moving engine parts; noise problems of combustion engines.
The Institute carries out independent research and development programmes for industry, public services and research associations.
Contract work: Yes

Institut für   1043
Naturwissenschaftlich-
Technische Dienste GmbH

– NATEC
[Institute for Scientific-Technical Services]
Address: Behringstrasse 154, D-2000 Hamburg 50
Telephone: (040) 08827 715
Telex: 2164293 unat d
Affiliation: Deutsche Unilever GmbH
Director: Professor Dr K.-F. Gander
Departments: Analytical chemistry, environmental research, Dr Vogt; Radiochemistry, metabolic studies, syntheses, Dr Figge; Microbiology, Mrs Zschaler; Packaging research and consultation, Dr Gartmann; Devices for mechanization and automation, Dr Thieme
Graduate research staff: 30
Contract work: Yes

Institut für Nuklearmedizin, 1044
Deutsches
Krebsforschungszentrum

[Nuclear Medicine Institute, German Cancer Research Centre]
Address: Postfach 101949, D-6900 Heidelberg 1
Telephone: (06221) 48 45 50
Telex: 461562dkfzd
Acting director: Professor Dr K.E. Scheer
Deputy director: Professor Dr W.J. Lorenz
Sections: Nuclear medicine and radiation therapy, Professor Dr K.E. Scheer
Diagnostic nuclear medicine, Professor Dr P. Georgi
Oncological diagnostics, Professor Dr G. van Kaick
Biophysics and medical radiation physics, Professor Dr W.J. Lorenz
Radiochemistry, radiopharmacology and radioimmunology, Dr W. Maier-Borst
Graduate research staff: 60
Annual expenditure: £501 000-2m
Activities: New forms of radiation therapy with incorporated radiation sources, external beam therapy and therapy with fast neutrons; development of methods for the identification and early detection of cancer as well as for tumour diagnostics (radioimmunology, nuclear medicine, radiophysics, biophysics, ultrasound, and radiopharmacology); experimental and clinical trace element studies; use of a cyclotron and reactor for biomedical applications.
Contract work: No

Institut für Seeverkehrswirtschaft 1045

[Shipping Economics Institute]
Address: Werderstrasse 73, D-2800 Bremen 1
Telephone: (0421) 500233
Director: Dr Hans Ludwig Beth
Activities: Market analysis and forecasting; research in economic problems; shipping and seaborne trade, shipbuilding, ports and sea canals.
Publications: Shipbuilding Statistics yearbook and monthly; series on maritime economics.

Institut für Sozialmedizin und Epidemiologie 1046

[Institute for Social Medicine and Epidemiology]
Address: Thielallee 88-92, Postfach 330013, D-1000 Berlin 33
Telephone: (030) 8308-0
Telex: 0184016 bgesa d
Parent body: Bundesgesundheitsamt
Head: Professor Dr H. Hoffmeister
Divisions: Public health; statistics; nutritional medicine; social medicine; epidemiology; applied diagnostic technology
Graduate research staff: 26
Annual expenditure: over £2m
Activities: Improvement of consumer protection, against health risks; reduction of environmental health hazards; research into the causes of diseases, early detection of diseases and disease control.
Contract work: No

Institut für Spektrochemie und angewandte Spektroskopie 1047

[Spectrochemistry and Applied Spectroscopy Institute]
Address: Bunsen-Kirchhoff-Strasse 11, Postfach 778, D-4600 Dortmund 1
Telephone: (0231) 12 90 01
Affiliation: Gesellschaft zur Förderung der Spektrochemie und angewandten Spektroskopie eV
Head of Institute: Dr K. Müller-Gliemann
Graduate research staff: 30
Annual expenditure: £501 000-2m
Activities: General analytical chemistry; optical emission and atomical absorption spectrochemical analysis; analytical X-ray spectroscopy; molecular spectroscopy; mass spectrometry; physics of light sources; data processing.
Contract work: No

Institut für Strahlenhygiene 1048

[Institute for Radiation Hygiene]
Address: Ingolstädter Landstrasse 1, D-8042 Neuherberg
Telephone: (089) 3874
Telex: 523125 stral d
Parent body: Bundesgesundheitsamt
Head: Professor Dr Alexander Kaul
Divisions: Radiation effects and radiation protection, Dr F. Kossel; medical radiation hygiene, Professor Dr A. Kaul; radioactive substances and environment, Dr J. Schwibach
Graduate research staff: 45
Annual expenditure: DM4m
Activities: Interests include radiation effects and protection: genetic effects; somatic effects; radiochemistry; radiation chemistry; radiopharmaceuticals; radiation physics; dosimetry; electromagnetic waves; ultraviolet irradiation; laser; ultrasonics. Medical radiation hygiene: nuclear medicine; X-ray diagnostics; radiotherapy; radiation in medical research; radiobiology; biokinetics of radionuclides; radiation hazards. Radionuclides and environment: natural and artificial radionuclides; protection of the population; emission-surveillance; radioecology.
WHO Collaborating Centre for Studies of Efficacy and Efficiency of Diagnostic Application of Radiation and Radionuclides.
Contract work: Yes

Institut für Umweltsschutz und Agrikulturchemie* 1049

[Environmental Protection and Agricultural Chemistry Institute]
Address: Am Vogelsang 14, Postfach 23, D-5628 Heiligenhaus
Director: Dr H. Berge
Sections: Chemistry, J. Peix; botany, K. Orgis; measurement techniques, H. Feldbaum, H. Heinen
Activities: Immission and emission control; gas, smoke, dust and noise measurements of all kinds; immission damage; investigation and evaluation of air and water pollution in arid and in humid zones.

Institut für Veterinärmedizin 1050

[Institute for Veterinary Medicine]
Address: Thielallee 88-92, D-1000 Berlin 33
Telephone: (030) 8308-0
Parent body: Bundesgesundheitsamt
Head: Professor Dr Dieter Grossklaus
Activities: Food hygiene; zoonoses and epizootics research; drugs, animal nutrition and residue research. FAO/WHO Collaborating Centre for Research and Training in Food Hygiene and Zoonoses.

Institut für Wasser-, Boden- 1051 und Lufthygiene

[Institute for Water, Soil and Air Hygiene]
Address: Corrensplatz 1, D-1000 Berlin 33
Telephone: (030) 8308-0
Parent body: Bundesgesundheitsamt
Head: Professor Dr Karl Aurand
Activities: Special problems of environmental hygiene, human ecology, and sanitary engineering; drinking-water hygiene; waste water and environmental hygiene in water pollution control, air hygiene; soil hygiene, hygiene of water catchment.

Institut für Zuckerrübenforschung 1052

[Sugar Beet Research Institute]
Address: Holtenser Landstrasse 77, D-3400 Göttingen
Telephone: (0551) 620 71
Affiliation: Verein der Zuckerindustrie, Bonn
Research director: Professor Dr Christian Winner
Sections: Crop production and statistics, Dr von Müller; chemistry, Dr Beiss; plant protection, Dr Schäufele; plant physiology, Dr Bürcky
Graduate research staff: 6
Activities: Seed quality and variety performance; chemical weed control; effectiveness of insecticides and fungicides; crop rotation systems; application of fertilizers and irrigation; soil and plant analysis; improvement of beet quality; economy of sugar beet production.
Contract work: No

Institute for Experimental 1053 Biology and Medicine

Director: Professor Dr J. Meissner
Scientific staff: 36
Activities: Clinical, experimental and scientific analysis; microbiology; pathology; immunology; biochemistry including pharmacokinetics; biophysics; radiation protection and microstructure analysis.

Internationale 1054 Forschungsgemeinschaft Futtermitteltechnik eV

[International Research Association for Fodder Technology]
Address: Fricken-Mühle, D-3300 Braunschweig-Thune
Telephone: (05307) 4682
Affiliation: Arbeitsgemeinschaft Industrieller Forschungsvereinigungen eV
Managing Director: Dr Ing W. Friedrich
Activities: Applied basic research into fodder-mixture technology.

Johann Wolfgang Goethe- 1055 Universität

[Frankfurt University]
Address: Senckenberganlage 31, D-6000 Frankfurt am Main 1
Telephone: (0611) 7981
Telex: 413932 unif d
President: Professor Dr H. Keln
Vice-Presidents: Professor Dr C. Winter, Professor Dr U. Loenenheim
Note: At Frankfurt University almost half of the research projects are supported by outside funds: in 1977 these amounted to 20 million DM. The major contributor is the Deutsche Forschungsgemeinschaft (DFG) in Bonn. In 1980 special research programmes have been supported by the DFG with 4.2 million DM. They are special collaborative programmes carried out by groups of scientists who have joined together with the approval of their universities for joint research, the universities recognizing that their research has common ground deserving support for a longer period of time.
See also entry for: Institute of Bee Science.

FACULTY OF BIOCHEMISTRY, 1056
PHARMACY AND FOOD CHEMISTRY

Dean: Professor Dr H. Niebergall

Institute of Biophysical Chemistry and 1057 Biochemistry

Address: Sandhofstrasse 3, D-6000 Frankfurt am Main
Research leader: Dr H. Schmidt
Projects: Sensitized photobiological reactions; aggregation of sensitizing dyes; Raman spectroscopy of proteins; structure of oxygen-developed system of photosynthesis membrane.

Institute of Food Chemistry 1058

Address: Robert-Mayer-Strasse 7-9, D-6000 Frankfurt am Main

Institute of Pharmaceutical Biology 1059

Research leaders: G. Willuhn, Professor Dr G. May
Projects: Antiviral effective plant substances; formation of steroids in Solanum dulcamara and in tissue cultures of this plant.

Institute of Pharmaceutical Chemistry 1060

Address: Georg-Voigt-Strasse 14, D-6000 Frankfurt am Main
Research leaders: Professor Dr H. Oelschläger, Professor Dr H. Linde, Professor Dr H. Janecke, Professor Dr H. Hoffmann
Projects: Presentation of new potential pharmaceutical substances; potentially therapeutic natural substances; new analytical methods for quality and quantity definition of pharmaceutically significant organic compounds with special regard to detecting small amounts of medical substances in single doses of medicaments; detection of drugs and their metabolism in biological substances, for example, blood or urine.
Collaboration with J. Heyrovsky Institute of Physical Chemistry and Electrochemistry, Czechoslovak Academy of Sciences; Komenskeho University, Bratislava; Institute of Chemistry, University of Århus; Chelsea College, University of London.

Institute of Pharmaceutical 1061 Technology

Research leader: K. Thoma
Projects: Colloid association of antihistamines; electrochemical standardization of diffusion films for the control of separation of effective medical substances from medicaments.

Institute of Pharmacology for 1062 Scientists

Address: Sandhofstrasse, D-6000 Frankfurt am Main
Research leaders: H.E. Geissler, G. Lambrecht, Professor Dr E. Mutschler
Projects: Synthesis and pharmacological testing of dopamin agonists; structure and conformation activity relationships of heterocyclic acetylcholinine analogues; development of a technique for measuring localized anaesthesia of the isolated nervus ischiadicus in frogs; local anaesthetic and antiarhythmic effects of indol and indoline compounds; drug interactions with azapropazon.

FACULTY OF BIOLOGY 1063

Dean: Professor Dr U. Halbach
Note: A special research programme has been set up in the Faculty of Biology on comparative neurobiology of animal behaviour. It consists of 24 research projects on special behaviour patterns of various kinds of animals; half are concerned with hearing only. The programme includes investigations into the 'language' of guinea-fowls and basic studies on hearing aids for the hard of hearing. It is carried out by 60 zoologists, medical scientists, physicists, communication engineers and system theoreticians, from the Institutes of Zoology of the University of Frankfurt, the Technische Hochschule Darmstadt, the Centre for Physiology of Human Medicine of the University of Frankfurt, and the Max Planck Institute of Brain Research in Frankfurt.

Botanic Institute (with Botanic 1064 Garden)

Address: Siesmayerstrasse 70, D-6000 Frankfurt am Main
Research leaders: H.W. Kohlenbach, Professor Dr G. Kahl, Professor Dr A.R. Kranz, Professor Dr H. Bücker, A. Ried
Projects: Physiology of anchogenesis; regulation of transcription in normal and tumourous plant tissues; gene physiology of photomorphogenetic effective pigment systems; aerospace experiments with the higher plant arabidopsis; regulation of distribution of stimulation energy in photosynthesis apparatus.

Institute of Anthropology and Human 1065 Genetics for Biologists

Address: Siesmayerstrasse 70, D-6000 Frankfurt am Main

Institute of Bee Science 1066

Address: Im Rotkopf 5, D-6370 Oberursel
Research leaders: Dr N. Königer, Professor Dr F. Ruttner
Projects: Incubation of young bees of Apis and Vespa; induction of egg deposition by the queen bee; thelytoke parthenogenesis of the honey bee.

Institute of Didactics of Biology 1067

Address: Sophienstrasse 1-3, D-6000 Frankfurt am Main

Institute of Microbiology 1068

Research leaders: Professor Dr M. Brendel, H. Dichtelmüller
Projects: Technique for isolation and characterization of thymidylate uptaking mutants in saccharomyces cerevisiae; molecular mechanism of differentiation processes.

Institute of Zoology 1069

Address: Siesmayerstrasse 70, D-6000 Frankfurt am Main
Research leaders: Professor Dr F.G. Barth, K. Brändle, Professor Dr V. Bruns, Professor Dr G. Fleissner, G. Neuweiler, Professor Dr W. Wiltschke, Professor Dr C. Winter
Projects: Sensory information from strains in the exoskeleton; changes of optical projection of the metamorphosis of the axon; echo orientation of bats; neurophysiological and behavioural analysis of the circadian rhythms of the arthropods; etho-ecology and neurobiology of echo-orientating bats in India; the significance of magnetic route information for the orientation of carrier pigeons; the development of sun orientation of birds; investigations into the primary processes of mechanoreceptors.

FACULTY OF CHEMISTRY 1070

Dean: Professor Dr W. Sterzel

Institute of Didactics of Chemistry 1071

Address: Robert-Mayer-Strasse 7-9, D-6000 Frankfurt am Main

Institute of Inorganic Chemistry 1072

Address: Niederurseler Hang, D-6000 Frankfurt am Main
Research leaders: H.U. Ehmcke, E. Rodek, M. Diehl, M. Aramak
Projects: Separation of isomeric benzenedisulfonic acids by high-pressure liquid chromatography; crystal structures and vibration spectra of inorganic platinum and palladium compounds; presentation, structures and compound relationships in inorganic ring compounds; unstable intermediate products.

Institute of Organic Chemistry 1073

Address: Niederurseler Hang, D-6000 Frankfurt am Main
Research leaders: Professor Dr H. Kessler, Professor Dr W. Ried, Professor Dr P. Rosenmund
Projects: Kinetics and thermodynamics of reversible ionization and dissociation reactions; investigations into reactivity of four-ring carbon cycles, especially of phenylcyclobutendion and tetragenal acid derivatives; new indole synthesis, indole dicarbonyls.

Institute of Physical and Theoretical Chemistry 1074

Address: Robert-Mayer-Strasse 11, D-6000 Frankfurt am Main
Research leaders: Professor Dr F. Becker, Professor Dr E. Brauer, Professor Dr H.-U. Chun, Professor Dr H. Kelm, Professor Dr H.-D. Brauer
Projects: Excess enthalpy of binary fluid systems with own associations of one component; electrochemical investigations of aluminium in neutral agents and seawater; dynamic behaviour of metal surfaces without top layer; mechanism of hydrogen diffusion in titanium and titanium alloy; X-ray and photoelectron spectroscopy of solid-state bodies; spectroscopic investigations of glass structures; kinetics of homogeneous catalytic isomerization of olefins by organometallic compounds; extinction of fluorescence emission of aromatic hydrocarbon by molecular oxygen.

FACULTY OF GEOSCIENCES 1075

Dean: Professor Dr H. Fuess

Geological-Palaeontological Institute 1076

Address: Senckenberganlage 32-34, D-6000 Frankfurt am Main
Research leaders: Professor Dr H. Murawski, Professor Dr G. Kowalczyk
Projects: Vertical movements and their causes with the example of the Rheinisches Schild (Germany); investiga-

tions into genetic interpretation of deterioration and crack formation in carboniferous rock; extent and kind of neotectonic movements on the Peloponnese (Greece).

Institute of Crystallography and Mineralogy 1077

Address: Senckenberganlage 30, D-6000 Frankfurt am Main
Research leader: Professor Dr H. Bartl
Projects: Neutron diffraction, automatic four-circle measuring device.

Institute of Geochemistry, Petrology and Science of Mineral Deposits 1078

Address: Senckenberganlage 28, D-6000 Frankfurt am Main
Research leaders: Dr M. Rosenhauer, Professor Dr E. Krum, Dr O. Spies
Projects: Polymorphic phase changes of carbonates at high pressures and temperatures, thermal and radiography measurements; main and trace elements in the serpentine body of Kraubath (Austria); postophiolytic vulcanite on the Iran geotraverse.

Institute of Meteorology and Geophysics 1079

Address: Feldbergstrasse 22, 47, D-6000 Frankfurt am Main
Research leaders: Dr B. Baier, Professor Dr H. Berckhemer, W. Jacoby, W. Fricke, Professor Dr H.W. Georgii
Projects: Rheinischer Schild - seismicity; earthquake research; relaxation and creeping behaviour of ground surface rock at high temperatures and pressures; photochemical smog formation in the Federal Republic of Germany; Iceland, Reykianic ridge: seismological geodynamic investigations of crust and upper surface (international project with a funding of DM2m in 1977); structure of the Ruhrcarbon, reflexion seismic measurements and gravimetry.
A special research programme has been set up for atmospheric trace elements. It has been divided into four main project areas: physico-chemical atmospheric processes, trace elements, aerosols, and palaeoatmosphere. The programme is to be executed by 17 scientists from the University of Frankfurt, the University of Mainz, and the Max Planck Institute of Chemistry in Mainz.

Institute of Physical Geography 1080

Address: Senckenberganlage 36, D-6000 Frankfurt am Main

FACULTY OF HUMAN MEDICINE 1081

Dean: Professor Dr H. Müller

Centre for Anaesthesiology and Resuscitation 1082

Address: Theodor-Stern-Kai 7, D-6000 Frankfurt am Main
Director: Professor Dr R. Dudziak

Centre for Dental Sciences 1083

Address: Theodor-Stern-Kai 7, D-6000 Frankfurt am Main

Centre for Dermatology and Venereology 1084

Address: Theodor-Stern-Kai 7, D-6000 Frankfurt am Main
Director: Professor Dr R. Milbradt
Research leaders: Professor Dr G. Keonhardi, Dr G. Reimer, Dr Ch. Schneider
Projects: Disc-electrophoretic separation of water-soluble proteins from scales of different forms of ichthyosis; DNA-related proteins in normal and pathological skin; influence on prognosis of melanoma patients of adaptive immunotherapy.

Centre for Ear, Nose and Throat Medicine 1085

Address: Theodor-Stern-Kai 7, D-6000 Frankfurt am Main
Director: Professor Dr H. Schaupp

Centre for Gynaecology and Obstetrics 1086

Address: Theodor-Stern-Kai 7, D-6000 Frankfurt am Main
Director: Professor Dr H. Schmidt-Matthiesen
Research leaders: Professor Dr H. Kuhl, Dr H. Schöndorf, Dr G. Bastert, Professor Dr H.-D. Taubert
Projects: Function of arylmidases in hypothalamus and in pituitary body of the rat with gonadotropine regulation; aspiration zytological cell measurement of malignant and non-malignant human mammary tumours; extensive investigation into individual and most effective therapy of gynaecological cancer including breast cancer; diagnostic and therapeutic use of highly effective LH-RH-analogue with cycle-disturbed women; investigations into operating mechanism of oral contraceptives.

Centre for Hygiene 1087

Address: Paul-Ehrlich-Strasse 40, D-6000 Frankfurt am Main
Director: Professor Dr H. Knothe

Centre for Internal Medicine 1088

Address: Theodor-Stern-Kai 7, D-6000 Frankfurt am Main
Director: Professor Dr K. Schöffling
Research leaders: Professor Dr A.W. Mondorf, Professor Dr K. Pirlet, Dr M. Bühring, Professor Dr G. Schultze-Werninghaus, Dr K.H. Ursel
Projects: Isolation and characterization of kidney membrane proteins and their detection in the urine as a parameter of inflammatory and toxic kidney damage; connection between diet and frequency of colon-carcinoma; immunological effect of whole-body hyperthermia; comparison between in vivo and in vitro tests with bronchial asthma; transplantation, foetal pancreas, diabetes.

Centre for Medical Information 1089

Address: Theodor-Stern-Kai 7, D-6000 Frankfurt am Main
Director: Professor Dr W. Giere

Centre for Morphology 1090

Address: Theodor-Stern-Kai 7, D-6000 Frankfurt am Main
Director: Professor Dr J. Winckler

Centre for Neurology and Neurosurgery 1091

Address: Schleusenweg 2-16, D-6000 Frankfurt am Main
Director: Professor Dr P.A. Fischer
Project: Long-term investigations into Parkinson syndrome.

Centre for Ophthalmology 1092

Address: Theodor-Stern-Kai 7, D-6000 Frankfurt am Main
Director: Professor Dr W. Doden

Centre for Paediatrics 1093

Address: Theodor-Stern-Kai 7, D-6000 Frankfurt am Main
Director: Professor Dr O. Hövels
Research leader: Professor Dr V.V. Loewenich
Project: Intrathecal treatment of neonatal meningitis.

Centre for Pharmacology 1094

Address: Theodor-Stern-Kai 7, D-6000 Frankfurt am Main
Director: Professor Dr D. Palm

Centre for Physiology 1095

Address: Theodor-Stern-Kai 7, D-6000 Frankfurt am Main
Director: Professor Dr W. Sinn
Research leaders: Professor Dr Hk. Müller, Professor Dr W. Röckemann
Projects: Orientation aid for the blind by acoustic space pictures; investigation into non-linearity of hearing in the ultrasonic region; mechanic properties of smooth muscles.

Centre for Psychiatry 1096

Address: Heinrich-Hoffmann-Strasse 10, D-6000 Frankfurt am Main
Director and research leader: Professor Dr H.J. Bocknik
Research leader: Professor Dr H. Hacker
Projects: Psychological and social consequences for the hard of hearing; epilepsy research; model scheme of outpatient psychiatric and psychotherapeutic/psychosomatic care.

Centre for Psychosocial Basis of Medicine 1097

Address: Theodor-Stern-Kai 7, D-6000 Frankfurt am Main
Director: Professor Dr V. Sigusch

Centre for Radiology 1098

Address: Theodor-Stern-Kai 7, D-6000 Frankfurt am Main
Director: Professor Dr F. Ball

Centre for Surgery 1099

Address: Theodor-Stern-Kai 7, D-6000 Frankfurt am Main
Director: Professor Dr W. Weber
Research leaders: Dr E. Elert, Dr J. Lucio, Dr A. Appel, Professor Dr A. Pannike
Projects: Myocardial protection, open heart surgery, cardioplegy; potency disturbance after colon surgery in childhood; new developments in surgical therapy of hydradenitis axillae; long-term investigations into bone metabolism after stomach surgery; fracture healing with primary and secondary osteosynthesis.

Gustav-Embden-Centre for Biological Chemistry 1100

Address: Theodor-Stern-Kai 7, D-6000 Frankfurt am Main
Director: Professor Dr L. Träger
Research leaders: Professor Dr P. Chandra, Professor Dr E. Heinz, Professor Dr H.J. Hohorst, Dr R. Peters, Professor Dr K. Ring, Professor Dr H. Fasold
Projects: Molecular-biological investigations into virus aetiology in human carcinogenesis; energetics of the amino acid transport; investigations into cytotoxic specificity of cancerotoxic selectivity of N-(2-chlorathyl)-amido-oxoza-phosphorines; function of the purple membrane of halobacteria; covalent synthesis of the transport proteins for nucleoside in tumour cells; reconstruction of the purple membranes in artificial and biological membrane systems.

Institute of Human Genetics 1101

Address: Paul-Ehrlich-Strasse 41-43, D-6000 Frankfurt am Main
Director: Professor Dr J. Svejcar
Research leaders: Professor Dr K.-H. Degenhardt, Dr J. Fränz, Dr M. Geisler, Professor Dr J. Kleinebrecht
Projects: Pregnancy progress and child development; cytogenetic effects of isoniazid (INH) on cell systems in mammals and humans; cytogenetic and histological experiments on embryos and placentas of spontaneous miscarriages; teratogenic and/or mutagenic effect of toxic substances; investigations into mucopolysaccharides and collagens in cartilage-bone biopsies of patients with hereditary skeletal dysplasia.

Institute of Immune Haematology 1102

Address: Sandhofstrasse 1, D-6000 Frankfurt am Main
Director: Professor Dr W. Spielmann

Orthopaedic University and Outpatients Clinic Friedrichsheim 1103

Address: Marienburgstrasse 2, D-6000 Frankfurt am Main
Research leaders: Professor Dr W. Heipertz, Dr A. Englehardt, Dr L. Zichner, Professor Dr H.-G. Willert
Projects: Development and testing of an adaptive artificial hand with myoelectric control and feedback; cementless anchoring, ceramic-coated endoprosthesis with quasi-physiological power initiation; ceramic and ceramic-coated bone replacement materials; wear characteristics of materials of artificial limbs.

Senckenberg Centre for Pathology 1104

Address: Theodor-Stern-Kai 7, D-6000 Frankfurt am Main
Director: Professor Dr K. Hübner

FACULTY OF MATHEMATICS 1105

Dean: Professor Dr G. Burde
Research leaders: Professor Dr F.W. Bauer, Professor Dr J. Bliedtner, Professor Dr F. Constantinescu, Professor Dr C.P. Schnorr, Professor Dr W. Pohlit
Projects: A shape theory with singular homology; potential theory and convexity; knots; stochastic processes and quantum fields; complexity theory; ionizing radiation as cancer therapy and its immediate effects.

FACULTY OF PHYSICS 1106

Dean: Professor Dr R. Bass
Note: A special research programme has been set up in solid-state spectroscopy; it has been divided into four project areas: electronic stimulations; magnetic ions in metallic environment; phase transfers; crystal growth and analysis. It is carried out by many scientists in various institutes of applied, experimental and theoretical physics both at the Technische Hochschule Darmstadt under Professor Dr B. Elschner, and at this University.
Financial aid for the overall programme: DM1 574 000.
Collaboration with Universität Stuttgart, MPI Festkorperförschung Stuttgart, ILL Grenoble, IAK Karlsruhe.

Institute of Applied Physics 1107

Address: Robert-Mayer-Strasse 2-4, D-6000 Frankfurt am Main
Research leaders: Dr H. Brehm, Professor Dr F. Granzer, Professor Dr H. Klein, Professor Dr D. Wolf
Projects: Spheric invariant signal sources; atomic circulation of crystal defects in ion crystals; sound emission at plastic deformation and during the development and deepening of cracks in metals; development and application of new techniques for the generation and speeding up of highly charged heavy ions; language signal processing, digital systems, linear predictions; noise causes in bipolar transistors; statistic properties of language signals.

Institute of Biophysics 1108

Address: Kennedyallee 70, D-6000 Frankfurt am Main
Research leaders: H.G. Burghoff, Professor Dr F. Hillenkamp, R. Nitsche, Professor Dr W. Pohlit
Projects: Conditions of water in cellulose-acetate membranes; development of a laser microprobe; max-

imum load of waste material at work; repair and recovery from radiation damages in living cells; immediate reactions to radiation with ionized particles.

Institute of Didactics of Physics   1109

Address: Gräfstrasse 39, D-6000 Frankfurt am Main

Institute of Nuclear Physics   1110

Address: August-Euler-Strasse 6, D-6000 Frankfurt am Main
Research leaders: Professor Dr K.O. Groeneveld, Dr H. Jex, M. Müller, Dr H. Schmidt- Böcking, Professor Dr E. Schopper conditions of light atoms after heavy ion bombarding; investigations into structure and dynamics of solid-state bodies with nuclear methods; inner shell stimulation at low disturbance; application of particle trace detectors in beam biophysics and in astronautics; high-energy core-core shock, compression waves.
Projects: Low electron conditions of light atoms after heavy ion bombarding; investigations into structure and dynamics of solid-state bodies with nuclear methods; inner shell stimulation at low disturbance; application of particle trace detectors in beam biophysics and in astronautics; high-energy core-core shock, compression waves.

Institute of Physics   1111

Address: Robert-Mayer-Strasse 2-4,8-10, D-6000 Frankfurt am Main
Research leader: Professor Dr W. Martienssen
Projects: Crystal preparations for colour centre lasers; production and optimization of gallium arsenide solar cells; realization of a light field with uncorrelated photons; interferometric evidence of weak phase modulations in light beams; holographic data logging.

Institute of Theoretical Physics   1112

Address: Robert-Mayer-Strasse 8-10, D-6000 Frankfurt am Main
Research leaders: Dr T.H. Rihan, H.M. Ruck, Professor W. Greiner, Professor Maruhn, Dr P.O. Hess
Projects: Atomic physics of heavy ions - quantum mechanism; relativistic wave equations for high spin; nuclear shock waves and properties of nuclear matter at high densities; collective nuclear models and their applications.

Johannes Gutenberg Universität Mainz   1113

[Johannes Gutenberg University Mainz]
Address: Saarstrasse 21, Postfach 3980, D-6500 Mainz

FACULTY OF BIOLOGY   1114

Address: Saarstrasse 21, D-6500 Mainz
Dean: Professor Dr H. Risler

Anthropology Institute   1115

Director: Professor Dr W. Bernhard

General Botany Institute   1116

Director: Professor Dr A. Wild

Genetics Institute   1117

Director: Professor Dr H. Laven

Microbiology and Wine Research Institute   1118

Director: Professor Dr F. Radler

Zoology Institute   1119

Director: Professor Dr H. Risler

FACULTY OF CHEMISTRY   1120

Address: Saarstrasse 21, D-6500 Mainz
Dean: Professor Dr W. Liptay

Biochemistry Institute   1121

Director: Professor Dr K. Dose

Inorganic and Analytic Chemistry Institute   1122

Director: Professor Dr G. Gattow

Nuclear Chemistry Institute   1123

Director: Professor Dr G. Herrmann

Organic Chemistry Institute   1124

Director: Professor Dr R.C. Schulz

Physical Chemistry Institute   1125

Director: Professor Dr H. Sillescu

FACULTY OF EARTH SCIENCES   1126

Address: Saarstrasse 21, D-6500 Mainz
Dean: Professor Dr M. Domrös

Geography Institute   1127

Senior staff: Professor Dr G. Abele, Professor Dr M. Domrös, Professor Dr H. Eggers, Professor Dr E. Gormsen, Professor Dr H. Hildebrandt, Professor Dr O. Kandler, Professor Dr W. Klaer, Professor Dr D. Uthoff

Geosciences Institute   1128

GEOLOGY DEPARTMENT   1129
Senior staff: Professor Dr S. Dürr, Professor Dr M. Fürst, Professor Dr D. Heim, Professor Dr A. Kröner, Professor Dr V. Lorenz

MINERALOGY DEPARTMENT   1130
Senior staff: Professor Dr W. Dosch, Professor Dr I. Keesmann, Professor Dr H. von Platen, Professor Dr E. Tillmanns, Professor Dr H.J. Tobschall

PALAEONTOLOGY DEPARTMENT   1131
Senior staff: Professor Dr D.E. Berg, Professor Dr J. Boy, Professor Dr K. Rothausen, Professor Dr N. Schmidt-Kittler

PRECIOUS STONES DEPARTMENT   1132
Head: Professor Dr J. Pense

FACULTY OF MATHEMATICS   1133

Address: Saarstrasse 21, D-6500 Mainz
Dean: Professor W. Bühler
Senior staff: Professor Dr B. Amberg, Professor Dr W. Börsch-Supan, Professor Dr K. Doerk, Professor Dr E. Gottschling, Professor Dr B. Gramsch, Professor Dr D. Held, Professor Dr A. Herzer, Professor Dr G. Hofmeister, Professor Dr B. Huppert, Professor Dr K. Kalb, Professor Dr P.P. Konder, Professor Dr M. Kreck, Professor Dr K.-J. Miescke, Professor Dr H. Mülthei, Professor Dr A. Pfister, Professor Dr H. Rüssmann, Professor Dr K.-J. Scheiba, Professor Dr G. Schleinkofer, Professor Dr U. Staude, Professor Dr K. Pommerening

History of Mathematics and Natural   1134
Sciences Team

Heads: Professor Dr F. Krafft, Professor Dr N. Stuloff

FACULTY OF MEDICINE   1135

Address: Langenbeckstrasse 1, D-6500 Mainz
Dean: Professor Dr Horst Leithhoff

Anaesthesiology Institute   1136

Address: Langenbeckstrasse 1, D-6500 Mainz
Director: Professor Dr R. Frey

Anatomy Institute   1137

Address: Saarstrasse 21, D-6500 Mainz
Directors: Professor Dr A. Mayet, Professor Dr L. Vollrath

Clinical Radiology Institute   1138

Address: Langenbeckstrasse 1, D-6500 Mainz
Director: Professor Dr M. Thelen

Dermatology Clinic   1139

Address: Langenbeckstrasse 1, D-6500 Mainz
Director: Professor Dr G.W. Korting

Diseases of the Teeth, Mouth and Jaw   1140
Clinic

Address: Augustusplatz 2, D-6500 Mainz
Department: Dental Materials and Technology, Professor Dr H. Marx

ORAL AND MAXILLO-FACIAL   1141
SURGERY INSTITUTE
Director: Professor Dr H. Scheunemann

ORTHODONTICS INSTITUTE   1142
Director: Professor Dr H.G. Sergl

PROSTHETIC DENTISTRY INSTITUTE   1143
Director: Professor Dr K. Fuhr

RESTORATIVE DENTISTRY INSTITUTE   1144
Director: Professor Dr W. Ketterl
dental prosthesis

Forensic Medicine Institute   1145

Address: Langenbeckstrasse 1, D-6500 Mainz
Director: Professor Dr H. Leithoff

History of Medicine Institute 1146

Address: Am Pulverturm, D-6500 Mainz
Director: Professor Dr G. Mann

Hygiene Institute 1147

Address: Obere Zahlbacherstrasse 67, D-6500 Mainz
Director: Professor Dr J. Borneff

Medical Clinic I and Outpatients Department 1148

Address: Langenbeckstrasse 1, D-6500 Mainz
Director: vacant
Department: Haematology, Professor Dr J. Fischer

Medical Clinic II and Outpatients Department 1149

Address: Langenbeckstrasse 1, D-6500 Mainz
Director: Professor Dr P. Schölmerich
Departments: Endocrinology, Professor Dr J. Beyer;
Physiotherapy and rheumatology, vacant; Pneumology,
Professor Dr R. Ferlinz

Medical Microbiology Institute 1150

Address: Obere Zahlbacherstrasse 67, D-6500 Mainz
Director: Professor Dr P. Klein

Medical Statistics and Documentation Institute 1151

Address: Obere Zahlbacherstrasse 69, D-6500 Mainz
Director: Professor Dr J. Michaelis

Neurology Clinic and Outpatients Department 1152

Address: Langenbeckstrasse 1, D-6500 Mainz
Director: Professor Dr H.Ch. Hopf

Neurosurgery Clinic 1153

Address: Langenbeckstrasse 1, D-6500 Mainz
Director: Professor Dr K. Schürmann

Obstetrics and Gynaecology Clinic 1154

Address: Langenbeckstrasse 1, D-6500 Mainz
Director: Professor Dr V. Friedberg

Occupational Medicine Institute 1155

Address: Langenbeckstrasse 1, D-6500 Mainz
Director: vacant

Ophthalmology Clinic 1156

Address: Langenbeckstrasse 1, D-6500 Mainz
Director: Professor Dr A. Nover

Orthopaedic Clinic 1157

Address: Langenbeckstrasse 1, D-6500 Mainz
Director: Professor Dr F. Brussatis

Otorhinolaryngology Clinic 1158

Address: Langenbeckstrasse 1, D-6500 Mainz
Director: Professor Dr J. Helms

Paediatric Clinic 1159

Address: Langenbeckstrasse 1, D-6500 Mainz
Director: Professor Dr J. Spranger

Pathological Anatomy Institute 1160

Address: Langenbeckstrasse 1, D-6500 Mainz
Director: Professor Dr W. Thoenes
Departments: Neuropathology, Professor Dr J.M.
Schröder; Paediatric pathology, Professor Dr H. Mün-
terfering

Pharmacology Institute 1161

Address: Obere Zahlbacherstrasse 67, D-6500 Mainz
Director: Professor Dr E. Muscholl
Departments: Toxicology, Professor Netter; Neuro-
pharmacology, vacant; Molecular pharmacology,
Professor Dr F. Oesch

Physiological Chemistry Institute 1162

Address: Saarstrasse 21, D-6500 Mainz
Directors: Professor Dr R. Zahn, Professor Dr K.-H.
Bässler

Physiology Institute 1163

Address: Saarstrasse 21, D-6500 Mainz
Directors: Professor Dr G. Thews, Professor Dr R.
Von Baumgarten

Psychiatric Clinic 1164

Address: Langenbeckstrasse 1, D-6500 Mainz
Director: vacant

Psychotherapy Clinic and Outpatients Department 1165

Address: Langenbeckstrasse 1, D-6500 Mainz
Director: vacant

Speech Disorders Clinic 1166

Address: Langenbeckstrasse 1, D-6500 Mainz
Director: Professor P. Biesalski

Surgical Clinic 1167

Address: Langenbeckstrasse 1, D-6500 Mainz
Director: Professor Dr F. Kümmerle

Urology Clinic 1168

Address: Langenbeckstrasse 1, D-6500 Mainz
Director: Professor Dr R. Hohenfellner

FACULTY OF PHARMACY 1169

Address: Saarstrasse 21, D-6500 Mainz
Telephone: (06131) 392519
Dean: Professor Dr Friedrich Moll

Pharmaceutical Biology Institute 1170

Address: Saarstrasse 21, D-6500 Mainz
Senior staff: Professor Dr Stopp, Professor Dr Eich

Pharmaceutical Chemistry Institute 1171

Address: Saarstrasse 21, D-6500 Mainz
Senior staff: Professor Dr Kreutzberger, Professor Dr Schunack, Professor Dr Back

Pharmaceutical Technology Institute 1172

Address: Saarstrasse 21, D-6500 Mainz
Head: Professor Dr F. Moll

Pharmacology Institute 1173

Address: Saarstrasse 21, D-6500 Mainz
Head: Professor Dr Wollert

FACULTY OF PHYSICS 1174

Address: Saarstrasse 21, D-6500 Mainz
Dean: Professor Dr Gernot Gräff

Meteorology Institute 1175

Director: Professor Dr Wilford Zdunkowski

Nuclear Physics Institute 1176

Director: Professor Dr H. Ehrenberg

Physics Institute 1177

Director: Professor Dr Florian Scheck

Justus Liebig-Universität Giessen 1178

[Giessen University]
Address: Postfach 111440, D-6300 Giessen
Telephone: (0641) 702-1
President: Professor Dr Karl Aleweh

FACULTY OF APPLIED BIOLOGY AND ENVIRONMENTAL PROTECTION 1179

Address: Bismarckstrasse 24, D-6300 Giessen
Telephone: (0641) 702 5960
Dean: Professor Dr Martin Zoschke

Microbiology and Land Cultivation Institute 1180

Address: Senckenbergstrasse 3, D-6300 Giessen
Telephone: (0641) 702 8330
Director: Professor Dr E. Küster
Sections: Agricultural microbiology, Professor Dr E. Ahrens
Land cultivation, Professor Dr R. Kowald

Phytopathology and Applied Zoology Institute 1181

Address: Ludwigstrasse 23, D-6300 Giessen
Telephone: (0641) 702 5965
Director: Professor Dr H. Schmutterer
Sections: Phytopathology, Professor Dr H. Schmutterer
Stock protection, Professor Dr W. Stein
Plant virology and molecular biology, Professor Dr H.-L. Sänger
Phytopathology and applied entomology in the tropics and subtropics, Professor Dr J. Kranz

GIESSEN RESEARCH STATION 1182

Address: Altersteinbacherweg 28, D-6300 Giessen
Telephone: (0641) 712 5973
Head: Dr J. Rössner

Plant Cultivation and Breeding   1183
Institute I

Address: Ludwigstrasse 23, D-6300 Giessen
Telephone: (0641) 702 5980
Director: Professor Dr W. Schuster
Sections: Plant cultivation and breeding in the tropics
and subtropics, Professor Dr J. Alkänaper

GIESSEN RESEARCH STATION   1184
Address: Weilburgergrenze 25, D-6300 Giessen
Telephone: (0641) 83236
Head: Professor Dr W. Jahn

GROSS-GERAN RESEARCH STATION   1185
Address: Am Woogsdammweg, D-6080 Gross-Geran
Telephone: (06152) 2694
Head: Professor Dr W. Schuster

RAUISCHOLZHAUSEN RESEARCH   1186
STATION
Address: Ebsdorfergrund 4, D-3557 Rauischolzhausen
Telephone: (06424) 2029
Head: Professor Dr M. Zoschke

Plant Cultivation and Breeding   1187
Institute II

Address: Ludwigstrasse 23 and 27, D-6300 Giessen
Telephone: (0641) 702 6010
Director: Professor Dr W. Gruppe
Sections: Pasture and fodder production, Professor Dr
U. Simon
Fruit cultivation and breeding, Professor Dr W. Gruppe
Biometry, Professor Dr W. Kohle

FRUIT CULTIVATION AND BREEDING   1188
RESEARCH STATION
Address: D-6369 Nidderau Heldenbergen
Telephone: (06187) 1437
Head: Professor Dr W. Gruppe

PASTURE AND FOOD PRODUCTION   1189
RESEARCH STATION
Address: Fannerweg 87, D-6301 Linden-Forst
Telephone: (06403) 61608
Head: Professor Dr U. Simon

Research Station for Vegetation   1190
Technology

Address: Gernarkung Am Rittergat, D-6301 Linden
Leihgestern

Soil Science and Conservation Institute   1191
Address: Wiesenstrasse 3-5, D-6300 Giessen
Telephone: (0641) 702 6081
Director: Professor Dr W. Moll
Section: Soil science and conservation in the tropics
and subtropics

FACULTY OF BIOLOGY   1192
Address: Heinrich-Buff-Ring 58, D-6300 Giessen
Telephone: (0641) 702 5825
Dean: Professor Dr Hans-Otto Schwantes

Animal Physiology Institute   1193
Address: Wartweg 95, D-6300 Giessen
Director: Professor Dr Günter Cleffmann
Sections: Cell and metabolic physiology, Professor Dr
Günter Cleffman
Brain physiology, Professor Dr Erick Schwartz

Anthropology Institute   1194
Address: Wartweg 49, D-6300 Giessen
Telephone: (0641) 702 5890
Director: Professor Dr Manfred Kunter

Botanical Garden   1195
Telephone: (0641) 702 8385
Head: Professor Dr Rüdiger Knapp

Edersee Ecological Research Station   1196
Telephone: (05634) 7373
Director: Dr Günter Fricke

General and Specialized Zoology   1197
Institute

Address: Stephanstrasse 24, D-6300 Giessen
Telephone: (0641) 702 5831
Director: Professor Dr Armin Wessing
Sections: Cytology and micromorphology, Professor
Dr Klaus-Jürgen Götting
Development and translocation of animals, Professor Dr
Armin Wessing
Specialized zoology, Professor Dr Gerhard Seifert
Ecology and animal systematics, Professor Dr Heinz
Scherf
Hydrobiology and ichthyology, Professor Dr Ernst F.
Killian

General Botany and Plant Physiology Institute   1198

Telephone: (0641) 702 8385
Director: Professor Dr Rudiger Knopp

GENERAL BOTANY   1199

Address: Senckenbergstrasse 17-25, D-6300 Giessen
Telephone: (0641) 702 8450
Head: Professor Dr F. Ringe
Sections: Morphology, anatomy, and development, Professor Dr F. Ringe
Systematic botany, Professor Dr Wolfgang Frey
Plant geography (geobotany) and hydrobotany, Professor Dr Rudiger Knapp
Membrane and movement physiology, Professor Dr Gottfried Wagner

PLANT PHYSIOLOGY   1200

Address: Heinrich-Buff-Ring 58, D-6300 Giessen
Telephone: (0641) 702 5935
Head: Professor Dr Klaus Zetsche
Sections: Metabolic and developmental physiology, Professor Dr Klaus Zetsche
Biochemistry of plants, Professor Dr Edwin Pahlich

Genetics Institute   1201

Telephone: (0641) 702 5900
Director: vacant

Plant Ecology Institute   1202

Telephone: (0641) 702 5865
Director: Professor Dr Lore Steubing
Sections: Experimental ecology, Professor Dr Hans-Jürgen Jäger
Ecology of microorganisms, Professor Dr Hans-Otto Schwantes

FACULTY OF CHEMISTRY   1203

Address: Heinrich-Buff-Ring 58, D-6300 Giessen
Dean: Professor Dr Rudolf Hoppe

Inorganic and Analytical Chemistry Institute   1204

Telephone: (0641) 702 5660
Director: Professor Dr Rudolf Hoppe

Inorganic Chemistry I   1205

Head: Professor Dr Christoph Hebecker

Inorganic Chemistry II   1206

Head: Professor Dr Reginald Gruehn

Organic Chemistry Institute   1207

Telephone: (0641) 702 5710
Director: Professor Dr Günther Maier

Physical Chemistry Institute   1208

Telephone: (0641) 702 5771
Director: Professor Dr Wolfhart Seidel

FACULTY OF FOOD ECONOMICS AND HOUSEHOLD SCIENCES   1209

Address: Bismarckstrasse 24, D-6300 Giessen
Telephone: (0641) 702 6180
Dean: Professor Dr Hartwig Spitzer

Agricultural Engineering Institute   1210

Address: Braugasse 7, D-6300 Giessen
Telephone: (0641) 702 8430
Director: Professor Dr Horst Eichhorn

Agricultural Management Institute   1211

Address: Senckenbergstrasse 3, D-6300 Giessen
Telephone: (0641) 702 8358
Director: Professor Dr Miklós-Géza Zitahi-Szabó

Agricultural Policy and Market Research Institute   1212

Address: Senckenbergstrasse 3, D-6300 Giessen
Telephone: (0641) 702 8300
Director: Professor Dr Egon Wöhlken

Home Economics and Consumer Research Institute   1213

Address: Diezstrasse 15, D-6300 Giessen
Telephone: (0641) 702 6100
Director: Professor Dr Jörg Bottler

Rural Communities Institute   1214

Address: Senckenbergstrasse 3, D-6300 Giessen
Telephone: (0641) 702 8350
Director: Professor Dr Horst Seuster

FACULTY OF GEOSCIENCES AND GEOGRAPHY 1215

Address: Schlossgasse 7, D-6300 Giessen
Telephone: (0641) 702 8214
Dean: Professor Dr Gert Jahn

Geology and Mineralogy Institute 1216

Address: Senckenbergstrasse 3, D-6300 Giessen
Telephone: (0641) 702 8360
Director: Professor Dr G. Strübel
Sections: General, historical and regional geology, Professor Dr F. Stibane
Palaeontology, Professor Dr W. Blind
Engineering geology and hydrogeology, Professor Dr K. Knoblich
Mineralogy and petrology, Professor Dr G. Strübel

FACULTY OF HUMAN MEDICINE 1217

Address: Rudolf-Buchheim-Strasse 8, D-6300 Giessen
Telephone: (0641) 702 3000
Dean: Professor Dr Dieter Ringleb

Anatomy and Cytobiology Institute 1218

Address: Aulweg 123, D-6300 Giessen
Telephone: (0641) 702 3940
Director: Professor Dr A. Oksche

Biochemistry Institute 1219

Address: Friedrichstrasse 24, D-6300 Giessen
Telephone: (0641) 702 4102
Director: Professor Dr G. Grundlach

Clinical Chemistry, Immunology, and Human Genetics Centre 1220

Telephone: (0641) 702 4180
Director: Professor Dr L. Róka

CLINICAL CHEMISTRY AND PATHOBIOCHEMISTRY INSTITUTE 1221

Address: Klinikstrasse 32b, D-6300 Giessen
Telephone: (0641) 702 4180
Director: Professor Dr L. Róka

HUMAN GENETICS INSTITUTE 1222

Address: Am Schlangenzahl 14, D-6300 Giessen
Telephone: (0641) 702 4145
Director: Professor Dr W. Fuhrmann

TRANSFUSION MEDICINE AND CLINICAL IMMUNOLOGY INSTITUTE 1223

Address: Langhanstrasse 7, D-6300 Giessen
Telephone: (0641) 702 4160
Director: Professor Dr C. Mueller-Eckhard

Dermatology, Andrology, and Venereology Centre 1224

Address: Gaffkystrasse 14, D-6300 Giessen
Telephone: (0641) 702 3520
Director: Professor Dr L. Illig
Sections: Dermatology, Professor Dr L. Illig
Andrology and venereology, Professor Dr W. Meyhöfer

Environmental Health Centre 1225

Telephone: (0641) 702 4210
Director: Professor Dr E.G. Beck

FORENSIC MEDICINE INSTITUTE 1226

Address: Frankfurterstrasse 58A, D-6300 Giessen
Telephone: (0641) 702 4225
Head: Professor Dr Dr G. Schewe

HYGIENE INSTITUTE 1227

Address: Friedrichstrasse 16, D-6300 Giessen
Telephone: (0641) 702 4210
Head: Professor Dr E.G. Beck

OCCUPATIONAL AND SOCIAL MEDICINE 1228

Address: Aulweg 129/III, D-6300 Giessen
Telephone: (0641) 702 4240
Head: Professor Dr H.-J. Woitowitz

Gynaecology and Obstetrics Centre 1229

Address: Klinikstrasse 32, D-6300 Giessen
Telephone: (0641) 702 3300
Director: Professor Dr W. Künzel
Sections: Gynaecology, Professor Dr W. Künzel
Gynaecological oncology and radiation therapy, Professor Dr H. Vahrson

Internal Medicine Centre 1230

Address: Klinikstrasse 36, D-6300 Giessen
Telephone: (0641) 702 3600
Director: Professor Dr H.G. Lasch
Sections: Medical clinic I, Professor Dr H.G. Lasch
Medical Clinic II, Professor Dr G. Schütterle
Medical Clinic III and Polyclinic, Professor Dr K. Federlin

Medical Microbiology Institute   1231

Address: Frankfurterstrasse 107, D-6300 Giessen
Telephone: (0641) 702 4530
Head: Professor Dr H.-J. Wellensiek

Medical Statistics and Documentation   1232
Institute

Address: Heinrich-Buff-Ring 44, D-6300 Giessen
Telephone: (0641) 702 4500
Director: Professor Dr J. Dudeck

Medical Technology Institute   1233

Address: Aulweg 123, D-6300 Giessen
Telephone: (0641) 702 2695
Director: Professor Dr Ing Werner Irnich

Neurology Centre   1234

Address: Am Steg 22, D-6300 Giessen
Telephone: (0641) 702 3900
Director: Professor Dr K. Kunze
Sections: Neurology, Professor Dr W. Dorndorf
Clinical neurophysiology, Professor Dr K. Kunze
Neuropathology, Professor Dr Dr H. Hager

Neurosurgery Centre   1235

Address: Klinikstrasse 29, D-6300 Giessen
Telephone: (0641) 702 4300
Director: Professor Dr Dr H.W. Pia

Orthopaedics Clinic   1236

Address: Freiligrathstrasse 2, D-6300 Giessen
Telephone: (0641) 702 4250
Director: Professor Dr H. Rettig

Otorhinolaryngology and   1237
Ophthalmology Centre

Address: Friedrichstrasse 18, D-6300 Giessen
Director: Professor Dr K.W. Jacobi
Sections: General ophthalmology, Professor Dr K.W. Jacobi
Pleioptics, orthoptics, and motor disturbances of the eye, Professor Dr H. Kaufmann
Ear, nose and throat clinic, Professor Dr K. Fleischer

Paediatrics Centre   1238

Address: Feulgenstrasse 12, D-6300 Giessen
Telephone: (0641) 702 4400
Director: Professor Dr H. Wolf
Sections: General paediatrics, Professor Dr H. Wolf
Paediatric Polyclinic, Professor Dr F. Lampert

Neonatology, Professor Dr H. Wolf
Child cardiology, Professor Dr H.W. Rautenburg
Paediatric neurology, Professor Dr G. Neuhäuser

Pathology Centre   1239

Address: Langhangstrasse 10, D-6300 Giessen
Telephone: (0641) 702 4070
Director: Professor Dr J. Kracht

Physical Medicine and Balneology   1240
Institute and Clinic

Address: Ludwigstrasse 37-39, D-6350 Bad Nauheim
Telephone: (06032) 8981
Director: vacant
Section: Water chemistry and chemical balneology, Dr D. Dreschler

Physiology Institute   1241

Address: Aulweg 129, D-6300 Giessen
Telephone: (0641) 702 4550
Director: Professor Dr K. Brück

Psychosomatic Medicine Centre   1242

Address: Ludwigstrasse 76, D-6300 Giessen
Telephone: (0641) 702 2463
Director: Professor Dr Dr H.-E. Richter
Sections: Psychosomatics and psychotherapy, Professor Dr Dr H.-E. Richter
Medical psychology, Professor Dr D. Beckmann
Medical sociology, Professor Dr U. Gerhardt

Radiology Centre   1243

Address: Klinikstrasse 29, D-6300 Giessen
Telephone: (0641) 702 3434
Director: Professor Dr S. Bayindir
Sections: Radiology clinic (radiation therapy), Professor Dr G. Barth
Radiation protection and biology, Professor Dr L. Rausch
Radiological surgery, Professor Dr S. Bayindir
Neuroradiology, Dr A.L. Aguoli
Paediatric radiology, Professor Dr W. Schuster
Internal medical radiology, Professor Dr J. Altaras

Rudolf-Buchheim Institute for   1244
Pharmacology

Address: Frankfurterstrasse 107, D-6300 Giessen
Telephone: (0641) 702 4135
Director: Professor Dr E.R. Habermann

Surgery Centre 1245

Address: Klinikstrasse 29, D-6300 Giessen
Telephone: (0641) 702 3400
Director: Professor Dr C.F. Rothauge
Sections: General surgery, Professor Dr K. Schwemmle
Cardiovascular surgery, Professor Dr F. Hehrlein
Accident surgery, Professor Dr H. Ecke
Anaesthesiology and intensive care, Professor Dr G. Hempelmann
Orology, Professor Dr C.F. Rothauge

Tooth, Mouth, and Jaw Centre 1246

Address: Schlangenzahl 14, D-6300 Giessen
Telephone: (0641) 702 3200
Director: Professor Dr H. Pantke
Sections: Conservative dentistry, Professor Dr H. Pantke
Parodontology, Professor Dr H.-C. Plagmann
Preventive and child dental care, vacant
Dental prosthesis, Professor Dr E. Pfutz
Dental surgery and polyclinic, Professor Dr H. Kirschner
Orthodontics, Professor Dr U.-G. Fammoscheit
Prosthetics, Professor Dr R. Horn
Dental surgery, Professor Dr Dr G.G. Lorber
Experimental conservative dentistry, Professor Dr H.-J. Oehmke

Virology Institute 1247

Address: Frankfurterstrasse 107, D-6300 Giessen
Telephone: (0641) 702 2870
Director: Professor Dr H. Bauer

FACULTY OF MATHEMATICS 1248

Address: Arndtstrasse 2, D-6300 Giessen
Telephone: (0641) 702 2530
Dean: Professor Dr Siegfried Fillipi

Mathematics Institute 1249

Telephone: (0641) 702 2545
Director: Professor Dr Dieter Gaier

FACULTY OF NUTRITIONAL SCIENCES 1250

Address: Bismarckstrasse 24, D-6300 Giessen
Telephone: (0641) 702 6020
Dean: Professor Dr Karl-Hermann Neumann

Animal Nutrition Institute 1251

Address: Senckenbergstrasse 5, D-6300 Giessen
Telephone: (0641) 702 8220
Director: Professor Dr Heinrich Brune

Nutritional Science Institute 1252

Address: Wilhelmstrasse 20, D-6300 Giessen
Telephone: (0641) 702 6025
Director: Professor Dr Erich Menden

Plant Nutrition Institute 1253

Address: Südantaye 6, D-6300 Giessen
Telephone: (0641) 702 8480
Director: Professor Dr Konrad Mengel

FACULTY OF PHYSICS 1254

Address: Heinrich-Buff-Ring 16, D-6300 Giessen
Telephone: (0641) 702 2750
Dean: Professor Dr Walter Biem

Applied Physics 1255

Telephone: (0641) 702 2791
Director: Professor Dr Christoph Heiden

Nuclear Physics Institute, Department 1256 of Heavy Apparatus, Biophysics Institute

See entry under: Radiation Centre.

Physics Institute I 1257

Address: Heinrich-Buff-Ring 14-20, D-6300 Giessen
Telephone: (0641) 702 2710
Director: Professor Dr Arthur Scharmann

Physics Institute II 1258

Address: Arndtstrasse 2, D-6300 Giessen
Telephone: (0641) 702 2760
Director: Professor Dr Hermann Wollnik

Theoretical Physics Institute 1259

Telephone: (0641) 702 2800
Director: Professor Dr Werner Scheid

FACULTY OF VETERINARY MEDICINE 1260 AND ANIMAL BREEDING

Address: Frankfurterstrasse 94, D-6300 Giessen
Telephone: (0641) 702 4700
Dean: Professor Dr Rudolf Wassmuth

Ambulatory and Obstetric Veterinary 1261 Clinic

Address: Frankfurterstrasse 106, D-6300 Giessen
Telephone: (0641) 702 4715
Director: Professor Dr H. Bostedt

Animal Breeding and Domestic Animal 1262 Genetics Institute

Address: Bismarckstrasse 16, D-6300 Giessen
Telephone: (0641) 702 6135
Director: Professor Dr K. Wassmuth
Sections: Animal breeding, Professor Dr K.-H. Finger
Milk production, Professor Dr E. Renner
Ecology of domestic animals in the tropics and subtropics, Professor Dr J. Steinbach

OBERER HARDTHOF TEACHING AND 1263 RESEARCH STATION
Head: Professor Dr R. Wassmuth

RUDLOS TEACHING AND RESEARCH 1264 STATION
Telephone: (06641) 2335
Head: Professor Dr R. Wassmuth

Bacteriology and Immunology Institute 1265

Address: Frankfurterstrasse 107, D-6300 Giessen
Telephone: (0641) 702 4831
Director: Professor Dr H. Blobel

Biochemistry and Endocrinology 1266 Institute

Address: Frankfurterstrasse 100, D-6300 Giessen
Telephone: (0641) 702 4841
Director: Professor Dr W. Schoner
Sections: Applied biology and clinical laboratory diagnosis, Professor Dr M. Sernetz
Biomathematics, Professor Dr N. Victor

Breeding Hygiene, Veterinary 1267 Genetics, and Tropical Veterinary Medicine Institute

BREEDING HYGIENE AND 1268 VETERINARY GENETICS

Address: Hofmannstrasse 10, D-6300 Giessen
Telephone: (0641) 702 6150
Director: Professor Dr G.W. Rieck

TROPICAL VETERINARY MEDICINE 1269

Address: Wilhelmstrasse 15, D-6300 Giessen
Telephone: (0641) 702 6155
Director: Professor Dr H. Fischer

Hygiene and Infectious Diseases of 1270 Animals Institute

Address: Frankfurterstrasse 89, D-6300 Giessen
Telephone: (0641) 702 4870
Director: Professor Dr T. Schliesser

Medical and Forensic Veterinary Clinic 1271 and Medical Polyclinic

INTERNAL VETERINARY MEDICINE I 1272

Address: Frankfurterstrasse 126, D-6300 Giessen
Telephone: (0641) 702 4764
Director: Professor Dr H. Eikmeier

INTERNAL VETERINARY MEDICINE II 1273 (RUMINANT DISEASES)

Address: Frankfurterstrasse 110, D-6300 Giessen
Director: Professor Dr H.-D. Gründer

Parasitology Institute 1274

Address: Rudolf-Buchheim-Strasse 2, D-6300 Giessen
Telephone: (0641) 702 4911
Director: Professor Dr G. Lämmler

Pharmacology and Toxicology Institute 1275

Address: Frankfurterstrasse 107, D-6300 Giessen
Telephone: (0641) 702 4950
Director: Professor Dr M. Frimmer

Poultry Diseases Institute 1276

Address: Frankfurterstrasse 85, D-6300 Giessen
Telephone: (0641) 702 4865
Director: Professor Dr H. Geissler

Surgical Veterinary Clinic and 1277 Polyclinic

Address: Frankfurterstrasse 108, D-6300 Giessen
Telephone: (0641) 702 4736
Director: Professor Dr R. Fritsch

Veterinary Anatomy, Histology, and Embryology Institute 1278

Address: Frankfurterstrasse 98, D-6300 Giessen
Telephone: (0641) 702 4806
Director: Professor Dr H. Goller

Veterinary Foodstuffs Science Institute 1279

Address: Frankfurterstrasse 92, D-6300 Giessen
Telephone: (0641) 702 4975
Director: Professor Dr R. Haddlok
Sections: Hygiene and milk technology, Professor Dr G. Kielwein

Veterinary Pathology Institute 1280

Telephone: (0641) 702 4925
Director: Professor Dr E. Weiss

Veterinary Physiology Institute 1281

Address: Frankfurterstrasse 100, D-6300 Giessen
Telephone: (0641) 702 4961
Director: Professor Dr H. Eder

Virology Institute 1282

Address: Frankfurterstrasse 107, D-6300 Giessen
Telephone: (0641) 702 4991
Director: Professor Dr R. Rott

UNIVERSITY CENTRES 1283

Computer Centre 1284

Address: Heinrich-Buff-Ring 44, D-6300 Gieasen
Director: Dr Joseph Hammerschick

Continental Agricultural and Economic Research Centre 1285

Address: Otto-Behaghel-Strasse 1O/D, D-6300 Giessen
Telephone: (0641) 702 2655
Director: Professor Dr E. Schinke
Sections: Soil science and conservation, Professor Dr J. Breburda
Plant cultivation and breeding, Professor Dr J. Breburda
Animal breeding and husbandry, Professor Dr K.H. Finger
Veterinary medicine, Professor Dr T. Schliesser
Agricultural and nutritional economy, Professor Dr E. Schinke

Radiation Centre 1286

Address: Leihgesternerweg 217, D-6300 Giessen
Telephone: (0641) 702 2590
Director: Professor Dr W. Lohmann
Sections: Radiation protection, Dr W. Reiser
Central department, Professor Dr E.L. Sattler
Linear accelerator, W. Arnold
Computing, Dr K. Huber

BIOPHYSICS INSTITUTE 1287

Telephone: (0641) 702 2600
Director: Professor Dr W. Lohmann

NUCLEAR PHYSICS INSTITUTE 1288

Telephone: (0641) 702 2655
Director: Professor Dr G. Clausnitzer
Section: Heavy apparatus (applied nuclear physics), Professor Dr H. Schneider

Tropics Institute of the Sciences Centre 1289

Address: Wilhelmstrasse 15, D-6300 Giessen
Telephone: (0641) 702 6155
Director: Professor Dr H. Fischer
Sections: Geography of the tropics, Professor Dr W. Haffner
Tropical veterinary medicine, Professor Dr H. Fischer
Tropical agricultural sciences, Professor Dr W. Moll

Kernforschungsanlage Jülich GmbH 1290

[Jülich Nuclear Research Centre]
Address: Postfach 1913, D-5170 Jülich
Director: H.H. Haunschild
Activities: Development of high-temperature reactor and its applications for producing electricity, district heating, and coal gasification; reactor development, reactor materials, reactor components, reactor experiments, fuel element technology, nuclear safety, nuclear physics, solid-state research, plasma physics, vacuum physics, interface research, nuclear technology; physical and analytical chemistry, medicine, biology, biochemistry, neurobiology, radio-agronomy, research reactors, applied mathematics, electronics, general technology, systems research and technology development.

CENTRAL DIVISION OF CHEMICAL ANALYSES 1291

Head: Professor B. Sanson

CENTRAL DIVISION OF FUEL ELEMENT AND IRRADIATION TECHNOLOGY   1292

Head: Dr S. Krawczynski

CENTRAL DIVISION OF GENERAL TECHNOLOGY   1293

Head: Dipl-Ing W. Lehrheur

CENTRAL DIVISION OF HEALTH PHYSICS   1294

Head: Dr M. Keller

CENTRAL DIVISION OF RESEARCH REACTORS   1295

Head: Dr H. Friedewold

CENTRAL INSTITUTE OF APPLIED MATHEMATICS   1296

Head: Dr F. Hossfeld

CENTRAL LABORATORY OF ELECTRONICS   1297

Heads: Dr K.K. Müller; Dipl-Ing K.F. Rittinghaus

INSTITUTE OF AGRONOMY   1298

Head: Professor Dr F. Führ

INSTITUTE OF CHEMICAL TECHNOLOGY   1299

Head: Professor Dr E. Merz

INSTITUTE OF CHEMISTRY   1300

Heads: Professor Dr D. Ehalt, Professor Dr H.W. Nürnberg, Professor Dr G. Stöcklin, Professor Dr D. Welte

INSTITUTE OF MEDICINE   1301

Head: Professor Dr L.E. Feinendegen

INSTITUTE OF NEUROBIOLOGY   1302

Head: Professor Dr H. Stieve

INSTITUTE OF NUCLEAR PHYSICS   1303

Heads: Professor Dr Claus Mayer-Böricke; Professor Dr O. Schult

INSTITUTE OF NUCLEAR SAFETY RESEARCH   1304

Head: Dr J. Fassbender

INSTITUTE OF PLASMA PHYSICS   1305

Heads: Dr E. Hintz, F. Wallbroeck, Dr G. Wolf

INSTITUTE OF REACTOR COMPONENTS   1306

Head: Professor C.B. von der Decken

INSTITUTE OF REACTOR DEVELOPMENT   1307

Heads: Dr R. Hecker; Professor R. Schulten

INSTITUTE OF REACTOR MATERIALS AND HOT CELLS   1308

Head: Professor H. Nickel

INSTITUTE OF SOLID-STATE RESEARCH   1309

Heads: Professor Dr G. Eilenberger, Professor Dr K. Binder, Professor Dr W. Schilling, Professor Dr H.H. Stiller, Professor Dr F. Pobell, Professor Dr W. Zinn, Dr H. Wenzl, Professor Dr M. Campagua

INSTITUTE OF SURFACE AND VACUUM RESEARCH   1310

Heads: Professor Dr G. Comsa, Dr H. Ibach

TECHNICAL SERVICES   1311

Head: W. Anger

Kernforschungszentrum Karlsruhe GmbH 1312

[Nuclear Research Centre Karlsruhe]
Address: Postfach 3640, D-7500 Karlsruhe
Telephone: (07247) 821
Telex: 7826484
Affiliation: Karlsruhe-Technische Hochschule
Chairman: Professor Dr R. Harde
Deputy Chairman of the Executive Board, Commercial and Administrative Matters, Infrastructure: Dr Hellmut Wagner
Graduate research staff: 830
Annual expenditure: DM470m
Activities: The Karlsruhe Nuclear Research Centre is mainly engaged in research and development, especially in the field of nuclear technology. This includes the construction of semitechnical pilot plants and their operation, sometimes in cooperation with industry.
Two-thirds of the research and development potential are reserved for project work carried out in close cooperation with national and international research institutions and partners from industry, or with authorities responsible for licensing and safety. The remaining capacity is used for basic and applied research, and for development in fields which could lead to future projects.
All research and development at the Nuclear Research Centre is combined in eleven main activities, which can be assigned to one or more of the following four objectives of research policies: securing the supply of nuclear fuel; back-end fuel cycle services; safety of nuclear facilities; generation of knowledge in basic research and for new technologies.
Note: The following Institutes are associated with the Centre: Institute for Food Preservation Technology European Transuranium Institute
Energy, Physics, Mathematics Information Centre.
Contract work: No
Publications: Research report.

EXECUTIVE DIVISION I: REACTOR DEVELOPMENT AND REACTOR SAFETY 1313

Head: Dr Hans-Henning Hennies

Department for Engineering 1314

Head: Dr Ing W.P. Schmidt

Department for Security 1315

Heads: Professor Dr H. Kiefer, Professor Dr Koelzer

Institute for Neutron Physics and Reactor Engineering 1316

Head: Dr Kessler

Institute for Reactor Components 1317

Head: Professor Dr U. Müller

Institute for Reactor Development 1318

Head: Professor Dr D. Smidt

Laboratory for Aerosol Physics and Filter Technology 1319

Heads: Dr Schikarski, Dr chem Wilhelm

Project - Fast Breeder 1320

Head: Dr W. Marth

Project - HDR Safety Programme 1321

Head: Dr D. Gupta

Project - Nuclear Safety 1322

Head: Dr Rininsland

EXECUTIVE DIVISION II: FUEL CYCLE AND MATERIALS RESEARCH 1323

Head: Professor Dr Horst Böhm

Institute for Hot Chemistry 1324

Head: Professor Dr Ebert

Institute for Materials and Solid-State Research 1325

Heads: Professor Dr F. Thümmler, Dr K. Kummerer, Dr Anderko

Institute for Nuclear Engineering 1326

Head: Professor Dr W.E. Becker

Institute for Radiochemistry 1327

Head: Professor Dr Seelemann-Eggebert

Institute for Waste Management Research 1328

Head: Dr H. Krause

Project - Reprocessing and Waste   **1329**
Management

Head: Dr R. Kroebel

Project - Uranium-Isotope Separation   **1330**

Head: Dr D. Schubert

EXECUTIVE DIVISION III: NEW   **1331**
TECHNOLOGIES AND BASIC
RESEARCH

Head: Professor Dr Wolfgang Klose

Department for Applied Systems   **1332**
Analysis

Head: Dr Paschen

Institute for Applied Nuclear Physics   **1333**

Heads: Professor Dr Schmatz, Professor Dr G. Schatz

Institute for Data Processing in   **1334**
Technology

Head: Professor Dr H. Trauboth

Institute for Genetics and Toxicology   **1335**
of Fissile Materials

Heads: Professor Herrlich, Professor Taylor

Institute for Nuclear Physics   **1336**

Heads: Professor Dr B. Zeitnitz, Professor Dr A. Citron

Institute for Technical Physics   **1337**

Head: Professor Dr W. Heinz

Laboratory for Isotope Technology   **1338**

Head: Dr H. Vogg

Fried Krupp GmbH   1339

Address: Altendorferstrasse 103, D-4300 Essen 1
Telephone: (0201) 1881
Telex: 857385
Member of the Executive Board (Research and Development): Dipl Volkswirt Helmut Metzger
Activities: Steelmaking and special alloys; mechanical

engineering and electronics; plantmaking for the mining, iron and steel, chemical and other industries; shipbuilding. Research and development is concentrated on improving and developing the products, processes and systems and on medium- and long-term research for future products. Research and development is carried out at the Krupp Forschungsinstitut, the Central Research and Development Institute, in charge of material research and engineering and process research, and also in the technological laboratories of the production units.
Contract work: No
Publications: Technische Mitteilungen Krupp - Forschungsberichte.

KRUPP RESEARCH INSTITUTE   1340

Address: Münchenerstrasse 100, D-4300 Essen 1
Research director: Dr Ing Jürgen Hartwig
Graduate research staff: 100
Annual expenditure: over £2m
Activities: Physics, including technical physics, electronics, and metals research; chemistry, including chemical and spectral analysis; metallurgy, including metallography, microprobes, structural experiments; specialized materials, including powder metallurgy, alloy technology and special alloys; magnets, including permanent and soft magnets; materials processing technology, including preparation of raw materials, thermal and mechanical processes, biotechnology and water treatment; metallurgical processing; process regulation and control, including measurement technology; apparatus construction, including applied mathematics, tension analysis, testing of building materials, technical mechanics; machine design, including transport systems, machine parts and systems, and testing installations; manufacturing technology, including welding and casting, bonding materials, and materials testing.

Kuratorium für Forschung   1341
im Küsteningenieurwesen

– KFKI
[Coastal Engineering Research Council]
Address: Feldstrasse 251/253, Postfach 4448, D-2300 Kiel 1
Telephone: (0431) 362061-200
Research director: Dr Ing Rohde
General Secretary: Dipl-Ing Sindern
Annual expenditure: £51 000-500 000
Activities: KFKI is an institution set up by the Federal Government to carry out the following tasks: to establish a comprehensive long-term programme for government-sponsored coastal engineering research and

data acquisition; to initiate and judge research proposals; to coordinate research projects; to arrange for the cooperation of different government institutions dealing with coastal engineering research and to submit its recommendations, as well as the related financial requirements, to the respective government departments.
Contract work: No
Publications: Die Küste (Archive for Research and Technology on the North Sea and Baltic Coast).

Landes- Lehr- und Forschungsanstalt für Landwirtschaft, Weinbau und Gartenbau 1342

[Education and Research Centre for Agriculture, Viticulture and Horticulture]
Address: Breitenweg 71, D-6730 Neustadt um der Weinstrasse-Mussbach
Telephone: (06321) 671
Affiliation: Ministerium für Landwirtschaft, Weinbau und Forsten, Rheinland-Pfalz
Director: Dr Karl Adams
Sections: Chemistry and oenology, Dr L. Jakob; botany and biochemistry, Dr N. Beran; plant protection, Dr K.W. Eichhorn; virus disease, Dr H. Brückbauer; viticulture, Dr W. Fader; horticulture, Dr K. Schwarz
Graduate research staff: 18
Annual expenditure: £50 000-500 000
Contract work: Yes
Publications: Annual report.

Landesamt für Wasserhaushalt und Küsten Schleswig-Holstein 1343

[Schleswig-Holstein Regional Office for Water Conservation and Coasts]
Address: Saarbrückenstrasse 38, D-2300 Kiel 1
Telephone: (0431) 66097
Telex: 0292751 melf Kiel
Affiliation: Ministerium für Ernährung, Landwirtschaft und Forsten des Landes Schleswig-Holstein
Research director: Peter Petersen
Sections: Water chemistry, Dr Erik Brandt; sand flats morphology, Dr Ing E. Renger
Annual expenditure: £51 000-500 000
Activities: Quality control of inland and coastal waters; precipitation, drainage, evaporation, ground water formation, sand flats morphology.

Contract work: No
Publications: Gewässerüberwachung, half yearly report.

AFFILIATED INSTITUTE: 1344

Regional Office for Nature and Landscape Conservation 1345

Address: Hansaring 3, D-2300 Kiel Wellsee

Landesanstalt für Fischerei Nordrhein-Westfalen 1346

[North Rhine-Westphalia Fisheries Department]
Address: D-5942 Kirchhundem 1 Albaum
Telephone: (02723) 2085
Parent body: Ministry for Alimentation, Agriculture and Forests of the State of North Rhine-Westphalia
Director: Dr Harald Ungemach
Sections: Sewage, Dr H. Ungemach; fish biology, Dr Schmidt; fish diseases, Dr Lehmann
Annual expenditure: £10 000-50 000
Activities: Ecological effects of sewage, fish-testing, tropical limnology electric fishing; inland fisheries, freshwater fish culture, trout genetics, fish diseases; water insects.
Contract work: No

Landesanstalt für Immissionsschutz des Landes Nordrhein-Westfalen 1347

[State Centre for Air Pollution Control and Prevention of Noise and Vibration in North Rhine-Westphalia]
Address: Wallneyer Strasse 6, D-4300 Essen-Bredeney
Telephone: (0201) 79951
President: Professor Dr H. Stratmann
Activities: Air quality surveillance, abatement of harmful emissions, effects of air pollutants, protection against noise and vibration.

Landesanstalt für Ökologie, 1348 Landschaftsentwicklung und Forstplanung des Landes NW, Abteilung Grünland- und Futterbauforschung

[North Rhine-Westphalia Department for Ecology, Environmental Development and Forest Planning, Pastures and Fodder Section]
Address: Zum Breijpott 15, D-4190 Kleve-Kellen
Research director: Dr Norbert Mott
Activities: Permanent pastures, cultivation of field forage crops including intercropping; fodder conservation; mapping of grassland vegetation.

Landesanstalt für 1349 Pflanzenbau und Tabakforschung Forchheim

[Forchheim Research Centre for Horticulture and Tobacco]
Address: Kutschenweg 10, D-7512 Rheinstetten 4
Telephone: (0721) 511 91
Parent body: Ministerium für Ernährung, Landwirtschaft, Umwelt und Forsten, Baden-Württemberg
Director: Dr Josef A. Schmidt
Sections:
Chemistry of tobacco and tobacco smoke, Dr Peter Range
Analysis of tobacco and pesticide residues, Dr Dieter Fischbach
Tobacco breeding, Dr Willy Reisch
Biology, microbiology and plant protection, Dr Friedrich Vogel
Horticulture, Dr Karl-Hermann Martin
Graduate research staff: 7
Annual expenditure: £51 000-500 000
Activities: Research into all areas of tobacco production and breeding; seed cultivation and analysis.
Contract work: Yes
Publications: Two yearly report.

Landesanstalt für 1350 Umweltschutz Baden-Württemberg

[Baden-Württemberg Centre for Environmental Protection]
Address: Griesbachstrasse 3, Postfach 21 07 52, D-7500 Karlsruhe 21
Telephone: (0721) 5986 1
Telex: 07-826715
Parent body: Bundesministerium für Ernährung, Landwirtschaft, Umwelt und Forsten, Baden-Württemberg
President: Dr Helmut Prassler
Graduate research staff: 110
Activities: Research into all areas of environmental protection.
Contract work: Yes

LAKES RESEARCH AND FISHERIES 1351 INSTITUTE

Address: Untere Seestrasse 81, D-7994 Langenargen
Telephone: (07543) 2013
Research director: Dr Zahner
Sections:
Pure and applied hydrology, Dr Zahner
Fisheries research, Dr Deufel
Graduate research staff: 18
Annual expenditure: £51 000-500 000
Activities: Hydrobiology, sedimentology, hydrochemistry, metabolism of nutrients, fisheries biology, fish pathology; eutrophication in lakes and its influences on fish; lake management.
Contract work: No

Landesinstitut für 1352 Arbeitsmedizin

[Occupational Medicine State Institute]
Address: Soorstrasse 83, D-1000 Berlin 19
Telephone: (030) 302 50 26
Research director: Dr med Reinhard Bauer
Graduate research staff: 3
Annual expenditure: £51 000-500 000
Activities: Occupational hygiene, occupational medicine, research into occupational diseases and people suffering from occupation-related conditions; advisory activities according to the Seventh Occupational Diseases Act; investigations into and clarification of particular occupational medicine questions.
Contract work: No

Lehr- und Versuchsanstalt 1353 für Gartenbau Ahlem

[Ahlem Experimental and Training Centre for Horticultural Science]
Address: Harenberger Strasse 130, D-3000 Hannover 91
Telephone: (0511) 1665751
Research director: Dr H.C. Scharpf
Sections: Ornamental plant cultivation; vegetable crop cultivation
Graduate research staff: 3
Activities: Horticultural substrates; fertilizer needs; irrigation systems; variety trials; temperature trials; culture method experiments; plant protection experiments; glasshouses.
Contract work: No

Lehr- und Versuchsanstalt 1354 für Gartenbau Wolbeck

[Wolbeck Horticultural School and Research Station]
Address: Münsterstrasse 24, D-4400 Münster
Telephone: (02506) 1041
Affiliation: Westphalia-Lippe Chamber of Agriculture
Research director: Dr M. Schenk
Graduate research staff: 4
Annual expenditure: £51 000-500 000
Activities: Evaluation of varieties and investigation of temperature effects on plants; plant nutrition; development of horticultural pot substrates; tray irrigation of pot plants; soilless culture of crops and pot plants; flower induction as affected by light and temperature.
Contract work: Yes

Linde Aktiengesellschaft 1355

Address: Abraham-Lincoln-Strasse 21, D-6200 Wiesbaden
Telephone: (06121) 7701
Telex: 4186833 lind d
Chairman of the Executives Board: Dr Meinhardt
Graduate research staff: 100
Annual expenditure: over £2m
Contract work: No
Publications: Linde-Berichte aus Technik und Wissenschaft; Linde-heute; Jahresbericht.

COLD STORES DIVISION 1356

Activities: Research and development of cold storage technology, including chilling, freezing and cold storage of foods and industrial products; fruit processing.

GÜLDNER ASCHAFFENBERG DIVISION 1357

Activities: Research and development of material handling equipment and hydraulic components, including combustion-engine fork lift trucks; electric-motor fork lift trucks; stackers; industrial tractors; platform trucks; hydrostatic transmissions; hydraulic valves and controls.

INDUSTRIAL GASES DIVISION 1358

Activities: Research and development of industrial gases, including oxygen, nitrogen, argon; shielding gases for welding; rare gases, high-purity gases and gas mixtures; medical gases; hydrogen; acetylene and other fuel gases; gas application processes, systems and equipment.

REFRIGERATION AND SHOP EQUIPMENT DIVISION 1359

Activities: Research and development of refrigeration plants, shop equipment, and reciprocating and turbo machinery, including space and process cooling; turnkey cold stores; energy recovery systems; heat pumps; air conditioning and ventilation systems; refrigerated and freezer display cabinets; walk-in refrigerators and freezers; non-refrigerated shop equipment; reciprocating gas compressors; turbocompressors; air and gas expansion turbines; reciprocating, screw-type and turbo refrigerating compressors; pneumatic tools; compressed air and gas valves and fittings.

TVT MÜNCHEN DIVISION 1360

Activities: Process plant construction and engineering, including chemical and petrochemical plants, gas generating and processing plants, synthetic gas plants, natural gas plants, air separation plants, nuclear plant systems, cryogenic plants and systems, environmental engineering; construction of liquified gas tanks, plant components and process units.

Lingner & Fischer Gmbh 1361

Address: Hermannstrasse 7, Postfach 1440, D-7580 Bühl, Baden
Telephone: (07223) 284 1
Telex: UHU D 78761
Parent body: Beecham Group
Research director: A.G. McGee
Section: Chemotechnical products, Dieter A. Hechenberger
Graduate research staff: 4
Annual expenditure: £51 000-500 000
Activities: Adhesives, sealers, fillers.
Contract work: No

Ludwig-Maximillians- 1362
Universität München

[Ludwig-Maximillians University Munich]
Address: Geschwister-Scholl-Platz 1, D-8000 München 22
Telephone: (089) 2180-1
Telex: 59860univmd
Rector: Professor Dr Nikolas Lobkowicz

FACULTY OF BIOLOGY 1363

Dean: Professor Dr Friedrich Schwarzfischer

Anthropology and Human Genetics 1364
Institute

Address: Richard-Wagner-Strasse 10, D-8000 München 8
Director: Professor Dr Hartwig Cleve

Botanical Institute 1365

Address: Menzingerstrasse 67, D-8000 München 19
Directors: Professor Dr Otto Kandler, Professor Dr Werner Rau, Professor Dr Walther Rüdiger

Genetics Institute 1366

Address: Maria-Ward-Strasse 1a, D-8000 München 19
Director: Professor Dr Fritz Kaudewitz

Systematic Botany Institute 1367

Address: Menzingerstrasse 67, D-8000 München 19
Directors: Professor Dr Hermann Merxmüller, Professor Dr Dieter Podleck

Zoological Institute 1368

Address: Luisenstrasse 14, D-8000 München 2
Senior staff: Professor Dr Bernd Linzen, Professor Dr Peter Bruckmoser, Professor Dr Jürgen Jacobs, Professor Dr Gerhard Neuweiler, Professor Dr Maximilian Renner, Professor Dr Friedrich Zettler

FACULTY OF CHEMISTRY AND 1369
PHARMACY

Dean: Professor Dr Gerhard Ertl

Biochemistry Institute 1370

Address: Karlstrasse 23, D-8000 München 2
Directors: Professor Dr Ernst-Ludwig Winnacker, Professor Dr Guido Hartmann

Inorganic Chemistry Institute 1371

Address: Meiserstrasse 1-3, D-8000 München 2
Directors: Professor Dr Armin Weiss, Professor Dr Wolfgang Beck, Professor Dr Heinrick Nöth, Professor Dr Hans-Peter Boehm, Professor Dr Alfred Schmidpeter, Professor Dr Friedrich Wiegel

Organic Chemistry Institute 1372

Address: Karlstrasse 23, D-8000 München 2
Directors: Professor Dr Rolf Huisgen, Professor Dr Rudolf Gompper, Professor Dr Gerhard Binsch, Professor Dr Rudolf Grashey, Professor Dr Klaus Gollnick

Pharmacology Institute 1373

Address: Karlstrasse 29, D-8000 München 2
Directors: Professor Dr Hildebert Wagner, Professor Dr Meinhart Zenk

Pharmacy and Food Chemistry 1374
Institute

Address: Sophienstrasse 10, D-8000 München 2
Directors: Professor Dr Fritz Eiden, Professor Dr Theodor Severin, Professor Dr Hans-Dietrich Stachel, Professor Dr Karl Thoma

FOOD CHEMISTRY DEPARTMENT 1375
Head: Professor Dr Theodor Severin

PHARMACEUTICAL CHEMISTRY 1376
DEPARTMENT
Senior staff: Professor Dr Fritz Eiden, Professor Dr Hans-Dietrich Stachel, Professor Dr Eberhard Reimann

PHARMACEUTICAL TECHNOLOGY DEPARTMENT   1377

Head: Professor Dr Karl Thoma

Physical Chemistry Institute   1378

Address: Sophienstrasse 11, D-8000 München 2
Directors: Professor Dr Jürgen Voitländer, Professor Dr Gerhard Ertt

FACULTY OF FORESTRY   1379

Address: Amalienstrasse 52, D-8000 München 40
Dean: Professor Dr Peter Schütt

Afforestation and Forest Planning Institute   1380

Telephone: (089) 2180-3159
Director: Professor Dr Peter Burschel

Anatomy, Physiology, and Pathology of Plants Institute   1381

Telephone: (089) 2180-3124
Directors: Professor Dr Peter Schütt, Professor Dr Werner Koch

Applied Zoology Institute   1382

Telephone: (089) 2180-3165
Director: Professor Dr Wolfgang Schwenke

Bioclimatology and Applied Metereology Institute   1383

Telephone: (089) 2180-3153
Director: Professor Dr Albert Baumgartner

Forest Expansion Science Institute   1384

Telephone: (089) 2180-3120
Director: Professor Dr Friedrich Franz

Forest Policy and Forest History Institute   1385

Address: Schellingstrasse 12, D-8000 München 40
Telephone: (089) 2180-3551
Directors: Professor Dr Richard Plochmann, Dr Dr Wolfgang Schröder

Forest Policy and Forest Management Institute   1386

Telephone: (089) 2180-3137
Director: Professor Dr Werner Kroth

Forestry Science and Production Technology Institute   1387

Address: Hohenlindenstrasse 5, D-8000 München 40
Telephone: (089) 912038
Director: Professor Dr Hans-Dietrich Löffler

Landscape Technology Institute   1388

Address: Winzererstrasse 45, D-8000 München 40
Telephone: (089) 30 30 13
Director: Professor Dr Ulrich Ammer

Seeds, Genetics and Breeding of Forest Trees Institute   1389

Telephone: (089) 2180-3130
Director: Professor Dr Alexander von Schönborn

Soil Science Institute   1390

Telephone: (089) 2180-3115
Director: Professor Dr Karl-Eugen Rehfuess

Wood Research Institute   1391

Address: Winzererstrasse 45, D-8000 München 40
Telephone: (089) 303013
Director: Professor H. Schulz
Sections: mechanical engineering, Dr Kufner; technology/fires, Dr Teichgräber; physics, Dr Schnieder; chemistry, Dr Fengel; anatomy, Dr Grosser
Graduate research staff: 15
Annual expenditure: £51 000-500 000
Contract work: Yes

BAVARIAN FORESTRY RESEARCH STATION   1392

See entry under: Bayerische Forstliche Versuchs- und Forschungsanstalt.

FACULTY OF GEOSCIENCES   1393

Dean: Professor Dr Johann Bodechtel

Applied Geophysics Institute   1394

Address: Theresienstrasse 41, D-8000 München 2
Director: Professor Dr Gustav Angenheister

Crystallography and Mineralogy Institute   1395

Address: Theresienstrasse 41, D-8000 München 2
Director: Professor Dr Heinz Jagodzinski

General and Applied Geology and Mineralogy Institute   1396

Address: Luisenstrasse 37, D-8000 München 2
Director: Professor Dr Klaus Schmidt

APPLIED GEOLOGY DEPARTMENT   1397
Head: Professor Dr Wolf-Dieter Grimm

GEOCHEMISTRY DEPARTMENT   1398
Head: Professor Dr Dietrich-Dankwart Klemm

PHOTOGEOLOGY DEPARTMENT   1399
Head: Professor Dr Johann Bodechtel

Geographical Institute   1400

Address: Luisenstrasse 37, D-8000 München 2
Directors: Professor Dr Friedrich Wilhelm, Professor Dr Hans-Günther Gierloff-Emden, Professor Dr Josef Birkenhauer

Mineralogy and Petrography Institute   1401

Address: Theresienstrasse 41, D-8000 München 2
Director: Professor Dr Hans-Gerhard Huckenholz

Palaeontology and Historic Geology Institute   1402

Address: Richard-Wagner-Strasse 10, D-8000 München 2
Directors: Professor Dr Dietrich Herm, Professor Dr Volker Fahlbusch

MICROPALAEONTOLOGY DEPARTMENT   1403
Head: Professor Dr Herbert Hagn

PALAEOBOTANY DEPARTMENT   1404
Head: Professor Dr Walter Jung

FACULTY OF MATHEMATICS   1405

Dean: Professor Dr Karl Stein

Mathematics Institute   1406

Address: Schellingstrasse 2-8, D-8000 München 13
Senior staff: Professor Dr Karl Stein, Professor Dr Friedrich Kasch, Professor Dr Günther Hämmerlin, Professor Dr Walter Roelcke, Professor Dr Ernst Wienholtz, Professor Dr Jürgen Batt, Professor Dr Peter Gänssler, Professor Dr Hans G. Kellerer, Professor Dr Ulrich Oppel, Professor Dr Horst Oswald, Professor Dr B. Pareigis, Professor Dr H.J. Schneider, Professor Dr M. Schottenloher, Professor Dr H. Schwichtenberg

INFORMATION SCIENCES DEPARTMENT   1407
Head: Professor Dr Gerhard Seegmüller

FACULTY OF MEDICINE   1408

Address: Goemestrasse 29, D-8000 München 2
Dean: Professor Dr Wolfgang Spann
Facilities: Computer centre.

Anatomy Institute   1409

Address: Pettenkoferstrasse 11, D-8000 München 2
Directors: Professor Dr med Hans Frick, Professor Dr H. Wetzstein

City Medical Clinic   1410

Address: Ziemssenstrasse 1, D-8000 München 2
Director: Professor Dr Eberhard Buehborn

Dermatology Clinic and Outpatients Clinic   1411

Address: Frauenlobstrasse 9, D-8000 München 15
Director: Professor Dr Otto Braun-Falco

Forensic Medicine Institute   1412

Address: Frauenlobstrasse 7, D-8000 München 15
Director: Professor Dr med Wolfgang Spann

Grosshadern Clinic   1413

Address: Marchioninistrasse 15, Postfach 70 12 60, D-8000 München 70
Telephone: (089) 7095-1
Telex: 5/212228 kmgh/d
Medical director: Professor Dr Dr Heinz Goerhe

ANAESTHESIOLOGICAL INSTITUTE   1414
Director: Professor Dr med Klaus Peter

Neurosurgical Anaesthesiology and Resuscitation Department   1415
Head: Professor Dr med Robert Enzenbach

CLINICAL CHEMISTRY INSTITUTE   1416
Director: Professor Dr med Maximilian Knedel

EAR, NOSE AND THROAT CLINIC AND POLYCLINIC   1417
Telephone: (089) 7095-2990/1
Director: Professor Dr med Heinz Naumann

GYNAECOLOGICAL CLINIC   1418
Director: Professor Dr med Kurt Richter

HEAT SURGERY CLINIC   **1419**
Telephone: (089) 7095-2951
Director: Professor Dr med Werner Klinner

MEDICAL CLINIC I   **1420**
Director: Professor Dr Gerhard Riecker

MEDICAL CLINIC II   **1421**
Director: Professor Dr Gustav Paumgartner

MEDICAL CLINIC III   **1422**
Director: Professor Dr med Wolfgang Wilmanns

MEDICAL DATA PROCESSING,   **1423**
STATISTICS AND BIOMATHEMATICS
INSTITUTE
Telephone: (089) 7095-4490
Director: Professor Dr med Karl Überla

NEUROLOGICAL CLINIC AND   **1424**
POLYCLINIC
Director: Professor Dr med Adolf Schrader

NEUROSURGICAL CLINIC   **1425**
Director: Professor Dr med Frank Marguth

ORTHOPAEDIC CLINIC   **1426**
Director: Professor Dr med Alfred Nikolans Witt

PHYSICAL MEDICINE CLINIC   **1427**
Director: Professor Dr med Heinrich Drexel

RADIOLOGY CLINIC AND POLYCLINIC   **1428**
Director: Professor Dr med Josef Lissner

SURGICAL CLINIC   **1429**
Director: Professor Dr med Georg Heberer

SURGICAL RESEARCH INSTITUTE   **1430**
Telephone: (089) 7095-4400
Director: Professor Dr med Walter Brendel

UROLOGICAL CLINIC AND   **1431**
POLYCLINIC
Telephone: (089) 7095-2971
Director: Professor Dr med Egbert Schmiedt

Infections and Tropical Diseases   **1432**
Institute
Address: Leopoldstrasse 5, D-8000 München 40
Director: Professor Dr med Werner Lang

Max von Pettenkofer Institute for   **1433**
Hygiene and Medical Microbiology
Address: Pettenkoferstrasse 9, D-8000 München 2
Director: Dr F. Deinherd

Medical Climatology and Balneology   **1434**
Institute
Address: Marchioninistrasse 17, D-8000 München 15
Director: Professor Dr H. Drexel

Medical Outpatients Clinic   **1435**
Address: Pettenkoferstrasse 8a, D-8000 München 2
Director: Professor Dr Walter Seitz

Medical Psychology Institute   **1436**
Address: Schillerstrasse 42, D-8000 München 2
Director: Professor Dr phil E. Pöppel

Obstetrics and Gynaecology Clinic   **1437**
Address: Maistrasse 11, D-8000 München 2
Director: Professor Dr Josef Zander

RADIOLOGY DEPARTMENT   **1438**
Director: Professor Dr Julius Ries

Ophthalmology Clinic   **1439**
Address: Mathildenstrasse 8, D-8000 München 2
Director: Professor Dr Otto-Erich Lund

Orthopaedic Outpatients Clinic   **1440**
Address: Pettenkoferstrasse 8a, D-8000 München 2
Director: Professor Dr Alfred Nikolans Witt

Paediatric Clinic   **1441**
Address: Lindwurmstrasse 4, D-8000 München 2

PAEDIATRIC MEDICAL CLINIC   **1442**
Director: Professor Dr Klaus Betke

Antimicrobial Therapy Department   **1443**
Head: Professor Dr Walter Marget

Neonatology Department   **1444**
Head: Professor Dr Klaus Riegel

Paediatric Cardiology Department   **1445**
Head: Professor Dr Konrad Bühlmeyer

Paediatric Haematology Department   **1446**
Head: Dr Fritz Lampert

PAEDIATRIC SURGICAL CLINIC   1447
Director: Professor Dr Waldemar Hecker

Paediatric Anaesthesiology Department   1448
Head: Dr Gettrud König-Westhues

Paediatric Plastic Surgery Department   1449
Head: Dr Ilse Coerdt

Paediatric Outpatients Clinic   1450

Address: Pettenkoferstrasse 8a, D-8000 München 2
Director: Professor Dr Heinz Spiess

Pathology Institute   1451

Address: Thalkirchner Strasse 36, D-8000 München 2
Director: Professor Dr med Max Eder

NEUROPATHOLOGY DEPARTMENT   1452
Head: Professor Dr Otto Stochdorph

Pharmacology Institute   1453

Address: Nussbaumstrasse 26, D-8000 München 2
Director: Professor Dr W. Farth

Physiological Chemistry and Physical   1454
Biochemistry Institute

Address: Goethestrasse 33, D-8000 München 2
Directors: Professor Dr Dr Theodor Bücher, Professor Dr Hans Georg Zachau, Professor Dr Martin Klingenberg

CELL BIOLOGY DEPARTMENT   1455
Head: Professor Dr med Fritz Miller

Physiology Institute   1456

Address: Pettenkoferstrasse 12, D-8000 München 2
Directors: Professor Dr med E. Gerlach, Professor Dr med Klaus Thurau, Professor Dr Bruggenlate

Prophylaxis of Circulatory Diseases   1457
Institute

Address: Pettenkoferstrasse 9, D-8000 München 2
Director: Professor Dr med Gustav Schimert

Psychiatric Clinic   1458

Address: Nussbaumstrasse 7, D-8000 München 2
Director: Professor Dr Hanns Hippius

FORENSIC PSYCHIATRY DEPARTMENT 1459
Head: Professor Dr Werner Mende

NEUROCHEMISTRY DEPARTMENT   1460
Head: Professor Dr Norbert Matussek

NEURORADIOLOGY DEPARTMENT   1461
Head: Professor Dr Kurt Decker

Radiation Biology Institute   1462

Address: Bavariaring 19, D-8000 München 2
Director: vacant

Radiology and Outpatients Clinic   1463

Address: Ziemssenstrasse 1, D-8000 München 2
Director: Professor Dr Josef Lissner

Social Paediatrics and Adolescent   1464
Research Centre

Address: Lindwurmstrasse 131, D-8000 München 2
Director: Professor Dr med Theodor Hellbrügge

Surgical Outpatients Clinic   1465

Address: Pettenkoferstrasse 8a, D-8000 München 2
Director: Professor Dr Fritz Holle

ANAESTHESIOLOGY DEPARTMENT   1466
Head: Professor Dr Alfred Doenicke

Tooth, Mouth and Jaw Diseases Clinic 1467
and Outpatients Department

Address: Pettenkoferstrasse 11, D-8000 München 2

CONSERVATIVE DENTISTRY   1468
DEPARTMENT
Head: Professor Dr E. Sonnabend

DENTAL SURGERY DEPARTMENT   1469
Head: vacant

ORTHODONTICS DEPARTMENT   1470
Head: Professor Dr Stahl

PROSTHETICS DEPARTMENT   1471
Head: Professor Dr Ewald Kraft

FACULTY OF PHYSICS   1472

Dean: Professor Dr Ulrich Berkhout

Astronomy and Astrophysics Institute 1473
and Observatory

Address: Scheinerstrasse 1, D-8000 München 80
Director: Professor Dr Peter Wellmann

Medical Optics Institute   1474

Address: Barbarastrasse 16, D-8000 München 40
Directors: Professor Dr Wolfgang Waidelich, Professor Dr Erwin Hartmann

Meteorological Institute   1475

Address: Schellingstrasse 12/IV, D-8000 München 13
Director: Professor Dr Gustav Hofmann

ATMOSPHERIC RADIATION AND   1476
SATELLITE METEOROLOGY
DEPARTMENT
Head: Professor Dr Hans-Jürgen Bolle

MICROMETEOROLOGY DEPARTMENT 1477
Head: Dr Helmut Kraus

Physics Departments: 1478

EXPERIMENTAL PHYSICS   1479
DEPARTMENT
Address: Am Coulombwall 1, D-8046 Garching
Senior staff: Professor Jorrit de Boer, Professor Dr Josef Brandmüller, Professor Dr Johann Peisl, Professor Dr Ulrich Meyer Berkhout, Professor Dr Herbert Walther, Professor Dr Rudolf Sizmann, Professor Dr Siegfried Skorka, Professor Dr Crtomir Zupancic

THEORETICAL PHYSICS   1480
DEPARTMENT
Address: Theresienstrasse 37, D-8000 München 2
Senior staff: Professor Harald Fritsch, Professor Dr Helmut Bross, Professor Dr Helmut Salecker, Professor Dr Herbert Wagner, Professor Dr Georg Süssmann

Theoretical Meteorology Institute   1481

Address: Haimhauser 4/I, D-8000 München 13
Directors: Professor Dr Günther Hollmann, Professor Dr Josef Egger, Professor Dr Heinrich Quenzel, Professor Dr Frank Schmidt

FACULTY OF VETERINARY MEDICINE 1482

Address: Veterinärstrasse 13, D-8000 München 22
Dean: Professor Dr Erwin Dahme

Animal Anatomy Institute   1483

Director: Professor Dr Peter Walter

Animal Breeding Institute   1484

Director: Professor Dr Horst Kräusslich

Animal Gynaecological and   1485
Outpatients Clinic

Address: Königstrasse 12, D-8000 München 22
Directors: Professor Dr Meinhard Rüsse, Professor Dr Werner Leidl

Animal Hygiene Institute   1486

Director: Professor Dr Johann Kalich

Animal Macroscopic Anatomy   1487
Institute

Director: Professor Dr Bernd Kollmerhans

Animal Medical Clinic   1488

Director: Professor Dr Wilfried Kraft

Animal Physiology Institute   1489

Director: vacant

Animal Surgical Clinic   1490

Director: Professor Dr Horst Schebitz

Domestic and Wild Birds Diseases   1491
Institute

Address: Mittenheimerstrasse 54, D-8042 Schleissheim
Director: Professor Dr Irmgard Gylstorff

Domestic Animal Genetics Institute   1492

Address: St-Hubertus-Strasse 2, D-8042 Oberschleissheim
Director: Professor Dr Frederik Bakels

General and Neuropathology Animal   1493
Institute

Director: Professor Dr Erwin Dahme

General Animal Pathology and   1494
Pathological Anatomy Institute

Director: Professor Dr Joachim von Sandersleben

Hygiene and Technology of Food of   1495
Animal Origin Department

Head: Professor Dr Ludwig Kotter
Section: Milk hygiene and technology, Professor Dr Gerhard Terplan

Microbiology and Infectious Diseases 1496
of Animals Institute

Director: Professor Dr Anton Mayr

Nutrition Physiology Institute 1497

Director: Professor Dr Dr Zucker

Palaeoanatomy and Domestication 1498
Research Institute

Address: Schellingstrasse 10, D-8000 München 13
Director: Professor Dr Joachim Boessneck

Pharmacology, Toxicology and 1499
Pharmacy Institute

Director: Professor Dr Dietmar Hegner

Veterinary Tropical Medicine Institute 1500

Address: Leopoldstrasse 5, D-8000 München 23
Director: Professor Dr Josef Boch

Zoology-Parasitology Institute 1501

Address: Kaulbachstrasse 37, D-8000 München 22
Director: Professor Dr Dr Ruf

MAN Maschinenfabrik 1502
Augsburg Nürnberg
Aktiengesellschaft

Address: Stadtbachstrasse 1, Postfach 10 00 80, D-8900
Augsburg
Telephone: (0821) 3221
Telex: 05 3751
Research director: Dr Dr Friedrich Laussermair
Graduate research staff: 500
Annual expenditure: over £2m
Activities: Research and development is carried out in
all MAN Product-Divisions, and is concentrated on
improving and developing the following products and
systems: diesel engines, gas engines, engine power plants,
steam power plants; road vehicles, omnibuses, automotive diesel engines, rail vehicles, transport technology;
cranes and conveyors; printing machines; steel structures, pumps, process equipment; plant and components
for coal gasification; plant and equipment for mining;
plant and equipment for the production of iron, steel and
non-ferrous metals.
Contract work: No
Publications: Research, Engineering, Manufacturing, annual research report.

ADVANCED TECHNOLOGY 1503
DIVISION

Address: Dachaner Strasse 667, D-8000 München 50
Sections: Nuclear engineering, Dipl-Ing Horst Rauck
Development, Dipl-Ing Jörg Feustel
Activities: Research projects on gas ultra-centrifuges;
modular cogeneration power stations; engine powered
heating systems; solar-thermal and electrical power stations; heat pump plants; gyroscopic energy storage
systems with recovery of brake energy; structural parts
for aeronautics and astronautics; emergency systems for
high-speed rail vehicles; hybrid propulsion for commercial vehicles; fast wheel/rail systems; pressure vessels
and machine components in advanced composite
designs; high-accuracy extrusion method for producing
high-strength quasi-fully-balanced hollow parts; 5-axle
NC-milling method; magnetic bearings; adaptable grip-
ping systems; handling systems; digital signal acquisition
systems.

COMMERCIAL VEHICLES DIVISION 1504

Address: Dachauer Strasse 667, D-8000 München 80
Head: Dr Ing Hans Hogen
Activities: Research and development of automotive
diesel engines with low toxicity level in exhaust gases;
natural-gas bus; electric-drive bus; gas turbine for commercial vehicles.

DIESEL ENGINES AND PRINTING 1505
MACHINERY DIVISION

Address: Katzwanger Strasse 101, D-8500 Nürnberg 44
Sections: Development, Dr Ing Klaus Wiebicke; basic
research, Ing Alfred Neitz
Activities: Research and development of total energy
plants; diesel and reciprocating gas engines for sewage
treatment plants.

Steam Power Plants 1506

Sections: Basic research, Dr Ing Gernot Mathias

MECHANICAL AND STRUCTURAL 1507
ENGINEERING DIVISION

Activities: Research and development of safety containers for nuclear power plants; emergency running
system for magnetic cushion vehicles; large antennae
systems for data transmission; pumps for sewage treatment plants; dry cooling systems for steam and nuclear
power plants.

MECHANICAL ENGINEERING AND PLANT CONSTRUCTION DIVISION   1508

Activities: Research and development of closed-cycle turbines and heat-exchangers for thermal power plants; reactor pressure vessels, steam generating and heating plants; steel flyovers and bridges; concrete bridges, bridge bearings, roadway extension joints; exhaust gas purification systems for oxygen blowing converters; dust removal systems for electric steel mills and ore sintering plants.

Materialprüfungs- und Versuchsanstalt GmbH Forschungsinstitut für Vulkan-Baustoffe   1509

[Materials Testing and Research Institute for Igneous Aggregates]
Address: 1 Sandkauler Weg, D-5450 Nauwied 1
Telephone: (02631) 22 22 78
Affiliation: Arbeitsgemeinschaft Industrieller Forschungsvereinigungen eV
Managing Director: Dipl-Ing P. Heinig
Scientific staff: 2
Activities: Recognition and research into the manufacture, use and processing of hydraulically compression-bonded building blocks and material by-products of fired processes.

Max-Planck-Gesellschaft zur Förderung der Wissenschaften eV   1510

[Max Planck Society for the Promotion of Sciences]
Address: Residenzstrasse 1a, Postfach 647, D-8000 München 1
President: Professor Dr Reimer Lüst
Vice-presidents: Professor Dr Helmut Coing, Professor Dr Benno Hess, Professor Dr Hans L. Merkle, Professor Dr Günther Wilke
General Secretary: Dietrich Ranft
Activities: The Society has fifty-three autonomous research centres which are divided into three sections: for biological and medical sciences; for chemical, physical and technical sciences; and for the arts.

ASSOCIATED INSTITUTES   1511

Garching Instrumente - Gesellschaft zur Industriellen Nutzung von Forschungsergebrissen mbH   1512

[Garching Instruments - Company for Industrial Applications of Research Results]
Address: Königinstrasse 19, D-8000 München 22
Telephone: (089) 288279
Telex: 5 215 493
Manager: Dr Heinrich Kuhn
Activities: The Company performs a variety of functions, including finding licensees for inventions originating from the Max Planck institutes, and developing scientific instruments.

Gesellschaft für Wissenschaftliche Datenverarbeitung mbH Göttingen   1513

[Scientific Data Processing Company Göttingen]
Address: Am Fassberg, D-3400 Göttingen-Nikolausberg
Telephone: (0551) 201510
Telex: 9 6 786
Managers: Dr Kurt Pfuhl, Dr Dieter Wall
Activities: The Company is a joint institution of the State of Lower Saxony (University of Göttingen) and the Max Planck Society. It works on the solution of problems for science by means of computers, carries out research in the field of computer science, and contributes to the training of data processing personnel.

Minerva Gesellschaft für die Forschung mbH   1514

[Minerva Research Society]
Address: Residenzstrasse 1a, Postfach 647, D-8000 München 1
Telephone: (089) 21081
Manager: Dietrich Ranft
Activities: Operation of research and supporting installations of all kinds.

KERCKHOFF-KLINIK   1515
[Kerckhoff Clinic]
Address: Benekestrasse 6-8, D-6350 Bad Nauheim
Telephone: (06032) 3451
Director: Professor Dr Martin Schlepper
Activities: Diagnostics and treatment of heart diseases. The clinic is a 100-bed research hospital confined to diagnosis and treatment of cardiac diseases in adults.

BIOLOGICAL AND MEDICAL SECTION   1516

Forschungsstelle für Psychopathologie 1517 und Psychotherapie in der Max-Planck-Gesellschaft

[Research Institute for Psychopathology and Psychotherapy in the Max Planck Society]
Address: Montsalvatstrasse 19, D-8000 München 40
Telephone: (089) 363037
Head: Professor Dr Paul Matussek
Activities: Research into psychic and mental disorders caused by emotional and environmental influences.

Friedrich-Miescher-Laboratorium in 1518 der Max-Planck-Gesellschaft

[Friedrich Miescher Laboratory in the Max Planck Society]
Address: Spemannstrasse 39, Postfach 2109, D-7400 Tübingen
Telephone: (07071) 601 460
Activities: Molecular genetics; molecular biology; functions of biological cells.

ANDERER DEPARTMENT   1519
Director: Professor Dr F. Alfred Anderer
Activities: Model systems of animal virology which permit the study of virus-induced cell transformation by DNA tumour viruses.

BIOLOGICAL RESEARCH GROUPS   1520
Group leaders: Dr Walter Birchmeier, Dr Rolf Kemler, Dr Matthias Wabl, Dr Christianne Nüsslein-Volhard
Activities: Molecular biology, with special emphasis on problems of cell differentiation and morphogenesis.

Klinische Forschungsgruppe für 1521 Blutgerinnung und Thrombose am Klinikum der Universität Giessen

[Clinical Research Unit for Blood Clotting and Thrombosis at the University Clinic, Giessen]
Address: Gaffkystrasse 11, D-6300 Giessen
Telephone: (0641) 7021
Head: Professor Dr Friedrich Begemann

Klinische Forschungsgruppe für 1522 Reproduktionsmedizin an der Frauenklinik der Universität Münster

[Clinical Research Unit for Reproductive Medicine at the Women's Hospital of the University, Münster]
Address: Steinfurter Strasse 107, D-4400 Münster
Head: Professor Dr Eberhard Nieschlag

Max-Planck-Institut für Biochemie 1523

[Max Planck Institute for Biochemistry]
Address: Am Klopferspitz 18a, D-8033 Martinsried bei München
Telephone: (089) 85851
Telex: 521 740
Managing director: Professor Dr Peter Hans Hofschneider
Activities: Studies of proteins and nucleic acids, their structure and function, and the stages of their formation in living substances; fundamental research in experimental medicine.

BIOCHEMICAL METHODS   1524 DEPARTMENT
Director: Professor Dr Kurt Hannig
Activities: Characterization of biological membranes, using free-flow electrophoresis.

CELL BIOLOGY DEPARTMENT   1525
Director: Professor Dr Günther Gerisch

CONNECTIVE TISSUE RESEARCH   1526 DEPARTMENT
Director: Professor Dr Klaus Kühn
Activities: Structure and function of connective tissues.

EXPERIMENTAL MEDICINE   1527 DEPARTMENT
Director: vacant
Activities: Cell ecology, especially new methods and equipment for measurement.

INDEPENDENT RESEARCH GROUPS   1528
Head: Dr Dietmar Kamp
Emeritus scientific member: Professor Dr Adolf Butenandt

MEMBRANE BIOCHEMISTRY   1529 DEPARTMENT
Director: Professor Dr Dieter Oesterhelt

MOLECULAR BIOLOGY OF GENE   1530 EXPRESSION DEPARTMENT
Director: Professor Dr Wolfram Zillig
Activities: Research into the expression of the genetic programmes of organisms.

PEPTIDE CHEMISTRY DEPARTMENT   1531
Director: Professor Dr Erich Wünsch
Activities: Synthesis of peptides, especially of biologically important natural products.

PROTEIN CHEMISTRY DEPARTMENT   1532
Head: Professor Dr Gerhard Braunitzer
Activities: Structural elucidation of the fibrinogen protein; development of a protein sequenator.

STRUCTURAL RESEARCH   1533
DEPARTMENT I
Director: Professor Dr Walter Hoppe
Activities: Determination of the spatial structure of small and large molecules, particularly those of biological importance.

STRUCTURAL RESEARCH   1534
DEPARTMENT II
Director: Professor Dr Robert Huber
Activities: Elucidation of the three-dimensional structure of proteins to improve understanding of biochemical problems.

VIROID RESEARCH DEPARTMENT   1535
Director: Professor Dr Heinz-Ludwig Sänger

VIRUS RESEARCH DEPARTMENT   1536
Director: Professor Dr Peter Hans Hofschneider
Activities: Replication of nucleic acids and gene expression are topics studied using viruses and plasmids as the model systems.

Max-Planck-Institut für Biologie   1537
[Max Planck Institute for Biology]
Address: Corrensstrasse 42, D-7400 Tübingen
Telephone: (07071) 6011
Director: Professor Dr Jan Klein
Emeritus scientfic member: Professor Dr Georg Melchers
Activities: Chromosome research; biological control mechanisms in genetics; and behaviour of genetic materials.

BEERMANN DEPARTMENT   1538
Address: Spemannstrasse 34, D-7400 Tübingen
Telephone: (07071) 601200
Director: Professor Dr Wolfgang Beermann
Activities: Elucidation of the structure and functions of chromosomes in higher organisms.

HENNING DEPARTMENT   1539
Address: Corrensstrasse 38, D-7400 Tübingen
Telephone: (07071) 601230
Director: Professor Dr Ulf Henning
Activities: Biochemical mechanics operative in the expression of the genetically determined cellular shape in bacteria; structure of the cell envelope of such organisms.

IMMUNOGENETICS DEPARTMENT   1540
Address: Corrensstrasse 42, D-7400 Tübingen
Telephone: (07071) 601290
Director: Professor Dr Jan Klein

OVERATH DEPARTMENT   1541
Address: Corrensstrasse 38, D-7400 Tübingen
Telephone: (07071) 601236
Director: Professor Dr Peter Overath
Activities: Investigation of the structure and function of biological membranes, using a combined genetic, biochemical and physical approach.

Max-Planck-Institut für Biologische   1542
Kybernetik
[Max Planck Institute for Biological Cybernetics]
Address: Spemannstrasse 38, D-7400 Tübingen
Telephone: (07071) 6011
Managing director: Professor Dr Werner Reichardt
Scientific members, directors: Professor Dr Valentin Braitenberg, Professor Dr Karl Georg Götz, Professor Dr Kuno Kirschfeld, Professor Dr Werner Reichardt
Activities: Control reactions in organisms; nervous systems and visual systems in insects.

Max-Planck-Institut für Biophysik   1543
[Max Planck Institute for Biophysics]
Address: Kennedyallee 70, D-6000 Frankfurt am Main 70
Telephone: (0611) 63031
Managing director: Professor Dr Karl Julius Ullrich
Activities: Material transport through membranes; desalination; hydrogen/ion and sodium transport in organs; and molecular mechanisms.

CELL PHYSIOLOGY DEPARTMENT   1544
Address: Heinrich-Hoffmann-Strasse   7,   D-6000 Frankfurt am Main 71
Telephone: (0611) 67041
Director: Professor Dr Hermann Passow
Activities: Kinetics of passive ion transport across cell membranes, notably the membrane of the red blood cell.

PHYSICAL CHEMISTRY DEPARTMENT 1545
Director: Professor Dr Reinhard Schlögl
Activities: The general physico-chemical principles of passive and active transport across membranes are formulated and applied to model systems.

PHYSIOLOGY DEPARTMENT   1546
Director: Professor Dr Karl Julius Ullrich
Activities: Transport of solutes through epithelial membranes (kidney, exocrine pancreas and intestine).

Max-Planck-Institut für Ernährungsphysiologie 1547

[Max Planck Institute for Nutrition Physiology]
Address: Rheinlanddamm 201, D-4600 Dortmund 1
Telephone: (0231) 12061
Telex: 8 227 147
Director: Professor Dr Benno Hess
Emeritus Scientific Member: Professor Dr Heinrich Kraut
Activities: Nutrition of men and animals; metabolism of proteins; and the structure and function of enzymes.

Max-Planck-Institut für Experimentelle Endokrinologie 1548

[Max Planck Institute for Experimental Endocrinology]
Address: Karl-Wiechert-Allee 9, Postfach 610 309, D-3000 Hannover 61
Telephone: (0511) 5325958
Director: Professor Dr Peter W. Jungblut

Max-Planck-Institut für Experimentelle Medizin 1549

[Max Planck Institute for Experimental Medicine]
Address: Hermann-Rein-Strasse 3, D-3400 Göttingen
Telephone: (0551) 3031
Telex: 96 626 exmed d
Managing director: Professor Dr Norbert Hilschmann
Graduate research staff: 100
Activities: Pharmacology; respiration and lung functions; molecular human genetics; chemistry and biochemistry of nucleic acids; antigens; molecular biology; biochemistry.
Contract work: No

BIOCHEMICAL PHARMACOLOGY DEPARTMENT 1550

Director: Professor Dr Walther Vogt
Activities: Biologically active substances generated in blood and tissues which seem to be significant in the mediation or control of physiological functions, of defence reactions and pathological processes.

CHEMISTRY DEPARTMENT 1551

Director: Professor Dr Friedrich Cramer
Activities: Investigation of the chemical structure and biological function of nucleic acids.

IMMUNOCHEMISTRY DEPARTMENT 1552

Director: Professor Dr Norbert Hilschmann
Activities: Chemical analysis of the specific immune response.

MOLECULAR BIOLOGY DEPARTMENT 1553

Director: Professor Dr Norbert Hilschmann
Activities: Biology of higher multicellular organisms.

MOLECULAR GENETICS DEPARTMENT 1554

Director: Professor Dr Heinrich Matthaei
Activities: Mechanisms of chemical information transfer in the central nervous system which are involved in psychic processes in man are investigated.

NEUROCHEMISTRY RESEARCH GROUP 1555

Head: Professor Dr Volker Neuhoff
Activities: Analysis of the cellular and molecular bases of the neuronal transfer of information.

PHYSIOLOGY DEPARTMENT 1556

Director: Professor Dr Johannes Piiper
Activities: Physiology of respiration.

Max-Planck-Institut für Hirnforschung 1557

[Max Planck Institute for Brain Research]
Address: Deutschordenstrasse 46, Postfach 710 409, D-6000 Frankfurt am Main 71
Telephone: (0611) 67041
Managing director: Professor Dr Rolf Hassler
Scientific member: Dr Heinz Stephan
Activities: Neurobiology; Parkinson's disease; neuropathology; diseases of the central nervous system; cancer research; and brain tumours.

CIRCULATION IN THE BRAIN RESEARCH UNIT 1558

Address: Ostmerheimer Strasse 200, D-5000 Köln 91
Telephone: (0221) 892091
Heads: Professor Dr Wolf-Dieter Heiss, Professor Dr Konstantin-Alexander Hossman

NEUROBIOLOGY DEPARTMENT 1559

Director: Professor Dr Rolf Hassler
Activities: Nerve conductions participating in the generation of involuntary movements and rigidity and their relief.

SINGER DEPARTMENT* 1560

Director: Professor Dr Wolf Singer

WÄSSLE DEPARTMENT* 1561

Director: Dr Heinz Wässle

Max-Planck-Institut für Immunobiologie   1562

[Max Planck Institute for Immunobiology]
Address: Stübeweg 51, Postfach 1169, D-7800 Freiburg
Telephone: (0761) 51081
Managing director: Professor Dr Klaus Eichmann
Scientific members, directors: Professor Dr Klaus Eichmann, Dr Otto Lüderitz
Activities: Immune reactions of men and animals against infections, cancer, etc; effects of vaccines.

Max-Planck-Institut für Limnologie   1563

[Max Planck Institute for Limnology]
Address: August-Thienemann-Strasse 2, Postfach 165, D-2320 Plön-Holstein
Telephone: (04522) 5021
Managing director: Professor Dr Hans Jürgen Overbeck
Emeritus scientific member: Professor Dr Harald Sioli
Activities: Tropical ecology, especially of Brazil; life conditions in lakes and rivers; and biological products in flowing waters.

BRANCH STATION   1564
Address: Damenweg 1, Postfach 260, D-6407 Schlitz/Hessen
Telephone: (06642) 383
Head: Professor Dr Joachim Illies

GENERAL LIMNOLOGY DEPARTMENT 1565
Director: Professor Dr Hans Jürgen Overbeck
Activities: Metabolic activity of bacteria in the ecosystems of lakes.

INDEPENDENT RESEARCH GROUPS   1566
Heads: Dr W. Junk, Dr W. Lampert

TROPICAL ECOLOGY DEPARTMENT   1567
Head: Professor Dr Hans Jürgen Overbeck
Activities: Studies of the equatorial lowland of Brazilian Amazonia and comparison with German ecosystems.

Max-Planck-Institut für Medizinische 1568 Forschung

[Max Planck Institute for Medical Research]
Address: Jahnstrasse 29, Postfach 103 820, D-6900 Heidelberg 1
Telephone: (06221) 4861
Telex: 461 505
Managing director: Professor Dr Wilhelm Hasselbach
Activities: Fundamental research into physiological and molecular biological processes.

BIOPHYSICS DEPARTMENT   1569
Director: Professor Dr Kenneth C. Holmes
Activities: Mechanism of action of the nucleotide binding proteins; new X-ray sources; advancement of kinetic procedures.

MOLECULAR BIOLOGY DEPARTMENT 1570
Director: Professor Dr Dr Hartmut Hoffmann-Berling
Activities: Mechanism of replication of DNA.

MOLECULAR PHYSICS DEPARTMENT 1571
Director: Professor Dr Karl Hermann Hausser
Activities: Methods of magnetic resonance and their application to molecules and molecular crystals.

ORGANIC CHEMISTRY DEPARTMENT 1572
Director: Professor Dr Dr Heinz A. Staab
Activities: Relation between the structure of organic molecules and their physical, chemical, and biological properties.

PHYSIOLOGY DEPARTMENT   1573
Director: Professor Dr Wilhelm Hasselbach
Activities: Mechanism of energy conversion in biological systems.

Max-Planck-Institut für Molekulare 1574 Genetik

[Max Planck Institute for Molecular Genetics]
Address: Ihnestrasse 63-73, D-1000 Berlin 33
Telephone: (030) 83071
Managing director: Professor Dr Thomas A. Trautner
Activities: Molecular mechanisms of DNA; genetic recombination; structure and function of ribosomes; and interactions of proteins and nucleic acids.
Contract work: No

INDEPENDENT RESEARCH GROUPS   1575
Heads: Dr Klaus Bister, Dr Reinhard Lührmann

SCHUSTER DEPARTMENT   1576
Director: Professor Dr Heinz Schuster
Activities: Molecular mechanism of DNA replication.

TRAUTNER DEPARTMENT   1577
Director: Professor Dr Thomas A. Trautner
Activities: The following are studied: mechanism of the initiation of DNA replication in E. coli; mechanism of conjugation in E. coli; mechanism of genetic recombination; DNA transport and processing; phototropism and photodifferentiation.

WITTMANN DEPARTMENT   1578
Director: Professor Dr Heinz-Günter Wittmann
Activities: Elucidation of the structure and function of ribosomes.

Max-Planck-Institut für Physiologische 1579 und Klinische Forschung, W.G. Kerckhoff-Institut

[Max Planck Institute for Physiological and Clinical Research, W.G. Kerckhoff Institute]
Address: Parkstrasse 1, D-6350 Bad Nauheim
Telephone: (06032) 6015
Managing director: Professor Dr Eckhart Simon
Emeritus scientific members: Professor Dr Rudolf Knebel, Professor Dr Rudolf Thauer
Activities: Basic physiology research in special fields not adequately represented at the universities; development of scientific cooperation in physiological and clinical research.

EXPERIMENTAL CARDIOLOGY 1580 DEPARTMENT

Address: Benekestrasse 2, D-6350 Bad Nauheim
Director: Professor Dr Wolfgang Schaper
Activities: Regeneration and degeneration of the heart and its blood supply.

PHYSIOLOGY DEPARTMENT I 1581

Director: Professor Dr Eckhart Simon
Activities: Investigation of temperature effects and temperature regulation in vertebrates, particularly in warm-blooded animals, including man.

PHYSIOLOGY DEPARTMENT II 1582

Director: Professor Dr Eberhard Dodt
Activities: The eye, its circulatory supply and the information gathered by the transformation of physical stimuli into electrical activity of photoreceptors and nerve cells propagated into, and conducted along, visual pathways which supply information from the outer world to nerve centres in the brain.

Max-Planck-Institut für Psychiatrie 1583 (Deutsche Forschungsanstalt für Psychiatrie)

[Max Planck Institute for Psychiatry (German Psychiatry Research Institute)]
Address: Kraepelinstrasse 2 und 10, Postfach 401 240, D-8000 München 40
Telephone: (089) 381021
Managing director: Professor Dr Detlev Ploog
Scientific member: Professor Dr Johannes Brengelmann
Emeritus scientific members; Professor Dr Gerd Peters, Professor Dr Horst Jatzkewitz
Activities: Theoretical and clinical investigation of problems of psychiatry, psychopathology and neurology.

CLINICAL INSTITUTE 1584

Director: Professor Dr Detlev Ploog

INDEPENDENT RESEARCH GROUPS 1585

Heads: Dr L.J. De Gennaro, Dr W. Huttner, Dr G. Isenberg

THEORETICAL INSTITUTE 1586

Director: Professor Dr Hans Thoenen
Scientific members, directors: Professor Dr Albert Herz, Professor Dr Georg Kreutzberg, Professor Dr Hans Dieter Lux, Professor Dr Hans Thoenen, Professor Dr Detlev Ploog

Max-Planck-Institut für 1587 Psycholinguistik

[Max Planck Institute for Psycholinguistics]
Address: Berg en Dalseweg 79, 6522 BC Nijmegen, Netherlands
Telephone: (003180) 230100
Managing director: Professor Dr Willem J.M. Levelt
Scientific members, directors: Professor Dr Wolfgang Klein, Professor Dr Willem J.M. Levelt

Max-Planck-Institut für 1588 Systemphysiologie

[Max Planck Institute for System Physiology]
Address: Rheinlanddamm 201, D-4600 Dortmund 1
Telephone: (0231) 12061
Telex: 8 227 147
Director: Professor Dr Dietrich Werner Lübbers
Activities: The oxygen supply of men and animals; reactions of individual organs and systems.

Max-Planck-Institut für 1589 Verhaltensphysiologie

[Max Planck Institute for Behavioural Physiology]
Address: D-8131 Seewiesen über Starnberg
Telephone: (08157) 291
Managing director: Professor Dr Dietrich Schneider
Emeritus scientific members: Professor Dr Jürgen Aschoff, Professor Dr Konrad Lorenz, Professor Dr Ernst Schütz
Activities: Behaviour of man and animals.

HUBER DEPARTMENT 1590

Director: Professor Dr Franz Huber
Activities: Connection between the expression of behaviour and the sensory and neurophysiological processes underlying it.

HUMAN ETHOLOGY RESEARCH GROUP 1591

Head: Professor Dr Irenäus Eibl-Eibesfeldt
Activities: Phylogenetic adaptation in human behaviour.

MITTELSTAEDT DEPARTMENT 1592

Director: Professor Dr Horst Mittelstaedt
Activities: Information flow systems of the individual.

RADOLFZELL ORNITHOLOGICAL STATION 1593

Address: Schloss Mögingen, D-7760 Radolfzell 16
Telephone: (07732) 10392; 10677
Head: Professor Dr Wolfgang Wickler
Head of station: Professor Dr Eberhard Gwinner
Activities: Bird migration; relationship between birds and their environment; acoustic communication and anatomical and behavioural adaptation.

SCHNEIDER DEPARTMENT 1594

Director: Professor Dr Dietrich Schneider
Activities: Olfaction in insects is studied as an example of the biological functional chain leading from the reception of the stimulus by the sense organ through the formation and processing of nervous pulses to the behavioural response of the animal.

WICKLER DEPARTMENT 1595

Director: Professor Dr Wolfgang Wickler
Activities: Comparative ethology, mainly in the field of socioecology.

Max-Planck-Institut für Virusforschung 1596

[Max Planck Institute for Virus Research]
Address: Spemannstrasse 35, Postfach 2109, D-7400 Tübingen
Telephone: (07071) 6011
Managing director: Dr Alfred Gierer
Graduate research staff: 37
Annual expenditure: £501 000-2m
Activities: The creation of tumour viruses; molecular problems of morphogenetics; control mechanisms in nucleic acid synthesis.
Contract work: No

BIOCHEMISTRY DEPARTMENT 1597

Director: Dr Uli Schwarz
Activities: Generation and controlled modification of cellular shape.

BIOLOGICAL MEDICINE DEPARTMENT 1598

Director: vacant
Activities: Virus-initiated tumours of mammals and birds, especially tumours caused by ribonucleic acid bearing viruses.

CELL BIOLOGY DEPARTMENT 1599

Director: Professor Dr Peter Hausen
Activities: Mechanism of ribonucleic acid synthesis in mammalian cells.

MOLECULAR BIOLOGY DEPARTMENT 1600

Director: Professor Dr Alfred Gierer
Activities: Physical principles and molecular processes in the development of higher organisms.

PHYSICAL BIOLOGY DEPARTMENT 1601

Director: Professor Dr Friedrich Bonhoeffer
Activities: Role of chromosomal proteins in the architecture of chromosomes and the regulation of gene activities; generation of regionally specific nerve cell connections during the development of the nervous system.

Max-Planck-Institut für Zellbiologie 1602

[Max Planck Institute for Cell Biology]
Address: Rosenhof, D-6802 Ladenburg bei Heidelberg
Telephone: (06203) 5097
Managing director: Professor Dr Peter Traub
Emeritus scientific member: Professor Dr Hans Bauer
Activities: Steroid hormones; interactions of cellular nuclei and cytoplasma; structure and function of ribosomes.

SCHWEIGER DEPARTMENT 1603

Director: Professor Dr Hans-Georg Schweiger
Activities: Biochemistry of 'nucleo-cytoplasmic' interactions, with particular reference to cell differentiation and the biological clock.

TRAUB DEPARTMENT 1604

Director: Professor Dr Peter Traub
Activities: Protein biosynthesis and its regulation in mammalian cells.

Max-Planck-Institut für Züchtungsforschung (Erwin-Baur-Institut) 1605

[Max Planck Institute for Plant Breeding Research (Erwin Baur Institute)]
Address: Egelspfad, D-5000 Köln 30
Telephone: (0221) 508044
Managing director: Professor Dr Jozef Schell
Scientific member: Professor Dr Heinz Saedler

Emeritus scientific members: Professor Dr Wilhelm Menke, Professor Dr Joseph Straub
Graduate research staff: 27
Annual expenditure: DM9 350 000
Activities: Genetic engineering of plants with the Ti-plasmids of agrobacteria; molecular analysis of tumour growth in plants; nitrogen fixation by rhizobia; molecular analysis of controlling elements in maize; insertion elements in bacteria.
Contract work: Yes

MOLECULAR PLANT GENETICS DEPARTMENT*   1606
Director: Professor Dr Heinz Saedler

PLANT BREEDING RESEARCH DEPARTMENT*   1607
Director: Professor Dr Jozef Schell

PLANT GENETICS DEPARTMENT*   1608
Director: Professor Dr Jozef Schell

CHEMICAL, PHYSICAL AND TECHNICAL SECTION   1609

Fritz-Haber-Institut der Max-Planck-Gesellschaft   1610

[Fritz Haber Institute of the Max Planck Society]
Address: Faradayweg 4-6, D-1000 Berlin 33
Telephone: (030) 83051
Telex: 185 676
Managing director: Professor Dr Heinz Gerischer
Scientific members, directors: Professor Dr Jochen Block, Professor Dr Elmar Zeitler
Emeritus scientific members: Professor Dr Ing Gerhard Borrmann, Professor Dr Rudolf Brill, Professor Dr Rolf Hosemann, Professor Dr Kurt Molière, Professor Dr Kurt Ueberreiter, Professor Dr Ing Ernst Ruska
Activities: Research in physical chemistry and electrochemistry using diffraction methods and electron microscopy; technical development of electron microscopes.

Gmelin-Institut für Anorganische Chemie und Grenzgebiete der Max-Planck-Gesellschaft   1611

[Gmelin Institute for Inorganic Chemistry and Related Fields in the Max Planck Society]
Address: Varrentrappstrasse 40-42, Postfach 900 467, D-6000 Frankfurt am Main 90
Telephone: (0611) 79171
Telex: 4 12 526
Director: Professor Dr Ekkehard Fluck

Emeritus scientific member: Professor Dr Margot Becke
Activities: The Institute is in charge of publishing the Gmelin Handbook of Inorganic Chemistry.

Max-Planck-Institut für Aeronomie   1612

[Max Planck Institute for Aeronomy]
Address: Postfach 20, D-3411 Katlenburg-Lindau
Telephone: (05556) 411
Telex: 9 65 527
Managing director: Professor Dr Helmut Rosenbauer
Scientific members, directors: Professor Dr W. Ian Axford, Professor Dr Vytenis M. Vasyliunas
Emeritus scientific members: Professor Dr Walter Dieminger
Activities: Physics of the ionosphere, stratosphere and magnetosphere; space research; satellite experiments.

Max-Planck-Institut für Astronomie   1613

[Max Planck Institute for Astronomy]
Address: Königstuhl, D-6900 Heidelberg 1
Telephone: (06221) 5281
Telex: 4 61 789
Managing director: Professor Dr Hans Elsässer
Scientific member, director: Professor Dr Guido Münch
Activities: Structure, matter, and magnetic fields of the galactic system; origin of stars. A joint German/Spanish centre is maintained at Calar Alto in Spain.

Max-Planck-Institut für Biophysikalische Chemie (Karl-Friedrich-Bonhoeffer-Institut)   1614

[Max Planck Institute for Biophysical Chemistry (Karl Friedrich Bonhoeffer Institute)]
Address: Am Fassberg, Postfach 968, D-3400 Göttingen-Nikolausberg
Telephone: (0551) 2011
Telex: 9 6 786
Managing director: Professor Dr Hans Strehlow
Sections: Neurobiology, Professor Dr Otto Detlev Creutzfeldt; biochemical kinetics, Professor Dr Manfred Eigen; molecular biology, Dr Thomas M. Jovin; phase development, Professor Dr Manfred Kahlweit; molecular system construction, Professor Dr Hans Kuhn; experimental methods, Professor Dr Leo C.M. De Maeyer; laser physics, Professor Dr Fritz Peter Schäfer; electrochemistry and reaction kinetics, Professor Dr Hans Strehlow; biochemistry, Professor Dr Klaus Weber; spectroscopy, Professor Dr Albert Weller; neurochemistry, Professor Dr Victor P. Whittaker
Activities: Dynamics of biological and chemical processes, including studies of the nervous system and of enzyme systems.

Max-Planck-Institut für Chemie (Otto- 1615 Hahn Institut)

[Max Planck Institute for Chemistry (Otto Hahn Institute)]

Address: Saarstrasse 23, Postfach 3060, D-6500 Mainz
Telephone: (06131) 3051
Telex: 4 187 674 mpch d
Managing director: Professor Dr Friedrich Begemann
Sections: Atmospheric chemistry, Professor Dr P. Crutzen; cosmo-chemistry, Professor Dr H. Wänke, Professor Dr F. Begemann; geochemistry, Dr A. Hoffmann; nuclear physics, Professor Dr Peter Brix, Professor Dr Bernhard Ziegler
Graduate research staff: 90
Annual expenditure: £501 000-2m
Activities: Abundance and distribution of atmospheric trace constituents, general circulation and development of the atmosphere; high sensitivity mass spectroscopy of stable and radioactive nuclear reaction products, isotope geology, age determination; study of cosmic ray produced isotopes in meteorites, using neutron activation; nuclear structure; nuclear reactions; photonuclear processes; polarization phenomena in nuclear reactions, high energy gamma spectroscopy.
Contract work: No

Max-Planck-Institut für Eisenforschung 1616 GmbH

[Max Planck Institute for Ferrous Metallurgy]

Address: Max-Planck-Strasse 1, Postfach 140 260, D-4000 Düsseldorf
Telephone: (0211) 67921
Telex: 8 586 762
Managing directors: Professor Dr Hans-Jürgen Engell, Dr Rolf Weidemann
Scientific members, directors: Professor Dr Oskar Pawelski, Professor Dr Wolfgang Pitsch, Professor Dr Hans-Jürgen Engell, Professor Dr Peter Neumann
Emeritus scientific member: Professor Dr Franz Wever
Activities: Fabrication procedures for steels and iron alloys; structure of materials and material properties.

Max-Planck-Institut für 1617 Festkörperforschung

[Max Planck Institute for Solid-State Research]

Address: Heisenbergstrasse 1, Postfach 800 665, D-7000 Stuttgart 80
Telephone: (0711) 68601
Telex: 7 255 555 mpis d
Managing director: Professor Dr Hans-Joachim Queisser
Scientific members, directors: Professor Dr Heinz Bilz, Professor Dr Ole Krogh Andersen, Professor Dr Manuel Cardona, Professor Dr Klaus Dransfeld, Professor Dr Peter Fulde, Professor Dr Ludwig Genzel,

Professor Dr Hans-Joachim Queisser, Professor Dr Albrecht Rabenau, Professor Dr Hans Georg V. Schnering, Professor Dr Arndt Simon
Graduate research staff: 150
Annual expenditure: DM7m
Activities: Crystalline and amorphous matter; semiconductors and dielectrics; optical, electrical, and magnetic properties. Investigations centre on the following general topics: the lattice dynamics of solids, semiconductors and materials of technical importance, new types of materials.
Contract work: No

Max-Planck-Institut für Kernphysik 1618

[Max Planck Institute for Nuclear Physics]

Address: Saupfercheckweg, Postfach 103 980, D-6900 Heidelberg 1
Telephone: (06221) 5161
Telex: 4 61 666
Managing director: Professor Dr Hans A. Weidenmüller
Scientific members, directors: Professor Dr Peter Brix, Professor Dr Hugo Fechtig, Professor Dr Bogdan Povh, Professor Dr Ulrich Schmidt-Rohr, Professor Dr Heinrich Völk, Professor Dr Hans A. Weidenmüller
Activities: Nuclear structure, nuclear reactions, nuclear binding forces, and cosmic chemistry.

Max-Planck-Institut für 1619 Kohlenforschung

[Max Planck Institute for Coal Research]

Address: Kaiser-Wilhelm-Platz 1, Postfach 011 325, D-4330 Mülheim/Ruhr
Telephone: (0208) 3061
Telex: 856 741
Director: Professor Dr Günther Wilke
Scientific member: Dr Roland Köster
Activities: Organometallic chemistry of highly reactive systems, in particular those in which boron, aluminium, titanium, cobalt or nickel are attached directly to the carbon atom of organic group.

Max-Planck Institut für Mathematik* 1620

[Max Planck Institute for Mathematics]

Address: Gottfried-Claren-Strasse 26, D-5300 Bonn 3
Telephone: (0228) 4021
Director: Professor Dr Friedrich Hirzebruch

Max-Planck-Institut für Metallforschung 1621

[Max Planck Institute for Metals Research]
Address: Seestrasse 92, D-7000 Stuttgart 1
Telephone: (0711) 20951
Telex: 7 23 742
Managing director: Dr Jörg Diehl
Activities: Configurations and atomic structures of metals and their alloys, and the relation between their internal structure and their physical, chemical, metallurgical and technical properties.

MATERIALS SCIENCE INSTITUTE 1622

Address: Seestrasse 92, D-7000 Stuttgart 1
Telephone: (0711) 20951
Telex: 7 23 742
Research director: Professor Dr Hellmut Fischmeister
Senior staff: Dr Jörg Diehl, Professor Dr Volkmar Gerold, Professor Dr Günter Petzow, Professor Dr Bruno Predel
Activities: Physical and atomic structure and properties of metals and alloys; solid-state physics.
Publications: Quarterly report.

PHYSICS INSTITUTE 1623

Address: Heisenbergstrasse 1, Postfach 800 665, D-7000 Stuttgart 80
Telephone: (0711) 68601
Telex: 7 255 555
Director: Professor Dr Alfred Seeger
Senior staff: Professor Dr Helmut Kronmüller, Professor Dr Manfred Wilkens
Activities: Development and application of experimental and theoretical methods to investigate properties of crystalline materials sensitive to structural and chemical defects.

Max-Planck-Institut für Meteorologie 1624

[Max Planck Institute for Meteorology]
Address: Bundesstrasse 55, D-2000 Hamburg 13
Telephone: (040) 41141
Telex: 2 11 092
Director: Professor Dr Klaus Hasselmann
Scientific member: Professor Dr Hans G.T. Hinzpeter
Activities: The development of theoretical climatic models; detailed examination of interaction processes in the global system made up of the oceans and the atmosphere.

Max-Planck-Institut für Physik und Astrophysik 1625

[Max Planck Institute for Physics and Astrophysics]
Address: Föhringer Ring 6, Postfach 401 212, D-8000 München 40

Telephone: (089) 318931
Telex: 5 215 619
Managing director: Professor Dr Joachim Trümper
Activities: Elementary particle physics; astrophysics; space research.

ASTROPHYSICS INSTITUTE 1626

Address: Karl-Schwarzschild-Strasse 1, D-8046 Garching bei München
Telephone: (089) 32990
Telex: 524 629
Director: Professor Dr Rudolf Kippenhahn
Scientific Members: Professor Dr Heinz Billing, Professor Dr Jürgen Ehlers, Professor Dr Rudolf Kippenhahn, Professor Dr Friedrich Meyer, Dr Hermann Ulrich Schmidt, Dr Eleonore Trefftz
Activities: Sunspots, solar flares, and the corona surrounding the sun; comets; inner structure and temporal evolution of stars.

EXTRATERRESTRIAL PHYSICS INSTITUTE 1627

Address: Karl-Schwarzschild-Strasse 1, D-8046 Garching bei München
Telephone: (089) 32990
Telex: 5 215 845
Managing director: Professor Dr Joachim Trümper
Scientific members, directors: Dr Gerhard Haerendel, Professor Dr Reimar Lüst, Professor Dr Klaus Pinkau
Emeritus scientific member: Professor Dr Ludwig Biermann
Activities: Properties and interactions of elementary particles; solar research; planets and cosmic research; satellites; and the ionosphere and magnetosphere.

WERNER-HEISENBERG PHYSICS INSTITUTE 1628

Managing director: Professor Dr G. Buschhorn
Scientific members, directors: Professor Dr G. Buschhorn, Professor Dr Hans-Peter Dürr, Professor Dr Klaus Gottstein, Professor Dr Norbert Schmitz, Professor Dr Ulrich Stierlin, Dr Leo Stodolsky, Professor Dr Wolfhart Zimmermann
Activities: Sunspots, solar flares, and the corona surrounding the sun; comets; inner structure and temporal evolution of stars.

Max-Planck-Institut für Plasmaphysik 1629

[Max Planck Institute for Plasma Physics]
Address: Boltzmannstrasse, D-8046 Garching bei München
Telephone: (089) 32991
Telex: 5 215 808
Scientific director and President: Professor Dr Klaus Pinkau
Manager: Dr Ernst-Joachim Meusel

Activities: The largest establishment for controlled thermonuclear fusion research in Germany. Since attaining temperatures necessary for fusion reaction is no longer the basic problem, interest is concentrated mainly on how to contain the hot plasma for a sufficiently long time. The Institute also works on the development of electron ring accelerators for heavy ions.

EXPERIMENTAL PLASMA PHYSICS I   1630
Director: Dr Michael Kaufmann

EXPERIMENTAL PLASMA PHYSICS II   1631
Director: Dr Günter Grieger

EXPERIMENTAL PLASMA PHYSICS III   1632
Director: Dr Gerhart Von Gierke

INFORMATION PROCESSING   1633
Director: Professor Dr Friedrich Hertweck

SURFACE PHYSICS   1634
Head: Professor Dr Dieter Pfirsch

TECHNOLOGY   1635
Director: Dipl-Ing Karl-Heinz Schmitter

THEORY I   1636
Director: Professor Dr Dieter Pfirsch

THEORY II   1637
Director: Professor Dr Arnulf Schlüter

Max-Planck-Institut für Quantenoptik   1638

[Max Planck Institute for Quantum Optics]
Address: D-8046 Garching bei München
Telephone: (089) 32991
Telex: 5 215 808
Managing director: Dr Siegbert Witkowski
Directors: Professor Dr Karl-Ludwig Kompa, Professor Dr Herbert Walther

Max-Planck-Institut für   1639
Radioastronomie

[Max Planck Institute for Radioastronomy]
Address: Auf dem Hügel 69, D-5300 Bonn 1
Telephone: (0228) 5251
Telex: 886440 astro d
Managing director: Professor Dr Ing Peter G. Mezger
Scientific members, directors: Professor Dr Ing Peter G. Mezger, Professor Dr Richard Wielebinski
Emeritus scientific member: Professor Dr Otto Hachenberg
Graduate research staff: 30
Annual expenditure: over £2m
Activities: The work of the Institute includes almost all astronomical problems which can be attacked by obser-

vational radioastronomy. Emphasis is put on radiospectroscopy; the structure, chemical composition and physical state of the interstellar gas are investigated along atomic and molecular lines. In addition, numerous new transitions of partly very complex molecules are being observed. The galactic continuum radio radiation provides information on HII regions, supernova remnants, and the galactic magnetic field. Pulsars are another field of detailed investigations. Radio radiation of extragalactic systems is likewise an object of investigation, for which the inclusion of the 100-metre radio telescope in an international network of radio telescopes (the so-called Very Long Baseline Interferometry), to achieve an extremely high angular resolution, plays an important role. In addition, theoretical work, particularly on the interstellar medium, is pursued.
Contract work: No
Publications: Annual report.

Max-Planck-Institut für Strahlenchemie 1640

[Max Planck Institute for Radiation Chemistry]
Address: Stiftstrasse 34-36, D-4330 Mülheim/Ruhr
Telephone: (0208) 31073
Telex: 856 741
Managing director: Professor Dr Dietrich Schulte-Frohlinde
Scientific members, directors: Professor Dr Kurt Schaffner, Professor Dr Oskar E. Polansky
Activities: Chemistry of metal-organic compounds; radiation chemistry of DNA and DNA model compounds and carbohydrates; pulse radiolysis; and ion-molecule and atom-molecule reactions.
Facilities: Two 3MV Van de Graaff electron accelerators.

Max-Planck-Institut für   1641
Strömungsforschung

[Max Planck Institute for Hydrodynamic Research]
Address: Böttingerstrasse 6-8, D-3400 Göttingen
Telephone: (0551) 7091
Telex: 9 6 768
Managing director: Professor Dr Heinz-Georg Wagner
Activities: Fluid dynamics of liquids and gases; atomic and molecular collision reactions; atmospheric properties.

ATOMIC AND MOLECULAR PHYSICS   1642
DEPARTMENT
Director: Professor Dr Hans Pauly
Activities: Collisions between atoms and molecules over a broad range of energies.

DYNAMIC COMPRESSIBLE MEDIA DEPARTMENT 1643

Director: Professor Dr Ernst-August Müller
Activities: Shock wave oscillations in supersonic flows; production, propagation and damping of weak shock waves or sound waves in supersonic and subsonic flows, with feedback mechanisms taken into account; interaction of flow, combustion and sound in flame jets; turbulent flows, vortex motion and condensation.

MOLECULAR INTERACTIONS DEPARTMENT 1644

Director: Professor Dr Jan-Peter Toennies
Activities: Elementary collision processes between molecules.

REACTION KINETICS DEPARTMENT 1645

Director: Professor Dr Heinz-Georg Wagner
Activities: Absolute rate coefficients, reaction products, distribution of reaction energies over the products, and the interaction of such reactions with transport and flow processes under thermal equilibrium and nonequilibrium conditions.

Max von Pettenkofer- 1646 Institut

[Max von Pettenkofer Institute]
Address: Unter den Eichen 82-84, D-1000 Berlin 45
Telephone: (030) 8308-0
Parent body: Bundesgesundheitsamt
Activities: Pesticides, insecticides and wood preservation agents; general toxicology; chemistry of foods and surfaces in contact with foods, the human body, etc; toxicology of foods and surfaces in contact with foods, the human body, etc.

Medizinische Hochschule 1647 Hannover*

[Medical University of Hannover]
Address: Karl-Wiechert-Allee 9, DDR-3000 Hannover

PATHOLOGISCHES INSTITUT 1648

[Pathology Institute]
Address: Karl-Wiechert-Allee 9, D-3000 Hannover 61
Telephone: (0571) 532 4500
Telex: 922044 medho d
Research director: Professor Dr Georgii
Graduate research staff: 22

Activities: Oncology and neoplastic haematopathology.
Contract work: No

Messerschmitt-Bölkow- 1649 Blohm GmbH

– MBB
Address: Postfach 80 1109, D-8000 München 80
Telephone: (089) 600 01
Telex: 5287-0 mbb d
President and General Manager: Professor Gero Madelung
Executive Corporate Vice-President and Deputy General Manager: Sepp Hort
Department: Engineering and Technology (ZE), Dr-Ing Othmar Heise

COMMERCIAL AIRCRAFT DIVISION 1650 (UH)

Address: Kreetslag 10, Postfach 95 0109, D-2103 Hamburg 95
Telephone: (040) 74 70
Telex: 217 684 mbb h
Managing Director: Ernst-Georg Pantel
Activities: The Division is responsible for development, production and support of transport aircraft and is a partner of Deutsche Airbus GmbH.

DYNAMICS DIVISION (UA) 1651

Address: Postfach 80 1149, D-8000 München 80
Telephone: (089) 60 00-22 06
Telex: 5287-0 mbb d
Managing Director: Günther Kuhle
Activities: Develops, produces and supports modern defence systems, particularly missile systems. All areas of work are undertaken - theoretical principles, design, simulation, testing, production and support.

HELICOPTER AND TRANSPORT 1652 SYSTEMS DIVISION (UD)

Address: Postfach 80 1140, D-8000 München 80
Telephone: (089) 60 00-29 45
Telex: 5287-740 mbb d
Managing Director: Kurt Pfleiderer
Activities: The Division is responsible for development, production, support and world wide civil marketing of helicopters and rail vehicles. It also shares in aircraft and missile programmes for other Divisions. Production takes place at factories in Donauwörth and Laupheim

(aircraft interiors). The main programme is the MBB BO 105 utility helicopter, the first helicopter in the two-tonne class to have two turbine engines. Rail vehicle construction, particularly the development of light weight construction methods takes place at the Donauwörth factory. Power cars and passenger coaches for city transport systems, and high comfort tourist passenger trains are produced.

MILITARY AIRCRAFT DIVISION (UF) 1653

Address: Postfach 80 1160, D-8000 München 80
Telephone: (089) 60 00-59 16
Telex: 5287-910 mbb d
Managing Director: Oskar Friedrich
Activities: Develops, produces and supports high performance combat aircraft for flying units of the German Air Force and Navy and their allies.

OTTOBRUNN OPERATIONS DIVISION (B) 1654

Address: Postfach 80 1220, D-8000 München 80
Telephone: (089) 6000-2401
Telex: 5287-0 mbb d
Managing Director: Gunter Horstkotte

Central Laboratory 1655

Activities: Undertakes research and development in the areas of physics, acoustics, chemistry, plating, plastics, metals, and special materials. One centre of interest is the evolution of new methods of measuring and analysis, for example in acoustics, chemistry and non-destructive testing of parts.

SPACE DIVISION (UR) 1656

Address: Postfach 80 1169, D-8000 München 80
Telephone: (089) 60 000-2459
Telex: 5287-0 mbb d
Managing Director: Johannes Schubert
Activities: Develops satellites and probes, payloads such as the materials science laboratory for Skylab, data transmission systems and ground stations, propulsion systems for rocket stages and thrusters for the orbit and altitude control of long life applications satellites and interplanetary probes. Technologies evolved in space work are also used for the development of advanced transport systems and energy systems. The Division develops components and systems to generate heat and electricity through the use of solar energy. The basis for this work is contracts from the Federal Ministry of Research and Technology, the Federal Ministry of Economic Cooperation, the Commission of the European Communities, and foreign government agencies.

Mobil Oil AG in Deutschland, Forschung-Entwicklung-Anwendung 1657

Address: Tinsdaler Weg, D-2000 Wedel/Holstein
Telephone: (4103) 706314
Telex: 2189566
Director: Dr W.K. Thiemann
Departments: Fuels division, Dr H. Rodenbusch; Lubricants and special products, Dr G.H. Nernst; Service division, Dr O. Janssen
Graduate research staff: 29
Annual expenditure: £501 000-2m
Activities: Research and development of fuels and lubricants.
Contract work: No

Motoren- und Turbinen- Union München GmbH 1658

– MTU
Address: Postfach 50 06 40, D-8000 München 50
Telephone: (089) 14891
Telex: 5215603 mtu
Research director: Dr Paul Esslinger
Sections: Materials, Dr Helmut Huff; processing, Dr Peter Adam; chemistry, Dr Harald Simon
Activities: Research and development of jet engines and turbines.

Niedersächsisches Landesamt für Bodenforschung 1659

[Geological Survey of Lower Saxony]
Address: Stilleweg 2, Postfach 51 01 53, D-3000 Hannover Buchholz
President: Professor Dr F. Bender
Activities: Geophysics, petroleum geology, soil research, geological mapping, natural resource planning, hydrogeology, peat research, engineering geology, environmental geosciences, geoscientific data processing.

INSTITUTE FOR SOIL TECHNOLOGY   1660

Address: Friedrich-Missler-Strasse 46-8, D-2800 Bremen 17
Director: Professor Dr Herbert Kuntze
Activities: Soil science and technology, peat research, water management, grassland research, soil reclamation and improvement.

Obstbauversuchsanstalt   1661
Jork

[Jork Fruit Growing Experimental Station]
Address: Westminnerweg 22, D-2155 Jork
Affiliation: Hannover Chamber of Commerce
Research director: Dr K.-H. Tiemann
Activities: Tree nursery research; selection of varieties; methods of fruit growing; hormone research; virus, mycoplasma, bacteria and fungi research; bees in fruit growing; pest control research; air pollution research; studies on fruit crop nutrition; chemical weed control; fruit storage research; techniques in fruit production.

Papiertechnische Stiftung   1662
für Forschung und
Ausbildung in
Papiererzeugung und
Papierverarbeitung

[Paper Technology Foundation, for Research and Development of Paper Production and Manufacture]
Address: Hess-Strasse 130a, D-8000 München 40
Telephone: (089) 195404
Telex: 5233088 pts
Research director: Dr Ing H.L. Baumgarten
Graduate research staff: 7
Annual expenditure: £501 000-2m
Activities: Pulp, paper, and board producing and converting technology; materials testing; water and wastewater research.
Contract work: Yes

Paul-Ehrlich-Institut   1663
Bundesamt für Sera und
Impfstoffe

[Paul Ehrlich Federal Institute for Serums and Vaccines]
Address: Paul-Ehrlich-Strasse 42-44, D-6000 Frankfurt am Main 70
Telephone: (0611) 636016
President: Professor Dr med H.D. Brede
Sections: Immunology; microbiology; standardization; virology
Graduate research staff: 48
Activities: Standardization and control of serums and vaccines.
Contract work: Yes
Publications: Arbeiten aus dem Paul-Ehrlich-Institut (Bundesamt für Sera und Impfstoffe), dem Georg-Speyer-Haus und dem Ferdinand-Blum-Institut.

Philipps-Universität   1664
Marburg-Lahn

[Marburg University]
Address: Biegenstrasse 10, D-3550 Marburg Lahn
Telephone: (0641) 281
Telex: 482372
President: Professor Dr Walter Kröll

DEPARTMENT OF BIOLOGY   1665

Address: Lahnberge, D-3550 Marburg Lahn
Dean: Professor Dr Dietrich Werner
Sections:
Botany, Professor Dr Andreas Bertsch, Professor Dr Wilhelm Nultsch, Professor Dr Ekkehard Schönbohm, Professor Dr Horst Senger, Professor Dr Hans-Adolf von Stosch, Professor Dr Günter Throm, Professor Dr Werner Wehrmeyer
Comparative anatomy, Professor Dr Karl-August Seitz
Developmental physiology, Professor Dr Heinz-Werner Küthe
Ecology, Professor Dr Hermann Remmert
General zoology, Professor Dr Hans-Ulrich Koecke
Genetics, Professor Dr Paul Koch
Microbiology, Professor Dr Achim Kröger, Professor Dr Rudolf Thauer
Morphology, Professor Dr Ingeborg Lenski
Systematic botany, Professor Dr Aiono Henssen
Systematics and evolution of animals, Professor Dr Reinhard Remane
Zoology, Professor Dr Christiane Buchholtz, Professor

Dr Egbert Geyer, Professor Dr Klaus Kalmring, Professor Dr Christoph Kirchner
Zoology, evolution and human biology, Professor Dr Heinrich-Otto von Hagen

DEPARTMENT OF CHEMISTRY 1666

Address: Lahnberge, D-3550 Marburg Lahn
Dean: Professor Dr Dirk Reinen
Sections:
Biochemistry, Professor Dr Hartmut Follman, Professor Dr Bernard Kadenbach, Professor Dr Helmut Kindl
Chemistry, Professor Dr Jörg Lorberth
Inorganic and analytical chemistry, Professor Dr Horst Klamberg, Professor Dr Gottfried Stork
Inorganic chemistry, Professor Dr Dietrich Babel, Professor Dr Gerd Becker, Professor Dr Kurt Dehnicke, Professor Dr Christoph Elschenbroich, Professor Dr Ulrich Müller, Professor Dr Walter Siebert
Organic chemistry, Professor Dr Hans Günter Aurich, Professor Dr Armin Berndt, Professor Dr Gernot Boche, Professor Dr Reinhard W. Hoffman, Professor Dr Hartwig Perst, Professor Dr Manfred Reetz, Professor Dr Christian Reiehardt, Professor Dr Curt Wentrup, Professor Dr Friedrich-Wilhelm Steuber

DEPARTMENT OF GEOGRAPHY 1667

Address: Deutschhausstrasse 1a, D-3550 Marburg Lahn
Dean: Professor Dr Eckart Ehlers
Senior staff: Professor Dr Wolfgang Andres, Professor Dr Ekkehard Buckhofer, Professor Dr Horst Dickel, Professor Dr Hans-Jörg Dongus, Professor Dr Ingeborg Leister, Professor Dr Günter Mertins, Professor Dr Alfred Pletsch, Professor Dr Carl Schott

DEPARTMENT OF GEOSCIENCES 1668

Address: Lahnberge, D-3550 Marburg Lahn
Dean: Professor Dr Werner Fischer
Sections:
Crystallography, Professor Dr Peter Buck, Professor Dr Mauritius Renninger
Crystallography and mineralogy, Professor Dr Werner Fischer, Professor Dr Stefan Hafner, Professor Dr Rudolf Allmann
Geology, Professor Dr Maurits Lindström
Geology and palaeontology, Professor Dr Reinhold Huckriede Professor Dr Hans-J. Anderson, Professor Dr Willi Ziegler
Geology and sedimentology, Professor Dr Heinrich Zankl

Mineralogy, Professor Dr Erwin Hellner, Professor Dr Hans-Heinrich Lohse
Palaeontology, Professor Dr Gerhard Hahn

DEPARTMENT OF HUMAN MEDICINE 1669

Address: Robert-Koch-Strasse 3, D-3550 Marburg Lahn
Dean: Professor Dr Dr Hans-Jürgen Hering
Sections:
Anaesthesiology, Professor Dr Herbert Lennartz
Anatomy, Professor Dr Herfried Amon, Professor Dr Gerhard Aumüller, Professor Dr Gerlinde Ludwig, Professor Dr Hans-Georg Mannherz, Professor Dr Gerhard Petry, Professor Dr Klaus Unsicker
Applied physiology, Professor Dr Franz Josef Haberich
Biophysics, Professor Dr Leo Priebe
Clinical biochemistry and biochemical microbiology, Professor Dr Manfred Doss
Clinical chemistry and microscopy, Professor Dr Gerhard Sturm
Cytobiology and cytopathology, Professor Dr Horst-Franz Kern
Dentistry, Professor Dr Günther Ahrens, Professor Dr Heinz Bernhardt, Professor Dr Ilse Hennis, Professor Dr Walter Klötzer, Professor Dr Klaus Lehmann, Professor Dr Helmut Schmidt
Dermatology, Professor Dr Horst Eissner, Professor Dr Mladen Rupec
Dermatology and venereology, Professor Dr Hugo Constantin Friedrich
Experimental nuclear medicine, Professor Dr Klaus Joseph, Professor Dr Horst Kuni
Experimental surgery and pathological biochemistry, Professor Dr Wilfried Lorenz
Eye clinic, Professor Dr Wolfgang Straub
Forensic and social psychiatry, Professor Dr Helmut Erhardt
Forensic medicine, Professor Dr Irmgard Oepen, Professor D Reinhard Hitgermann
General pathology and pathological anatomy, Professor Dr Paul Schmitz-Moormann
Human genetics, Professor Dr Heinrich Oepen
Hygiene, Professor Dr Karl Heinz Knoll
Hygiene and bacteriology, Professor Dr Rudolf Siegert
Immunology, Professor Dr Klaus-Ulrich Hartmann
Internal medicine, Professor Dr Gerhard Baltzer, Professor Dr Christian Bode, Professor Dr Rudolf Egbring, Professor Dr Alfred Hardewig, Professor Dr Klaus Haremann, Professor Dr Hans Kaffarnik, Professor Dr Hans-Georg Knauff, Professor Dr Harold Lange, Professor Dr Gustav Adolf Martini, Professor Dr Sadegh Massarrat, Professor Dr Carl-Peter Sodomann
Medical data processing, Professor Dr Adolf Habermehl
Medical microbiology, Professor Dr Werner Slenczka

Medical microbiology and bacteriophysiology, Professor Dr Walter Mannheim

Medical microbiology and immunology, Professor Dr Wilhelm Schoff

Medico-biological statistics and documentation, Professor Dr Peter Ihm

Microbiology, Professor Dr Heinz Kohlhage

Neurology and neuropathology, Professor Dr Hans Solcher

Neurobiochemistry and physiological chemistry, Professor Dr Tilmann Otto Kleine

Neurology and psychiatry, Professor Dr Gert Huffman, Professor Dr Rainer Heene

Neurosurgery, Professor Dr Bernhard Bauer

Neuropsychiatry of children, Professor Dr Doris Weber

Nuclear biology, Professor Dr Erick Schaumlöffel

Obstetrics and gynaecology, Professor Dr Rudolf Buchholz, Professor Dr Erhard Daume, Professor Dr Peter Pots

Ophthalmology, Professor Dr Rüdiger Turss, Professor Dr Lutz Welge-Lüssen

Orthopaedics, Professor Dr Gerhard Exner, Professor Dr Friedrich Neurath

Otorhinolaryngology, Professor Dr Oskar Kleinsasser, Professor Dr Wolfhart Niemeyer, Professor Dr Elimar Schöndarl

Paediatrics, Professor Dr Joachim Dittrich, Professor Dr Carl Eschenbach, Professor Dr Ulrich Willenbockel

Parodontology, Professor Dr Lavinia Flores di Jacobi

Pathological anatomy, Professor Dr Heinrich Kalbfleisch

Pathology, Professor Dr Carlos Thomas

Pharmacology and toxicology, Professor Dr Karl Joachim Netter, Professor Dr Joachim Portig, Professor Dr Rolf Schulte-Hermann, Professor Dr Günther Fred Fuhrmann

Physical chemistry, Professor Dr Peter Karlson

Physiological chemistry, Professor Dr Miguel Beato, Professor Dr Dieter Gallwitz, Professor Dr Jürgen Niessing, Professor Dr Dietrich Schachtschabel, Professor Dr Heinrich Seifart, Professor Dr Wolfgang Wisemann, Professor Dr Herbert Wiegandt

Physiological chemistry and biochemistry, Professor Dr Friedhelm Schneider

Work physiology and rehabilitation research, Professor Dr Günther Hildebrandt, Professor Dr Peter Engel

Psychiatry and neurology, Professor Dr Albrecht Lütcke

Psychiatry and psychopathology, Professor Dr Wolfgang Blankenburg

Psychotherapy, Professor Dr Manfred Pohlen

Psychosomatics, Professor Dr Wolfram Schüffel

Radiology, Professor Dr Emil Heinz Graul, Professor Dr Hans-Georg Grundner

Roentgenology, Professor Dr Horst Dombrowski

Roentgenology and radiology, Professor Dr Friedhelm Hess

Surgery, Professor Dr Hans Koch, Professor Dr Dieter Maroski, Professor Dr Hans-Dietrich Röher

Toxicology and pharmacology, Professor Dr Wolfgang Koransky

Urology, Professor Dr Gerhard Rodeck

DEPARTMENT OF MATHEMATICS　1670

Address: Lahnberge, D-3550 Marburg Lahn
Dean: Professor Dr Werner Schraal
Senior staff: Professor Dr Vojislav G. Avakumovic, Professor Dr Klaus Böhmer, Professor Dr Manfred Breuer, Professor Dr Alexander Dressler, Professor Dr Wolfgang Gromes, Professor Dr Karl-Bernard Gundtach, Professor Dr Wolfgang Haneke, Professor Dr Horst Herold, Professor Dr Friedrich W. Knöller, Professor Dr Hans-Heinrich Körle, Professor Dr Volker Mammitzsch, Professor Dr Walter Miesner, Professor Dr Claude Portenier, Professor Dr Manfred Renfel, Professor Dr Peter Georg Schmidt, Professor Dr György Targonski

DEPARTMENT OF PHARMACY AND　1671 FOOD CHEMISTRY

Address: Wilhelm-Roser-Strasse 2, D-3550 Marburg Lahn
Dean: Professor Dr B. Unterhalt
Sections:

Pharmaceutical and food chemistry, Professor Dr Horst Böhme

Pharmaceutical biology, Professor Dr Josef Hölzl, Professor Dr Max Wiehtl

Pharmaceutical chemistry, Professor Dr Siegfried Ebel, Professor Dr Manfred Haake, Professor Dr Klaus Hartke, Professor Dr Uwe Kuckländer, Professor Dr Gunther Seitz

Pharmaceutical chemistry and technology, Professor Dr Paul Heinz List

Pharmaceutical microbiology, Professor Dr Gerlind Eger-Hummel

Pharmacology and toxicology, Professor Dr Josef Krieglstein

DEPARTMENT OF PHYSICAL　1672 CHEMISTRY

Address: Lahnberge, D-3550 Marburg Lahn
Dean: Professor Dr Heinz Bässler
Sections:

Biopolymers, Professor Dr Gotthold Ebert

Nuclear physics, Professor Dr Reinhard Brandt, Professor Dr Paul Patzelt

Physical chemistry, Professor Dr Horst-Dieter Försterling, Professor Dr Friedrich Hensel, Professor Dr Werner Luck, Professor Dr Armin Schweig

Polymer chemistry, Professor Dr Walter Heitz, Professor Dr Horst F. Müller, Professor Dr Wilhelm Ruland

DEPARTMENT OF PHYSICS 1673

Address: Renthof 5-7, D-3550 Marburg Lahn
Dean: Professor Dr Falk Pïchlhofer
Sections:
Applied physics, Professor Dr Herbert Reitböck
Experimental physics, Professor Dr Hans Ackerman, Professor Dr Rudolf Bock, Professor Dr Ulrich Cappeller, Professor Dr Matthias Elbel, Professor Dr Dieter Fick, Professor Dr Roland Fischer, Professor Dr Wolfgang Fischer, Professor Dr Walter Fuhs, Professor Dr Eberhard Ganssauge, Professor Dr Harry Hühnermann, Professor Dr Friedrick W. Richter, Professor Dr Hans-Jürgen Stöckmann, Professor Dr Josef Stuke, Professor Dr Wilhelm Walcher, Professor Dr H.-W. Wassmuth, Professor Dr Gerhard Weiser, Professor Dr W. Zimmerman
Theoretical physics, Professor Dr Wolfgang Bestgen, Professor Dr Gerald Grawert, Professor Dr Siegfried Grossman, Professor Dr Frankesik Jenc, Professor Dr Werner Kerler, Professor Dr Günther Ludwig, Professor Dr Wolfgang Maas, Professor Dr Otfried Madelung, Professor Dr Olaf Melsheimer, Professor Dr Dvan Movaghar, Professor Dr Holger Neumann, Professor Dr Joachim Petzgold, Professor Dr Peter Thomas, Professor Dr Richard Weiner, Professor Dr Christian Wissel, Professor Dr Werner Zickendrant

DEPARTMENT OF PSYCHOLOGY 1674

Dean: Professor Dr Hans Schauer

Psychology Institute 1675

Address: Gutenbergstrasse 18, D-3550 Marburg Lahn
Senior staff: Professor Dr Heinrich Düker, Professor Dr Theodor Ehlers, Professor Dr Irmela Florin, Professor Dr Otto Lane, Professor Dr Ernst Liebhart, Professor Dr Ferdinand Merz, Professor Dr Hans Schauer, Professor Dr Hartmann Scheiblechner, Professor Dr Klaus Schneider, Professor Dr Bert Sommer, Professor Dr Ingeborg Stelzl, Professor Dr Lothar Tent, Professor Dr Manfred Ritter

Philips GmbH Forschungslaboratorium Aachen* 1676

Address: Weisshausstrasse, Postfach 1980, D-5100 Aachen
Head: Professor Dr E. Kauer
Activities: Electronic devices and systems.

Philips GmbH Forschungslaboratorium Hamburg* 1677

Address: Vogt-Kölln-Strasse 30, Postfach 540840, D-2000 Hamburg 54
Head: Dr K.J. Schmidt-Tiedemann
Activities: Electronic devices and systems.

Physikalisch-Technische Bundesanstalt Braunschweig und Berlin 1678

– PTB
[Federal Physical-Technical Establishment in Braunschweig and Berlin]
Address: Bundesallee 100, D-3300 Braunschweig
Telephone: (0531) 5921
Telex: 9-52822 (pth d)
Parent body: Bundesminister für Wirtschaft
President: Professor Dr D. Kind
Vice-president: Professor Dr H.-J. Schrader
Member of the Presidential board: Professor Dr S. German
Graduate research staff: 350
Activities: PTB is a national institute for science and technology and the highest technical authority for metrology in the Federal Republic of Germany. Its interests cover metrology and basic research in the field of mechanics, electricity, heat, optics, acoustics, atomic and nuclear physics; testing and approval of measuring instruments, apparatus and materials.
Contract work: Yes
Publications: Annual report.

ACOUSTICS DIVISION 1679

Head: Professor Dr H.-G. Diesel
Sections: Physical acoustics, Dr P. Dämmig; audio acoustics, Professor Dr R. Martin

ATOMIC PHYSICS DIVISION 1680

Head: Professor Dr S. Wagner
Sections: Ion physics, Professor Dr E. Waibel; electron beams and X-rays, Professor Dr K.-J. Hanssen; radioactivity, Professor Dr H.-M. Weiss; photon and electron dosimetry, Professor Dr H. Reich; neutron dosimetry, Professor Dr R. Jahr; metrology of radiation protection, Dr W. Kolb

BERLIN INSTITUTE 1681

Address: Abbestrasse 2-12, D-1000 Berlin 10
Telephone: (030) 34811
Head: Professor Dr G. Sauerbrey
Sections: Mechanics and thermal engineering, Professor Dr G. Sauerbrey; high-temperature and vacuum physics, Professor Dr B. Wende; low-temperature physics, Professor Dr H.-D. Hahlbohm, Dr K. Grohmann, Dr F. Thurley; medical measuring techniques, Dr R. Nink

ELECTRICITY DIVISION 1682

Head: Professor Dr V. Kose
Sections: Electrical units, Professor Dr F. Melchert; precision electrical measurements, Professor Dr H. Capptuller; electrical energy measurements, Professor Dr R. Friedl, Dr D.-W. Peier; electrophysics, Professor Dr V. Zehler, Dr E. Braun, Dr J.D. Sievert

GENERAL TECHNICAL AND 1683 SCIENTIFIC SERVICES DIVISION

Head: Professor Dr W. Mühe
Sections: Fundamental Physics, Professor Dr B. Kramer; technical administration, Dr N. Helwig; technical and scientific coordination, Professor Dr L. Wiedecke; data processing, Professor Dr W. Gitt

HEAT DIVISION 1684

Head: Professor Dr S. German
Sections: Basic thermodynamics, Professor Dr W. Thomas; thermodynamic transport quantities, Professor Dr W. Rühl, Dr K.-H. Bode; physical chemistry, Professor Dr H.-H. Kirchner; basic physical safety research, Dr H. Steen; explosion - protection of electrical equipment, Professor Dr H. Dreier

LONG-TERM STORAGE AND FINAL 1685 DISPOSAL OF RADIOACTIVE WASTE DIVISION

Head: Professor Dr W. Heintz
Sections: Science and technology, Professor Dr H. Röthemeyer; law, industrial economics and administration, Dr P.-G. Gutermuth; nuclear fuels, Professor Dr W. Heintz

MECHANICS DIVISION 1686

Head: Professor Dr J. Bortfeldt
Sections: Length, Professor Dr F. Bayer-Helms; time, frequency, Dr H. De Boer; mass, Dr M. Kochsiek; force, Professor Dr W. Weller; liquids, gases, Professor Dr L. Narjes; industrial metrology, Professor Dr F. Lebowsky; industrial metrology, machine elements, Professor Dr H. Kunzmann

OPTICS DIVISION 1687

Head: Professor Dr D. Hahn
Sections: Light and radiation, Professor Dr K. Bischoff, Dr W. Erb; image and wave optics, Professor Dr G. Vieth

REACTOR RADIATION DIVISION 1688

Head: Professor Dr V. Siegel
Sections: Reactor technology, Dr H.-J. Kriks; metrology of reactor neutrons, Professor Dr H. Ramthun; reactor experiments, Professor Dr R. Scherm; theory and on-line data processing, Professor Dr K. Weise

Rheinisch-Westfälische 1689 Akademie der Wissenschaften

[Rhineland-Westphalia Academy of Sciences]
Address: Palmenstrasse 16, D-4000 Düsseldorf 1
Telephone: (0211) 342051
President: Professor Dr Franz Grosse-Brockhoff
Managing secretary: Professor Dr Gerhard Kegel
Secretary, Natural Sciences, Engineering and Economics Section: Professor Dr Werner Schmeyer
Activities: Founded in 1969, the Academy is the youngest in the Federal Republic of Germany. It has two sections, one for the human sciences, and one for natural sciences, engineering and economics.

Rheinisch-Westfälische Technische Hochschule Aachen

1690

– RWTH
[Aachen Technical University]
Address: Templergraben 55, D-5100 Aachen
Rector: Professor Dr Günter Urban

FACULTY OF ARCHITECTURE AND CIVIL ENGINEERING

1691

Dean: Professor Dr Ing Gerhard Rouvé

Architecture Division

1692

BUILDING CONSERVATION

1693

Head: Professor Dr Ingeborg Schild

BUILDING CONSTRUCTION I (STRUCTURE)

1694

Head: Professor Dr Franz Krauss

BUILDING CONSTRUCTION II (BUILDING SERVICES)

1695

Head: Professor Wolfgang Döring

BUILDING CONSTRUCTION III (BUILDING PHYSICS AND ENVIRONMENTAL DESIGN)

1696

Head: Professor Dr Erich Schild

CONSTRUCTION PRINCIPLES OF DESIGN

1697

Head: Professor Horst Kohl

FUNDAMENTALS OF BUILDING TYPOLOGY

1698

Head: Professor Dr Peter Fuhrmann

HOUSING DESIGN

1699

Head: Professor Günther Schöfl

INDUSTRIAL AND SCHOOL DESIGN (BUILDING TYPOLOGY)

1700

Head: Professor Fritz Eller

INTERIOR DESIGN AND FURNISHING

1701

Head: Professor Marijke van Moorsel

LANDSCAPE ARCHITECTURE

1702

Head: Professor Hermann Birkigt

LANDSCAPE ECOLOGY AND DESIGN

1703

Head: Professor Wolfram Pflug

PLANNING THEORY

1704

Head: Professor Dr Gerhard Fehl

THEORY OF ARCHITECTURE

1705

Head: Professor Dr Manfred Speidel

TOWN AND REGIONAL PLANNING

1706

Head: Professor Gerhard Curdes

URBAN DESIGN

1707

Head: Professor Gottfried Böhm

Civil Engineering Division

1708

BUILDING MACHINES AND OPERATIONS INSTITUTE

1709

Address: Mies-van-der-Rohe-Strasse, D-5100 Aachen
Director: Professor Dr Ing G. Pohle

BUILDING MATERIALS INSTITUTE

1710

Address: Schinkelstrasse 3, D-5100 Aachen
Director: Professor Dr Ing Karlhans Wesche

CONCRETE CONSTRUCTIONS INSTITUTE

1711

Address: Mies-van-der-Rohe-Strasse, D-5100 Aachen
Director: Professor Dr Ing Heinrich Trost
Sections: Building statics, Professor Dr Ing Jürgen Kammenhuber; steel constructions, Professor Dr Ing Philipp Stein; general construction engineering, Professor Dr Ing Helmut Domke

GEODETICS INSTITUTE I

1712

Director: Professor Dr Fritz Löschner

GEODETICS INSTITUTE II

1713

Director: Professor Dr Ing Erich Hektor

HOUSING ESTATES WATER SUPPLY INSTITUTE

1714

Address: Mies-van-der-Rohe-Strasse, D-5100 Aachen
Director: Professor Dr Ing Botho Böhnke

HYDRAULIC ENGINEERING AND WATER SUPPLY INSTITUTE

1715

Director: Professor Dr Ing G. Rouvé

ROADS AND TUNNELS CONSTRUCTION INSTITUTE

1716

Address: Mies-van-der-Rohe-Strasse, D-5100 Aachen
Director: vacant

TRANSPORT AND RAILWAY ENGINEERING INSTITUTE

1717

Address: Mies-van-der-Rohe-Strasse, D-5100 Aachen
Director: Professor Dr Ing Hermann Nebelung

URBAN BUILDING INSTITUTE   **1718**
Address: Mies-van-der-Rohe-Strasse, D-5100 Aachen
Director: Professor Dr Ing Paul A. Mäcke

WATERWAY ENGINEERING,   **1719**
FOUNDATIONS AND SOIL MECHANICS
INSTITUTE
Address: Mies-van-der-Rohe-Strasse, D-5100 Aachen
Director: Professor Dr Ing Werner Wittke

FACULTY OF ELECTRICAL   **1720**
ENGINEERING
Dean: Professor Dr Ing Klaus Möller

Control Engineering   **1721**
Director: Professor Dr Heinrich Meyr

Electrical Engineering Materials   **1722**
Institute
Directors: Professor Dr Karl-A. Hempel, Professor Dr
Gottfried Arlt

Electrical Machines Institute   **1723**
Directors: Professor Dr Ing Philipp Klaus Sattler,
Professor Dr Ing Johannes Schroeder

Electrical Power Transmission and   **1724**
Distribution Institute
Director: Professor Dr Kurt Edwin

Electrical Telecommunication   **1725**
Engineering Institute
Director: Professor Dr Ing Hans Dieter Lüke

High Frequency Technology Institute   **1726**
Director: Professor Dr Ing Hans Jürgen Schmitt

High Tension Engineering Institute   **1727**
Directors: Professor Dr Ing Klaus Möller, Professor
Dr Gerhard Pietsch

Institute of Semiconductor Electronics   **1728**
Directors: Professor Dr Heinz Beneking, Professor Dr
Pieter Balk Professor Dr Dieter Bimberg

Metrology   **1729**
Director: Professor Dr von Basel

Operating Systems   **1730**
Director: Professor Dr Dieter Haupt

Power Electronics and Electrical   **1731**
Drives Institute
Director: Professor Dr Ing Hans Christoph Skudelny

Rogowski Institute for Electrical   **1732**
Engineering
Director: Professor Dr Ing Walter Ameling

Signalling Equipment and Data   **1733**
Processing Institute
Director: Professor Dr Ing Hans Jörg Tafel

Technical Acoustics Institute   **1734**
Director: Professor Dr Heinrich Kuttruff

Technical Electronics Institute   **1735**
Director: Professor Dr Heinz Lueg

Theoretical Electrical Engineering   **1736**
Institute
Director: Professor Dr Walter Engl

FACULTY OF MATHEMATICS AND   **1737**
NATURAL SCIENCES
Dean: Professor Dr Peter Grosse

Chemistry and Biology Division   **1738**

BOTANICAL INSTITUTE   **1739**
Address: Worringer Weg, D-5100 Aachen
Director: Professor Dr Hans-Günther Aach
Sections: Systematic and geobotany, Professor Dr
Ludwig Aletsee; plant morphology, Professor Dr Hans
Albrecht Froebe

ECOLOGICAL INSTITUTE   **1740**
Address: Kopernikusstrasse 16, D-5100 Aachen
Director: Professor Dr Heinrich Kaiser

FUEL CHEMISTRY AND PHYSICO-   **1741**
CHEMICAL PROCESS ENGINEERING
INSTITUTE
Address: Worringer Weg 1, D-5100 Aachen
Director: Professor Dr Ing Hans Hammer

GERMAN WOOL RESEARCH INSTITUTE   1742
Address: Veltmanplatz 8, D-5100 Aachen
Director: Professor Dr Ing Drs Helmut Zahn

INORGANIC CHEMISTRY INSTITUTE   1743
Address: Professor-Pirlet-Strasse 1, D-5100 Aachen
Sections: Inorganic and analytical chemistry, Professor Dr Welf Bronger; inorganic chemistry, Professor Dr Gerhard Herberich; inorganic and electrochemistry, Professor Dr Peter Paetzold, Professor Dr Herbert Jacobs, Professor Dr Peter Laur

MACROMOLECULAR CHEMISTRY AND TEXTILE CHEMISTRY INSTITUTE   1744
Address: Worringer Weg 1, D-5100 Aachen
Sections: Macromolecular chemistry, Professor Dr Ernst Klesper; textile chemistry and macromolecular chemistry, Professor Dr Ing Drs Helmut Zahn, Professor Dr Hanno Baumann

MICROBIOLOGICAL INSTITUTE   1745
Address: Worringer Weg, D-5100 Aachen
Director: Professor Dr Carl-Christian Emeis

NEUROBIOLOGY INSTITUTE   1746
Address: KFA Jülich, Postfach, D-5170 Jülich
Director: Professor Dr H. Stieve

ORGANIC CHEMISTRY INSTITUTE   1747
Address: Professor-Pirlet-Strasse 1, D-5100 Aachen
Senior staff: Professor Dr Hermann Stetter, Professor Dr Hans-Dieter Scharf, Professor Dr Franz Dallacker, Professor Dr Jörg Fleischhauer, Professor Dr Hans Günther Thomas

PHYSICAL CHEMISTRY INSTITUTE I   1748
Address: Templergraben 59, D-5100 Aachen
Director: Professor Dr Manfred Zeidler
Section: Physical chemistry of biopolymers, Professor Dr Hansjürgen Schönert

PHYSICAL CHEMISTRY INSTITUTE II   1749
Address: Templergraben 59, D-5100 Aachen
Director: Professor Dr Rolf Haase
Section: Physical chemistry of ionic liquids, Professor Dr Joachim Richter

PLANT PHYSIOLOGY INSTITUTE   1750
Address: Worringer Weg, D-5100 Aachen
Director: Professor Dr Hans-Joachim Reisener

TECHNICAL CHEMISTRY AND PETROCHEMISTRY INSTITUTE   1751
Address: Worringer Weg 1, D-5100 Aachen
Directors: Professor Dr Wilhelm Keim, Professor Dr Bernhard Fell

ZOOLOGY INSTITUTE   1752
Address: Kopernikusstrasse 16, D-5100 Aachen
Director: Professor Dr Friedrich-Wilhelm Schlote
Sections: Morphology and developmental biology, Professor Dr Martin Scriba; general zoology, Professor Dr Peter Schmidt

Mathematics and Physics Division   1753

APPLIED MATHEMATICS AND COMPUTER SCIENCE DEPARTMENT   1754
Address: Templergraben 64, D-5100 Aachen
Head: Professor Dr Walter Oberschelp

COMPUTER SCIENCE DEPARTMENT I   1755
Head: Professor Dr Jürgen Merkwitz

COMPUTER SCIENCE DEPARTMENT II   1756
Head: Professor Dr Klaus Indermark

COMPUTER SCIENCE DEPARTMENT III   1757
Head: Professor Dr Hartmut Noltemeier

EXPERIMENTAL PHYSICS INSTITUTE I   1758
Address: Sommerfeldstrasse, D-5100 Aachen
Directors: Professor Dr Dr Peter Grosse, Professor Dr Dr Klaus Lübelsmeyer, Professor Dr Detlef Schmitz

EXPERIMENTAL PHYSICS INSTITUTE II   1759
Address: Sommerfeldstrasse, D-5100 Aachen
Directors: Professor Dr Dr Gerhard Heiland, Professor Dr Dr Wilhelm Sander

EXPERIMENTAL PHYSICS INSTITUTE III   1760
Address: Sommerfeldstrasse, D-5100 Aachen
Directors: Professor Dr Dr Helmut Faissner, Professor Dr Martin Deutschmann
Section: Theoretical elementary particle physics, Professor Dr Rudolf H.A. Rodenberg

GENERAL MECHANICS INSTITUTE   1761
Address: Templergraben 64, D-5100 Aachen
Director: Professor Dr Ing Gerhard Adomeit

GEOMETRY AND PRACTICAL MATHEMATICS INSTITUTE   1762
Address: Templergraben 55, D-5100 Aachen
Director: Professor Dr Rolf Jeltsch

MATHEMATICS DEPARTMENT A   1763
Address: Templergraben 55, D-5100 Aachen
Head: Professor Dr Paul Leo Butzer

MATHEMATICS DEPARTMENT B   **1764**
Address: Templergraben 64, D-5100 Aachen
Head: Professor Dr Heinz Schöneborn

MATHEMATICS DEPARTMENT C   **1765**
Address: Templergraben 55, D-5100 Aachen
Head: Professor Dr Friedhelm Erwe

MATHEMATICS DEPARTMENT D   **1766**
Address: Templergraben 64, D-5100 Aachen
Head: Professor Dr Joachim Neubüser

MATHEMATICS DEPARTMENT I   **1767**
Address: Augustinerbach 2a, D-5100 Aachen
Head: Professor Dr Horst Niemeyer

MATHEMATICS DEPARTMENT II   **1768**
Address: Wüllnerstrasse zwischen 5 und 7, D-5100
Aachen
Head: Professor Dr Klaus Habetha

MATHEMATICS INSTITUTE   **1769**
Address: Templergraben 55, D-5100 Aachen
Director: Professor Dr Günter Hellwig

MECHANICS INSTITUTE   **1770**
Address: Templergraben 64, D-5100 Aachen
Director: Professor Dr Carl Heinz

OPERATIONAL RESEARCH   **1771**
DEPARTMENT
Address: Templergraben 64, D-5100 Aachen
Head: Professor Dr Rolf Kaerkes

PURE AND APPLIED MATHEMATICS   **1772**
INSTITUTE
Address: Templergraben 55, D-5100 Aachen
Director: Professor Dr Claus Müller

STATISTICS DEPARTMENT I   **1773**
Address: Wüllnerstrasse 3, D-5100 Aachen
Head: Professor Dr Burkhard Rauhut

STATISTICS DEPARTMENT II   **1774**
Address: Wüllnerstrasse 3, D-5100 Aachen
Head: Professor Dr Olaf Krafft

TECHNICAL MECHANICS INSTITUTE   **1775**
Address: Templergraben 64, D-5100 Aachen
Director: Professor Dr Georg Rieder

THEORETICAL PHYSICS INSTITUTE   **1776**
Address: Sommerfeldstrasse, D-5100 Aachen
Directors: Professor Dr B. Ubbo Felderhoff, Professor
Dr Dr Friedrich Schlögl, Professor Dr Horst-Dietrich
Dietze, Professor Dr Jürgen Schnackenberg, Professor
Dr Hans A. Kastrup

FACULTY OF MECHANICAL   **1777**
ENGINEERING

Aerodynamics Institute   **1778**
Director: Professor E. Krause
Sections: Non-stationary gas dynamics, Professor Dr
Ing Zeller; aerodynamics of flying, Professor Dr Dr
Nastase

Air and Space Travel Institute   **1779**
Director: Professor Dr Ing Staufenbiel

Applied Thermodynamics Institute   **1780**
Director: Professor Dr Pischinger

Automobile Institute   **1781**
Director: Professor Dr Ing Helling

Chemical Engineering Institute I   **1782**
Director: Professor Dr Ing Rautenbach
Section: Mathematical methods in chemical engineering, Professor Dr Schümmer

Chemical Engineering Institute II   **1783**
Director: Professor Dr Ing Hartmann

Control Engineering Institute   **1784**
Director: Professor Dr Ing Rake
Section: Process computer application and process
control, Professor Dr Ing Plessmann

Gear Design and Machine Dynamics   **1785**
Institute
Director: Professor Dr Ing Dittrich

General Mechanical Engineering   **1786**
Institute
Director: Professor Dr Ing Koller

Heat Transfer and Air Conditioning   **1787**
Institute
Director: Professor Dr Ing Renz

Hydraulic and Pneumatic Drive and   **1788**
Control Systems Institute
Director: Professor Dr Ing Backé

Institut für Kunststoffverarbeitung in Industrie und Handwerk — 1789

- IKV
[Plastics Technology Institute]
Address: Pontstrasse 49, D-5100 Aachen
Telephone: (0241) 803806
Telex: 832358 ikv d
Affiliation: Vereinigung zur Förderung des Instituts für Kunststoffverarbeitung
Director: Professor Dr Ing Georg Mendes
Section: Materials technology, Dr Ing V. Thebing
Graduate research staff: 65
Activities: The IKV carries out research into extrusion, including process control and screw and extruder design; injection moulding, including the development of control parameters and measurement technology; foamed plastics; fibre-reinforced plastics, including the automation of compression moulding, hand lamination and winding; joining techniques, including polyolefins for glueing, printing and painting; materials technology, including plastics corrosion.
Contract work: Yes
Publications: IKV - Communications.

Jet Propulsion and Turboengines Institute — 1790

Director: Professor Dipl-Ing David
Sections: Aircraft engines, Professor Dr Ing Gallus; electrical drives in space, Professor Dr Ing Beylich

Labour Science Institute — 1791

Director: Professor Dr Ing Hackstein
Section: System technology, Professor Dr Ing Hildebrandt

Light Construction Institute — 1792

Director: Professor Dr Ing Öry

Machine Elements and Design Institute — 1793

Director: Professor Dr Ing Peeken
Section: Machine elements, Professor Dr Ing von den Osten-Sacken

Machine Tools Laboratory — 1794

Sections: Machine tools, Professor Dr Ing Weck; technology for production engineering, Professor Dr Ing König; production systematology, Professor Dr Ing Eversheim; measuring technique, Professor Dr Ing Pfeifer

Materials Science Institute — 1795

Director: Professor Dr Knotek
Section: Materials science, Professor Dr Lugscheider

Materials Science Institute — 1796

Director: Professor Dr Ing Troost
Sections: Materials science, Professor Dr Ing El-Magd; materials technology, Professor Dr Ing Broichhausen

Missile Dynamics Institute — 1797

Director: Professor Dr Ing Thomae
Section: High-temperature gas dynamics, Professor Dr Grönig

Reactor Materials and Fuel Elements Institute — 1798

Director: Professor Dr Nickel

Reactor Structural Elements and Reactor Security Institute — 1799

Director: Professor Dr van den Decken

Reactor Technology Institute — 1800

Director: Professor Dr Schulten

Shipbuilding, Construction and Statics Institute — 1801

Director: Professor Dr Ing Schultz

Shipbuilding, Design and Dynamics Institute — 1802

Director: Professor Dr Ing Schneekluth
Section: Offshore technology, Professor Dr Ing Kokkinowrachos

Steam and Gas Turbines Institute — 1803

Director: Professor Dr Ing Dibelius

Technical Thermodynamics Institute — 1804

Director: Professor Dr Ing Knoche

Textile Technology Institute — 1805

Director: Professor Dr Ing Lünenschloss

Transportation and Rail Vehicles Institute   1806

Director: Professor Dr Ing Frederich
Sections: Analytical methods in vehicle and transport technology, Professor Dr Ing Krettek; wear of materials, Professor Dr Ing H. Krause

Welding Technology Institute   1807

Director: Professor Dr Ing Eichhorn
Section: Process controlling device in welding, Professor Dr Ing Drews

FACULTY OF MEDICINE   1808

Dean: Professor Dr W. Kühnel

Anatomy Department   1809

Address: Melatener-Strasse 211, D-5100 Aachen

Biophysics Department   1810

Address: Postfach 360, D-5170 Jülich
Director: Professor Dr Klaus Wagener

Central Clinical Chemistry Laboratory   1811

Address: Goethestrasse 27-29, D-5100 Aachen
Director: Professor Dr Helmut Greiling

Dentistry (Prosthetics)   1812

Address: Goethestrasse 27-29, D-5100 Aachen
Director: Professor Dr Hubertus Spiekermann

Dermatology Department   1813

Address: Goethestrasse 27-29, D-5100 Aachen
Director: Professor Dr Wolf Meinhof

Ear, Nose and Throat Department   1814

Address: Goethestrasse 27-29, D-5100 Aachen
Director: Professor Dr Georg Schlöndorff

Forensic Medicine Department   1815

Address: Lochnerstrasse 4-20, D-5100 Aachen
Director: Professor Dr Helmut Althoff

Gynaecology and Obstetrics Department 1816

Address: Goethestrasse 27-29, D-5100 Aachen
Director: Professor Dr Hugo Jung

Hygiene and Occupational Medicine Department   1817

Address: Lochnerstrasse 4-20, D-5100 Aachen
Director: Professor Dr Hans Joachim Einbrodt

Internal Medicine Department I   1818

Address: Goethestrasse 27-29, D-5100 Aachen
Director: Professor Dr Sven Effert

Internal Medicine Department II   1819

Address: Goethestrasse 27-29, D-5100 Aachen
Director: vacant

Maxillo-Facial and Plastic Surgery of the Face   1820

Director: Professor Dr Wolfgang Koberg

Medical Microbiology Department   1821

Address: Goethestrasse 27-29, D-5100 Aachen
Director: Professor Dr Günther Gillissen

Medical Psychology   1822

Address: Gut Kullen (Schwesternwohnheim), D-5100 Aachen
Director: Professor Dr Andreas Ploeger

Medical Statistics and Documentation 1823

Address: Goethestrasse 23, D-5100 Aachen
Director: Professor Dr Rudolf Repges

Neurology Department   1824

Address: Goethestrasse 27-29, D-5100 Aachen
Director: Professor Dr Klaus Poeck

Neuropathology   1825

Address: Goethestrasse 27-29, D-5100 Aachen
Director: Professor Dr Michael Schröder

Neurosurgery   1826

Address: Goethestrasse 27-29, D-5100 Aachen
Director: Professor Dr Werner Krenkel

Ophthalmology Department   1827

Address: Goethestrasse 27-29, D-5100 Aachen
Director: Professor Dr Martin Reim

Orthopaedics Department 1828

Address: Goethestrasse 27-29, D-5100 Aachen
Director: Professor Dr Jochen Ohnsorge

Paediatric Cardiology 1829

Address: Goethestrasse 27-29, D-5100 Aachen
Director: Professor Dr Götz von Bernuth

Paediatrics Department 1830

Address: Goethestrasse 27-29, D-5100 Aachen
Director: Professor Dr Hans Schönenberg

Pathology Department 1831

Address: Goethestrasse 27-29, D-5100 Aachen
Director: Professor Dr Christian Mittermayer

Pharmacology Department 1832

Address: Melatenerstrasse 211, D-5100 Aachen
Director: Professor Dr Otto Heidenreich

Physiological Chemistry Department 1833

Address: Melatenerstrasse 211, D-5100 Aachen
Director: Professor Dr Hans-Dieter Ohlenbusch

Physiology Department 1834

Address: Melatenerstrasse 211, D-5100 Aachen
Director: Professor Dr Holger Schmid-Schönbein

Psychiatry Department 1835

Address: Goethestrasse 27-29, D-5100 Aachen
Director: Professor Dr Wolfgang Klages

Radiology Department 1836

Address: Goethestrasse 27-29, D-5100 Aachen
Director: Professor Dr Wolfgang Frik

Surgery Department 1837

Address: Goethestrasse 27-29, D-5100 Aachen
Director: Professor Dr Martin Reifferscheid

Urology Department 1838

Address: Goethestrasse 27-29, D-5100 Aachen
Director: Professor Dr Wolfgang Lutzeyer

FACULTY OF MINING AND METALLURGY 1839

Dean: Professor Dr Ing Ernst-Ulrich Reuther

Earth Sciences Division 1840

APPLIED GEOPHYSICS 1841
Address: Jägerstrasse 17-19, D-5100 Aachen
Director: Professor Dr Jürgen Wohlenberg

CRYSTALLOGRAPHY INSTITUTE 1842
Address: Jägerstrasse 17-19, D-5100 Aachen
Director: Professor Dr Theo Hahn

GEOLOGY AND PALAEONTOLOGY INSTITUTE 1843
Address: Wüllnerstrasse 2, D-5100 Aachen
Director: Professor Dr R. Walter
Sections: Geology of solid fuels, vacant; palaeontology, vacant

MINERALOGY AND STRATIGRAPHY INSTITUTE 1844
Address: Wüllnerstrasse 2, D-5100 Aachen
Director: Professor Dr Günther Friedrich
Section: Applied stratigraphy, Professor Dr Gunther Friedrich.

REGIONAL AND APPLIED GEOLOGY RESEARCH UNIT 1845
Address: Lochnerstrasse 4-20, D-5100 Aachen
Director: Professor Dr Karl-Heinrich Heitfeld

Metallurgy Division 1846

ATOMIC FUELS AND THEORETICAL METALLURGY INSTITUTE 1847
Address: Kopernikusstrasse 16, D-5100 Aachen
Director: Professor Dr Ottmar Knacke
Section: Theoretical metallurgy, Professor Dr Hans Adolf Friedrichs

FERROUS METALLURGY INSTITUTE 1848
Address: Intzestrasse 1, D-5100 Aachen
Telephone: (0241) 805782
Telex: 832704 thacd
Director: Professor Dr Winfried Dahl
Sections: Process metallurgy, Professor Dr Gudenau; metallurgy, Professor Dr Tarek El Gammal, Professor Dr Klaus Lange; materials science, Professor Dr Winfried Dahl
Graduate research staff: 75
Annual expenditure: £500 000-2m
Activities: The Institute carries out teaching and research in the field of iron and steel metallurgy.

Research work is directed towards the improvement of steelmaking processes and the properties of steel. This also includes developments in closely allied fields, such as coal gasification. All research projects are conducted in close cooperation with the Verein Deutscher Eisenhüttenleute (German Iron and Steel Institute) and with industry, emphasis being placed on the investigation of fundamental principles and their application to the technical problems of iron- and steelmaking.

Facilities: Electric arc furnace, 150 kg; various pilot plants for coal gasification; vacuum induction furnace, 100 kg; X-ray flash equipment with induction furnace; ESR equipment, 50 kg; Duffers Gleeble; various servohydraulic material-testing machines 60 kN up to 1 000 kN; servohydraulic resonant/non-resonant testing machine 12 000 kN.

Contract work: Yes

FOUNDRY INSTITUTE 1849

Address: Intzestrasse 5, D-5100 Aachen
Director: Professor Dr Peter R. Sahm
Sections: Moulding materials science and foundry matters, Professor Dr Dietmar Boenisch; foundry matters, Professor Dr Siegfried Engler

INDUSTRIAL FURNACES AND 1850 THERMAL ENGINEERING IN METALLURGY INSTITUTE

Address: Kopernikusstrasse 16, D-5100 Aachen
Director: Professor Dr Herbert Wilhelmi
Sections: Industrial furnaces and thermal engineering in ferrous metallurgy, Professor Dr Günther Woelk; energy and mass transport, Professor Dr Heinrich Köhne

METAL FORMING INSTITUTE 1851

Address: Intzestrasse 10, D-5100 Aachen
Director: Professor Dr Reiner Kopp

METALLOGRAPHY AND METAL 1852 PHYSICS INSTITUTE

Address: Kopernikusstrasse 14, D-5100 Aachen
Director: Professor Dr Kurt Lücke
Sections: Applied metallography of non-ferrous metals, Professor Dr Wolfgang Bunk; metallography and metal physics, Professor Dr Josef Schlipf

METALLURGY AND 1853 ELECTROMETALLURGY INSTITUTE

Address: Intzestrasse 3, D-5100 Aachen
Director: Professor Dr Joachim Krüger

ROCK METALLURGY INSTITUTE 1854

Address: Mauerstrasse 5, D-5100 Aachen
Director: Professor Dr Piet Reynen
Sections: Bonding materials, Professor Dr Udo Ludwig; metallurgical and ceramic thermochemistry,

Professor Dr Franz Müller; glass and glass metallurgy, Professor Dr Ludwig Zagar; physico-chemical basis of ceramics, Professor Dr W. Krönert; mineralogy and petrography, Professor Dr O.E. Radezewski

Mining Division 1855

COKING AND BRIQUETTING MINERAL 1856 PROCESSING INSTITUTE

Address: Wüllnerstrasse 2, D-5100 Aachen
Director: Professor Dr Ing Heinz Hoberg

MINE SURVEYING, MINING DAMAGE, 1857 AND GEOPHYSICS IN MINING INSTITUTE

Address: Wüllnerstrasse 2, D-5100 Aachen
Director: Professor Dr Ing Adolf Spettmann

MINING AND METALLURGICAL 1858 MACHINERY INSTITUTE

Address: Wüllnerstrasse 2, D-5100 Aachen
Director: Professor Dr Ing Hermann Fauser

MINING INSTITUTE I 1859

Address: Wüllnerstrasse 2, D-5100 Aachen
Director: Professor Dr Ing Ernst-Ulrich Reuther

MINING INSTITUTE II 1860

Address: Lochnerstrasse 4-20, D-5100 Aachen
Acting director: Professor Dr Ing Sann

MINING INSTITUTE III 1861

Address: Lochnerstrasse 4-20, D-5100 Aachen
Director: Professor Dr Ing Hans Goergen

FACULTY OF PHILOSOPHY 1862

Dean: Professor Dr Karl Georg Zinn

Geographical Institute 1863

Address: Templergraben 55, D-5100 Aachen
Directors: Professor Dr Felix Monheim, Professor Dr Friedrich Stang, Professor Dr Frank Ahnert
Sections: Climatology, Professor Dr Dieter Havlik; regional geography and geography of the Rhineland, Professor Dr Reinhart Zschocke; social geography, vacant

Rheinische Braunkohlenwerke AG

1864

– Rheinbraun
Address: Stüttgenweg 2, D-5000 Köln 41
Telephone: (0221) 480-1
Telex: 8883011
Director: Dr Hans Teggers
Sections: Coking and chemistry, Dr Böcker; gasification, Dr Theis; nuclear process-heat, Dr Scharf
Graduate research staff: 25
Annual expenditure: over £2m
Activities: A lignite mining company, research work includes coal analysis and chemistry, the development of a special coking process for Rhenish brown coal and the substitution of oil and gas in industrial heating processes by dried brown coal dust. Main activities are directed to the gasification and liquefaction of brown coal. The high-temperature Winkler coal gasification process for the production of synthesis gas is being developed. A pilot plant has operated since 1978, and the plant will be ready in early 1984. For the production of synthetic natural gas (SNG) the hydrogasification of brown coal in a fluidized bed was developed. A semi-technical plant operated since 1975 and a pilot plant is now under construction. This process can be applied both for the conventional SNG production in connexion with a high-temperature Winkler plant for the necessary hydrogen supply and for the nuclear SNG production by means of a high-temperature nuclear reactor. This nuclear production of SNG is developed with four other German FR companies within the Prototype Nuclear Process Heat (PNP) project. In the field of coal liquefaction the hydrogenation technology of Bergius-Pier was improved. A continous test unit has been in operation since 1978 and the basic engineering for a pilot plant has been initiated. Together with the Nuclear Research Center (KFA), Jülich, the Nuclear Long Distance Energy System (NFE) within the NFE-Project is being developed. A small pilot plant, applying this system, has been in operation since 1979, and a full-scale experimental plant started in 1981. In addition, methanation catalysts for the special NFE-requirements are tested. A special programme for the testing and qualification of high-temperature materials, which includes stress tests, corrosion tests and creep rupture tests, has been installed.
Contract work: No

Rheinische Friedrich-Wilhelms Universität Bonn

1865

[Bonn University]
Address: Regina-Pacis-Weg 3, D-5300 Bonn
Rector: Professor Dr Hans Jacob Krümmel

FACULTY OF AGRICULTURE

1866

Address: Meckenheimer Allee 174, D-5300 Bonn
Dean: Professor Dr Klaus-Ulrich Heyland

Agrarian Policy, Market Research and Economic Sociology Institute

1867

Address: Nussallee 21, D-5300 Bonn
Directors: Professor Herbert Kötter, Professor Henrichsmeyer, Professor Wolffram

Agricultural Botany Institute

1868

Address: Meckenheimer Allee 176, D-5300 Bonn
Director: Professor Wolfgang Franke

Agricultural Chemistry Institute

1869

Address: Meckenheimer Allee 176, D-5300 Bonn
Director: vacant

Agricultural Engineering Institute

1870

Address: Nussallee 5, D-5300 Bonn
Director: Professor Wolfgang Brinkmann

Agricultural Management Institute

1871

Address: Meckenheimer Allee 174, D-5300 Bonn
Directors: Professor Werner Skomroch, Professor Günther Steffen

Agricultural Zoology and Bee Research Institute

1872

Address: Melbweg, Gutshaus, D-5300 Bonn
Director: Professor Bick

Animal Breeding and Fodder Institute

1873

Address: Endenicher Allee 15, D-5300 Bonn
Director: Professor Schmitter
Department:
Small animal breeding and behaviour, Professor Petersen

Animal Nutrition Institute 1874

Address: Endenicher Allee 15, D-5300 Bonn
Director: Professor Pfeffer

Cartography and Topography Institute 1875

Address: Meckenheimer Allee 172, D-5300 Bonn
Director: Professor Aloys Heupel

Domestic Animals Anatomy and 1876 Physiology Institute

Address: Katzenburgweg 7-9, D-5300 Bonn
Director: Professor H. Sommes

Food Sciences Department 1877

Address: Katzenburgweg 3 and 2, D-5300 Bonn
Director: Professor Konrad Pfeilsticker

Forestry Research Establishment and 1878 Collection

Address: Beethovenstrasse 30, D-5300 Bonn
Director: Professor Herbert Hesmer

Fruit and Vegetable Cultivation 1879 Institute

Address: Auf dem Hügel 6, D-5300 Bonn
Director: Professor Lanz

Geodetic Institute 1880

Address: Nussallee 17, D-5300 Bonn
Director: Professor Seeger

Mathematics Seminar 1881

Address: Nussallee 15, D-5300 Bonn
Director: Professor Hilmar Wendt

Nutrition Sciences Institute 1882

Address: Endenicher Allee 11-13, D-5300 Bonn
Director: Professor Dieter Hotzel

Photogrammetry Institute 1883

Address: Nussallee 15, D-5300 Bonn
Director: Professor Günther Kupfer

Plant Cultivation Institute 1884

Address: Katzenburgweg 5, D-5300 Bonn
Directors: Professor Peter Boeker, Professor Klaus-Ulrich Heyland

Plant Diseases Institute 1885

Address: Nussallee 9, D-5300 Bonn
Director: Professor Weltzien
Department:
Microbiology, Professor Krämer

Soil Science Institute 1886

Address: Nussallee 13, D-5300 Bonn
Director: Professor Zakosek
Department:
Tropical soils and soil radiometry, Professor Hans-Wilhelm Scharpenseel

Theoretical Geodesy Institute 1887

Address: Nussallee 17, D-5300 Bonn
Director: Professor Koch

Urban Building, Housing and Modern 1888 Living Institute

Address: Nussallee 1, D-5300 Bonn
Directors: Professor Borchers, Professor Seele

FACULTY OF MATHEMATICAL AND 1889 NATURAL SCIENCES

Address: Wegelerstrasse 10, D-5300 Bonn
Dean: Professor Dr Theo-Mayer-Kuckuk

Applied Mathematics and Informatics 1890 Institute

Address: Wegelerstrasse 6 and 10, D-5300 Bonn
Directors: Professor Frehse, Professor Dr Rolf Leis, Professor Dr Walter Vogel, Professor Dr Werner
Departments:
Functional analysis and numerical mathematics, Professor Dr Werner
Informatics, Professor Dr Karl-Heinz Böhling
Mathematical methods in physics, Professor Dr Rolf Leis
Theory of probabilities and mathematical statistics, Professor Dr Walter Vogel

Applied Physics Institute 1891

Address: Wegelerstrasse 8, D-5300 Bonn
Director: Professor Wiegfried Penselin

Applied Zoology Institute 1892

Address: An der Immenburg 1, D-5300 Bonn-Endenich
Director: Professor Werner Kloft

Astronomy Institute　　　1893

Address: Aug dem Hügel 71, D-5300 Bonn
Directors: Professor Wolfgang Priester, Professor Hans Schmidt

ASTROPHYSICS AND　　　1894
EXTRATERRESTRIAL RESEARCH INSTITUTES
Head: Professor Wolfgang Priester

OBSERVATORY　　　1895
Head: Professor Hans Schmidt

RADIOASTRONOMY INSTITUTE　　　1896
Head: vacant

Biological Institutes　　　1897

BIOREGULATION DEPARTMENT　　　1898
Address: Kirschallee 1, D-5300 Bonn
Head: Professor Augustin Betz

BOTANICAL INSTITUTE AND GARDEN　　1899
Address: Meckenheimer Allee 170, D-5300 Bonn
Director: Professor Dr Sievers

CYTOLOGY DEPARTMENT　　　1900
Address: Venusbergweg 22, D-5300 Bonn
Head: Professor Andreas Sievers

EXPERIMENTAL ECOLOGY　　　1901
DEPARTMENT
Address: Meckenheimer Allee 170, D-5300 Bonn
Director: Professor Brinkmann

SYSTEMATICS DEPARTMENT　　　1902
Address: Meckenheimer Allee 170, D-5300 Bonn
Head: vacant

Chemical Institutes　　　1903

Address: Meckenheimerallee 158, D-5300 Bonn
Overall director: Professor Rudolf Tschesche
Departments:
Technical chemistry, Professor Hermann Josef Antweiler
Heterocyclic chemistry, Professor Joachim Goerdeler
Theoretical chemistry, Professor Dr S. Peyerimhoff
Electrochemistry, Professor Dr Wolf Vielstich
Nuclear chemistry, vacant

INORGANIC CHEMISTRY INSTITUTE　　1904
Head: Professor Rolf Appel

ORGANIC CHEMISTRY AND　　　1905
BIOCHEMISTRY INSTITUTE
Head: Professor Dr W. Steglich

PHYSICAL CHEMISTRY INSTITUTE　　1906
Heads: Professor Dr S. Peyerimhoff, Professor Dr Wolf Vielstich

Cytology and Micromorphology　　1907
Institute

Address: Ulrich-Haberland-Strasse 61a, D-5300 Bonn
Director: Professor Karl-Ernst Wohlfarth-Bottermann
Department:
Cytochemistry, Professor Dr Hans Komnick

Endenich Pharmaceutical Institute　　1908

Address: An den Immenburg, D-5300 Bonn
Director: Professor Dr Hermann J. Roth

PHARMACEUTICAL TECHNOLOGY　　1909
DEPARTMENT
Address: Endenicher Allee 11-13, D-5300 Bonn
Head: Professor Dr Fritz Müller

Genetics Institute　　　1910

Address: Kurfürstenstrasse 74, D-5300 Bonn
Director: Professor Werner Gottschalk

Geography Institutes　　　1911

Address: Franziskanerstrasse 2, D-5300 Bonn
Directors: Professor Helmut Hahn, Professor Peter-Wilhelm Höllermann, Professor Wolfgang Kuls, Professor Wilhelm Lauer, Professor Boesler, Professor Fehn
Department:
Applied geography, Professor Gerhard Aymans

ECONOMIC GEOGRAPHY INSTITUTE　　1912
Heads: Professor Helmut Hahn, Professor Boesler

SPECIAL AND APPLIED PHYSICAL　　1913
GEOGRAPHY DEPARTMENT
Address: Giergasse 11, D-5300 Bonn
Head: vacant

Geology Institute　　　1914

Address: Nussallee 8, D-5300 Bonn
Director: Professor Paul Wurster
Department:
Tectonics, Professor Wilhelm Meyer

Mathematical Institute 1915

Address: Wegelerstrasse 10, D-5300 Bonn
Directors: Professor Dr Stefan Hildebrandt, Professor Dr Friedrich Hirzebruch, Professor Dr Wilhelm Klingenberg, Professor Dr Rolf Leis, Professor Dr Brieskorn
Department:
Basic mathematical research, Professor Wolfram Schwabhäuser

Meteorology Institute 1916

Address: Auf dem Hügel 20, D-5300 Bonn
Director: Professor Dr H. Kraus

Mineralogy and Petrology Institute 1917 and Museum

Address: Poppelsdorfer Schloss, D-5300 Bonn
Directors: Professor Dr Georg Will, Professor Dr G. Voll
Departments:
Petrology, Professor Dr G. Voll
Crystal structure, Professor Karl-Friedrich Seifert
Mineral deposits and geochemistry, Professor Dr Georg Will

NEUTRON DIFFRACTION RESEARCH 1918 SECTION AT JÜLICH
Head: Professor Dr Georg Will

Palaeontology Institute 1919

Address: Nussallee 8, D-5300 Bonn
Director: Professor Heinrich K. Erben
Departments:
Palaeontology, Professor Heinrich K. Erben
Palaeobotany, Professor Hans-Joachim Schweitzer
Applied palaeontology, Professor K.J. Müller

Pharmacognosy Institute 1920

Address: Nussallee 6, D-5300 Bonn
Director: Professor Dr Kating

Physics Institute 1921

Address: Nussallee 12, D-5300 Bonn
Directors: Professor Karl-Heinz Althoff, Professor Klaus Dietz, Professor Gerhard Knop, Professor Kurt Meetz, Professor Gerhard Nöldeke, Professor Wolfgang Paul, Professor Horst Rollnik
Sections:
Theoretical physics, Professor Klaus Dietz, Professor Horst Rollnik, Professor G. von Gehlen, Professor von Rittenberg
Experimental physics, Professor Karl-Heinz Althoff,

Professor Gerhard Knop, Professor Gerhard Nöldeke, Professor Wolfgang Paul, Professor H. Fischer, Professor Wedemeyer, Professor von Zahn

Poppelsdorf Pharmaceutical Institute 1922

Address: Kreuzbergweg 26, D-5300 Bonn
Director: Professor Dr Hermann J. Roth

Radiation and Nuclear Physics 1923 Institute

Address: Nussallee 14-16, D-5300 Bonn
Directors: Professor Erwin Bodenstedt, Professor Theo-Mayer-Kuckuk

Theoretical Nuclear Physics Institute 1924

Address: Nussallee 14-16, D-5300 Bonn
Director: Professor Dieter Schütte

Zoological and Comparative Anatomy 1925 Institute

Address: Poppelsdorfer Schloss, D-5300 Bonn
Director: Professor Hans Schneider
Departments:
Evolution history, Professor Norbert Weissenfels
Physiology, Professor Ernst Wendt
Protozoology, Professor Erich Scholtyseck

FACULTY OF MEDICINE 1926

Dean: Professor Dr Friedrich Krück

Anatomy Institute 1927

Address: Nussallee 10, D-5300 Bonn
Directors: Professor Dr Kurt Fleischhauer, Professor Dr Hubert Wartenburg
Departments:
Neuroanatomy, Professor Fleischhauer
Experimental biology, Professor H. Wartenburg

Biophysics Institute 1928

Address: Sigmund-Freud-Strasse 15, D-5300 Bonn Venusberg
Acting director: Professor Hans-Dietrich Bergeder

Clinical Biochemistry Institute 1929

Address: D-5300 Bonn Venusberg
Director: Professor Heinz Breuer

Dermatology and Venereology Clinic 1930 and Polyclinic

Address: D-5300 Bonn Venusberg
Director: Professor Dr H.W. Kreysel

Experimental Haematology and Blood 1931 Transfusion Institute

Address: Sigmund-Freud-Strasse, D-5300 Bonn Venusberg
Director: Professor Hans Egli

Experimental Ophthalmology Clinical 1932 Institute

Address: Abbestrasse 2, D-5300 Bonn Venusberg
Director: Professor Erich Weigelin
Department:
Eye biochemistry, Professor Otto Hockwin

Forensic Medicine Institute 1933

Address: Stiftsplatz 12, D-5300 Bonn
Director: Professor, U. Heifer
Department:
Forensic toxicology, Professor Dr Walter Paulus

History of Medicine Institute 1934

Address: Sigmund-Freud-Strasse 25, D-5300 Bonn Venusberg
Director: Professor Dr Nikolaus Mani

Human Genetics Institute 1935

Address: Wilhelmsplatz 31, D-5300 Bonn
Director: Professor Heinz Weicker

Hygiene Institute 1936

Address: D-5300 Bonn Venusberg
Director: Professor Elgar Thofern

Medical Clinic 1937

Address: D-5300 Bonn Venusberg
Director: vacant
Departments:
Cardiology, Professor Dr Adalbert Schaede
Internal diseases of the vegetative nervous system, and psychosomatic diseases, Professor Dr August Wilhelm von Eiff
Medical statistics, documentation and data processing, Professor Dr Gerhard Oberhoffer

Medical Microbiology and 1938 Immunology Institute

Address: D-5300 Bonn Venusberg
Director: Professor Dr Henning Brandis

Medical Parasitology Institute 1939

Address: D-5300 Bonn Venusberg
Director: Professor Dr H.M. Seitz

Medical Polyclinic 1940

Address: Wilhelmstrasse 35-37, D-5300 Bonn
Director: Professor Dr W. Burmeister

Mouth, Tooth and Jaw Diseases Clinic 1941 and Polyclinic

Address: Hans-Böcker Strasse 5, D-5300 Bonn
Director: Professor Dr Lorenz Hupfauf
Departments:
Conservative dentistry and paradontology, Professor Ernst Sauerwein
Dental prosthesis, Professor Dr Lorenz Hupfauf
Dental and jaw surgery, Professor Dr Eberhard Krüger
Dental orthopaedics, Professor Dr Gottfried Schmuth
Clinical and experimental materials, vacant

Neurology Clinic and Polyclinic 1942

Address: Annaberger Weg, D-5300 Bonn Venusberg
Director: Professor Hans Georg Weitbrecht
Departments:
Clinical neurophysiology and experimental neuropsychiatry, Professor Dr Heinz Penin
Psychotherapy and depth psychology, Professor Dr Hans Quint
Medical psychology, Professor Dr Wilhelm Zeh

Neuropathology Institute 1943

Address: D-5300 Bonn Venusberg
Director: Professor Dr Günter Kersting

Neurosurgical Clinic 1944

Address: Annaberger Weg, D-5300 Bonn Venusberg
Director: Professor Dr Rolf Wüllenweber
Departments:
Anaesthesiology, Dr Wolfgang Entzian
Neuroradiology, Professor Dr Josef Wappenschmidt
Clinical neurophysiology, Professor Dr Hans-Joachim Hufschmidt

Obstetrics and Gynaecology Clinic and Polyclinic 1945

Address: D-5300 Bonn Venusberg
Director: Professor Dr Ernst-Jürgen Plotz
Departments:
Outpatients, Professor Dr Wolfgang Korte
Gynaecological endocrinology, Dr Wolfgang Nocke
Radiology, Dr Windemuth

Ophthalmology Clinic and Polyclinic 1946

Address: D-5300 Bonn Venusberg
Acting director: Professor Dr E. Weigelin
Department:
Eye microsurgery, Professor Dardenne

Orthopaedic Clinic 1947

Address: D-5300 Bonn Venusberg
Director: Professor Dr Helmut Rössler

Otorhinolaryngology Clinic and Polyclinic 1948

Address: D-5300 Bonn Venusberg
Director: Professor Dr Walter Becker

Paediatrics Clinic and Polyclinic 1949

Address: Adenauerallee 119, D-5300 Bonn
Director: Professor Dr W. Burmeister

Pathology Institute 1950

Address: D-5300 Bonn Venusberg
Director: Professor Dr Peter Gedigk
Departments:
Child pathology, Professor Dr H.J. Födisch

Pharmacology Institute 1951

Address: Reuterstrasse 26, D-5300 Bonn
Director: Professor U. Schwabe

Physiological Chemistry Institute 1952

Address: Nussallee 11, D-5300 Bonn
Director: Professor Dr Fritz Zilliken
Departments:
Physical biochemistry, Professor Karl Oscar Mosebach
Enzymology, Professor Klaus Otto

Physiology Institute 1953

Address: Nussallee 11, D-5300 Bonn
Director: Professor Dr Josef Peter Pichotka

Radiology Clinic 1954

Address: D-5300 Bonn Venusberg
Director: Professor Peter Thurn
Department:
Nuclear medicine, Professor Dr Cuno Winkler

Surgical Clinic and Polyclinic 1955

Address: D-5300 Bonn Venusberg
or: (Polyclinic) Wilhelmstrasse 31, D-5300 Bonn
Director: Professor Dr Friedrich Krück
Department:
Anaesthesiology, Professor Leo Havers

Urology Clinic 1956

Address: D-5300 Bonn Venusberg
Director: Professor Dr Winfried Vahlensieck

Robert Koch-Institut 1957

[Robert Koch Institute]
Address: Nordufer 20, D-1000 Berlin 65
Telephone: (030) 4503-1
Parent body: Bundesgesundheitsamt
Head: Dr med Wilhelm Weise
Activities: Virology; bacteriology; immunology; biochemistry; cytology.
On the recommendation of the World Health Organization, several special units of the Institute have been appointed reference centres: national influenza reference centre; national vibrio reference laboratory; national salmonella centre; national reference laboratory for blood grouping; laboratory for yellow fever vaccine production.

Ruhr-Universität Bochum 1958

[Ruhr University of Bochum]
Address: Postfach 10 21 48, D-4630 Bochum
Telephone: (0234) 7001
Telex: 8 25 860
Rector: Professor Dr Knut Ipsen

DEPARTMENT OF BIOLOGY 1959

Dean: Professor Dr Hans-Christoph Lüttgau
Sections: General botany, Professor Dr Karl Esser; general zoology, Professor Dr Johann Schwartzkopff, Professor Dr Hans Machemer (primary processes and receptors); special zoology, Professor Dr Hans Mergner, Professor Dr Konrad Märkel; plant physiology,

Professor Dr Nikolaus Amrhein; animal physiology, Professor Dr Helmut Langer, Professor Dr Kurt Hamdorf, Professor Dr Werner Rautenberg (temperature regulation), Professor Dr Volker Blüm; cell physiology, Professor Dr Hans-Christoph Lüttgau, Professor Dr Helfried Glitsch (muscle physiology); cell morphology, Professor Dr August Ruthmann, Professor Dr Wolfgang Scheuermann (molecular plant cytology); plant biochemistry, Professor Dr Achim Trebst, Professor Dr Karlheinz Altendorf, Professor Dr Richard Berzborn; microorganisms biology, Professor Dr Ulrich Winkler, Professor Dr Wolfgang Hengstenberg, Professor Dr Wolfgang Rüger (molecular genetics); special botany, Professor Dr Ulrich Hamann; behavioural research, Professor Dr Eberhard Curio

DEPARTMENT OF CHEMISTRY 1960

Dean: Professor Dr Olaf Pongs
Sections: Inorganic chemistry, Professor Dr Hermann Specker, Professor Dr Horst Sabrowsky, Professor Dr Dr Alois Haas
Organic chemistry, Professor Dr Wolfgang R. Roth, Professor Dr Peter Welzel, Professor Dr Frank-Gerrit Klärner
Physical chemistry, Professor Dr Heinrich Richtering, Professor Dr Friedrich Stuhl, Professor Dr Gerhard M. Schneider, Professor Dr Gerhard Findenegg
Biochemistry, Professor Dr Olaf Pongs
Analytical chemistry, Professor Dr Gerhard Bergmann, Professor Dr Ewald Jackwerth
Theoretical chemistry, Professor Dr Werner Kutzelnigg
Structural chemistry, Professor Dr Günther Snatzke
Technical chemistry, Professor Dr Manfred Baerns

DEPARTMENT OF CIVIL ENGINEERING 1961

Dean: Professor Dr Ing Gert A. Schulz

Construction Engineering Institute 1962

Director: Professor Dr Ing Karlheinz Roik
Departments: I, Professor Dr Ing Wolfgang Zerna; II, Professor Dr Ing Karlheinz Roik; III, Professor Dr Ing Wilfried B. Kratzig; IV, Professor Dr Ing Walter Wunderlich; V, Professor Dr Ing Bernhard Maidl
Groups: Applied informatics, vacant; system mechanics and applied informatics, Professor Dr Ing Karl-Heinrich Schrader; building constructions and wood structures, Professor Dr Ing Elmar Krabbe

Foundations, Water and Traffic Institute 1963

Director: Professor Dr Ing Wilhelm Schäfer
Departments: Foundations and soil mechanics, Professor Dr Ing Hans-Ludwig Jessberger; traffic, Professor Dr Ing Wolfgang Teichgräber
Group: Surveying, Professor Dr Ing Wilhelm Schäfer

Mechanics Institute 1964

Director: Professor Dr Ing H. Stumpf
Departments: Mechanics I, Professor Dr Ing Th. Lehmann
Mechanics II, Professor Dr Ing H. Stumpf
Groups: Experimental continuum mechanics, Professor Dr Horst Schwieger; numerical methods in mechanics and simulation techniques, Professor Dr Ing Heinz Waller

DEPARTMENT OF ELECTRICAL ENGINEERING 1965

Dean: Professor Dr Ing F. Haberey

Basic Electrical Engineering Institute 1966

Directors: Professor Dr Ing Jens Blauert, Professor Dr Siegfried Blume, Professor Dr Ing Manfred Depenbrock
Departments: General electrical engineering and electro-acoustics, Professor Dr Ing Jens Blauert; general and theoretical electrical engineering, vacant; generation and utilization of electrical energy, Professor Dr Ing Manfred Depenbrock, Professor Dr Ing Johannes Buter; theoretical electrical engineering, Professor Dr Siegfried Blume; information processing, Professor Dr Alfred Fettweis; electrical control and regulation, Professor Dr Ing Heinz Unbehauen; data processing, Professor Dr Ing Wolfgang Weber
Groups: Processing, Professor Dr Ing F. Depping; electronic metrology, Professor Dr Ing Burkhard Schick

Electrical Materials Institute 1967

Senior staff: Professor Dr Eckart Kneller

Electronics Institute 1968

Senior staff: Professor Dr Berthold Bosch, Professor Dr Ing Jurgen-Winfried Klein, Professor Dr Ing Hans-Martin Rein

High Frequency Institute 1969

Senior staff: Professor Dr Hans Severin

DEPARTMENT OF EXTRATERRESTRIAL PHYSICS   1970

Head: Professor Dr Richard-Heinrich Giese

Biophysics Institute   1971

Director: Professor Dr Albrecht Redhardt
Dean: Professor Dr Dr Karlheinz Hottes

Geography Institute   1972

Director: Professor Dr Hans-Jürgen Klink
Senior staff: Professor Dr Karlheinz Hottes, Professor Dr Herbert Liedtke, Professor Dr Peter Schöller, Professor Dr Zlatko Graĉanin, Professor Dr Eberhard Kross, Professor Dr Werner Rutz, Professor Dr Detlef Schreiber, Professor Dr Manfred Büttner, Professor Dr Horst Förster

Geology Institute   1973

Director: Professor Dr Hans Füchtbauer
Senior staff: Professor Dr Rolf Hoeppener, Professor Dr Ing Klaus W. John
Groups: Palaeontology, Professor Dr Hans Mensink, historic and regional geology, Professor Dr Bernt Schröder, rock mechanics, Professor Dr Herbert Kutter

Geophysics Institute   1974

Director: Professor Dr Hans-Peter Harjes
Senior staff: Professor Dr Lothar Dresen

Mineralogy Institute   1975

Director: Professor Dr O.W. Flörke
Senior staff: Professor Dr W. Schreyer, Professor Dr Niranjan Deb Chatterjee, Professor Dr Kurt Sahl, Professor Dr Hans-Ulrich Schmincke, Professor Dipl-Ing Dr E. Gugel

DEPARTMENT OF MATHEMATICS   1976

Dean: Professor Dr Eduard Zehnder

Mathematics Institute   1977

Director: Professor Dr Heiner Zieschang
Senior staff: Professor Dr Sergio Albeverio, Professor Dr Volker Baumann, Professor Dr Reinhold Böhme, Professor Dr Dietrich Braess, Professor Dr Hartmut Ehlich, Professor Dr Günter Ewald, Professor Dr Lothar Gerritzen, Professor Dr Rolf Reissig, Professor Dr Friedrich Sommer, Professor Dr Karlheinz Spallek, Professor Dr Gordon Wassermann, Professor Dr Wolfgang Bartenwerfer, Professor Dr Erwin Böger,

Professor Dr Andrei Duma, Professor Dr Sigurd Elliger, Professor Dr Volker Enss, Professor Dr Frank Levin

DEPARTMENT OF MECHANICAL ENGINEERING   1978

Dean: Professor Dr Friedrich Kohler

Automation Engineering Institute   1979

Director: Professor Dr Karl-Heinz Fasol
Group: Metrology, Professor Dr Werner Tielsch

Construction Technology Institute   1980

Director: Professor Dr Ing Hans Seifert
Senior staff: Professor Dr Ing Friedrich Jarchow, Professor Dr Ing Ernst-Otto Schneidersmann, Professor Dr Ing Erich Pollmann
Department: Machine elements and construction, Professor Dr Ing Andreas E. Kanarachos

Materials Institute   1981

Directors: Professor Dr Ing Erhard Hornbogen, Professor Dr Hans Berns
Senior staff: Professor Dr Gerd Lütjering

Power Engineering Institute   1982

Director: Professor Dr Ing Werner Fister
Departments: Hydraulic machines, Professor Dr Ing Werner Fister; reactor engineering, Professor Dr Albert Ziegler; power installations, Professor Dr Ing Hans Kremer
Groups: Steam and gas turbines, Professor Dr Ing Heiner Pfost

Thermo- and Fluid Dynamics Institute   1983

Director: Professor Dr Ing Klaus Gersten
Departments: Hydromechanics, Professor Dr Ing Klaus Gersten; thermal materials, Professor Dr Ing Reinhard Billet; thermodynamics, Professor Dr Friedrich Kohler; heat transfer, Professor Dr Ing Martin Fiebig
Groups: Experimental gas dynamics, Professor Dr Wolfgang Merzkirch; experimental thermodynamics, Professor Dr Ing Wolfgang Wagner

DEPARTMENT OF PHYSICS AND ASTRONOMY   1984

Dean: Professor Dr Haro von Buttlar

Astronomical Institute 1985

Director: Professor Dr Kristen Rohlfs
Senior staff: Professor Dr Theodor Schmidt-Kaler, Professor Dr Joachim Dachs, Professor Dr Michael Reinhardt

Experimental Physics Institute 1986

Director: Professor Dr Hans Schlüter
Senior staff: Professor Dr Haro von Buttlar, Professor Dr Detlef Kamke, Professor Dr Hans-Joachim Kunze, Professor Dr Siegfried Methfessel, Professor Dr Michai Rosenberg, Professor Dr Hans Schlüter, Professor Dr Bernhard Gonsior, Professor Dr Benedikt Kronast, Professor Dr Josef Pelzl, Professor Dr Klaus Wiesemann, Professor Dr Paul Heinrich Heckmann, Professor Dr Hartwig Freiesleben, Professor Dr Eduard Hintz, Professor Dr Henning Neddermeyer

Theoretical Physics Institute 1987

Director: Professor Dieter Wagner
Senior staff: Professor Dr Günter Ecker, Professor Dr Karl Schindler, Professor Dr Dieter Wagner, Professor Dr Klaus Elsässer, Professor Dr Walter Glöckle, Professor Dr Jürgen Kübler, Professor Dr Manfred Gari, Professor Dr Hermann Kümmel

DEPARTMENT OF SCIENTIFIC MEDICINE 1988

Dean: Professor Dr Holger Preuschoft

Anatomy Institute 1989

Director: Professor Dr Karl-Hermann Andres
Departments: Anatomy I, Professor Dr Klaus Hinrichsen; Anatomy II, Professor Dr Karl-Hermann Andres, Professor Dr Monika von Düring
Groups: Experimental cytology, Professor Dr Karl Meller; functional morphology, Professor Dr Holger Preuschoft; micromorphology, Professor Dr Peter Stanka

Genetics Institute 1990

Director: Professor Dr Walter Scholz
Department: Genetics, Professor Dr Hans-Günther Keyl
Group: Human cytogenetics and clinical genetics, Professor Dr Walter Scholz

Physiological Chemistry Institute 1991

Director: Professor Dr August W. Holldorf
Departments: Physiological chemistry I, Professor Dr Ludwig Heilmayer; physiological chemistry II, Professor Dr August W. Holldorf
Groups: Enzymology, Professor Dr Wolfgang Duntze; bio-organic chemistry, Professor Dr Wolf-H. Kunau; cell chemistry, Professor Dr Walter Hanstein

Physiology Institute 1992

Director: Professor Dr Dietrich Trincker
Departments: Physiology I, Professor Dr Hans H. Loeschcke; Physiology II, Professor Dr Dietrich Trincker
Groups: Membrane physiology, Professor Dr Wolfgang Karger; regulation physiology, Professor Dr Marianne Schläfke; vegetative physiology, Professor Dr Dr Walter Niesel

DEPARTMENT OF THEORETICAL MEDICINE 1993

Dean: Professor Dr Herbert Viefhues

Hygiene Institute 1994

Director: Professor Dr Fidelis Selenka

Medical Microbiology Institute 1995

Director: Professor Dr Wolfgang Opferkuch
Departments: Bacteriology, Professor Dr Wolfgang König; virology, Professor Dr Hermann Werchau

Pathology Institute 1996

Director: Professor Dr Wolfgang Hartung
Departments: Pathology I, Professor Dr Wolfgang Hartung; pathology II, Professor Dr Konrad Morgenroth

Pharmacology and Toxicology Institute 1997

Director: vacant
Group: Biochemical pharmacology, Professor Dr Fritz Lauterbach

Social Medicine Department 1998

Head: Professor Dr Herbert Viefhues

Ruhrchemie AG 1999

– RCH
Address: Postfach 130160, D-4200 Oberhausen-Holten
Telephone: (0208) 6931
Telex: 856867
Research Director: Dr B. Cornils
Sections: Organic chemicals; coal conversion techniques; plastics; catalysts
Graduate research staff: 30
Annual expenditure: over £2m
Activities: Organic chemicals, basing mainly on hydroformylation products; coal conversion techniques and synthesis gas chemistry; plastics, mainly polyethylenes; catalysts, mainly supported catalysts; metal organic chemistry, especially homogeneous catalysis; petrochemicals.
Contract work: Yes

Ruhrstahl* 2000

Address: Eberhardstrasse 12, D-4600 Dortmund
Activities: This Company comprises the merged assets of a large part of the steel-related work of Estel-Hoesch Werke and Krupp Stahl. The steelmaking, sheeting and coating operations, and some further activities are combined into Ruhrstahl, and Estel-Hoesch Werke and Krupp Stahl hold an equal share. The full merger combines production of about 11 million tonnes of crude steel per annum. New investments include the construction of a 3.5 million tonne-a-year oxygen steelworks at Dortmund and additional investment at a cold rolling mill at Bochum. Surface finishing and coating of sheet steel is concentrated at Hoesch's works at Dortmund.

Ruhrverband 2001

[Ruhr River Association]
Address: Kronprinzenstrasse 37, Postfach 103242, D-4300 Essen
Telephone: (0201) 1781
Telex: 0 857 414 esn
Directors: Dr rer pol Fritz Bergmann, Dr Ing Klaus R. Imhof
Activities: Water quality management in the Ruhr basin.

RUHR RESERVOIRS ASSOCIATION 2002

Activities: Water quantity management in the Ruhr river basin.

Ruprecht-Karl-Universität Heidelberg 2003

[Ruprecht-Karl University Heidelberg]
Address: Grabengasse 1, Postfach 105760, D-6900 Heidelberg 1
Telephone: (06221) 541
Telex: 461 515
Rector: Professor Dr Adolf Laufs

FACULTY OF BASIC MEDICAL SCIENCES 2004

Anatomy Institute 2005

Address: Im Neuenheimer Feld 307, D-6900 Heidelberg
Directors: Professor Dr H.W. Kriz, Professor Dr D.H. Fahimi

Biochemistry Institute I 2006

Address: Im Neuenheimer Feld 328, D-6900 Heidelberg
Director: Professor Dr Hans Schimassek

Biochemistry Institute II 2007

Address: Im Neuenheimer Feld 328, D-6900 Heidelberg
Director: Professor Dr Reinhard Brossmer

Central Research Station of the Medical Faculties 2008

Address: Kirchheimer Mühle, D-6902 Sandhausen
Head: Professor Dr W. Hardegg

Physiology Institute I 2009

Address: Im Neuenheimer Feld 326, D-6900 Heidelberg
Director: Professor Dr Horst Seller

Physiology Institute II 2010

Address: Im Neuenheimer Feld 326, D-6900 Heidelberg
Director: Dr Casper Rüegg

FACULTY OF BIOLOGY 2011

Biological Chemistry Institute 2012

Address: Im Neuenheimer Feld 501, D-6900 Heidelberg
Director: Professor Dr Joachim Knappe

Botanical Garden 2013

Address: Im Neuenheimer Feld 340, D-6900 Heidelberg
Director: Professor Dr Werner Rauh

Botany Institute 2014

Address: Im Neuenheimer Feld 360, D-6900 Heidelberg
Director: Professor Dr Martin Bopp

Cytology Department 2015

Address: Im Neuenheimer Feld 230, D-6900 Heidelberg
Director: Professor Dr Eberhard Schnepf

Microbiology Institute 2016

Address: Im Neuenheimer Feld 280, D-6900 Heidelberg
Director: Professor Dr Heinz Schaller

Molecular Genetics Institute 2017

Address: Im Neuenheimer Feld 230, D-6900 Heidelberg
Director: Professor Dr Ekkehard Bautz

Systematic Botany Institute 2018

Address: Im Neuenheimer Feld 280, D-6900 Heidelberg
Director: Professor Dr Werner Rauh

Zoology Institute 2019

Address: Im Neuenheimer Feld 230, D-6900 Heidelberg
Director: Professor Dr Werner Müller

FACULTY OF CHEMISTRY 2020

Inorganic Chemistry Institute 2021

Address: Im Neuenheimer Feld 270, D-6900 Heidelberg
Director: Professor Dr Hans Siebert

Organic Chemistry Institute 2022

Address: Im Neuenheimer Feld 270, D-6900 Heidelberg
Director: Professor Dr Hermann Schildknecht

Physical Chemistry Institute 2023

Address: Im Neuenheimer Feld 293, D-6900 Heidelberg
Director: Professor Dr Lorenz Cederbaum

FACULTY OF CLINICAL MEDICINE 2024

Address: Theodor-Kutzer-Ufer, D-6800 Mannheim 31

Anaesthesiology and Reanimation Institute 2025

Head: Professor Dr Horst Lutz

Dermatology Clinic 2026

Head: Professor Dr Ernst Jung

Hygiene Institute 2027

Head: Professor Dr Willhelm Wundt

Medical Clinic I 2028

Head: Professor Dr Dieter Heene

Medical Clinic II 2029

Address: Marburger Strasse, D-6800 Mannheim 31
Director: Professor Dr Heinz Harald Hennemann

Neurological Clinic 2030

Head: Professor Dr Otto Hallen

Obstetrics and Gynaecology Clinic 2031

Head: Professor Dr Peter Stoll

Ophthalmology Clinic 2032

Head: Professor Dr Hans Liesenhoff

Orthopaedic Clinic 2033

Address: Meerfeldstrasse, D-6800 Mannheim-Lindenhoff
Director: Professor Dr Günter Jentschura

Otorhinolaryngology Clinic 2034
Head: Professor Dr. Ulrich Legler

Paediatric Clinic 2035
Head: Professor Dr Erich Huth

Pathology Institute 2036
Head: Professor Dr Uwe Bleyl

Pharmacology and Toxicology Institute 2037
Head: Professor Dr Klaus Dietrich Friedberg

Preventive Oncology Institute 2038
Head: Professor Dr Ferdinand Schmidt

Radiology Institute 2039
Head: Professor Dr Max Georgi

Social Psychiatric Clinic 2040
Head: Professor Dr Heinz Häfner

Surgical Clinic 2041
Head: Professor Dr Michael Trede

Urology Clinic 2042
Head: Professor Dr Joachim Potempa

FACULTY OF CLINICAL MEDICINE I 2043

Medical Outpatients Clinic 2044
Address: Hospitalstrasse 3, D-6900 Heidelberg
Director: Professor Dr Werner Hunstein
Departments Endocrinology, Professor Dr R. Ziegler; Thannhauser Metabolism Research, Professor Dr Helmut Weiker

Medical University Clinic 2045
Address: Bergheimer Strasse 68, D-6900 Heidelberg
Director: Professor Dr Gotthard Schettler
Departments: Social Clinical Medicine, Professor Dr Friedrich Egbert Nüssel; Gastroenterology, Professor Dr Burkhard Kommerell; Cardiology, Professor Dr Wolfgang Kübler

Obstetrics and Gynaecology Clinic 2046
Address: Vosstrasse 9, D-6900 Heidelberg
Director: Professor Dr Fred Kubli

Orthopaedic Clinic 2047
Address: Schlierbacher Landstrasse 200a, D-6900 Heidelberg
Director: Professor Dr Horst Cotta

Paediatric Clinic 2048
Address: Im Neuenheimer Feld 150, D-6900 Heidelberg
Director: Professor Dr Horst Bickel

Surgical Clinic 2049
Address: Im Neuenheimer Feld 110, D-6900 Heidelberg
Director: Professor Dr Otto Just
Departments: Anaesthesiology, Professor Dr Otto Just; Urology, Professor Dr Lars Röhl; Neurosurgery, Professor Dr Helmut Penzholz; Special Thoracic Surgery, Professor Dr Wolfgang Schmitz; Paediatric Surgery, Professor Dr Roland Daum; Radiology, Professor Dr Paul Gerhardt; Experimental Surgery, Professor Dr Ulrich Mittmann; Clinical Laboratory, Dr Hans Peter Geisen

FACULTY OF CLINICAL MEDICINE II 2050

Dermatology Clinic 2051
Address: Vosstrasse 2, D-6900 Heidelberg
Director: Professor Dr Detlef Petzoldt

Neurology Clinic 2052
Address: Vosstrasse 2, D-6900 Heidelberg
Director: Professor Dr Heinz Gänshirt

Ophthalmology Clinic 2053
Address: Bergheimer Strasse 20, D-6900 Heidelberg
Director: Professor Dr Wolfgang Jaeger

Otorhinolaryngology Clinic 2054
Address: Vosstrasse 5-7, D-6900 Heidelberg
Director: Professor Dr Hans-Georg Boenninghaus

Psychiatric Clinic   2055

Address: Vosstrasse 4, D-6900 Heidelberg
Director: Professor Dr Werner Janzarik
Department: Child Psychiatry, Professor Dr Manfred
Müller-Küppers

Psychosomatic Clinic   2056

Address: Vosstrasse 2, D-6900 Heidelberg
Director: Professor Dr Walter Bräutigam

Radiation Clinic (Czerny Hospital)   2057

Address: Vosstrasse 3, D-6900 Heidelberg
Director: Professor Dr Karl zum Winkel

Stomatology Clinic   2058

Address: Hospitalstrasse 1, D-6900 Heidelberg
Director: Professor Dr Kurt Kristen

FACULTY OF EARTH SCIENCES   2059

Geography Institute   2060

Address: Im Neuenheimer Feld 348, D-6900
Heidelberg
Director: Professor Dr Dietrich Barsch
Departments: Rhine-Neckar Research, Professor Dr
Werner Fricke; Geomorphology, Professor Dr Dietrich
Barsch

Geology and Paleontology Institute   2061

Address: Im Neuenheimer Feld 234, D-6900
Heidelberg
Director: Professor Dr Wilhelm Simon

Mineralogy and Petrography Institute   2062

Address: Im Neuenheimer Feld 236, D-6900
Heidelberg
Director: Professor Dr G. Christian Amstutz

Sedimentology Research Institute   2063

Address: Im Neuenheimer Feld 236, D-6900
Heidelberg
Director: Professor Dr German Müller

GEOCHRONOLOGY LABORATORY   2064
(ISOTOPE-GEOPHYSICS)
Head: Professor Dr Hans Joachim Lippolt

FACULTY OF MATHEMATICS   2065

Applied Mathematics Institute   2066

Address: Im Neuenheimer Feld 294, D-6900
Heidelberg
Director: Professor Dr Wilhelm von Waldenfels

Mathematics Institute   2067

Address: Im Neuenheimer Feld 288, D-6900
Heidelberg
Director: Professor Dr Eberhard Freitag

FACULTY OF PHARMACY   2068

Pharmaceutical Chemistry Institute   2069

Address: Im Neuenheimer Feld 364, D-6900
Heidelberg
Director: Professor Dr Richard Neidlein

Pharmaceutical Technology Institute   2070

Address: Im Neuenheimer Feld 366, D-6900
Heidelberg
Director: Professor Dr Herbert Stricker

FACULTY OF PHYSICS AND   2071
ASTRONOMY

Applied Physics Institute I   2072

Address: Albert-Überle-Strasse 3-5, D-6900
Heidelberg
Director: Professor Dr Josef Bille

Applied Physics Institute II   2073

Address: Albert-Überle-Strasse 3-5, D-6900
Heidelberg
Director: Professor Dr Konrad Tamm

Astronomical Computing Centre   2074

Address: Mönchhafstrasse 12-14, D-6900 Heidelberg
Director: Professor Dr Walter Fricke

Heidelberg-Königstuhl Observatory   2075

Address: Königstuhl, D-6900 Heidelberg
Director: Professor Dr Immo Appenzeller

High-Energy Physics Institute 2076

Address: Albert-Überle-Strasse 2, D-6900 Heidelberg
Director: Professor Dr Klaus Tittel

Physics Institute 2077

Address: Philosophenweg 12, D-6900 Heidelberg
Director: Professor Dr Hans-Joachim Specht

Theoretical Astrophysics Department 2078

Address: Im Neuenheimer Feld 294, D-6900 Heidelberg
Director: Professor Dr Bodo Baschek

Theoretical Physics Institute 2079

Address: Philosophenweg 16, D-6900 Heidelberg
Director: Professor Dr Franz Wegner

FACULTY OF THEORETICAL MEDICINE 2080

Anthropology and Human Genetics Institute 2081

Address: Im Neuenheimer Feld 328, D-6900 Heidelberg
Director: Professor Dr Friedrich Vogel

Forensic Medicine Institute 2082

Address: Vosstrasse 2, D-6900 Heidelberg
Director: Professor Dr Georg Schmidt

Hygiene Institute 2083

Address: Im Neuenheimer Feld 324, D-6900 Heidelberg
Director: Professor Dr Herbert Barth
Department: Tropical Hygiene and Public Health, Professor Dr Hans Jochen Diesfeld

Immunology and Serology Institute 2084

Address: Im Neuenheimer Feld 305, D-6900 Heidelberg
Director: Professor Dr Klaus Rother
Department: Medical Virology, Professor Dr Klaus Munk

Pathology Institute 2085

Address: Im Neuenheimer Feld 220-221, D-6900 Heidelberg
Director: Professor Dr Wilhelm Doerr
Departments: Neuropathology, Professor Dr Günter Ule; Pathological Chemistry and General Neurochemistry, vacant; Comparative and Experimental Pathology, Professor Dr Klaus Goerttler; Forensic Pathology, Professor Dr Georg Schmidt; Traffic Medicine, Professor Dr Georg Schmidt

Pharmacology Institute 2086

Address: Im Neuenheimer Feld 366, D-6900 Heidelberg
Director: Professor Dr Franz Gross
Department: Medical Documentation and Statistics, Professor Dr Herbert Immich

INSTITUTES ATTACHED TO THE UNIVERSITY 2087

German Cancer Research Centre 2088

Address: Im Neuenheimer Feld 280, D-6900 Heidelberg
Chairman: Professor Dr Klaus Munk

BIOCHEMISTRY INSTITUTE 2089
Head: Professor Dr Erich Hecker

DOCUMENTATION, INFORMATION AND STATISTICS INSTITUTE 2090
Head: Professor Dr Gustav Wagner

EXPERIMENTAL CANCER RESEARCH INSTITUTE 2091
Acting director: Dr Dieter Werner

EXPERIMENTAL PATHOLOGY INSTITUTE 2092
Head: Professor Dr Klaus Goerttler

NUCLEAR MEDICINE INSTITUTE 2093
Head: Professor Dr W.J. Lorenz

TOXICOLOGY AND CHEMOTHERAPY INSTITUTE 2094
Head: Professor Dr Dietrich Schmähl

VIRUS RESEARCH INSTITUTE 2095
Head: Professor Dr Klaus Munk

Karlsruhe Nuclear Research Centre   2096

Address: Postfach 3640, D-7500 Karlsruhe 1

**APPLIED NUCLEAR PHYSICS   2097
INSTITUTE**
Head: Professor Dr Gerd Schatz
nuclear physics   applied

**HIGH-TEMPERATURE CHEMISTRY   2098
INSTITUTE**
Head: Professor Dr Klaus Ebert

RADIATION BIOLOGY INSTITUTE   2099
Head: Professor Dr Karl Günther Zimmer

Schering Aktiengesellschaft   2100

Address: Müllerstrasse 178, 1 Berlin 65
Telephone: (030) 468-4681
Telex: 1820325 sch d
Research director: Dr Herbert Asmis
Divisions: Pharmaceuticals; Agrochemicals; Industrial Chemicals, Adhesives and Building Protectants; Electroplating
Graduate research staff: 350
Annual expenditure: DM250m
Activities: Research, manufacture and distribution of pharmaceuticals and chemicals in 120 plants and subsidiaries located in all five continents.
Pharmaceuticals - particular emphasis is placed in the fields of cardiovascular diseases, antipsychotic drugs, X-ray contrast media, hormonal contraception, gynaecological diseases, novel anti-inflammatory substances.
Agrochemicals - combating plant diseases and specific pests; weed control.
Industrial chemicals, adhesives and building protectants - synthesis and testing of reactive and thermoplastic synthetic resin and organometallic compounds; special polyurethane sealants for the building industry; use of organic magnesium compounds in catalysts for production of high-density polyethylene and polypropylene; organic tin compounds.
Electroplating - development of non-polluting processes; electronic circuitry; electrolytes.
Contract work: No
Publications: Annual report.

Schweisstechnische Lehr-   2101
und Versuchsanstalt
Duisburg

[Welding Technology Teaching and Research Institute Duisburg]
Address: Postfach 10 02 01, Bismarckstrasse 85, D-4100 Duisburg
Telephone: (0203) 35 30 55
Telex: 8551331 slvd d
Affiliation: Arbeitsgemeinschaft Industrieller Forschungsvereinigungen eV
Scientific Director: Professor Dr H. Thier
Scientific staff: 23
Activities: Mechanized light arc and resistance welding; metallurgy of welding processes; material transfer; development of new hard-facing materials; crack formation by hydrogen; hot cracking; void formation; long-term storage of electrodes.

Siemens Aktiengesellschaft   2102

Annual expenditure: over DM3 000m
Activities: Siemen's largest research laboratories are in West Berlin, Erlangen, Karlsruhe and Munich and are not organizationally integrated with the six product groups. Development needs to maintain close contact with both production and customers so the choice of development projects is the sole responsibility of the six product groups, each of which has its own development laboratories. The product groups are components, data and information systems, power engineering, electrical installations, medical engineering, and communications. In 1978/79 Siemens spent on research and development an amount equal to about 9 per cent of world sales. Siemens estimates that about half of its research and development spending has been devoted to microelectronics. The Federal Ministry of Research and Technology has provided substantial grants in the areas of microelectronics and data processing research and development from 1975 to 1980, some of which were received by Siemens, which is active worldwide in 127 countries outside the Federal Republic of Germany. There are Siemens companies in Argentina, Australia, Austria, Belgium/Luxembourg, Brazil, Canada, Columbia, Costa Rica, Denmark, Ecuador, El Salvador, Finland, France, Greece, Guatemala, Honduras, India, Iran, Ireland, Italy, Japan, Mexico, Morocco, Netherlands, Nicaragua, Nigeria, Norway, Pakistan, Portugal, South Africa, Spain, Sweden, Switzerland, Turkey, United Kingdom, United States of America, Venezuela and Zaïre.

CENTRAL TECHNOLOGY DIVISION   2103

Address: Büro der Leitung, Postfach 832740, D-8000 München 83

Research and Engineering Centre I   2104

Address: Otto-Hahn-Ring 6, Postfach 832740, D-8000 München 83
Telephone: (089) 636-1
Telex: 52109-0 sie d
Research director: Professor Dr W. Heywang
Sections: Analysis and materials research, Dr Pfisterer; applied physics, Dr Gremmelmaier; plastics and electrochemistry, Dr Kleeberg; solid-state electronics, Dr Winstel, Dr Zerbst; communications, general information, Dr Wille
Graduate research staff: 500
Annual expenditure: over £2m
Activities: Metals research; superconductivity; plasma physics; chemical analysis; electrochemistry; power engineering; plastics; semiconductor detectors; optics; semiconductor research; piezoelectrics; materials physics; systems research; computer architectures; semiconductor integrated circuits; scanning electron microscopy.
Contract work: No

Research and Engineering Centre II   2105

Address: Paul-Gossen-Strasse 100, Postfach 32 40, D-8520 Erlangen
Telephone: (09131) 7-1
Telex: 62921-0 sie d

COMMUNICATIONS GROUP   2106

Address: Hofmannstrasse 51, D-8000 München 70
Telephone: (089) 722-1
Telex: 5 288-0 sie d
Activities: Communication terminals; private and special purpose communication networks; public communication networks; safety and security systems.

COMPONENTS GROUP   2107

Address: Balanstrasse 73, Postfach 80 17 09, D-8000 München
Telephone: (089) 4144-1
Telex: 52108-0 sie d
Activities: Integrated circuits; discrete semiconductors; passive devices; tubes; special fields.

DATA AND INFORMATION SYSTEMS   2108 GROUP

Address: Otto-Hahn-Ring 6, Postfach 8329 40, D-8000 München
Telephone: (089) 636-1
Telex: 52109-0 sie d
Activities: Data processing systems; small computers and peripherals; application software.

DISCRETE SEMICONDUCTORS   2109 RESEARCH STATION

Address: Frankfurter Ring 152, Postfach 46 07 05, D-8000 München
Telephone: (089) 3500-1
Telex: 52108-70/73 sie d

ELECTRIC POWER RESEARCH   2110 STATION

Address: Nonnendammallee 62-79, Postfach 169, D-1000 Berlin 13
Telephone: (030) 386-1
Telex: 1 810253 sie d

ELECTRICAL INSTALLATIONS GROUP   2111

Address: Werner-von-Siemens-Strasse 50, Postfach 3240, D-8520 Erlangen
Telephone: (09131) 7-1
Telex: 62921-0 sie d
Activities: Power cables and insulated wires; wiring devices, lighting systems, and automotive electrical components; installation equipment and heating/air conditioning systems; electricity meters.

MEDICAL ENGINEERING GROUP   2112

Address: Henkestrasse 127, Postfach 3260, D-8250 Erlangen
Telephone: (09131) 84-1
Telex: 62920-0 sie d
Activities: Radiology; electromedicines; dentistry; electro-acoustics.

POWER ENGINEERING GROUP   2113

Address: Werner-von-Siemens-Strasse 50, Postfach 3240, D-8520 Erlangen
Telephone: (09131) 7-1
Telex: 62921-0 sie d
Activities: Power generation and distribution; transportation and public authorities; instrumentation and control; basic industries; manufacturing industries; standard products.

POWER ENGINEERING RESEARCH STATION 2114

Address: Östliche Rheinbrückenstrasse 50, Postfach 211262, D-7500 Karlsruhe
Telephone: (0721) 595-1
Telex: 78255-0 sie d

SWITCHGEAR RESEARCH CENTRE 2115

Address: Nonnendammallee 104-1 10, Postfach 140, D-1000 Berlin 13
Telephone: (030) 386-1
Telex: 1 810-259 sie d

TUBES-SPECIAL FIELDS RESEARCH STATION 2116

Address: St-Martin-Strasse 76, Postfach 80 17 01, D-8000 München
Telephone: (089) 4133-1
Telex: 52108-81/84 sie d

Sigmund Freud Institut - Ausbildungs- und Forschungsinstitut für Psychoanalyse 2117

[Sigmund Freud Institute - Training Centre and Research Institute for Psychoanalysis]
Address: Myliusstrasse 20, D-6000 Frankfurt-am-Main
Affiliation: Hesse Land Institute
Director: Professor Dr med Clemens de Boor
Activities: Psychoanalysis, psychosomatic medicine, and social and clinical psychology.

Staatliche Landwirtschaftliche Untersuchungs- und Forschungsanstalt Augustenberg 2118

[Augustenberg Experimental Centre for Agricultural Research]
Address: Nesslerstrasse 23, D-7500 Karlsruhe 41
Telephone: (0721) 48521
Parent body: Bundesministerium für Ernährung, Landwirtschaft, Umwelt und Forsten, Baden-Württemberg

Director: Professor Dr Georg Hoffmann
Sections:
Soil studies, Dr E. Wiechens
Agricultural chemistry, Dr H. Rückemann
Trace elements, heavy metals, radioagronomy, Dr W. Scholl
Seeds and applied botany, Dr B. Schmidt
Microbiology, Dr A. Thalmann
Environmental research, Dr P. Schweiger
Graduate research staff: 14 (part-time)
Annual expenditure: £10 000-50 000
Activities: Chemical testing of soils, feedstuffs, and fertilizers, including measurement of radioactivity levels; plant and animal nutrition; seed control and technology; environmental research.
Contract work: Yes

Staatliche Lehr- und Versuchsanstalt für Milchwirtschaft und Molkereiwesen 2119

[Dairy Industry State Training and Experiment Centre]
Address: Auf dem Bühl 84, D-8960 Kempten-Allgäu
Telephone: (0831) 75 412
Research director: Helmut Schöner
Sections: Cheese-making technology, Herr Bochtler, Herr Peschek; natural sciences, Herr Fickel, Herr Peschek
Activities: Education of dairymen and dairy technicians; research in dairy technology, especially cheese-making.
Contract work: No

Staatliches Veterinäruntersuchungsamt Arnsberg 2120

[State Veterinary Diagnostic Laboratory Arnsberg]
Address: Zur Taubeneiche 10-12, D-5760 Arnsberg 2
Telephone: (02931) 1805
Director: Dr E. Schaal
Section: Coronavirus infections of swine, Dr K.H. Witte
Annual expenditure: DM15 000
Activities: Aetiology, clinical picture, and pathology of epizootic viral diarrhoea of pigs; swine influenza.
Contract work: No

Standard Elektrik Lorenz AG   2121

– SEL
Address: Hellmuth-Hirth-Strasse 42, D-7000 Stuttgart 40
Telephone: 821-1
Telex: 7211-0
Affiliation: International Telephone and Telegraph Corporation, USA
Research Director: Dr Horst Ohnsorge
Sections: Components and technologies, Dr H. Ohnsorge; communication systems, Dr D. Becker; advanced terminals, Dr B. Cramer
Graduate research staff: 150
Annual expenditure: DM300m
Activities: Materials and components; production and system technology; telecommunication systems; transmission systems; data terminals and services; industry and consumer electronics; fundamentals of user equipment.
Contract work: No

Steinhandel Becker, Essen   2122

Address: Huttropstrasse 29, D-4300 Essen
or: Alte Schulstrasse 3-5, D-5461 Kalenborn/Linz
Telephone: (02645) 3092
Telex: 863021 stbe
Research director: Dr Ing Rolf Becker
Graduate research staff: 1
Annual expenditure: £10 000-50 000
Activities: Materials application: oxide and non-oxide ceramics, surface technology.
Contract work: No

Stifterverband für die Deutsche Wissenschaft eV   2123

[Donors' Association for the Promotion of Sciences and Humanities in Germany]
Address: Brucker Holt 50-60, Postfach 230360, D-4300 Essen 1
Telephone: (0201) 711051
Telex: 0857/544
General Secretary: Dr Horst Niemeyer
Director of Grant-Making: Dr H.-H. Pistor
Annual expenditure: over £2m
Activities: The Association administers funds and trusts donated by the German business community for the advancement of scientific research, teaching and training.

Contract work: No
Publications: Annual report.

Stiftung Institut für Härterei-Technik   2124

[Heat Treatment Foundation]
Address: Postfach 770207, D-2820 Bremen 77
Telephone: (0421) 630007
Telex: 245579
Research director: Professor Dr Otto Schaaber
Graduate research staff: 8
Activities: Production and investigation of surface layers of high wear and/or corrosion resistance; precipitation hardening and investigation of aluminium alloys.
Facilities: Heat treatment centre, testing machines, REM and ESMA equipment.
Contract work: Yes

Süddeutsche Zucker AG   2125

Address: Maximilianstrasse 10, D-6800 Mannheim 1
Research Director: Dr K.H. Fasol

CENTRAL LABORATORY   2126

Address: Wormser Strasse 11, D-6719 Obrigheim
Telephone: (06359) 803298
Telex: 451218 szof d
Development head: Dr H. Schiweck
Sections: Sugar production technology; biotechnology; carbohydrate chemistry; environmental protection
Graduate research staff: 12
Annual expenditure: £501 000-2m
Contract work: No

Süddeutsches Kunststoff-Zentrum   2127

– SKZ
[South German Plastics Centre]
Address: Frankfurter Strasse 15, D-8700 Würzburg
Telephone: (0931) 44081
Telex: 068 448 skzd
Research director: Professor Dr Ing W. Woebcken
Sections: Department of Education and Training, Dr Ing O. Schwarz; Department of Testing and Research, Dr Ing J. Zöhren
Activities: Research and testing of all kinds of plastics.

Publications: Informationen - Süddeutsches Kunststoff-Zentrum; *SKZ-Brücke*, for participants from underdeveloped countries.

Technische Hochschule Darmstadt 2128

[Darmstadt Institute of Technology]
Address: Karolinenplatz 5, D-6100 Darmstadt
Telephone: (06151) 161
Telex: 419 579 th d
President: Professor Dr Helmut Böhme

FACULTY OF ARCHITECTURE 2129

Dean: Professor Dr Georg Friedrich Koch
Sections:
Building production and industrial architecture, Professor Günter Behnisch, Professor Hans-Jacob Führer
Design and architecture, Professor Dipl-Ing Jürgen Bredow, Professor Dipl-Ing Hans-Georg Waechter
Interior decoration, Professor Max Bächer, Professor Dipl-Ing Peter Färber, Professor Dipl-Ing Fritz Seelinger
Surface constructions I, Professor Peter Steiger
Surface constructions II, Professor Dipl-Ing Walter Belz
Surface construction technology, Professor Dr Ing Gerd Fesel
Town planning and constructions, Professor Dipl-Ing Martin Einsele, Professor Dipl-Ing Thomas Sieverts
Building constructions, Professor Dipl-Ing Helmut Striffler
Statics of surface constructions, Professor Dr Ing Walther Mann, Professor Dr Ing Jürgen Stöffler
Planning and constructions in developing countries, Professor Dipl-Ing Arnold Körte
Mathematics for architects, Professor Dr Helmut Emde
Landscape design, Professor Dipl-Ing Robert Mürb

FACULTY OF BIOLOGY 2130

Dean: Professor Dr Wolfram Ullrich
Sections:
Botany, Professor Dr Gisbert Grosse-Brauckmann, Professor Dr Manfred Kluge, Professor Dr Diethard Köhler, Professor Dr Ulrich-Ernst Lüttge, Professor Dr Wolfram Ullrich, Professor Dr Josef Weigl, Professor Dr Eckhard Wollenweber, Professor Dr Maria Fekete (Chemical Plant Physiology)
Microbiology, Professor Dr Hans Jürgen Kutzner, Professor Dr Hans Herbert Martin, Professor Dr Kathryn Nixdorff, Professor Dr Hans-Jürgen Preusser, Professor Dr Friedrich K. Zimmermann

Zoology, Professor Dr Alfred Buschinger, Professor Dr Ute Gröschel-Stewart, Professor Dr Hans Emmerich, Professor Dr Werner Himstedt, Professor Dr Walter Kaiser, Professor Dr Dietrich Magnus, Professor Dr Herbert Miltenburger, Professor Dr Henning Scheich

FACULTY OF CONTROL AND COMPUTER ENGINEERING 2131

Dean: Professor Dr Hans Strack
Sections:
Control engineering, Professor Dr Ing Rolf Isermann, Professor Dr Henning Tolle
Computer engineering, Professor Dr Ing Wolfgang Hilberg, Professor Dr Ing Robert Piloty
Network and signal theory, Professor Dr Ing Georg Bosse, Professor Dr Ing Eberhard Hänsler
Semiconductor technology, Professor Dr Arno Kostka, Professor Dr Werner Langheinrich, Professor Dr Hans Strack

FACULTY OF EARTH SCIENCES AND GEOGRAPHY 2132

Dean: Professor Dr Otmar Seuffert
Sections:
Geography, Professor Dr Heinz-Dieter May, Professor Dr Manfred Schick, Professor Dr Otmar Seuffert
Geology and palaeontology, Professor Dr Egon Backhaus, Professor Dr Götz Ebhardt, Professor Dr Klaus Fahlbusch, Professor Dr Georg Kleinschmidt, Professor Dr Kurt Schetelig, Professor Dr Dietrich Schumann
Mineralogy and applied petrology, Professor Dr Wolfgang F. Müller, Professor Dr Peter Paulitsch geography

FACULTY OF ELECTRICAL POWER ENGINEERING 2133

Dean: Professor Dr Ing Wolfgang Pfeiffer
Sections:
Electrical energy conversion, Professor Dr Ing Egon Andresen, Professor Dr Wilhelm Müller
Electricity supply, Professor Dr Ing Hans-Jürgen Koglin, Professor Dipl-Ing Dietrich Oeding
Rectifiers and gas discharge, Professor Dr Ing Karl Hasse, Professor Dr Ing Robert Jötten, Professor Dr Ing Helmut Zürneck
High tension engineering and metrology, Professor Dr Ing Dieter König, Professor Dr Ing Wolfgang Pfeiffer

FACULTY OF INFORMATION SCIENCES   2134

Dean: Professor Dr Helmut Jürgensen
Sections:
Theoretical computer science, Professor Dr Britta Schinzel, Professor Dr Hans Tzschach, Professor Dr Helmut Waldschmidt, Professor Dr Hermann Walter
Practical computer science, Professor Dr Wolfgang Henhapl, Professor Dr Ing Hans-Jürgen Hoffmann, Professor Dr Ing Rolf Hoffmann
Information processing and interactive systems, Professor Dr Ing José Encarnacao, Professor Dr Gerhard Lustig, Professor Dr Ing Wolfgang Strasser

FACULTY OF INORGANIC AND NUCLEAR CHEMISTRY   2135

Dean: Professor Dr Herbert Schäfer
Sections:
Inorganic chemistry, Professor Dr Johann Buchler, Professor Dr Horst Elias, Professor Dr Joseph Grobe, Professor Dr Günter Joppien, Professor Dr Friedhelm Kober, Professor Dr Herbert Schäfer
Inorganic and nuclear chemistry, Professor Dr Karl-Heinrich Lieser
Nuclear chemistry, Professor Dr Ing Knut Bächmann, Professor Dr Helmut Münzel

FACULTY OF MATHEMATICS   2136

Dean: Professor Dr Erhard Meister
Senior staff: Professor Dr Benno Artmann, Professor Dr Gerhard Bruhn, Professor Dr Peter Burmeister, Professor Dr Karl Graf Finck zu Finckenstein, Professor Dr Bernhard Ganter, Professor Dr Hans-joachim Groh, Professor Dr Erhard Heil, Professor Dr Josef Hoschek, Professor Dr Hubert Kalf, Professor Dr Klaus Keimel, Professor Dr Eberhard Klingbeil, Professor Dr Werner Krabs, Professor Dr Detlef Laugwitz, Professor Dr Jürgen Lehn, Professor Dr Wolfgang Luh, Professor Dr Helmut Mäurer, Professor Dr Wolfgang Nolte, Professor Dr Vasco Osório, Professor Dr Egon Scheffold, Professor Dr Helmut Schellhaas, Professor Dr Gunter Stein, Professor Dr Willi Törnig, Professor Dr Walter Trebels, Professor Dr Peter Spellucci, Professor Dr Helmut Wegmann, Professor Dr Wolfgang Wendland, Professor Dr Rudolf Wille
Working groups: General algebra; geometry and algebra; differential geometry and kinematics; analysis and geometry; functional analysis; partial differential equations and applicable analysis; analysis and applications; numerical mathematics; operations research, statistics and theory of probabilities; approximation theory and optimal control; mathematics education; mathematical methods of physics.

FACULTY OF MECHANICAL ENGINEERING   2137

Dean: Professor Dr Erwin Krämer
Sections:
Labour sciences, Professor Dr Ing Walter Rohmert
Printing machines and processes, Professor Dipl-Ing Karl R. Scheuter
Motor vehicle technology, Professor Dr Ing Bert Breuer
Flight propulsion, Professor Dipl-Ing Friedrich Wazelt
Aeronautics, Professor Dr Ing Xaver Hafer
Conveyers and cranes, Professor Dr Ing Rudolf Neugebauer
Hydraulic machines and plant, Professor Dipl-Ing Jörg Osterwalder
Structures, Professor Dr Ing Johannes Wissmann
Machine components, Professor Dr Ing Herbert Müller, Professor Dr Ing Gerhard Pahl
Machine components and mechanics, Professor Dr Ing Walter Raab
Machine dynamics, Professor Dr Erwin Krämer
Mechanical technology, machine tools, Professor Dr Ing Friedrich Eckstein
Paper manufacturing, Professor Dr Ing Lothar Göttsching
Reactor engineering, Professor Dr Walter Humbach
Hydro- and aerodynamics, Professor Dr Ing Joseph H. Spurk
Steam turbines and plant, Professor Dr Ing Horst Pfeil
Thermal process technology and heat engineering, Professor Dr Ing Werner Kast
Metal forming, Professor Dr Ing Dieter Schmoeckel
Internal combustion engines, Professor Dr Ing Erhard Mühlberg
Heat theory, Professor Dr Ing Hans Beer
Thermodynamics, Professor Dr Ing Fritz Brandt
Materials science, Professor Dr Ing Helmut Speckhardt, Professor Dr Ing Karl-Heinz Kloos

FACULTY OF MECHANICS   2138

Dean: Professor Dr Walter Schnell
Sections:
Mechanics, Professor Dr Ernst Becker, Professor Dr Dietmar Gross, Professor Dr Ing Peter Hagedorn, Professor Dr Werner Hauger, Professor Dr Ing Peter Haupt, Professor Dr Ing Karl Roesner, Professor Dr Walter Schnell, Professor Dr Ing Hans-Theo Woernle
Meteorology, Professor Dr Werner Klug, Professor Dr Gerhard Manier, Professor Dr Friedrich Wippermann

FACULTY OF ORGANIC AND MACROMOLECULAR CHEMISTRY 2139

Dean: Professor Dr Hans Neunhoeffer
Sections:
Organic chemistry I-IV, Professor Dr Peter Eilbracht, Professor Dr Hans Günter Gassen, Professor Dr Bernd Giese, Professor Dr Frieder W. Lichtenthaler, Professor Dr Hans Jörg Lindner, Professor Dr Hans Neunhoeffer
Macromolecular chemistry, Professor Dr Dietrich Braun, Professor Dr Eckart Heidemann, Professor Dr Thomas Krause

FACULTY OF PHYSICAL CHEMISTRY AND CHEMICAL TECHNOLOGY 2140

Dean: Professor Dr Ing Johann Gaube
Sections:
Physical chemistry I-III, Professor Dr Jürgen Brickmann, Professor Dr Walter Eichenauer, Professor Dr Siegfried Göttlicher, Professor Dr Wolfgang Haase, Professor Dr Klaus-Heinrich Homann, Professor Dr Konrad-Georg Weil, Professor Dr Alarich Weiss, Professor Dr Erich Wölfel
Chemical technology, Professor Dr Fritz Fetting, Professor Dr Johann Gaube, Professor Dr Ing Gerhard Luft, Professor Dr Hartmut Wendt

FACULTY OF PHYSICS 2141

Dean: Professor Dr Gerd Herziger
Sections:
Applied physics, Professor Dr Heinz Finkenrath, Professor Dr Gerd Herziger, Professor Dr Herbert Pagnia, Professor Dr Harald Rose, Professor Dr Ing Wolfgang Seelig
Solid-state physics, Professor Dr Eugen Fick, Professor Dr Bruno Elschner, Professor Dr Johann Heber, Professor Dr Günter Sauermann, Professor Dr Herwig Sauermann, Professor Dr Frank Steglich, Professor Dr Günter Weber
Nuclear physics, Professor Dr Friedrich Beck, Professor Dr Hans-Georg Clerc, Professor Dr Helmut Frank, Professor Dr Eberhard Hilf, Professor Dr Egbert Kankeleit, Professor Dr Alfred Kording, Professor Dr Panagiotis Manakos, Professor Dr Achim Richter, Professor Dr Jürgen Theobald, Professor Dr Karl Wien

FACULTY OF STRUCTURAL ENGINEERING 2142

Dean: Professor Dr Ing Horst G. Schäfer
Sections:
Soil mechanics and foundations, Professor Dr Ing Eberhard Franke
Reinforced and prestressed concrete, Professor Dr Ing

Gert König, Professor Dr Ing Gerhard Mehlhorn, Professor Dr Ing Horst G. Schäfer, Professor Dr Ing Helmut G. Weigler
Site management and information processing, Professor Dr Ing Eberhard Schubert, Professor Dr Ing Heinz Schwarz
Statics, Professor Dr Ing Heinz Ebel, Professor Dr Helmut Saal, Professor Dr Ing Richard Schardt
Steel constructions and material mechanics, Professor Dr Ing Harald Friemann, Professor Dr Ing Otto Jungbluth, Professor Dr Ing Timm Seeger, Professor Dr Ing Wolfhart Uhlmann

FACULTY OF SURVEYING 2143

Dean: Professor Dr Ing Otfried Wolfrum
Sections:
Geodesy, Professor Dr Ing Gerhard Eichhorn, Professor Dr Ing Hansdieter Grosse, Professor Dipl-Ing Günter Paul, Professor Dr Ing Otfried Wolfrum
Photogrammetry and cartography, Professor Dr Ing Herman Deker
Astronomic and satellite geodesy, Professor Dr Ing Erwin Groten, Professor Dr Ing Carl-Erhard Gerstenecker

FACULTY OF TELECOMMUNICATIONS ENGINEERING 2144

Dean: Professor Dr Ing Hans L. Hartnagel
Sections:
Electromechanical constructions, Professor Dr Ing Curt Brader, Professor Dr Ing Heinrich Buschmann, Professor Dr Ing Heinz Weissmantel
Telecommunications and electro-acoustics, Professor Dr Ing Karl Hoffmann Professor Dr Gerhard Sessler, Professor Dr Wilmut Zschunke
High-frequency engineering, Professor Dr Ing Hans L. Hartnagel, Professor Dr Ing Alfons Kessler, Professor Dr Ing Anton Vlcek
Theoretical electrical engineering, Professor Dr Ing Gerhard Piefke

FACULTY OF WATER AND TRAFFIC 2145

Dean: Professor Dr Ing Günter Rincke
Sections:
Water supply, waste-water disposal, and municipal engineering, Professor Dr Ing Karl-Heinz Jacobitz, Professor Dr Ing Günther Rincke, Professor Dr Norbert Wolters
Traffic, Professor Dr Ing Walter Durth, Professor Dr Ing Edmund Mühlhans, Professor Dr Ing Gerhard Paulmann, Professor Dr Ing Hans-Georg Retzko
Hydraulic engineering, Professor Dr Ing Georg Euler,

Professor Dr Ing Hannes Lacher, Professor Dr Ing Josef Mock, Professor Dr Ing Ralph Schröder, Professor Dr Ing Wolfgang Schröder, Professor Dr Ing Walter Tiedt

Technische Universität Berlin 2146

[Berlin Technical University]
Address: Strasse des 17 Juli 135, D-1000 Berlin 12
Telephone: (030) 314 1
President: Professor Dr Jürgen Starnick
Note: The University collaborates with: Hahn-Meitner Institut für Kernforschung GmbH Berlin; Institut für Turbulenzforschung.

FACULTY OF AGRICULTURE 2147

Institute of Agriculture 2148
Director: Professor Dr Joachim Wesche

Institute of Cultivation and Pasture Economy 2149
Director: Professor Dr Konrad Merkel

Institute of Ecology 2150
Director: Professor Dr Waldemar Heinze

Institute of Landscape Gardening and Horticulture 2151
Director: Professor Jürgen Wenzel

FACULTY OF CONSTRUCTION AND PROCESS ENGINEERING 2152

Institute of Engineering Design and Thermal Engineering 2153
Director: Professor Dr Klaus Mollenhauer

Institute of Machine Tool and Processing Technology 2154
Director: Professor Dr G. Spur

Institute of Mechanical Engineering 2155
Director: Professor Dr H. Göhlich

Institute of Precision and Biomedical Engineering 2156
Director: Professor Dr Walter Schweizer

FACULTY OF CONSTRUCTION ENGINEERING AND SURVEYING 2157

Institute of Building Construction Statistics and Mechanical Engineering 2158
Director: Professor Dr Hanno Müller-Kirchenbauer

Institute of Building Materials Testing Methods 2159
Director: Professor Dr Franz Pilny

Institute of General Construction Engineering 2160
Director: Professor Dr Gebhard Hees

Institute of Hydromechanics and Hydrology 2161
Director: Professor Dr Carlwalter Schreck

FACULTY OF ELECTRICAL ENGINEERING 2162

Institute of Electrical Materials 2163
Director: Professor Dr Hans Günther Wagemann

Institute of Electronics 2164
Director: Professor Dr Karl Wolters

Institute of High Frequency Engineering 2165
Director: Professor Dr Walter John

Institute of High Voltage and Power Plant Engineering 2166
Director: Professor Dr Rudolf Gärtner

Institute of Telecommunications 2167
Director: Professor Karlheinz Manz

Institute of Theoretical Electrical Engineering 2168

Director: Professor Dr Ludwig Hannakam

FACULTY OF ENVIRONMENTAL SCIENCES 2169

Hermann-Rietschel Institute of Heating and Ventilation 2170

Director: Professor Dr Horst Esdorn

Institute of Illumination Engineering 2171

Director: Professor Dr Klaus Stolzenberg

Institute of Technical Acoustics 2172

Director: Professor Dr Manfred Heckl

Institute of Technical Environmental Science 2173

Director: Professor Dr Karl Joachim Thome-Kozmiensky

FACULTY OF FOOD CHEMISTRY AND TECHNOLOGY 2174

Institute of Fermentation and Brewery Technology 2175

Director: Professor Dr Eckard Krüger

Institute of Food Chemistry 2176

Director: Professor Dr Klaus Rubach

Institute of Food Technology 2177

Director: Professor Dr Hans Joachim Bielig

FACULTY OF INDUSTRIAL PROCESS ENGINEERING 2178

Institute of Chemical Engineering 2179

Director: Professor Dr Wolfgang Simonis

Institute of Metrology and Control Engineering 2180

Director: Professor Dr Irmfried Hartmann

Institute of Nuclear Engineering 2181

Director: Professor Dr Gerhard Memmert

Institute of Thermodynamics and Systems Engineering 2182

Director: Professor Dr Horst Gelbe

FACULTY OF INTERNATIONAL AGRICULTURAL DEVELOPMENT 2183

Institute of Animal Husbandry 2184

Director: Professor Dr Joachim Hans Weniger

Institute of Plant Cultivation Research 2185

Director: Professor Dr G. Krzysch

FACULTY OF MATERIALS SCIENCES 2186

Institute of Materials Technology 2187

Director: vacant

Institute of Metal Research 2188

Director: Professor Dr Hans Wever

Institute of Metallurgy 2189

Director: Professor Dr Martin G. Frohberg

Institute of Non-metallic Materials 2190

Director: Professor Dr Ulrich Hildebrandt

FACULTY OF MINING AND EARTH SCIENCES 2191

Institute of Applied Geophysics, Petrology and Mineral Deposits Research 2192

Director: Professor Dr Ludwig Hertel

Technische Universität Clausthal 2220

[Clausthal Technical University]
Address: Adolf-Römer-Strasse 2a, Postfach 230, D-3392 Clausthal -Zellerfeld
Telephone: (05323) 72 1
Telex: 09-53 828 tu clz d
Rector: Professor Dr Ing R. Jeschar

FACULTY OF MINING, METALLURGY AND MINING ENGINEERING 2221

Dean: Professor Dr Ing H.W. Hennicke

Apparatus and Plant Engineering Institute 2222

Address: Leibnitzstrasse 22, D-3392 Clausthal -Zellerfeld
Director: Professor Dr Theodor Tellkamp

Chemical and Fuel Technology Institute 2223

Address: Erzstrasse 18, D-3392 Clausthal -Zellerfeld
Director: Professor Dr Hans-H. Oelert

CHEMICAL ENGINEERING DEPARTMENT 2224

Head: Professor Dr Ing Ulrich Hoffmann

FUEL TECHNOLOGY DEPARTMENT 2225

Head: Professor Dr Otto Abel

Deep Well Drilling and Petroleum Engineering Institute 2226

Address: Agricolastrasse, D-3392 Clausthal -Zellerfeld
Director: Professor Dr Ing Claus Marx

Deformation and Rolling Mills Institute 2227

Address: Agricolastrasse 6, D-3392 Clausthal -Zellerfeld
Director: Professor Dr Ing Paul Funke

Electrical Engineering Institute 2228

Address: Leibnizstrasse 28, D-3392 Clausthal -Zellerfeld
Director: Professor Dr Ing Karlheinz Bretthauer

CONTROL ENGINEERING AND ELECTRONICS DEPARTMENT 2229

Head: Professor Dr Ing Kurt Lamberts
Senior staff: Professor Dr Ing Eike Muhlenfeld

Ferrous Metallurgy Institute 2230

Address: Robert-Koch-Strasse 14, D-3392 Clausthal -Zellerfeld
Director: Professor Dr Ing Eberhard Schürmann

METALLURGICAL PROCESSES DEPARTMENT 2231

Head: Professor Dr Ing Klaus Koch

Foundry Technology Institute 2232

Address: Agricolastrasse 2, D-3392 Clausthal -Zellerfeld
Director: Professor Dr Ing Eberhard Schürmann

Friction Technology and Machine Kinetics Institute 2233

Address: Agricolastrasse, D-3392 Clausthal -Zellerfeld
Director: Professor Dr Ing Jörn Holland

Heat Engineering and Industrial Furnaces Institute 2234

Address: Agricolastrasse, D-3392 Clausthal -Zellerfeld
Director: Professor Dr Ing Rudolf Jeschar

Heat Process Engineering Institute 2235

Address: Agricolastrasse 2, D-3392 Clausthal -Zellerfeld
Director: Professor Dr Ing Alfons Vogelpohl

MECHANICAL PROCESS ENGINEERING DEPARTMENT 2236

Address: Zellbach 5, D-3392 Clausthal -Zellerfeld
Head: Professor Dr Ing K. Leschonski

Mechanical Engineering Institute 2237

Address: Robert-Koch-Strasse 4, D-3392 Clausthal -Zellerfeld
Director: Professor Dr Ing Peter Dietz

Metallography and Metal Physics Institute 2238

Address: Grosser Bruch 23, D-3392 Clausthal -Zellerfeld
Director: Professor Dr Hans-Joachim Bunge
Senior staff: Professor Günter Wassermann

INDEPENDENT CORROSION DEPARTMENT   **2239**

Address: Robert-Koch-Strasse 14, D-3392 Clausthal -Zellerfeld
Head: Professor Dr Konrad Heusler

MATERIALS SCIENCE AND TECHNOLOGY DEPARTMENT   **2240**

Head: Professor Dr Ing Werner Heye

Metallurgy and Electrometallurgy Institute   2241

Address: Adolf-Römer-Strasse 2a, D-3392 Clausthal -Zellerfeld
Director: Professor Dr Ing Ulrich Kuxmann

Mine Surveying Institute   2242

Address: Erzstrasse 18, D-3392 Clausthal -Zellerfeld
Director: Professor Dr Ing Walter Haupt

Mining and Mining Economy Institute   2243

Address: Erzstrasse 20, D-3392 Clausthal -Zellerfeld
Director: Professor Dr Ing Walter Knissel
Senior staff: Professor Dr Ing F. Ludwig Wilke, Professor Dr Ing Siegfried von Wahl

Mining and Power Law Institute   2244

Address: Erzstrasse 51, D-3392 Clausthal -Zellerfeld
Director: Professor Dr Günter Kühne

Mining Institute   2245

Address: Erzstrasse 20, D-3392 Clausthal -Zellerfeld
Director: Professor Dr Ing H.J. Lürig

ROCK MECHANICS DEPARTMENT   **2246**

Head: Professor Dr Wolfgang Dreyer

Plant Engineering Institute   2247

Address: Robert-Koch-Strasse 4, D-3392 Clausthal -Zellerfeld
Director: Professor Dr Ing Friedrich Wilhelm Griese
Senior staff: Professor Dr Ing Hans-Joachim Torke

Processing Institute   2248

Address: Erzstrasse 20, D-3392 Clausthal -Zellerfeld
Director: Professor Dr Ing Martin Clement

WASTE-WATER TECHNOLOGY DEPARTMENT   **2249**

Head: Professor Dr Ing Albert Bahr

Rocks and Soils Institute   2250

Address: Zehntnerstrasse 2a, D-3392 Clausthal - Zellerfeld
Telephone: (05323) 722354
Telex: tu c/2/Steine und Erden
Director: Professor Dr Hans Walter Hennicke
Senior staff: Ceramics and enamels, Professor Dr H.W. Hennicke; glass, Professor Dr G. Frischat; cements and construction materials, Professor Dr I. Odler; raw materials, Dr H. Urban; testing analyses, Professor Dr Leers
Activities: Mechanical properties (strength, plasticity, elasticity); manufacturing properties (extrusion, forging); insulating properties; surface studies; corrosion resistance; powder behaviour and recycling of: ceramics, vitreous enamels, glass, cement and construction materials, raw materials.
Facilities: Scanning electron microscope, microprobe, surface mensuration and porosity testing, fracture testing of various raw materials, testing at high temperatures (1 200°C).

Technical Mechanics Institute   2251

Address: Graupenstrasse 3, D-3392 Clausthal -Zellerfeld
Director: Professor Dr Manfred Schäfer
Senior staff: Professor Dr Dietrich Behr, Professor Dr Bernhard Zimmermann

Theoretical Metallurgy and Applied Physical Chemistry Institute   2252

Address: Agricolastrasse 6, D-3392 Clausthal -Zellerfeld
Director: Professor Dr Klaus Schwerdtfeger

Welding Technology and Production Engineering Institute   2253

Director: Professor Dr Ing Wolfgang Drangelates

FACULTY OF NATURAL SCIENCES   2254

Dean: Professor Dr Horst Quade

Applied Physics Institute   2255

Address: Arnold-Sommerfeld-Strasse 1, D-3392 Clausthal -Zellerfeld
Director: Professor Dr Reiner Labusch

Economics Institute 2256

Address: Adolf-Römer-Strasse 2a, D-3392 Clausthal - Zellerfeld
Head: Professor Dr Rolf Schwinn

Geology Institute 2257

Address: Leibnitzstrasse 10, D-3342 Clausthal -Zellerfeld
Directors: Professor Dr Heinz Beckmann, Professor Dr Andreas Pilger

ENGINEERING GEOLOGY DEPARTMENT 2258
Head: Professor Dr Heinz Bottke

GEOLOGY AND PALAEONTOLOGY DEPARTMENT 2259
Head: Professor Dr Klaus Schwab
Senior staff: Professor Dr Rudolf Adler, Professor Dr Peter Kronberg, Professor Dr Kurt Mohr

NON-EUROPEAN GEOLOGY DEPARTMENT 2260
Head: Professor Dr Horst Quade

PETROLEUM GEOLOGY DEPARTMENT 2261
Head: Professor Dr Heinz Beckmann

Geophysics Institute 2262

Address: Arnold-Sommerfeld-Strasse 1, D-3392 Clausthal -Zellerfeld
Director: Professor Dr Reinhard K. Bortfeld

Inorganic Chemistry Institute 2263

Address: Paul-Ernst-Strasse 4, D-3392 Clausthal - Zellerfeld
Directors: Professor Dr Werner Bues, Professor Dr Eberhard Stumpp

Mathematics Institute 2264

Address: Erzstrasse 1, D-3392 Clausthal -Zellerfeld
Directors: Professor Dr Julius Albrecht, Professor Dr Bernhard Hornfeck, Professor Dr Lothar Jantscher, Professor Dr Stefan Schottlaender, Professor Dr Hanns Weinert

ANALYTICAL MATHEMATICS DEPARTMENT 2265
Head: Professor Dr Ulrich Mertins

ARITHMETIC DEPARTMENT 2266
Head: Professor Dr Klaus Ecker, Professor Dr Lutz Lucht

ELEMENTARY MATHEMATICS DEPARTMENT 2267
Head: Professor Dr Erich Glock

FUNCTIONAL ANALYSIS DEPARTMENT 2268
Head: Professor Dr Hans-Heinrich Kairies

Mineralogy and Crystallography Institute 2269

Address: Sägemüllerstrasse 4, D-3392 Clausthal - Zellerfeld
Director: Professor Dr Bruno Brehler

ORE DEPOSITS AND RAW MATERIALS DEPARTMENT 2270
Address: Adolf-Römer-Strasse 2a, D-3392 Clausthal - Zellerfeld
Head: Professor Dr Ing Hans Krause

Mineralogy and Petrography Institute 2271

Address: Adolf-Römer-Strasse 2a, D-3392 Clausthal - Zellerfeld
Director: Professor Dr Georg Müller

APPLIED MINERALOGY, GEOCHEMISTRY, AND RAW MATERIALS DEPARTMENT 2272
Head: Professor Dr Peter Halbach

Organic Chemistry Institute 2273

Address: Leibnizstrasse 6, D-3392 Clausthal -Zellerfeld
Directors: Professor Dr Karl-Dietrich Gundermann, Professor Dr Friedrich Boberg

Physical Chemistry Institute 2274

Address: Adolf-Römer-Strasse 2a, D-3392 Clausthal - Zellerfeld
Director: Professor Dr Günther Rehage
Senior staff: Professor Dr Peter Zugenmaier

Physics Institute 2275

Address: Leibnizstrasse 4, D-3392 Clausthal -Zellerfeld
Director: Professor Dr E.G. Bauer
Senior staff: Professor Dr Hans Oechsner, Professor Dr Ulrich Gradmann

Theoretical Physics Institute 2276

Address: Leibnitzstrasse 4, D-3392 Clausthal -Zeller-feld
Directors: Professor Dr Heinz Doebner, Professor Dr Lothar Fritsche

LEARNING THEORY DEPARTMENT 2277
Head: Professor Dr Dr Werner Wiater

Technische Universität München 2278

[Munich Technical University]
Address: 21 Arcisstrasse, Postfach 202420, D-8000 München 2
Telephone: (089) 210 51
Telex: 0522854 tumue d
President: Professor Dr W. Wild

FACULTY OF AGRICULTURE AND HORTICULTURE 2279

Dean: Professor Dr W. Rothenburger

FACULTY OF ARCHITECTURE 2280

Dean: Professor J.C. Ottow

FACULTY OF BREWERY, FOOD TECHNOLOGY AND MILK SCIENCES 2281

Dean: Professor Dr W. Postel

FACULTY OF CHEMISTRY, BIOLOGY AND GEOSCIENCES 2282

Dean: Professor Dr H. Schmidbauer

FACULTY OF CIVIL ENGINEERING AND SURVEYING 2283

Dean: Professor Dr H. Grundmann

FACULTY OF ELECTROTECHNOLOGY 2284

Dean: Professor Dr R. Saal

FACULTY OF MATHEMATICS 2285

Dean: Professor R. Bayer

FACULTY OF MECHANICAL ENGINEERING 2286

Dean: Professor Dr H. Lippmann

Metals Science and Metallurgy Department 2287

Telephone: (089) 210 525 44
Telex: tu mue d 522854
Head: Professor Dr Ing Karlheinz G. Schmitt-Thomas
Total r&d staff: 50
Activities: Failure investigation; failure prevention; technical reliability of materials; soldering; non-destructive testing; acoustic emission analysis; X-ray stress analysis; corrosion and corrosion control.
Facilities: Electron microscopy; microanalyser; acoustic emission devices; testing material devices.

FACULTY OF MEDICINE 2288

Dean: Professor Dr M. Reiter

FACULTY OF PHYSICS 2289

Dean: vacant
Deputy Dean: Professor Dr D. Menzel

SPECIAL RESEARCH PROGRAMMES 2290

Cybernetics 2291

Address: 21 Arcisstrasse, D-8000 München 2
Manager: U. Lupp
Activities: Research into visual, audio, somatic-sensory systems.

Programming Technology 2292

Address: 21 Arcisstrasse, D-8000 München 2
Head: Professor Dr F.L. Bauer

Satellite Geodesy 2293

Address: 21 Arcisstrasse, D-8000 München 2
Manager: Professor Dr M. Schneider

UNIVERSITY AFFILIATED INSTITUTES 2294

Central Institute for Space Planning and Environmental Research   2295

Address: 30/II Gabelsbergerstrasse, D-8000 München 2

Elementary Surface Stimulations   2296

Address: Physikalisch-Chemisches Institut der Ludwig-Maximilians-Universität, 11 Sophienstrasse, D-8000 München
Head: Professor Dr G. Ertl

German Food Chemistry Research Centre   2297

Address: Lichtenbergstrasse 4, D-8046 Garching
Telephone: (089) 32 09; 51 70
Research director: Professor Dr H.-D. Belitz
Senior staff: Professor Dr W. Grosch
Annual expenditure: £10 000-50 000
Activities: Proteins and enzymes of foodstuffs; fat oxidation; analysis of foodstuffs.
Contract work: No

Gutters Drainage   2298

Address: 21 Arcisstrasse, D-8000 München 2
Manager: Professor Dr P.-G. Franke

Institute of Preventive Medicine   2299

Address: 15 Ismaninger Strasse, D-8000 München 80
Managers: Professor Dr W. Vaillant, Professor Dr O. Messerschmidt

Production Technology of Cattle Breeding   2300

Address: 36 Vöttinger Strasse, D-8050 Freising
Manager: Dr M. Schurig

Reaction and Exchange Technology of Dispersing Two-Phase Systems   2301

Address: 21 Arcisstrasse, D-8000 München 2
Manager: Dr T. Pilhofer

Reliability Theory of Buildings   2302

Address: 21 Arcisstrasse, D-8000 München 2

South-German Research Institute for Milk Production, Weihenstephan   2303

Address: 45 Vöttinger Strasse, D-8050 Freising-Weihenstephan
Director: Dr Haisch

State-Research Institute for Applied Mineralogy, Regensburg   2304

Address: 2 Kumpfmühler Strasse, 2 Dörnberg-Palais, D-8400 Regensburg
Director: Professor Dr A. Forster

Textilprüfstelle Nagold   2305

[Nagold Textile Testing Institute]
Address: Postfach 246, D-7270 Nagold Schwarzwald
Telephone: (07452) 66088
Affiliation: Textilprüfstelle des Deutschen Textil-Einzelhandels
Research director: Herbert Stiegler

Thyssen Aktiengesellschaft vorm. August Thyssen-Hütte   2306

Address: Kaiser-Wilhelm-Strasse 100, D-4100 Duisburg 11
Telephone: (0203) 521
Telex: 855401 thy d, 855483 tvk d
Director, Research, Quality and Chemical Laboratories: Dr-Ing Ch. Schneider
Director, Research Department: Dr-Ing H. Rellermeyer
Sections: Chemical metallurgy, Dr-Ing R. Hammer; hot rolled products, Dr rer nat J. Degenkolbe; cold rolled products, Professor Dr-Ing Ch. Strassburger; system techniques, Dr rer nat E. Büchel
Graduate research staff: 145
Annual expenditure: over £2m
Activities: Blast furnace metallurgy; steelmaking metallurgy; refractories; by-products; development of unalloyed, micro-alloyed and alloyed steels; physical metallurgy; fabrication technology; surface techniques; measuring techniques; analyzing techniques; physical techniques; mathematical operations.
Contract work: No
Publications: Thyssen Technische Berichte
Additional information: The company was formerly called August Thyssen-Hütte.

Fritz Thyssen Stiftung 2307

[Fritz Thyssen Foundation]
Address: Am Römerturm 3, D-5000 Köln 1
Telephone: (0221) 234471
Chairman, Board of Trustees: Dr Kurt Birrenbach
Chairman, Scientific Advisory Board: Professor Dr Helmut Coing
Director: Dr Rudolf Kerscher
Activities: Established in 1959 by Mrs Amélie Thyssen and her daughter Anity, Countess Zichy-Thyssen, in memory of August Thyssen and Fritz Thyssen, the Foundation is devoted to the advancement of research and learning in universities and research institutes, particularly in Germany. Grants are awarded mainly in the following areas: basic research in the humanities; international relations; state, economy, and society; medicine and the natural sciences. None of the projects supported by the Foundation is concerned with areas from which the income of the Foundation is derived.

Tierärztliche Hochschule Hannover 2308

[Hannover School of Veterinary Medicine]
Address: Bischofsholer Damm 15, D-3000 Hannover 1, Niedersachsen
Telephone: (0511) 8561
Telex: 922034 tiho d
Vice-chancellor: Professor Dr Horst Frerking
Graduate research staff: 120

ANATOMY INSTITUTE 2309

Director: Professor Dr Helmut Wilkens

ANDROLOGY AND INSEMINATION OF DOMESTICATED ANIMALS CLINIC 2310

Director: Professor Dr Hans Merkt

ANIMAL HUSBANDRY AND GENETICS INSTITUTE 2311

Director: Professor Dr Christian Gall

ANIMAL HYGIENE INSTITUTE 2312

Director: Professor Dr Hans Georg Hilliger

ANIMAL NUTRITION INSTITUTE 2313

Director: Professor Dr Hans Meyer

BOTANY INSTITUTE 2314

Director: vacant

CATTLE DISEASES CLINIC 2315

Director: Professor Dr Mattheus Stöber

CATTLE OBSTETRICS AND GYNAECOLOGY CLINIC 2316

Director: Professor Dr Eberhard Grauert

CHEMISTRY INSTITUTE 2317

Director: Professor Dr G. Habermahl

EQUINE CLINIC 2318

Director: Professor Dr Rudolf Zeller

FISH DISEASES RESEARCH UNIT 2319

Head: Professor Dr Wolfgang Körting

FOOD SCIENCE AND MEAT TECHNOLOGY AND HYGIENE INSTITUTE 2320

Director: Professor Dr Siegfried Wenzel

HISTORY OF VETERINARY MEDICINE - SPECIAL STUDY AREA 2321

Director: Professor Dr Ernst-Heinrich Lochmann

MEDICAL PHYSICS DEPARTMENT 2322

Head: Professor Dr Werner Giese

MICROBIOLOGY AND EPIDEMIOLOGY INSTITUTE 2323

Director: Professor Dr Wolfgang Bisping

**MILK HYGIENE AND TECHNOLOGY   2324
INSTITUTE**

Director: Professor Dr Hans-Ulrich Wiesner

PARASITOLOGY INSTITUTE   2325

Director: Professor Dr Michel Rommel

PATHOLOGY INSTITUTE   2326

Director: Professor Dr Leo-Clemens Schulz

**PHARMACOLOGY, TOXICOLOGY   2327
AND PHARMACY INSTITUTE**

Director: Professor Dr Kurt Kaemmerer

**PHYSIOLOGICAL CHEMISTRY   2328
INSTITUTE**

Director: Professor Dr Jürgen Schole

PHYSIOLOGY INSTITUTE   2329

Director: Professor Dr Wolfgang Von Engelhardt

POULTRY CLINIC   2330

Director: Professor Dr Otfried Siegmann

SMALL ANIMALS CLINIC   2331

Director: Professor Dr Wilhelm Brass

**SMALL HOOFED ANIMALS CLINIC,   2332
FORENSIC MEDICINE AND
AMBULATORY CLINIC**

Director: Professor Dr Wilhelm Schulze

**STATISTICS AND BIOMETRY   2333
INSTITUTE**

Director: Professor Dr Hans Rundfeldt

VIROLOGY INSTITUTE   2334

Director: Professor Dr Bernd Liess

ZOOLOGY INSTITUTE   2335

Director: Professor Dr Manfred Röhrs

Special Research Projects: 2336

Note: The School of Veterinary Medicine is also engaged in the following Special Research Projects, which are partly financed by federal and regional government through the Deutsche Forschungsgemeinschaft:

**SPECIAL RESEARCH PROJECT 146 -   2337
EXPERIMENTAL ANIMAL RESEARCH**

Director: Professor Dr Klaus Gärtner

**SPECIAL RESEARCH PROJECT 54 -   2338
RHEUMATOID DISEASES IN ANIMALS**

Director: Professor Dr Helmut Deicher

**WHO Collaborating Centre: 2339
Veterinary Public Health**

Tiergesundheitsamt der   2340
Landwirtschaftskammer
Weser-EMS

**[Animal Health Bureau of the Weser-Ems
Chamber of Agriculture]**
Address: Mars-la-Tour-Strasse 1, Postfach 2545, D-2900 Oldenburg
Research director: Professor Dr V. Reuss
Activities: Diagnostic examinations in order to establish diseases and causes of death by means of histological, bacteriological, parasitological, serological, haematological, chemical and virological research. Health offices are maintained for cattle, pig, sheep, poultry, fur-bearing animals, and the health of freshwater fish. Particular work is directed to the supervision of brucellosis in cattle, bovine leukaemia, mastitis in cattle, parasites of cattle and sheep, swine pest, pseudo-rabies and atrophic rhinitis in pigs.

Unilever Forschungsgesellschaft mbH* 2341

Address: Behringstrasse 154, D-2000 Hamburg 50
Head: Dr K.-F. Gander
Activities: Research into foods (mainly edible fats) and analysis.
Note: See also Unilever PLC, United Kingdom; Unilever NV, Netherlands.

Union Rheinische Braunkohlen Kraftstoff Aktiengesellschaft 2342

Address: Postfach 8, D-5047 Wesseling
Telephone: (02236) 791
Telex: 888 69 47 ukw d
Parent body: Hoechst Aktiengesellschaft
Research director: Karl-Heinz Keim

Universität Bayreuth 2343

[Bayreuth University]
Address: Münzgasse 9, Postfach 3008, D-8580 Bayreuth
Telephone: (0921) 60 81
President: Dr K. D. Wolff

BIOLOGY, CHEMISTRY, EARTH SCIENCES DEPARTMENT 2344

Dean: Professor Dr E. Beck
Representative: Professor Dr Jörg Maier

MATHEMATICS AND PHYSICS DEPARTMENT 2345

Dean: Professor Dr L. Kramer

Computer Centre 2346

Head: Jürgen Kettler

Universität Bielefeld* 2347

[Bielefeld University]
Address: Universitätsstrasse, D-4800 Bielefeld

FACULTY OF BIOLOGY* 2348

Dean: Professor W. Kowallik

FACULTY OF CHEMISTRY* 2349

Dean: Professor A. Müller

FACULTY OF MATHEMATICS* 2350

Dean: Professor C. Klessmann

FACULTY OF PHYSICS* 2351

Dean: Professor D. Beck

Universität des Saarlandes* 2352

[Saar University]
Address: Im Stadtwald, 66 Saarbrücken
Telephone: (0681) 3021

FACULTY OF MEDICINE* 2353

Head: Professor Dr Hermann-Josef Haas

FACULTY OF NATURAL SCIENCES* 2354

Head: Professor Dr Friedrich Tomi

Universität Dortmund 2355

[Dortmund University]
Address: Postfach 500500, D-4600 Dortmund 50
Telephone: (0231) 7551
Telex: 822465 unido d
Rector: Professor Dr rer pol Velsinger
Head of Research: Professor Dr Ufo U. Bonse

DEPARTMENT OF ARCHITECTURE AND CONSTRUCTION ENGINEERING 2356

Telephone: (0231) 7551
Telex: 822465 unido d
Dean: Professor Dr Ing Josef Eibl
Sub-Dean: Professor Dipl Ing Herbert Pfeiffer
Graduate research staff: 54

DEPARTMENT OF CHEMICAL ENGINEERING   2357

Telephone: (0231) 7551
Telex: 822445 unido d
Dean: Professor Dr rer nat H. Giesekus
Sub-Dean: Professor Dr Ing J. Hapke
Graduate research staff: 56

DEPARTMENT OF CHEMISTRY   2358

Telephone: (0231) 7551
Telex: 822445 unido d
Dean: Professor Dr rer nat D. Naumann
Sub-Dean: Professor Dr rer nat B. Boddenberg

Institute of Chemistry   2359

Telephone: (0231) 755 3730
Director: Professor Dr rer nat Theophil Eicher
Graduate research staff: 77

DEPARTMENT OF COMPUTER SCIENCE   2360

Telephone: (0231) 7551
Telex: 822465 unido d
Dean: Professor Dr Volker Claus
Sub-Dean: Professor Dr Hans-Dieter Enrich
Graduate research staff: 66

DEPARTMENT OF EDUCATION AND BIOLOGY   2361

Telephone: (0231) 7551
Dean: Professor Dr phil K.-H. Schäfer
Sub-Dean: Professor Dr rer nat Ch. Ullrich

DEPARTMENT OF ELECTRICAL ENGINEERING   2362

Telephone: (0231) 7551
Telex: 822465 unido d
Dean: Professor Dr Ing Rudolf Schehrer
Sub-Dean: Professor Dr techn Kurt Oberrett
Graduate research staff: 68

DEPARTMENT OF MATHEMATICS   2363

Telephone: (0231) 7551
Telex: 822465 unido d
Dean: Professor Dr G. Frank
Sub-Dean: Professor Dr K.H. Mayer

Institute of Mathematics   2364

Telephone: (0231) 755 3136
Director: Professor Dr G. Frank
Graduate research staff: 74

DEPARTMENT OF MECHANICAL ENGINEERING   2365

Telephone: (02331) 7551
Telex: 822465 unido d
Dean: Professor Dr Ing K. Thermann
Sub-Dean: Professor Dr Ing Eberhard von Finckenstein
Graduate research staff: 95

DEPARTMENT OF PHYSICS   2366

Telephone: (0231) 7551
Telex: 822445 unido d
Dean: Professor Dr Ewald Reya
Sub-Dean: Professor Dr Joachim Treusch

Institute of Physics   2367

Telephone: (0231) 7551
Director: Professor Dr Dietrich Wegener
Graduate research staff: 85

DEPARTMENT OF STATISTICS   2368

Telephone: (0231) 7551
Telex: 822445 unido d
Dean: Professor Dr F. Hering
Sub-Dean: Professor Dr Siegfried Heller
Senior staff: Professor Dr rer nat Friedhelm Eicker, Professor Dr phil Siegfried Schath, Professor Dr rer nat Joachim Hartung, Professor Dr rer nat F. Hering
Graduate research staff: 16

DEPARTMENT OF URBAN AND REGIONAL PLANNING   2369

Telephone: (0231) 7551
Telex: 822465 unido d
Dean: Professor Dr rer nat Volker Kreibich
Sub-Dean: Professor Dr rer nat Lothar Finke

Institute of Urban and Regional Planning   2370

Head: Professor Dr tech Klaus R. Kunzmann
Graduate research staff: 76

INSTITUTE OF ENVIRONMENTAL   2371
PROTECTION

Telephone: (0231) 7551
Telex: 822445 unido d
Head: Professor Dr J. Karpe
Graduate research staff: 12

INSTITUTE OF OCCUPATIONAL   2372
PHYSIOLOGY

Address: Postfach 1508, D-4600 Dortmund 1
Telephone: (0231) 1084 1
Head: Professor C.R. Cavonius

INSTITUTE OF SPECTROCHEMISTRY   2373
AND APPLIED SPECTROSCOPY

Address: Bunsen-Kirchhoff-Strasse 11, D-4600 Dortmund 1
Telephone: (0231) 12 90 01
Director: vacant

Universität Duisburg -   2374
Gesamthochschule

[Duisburg University]
Address: Lotharstrasse 65, D-4100 Duisburg 1
Telephone: (0203) 3050
Telex: 855 733 uni du d
President: Professor Dr Adam Weyer

FACULTY OF BIOLOGY, CHEMISTRY   2375
AND GEOGRAPHY

Dean: Professor Dr V. Buss
Activities: A special research programme for the optimization of molecular-chemical processes and recycling is conducted by members of the Faculty under the leadership of Professor Dr E.-A. Hemmer.

Department of Applied Chemistry   2376

Address: Lotharstrasse 63, D-4100 Duisburg 1
or: Ruhrorterstrasse, D-4100 Duisburg 1
Head: Professor Dr A. Saus

Department of Applied Physical   2377
Chemistry

Address: Bismarckstrasse 90, D-4100 Duisburg 1
Head: Professor Dr W. Borchard

Department of Botany   2378

Head: Professor Dr R. Düll

Department of Didactics of Chemistry 2379

Head: Professor Dr R. Metze

Department of Electrochemistry   2380

Address: Lotharstrasse 63, D-4100 Duisburg 1
Head: Professor Dr F. Beck

Department of General Biology and   2381
Human Biology

Head: Professor Dr I. Danneel

Department of Geography and its   2382
Didactics

Address: Lotharstrasse 63, D-4100 Duisburg 1
Head: Professor Dr H. Beck

Department of Inorganic Chemistry   2383

Address: Bismarckstrasse 90, D-4100 Duisburg 1
Head: Professor Dr P. Sartori

Department of Instrumentation   2384

Head: Professor Dr A. Golloch

Department of Organic Chemistry   2385

Address: Bismarckstrassc 81, D-4100 Duisburg 1
Head: Professor Dr D. Döpp

Department of Physical Chemistry   2386

Address: Bismarckstrasse 90, D-4100 Duisburg 1
Head: Professor Dr R. Kosfeld

Department of Theoretical Chemistry   2387

Address: Bismarckstrasse 90, D-4100 Duisburg 1
Head: Professor Dr V. Buss

FACULTY OF ELECTRICAL   2388
ENGINEERING

Address: Bismarckstrasse 81, D-4100 Duisburg 1
Dean: Professor Dr P.M. Frank

Department of Aerosol Technology   2389

Address: Bismarckstrasse 90, D-4100 Duisburg 1
Head: Professor Dr H. Fissan

Department of Control Technology   2390

Address: Kommandantenstrasse 60, D-4100 Duisburg 1
Head: Professor Dr P. Frank

Department of Data Processing   2391

Address: Lotharstrasse 63, D-4100 Duisburg 1
Head: Professor Dr W. Geisselhardt

**Department of Electrical Energy   2392
Transmission**

Address: Bismarckstrasse 90, D-4100 Duisburg 1
Head: Professor Dr W. Rasquin

**Department of Electrical Machines   2393
and Drives**

Address: Bismarckstrasse 90, D-4100 Duisburg 1
Head: Professor Dr W. Fritz

Department of Electrical Materials   2394

Address: Kommandantenstrasse 60, D-4100 Duisburg 1
Head: Professor Dr E. Kubalek

**Department of Electrical Plant and   2395
Distribution Network**

Address: Grabenstrasse 93, D-4100 Duisburg 1
Head: Professor Dr D. Rumpel

**Department of Electroacoustics and   2396
Ultrasonic Technology**

Address: Bismarckstrasse 119, D-4100 Duisburg 1
Head: Professor Dr J. Herbertz

**Department of Electromechanical   2397
Construction**

Head: Professor Dr E. Gerhard

**Department of General and   2398
Theoretical Electrical Engineering**

Head: Professor Dr I. Wolff

**Department of High and Very High   2399
Frequency Technology including
Digital Technology**

Head: Professor Dr A. Ziermann

**Department of Information Handling   2400
and Equipment**

Address: Lotharstrasse 63, D-4100 Duisburg 1
Head: Professor Dr G. Dickopp

**Department of Information   2401
Technology**

Address: Bismarckstrasse 90, D-4100 Duisburg 1
Head: Professor Dr H. Luck

**Department of Operational   2402
Technology for the Electrical Industry**

Head: Professor Dr G. Selbach

**Department of Semiconductor   2403
Technology**

Address: Kommandantenstrasse 60, D-4100 Duisburg 1
Head: Professor Dr K. Heime

FACULTY OF MATHEMATICS   2404

Address: Lotharstrasse 63, D-4100 Duisburg 1
Dean: Professor Dr M. Leppig

**FACULTY OF MECHANICAL   2405
ENGINEERING**

Dean: Professor Dr D. Wünsch
Activities: A special research programme, entitled
'Water-Air-Noise' is conducted jointly by members of
the Faculty of Mechanical Engineering and the Faculty
of Electrical Engineering, under the leadership of Dipl-
Ing W. Baersch. The project involves theoretical and
control-technical studies of detection, spreading, reduction, control and consequences of pollution and noise.

Department of Control Engineering   2406

Head: Professor Dr H. Schwarz

Department of Energy Technology   2407

Head: Professor Dr K. Kugeler

Department of Finishing Technology   2408

Head: Professor Dr D. Elbracht

Department of Fluid Flow Technology 2409

Head: Professor Dr P. Roth

Department of Installation and   2410
Systems Technology and Department
of Forming Technology-Metallurgy

Head: Professor Dr J. Elfert

Department of Material Technology   2411

Head: Professor Dr H.G. Mosle

Department of Mechanical Handling-   2412
Steel Construction

Head: Professor Dr J. Oser

Department of Mechanics   2413

Head: Professor Dr M. Frik

Department of Shipbuilding   2414

Head: Professor Dr P. Hagen

Department of Thermodynamics   2415

Head: Professor Dr K. Lucas

Department of Turbines and   2416
Reciprocating Engines

Head: Professor Dr K. Grahl

FACULTY OF METALLURGY AND   2417
FOUNDRY TECHNOLOGY

Address: Bismarckstrasse 118, D-4100 Duisburg 1
Dean: Professor Dr G. Dietzel

Department of Foundry Materials   2418

Head: Professor Dr G. Dietzel

Department of Glass and Ceramic   2419
Materials Production

Head: Professor Dr H. von Kamptz

Department of Metal Science   2420

Head: Professor Dr H. Hasenkox

Department of Metallurgy   2421

Head: Professor Dr J. Agst

Department of Operating Technology   2422
for Foundries

Head: Professor Dr W. Gesell

Department of Plastic Moulding   2423

Head: Professor Dr H.-O. Lemper

FACULTY OF PHYSICS AND   2424
TECHNOLOGY

Address: Lotharstrasse 63, D-4100 Duisburg 1
Dean: Professor Dr K. Usadel

Department of Experimental Solid-   2425
State Physics

Address: Bismarckstrasse 81, D-4100 Duisburg 1
Head: Professor Dr W. Mönch

Department of Technology and   2426
Didactics of Technology

Address: Lotharstrasse 65, D-4100 Duisburg 1
Head: Professor Dr H. Sanfleber

Department of Theoretical Low   2427
Temperature Physics

Address: Bismarckstrasse 90, D-4100 Duisburg 1
Head: Professor Dr K. Usadel

Department of Theoretical Solid-State 2428
Physics

Address: Bismarckstrasse 90, D-4100 Duisburg 1
Head: Professor Dr R. Feder

Laboratory for Applied Physics   2429

Address: Lotharstrasse 65, D-4100 Duisburg 1
Head: Professor Dr W. Keune

Laboratory for Low Temperature and   **2430**
Experimental Low Temperature
Physics

Address: Lotharstrasse 65, D-4100 Duisburg 1
or: Kommandantenstrasse 60, D-4100 Duisburg 1
Head: Professor Dr E. Wassermann

Research Station for Shipbuilding for   **2431**
Inland Waterways

Address: Oststrasse 77, D-4100 Duisburg 1

Welding Technology Teaching and   **2432**
Research Centre

Address: Bismarckstrasse 85, D-4100 Duisburg 1

Universität Düsseldorf   2433

[Düsseldorf University]
Address: 1 Universitätsstrasse, D-4000 Düsseldorf 1
Telephone: (0211) 31 11
Telex: 8587348 uni d
President: Professor Dr P. Hüttenberger
Vice-President: Professor Dr M.-W. Schlipköter
See also entry for: Deutsches Krankenhaus Institut.

FACULTY OF MATHEMATICS AND   **2434**
NATURAL SCIENCES

Dean: Professor Dr J. Uhlenbusch

Institute of Applied Physics   **2435**

Director: Professor Dr J. Kranz

Institute of Botany   **2436**

Directors: Professor Dr W. Stubbe, Professor Dr K.A.
Santarius

Institute of Genetics   **2437**

Director: Professor Dr O. Hess

Institute of Geography   **2438**

Director: Professor Dr H.G. Steinberg

Institute of Inorganic Chemistry and   **2439**
Structural Chemistry

Director: Professor Dr W. Kuchen

Institute of Mathematics   **2440**

Director: Professor Dr B. Döring

Institute of Microbiology   **2441**

Director: Professor Dr C.P. Hollenberg

Institute of Organic Chemistry I   **2442**

Director: Professor Dr M.-D. Martin

Institute of Organic Chemistry II   **2443**

Director: Professor Dr G. Wulff

Institute of Pharmaceutical Biology   **2444**

Director: Professor Dr G. Willuhn

Institute of Pharmaceutical Chemistry   **2445**

Director: Professor Dr H. Möhrle

Institute of Pharmaceutical   **2446**
Technology

Director: Professor Dr B.C. Lippold

Institute of Physical Biology   **2447**

Director: Professor Dr D. Riesner

Institute of Physical Chemistry I and II 2448

Directors: Professor Dr H.-H. Perkampus, Professor
Dr J.W. Schultze

Institute of Physics   **2449**

Directors: Professor Dr G. Decker, Professor Dr A.
Otto, Professor Dr D. Schmid, Professor Dr J. Uhlenbusch

Institute of Psychology   **2450**

Director: Professor Dr J.P. Huston

Institute of Statistics and   **2451**
Documentation

Director: Professor Dr H. Klinger

Institute of Theoretical Chemistry   **2452**

Director: Professor Dr H.-H. Schmidtke

Institute of Theoretical Physics　　　2453

Directors:　Professor Dr R. Bausch, Professor Dr N.-R. Janssen

Institute of Zoology　　　2454

Directors:　Professor Dr W. Peters, Professor Dr G. Schneider, Professor Dr K.-D. Spindler

FACULTY OF MEDICINE　　　2455

Address:　5 Moorenstrasse, D-4000 Düsseldorf
Dean:　Professor Dr M. Strasburg

C. u. O. Vogt-Institute of Brain Research　　　2456

Director:　Professor Dr A. Hopf

Central Institute of Clinical Chemistry and Laboratory Diagnostics　　2457

Director:　Professor Dr W. Rick

Clinic and Outpatients Clinic of Dentistry (Westdeutsche Kieferklinik)　　2458

Directors:　Professor Dr H. Böttger, Professor Dr F. Schübel

Clinic of Dental and Plastic Surgery (Westdeutsche Kieferklinik)　　2459

Director:　Professor Dr J. Lentrodt

Clinic of Dermatology　　　2460

Director:　Professor Dr A. Greither

Clinic of Gynaecology　　　2461

Director:　Professor Dr L. Beck

Clinic of Neurology　　　2462

Director:　Professor Dr H.-J. Freund

Clinic of Nuclear Medicine　　　2463

Director:　Professor Dr L. Feinendegen

Clinic of Ophthalmology　　　2464

Director:　Professor Dr H. Pau

Clinic of Orthopaedics　　　2465

Director:　Professor Dr K.P. Schulitz

Clinic of Paediatrics　　　2466

Director:　Professor Dr G.A. van Harnack

Clinic of Psychiatry (Rheinische Landesklinik)　　2467

Director:　Professor Dr K. Heinrich

Clinic of Psychotherapy (Rheinische Landesklinik)　　2468

Director:　Professor Dr A. Heigl-Evers

Clinic of Urology　　　2469

Director:　Professor Dr H. Dettmar

Institute and Clinic for Medical Radiation　　2470

Director:　Professor Dr H. Vieten

Institute of Anaesthesiology　　　2471

Director:　Professor Dr M. Zindler

Institute of Anatomy　　　2472

Director:　Professor Dr H.G. Goslar

Institute of Biophysics and Electron Microscopy　　2473

Director:　Professor Dr W. Vogell

Institute of Diabetes Research (Clinical Biochemistry)　　2474

Director:　Professor Dr H. Reinauer

Institute of Diabetes Research: Internal Medicine　　2475

Director:　Professor Dr F.A. Gries

Institute of Experimental Surgery　　　2476

Director:　Professor Dr G. Arnold

Institute of Human Genetics and Anthropology　　2477

Director:　Professor Dr G. Röhrborn

Institute of Hygiene 2478

Director: Professor Dr H.-W. Schlipköter

Institute of Medical Microbiology and 2479
Virology

Director: Professor Dr P. Naumann

Institute of Medical Psychology 2480

Director: Professor Dr H.-J. Steingrüber

Institute of Neuropathology 2481

Director: Professor Dr W. Wechsler

Institute of Pathology 2482

Director: Professor Dr W. Hort

Institute of Pharmacology 2483

Director: Professor Dr K. Greeff

Institute of Physiological Chemistry 2484

Directors: Professor Dr W. Staib, Professor Dr H. Sies

Institute of Physiology 2485

Director: Professor Dr J. Haase

Institute of Thrombosis and 2486
Transfusion Medicine

Director: Professor Dr H.T. Brüster

Institute of Toxicology 2487

Director: Professor Dr F.K. Ohnesorge

Medical and Outpatients Clinic 2488

Director: Professor Dr G. Strohmeyer

Surgical and Outpatients Clinic 2489

Directors: Professor Dr K. Kremer, Professor Dr W.
Bircks

Universität Essen 2490
Gesamthochschule

[Essen University]
Address: Universitätsstrasse 2, Postfach 103764, D-
4300 Essen
Telephone: (0201) 183 1
Telex: 8579091
President: Professor Dr Peter Neumann-Mahlkau

FACULTY OF ARCHITECTURE, 2491
BIOSCIENCES AND GEOSCIENCES

Address: Universitätsstrasse 15-17, D-4300 Essen 1
Telephone: (0201) 183 32 13
Dean: Professor Johannes Biecker

FACULTY OF CHEMISTRY 2492

Address: Universitätsstrasse 5-7, D-4300 Essen 1
Telephone: (0201) 183 31 94
Dean: Professor Dr Günter Schön

FACULTY OF ENERGY, PROCESS AND 2493
ELECTRICAL ENGINEERING

Address: Universitätsstrasse 2, D-4300 Essen 1
Telephone: (0201) 183 27 14
Dean: Professor Dr Thomas Bohn

FACULTY OF ENGINE TECHNOLOGY 2494

Address: Schützenbahn 70, D-4300 Essen 1
Telephone: (0201) 183 29 31
Dean: Professor Dr Michael Jischa

FACULTY OF MATHEMATICS 2495

Address: Universitätsstrasse 1-3, D-4300 Essen 1
Telephone: (0201) 183 23 88
Dean: Professor Dr Laurie Davies

FACULTY OF PHYSICS 2496

Address: Universitätsstrasse 3-5, D-4300 Essen 1
Telephone: (0201) 183 24 80
Dean: Professor Dr Hans-Friedrich Dobele

FACULTY OF PRACTICAL MEDICINE 2497

Address: Hufelandstrasse 55, D-4300 Essen 1
Telephone: (0201) 7 99 11
Dean: Professor Dr Dietrich Schettler

FACULTY OF THEORETICAL MEDICINE   2498

Address: Hufelandstrasse 55, D-4300 Essen 1
Telephone: (0201) 7 99 11
Dean: Professor Dr Lutz-Dietrich Leder

Universität Fridericiana Karlsruhe - Technische Hochschule   2499

[Karlsruhe Technical University]
Address: Kaiserstrasse 12, D-7500 Karlsruhe
Telephone: (0721) 60 81
Telex: 07-826521 Uni Karlsruhe
Rector: Professor Dr H. Draheim
See also entries for: Kernforschungszentrum Karlsruhe
Bundesforschungsanstalt
Forschungs - und Materialprüfungsanstalt Baden-Württemberg.

AFFILIATED RESEARCH CENTRES   2500

Fire Protection Research Centre   2501

Address: Hertzstrasse 16, Postfach 6380, D-7500 Karlsruhe 21
Telephone: (0721) 608 44 73
Research director: Dr Ing P.G. Seeger
Activities: Research on fire protection; ignition and growth of a fire; fire fighting, methods of fire extinguishing and extinguishing agents, and provisions for the escape from fires.

FACULTY OF BIOLOGY AND GEOSCIENCES   2502

Dean: Professor Dr E. Oldemeyer
Senior staff: Mineralogy, Professor E. Althaus
Zoology, Professor E. Hanke, Professor G. Kümmel
Genetics and toxicology, Professor P. Herrlich
Geology, Professor H. Illies, Professor V. Maurin
Geography, Professor A. Kilchenmann, Professor A. Wirthmann
Botany, Professor H. Lichtentaler
Botany and pharmacology, Professor M. Weisenseel
Petrography, H. Puchelt

FACULTY OF CHEMICAL ENGINEERING   2503

Dean: Professor Dr K. Griesbaum
Senior staff: Technical thermodynamics, Professor K. Bier
Mechanical engineering, Professor N. Buggisch
Petrochemical and organic technology, Professor Dr K. Griesbaum
Chemistry and technology of gas, petroleum, coal, Professor K. Hedden
Heating technology, Professor W. Leuckel
Food processes, Professor M. Loncin
Chemical processes, Professor L. Riekert
Thermotechnics, Professor E.U. Schlunder
Hydrochemistry, Professor H. Sontheimer

FACULTY OF CHEMISTRY   2504

Dean: Professor Dr W. Seelmann-Eggebert
Senior staff: Inorganic chemistry, Professor G. Fritz
Inorganic chemistry II, Professor H. Barnighausen
Theoretical chemistry, Professor R. Ahlrichs
Chemical technology, Professor R. Fitzer
Physical chemistry, Professor E.U. Franck, Professor G. Hertz, Professor U. Schindewolf
Analytical chemistry, Professor K. Krogmann
Organic chemistry, Professor H. Musso
Organic chemistry II, Professor G. Schröder
Biochemistry, Professor J. Retey
Radiochemistry, Professor Dr W. Seelmann-Eggebert
Macromolecular chemistry, Professor B. Vollmert
Chemistry of foodstuffs, vacant

FACULTY OF CONSTRUCTION ENGINEERING   2505

Dean: Professor Dr H.H. Hahn
Senior staff: Building construction, Professor W. Baehre
Geodesy, Professor H. Draheim, Professor J. Van Mierlo
Soil mechanics and foundation construction, Professor G. Gudehus
Waterworks, Professor Dr H. H. Hahn, Professor E. Plate, Professor E. Naudascher
Engineering biology, Professor I. Hartmann
Town and country planning, Professor C. Heidemann, Professor G. Lammers
Building materials, Professor H. Hilsdorf
Topography, Professor W. Hofmann; Professor E. Kuntz
Transport, Professor W. Leutzbach
Geodynamics, Professor H. Malzer
Steel and cement constructions, Professor F.P. Müller
Rock mechanics, Professor O. Natau
Transport and traffic systems, Professor G. Schweizer
Construction statistics, Professor U. Vogel
Mechanics, Professor J. Wittenburg

FACULTY OF ECONOMICS 2506

Dean: Professor Dr G. Hammer
Senior staff: Economics, Professor W. Eichhorn, Professor R. Funck
Industrial economics, Professor G. Kuhl
Political economics, Professor R. Henn
Industrial management, Professor H. Goppl
Operations research, Professor Dr G. Hammer, Professor K. Neumann
Econometrics and statistics, Professor M. Rutsch
Computer sciences and formal description methods, Professor Th. Ottmann, Professor W. Stucky

FACULTY OF ELECTRICAL 2507
ENGINEERING

Dean: Professor Dr H. Kronmüller
Senior staff: Control and steering methods, Professor O. Föllinger
Electronics, Professor H. Friedburg
Electronics in computer engineering, Professor W. Jutzi
High-frequency techniques, Professor G.K. Grau
Process measuring techniques, Professor Dr H. Kronmüller
Theoretical electronics and measuring, Professor D. Mlynski
Lighting techniques, Professor H.P. Popp
Applied lighting techniques, Professor H.W. Bodmann
High voltage techniques, electrical drive, Professor A. Schwab
Biological cybernetics and physiology, Professor G. Vossius
Communication systems, Professor H. Wolf
Electrical technology, vacant

FACULTY OF INFORMATION 2508
SCIENCES

Dean: Professor Dr P. Lockemann
Senior staff: Professor P. Deussen, Professor W. Görke, Professor G. Goos, Professor G. Krüger, Professor P. Lockemann, Professor W. Menzel, Professor W. Rembold, Professor D. Schmid, Professor A. Schmitt, Professor A. Schreiner, Professor H. Wettstein

FACULTY OF MATHEMATICS 2509

Dean: Professor Dr U. Kulisch
Senior staff: Theoretical mechanics, Professor W. Bürger
Mathematics, Professor H. Hauser, Professor H. Kunle, Professor H.W. Leopoldt, Professor E. Martensen, Professor M. Schneider, Professor W. Walter

Applied mathematics, Professor U. Kulisch, Professor J. Weissinger
Mathematical statistics, Professor W. Fieger, Professor K. Hinderer
Practical mathematics, Professor W. Niethammer

FACULTY OF MECHANICAL 2510
ENGINEERING

Dean: Professor Dr R. Haller
Senior staff: Haulage, Professor E. Bahke
Nuclear engineering, Professor E.W. Becker
Technical thermodynamics, Professor G. Ernst
Use of computers in machine construction, Professor H. Grabowski
Machine construction and heavy vehicles, Professor Dr R. Haller
Combustion engines, Professor G. Jungbluth
General machine construction, Professor P. Kuhn
Raw materials I, Professor E. Macherauch
Raw materials II, Professor F. Thümmler
Measurement and regulation in machine construction, Professor F. Mesch
Machine testing and defects, Professor D. Munz
Machine technology and resistance, Professor E. Schnack
Reactor techniques, Professor D. Smidt
Technical mechanics, Professor F. Weidenhammer
Thermal electric machines, Professor S Wittig
Flow, J Zieref
Machine tools and workshop techniques, vacant

Materials Science and Engineering 2511
Department

Telephone: (0721) 608 23 45
Research director: Professor Dr E. Macherauch
Departments: Technology, Professor Dr H. Müller; plasticity, Professor Dr O. Vöhringer; oscillations, Dr P. Mayr
Total r&d staff: 52
Activities: Mechanical properties, plasticity, fatigue, heat treatment, residual stresses - metals (steel, aluminium and titanium alloys).
Publications: Research reports.

FACULTY OF PHYSICS 2512

Dean: Professor Dr G. Falk
Senior staff: Experimental physics, Professor W. Buckel, Professor H.G. Kahle
Experimental nuclear physics, Professor A. Citron, Professor W. Heinz, Professor W. Schmatz, Professor B. Zeitnitz
Physics Education, Professor Dr G. Falk
Meteorology, Professor F. Fiedler

Theoretical nuclear physics, Professor G. Hohler
Applied physics, W. Ruppel, Professor F. Stöckmann
Condensed matter physics, Professor A. Schmid
Theoretical physics, Professor J. Wess
Crystallography, Professor H. Wondratschek
Geophysics, Professor K. Fuchs

Universität-   2513
Gesamthochschule-
Paderborn

[Paderborn University]
Address: Warburger Strasse 100, D-4790 Paderborn
Telephone: (05251) 601
Telex: 936776 unipb d
Rector: Professor Dr Friedrich Buttler

AGRICULTURE   2514

Agriculture Department   2515

Dean: Professor Dr Werner Röper

ENGINEERING   2516

Architecture Department   2517

Dean: Professor Dipl-Ing Karl-Ludwig Medefindt

Computer Science Department   2518

Dean: Professor Dr Klaus-Dieter Bierstedt
Senior staff: Professor Dr Burkhard Monien

Electric Power Engineering   2519
Department

Dean: Professor Dipl-Ing Jürgen Grüneberg

Electronics - Electrical Engineering   2520
Department

Dean: Professor Dr Wido Kumm
Research coordinator: Professor Dr H. Moczala
Senior staff: Professor Dr Dieter Barschdorff,
Professor Dr Frank Dörrscheidt, Professor Dr Nicolas
Dourdoumas, Professor Dr Georg Hartmann, Professor
Dr Wolfgang Latzel
Special research programme: Small electric drives.

Mechanical Engineering Department I   2521

Dean: Professor Dr Fritz Dohmann
Senior staff: Professor Dr Dieter Gorenflo, Professor
Dr Ortwin Hahn, Professor Dr Klaus Herrmann,
Professor Dr Walter Jorden, Professor Dr Joachim
Lückel, Professor Dr Manfred Pahl, Professor Dr
Helmut Potente, Professor Dr Rolf Rennhack

Mechanical Engineering Department II   2522

Dean: Professor Dipl-Ing Meinolf Schweins

Mechanical Engineering Department   2523
III

Dean: Professor Dipl-Ing Günter Havenstein

Structural Engineering Department   2524

Dean: Professor Dr Friedrich-Karl Ewert

SCIENCE   2525

Chemistry Department   2526

Dean: Professor Dr Antonius Kettrup
Research coordinators: Professor Dr Horst
Stegemeyer, Professor Dr Joachim Schröter
Senior staff: Professor Dr Dietmar-Christian Hempel,
Professor Dr Horst Langemann, Professor Dr Heinrich
Marsmann, Professor Dr Peter Pollmann, Professor Dr
Eckhard Schlimme, Professor Dr Dieter Sellmann,
Professor Dr Wolfgang Sucrow
Special research programmes: Intermolecular ex-
changes in anisotropic matter; membrane research.

Mathematics Department   2527

Dean: Professor Dr Klaus-Dieter Bierstedt
Research coordinator: Professor Dr Helmut Lenzing
Senior staff: Professor Dr Klaus Deimling, Professor
Dr Benno Fuchssteiner, Professor Dr Karl-Heinz Ind-
lekofer, Professor Dr Eberhard Kaniuth, Professor Dr
Karl-Heinz Kiyek, Professor Dr Raimund Rautmann,
Professor Dr Hans-Dieter Rinkens, Professor Dr Her-
mann Sohr, Professor Dr Hartmut Spiegel
Special research programmes: Analysis of model
system, in natural sciences and technology, mathemati-
cal structures with special attention to information processing systems.

Physics Department   2528

Dean: Professor Dr Johann-Martin Spaeth
Senior staff: Professor Dr Margareta Erber, Professor Dr Wilfried Holzapfel, Professor Dr Wolfgang Kleemann, Professor Dr Wolf Von Der Osten, Professor Dr Harald Overhof, Professor Dr Josef Schmitz, Professor Dr Joachim Schröter, Professor Dr Horst Ziegler

Universität-Gesamthochschule-Siegen   2529

[Siegen University]
Address: Hölderlinstrasse 3, 500 Siegen 21
Telephone: (0271) 740-1
Telex: 872337

FACULTY OF CONSTRUCTION ENGINEERING   2530

Dean: Professor Dr Eberhard Keller

FACULTY OF ELECTRICAL ENGINEERING I (SIEGEN)   2531

Dean: Professor Dr Paul Kühn

FACULTY OF ELECTRICAL ENGINEERING II (GUMMERSBACH)   2532

Dean: Professor Dipl-Ing Paul Kalbhen

FACULTY OF MATHEMATICS   2533

Dean: Professor Dr Volker Klotz

FACULTY OF MECHANICAL ENGINEERING I (SIEGEN)   2534

Dean: Professor Dr Hans Schulze

FACULTY OF MECHANICAL ENGINEERING II (GUMMERSBACH)   2535

Dean: Professor Dipl-Ing Erich Boos

FACULTY OF NATURAL SCIENCES I (PHYSICS)   2536

Dean: Professor Dr Günter Zech

FACULTY OF NATURAL SCIENCES II (CHEMISTRY, BIOLOGY)   2537

Dean: Professor Dr Roger Blachnik

Universität Hamburg   2538

[Hamburg University]
Address: 1 Edmund-Siemers-Allee, D-2000 Hamburg 13
Telephone: (040) 4123
Telex: 2 14732
President: Dr P. Fischer-Appelt

DEPARTMENT OF BIOLOGY   2539

Address: Moorweidenstrasse 9, D-2000 Hamburg 13
Chairman: Professor Dr Rainer Knussmann

Anthropology Institute   2540

Address: Von-Melle-Park 10, D-2000 Hamburg 13
Director: Professor Dr Rainer Knussmann
Senior staff: Professor Dr Virendra Chopra

Applied Botany Institute   2541

Address: Marseiller Strasse 7, D-2000 Hamburg 36
Director: Professor Dr Konrad Von Weihe
Scientific staff: 26
Annual expenditure: DM408 000 (1977)
Activities: Useful plants and their products; feed stuff.

PHARMACOGNOSY DEPARTMENT   2542
Heads: Professor Dr Ewald Sprecher, Dr Ljubomir Kraus

General Botany Institute and Botanical Garden   2543

Address: Junguisstrasse 6, D-2000 Hamburg 36
Director: Professor Dr Wolfgang Abel
Senior staff: Professor Dr Eberhard Bock, Professor Dr Michael Böttger, Professor Dr Karl Dörffling, Professor Dr Peter Fortnagel, Professor Dr Georg Heinrich, Professor Dr Hans-Dieter Ihlenfeldt, Professor Dr Ludwig Kies, Professor Dr Udo Kristen, Professor Dr Klaus Kubitzki, Professor Dr Dieter Mergenhagen, Professor Dr Marianne Mix, Professor Dr Alexander Schmidt, Professor Dr Adolf Weber
Scientific staff: 33
Annual expenditure: DM1 274 700 (1977)
Activities: Effect of plant hormones on growth and development; ecology of algae, especially effect of heavy metals (lead, cadmium, manganese); metabolism of plant glands; cell wall formations of algae; effect of

substances on cell division; cultivation of plant cells; ecology of bacteria; effect of chemically altered antibiotics on bacteria.

Hydrobiology and Fisheries Science Institute   2544

Address: Olbersweg 24, D-2000 Hamburg 50
Director: Professor Dr Kurt Lillelund
Senior staff: Professor Dr Dietrich Schnack, Professor Dr Hjalmar Thiel
Scientific staff: 21
Annual expenditure: DM3 482 500 (1977)
Activities: Effects of industrial waste water on aquatic plant systems; ecological aspects of egg and larva development of fish; ichthyopathological effects in aquacultivation, stress symptoms; pesticides in food chains; respiration measurements in deep sea.

FISHERIES SCIENCE DEPARTMENT   2545
Head: Professor Dr Erich Braum

HYDROBIOLOGY DEPARTMENT   2546
Address: Zeiseweg 9, D-2000 50
Senior staff: Professor Dr Dietrich Schnack, Professor Dr Hjalmar Thiel

Wood Biology Department   2547

Address: Leuschnerstrasse 91, D-2050 Hamburg 80
Senior staff: Professor Dr Joseph Bauch, Professor Dr Dieter Eckstein, Professor Dr Walter Liese
Scientific staff: 4
Annual expenditure: DM207 800 (1977)
Activities: Crossbreeding; selection and resistance breeding of forestry plants; wood biology, anatomy, damage and protection; wood chemistry; utilization of lignose, cellulose, paper, fibres, isotope techniques and analysis.
Note: This Department and the two following Departments carry out research which is inseparably linked to that carried out at Bundesforschungsanstalt für Forst- und Holzwirtschaft, at the same address.

Wood Technology Department   2548

Address: Leuschnerstrasse 91, D-2050 Hamburg 80
Senior staff: Professor Dr Arno Frühwald, Professor Dr Detlef Noack, Professor Dr Rudolf Patt

World Forest Economy Department   2549

Address: Leuschnerstrasse 91, D-2050 Hamburg 80
Senior staff: Professor Dr Eberhard Brüning, Dr Gerhard Kaminsky, Professor Dr Claus Wiebecke

Zoology Institute and Zoological Museum   2550

Address: Martin-Luther-King-Platz 3, D-2000 Hamburg 13
Director: Professor Dr Gerhard Hartmann
Senior staff: Professor Dr Rudolf Abraham, Professor Dr Wilhelm Becker, Professor Dr Michael Dzwillo, Professor Dr Dierk Franck, Professor Dr Olaf Giere, Professor Dr Hans-Wilhelm Koepcke, Professor Dr Otto Kraus, Professor Dr Jakob Parzefall, Professor Dr Nicolaus Peters, Professor Dr Lothar Renwrantz, Professor Dr Walter Rühm, Professor Dr Harald Schliemann, Professor Dr Hans Strümper, Professor Dr Wolfgang Villwock, Professor Dr Federico Wenzel, Professor Dr Horst Wilkens, Professor Dr Claus-Dieter Zander, Professor Dr Eckart Zeiske
Scientific staff: 41
Annual expenditure: DM815 400 (1977)
Activities: Regressive evolutionary processes (eg scale and fin reduction in fish); genetics; ecology (eg aspects of environmental planning and water protection); metabolism physiology; invertebrate-immunology; carbohydrate metabolism.

DEPARTMENT OF CHEMISTRY   2551

Address: Martin-Luther-King-Platz 6, D-2000 Hamburg 13
Chairman: Professor Dr Fritz Thieme

Inorganic and Applied Chemistry Institute   2552

Address: Martin-Luther-King-Platz 6, D-2000 Hamburg 13
Director: Professor Dr Heindirk Tom Dieck
Senior staff: Professor Dr Rainer Dietrich Fischer, Professor Dr Walter Kaminsky, Professor Dr Günter Klar, Professor Dr Reinhard Kramolowsky, Professor Dr Erwin Weiss
Scientific staff: 17
Annual expenditure: DM3 055 800 (1977)
Activities: Polyreactions; optimization of polyreactions, regarding molecular weight distribution, sequency-length distribution; analysis of polymers; connection between structure and properties of plastics; pyrolytics of plastics and used tyres.

APPLIED CHEMISTRY DEPARTMENT   2553
Head: Professor Dr Gerhard Zachmann

SPECIAL INORGANIC AND ANALYTICAL CHEMISTRY DEPARTMENT   2554
Head: Professor Dr Erwin Weiss

Organic Chemistry and Biochemistry Institute   2555

Address: Martin-Luther-King-Platz 6, D-2000 Hamburg 13
Director: Professor Dr Wolfgang Walter,
Senior staff: Professor Dr Günther Gercken, Professor Dr Joachim Jentsch, Professor Dr Wilfried A. König, Professor Dr Hubert Köster, Professer Dr Adolf Krebs, Professor Dr Heinz Kropf, Professor Dr Ferdinand Liemann, Professor Dr Armin De Meijere, Professor Dr Hans Paulsen, Professor Dr Ernst Schaumann, Professor Dr Joachim Thiem, Professor Dr Jürgen Voss
Scientific staff: 18
Annual expenditure: DM1 552 800 (1977)
Activities: Natural substances with view to synthetic and biochemical properties; highly-strained ring systems; organic sulphur compounds (thiomides); stereochemical investigations; monomolecular surface films; oxydation and antioxydation processes under catalysis by phtalocyanine.

BIOCHEMISTRY DEPARTMENT   2556
Head: Professor Dr Werner Thorn

CHEMICAL INVESTIGATION OFFICE   2557
Head: Professor Dr Alfred Montag

FOOD CHEMISTRY DEPARTMENT   2558
Head: Professor Dr Alfred Montag

THEORETICAL ORGANIC CHEMISTRY DEPARTMENT   2559
Senior staff: Dr Wolfgang Walter, Dr Ernst Schaumann, Dr Jürgen Voss

Pharmaceutical Chemistry Institute   2560

Address: Laufgraben 28, D-2000 Hamburg 13
Director: Professor Dr Norbert Kreutzkamp
Senior staff: Professor Dr Wolfgang Hanefeld, Professor Dr Klaus Lührs, Professor Dr Kieter Matthies, Professor Dr Jobst Mielck
Scientific staff: 7
Annual expenditure: DM218 100 (1977)
Activities: Structure interactions of medicaments in order to optimize the effects by synthesis of new compounds; development of chemical transport agents for biological active molecules; investigations of chemical reactions for the analysis of medicaments; testing of germinized compounds for their effective substance.

PHARMACEUTICAL TECHNOLOGY DEPARTMENT   2561
Head: Professor Dr J. Mielck

Physical Chemistry Institute   2562

Address: Laufgraben 24, D-2000 Hamburg 13
Director: Professor Dr Bertel Kastening
Senior staff: Professor Dr Horst Förster, Professor Dr Walter Gunsser, Professor Dr Adolf Knappwost, Professor Dr Hans Lechert, Professor Dr Klaus Nagorny, Professor Dr Friedrich Steinbach, Professor Dr Fritz Thieme
Scientific staff: 23
Annual expenditure: DM1 356 400 (1977)
Activities: Thermodynamics and kinetics of surface reactions regarding the smooth and abrasion-resistant running of machine components; corrosion problems; mineral metabolism; structure and formation of solid-state bodies.

DEPARTMENT OF COMPUTER SCIENCES   2563

Address: Schlüterstrasse 70, D-2000 Hamburg 13
Chairman: Professor Dr Joachim Schmidt
Senior staff: Professor Dr Wilfried Brauer, Professor Dr Klaus Brunstein, Professor Dr Hermann Flessner, Professor Dr Werner Grass, Professor Dr Eike Jessen, Professor Dr Karl Kaiser, Professor Dr Manfred Kudlek, Professor Dr Ingbert Kupka, Professor Dr Klaus Lagemann, Professor Dr Hans-Hellmut Nagel, Professor Dr Frieder Schwenkel, Professor Dr Rüdiger Valk

DEPARTMENT OF EARTH SCIENCES   2564

Address: Bundesstrasse 55, D-2000 Hamburg 13
Chairman: Professor Dr Klaus Fiedler

Geography and Economic Geography Institute   2565

Address: Bundesstrasse 55, D-2000 Hamburg 13
Director: Professor Dr Gerhard Sandner
Senior staff: Professor Dr Günter Borchert, Professor Dr Eckhard Grimmel, Professor Dr Horst Mensching, Professor Dr Helmut Nuhn, Professor Dr Gerhard Sendler, Professor Dr Hans-O. Spielmann, Professor Dr Fritjof Voss

Geology and Palaeontology Institute and Museum   2566

Address: Bundesstrasse 55, D-2000 Hamburg 13
Director: Professor Dr Friedhelm Thiedig
Senior staff: Professor Dr Gerhard Alberti, Professor Dr E.T. Degens, Professor Dr Klaus Fiedler, Professor Dr Gero Hillmer, Professor Dr Christian Spaeth, Professor Dr Ida Valeton, Professor Dr How Kin Wing
Scientific staff: 18

Annual expenditure: DM4 119 500 (1977)
Activities: Organic geochemistry and sedimentology; palaeontology; alpine and saxonic tectonics; carbon circulation in the sea; young sediments of oceans and inland lakes.

Geophysics Institute   2567

Address: Bundesstrasse 55, D-2000 Hamburg 13
Director: Professor Dr Janis Makris
Senior staff: Professor Dr Alfred Behle, Professor Dr Seweryn Duda
Scientific staff: 26
Annual expenditure: DM2 606 200 (1977)
Activities: Refraction seismics at sea, reflection seismics at sea; gravitation; magnetics; refraction and reflection seismics; land seismics; geoelectrics; electromagnetic methods (used for ore prospecting); water prospecting; soil mechanical investigation; development of microwave telemetry for sea motion measurments; ocean acoustics.

Meteorology Institute   2568

Address: Bundesstrasse 55, D-2000 Hamburg 13
Director: Professor Dr Hans Hinzpeter
Senior staff: Dr Günter Fischer, Dr Gerd Stilke
Scientific staff: 25
Annual expenditure: DM126 700 (1977, excluding external funding)
Activities: Development of meteorological models for general circulation, climate, meteorology and storm floods; spreading of trace elements (environmental protection); turbulent processes in atmospheric boundary layer (lower 1 000 m); development of convection and clouds; reciprocal action between ocean and atmosphere.

HELIGOLAND METEOROLOGICAL   2569
OBSERVATORY

Address: Mittelland, D-2192 Heligoland
Head: Dr Helmut Jeske

Mineralogy and Petrography Institute   2570

Address: Grindelallee 48, D-2000 Hamburg 13
Director: Professor Dr Horst Saalfeld
Senior staff: Professor Dr Otto Jarchow, Professor Dr Dieter Jung, Professor Dr Dieter Pohl, Professor Dr Robert Rath, Professor Dr Mahmud Tarkian
Scientific staff: 18
Annual expenditure: DM420 000 (1977)
Activities: Crystal growth and breeding; formation of andesite vulcanismus; geochemistry and genesis of non-ferrous metals in magmatic deposits.

Observatory of the Geophysical   2571
Institutes

Address: Kuhtrift 18, D-2100 Hamburg 90
Head: Professor Dr Gerd Stilke

Oceanography Institute   2572

Address: Heimhuder Strasse 71, D-2000 Hamburg 13
Director: Professor Dr Jürgen Sündermann

Soil Science Department   2573

Address: Von-Melle-Park 10, D-2000 Hamburg 13
Head: Professor Dr Hans-Wilhelm Scharpenseel
Senior staff: Professor Dr Günter Miehlich
Scientific staff: 9
Annual expenditure: DM481 600 (1977)
Activities: General and regional soil sciences; tropical soil science; environmental protection, eg waste water filtering, heavy metals, chlorinated hydrocarbons; soil ecology and soil-radioecology; ground water data.

DEPARTMENT OF MATHEMATICS   2574

Address: Bundesstrasse 55, D-2000 Hamburg 13
Chairman: Professor Dr Carl Geiger

Applied Mathematics Institute   2575

Director: Professor Dr Reiner Hass
Senior staff: Professor Dr Rainer Ansorge, Professor Dr Ulrich Eckhardt, Professor Dr Carl Geiger, Professor Dr Klaus Glashoff, Professor Dr Wolf Dietrich Hofmann, Professor Dr Hubertus Jongen, Professor Dr Gerhard Opfer, Professor Dr Bodo Werner

Mathematical Stochastics Institute   2576

Director: Professor Dr Konrad Behnen
Senior staff: Professor Dr Wolf-Rüdiger Heilmann, Professor Dr Gerhard Hübner, Professor Dr Georg Neuhaus

Mathematics Seminar   2577

Director: Professor Dr Helmut Brückner
Senior staff: Professor Dr Walter Benz, Professor Dr Rolf Berndt, Professor Dr Helene Braun, Professor Dr Rudolf Halin, Professor Dr William Kerby, Professor Dr Egmont Köhler, Professor Dr Helmut Krämer, Professor Dr Hanspeter Kraft, Professor Dr Kurt Legrady, Professor Dr Johannes Michaliček, Professor Dr Helmut Müller, Professor Dr Oswald Riemenschneider, Professor Dr Hellmut Schaeffer, Professor Dr Eberhard Schröder, Professor Dr Werner Seier, Professor Dr Helmut Strade

DEPARTMENT OF MEDICINE　2578

Address: Martinistrasse 52, D-2000 Hamburg 20
Chairman: Professor Dr K.-H. Hölzer

Anatomy Institute　2579

Director: Professor Dr W. Lierse
Scientific staff: 19
Annual expenditure: DM313 000 (1977)
Activities: Embryological studies on central nervous system, the eye, male sex organs, placenta; morphological studies on smooth-muscular hollow organs, fertilization; blood morphology, anatomic basis for sensibility; effects of ionizing rays and antimetabolites on the central nervous system, distribution of transfer agents in the nervous system.

Biophysics and Radiation Biology　2580
Institute

Director: Professor Dr H. Jung
Scientific staff: 7
Annual expenditure: DM246 100 (1977)
Activities: Proliferation kinetics of cells and tumours; influence of radiation sensitivity; application of biophysical testing methods for clinical problems.

Dental Clinic　2581

Director: Professor Dr B. Rottke

CONSERVATIVE DENTISTRY　2582
DEPARTMENT
Head: Professor Dr J. Franke

JAW ORTHOPAEDICS DEPARTMENT　2583
Head: Professor Dr E. Hausser

PROSTHESIS DEPARTMENT　2584
Head: Professor Dr H. Ritze

SURGICAL DEPARTMENT　2585
Head: Professor Dr G. Pfeifer

Dermatology Clinic　2586

Director: Professor Dr T. Nasemann

Ear, Nose and Throat Clinic　2587

Director: Professor Dr H. Rollin

Forensic Medicine Institute　2588

Director: Professor Dr W. Janssen

Heinrich-Pette-Institut für　2589
experimentelle Virologie und
Immunologie

[Heinrich Pette Institute for Experimental Virology and Immunology]
Sections: General virology, Professor O. Drees; Virus biochemistry, Professor Dr R. Drzeniek; membrane research, Professor Dr R. Jaenisch; immunology, Professor Dr W. Ostertag; clinical virology, Professor Dr F. Lehmann-Grube; cytology, virology, Professor Dr K. Mannweiler
Scientific staff: 70
Annual expenditure: DM270 00 (1977)
Activities: Virus structures and functions of their components; direct and indirect virus effects as decisive factors in virus infections; membranes of animal cells; leukaemia virus, cell differentiation and tumour genesis; immunological tolerance against virus and membrane antigens.

Human Genetics Institute　2590

Director: Professor Dr W. Goedde
Scientific staff: 7
Annual expenditure: DM230 600 (1977)
Activities: Metabolism disorders; hereditary diseases; early diagnosis and proof of genetic defects; prenatal diagnosis, chromosome investigations; hereditary biology; sero-genetic and twin research.

Mathematics and Computer Sciences　2591
in Medicine Institute

Director: Dr Jürgen Berger

Medical Clinics　2592

Directors: Professor Dr H.G. Thiele; Professor Dr H. Frahm
Scientific staff: 27
Annual expenditure: DM2 751 500 (1977)
Activities: Clinical and experimental endocrinology, haematology, fats metabolism disorders; diagnosis and therapy of hormone dependent tumours; malignant diseases of haematological and lymphatic systems; myocardial blood circulation and metabolism.

Medical Microbiology and　2593
Immunology Institute

Director: Professor Dr C. Hiller
Scientific staff: 15
Annual expenditure: DM558 400 (1977)
Activities: Antibiotics - resistance and mechanism of antibiotics; formationof multi-resistance of bacteria and sensitivity of clinical bacteria-isolatorsagainst antibiotics.

Neurology Clinic   2594

Director: Professor Dr K.H. Puff
Scientific staff: 26
Annual expenditure: DM2 012 700 (1977)
Activities: Neurotraumatology; metabolic disorders of the nervous system; circulatory disturbances of the nervous system; diseases of the skeleton and their effects on the nervous system; epileptology; neuromuscular diseases; neurological intensive care; neuro-ophthalmology; neuro-otology; neurochemistry.

NEURORADIOLOGY DEPARTMENT   2595
Head: Professor Dr A. Tänzer

NEUROSURGERY DEPARTMENT   2596
Head: Professor Dr R. Kautzky

Obstetrics and Gynaecology Clinic   2597

Director: Professor Dr K. Thomsen
Scientific staff: 25
Annual expenditure: DM2 022 300 (1977)
Activities: Physiology and pathology of ovarian function and reproduction;mammary and ovarian carcinoma.

Ophthalmology Clinic   2598

Director: Professor Dr H. Sautter

Orthopaedic Clinic   2599

Director: Professor Dr Günter Dahmen
Senior staff: Professor Dr Von Torklus

Paediatric Clinic   2600

Director: Professor Dr F. Bläker
Scientific staff: 29
Annual expenditure: DM5 097 700 (1977)
Activities: Leukemia; endocrinology; psychosomatic disorders.

Pathology Institute   2601

Director: Professor Dr G. Seifert
Scientific staff: 28
Annual expenditure: DM347 900 (1977)
Activities: Pre- and early stages of tumours, molecular-pathological endo- and exocrine metabolism breakdowns, eg rheumatism, diabetes mellitus, geriatrics; tumour classification in correlation to therapeutic effects and research of environmental factors causing or influencing human diseases.

Pharmacology Institute   2602

Director: Professor Dr W. Braun
Scientific staff: 12
Annual expenditure: DM260 900 (1977)
Activities: Metabolism of medicaments and other foreign materials in order to find an answer to interactions in metabolism processes leading to an improved action of drugs, including mechanisms of reabsorption, separation and toxicology; investigations into action mechanism of individual medicament toxicology, eg with the aim of optimizing treatment for poisoning; environmental-toxicological investigations into carcinogenetic and mutagene effects.

Physiological Chemistry Institute   2603

Director: Professor Dr H. Hilz
Scientific staff: 24
Annual expenditure: DM1 004 600 (1977)
Activities: Time-dependent translocation of protein kinase in liver of Glucagon-treated rats; chemical sequestration of cAMP, protein kinase activation and hormonal response; supranucleosomal structure of chromatin; absorption and theapeutic effect of iron-(III)-citrate and iron-(III)-hydroxide-carbohydrate complexes containing trivalent iron; food-dependent regulation of the intermediary metabolism.

Physiology Institute   2604

Director: Professor Dr B. Bromm
Scientific staff: 14
Annual expenditure: DM249 900 (1977)
Activities: Adaptation of heart action to the peripheral circulation; biological regulation, especially with thermoregulation; transport processes in biological membranes, especially in the kidney; excitation mechanisms in peripheral nerves; perception through skin senses; psychophysical symptom with sensation of pain.

Psychiatric Clinic   2605

Director: Professor Dr J. Gross

Radiology Clinic and Radiation   2606
Institute

Director: Professor Dr E. Bücheler
Scientific staff: 40
Annual expenditure: DM3 188 500 (1977)
Activities: Computer tomography; sonography; operated digestive tract; inflammatory intestinal changes; angiography; radiation protection.

Surgical Clinic   2607

Director: Professor Dr G. Rodewald

Urology Clinic 2608

Director: Professor Dr H. Klosterhalfen

DEPARTMENT OF PHYSICS 2609

Address: Moorweidenstrasse 9, D-2000 Hamburg 13
Chairman: Professor Dr Harry Lehmann

Applied Physics Institute 2610

Address: Jungiusstrasse 11, D-2000 Hamburg 36
Director: Professor Dr Manfred Harsdorff
Senior staff: Professor Dr Hans Günter Danielmeyer, Professor Dr Douglas A. Fay, Professor Dr Günter Huber, Professor Dr Jörg Peter Kotthaus, Professor Dr Werner Legler, Professor Dr Kurt Scharnberg; theoretical solid-state physics, Professor Dr Ludwig Tewordt
Scientific staff: 27
Annual expenditure: DM1 089 100 (1977)
Activities: Solid-state lasers; coherent optics and picture processing; slow electrons; inelastic electron scattering; gas discharging and laser sparks; quantum fluids; superconduction and lattice dynamics.

Experimental Physics Institute I 2611

Address: Jungiusstrasse 9, D-2000 Hamburg 36
Director: Professor Dr Gunnar Anderson-Lindström
Senior staff: Professor Dr Hanno Brückmann, Professor Dr Hans-Heinrich Duhm, Professor Dr Heinrich Viktor Von Geramb, Professor Dr Rudolf Langkau, Professor Dr Albrecht Lindner, Professor Dr Wolfgang Scobel, Professor Dr Udo Strohbusch
Scientific staff: 30
Annual expenditure: DM1 390 800 (1977)
Activities: Isochron-cyclotron studies; basic research into experimental low energy physics; theoretical nuclear physics; nuclear testing and measurement and applied nuclear physics; experimental nuclear and molecular physics and its application.

Experimental Physics Institute II 2612

Address: Luruper Chaussee 149, D-2000 Hamburg 50
Director: Professor Dr Peter Stähelin
Senior staff: Professor Dr Volker Blobel, Professor Dr Friedrich Wilhelm Büsser, Professor Dr Erich Gerdau, Professor Dr Martin Holder, Professor Dr Christof Kunz, Professor Dr Erich Lohrmann, Professor Dr Peter Schmüser, Professor Dr Herwig Schopper, Professor Dr Bernd Sonntag, Professor Dr Hartwig Spitzer, Professor Dr Gustav Weber, Professor Dr Georg Zimmerer
Scientific staff: 49
Annual expenditure: DM3 699 300 (1977)
Activities: Elementary meson physics with the aid of an electron synchrotron (accelerator); synchrotron radiation in nuclear, molecular, surface and solid-state physics.

Hamburg Observatory 2613

Address: Gojenbergweg 112, D-2050 Hamburg 80
Director: Professor Dr Heinrich Wendker
Senior staff: Professor Dr Ulrich Haug, Professor Dr John Hazlehurst, Professor Dr Sjur Refsdal, Professor Dr Dieter Reimers, Professor Dr Christian De Vegt, Professor Dr Heinrich Wendker
Scientific staff: 15
Annual expenditure: DM626 800 (1977)
Activities: Single stars; non-radial oscillation of stars; contact systems; gravitation lens effects; physical and astronometric studies of comets and asteroids; kinematics of the Milky Way in the Sun's environment up to 1 000 parsec distance; radiation from stars; frequency of helium in the galaxy.

Theoretical Physics Institute I 2614

Address: Jungiusstrasse 9, D-2000 Hamburg 36
Director: Professor Dr Joachim Appel
Senior staff: Professor Dr Dietmar Geissler, Professor Dr Heinrich Heyszenau, Professor Dr Hartwig Schmidt, Professor Dr Kurt Schönhammer
Scientific staff: 14
Annual expenditure: DM307 100 (1977)
Activities: Electrical properties of metal surfaces and semiconductor surfaces; superconduction of transfer metals; optical and electrical properties of ferroelectrical semiconductors and metals; microscopic theory of quantum fluids.

Theoretical Physics Institute II 2615

Address: Luruper Chaussee 149, D-2000 Hamburg 50
Director: Professor Dr Frank Steiner
Senior staff: Professor Dr Joachim Bartels, Professor Dr Detlev Buchholz, Professor Dr Rudorf Haag, Professor Dr Gustav Kramer, Professor Dr Gerhard Mack
Scientific staff: 15
Annual expenditure: DM184 700 (1977)
Activities: Quadrant theory of fields and elementary mesons.

UNIVERSITY RESEARCH INSTITUTE 2616

Institute for Shipbuilding   2617

Address: Lämmersieth 90, D-2000 Hamburg 60
Director: Professor Dr Ing Hansjörg Petershagen
Senior staff: Professor Dr Klaus Eggers, Professor Dr Ing Wolfgang H. Isay, Professor Dr Ing O. Krappinger, Professor Dr Ing Heinrich A. Schimmöller, Professor Dr Ing Heinrich Söding, Professor Dr Karl Wieghardt
Note: The Institute cooperates very closely with Hamburgische Schiffbau-Versuchungsanstalt GmbH.

Universität Hannover*   2618

[Hannover University]
Address: Welfengarten 1, D-3000 Hannover
Telephone: (0511) 7621

FACULTY OF CIVIL ENGINEERING*   2619

Dean: Professor R. Kracke

FACULTY OF HORTICULTURE AND SOIL CONSERVATION*   2620

Dean: Professor Von Reichenbach
Departments: Horticulture; soil husbandry; biology and meteorology

FACULTY OF MATHEMATICS AND NATURAL SCIENCES*   2621

Dean: Professor H.J. Barthold
Departments: Mathematics; physics; chemistry; earth sciences

FACULTY OF MECHANICAL ENGINEERING*   2622

Dean: Professor H.G. Musmann
Note: Incorporating electrical studies.

Universität Hohenheim   2623

[Hohenheim University]
Address: Postfach 700562, D-7000 Stuttgart 70
Telephone: (0711) 4501-1
Activities: The University of Hohenheim conducts research in all branches of science and technology, with particular emphasis on the following special subject areas: agricultural technology, including the development and design of agricultural machinery, and harvesting and drying technologies for cereals; the nutritional qualities of agricultural products, including the investigation of protein yields in maize and other crops, and the study of fat synthesis and trace element absorption in animals.
In 1980 the University decided to coordinate many already existing programmes of research as a Centre for Tropical and Subtropical Agriculture, under the leadership of Professor Dr Erwin Reisch. The Centre directs an extensive research programme into all areas of agricultural science and production in tropical climates, including animal husbandry, crop fertilization and productivity, ecological protection, and many specialized regional projects.

FACULTY OF AGRICULTURAL SCIENCES I (PLANT PRODUCTION AND LANDSCAPE ECOLOGY)   2624

Dean: Professor Dr F. Grossmann

Institute of Fruit, Vegetables and Wine Growing   2625

Address: 25 Emil-Wolff-Strasse, D-7000 Stuttgart
Director: Professor Dr G. Buchloh

Institute of Land Cultivation and Plant Ecology   2626

Address: Schloss, D-7000 Stuttgart
Director: Professor Dr A. Kohler

Institute of Phytomedicine   2627

Address: 5 Otto-Sander-Strasse, D-7000 Stuttgart
Director: Professor Dr G. Grossmann

Institute of Plant Cultivation, Seed Research and Population Genetics   2628

Address: 9 and 17 Garbenstrasse, D-7000 Stuttgart
Director: Professor Dr H.H. Geiger

Institute of Plant Feeding   2629

Address: 20 Fruwirthstrasse, D-7000 Stuttgart
Director: Professor Dr H. Marschner

Institute of Plant Production   2630

Address: Fruwirthstrasse 23, Postfach 700562, D-7000 Stuttgart 70
Telephone: (0711) 4501 2382
Telex: 7-22959 uniho d
Head: Professor Dr G. Kahnt
Graduate research staff: 8
Annual expenditure: £10 000-50 000

Activities: Soybean-production-systems; crop-rotation effects, green manuring; soil tillage; organic farming systems.
Contract work: Yes .
Publications: Agronomy without Ploughing; Green Manuring.

DEPARTMENT OF AGRONOMY AND CROP SCIENCE 2631

Address: Postfach 700562, D-7000 Stuttgart 70
Telephone: (0711) 4501 2382
Telex: 7-22959 unihod
Head: Professor Dr G. Kahnt
Senior staff: Dr Gutzmann, Dr Kübler, Dr Tekete
Graduate research staff: 8

Institute of Soil Science and Location Science 2632

Address: 27 Emil-Wolff-Strasse, D-7000 Stuttgart
Director: Professor Dr E. Schlichting

Research Centre for Fruit Growing and Horticulture 2633

Address: Hohenheim 2
Head: A. Mohr

Research Centre for Intensive Culture and Agrarian Ecology 2634

Address: Schuhmacherhof 1, D-7980 Ravensburg 1
Director: Professor Dr F. Winter

Research Centre for Plant Cultivation 2635

Address: Maiszuchtstation Eckartsweier, D-7601 Willstätt
Head: Dr D. Klein

Research Centre for Plant Cultivation 2636

Address: Heidfeldhof, Hohenheim 3
Head: Dr U. Posselt

Research Centre for Plant Production and Plant Protection 2637

Address: Ihinger Hof, D-7253 Renningen
Director: Dr G. Renz

FACULTY OF AGRICULTURAL SCIENCES II (AGRICULTURAL ECOLOGY, TECHNOLOGY AND ANIMAL PRODUCTION) 2638

Dean: Professor Dr J. Zeddies

Institute of Agricultural Technology 2639

Address: 9 Garbenstrasse, D-7000 Stuttgart
Director: Professor Dr H.-D. Kutzbach

Institute of Animal Feeding 2640

Address: D-7000 Stuttgart
Director: Professor Dr K.H. Menke

Institute of Animal Husbandry 2641

Address: 17 Garbenstrasse, D-7000 Stuttgart
Director: Professor Dr S. Scholtyssek

Institute of Veterinary Medicine and Hygiene 2642

Address: 35 Fruwirthstrasse, D-7000 Stuttgart
Director: Professor Dr D. Strauch

Research Centre for Animal Husbandry and Animal Breeding 2643

Address: Unterer Lindenhof, D-7412 Eningen bei Reutlingen
Director: Dr J. Lorenz

Research Centre for the Breeding of Small Animals 2644

Address: Unterer Lindenhof, D-7412 Eningen bei Reutlingen
Head: Dr J. Gerlach

REGIONAL INSTITUTE OF AGRICULTURAL CHEMISTRY 2645

Address: 14 Emil-Wolff-Strasse, D-7000 Stuttgart
Manager: Professor Dr R. Seibold

REGIONAL INSTITUTE OF AGRICULTURAL MACHINERY AND DESIGN 2646

Address: 9 Garbenstrasse, D-7000 Stuttgart
Director: Professor Dr Th. Bischoff

REGIONAL INSTITUTE OF BEEKEEPING 2647

Address: 13 August-von-Hartmann-Strasse, D-7000 Stuttgart
Director: Professor Dr G. Buchloh

REGIONAL INSTITUTE OF SEED GROWING 2648

Address: 14-16 and 25 Fruwirthstrasse, D-7000 Stuttgart
Director: Professor Dr H.H. Geiger

FACULTY OF BIOLOGY 2649

Dean: Professor Dr W. Frank

Institute of Botany 2650

Address: 30 Garbenstrasse, D-7000 Stuttgart
Director: Professor Dr B. Frenzel
Senior staff: Dr B. Becker, Dr R. Geranmayeh, Dr E. Götz, Dr K. Haas, Professor Dr Körber-Grohne, Dr M. Küttel, Dr K. Loris, Dr P. Peschke, Dr G. Röderer
Activities: Palaeoecology of Central Europe during the ice-age and post ice-age; ice-age vegetation of Central Europe; influence of primitive man on the palaeoecology of Central Europe; palaeoclimatology; chronological process of the ice retreat during the last large glaciation of the Northern and Central Alps; correlation between pleistocene warm and cold ages of the Alps and Northern Germany; full oak-year-ring chronology of the post-glacial period; regulating mechanism in forest ecosystems; physiology of resistance of plants against heat, cold and drought; palaeoethnobotany and vegetation history of the postglacial period; effect of inorganic and organic lead compounds on single-cell algae; systematics of the angiosperms; radial thickness growth of a tropical wood on the Philippines.

Institute of Genetics and Plant 2651 Physiology

Address: 30 Garbenstrasse, D-7000 Stuttgart
Director: Professor Dr F. Mechelke
Senior staff: Professor Dr Bayreuther, W. Blaschek, C. Donn, K. Dressler, Dr R. Endress, Dr E.-M. Götz, H. Grossberger, Professor Dr C. Hesemann, Professor Dr D. Hess, R.-D. Illg, K. Jenne, M. Komp, B. Liebke, H. Lorenz, B. Lustig, F. Meiss, W. Plischke, C. Schetter
Activities: Genetics of mistletoe, viscum album; differentiation processes of apple blossoms; heterochromatic structures of higher plants; methodology of zytochemical analysis of plant cells; culture and fusion of vicia protoplasts; influence of extreme feeding conditions on the development of the antherentapetum of the antirrhinum; gene manipulations, transfer of genes; molecular biology of cell ageing; biological nitrogen fixing in associations between tropical and subtropical grasses and rhizobes.

Institute of Microbiology 2652

Address: 30 Garbenstrasse, D-7000 Stuttgart
Director: Professor Dr F. Lingens
Senior staff: H. Blecher, Dr J. Eberspächer, C. Fröhner, H. Ginsch, S. Haug, Dr E. Keller, U. Koch, G. Krauss, Dr R. Muller, G. Rosenberg, K. Sauber, Dr R. Süssmuth
Activities: Chloridazon-reducing bacteria of African soil; dioxygenase of pyramin-reducing bacteria; bacteria reduction of antipyrin; bacteria reduction of caffeine; mutation mechanisms, ray-resistance of micrococcus radioduran; chloramphenicol-resistant flavobacteria; mechanism of chorismatmutase reaction; synthesis of prephen acid with immobilized chorismatmutase; reaction mechanism of histidinol-dehydrogene.

Institute of Zoology 2653

Address: 30 Garbenstrasse, D-7000 Stuttgart
Director: Professor Dr H. Rahmann
Senior staff: G. Bässler, H. Beuttler, Professor Dr H. Bosch, Dr H. Brehm, W. Epple, Dr R. Hilbig, G. Jeserich, V. Kajubiri, Dr B. Loos-Frank, R. Lucius, M. Mühleisen, Dr W. Probst, W. Reckhaus, H. Römer, Professor Dr H. Rösner, Dr G. Schubert, G. Schwarzmann, K. Segler, H. Wiegandt, W. Zeese, I. Zeutzius, E. Zeyhle
Activities: Influence of gangliosides on the process of nerve-neuronal regeneration; behaviour-physiological experiments on the ontogenesis of visual perception of trouts under normal and experimental conditions; insertion of gangliosid metabolites into the retina of goldfish; synaptgenesis of the tectum opticum of the rainbow trout; correlations between morphogenesis, gangliosid, synthesis and acetylcholinesterasis-activity; temperature influence on the bioelectricity of the central nervous system of fish; investigations into bioelectrical activity of the electrofish (Gnathonemus Petersi); brain gangliosid metabolism of mice during ontogenesis; regional differences in brain gangliosid patterns of vertebrates; gangliosides and electrical potential in the central nervous system; variability of neuronal gangliosides during hibernation of warm-blooded vertebrates; ecophysiological adaptation of brain gangliosides of alternating warm-cold vertebrates; interaction between gangliosides and cations; comparative moving mechanism of the jaw of vertebrates; fish diseases especially of ornamental tropical fish; behaviour system of the owl (Tyto Alba); the small parasite Dicrocoelium dentriticum in West Africa; sarcocystis infections of reptiles; 'Dogworm-similar', Echinococcus Multilocularis, infections in South Germany; ekto- and endoparasites on reptiles; the worm problem of Helminthen fauna on the fox; biology and economical significance of Dicrocoelium Hospes in West Africa and Uganda; parasite fauna of small mammals with regard to their reservoir host function; research into control of hydatid disease; reservoir host function of reptiles, especially with regard to the Leishmaniosis in South Sudan.

Institute of Zoophysiology 2654

Address: 30 Garbenstrasse, D-7000 Stuttgart
Director: Professor Dr H. Hörnicke
Senior staff: Dr W. Clauss, Professor Dr H.-J. Ehrlein, Professor Dr W. von Engelhard, U. Ensinger, Professor

Dr H. von Faber, Professor Dr D. Fewson, B. Grässle, D.L. Hartner, S. Hinderer, R. Meixner, G. Rechkemmer, E. Rogdakis, Dr K. Rüsamen, U. Schreiber, E. Wipper, K. Wirthensohn

Activities: Sport physiology of the horse; digestive tract of the rabbit; 24-hour rhythms of rabbits; stomach mechanism of the rabbit; rat-sized rabbits whose habitat is the Himalayas and Rocky Mountains, used for experimental purposes; stomach functions of the kangaroo; functions of sections of the first stomach of the llama; urine metabolism and urea utilization in llamas by adaptation of a protein-low diet; water management, energy metabolism and body temperatures of 'klippschliefers' in Africa; mechanisms of resorption of short-chained fatty acids in the colon of herbivores; influence of mucosubstances on the resorption process in the colon; the effects of hormones on the quality of pig meat; the effects of chlorinated hydrocarbons on the quality of birds' eggshells.

FACULTY OF GENERAL AND APPLIED NATURAL SCIENCES   2655

Dean: Professor Dr W. Kraus

Institute of Applied Mathematics and Statistics   2656

Address: Schloss, Westhof-Süd, D-7000 Stuttgart
Director: Professor Dr G. Bach
Senior staff: Professor Dr K. Bosch, Dr U. Jensen, Dr K. Sandau, Dr E. Schumacher, Professor Dr H. Thöni, H.E. Wichert
Activities: Generalization of the Kendall parameter; investigation into new forms of linear regression calculation; functions of homogeneous Markoff series; renewal processes of maintenance strategies, models for service and maintenance processes; renewal processes with guarantee strategies; inspection strategies; stochastic models for maintenance processes; evaluation of longitudinal data; experiments in the field of dimension theories.

Institute of Biological Chemistry and Food Science   2657

Address: 30 Garbenstrasse, D-7000 Stuttgart
Director: Professor Dr P. Pfaender
Senior staff: Professor Dr J. Koch, Dr B. Baumann, G. Siebert
Activities: Molecular mechanism of trypanozide diamidines; protein reevaluation.

Institute of Chemistry   2658

Address: 30 Garbenstrasse, D-7000 Stuttgart
Director: Professor Dr W. Kraus
Senior staff: M. Bokel, J. Buhlert, Dr R. Cramer, A. Eckstein, Dr G. Eulenberger, W. Frenger, Professor Dr H. Geiger, Dr G. Greiner, W. Grimminger, R. Hagenbruch, Dr H. Hahn, M. Hörmann, M.Z. Jandali, G. Klein, A. Kunze, K. Kypke, H. Michel, H. Nitsch, B. Oechsle, H. Patzelt, Dr H. Sadlo, Dr G. Sawitzki, Dr E. Schill, Professor Dr H. Rah, Dr D. Spitzner, W. Weber, Binary, tertiary and quaternary chalcogenide; heteropolar acids of molybdenum, tungsten and vanadium; stretched alkyl cations; cycling of alkinyl carbon acid chlorides; components of meliaceen, a high-grade timber in the tropics, subtropics and warmer temperate regions; terpenoid synthesis; synthesis of tricyclic sesquiterpene, a natural substance with a 15-carbon-skeleton, extracted from exotic plants in the Seychelles; photodynamic effective substances from taxodiaceae components; spectroscopy and photochemistry of azo compounds; energy transfer of an optically active donor of racemic compositions.

Institute of Food Technology   2659

Address: 25 Garbenstrasse, D-7000 Stuttgart
Director: Dr K. Gierschner
Senior staff: R. Herbst, M. Goldbach, M. Haug
Activities: Bulb almond technology; fruit juice extraction; monomerous plant phenol content in fruit juice extraction.
Affiliated institutes: Versuchs- und Lehrbrennerei (Research and Training Distillery); Versuchs- und Lehrmolkerei (Research and Training Dairy).

Institute of Physics   2660

Address: 30 Garbenstrasse, D-7000 Stuttgart
Director: Professor Dr H. Seiler
Senior staff: J. Baumüller, Dr V. Cercasov, D. Eckstein, Dr A. Hierlemann, Dr W. Rentschler, Professor Dr H. Schreiber, Dr P.H. Wieser, Dr R. Wurster
Activities: Determination of the size of aerosol particles by electron microscopy; investigations into the physical properties of aerosol particles by size-dispersive extraction process; connection between optics and geometrical size for atmospheric aerosol particles; content of aerosol just above soil level in short-lived metabolon radon and thoron; measurement of alpha-radiation of airfilter samples; separation and adhesion of aerosol particles on leaves and absorption of noxious substances; structure and formation of surface growth on leaves.

Universität Kaisersläutern* 2661

[Kaisersläutern University]
Address: Pfaffenbergstrasse, D-6750 Kaisersläutern

Universitat Konstanz 2662

[Konstanz University]
Address: Postfach 5560, D-7750 Konstanz
Telephone: 07531/88-1
Telex: 0733359

ENERGY RESEARCH CENTRE 2663

Professors: Dr Peter Böger, Dr Hans E. Bömmel, Dr Ernst Bucher, Dr Jürgen Felach

FACULTY OF BIOLOGY 2664

Dean: Professor Dr Eberhardt Weiler
Departments: Animal behaviour, Professor Dr Hubert Markl; animal physiology and neurobiology, Professor Dr Werner Rathmayer, Professor Dr Wolfram Kutsch; animal physiology and neuropharmacology, Professor Dr Ernst Florey; bio(in)organic chemistry, Professor Dr Peter Hemmerich, Professor Dr Sandro Ghisla; cytology, Professor Dr Ernesto Bade; developmental biology, Professor Dr Dieter Malchow; enzyme and protein chemistry, Professor Dr Horst Sund; functional ultrastructural research, Professor Dr Helmut Plattner; immunobiology, Professor Dr Eberhardt Weiler; limnology, Professor Dr Max Tilzer, Professor Dr Jürgen Schwoerbel; membrane biophysics, Professor Dr Peter Läuger, Professor Dr Gerold Adam, Professor Dr Gunther Stark; microbiological genetics and biochemistry, Professor Dr Winfried Boos; microbiological ecology, Professor Dr Norbert Pfenning; molecular genetics, Professor Dr Rolf Knippers; physical biochemistry, Professor Dr Fritz Pohl; physiological chemistry, Professor Dr Dirk Pette; physiology and biochemistry of plants, Professor Dr Peter Böger, Professor Dr Herbert Böhme, Professor Dr Dieter Müller; phytopathology, Professor Dr Kurt Mendgen

FACULTY OF CHEMISTRY 2665

Organic Chemistry: Professor Dr Johannes Jochims, Professor Dr Richard R. Schmidt
Inorganic Chemistry: Professor Dr Gottfried Huttner, Professor Dr Hans Brintzinger
Chemistry of Natural Substances: Professor Dr Wolfgang Pfleiderer
Physical Chemistry Professor Dr Ewald Daltrozzo, Professor Dr Wolf Weyrich

FACULTY OF MATHEMATICS 2666

Professors: Dr Erich Bohl, Dr Hans-Berndt Brinkmann, Dr Wilhelm Fürst, Dr Rudolf Fritsch, Dr Dieter Hoffmann, Dr Ludger Kaup, Dr Gerhard Neubauer, Dr Alexander Prestel, Dr Volker Puppe, Dr Friedrich Wilhelm Schäfke, Dr Hanns-Jörg Stoss, Dr Wolfgang Watzlawek

FACULTY OF PHYSICS 2667

Solid-State Physics: General solid-state physics, Professor Dr Hans E. Bömmel, Professor Dr Dietrich Korn; nuclear solid-state physics, Professor Dr Ekkehard Recknagel, Professor Dr Günther Schatz; theoretical solid-state physics, Professor Dr Rudolf Klein, Professor Dr Wolfgang Dieterich, Professor Dr Josef Jäckle; applied solid-state physics, Professor Dr Ernst Bucher, Professor Dr Reinhardt Weber
Theoretical Physics: Professor Dr Heinz Dehnen, Professor Dr Jürgen Audretsch

Universität Oldenburg 2668

[Oldenburg University]
Address: Ammerländer Heerstrasse 67-99, Postfach 2503, D-2900 Oldenburg
Telephone: (0441) 798-1
Telex: 25655 unol d Q(0441)798-406
President: Dr Horst Zillessen

FACULTY OF MATHEMATICS AND 2669 NATURAL SCIENCES

Chairman: Professor Dr Joachim Luther

Biology Department 2670

Sections: Botany, Professor Dr W. Eber
Didactics of biology, Professor Dr D. Eschenhagen
Applied biology, Professor Dr R. Megnet
Biochemistry, Professor Dr Th. Höpner
Microbiology, Professor Dr S. Jannsen
Zoology, Professor Dr A. Willig
Neurobiology, Professor Dr H. Zimmermann
Earth science, Professor Dr H. Gebhardt
Zoology/morphology, Professor Dr H.K. Schminke
Plant physiology, Professor Dr H. Stabenau
Zoology/entomology, Professor Dr V. Haeseler
Geomicrobiology, Professor Dr W. Krumbein

Chemistry Department   2671

Sections: General physical chemistry, Professor Dr Schuller
General and applied physical chemistry, Professor Dr E. Zeeck
Electrochemistry, Professor Dr C.H. Hamann
Organic chemistry, Professor Dr P. Köll
Inorganic chemistry, Professor Dr M. Weidenbruck
Didactics of chemistry, Professor Dr W. Jannsen

Geography Department   2672

Sections: Geography, Professor Dr R. Krüger
Geosciences and didactics, Professor Dr G. Jannsen
Social geography, Professor Dr J. Strassel
Geography, Professor Dr G. Jung

Mathematics Department   2673

Sections: Mathematics, Professor Dr H. Späth, Professor Dr W. Ebenhöh, Professor Dr O. Emrich, Professor Dr B. Eifrig, Professor Dr J. Herzberger, Professor Dr U. Knauer, Professor Dr I. Pieper-Seier, Professor Dr W. Schmale, Professor Dr W. Leissner
Applied information science, Professor Dr P. Gorny, Professor Dr W. Möbus
Didactics of mathematics, Professor Dr W. Sprockhoff, Professor Dr H. Besuden

Physics Department   2674

Sections: Theoretical physics, Professor Dr K. Haubold
Experimental physics, Professor Dr J. Luther, Professor Dr K. Maier, Professor Dr W. Schmidt, Professor Dr K. Hinsch
Applied physics, Professor Dr V. Mellert
Didactics of physics, Professor Dr V. Ruth

Universität Osnabrück   2675

[Osnabrück University]
Address: Neuer Graben/Schloss, Postfach 4469, D-4500 Osnabrück
or: Abteilung Vechta, Driverstrasse 22, D-2848 Vechta
Telephone: (0541) 608-1
Telex: 940 850 uni os d
President: Professor Dr M. Horstmann

FACULTY OF MATHEMATICS -   2676
PHILOSOPHY: STRUCTURES AND
QUANTIFICATION

Telephone: (0541) 608-2514
Dean: Professor Dr Elmar Cohors-Fresenborg
Activities: Algebra; topology; analysis; geometry; rudiments of mathematics; didactics of mathematics.

FACULTY OF NATURAL SCIENCES: 2677
MATHEMATICS - DYNAMICS
SYSTEMS

Telephone: (0541) 608-4241
Dean: Professor Dr Eckhard Werries
Activities: Theoretical physics; mathematical physics; theory of rule systems; applied mathematics; instrumental and numerical mathematics; functional analysis; differential equations; differential geometry; statistics; theoretical chemistry; biology.

FACULTY OF NATURAL SCIENCES: 2678
SOLIDS AND SOLID-STATE
TECHNOLOGY

Telephone: (0541) 608-2435
Dean: Professor Dr Gerhard Meyer-Ehmsen
Activities: Experimental physics (solid-state physics); applied physics (electronics and quantum electronics); solid-state chemistry; didactics of physics.

Universität Regensburg   2679

[Regensburg University]
Address: Postfach 937, D-8400 Regensburg 2
Telephone: (0941) 9431
Telex: 06 5 658 unire d

FACULTY OF NATURAL SCIENCES I -   2680
MATHEMATICS

Senior staff: Professor Dr rer nat Dietrich Bierlein, Professor Dr rer nat Jürgen Bingener, Professor Dr rer nat Theodor Bröcker, Professor Dr rer nat Wolfgang Hackenbroch, Professor Dr rer nat Klaus Jänich, Professor Dr rer nat Manfred Knebusch, Professor Dr rer nat Knut Knorr, Professor Dr rer nat Ernst Kunz, Professor Dr phil Hermann Maier, Professor Dr rer nat Reinhard Mennicken, Professor Dr rer nat Jürgen Neukirch, Professor Dr rer nat Günter Tamme, Professor Dr rer nat Richard Warlimont

FACULTY OF NATURAL SCIENCES II - 2681 PHYSICS

Senior staff: Professor Dr Ing Richard Bonart, Professor Dr phil Matthias Brack, Professor Dr rer nat Martin Creuzburg, Professor Dr rer nat Wolfgang Gebhardt, Professor Dr rer nat Dietmar Göritz, Professor Dr rer nat Horst Hoffmann, Professor Dr phil nat Joachim Keller, Professor Dr rer nat Uwe Krey, Professor Dr rer nat Max Maier, Professor Dr rer nat Gustav Obermair, Professor Dr phil Henning von Philipsborn, professor Dr rer nat Karl Renk, Professor Dr rer nat Ulrich Rössler, Professor Dr rer nat Alfons Penzkofer, Professor Dr rer nat Wilhelm Prettl, Professor Dr rer nat Ulrich Schröder, Professor Dr phil nat Dieter Strauch, Professor Dr rer nat Wolfram Weise

FACULTY OF NATURAL SCIENCES III 2682 - BIOLOGY AND CLINICAL MEDICINE

Sections: Physiology, Professor Dr med Claus Albers, Professor Dr med Christian Bauer, Professor Dr med Waldemar Moll, Professor Dr med Klaus Schnell
Zoology, Professor Dr rer nat Helmut Altner, Professor Dr rer nat Jürgen Boeckh, Professor Dr rer nat Dietrich Burkhardt, Professor Dr phil Benno Darnhofer-Demar, Professor Dr rer nat Klaus-Dieter Ernst, Professor Dr rer nat Kai Hansen, Professor Dr rer nat Bernd Kramer
Botany, Professor Dr rer nat Andreas Bresinsky, Professor Dr phil Günter Hanska, Professor Dr rer nat Hans-Peter Molitoris, Professor Dr rer nat Widmar Tanner
Anatomy, Professor Dr med vet Armin E. Friess, Professor Dr Dr Karl-Heinz Wrobel
Morphology and anatomy, Professor Dr med Erich Lindner
Biochemistry, Professor Dr rer nat Manfred Sumper, Professor Dr phil nat Rainer Jaenicke, Professor Dr med Georg Löffler
Biophysics, Professor Dr rer nat Jürgen Hüttermann, Professor Dr rer nat Adolf Müller-Broich
Didactics of biology, Professor Dr phil nat German Reng
Genetics, Professor Dr rer nat Rüdiger Schmitt
Medical psychology, Professor Dr med Gert W. Speirer
Microbiology, Professor Dr Karl Otto Stetter

FACULTY OF NATURAL SCIENCES IV 2683 - CHEMISTRY AND PHARMACY

Sections: Inorganic chemistry, Professor Dr rer nat Henri Brunner, Professor Dr rer nat Wolfgang Anton Hermann, Professor Dr Ing Klaus Gustav Heumann, Professor Dr rer nat Klaus-Jürgen Range, Professor Dr rer nat Arnd Vogler

Organic chemistry, Professor Dr rer nat Jörg Daub, Professor Dr rer nat Gothfried Märkl, Professor Dr rer nat Albrecht Mannschreck, Professor Dr rer nat Andreas Merz, Professor Dr rer nat Jürgen Sauer
Pharmaceutical biology, Professor Dr rer nat Gerhard Franz
Pharmaceutical chemistry, Professor Dr rer nat Helmut Schönenberger, Professor Dr rer nat Wolfgang Wiegrebe
Pharmaceutical technology, Professor Dr rer nat Herbert Rupprecht
Pharmacology for natural sciences, Professor Dr med Horst Grobecker
Physical chemistry, Professor Dr rer nat Josef Barthel, Professor Dr rer nat Valentin Friese, Professor Dr rer nat Klaus Dietrich Heckmann, Professor Dr rer nat Rudolf Wachter
Physiological chemistry, Professor Dr rer nat Manfred Liefländer
Theoretical chemistry, Professor Dr phil nat Günter Gliemann
Theoretical and physical chemistry, Professor Dr phil nat Otto Steinborn

Universität Stuttgart 2684

[Stuttgart University]
Address: Keplerstrasse 7, D-7000 Stuttgart
Telephone: (0711) 20731
Telex: 07 21703
Rector: Professor Dr rer nat Hartmut Zwicker
Note: Stuttgart University is organized in thirteen faculties: only those concerned with scientific and technical disciplines are listed below.

FACULTY I - ARCHITECTURE AND 2685 TOWN PLANNING

Address: Keplerstrasse 11, D-7000 Stuttgart 1
Dean: Professor Dr Rittel

Building Construction Institute 2686

Building Economics Institute 2687

Address: Goethestrasse 2, D-7000 Stuttgart
Director: Professor Dr Horst Küsgen

Building Materials, Construction 2688 Physics, Technical Development and Planning Institute

Design and Modelling Institute　　　2689

Director:　Professor Dr Johannes Uhl

Interior Construction and Design　　2690
Institute

Director:　Professor Dipl-Ing Hans Kammerer

Landscape Planning Institute　　　2691

Load-Bearing Constructions and　　2692
Constructional Planning Institute

Municipal Buildings Institute　　　2693

Principles and Design in Modern　　2694
Architecture Institute

Director:　Professor Dr Ing Jürgen Joedicke

Principles of Planning in Architecture　2695
Institute

Public Buildings and College Design　2696
Institute

Rural Estates Planning Institute　　2697

School Buildings Institute　　　　2698

Address:　Ossietzskystrasse 4, D-7000 Stuttgart
Director:　Professor Dipl-Ing Walter Kröner

FACULTY II - CONSTRUCTION　　　2699
ENGINEERING AND SURVEYING

Address:　Pfaffenwaldring　7,　D-7000　Stuttgart
Vaihingen
Dean:　Professor Dr R.K. Müllar

Air Navigation Institute　　　　　2700

Address:　Keplerstrasse 11, D-7000 Stuttgart
Director:　Professor Dr Ing Karl Ramsayer
Departments:
Navigation, Professor Dr Ing Karl Ramsayer
Navigational instruments, Dr Ing Eberhard Wilder-
muth

Applied mathematics and data processing, Dipl-Math
Walter Kiechle
Airborne digital computer technology, Dipl-Ing Karl
Potthast

Applications of Geodesy in the　　2701
Building Industry Institute

Address:　Keplerstrasse 10, D-7000 Stuttgart
Director:　Professor Dr Ing Klaus Linkwitz

Building Materials Institute　　　2702

Address:　Pfaffenwaldring 4, D-7000 Stuttgart
Director:　Professor Dr Ing Karl-Friedrich Henke

Building Statics Institute　　　　2703

Construction and Design Institute　2704

Address:　Keplerstrasse 11, D-7000 Stuttgart
Director:　Professor Dipl-Ing K. Ackermann

Construction Management Institute　2705

Address:　Keplerstrasse 10, D-7000 Stuttgart
Director:　Professor Dr Ing Gerhard Drees

Domestic Water Supply, Installations,　2706
and Wastewater Technology Institute

Address:　Bandtäle 1, D-7000 Stuttgart 80 (Büsnau)
Director:　Professor Dr Karl-Heinz Hunken
Departments:
Wastewater technology, Dipl-Ing Karl-Heinz Krauth
Water supply, Professor Dr Baldefrid Hamish
Biology, Dr Dieter Bardtke
Chemistry, Dipl-Chem, Dr Rudolf Wagner
Research and metrology, Dr Helmut Steinecke
Water management, Dr Dieter Groche

Foundations and Soil Mechanics　　2707
Institute

Address:　Pfaffenwaldring　35,　D-7000　Stuttgart
Vaihingen 80
Director:　Professor Dr Ing Ulrich Smoltczyk

Geodesy Institute　　　　　　　2708

Address:　Keplerstrasse 17, D-7000 Stuttgart
Director:　Professor Dr Ing Graferend

Hydraulics Institute 2709

Address: Keplerstrasse 1, D-7000 Stuttgart
Directors: Professor Dr Ing Jürgen Giesecke, Professor Dr Kobus

Lightweight Supporting Surfaces Institute 2710

Address: Pfaffenwaldring 14, D-7000 Stuttgart
Director: Professor Dr Ing Frei Otto

Mechanics Institute 2711

Address: Keplerstrasse 11, D-7000 Stuttgart
Director: Professor Dr Ing Hans Bufler
Departments:
Experimental mechanics, Dr Ing Günther Brinkman
Numerical methods in mechanics, Dr Ing Siegfried Gurr

Model Statics Institute 2712

Address: Keplerstrasse 11, D-7000 Stuttgart
Director: Professor Dr Ing Robert K. Müller

Photogrammetry Institute 2713

Address: Keplerstrasse 17, D-7000 Stuttgart
Director: Professor Dr Ing Friedrich Ackermann

Railways and Transport Systems Institute 2714

Address: Keplerstrasse 11, D-7000 Stuttgart
Director: Professor Dr Ing Georg Heimerl

Roads and Transport Systems Institute 2715

Address: Keplerstrasse 11, D-7000 Stuttgart
Director: Professor Dr Ing Gerd Steierwald

Solid Structures Institute 2716

Spatial Organization and Development 2717 Planning Institute

Steel and Wood Constructions Institute 2718

Address: Keplerstrasse 11, D-7000 Stuttgart
Director: Professor Dr Ing Josef Oxfort

FACULTY III - CHEMISTRY 2719

Address: Pfaffenwaldring 55, D-7000 Stuttgart Vaihingen
Dean: Professor Dr Gerold

Food Chemistry Institute 2720

Address: Keplerstrasse 17, D-7000 Stuttgart
Director: Professor Dr Karl-Gustav Bergner

Inorganic Chemistry Institute 2721

Address: Schellingstrasse 26, D-7000 Stuttgart
Directors: Professor Dr Eckhard Allenstein, Professor Dr Ekkehard Fluck

Metallurgy Institute 2722

Address: Seestrasse 75, D-7000 Stuttgart
Director: Professor Dr Volkmar Gerold

Organic Chemistry, Biochemistry and 2723 Isotope Research Institute

Address: Azenbergstrasse 14, D-7000 Stuttgart
Director: Professor Dr F. Effenberger

Physical Chemistry Institute 2724

Address: Widerholdstrasse 18, D-7000 Stuttgart
Director: vacant

Technical Chemistry Institute I 2725

Address: Böblingerstrasse 70, D-7000 Stuttgart
Director: Professor Dr Wilhelm Brötz

Technical Chemistry Institute II 2726

Address: Widerholdstrasse 10, D-7000 Stuttgart
Director: vacant

Textile and Fibres Chemistry Institute 2727

Address: Ulmerstrasse 227, D-7000 Stuttgart Wangen 60
Director: Professor Dr Heinz Herlinger

DEPARTMENT OF TEXTILE 2728 TECHNOLOGY

Address: Burgstrasse 29, D-7410 Reutlingen 1
Telephone: (07121) 4 40 97
Telex: intex d 7-29 880
Research director: Dr Ing Gerhard Egbers
Graduate research staff: 65
Annual expenditure: £501 000-2m
Activities: The Department conducts research projects

in the following areas: problems of high-productivity ring spinning and twisting; development of spinning machinery and new spinning processes; solutions for processing problems in rotary spinning; optimization of dressing processes; optimization of weaving and new weaving methods; processing problems in knitwear manufacture; determination of physical properties of fibre surfaces; adhesion problems in fibre and thread systems; process control of textile machinery; applications of textiles in medicine; environmental protection, including oil separation from wastewater, wastewater purification, noise control precautions; raw material processing; data collection; thread manufacture.
Contract work: Yes

Denkendorf Research Station 2729
Address: Körschtalstrasse 26, D-7306 Denkendorf
Telephone: (0711) 34 40 41
Telex: denkd 7-256 554

Theoretical Chemistry Institute 2730
Address: Relenbergstrasse 32, D-7000 Stuttgart
Director: Professor Dr Heinzwerner Preuss

FACULTY IV - ELECTRICAL ENGINEERING 2731
Address: Breitscheidstrasse 2, D-7000 Stuttgart 1
Dean: Professor Dr von Münch

Communications and Data Processing Institute 2732
Address: Seidenstrasse 36, D-7000 Stuttgart
Director: Professor Dr Alfred Lotze

Communications Transmission Institute 2733
Director: Professor Dr Ing Wolfgang Kaiser

Electrical Engineering Theory Institute 2734
Address: Breitscheidstrasse 3, D-7000 Stuttgart
Director: Professor Dr Ing G. Lehner

Electrical Installations Institute 2735
Address: Breitscheidstrasse 3, D-7000 Stuttgart
Director: Professor Dr Ing Rudolf Lauber

Electrical Machines and Drives Institute 2736
Director: vacant
Departments:
Small electric machines, Dr Ing Walter Tiexinger
Special machine construction and testing, Dr Ing H. Moser

Energy Transmission and High Tension Engineering Institute 2737
Director: Professor Dr Ing Helmut Böcker
Department:
Electrical transmission, Dr Ing Heinz Maier

High Frequency Engineering Institute 2738
Address: Seidenstrasse 36, D-7000 Stuttgart
Director: Professor Dr Alois Egger

Networks and Systems Theory Institute 2739
Address: Seidenstrasse 36, D-7000 Stuttgart
Director: Professor Dr Ing Ernst Löder

Physical Electronics Institute 2740
Address: Böblingerstrasse 70-72, D-7000 Stuttgart
Directors: Professor Dr Ing Werner H. Bloss, Professor Dr Ing A. Böehringer
Departments:
Gas and surface electronics, Dr Ing Hans Albrecht
Electronic optics, Dr Ing Hermann App
Photo-electronics, Dipl phys Gert Hewig

Plasma Research Institute 2741
Address: Pfaffenwaldring 31, D-7000 Stuttgart
Director: Professor Dr H. Zwicker
Departments:
Plasma flow, Professor Dr Rudolf Wienecke
Plasma heating, Dipl phys Eberhard Räuchel
Lasers, Dr Hans Friedrich Dobele

Process Control and Automation Technology Institute 2742

Semiconductor Technology Institute 2743
Director: Professor Dr von Münch

Telecommunications Engineering Institute 2744
Director: Professor Dr Ing Gerhard Kohn

FACULTY V - POWER ENGINEERING 2745

Address: Pfaffenwaldring 9, D-7000 Stuttgart Vaihingen
Dean: Professor Dr Kussmaul

Hydraulic Power Engines and Pumps 2746 Institute

Address: Holzgartenstrasse 15, D-7000 Stuttgart

Internal Combustion and Industrial 2747 Engines Institute

Address: Pfaffenwaldring 6, D-7000 Stuttgart

Internal Combustion Engines and 2748 Automobiles Science Institute

Address: Keplerstrasse 17, D-7000 Stuttgart
Director: Professor Dr Ing Ulf Essers

Nuclear Power and Systems Institute 2749

Address: Pfaffenwaldring 31, D-7000 Stuttgart Vaihingen
Director: Professor Dr Karl-Heinz Höcker

Process Technology and Steam 2750 Engines Institute

Address: Pfaffenwaldring 23, D-7000 Stuttgart Vaihingen
Director: Professor Dr Ing Dolezal

State Materials Testing Department at 2751 Stuttgart University

Address: Pfaffenwaldring 32, D-7000 Stuttgart Vaihingen
Director: Professor Dr Ing Kussmaul

Thermal Hydraulic Engines and 2752 Machines Laboratory

Address: Pfaffenwaldring 6, D-7000 Stuttgart Vaihingen
Director: Professor Dr Ing Jakob Wachter

Thermodynamics and Heat 2753 Technology Institute

Address: Seidenstrasse 36, D-7000 Stuttgart
Director: Professor Dr Ing E. Hahn

FACULTY VI - MANUFACTURING 2754 TECHNOLOGY

Address: Pfaffenwaldring 9, D-7000 Stuttgart Vaihingen
Dean: Professor Dr Langenbeck

Control Engineering for Machine Tools 2755 and Production Equipment Institute

Address: Seidenstrasse 36, D-7000 Stuttgart
Director: Professor Dr Ing Gottfried Stute

Conveyors, Gears, and Building 2756 Machines Institute

Address: Holzgartenstrasse 15b, D-7000 Stuttgart
Director: Professor Dr Ing Franz Beisteiner

Horology and Precision Engineering 2757 Institute

Address: Breitscheidstrasse 2b, Postfach 560, D-7000 Stuttgart 1
Telephone: (0711) 2073 505
Telex: 0721703
Director: Professor Dr Phil Günther Glaser
Graduate research staff: 10
Activities: Micromechanics, horology, electronics, integrated circuits, oscillators, atomic time control, technical measurements.
Contract work: Yes

Industrial Manufacture and Factory 2758 Management Institute

Address: Holzgartenstrasse 17, D-7000 Stuttgart
Director: Professor Dr Ing Hans-Jürgen Warnecke

Machine Construction and Gear 2759 Assembly Institute

Machine Elements and Design 2760 Institute

Address: Keplerstrasse 17, D-7000 Stuttgart
Director: Professor Dr Ing Langenbeck

Machine Tools Institute 2761

Address: Holzgartenstrasse 17, D-7000 Stuttgart
Director: Professor Dipl-Ing Karl Tuffentsammer

Mechanics Institute B 2762

Address: Keplerstrasse 17, D-7000 Stuttgart

Precision Engineering Construction and Production Institute　　2763

Address: Keplerstrasse 17, D-7000 Stuttgart
Director: Professor Dr Ing Jung

Technical Optics Institute　　2764

Address: Keplerstrasse 17, D-7000 Stuttgart
Director: Professor Dr Tiriani

Transformers Technology Institute　　2765

Address: Holzgartenstrasse 17, D-7000 Stuttgart
Director: Professor Dr Ing Kurt Lange

FACULTY VII - BIOLOGY AND GEOSCIENCES　　2766

Address: Pfaffenwaldring 55, D-7000 Stuttgart Vaihingen
Dean: Professor Dr Walente

Biology Institute　　2767

Address: Ulmerstrasse 227, D-7000 Stuttgart
Departments:
Plant physiology, Professor Dr Strasser
Animal physiology, Professor Dr P. Kunze
Zoology, Professor Dr Kurt Kühler
Botany, Professor Dr Karl-Wolfgang Mundry

Geography Institute　　2768

Address: Silcherstrasse 9, D-7000 Stuttgart
Directors: Professor Dr Christoph Borcherdt, Professor Dr Wolfgang Meckelein

Geology and Palaeontology Institute　　2769

Address: Böblingerstrasse 72, D-7000 Stuttgart
Departments:
Palaeontology, Professor Dr Bernhard Ziegler
Biostratigraphy and historical geology, Professor Dr Otto Franz Geyer
Regional geology, Professor Dr M.P. Gwinner

Geophysics Institute　　2770

Address: Richard-Wagner-Strasse 44, D-7000 Stuttgart
Director: Professor Dr Klaus Strobach

Mineralogy and Crystal Chemistry Institute　　2771

Address: Herdeweg 5, D-7000 Stuttgart
Director: Professor Dr Walente

FACULTY IX - AERONAUTICS AND ASTRONAUTICS　　2772

Address: Pfaffenwaldring 31, D-7000 Stuttgart Vaihingen
Dean: Professor Dr Frohn

Aerodynamics and Gas Dynamics Institute　　2773

Address: Pfaffenwaldring 21, D-7000 Stuttgart Vaihingen 80
Director: Professor Dr Ing Franz Xavier Wortmann

Aircraft Construction Institute　　2774

Director: Professor Dr Arends

Aircraft Propulsion and Turbo Engines Institute　　2775

Address: Pfaffenwaldring 6, D-7000 Stuttgart Vaihingen 80
Director: Professor Dr Rolf D. Bühler

Space Propulsion Institute　　2776

Director: Professor Dr Rolf D. Bühler

Statics and Dynamics of Aero and Space Constructions Institute　　2777

Address: Pfaffenwaldring 27, D-7000 Stuttgart Vaihingen 80
Director: Professor Dr John H. Argyris

Thermodynamics of Air and Space Travel Institute　　2778

Director: Professor Dr Ing A. Frohn

FACULTY X - MATHEMATICS AND COMPUTER SCIENCE　　2779

Address: Pfaffenwaldring 57, D-7000 Stuttgart Vaihingen
Dean: Professor Dr Bodo Volkmann

Computer Sciences Institute 2780

Address: Herdweg 51, D-7000 Stuttgart
Director: Professor Dr Gunsenhauser

Mathematics Institute A 2781

Address: Herdweg 21-23, D-7000 Stuttgart
Directors: Professor Dr Peter Lesky, Professor Dr Klaus Kirchgässner, Professor Dr Werner Meyer-König, Professor Dr Bodo Volkmann, Professor Dr Peter Werner

Mathematics Institute B 2782

Address: Herdweg 21-23, D-7000 Stuttgart
Directors: Professor Dr Wendelin Degen, Professor Dr Kurt Leichtweiss, Professor Dr Hermann Schaal

FACULTY XII - PHYSICS 2783

Address: Pfaffenwaldring 57, D-7000 Stuttgart Vaihingen
Dean: Professor Dr Wolf

Physics Institute I 2784

Address: Wiederholdstrasse 13, D-7000 Stuttgart
Director: Professor Dr Wolfgang Eisenmenger

Physics Institute II 2785

Address: Azenbergstrasse 12, D-7000 Stuttgart
Director: Professor Dr Heinz Pick

Physics Institute III 2786

Address: Azenbergstrasse 12, D-7000 Stuttgart
Director: Professor Dr Hans-Christian Wolf

Physics Institute IV 2787

Address: Weiderholdstrasse 13, D-7000 Stuttgart
Director: Professor Dr Manfred Pilkuhn

Radiation Physics Institute 2788

Address: Seestrasse 71, D-7000 Stuttgart
Director: Professor Dr Klaus-Werner Hoffmann

Theoretical and Applied Physics Institute 2789

Address: Azenbergstrasse 12, D-7000 Stuttgart
Director: Professor Dr Ekkehard Kröner

Theoretical Physics Institute 2790

Address: Azenbergstrasse 12, D-7000 Stuttgart
Director: Professor Dr Hans Risken

FACULTY XIII - PROCESSING TECHNOLOGY 2791

Address: Pfaffenwaldring 9, D-7000 Stuttgart Vaihingen
Dean: Professor Dr Sorg

Chemical Process Engineering Institute 2792

Address: Böblingerstrasse 72, D-7000 Stuttgart
Director: Professor Dr Heinz Blenke

Mechanical Process Engineering Institute 2793

Address: Böblingerstrasse 72, D-7000 Stuttgart
Director: Professor Dr Christian Alt

Mechanics Institute A 2794

Address: Keplerstrasse 17, D-7000 Stuttgart
Director: Professor Dr Richard Eppler

Plastics Technology Institute 2795

Address: Böblingerstrasse 70, D-7000 Stuttgart

Polymer Testing and Polymer Science Institute 2796

– IKP
Address: Pfaffenwaldring 32, D-7000 Stuttgart 80
Telephone: (0711) 784 2667
Telex: 07-7255764 mpa
Director: Professor Dr Ing P. Eyerer
Departments:
Manufacturing properties of polymers, Dr Ing U. Delpe
Polymer physics, Dipl-Ing G. Fischer
Polymer chemistry, Dr rer nat A. Franck
Pipes and friction materials, Dr Ing P. Stockmayer
Mechanical properties of polymers, Dipl-Ing P. Pöllet
Annual expenditure: £501 000-2m
Activities: Investigation and testing of all types of polymers.
Facilities: Apparatus for all types of polymer testing.

Systems Dynamics and Control Engineering Institute 2797

Address: Keplerstrasse 17, D-7000 Stuttgart
Director: Professor Dr Ernst-Dieter Gilles

Technical Thermodynamics and Heat   2798
Process Engineering Institute

Address: Keplerstrasse 7, D-7000 Stuttgart
Director: Professor Dr K. Stephan

Universität Ulm*   2799

[Ulm University]
Address: Postfach 1 130, Oberer Eselberg, D-7900 Ulm
Telephone: (0731) 1781

FACULTY OF CLINICAL MEDICINE*   2800

FACULTY OF NATURAL SCIENCES   2801
AND MATHEMATICS*

FACULTY OF THEORETICAL   2802
MEDICINE*

Universität zu Köln*   2803

[Cologne University]
Address: Albertus-Magnus-Platz, D-5000 Köln Indenthal 41
Telephone: (0221) 4701

FACULTY OF MATHEMATICS AND   2804
NATURAL SCIENCES*

Dean: Professor Dr Helmut Happ

Biochemistry Institute*   2805

Botanical Institute*   2806

Crystallography Institute*   2807

Developmental Physiology Institute*   2808

Genetics Institute*   2809

Geological Institute*   2810

Geophysics and Meteorology   2811
Institute*

Inorganic Chemistry Institute*   2812

Mathematical Institute*   2813

Mineralogical Petrographical Institute*   2814

Nuclear Chemistry Institute*   2815

Nuclear Physics Institute*   2816

Organic Chemistry Institute*   2817

Petrarca Institute*   2818

Physical Chemistry Institute*   2819

Physics Institute I*   2820

Physics Institute II*   2821

Psychological Institute*   2822

Theoretical Physics Institute   2823

Address: Zülpicherstrasse 77, D-5000 Köln 41
Directors: Professor Dr J. Hajdu, Professor Dr P. Mittelstaedt, Professor Dr B. Mühlschlegel, Professor Dr J. Zittartz, Professor Dr E. Müller-Hartman
Senior staff: Professor Dr F.W. Hehl, Professor Dr M.L. Ristig, Professor Dr D. Stauffer

Zoological Institute*   2824

FACULTY OF MEDICINE   2825

Address: Joseph-Stelzmann-Strasse 9, D-5000 Köln 41
Dean: Professor Dr Wolfgang Kaufmann

Anaesthesiology Institute   2826

Address: Joseph-Stelzmann-Strasse 9, D-5000 Köln 41
Director: Professor Dr K. Bonhöffer
Senior staff: Professor Dr G. Loeschcke

Anatomy Institute   2827

Address: Joseph-Stelzmann-Strasse 9, D-5000 Köln 41
Director: Professor Dr B. Kummer
Departments: Electronmicroscopy, Professor Dr K.
Addicks; Angioanatomy and tissue fertilization, vacant

Cardiac Surgery Institute   2828

Address: Joseph-Stelzmann-Strasse 9, D-5000 Köln 41
Director: Professor Dr H. Dalichau

TRANSFUSIONAL MEDICINE   2829
DEPARTMENT
Address: Joseph-Stelzmann-Strasse 9, D-5000 Köln 41
Head: Professor Dr J. Krüger

Clinical and Experimental Nuclear   2830
Medicine Institute

Address: Joseph-Stelzmann-Strasse 9, D-5000 Köln 41
Director: Professor Dr H. Kutzim

Clinical Chemistry Department   2831

Address: Joseph-Stelzmann-Strasse 9, D-5000 Köln 41
Director: Professor Dr K. Oette

Dermatology Clinic   2832

Address: Joseph-Stelzmann-Strasse 9, D-5000 Köln 41
Director: Professor Dr G.K. Steigleder

Experimental Medicine Institute   2833

Address: Robert-Koch-Strasse 10, D-5000 Köln 41
Director: Professor Dr W. Isselhard

Forensic Medicine Institute   2834

Address: Metatengürtel 60-62, D-5000 Köln 30
Director: Professor Dr M. Staak
Department: Forensic psychology and psychiatry,
Professor Dr Dr H. Bresser

Gynaecology Clinic   2835

Address: Kerpenerstrasse 34, D-5000 Köln 41
Directors: Professor Dr R. Kaiser, Professor Dr A.
Bolte
Departments: Morphological laboratory, Professor Dr
P. Citoler; Endocrinological laboratory, Professor Dr
W. Geiger; Perinatology, Professor Dr A. Bolte

History of Medicine Institute   2836

Address: Franzstrasse 16, D-5000 Köln 41
Director: Professor Dr med D. Jetter

RESEARCH CENTRE   2837
Address: Robert-Koch-Strasse 10, D-5000 Köln 41
Head: Professor Dr med D. Jetter

Hygiene Institute   2838

Address: Goldenfelsstrasse 21, D-5000 Köln 41
Director: Professor Dr G. Pulverer

Internal Medicine Institute II   2839

Address: Medizinische Poliklinick und Medizinische
Klinik, Städtischen Krankenhaus Köln-Merheim,
D'5000 Köln
Director: Professor Dr W. Kaufmann

Internal Medicine Institute III   2840

Address: Joseph-Stelzmann-Strasse 9, D-5000 Köln 41
Department: Cardiology, Professor Dr H.H. Hilger

Medical Clinic   2841

Address: Joseph-Stelzmann-Strasse 9, D-5000 Köln 41
Director: Professor Dr R. Gross
Department: Experimental Internal Medicine,
Professor Dr G. Uhlenbruck

Medical Documentation and Statistics 2842

Address: Joseph-Stelzmann-Strasse 9, D-5000 Köln 41
Director: Professor Dr V. Weidtman

Nervous Diseases Clinic   2843

Address: Joseph-Stelzmann-Strasse 9, D-5000 Köln 41
Directors: Professor Dr A. Stammler, Professor Dr
U.H. Peters, Professor Dr Ellen Gibbels
Departments: Neuropsychiatric research, Professor Dr
K. Felgenhauer; Virology, Professor Dr Ackerman

Neurosurgical Clinic 2844

Address: Joseph-Stelzmann-Strasse 9, D-5000 Köln 41
Director: Professor Dr R.A. Frowein
Department: Stereotaxy, Professor Dr Nitter

Occupational and Social Medicine 2845
Institute and Polyclinic

Address: Joseph-Stelzmann-Strasse 9, D-5000 Köln 41
Director: Dr A. Buchter

Ophthalmology Clinic 2846

Address: Joseph-Stelzmann-Strasse 9, D-5000 Köln 41
Director: Professor Dr H. Neubaner
Departments: Ophthalmology II, Professor Dr K. Heimann; Occular motor disturbances and neuro-ophthalmology, Professor Dr W. Rüssmann

Orthopaedics Clinic 2847

Address: Joseph-Stelzmann-Strasse 24, D-5000 Köln 41
Directors: Professor Dr M.H. Hackenbroch

Otorhinolaryngology Clinic 2848

Address: Joseph-Stelzmann-Strasse 9, D-5000 Köln 41
Director: Professor Dr Dr F. Wustrow

Paediatric Clinic 2849

Address: Joseph-Stelzmann-Strasse 9, D-5000 Köln 41
Director: Professor Dr E. Gladtke
Departments: Outpatient social paediatrics, Professor Dr K. Wechselberg; Endocrinological laboratory, vacant

Pathology Institute 2850

Address: Joseph-Stelzmann-Strasse 52, D-5000 Köln 41
Director: Professor Dr R. Fischer
Departments: Microstructural pathology, Professor Dr H.E. Schaefer; Neuropathology laboratory, Professor Dr Dr W. Müller; Immunopathology laboratory, Professor Dr G. Krüger

Pharmacology Institute 2851

Address: Gleueler Strasse 24, D-5000 Köln 41
Director: Professor Dr W. Klaus

Physiological Chemistry Institute 2852

Address: Joseph-Stelzmann-Strasse 52, D-5000 Köln 41
Director: Professor Dr W. Stoffel
Senior staff: Professor Dr Hildegard Debuch

Plastic Surgery Department 2853

Address: Robert-Koch-Strasse 10, D-5000 Köln 41
Head: Professor Dr Dr J. Schrudde

Psychosomatic Department 2854

Address: Joseph-Stelzmann-Strasse 9, D-5000 Köln 41
Head: Professor Dr R. Lohmann

Pure and Pathological Physiology 2855
Institute

Address: Robert-Koch-Strasse 39, D-5000 Köln 41
Directors: Professor Dr H. Hirsch, Professor Dr H. Hirche, Professor Dr F.W. Klussmann

Radiation Therapy Clinic 2856

Address: Joseph-Stelzmann-Strasse 9, D-5000 Köln 41
Director: Professor Dr H. Kutzim
Department: Radiation physics, Dr N. Thesen

Radiological Institute and Polyclinic 2857

Address: Joseph-Stelzmann-Strasse 9, D-5000 Köln 41
Director: Professor Dr G. Friedmann

Rehabilitation Centre 2858

Address: Lindenburger Allee 44, D-5000 Köln 41
Head: Professor Dr K.-A. Jochheim

Surgical Clinic and Polyclinic 2859

Address: Joseph-Stelzmann-Strasse 9, D-5000 Köln 41
Director: Professor Dr Dr H. Pichlmaier
Departments: Accident surgery, Professor Dr W. Reichmann; Surgical radiology, Dr Kallenberg; Immunological laboratory, Professor Dr Dr G. Hermann

Surgical Institute at the Köln-Merheim 2860
Clinic, Köln-Merheim Municipal
Hospital

Address: Ostmerheimer Strasse 200, D-5000 Köln 91
Director: Professor Dr G.H. Engelhardt
Departments: Biochemical and experimental laboratory, Professor Dr H. Struck; Anaesthesiology, Professor Dr Matthes

Tooth and Jaw Clinic 2861

Address: Kerpener Strasse 32, D-5000 Köln 41
Directors: Professor Dr R. Voss, Professor Dr F.F. Eifinger, Professor Dr C.W. Schwarze, Professor Dr Dr H.-D. Pape
Departments: Dental prosthesis, Professor Dr R. Voss; Preclinical dental care, Professor Dr T. Kerschbaum; conservative dentistry, Professor Dr F.F. Eifinger; Orthopaedics of the jaw, Professor Dr C.W. Schwarze; Dental surgery, and mouth and jaw surgery, Professor Dr Dr H.-D. Pape

Urology Clinic 2862

Address: Joseph-Stelzmann-Strasse 9, D-5000 Köln 41
Director: Professor Dr R. Engelking

Virology Institute 2863

Address: Fürst-Pückler-Strasse 56, D-5000 Köln 41
Director: Professor Dr Hans J. Eggers

Veba Oel AG 2864

Address: Postfach 45, D-4660 Gelsenkirchen-Buer
Telephone: (0209) 3661
Telex: 824 881
Parent body: Veba AG
Chairman, Board of Directors: Dr Fritz Oschmann
Deputy Chairman, Board of Directors: Dipl-Ing Wilhelm Bonse
Directors of Research: Dipl-Ing Wilhelm Bonse; Dr Hubert Heneka
Sections: Product development, analytic, environmental protection, Dr Bruderreck; production, heavy oil, Dr Cornelius; technical development, alternative energies, Dr Escher
Graduate research staff: 75
Annual expenditure: DM67m
Activities: Earth sciences; geology; geochemistry; exploration and production; crude oil; coal and other energy resources; mineral oil products.
Contract work: No
Additional information: The company was formerly called Veba-Chemie AG.

DEMINEX-DEUTSCHE 2865 ERDÖLVERSORGUNGS-GESELLSCHAFT MBH

Address: Dorotheenstrasse 1, D-4300 Essen
Telephone: (0201) 726-1
Telex: 853-1141

Activities: Exploration and production of crude oil world wide.

VEBA OEL ENTWICKLUNGS- 2866 GESELLSCHAFT MBH

Address: Postfach 45, D-4660 Gelsenkirchen-Buer
Managing Director: Dr Ing Gerd Escher
Activities: Process development in the fields of alternative energies such as the recovery and upgrading of heavy crudes, shale oils, tar sands, bitumen, and the liquefaction of coal.

Verband Deutscher 2867 Landwirtschaftlicher Untersuchungs- und Forschungsanstalten

– VDLUFA
[German Agricultural Research Institutes Association]
Address: 41a Bismarckstrasse, D-6100 Darmstadt
Telephone: (06151) 21618
President: Professor Dr H. Vetter
General secretary: H. Zarges
Activities: The Association consists of 104 different agricultural research institutes, university institutes and industrial research laboratories.
There are 11 different working parties carrying out research in the following areas of activities: further development of basic research in soil sciences, food for plants, soil fertilizing; soil research; fertilizers; seeds; animal feeding; feedstuffs; milk; plant quality; agricultural microbiology; soil productivity; environmental analysis.
The main contribution of the VDLUFA lies in its informative service to the various members of the progress and new findings in the different fields of research activities; introduction and application of unified research techniques; summarized evaluation of research results; advice, seminars and publishing of journals and reports; awarding of prizes to deserving scientists and constant contact with scientific associations at home and abroad.
Contract work: No

Verein Deutscher Eisenhüttenleute   2868

– VDEh

[Association of German Iron and Steel Engineers]
Address: Breite Strasse 27, Postfach 8209, D-4000 Düsseldorf 1
Telephone: (0211) 8894-1
Telex: 8 582 512 vdeh
President: Dr Ing Franz-Josef Hufnagel
General Secretary: Dr Ing Klaus Nümberg
Graduate research staff: 100
Activities: Promotion of research and development covering the whole field of iron and steel technology; research development projects for industrial application in the fields of plant engineering, process technology and control, environmental control, measuring and materials testing; basic scientific research into the fundamental properties of iron and steel.
Contract work: No
Publications: Stahl und Eisen; Archiv für das Eisenhüttenwesen.

INSTITUTE OF APPLIED RESEARCH   2869

Director: Professor Dr Ing Karl-Heinz Mommertz

Verein für Technische Holzfragen eV   2870

[Wood Technology Association]
Address: 54 E. Bienroder Weg, D-3300 Braunschweig-Kralenriede
Telephone: (0531) 35 00 98
Affiliation: Arbeitsgemeinschaft Industrieller Forschungsvereinigungen eV
Managing Director: G. Kammerer
Activities: Increased and improved utilization of wood.

Vereinigte Aluminium-Werke Aktiengesellschaft   2871

– VAW

Address: 25 Georg-von-Boeselager-Strasse, Postfach 2468, D-5300 Bonn 1
Telephone: (02221) 5521
Telex: 8-869 607
Chairman of the Board of Directors: Dr R. Escherich
Activities: Further development of process control, data transfer and information systems; new instruments for trace analysis; quality control for the safety of ultrapure aluminium 'Kryal'; optimization of foundry technology, alloy compounds, metalworking and recycling of aluminium scrap; extensive model calculations on electromagnetic field effects in metal melt for further improvement and energy-saving in electrolytic process engineering; development of special hydroxides and oxides; technical experiments for the production of hydroglasses using a tube reactor and zeolite materials.
Note: VAW is made up of 28 companies in Germany and a further 10 outside Germany, in Europe and overseas. The total turnover of the VAW Group for 1980 amounted to DM2 931m.

Vereinigte Deutsche Metalwerke AG *   2872

Address: Zeilweg, D-6000 Frankfurt-Main 50
Activities: Development and production of copper and copper alloy wrought products.

Versuchs- und Lehranstalt für Brauerei in Berlin am Institut für Gärungsgewerbe und Biotechnologie   2873

[Research and Teaching Institute for Brewery in Berlin at the Fermentation and Biotechnology Institute]
Address: 13 Seestrasse, D-1000 Berlin 65
Telephone: (030) 45 30 11
Telex: 181734 igaer d
Affiliation: Arbeitsgemeinschaft Industrieller Forschungsvereinigungen eV
Scientific Director: Professor Dr R. Schildbach
Scientific staff: 42
Activities: Basic and applied research on brewery and malthouse products; special contract research; raw materials; intermediate and finished brewery products.

Versuchs- und Lehranstalt　2874
für Spiritusfabrikation und
Fermentations-Technologie
in Berlin

[Research and Teaching Institute for Alcohol
Production and Fermentation Technology in Be-
rlin]
Address: 13 Seestrasse, D-1000 Berlin 65
Telephone: (030) 45 30 11
Telex: 181734 igaer d
Affiliation: Arbeitsgemeinschaft Industrieller For-
schungsvereinigungen eV
Managing Technical Director: Dr R. Wiesenack
Activities: Alcohol production; yeast and foodstuff
yeast production; processing and other fermentation;
development of modern fermentation processes regard-
ing the production of vitamins, enzymes and other
metabolism products.

Versuchsanstalt der　2875
Hefeindustrie eV

[Yeast Industry Testing Laboratory]
Address: 13 Seestrasse, D-1000 Berlin 65
Telephone: (030) 45 30 11
Telex: 181734 lgaer d
Affiliation: Arbeitsgemeinschaft Industrieller For-
schungsvereinigungen eV
Managing Director: K.-D. Schünemann
Activities: Baking-yeast technology.

Versuchsanstalt für　2876
Binnenschiffbau eV

[Inland Shipbuilding Research Association]
Address: Postfach 10 12 28, 77 Klöcknerstrasse, D-
4100 Duisburg
Telephone: (0203) 35 30 96
Telex: 8551288 vbdud
Affiliation: Arbeitsgemeinschaft Industrieller For-
schungsvereinigungen eV
Director: Professor Dr H.H. Heuser
Activities: Basic research and specialized contract
research; shipbuilding-technical models and large-scale
experiments; development of special measuring instru-
ments.

Versuchsanstalt für　2877
Geflügelwirtschaft und
Kleintierzucht,
Beispielsbetrieb für
Absatzförderung

[Poultry and Small Animal Breeding Experimental
Station]
Address: Hüttenallee 235, D-4150 Krefeld Grosshüt-
tenhof
Telephone: (02151) 53533; 55300
Affiliation: Bouw Chamber of Agriculture
Research director: Dr Raimund Tüller
Graduate research staff: 1
Annual expenditure: £51 000-500 000
Activities: Housing and nutrition of laying hens,
turkeys, broilers, ducks, quails, pigeons, and geese;
marketing and economic studies. There is a specialist
centre for practical marketing.
Contract work: No

Versuchsanstalt für　2878
Wasserbau und Schiffbau

[Berlin Model Basin]
Address: Müller-Breslau-Strasse, Schleuseninsel, D-
1000 Berlin 12
Telephone: (030) 3184 1
Telex: 18 40 10
Research director: Professor Dr Ing Siegfried Schuster
Activities: Model and full-scale tests; research and
development in ship hydrodynamics and coastal
engineering.

Versuchsgrubengesellschaft　2879
mbH

Address: Tremoniastrasse 13, D-4600 Dortmund 1
Telephone: (0231) 143786
Research director: Kurt Reinke
Sections: Explosion and explosives technology, Dr Ing
Meerbach; mining fires and occupational protection,
Dipl-Ing Grumbrecht; pit-hauling and machine technol-
ogy, Dipl-Ing Slonina; measurement and calculation, Dr
Fischer; documentation, Dipl-Ing Hess
Activities: Research on safety in mines to prevent acci-
dent hazards and occupational diseases, by scientific
study under appropriate conditions.
Contract work: Yes

VGB - Technische Vereinigung der Grosskraftwerksbetreiber eV 2880

[VGB - Technical Association of Large Power Station Operators]
Address: Klinkestrasse 27-31, Postfach 103932, D-4300 Essen 1
Telephone: (0201) 1981
Telex: 0857507 vgbd
Director: Dr O. Schwarz
Department: Research, Professor H. Kirsch
Graduate research staff: 5
Annual expenditure: £51 000-500 000
Activities: Improvement and increase of operational security and availability of thermal power plants; cooperation on technical rules and in standardization; examination of damage; advice in planning, erection and operation of thermal power plants.
Contract work: Yes

Volkswagenwerk AG* 2881

– VW
Address: Postfach, D-3180 Wolfsburg 1
Telephone: (05361) 90
Telex: 09 586-0 VWW d
Head, Research Division: Dr U. Seiffert
Research staff: 630
Activities: Automotive research and development. In 1981 VW received DM500 000 for engine, handling and emission testing of the Auto 2000 car. VW is also receiving government financial assistance for research programmes covering electronics, noise and ceramics for use in gas turbines. VW has developed a computer-aided styling sketches system to aid the design of vehicles: the computer output allows VDU output to be translated directly into quarterscale three-dimensional models.

von Heyden GmbH 2882

Address: Postfach 177, D-8400 Regensburg 1
Telephone: (0941) 490335
Telex: 065804 vheyd d
Parent body: E.R. Squibb & Sons, Incorporated, USA
Research director: Dr rer nat Hermann Breuer
Sections: Organic chemistry, Dr rer nat Hermann Breuer; process development, Dr Ing Hans-Joachim Schneider; pathology/toxicology, Dr rer nat Harriet Mary Parish
Graduate research staff: / 12

Annual expenditure: £501 000-2m
Activities: Major research emphasis is directed towards the discovery and development of new therapeutic agents. These efforts involve synthesis of anti-infective agents, compounds with cardiovascular activity, and anti-inflammatory substances. In addition to chemical synthesis, process development, and biological screening, a variety of toxicological and pathological studies are performed; these include carcinogenicity, teratology, irritation, and chronic toxicity investigations.
Contract work: Yes

Wacker-Chemie GmbH 2883

Address: Prinzregentenstrasse 22, D-8000 München 22
Directors: Walter Dobmaier, Ekkehard Maurer, Dr Rudolf Mittag
Activities: Vinyl chloride and vinyl acetate plastics; low pressure polyethylene, silicones, chlorine-hydrocarbons; acetaldehyde solvents; caustic soda; plant protection chemicals; pyrogenic high dispersion silicic acid; organic intermediates and rock salt.

Westfälische Berggewerkschaftskasse 2884

[Westphalian Mining Fund]
Address: Herner Strasse 45, Postfach 10 27 49, D-4630 Bochum 1
Director: Franz-Rudolf Limper

APPLIED GEOLOGY INSTITUTE 2885
Director: Professor Dr Rolf Schmidt

CHEMISTRY INSTITUTE 2886
Director: Dr Hans Mertens

EXPLOSIVES PROTECTION AND TECHNOLOGY INSTITUTE 2887
Address: Beylingstrasse 65, D-4600 Dortmund 14
Director: Georg Seeger
Activities: Testing and research for explosion prevention (firedamp, coal dust, industrial dusts). Official test station for industrial explosives, and for electrical equipment for use in explosive gas and dust atmospheres.

GEOPHYSICS VIBRATION, AND SOUND TECHNOLOGY INSTITUTE 2888
Director: Dr Horst Rüter

GERMAN MINING MUSEUM 2889
Address: Vödestrasse 28, D-4630 Bochum 1
Director: Hans-Gunther Conrad

MACHINE TECHNOLOGY DEPARTMENT 2890
Director: Dipl Ing Karl Schriever

MINING VENTILATION TEST AUTHORITY 2891
Director: Dipl-Ing Eduard Schubert

PROPERTY BOUNDARY INSTITUTE 2892
Director: Dipl-Ing Helmut Vosen

ROPE TESTING AUTHORITY 2893
Address: Dinnendahlstrasse, D-4630 Bochum 1
Director: Dr Ing Hartmut Arnold

Westfälische Wilhelms-Universität Münster 2894

[Westfälische Wilhelms University Munster]
Address: Schlossplatz 2, D-4400 Münster
Telephone: 4901
Rector: Professor Dr Werner Müller-Warmuth

FACULTY OF MATHEMATICS AND NATURAL SCIENCES 2895
Dean: Professor Dr Wolfgang Hellenthal

Biology Department 2896
Dean: Professor Dr Klaus Heckmann

APPLIED BOTANY INSTITUTE 2897
Address: Hindenburgplatz 55, D-4400 Münster
Director: vacant

Biochemistry of Plants Chair 2898
Address: Hindenburgplatz 55, D-4400 Münster
Director: Professor Dr Wolfgang Barz

BOTANY INSTITUTE 2899
Address: Schlossgarten 3., D-4400 Münster
Director: Professor Dr Erwin Latzko

MICROBIOLOGY INSTITUTE 2900
Address: Tibusstrasse 7-15, D-4400 Münster
Director: Professor Dr Hans-Jürgen Rehm

ZOOLOGY INSTITUTE 2901
Address: Badestrasse 9, D-4400 Münster
Directors: Professor Dr Pio Fioroni, Professor Dr Klaus Heckmann, Professor Dr Ulrich Thurm, Professor Dr Ernst Zebe
Departments: Zoophysiology, Professor Dr Ernst Zebe; Histophysiology, Professor Dr Angela Nolte; Special zoology, Professor Dr Pio Fioroni; General zoology, Professor Dr Klaus Heckmann; Molecular biology, Professor Dr Karl Müller; Neurophysiology, Professor Dr Ulrich Thurm; Physiology and ecology, Professor Dr Rudolf Altevogt; Behavioural research, Professor Dr Gertrud Dücker

Chemistry Department 2902
Dean: Professor Dr Wilhelm Flitsch

BIOCHEMISTRY INSTITUTE 2903
Address: Orléans-Ring 23a, D-4400 Münster
Director: Professor Dr H. Witzel
Senior staff: Professor Dr Axel Lezius

FOOD CHEMISTRY INSTITUTE 2904
Address: Piusallee 7, D-4400 Münster
Director: Professor Dr Hans-Peter Thier

INORGANIC CHEMISTRY INSTITUTE 2905
Address: Gievenbecker Weg 9, D-4400 Münster
Directors: Professor Dr Hermann-Josef Becher, Professor Dr Bernt Krebs, Professor Dr Fritz Umland
Senior staff: Professor Dr Rainer Mattes, Professor Dr Robert Schöllhorn

MINERALOGICAL INSTITUTE AND MINERALOGICAL MUSEUM 2906
Address: Gievenbecker Weg 61, D-4400 Münster
Directors: Professor Dr Hans Ulrich Bambauer, Professor Dr Bernhard Grauert, Professor Dr Wolfgang Hoffmann

ORGANIC CHEMISTRY INSTITUTE 2907
Address: Orléans-Ring 23, D-4400 Münster
Directors: Professor Dr Burchard Franck, Professor Dr Thomas Kauffmann, Professor Dr Martin Klessinger, Professor Dr Hans J. Schäfer
Senior staff: Professor Dr Ingolf Dyong, Professor Dr Wilhelm Flitsch, Professor Dr Albert Heesing, Professor Dr Almuth Klemer

PHARMACEUTICAL BIOLOGY AND PHYTOCHEMISTRY INSTITUTE   2908
Address: Hittorfstrasse 56, D-4400 Münster
Director: Professor Dr Hilmar Friedrich

PHARMACEUTICAL CHEMISTRY INSTITUTE   2909
Address: Hittorfstrasse 58-62, D-4400 Münster
Director: vacant
Department: Drug analysis, Professor Dr Johannes Reisch

PHARMACEUTICAL TECHNOLOGY INSTITUTE   2910
Address: Hittorfstrasse 58-62, D-4400 Münster
Director: Professor Dr Theodor Eckert

PHYSICAL CHEMISTRY INSTITUTE   2911
Address: Schossplatz 4, D-4400 Münster
Directors: Professor Dr Ewald Wicke, Professor Dr Werner Müller-Warmuth

Earth Sciences Department   2912
Dean: Professor Dr Julius Werner

GEOGRAPHY INSTITUTE   2913
Address: Robert-Koch-Strasse 26-28, D-4400 Münster
Directors: Professor Dr Wilfried Bach, Professor Dr Heinz Heineberg, Professor Dr Karl-Friedrich Schreiber, Professor Dr Peter Weber
Senior staff: Professor Dr Friedrich Karl Holtmeier, Professor Dr Cay Lienau, Professor Dr Aloys Mayr, Professor Dr Ulrich Streit, Professor Dr Ingrid Henning

GEOLOGY AND PALAEONTOLOGY INSTITUTE   2914
Address: Gievenbecker Weg 61, D-4400 Münster
Director: Professor Dr Hubert Miller
Senior staff: Professor Dr Lutz Bischoff, Professor Dr Matthias Kaever, Professor Dr Eckehard Löhnert, Professor Dr Winfried Remy, Professor Dr Ulrich Rosenfeld

Mathematics Department   2915

COMPUTER CENTRE   2916
Address: Roxeler Strasse 60, D-4400 Münster
Director: Professor Dr Helmut Werner

MATHEMATICAL LOGIC AND FUNDAMENTAL RESEARCH INSTITUTE   2917
Address: Roxeler Strasse 64, D-4400 Münster
Directors: Professor Dr Dieter Rödding, Professor Dr Justus Diller

MATHEMATICAL STATISTICS INSTITUTE   2918
Address: Roxeler Strasse 64, D-4400 Münster
Directors: Professor Dr Detlef Plashky, Professor Dr Norbert Schmitz

MATHEMATICS INSTITUTE   2919
Address: Roxeler Strasse 64, D-4400 Münster
Senior staff: Professor Dr Otto Forster, Professor Dr Georg Maltese, Professor Dr Wolfgang Meyer, Professor Dr Hans-Joachim Nastold, Professor Dr Reinhold Remmert, Professor Dr Winfried Scharlau, Professor Dr Heinz-Günter Tillmann, Professor Dr Gunter Bengel, Professor Dr Siegfried Bosch, Professor Dr Ludwig Bröcker, Professor Dr Jürgen Elstrodt, Professor Dr Helmut Ischebeck, Professor Dr Heinrich Lang, Professor Dr Klaus Langmann, Professor Dr Falko Lorenz

NUMERICAL AND INSTRUMENTAL MATHEMATICS INSTITUTE   2920
Address: Roxeler Strasse 64, D-4400 Münster
Director: vacant
Senior staff: Professor Dr Hans-Peter Helfrich, Professor Dr Helmut Maurer

Physics Department   2921
Dean: Professor Dr Wolfgang Ludwig

APPLIED PHYSICS INSTITUTE   2922
Address: Roxeler Strasse 70-72, D-4400 Münster
Directors: Professor Dr Wilfried Hampe, Professor Dr Hans-Georg Purwins
Senior staff: Professor Dr Leo Storm

ASTRONOMY INSTITUTE   2923
Address: Steinfurter Strasse 60, D-4400 Münster
Director: Professor Dr Waltraud C. Dürbeck

GEOPHYSICS INSTITUTE   2924
Address: Gievenbecker Weg 61, D-4400 Münster
Director: Professor Dr Jürgen Untiedt
Department: Geophysics of the arctic zone and applied geophysics, Professor Dr Franz Thyssen

METAL RESEARCH INSTITUTE   2925
Address: Domagkstrasse, D-4400 Münster
Director: Professor Dr Theodor Heumann
Senior staff: Professor Dr Eckhard Nembach

NUCLEAR PHYSICS INSTITUTE   2926
Address: Corrensstrasse, D-4400 Münster
Directors: Professor Dr Rainer Santo, Professor Dr Jürgen Andrä

PHYSICS INSTITUTE 2927

Address: Domagkstrasse, D-4400 Münster
Directors: Professor Dr Alfred Benninghoven, Professor Dr Fred Fischer, Professor Dr Joachim Kessler
Senior staff: Professor Dr Ludwig Merten, Professor Dr Horst Merz

THEORETICAL PHYSICS INSTITUTE I 2928

Address: Corrensstrasse, D-4400 Münster
Directors: Professor Dr Are Mann, Professor Dr Achim Weiguny
Senior staff: Professor Dr Josef Kamphusmann, Professor Dr Manfred Stingl

THEORETICAL PHYSICS INSTITUTE II 2929

Address: Steinfurter Strasse 107, D-4400 Münster
Directors: Professor Dr Otto Krisement, Professor Dr Wolfgang Ludwig
Senior staff: Professor Dr Roland Wehner

UNIVERSITY AFFILIATED 2930 INSTITUTES*

Spectrochemistry and Applied Spectroscopy 2931 Institute
Address: Bunsen-Kirchhoff-Strasse 11, D-4600 Dortmund
Director: Professor Dr K. Müller-Gliemann
Departments: Analytical chemistry, vacant; Atom absorption and fluorescence analysis, Dr H. Massmann; Emission spectroscopic analysis, Professor Dr K. Laqua; X-ray spectroscopy, Dr R. Klockenkämper; Source of light physics, Dr Wolf D. Hagenah; Organic chemistry, Dr J. Buddrus; Molecular spectroscopy, Dr E.H. Korte; Mass spectrometry and chromatography, vacant; Data processing, Dr D. Stüwer

FACULTY OF MEDICINE 2932

Dean: Professor Dr Hermann Themann

Clinical Medicine Department 2933

Dean: Professor Dr Harald Feldmann

ANAESTHESIOLOGY AND OPERATIVE 2934 INTENSIVE MEDICINE CLINIC

Address: Jungeblodtplatz 1, D-4400 Münster
Director: Professor Dr Peter Güth

DERMATOLOGY CLINIC 2935

Address: Von-Esmarch-Strasse 56, D-4400 Münster
Directors: Professor Dr Egon Macher, Professor Dr Hans Niermann
Departments: Experimental dermatology, Professor Dr Egon Macher, Professor Dr Clemens Sorg; Andrology, Professor Dr Hans Niermann; Allergology and occupational dermatology, Professor Dr Günther Frock; Dermatomicrobiology, Professor Dr Siegfried Nolting

GYNAECOLOGY CLINIC 2936

Address: Westring 11, D-4400 Münster
Directors: Professor Dr Fritz K. Beller, Professor Dr Hermann P.G. Schneider

MEDICAL CLINIC AND OUTPATIENTS 2937 DEPARTMENT

Address: Westring 3, D-4400 Münster
Directors: Professor Dr Franz Bender, Professor Dr Ulrich Gerlach, Professor Dr Jürgen van de Loo

MEDICAL INFORMATION AND 2938 BIOMATHEMATICS INSTITUTE

Address: Hüfferstrasse 75, D-4400 Münster
Director: Professor Dr Friedrich Wingert
Senior staff: Professor Dr Helmut Göttsche

MEDICAL POLYCLINIC 2939

Address: Westring 3, D-4400 Münster
Director: Professor Dr Heinz Losse

OPHTHALMOLOGY CLINIC 2940

Address: Westring 15, D-4400 Münster –
Director: Professor Dr Hans Joachim Küchle

ORTHOPAEDIC CLINIC AND 2941 OUTPATIENTS DEPARTMENT

Address: Hüfferstrasse 27, D-4400 Münster
Director: Professor Dr Hans-Henning Matthias
Senior staff: Professor Dr Paul Brinkmann, Professor Dr Volker Güth, Professor Dr Jürgen Polster; Technical orthopaedics and rehabilitation, Professor Dr Goetz Gerd Kühn

OTORHINOLARYNGOLOGY CLINIC 2942

Address: Kardinal-von-Galen-Ring 10, D-4400 Münster
Director: Professor Dr Harald Feldmann
Senior staff: Professor Dr Eckhard Nessel, Professor Dr Walter Kumpf, Professor Dr Hermann Kraus, Professor Dr Manfried Hoke

PAEDIATRICS CLINIC 2943

Address: Robert-Koch-Strasse 31, D-4400 Münster
Directors: Professor Dr Klaus-Ditmar Bachmann, Professor Dr Günther Schellong, Professor Dr Fritz Hilgenberg

Sections: Outpatients Clinic, Professor Dr Günther Schellong; cardiology, Professor Dr Fritz Hilgenberg; psychosomatics, Professor Dr Ingeborg Jochmus; neurology, Professor Dr Dietrich Palm; nephrology, Professor Dr Leonhard Diekmann

PSYCHIATRIC AND NEUROLOGY CLINIC 2944
Address: Roxeler Strasse 131-141, D-4400 Münster
Directors: Professor Dr Günter Brune, Professor Dr Rainer Tölle
Senior staff: Professor Dr Hans Kehrer, Professor Dr Bernhard Pauleikhof, Professor Dr Dietrich Habeck

RADIOLOGY CLINIC 2945
Director: Professor Dr Elmer Schnepper

SPECIAL CLINIC FOR TUMOURS AND TUBERCULOSIS 2946
Director: Professor Dr Franz Ehring

SURGICAL CLINIC AND OUTPATIENTS DEPARTMENT 2947
Address: Jungeblodtplatz 1, D-4400 Münster
Directors: Professor Dr Hermann Bünte, Professor Dr Herbert Dittrich, Professor Dr Werner Schmandt, Professor Dr Wendelin Walter
Sections: Urology, Professor Dr Werner Schmandt; Neurosurgery, Professor Dr Wendelin Walter; Universal Surgery, Professor Dr Hermann Bünte

TOOTH, MOUTH AND JAW DISEASES CLINIC AND OUTPATIENTS DEPARTMENT 2948
Address: Waldeyerstrasse 30, D-4400 Münster
Directors: Professor Dr Rüdiger Becker, Professor Dr Wolfgang Büttner, Professor Dr Rudolf Karwetzky, Professor Dr Reinhard Marxkors, Professor Dr Hans-Dieter Lange
Departments: Prosthesis, Professor Dr Reinhard Marxhors; Surgical, Professor Dr Rüdiger Becker; Conservative Dentistry, Professor Dr Wolfgang Büttner; Orthodontics, Professor Dr Rudolf Karwerzky; Paradontology, Professor Dr Hans-Dieter Lange; Experimental dental surgery, Professor Dr Johanna Vahl; Radiography, Professor Dr Walter Ritter; Outpatients, Professor Dr Karl-Heinz Austermann

UNIVERSITY AFFILIATED INSTITUTES 2949

Arteriosclerosis Research Institute 2950
Address: Westring 3, D-4400 Münster
Directors: Professor Dr Jürgen van de Loo, Professor Dr Eckhart Buddecke, Professor Dr Ulrich Gerlach

Erich-Schütz Research Institute for Preventive Medicine and Physiotherapeutic Rehabilitation 2951
Address: Parkstrasse 37, D-4902 Bad Salzuflen
Director: Professor Dr Ernst G. Schmidt

Preclinical and Theoretical Medicine Department 2952
Dean: Professor Dr Dietrich Eichner

ANATOMY INSTITUTE 2953
Address: Vesaliusweg 2-4, D-4400 Münster
Director: Professor Dr Heinz Rollhäuser

FORENSIC MEDICINE INSTITUTE 2954
Address: Von-Esmarch-Strasse 86, D-4400 Münster
Director: vacant

HISTORY OF MEDICINE INSTITUTE 2955
Address: Waldeyerstrasse 27, D-4400 Münster
Director: Professor Dr Richard Toellner

HUMAN GENETICS INSTITUTE 2956
Address: Vesaliusweg 12-14, D-4400 Münster
Director: Professor Dr Widukind Lenz
Departments: Population genetics and mutation statistics, Professor Dr Wilhelm Tünte; Clinical and cytogenetics, Professor Dr Ivar-Harry Pawlowitzki; Cell genetics, Professor Dr Karl-Heinz Grzeschik

HYGIENE INSTITUTE 2957
Address: Westring 10, D-4400 Münster
Directors: Professor Dr Eckehart Kölsch, Professor Dr Wolfgang Ritzerfeld

MEDICAL PHYSICS INSTITUTE 2958
Address: Hüfferstrasse 68, D-4400 Münster
Director: Professor Dr Gerhard Pfefferkorn
Departments: Medical aerosol research, Professor Dr Werner Stöber; Microanalysis, Professor Dr Hans-Jürgen Höhling; Analytical electron microscopy, Professor Dr Hans-Georg Fromme

MEDICAL PSYCHOLOGY DEPARTMENT 2959
Address: Hüfferstrasse 75, D-4400 Münster
Director: Professor Dr Wolfgang M. Pfeiffer

PATHOLOGY INSTITUTE 2960
Address: Westring 17, D-4400 Münster
Director: Professor Dr Ekkehard Grundmann
Senior staff: Professor Dr Rotraud Gieseking, Professor Dr Heinrich Nienhaus, Professor Dr Klaus-Michael Müller, Professor Dr Götz Freytag

PHARMACOLOGY AND TOXICOLOGY 2961
INSTITUTE
Address: Westring 12, D-4400 Münster
Director: Professor Dr Fritz Kemper

PHYSIOLOGICAL CHEMISTRY 2962
INSTITUTE
Address: Waldeyerstrasse 15, D-4400 Münster
Director: Professor Dr Eckhart Buddecke
Department: Experimental cell research, Professor Dr Michael Cantz

PHYSIOLOGY INSTITUTE 2963
Address: Westring 6, D-4400 Münster
Directors: Professor Dr Heinz Caspers, Professor Dr Heinz Schröer

RADIATION BIOLOGY INSTITUTE 2964
Address: Hittorfstrasse 17, D-4400 Münster
Director: Professor Dr Wolfgang Dittrich

SILICOSIS AND OCCUPATIONAL 2965
MEDICINE INSTITUTE
Address: Westring 10, D-4400 Münster
Director: Professor Dr K. Norpoth

SPORTS MEDICINE INSTITUTE 2966
Address: Horstmarer Langweg 39, D-4400 Münster
Director: Professor Dr Eberhard Zipf

RESEARCH PROJECTS 2967

Geochronology Central Laboratory 2968
Address: Gievenbecker Weg 61, D-4400 Münster
Leader: Professor Dr Borwin Grauert

Human Reproduction 2969
Address: Westring 11, D-4400 Münster
Leader: Professor Dr E. Nieschlag

Melanoimmunology 2970
Address: Von-Esmarch-Strasse 56, D-4400 Münster
Leaders: Professor Dr Egon Macher, Professor Dr Clemens Sorg

Mesenchyme Research 2971
Address: Waldeyer Strasse 15, D-4400 Münster
Spokesman: Professor Dr Eckhart Buddecke

Secondary Natural Substances - All 2972
Cultures
Address: Hindenburgplatz 55, D-4400 Münster
Spokesman: Professor Dr Wolfgang Barz

Teratological Research and 2973
Rehabilitation of Multiply-
Handicapped People
Address: Hüfferstrasse 27, D-4400 Münster
Spokesman: Professor Dr Manfried Hoke

Wieland Werke AG* 2974

Address: Berliner Platz, D-7900 Ulm-Donau
Activities: Development and production of copper and copper alloy wrought products.

Wilhelm-Foerster- 2975
Sternwarte eV mit Zeiss-
Planetarium

[Wilhelm Foerster Observatory and Zeiss Planetarium]
Address: Munsterdamm 90, D-1000 Berlin 41
Telephone: (030) 796 20 29
Research director: A. Kunert
Graduate research staff: 2
Annual expenditure: £10 000-50 000
Activities: The introduction of new methods of education in astronomy, and the production of educational films; research programmes in astrometry, variable stars, and the sun.
Facilities: Telescopes; optical laboratory; computer on line automatic coordinate measurement system; photoelectric photometer.
Contract work: Yes
Publications: Veröffentlichungen der Wilhelm Foerster Sternwarte; Protokoll der Gruppe Berliner Mondbeobachter.

Wintershall AG 2976

Address: Postfach 104020, D-3500 Kassel
Telephone: (0561) 301
Telex: 99632
Chairman: Dr Ronaldo Schmitz
Activities: Oil and gas production, processing and marketing; fertilizers; chemicals and salt.

Zentralinstitut für Versuchstiere   2977

[Central Institute for Laboratory Animals]
Address: 57 Lettow-Vorbeck-Allee, D-3000 Hannover 91
Affiliation: Deutsche Forschungsgemeinschaft
Head: Professor Dr W. Heine
Activities: Basic and applied research in the experimental use of animals, including the breeding of small genetically-defined, standardized laboratory animals; especially specified-pathogen-free and gnotobiotic mice and rats.

Zentralstelle für Pilzforschung und Pilzverwertung   2978

Address: Garbenstrasse   13,   D-7000   Stuttgart Hohenheim
Telephone: (0711) 455063/64
Research director: Dr Werner Bötticher
Activities: Mushroom research and utilization.
Contract work: No

Zoologisches Forschungsinstitut und Museum Alexander Koenig   2979

[Alexander Koenig Zoological Research Institute and Museum]
Address: Adenauerallee 150-164, D-5300 Bonn 1
Parent body: Wissenschaftsministerium des Landes Nordrhein-Westfalen

Research director: Professor Dr Günter Nobis
Activities: Mammals, birds, reptiles, amphibians, fishes, arthropods; systematics and taxonomy, animal geography, evolution, ecology.

Zuendapp-Werke GmbH   2980

Address: Anzingerstrasse 1-3, D-8000 München 80
Telephone: (089) 411 3390
Telex: 05/23335

RESEARCH AND DEVELOPMENT DIVISION   2981

Research director: Karl-Heinz Menzl
Annual expenditure: £51 000-500 000
Activities: Combustion engines; noise control of two-wheeled vehicles and lawn mowers; wear reduction and exhaust gas control of high-speed Otto engines; assembly and construction of motorcycle plants.
Contract work: No

GREECE

Academy of Athens   1

Address: 28 El. Venizelou Avenue, Athinai 143
General Secretary: Professor I. Theodoracopoulos
Committees: Greek National Committee for Astronomy, President: Professor I. Xanthakis; Greek National Committee for Space Research, President: Professor I. Xanthakis; Greek National Committee for Mathematics, President: Professor Ph. Vassiliou

RESEARCH CENTRE FOR   2
ASTRONOMY AND APPLIED
MATHEMATICS

Address: 14 Anagnostopoulou Street, Athinai 136
Supervisor: Professor I. Xanthakis
Publications: Annual report.

RESEARCH CENTRE FOR   3
ATMOSPHERIC PHYSICS AND
CLIMATOLOGY

Address: 131 3rd September Street, Athinai
Supervisor: Professor El Mariolopoulos

Athens National and   4
Capodistrian University*

Address: Odos Panepistimiou 30, Athinai 143
Telephone: (01) 3620003

FACULTY OF DENTISTRY*   5

Dean: K. Kopsiaftis

FACULTY OF MATHEMATICS AND   6
PHYSICAL SCIENCES*

FACULTY OF MEDICINE*   7

Dean: K. Papadatos

SCHOOL OF PHARMACY   8

Address: 30 E. Benaki, Athinai 142
Telephone: (01) 3609108
Director: Professor N.H. Choulis
Graduate research staff: 5
Annual expenditure: £10 000-50 000
Activities: Drug level studies; narcotics and drug abuse; tablet formulations; Greek chlora; isolation of active substances from natural products.
Contract work: Yes

Athens National Technical   9
University*

Address: Odos Patission 42, Athinai 147
Telephone: (01) 3691281

FACULTY OF CHEMICAL   10
ENGINEERING*

Dean: Professor J. Marangotis

FACULTY OF CIVIL ENGINEERING*   11

Dean: Professor Th. Tassios

Benaki Phytopathological   15
Institute

Address: 8 Delta Street, Kiphissia, Athinai
Telephone: 8012 376; 8019 861
Affiliation: Ministry of Agriculture
Director: D.S. Vassilopoulos
Deputy director: Dr P.A. Mourikis
Activities: Plant protection problems (fungi, virus, bacteria, non-parasitic diseases, insect and animal pests, biological control, and phytopharmacy).
Publications: Annual report.

DEPARTMENT OF ENTOMOLOGY   16
AND AGRICULTURAL ZOOLOGY

Telephone: 8019 861
Head: Dr P.A. Mourikis

Agricultural Entomology Laboratory   17

Senior staff: Dr P.A. Mourikis, P. Vassilaina-Alexopoulou, Dr A.S. Drosopoulos

Agricultural Zoology, Nematology and   18
Acarology Laboratory

Senior staff: Dr K.Th. Buchelos, Cl. Kalyviotis-Gazelas, P. Papaioannou Souliotis, V.G. Vlachopoulos

Biological Control Laboratory - A   19

Senior staff: Dr Loukia Ch. Argyriou

Biological Control Laboratory - B   20

Senior staff: Dr H. Pavlopoulou-Stavraki

Insect Microbiology and Pathology   21
Laboratory

Senior staff: Dr Ch. N. Yamvrias

Insect Physiology Laboratory   22

Senior staff: Dr E.A. Fytizas, C. Soultanopoulou-Mantaka

DEPARTMENT OF PESTICIDE   23
CONTROL

Telephone: 8010 376
Head: Dr P.G. Patsakos
Senior staff: P.E. Kalmoukos

Pesticide Residues Laboratory   24

Senior staff: Dr P.G. Patsakos, Dr M.L. Anagnostopoulos, P.G. Aplada

Pesticide Toxicology Laboratory   25

Senior staff: Dr R. Fytiza-Danielidou, Dr G.V. Vassiliou

Pesticides Efficiency Evaluation   26
Laboratory

Senior staff: P.E. Kalmoukos, Dr C.N. Giannopolitis, Dr M. Chrysayi-Tokousballidi

Physical and Chemical Examination of   27
Pesticides Laboratory

Senior staff: G.S. Spyropoulos, Dr E. Anagnostopoulou-Tsorbatzoudi, Dr A. Rokophyllou-Chourdaki

DEPARTMENT OF PHYTOPHARMACY   28

Telephone: 8014 266
Head: Dr M.E. Damanakis

Biological Laboratory   29

Senior staff: E.G. Kapetanakis, A.J. Vatos

Chemical Analysis of Pesticides   30
Laboratory

Senior staff: N.Ch. Adam, C.Z. Zaphiriou

Fungicides Laboratory   31

Senior staff: Dr N. Panayotarou-Petsikou

AUTOMATIC CONTROL SYSTEMS 61
Head: Professor P. Paraskevopoulos

ELECTRICAL POWER SYSTEMS 62
Head: Professor D. Tsanakas

ELECTROMAGNETIC THEORY 63
Head: Professor E.T. Sarris

ELECTRONICS LABORATORY 64
Telephone: (0541) 26474
Director: Professor Dr Chris J. Georgopoulos
Sections: Fibre optics and infrared technology, C. Koykoyrlis; telecommunications, A. Athanasiadis
Graduate research staff: 10
Annual expenditure: £10 000–50 000
Activities: Communications circuits and systems using fibre optics and infrared technology; phased array radars and electronic control systems.
Contract work: Yes

ELECTROTECHNICAL AND 65
ELECTRONIC MATERIALS
TECHNOLOGY
Head: Professor A. Thanailakis

GENERAL PHYSICS 66
Heads: Professor J. Yakinthos, Dr H. Simantiri

MICROWAVES 67
Head: Professor J. Sahalos

NUCLEAR TECHNOLOGY 68
Head: Professor N. Tsagas

SPECIAL MECHANICAL ENGINEERING 69
Head: Professor P. Sparis

TELECOMMUNICATION SYSTEMS 70
Head: Professor N. Voulgaris

Environmental Pollution 71
Control Project - Athens

Address: 147,28 Octovriou Street, Athinai 814
Telephone: 86 50 111; 86 50 476; 86 50 053; 86 50 334
Telex: 216028 DYPP GR
Affiliation: Ministry of Social Services
Project manager: Professor Gr. Markantonatos John Vournas
Sections: Air pollution control, M. Spyropoulos; water pollution control, M. Panagiotidis; noise abatement, M. Simandonis; solid wastes management, M. Bourkas; epidemiological surveys, M. Zaphiropoulos
Graduate research staff: 37

Annual expenditure: £51 000–500 000
Activities: Pollution problems in Greater Athens area.
Facilities: Air pollution monitoring network.
Contract work: No
Publications: Interim Technical Report, (4 volumes).

Hellenic Pasteur Institute 72

Address: 127 Vassilissis Sofias Avenue, Athinai 618
Telephone: (64) 62 281; (64) 65 905
Telex: 221188 IPH
Director: Professor Charles Serie
Departments: Bacteriology, Dr L. Mavrommatis; Biochemistry, Dr C. Stournaras; Immunology, Dr E. Patéraki; Parasitology, Dr A. Garyfallou; Virology, Dr J. Vincent, Dr N. Spyrou; Vaccines, Dr E. Patéraki; BCG, Dr E. Patéraki
Reference Centres: Influenza, Dr J. Vincent; Enterovirus, Dr J. Vincent; Neisseria, Dr L. Mavrommatis
Activities: Viral infections, mostly respiratory and intestinal viruses; bacterial infections, mostly Neisseria gonorrhea; parasitological infections, mostly Leishmania and Toxoplasmosis.
Publications: Yearly periodical.

Institute of Geology and 73
Mineral Exploration

– IGME
Address: 70 Messoghion Avenue, Athinai 608
Telephone: (01) 7798412/17
Telex: 6357 IGME GR
Affiliation: Ministry of Industry and Energy
Director of research: N. Apostolides
Graduate research staff: 250
Annual expenditure: over £2m
Activities: Investigation of mineral wealth; energy resources; underground water reserves; geological, geophysical, geotechnical, hydrogeological maps; ore dressing; water and ore chemical analysis; mineralogy; geochemistry; micropaleontology; microprobe techniques; thermal analysis; submarine geology; feasibility studies.
Contract work: Yes

GENERAL GEOLOGY AND 74
ECONOMIC GEOLOGY DIVISION

Departments: General Geology and Geological Mapping; Engineering Geology; Economic Geology; Energy Resources

GEOCHEMICAL EXPLORATION DEPARTMENT 75

GEOPHYSICAL EXPLORATION DEPARTMENT 76

HYDROGEOLOGY DEPARTMENT 77

LABORATORIES DIVISION 78

Departments: Chemistry; Mineralogy and Petrography; Ore Dressing and Metallurgy

MINERAL EXPLORATION AND CONTROL OF MINING ACTIVITIES DIVISION 79

Departments: Mineral Exploration; Technical and Feasibility Studies; Mining Activities Control

Institute of Oceanographic and Fisheries Research 80

Address: Aghios Kosmas Hellinikon, Athinai
Telephone: 98 20 214
Affiliation: Ministry for Coordination
President: Professor Dr Vassilios Kiortsis
Director General: Dr Constantine Vamvakas
Sections: Fisheries, Dr N. Tsimenidis; chemistry, Dr N. Frilingos; biology, Dr C. Vamvakas; physics, E. Balopoulos; aquaculture, S. Klaoudatos; experimental food, Professor S. Papoutsoglou
Graduate research staff: 35
Annual expenditure: £51 000-500 000
Activities: Applied oceanographic and fish research (marine and freshwater); biology, geology, chemistry, physical oceanography, pollution, aquaculture, primary production, ecology and environment.
Facilities: Two vessels and a 4 000 volume library.
Contract work: Yes
Publications: Talassographica.

Ministry of Agriculture 81

Address: 2-6 Acharnon Street, Athinai
See separate entry for: Benaki Phytopathological Institute.

AGRICULTURAL RESEARCH SERVICE 82

Address: 6 Kapnokoptiniou Street, Athinai 103
Telephone: (01) 8232002
Director: Dr Angelos Chlichlias
Sections: Plant production research, A. Angelides; animal production research, A. Houliaras; programme and valorization of agricultural research, E. Youyas; agricultural meteorology and environmental research, A. Athonassopoulos
Graduate research staff: 300
Annual expenditure: over £2m
Activities: The Agricultural Research Service is a central service of the Ministry of Agriculture which supervises and coordinates the research activities of the institutions belonging to five agricultural research centres throughout Greece. These institutions carry out research programmes in the following fields: improvement of plant varieties; different practices and systems of crop and tree cultivation; soil and plant nutrition; mechanical picking and harvesting methods; pest control; out of season vegetable production; irrigation methods; animal nutrition and breeding; postharvest technology for agricultural products; improvement and management of pastures.
Contract work: Yes
Publications: Quarterly report.

Agricultural Engineering Institute 83

Address: 61 Democratius Street, Aghii Anargyri, Attica
Telephone: (01) 2611011
Director: George Souvatzis
Activities: Agricultural machinery; study of new types of equipment.

Agricultural Research Station of Ioannina 84

Address: Ioannina
Director: Andonios Manzios
Activities: Regional research with emphasis on livestock nutrition and fodder plants.

Agricultural Research Station of Komotini 85

Address: Komotini
Director: Stavros Pappas
Activities: Regional research in animal husbandry.

Aliartos Station of Agricultural Research 86

Address: Aliartos, Veotia
Director: Christos Georgiades
Activities: Regional experiments on behalf of the various plant research institutes; research on local problems conducted independently by the station; research on aromatic plants and fodder beets.

Animal Breeding and Nutrition Institute 87

Address: Yannitsa
Director: Stergios Kydonas
Activities: The improvement of animal husbandry in Greece; improvement of animals, feeding methods, pastures and meadows.

Arta Station of Agricultural Research 88

Address: Arta, Epirus
Director: George Kalyvas
Activities: Conducting regional research on local problems either independently or in cooperation with the plant research institutes. It is mainly concerned with citrus trees.

Cereals Institute 89

Address: Salonica
Director: Ioannis Karayannis
Activities: Cereal breeding and research on the agronomic and technical problems of their cultivation; supervising the production to supply the growers; improvement of fresh vegetable crops in Northern Greece.

Chalkidiki Station of Agricultural Research 90

Address: Aghios Mamas, Chalkidiki
Director: Evangelos Tsimbouris
Activities: Conducting regional experimentation on behalf of the plant research institutes; breeding of livestock and poultry and propagation of improved breeds; feeding and maintenance of farm animals.

Citrus and Subtropicals Research Institute 91

Address: Chanea, Crete
Director: Nicos Psellakis
Activities: Primarily the study of problems of olive tree growing on the island of Crete and secondarily the study of other trees (citrus trees mainly) and vines.

Citrus Station of Poros 92

Address: Poros
Director: N. Nikolakos
Activities: Research on problems arising in growing citrus fruit trees.

Cotton and Industrial Plants Institute 93

Address: Sindes, Salonica
Director: Ioannis Klavanidis
Activities: Cotton breeding and research on cotton growing problems; first-stage multiplication of seeds of improved cotton varieties; improved cultivation of flax and oleaginous plants.

Fodder Crops Institute 94

Address: Larissa
Director: Evangelos Stylopoulos
Activities: Field and plant techniques regarding fodder crops and pulses; breeding of new varieties.

Heracleion Institute of Vegetable and Floriculture Research 95

Address: Heracleion, Crete
Director: Marcos Petrakis
Activities: Regional experiments on behalf of the plant research institutes; independent research on growing vegetables (tomatoes, cucumbers, etc) under cover and flowers.

Land Reclamation Research Institute 96

Address: Sindos, Salonica
Director: Savas Athanassiadis
Activities: Experimental work on irrigation, drainage improvement of saline-alkali soils, sandy soils, weed control in ditches.

Lesvos Station of Agricultural Research 97

Address: Mytilini
Director: Efstiatios Tsirtsis
Activities: Problems of olive tree cultivation on the island of Lesvos.

North-East Pelopennesus Institute of Agricultural Research 98

Address: Amalias, Pyrgos
Director: Constantinos Dimitrakis
Activities: Conducting regional research on local problems either independently or in cooperation with other research institutes. It is mainly concerned with research on plant water requirements, irrigation methods, suitability of the available water for irrigation, water

losses in irrigation under the ecological conditions of the valley of Pinios. Also with citrus trees, vegetables, vines and other crops which are best adapted to the ecological conditions of North-East Peloponnesus.

Olive Institute   99

Address: Corfu
Director: George Karvounis
Activities: Olive tree growing.

Plant Products Technology Institute   100

Address: Lycovryssi, Attica
Director: Mechael Kodouny
Activities: Technological problems of Greek plant products in general; preservation of fresh fruits and vegetables, processing and manufacture of fruits and juices from fruits; preparation of new types of processed products and application of new methods; utilization of waste from the processing of plant products.

Plant Protection Research Institute of   101
Heraclion

Address: Heraclion, Crete
Director: John Chardakis

Plant Protection Research Institute of   102
Patras

Director: Kostas Thanassoulopoulos
Activities: Study of problems related to crop pests and diseases.

Plant Protection Research Institute of   103
Salonica

Address: Salonica
Director: George Themelis
Activities: Problems related to crop pests and diseases.

Plant Protection Research Institute of   104
Volos

Director: John Ioannides
Activities: Study of problems related to crop pests and diseases.

Pomology Institute   105

Address: Naoussa, Macedonia
Director: George Siryannidis
Activities: Problems arising in growing deciduous fruit trees.

Ptolemais Station of Agricultural   106
Research

Address: Ptolemais
Director: Vassilios Michailidas
Activities: Conducting regional experimentation on behalf of the various plant research institutes; independent research for the study of local problems of West Macedonia.

Rhodes Station of Agricultural   107
Research

Address: Vaghies, Rhodes
Director: Apostolos Kostadakis
Activities: Conducting regional research on local problems either independently or in cooperation with the plant research institutes. The station is mainly concerned with citrus trees, fruit trees, olive trees, vines and fresh vegetables.

Serres Agricultural Research Station   108

Address: Serres
Director: Sakis Kaftanzis
Activities: Applied livestock research on problems of nutrition, raising, fattening and breeding of animals; applied regional research on crop varieties and cultivation methods in cooperation with the plant research institutes.

Soils and Fertilizers Research Institute   109
of Salonica

Address: Salonica
Director: Nicos Koroxenidis
Activities: Soils of Northern Greece: soil surveys and soil and water samples analyses needed by various services of the Ministry; research on crop requirements in fertilizers.

Soils and Fertilizers Research Section   110
of Thessaly

Address: Larissa
Director: Panayotis Tzolas
Activities: To collect data from soil analyses for the preparation of soil maps and to study problems related to fertilizing.

Soils, Fertilizers and Climate Institute   111

Address: Lycovryssi, Attica
Director: Athanasios Koutalos
Activities: To study, classify and map out the soils of the country; to study the fertilizer requirements of the crops on various types of soils experimentation; to examine irrigation waters.

Vardates Station of Agricultural Research   112

Address: Vardates, Pthiotis
Director: Nicos Katranis
Activities: Conducting regional experimentation on behalf of the institutes of plant research.

Vine Institute   113

Address: Lycovryssi, Attica
Director: Nikos Karadonis
Activities: Any subject related to the growing of grape vines.

Wine Institute   114

Address: Lycovryssi, Attica
Director: Stavroula Kouracou
Activities: Study of all problems related to wine (wine standardization, improvement in grade, methods of wine making and processing, fermentation techniques and composition of Greek wine).

Xanthi Station of Agricultural Research   115

Address: Xanthi
Director: Soultana Kimoundri
Activities: Regional field experiments for the various plant research institutes.

DIVISION OF AGRICULTURAL ECONOMIC STUDIES AND PLANNING   116

Address: 2-4 Acharnon Street, Athinai
Director: Athanasios Stoukas
Activities: Agricultural economic surveys, vertical and horizontal planning, production and price statistics; relations with specialized national and international institutions; follow-up of trends and evolutions in agriculture; management of the library of the Ministry of Agriculture.

DIVISION OF CEREALS AND LEGUMES   117

Address: 2-4 Acharnon Street, Athinai
Director: Triant Karalafos
Activities: Production and protection of cereals, cattle-fodder plants and legumes; planning and producing of grains and seeds of cereals, legumes and vegetables, conducted throughout the country, of 50 seed and grain producing centres.

DIVISION OF PLANT PATHOLOGY   118

Address: 2-4 Acharnon Street, Athinai
Director: E.E. Psarros
Activities: Coordination of research on plant pests and diseases and their control.

DIVISION OF VETERINARY SERVICE   119

Activities: Control of infectious and parasitic diseases; measures for protection and control of animal infections; organization and supervision of diagnostic laboratories; research into and supply of biological products; police veterinary service; health control of animal products; veterinary assistance; drugs.

Animal Origin Food Control Laboratory   120

Address: Botanical Garden, Athinai
Activities: Control of all foods of animal origin.

Livestock Division   121

Address: Acharnon Street 2-4, Athinai
Activities: Development and improvement of livestock.
Facilities: Animal reproduction stations at Rhodos, Drama, Kozani, Karditsa and Pyrgos.

Veterinary Institute of Foot and Mouth Disease   122

Address: Aghia Paraskevi, Attikis
Activities: Production of foot and mouth disease vaccines; research and control of foot and mouth disease.

Veterinary Laboratory for Physiology and Pathology Research on Animal Reproduction   123

Address: Aghia Paraskevi, Attikis
Activities: Research and diagnosis on reproductive diseases of animals.

Veterinary Microbiological Institute   124

Address: Botanical Garden, Athinai
Activities: Research and diagnosis of infectious and parasitic diseases of domestic animals; preparation of biological products.

Veterinary Microbiological Laboratory   125

Address: 26th October Street 66, Salonica
Activities: Research and diagnosis of infectious and parasitic diseases of domestic animals.

Veterinary Microbiological Laboratory 126
of Diagnosis and Research

Address: Komotini
Activities: Diagnosis of infectious and parasitic diseases of domestic animals.

Veterinary Microbiological Laboratory 127
of Diagnosis and Research

Address: Larissa
Activities: Diagnosis of infectious and parasitic diseases of domestic animals.

Veterinary Microbiological Laboratory 128
of Diagnosis and Research

Address: Chania, Crete
Activities: Diagnosis of infectious and parasitic diseases of domestic animals.

Veterinary Microbiological Laboratory 129
of Diagnosis and Research

Address: Giannina
Activities: Diagnosis of infectious and parasitic diseases of domestic animals.

Veterinary Microbiological Laboratory 130
of Diagnosis and Research

Address: Patras
Activities: Diagnosis of infectious and parasitic diseases of domestic animals.

FOREST DIRECTORATE 131

Forestry Development, Planning and 132
Research Division

Address: 22 Menandrou Street, Athinai 112
Director: Demos P. Siderides

FOREST RESEARCH INSTITUTE 133
Address: Terma Alkmanous, Kouponia, Athinai 615
Telephone: (01) 7784850
Director: Nicolaos Panayotides
Activities: Applied research in forest soils, forest ecology, genetics, silviculture, management, wood technology, forest hydrology, forest protection and forest utilization.

NORTHERN GREECE FOREST 134
RESEARCH CENTRE
Address: Megalou Alexandrou 106, Salonica
Director: Orestis Katsanos
Activities: Applied research in poplar cultivation and range management.

LAND RECLAMATION SERVICE 135

Address: 22 Menandrou Street, Athinai 112
General Director: Amt. Psarrakis
Activities: Experimental work on irrigation, drainage, improvement of saline-alkali soils, sandy soils, weed control in ditches.

Patras University 136

Address: Patras
Telephone: (061) 991 822
Rector: George Maniatis
Publications: Annual bulletin.

FACULTY OF ENGINEERING 137

Dean: Professor Vasilios Makios
Sections: Synthesis of Structure II, Professor Demitrios Beskos; inorganic chemical technology, Professor Grigorios Botsaris; machine design, Professor Andreas Demarogonas; organic chemical technology, Professor Anastasios Dodos; mechanical engineering, Professor Panayiotis Drakatos; power system engineering, professor Glafkos Galanos; general electrotechnology, Professor Antonios Grammaticos; environmental technology, Professor Sotirios Grigoropoulos; structural analysis, earthquake engineering, Professor Aristarchos Iconomou; material science and strength of materials, Professor Theodoros Kermanides; wire telecommunication, Professor George Kokkinakis; industrial management, Professor Antonios Kontaratos; engineering economics and project management, Professor Vasilios Kouskoulas; pattern recognition, Professor Demitrios Lainiotis; applied electronics optics, Professor Panayiotis Lambropoulos; construction equipment, Professor Evangelos Lazaris; mechanical engineering, Professor Constantine Lefas; electromagnetic theory B, Professor Vasilios Makios; mathematics A, Professor Vasilios Markellos; machine theory and design, Professor Andreas Mavromatis; high pressures, Professor Efstathios Menemenlis; biomechanics, Professor John Missirlis; wireless telecommunication, Professor John Nicolis; technical mechanics and vibration, Professor Stefanos Paipetis; applied electronics, Professor George Papadopoulos; technical mechanics and application, Professor Demosthenis Papailiou; metal science, Professor Demitrios Papamantellos; fluid

mechanics and application, Professor Demitrios Papanikas; chemical thermodynamics, Professor George Papatheodorou; chemical mechanics A, Professor Alkiviadis Payiatakis; thermal engines, Professor Panayiotis Razelos; electromechanical energy conversion, Professor Athanasios Safacas; nuclear technology, Professor Constantine Syros; electromagnetic theory A, Professor George Theodorides; information theory, Professor Nicolaos Tzannes; automatic control systems, Professor Spyridon Tzafestas; chemical mechanics B, Professor Constantine Vagenas

Activities: The Faculty has departments of electrical, mechanical, civil and chemical engineering, and a department of computer informatics.

FACULTY OF MEDICINE   138

Dean: Professor Theodoros Papapetropoulos
Sections: Surgery, Professor John Androulakis; paediatrics, Professor Nicolaos Beratis; pathologic anatomy, Professor Dionisios Bonicos; psychiatry, Professor Petros Chartocollis; radiology, Professor John Demopoulos; public health, Professor Gerasimos Kondakis; biological chemistry, Professor Charalambos Koutsogeorgopoulos; physiology, Professor Elias Kouvelas; general biology, Professor George Maniatis; general pharmacology, Professor Michael Maragoudakis; gynaecology, Professor George Maroulis; neurology, Professor Theodoros Papapetropoulos; medical physics, Professor Vasilios Proimos; internal medicine, Professor Apostolos Vagenakis

FACULTY OF NATURAL SCIENCES   139

Dean: Professor Theodoros Deligiannis
Sections: Biochemistry, Professor Stylianos Actipis; mathematics A, Professor Nicolaos Artemiadis; palaeontology and historical geology, Professor George Christodoulou; biology, Professor Constantine Christodoulou; electronics, Professor Theodoros Deligiannis; radiochemistry and X-ray chemistry, Professor Paul Demotakis; mathematics B, Professor Lambros Dokas; botany, Professor Demitrios Fitos; inorganic chemistry, Professor Andreas Galinos; plant physiology, Professor Nicolaos Gavalas; theoretical physics, Professor Stergios Giannoussis; mechanics, Professor Constantine Goudas; mathematics for physics, Professor Evangelos Ifantis; mathematics D, Professor Stavros Iliadis; physics of the atmosphere, Professor Demitrios Illias; numerical analysis and programming, Professor Kosmas Iordanides; physical chemistry, Professor Nicolaos Katsanos; pharmaceutical chemistry, Professor Panayiotis Katsoulakos; oryctology-petrology, Professor George Macheras; set theory and logic, Professor George Mitakides; zoology, Professor John Ontrias; genetics, Professor Michael

Pelekanos; physics B, Professor Rigas Rigopoulos; physics C, Professor Minas Roilos; applied mathematics A, Professor George Roussas; organic chemistry, Professor Demitrios Theodoropoulos; physics A, Professor Alexander Theodossiou; chemical technology, Professor Alexander Tsolis; human and animal physiology, Professor Theoni Valcana

Activities: The Faculty has departments of mathematics, physics, chemistry, biology, geology, and pharmacy.

Scientific Group for Space   140
Research

Address: 43 Ellanikou Street, Athinai 501/1
Telephone: 719-893
Research Director: Dr Constantin Kourogenis
Sections: Astronomical observations, D.P. Elias, C. Damilatis; artificial satellites (observations), D.P. Elias; solar radiation, A.Ch. Frangos; meteors and meteorites, M. Nikiforakis; earth sciences, Dr C. Kourogenis
Graduate research staff: 10
Annual expenditure: £10 000-50 000
Contract work: No

Scientific Research and   141
Technology Agency

Address: 48 Vassileos Constantinou Avenue, Athinai 501
Telephone: (01) 741937
Telex: 214074 YEET GR
Parent body: Ministry of Coordination
Director, Documentation and Information Directorate: Dr M. Petrakis
Activities: The promotion and coordination of most government research projects is carried out by the Agency.

Thessaloniki Aristotelion   142
University*

Address: Thessaloniki
Telephone: (031) 2392 2251

FACULTY OF AGRICULTURE AND   143
FORESTRY*

Dean: Professor I.-M. Tjarakakis

FACULTY OF DENTISTRY*   144

Dean: Professor E. Stasinopoulos

FACULTY OF MEDICINE*   145

Dean: Professor N. Kardraviotis

FACULTY OF SCIENCES*   146

Dean: Professor D. Yassakoudakis

FACULTY OF TECHNOLOGY*   147

Dean: Professor; G. Tsargas

FACULTY OF VETERINARY   148
MEDICINE*

Dean: Professor A. Spais

Tobacco Institute of Greece   149

Address: Drama
Telephone: 224 45
Affiliation: National Tobacco Board of Greece
Director: A.G. Sficas
Graduate research staff: 32
Annual expenditure: £501 000-2m
Activities: The study and application of all appropriate measures to improve the physical, agrotechnical and agroeconomical conditions of production with the ultimate objective an increased yield, improvement of quality and the reduction of production cost.
Contract work: No
Publications: Annual report.

DEPARTMENT OF CHEMICAL   150
RESEARCH

Laboratories: Tobacco Chemistry; Tobacco Technology
Activities: Chemical constitution of Greek tobacco; relation of chemical constituents to the quality of the tobacco leaf; constituents of tobacco smoke.

DEPARTMENT OF   151
PHYTOPATHOLOGY

Laboratories: Entomology; Plant Pathology
Activities: Tobacco protection problems in seedbeds, fields and warehouses.

DEPARTMENT OF TOBACCO   152
PRODUCTION

Laboratories: Plant Breeding; Variety Testing; Agrotechnical; Seed Production
Activities: Breeding of new varieties; seed production; research on all production phases (seedbeds, transplanting, fertilization, irrigation, etc) as well as the study of curing, manipulation, and storage problems of raw tobacco.

University of Ioannina   153

Address: Ioannina
Telephone: (0651) 21805
Telex: 0322160

FACULTY OF SCIENCE   154

Chemistry Department   155

Senior staff: Professor C. Polydoropoulos, Professor J. Tsamgaris, Professor A. Kosmatos, Professor E. Boudouris, Professor A. Sdoukos, Professor M. Karayannis, Professor V. Kapoulas
Graduate research staff: 34

Mathematics Department   156

Senior staff: Professor G. Tzivanidis, Professor V. Staikos, Professor A. Hadjidimos, Professor P. Bozonis, Professor J. Sficas, Professor T. Papaioannou, Professor A. Katsarocs, Professor E. Smyrnelis, Professor D. Koutroufiotis, Professor S. Bozapalidis
Graduate research staff: 35

Physics Department   157

Senior staff: Professor N. Gangas, Professor G. Andritiopoulos, Professor D. Metaxas, Professor G. Banos, Professor D. Miliotis, Professor Chr. Papageorgopoulos, Professor N. Alexandropoulos, Professor P. Assimacopoulos, Professor J. Vergados, Professor F. Triantis
Graduate research staff: 32

MEDICAL SCHOOL   158

Telephone: (0651) 21802

Anatomy   159

Head: Dr O.B. Kotoulas

HUNGARY

Agrártudományi Egyetem Gödöllő   1

[Agricultural University, Gödöllő]
Address: Páter Károly Útca 1, H-2103 Gödöllő
Telephone: Gödöllő 1
Telex: 22 48 92
Rector: Professor László Cselőtei
Pro-rectors: Professor László Lőkös, Professor Károly Kocsis, Professor László Udvari
Director, University Experimental Farm: Dr Attila Puskás

FACULTY OF AGRICULTURAL ENGINEERING   2

Dean: Professor István Huszár
Sub-deans: Professor János Váradi, Professor György Beer, Professor János Bánházi

Agricultural Architecture Department   3

Head: Assistant Professor László Tomory

Agricultural Electrification and Animal Breeding Machinery Department   4

Heads: Professor István Mikecz, Professor Károly Kocsis

Agricultural Machinery Operations Department   5

Head: Professor Vilmos Tibold

Agricultural Machinery Repairs Department   6

Heads: Professor György Beer, Professor József Janik

Agricultural Mechanics Institute   7

Director: Professor László Lehoczky
Departments: Agricultural Machinery, Professor László Lehoczky, Professor János Bánházi, Professor Pál Soós; General Agricultural Mechanics, Assistant Professor László Király

Agriculture Department   8

Head: Professor József Czakó

Mathematics and Computation Technology   9

Director: Professor Gyula Obádovics
Department: Mathematics, Professor Gyula Obádovics; University Computation Centre, Lajos Szóda

Mechanics Department   10

Head: Professor István Huszár

Physics Department   11

Head: Professor Árpád Nagy

Tractors and Cars Department   12

Heads: Professor János Váradi, Professor György Komándi

FACULTY OF AGRICULTURAL SCIENCES   13

Dean: Professor József Lorincz
Sub-deans: Professor István Petróczi, Assistant Professor Pál Széky, Professor Ambrus Burgán

Agricultural Chemistry Department 14

Head: Professor Béla Debreczeni

Agricultural Economics Department 15

Head: Professor László Lőkös

Agricultural Management Department 16

Heads: Professor Mihály Tóth, Professor Károly Dobos

Animal Breeding Department 17

Heads: Professor Dr András Magyari, Professor Nándor Nagy
Research Station, Babatpuszta: Goose breeding, Dr Imre Kozák

Dairy Farming and Foraging Department 18

Head: Professor Lajos Fekete

Educational Department of Tropical Agriculture 19

Head: Assistant Professor Sándor Héjja

Farming and Plant Cultivation Department 20

Heads: Professor József Lörincz, Professor József Antal, Professor Sándor Sipos

Horticulture Department 21

Head: Professor László Cselőtei

Microbiology Department 22

Head: Assistant Professor Ferdinánd Buday

Pedology Department 23

Head: Professor Pál Stefanovits

Phytology and Plant Physiology Department 24

Head: Dr Albert Koltay

Plant Breeding Department 25

Head: Professor Andor Bálint

Plant Protection Department 26

Head: Dr István Petróczi

Statistics Department 27

Head: Assistant Professor Jenő Manczel

Water Supply and Melioration Department 28

Head: Professor Imre Petrasovits

Work Organization and Labour Safety Institute 29

Director: Professor László Udvari

WORK ORGANIZATION DEPARTMENT 30
Head: Professor László Udvari
Sections: Technology of Production, Dr András Szabó; Investigation of Labour Safety, Géza Fialka; Development of Production, Dr Pál Kiss

Zoobiology and Veterinary Hygiene Department 31

Head: Professor Béla Tóth

Zoology Department 32

Head: Professor Emil Nagy
Research Station: Biology of Wild Animals, Dr István Heltai

Agrártudományi Egyetem Keszthely* 33

[Keszthely Agricultural University]
Address: Deák Fereic utca 16, H-8361 Keszthely
Telephone: 12 330

KESZTHELY FACULTY OF AGRICULTURAL SCIENCES* 34

Head: Dr Z. Kardos
Activities: Soil science, botany and plant physiology, zoology, horticulture.

MOSONMAGYARÓVÁR FACULTY OF AGRICULTURAL SCIENCES* 35

Head: Dr J. Schmidt
Activities: Dairy farming, horticulture, rural economy, animal husbandry.

Agrobotanikai Központ   36

[Research Centre for Agricultural Botany]
Address: H-2766 Tápiószele
Telephone: Tápiószele 41
Telex: agbot h 226981
Parent body: National Institute for Agricultural Variety Testing, Budapest
Research Director: Dr J. Unk
Sections: Gene bank, Dr L. Holly; applied botany, J. Mesch; physiology, Zs. Horváth
Graduate research staff: 20
Annual expenditure: £51 000-500 000
Activities: Collection of land-races, ecotypes of cultivated field and vegetable crops and their wild relatives. Preservation and evaluation of crop plant collections; their conservation as genetic resources and distribution among breeders as raw material for breeding programmes.
Contract work: No
Publications: Fajtakisérletezés (Plant Variety Testing).

Állatorvostudományi Egyetem   37

[Veterinary Science University of Budapest]
Address: Landler Jenő Útca 2, Postafiók 2, H-1400 Budapest VII
Telephone: (01) 222-660
Telex: 22-44-39
Rector: Professor L. Várnagy
Pro-rector of Research: Professor F. Kovács
Pro-rector of Postgraduate Building and International Affairs: Professor F. Karsai
General Secretary: L.M. Kovács
Activities: Research activities conducted in the various departments are centred on basic research related to complex measures for the prevention and control of infectious and non-infectious diseases in farm animals.

ANATOMY AND HISTOLOGY DEPARTMENT   38

Head: Professor Gy. Fehér
Sections: Anatomy and embryology, Professor Gy. Fehér; histology, E. Tury

ANIMAL HUSBANDRY DEPARTMENT   39

Head: Professor J. Dohy

ANIMAL HYGIENE DEPARTMENT   40

Head: Professor F. Kovács

ANIMAL NUTRITION DEPARTMENT   41

Head: Professor J. Bokori

ANIMAL PHYSIOLOGY DEPARTMENT   42

Head: Professor Gy. Pethes
Sections: Physiology, Professor Gy. Pethes; biochemistry, F. Kutas

ASSOCIATED INSTITUTE   43

Állatégészségügyi Főiskolai Kar   44

[Higher Institute of Veterinary Medicine]
Address: Lenin Útca 15, H-6800 Hódmezővásárhely
Director: Professor F. Korell

BOTANY DEPARTMENT   45

Head: E. Haraszti

CHEMISTRY DEPARTMENT   46

Head: Professor K. Nádor
Sections: Chemistry, Professor K. Nádor; physics, P. Scheiber

EPIDEMIOLOGY AND MICROBIOLOGY DEPARTMENT   47

Head: Professor T. Szent-Iványi
Reader: S. Tuboly

FOOD HYGIENE DEPARTMENT   48

Head: G. Biró

INTERNAL MEDICINE DEPARTMENT AND CLINIC   49

Head: Professor Z. Horváth
Sections: Internal medicine, Professor Z. Horváth; pathophysiology, Professor F. Karsai

OBSTETRICS AND REPRODUCTION BIOLOGY DEPARTMENT AND CLINIC 50

Head: Professor J. Haraszti
Leader, Laboratory of Udder Diseases: Professor Gy. Horváth

OUTPATIENT CLINIC 51

Head: F. Felkai

PARASITOLOGY DEPARTMENT 52

Head: Professor T. Kobulej
Leader, Laboratory for Helminthology: Professor T. Kassai

PATHOLOGICAL ANATOMY DEPARTMENT 53

Head: Professor A. Kardeván
Leader, Laboratory of Electron Microscopy: P. Kapp

PHARMACOLOGY DEPARTMENT 54

Head: F. Simon

VETERINARY SURGERY DEPARTMENT 55

Head: Professor A.B. Kovács
Reader: L. Tamás

Allatorvostudományi Kutatóintézete 56

[Veterinary Medical Research Institute,]
Address: Hungária Korut 21, H-1581 Budapest XIV
Telephone: (01) 842-1 15
Parent body: Magyar Tudományos Akadémia
Director: Dr János Mészáros
Deputy Director: Dr L. Pesti
Departments: Bacteriology, Dr Gábor Semjén; Virology, Dr Adorján Bartha; Immunology, Parasitology, Dr Istvan Nemeth
Graduate research staff: 35
Annual expenditure: £51 000-500 000
Activities: Basic and applied research in bacteriology, immunology, virology and parasitology in the field of infectious diseases of mammals and birds (E. coli infections, swine dysentery, Aujeszky disease, Newcastle disease, etc).
Contract work: Yes

Atommag Kutató Intézete 57

– ATOMKI
[Nuclear Research Institute]
Address: 18c Bem tér, Postafiók 51, H-4001 Debrecen
Telephone: (052) 17-266
Telex: 72210 atomki h
Parent body: Magyar Tudományos Akadémia
Director: Professor D. Berényi
Sections: Nuclear Methods Department, Dr G. Somogyi; Technical Physics Department, Dr I. Berecz; Electrostatic Accelerators Department, Professor E. Koltay; Nuclear Electronics Department, Dr G. Mathé; Nuclear Atomic Physics Department, Professor D. Berényi; Cyclotron Department, Dr A. Valek; theoretical nuclear physics and computation group, Dr B. Gyarmati; interdisciplinary research group, Professor A. Szalay; nuclear spectroscopy group, Professor T. Fényes; atomic collisions research group, Dr B. Schlenk
Graduate research staff: 110
Activities: Fundamental and applied research work in the field of nuclear physics and atomic physics; producing the instrumental conditions of these research activities. Among the research tasks of the Institute the interdisciplinary research work and the widespread application of nuclear methods in other sciences and also in practice are involved.
Facilities: 5 MV Van de Graaff accelerator; 700 keV Cockcroft Walton accelerator; 300 keV neutron generator.
Contract work: Yes
Publications: *ATOMKI Közlemények* (ATOMKI Bulletin), quarterly, in Hungarian, English and Russian.

Autóipari Kutató Intézet 58

– Autókut
[Automotive Industry Research Institute]
Address: Csóka Útca 7-13, Postafiók 25, H-1502 Budapest XI
Telephone: (01) 666-968
Telex: 226587 atkut h
Research director: Dr István Ratskó
Sections: Engine, Dr Gyula Cser; main components, Sándor Szabó; vehicle, Lászlo Székely
Graduate research staff: 200
Annual expenditure: £501 000-2m
Activities: Engines: turbo, resonance and combined charging, non-steady flow, noxious emissions. Vehicle: studies on bus coach design, collision analysis of bus coaches. Power steering: all aspects. Suspension: especially heavy vehicles, buses. Noise-control: especially automotive related. Tribology: radioisotope analysis and diagnosis.
Facilities: Special and standard equipment to perform all tasks related to research in the automotive industry.
Contract work: Yes

Biológiai Kutatóintézete 59

[Biological Research Institute]
Address: Fürdőtelep 56, H-8237 Tihany
Telephone: (080) 44-038
Telex: 32427 mtabk
Parent body: Magyar Tudományos Akadémia
Director: Professor János Salánki
Graduate research staff: 24
Contract work: No

HYDROBIOLOGY DEPARTMENT 60

Head: J. Ponyi
Activities: The Lake Balaton establishment covers research in both the quantitative and qualitative conditions of the phytoplankton, the horizontal distribution of zooplankton, and questions concerning the feeding and growth of fishes.

ZOOLOGY DEPARTMENT 61

Head: Professor János Salánki
Activities: Comparative physiology of invertebrates. Studies are focused on research of neurohumoral regulating mechanisms on the level of cells, organs and organisms.

Botanikai Kutatóintézete 62

[Research Institute for Botany]
Address: H-2361 Vácrátót
Telephone: Vácrátót 2
Telex: 282201
Parent body: Magyar Tudományos Akadémia
Director: Professor A. Berczik
Departments: Plant Ecology, Professor G. Fekete, Dr M. Kovács, Dr I. Máthé; Botanic Garden, Dr T. Pócs
Graduate research staff: 30
Annual expenditure: £51 000-500 000
Activities: Ecology of urban ecosystems (Budapest), niche-ecology, biological degradation, mapping of Hungarian flora, flora of Cuba, tropical ecology. Plant chemistry (medicinal plants) genetic aspects of microevolution of higher plants. Hydrobiology of the Danube river.
Facilities: Botanic Garden of 25 hectares; plant ecological laboratory with phytotron; library and herbarium.
Contract work: Yes

HUNGARIAN DANUBE RESEARCH 63 STATION

Head: Professor A. Berczik

Budapesti Műszaki 64 Egyetem *

– BME
[Technical University of Budapest]
Address: Müegyetem Rakpart 3, H-1111 Budapest XI
Telephone: (01) 664-011
Telex: 22-5931 MUEGY H
Rector: Professor K. Polinszky
Pro-rector: Professor Imre Szabó
Publications: Periodica Polytechnica.

FACULTY OF CHEMICAL 65 ENGINEERING*

Dean: Professor L. Fodor

FACULTY OF CIVIL ENGINEERING* 66

Dean: Professor O. Halász

FACULTY OF ELECTRICAL 67 ENGINEERING*

Dean: Professor I. Vágó

FACULTY OF MECHANICAL 68 ENGINEERING*

Dean: Dr Gy. Strommer

FACULTY OF TRANSPORT 69 ENGINEERING*

Dean: Professor Z. Lévai

Csillagvizsgáló Intézete* 70

[Konkoly Observatory]
Address: Konkoly Thege Útca 13-17, H-1121 Budapest
Parent body: Magyar Tudományos Akadémia

Cukortermelési Kutató Intézet　　71

[Sugar Industry Research Institute]
Address: Vörös Hadsereg Útca 31, Postafiók 9, H-5001 Szolnok
Telephone: (056) 12 016
Telex: 23-425
General Manager: Dr Karoly Hangyál
Sections: Agricultural and biological research; sugar industrial research
Graduate research staff: 35
Annual expenditure: £501 000-2m
Activities: Agricultural and biological research: refinement of sugar beet; production of beet seed; protection of plant; agrotechnical research. Sugar industrial research: reducing sugar losses; improvement of heat engineering of sugar production; regulation of technological procedure of sugar production.
Contract work: No

Debreceni Agrártudományi Egyetem　　72

[Debrecen University of Agrarian Sciences]
Address: Böszörményi Útca 138, Postafiók 36, H-4015 Debrecen
Telephone: (052) 15-873
Telex: 72-211
Rector: Professor József Tóth

FACULTY OF AGRONOMY　　73
Dean: Professor Jakab Loch

Agricultural Economics Department　　74
Head: Professor Miklós Bodnár

Agricultural Mechanics Department　　75
Head: Professor Frigyes Varga

Agricultural Water Management Department　　76
Head: Professor Gusztáv Sziki

Animal Husbandry Department　　77
Head: Professor István Kiss

Animal Physiology and Hygiene Department　　78
Head: Professor Ferenc Munkácsi

Applied Farm Management Department　　79
Head: Professor Gyula Kurucz

Botany and Plant Physiology Department　　80
Head: Professor Menyhért Pethő

Chemistry Department　　81
Head: Professor Jakab Loch

Farm Management Department　　82
Head: Professor Béla Kádár

Horticulture Department　　83
Head: Professor Ferenc Pethő,

Mathematics-Physics Department　　84
Head: Professor János Nagy

Plant Production Department　　85
Head: Professor Erno Bocz

Plant Protection Department　　86
Head: Professor István Szepessy

Soil Science and Microbiology Department　　87
Head: Professor Balázs Helmeczi

Zoology Department　　88
Head: vacant

UNIVERSITY INSTITUTES　　89

Agricultural College Szarvas　　90
Address: Szabadság Útca 1-3, Szarvas

Agricultural Extension Institute 91

Director: Professor Joszef Ecsedi

Agricultural Technology Institute 92

Address: Tolbuchin Útca 2, H-5400 Mezotur
Telephone: Mezotur 70
Director: Dr István Patkós

AGRICULTURAL MACHINES 93
DEPARTMENT
Head: Dr András Dávid
Graduate research staff: 4

AGRICULTURE DEPARTMENT 94
Head: Dr Károly Varga
Graduate research staff: 3

FARMBUILDING MACHINERY 95
DEPARTMENT
Head: Dr István Patkós
Graduate research staff: 5

OVERHAUL DEPARTMENT 96
Head: Dr István Toth
Graduate research staff: 4

POWER MACHINES DEPARTMENT 97
Head: Dr Dezső Jaksits
Graduate research staff: 5

Soil Cultivation Research Institute 98

Address: H-5300 Karcag
Director: Dr János Borsos

Debreceni Orvostudományi 99
Egyetem *

[Debrecen University of Medicine]
Address: Nagyerdei Körút 98, H-4012 Debrecen
Telephone: (052) 11-600
Rector: Dr L. Karmazsin

Dohánykutató Intézet 100

[Tobacco Research Institute]
Address: Attila tér 3, H-4029 Debrecen
or: Postafiók 66, H-4002, Debrecen 2
Telephone: (052) 12-633
Telex: 072-341
Parent body: Ministry of Food and Agriculture
Director: Dr Laszló Nemethi

Scientific Deputy Director: Dr György Kandra
Sections: Tobacco breeding and cultivation, Dr Viktor Kővári; tobacco manufacturing, Dr Sándor Nemes
Graduate research staff: 36
Annual expenditure: Ft25m
Activities: Genetic and breeding work on tobacco: seed production and variety maintenance; development of cultivation and mechanization; plant protection; tobacco curing. Development of industrial tobacco manufacturing: development of products; qualification and standardization.
Facilities: Standard instruments and facilities for small plot and field experiments are used. Special measuring instruments (smoking machine, tensimeter, etc). Laboratory instruments (gas chromotograph, spectrophotometer, auto-analyser, etc). Pilot plant tobacco manufacturing line.
Contract work: No
Publications: Quarterly periodical.

Dunántuli Tudományos 101
Intézete

[West Hungarian Research Institute]
Address: Kulich Gy. Útca 22, Postafiók 199, H-7601 Pecs
Telephone: (072) 12-755
Telex: 12-475 DUTT H
Parent body: Magyar Tudományos Akadémia
Research director: Dr Ottó Bihari
Sections: Economy and law, Dr Béla Sas; geology, Dr István Fodor; history, Dr Lajos Ruzsas
Graduate research staff: 20
Annual expenditure: £51 000-500 000
Activities: Regional researches for the development of the country; agglomerations, their sociological-ecological features; protection of surroundings, ecological and legal questions. Sociology and ethnography of county Baranya, etc.
Contract work: Yes

Élelmiszeripari Főiskola, 102
Szeged

[Szeged School of Food Technology]
Address: Marx tér 7, H-6724 Szeged
Telephone: (062) 14-134
Telex: 82-445
Rector: Professor Elisabeth Gábor

MECHANICS AND AUTOMATION 103
INSTITUTE

Engineering Department 104

Head: Professor Ferenc Bráda
Activities: Different machines, mechanization of food industry.

Instruments and Regulation 105
Technology Department

Head: József Gyöngyösi
Activities: Different solutions of regulation and applied instruments in food technology.

Mathematics Department 106

Head: Professor József Kispéter
Activities: Applied mathematical solutions of different food operations, especially food drying.

SOCIAL STUDIES INSTITUTE 107

Economics Department 108

Head: Assistant Professor József Virág
Activities: New economic factors of different food technologies.

TECHNOLOGY INSTITUTE 109

Chemistry Department 110

Head: Professor Elisabeth Gábor
Activities: Antioxidant activity of different flavonoid compounds in fats and towards vitamin C; food analysis (vitamins, proteins, fats).

Microbiology Department 111

Head: Professor Károly Horváth
Activities: Methods of microbiological analysis of foods; hygiene of food technology.

Operations Department 112

Head: Professor Dr Herbert Sárosi
Activities: Different methods of food drying.

Technology Department 113

Head: Professor Tibor Huszka
Activities: Poultry industry; red pepper (milling and quality control); milk and milk products; meat and meat products; wheat quality and milling.

Eötvös Loránd 114
Tudományegyetem*

[Eötvös Loránd University]
Address: Egyetem tér 1-3, H-1364 Budapest
Telephone: (01) 18 0820

AFFILIATED INSTITUTE* 115

Biological Experiment Station* 116

Address: Javorka utca 14, 2131 Göd
Head: Dr J. Gergely

FACULTY OF SCIENCE* 117

Address: Muzeum Körut 6-8, Budapest
Head: Professor I. Kubovics
Activities: Astronomy, geology, mathematics, physics, chemistry.

Erdészeti és Faipari 118
Egyetem

[Forestry and Wood Sciences University]
Address: Bajcsy-Zsilinszky Útca 4, H-9400 Sopron
Telephone: (099) 11-100
Telex: 24-9126
Rector: Professor Sándor Kecskés

FACULTY OF FORESTRY 119

Dean: Professor Imre Herpay

Afforestation Department 120

Head: Professor János Gál
Activities: Problems of mending shelter forest belts; examination of willow clones; serviceable formation of the green belt around Lake Balaton. Utilization of marshy areas in forestry.

Botany Department 121

Head: Professor László Gencsi
Activities: Examination of methods and ecology of natural reafforestation, with special regard to oak woods; within the scope of deciduous tree breeding, the possibilities of autovegetative propagability of oak; examination of crown structure, types and physiological activities of Scotch fir; elucidation of the relationship between anatomical and technical characteristics.

Chemistry Department   122

Head: Professor István Szendrey
Activities: Application of radioisotopes in forestry and timber industry; technological examination of modern adhesives and surface treatment materials in timber industry by chemical methods.

Forest Utilization Department   123

Head: Professor Imre Herpay
Activities: Work organization and its reference to planning in timber utilization; profitable exploitation of secondary forestry products.

Forestry Economics Department   124

Head: Professor Elemér Somkuti
Activities: Problems of optimization of forestry and timber industry on national economy and enterprise levels; complex examination of forestry management; possibilities of application of electronic data processing in forestry and timber industry.

Forestry Management Department   125

Head: Professor Dr László Király
Activities: Exploration of the laws of growth and development of tree species and wood stands respectively, in order to construct devices of forest management by means of which the wood stand can be surveyed in detail and methodically transformed.

Forestry Mechanics Department   126

Head: Professor József Káldy
Activities: Construction of wood peeling machines for pulpwood from deciduous trees; machines of centrally manipulated and woodworking plants and their technology; examination of groups of machines used in thinning; comparative examination of stump drawing machines.

Forestry Protection Department   127

Head: Professor Zoltán Igmándy
Activities: Biology of the commoner fungi damaging the dominant tree species and prophylactic methods; biology of great butterflies damaging oak stands and prophylactic and preventive methods; preventive methods against fungi and insects damaging timber.

Forestry Surveying and Mapping   128
Department

Head: Professor László Bácsatyay
Activities: Possibilities of making nadir pictures with perpendicular axes, using registered nadir points; application of aerophotogrammetry to stand estimation with true colour negative materials; microphotogrammetric examination of targeting; determination of the 'load-curve' of a cableway through earth photogrammetry.

Forestry Transport Department   129

Head: Professor Sándor Kecskés
Activities: Complex examination of the economical character of conveyance of materials; application of soil stabilization in the making of forests; planning and building of roadway structures adequate to the forestry service.

Mathematics Department   130

Head: Professor Artur Moór
Activities: Spaces of recurrent curvature in differential geometry; relation between functional and differential equations; mathematical statistics applied to forestry and timber industry; application of nomography to timber estimation.

Silviculture Department   131

Head: Professor Antal Majer
Activities: Modern methods of cultivation of stands; comparative examination of wood stands with excellent structure and methods of their formation; cultivation problem of young woods at the age of thinning; timber yield and economics of certain types of forests.

Soil Science Department   132

Head: Professor György Pántos
Activities: Degree of efficiency of natural manure and artificial fertilizers in nursery gardens with poplars; interrelationship between higher plants and microorganisms living in their rooting zones; research section for soil microbiology.

Wildlife Management Department   133

Head: Professor Tamás Kőhalmy
Activities: Connection between wild animals and their environment, prevention and estimation of damages done by wild animals to forestry and agriculture.

FACULTY OF WOOD TECHNOLOGY   134

Address: Bajcsy Zsilinszky Útca 7, H-9400 Sopron
Dean: Dr Ferenc Béldi
Activities: Research into properties of wood and wood-based materials and structures.

Descriptive Geometry Department   135

Head: Professor Mihály Gunda
Activities: Distortions of angles and areas with central projections; geometry of transit surfaces of roads.

Electrical Physics Engineering Department   136

Head: Professor Ferenc Béldi
Activities: Electrophysical characteristics of the species of trees in Hungary; determination of the electrophysical, acoustic and thermologic characteristics of panels used as constructional elements.

Forestry Architecture Department   137

Head: Professor Mihály Kubinszky
Activities: Elaboration of data necessary for the principles of designing wood-working factories, reconciling the technological and architectural requirements; satisfactory ways of designing and manufacturing wooden structures with prefabricated walls and roofs.

Furniture Manufacturing Department   138

Head: Professor Lajos Czagány
Activities: Improvement of door and window structures; modernization of built-in furniture; application of new technology in using adhesives and surface treatment.

Mechanics Department   139

Head: Professor Ferenc Rónai
Activities: Mechanical tests of structures in timber industry (constructional joinery and building industry); shaping and designing glued trusses in the building industry; mechanical and vehicle-mechanical problems of motor traction in forestry; examination of optimum traction characteristics of wheeled traction engines in forestry.

Mechanics of Timber Industry Department   140

Head: Professor György Sitkei
Activities: Cutting of chip board and fibre board; effect of physical and mechanical qualities on resistance to cutting and on blunting of tools; application of the most up-to-date conveyors used in furniture manufacturing and constructional joinery; working of precipitation apparatus with mechanical separation in function of granulation of powder and chip; drying of artificial lacquer; noise and vibration tests of machines used in timber industry; application of pneumatic automation in timber industry technology.

Panel Manufacturing Department   141

Head: Professor József Cziráki
Activities: Testing the quality criteria of chip and chaff board, fibre board and plywood; reduction of water-absorption by adding waste materials and synthetic resins; effect of granulation on chip and chaff board; modernization and development of drying techniques and devices.

Timber Technology Department   142

Head: Professor Illés Kovács
Activities: Physical and mechanical qualities of timber; development of woodworking industry, with special emphasis on increase in yield.

Erdészeti Tudományos Intézet   143

[Forest Research Institute]
Address: Frankel Leó Útca 42-44, H-1023 Budapest
Telephone: (01) 150-624
Telex: 22 6914
Research director: Dr Béla Keresztesi
Secretary for Environmental Protection: Dr János Bogyai
Sections: Ecology, selection, breeding and afforestation, Dr Zoltán Járo; work organization, ergonomics and economics, Dr Tibor Szász; technical development, Dr László Szepesi; silviculture, forest protection and management, Dr Rezső Solymos
Graduate research staff: 70
Activities: Forestry: site conditions, tree-breeding, seed and seedling production, afforestation, tending of young stands, clearing, thinning, wood production, stand structure, protection, utilization, mechanization, economics, work organization, ergonomics, environmental protection.
Contract work: Yes
Publications: Erdészeti Kutatasok; Proceedings of the Húngarian Forest Research Institute, every five years; *Az Erdő*, (The Forest), monthly

Földrajztudományi Kutatóintézete* 144

[Geographical Research Institute]
Address: Népköztársaság Útca 62, H-1062 Budapest
Parent body: Magyar Tudományos Akadémia

Geodéziai és Geofizikai Kutatóintézete* 145

[Geodetical and Geophysical Research Institute]
Address: Muzeum Útca 6-8, H-9400 Sopron
Parent body: Magyar Tudományos Akadémia

Geokémiai Kutatólaboratóriuma 146

[Geochemical Research Laboratory]
Address: Budaörsi Útca 45, H-1112 Budapest
Telephone: (01) 851-781
Parent body: Magyar Tudományos Akadémia
Scientific Director: Dr György Pantó
Sections: Inorganic geochemistry, Dr Gy. Pantó; organic geochemistry, Dr E. Dudich; petrology, Dr P. Árkai; experimental petrology, Dr L. Pesty
Graduate research staff: 16
Activities: Investigation into the genetical relations of the sedimentary, igneous and metamorphic stages of rock evolution; methodological development in the fields of geochemistry and petrology as to the regularities of accumulation and distribution of elements in order to solve genetical problems of mineral resources; development of organic geochemical and geo-microbiological methods and their application to hydrocarbon prospecting; ore processing and environment protection; multilateral geochemical investigation of mineral raw materials in view of their complex utilization; modelling in laboratory of rock formation and transformation processes under high pt conditions.
Contract work: Yes

Gépipari és Automatizálási Műszaki Főiskola 147

– GAMF
[Mechanical Engineering and Automation College]
Address: Izsáki Útca 10, Postafiók 91, H-6001 Kecskemét
Telephone: (078) 115-27
Principal: Dr Sándor Kapitány

BASIC TECHNICAL DEPARTMENT 148
Head: János Silling

ELECTRICAL ENGINEERING AND CYBERNETICS DEPARTMENT 149
Head: Dr Clara Vágó

MACHINE INDUSTRY AUTOMATION DEPARTMENT 150
Head: Dr János Davidesz

MATHEMATICS AND PHYSICS DEPARTMENT 151
Head: Sándor Kalmár

MECHANICAL TECHNOLOGY DEPARTMENT 152
Head: Dr Sándor Kapitány

PLASTICS PROCESSING AND TECHNOLOGY DEPARTMENT 153
Head: Dr Lászlo Varga

PRODUCTION TECHNOLOGY DEPARTMENT 154
Head: Dr Benedek Molnár

Gyógynövény Kutató Intézet 155

[Medicinal Plants Research Institute]
Address: József Attila Útca 68, Postafiók 11, H-2011 Budakalász
Telephone: 688-042; 882-180
Telex: 224829
Director: Professor P. Tétényi
Research director: Dr J. Bernáth
Graduate research staff: 32
Annual expenditure: Ft40m
Activities: Research on the cultivation, propagation, utilization, biology, inheritance, improvement of medicinal plants, of plants furnishing volatile oils or drugs and as a consequence of this research the introduction of novel methods and procedures, the preparation of propagation material, the conservation of species and the production of novel species, chemical, analytical, pre-

parative and technological research on active agents of medicinal plants, qualification of medicinal plants, drugs and volatile oils.
Contract work: Yes
Publications: Herba Hungarica.

MICROPHYTOTRON UNIT   156

Activities: The study of natural biological rhythms, of the formation of active agents, of the metabolism and genetic properties of various species of medicinal plants in controlled conditions. This experimental work is complemented by a study of active agent production in vegetable tissue cultures.

Gyümölcs és   157
Disznövénytermesztési
Kutató Intézet

[Fruit Growing and Ornamentals Research Institute]
Address: Budafok 1.1775, Postafiók 108, Budapest
or: Park Útca 2, H-1223 Budapest
Telephone: (01) 385-787
Telex: 22-4790 gydki h
Director: Dr Béla Molnár
Sections: Fruit growing, Dr Péter Vigù; Ornamentals, Dr Zoltán Kováts
Graduate research staff: 67
Annual expenditure: £501 000-2m
Activities: Breeding, adaptation and maintenance of different fruit species and rootstocks - agrotechnology and plant protection. Problems of mechanization, storage and economics of fruit growing. Breeding, adaptation and maintenance of annual flowers, roses, and flower seed production.
Contract work: No

CEGLéD RESEARCH STATION   158

Address: Cegléd
Head: Ferenc Nyujtó

FERTöD RESEARCH STATION   159

Address: Fertöd
Head: Dr Kalman Szilágyi

UJFEHéRTÓ RESEARCH STATION   160

Address: Ujfehértó
Head: Dr László Harmat

Izotópintézete   161

[Isotopes Institute]
Address: Postafiók 77, H-1525 Budapest
Telephone: (01) 166-648
Telex: 22-5360 izot h
Parent body: Magyar Tudományos Akadémia
Director: Dr Árpád Veres
Sections: Isotope chemistry, Dr T. Lengyel; physical chemistry, Dr G. Földiák; physics, Dr T. Biró; isotope technology, Dr J. Hirling
Graduate research staff: 100
Annual expenditure: £501 000-2m
Activities: Radiochemical separation, ion exchange; synthesis of organic compounds labelled with radioisotopes for plant physiological studies, metabolism of herbicides and growth regulations; development of kits in vivo and in vitro for nuclear medicine; catalytic studies with isotopic tracers; basic and applied investigation of nuclear photoeffect gamma-activation; thermoluminescence and X-ray fluorescence methods; low activity measurements; use of radioactive tracers in industry, agriculture, medicine, food production and environmental research; physical and chemical dosimetry; radiation and photochemistry; research and pilot plant irradiation with a high activity cobalt facility; construction of irradiators; development of industrial nuclear gauges and control systems; health physics; computer techniques.
Contract work: Yes

József Attila   162
Tudományegyetem

[József Attila University]
Address: Dugonics Tere 13, H-6701 Szeged
Telephone: (062) 11-251
Rector: Professor Gy. Antalffy
Pro-rector, Scientific Affairs: Professor Gyula Krajkó
Pro-rector, Educational Affairs: Professor Gyula Kristó

FACULTY OF SCIENCE   163

Address: Aradi Vértanúk Tere L, H-6700 Szeged
Dean: Professor Károly Tandori
Pro-deans: Associate Professor Imre Hevesi, Associate Professor Irén Vincze, Associate Professor Sándor Gulyás

Anthropology Department   164

Address: Egyetem Útca 2, Szeged
Head: Professor Pál Lipták
Activities: Palaeoanthropology; new methods for the chemical analysis of skeletons.

Applied Chemistry Department   165

Address: Béke Epület, H-6700 Szeged
Head: Professor Pál Fejes
Activities: The connection between chemical structure and reactivity, especially concerning Darsens condensation; biochemical research in protein chemistry; the catalytic effect of pulverized metals is studied and equipment is designed for producing pulverized metals.

Biochemistry Department   166

Address: Középfasor 50-51, Szeged
Head: Professor László Boross
Head, Isotope Laboratory: Associate Professor Béla Matkovics

Biophysics Department   167

Address: Egyetem Útca 2, Szeged
Head: Professor László Szalay
Activities: Utilization of molecular luminescence in biological systems; migration of electron-generating energy between photosynthetic pigments.

Bolyai Institute   168

Address: Aradi Vértanúk Tere 1, H-6700 Szeged
President, Institute Council: Professor László Leindler
Secretary, Institute Council: Associate Professor Lajos Pintér
Departments: Algebra and number theory, Professor Béla Csákány; Analysis, Professor Béla Szökefalvi-Nagy; Computation, Professor László Lovász; Applications of analysis, Professor Károly Tandori; Theory of sets and mathematical logic, Professor László Leindler

Botany Department and Botanical   169
Gardens

Address: Egyetem Útca 2, Szeged
Head: Professor Pál Simoncsics

Climatology Department   170

Address: Egyetem Útca 2, Szeged
Head: Professor G. Péczely
Activities: Micro- and bioclimatology; agro-meteorological research relative to rice fields; meteorological observatory.

Colloid Chemistry Department   171

Address: Aradi Vértanúk Tér 1, H-6700 Szeged
Head: Professor Ferenc Szantó
Activities: Sedimentary and rheological properties of suspensions; research on organophilic clay minerals and pigments for the dye and synthetic materials industry and also applied to the oil industry; preparation and separation of bentonites and kaolins; industrial synthetic resins; molecular characteristics of humus components.

Comparative Physiology Department   172

Address: Középfasor 50-52, Szeged
Head: Professor Otto Fehér

Economic Geography Department   173

Address: Egyetem Útca 2, Szeged
Head: Professor Gyula Krajkó
Activities: Complex research of the southern Great Plain with a view to possibilities of industrial and agricultural development.

Experimental Physics Department   174

Address: Dóm Tér 9, H-6700 Szeged
Head: Professor István Ketskemétry
Activities: Luminescent and optical properties of solid inorganic systems; surface properties of semiconductors; physical investigation of lasers.

General and Physical Chemistry   175
Department

Address: Béke Epület, H-6700 Szeged
Head: Professor József Császár
Senior staff: Professor Ferenc Márta; Professor Miklós Bán
Activities: The Department includes an academic research group for gas reaction kinetics; thermal decomposition of aliphatic hydrocarbons and their inhibition in the gaseous phase, and the oxidation of organic compounds in the liquid phase when catalysed by metal ions. Elucidation of the decomposition mechanism of metal chlorites, chlorates and perchlorates; catalytic and electric properties of semiconducting oxides related to the catalytic effect of metal oxides on the gaseous phase decomposition of perchloric acid. Mo'ecular structure research to determine the chief characteristics of complex compounds of intermediate metal ions. Electrochemical Kinetic research

Genetics Department   176

Address: Középfasor 50-52, Szeged
Head: Associate Professor László Orosz

Geology Department   177

Address: Egyetem Útca 2, Szeged
Head: Associate Professor Béla Molnár
Activities: Sedimentology of carbonated and detritic rocks of the Pannonian Basin.

Inorganic and Analytical Chemistry   178
Department

Address: Dóm Tér 7, H-6700 Szeged
Head: Professor Péter Huhn
Activities: Chemistry of inorganic radicals and ions in unstable valency conditions, as well as the mechanism of induction and oxidation reduction reactions taking place through intermediates; analytical, electrochemical and coordinative chemical examinations; reactions occurring in the gaseous phase in order to clarify the mechanism of the thermal decomposition of simple hydrocarbons initiated with alkyl and alkoxy radicals.

Microbiology Department   179

Address: Középfasor 50-52, Szeged
Head: Associate Professor Lajos Ferenczy

Mineralogy, Geochemistry and   180
Petrography Department

Address: Egyetem Útca 2, Szeged
Head: Professor Gyula Grasselly
Activities: Geochemical examination of sedimentary rocks rich in organic matter; genetical and geochemical investigation of manganese ore deposits; stability and absorption properties of manganese minerals; petrological study of the metamagmatites of the Mátra Mountains and the connection between ore genesis and potassium metasomatism.

Organic Chemistry Department   181

Address: Dóm Tér 8, H-6700 Szeged
Head: Professor M. Bartok
Activities: Synthesis, pharmacological and chemical properties of amines and acylamines and their derivatives affecting the central and vegetative nervous systems; transformation of iols and aminoalcohols, stereochemical research and synthesis of compounds of isoquinoline and phenanthrolysidine structure; synthesis of biologically active peptides and tiopeptides; synthesis and sterochemical research of steroid modifications.

Physical Geography Department   182

Address: Egyetem Útca 2, Szeged
Head: Professor László Jakucs
Activities: Morphogenetic analysis of karstic processes and phenomena; climatogenetic regulation of karsts; physicogeographical conditions of the southern Great Plain.

Plant Physiology Department   183

Address: Egyetem Útca 2, Szeged
Head: Associate Professor E. Sirokmán

Radiochemistry Department   184

Address: Aradi Vértanúk Tere 1, H-6700 Szeged
Head: Professor Pál Fejes
Activities: Reactivity and exchange reactions of carbon compounds in the case of differently substituted cycloalkyl haloids; synthesis and effect mechanism of biologically active C14 labelled organic compounds; kinetic study of reactions of radicals in homogeneous gas phase; study of thermal decomposition of different hydrocarbons.

Theoretical Physics Department   185

Address: Aradi Vértanúk Tere 1, H-6700 Szeged
Head: Associate Professor Ferenc Gilde
Activities: Multibody problem of quantum mechanics; electron structure of complex molecules; development of the method of interaction of configurations by the use of spin operators.

Zoology Department   186

Address: Egyetem Útca 2, Szeged
Head: Professor László Móczár
Activities: Comparative anatomy, taxonomy and ecology; taxonomy, autoecology and systematics of insects, especially of hymenoptera; cytology of protozoa, their role in waters and soils; innervation of the organs of vertebrates, the structure of their peripheral nervous system; the central nervous system of insects.

Kandó Kálmán Villamosipari Műszaki Főiskola* 187

[Kandó Kálmán College of Electrical Engineering]
Address: Tavaszmző Útca 17, H-1084 Budapest VIII
Telephone: 341-908
Telex: 22-4897 kkvmf
Director: Professor Sándor Domonkos
Research leader: Professor István Bakos
Activities: Electrical generator research - research and development of synchronizing generators for operating technology of power stations, and for giving dynamic versions of power characteristics built in per unit system, considering the influence of stimulator systems.

Kertészeti Egyetem 188

[Horticulture University]
Address: Villanyi Útca 35-43, H-1118 Budapest
Telephone: (01) 850-666
Telex: UHORT 226011
Rector: Professor Imre Dimény

COLLEGE FACULTY OF HORTICULTURAL PRODUCTIONS 189

Director: Professor István Filius

FACULTY OF FOOD PROCESSING 190

Head: Professor Kálmán Gasztonyi

Chemistry Department 191

Head: Professor István Pais

Food Technology and Microbiology Department 192

Head: Dr Elemér Almási

Mathematics and Physics Department 193

Head: Professor Zoltán Szabó

Wine Department 194

Head: Professor Gyula Kádár

FACULTY OF PLANT PRODUCTION 195

Dean: Professor János Karai

Economics Institute 196

Director: Professor Imre Dimény

AGRARIAN ECONOMY DEPARTMENT 197
Head: Professor Anna Burger

AGRICULTURE DEPARTMENT 198
Head: Associate Professor Vencel Balla

COMPUTING DEPARTMENT 199
Head: Associate Professor Otto Pozsgay

ECONOMICS DEPARTMENT 200
Head: Professor Imre Dimény

FOOD PROCESSING ORGANIZATION DEPARTMENT GROUP 201
Head: Associate Professor Pál Szilágyi

Vegetable Crops Institute 202

Director: Professor András Somos

BOTANY DEPARTMENT 203
Head: Professor András Terpó

FRUIT GROWING DEPARTMENT 204
Head: Professor Ferenc Gyúró

GARDEN ARCHITECTURE DEPARTMENT 205
Head: Associate Professor László Csóti

NURSERY DEPARTMENT 206
Head: Professor Andre Proboeskai

ORNAMENTAL PLANTS AND DENDROLOGY DEPARTMENT 207
Head: Professor Béla Nagy

PLANT DRUGS DEPARTMENT 208
Head: Associate Professor László Hornok

PLANT GENETICS AND BREEDING DEPARTMENT 209
Head: Professor Istvan Tamássy

PLANT PROTECTION DEPARTMENT 210
Head: Professor Sándro Bognár

SOIL SCIENCE DEPARTMENT 211
Head: Professor Lászlo Hargitai

TECHNICS DEPARTMENT 212
Head: Professor János Karai

VEGETABLE GROWING DEPARTMENT 213
Head: Professor András Somos

VITICULTURE DEPARTMENT 214
Head: Professor Pál Kozma

POSTGRADUATE TRAINING DEPARTMENT 215
Head: Professor Péter Sárközy

Kisérleti Orvostudományyi Kutatóintézete* 216

[Experimental Medicine Research Institute]
Address: Szigony Útca 43, H-1083 Budapest
Parent body: Magyar Tudományos Akadémia

Kossuth Lajos Tudományegyetem* 217

[Kossuth Lajos University]
Address: H-4010 Debrecen
Telephone: (052) 16 666

FACULTY OF SCIENCE* 218
Head: Dr P. Nánási

Közponi Élelmiszeripari Kutató Intézet 219

– KEKI
[Central Food Research Institute]
Address: Herman Ottó Útca 15, H-1525 Budapest
Telephone: (01) 158-674
Telex: OSZBOKI 224 709
Director: Professor K. Vas
Deputy Director: Professor J. Farkas
Managing Director: Dr I. Orbányi
Graduate research staff: 60
Annual expenditure: £51 000-500 000
Activities: Research on topics of interest to the food industry; development of future technologies of food production by basic and applied research. The Institute concentrates on the following research topics: economical and substantial development of food supplies by new technologies; utilization of available and potential basic materials in the development of a wide range of foodstuffs, complying with the demands of modern nutrition; preservation of existing food supplies for the longest possible period with minimum loss; development of new procedures for feed protein production on an industrial scale.
Contract work: Yes
Publications: Acta Alimentaria, quarterly.

FOOD SCIENCE DIVISION 220
Head: Dr A. Halász
Sections: Analytical chemistry, M. Petró-Turza; enzymology, Dr L. Vámos-Vigyázo; microbiology, Dr I. Kiss; biochemistry, Dr A. Halász; biology, Dr J. Barna

FOOD TECHNOLOGY DIVISION 221
Head: Professor Gy. Kárpáti
Sections: Bioengineering, Dr K. Zetelaki-Horváth; measuring and control engineering, Dr K. Kaffka; process development, Dr M. Demeczky; product development, Professor Gy. Kárpáti

Központi Fizikai Kutató Intézete 222

– KFKI
[Physics Central Research Institute]
Address: 114 Postafiók 49, H-1525 Budapest
Telephone: (01) 166-547
Telex: KFKI H 224722
Parent body: Magyar Tudományos Akadémia
Director in Chief: Ferenc Szabó
Deputy Director in Chief: Dezső Kiss
Graduate research staff: 448
Annual expenditure: Ft330m
Contract work: No

ATOMIC ENERGY RESEARCH INSTITUTE 223
Director: Z. Gyimesi
Activities: Experimental equipment - research reactor; reactor physics; reactor thermohydraulics; reactor electronics; health physics; chemical analysis; radiation and electron chemistry.

COMPUTING CENTRE   224

Head: Gy. Lőcs
Activities: Computing technical tasks for research
requirements; research into computer applications;
research into system programming.

DEVELOPMENT ENGINEERING   225

Head: F. Szlávik
Activities: Development of research apparatus;
development of measurement methods; production of
instruments, individual and small series.

MEASUREMENT AND COMPUTING   226
TECHNIQUES RESEARCH INSTITUTE

Director: F. Törő
Activities: Research and development of hardware
and software for small computer systems; practical
applications of the above results.

PARTICLE AND NUCLEAR PHYSICS   227
RESEARCH INSTITUTE

Director: K. Szegő
Activities: Theory of relativity and astrophysics;
particle physics - theory and experiment; cosmic ray
and space research; nuclear reactions; controlled
thermonuclear reactions.

SOLID-STATE RESEARCH INSTITUTE   228

Director: E. Krén
Activities: Theoretical solid-state physics; magnetism;
metal physics; partially ordered systems, amorphous
semiconductors, organic conductors and
semiconductors, liquid crystals; investigation of solids
by using neutrons and photons; laser physics and
applications; solid-state technology - research and
development; micro circuit technology; magnetic
bubble memory research; optical memory research.

Központi Kémiai Kutató   229
Intézete

[Central Chemistry Research Institute]
Address: Pusztaszeri Útca 59-67, H-1025 Budapest
Telephone: (01) 353-735
Telex: 226686 kemia h
Parent body: Magyar Tudományos Akadémia
General Director: Professor Ferenc Márta
Deputy General Director: Professor János Holló
Sections: Organic and bioorganic chemistry, Professor

László Ötvös; physical chemistry, Professor Sándor
Lengyel
Graduate research staff: 220
Annual expenditure: Ft140m
Activities: Study of biologically active substances;
synthesis of organic compounds; bioorganic investigations; investigation of pesticides; physical chemistry -
heterogeneous catalysis, homogeneous catalysis,
macromolecular chemistry, kinetics of elementary reactions; structural and theoretical investigations, spectroscopy and diffraction, quantum chemistry.
Contract work: Yes

Kristályfizikai   230
Kutatólaboratórium

[Crystal Physics Research Laboratory]
Address: Budaörsi Útca 45, H-1112 Budapest
Telephone: (01) 851-784
Parent body: Magyar Tudományos Akadémia
Research director: Dr Rudolf Voszka
Groups: Crystal technology, Dr István Földvári; Crys-
tal physics, Dr József Janszky
Graduate research staff: 16
Annual expenditure: £51 000-500 000
Activities: Growth and study of optical crystals, eg of
alkali halides; lithium niobate, tellur dioxide, bismuth
germanate, bismuth silicate, etc. Investigation of growth
and radiation defects, basic and applied research.
Contract work: Yes.

Lumineszcencia és   231
Félvezető Kutatócsoport

[Luminescence and Semiconductors Research
Group]
Address: Dóm tér 9, H-6720 Szeged
Telephone: (062) 11-154
Parent body: Magyar Tudományos Akadémia
Research director: Professor István Ketskeméty
Graduate research staff: 12
Activities: Molecular luminescence; dye lasers; optical
properties of vanadium pentoxide.
Contract work: Yes

Magyar Állami Eötvös   232
Loránd Geofizikai Intézet*

[Loránd Eötvös Hungarian Geophysical Institute]
Address: Columbus Útca 17-23, H-1145 Budapest XIV

GEOFIZIKAI OBSZERVATORIUM 233

[Geophysical Observatory, Tihany]
Address: Kossuth Útca 81-83, H-8237 Tihany
Telephone: (080) 44-029
Telex: 32-294
Director: Dr Péter Tóth
Annual expenditure: £10 000-50 000
Activities: Earth magnetism; palaeomagnetism; earth tides; space research; rock physics.
Contract work: Yes
Publications: Annual and monthly reports.

Magyar Állami Földtani 234 Intézet

– MÁFI
[Hungarian Geological Institute]
Address: Népstadion Útca 14, Postafiók 106, H-1442 Budapest
Telephone: (01) 836-912
Telex: H 225 200
Director: Dr Géza Hámor
Deputy Director: Dr E. Dudich
Departments: Geological Mapping, E. Nagy; Laboratories, I. Csalagovits; Documentation, I. Nagy; Mineral Resources Prognostics, L. Szebényi; Regional Geological Services, Gy. Zsilák
Graduate research staff: 205
Activities: The Institute performs the geological surveying of Hungary with all material testing involved; gathers and stocks in the Central Archives all geological documentation of the country; takes part in the reconnaissance survey, estimation and calculation of mineral resources.
Contract work: Yes
Publications: Annual reports.

Magyar Ásványolaj és 235 Földgáz Kisérleti Intézet

– MÁFKI
[Hungarian Oil and Gas Research Institute]
Address: József Attila Útca 34, H-8200 Veszprém
Telephone: (080) 12-440
Telex: 32288
Director: Dr Rezső Csikós
Departments: Bench Test, Dr A. Zalai; Physical Chemistry, Dr Z. Nagy; Technology for Mineral Oil, Dr A. Fehervári; Organic Chemistry, Dr J. Bathory; Analytical Chemistry, Dr E. Kerenyi; Olefin Chemistry, L. Farkas; System Engineering, F. Simon
Graduate research staff: 120

Activities: Research, development, advisory, and documentation and information services are undertaken on behalf of the petroleum, natural gas and petrochemical industries. Research activities include: solvent technology of lubricating oils; paraffin and asphalt technology; production of electrical insulating liquids and materials; quality development of motor fuels, motor oils, and transmission oils; development of new additives; production of plastifiers; production of synthetic detergents; production of ethylene; research on cracking and pyrolysis; olefin chemistry; processing of pyrolysis heavy residues; production of plastics and basic materials for artificial resins; production of normal hydrocarbons; production of intermedia organic compounds; production of special anticorrosion insulating systems; research on catalysts; rheological research; structure determination of complex products; mathematical modelling and system engineering of units, processes and plants in the chemical and petroleum industries; protection of environment. Manufacturing activities include: special gasolines; narrow cut petroleum products; liquid normal hydrocarbons, pure hydrocarbon gases; catalysts; special heat resisting lubricating greases; special vaselines and paraffins; macro- and microcrystalline paraffins and kerosenes; high efficiency rectification units and packing elements; and isotope analytic instruments for intermittent and continuous operation.
Contract work: Yes

Magyar Népköztársaság 236 Meteorológiai Szolgálata

[Meteorological Service of the Hungarian People's Republic]
Address: Postafiók 38, H-1525 Budapest 114
Telephone: (01) 353-500
Telex: 22-6527
President: Professor R. Czelnai
Activities: Basic and applied research in meteorology; weather modification (hail suppression).

KÖZPONTI CÉGKÖRFIZIKAI INTÉZET 237

[Central Institute for Atmospheric Physics]
Address: Péterhalmi Útca 1, H-1675 Budapest XVIII
Director: Dr E. Mészávos
Activities: Cloud physics; atmospheric chemistry; use of satellite information; radiation; ozone; ionosphere; heat and water balance; irrigation problems.

KÖZPONTI ELÖREJELZÖ INTÉZET   238

[Central Forecasting Institute]
Address: Tatabánya tér 15-18, H-1675 Budapest XVIII
Director: Dr Z. Varga-Haszonits
Activities: Short and medium range, and agrometeorological forecasting research.

KÖZPONTI METEOROLÓGIAI   239
INTÉZET

[Central Meteorological Institute]
Address: Kitaibel Pál Útca 1, H-1024 Budapest II
Director: Dr P. Ambrózy
Activities: Stochastic and dynamic modelling: hydrometeorological research; long range forecasting research.

Magyar Szénhidrogénipari   240
Kutató-Fejlesztö Intézet

[Hungarian Hydrocarbon Institute]
Address: Postafiók 32, H-2443 Százhalombatta
Telephone: 260-674
Telex: 22-6636
Director: Dr S. Doleschall
Graduate research staff: 250
Activities: Research and development of hydrocarbon production, storage and transportation; petroleum processing, petrochemistry, geological researches and drilling; quality control, technical and technological application of hydrocarbon products; air and water conservation; corrosion problems; computer techniques; natural and town gas supply; combustion techniques.
Contract work: Yes

Magyar Tudományos   241
Akadémia

– MTA
[Hungarian Academy of Sciences]
Address: Roosevelt tér 9, Postafiók 6, H-1361 Budapest
Telephone: (01) 113-400
President: János Szentágothai
See separate entry for:
Allatorvostudományi Kutatóintézete
Atommag Kutató Intézete
Biokémiai Intézet
Biofizikai Intézet
Biologiai Kutatóintézete
Botanikai Kutatóintézete
Csillagvizsgáló Intézete
Dunántuli Tudományos Intézete

Enzimológiai Intézet
Genetikai Intézet
Földrajztudományi Kutatóintézete
Geodéziai és Geofizikai Kutatóintézete
Geokémiai Kutatólaboratóriuma
Izotópintézete
Kisérleti Orvostudományi Kutatóintézete
Központi Fizikai Kutató Intézete
Központi Kémiai Kutató Intézete
Kristályfizikai Kutatólaboratórium
Luminészcencia és Felvezető Kutatócsoport
Matematikai Kutatóintézete
Mezőgazdasági Kutatóintézete
Mikrobiológiai Kutatócsoportja
Műszaki Fizikai Kutató Intézete
Műszaki Kémiai Kutató Intézet
Napfizikai Obszervatóriuma
Növényélettani Intézet
Olajbányászati Kutatólaboratóriuma
Számitástechnikai és Automatizálási Kutató Intézete
Szeged Biologiai Központja
Talajtani és Agrokémiai Kutatóintézete.

Matematikai   242
Kutatóintézete*

[Mathematical Research Institute]
Address: Reáltanoda Útca 13-15, H-1529 Budapest
Parent body: Magyar Tudományos Akadémia

Mecseki Szénbányák   243
Kutatási Osztálya

[Mecsek Coal Mines Research Department]
Address: Postafiók 104, H-7601 Pécs
Telephone: (072) 11-153
Telex: 012242
Research director: Dr Mihály Bánhegyi
Sections: Prevention of gas hazards, Jozsef Nyers; mining geophysics, Jozsef Verbőci; rock mechanics, János Bakai; protection against air pollution, Dr István Gyurkó; technical prevention of coal dust, Dr Henrik Vékény; prevention of explosion and fire hazards, Andor Gombo; medical biology, Dr Viktor Seres
Graduate research staff: 25
Annual expenditure: £225 000
Activities: Prevention of gas outbursts, fire and explosion hazards, pneumoconiosis and pollution of the environment in the mining area.
Contract work: Yes
Publications: Yearbook.

Mezőgazdasági Kutatóintézete 244

[Agricultural Research Institute]
Address: Postafiók 19, 2462 Martonvásár
Telephone: Martonvásár 119
Telex: H-224008
Parent body: Magyar Tudományos Akadémia
Research director: Dr Béla Győrffy
Sections: Plant breeding, Dr István Kovács; crop production, Dr Béla Győrffy; phytotron research, Dr Sándor Rajki; biochemistry and plant physiology, Dr László Gáspár
Graduate research staff: 33
Activities: Most of the research conducted by the Institute and its experimental farm is connected with Hungary's two main agricultural plants, wheat and maize. This research represents the whole spectrum of basic and applied research, from genetics and physiology to plant breeding and seed production and the development of farming techniques for the successful use of selected seed.
Contract work: No
Publications: Acta Agronomica Academiae Scientiarum Hungaricae.

Mikrobiológiai Kutatócsoportja 245

[Microbiological Research Group]
Address: Pihenő Útca 1, H-1529 Budapest
Telephone: (01) 365-527
Parent body: Magyar Tudományos Akadémia
Director: Professor István Földes
Sections: Virology, Dr Margarita Tálas; immunology, Dr István Jókay; chemistry, Dr Gyula Nagy; biochemistry, Pál Somogyi; experimental oncology, Professor István Földes
Graduate research staff: 14
Annual expenditure: Ft5m
Activities: Experimental oncology with special regard to virus tumours; basic immunology; interferon research; molecular biology of viruses and phages.
Contract work: Yes

Műszaki Fizikai Kutató Intézet 246

– MFKI
[Technical Physics Research Institute]
Address: Ujpest L, Postafiók 76, H-1325 Budapest
Telephone: (01) 692-100

Telex: 225197 mohps h
Parent body: Magyar Tudományos Akadémia
Director: Elemér Nagy
Deputy Director: Dr I.C. Szép
Divisions: Semiconductor research, Dr E. Lendvay; Metal research, Dr L. Bartha; Structure research, Dr L. Zsoldos; Optics and electronics, Dr J. Schanda
Graduate research staff: 116
Annual expenditure: £50 000-100 000
Activities: Basic and applied research in the field of refractory metals and alloys (tungsten, molybdenum, iron), powder metallurgy, semiconductor materials and device structures, structural properties of solids, thin film physics, measurement of light and radiation, photometry of light sources, including light emitting diodes.
Facilities: X-ray diffraction, transmission and scanning electron microscopy, thermal analysis, electron and optical spectroscopy; cryogenic laboratory, workshops for building mechanical and electronic equipment to support the research activities. Special purpose original measuring equipment (eg gonio-photometers, thermogravimetric microbalance, apparatus for deep level transient spectroscopy, automatic flatness control equipment for rolled steel) is also built and supplied on order.
Contract work: Yes.
Publications: MFKI Yearbook, biannual in English.

Műszaki Kémiai Kutató Intézet 247

– MÜKKI
[Research Institute for Technical Chemistry]
Address: Schönherz Z. Utca 2, Postafiók 125, H-8201 Veszprém
Telephone: (080) 13-150
Telex: 32311
Parent body: Magyar Tudományos Akadémia
Director: Dr Tibor Blickle
Sections: Unit operation, A. Ujhidy; chemical procedures, Z. Ormós; chemical equipment, J. Fülöp; fluid mechanics, J. Gyenis; modelling and systemology, Dr T. Blickle; holography laboratory, J. Timkó
Graduate research staff: 91
Annual expenditure: £51 000-500 000
Activities: Research programme: industrial chemical operation systems and their optimization; operation research of medicine, insecticide, and intermediary production; examination of reductive chlorination of metal oxides.
Contract work: Yes
Publications: Kutatási Eredmények Research Results 1971-80/Kutatási Célkitüzések Research Programme 1981-85, in English.

Munkavédelmi Tudományos Kutató Intézet   248

[Labour Safety Scientific Research Institute]
Address: Postafiók 7, H-1281 Budapest
Telephone: (01) 164-440
Telex: 227079
Parent body: Hungarian Trade Unions Council
Scientific Director: Lajos Hirsch
Graduate research staff: 100
Annual expenditure: Ft16m
Activities: Research in: devices, systems, equipment; their testing and propagation; human macro- and microenvironment to control and prevent harmful effects; developing personal protective equipment; investigation and analysis of accident causes; establishing healthy, safe and pleasant working conditions; modernizing means of labour safety propaganda, information and education. Theoretical and applied research for explosion and fire prevention.
Contract work: Yes
Publications: Munkavédelem (Labour Safety); *Labour Safety Publications.*

Napfizikai Obszervatóriuma   249

[Heliophysical Observatory]
Address: Postafiók 30, H-4010 Debrecen
Telephone: (052) 11-015
Telex: 72517 deobs h
Parent body: Magyar Tudományos Akadémia
Director: Professor L. Dezső
Graduate research staff: 12
Activities: Solar activity studies, mainly sunspots, prominences and flares. The Observatory is engaged in some cooperative international research programmes: International Astronomical Union, Special Committee on Solar Terrestial Physics, Committee on Space Research, Council on International Cooperation in Research and uses of Outer Space.
Contract work: No
Publications: Publications of Debrecen Heliophysical Observatory.

Nehézipari Müsaki Egyetem   250

[Technical University of Heavy Industry]
Address: 3515 Miskolc-Egyetemváros
Telephone: 13-691
Telex: 62 223
Rector: Professor Dr T. Czibere
Annual expenditure: Ft50m

FACULTY OF MECHANICAL ENGINEERING   251

Dean: Professor Dr I. Lévai

Analysis Department   252

Head: Professor Dr E. Vincze

Chemical Machinery Department   253

Head: Dr G. Fejes
Activities: Investigations into basic chemical processes; chemical system safety.

Computer Engineering Department   254

Head: Professor Dr E. Klafszky

Descriptive Geometry Department   255

Head: Professor Dr I. Drahos
Activities: Geometry of machine construction; processing geometry of machine components.

Electrical Engineering Department   256

Head: Professor Dr I. Szentirmai

Fluid and Thermal Engineering Department   257

Head: Professor Dr T. Czibere
Activities: Research in the following areas: flows in bladed area of fluid machinery; development of fluid measuring equipment and calibration methods; heat transfer processes in thermal machinery and plant; working processes in piston engines.

Industrial Economics Department   258

Head: Professor Dr J. Susánsky

Machine Building Technology Department   259

Head: Professor Dr L. Gribovszki
Activities: Research in the following areas: precision working of machine tools; effect of end processing on surface quality and durability; computer application in technological planning and design; product quality control.

Machine Elements Department   260

Head: Professor Dr Z. Terplán
Activities: Research into mechanical gear units (gear wheels, planetary gearing, worm drive, wave gear, couplings, gaskets).

Machine Tools Design Department   261

Head: Professor Dr J. Tajnaföi
Activities: Construction development of NC machines; planning of CNC systems; theoretical and experimental investigations of machine components such as drives, positioning systems, electronic kinematic control links.

Mechanical Technology Department   262

Head: Professor Dr P. Romvári
Activities: Areas of research include: fracture mechanics; weldability of materials; high-efficiency welding and thermal cutting methods; welding of rails; friction welding; plastic forming procedures; modern heat treatment, for example gas nitriding.

Mechanics Department   263

Head: Professor Dr I. Kozák
Activities: Analysis of stress and strain of structures using the distortion finite-element technique; kinematic, dynamic and vibration mathematical models; theory and methods of elasticity; photoelasticity.

Physics Department   264

Head: Professor Dr J. Szabó
Activities: Plasma physics; measurement of magnetic permeability of materials.

Transport Equipment Department   265

Head: Professor Dr I. Lévai

FACULTY OF METALLURGICAL ENGINEERING   266

Dean: Professor Dr B. Vossatz

Automation Department   267

Head: Professor Dr F. Sulcz
Activities: Research into regulation systems of arc-furnaces and regulation of low pressure gas networks.

Ferrous Metallurgy Department   268

Head: Professor Dr S. Simon
Activities: Research in the following areas: metallurgical problems of sinters, raw iron, and steel production; metallurgical use of rare earths; continuous casting; production of ferroalloys; metallurgical use of radioactive isotopes.

Foundry Technology Department   269

Head: Professor Dr Gy. Nándori
Activities: Topics of research include: forms of various consistencies exposed to high temperatures; volume changes of alloys, especially cast-iron, during crystallization; alloys with rare earths in cast-iron; crystallization properties of nodular cast-iron.

Fuel Engineering Department   270

Head: Dr Farkas

General and Physical Chemistry Department   271

Head: Professor Dr E. Berecz

Hot Metal Working and Plastic Deformation Department   272

Head: Professor Dr E. Kiss

Inorganic and Analytical Chemistry Department   273

Head: Professor Dr B. Vorsatz
Activities: Research in the following areas: production and use of rare earths; origin of nonmetallic inclusion agents in pure aluminium and its alloys.

Non-ferrous Metallurgy Department   274

Head: Professor Dr Z. Horváth

Physical Metallurgy Department   275

Head: Professor Dr M. Káldor

FACULTY OF MINING ENGINEERING   276

Dean: Professor Dr E. Takács

Geodesy and Mine Surveying Department   277

Head: Dr G. Kolozsvári
Activities: Surveying of high precision of mining and other industrial plant; new surveying methods and instruments; survey guidelines; rock movement; mine damage; mining layout.

Geology and Mineral Deposits Department   278

Head: Dr Z. Némedi Varga

Geophysics Department   279

Head: Professor Dr J. Csókás
Activities: Introduction and further development of telluric and magnetotelluric methods in Hungary; geo-electrical mining method; archaeo-geophysics.

Mineral Processing Department   280

Head: Professor Dr I. Tarján
Activities: Research in the following areas: modern mining of minerals in Hungary; development of new plant for mineral processing; filters for turbid and polluted liquids; models and computer-process control of separation and homogenization processes; hydraulic and pneumatic conveyance; production and use of compressed air; compressor plant for the gas industry; air conditioning for mines.

Mineralogy and Petrography Department   281

Head: Dr T. Pojják
Activities: Areas of research include: mineral-genetic processes; mineral analysis of Redox-processes; theoretical investigations and practical application of water/mineral interaction, development of X-ray analysis methods with respect to structural properties of X-ray amorphous materials.

Mining Exploitation Department   282

Head: Professor Dr J. Zambó

Mining Machines Department   283

Head: Professor Dr J. Bocsáncy
Activities: Subjects of research include: construction and operation of mining machines; flexible traction components (conveyer belts, wire ropes); reliability of production systems.

Oil Production Department   284

Head: Professor Dr A.P. Szilas
Activities: Research in the following areas: deep drilling safety; oil yield enhancement; rock structure; underground gas deposits; fluid extraction with probes; transport of non-Newtonian oils; flow in town and long-distance gas pipeline networks; geothermal energy recovery.

UNIVERSITY ASSOCIATED INSTITUTES   285

Higher Institute of Digital Control for Chemical Engineering   286

Address: Lenin utca 1, 3701 Kazincbarcika
Director: Professor M. Cservenka

Higher Institute of Metallurgical Technology   287

Address: Táncsics M. utca 1, 2401 Dunanjvásos
Director: Professor Dr L. Molnár

Nehézvegyipari Kutató Intézet   288

[Heavy Chemical Industries Research Institute]
Address: Wartha Vince Útca 1, H-8200 Vesprém
Telephone: 12-480
Director: Dr András Szántó
Scientific Deputy Director, Dr M. Nadasy
Activities: Inorganic and agricultural chemistry: fertilizers, plant protecting materials; instrumentation control; corrosion and its prevention; air pollution; radioisotopes.

Növényolaj és Mososzeripari Kutató Intezét*   289

[Institute for the Vegetable Oil and Detergent Industry]
Address: Maglódi utca, H-1106 Budapest

Növényvédelmi és Agrokémiai Központ 290

[Plant Protection and Agrochemistry Centre]
Address: Budaörsti Útca 141-145, Postafiók 127, H-1502 Budapest
Telephone: (01) 851-17
Telex: 226393
Parent body: Ministry of Agriculture and Food, Plant Protection and Agrochemistry Department
General Director: Dr Imre Kovács
Activities: The tasks of the Centre are to organize, develop and manage the plant protection and agrochemistry activities of farms and to test the chemicals in use. The Centre has an administrative authority to supervise pest and/or soil management under statutory rules. This requires administrative extension and various other operational activities which are carried out as state measures or arrangements; however, specific problems are solved on farm orders, too. The most important duties are performed either directly by the Centre itself or by its special laboratories on a national or on a regional level. On the other hand, local management, extension, forecasting, education activities, quarantine and laboratory services are carried out by plant protection and agrochemistry stations.
Main spheres of activitity of the Centre are: state inspection on the biological efficacy of pesticides and fertilizers for registration purposes; quality testing on pesticides and fertilizers; supervision of storing and use of registered pesticides in farms; inspection of storing, handling and use of fertilizers, manures, and liquid manures in farms; extension on pest control problems to state/cooperative farms and private growers; forecasting the expected density distributions and the correct timing of control of pests and diseases at regional and/or county level; testing soil nutrient levels of farm fields for reasonable soil management purposes; extension on plant nutrition based on laboratory tests; control of soil melioration activities and preparing opinions on related schedules; preparing opinion on projects for improving physical and chemical soil properties; elaborating and improving complex pest management and soil nutrient replacement technologies.
Contract work: No

AGROCHEMISTRY DIVISION 291

Director: Margit Fórizs
Departments: Soil management, Dr István Buzás; Soil science, Ferenc Jassó; Data processing and extension, Attila Fekete; Supervising soil melioration projects, Dr Jenő Horváth

CHEMISTRY DIVISION 292

Head: Sándor Gaál
Departments: Analytical, Árpád Ambrus; Metabolite analysis, Dr Katalin Görög; Quality testing on pesticides and fertilizers, János Karlinger

ENGINEERING DIVISION 293

Head: László Trefán
Department: Technical development, Károly Márfi

PLANT PROTECTION DIVISION 294

Director: Imre Koncz
Departments: Phytopathology, István Kajati; Entomology, Imre Seprős; Testing pesticides and fertilizers, György Kis; Forecasting, Dr Pál Benedek; Plant protection technology, Sándor Balogh

SUPERVISION AND ORGANIZATION DIVISION 295

Head: Mihály Ötvös
Departments: Quarantine, István Fésüs; Supervision and administration, László Szepesvári; Information and documentation, Marié Somi Kovács; International affairs, Péter Zsidó

Plant Protection and Agrochemistry Station, County Bács 296

Address: Postafiók 16, H-6090 Kunszentmiklós
Telephone: Kunszentmiklós 16
Telex: 026-382 noeval h
Head: Béla Balog

Plant Protection and Agrochemistry Station, County Barahya 297

Address: Postafiók 13, H-7615 Pécs 15
Telephone: (072) 10-801; 10-299; 10-793; 10-940; 10-752
Telex: 012-417 danoev h
Head: Dr Károly Szűcs

BACTERIOLOGY LABORATORY 298
Head: Erzsébet László

Plant Protection and Agrochemistry Station, County Békés 299

Address: Postafiók 28, H-5602 Békéscsaba
Telephone: Békéscsaba 11-637; 11-168; 12-056
Telex: 083-284 noev h
Head: Dr Gábor Kovács

**Plant Protection and Agrochemistry 300
Station, County Borsod**

Address: Postafiók 197, H-3501 Miskolc
Telephone: (046) 15-296; 15-288; 35-721; 35-722
Telex: 062-408 nvedoe h
Head: Miklós Nádler

**INSECT MASS BREEDING 301
LABORATORY**
Head: Péter Gyulai

**Plant Protection and Agrochemistry 302
Station, County Csongrád**

Address: Postafiók 99, H-6801 Hódmezővásárhely
Telephone: Hódmezővásárhely 11-677; 11-376; 11-576
Telex: 084-224 noeval h
Head: Róbert Surányi

BIOLOGICAL CONTROL LABORATORY 303
Head: János Szántó

NEMATOLOGY LABORATORY 304
Head: Dr Csaba Budai

**Plant Protection and Agrochemistry 305
Station, County Fejér**

Address: Fő Útca 230, H-2481 Velence, Kápolnásnyék
Telephone: Kápolnásnyék 34; 35
Telex: 021-282 noev h
Head: Géza Major

PLANT VIROLOGY LABORATORY 306
Head: Emil Pocsai

**Plant Protection and Agrochemistry 307
Station, County Győr-Sopron**

Address: Avató Útca 5, H-9018 Győr
Telephone: (096) 15-469
Telex: 024-376 nvagyr h
Head: Antal Varga

LABOUR SAFETY LABORATORY 308
Head: Lajos Kovács

**Plant Protection and Agrochemistry 309
Station, County Hajdu-Bihar**

Address: H-4271 Mikepércs
Telephone: Sáránd 26; 34
Head: Péter Berecz

**IRRIGATED CROPS PEST CONTROL 310
LABORATORY**
Head: Ferenc Antal

**Plant Protection and Agrochemistry 311
Station, County Heves**

Address: Postafiók 218, H-3301 Eger
Telephone: 10-35; 10-43
Telex: 063-311 noval h
Head: István Kovács

**Plant Protection and Agrochemistry 312
Station, County Komárom**

Address: Postafiók 50, H-2891 Tata
Telephone: 315
Telex: 027-220 kmatt h
Head: Zoltán Szentkirályi

**Plant Protection and Agrochemistry 313
Station, County Nógrád**

Address: Postafiók 69, H-2661 Balassagyarmat
Telephone: 572
Telex: 028-2232 naabgy h
Head: László Tóth

**Plant Protection and Agrochemistry 314
Station, County Pest**

Address: Postafiók 52, H-1780 Budapest
Telephone: (01) 264-671; 464-205; 264-217
Head: Balázs Magyar

HYDROBIOLOGY LABORATORY 315
Address: H-2440 Százhalombatta
Head: Dr Bethen Pénzes

**Plant Protection and Agrochemistry 316
Station, County Somogy**

Address: Postafiók 55, H-7401 Kaposvár
Telephone: (082) 13-430; 13-431; 12-179
Telex: 013-303 noeva h
Head: Máté Szili

**Plant Protection and Agrochemistry 317
Station, County Szabolcs-Szatmár**

Address: Postafiók 124, H-4401 Nyíregyháza
Telephone: (042) 11-866, 11-867
Telex: 073-201 nany h
Head: József Keresztély

Plant Protection and Agrochemistry 318
Station, County Szolnok

Address: Postafiók 14, H-5331 Kenderes
Telephone: 26; 29
Telex: 023-372 rnaa h
Head: Dr Lajos Pásti

GREAT PLAIN SECTION OF PLANT 319
PROTECTION ECONOMICS
Head: Ádám L. Kovács

Plant Protection and Agrochemistry 320
Station, County Tolna

Address: Postafiók 104, H-7101 Szekszárd
Telephone: 12-839,12-868
Telex: 014-254 noeval h
Head: Dr Elemér Nagy

Plant Protection and Agrochemistry 321
Station, County Vas

Address: Ambrozi Sétány, H-9762 Tanakajd
Telephone: 2
Telex: 037-310 noeval h
Head: Dr Endre Sipos

Plant Protection and Agrochemistry 322
Station, County Veszprém

Address: Kishelyi Útca 15, H-8229 Csopak
Telephone: (080) 46-515; 46-563
Telex: 032-336 nvall h
Head: Kálmán Siető

TOXICOLOGY LABORATORY 323
Address: H-8360 Keszthely
Head: Dr Attila Antal

Plant Protection and Agrochemistry 324
Station, County Zala

Address: Postafiók 9, H-8901 Zalaegerszeg
Telephone: (092) 11-053; 11-054; 11-055; 11-057
Telex: 033-286 nazeg h
Head: Dr Ferenc Tihanyi

ACAROLOGY LABORATORY 325
Head: Dr József Bozai

CHESTNUT AND FOREST PEST 326
CONTROL LABORATORY
Head: István Eke

TRANSDANUBIAN SECTION OF PLANT 327
PROTECTION ECONOMICS
Head: Dr Ilona Peti

Plant Protection and Agrochemistry 328
Station of the State Capital

Address: Keleti Károly Útca 24, H-1024 Budapest II
Telephone: (01) 353-709
Telex: 22-6906 nvkem h
Head: Janós Kiss

Növényvédelmi Kutató 329
Intézet

[Research Institute for Plant Protection]
Address: Herman Ottó Útca 15, Postafiók 102, H-1525
Budapest II
Telephone: Budapest 151-460
Director: Zoltán Király
Managing Director: Gyula Benke
Deputy Director: Dr Odön Szatala
Graduate research staff: 52
Contract work: No

BIOCHEMISTRY AND ANALYTICAL 330
CHEMISTRY DEPARTMENT
Head: Dr Gy. Josepovits
Activities: Analytical control methods for pesticides;
biochemical bases of the selectivity of fungicidal
action and resistance to fungicides; mode of action of
pesticides and fungicides.

ORGANIC CHEMISTRY DEPARTMENT 331

Head: Dr Gy. Matolcsy
Activities: Synthesis of pesticide molecules,
optimization; design, synthesis and evaluation of
compounds acting as inhibitors of insect hormone
biosynthesis; design and synthesis of insect juvenile
hormone analogues; new methods for the synthesis of
pesticide molecules; laboratory and glasshouse and
field trials with putative fungicides; new methods of
toxicology; synthesis and evaluation of potential
systemic fungicides of the azole type; mode of action
of newly synthesized compounds; management of
development of new compounds; biometrics and
quantitative structure activity studies.

PATHOPHYSIOLOGY AND DISEASE 332
RESISTANCE DEPARTMENT

Head: Dr Z. Király
Activities: Replication of plant viruses; biochemistry of defence reactions to rusts; rust diseases; physiology and biochemistry of virus infected plants; physiology of plant resistance to bacterial infections; biochemistry and physiology of disease resistance; physiology of bacterial plant diseases. Methods in phytobacteriology; biological control of crown-gall; role of different hormones in pathogenesis; toxins produced by bacteria.

PLANT PATHOLOGY DEPARTMENT 333

Head: Dr J. Vörös
Activities: Virus diseases of leguminous plants; virus characterization, serology; virus diseases of grapevine; virus diseases of vegetable crops; physicochemical characterization of plant viruses; soybean diseases; serotaxonomy and serological identification of fungi; soil-borne plant pathogens; sunflower diseases; powdery mildews; die back, bark necrosis and canker of stone fruit trees; chemotaxonomy of fungi; bark necrosis and canker of apple and pear trees; downy mildew of sunflower and other crops; fungal diseases of sunflower and medicinal plants.

WEED RESEARCH DEPARTMENT 334

Head: Dr Ö. Szatala
Activities: Investigations on the threshold of the dangerous number of weed species in the main cultivated crops; influence of light, rain and temperature factors on the efficiency of soil-acting and foilage-contact herbicides; weed-competition in corn fields; ecological, cenological and herbological studies on Amaranthus and Chenopodium species; biology of Cuscuta species; germination, ontogenesis, flowering and seed production of Polygonum species; biological aspects of annual grasses.

ZOOLOGY DEPARTMENT 335

Head: Dr F. Kozár
Activities: Ecosystem research in apple orchards; maize ecosystem research; antifeedant effects of substances of plant origin on phytophagous insects; biology of pests infesting lucerne and other fodder crops; population dynamics of Coccidae; polyphagous predators in agroecosystems (apple and maize). Ecology and faunistics of ground beetles; host plant pattern of the European corn borer and codling moth. Hemp pests; insect pathology; ethology of insect/host plant relationships, oviposition behaviour of the bean weevil; mathematical statistical analysis of light trap

data; lepidopterous sex pheromones and attractants; rearing methods of Noctuidae on semisynthetic diets; sex pheromone-related behaviour of Noctuidae and Tortricidae. Laboratory and field testing of lepidopterous sex attractants and inhibitors; insect hormones (juvenile hormone and its analogues, antihormones).

Olajbányászati 336
Kutatólaboratóriuma

[Petroleum Engineering Research Laboratory]
Address: Postafiók 2, H-3515 Miskolc-Egyetemváros
Telephone: (046) 14-841
Telex: 62421
Parent body: Magyar Tudományos Akadémia
Director: Dr József Tóth
Departments: Physical chemistry and analytical chemistry, Dr István Lakatos; reservoir engineering, Dr Gyula Milley
Graduate research staff: 17
Annual expenditure: £51 000-500 000
Activities: Theoretical and applied research in the field of enhanced hydrocarbon recovery focused mainly on chemical methods (application of polymers, surfactants, silicates, etc. in flooding and well treating). Laboratory and mathematical simulation of microhydraulic and displacement processes (water and chemical flooding). Investigation of intensive fluid technique of ore and mineral mining. Development and manufacturing of special laboratory instruments and apparatus.
Contract work: Yes

Öntözési Kutató Intézet 337

– OKI
[Irrigation Research Institute]
Address: Szabadság Útca 2, H-5540 Szarvas
Telephone: Szarvas 214
Telex: 82471
Parent body: Ministry of Food and Agriculture
Director: Dr Károly Kiss
Sections: Water economy of plants and irrigated farming; grassland cultivation; rice production
Graduate research staff: 52
Annual expenditure: Ft12m
Activities: Research in agrochemistry, water economy, agronomy, engineering, economics, grassland cultivation and rice production. This research is carried out on research stations and in cooperation with a number of production farms.
Contract work: Yes

Országos Csecsemő és Gyermekegészségügyi Intézet 338

[National Institute for Infant and Child Health]
Address: Tüzoltó Útca 7-9, H-1094 Budapest
Telephone: (01) 341-985
Parent body: Ministry of Health
Director: Professor Dezső Schuler
Sections: Cardiology, Dr K. Lozsádi; biometry; Dr R. Agfalvy; haematology-oncology, Dr T. Révesz; endocrinology, Dr G. Gács
Graduate research staff: 8
Annual expenditure: £10 000-50 000
Activities: Neonatal cardiology; biometry; endocrinology; haematology-oncology - cytogenetics, immunology, therapy.
Contract work: No

Országos Élelmezés és Táplálkozástudományi Intézet 339

[Institute of Nutrition]
Address: Gyáli Útca 3/a, H-1097 Budapest
Telephone: (01) 334-130
Telex: 226001
Parent body: Ministry of Health
Scientific Secretary: Dr Endre Morava
Sections: Organization and method, Dr T. Novotny; food microbiology, Dr L. Ormay; toxicological chemistry, Dr V. Cieleszky; physiology and pathology of nutrition, Dr M. Bedő; food chemistry, Dr Ö. Gaál; people's nutrition, Dr D. Bouquet
Activities: Physiology and pathophysiology of human nutrition; nutritional toxicology; nutritional field surveys; food composition tables; dietetic foods; analysis and evaluation of food additives, pesticide residues and other food contaminants; food microbiology; hygienic and nutritional evaluation of foods.

Országos Frédéric Joliot-Curie Sugárbiologiai és Sugáregészségügyi Kutató Intézet 340

[Frédéric Joliot-Curie National Research Institute for Radiobiology and Radiohygiene]
Address: Postafiók 101, H-1775 Budapest
Telephone: (01) 264-856
Telex: 22-5103 osski h

Director: Professor László B. Sztanyik
Scientific Deputy Director: Dr György J. Köteles
Departments: Radiobiology; Radiohygiene; Radiation and radioisotope application
Graduate research staff: 70
Activities: Radiohygiene, including the radiation protection of workers and the population in and around nuclear facilities, especially nuclear power stations. Radiobiology studies are conducted at the levels of cells and whole organisms concerning the early and late effects of ionizing radiations and incorporated radioisotopes. Radiation and radioisotope applications involve preservation of biological tissues, sterilization and detoxification of drugs, toxins and vaccines, as well as preparation of radiopharmaceuticals for the in vivo and in vitro uses in nuclear medicine.
Contract work: Yes

Országos Gyógyszerészeti Intézet 341

[National Institute of Pharmacy]
Address: Postafiók 450, H-1372 Budapest
Telephone: (01) 174-044
Telex: 224656 ogyi h
Activities: Chemical analytical, biological, microbiological, pharmaceutical and biopharmaceutical investigation, evaluation and standardization of new drugs and pharmaceutical preparations.
Contract work: No

Országos Husipari Kutatóintézet 342

[Hungarian Meat Research Institute]
Address: Gubacsi Útca 6/b, H-1097 Budapest
Telephone: (01) 336-770
Telex: 224980 ohki h
Parent body: Trust for Livestock Trade and Meat Industry
Director: Endre Zukál
Departments: Technology, S. Simon; Economics and Raw Materials, O. Vágvölgyi; Chemistry and Biology, Dr K. Incze; Machine Designing, J. Foltányi
Graduate research staff: 85
Activities: Research in raw materials for the meat industry; modernization of slaughter technology; development of a continuous sausage technology and mechanization of the production process. Development of up-to-date and new products; research in new laboratory methods as well as in grading and quality control; modernization of material transport in the slaughter house and in the packing plant.
Contract work: Yes

Országos Reuma és 343
Fizioterápiás Intézet

[National Institute of Rheumatism and Physiotherapy]
Address: Postafiók 54, H-1525 Budapest 114
Telephone: (01) 159-850
Telex: 22-4706
Research director: Professor S. Bozsóky
Sections: Morphology, histochemistry, Dr D. Tanka; medical hydrology, Dr A. Richter; immunology, Dr K. Merétey; genetics, Dr B. Gömör
Graduate research staff: 5
Activities: Morphological, histological, ultrastructural, biochemical, immunological and genetical aspects of problems of rheumatic diseases; research work in the clinical field; control of drug treatment. Physiotherapy, medical hydrology, spa treatment and rehabilitation.

Orvostovábbképzo 344
Intézet*

[Postgraduate Medical School]
Address: Szabolcs utca 35, H-1135 Budapest
Rector: Professor Dr E. Endröczi
Activities: All medical specialities.

Papiripari Vállalat 345
Kutatóintézete

[Paper Industries Research Institute]
Address: Duna Útca 57, Postafiók 86, 1751 Budapest
Telephone: (01) 570-703
Telex: 22-4017 pv bp h
Parent body: Hungarian Paper Industries Company
Deputy Director General: Dr Sándor Annus
Scientific Deputy Director: Dr Sándor Hernadi
Sections: Fibrous materials, Attila Rab; paper technology, Sándor Térpál; paper conversion, Dr Klara Helyes
Graduate research staff: 15
Annual expenditure: £51 000-500 000
Activities: New raw materials for the pulp and paper industry, up-to-date converted products, new products in the conversion industry.
Facilities: Pilot cooking equipment; laboratory paper machine; coating equipment.
Contract work: Yes

Pécsi Orvostudományi 346
Egyetem*

[Pecs Medical University]
Address: Szigeti ut 12, H-7643 Pécs
Telephone: (072) 14 086
Rector: Professor Dr B. Flerkó
Activities: Medicine, pharmacy and dentistry.

Posta Kisérleti Intézet 347

[Post Office Research Institute]
Address: Postafiók 2, H-1456 Budapest
Telephone: (01) 471 560
Telex: 22-1140
Research director: Dr György Lajtha
Sections: Transmission system, V. Farkas; radio relay link, S. Czigány; broadcasting, L. Böti; network planning, S. Gránásy; switching; Dr P. Molnár; installation T. Verebélyi
Graduate research staff: about 250
Annual expenditure: £501 000-2m
Activities: The main task of the Institute is to develop the theoretical background of the installation and maintenance work of the Post Office. Work includes computer-aided planning, special measurements, reliability tests, specifications for industrial development.
Contract work: Yes
Publications: Proceedings of the Research Institute; papers - in BUDAVOX Telecommunication Review, in English; in POSTA, in Hungarian.

Semmelweis 348
Orvostudományi Egyetem

[Semmelweis Medical University]
Address: Ullői Útca 26, H-1085 Budapest VIII
Telephone: (01) 134-610
Telex: 226720 bpsur h

FACULTY OF MEDICINE 349

Anatomy, Histology and Embryology 350
Department

Head: Professor B. Halász; Professor T. Tömböl

Biochemistry Department 351

Head: Professor I. Horváth

Biology Department   352
Head: Professor Gy. Csaba

Biophysics Department   353
Head: Professor I. Tarján

Dermatology Clinic   354
Head: Professor I. Rácz

Forensic Medicine Department   355
Head: Professor E. Somogyi

General Pathology Department   356
Head: Professor K. Lapis

Institute of Pathology and   357
Experimental Cancer Research

Telephone: (01) 138-669
Research director: Professor K. Lapis
Laboratories: Electronmicroscopy, Dr Zsuzsa Schaff;
Otology, Dr Béla Szende; Biochemistry, Dr András
Jeney
Graduate research staff: 10
Annual expenditure: £10 000-50 000
Activities: Surgical pathology and morbid anatomy;
human kidney pathology; liver pathology - human and
experimental; tumour research - electron microscopy of
human tumours, biological characterization of tumours,
studies on MC-29 virus-induced chicken hepatoma;
tumour   chemotherapy   -   xenotransplantation,
metastasis; carcinogenesis.
Contract work: Yes

Medical Chemistry Department   358
Head: Professor F. Antoni

Medical Clinics   359
Heads: Professor I. Magyar; Professor G. Petránui;
Professor F. Gráf; Professor Romoda

Microbiology Department   360
Head: Professor I. Nász

Neurology and Psychiatry Clinic   361
Heads: Professor E. Csanda (Neurology); Professor P.
Juhász (Psychiatry)

Obstetrics and Gynaecology Clinic   362
Heads: Professor S. Csömör; Professor B. Zsolnai

Ophthalmology Clinic   363
Heads: Professor M. Radnot; Professor B. Németh

Orthopaedics Clinic   364
Head: Professor R. Glauber

Otorhinolaryngology Clinic   365
Head: Professor Gy. Réuész

Paediatrics Clinic   366
Heads: Professor F. Gerlóczy, Professor D. Schuler

Pathological Anatomy Department   367
Head: Professor H. Jellinek

Pharmacology Department   368
Head: Professor J. Knoll

Physiology Department   369
Head: Professor P. Bálint

Public Health Department   370
Head: Professor I. Vedres

Pulmonary Diseases Clinic   371
Head: Professor G. Miskovits

Radiology Clinic   372
Head: Professor I. Török

Social Medicine Department   373
Head: Professor Gy. Aczél

Surgical Clinics   374
Heads: Professor A. Szécsény, Professor J. Stefanics,
Professor T. Marton, Professor L. Soltész (Vascular
surgery)

Urology Department   375
Head: Professor F. Balogh

FACULTY OF ODONTOLOGY 376

Conservative Dentistry Department 377
Head: Professor J. Bánóczy

Oral Surgery Department 378
Head: Professor Á. Csiba

Orthodontics and Children's Dentistry Department 379
Head: Professor J. Dénes

Prosthetic Dentistry Department 380
Head: Professor T. Fábián

FACULTY OF PHARMACY 381

Pharmaceutical Chemistry Department 382
Head: Professor Gy. Szász

Pharmaceutical Organic Chemistry Department 383
Head: Professor L. Szabó

Pharmaceutics Department 384
Head: vacant

Pharmacodynamics Department 385
Head: Professor K. Magyar

Pharmacognosy Department 386
Head: Professor G. Petri

Számitástechnikai és Automatizálási Kutató Intézete 387

– SZTAKI
[Computer and Automation Institute]
Address: Kende Útca 13-17, H-1502 Budapest XI
Telephone: (01) 665-435
Telex: 22-5066 akibp h
Parent body: Magyar Tudományos Akadémia
Director: Professor Tibor Vámos

Sections: Applied mathematics, András Prékopa; automation, János Somló; electronics, Pál Verbély; process control, Károly Hamar; mechanical engineering and automation, László Nemes; computer and network, Péter Bakony; computer science, János Demetrovics
Graduate research staff: 300
Annual expenditure: £2m
Activities: Research on computer applications, methods and components, the mathematical methods, programming techniques, equipment and facilities required for these purposes.
Contract work: Yes
Publications: Computational Linguistics and Computer Languages; *SZTAKI Kozlemények* (Proceedings); *SZTAKI Tanulmányok* (Studies).

Szegedi Biologiai Központja 388

– SZBK
[Szeged Biological Research Centre]
Address: Odesszai Körút 62, Postafiók 521, H-6701 Szeged
Telephone: (062) 13-911
Telex: 82442 bioce
Parent body: Magyar Tudományos Akadémia
Activities: Fundamental research and long term applied aspects for the agriculture, food and pharmaceutical industries.

BIOFIZIKAI INTÉZET 389
[Biophysics Institute]
Director: Lajos Keszthelyi
Sections: Chirality laboratory, Lajos Keszthelyi; Laboratory for membrane research and biological transport, Béla Karvaly; molecular neurobiology group, Ference Joó; Laboratory of nucleotide chemistry, Jenő Tomasz

BIOKÉMIAI INTÉZET 390
[Biochemistry Institute]
Director: Dr Maria Wollemann
Sections: Nucleic acid research, Dr Pál Venetianer; membrane research, Dr Tibor Farkas
Graduate research staff: 25
Annual expenditure: Ft6.5m

ENZIMOLÓGIAI INTÉZET   391

[Enzymology Institute]
Address: Karolina Útca 29, Budapest XI
Director: F. Bruno Straub
Deputy Director: Tamas Keleti
Activities: Stability and dynamics of protein structure studies by physical methods; enzyme action and regulation at near physiological high-enzyme concentrations; supramolecular organization of erythrocyte glycolysis and molecular sieving effect of erythrocyte membrane; symmetry of oligomenic proteins; nitrogenase and nitrate reductase from Rhizobium meliloti; development of protein analytical techniques; organic and stereochemistry of enzyme action; experimental and theoretical enzyme kinetics.

GENETIKAI INTÉZET   392

[Genetics Institute]
Director: Lajos Alfoldi;
Deputy Director: Tibor Sik
Laboratories: Bacterial genetics I, Adam Kondorosi; II, Tibor Sik; III, Lajos Alfoldi; IV, Csaba Kari; Plant cell genetics, Dénes Dudits; Plant genetics, Adonisz Belea; Mammalian cell genetics, Istvan Raskó; Steroid hormone action on mammalian cells, Aniko Venetianer; Immunogenetics, József Fachet

NÖVÉNYÉLETTANI INTÉZET   393

[Plant Physiology Institute]
Director: Gábor L. Farkas
Deputy Director: Agnes Faludi-Dániel
Laboratories: Blue-green algae and algae viruses, György Borbely; Plant virus research, Gábor L. Farkas; Photosynthesis, Agnes Faludi Dániel; Plant cell genetics, Pál Maliga

Szegedi Orvostudományi   394
Egyetem

[Szeged University of Medicine]
Address: Dugonics Tér 13, H-6720 Szeged
Telephone: (062) 12-729
Rector: Professor Gábor Petri
Vice-rectors: Professor István Cserháti, Professor Ferenc Guba, Professor János Szilárd

FACULTY OF GENERAL MEDICINE   395

Dean: Professor Vilmos Földes

Anatomy, Histology and Embryology   396
Institute

Address: Kossuth Lajos Sgt 40, H-6724 Szeged
Director: Professor Bertalan Csillik
Activities: Neurohistological, cytochemical, electron-microscopic and autoradiography studies carried out at the level of molecular anatomy to reveal the ultrastructural basis of synaptic impulse transmission in the nervous system.

Biochemistry Institute   397

Address: Dóm Tér 9, H-6720 Szeged
Director: Professor Ference Guba
Activities: Methodology; differentiation of muscle cell and the organization and behaviour of structural proteins.

Dentistry and Oral Surgery Clinic   398

Address: Lenin Körút 64, H-6720 Szeged
Director: Professor Károly Tóth
Activities: Epidemiology and prevention of dental caries by domestic salt fluoridation; periodontitis; benign and malignant tumour therapy and surgery.

Dermatology and Venereology Clinic   399

Address: Korányi Fasor 8-10, H-6720 Szeged
Director: Professor Miklós Simon
Activities: Porphyrinopathies;   immunology; reconstructive plastic surgery; malignant melanoma; mycology.

Experimental Surgery Institute   400

Address: Pécsi Útca 4, H-6720 Szeged
Director: Professor Gábor Petri
Activities: Circulatory shock; transplantation and tumour immunology; cellular biochemistry.

Forensic Medicine Institute   401

Address: Kossuth Lajos Sgt 40, H-6724 Szeged
Director: Professor Vilmos Földes
Activities: Investigation of the inorganic material content of bone to determine its chronological age; paternity tests and criminological serological investigations; studying the measurements of foetal bones; medico-legal problems; pathological and differential diagnostics of trauma.

Internal Medicine Clinic I 402

Address: Korányi Fasor 8, H-6720 Szeged
Director: Professor Vince Varró
Activities: Experimental and clinical gastroenterology, endocrinology, nephrology; clinical pharmacology; clinical immunology.

Internal Medicine Clinic II 403

Address: Korányi Fasor 8, H-6720 Szeged
Director: Professor István Cserháti
Activities: Clinical and experimental haematology and cardiology.

Medical Biology Institute 404

Address: Somogyi B. Útca 4, H-6720 Szeged
Director: Professor János Molnár
Activities: Processing and transport of eukaryotic mRNA and cytogenetics.

Medical Chemistry Institute 405

Address: Dóm Tér 8, H-6720 Szeged
Director: Professor Kálmán Kovács
Activities: Syntheses of peptides with hormone activity; syntheses of polypeptides with unnatural (non-proteinogenic) amino acids.

Microbiology Institute 406

Address: Dóm Tér 10, H-6720 Szeged
Director: Professor Ilona Béládi
Activities: Medical aspect of microbiology; virology; interferon research.

Neurology and Psychiatry Clinic 407

Address: Korányi Fasor 15, H-6720 Szeged
Director: Professor János Szilárd
Activities: Molecular mechanism of transport phenomena on different membranes and sarcoplasmis reticulum of skeletal muscles; pathochemical research concerned with tissue-cultures of central nervous system; analysis of psychological metabolism in schizophrenia - pathochemical, psychologic and social psychiatric research of affective disorders; psychiatric disorders in childhood.

Obstetrics and Gynaecology Clinic 408

Address: Semmelweis Útca 1, H-6725 Szeged
Director: Professor Mihály Sas
Activities: Sterility and fertility (male and female); reproductive endocrinology; intrauterine physiology; pathology in pregnancy; perinatal medicine.

Ophthalmology Clinic 409

Address: Korányi Fasor 12, H-6701 Szeged
Director: Professor Agost Kahán
Activities: Neurohormones in pathogenesis and therapy; disorders of intra-ocular fluid circulation; investigation of immunological eye disorders; application of immunological methods to obtain aetiological diagnosis.

Otorhinolaryngology Clinic 410

Address: Lenin Körút 111, H-0725 Szeged
Director: Professor Ottó Ribári
Activities: Surgery, histopathology and medical treatment of otosclerosis; transplantation of the middle ear; study of laser effect in otolaryngology; audiology; prevention of occupational diseases; possible rehabilitation of damaged hearing; problems of diagnostic and modern therapy of allergic diseases in the nose and the nasal sinuses; optimal therapeutical possibilities of malign tumours in the field of otorhinolaryngology.

Paediatrics Clinic 411

Address: Korányi Fasor 18, H-6725 Szeged
Director, Professor Domokos Boda
Activities: Pathology of newborn and premature infants, acute severe diseases; congenital heart complaints; respiratory deficiency, paediatric immunology and metabolism; clinical pharmacology.

Pathological Anatomy Institute 412

Address: Kossuth Lajos Sgt 40, H-6724 Szeged
Director: Professor Jenő Ormos
Activities: Human and experimental pathology, especially diseases of the kidney, cardiovascular system and liver; functional morphology of the hypothalamic-hypophyseal system and nervous system; diagnostic electron microscopy.

Pathophysiology Institute 413

Address: Semmelweis Ignác Útca 1, H-6725 Szeged
Director: Professor Gyula Telegdy
Activities: Neuroendocrinology; the role of peptides (neuropeptides and peptide hormones) and prostaglandins in the regulation of endocrine system and behaviour.

Pharmacological Institute 414

Address: Dóm Tér 12, H-6701 Szeged
Director: Professor László Szekeres
Activities: Pharmacological study of drugs affecting the cardiovascular system.

Physiological Institute   415

Address: Dóm Tér 10, H-6720 Szeged
Director: Professor Ferenc Obál
Activities: Functions of the central nervous system; sleep-waking rhythm, thermoregulation carried out with electrophysiological conditioning; biochemical and computer techniques.

Public Health and Epidemiology   416
Institute

Address: Dóm Tér 10, H-6720 Szeged
Director: Professor György Berencsi
Activities: Research on toxico-hygiene; the relation of chemistry and different toxicological effects (carcinogenesis, mutagenesis, teratogenesis and allergy, etc).

Radiology Clinic   417

Address: Korányi Fasor 8, H-6720 Szeged
Director: Professor János Kelemen
Activities: Experimental and clinical investigations with the effects of vasoactive humoral agents on blood circulation; biological effects of ionizing radiation (radiation damage and radioprotection); therapeutic dose planning based on various computer systems.

Social Medicine and Organization of   418
Health Service Institute

Address: Kossuth Lajos Sgt 35, H-6724 Szeged
Director: Professor Sámuel Zalányi
Activities: Morbidity investigations of in-and out-patients; accident prevention and safety regulations, improvement of working conditions; life and working conditions of health service personnel; organization and management of labour in pharmacy; health education; medical sociology.

Surgery Clinic I   419

Address: Pécsi Útca 4, H-6720 Szeged
Director: Professor Gábor Petri
Activities: Haemodynamics of the systemic and lesser circulations; ileus; renal insufficiency; clinical septic complications in surgical patients by active immunization.

Surgery Clinic II   420

Address: Pécsi Útca 4, H-6720 Szeged
Director: Professor György Fényes
Activities: Diagnostical and therapeutical problems of brain tumours and congenital malformations of brain vessels; cerebral angiographies; diagnostical and therapeutical problems of closed skull fractures; surgical treatment of intractable pain and epilepsy; general traumatology; reconstructive surgery of extremities; micro-, neuro- and vascular surgery.

FACULTY OF PHARMACY   421

Address: Eötvös Útca 6, H-6720 Szeged
Dean: Professor Emil Minker

Pharmaceutical Chemistry Institute   422

Address: Eötvös Útca 6, H-6720 Szeged
Director: Professor Gábor Bernáth
Activities: Drug synthesis; synthesis and conformational analysis of condensed skeleton saturated heterocycles containing nitrogen and oxygen.

Pharmaceutical Technology Institute   423

Address: Eötvös Útca 6, H-6720 Szeged
Director: Professor György Kedvessy
Activities: Colloid-physical properties of pharmaceutical preparations; principles of the release of active factors in various forms of pharmaceutical products.

Pharmacodynamics Institute   424

Address: Eötvös Útca 6, H-6720 Szeged
Director: Professor Emil Minker
Activities: Pharmacology and modulation of synaptic transmission in autonomic ganglia; pharmacology of smooth muscle; pharmacology of anti-inflammatory agents; biopharmacy of antimalars; general chronological effects of flavonoids and pharmacology of capillary resistance.

Pharmacognosy Institute   425

Address: Eötvös Útca 6, H-6720 Szeged
Director: Professor Kálmán Szendrei
Activities: Scientific evaluation of popular medicinal herbs and their possible use in medicine; research on biologically active new natural (plant) products; chemotaxonomy.

Szilikátipari Központi Kutató és Tervező Intézet   426

– SZIKKTI
[Central Research and Design Institute for Silicate Industry]
Address: Postafiók 112, H-1300 Budapest
Telephone: (01) 684-000; 684-060
Telex: 22-4367; 22-5269
Director: Professor József Talabér
Head, Research Department, Dr József Matrai
Sections: Silicate chemistry, Dr Tamás Träger; cement, Dr Károly Dolezsai; concrete, Dr Ádám Székely; structural, ceramics and thermal insulation, Dr Kálmán Tóth; fine ceramics, Dr Endre Wágner; special ceramics, Dr Lidia Kacsalova; glass, Dr Imre Bocsi; power engineering and environmental sciences, Dr Ferenc Szijj; scientific perspective development, Dr Árpád Kunvári; automation, Antal Fehér
Graduate research staff: 120
Annual expenditure: Ft80m
Activities: Basic research; geological prospecting; mineralogical and chemical examination of raw materials; new analytical methods; substitution of imported raw materials with Hungarian ones; new technological processes; power engineering methods and systems for economic energy consumption; anti-pollution measures; new building materials, silicate products and their practical applications; pilot plant production of special substances; cooperation with foreign countries - research, standards.
Contract work: Yes
Publications: Tudományos Közlemények (Transactions), in Hungarian, summaries in English, French, German and Russian, 5 or 6 issues a year.

Szőlészeti és Borászati Kutató Intézet   427

[Viticulture and Oenology Research Institute]
Address: Katona József Tér 8, H-6000 Kecskemét
Telephone: (076) 12-748
Telex: 26 518
Director General: Ferenc Magyar
Departments: Viticulture, Dr László Oláh; oenology; Dr Sándor Török
Graduate research staff: 56
Annual expenditure: Ft10m
Activities: Establishment of new species of vines; agrotechnics; application of organic and inorganic fertilizers; development of irrigation; modern methods of plant protection; virus diseases of vines; vinification; winemaking, treatment of wines; utilization of by-products of viti-viniculture; mechanization; economics.
Contract work: No
Publications: Szőlőtermesztés.

Talajtani és Agrokémiai Kutatóintézete*   428

[Research Institute for Soil Science and Agricultural Chemistry]
Address: Hermann Ottó Útca 15-17, H-1022 Budapest
Parent body: Magyar Tudományos Akadémia

Textilipari Kutató Intézet   429

[Textile Research Institute]
Address: Postafók 6, H-1475 Budapest
Telephone: (01) 472-300
Telex: 224698 texki
Deputy Director: Tibor Hajmásy
Departments: Mechanics, Gy. Vass; Chemistry, Gy. Bercsényi; Testing and Measurements, I. Králik; Textile and Clothing Development, B. Alpár; Engineering and Automation, T. Katona; Research Organization, J. Horváth
Graduate research staff: 100
Annual expenditure: £501 000-2m
Activities: Central research and development body of the Hungarian textile and textile clothing industry; also provides services, instrument development and production work to the industry. Research into all types of raw materials, techniques, and end products of textile clothing making-up industry; utilization of raw materials of natural origin; applicability of man-made fibres; industrial applications of permanent finishing processes; high capacity yarn and fabric producing technologies and machinery.
Contract work: Yes
Publications: Textilipari Kutató Intézet Közleményi; Textilipari Kutató Intézet Tájékoztatója; Textilipari Kutató Intézet Tevékenysége.

Tungsram Egyesült Izzólámpa-és Villamossági Rt   430

Address: Váci Útca 77, H-1340 Budapest
Telephone: (01) 692-800; 693-800
Telex: 22-5058 TUNGS H
Director, Research Institute: E. Barla
Technical Director for r&d: J. Molnár
Sections: Light sources, P. Billing; semiconductors, T. Zanati; electron tubes, E. Kis-Halas; machinery and equipment, Dr L. Horváth
Graduate research staff: 1000
Annual expenditure: over £2m
Activities: Production, research and development in

the fields of lighting, vacuum technical machinery, and electronics. Design, development and production of machines and machine lines for manufacturing and assembling parts for mass production, including planning and assembling turnkey factories. Electron tube production: radio and television receiving tubes, rectifiers, cathode ray and monitor tubes, vacuum gauges. Production of semiconductors, reed relays, thermoprobes, ballasts for fluorescent lamps and high pressure mercury vapour lamps, glass bulbs, glass tubes, tungsten wires and filaments, phosphors, electrodes, exhaust tubes, and caps for light sources.
Contract work: No
Publications: Tungsram Technical Review.

Veszprémi Vegyipari Egyetem 431

[Veszprém University of Chemical Engineering]
Address: Schönherz Soltán Útca 10, H-8201 Veszprém
Telephone: (080) 12-550
Telex: vegye-h 32397
Rector: Professor János Inczedy

ANALYTICAL CHEMISTRY DEPARTMENT 432

Head: Professor Janós Inczedy

CHEMICAL ENGINEERING CYBERNETICS DEPARTMENT 433

Head: Professor P. Árva

CHEMICAL ENGINEERING DEPARTMENT 434

Head: Professor P. Szolcsányi
Senior staff: Professor M. Bakos; Professor A. Lászlo

CHEMICAL TECHNOLOGY DEPARTMENT 435

Head: Professor P. Kaldi

ECONOMICS DEPARTMENT 436

Head: Professor M. Vándor

HYDROCARBON AND COAL PROCESSING DEPARTMENT 437

Head: Professor L. Péchy

INDUSTRIAL ENGINEERING AND MANAGEMENT DEPARTMENT 438

Head: Professor L. Bene

INORGANIC CHEMISTRY DEPARTMENT 439

Head: Professor E. Bodor
Senior staff: Professor B. Mohai

MATHEMATICS DEPARTMENT 440

Head: Professor Z. László

MECHANICAL ENGINEERING DEPARTMENT 441

Head: Professor A. Halász

MINERALOGY DEPARTMENT 442

Head: Professor E. Nemecz

ORGANIC CHEMISTRY DEPARTMENT 443

Head: Professor L. Markó
Senior staff: Professor B. Heil

PHYSICAL CHEMISTRY DEPARTMENT 444

Head: Professor F. Ratkovics

RADIOCHEMISTRY DEPARTMENT 445

Head: Professor T. Lengyel
Senior staff: Professor E. Hazi; Professor Gy. Straub

SILICATE CHEMISTRY DEPARTMENT 446

Head: Professor M. Déri

Vizgazdálkodási Tudományos Kutató Központ　447

– VITUKI

[Research Centre for Water Resources Development]

Address: Postafiók 27, H-1453 Budapest 92
Telephone: 338-160
Telex: 224959-h
Research director: Dr György Kovács
Institutes: Hydrology, Dr L. Goda,
Hydraulic Constructions, Dr O. Starosolszky,
Water Quality Protection, Dr P. Benedek,
Technical Development, Dr Gy. Bognár
Graduate research staff: 200
Activities: Investigations for water resources development; collection, processing and publication of data on surface and groundwater resources for systematic water management; investigation of hydrological events; quality research in surface and subsurface waters; commercial, industrial and agricultural use of waters; research into self-purification of water courses; purification of wastewaters before emission into streams or lakes; determination of radiation pollution of waters; carrying out of hydrotechnical research and experiments; development of modern instruments and methods in connection with the above tasks.
Contract work: Yes

Zöldségtermesztési Kutató Intézet　448

[Vegetable Crops Research Institute]

Address: Postafiók 116, H-6001 Kecskemét
Telephone: (076) 13-680
Telex: H-26330
Director-general: Dr Sandor Balázs
Activities: Research on vegetables, including genetics, breeding, modernization of cultural methods, plant protection, processing technology, economics of tomato, cucumber, onion, sweet and red pepper, green peas, snap bean, watermelon, muskmelon and brassicas, is carried on or coordinated in the Institute.